Ghost Towns of The West

Ghost Towns
of The West

by Lambert Florin

PROMONTORY PRESS

A Promontory Press book
Published in the United States of America by
Galahad Books
149 Madison Ave.
New York, NY 10016

Published by arrangement with Superior Publishing Company

Library of Congress Catalog Card Number 73-90741

ISBN 0-88394-013-2

Printed in the United States of America

WHAT IS A GHOST TOWN?

One of several dictionary definitions of "ghost" is "a shadowy semblance of its former self." We have elected to prefer this somewhat ambiguous phrase, because it accurately describes many towns on the borderline of being dead or alive. Most of the towns described and pictured in this book are "dead" ghosts, but some still have life, though nothing to compare with the lusty vigor they enjoyed in their heyday.

Some even have a future, and the shadowy remnants of a fascinating past are being sacrificed on the altar of a new strike, possibly of a newer metal such as Molybdenum. An example of this is Kokomo, Colorado. Here is a town full of interesting relics of Colorado's early mining days with a corner full of new buildings and developments.

Some have never really died but are much smaller than before, with a population sufficient to keep up a post office, a store or two and an eating place (and, of course, a tavern). Examples a r e Skamokawa, Washington; Shaniko, Oregon and Gem, Idaho. Many others still have a community spirit and hopes for a brighter future, perhaps more brilliant than the past.

Some are even crowded with people. The saloons are "revived," some buildings "restored" and in general are inflated with a sort of artificial respiration. Examples are Virginia City, Nevada and the town with the same name in Montana. These are well worth while, easily accessible and full of diversion, but they lack the charm of the deserted or nearly deserted places, for some, at least.

Our ideal is a town completely abandoned by all business and permanent residents, and many of the subjects included fall into this category.

GHOST TOWN ETIQUETTE

Such souvenirs as are found in the brush by the side of the road are legitimately carried home. Parts of buildings still standing, or furniture in them, we don't include in the souvenir category, however. The old towns are melting away too fast as it is.

One of the towns in our book, Shaniko, Oregon was written up in a local newspaper this year, and about the same time was a subject for a T. V. program. The results to the town were drastic. One of the tiny group of remaining inhabitants wrote to the newspaper as follows—"Today, your cameraman would find something new added to the panorama he viewed a few weeks ago," reads the letter. "The inhabitants have been forced to tack up 'No trespassing' signs, in order to preserve a bit of privacy and rights as property owners. Why? Because the public is carrying Shaniko away, piece by piece. . . . Among us are several who have had belongings of varied value, both sentimental and intrinsic, taken from their property, and the schoolhouse and surroundings have been devastated by souvenir-seekers. In short, our privacy has been invaded and we are irked to say the least . . ."

CONTENTS

Alaska, the Yukon, British Columbia   1

Arizona 73

California 153

Colorado and Utah 281

Montana, Idaho, and Wyoming 393

Nevada 505

New Mexico and Texas 601

Oregon 681

Washington .777

ALASKA, THE YUKON
BRITISH COLUMBIA
GHOST TOWNS

BY

LAMBERT FLORIN

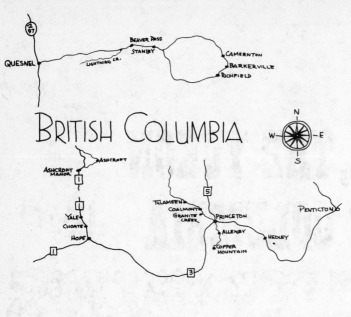

BRITISH COLUMBIA

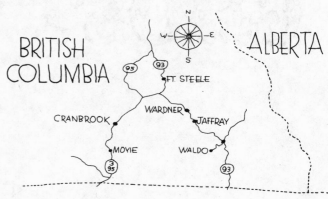

BRITISH COLUMBIA   ALBERTA

BRITISH COLUMBIA

CANADA

WASHINGTON

CONTENTS

CITY	Page	CITY	Page
Allenby	24	Hedley	34
Ashcroft Manor	6	Moyie	36
Barkerville	8	Richfield	37
Bennett	15	Sandon	39
Cameronton	18	Skagway	67
Coalmont	21	Stanley	45
Copper Mountain	24	Waldo	47
Dawson City	52	Whitehorse	62
Fisherville	29	Wild Horse	29
Fort Steele	29	Yale	49
Granite Creek	32	Ymir	51

CITY HALL was built immediately after great fire of 1900, survived equally destructive flood of 1955, though previously long deserted. As town declined school in higher Sunnyside was abandoned for lack of pupils, reestablished on lower floor of City Hall. It was attended by George Stewart who was born in Sandon and daughter Ivy went to first grade here before family left town. City offices at first filled entire structure, later shriveled to one room on upper floor reached by inside stairway, one shown here used for fire escape. Similar one on another building was first to burn in fire, cutting off escape by tenants.

4

GAUNT BUILDING forms frame for most conspicuous peak in this part of Steeples Range, spur of Rocky Mts. Fisher Peak, 9,200,' retains some snow in sheltered ravines all summer. Mountain presents climbing problems. Ascent demands expert technique in rock work, first ascent made without technical aids by "Red" Nichol, big game guide for many years. He had rugged physical constitution to make up for lack of ropes, pitons.

ASHCROFT MANOR, B.C.

The Cornwall brothers, Henry Alan and Clement Francis, established Ashcroft Manor, the very successful stopping place on the road to Barkerville. Being good Englishmen, they brought familiar customs with them and wanted to start a few old country sports. To this end, they imported some English hunting horses, fine Arab stallions and bought from the Duke of Beaufort twenty foxhounds.

Earlier, in 1862, the brothers had imported some cattle from Oregon. This meant cowboys, and there being none locally, they got these also from the States. And for a proper fox hunt who would ride the English hunters? Who else but the cowboys? Since there were no foxes in the country, coyotes would have to do. But on one point the Cornwalls insisted there would be no deviation. The proper terms for all phases of the hunt must be used.

The Americans sat in a row on a rail fence while instructed in all these proper terms. The first man sighting the quarry was to call out - "Where away!" When the direction taken by the "fox" was determined, the spotter was to cry - "Yoicks!" as a signal to get ready. Then all riders would take off at the shout— "Tally Ho!" But the Cornwall brothers were to suffer deep chagrin. The actual hunt went according to the best tradition up to the time the first coyote was sighted by a leathery cowhand from Wyoming. All the training in hunt vernacular went skittering over the sagebrush when he yelled out—"There goes the so-and-so—Now!"

Another story about these "fox hunts" is told by Mr. J. Alan Parker, the present occupant of the hundred-year-old hostelry — Ashcroft Manor. The hunting party was on its way to the huge Roper ranch on Cherry Creek in the direction of Kamloops, making an overnight stop at Christian's Hotel. There was no place to put the twenty foxhounds except in the pig pen, occupied by two immense sows. When the dogs were let out the next morning, they were so stuffed that even with whippings they would not pursue the quarry. There was no hunting that day and the stopover cost the party an extra twenty dollars for the sows.

The Cornwall brothers each kept diaries. "Their versions didn't always agree as to details," says Mr. Parker, "but the books do tell a lot of history written in faded old ink with quill pens." These documents are treasured in the Provincial Archives at Victoria but Mr. Parker is familar with their content.

"The Cornwall brothers came to the Crown Territories from Panama in 1858. Landing at Victoria they took another steamer up the Fraser River to New Westminster where they hired horses and rode north through Pemberton Meadows via Lillooet, over the Pavilion Mountains and came down into this beautiful valley."

The brothers liked what they saw—a paradise for horses. The bunch grass stood knee-high and water in the stream, later called Cornwall Creek, was so abundant the horses had to swim across it. The creek is now dry, being diverted for irrigation.

Henry and Clement returned to New Westminster and purchased a thousand acres of the valley land, presumably with some influence as the Surveyor General of the Crown Territories, Sir William Trutch, was induced to lay out the boundaries of the new domain and start proceedings to get a road built over a new route to avoid the dangerous mountains the Cornwalls had been forced to cross.

The road was all-important, the Cornwall plan being to build a comfortable inn for travelers on their way to the Barkerville gold fields. All went well and the Manor was built, at first called 103 Miles House in the

ST. JOHN'S CATHOLIC CHURCH stands on the Lillooet Indian Reservation near Cache Creek and Ashcroft. Complete isolation makes it most conspicuous sight for miles. First church built by whites in early 1860s was Protestant Anglican, one erected originally at Ashcroft Manor, later moved to edge of cliff above town of Ashcroft. Until 1955 Catholics of Ashcroft traveled to church below, then temporary Catholic house of worship was set up in old building at Ashcroft, served until 1961 when new church was built in town. Bonapart River flows past old edifice shown here, joins Thompson River near Ashcroft which enters Fraser in canyon below.

prevailing fashion indicating distance from Yale, head of navigation on the Fraser.

The hostelry was stoutly built and it is as sound today, constructed of the only material available— logs. The roof was covered with hand-split shakes, the floors made of one-and-a-half-inch planks. Additional buildings were put up close by for accommodation of the help and to corral the horses and bull teams of travelers and pack trains. Ashcroft Manor became a busy little community soon requiring a post office and church.

In cases of transgressions against the law, justice was meted out in a room of the Manor, designated as a Court of Law, with Clement Cornwall as Justice. There being no jail, prisoners were shackled to leg irons and allowed their freedom. None tried to get away as there was no place to go. One case mentioned in Clement's diary concerned a Pierre Philendreen accused of selling liquor to an Indian who subsequently fell from his horse and was killed. The accused was convicted, fined $200 and costs.

About this time a sawmill was built, powered by a waterwheel operating in Cornwall Creek. From then on, buildings of whipsawn lumber were rapidly added to the community. Farmers and ranchers were settling in the valley and a flour mill also powered by the stream was erected for their convenience. For every two sacks of wheat they received one sack of flour, the diary states. The grinding stone, oldest in British Columbia, still stands near where it was used.

In 1886 the Canadian Pacific extended its rails to a spot in the river valley below the Manor, the terminal called Ashcroft Station. Two men, Harvey and Bailey, formed a partnership and started a store across the street from the new depot. It was around this nucleus the town of Ashcroft sprang up, a flourishing place today.

The original community at the old hotel has all but vanished, only the Manor and outbuildings remaining. The little Anglican Church has been moved away, though still in sight, corrals and barns gone, post office moved down the steep hill to town. Sturdy old Ashcroft Manor conceals its ancient logs behind a facelift of boards, even these dating back to 1902. The shakes were replaced by shingles which lasted 40 years. The composition roof is new and surmounted by a T.V. aerial. But the rooms retain the original atmosphere, though kept immaculate for visitors.

ONE OF ORIGINAL LOG CABINS put up 100 years ago as auxiliary quarters for help at Ashcroft Manor, built before Cornwall sawmill, powered by now dry Cornwall Creek. Original domestics were Indians. Later, when Canadian Pacific Railway came as far as Ashcroft, construction crews brought many Chinese which were stranded at end of rail laying. Some found employment at bustling Ashcroft Manor, among them Wing Wo Ling, affectionately known as "Old Loy." Arriving at Manor about 1882, he soon showed skill as cook, presided over huge wood range many years. Buildings are surrounded by miles of sagebrush, not indigenous to area, brought in on hooves of cattle driven from Oregon, according to Mr. Parker, owner of Manor.

BARKERVILLE, B.C.

Canada was great green banks of timber ripe for the cutting. It was rivers teeming with salmon. It was mountains and creek beds glittering with golden gravel. And all of it was accepted as food and cover and for building canoes by a few Indians—a limitless supply for themselves and future generations.

To the browbeaten, half-starved English sailors whose ships ventured into West Coast coves, the wonderland was something else. It was freedom. Billy Barker was one of them. He was hungry for a new life and jumped ship when he heard the news about gold along the Fraser and its tributaries. Billy was tough. He got to the diggings on Williams Creek and set to work in his own unorthodox way to make a fortune. No geologist, he sank a shaft some distance from the stream itself, prompted by some inner light to explore the possibilities of a prehistoric stream bed or because it was the only spot available.

Billy and six partners, all Englishmen and most of them ex-seamen, began to dig August 13, 1862. When the hole reached 35 feet, a few superstitious ones wanted to quit. It was the 13th, a bad day. Their funds had run out, but lucky for them and the future of Barkerville, an "angel" who was reputed to be Judge Begbie of Richfield, staked them for a few more days.

At 50 feet down the men struck an old river channel. A shovel full of gravel was sent up and panned in the creek. It yielded $5. Struggling to control their elation, the men at the bottom filled the hoist bucket to the brim. This panned out $1,000. In the panic that followed everything came to a stop, except the men's feet which, after dancing, were headed for neighboring Richfield and its saloon.

The lack of one of these in the new camp was soon remedied. In less than a year there were half a dozen drink emporiums for the population of some 10,000. Since winter began to set in soon after the big discovery, and winter in the Cariboo was 40 below with deep snow, the first buildings were of logs, later of whipsawn lumber. Except for Chinatown on a short side street, all of Barkerville was strung along one single street. Buildings were elevated a few feet,

DENTIST'S OFFICE showing lifelike display — exhibit created with help of B. C. Dental Association and Dr. Lloyd Day of Quesnel.

EXHIBIT IN ORIGINAL DOCTOR'S OFFICE brings to life scene enacted many times when injuries were frequent. Figures were created by artist Mrs. Herbert T. Cowan of North Vancouver after detailed study of old days.

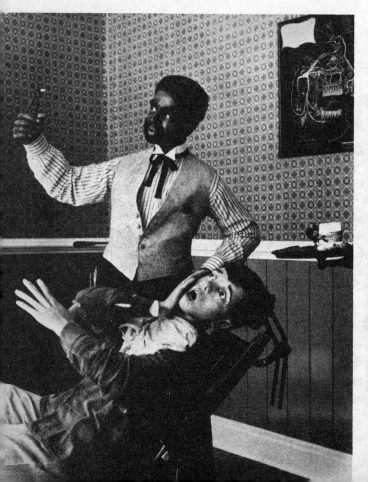

as were sidewalks, because miners would frequently dam the creek for a time in their hasty searchings of the gravel and Williams Creek would head for its former channel and tend to inundate Barkerville. And there were other hazards in the street. Oxen and other beasts of burden were not too sanitary, garbage was left anywhere and, except for August, the mud was kneedeep.

Billy Barker could take no real pride in all this growth. He was a worried man. The January after his strike he decided he could afford to be married since gold was pouring from the shaft in a blinding flood. On another 13th he married a widow in Victoria and brought her to camp. It is presumed the new Mrs. Barker had heard more than rumors of her husband's wealth, that his looks had not attracted her. At 42 he was wide and stubby, bowlegged and bearded. Most of the other miners were younger, better looking and Billy found it increasingly necessary to spend huge sums on his bride to bring back her attentions.

Although his company soon took some $600,000 from the hole in the creek bed, Billy went through his share quickly, dividing it between his wife and the saloons. As soon as it became evident his resources had struck bottom, his mate left the camp for greener pastures in company with a younger man. Abandoned and lonely, Billy soon spent what little was left and when the mine failed, he made a living cooking for road crews. Drinking and a persistent sore on his lip cost him one job after another and he wound up in the Old Men's Home in Victoria, dying of cancer July 11, 1894.

Meanwhile, Barkerville was mushrooming with new discoveries. The nearby Grizzly mine had a weekly payroll of $10,000. One "clean up" at the Raby claim yielded twenty pounds of gold and this was not unusual. The Caledonian at the edge of town brought in more than $5,000 a day for a time, the Ericson turning out nearly ninety pounds of gold every week. In 1865 this working paid a dividend of $14,000 a share.

Since the area not actually occupied by the town was packed solid with claims of this kind, Barkerville flourished and in the heedless rush burned to the ground in September, 1868. Flimsy stovepipes projected shakily through the tinder-dry roofs of late summer and showered sparks on the shingles. When rebuilt, the town resembled its earlier self except that spaces were left for side streets and walks in front of business establishments were connected at a level.

Some time before the fire, Barkerville had acquired a newspaper which was to exert a strong influence on the life of the camp—the *Cariboo Sentinel*. Items gleaned from its files reflect the feelings of the

day. Reports were coming in constantly of new strikes, the issue of May 10, 1866 carrying this item:

"We have been permitted to peruse a letter received by a gentleman on the creek from a friend, an old Cariboo miner who has been to the Blackfoot country. Writing from Walla Walla he says—'I have been to the Blackfoot mines. They are better in my opinion than Cariboo ever was and much more extensive the gold being of a much finer quality and all of it of a course (sic) nature, bringing readily $18 per ounce. The country is very accessible to the miner, he can pack his tools and grub on a horse, get astride of another and go just where he pleases. He can kill all the game he wants; I think the deer are in greater abundance than they are around Victoria. Bear, elk and mountain sheep are plentiful; the winter has been severe for this part of the country, the snow has been two feet deep.'" The writer of this letter was probably as much bemused by the ease of transportation as anything else for getting around in the Cariboo was notoriously difficult. However, the Blackfoot diggings were apparently something less than expected. An item from Cache Creek dated May 18 stated: "A good number of miners are on the way back from Big Bend and they give a horrid account of it."

Hard rock mining was attempted from time to time with discouraging results. Said the *Sentinel*: "Last fall some little noise was created by the discovery of a lode on the ridge that divides Williams

REMAINS OF ANCIENT SLEIGH, essential to long, hard winter life. Mining came to halt when wet gravel froze hard and water was not available for washing and panning. *Cariboo Sentinel* of May 14, 1866 reported: "Symptoms of a change in the weather — rained heavily whole afternoon. Apprehension felt for sudden rising of creek." Next issue said: "The creek is beginning to resume its appearance of summer activities and in another week, when the time of layover expires, we expect to see every old claim at work in a fair way of taking out pay . . . The banks are not yet thawed out to allow hydraulic washing to commence." Next week paper warned: "Miners would do well to bear in mind the period to which the claims were laid over by the Gold Commissioner expires on Sunday next, 20th inst. and that all ground must be represented by that date."

OLD BARKERVILLE welcomes arrival of fresh beef. Cattle are being driven up main street in old picture from Provincial Archives taken nearly 100 years ago. Water was not piped to individual houses but conveyed in wooden troughs to barrels in street (foreground). Some buildings are identifiable today, notably Anglican Church at end of street.

Creek from Grouse Creek . . . A shaft was sunk on the ledge to some depth and a ton of rock was got out and transmitted to San Francisco for assay; up to the present moment however nothing further is known respecting it; it is even asserted that the rock still lies on the wharf where it was landed in San Francisco untouched." The item ends on a querulous note: "Shall we ever get satisfactory results at that rate?" Apparently not, a later paragraph states. "A return has been received to the assay of the portion of the quartz sent to San Francisco last fall. The results have not been learned."

Although there was plenty of gold in Barkerville, the terrible road conditions in winter often kept food out and the *Sentinel* tells of near-famine: "There is not a pound of beef or mutton to be procured at any of the butchering establishments on the creek. At Richfield, we believe, there is a small quantity of fresh pork which sells readily at 62 cents a pound, Mr. Toomey and Mr. Clark are both out after cattle and are expected back in a few days; until then we will have to betake ourselves to the old fare of earlier times, beans and bacon, for a change." But even

beans and bacon were not always available and sometimes neither were such staple articles as candles. Again the *Sentinel*: "In consequence of the scarcity of candles, we notice several persons are availing themselves of a large quantity of beef tallow accumulated by them during the winter and are now busy converting it into candles which they readily sell at $1 per pound."

The advent of the first pack trains in spring was also news. The issue of June 4, 1866, joyously proclaimed: "A train of 20 pack animals being the first arrival for the season got in yesterday morning . . . brought in a load of potatoes which are being sold for 15 cents a pound." This cost must have been prohibitive for a later report had it: "The trail is in a very bad state but the expected arrivals of several later trains is expected to bring prices down considerably." A late storm delayed the trains and the next issue's column "From the Outside" carried the illuminating statement: "Due to wires being down we have no news."

The *Sentinel's* advertising columns also show an image of life as it was. Restaurants, saloons and

MAIN STREET OF TOWN is deserted in early morning. Town enjoyed main prosperity in 1860s and early '70s, was genuine ghost town for many years, reviving temporarily during excitement of dredge operations on neighboring Antler Creek in 1920s and on Pine Creek 1948-50. Other spurts came when Cariboo Quartz Mine opened for short life in '33 and gold mining in neighboring new town of Wells when Barkerville was home for workers. When restoration began some four years ago, about 20 people lived in once teeming city.

cafes were regular advertisers and not given to undue modesty. One stated: "Occidental Hotel and Restaurant—Thurbers and Lawlors, Props. This house has been fitted up on the restaurant principle with a view to the comfort of the public and will be conducted in a manner to ensure the satisfaction of those who are disposed to favor the proprietors with their patronage. Meals at all hours. Good beds. The bar is furnished with the best selection of Liquors and Segars."

The Oppenheimer Co. had a clearance sale and told the public: "Provisions, Liquors, Segars, Clothing, Boots, Shoes, Mining Tools, etc., at COST PRICE! to make room for new stock to arrive as soon as the roads are open." Saloons were also regular advertisers. Said one: "Great attraction! Every night at the Fashion Saloon. All lovers of the Terpsichorean Art are invited to call and enjoy themselves, when a hearty welcome to all will be extended. Good order observed."

Saloons and dancehalls maintained an attraction known as "Hurdy Gurdy Girls." The *Sentinel* describes them with something of a sniff: "They are

unsophisticated maidens of Dutch extraction, from 'poor but honest' parents, and morally speaking they are not what they are generally put down for. They are generally brought to America by some speculating, conscienceless scoundrel of a being commonly called a 'Boss Hurdy.' This man binds them in his service until he has received about a thousand percent for his outlay. The girls receive a few lessons in the terpsichorean art and are put into some kind of uniform with a headdress resembling in shape the top-knot of a male turkey. The Hurdy Gurdy style of dancing differs from all other schools . . . the more muscular the partner, the nearer the approximation of the ladies' pedal extremities to the ceiling, and the gent who can hoist the 'gal' the highest is considered the best dancer." It was generally known that these girls, besides cavorting publicly with the miners also indulged in some remunerative extracurricular activities in the backroom. It was said that during one such session an over-eager lover upset the heating stove and thus started the fire that devastated the town in 1868.

Remarkable and somewhat unique in a mining camp was the almost total absence of violence, shoot-

11

BILLY BARKER AND HIS TREASURED WATCH, a display in museum now maintained in Barkerville. Billy rests in Ross Bay cemetery at Victoria where he died. On evening of July 11, 1962 simple ceremony was held there honoring his memory in connection with dedication of Barkerville as Provincial Historic Park. Native of Barkerville, Miss Lottie Bowron pulled cord to unveil plaque. Service extolled Billy's generosity to out-of-luck miners, omitted his prodigality in saloons which resulted in dissipation of fortune taken from Williams Creek.

M.D.'S EQUIPMENT as found in old buildings of camp searched by restorers.

ings and lynchings in Barkerville, and this in spite of a population made up of youngish, mostly single miners from every walk of life and several countries. This was probably not due to more brotherly love than usual but because getting in and out of town was so hard. It was a task in summer and a quick getaway in winter was next to impossible. A man might think twice before pulling a gun.

There was some friction between the numerous Americans and the big segment from the British Isles. When nationalities conflicted, it was usually due to the inherent desire of the Americans to have the biggest and best of everything—but a sense of humor on both sides usually saved the day.

In point, was the flagpole incident. Martin's American-owned saloon boasted the tallest flagpole in town. From it waved the Stars and Stripes which the Canadians did not mind until the holiday celebrating the admission of British Columbia as a province into the Dominion drew near—the First of July. The day before, a few young Canadians went into the woods and found a tree that would make a taller flagpole than Martin's. They cut and dressed it, waited

for darkness and dug a ten-foot hole, erected the pole and rigging it with pulley and rope. Daylight revealed the new Canadian flag flying several feet higher than the American one. When the amazed Americans saw it, Martin was the first to break into a hearty laugh. He opened his saloon, invited everybody in and set up free drinks with Canadians as guests of honor. An international incident was averted.

It was a time when people favored every new nostrum and patent medicine and a profitable section in the *Sentinel* advertised these cure-alls. Wellington Delaney Moses, Barkerville's colored barber, was a steady contributor. His notice in the issue June 21, 1866, read:

"Moses Hair Invigorator—to prevent baldness, restore hair that has fallen out or become thin and to cure effectively Scurf or Dandruff. It will also relieve headaches and give the hair a darker and glossy color and the free use of it will keep both hair and skin in healthy state. Ladies will find the Invigorator a great addition to the toilet, both in consideration of the agreeable and delicate perfume and the great facility it affords in dressing the hair which when moistened with it can be dressed in any desired form, so as to preserve its place whether plain or in curls. When used on children's heads, it lays the foundations for a good head of hair."

Though Mr. Moses promised much he publicized evidence of miracles performed to back him up. "Sir," one letter he had received read, "in the years 1860 and '61, from long and severe illness my hair became very weak and was falling out in a most fearful manner. I was in dread of becoming entirely bald. After a few applications by you, and after using three bottles of the Invigorator my hair was restored and is becoming thick and strong as it ever was before."

Mr. Moses, emboldened by his success, ventured to install Barkerville's first bathtub. It was placed in the back room of his Shaving Salon and although everyone in town was aware of the novelty, its owner celebrated the great occasion by publicly inviting all to the "opening of the new Bathroom," adding discreetly—"Private entrance for ladies."

EXTERIOR OF ST. SAVIOUR'S. Building was started in 1869 with long period of sacrifice of personal health and finances of Rev. James M. Reynard. Arriving from Yorkshire about 1865, Reynard was aghast at lack of morals and worship, set to work with zeal that sapped his strength. With meagre funds, saloon was purchased, used as church Sundays, school weekdays. Fire of '68 destroyed it. Reynard wrote: "All my efforts and expenditures have been in vain." For a time he came close to giving up struggle for new church, then tried personal solicitation of merchants to no avail. Suddenly Barkerville had a change of heart, people and merchants rallying around pastor with funds. On Sunday, Sept. 24, 1870 first services were held in now venerable structure. Later near starvation and rigors of Cariboo winters without proper heat and clothing broke Reynard's health to point he was forced to leave pastorate, dying in '75. Church is almost same as he left it. Though it was not part of official restoration, the committee carefully added few boards and panes of glass. Plans under way for new foundation.

Prosperity could be read into the *Sentinel's* columns but the day came when it was painfully evident gold in Williams Creek was not going to last forever and the hopes for some fantastic lode in quartz outcroppings grew more and more remote. In June of 1868 L. A. Blanc had confidently held up his business as: "Photographer Artist. Cartes de Visita. Timbre de Poste, Portraits, Ambrotypes, Leather Pictures, Milanotypes, Views of Houses, Claims, etc. Single or Stereoscopic Portraits taken on White Silk, Linen or Cotton Cloth." In the '70s his newspaper insertions had fallen to "Great reduction in prices. L. A. Blanc wishes to inform his friends and the public that he has for a few months only Greatly Reduced His Prices to suit the times. Miners leaving for the new mines on the Peace River will do well to take advantage of this opportunity," and in the same issue appeared another notice: "All parties desirous of obtaining copies of their prescriptions for having them refilled will please call soon as I intend leaving for the Peace River mines." A line in smaller type followed hopefully: "Parties owing small accounts

INTERIOR OF ST. SAVIOUR'S ANGLICAN CHURCH. Beautiful vaulting of natural wood ceiling in Gothic design over apsidal recess was patterned after that in some English cathedrals. Bishop's chair is accurately fitted together without nails. Sacred structure is not exempt from vandalism, brass cross surmounting edifice for many years having been stolen in 1961. Cigarette butts are frequently thrown on floor.

will please call and settle same. James P. Taylor Drug Store."

In '66 a claim in the area could not be purchased at any price but the time came when they were hard to dispose of and such advertisements as this were common: "For Sale—one full interest in the MacLaren Claim." The MacLaren had been one of the best producers. During the Barkerville heyday, this news had appeared: "Above 160,000 taken out in two weeks. 1132 ounces washed up July 30. 2,620 ounces taken out in one week. The prestige of Cariboo is well sustained." Now, struggling to maintain optimism, the news ran: "The Mucho Oro Co. in Stout Gulch made expenses this week. The Good Hope Co. made wages for the week." Then the *Sentinel* became frankly despairing: "The Hope Co. have abandoned their ground."

A dwelling was not to be purchased for any money in '66 but as decay set in advertisements like these were placed in the paper. "For Sale—well built house pleasantly situated at the head of Stout's Gulch. Two rooms, woodshed and carriage house." And: "For Sale, a first class cabin near Barkerville, suitable for winter as it has a double roof."

More claims petered out, businesses failed as the population moved to the more promising Peace River diggings. Just as the camp had been filled with miners abandoning the California gold fields, Barkerville was now losing its people to a more glittering prospect. Before long even the loyal *Sentinel* was discontinued and that marked the end. Barkerville stood empty, forlorn.

In late years the Province of British Columbia became aware of the historical importance of the old camp and began a program of restoration. This has been carried on with attention to the minutest detail, hulks of buildings bolstered up without obvious changes, stairways long dangerous have been replaced with weathered and unpainted but stout boards to resemble the originals, countless other unobtrusive repairs and replacements made.

In August, 1962, just 100 years from the day Billy Barker made his big strike on Williams Creek, the Centennial Celebration was held in the old town, a fine museum dedicated by Premier A. C. Bennett marking the official opening of Barkerville Historic Park, after which the crowd pressed into the newly restored Theatre Royal to watch a special performance of "The Rough Diamond."

DEBRIS OF BUSY TIMES in Barkerville is piled in rear of firehouse and Theatre Royal. Fire protection was not thought vital in early days, town leveled in '68. Shortly before fire, Theatre Royal advertised "The Cariboo Amateurs will perform Blackstone's laughable farce 'A Kiss in the Dark' — interlude — Glees, Duets and Songs to conclude with Joseph Lynn's farce 'Fish Out of Water.' Adm. $1." Restoration started search through attics and storehouses of old camp, brought to light most furnishings of old theater. First play presented after refurbishing was "A Diamond in the Rough," produced from script in possession of Mrs. Joseph Wendle, longtime resident of town. Yellowed sheets bore lead pencilled note — "No good." Modern producers disagree. Play first staged in New York in 1841 brought howls of laughter for quaintness.

BENNETT, B.C.

How to get to the Klondike? The White Pass route from Skagway to Lake Bennett and down the mighty Yukon River was only one of several ways. At least six "trails" were available, most of them not fit for travel. If a man decided against gaining the headwaters of the Yukon, he could go up river, if the season was right and he could get passage, which the earliest rushers could not.

The Yukon River, after passing the site of Dawson City at the mouth of the Klondike, flows on into Alaska and thence to the Bering Sea via Norton Sound. This is north of the Aleutian Islands which separate all-year open waters from those closed by ice much of the year. In summer boats could slip through the Aleutians into Bering Sea, Norton Sound and the mouth of the Yukon via St. Michael which was usually free of ice by the middle of May. If the steamer was powerful enough to buck the seaward current she could proceed to Dawson City, a distance of about 1600 turbulent miles. Such a trip required at least three months from Seattle. This route was in use after the first year but could be used for only a few months, and by the time regular service — within seasonal limitations — was established the real rush was over.

Eastern Canadian newspapers advertised the "All Canadian" route overland from Edmonton and there was the Dalton Trail. Among the objections to these were their lengths. Without transportation a man could not bring his ton of supplies, which the Canadian authorities required for entry, let alone food and other immediate necessities.

There remained the two popular routes — Chilkoot Pass leading from Dyea and White Pass, beginning at Skagway. The Chilkoot began in a narrow gorge, rising steeply in 35 miles to a summit of 3,500 feet. White Pass took another ten miles to stretch more gently from Skagway to a ridge of 2,400 feet.

Here is a plateau dividing Alaska from Canadian British Columbia. After crossing the forbiddingly cold, windy area the plodding thousands again encountered small streams flowing north into myriad lakes forming the headwaters of the Yukon River, the largest of them Lake Lindeman and Lake Bennett. Most miners stopped at the latter to build their boats, others choosing to avoid the treacherous White Horse Rapids by traveling on foot to the end of the trail at Lake Laberge.

There were many ways to get up to either pass, some fantastically impractical. The simplest and surest was to climb on foot but this was a herculean job. A man could get himself up easily enough but he had to show a ton of supplies to the Canadian police at the boundary or be turned back as a potential indigent. This meant shouldering as much of the ton as possible, carrying the pack a mile or two, deposit it beside the trail while returning for a second load and then repeat the process until all supplies were produced for inspection at the summit.

CARCROSS was original home of Tagish Kate who with husband George Carmack made big strike. Suddenly wealthy, couple went to San Francisco to splurge in fancy living. Kate, left alone one day became lost but was found by blazes she notched in mahogany banisters. Deserted by Carmack, she returned to Carcross, lived in simple log cabin, wore cotton dresses, but retained necklace of gold nuggets from claim. She died in 1917. A brother, Tagish Charlie, also in on Carmack strike, was honored by government, being given Canadian citizenship and white man's privileges in saloons. With plenty of money he treated everyone and himself to point where he was spending whole time in jail, winding up broke in old Carcross home. Railroad bridge crosses lake at same point caribou did. While in cups one night, Charlie toppled from bridge drowning in cold lake waters.

OLD CHURCH, now in near ruin, is beautifully situated with view looking north down Lake Bennett. Picture was made in middle of June. About end of August snow will fall, lake freezing deeply for many months. Avalanches frequently roar down steep mountain sides, especially as spring approaches in May.

Naturally horses were in great demand but the few available were unsuited to the slippery, jagged ice, mud and mossy rocks. At some steep points where the trail rounded precipitous cliffs hundreds of animals were lost, falling to their deaths or mangled and abandoned. At one spot during the height of the rush the rocks at the bottom of the cliff were covered by dead and dying horses.

One fantastic scheme to ease transportation of gear was dreamed up by some high U.S. Government source. Helpful Uncle Sam sent agents to Norway for 500 reindeer and shipped them to New York at great cost. $10,000 more was paid to get them to Seattle where a chartered ship rushed them to Haines, near Skagway. It was another bureaucracy fumble. The reindeer could pull and pack men and supplies on level tundra but not on steep mountain passes — and there was no natural food

like lichens. In a few months most of them died of starvation, exhaustion and injuries. The fiasco would have created a national scandal had not the battleship *Maine* been blown up in Havana harbor and diverted public attention.

The Seattle Chamber of Commerce was flooded with letters from promoters, schemers and plain crackpots. One man said if the Chamber would help him financially he could quickly perfect his invention of an airplane that could fly forward, backward, straight up or down. Another man was building a covered "ice wagon" in which two men could sleep while two others pushed. But even without these idealistic contraptions many thousands did make it to the summit and on down to Lake Bennett.

This lake with its neighbor Lindeman at the head of the 2300 mile long Yukon offered a down-river route to Dawson City, 550 miles away, but

16

how about a boat? Few knew a boat from a bicycle let alone how to build one especially when they had to start with standing trees. And even they were scarce having been cut so far from the shore hauling was a problem. A few skilled boat builders made so much money showing others the tricks, they stayed on and were delayed getting to pay dirt.

Before the rush there was not one man on the bleak, wind-swept, icy shores of Lake Bennett. In one year there were 10,000 stampeders at the head of the lake. It was easily the largest tent city in the world. In the midst of all the boat building Mike King arrived with sawmill parts which he assembled and cut lumber for $250 a thousand feet which went fast to those who had the money.

Although snow and ice remained at the summit until the end of June it began to melt at the lake by the middle of May, after which the lake ice grew mushy and opened up in spots. As soon as chunks were floating clear there was an exodus of a vast fleet — skiffs, scows, dories and what have you. In a few days they had floated into Yukon Territory.

At one point the lake narrowed so much that immense herds of caribou were able to swim across. Tagish Indians lived here and shot game, the village called Carcross by the whites. It was here Carmack had met the attractive Indian girl Kate who shared his later discovery of gold on Bonanza Creek.

After negotiating these narrows, boats proceeded down the long lake encountering little trouble unless they were too early and met ice floes. Many crudely built barges fell apart when squeezed between the bigger chunks. However those who did start early, if they survived the ice hazards, were spared some torment caused by swarms of mosquitoes. Few men had the forethought to bring netting and those who did lived day and night with it draped from their hats. Yet far greater hazards were ahead. First came the narrow gorge called Miles Canyon, followed almost immediately by the much feared stretch of foaming water aptly named White Horse Rapids.

With all these problems and dangers many enterprising men not interested in mining itself began working on plans to make money by expediting travel from the head of Lynn Canal to the summits of the passes. The first of these ventures was a short railroad from Dyea to the head of the steep-walled gorge back of the town, the starting point of the Chilkoot Pass route. Next was the building of a steam operated tramway. Incredibly, dismantled steamboats were transported by this means to the head of Lake Bennett and reassembled for service to the lower outlet.

But the whole picture was even more radically changed by the White Pass and Yukon Railroad, promoted in England when efforts failed in the United States, the capital provided by Close Brothers of London. A Canadian railroad expert Michael J. Heney surveyed and planned the route with most of the work carried out by American engineers and contractors. The project was one of the most difficult and spectacular feats of railroading, right of way hacked out of vertical cliffs, across swamps, ice fields, deep canyons and house-sized boulders, in some places the grade being as much as four percent.

With no heavy construction equipment, all work was done by men, horses, shovels and black powder. In one instance an entire cliff, 120 feet high, 70 feet deep and 20 feet wide, was blasted completely away. All men and supplies had to be transported by boat from Seattle to Skagway, all communications carried the same way. As rails were laid down from Skagway, they carried material to the end of steel.

Much of the line was laid along the sides of steep slopes, workmen often plagued by thundering avalanches of snow which buried everything. At one spot near the bottom of a gorge an enormous rock, estimated at 100 tons, fell upon two men. The weight was impossible to lift or move and all that could be done for the men was to erect a cross on the boulder to mark their tomb.

Construction was proceeding simultaneously from the Whitehorse end and the rails met at Carcross, July 29, 1900. A gala celebration was scheduled, the last spike tapped in. Top-hatted dignitaries gathered to watch the invited guests, led by a senior army officer, drive the spike home, each taking a swing.

Aim was possibly affected by pre-ceremony quaffing. The first blow glanced off the steel, the next knocked the spike aslant. Wild cheers rose from the crowd which was well lubricated. After several more dainty or dubious blows, the spike "bloody but unbowed", the visitors adjourned to the nearest Carcross saloon and the trackmen took a new spike and did the job properly. The next month saw trains running and while the main rush was over, the line was busy with organized travel and freight transportation.

It operates a regular service today, carrying large freight tonnage over White Pass. Passengers express gasps as the little cars — the original ones — careen wildly over the narrow gauge tracks.

CAMERONTON, B.C.

It was a strange procession that moved down the ruggedly primitive trail. First came a man leading a horse hitched to a sleigh and on it, a wooden coffin. Inside this was a slightly smaller tin one holding the frozen remains of the woman who had married John Cameron and came with him to the Cariboo to find gold. The last member of the group struggling through the snow was John himself, both hands busy trying to keep the coffin from tipping over every time the sleigh careened over rocks or logs and steadying the bags of food and fifty-pound sack of gold on top of the coffin.

John and Sophia Cameron had been married in Cornwall, Ontario. They had set out for the new world, the West that was very far west, arriving in Victoria in March, 1862. They took the Cariboo Trail, reaching the site of what would be the boom town of Cameron in August.

Also heading for the gold fields along Williams Creek was Robert Stevenson. Along the way he had bought a bunch of horses in the Okanogan country, sold them in Lillooet for $10,000 and arrived on the creek as the only person likely to be endowed with money. He had prospected without settling on a claim for a month when the Camerons arrived. They became acquainted and were shortly partners. The association was a stormy one, marked by many quarrels and fallings out, but when the test came Stevenson was the only one to come to the aid of John Cameron.

There were other members of the company formed to pool resources and labor—Sophia and five more. When the time came to stake out the claim, its location was decided upon only after heated arguments and Cameron was all for backing out. It was Friday and he said he would start no venture on such an unlucky day. Persuaded to go ahead, he insisted on a location on the left side of the creek, Stevenson holding out for the right. Later this man wrote: "If he (Cameron) had followed my advice the claim would have paid double the million dollars it did." The

LEGENDS ON MANY HEADBOARDS in old Cameronton cemetery are indistinct, others speaking clearly of tragedies of long ago. Cameron himself chose site. Someone wrote of first burial — for Peter Gibson, July 24, 1863: "One of Cariboo Cameron's men died and they hauled him up on the side of the hill and buried him there." Marker at left in photo reads: "In memory of Chartres Brew, born at Corsefin, County Clare, Ireland, 31 Dec. 1815. Died at Richfield 31 May 1870. Gold Commissioner and County Court Judge. A man imperturbable in courage and temper endowed with a great and varied administration capacity. A most ready wit, a most pure integrity." Burial ground is only evidence of Cameronton. Decayed remnants of once roaring camp persisted on banks of creek, were finally engulfed in maw of dredge.

location was at last agreed upon and named The Cameron August 22, 1862. On the same date in December, Stevenson said: "We struck it very rich at 22 feet. It was thirty below. Dick Rivers was in the shaft and Halfpenny and I were at the windlass. Rivers called up from the shaft: 'The place is yellow with gold. Look here, boys. He held up a piece of rock the size of a dinner pail. I laid down on the platform and peered into the shaft. I could see gold standing out on the rock as he held it." Chunks of frozen rock and gravel came up in the bucket with frenzied speed to be thrown into the meagre flow of the stream to get it thawed out for panning. What little water they had froze in the intense cold of the Cariboo winter and though the wealth of the claim had been established, operations had to be suspended.

But Sophia never learned of the gold pouring into her husband's pockets. After only a few months which seemed like years to her "in this God-forsaken wilderness" she had died and was buried inside a small cabin, the first of a series of her tombs. Over her grave her husband swore she would not have to rest in this "womanless land" any longer than necessary and set to work feverishly to harvest as much gold as he could.

In the middle of winter he decided the time had come, removed the body of his wife from the grave and tried to find someone to help him get it to Victoria, offering $12 a day and a prize of $2,000 to anyone who would aid him. There were no takers. It was then his partnership with Robert Stevenson panned out. "Bob" offered to go along on the dangerous trip "but not for gold." Cameron collected all the gold he could, the supply augmented by a sizable amount

WATER SEEPAGE FROM HIGHER Williams Creek was constant hazard in mine shafts, removed by pumps operated by Davis or Cornish water wheels like this one on Morning Star claim. Flume, at top, carried water to buckets. Central shaft worked pump as with windmill.

Billy Barker raised by public subscription in Barkerville, just above Cameronton. Only Cameron knew how much he was taking along for expenses but the bag was supposed to weigh fifty pounds. This, with supplies, was placed on top of the coffin and the partners set out. In many places the trail angled so sharply stakes had to be driven in a row on the bank to keep the sleigh with its precious burden from overturning. When it did slide off the trail, both men struggled mightily to get the four-hundred-pound vehicle and load back on track and headed in the right direction. At one bad spot the men met a miner who volunteered his services in getting the load the rest of the way. With only a few upsets, the party finally arrived at Fort Douglas where they boarded a steamer. But even the boat had trouble. Unable to buck a squall, it had to lay to in a cove to wait for better weather.

In all, the trip to Victoria required 36 days, the arrival being at the end of April. Another funeral and burial was held for Sophia, with Cameron and Stevenson as the only mourners. The latter returned to the diggings but Cameron waited for the November arrival of a ship to take him and the body to Panama. Once again his wife's remains were exhumed and from Panama taken to Cornwall.

Upon arrival at Christmastime, there was another funeral service at which most of Sophia's relatives were present but she was not yet to rest undisturbed. A vicious rumor was circulated purporting Cameron had killed his wife, disposed of her body and smuggled a cache of gold back home in the coffin. So again the casket was opened to the light of day showing Sophia well preserved by the combination of freezing weather and liquid spirits in the tin liner. The fourth burial was the final one.

While Cameron was establishing a farm near the grave, spending much of the gold dust which had come on the long trail with his wife's body, events were happening fast in the British Columbia town that bore his name. In the boom, Cameronton had extended itself to the edge of Barkerville which had likewise grown to fuse with Richfield. These three towns along Williams Creek made a continuous street some three miles long with no appreciable indication of the beginning or end of any one. Barkerville had the newspaper, the *Cariboo Sentinel* and carried news and advertising from Cameronton as freely as those more local. One paid notice dated May 10, 1866 read: "Cameronton Reading Room and Circulating Library—$2 per month. Parties are solicited to subscribe. John Bowron, Librarian." Another in the same issue stated: "Billiard and Bowling Saloon. C. Fulton, Prop. There is no distillery in this establishment. Strychnine and rotgut find no place here."

Sporting events were duly chronicled. A display appeared May 10: "Grand Entertainment—Best Layout of the Season! No Humbug! No Bilk! A grand exhibition of the noble art of self-defense will be given at Loring's Saloon, Cameronton, May 12, 1866, on which occasion the following gentlemen will appear—Mr. George Wilson in glove fight with any man in Cariboo for the sum of $500. Harry Shannon will be matched with George Fairbrother to be followed by four other fights. The entertainment will be interspersed with Songs and Music suitable for the occasion. Big Time. Everybody Come. Admission—Front Seats $2 Back Seats $1. Doors open 7 ½ o'clock Commence at 8 o'clock." Shortly after this a "Society Item" was seen in the columns of the *Sentinel*, headed: "Sparring Exhibition. We understand the entertainment came off on Saturday evening last, at Cameronton, and was well patronized by lovers of the manly art. The affair passed off very satisfactorily and was the source of some little profit to the manager."

On May 17, 1866 this notice appeared: "Miners' Ball and Concert on the Queen's Birthday, May 24th. Mrs. Clunes begs to inform the miners of Williams Creek, Lowhee Creek, Grouse Creek and Van Winkle that she intends giving a Benefit Ball and Concert on the 24th of May, the best ever given on Williams Creek when she respectfully solicits the patronage of the public." The report on this festive affair appeared May 28. "Mrs. Clunes Ball and Concert came off at Cameronton on the Queen's Birthday and was well attended. The music was first class and the dancing was kept up to a late hour in the morning, everything passed off pleasantly."

Meanwhile in the Old Country, Cameron was not doing at all well with his farm. He had spent almost all the fifty pounds of gold but while there was still some left, he gave up and returned to the diggings to recoup his fortune. But things were different on Williams Creek now. The old days of scooping up gravel laden with nuggets were long gone. The ones of mechanized mining had arrived and Cameron did not have the cash for a new start. The good claims were taken up and there was no place for the stranger he had now become.

Unexplained is what happened to his interests in Cameronton. There seems to be no record of money being sent to him while in Cornwall or any waiting for him on his return to the claim. It is supposed he sold everything before he left the creek. But it is recorded he became a broken wreck of a man and died exactly fifteen years from the day he left Victoria with Sophia's body. He was buried in the cemetery overlooking the scene of his sudden rise to wealth and of his heartbreak.

COALMONT, B.C.

Just previous to November 19, 1858, when the British Columbia mainland across the straits from Vancouver Island was proclaimed a Crown Colony, an exploration by John Alison turned up an open outcropping of coal in the banks of the Similkameen River. "The vein was fully exposed," he reported. "It was very thick with interlaced seams of resin all through it. You could set it afire with a match. It seems strange that nature had not done it with a bolt of lightning long ago." Trappers and homesteaders hastened to load toboggans and sleighs to transport the new and free fuel home.

This was in an untouched wilderness, teeming with wild animals. Walter Moberly in his *Rocks and Rivers of British Columbia* gives a vivid picture of an encounter with one of them. In the spring of 1860 he "had entered into a contract in partnership with Mr. Edgar Dewdney to build a trail from Fort Hope on the Fraser River to the Similkameen River on the east side of the Cascade Range, in order to reach the diggings on the latter river where gold of fine quality had been discovered.

"Meeting with a very severe accident, I was laid up for some days in a miserable swamp, with only an Indian boy for my companion. When I felt a little better, I rode a mule down to a small log storehouse which we had at a little lake.

"I arrived in the evening and soon lay down to rest in the lower of two bunks in one corner of the house. As I lay there watching the moon shine through a large square opening in the roof that served the purpose of a chimney, I heard something walking on the mud-covered roof and quietly got up with my revolver. I thought it might be an Indian intent on stealing some of our supplies or rum, of which we kept a good supply in the house. I saw what I took to be a hand coming down through the opening, evidently feeling what was below. This was repeated several times, when I managed to get into such a position as to leave the moonbeam between myself and the invader. Instead of an Indian I made it out to be a panther, this making me very uncomfortable. As soon as the moonlight came between us I fired, and as I found in the morning some blood on the roof, I must have hit the brute."

One cougar shot in the area by Charlie Shuttleworth measured 9 feet, 2 inches in length. It weighed 240 pounds and "was rolling in fat." The hunter said the animal would kill an average of two deer a week. Encounters with bears were frequent. Trapper Frank Le Farge was walking toward Hope one evening as darkness was settling. He vaulted over a large log on the trail, landing squarely on a bear's back. He backed off and although the bear was as startled as he was, it charged. La Farge was forced away from his gun but somehow managed to get at his knife as he tried to scrape loose from the slavering jaws and sharp claws. He stabbed frantically and finally struck a vital spot, both he and the bear collapsing. Only the bear died. Another trapper, George Aldous, happened along shortly to help La Farge to the little hospital at Chilliwack where he recovered in a few weeks.

Before the turn of the century, Henry Younger Lowe was freighting on the old Cariboo road to the north and not having much work as the gold mines were just about depleted. When he left home in Wales he had told the folks: "I won't be back until I have made my fortune," and since he had not, he drifted south to the scenic valleys of the Similkameen and Tulameen.

Acquiring some land near Otter Lake about 1905, he built a log house in which he lives today. Others stopped at the site on a level piece of ground at first called Otter Flat, then Tulameen. Most of the Lillooet Indians picking berries and hunting in the area were friendly and remained for a time, slowly drifting away as more settlers came in. Hank Lowe built houses, among them the first board house in the growing town, selling them to the new people.

He spent much time hunting, ranging the hills and valleys, and when the Great Northern Railway needed coal to fire the locomotives of trains for the projected route to a point 26 miles north at Blakemere, the line sought out the man who knew the country best—Henry Lowe. The young Welshman soon convinced the man he refers to affectionately as "Sam Hill" there was plenty of coal available, sufficient to fuel the locomotives at this point for many years to come.

Henry is vague about details of what happened in the ensuing struggle for power between the Great Northern and Canadian Pacific, saying only: "The C.P.R. won out and that was the end of Sam Hill." The new line continued to take most of the coal.

During the early days of railroad construction, Tulameen and Coalmont boomed. Young Lowe took on other jobs such as laying the foundations for the pretentious new Dominion Hotel in 1912. It was built by a man named McRea, usually called "Mac." He had espoused a wealthy English widow for his second wife and it was she who financed the enterprise.

After several years of successful operation, the hotel began to lose patronage, because Mac was "acting queerly," it seemed. Then for several days the proprietor was not seen around the hotel. Hank and several others broke into the now shabby and empty Dominion and found Mrs. McRea lying on a bed, blind from cataracts. She had no idea where her husband was.

Hank took to the mountains and finally came upon McRea. "The man had no gun and no haversack," he relates, "and he stared at me like a wild man. I said to him, 'Mac, what's the matter with you? Why don't you come down to the hotel with me?' He stared some more without a word and turned away. I said to him, 'The hell with you then,' and left him. He was never seen again."

A large coal mining operation was started on the mountain directly above nearby Coalmont and Granite Creek. The latter had been a fabulous gold camp and now on the decline, offered a ready-made bunch of miners who had only to change their trade skills for coal. Perry Wilson and Blake Burns were friends and partners, holding the most shares in the new venture, and gave parts of their names to the town developing on the mountain—Blakeburn.

COALMONT IS SLEEPIER today than in 1912 when *Coalmont Courier* was distributed on streets. Paper carried banner head on front page —"Circulates in every home in Princeton, East Princeton, Tulameen, Aspen Grove, Merrit, Nicola, Hedley and Keremeos and around the Terrestrial Globe." Editor Ed Clark confidently predicted Coalmont "is the city of destiny, the coming coal metropolis of Southern British Columbia, with a population of 10,000 in the near future." One advertisement urged hesitant buyers of Coalmont real estate: "Take time by the forelook — she has no back hair." Although several streams ran close to community they were usually contaminated by mining operation so water supply came from wells like this one in center of town. (Little black dog, Toody, author's constant —and hammy — companion, managed to sneak into picture as signature.)

Hank Lowe was in on that town's beginnings. "I hauled the first frame bunkhouse up there," he said, "before there was any road. I'd haul up supplies, too. If there was heavy fall of snow when I was up there, I'd fill about eight sacks full of coal, pile them on a toboggan made of a twelve-inch piece of lumber, let out a whoop and a holler and the horses would tear down the hill, making a trail for the rest of them." The bakery had remained in Granite Creek and owner F. M. Cook continued to bake bread, carrying it up the Blakeburn miners.

Lowe had located four veins at Blakeburn, each known by a numeral in order of their operation. As the vein was penetrated the "hanging wall" or roof was supported by pillars of coal, two or more feet thick. When the end of the vein was reached, further exploration was made to determine whether the vein was only "faulted," continuing in another direction a few feet away, or whether there was no more coal. If the latter, equipment and men were withdrawn from the workings, the pillars mined out as the men re-treated. This naturally caused collapse of the hanging wall.

The quality of Similkameen coal which made it unsafe to stockpile at the mills because of spontaneous combustion, now worked to cause the province's worse disaster. Veins 1, 2, and 3 had been finished without incident but 4 lay smouldering, and on August 13, 1930, all hell broke loose. Hank Lowe tells the story.

"I was up on the mountain when I heard the noise but at first I didn't know what it was. I hurried down to Tulameen and met Mrs. McIntosh on the street. I asked her what was the matter. She threw her apron over her head and burst into sobs, saying: 'They're all dead.' I knew then because we had disasters like that in the mines in Wales, my uncle killed in one. I hurried to the store and found a list posted with the names of all the young fellows that had been in the mine at the time, 48 of them. Next day we knew they were all dead for sure, suffocated by deadly carbon monoxide fumes."

The men were buried in the Princeton cemetery with services by Catholic and United Churches, the sad series of funerals beginning with Albert Cole, 19, and ending with John Smith, 36. For their families a relief fund of $33,000 was raised in Princeton. It helped greatly but now the "Hungry Thirties" had begun. Blakeburn mines were closed after the disaster, never to reopen. The collieries at Coalmont at the bottom of the "mountain of coal" ceased to work when the coal supply was shut off. Tulameen, with its beautiful Otter Lake which area had served as a residential section for the men and families also died when they went elsewhere to work. Granite Creek was already long dead, the ring of ghost towns now in full circle.

OLD DOMINION HOTEL rears its bulk in lonely isolation at Tulameen which was close enough to serve Coalmont as residental section. Was built by "Mac" McRae in wildly turbulent, prosperous period of railroad construction. Smaller hotel nearby was put up by Lars Anderson. Until railroad tracks were completed, bars in both were three deep with thirsty workers. Depression came with end of railroad building, smaller hotel burning to ground, perhaps man-fired. Asked if he thought Dominion's owner was responsible, oldest inhabitant Hank Lowe said in lowered voice: "Son, as sure as you're born, he did it. Maybe not himself but in those rough days it was easy enough to get a couple of transients drunk and they'd do anything." Tulameen, dead as coal mining town, lives meagerly as resort. Beautiful Otter Lake is close by, cottages lining shore whose occupants fish in summer, hunt in fall.

COPPER MOUNTAIN AND ALLENBY, B.C.

"It was the middle of the night. Flames lit the sky and people were screaming so that in no time everyone in camp was awake and saw the big three-story bunkhouse was afire. There was a balcony on the third floor, a man on it begging for someone to catch him when he jumped but he was so large and heavy no one was willing. He just went back into the flames to die. Several others were trapped and burned to death. These and the men killed fighting the flames made eight lives lost. And in the morning when the ashes were cool enough to investigate it was found a ninth man had been dead before the fire started. He lay on his cot, a knife in his back."

Those are Etta Ferguson's words describing her experiences in the devastation at Copper Mountain on March 18, 1928. She was born in the mining camp and spent all her early life in the rough-and tumble before the huge Granby Mining Company expanded the "hole in the ground" operation. And the stirring events that occurred before her father came to work in the mine were told and retold as she walked her dolls over the ore tailings. Etta is Mrs. William Ferguson now living with her husband and three teen-age children on a farm at the base of the last steep grade up Copper Mountain.

"Thirty-five years ago," she continues, "mining there was very much different from the big Granby operation. All the copper was taken out of a deep shaft, the opening just a hole in the ground. When I was a little girl, my mother would let me walk to work with my father, whose name was Alexander Corci. And how I shuddered and cried with fright when I saw him crawl down into that black hole on a flimsy rope ladder. After that mother discouraged my going and I'm glad she did because one day father stumbled and fell a long way down. He was badly hurt and suffered for years before he died."

The area along the river called Similkameen is rich in Indian legend and the stream links the many mining towns from near Hedley on the south to Tulameen on the north. Before the river existed cataclysmic upheavals formed the mineral deposits and then came violent volcanic outburst which lifted the very rugged ridges including Copper Mountain. Then deep valleys were gouged out in an icy glacial period, one of the long troughs occupied by the rushing Similkameen.

The first white men in the Similkameen, Okanogan and Tulameen Valleys were fur traders, including those of the Hudson's Bay Co., organized in 1670. The period when fur was king extended well into the 1800s. One of the trappers was James Joseph Jameson, born in Kentucky in 1828, who had ten children, James, Jr., being born in the Kamloops, B.C., area August 26, 1864. The father and family settled in the Similkameen Valley in '82. Out of his life came the discovery of copper in the area.

OPEN-PIT OPERATION introduced dangers to aboveground population, not existing in days of deep shaft mining when hazards were confined to miners in underground passages.

The elder and junior Jamesons were hunting on the mountain and although they had plenty of meat for their first winter both had new rifles and wanted to try them out. After some hours without success on the rough and heavily timbered peak both saw a deer and both fired at the same moment. The deer went down and lay still until James, Jr., walked almost up to it, when it scrambled up and disappeared into the timber. Chagrined, the hunters stared at the spot where the deer had lain and the father continued to stare after the son had turned away. Plain to be seen in the rock was the bright greenish tinge of copper.

The Jameson family seems to have "sat on" their find for ten years until their friend, R. A. Brown, interested in trapping, visited at the home and learned of the discovery. The claim was recorded by Brown and Jameson in October, 1892, and the first mine worked was the Sunset, followed in rapid succession by the Oriol, Jennie Silkman, King Solomon and others.

All these were ordinarily successful but because the ore was refractory, treatment difficulties prevented any big success. But by 1914, when Pardoe Wilson surveyed for a railway line to Copper Mountain and Princeton at the junction of the Similkameen and Tulameen, things began to look up. Labor troubles, which were to harass operations at intervals to the very end, delayed actual shipping of the ore until October, 1920. The war then forced closure by dropping prices to an unprofitable thirteen cents.

The nearby town of Princeton (so named because the Prince of Wales stopped there) was suffering ups and downs with the fortunes of the copper mines and had become a virtual ghost town with the low ebb suffered by the Canada Copper Corporation which had acquired the controlling interest in the mines.

In 1923, the giant in Canadian mining operations, Granby Smelting and Power Company, Ltd., was running out of raw material in its massive holdings at various locations and sent men to look into the possibilities of exploiting the undeniably rich deposits on Copper Mountain. When this news leaked out, Princeton began to breathe again. Actual activity began when Canada Copper Corporation was absorbed

HEADQUARTERS AND RESIDENCE for mine superintendents overlooks densely forested hills around Copper Mountain. Copy of picture was currently sent to former resident, Mrs. Etta Ferguson who replied: "You can imagine how I will treasure my picture since the beautiful bungalow burned to the ground after you were here."

COPPER MOUNTAIN STREET SCENE. Enough old residences remained at time of photographer's visit in August of 1962 to to give town form, have since been leveled by fire along with predecessors.

MESS HALL AND COOKHOUSE, latter with enormous ranges, stand among wreckage of other buildings. Tree is *Pseudotsuga douglasi,* commonly Douglas "fir," distinguished from true fir by cones hanging beneath branches instead of growing erect.

25

by the Granby interests and one of its subsidiaries, Allenby Copper Co., developed huge smelting plants at Allenby near Princeton at the bottom of the steep grade from the mines. Raw ores were now loaded directly into railway cars at the lower level opening of the mine and run by gravity to the refinery.

Mines and smelters were brought to full capacity in 1926 and the following years were golden ones for all concerned. Temporarily there were no labor disputes and prices were satisfactory. Little shaft mining was done, during the summer months half the ore taken out of the Mountain coming from three open pits or "glory holes." In 1926, 665,000 tons of ore went down the steep grade to the Allenby mills.

There were 44 individual houses for families of miners on the peak as well as bunkhouses, mess halls and showers, etc., for 218 single men. A huge company store stood on an eminence, rented to a Princeton man, W. A. Wagenhauser. Large office buildings and machinery houses were built and the mountaintop camp took on the aspect of a good-sized city. Then on March 18, 1928 came the tragedy of fire which Etta Ferguson experienced.

All the victims were buried in Princeton cemetery on March 23 except one which was sent to Penticton. An investigation was launched into the murder without conclusive results yet a few facts were turned up. The victim, Ralph P. Bassett, had won a lot of money in a poker game the previous evening and a man known to have quarreled with him was seen to remove his belongings from the bunkhouse before the fire and leave town in a hurry the morning after. This man was never tracked down. Confusing was the sidelight that, a few days later, the body of a Chinese worker was found hanging from a beam. It was apparently a suicide, nothing definite linking him to the murder.

Etta Ferguson relates another incident of the raw life. "It was gruesome but no more so than many other accidents in the mines. Wally Beckman, a man independent and intolerant of company rules, refused to wear his safety belt while shoveling ore down the last chute at the top of the vertical shaft leading to the ore cars below. One day the man guiding the down-coming ore so it would be spread evenly, noticed the shoveler's hat coming down. Then came his head and other parts until the whole body arrived."

MINERS PASSED THROUGH this building on way to shaft opening. In spite of some serious accidents, overall safety factor in mines was high. When shaft was abandoned in favor of open pit, it was blasted shut but continues to sink. Town is now posted as being extremely dangerous.

ONE OF "GLORY HOLES" resulting from open-pit operation. As vein was opened up, operation became increasingly expensive as ground on top, "overburden," had to be removed in ever-increasing amounts. Nevertheless, with modern machinery, this type of mining is still more economical than deep shaft.

26

ALLENBY, some 10 miles below Copper Mountain mines, in middle distance of photo, may seem like thriving city but is entirely abandoned except for skeleton crew maintaining and guarding expensive machinery. About one-fourth of workers in heyday resided in company-built section complete with movie house and stores, now all moved or destroyed. One-fourth of workers lived in nearby Princeton.

And a brighter note. A big celebration was held on the Mountain Friday, April 11, 1930, when the long-planned-for community hall was dedicated. In the beautiful dance area, 72' x 42', speeches were made, a bountiful repast served and the big dance lasted all night. This happy spirit of fiesta held over for several weeks but in May, Lt.-Gov. R. R. Bruce, at a reception given for him on the Mountain, announced a fact already whispered, that the mines would soon be closing. Again labor troubles, falling copper prices and depression had won out. He voiced the hope that "the trade winds will soon blow again."

The years following were ones of desperate effort for miners and smelter men just to stay alive. Work of any kind was almost impossible to get. Yet on June 12, 1937, the work whistle blew once more. Amid general rejoicing a trainload of ore left the mountaintop and was sent to Allenby where the smelters were fired up and ready. The activity was marred by a bad accident in August, at four in the afternoon, when a

man cage crashed to the bottom of a shaft due to failure of the hoist apparatus. Drs. R. J. Wride and Paul Phillips are given credit for saving the lives of all but one of the seriously injured men. But the mines were operating again, the people making livings and almost everyone was happy.

The exception was the company itself. Granby was having a hard time in the fall of 1939 to defend the fact it was shipping copper concentrates to Japan. There was little consolation in the fact that the Canadian and British governments were giving full approval to the deal.

Criticism was not too blatant for Granby meant too much to the community. Since it had reactivated the mines and smelters in 1937, wages alone amounted to $4 million and millions more had been spent for equipment, in income taxes, etc. However, when Japan attacked Pearl Harbor, Canada was soon at war and shipments came to an end.

During 1952 the crew working on the mountaintop

27

totaled 560 with 431 underground. Together with the men working in the Allenby smelters, the grand total on the Granby payroll was 853. Yet the rosy picture was not to last. In April of '53, General Manager J. A. C. Ross announced that due to poor prices, the entire operation would cease forthwith. This meant complete abandonment of Copper Mountain and Allenby, a crushing blow to Princeton as well. All buildings on the Mountain have since been destroyed, all residences at Allenby removed, the permanent buildings at the smelter remaining.

The one-time big town on Copper Mountain with its schools, stores and other buildings now presents a "scorched earth" aspect. Etta Ferguson presumes the company, if it ever does resume operations, will scoop up the whole place in open pit ore removal. "But," she adds, "it is beginning to look as though that will never happen. For a while we were looking forward to seeing the cars going up the mountain grade again. Now we feel it would be too bad if they did. Things are very peaceful here as it is."

CORE SAMPLINGS by the hundreds of thousands filled two buildings, made at frequent intervals over many years to determine direction of vein. Cylindrical cores were split in two, carefully laid in grooves in drawers and numbered to be compared with records.

SETTLING LAKE created by retaining dike, when tailings began to foul sparkling waters of Similkameen River. Solids have appearance of fine sand, are ground residue when copper concentrates removed from finely crushed ore.

WILD DAYS IN THE BUSH

Fort Steele, Fisherville, Wild Horse, B.C.

It was the biggest Independence Day celebration held in Canada and very possibly the last. Montana liquor was flowing freely before July 4 and a good share of it into one Walker and "Yeast Powder" Bill. They agreed to disagree very violently and the crowd demanded a shoot-out. Bill's first shot went wild and Walker's first took Bill's thumb. This aggravated him mightily and he shot Walker dead.

Yankee prospectors smelling gold paid little heed to international boundaries in 1863. The story of how a party from notorious Hell Gate, Montana, founded a mining camp in British Columbia, would long ago have been forgotten but for a journalistic curiosity, the Fort Steele *Prospector*.

The long defunct paper was produced on a typewriter and reproduced by mimeograph. A complete file is owned by Basil G. Hamilton, of Invermere, B.C. The copy dated 18 April, 1896 begins: "The following facts relating to the early days on Wild Horse Creek have been learned from some of the old timers still living in the country."

The article tells of a half-breed named Findlay and two companions hailing from Frenchtown, fifteen miles northwest of Missoula, roaming the Kootenay country in hopes of finding placer gold. The men did discover a rich deposit in the shape of "pumpkin seeds" (perhaps the same type of nuggets called "melones" by Mexicans in Sierra streams. By late summer the party gleaned $700 worth of the little flat nuggets and with the first flakes of snow, packed up and headed for home, fearing to be trapped in the wild, inaccessible country.

They stopped at the Hudson's Bay post on the Tobacco Plains and found a buyer for their gold in the factor, a man named Linklater. Although the only white resident there he must have spread the news for the next spring several parties formed in the area and headed for the upper Kootenay country to search for Findlay's find.

Perhaps with inside information, one party of fifteen from Hell Gate found the place called Findlay Creek. It was still covered with snow and lacked pasturage for their mounts so the men retraced their tracks to a lower elevation where the

WINDSOR HOTEL was built in 1895 as Delgardno House by Robert D. Mather. Registers contain such illustrious names as Benjamin Harrison, Grover Cleveland, William McKinley, Sir William Laurier-Jones Skinflint, Paris, France(?). Present official status is as Fort Steele Historic Park. In early days building was encircled by fancy-trimmed balcony.
One year was enough for Northwest Mounted Police headed by Major Sam Steele to pacify disgruntled natives without aid of stockade or mounted guns. His tact and understanding receives most credit for success. Brief presence of Mounties was responsible for founding of busy town that survived as long as river traffic was most important means of transportation and gold was found in paying quantities.

grass was already several inches high. They all went to work in the creek, finding a little color and more as they worked upstream. Then they hit the bonanza, a deposit that kept them all busy right there, nobody going up to Findlay Creek even when the snow there melted. One man heard a sound on the bank, looked up from his pan to see a fine shiny black cayuse stud horse. "Stud Horse Creek," the place became.

Amounts of gold taken from the river are almost unbelievable. One claim alone, staked by Bob Dore, yielded $7,000 in a single day. Even ordinary days averaged $3,500. Yet the miners could not eat the gold. With unlimited resources food was so scarce some men almost starved. In the early spring of 1865 flour sold there for $1.25 a pound when it could be found, tobacco $15 and all else in proportion. Beef became unobtainable. A herd of sheep was driven in and they sold for 50c a pound on the hoof. Of a total summer population of 3,000, 800 miners wintered over. Drivers of the first trains with food supplies from the Flathead Mission in Montana found on May 15 only 400 men in camp, the others out hunting or fishing for food.

A year or two later found better conditions at the camp called Fisherville, after Jack Fisher, a prominent member of one of the first parties. In that first village a double row of log cabins was built almost on top of the first diggings and when it was found the best ground extended beneath them, Fisherville had to go. Without too much regret, as annual freshets had undermined them

anyway, the miners tore the buildings down as fast as digging advanced.

In the meantime a new town was going up on a higher bench above Stud Horse Creek. Miners thought it should be named after the creek but by now there was government of a sort, more or less under control of P. O. Reilly, Gold Commissioner. Said Reilly, "This will be a permanent city. Although we are a womanless community of 3,000 men, the ladies are bound to come in eventually. Think how embarrassing the name Stud Horse would be to them." His solution was a compromise acceptable to the majority, the less rugged "Wild Horse."

Although the new camp proved as transient as its predecessor, it is estimated hundreds of men were making $3,000 to $6,000, some up to $20,000, in the few months of good weather. Fisher's company with six partners took $1 million in 1865, Dore Company with ten, $150,000. Hundreds of nuggets here far exceeded the little pumpkin seeds, ranging up to a pound, one a giant of 32 ounces. As most of the miners were Americans an estimated total of $5 million was going to Walla Walla and Missoula. Again estimating, a conservative total of $17 million was harvested up to 1896.

In one of those big production years came the Fourth of July bust that found "Yeast Powder" Bill a murderer. Whatever his true name (some accounts call him "Yeast Porter" Bill) he got away, making camp near Brewery Creek where he was found asleep, rolled up in a blanket. Bob Dore pulled a gun on him and herded him back to town,

VERY OLD STORES strung along north side of road leading to Wild Horse Creek, mecca of trout fishermen. At extreme left is glimpse of ferry office, possibly oldest building in Fort Steele and typical of early log structures.
Larger complex was also by Galbraith brothers, replacing earlier log buildings in 1890s. Building with porch was store, in between saloon and right, hardware, feeds, livery stables. View looks northeast, road leading left into gulch of Kootenay River.

the miners electing a sheriff, judge and jury for trial purposes. It lasted only a few minutes, Y. P. Bill being acquitted on condition he leave the country forthwith. Not long after this Constable John Lawson was killed while attempting to arrest a horse thief named Brown who was later caught at a creek near Bonner's Ferry, Idaho, and slain, the creek still bearing the name Brown.

Wild Horse was the seat of government some twenty years, though without permanent officers of the law, circuit judges stopping at intervals to take care of accumulated cases of transgression. Gold mining gradually changed from panning the placers to deeper digging, then to hydraulic operations on a vast scale. When the yield became scanty the companies closed down and miners began to move away until in 1882 there were only eleven whites working their claims. Following the universal pattern, more easily satisfied Chinese then took over the placers.

One of the first miners here was John Galbraith who held land claims from Wild Horse Creek to the Kootenay River. In 1865 he decided to get out of the icy waters of the creek, obtaining a charter to operate a ferry across the river and run a pack train into the camp nearby. He opened a store on the river bank, established a post office next door and others came in to set up businesses. As a settled community it naturally took the name of Galbraith's Ferry. In 1874 brother Robert joined him and then took over John's interests to become a member of legislature representing East Kootenay.

Relations with the Kootenay Indians were on a steady if not cordial basis until 1884 when there was an incident that placed the whole country in danger and resulted in the founding of Fort Steele. Head of the Indian tribes was Chief Isadore. One of his men was charged with the murder of two white placer miners on the trail between Wild Horse and Deadman's Creek. A posse of miners overtook and captured the tribesman, Kapula, lodging him in the Wild Horse jail, less than seven miles from Galbraith's Ferry. Isadore and braves broke open the calaboose, took Kapula, the chief warning the provincial constable to get out of the country. Alarmed officials persuaded Isadore to return Kapula, promising him safe conduct at least until after the trial. Then they sent for Northwest Police, particularly Major Sam Steele.

Steele was the perfect man for the job, just and sympathetic to the Indian viewpoint. He came to Wild Horse, held a hearing of evidence from all concerned and decided the actual murderers of the miners were white renegades who blamed the Indian. Kapula was immediately freed and to further

BUILDING housed executive offices, constructed when Fort Steele was center of government for all East Kootenay. With decline of river town as metropolis, offices were moved to Cranbrook, building then reverting to use as hotel. Under protection now as relic it will be restored as government building.

cement relations, Steele arranged for establishment of Indian schools and agricultural aid. As a safety measure a fort was built on the arid elevated plain above Galbraith's Ferry and called Fort Steele.

Barracks buildings were constructed of yellow pine logs, partly hewn, sheeted and floored with common lumber, according to Major Steele's report. They had to be large enough to quarter a whole division without crowding. Stables for seventy-five horses had saddle and harness rooms under the same roof. There was a hospital 25 ft. x 40 ft., officers' quarters, guard room cells, casualty store and orderly room. In addition there were sergeants' mess, kitchen and staff sergeant's quarters, stores, horse shoeing and carpenter's shops and other structures. Steele included the note, "A sufficient quantity of beef, potatoes and fuel is obtainable here of good quality and reasonable prices. Twenty-two thousand pounds of oats have been purchased . . . but the hay is of poor quality."

Interviewed for the *Daily Colonist* of January in 1963, was "Red" Nichol, then over 80 years of age. After serving in the Boer War he came to Fort Steele in 1902 and for more than 50 years served as big game hunter for parties from all over the world. When he came to the fort on the Kootenay River, he said, there were seven hotels with drinking and gambling freely flourishing in all. He remembered especially the Del Gardno, Windsor, Imperial, Fort Steele and Strathcona. "There were lots of wild women too, but we kept them all across the river." At the end of the interview Red was silent for a time, then concluded, "Fort Steele must be at its lowest ebb now. There isn't even a bootlegger left any more."

GRANITE CREEK, B.C.

John Chance was out to make some money. He figured that taking a bunch of horses from Washington state to the raw frontier town of New Westminster, B.C., was maybe a little easier than driving a swarm of bees, but he had a hankering to do it.

He had the iron nerve, too. And by veering from the regular route, he set off a gold rush that made the wild spot along Granite Creek boom into the third largest city in the Province of British Columbia.

Local historian John Goodfellow pins it down in his *The Story of Similkameen*. . . . "For some unaccountable reason, after he (Chance) reached Princeton, he did not follow the Dewdney Trail but went up the Tulameen past Aspen Grove and followed the old Coquihalla Trail."

The memories of Henry Younger Lowe of Tulameen go back to the turn of the century when he arrived from Wales to set up a log cabin on the lower level area near Otter Lake, called Otter Flat and later to be known as Tulameen. Henry was a friend to all the Chinook Indians thereabout. Since his arrival was only a few years after that of John Chance, he gives his reason for the horse wrangler going the way he did.

"Some of those poor devils hadn't seen a woman for months. They were well aware the Chinooks spent the summer berry season in this valley along the Tulameen and Granite Creek. They also knew the squaws were left more or less alone to do the picking while the braves hunted in the mountains. Also that their chief was willing to allow the girls to extend hospitality to the roving young white men, assuming there would be a consideration of some beans, tea and flour. John Chance was after klootchman and that's how come he went so far out of his way."

Even after such dalliance Chance was not quite ready to get back to the business of pushing his horses on toward the Coast. Like every other wanderer of the day, he was part prospector and could not resist dipping his pan into the little creek that flows into the Tulameen at this point.

What he found made him "whoop and holler." The sounds scared the horses but Chance couldn't care less. He washed pan after pan until he had a goodly pinch of gold dust, then hurried on to New Westminster with his animals and disposed of them for funds to purchase supplies. He registered his claim, making every effort to keep it secret, but the word was out that John Chance had discovered gold and he was followed by an eager band of hopefuls. They staked out claims along the creek and as the time was July, slept on the ground, too busy to build cabins.

Chance and his new-found friends panned plenty of the "maddening stuff" and the little group expanded into a horde that needed shelter when the nights grew cold. Logs were the only building material available

PLAQUE ON MONUMENT beside waters of creek where Chance found gold. The *Similkameen Star* of Sept. 10, 1915 wrote of Granite Creek in prosperous times: "E. P. Cook, the pioneer merchant of Granite Creek, was to Princetown last Friday. In 1885 when he walked into Granite Creek carrying his blankets it was with difficulty that he made his way along the crowded main street. Twelve saloons did a flourishing business and closing hours were unknown. The town was the third largest in B. C., being only exceeded by Victoria and New Westminster. Kamloops would probably come next in size. Placer miners in 1885-6 took probably $800,000 in gold and platinum out of Granite Creek." John Goodfellow thinks this is exaggerated, the actual amount somewhere between this and the sum officially reported.

FRONT DOOR DETAIL of "house of pleasure." Structure extended back to shed and attached outhouse, had basement as well. Method of notching ends of logs is varied, chinks first filled with chips and scraps, then clay.

"FANCY HOUSE" in Granite Creek had second floor where girls cooperated. Woodshed at rear is covered by hop vines, persisting from early days. Addition is of whipsawn lumber but no entire building so constructed remains on Creek. All structures, some 15, are of logs, some retaining roofs, one occupied. Beyond is Douglas fir forest.

and cabins sprang up along three "streets" parallel with the creek on one bank only where the walls were not too steep.

Rev. George Murray was the first preacher to hold a church service in Granite Creek. Since the scene is described as having "tents aplenty but really no houses," the event took place about August that first year, 1885. One log building was being built for a saloon. At three logs in height, the Rev. Murray appropriated it and after services the hat was passed for gold dust. When a real church was built, the log cabin reverted to its original mundane status, a saloon called the Adelph.

Walton Hugh Holmes, born in England in 1853, made a visit to Granite Creek in '85 and wrote: "On leaving Tulameen we began to meet people and six miles farther on when we came in sight of Granite Creek, it looked like an anthill. Several hundred men of all sorts, saddle horses and pack animals, tents on both sides of the river. What a sight! All available space taken up for tents. Camp fires everywhere. There was one small cabin built by Mr. Alison for a store but there were no supplies in it. Only some tin plates and iron knives and forks: no provisions procurable and they were badly needed. We found our pack

trains would be welcome when they arrived. The most of Granite Creek was staked off for claims. They were only 100 feet long from high water mark across the creek. There was no government office to record them, so it was not long before we had to appoint a recorder, a Mr. H. Nicholson, pro tem, until a government agent was sent in 1886. . . . By that time Granite Creek was quite a town, all log houses."

Through July, September and October the workers received $90,000 in gold. There were 62 claims of 300 feet each, and the population totaled almost a thousand, one-third Chinese. In January of the next year, the gold commissioner, G. C. Tunstal, said there were 40 houses, six saloons, hotels and seven stores. The year 1886 was the year of peak production of gold and platinum, officially reported to the Commissioner as being $193,000. Humans being what they are, it is safe to assume the actual figure was much larger.

When the easily garnered wealth began to thin out and no lodes were found, people began to move away, some to dig for the much less glamorous coal then being mined in the area. Fifteen years after John Chance had found his gold, Granite Creek was a ghost town.

HEDLEY, B.C.

The Indians along the Similkameen and its creeks had no use for gold and no incentive to work for it. In the '60's they watched the white man sloshing gravel around in big pans, picking out flakes of something yellow and went back to their tipis, giving thanks to the Great Mystery that they were not that hungry.

Yet the white men, they saw, needed Indian furs and in a spirit of barter instead of fight some awkward trading was done, neither faction being able to understand the other's words. When the trade language known as Chinook jargon infiltrated from the lower Columbia River where sailors were fraternizing briskly with the local tribes, the B.C. miners were able to say "Hyas kloshe" and settle down to some plain and fancy horse trading.

The *British Columbia Quarterly* of April, 1948, describes the location of Hedley as "lying at a point where Twenty Mile Creek, after swinging around the western base of Nickel Plate Mountain, emerges from its canyon to cut a boulder-strewn channel through the river benches to flow into the Similkameen River a short distance below the town."

The name Hedley is very common in Britain and Canada and several men of that name were connected with the early history of the mining camp. Rev. J. W. Hedley served the Keremeos area as minister and moved to Hedley Camp in 1902 which was probably named for R. Robert Hedley, manager of the Hall Mines Smelter at Nelson, B.C. This Hedley had grubstaked Peter Scott, the first man to get things going in the lode mines along the Similkameen in 1896. Earlier efforts to work claims had failed for lack of finances, notably those of George Alison, James Riordan, Edgar Dewdney and J. Coultard.

Peter Scott had a vast ambition to make his newly located Rolle the biggest thing in mining history and, with Robert Hedley's money, set about to do it. Other claims were taken up in rapid succession, among them the Mound, Copper Cleft, Horsefly, Bulldog, Nickel Plate and Copperfield. And it was the Nickel Plate, not the Rolle, which turned out to be the most successful—the first producing lode mine in the Similkameen.

This one was started by a combination of circumstances. One was the staging of a fair at New Westminster, at that time the metropolis on the Coast, later swallowed up by a faster-growing Vancouver. Another was the fact that New Westminster was hosting a distinguished visitor, M. K. Rodgers, moving force of the vast Marcus Daly outfit in Butte, Montana. All that remained for a catalyst was for Wollaston and Arundel, owners of the struggling Nickel Plate, to bring a few chunks of its ore to the fair and let events take their course.

Rodgers was actually on his way to Cassiar, due to sail the next day from Victoria, but he had a few hours to spend and "took in" the New Westminster Fair. When he saw the Nickel Plate ore samples, his eyes bugged out. Cagily, however, he examined the samples carefully, concluding they must be "salted," referring to the artificial enriching of ore to give a false impression of value. After locating the mine's owners who were standing by, he was willing to believe the samples were genuine, cancelled his sailing arrangements and was on his way next morning to the mines on the Similkameen.

Rodgers took a look at the mine, accepted a few pieces of ore and took them to be assayed. The results were so high he felt Wollaston and Arundel had handed him something special, went back to make a few choices of his own. What happened after his private assay made history for Hedley.

Wollaston and Arundel were "fit to be tied" while Rodgers was "fooling around," so cagily had he concealed his intense interest. The owners' funds were running low and they began to fear a collapse of their hopes. Then one day as Arundel was walking dejectedly along the board sidewalk in front of the bank, a hand reached out and touched his shoulder, then a familiar voice: "I'd like to complete the deal we mentioned the other day." Arundel was stunned at the sight and sound of the Butte man. He went inside the bank in a daze and was handed a check for $79,000.

In January money began to flow into the camp and the first large expenditure was for a tramway. The mine openings were located in "impossible" places, clinging like flies to vertical faces of cliffs hundreds of feet above the town. With the tramway completed in October, 1902, the "muck" could fly down on a spider web of cable. At the landing place a large stamp mill for crushing and a cyanide plant for refining were built and milling began in May, 1904.

The camp had always been inaccessible. The first sizable shipment of supplies came in 1898 from Fairview, when George Cahill, one of the first owners of a Hedley claim, brought in a 35-horse pack train. As the camp grew larger, ways of getting supplies in had to be worked out. A 15-mile cut-off was built from Keremeos road, shortening the distance from the coast to Princeton and Hedley.

The camp was now in the throes of a boom and enjoying it. In 1904 the big Similkameen Hotel was

MINE BUILDINGS of Hedley Mascot cling precariously to steep cliffs (upper left). Hedley rose in importance as mining camp when Granite Creek placers declined, was for many years most important gold center in entire Similkameen area. Lode mines like this resulted from discoveries in rich veins after depletion of deposits in gravels of Similkameen River at mouth of tributary, Twenty Mile Creek, now called Hedley Creek. Elevation of town at base of cliffs is 1,700 feet, mines on overhanging mountain sides 3,000 feet higher.

built, the first good stopping place and an elegant one. The New Zealand Hotel went up in 1905; both hotels were destroyed by fire, the latter in 1911, former in 1916. The town had general stores, butcher shops and all kinds of mercantile establishments. One structure had no need for advertising—the three-story one down on the point where Twenty Mile Creek enters the Similkameen, where the workers could spend their money on all pleasures of the flesh.

More respectable were the Bank of British North America, first in the Similkameen, telephone office and imposing school on the hill replacing the original, a room at the rear of the Methodist Church. The school also suffered disaster, demolished by a massive earth slide.

There were many golden years for the community but in 1930 ore became so poor operations were suspended. Hedley, like many other one-industry towns, suffered severe depression pangs. In 1932 the mine was sold to John Mercer Exploration Company

which found a new paying lead, extending Hedley's lease on life. A modern village was built around the mine on the 5,000-foot perch, connected with east-west highway by a mountain road.

But, had everyone read the production report of the Hedley Mascot, the other big mine, they would have known the town was doomed. The report started out bravely but carried a stinger: "During the thirteen years ending April, 1949, the Hedley Mascot fractional claim yielded over $8,500,000 in gold. Exhaustive explorations elsewhere on the property yielded interesting indications but sufficient ore was not found to warrant continuation of milling."

The next year saw the closure of the Hedley Mascot and 1955 was the end of the fabulous Nickel Plate and the little town of the same name in the clouds. Hedley was on its way to becoming a ghostly spectre. Flood and fire had always beset the town and in 1956 a searing blast took down several hotels and other structures. The ones remaining are largely empty and faded.

35

AND INDIAN PETER GOT RICH

Moyie, B.C.

During the brief period Fort Steele was "occupied" by Northwest Mounties, commanding officer Major Sam Steele was able to conciliate the Indians of the Kootenay to the point where whites no longer felt the danger of a general uprising. The truce however was an uneasy one as far as native leader Chief Isadore was concerned.

Father Coccola and other priests from the mission established a short distance north in Mary's Valley had been working hand in hand with Major Steele to bring about a general peace. Since the Indians were suspicious of the strong combination, the departure of the Mounties actually helped smooth relations with the tribes, only Isadore remaining implacable. When Father Coccola tried to move him to the mission he replied, "No. You can even threaten me with attack by soldiers, but next spring I will plow my land as usual. I would rather die of bullets than by starvation." But by the fall of 1888, Isadore too was persuaded and total peace reigned.

It was true funds provided by the government helped sustain the mission school. Parents grudgingly acknowledged that children attending were "fat and healthy" but not all the adult Indians were so well looked after. When a hungry group of them came to Coccola for help one day the desperate priest made a suggestion. "Until we get enough money to help your people more fully, why don't your men go out in the hills to see if you can find a silver mine as some white men have been doing?"

Several Indians did exactly that. After a few weeks one native named Indian Pete returned to the mission to see Father Coccola in private. Alone with the priest he opened a little rawhide bag and took out a chunk of almost solid silver the size of an egg. The dazzled Coccola sent for James Cronin, a mining expert visiting at the mission. A small party was organized to go to the spot where the galena was found, Indian Pete leading the way. The vein ultimately became the famous St. Eugene silver mine at Moyie, at its height the largest producer in the country, in ten years yielding over $11 million.

The location was immediately developed under direction of the man who knew how to do it, technician James Cronin, one claim staked out to Indian Peter, the next to Father Coccola. When work began it was discovered the St. Eugene (Coccola) vein dipped into Peter's, all agreeing the two properties be worked as a unit. Deeper penetration in 1895 exposed a vein of silver-lead eight feet wide and it was obvious the mine was bigger than the priest could manage with small funds available. He sold out to financier John A. Fich of Spokane for $120,000, divided it with Indian Peter and returned to his mission.

The Indian bought a plot of good farm land, had a home and barn erected on it, stocked it with cattle, horses and sheep. Coccola spent his share on a fine new church, St. Eugene, at the mission and finished paying for the hospital previously constructed mostly on hope. There was enough left to care for and feed his parishioners for some time.

MAIN BUILDING, head frame of famous old St. Eugene workings. Overall production of $11 million is amazing in view of many difficulties, closures. Last activity lasted from 1911 to 1919. Ore contained 10 ounces of silver to 1 of lead with lesser amounts of zinc. Mine workings had 30 different levels, some upper ones penetrating deeply into mountain, lower ones extending under Lake Moyie.

RICHFIELD, B.C.

"Dutch William, restless and enterprising, left the others basking before the burning logs and traveled up the creek until he found the bare bedrock cropping up in the stream. He tried one panful of gravel but obtained none of the precious metal. He tried another from the side where there was a high ledge and to his great delight found himself rewarded with a dollar to the pan. The gravel was hard frozen to the rock and when detached with difficulty was thawed in the cold stream. Time passed quickly and he was soon forced by darkness to return to the campfire. He showed his companions the prize he had obtained but possibly they discredited his statement for they determined to return to the Forks. Having no pick, Dutch William was obliged, unwillingly, to return with them though he had provisions for some days more."

So were the events on Williams Creek in February of 1861 chronicled in the *Victoria Colonist* of Nov. 5, 1863. It then appeared Dutch William Dietz scoured the camp of Antler for a few tools of his own, confided in three other men more willing to believe in his find than his erstwhile companions and returned to the area with them. They found plenty to confirm the story but the three new men returned to Red-Headed Davis' store for supplies, taking precautions to leave a man on guard just in case the secret leaked out. It was a useless gesture. Although the supply trip was made on snowshoes in record time, "the whole creek was staked off into claims over ground covered by eight feet of snow." Leaving his partners hacking at the frozen gravel, Dutch returned to Antler for a rocker which he carried to the diggings

RICHFIELD COURTHOUSE is only building of camp remaining. When hanging was ordered, temporary scaffold was erected in front of it. On one occasion double gallowses were set up, one victim of justice being James Berry who had shot James Morgan Blessing on road to diggings. Loot was roll of $20 notes and stickpin of unique design, later noticed in Berry's tie by Barkerville's colored barber, Wellington Delaney Moses, a friend of Blessing. At trial, evidence of stickpin (with tiny human head accidentally mounted upside down) was sufficient to convict. Other man on double gibbet was Indian convicted of murdering white man at Soda Creek, way station on road to mines.

on his back. Open-heartedly he stopped frequently to chop out brush so others, though uninvited, might follow more easily.

The first straggling assemblage of tents and shacks began to take form on one side of the stream now called Williams Creek and when the need for a gold commissioner was filled by Thomas Elwyn, the growing camp was referred to as Elwyntown. The name seemed inappropriate to miners proud of the golden wealth pouring out of the riverbed and they came up with the more satisfying one of Richfield.

The raw camp spawned troubles in the form of murder and violence. Trials had to be held for the miscreants and a substantial log cabin was commandeered for courthouse until it became inadequate and a new one was built. The judiciary was even responsible for expediting travel into the town, judging from an item in the *Cariboo Sentinel* of June 11, 1866: "We understand Judge Cox had to pay $250 for shoveling snow from between Van Winkle and Richfield so as to enable trains to get in" . . . the trains being strings of pack animals.

Another new structure in Richfield was heralded in the July 13 issue, two years later, headed: "St. Patrick's Catholic Church. His Lordship the Right Rev. Bishop De Heromes, D.D., will perform the ceremony of the Benediction of the above church and bell on Sunday next, 19th, services to commence at 10 o'clock A.M."

Gold commissioner Elwyn was replaced by Chartres Brew who died May 31, 1870. The June 14 *Cariboo Sentinel* displayed on its front page a black-bordered obituary: "On Tuesday last Mr. Chartres Brew died at Richfield. In the early part of last winter Mr. Brew had been taken ill. He was born, we believe, in Limerick, Ireland, and was about 59 years old. He was buried in the Cameronton cemetery on Williams Creek on Thursday last. A large procession followed the remains to the grave."

Immediately below the notice was an advertisement making the most of the lugubrious details. "Memory presides over the past—Fell's Coffee over the present. It has but one shrine and that is every breakfast table. Its aroma walks the earth like a spirit and can be found at respectable dealers in British Columbia. BEWARE OF SPURIOUS IMITATIONS!"

Richfield had a short life and a merry one, its gaiety being stimulated by potations in numerous saloons along the creek banks, the sudden demise taking place when the golden wealth was suddenly pinched off. The rest of the nuggets were securely buried farther down, and deeper in the gravels, in one side of the stream in what had been in the bed in prehistoric days. But before these were discovered, Richfield as a city died, its inhabitants going to other strikes and other saloons.

Dutch William, the man who sparked the brief and fiery history of Richfield as well as the whole pageant of other and larger gold strikes in the Cariboo never shared in the wealth resulting from his discovery. Poor food and the deprivations of the raw frontier took early toll. While the story of his find was being hailed and discussed in Victoria, he was lying there in a sickbed. He died a pauper in 1877.

STOUT'S GULCH, just below Richfield and just above confluence with slightly broader canyon of Williams Creek seen at right angles in middle distance. Edward Stout was Indian fighter in youth, one of party attacked in Fraser River canyon in wars of 1858. Indians had used up arrows poisoned with rattlesnake venom and Stout was hit with regular one, lived to become one of prospecting party discovering Williams Creek. After active life in gold fields, he retired to live in Yale, dying at 99. Stout always maintained he owed his long life to never having touched liquor. He did not mention scarcity of snake venom.

SANDON, BRITISH COLUMBIA

Midnight of May 3, 1900, in the mountain-girt mining town of Sandon, was very quiet. The evening before was one of the gayest in the town's history, a traveling stock company presenting the play *Bitter Atonement* at Spencer's Virginia Hall. The house was filled to capacity and the audience gave the actors a standing ovation when the curtain fell. Then between curtain calls one of the actors dropped a burning cigarette in a waste basket.

At 12:30 fire alarm bells began ringing wildly. Most of the population of the isolated town rushed to the scene of the blaze, attempting to remove belongings and furniture from neighboring, closely packed buildings but it was soon obvious that the town was doomed, with flames leaping from one frame building to the next. Sandon's upstream "suburb" was saved only by the dynamiting of the Canadian Pacific's station which stood at the upper end of the gutted section, the fire not being able to jump the gap. Next morning the entire business section was in ashes. All hotels, theaters, banks and stores had burned away, Victoria's *Daily Chronicle* listing more than fifty buildings destroyed.

All this happened eight years after J. M. "Johnny" Harris discovered silver here, started his fabulous climb to riches and setting a mining boom in action. The mining district once known as the "Silvery Slocans" lies in high, timber-clad country in the fork of the Columbia and Kootenay Rivers, bounded on the east by Kootenay Lake, on the west by parallel Slocan Lake. The whole country is a jumble of mountains, many bearing glaciers, and one of the streams draining into Slocan Lake is the Sandon. A fork of the main stream is Carpen-

ter Creek, the steep hills above it still loaded with silver. The first men to tap this mineral wealth were Jack Seaton and Eli Carpenter who would have reaped great reward had they not quarreled over partnership details and parted in bitterness. Others worked their claims and several more rich deposits in the Silvery Slocans but none developed in spectacular fashion. It fell to J. M. "Johnny" Harris to become the silver magnate of the country.

Johnny spent his early boyhood in the tobacco and cotton fields of Virginia, succumbed to wanderlust at a tender age and wound up in Idaho in 1884. He worked in the gold mines there, still only a boy, then discovered he could sell real estate and opened an office. That lasted until a prospector from the wild country north of Nelson brought him a piece of ore shining with veins of silver. Johnny Harris then knew where his heart's desire lay—in the prospecting tradition—and he headed for the new strike.

He stopped first in Nelson which was in the throes of a mining boom, then moved on up into the really wild country to the north, arriving with a companion at the lower end of Slocan Lake where there was no trail, the shoreline vertical cliffs. The two procured a canoe and started for the outpost camp of New Denver, 35 miles up the lake. Just short of the town, a sudden storm overturned the flimsy craft and they had to swim for it, a day later being lodged in the swankiest flophouse in New Denver. The slighty built Virginian then started hiking up the Sandon River, reached the tributary Carpenter Creek, started digging and almost at once uncovered a fabulous vein of silver. The date was April 7, 1892.

THIS AREA IN SANDON was separated from rest of town for entertainment of single men. Being built on higher ground at lower end it escaped floods that devastated more respectable section. Author drove camper into level area for night to be on hand for morning light, was questioned by town guard then welcomed with apologies. Many relics have been carried off by vandals, thieves.

With the money from the claim Johnny purchased a third interest in an even more promising mine, the Reco. Before the boom was over the area's mines had produced millions and a flourishing town named for Sandon Creek grew up along the canyon. The town was Johnny's baby as was much of the wealth that came out of the ground around it.

At first the silver-lead ore was hauled down a rough, hacked-out trail to New Denver by the crude method of rawhiding—two cowhides wrapped around twin loads balanced on mules and tied to wooden pack saddles. But as Sandon boomed and the silver mines produced tons of rich ore, the need for a railroad became imperative. Two railroads began laying track simultaneously in a race to reach the camp in the mountains. One was a spur of the Great Northern, United States railroad bossed by tough, Canadian-born Jim Hill, the other a branch of the Canadian Pacific, the Kaslo-Slocan Line. The latter, confident of reaching Sandon first, built an elaborate station there in advance. Just as the K-S line drove the last spike beside it, an engine of the competition chugged around the last bend below town. While the K-S bosses and crew celebrated roundly and went to bed, the G N men "accidentally" got a chain around the shiny new station, hooked it to their new engine and dragged it down the tracks a few hundred feet, toppling the proud little edifice into Carpenter Creek. At it turned out, after hostilities were settled and damages paid, there was plenty of ore for both lines to haul and both served the town for several years.

Before the fire Sandon was a city of more than 3,000, a metropolis in the otherwise unpopulated mountains. One of the showplaces was the Reco, built by Johnnny Harris, named for the mine and attracting the elite of the mining world. Another was the Miners' Union Hall, with hardwood dance floor and stage complete with elaborate scenery. There was the Harris Power and Light Building, two newspapers — MINING REVIEW and PAYSTREAK — two banks, two drug stores and Sandon Hospital. This building was in the upper Gulch section and escaped the big fire in 1900 but was consumed by another blaze six years later that took out the Gulch. The town was proud of its ice rink with a hockey team that consistently took first place in British Columbia leagues. The rink had a separate section for curling and there was a ski jump which brought visiting teams from Revelstoke, Nelson and elsewhere. But the fire at the turn of the century wiped out all this.

The town was originally built on one side of one street; Carpenter Creek, the narrow canyon bottom allowing no more. After the fire Sandon was promptly rebuilt but by confining the stream to a planked flume and covering it with heavy planks, the street had two solid lines of buildings facing it. This double row continued up the broader section of the canyon about a quarter mile, terminating at the narrower Gulch where a more conventional road wound on for several blocks, this too lined solidly with business structures.

The fire was in May, 1900, and in September little eleven-year old Minnie Stewart arrived in Sandon with her mother and stepfather, James Thompson. Born in another famous camp, Georgetown, Colorado, Minnie did not find her new situation too strange except for the frenzy of rebuilding. The family settled in the Gulch section and Minnie started school in a large tent, since the regular school house had burned to the ground. Now 76 years old and living in New Denver, Minnie relates the details with some feeling of nostalgia. The school's walls were boards part way up, the rest of canvas, as was the roof. It housed about 30 pupils, Mr. Barron's upper classes and Miss English's lower. In the center was a wood-burner stove enclosed in a sheet metal circulator. A permanent school was soon built on the side hill and the site of the tent school became that of the new M. E. church in a section called Sunnyside. Then came the 1906 fire in the Gulch, burning out almost all the crowded buildings there. When they were rebuilt, water mains were connected to fire hydrants which extended high in the air above deep winter snows.

Not long after Minnie came to Sandon she met Collin Stewart, then 19 and working in the mines. Seven years later they were married and Minnie

ASPEN TREE is shown with sun just clearing high mountain horizon in mid-morning.

did not have to change her name. When their first born son George grew older he too worked in the silver mines around Sandon and was married there. His daughter Ivy was born in 1936 and went to school there until 1942 when the entire family group moved to New Denver. Ivy was married there to Perry Anderson of the old mining camp of Ymer, B.C. and the couple has three children. Now the whole line from great-grandmother Minnie Stewart on down lives in one New Denver house. This near ghost town lies on the shore of beautiful Slocan Lake almost in the shadow of a mountain topped by the extensive Lucerne Glacier.

Sandon would likely never have rebuilt after the fire but for the drive of Johnny Harris who could see nothing but a rosy future for his town. The rush to the Klondike had drained away many miners dissatisfied with returns after the silver panic although there was still plenty of the metal left in

the Slocans. The city had seen its best days but Harris kept it going even helping finance some slipping mines and there were still some lively events.

One miner's house was built at the edge of Carpenter Creek, just above the flume entrance. His wife tried to talk with her neighbor across the stream, leaned too far out to catch some bit of gossip, lost her balance and fell. She was swept into the flume and down the canyon under the planked street, drowning before reaching the lower open end. And several times sudden melting of snows swelled the stream to proportions that wrecked a building or two and undermined sections of track, leaving rails and ties dangling.

Yet these were minor disasters compared with the news that Johnny Harris was going to make his last home in his native Virginia. Once there in a fine house with luxurious furniture, he wrote Sandon friends he was glad he had returned to his birthplace, that he was enjoying his new life. But in a short time he was back in B.C. "Too many relatives moved in with me," he said.

Sandon was fast fading away but Harris kept up a pretense that the place would one day boom again, and maintained his once plush Reco Hotel to be ready for it. He even retained his electric plant, saying he wanted to have the lights ready when the guests arrived. In September of 1950 he told a Vancouver SUN reporter, Jim Hazelwood: "When big money starts rolling again, Sandon will come to life with a bang." But Hazelwood and his bride, in the town on their honeymoon, were almost the last guests in the old hostelry. Johnny was still full of faith in a comeback for his city when he died there in 1953 at 89.

His death spared him the sight of Sandon's nearly complete destruction two years later. Snows had attained an unusually heavy pack in the winter of 1954-55 and it was slow melting that spring, meeting in June a tremendous electric storm with a deluge of warm rain. A log jam twenty feet high formed in the canyon above Sandon and then broke, releasing a torrent that carried trees, rocks and mud down on the nearly deserted town. The flume was entirely destroyed and almost all buildings carried away or shattered. Johnny's pride, the Reco Hotel, was wrecked, foundations and lower floor carried away, remaining upper floors tipped crazily into the roaring waters. The few remaining inhabitants escaped on foot, crossing the canyon farther down on a railway trestle that was "vibrating and shivering

OLD STRUCTURE in Gulch section above main business section escaped both fire and floods, was office for one of Sandon's physicians, Dr. Gomm. Fire hydrant is barely accessible in summer, more so when snow was deep. Water still trickles from this one.

something awful", according to one of the refugees. The entire canyon was filled with the wreckage of the city and much of the debris remains.

Sandon today is peaceful, though Carpenter Creek still roars down the canyon. The few buildings spared by the flood of June 22, 1955, stand scattered along the stream like the snaggled remnants of an old crone's teeth. In summer half a dozen people live in small houses farther back from the creek in the Gulch, one of them a watchman for remaining mine properties. Visitors are welcome but kept under his scrutiny because of vandalism. The road from Nelson is paved most of the way, becoming narrow but fairly good dirt and gravel near Slocan at the foot of Slocan Lake. The road then follows along the water, often at the very edge, and in one stretch is one-way, squeezed between rock walls and through a rather small tunnel. A sign along the way reads with some understatement: "Pass with caution". There is a five-mile stretch of pavement between Silverton and New Denver, then dirt again and narrower, is strictly one-way in spots to Sandon.

STANLEY, B.C.

Fantastic tales of enormous amounts of gold taken out of Williams Creek and other streams of the Cariboo pop up out of the dust and rock. The claim of Bill Dillar and his partners produced in one working day 102 pounds of the yellow metal. Even at the going price of $20 an ounce, Dillar piled up a fortune, dutifully paying off his stockholders at $10,000 a share every Sunday.

Many other claims produced in like fashion, creating the impression every prospector who clawed his way over the infamous Cariboo Trail struck it rich. The facts are far from this. It is said the actual average "take" of the eager gold-seeking thousands during the palmiest days along the upper Fraser and its tributaries was little more than $600 a year.

One of these who fell into the average category was Samuel Montgomery. His headboard, still standing in the Cameronton cemetery, states he was born in Enniskillen Fermanagh, Ireland, on Oct. 28, 1814. A sailor for some fifteen years, he became involved in the rush to the Sierra gold fields, drifting on to the Cariboo when the California gold supply began to fail.

The ex-argonaut settled on the banks of Lightning Creek and never went "outside" for forty-two years. Sam found a little gold, enough to keep him from starvation. At 82 he made what he said would be his last effort, took hold of a claim on Van Winkle Creek, a tributary of Lightning, and on it sank a seventy-eight foot shaft. At the bottom, he dug horizontally as far as he was able, hoisting every bucket of dirt himself. The result of all this effort was almost complete failure and Sam was a broken old man.

During the years he had been grubbing away, other miners around him had been more successful, some spectacularly so. Two cities had sprung up around Montgomery, almost without his noticing them—Stanley at the Lightning's confluence with Chisholm Creek and Van Winkle having its short, happy life two miles farther on where Van Winkle Creek came in. Over the years the Stanley area yielded more than $10 million but old Sam got none of it.

About the turn of the century, a group of more successful gold diggers—Harry Jones (who told the story) with George Rankin, Fred Tregillis and Joe Spratt—formed a company to explore an old claim, once a part of the South Wales workings but declared worthless. More out of pity than any other reason, and almost too late, the partners decided to "include in" old Sam Montgomery. The outfit was formally

called the Little Van Winkle but in deference to the well-loved senior partner was familiarly referred to as the Montgomery.

Now came the climax of Sam's long, hard years of labor. In 1902 the Montgomery drift penetrated a piece of ground so rich the usual "clean up" had to be held every day, wages paid out of the resulting pile of dust and nuggets, the remainder divided between the partners. This method of paying off eliminated detailed bookkeeping and satisfied everybody. But poor old Sam could not take the sudden prosperity. He soon died from an excess of regular eating, wearing decent clothes and keeping himself comfortably warm. He was buried on the hillside with many of his cronies. A picture taken in 1862 shows Van Winkle as a huddle of some dozen log buildings. These constituted the "downtown core" and included tin shops, bakeries, blacksmiths and the usual assortment of saloons and gambling houses.

In those early Cariboo days it was the custom for a poker player, disgusted with a run of bad hands, to blame the deck and throw the whole deck over his shoulder, cards strewn all over the floor. It was said the practice was carried on to such an extent the floor would be "ankle deep in cards" when the players

THOMPSON ROAD STEAMERS as advertised in Victoria *Colonist*, were utter failures on the Cariboo's rugged roads.

LY BRITISH COLONI
d Victoria Chronicle.

, BRITISH COLUMBIA, THURSDAY MORNING, MARCH 23, 1871.

New Advertisements.

STEAM TO CARIBOO!

The British Columbia
GENERAL TRANSPORTATION COMPANY

Will place Four of THOMSON'S PATENT ROAD STEAMERS on the route between Yale and Barkerville in the First Week in April, and will be prepared to enter into Contracts for the conveyance of Freight from Yale to Soda Creek in EIGHT DAYS. Through Contracts will be made as soon as the condition of the road above Quesnelmouth permits.
Rates of Passage will be advertised in due time.
BARNARD & BEEDY, anagers.

quit. Since no freight of any kind could get to town during the long winter, miners eventually ran out of cards. At this point, the discarded decks would reappear, thriftily salvaged and sorted by the saloon swamper who sold them once again.

Since most Lightning gold was found near Stanley, Van Winkle clung to life for a while as a supply depot for the bigger centers, including Barkerville farther on, eventually dwindling away. Hardly a trace of the town remains today.

Its neighbor had been named for Edward Henry Stanley, brother of the Frederick Arthur for whom Vancouver's Stanley Park was named. The town was more solid and wealthy than Van Winkle—and wilder. A man visiting in one of its brothels had to take every precaution against being rolled, making real relaxation impossible. Most of the hotels and all the dancehalls were either illicit houses or meeting places for them. The old Lightning Hotel was the last to close its doors, having lasted long beyond the life of the town.

One enterprising individual, not cut out for a miner, more fitted for promoting and merchandising, and who ended his days in Van Winkle, was Josiah Crosby Beedy. Beedy's most spectacular venture was his fleet of fantastic vehicles to take over the onerous task of transporting freight from Yale, the head of navigation. In 1871, Beedy with partner Francis Jones Barnard of Barnard's Express, applied to the legislature for a charter to run a train of "Thompson's Patent Road Steamers" over the Cariboo road. In the petition he stated optimistically: "There seems to be little doubt of the road steamer carriage being far safer than the stages drawn by horses. The drivers are to be sent from England and are to be men picked for the service."

Six of the outlandish contraptions, crosses between steam rollers and tractors with treads, arrived from England and two were actually started on the road. Difficulties beset the rigs from the start. For the sharp turns on the switchbacks, they did not have the flexibility of horse-drawn vehicles and narrow turns had to be widened. But the obstacle that stopped them for good was the steep grade up Jackass Mountain. The rigs could possibly have made it without loads and with the aid of horses but no extra animals were available. The costly experiment was a failure. At least one of the steamers was kept in British Columbia to replace oxen in logging operations.

Beedy returned to the Stanley area after that fiasco for a retail venture with a man named Townsend. It was called the Van Winkle Store, and according to its advertisement in the Cariboo *Sentinel*, carried "everything required in a mining camp."

GRAVE OF JOSIAH CROSBY BEEDY, one of promoters of "road steamers," in old Stanley cemetery, has survived crumbling shells of log and frame.

British Columbia

TAMING THE TALL UNCUT

Waldo, B.C.

If three men and their homes constitute a settlement, old Crow's Nest Landing was one, the spot a lonely one in 1905. W. W. Waldo, from south of the border, was one, owning a shack on the bank of the Kootenay River near the place where steamers from "down in the States" bound for Fort Steele could land at the muddy banks. The boats started at Jennings, Montana, with supplies hauled there by wagon. The other settlers were Jim Squiers and Newt Berry, famed horse ranchers, who had their home across the river from Waldo's. Many fine blooded horses came from their ranch.

In February of 1905 the brothers Hales H. and Joseph W. Ross came out to the Kootenay country from Whitemouth, Manitoba. They purchased a small sawmill from a company in Fernie to the north, installing it at the point where Elk River flows into the larger Kootenay. After operating it for a time the brothers looked around for a site to suit their fast growing ambitions, bought Waldo's property and began to develop the area as a sawmill town. Waldo returned to the States.

Next year the Ross brothers built a large sawmill near the river where lumber could be loaded on the *S.S. Waldo Belle*, just put into regular service. Many of the large frame buildings erected in the Kootenay country around 1907 were built with Ross Brothers' lumber from Waldo. When the Great Northern ran a line through there from Rexford, Montana, to the coal fields at Fernie and

Michel, the Canadian Pacific followed with a spur to Waldo. The wagon road was still a slightly improved Kalispell Trail, the old route from Montana to the gold camps of Fisherville, Wild Horse and later Fort Steele.

The Baker sawmill was the second large one in the town which thrived and grew yet never be-

GROUP OF EQUISETUM—mare's tail or scouring rush—lifted at site of long vanished Davis sawmill, brought to studio for photographing. Altho exquisitely proportioned, plants become invasive, pernicious weeds in gardens. Lovers of damp places, these "rushes" lived as giants 100′ tall in marshes when world was young, fossilized remains constituting appreciable portion of most coal.

47

came a boom town. Dr. T. Saunders and his faithful nurse took care of all physical ills without the convenience of a regular hospital. Veterinarian Dr. Rutledge came regularly from Cranbrook to maintain the health of numerous horses used in the bush around the mills, also willing to make "house calls" in emergencies. One popular traveling man was "Whistling" Powell who came regularly in his chain-drive automobile to service sewing machines, a valuable effort in a community where no "store bought" clothing was available. And on one gala occasion an organ grinder came to Waldo, complete with a jaunty-capped monkey. Exciting too was a visit by a band of gypsies who camped in their covered wagons at the river. Children were fascinated by their fires burning most of the night and some adventurous adults had their fortunes told at the camp, for a fee of course. Then there was Mr. Rahal, the "jeweler," who periodically appeared in Waldo with two large leather packs on his back, selling watches, rings, cheap jewelry. He later established a conventional jewelry store in Fernie.

With the growth of the Ross brothers business, the partners took in another who had been an outside salesman, one Telford, from Saskatoon. He sold much lumber there and the sawmill name was changed to Ross-Saskatoon Lumber Co. Ltd. The two mills served the town until well into the 1920s when both closed down. Waldo, like other one industry communities, quietly disintegrated. Fires took out many buildings, leaving only a few like snaggle teeth along the old Kalispell Trail.

The railroad tracks have long since been torn up leaving lush pasturage and no stock to graze it. Down along the banks of the Kootenay River the famous mosquitoes of the region remain traditionally huge and vigorous. Crow's Nest Landing and Pigeon's Landing a mile upstream are now strictly for the birds.

KRAG HOTEL was one of the three in Waldo, this only remaining. Another, McConnell's, was used for hay storage for some years. Krag facade faces open meadows filled with blooming clover which formerly was main road thru town following old Kalispell Trail. Present road runs along rear. Nearby were tracks of long abandoned Great Northern line.

Beginning at right front was bar extending full length of north wall. Bartender Billy Palmer, one of four sons of owner, had long standing quarrel with fellow townsman Martin Heller and kept sawed-off shotgun under bar. One day Heller strode in suddenly and without giving Palmer chance to grab gun, shot him dead.

Immediately organized posse pursued murderer, overtaking him near Kootenay River bank. When Heller raised gun to fire at pursuers, posse members fired first, wounding him so severely he died on way to hospital. Story was related by one time resident, Douglas Ross, born at Waldo in 1909, now of Vernon, B.C.

48

YALE, B.C.

The violent river was called the Fraser. Fifty years before, the first white man to make an attempt to navigate it was the explorer Simon Fraser and about it he wrote: "The water which rolls down this extraordinary passage in tumultuous waves and with great velocity had a frightful appearance." Draining a vast area of snow-packed mountains the river is dangerous, even at lowest levels when little snow is melting. With spring freshets extending over a long time because of the varied terrain, it can rise a hundred feet and carry everything loose before it.

The Fraser canyon above New Westminster is somewhat deeper and broader, the waters roll with less violence and, in the early days, ships were able to make headway as far as the raw frontier town of Yale nestled on a narrow shelf on the north bank. Vancouver, as such, did not then exist, the small community being referred to as "Gastown." From Yale all traffic for the gold fields took whatever means was available for the even rougher land journey, the means including all manner of strange conveyances.

One primitive method of transporting the prospector's worldly goods was by the trundle barrow. A four-foot wheel was equipped with a rack on each side, wheelbarrow handles front and rear, the load evenly divided on the racks. One man got between each set of handle grips and away they went. Several hundred miles of this took heavy toll of the prospectors but some made it to Barkerville.

Other methods of trail transport were the fire-breathing behemoths, Thompson Patent Road Steamers which never got over Jackass Mountain and the even more exotic camels which frightened other animals to the point of jumping over cliffs into the river far below. More stable and dependable were the oxen or bulls, mules and horses.

At first these pack trains did not have far to go as the early strikes of gold were on the Fraser itself. The gravel bars extending into the rapids were loaded with it but the panning could only be done when the water was low. One method of locating the richer deposits was to dump a quantity of leaves into the stream and follow them. Where they tended to bunch up in eddies, circles were staked off as likely spots where gold particles might have landed.

A man standing exposed on one of these bars was a prime target for the arrows or bullets of ever-present Indians who resented the white man's invasion. One gold seeker was working the gravels with a rocker on a bar near Yale when he was startled by a shot. There was a hole through his rocker and it seemed the next one would be through him. Having no place to hide, all he could do was watch the Indian raise his rifle for another shot. There was a shot, not from the Indian but from a prospector on the shore. The Indian toppled into the river and the miner went on with his panning.

Before long the placer gold in the Fraser's banks was exhausted but then came reports of fabulous amounts of the yellow metal being taken out of Williams Creek and the streams at Quesnel Forks and Horsefly. The real rush out of Yale now set in and the town saw its heyday as a shipping point.

The prospector going north found Yale the last place to get liquor, women and gambling and those coming "outside" found freedom and license after long months of enforced abstinence. With no restraints, Yale became another Barbary Coast. It was considered the most wicked spot on the Coast, San Francisco having tamed down some with the end of the Sierra gold rush. In fact, it was the wilder element from the California town that came to Yale and gave it an impetus to lawlessness.

OLD ANGLICAN CHURCH OF ST. JOHN THE DIVINE, only remaining relic of roistering old Yale. Religious services were first held in old store by W. Burton Crickmer, June 10, 1860. New church was built one block away in 1863. Age and long periods of disuse caused such deterioration that in 1952 structure was condemned, causing such a furor campaign extended across Dominion to raise funds for restoration. Original logs now covered by boards, new foundation placed and even pulpit provided, convenience lacking in all years of history. Original wooden cross, rotted at base, was sent to Provincial Archives at Victoria for preservation. Verdure so conceals edifice visitor must look twice to find it.

One unholy pair, Ned McGowan and John Bagley, refugees from the California Vigilantes, teamed up with one Hicks, the Yale Gold Commissioner. Through his position the latter got hold of a fifty-year lease on the best placering grounds near Yale, then gouged the miners for short-term rentals. With the strong-arm help of his cohorts, he then extorted these miners with a "protection" racket. Miners who couldn't afford or refused to go along were brutally tortured or murdered. Killings in the saloons and brothels were common, bodies dumped into the turbulent Fraser. If they showed up downstream, they were considered victims of Indian outrage.

Shipments of gold from Williams Creek usually came down the Fraser canyon on muleback, later by horse-drawn stages. The bags and boxes of treasure were reloaded on boats and barges at Yale and this shift was more hazardous than the whole trip south with all the road agents it engendered. Once this hurdle was surmounted, the gold was considered safe in New Westminster. It was melted into bars here and as much as $100,000 might be piled on a table in a bank awaiting shipment to San Francisco.

Yale suffered a slump between the periods of Fraser wealth and the Williams Creek boom but that was nothing compared to the doldrums the town endured in the late 1870s when the main Cariboo rush ended. The once wild stopping place became a virtual ghost town. New life was breathed into it when the Canadian Pacific Railway began construction of its western end in the early '80s. With the arrival of 2,500 white rail construction workers and 6,500 Chinese laborers came a bigger boom than before and once again vice was rampant. A huge red-light district was organized. There were no restrictions to prevent rollings and murders, miners patronizing the girls at the risk of their lives. This seemed to be accepted, however, for Yale supported at least twenty "madames" each of whom managed many "frail sisters," not to mention the many girls in business for themselves. Faro, chuck-a-luck and keno in the gambling dens offered easy ways to spend railroad wages. No one gambling dared protest if he felt cheated. He was always aware of the raging Fraser a few feet from the door.

With the completion of rail laying, peace descended. Modern laws were less tolerant of gambling and violence with the result of greater prosperity. Yale dozes now, as deeply as it can, being only a stone's throw from a fine new highway up the Fraser Canyon.

YALE OF GOLD RUSH DAYS on narrow shelf beside boiling Fraser River pictured in old photo from Archives in Victoria. Main street was on waterfront where violence centered, a continuous row of false fronts. Up to Yale Fraser was navigable, above it canyon narrowed to funnel river into roaring rapids. To go overland, trails and "roads" were hacked out of canyon sides, traffic continuing to gold fields at risk of life and limb.

PROVINCIAL ARCHIVES

"IT WAS LIKE THIS, SON..."

Ymer, B.C.

"There was a lot going on when I first went to work as a miner here," the last old timer remaining in the former gold camp of Ymer (Wi-mer) told the author in 1965. "I was born on Prince Edward Island on June 9, 1882. My name is Alexander MacDonald, but why don't you just call me Alec?

"No, there never was any placering. Maybe once in a while somebody would find a little nugget in the creek, but it really was all hard rock mining. The man that found the lode was a Frenchman, he was a real geologist prospector, not the kind that goes around with a pan.

"The name of the town? Well the Frenchman named his mine the Ymer, so they called the town by that name. I don't know exactly, but if you want to go to the trouble to look through the Bible its there somewhere, the name of a Greek giant, I think.

"They built an 80 stamp mill up there on the hill next to the mine, it was the biggest stamp mill in the British Empire at that time and I think maybe since, too. Yes there were a few silver mines around here, but they weren't so much, you know. The Yankee Girl was the biggest, it was down there across the creek. You don't hardly ever find any gold without some silver, lead and zinc along with it, you know.

"There were about 200 single men working around at the Ymer and maybe another 200 in smaller camps not too far away. We had about 14 whiskey joints here, and maybe five hotels, but they never had girls in any of them. Oh, yes, we had 'em, alright, but they were in a house by themselves across the creek. It was real handy for the Yankee Girl boys, maybe about 11, they depended on the mine boys for a living, of course, and when there weren't enough to keep 'em busy,

some moved to another camp somewhere. Then when we had a boom like we did several times, they'd come back. The boys threw a party for Sally when she came back, they liked her real well.

"The miners had to stay in the boarding houses at the mines until Friday night, then they'd come down here to get drunk and son, you know, they wouldn't go back until Monday morning. Sometimes they couldn't make it and sometimes they never got back at all. The boarding house owners up there got mad, the cooks got paid in the number of meals they fed the men, so some closed down. Then the men had to go back and forth from here, but they brought it on themselves. Oh, they always traveled on saddle horses, though sometimes they caught a ride with other fellows in a buggy. A lot of them were fine men, mostly all young. I've lived here almost sixty years and I made a lot of friends among them, but of course they are all dead now, or else moved away. And no young men come to the town to stay any more, they won't stay at the mine boarding houses any more, either. They have cars now, and what men will work around in the mines or woods either, they can drive back and forth to Salmo or somewhere.

"Oh the mines have mostly shut down long ago, maybe twenty years. There was a boom for a while, and four mills were working for a while but they shut down too. One mill works sometimes, the concentrates they turn out go down to Salmo.

"Small mines don't have a chance any more, those big companies, all they are interested in is a million dollars or so, they won't bother with putting in machinery for a few thousand. There is a lot of gold and silver around still, but its so scattered in small deposits that it never will be mined, don't you know."

DAWSON CITY, Y.T.

Winters in Dawson City are and were cold, dark and long. Here in the sub-arctic Yukon Basin the sun describes an apparent circle around the horizon the year around. In summer the circle is above it, in winter below, always dipped a little downward in the north and upward in the south. About Christmas time at Dawson City the sun shows barely an edge above the southern horizon for a matter of minutes, then gaining in boldness it exposes a bit more surface for a few more minutes each day. In about two weeks the full orb shines for half an hour as it rolls along the horizon. Although seemingly cold, even this brief appearance raises temperatures several degrees.

During the sun's short visitation there is a gray half light. The remaining hours are dark but seldom "black" because the sun is just below the horizon and the stars, moon or crackling northern lights reflect their lustre from the snow. Precipitation being comparatively light in this inland basin, cloudy skies are infrequent. Snow depths are seldom over three feet although strong winds often produce deep drifts, exposing the hard-frozen ground elsewhere.

Temperatures in winter average -16 degrees. The actual range is from an extreme low of -81 to a high of near zero. During extreme cold spells when lights burn constantly the air is filled with minute ice crystals and clouds of steam rise from poorly insulated roofs. There will often be a week or two in mid-winter when the mercury runs between the -50s and -40s and there will be mild spells when it rises to zero or even above for a while. This long period of freezing causes the ground to become so hard that even in mid-summer it thaws not more than a foot on south-facing slopes, causing the condition known as "perma-frost."

Those stampeders arriving safely at Dawson City in the fall of 1897 in the face of this kind of winter were lucky in several respects. They were early enough to find good claims along the creeks, although the best had already been taken, and most of them found space to live on, no matter how limited. When all available ground for quarters was gone at Dawson, the men quickly began to "squat" at the newer settlement on the other side of the Klondike River where it entered the Yukon. Housing was a serious problem with no lumber available except the little shipped in by boat between the ice breakup in late May and the freezeup in October or earlier.

Most men who had come over the passes and down the river in boats they had built at one of the upper lakes, planned to return to the outside by steamboat downriver to St. Michael. So now they proceeded to tear apart the boats they had labored desperately to throw together. The lumber went into houses or flimsy shelters depending on how skilled

DAWSON CITY IN EARLY DAYS— Low, rounded hill in background is "dome" typical of region. Light patch is scar of earth slide in distant past, called Moose Slide because of shape, small stream on far slope bearing same name. Indian legend says slide obliterated flourishing village.

DAWSON CITY TODAY—This was main street, Third Avenue. Modern school, post office, museum are several blocks to right. Town was built on delta of Klondike River, ground swampy in summer, roads and wooden sidewalks elevated above mud. Soft earth extends only about a foot down, icy earth below even in summer—called perma-frost. Sun, in nearly horizontal orbit (in appearance) goes behind dome at back of town, produces light "dusk" at midnight when printed matter can easily be read. Situation produced long day of picture taking for photographer, with frequent interruptions by clouds or drizzle. Temperatures were in 40 to 65 range, in contrast to those of winter when mercury drops to 75 below zero.

or ingenious the builders were. The simplest ones were those put up by men who had hitch-hiked and had nothing to build anything with. They made walls of rough, unhewn logs, chinked them with moss and mud and smoothed off the ground a little for floors. Roofs were of aspen boughs plastered with mud and windows, if any, a row of bottles set in mud. Other shacks were respectable enough, made of ship lumber, usually ten to twelve feet.

Under all the talk and activity of putting up shelter, the new miners became aware of uneasiness among "old timers" who had arrived a few months earlier. The fact uncovered was — the two supply ships due in early autumn had not arrived and the gold-hungry population now faced the very real specter of belly hunger. A few had brought garden

seeds and planted radishes and lettuce on warm earthen roofs in the spring but this fall almost everyone watched the pancake ice coming down the Yukon with great misgivings. The chunks would soon begin freezing together and thickening and that would be the end of travel for the season. Dawson City would be isolated from the outside world until the breakup.

Late in October the superintendent of the Northern Commercial Company held an emergency meeting in front of the Dominion Saloon, and the men heard their worst fears confirmed — the *Porteus B. Weir* and her sister ship *Bella,* due in August, had been held up by low water and more than likely would be frozen in downriver. All men without sufficient food for the winter were advised to hurry

CONFLUENCE OF RIVERS shown in view taken from near summit of dome. Main stream is Yukon flowing from south in distance. Klondike enters at left, waters of different shade coloring Yukon for some distance. Point of level land in left middle distance at junction is site of Louse Town with its once notorious White Chapel red light section. Traffic across river was by boat, then foot bridge, then three-lane, steel railroad bridge. Yukon is not spanned in entire 2,300 mile length except near Whitehorse, some 500 miles above here. Ferry crosses it here in summer, traffic crosses on ice in winter. Dawson City shows blocks sharply delineated by elaborate system of board walks where wide cracks discourage spike heels, rare in town.

down to Fort Yukon which had enough supplies. Then a piercing whistle blast was heard. Everyone rushed to the river bank to cheer the arrival of the boats which had managed to get off the sand bar.

And everyone turned to and helped unload provisions so the two vessels could get back down to St. Michael safely. In two days they left with a full load of passengers who would not chance a Klondike winter. Those remaining could concentrate on digging for gold and squandering it in the bistros.

Enforcement of law and order was strict in Dawson City. Buttermilk was not the prevailing beverage and men did not play tiddlywinks in their spare time or remain celibate. They were all tough adventurers yet killings were few, robberies rare.

While the Royal Canadian Mounted Police recognized saloons, gambling houses and women were all necessary, they were kept under surveillance and any undue rowdyism was subdued right now.

It might have been different if the strike on Bonanza Creek had been the first magnet in the area but earlier was the rich discovery at Forty Mile Creek downstream from Dawson, just a few miles inside the Canadian-Alaskan border. On September 7, 1886, partners Franklin and Madison had struck it after the failure of many including Ed Schieffelin of earlier Tombstone fame. A boom developed at Forty Mile which was just beginning to fade when the Klondike hysteria broke out. A ready-made population complete with police force of twenty men moved up to the new location to be

54

joined by an additional twenty. The really rough element never had a chance.

The police combined several red-light districts in one, total membership 400 girls, establishing a new addition to the thinly populated Klondike City across that river. It was also known as South Dawson and the two-block, double line of cribs as White Chapel. The little cabins were fronted by wooden walks, the street being an impassable morass in summer. In a few months the whole place became known derisively as Louse Town and the editor of the DAWSON NUGGET, with a flair for hyperbole, reported: "The residents of Louse Town have made a big thing of what used to be a nuisance. They are holding louse races and betting large sums on the outcome. One man claims to have developed a speedier strain and offers stud service."

All ordinary price standards for services and goods went by the board due to freighting difficulties and the scarcity of men not engaged in prospecting or mining. Although wages were high, food and supplies were sky-high compared to prices outside. Shovels and underwear, both of the long-handled variety, were $20. Flour cost $400 a barrel. Eggs were $1 apiece, the supply depending on the caprice of two hens. Five minutes in the tub of the bath house cost $1.50 with a change of water, less for that already used and still warm.

Ways of making money were plentiful, when ingenuity was used. One good-looking girl auctioned herself to the highest bidder, the money to be held in trust by the Alaska Commercial Company until breakup. For $5,000 the successful bidder enjoyed

VIEW FROM DOME in southeasterly direction shows spot where fabled Bonanza Creek flows into Klondike, percolating through dredge dumps from left to right. Original discovery of gold that sparked world into Klondike rush was made on Bonanza in middle distance. After miners got out all gold possible by hand methods in network of creeks, dredges came in and at one point on Hunker Creek are still operating on third going-over, each time finding gold in finer flakes.

OLD POST OFFICE was imposing with elaborate tower. Here it is reflected in window full of house plants treasured in long, cold, winters. Months with little sunshine make artificial light necessary for plants' survival. One hanging is **Campanula Isophylla** blooming freely here in twenty-four hour summer daylight.

the young lady's snug companionship all that cold winter.

Those severe winters profoundly affected the course of living and mining in Dawson City. No buildings could be placed on conventional foundations which would shift on ice. Pilings were driven and many proved to be permanent, persisting to the present day. Pilings for the old post office for instance are decaying yet holding up the long abandoned structure.

Early Dawson had no underground sewage system or any provision for sanitation except a few outhouses which required difficult pit digging in solid ice. Public latrines came later, scattered through town with tickets sold for their use. In a year or so authorities worked out a novel system. A gang of guarded convicts followed a dog sled with tank up and down the streets, stopping at each house and business address. On collecting days, if the owner was absent, he would leave the door unlocked. The men would enter, pick up the "slop jar", carry it out to be dumped and return it. When full the tank was hauled out and emptied on the frozen Yukon.

Prospecting along the creeks of the Yukon basin was done in summer and all mining, following the first discoveries, used methods which involved washing the gravel, allowing the heavier gold to settle out either in the simple pan or in sluices or rockers. In winter this kind of elementary recovery stopped abruptly. Since the ground thawed only a foot or so, not much freezing was required to establish perma-frost at the surface which stopped the flow of water and congealed gravel as hard as rock. It then became necessary to thaw a section, remove the softened material and pile it at one side where it was frozen in minutes. When the breakup of the rivers came in May, accumulated piles of gravel were run through sluices and values recovered.

This was the procedure as long as surface gold-bearing gravel was available, which with all the miners working it, was not long. Deeper penetration by sinking a shaft was then required, generally by an elaboration of the easier method. Gold was not evenly distributed, allowing simple removal of over-burden or pit mining. This was uneconomical because the desired metal was found in pockets or concentrations usually running horizontally on layers of gravel laid down in flows of years before. So shafts had to be dug to reach them, every foot gained by thawing, summer or winter. A fire was built on the spot to be worked and after the smoke had cleared out, digging was resumed. Then the whole process was repeated time and again.

When the shaft reached bedrock below all old stream flows, streaks of gold-bearing gravel were followed horizontally either to their conclusion or the limits of the owner's claim — and sometimes beyond. Trouble followed if the infringement was discovered, usually settled by litigation. Sudden death, as in similar U.S. cases, was frowned upon by the Canadian authorities.

Thawing was greatly aided by the "steam point" brought into general use after the first year or two. Steam boilers were brought up on ships and placed at the top of the shafts. A hose carrying a head of steam led down to the working level, ending in a

sort of nozzle with a small opening. A miner could direct a jet of live steam at any point, thawing the material in minutes. The released gravel was lifted out in buckets by means of a winch and piled as before. With the faster system the piles grew larger, often reaching a height of twenty-five feet or more by spring.

Breakup was the biggest event in the calendar, huge bets placed on the exact date and hour the river would open. During the winter several stakes were driven across the river in a straight line. About the second week of May excitement would mount as the time came closer, a man being kept on constant watch for the first shifting of the markers. When this happened everybody would knock off work to watch. In about an hour there would be a loud explosion, followed by several smaller ones, and a narrow crack of black water would become visible. Other cracks developed quickly until the river became a heaving, jumbled mass of house-sized blocks of ice, moving slowly at first, then picking up speed. In about two weeks the river was clear but for another week or two the beach would be cluttered with bergs pushed ashore.

TERRITORIAL AUTHORITIES are making effort to revive Dawson as tourist attraction, largest accomplishment so far being restoration of old Palace Grand Theater where visitors attend plays during summer celebration—Gold Rush Festival. Another project, less publicized, is renovation of pioneer cemetery. This photo made in old Royal Canadian Mounted Police barracks shows weathered headboards brought in for repainting. When board is removed from grave, legend is copied, placed in corked bottle and partly buried at location. Lush summer vegetation soon covers all other marks. Boards are painted snowy white, letters black. Still visible on boards in photo are letters Y.O.O.P.—Yukon Order of Pioneers.

RELICS OF RUSH DAYS are still found but rapidly falling into decay. This store was still filled with stock left when abandoned. Being hundreds of miles from paved highways has saved relic from vandals.

With the breakup came spring and its long hours of daylight and by the middle of June those hours had extended over twenty-four and on the several nights around the 21st, the sun did not set at all. At Dawson City itself however, it passed almost horizontally behind a low peak, the Dome, directly back of and to the north of the city. From about eleven o'clock at night until two, a kind of dusk settled, affording a psuedo nighttime period.

The night of the 21st provided an annual excuse for picnics on the summit of the Dome to watch the midnight sun descend far enough to skim the Ogilvie Range to the north and on the stroke of twelve to be almost eclipsed for a moment behind the highest peak. Nights were warm but there would be big bonfires all over the level plateau.

This was the time of year nature relented, holding back the frosts, ice and snow to allow flowers to bloom by millions. Square miles of wild roses covered the tundra, punctuated here and there by groves of greening aspens and spruces. Every open glade between these stunted trees was filled with sheets of blue lupine and *mertensia*, locally called bluebells. Continuous hours of daylight allowed uninterrupted growth and quick maturity, forming seed before the early winter.

The same respite saw feverish activity in the mines. The very first trickles of water were used to run accumulated gravel through the sluices, the owner full of pent up anxiety to know if he was going to be rich or "skunked". After a few impatient trials, a semi-permanent set up allowed more water

to enter the upper ends of the sluices. Streams high up were usually small and often shared by several claims, used and reused until the once-clear water was liquid mud by the time it reached the bottom. Gold was allowed to accumulate on the riffles, the small cross bars on the bottoms of the sluice boxes, and after a few days a clean up was made.

The annual spring clean up varied in value from nothing at all to those like the fabulous one of Alex McDonald, who in June 1899, after scraping out the crevices behind his riffles, found he had so much gold it took twenty-nine mules to pack it into town. Nuggets were often detected as the gravel was dug, if large enough, or exposed in washing. Now and then some lucky miner found a streak along bedrock where there was a gleaming deposit, more gold than gravel. Many claims were abandoned or sold as worthless, the next owner finding a fortune nearer bedrock. Several of these yielded more than a million dollars.

But the river bed gravels were finally exhausted and things slowed up. When some late arriving "cheechahkos", or newcomers, asked where they might find some gold, they were told with sneers to try "up there on the hill." They did and excitement started all over again. They had struck prehistoric gravels where the stream once flowed and there was as much gold there as in the more modern beds. During the big year of 1898 the Klondike and its tributaries yielded $10 million.

During the early boom almost all trade in Dawson was carried on with gold dust as the medium of exchange at $17 per ounce. The supply of the glittering stuff was carried around in pokes, made of caribou or moose hide with draw strings or thongs. Most dust and nuggets, over and above that needed for immediate use, found its way to the bank to be melted and formed into bars. There was about 2% weight loss in the fluxing process where copper and iron were sloughed off. The pure bars were then assayed, since the "fineness" varied, the best being worth $20 per ounce, and the silver that most of them contained allowed for at 67 cents per ounce.

Bars were packed into heavy wooden boxes reinforced with metal straps and shipped down the Yukon to Seattle. One such shipment, made from the Alaska Commercial Company's dock, June 9, 1901, weighed a ton and a half. The early and grossly exaggerated reports of boats carrying a "Ton of Gold" were then to become fact.

There were several small fires in Dawson's first year. In the frigid temperature most of the stoves were fired to a cherry red and kept that way with flimsy stove pipes sticking through wooden roofs. When the situation became extremely hazardous, police stepped in. They made a thorough examination of all premises, pointing out the worst fire dangers and giving occupants twenty-four hours to make alterations. It stopped most of the fires until a big one gutted the entire business section.

This did not start from some foreseeable condition. Above one saloon was a cubicle rented to "one of the girls" and among her many customers was one gentleman valued for more than his money. The girl heard rumors he was sharing his attentions with another but he denied the accusation. The argument waxed above the boiling point and the girl flung a lighted kerosene lamp at him. The bonfire turned into a holocaust of massive destruction and in the rebuilding, all prostitutes were banished to Louse Town. This may have accelerated the construction of a footbridge to replace the use of boats. Bitter complaints by the girls were soon heard. They claimed that during the summer period when daylight prevailed the clock around, their customers felt conspicuous parading across the bridge on errands with obvious purpose and reduced their visits which put a crimp in the "cribbage".

For a few years Dawson City enjoyed a boom never before seen. But the "little man", with his pan and pick, and the slightly better equipped one with shovels and sluice boxes, soon faded into history. The rich and easy diggings were becoming exhausted, and while there was still plenty of gold it was necessary to use larger and more mechanized equipment. "Big business" had come into the picture. Knocked down dredges were shipped up the Yukon, put together at Dawson and were soon operating on the rivers. One of these monsters with a small crew could replace hundreds of men working by hand and the glory of Dawson went with the miners. Not all the men went outside, for the "Golden Sands" of Nome's beaches were beckoning. The new boom town located near where Anvil

ROBERT WILLIAM SERVICE, born in England in 1874, moved to Canada in '97, eventually settling on Vancouver Island farm. Traveling widely over Western Canada he worked as bank clerk in Dawson City and Whitehorse long enough to absorb "atmosphere" of north country, wrote many poems and novels. This cabin, in profusion of aspens and spruce, was his home in Dawson. On slight elevation at base of dome back of town near pioneer cemetery, it gave him fine view of town and river. Interior is simply furnished.

GROUP OF GIRLS celebrate in front of crib in notorious White Chapel section of Louse Town, "suburb" of Dawson City. District was exiled from town proper when one girl flung kerosene lamp at customer in fit of temper, setting entire city aflame.

Creek drains into Bering Sea was soon populated with men drained from Dawson.

There were still occasional bursts of excitement over some new strike but the big frenzy was over. There had been a time when an ounce of dust was standard pay for a day's work but now it was six dollars in paper or cheechahko money. Many of those who had packed their outfits so painfully over the passes and floated them so dangerously down the Yukon to Dawson City would never make good now. Some who had brought a little money with them spent their time in the bars until it was gone. Others held auction sales, disposing of the belongings to those headed for Nome or some other strike, then left for home. And Dawson City settled down like a city come of age.

There were still enough people to keep the dance halls, saloons and gambling rooms going on the same twenty-four hour basis. The Palace Grand Theater where Alexander Pantages first made his name still offered programs with such stars as Marjorie Rambeau. Where a newspaper was a rarity to be read to assembled crowds by somebody standing on a bar, there were now several regular weeklies, the best known, the KLONDIKE NUGGET.

And there were still such characters as One Eyed Riley who won $17,000 in a single poker game. Going outside while he was ahead, he fell in with "friends" at Whitehorse on the way and lost $3,000

BELLE OF THE YU 1898

PHOTO of classically draped female was displayed in every saloon in town. Subject seems to show effects of long winter diet of salt pork, beans and flapjacks.

60

in a game of stud. In Skagway he decided to indulge in another hand or two and lost the rest of his stake. The next morning he was headed back to the Klondike to recoup his losses.

There was always scurvy, sometimes approaching epidemic proportions, the waves following the lack of fruits and vegetables. The regulation "ton of provisions" brought in by one Englishman was composed largely of orange marmalade. He soon discovered the rare delicacy could be sold at outrageous prices and disposed of every tin for enough to buy a claim.

And there were still strange sights to be seen in Dawson City. One man brought a string of milk goats to Skagway to help pull his sled load up the pass and down to Lake Bennett. Many superfluous animals were butchered for food but the goats were pets and went on to Dawson City as the first such animals in the Yukon. In a town where only canned milk was available, the fresh supply from goats was worth a fortune. However when a friend brought in an orphaned moose calf, one of the goats was set to nursing it — with difficulties. The "child" towered over the foster mother and was unable to reach the source of supply. The problem was solved by standing the goat on a table.

Dan McDonald was one of the thousands who poured into Dawson City in the big rush period but instead of leaving after the bonanza days, he stayed on to make a home on the bank of the Yukon. He enjoys telling of the old days, particularly the building and operating of Dawson's railroad.

The maze of gold bearing creeks and their equally rich tributaries flowing north into the Klondike have their sources in a range of mountains to the southeast of the town. A pair of humps, characteristic of the region, are set on the summit of the ridge — King Dome and Queen Dome. The streams flowing on the far slopes run into the Stewart River and eventually the Yukon. They were also rich in gold, particularly the Dominion. In this area were concentrated thousands of mines, all clamoring for some easy way to get supplies in and gold out. A group of English financiers saw in the situation a chance to reap some of the fabled Klondike gold. They formed a company which bought engines and track materials for a narrow gauge railway, shipping them to Seattle and Skagway, over the newly built White Pass and Yukon Railroad and at Whitehorse transferring them to boats which delivered them at Dawson City.

In the meantime one crew of local laborers, most of the men disappointed miners, were cutting ties from native trees and the Dominion Bridge and Construction Company started a three-span bridge to carry the tracks across the Klondike.

The first trip on the new line in 1906 was a gala affair. The train, named "Pow Wow", started at the station which was half a block upstream from the Bank of Commerce and ran to Hunker Summit, almost in the center of the teeming mining district. The main attraction here was a roadhouse operated by a Jakie Hartman, a favorite stopping place for those on their way to Sulphur, Goldbottom and Goldrun, small mining towns. The train passengers soothed throats made hoarse by cheering and several who wanted to make the return trip hanging to the outside of the engine had to be forcibly removed.

INTERIORS OF OLD BUILDINGS show great variety of objects. This curiosity on counter caused photographer many hours of research, leads resulting in no positive identification. Possible solution is in old Smithsonian photo of Beach typewriter of about 1860 in wooden case. Machine here could be "innards" of similar model. Keys were thrust into center to make contact with two-inch strip of paper running over spools at right and left.

LITTLE ENGINE, smaller than most, served as work horse in hauling dirt, gold bearing gravel, to localities more convenient for washing. It burned wood cut from nearby hills which was hauled behind in tender. Note "spike coupling" in front, requiring manual insertion of pin to connect extra engine or car to be pushed. At lower right behind bumper can be seen steam cylinders and piston drivers. Larger engines burned coal in plentiful supply from open pits at Carmack, some distance up Yukon, supply shipped down on river barges. Dawson City never had rail connection to outside world, line local only to serve mines.

After the festivities the railroad settled down to hauling gold and freight although a regular passenger service was maintained and an excursion run made each year to watch the midnight sun from the summit of King Solomon's Dome. One cargo consignment was a huge, knocked-down dredge for Goldrun. Gold was shipped in heavy strongboxes by the new Klondike Mines Railway Express. With all the labor and expense of building and maintaining the railroad it lasted only eight years when gold production dropped.

Dan McDonald, who had been connected with the railroad in one way and another since its inception, on such jobs as working for Guggenheim and Co. loading trains with their derrick system, was on the last train in 1914. "Some of us had tears in our eyes," he recalls, "and some who were celebrating too hard actually bawled. It was really a sad affair and should have been carried off with some dignity. But a roaring argument got started among some of the boys and we almost had a knockdown fight on our hands at the finish."

The end of the railroad was a strong indication of the way things were going for Dawson City as well. It was never the same. Theaters, saloons and gay spots turned off their lights one by one and a fabulous era was finished.

WHITEHORSE, Y.T.

The modern city of Whitehorse is anything but a ghost town. It has a population of 8,000, most of the people in the entire Territory. It is the capitol of Yukon, having taken that honor from Dawson City which boasted of 30,000 people in gold rush days and has fine air fields, hotels, restaurants and all conveniences of a thriving city. Whitehorse began to boom at the turn of the century when the narrow gauge railroad was built over White Pass, from tidewater at Skagway to the interior terminus at Whitehorse, and kept on growing slowly until the Alaska Highway was built in the exigencies of the second World War when Alaska and Yukon were exposed to attack from nearby Siberia.

As a supply center in a remote gold rush region Whitehorse became a real boom town, with all the roistering aspects expected with a flood of single men. After this impact the town had a more normal growth as the main stop on the long Alaska Highway.

YUKON RIVER flows swiftly past old docks at Whitehorse. In busy days of water traffic steamers tied up here, unloaded or took on cargo for points below. Concrete platform, middle left, supported large crane. Across river is site of old Closeleigh, original town in area. Above this point entire flow of river is confined between rocky walls of Miles Canyon only 30 feet apart in some places, torrent of foaming water rushing through gorge. Yukon here flows north to enter last of series of long, narrow lakes—Lake La Barge—then heads for Alaska, eventually spreading out over 75 mile wide delta to enter Bering Sea. Total length is over 2,000 miles.

But prospering Whitehorse does not forget or neglect its historic single street along the waterfront. On the river side are such remnants as old loading wharves and hulks of steamboats they served. Scattered opposite are greying, false-fronted buildings remaining from the days when hordes of gold-hungry stampeders came swarming over the passes from Skagway and Dyea, then by boat down the twenty-five mile length of Lake Bennett into the upper end of shorter Lake Tagish.

At the foot of Tagish a post of Royal Canadian Mounted Police made a second check — the first having been made at the summit of the pass — to see that no one went on down the Yukon without the required amount of food. And this was something of a bottleneck, impatient prospectors chafing at the delay while police opened and checked bags of beans, rice, flour, sugar, ham, bacon, tea, coffee, condensed milk and dried fruit.

RELIC OF GOLD RUSH DAYS is tram car, built to run on wooden poles instead of rails. Two tram lines were built to by-pass treacherous Miles Canyon water. The Hepburn ran along the west bank of the river, the other built by originator of idea Norman Macauley, followed east side ending at Closeleigh, long vanished, across river from Whitehorse. Cleared lanes for tram lines are still visible along canyon, as are rotting remnants of pole rails.

The next hurdle was a rough stretch of water into Lake Marsh, in itself easy going but its outlet one of the most feared stretches on the entire waterway, Miles Canyon. Here the flow of water from all the lake basins were confined to a gorge whose vertical rock walls were only thirty feet apart in places, forming a torrent of white water sweeping at express train speed. Pressure caused a high ridge to form in the middle to which boats must cling or be crushed to kindling wood against the rocky walls. In some spots the channel was deep with spinning whirlpools and in others rocky shelves almost broke the surface, causing water to lunge forward in a series of cascades. Squaw Rapids was the first of these, then mile-long White Horse Rapids where the foamy, snowy crests resembled charging ranks of white stallions.

The story is told of one man's adventure in the canyon. He had made the arduous trip over the

NOVEL SITE chosen for nest building by eave swallows. Sometimes called cliff swallows, they prefer locations near water for greater supply of insects which are caught on wing. Birds are expert masons, building nests of mud in closely packed ranks, equipping each with entrance spout for greater privacy.

SLEIGH was in regular mail service many years, equipped with double set of runners to facilitate turning. Museum is one of original buildings remaining in old, ghostly section of Whitehorse. Dog sled on roof is not relic, merely stored for summer. Sleds are still much used in long, snowy winters and dog sled races are held in Whitehorse annually, attracting participants from entire northland.

pass, labored hard to build his boat, loaded it with all his supplies and in this welter of white danger with the end of his trip almost in sight, came crashing up against a projecting rock, losing everything but his life.

Half a mile downstream he struggled ashore and dried his clothes at a campfire. Gathering all the courage he could muster he set out on foot back to Skagway. The next season he had a new outfit in another boat but headed down the same canyon like a cork at the mercy of vicious water. And his boat struck the same rock. He made it to shore again but this time he would change the pattern. He pulled out a gun and shot himself.

At the end of this run men were only too glad to haul out on shore to catch their breath, rebuild or repair their crafts. The rapids were a proving ground, exposing poor or too hasty construction at Lake Bennett — especially the sparing of nails, scarcest item of all. One man who had brought plenty of them had some left over but instead of selling them for a fancy price at the lake, cannily took them with him down river and sold them for even more at the end of White Horse Rapids. Leaks in many boats were due to hulls improperly caulked. This was usually done with rags soaked in spruce pitch but it was natural to skimp on this item as spruce became harder to find every week.

Some of the rushers chose to stay at this resting spot until they were sure boats and themselves could make the rest of the river. Some enterprising individual set up a saloon and the crude shack soon had the company of a whacked-together hotel and other structures until the collection bore the aspects of a frontier town, acquiring the name of Closeleigh. Though roughly primitive, Closeleigh was never violent during its short life as the Royal Canadian Mounted Police discouraged any incipient rough stuff.

Then came the building of the tram lines — two parallel lines running along the sides of Miles Canyon, eliminating the danger for those who could afford the ride. The one on the east bank terminated at Closeleigh, the other at a point across the river where a twin town began to grow. It was quickly seen a single town had all the advantages in this country of short supply, so the only building in Closeleigh worth moving was taken across the frozen Yukon to the west bank town. This was named Whitehorse and Closeleigh was relegated to history.

BUSY, REGULAR STEAMSHIP service was maintained from here to St. Michael on Norton Sound. Water traffic was possible only in short summer period, Yukon itself is frozen almost solid in long winter, as is Bering Sea north of Aleutians. This chain of islands is geographical divider of climate, shunting southward warmer Japanese current, keeping ocean free of ice along Alaska's Panhandle. Each autumn before freeze up Yukon steamers were pulled up on bank to keep hulls clear of crushing ice. When river traffic became unprofitable, partly because of completion of Alaska Highway, boats were not returned to river in spring. Most are rotting, one converted to museum.

CHAIN OF EVENTS leading to writing of **Cremation of Sam Magee** by Robert W. Service began with steamer **Olive May's** being stuck on mud flats at head of Lake Laberge. She was caught in fall freeze up, became enforced home for crew for winter. Nearby was cabin of old trapper seriously ill with scurvy. Dr. Sugden came from Tagish near Whitehorse but found the man dead. Unable to bury him in frozen ground, doctor borrowed firebox of **Olive May**, cremated remains, turned ashes over to police. Later Dr. Sugden, while living with Whitehorse bank clerk Service, related story to him and poem was written, Service borrowing name of Sam Magee from friend in nearby cabin. Real Magee lived until 1940, dying in Calgary. This cabin was part of original Whitehorse and has been preserved.

SKAGWAY, ALASKA

If ever there was a "jumping off" place, Skagway took all the honors. The end of a hazardous sea voyage up the Inside Passage, the beginning of the devil knew what. It had all the confused excitement of a gold camp, all the panic and breathless anxiety, all the nervous expectancy, yet it was only a kind of shakedown stage in the journey to danger and adventure, the gateway to Dawson City and beyond.

Skagway lay at the extreme north tip of Lynn Canal, an inlet penetrating a maze of islands right up to the very foot of towering mountain peaks on Alaska's mainland. Strongly resembling a Norwegian fjord, the water way ended in an almost level delta of soil and gravel brought down the canyons by tumultuous streams.

The same geographic feature that provided space for a town to grow on made impossible any near approach for incoming ships. All steamers were forced to stay far outside, unloading passengers and freight on lighters, most of them at first little more than rafts. Huge piles of supplies bought in Seattle by Yukon-bound passengers were hastily dumped on the nearly flat beach to be searched out and claimed by their owners. Often before the bewildered gold seeker could locate his belongings a high tide carried them away. Replacing anything was next to impossible in Skagway and many a luckless stranger was stranded without passage money home.

If he did rescue his gear he had two choices of routes to the lakes on the other side of the mountains which were the headwaters of the mighty Yukon River, this the only inland way to the gold fields. There was White Pass, starting directly out of Skagway and Chilkoot Pass, beginning at Dyea, an old Indian settlement a few miles from Skagway. Until the gold rush began there had been only one white man at Dyea, Sam Heron, operating the Healy and Wilson Trading Post. Indians working in a fish cannery at nearby Chilkat spent their money at Heron's post and on rare occasions a white trapper or prospector would come through. A year after the rush began the village had changed to a city of tents and a few frame buildings. After the turn of the century, when the railroad chose the other pass for the right of way, Dyea's buildings rotted and collapsed under the heavy snows. Today there is hardly a trace of the town, said to have more wickedness to the square block than Skagway, something difficult to comprehend.

Skagway, at first spelled Skaguay, differed in some ways from an actual gold camp. Where it offered two kinds of a living, one hard working and

"SOAPY" SMITH (fourth from right) in Skagway with some of his cohorts about 1897.

ONE TIME FIREHOUSE stands with gaping windows. Many such deserted buildings in Skagway are in imminent danger of collapse or are being wrecked. Low level of timberline on closely surrounding mountains is evident here, Skagway being at sea level. Short climb up slopes brings into view numerous glaciers and ice fields.

rs. Pullen and Pullen House Bus in Early Days

"MA" PULLEN, one of best known and most loved women in Alaska. She met each incoming steamer with carriage drawn by best of her seven horses brought from her former ranch in Washington state.

morally upright, the other preying on the prosperity and lusts of the diligent, in Skagway there was no choice. Everybody was there for one purpose, to get out as quickly as possible. There was no "respectable" section and if there had been any street lights they would all have been red. The legitimate stores, hotels, offices were all but obscured by the brothels, saloons and vicious gambling halls. Parasite or host — which was which? Many times the knowledge came too late.

The probable reason for all the unrestrained depravity was Skagway's remoteness. Although in American territory the place had its birth without federal or territorial benefit or regulations of any sort. Then again a large part of Skagway's sudden population was made up of escapists and the worst kind of criminals looking for a place to operate. The innocent, confused and timid were their easy prey.

Many of the criminal predators were on their way somewhere just as their victims were. The boom camp of Dawson City was full of newly rich miners eager for a good time with wide-open gold

pokes. But both spider and fly came up against Canadian vigilance. At the top of the pass was the border and the harpies were stopped, the Royal Canadian Mounted Police not about to permit an invasion of known criminals into British Columbia or the slightly more distant Yukon Territory, part of Northwest Territory. Frustrated crooks and toughs of all sorts had no recourse but to return to Skagway and set up business.

Jefferson Randal Smith, a suave, cultured Southern gentleman, was reputedly the most notorious of such bad men. Nicknamed "Soapy" from a come-on game of selling bars of soap on street corners with the spiel that some were wrapped in dollar bills, Smith was fresh from the fading gold towns of Colorado.

He found Skagway his succulent oyster. More than a thousand lots were sold the first few months. Hotels, stores, restaurants were springing up, sold and resold at fantastic figures. The Skagway water was too cold to drink so sixty-seven saloons offered suitable substitutes.

ONCE FAMED all over Alaska, Pullen House now stands in decrepit solitude. This picture was taken from railroad track. Behind photographer was simple marble monument marking grave of Harriet Smith Pullen. Although time was late June, apple tree in full bloom shows lateness of northern season.

The bunco man bought one of them in the fall of 1897 and found work for the shills and confederates he had brought with him, an unholy lot of footpads, thugs, ruffians, harlots and card sharps. From the prospects already in town he expanded his gang to around three hundred members, each proficient in his particular field of chicanery. Contact men and bunco steerers met every boat, glad handed passengers, weeded out the well-heeled with practiced eye and steered them to Soapy's Saloon where a free drink was the starter. A good percentage of such tenderfeet soon found themselves out on the street with a cracked skull and stripped pockets. Smith himself was never in evidence when such things happened, remaining a power in the back room. He emerged however to pose as a public benefactor at public celebrations, making a great show of helping widows, orphans and the sick. These deeds masked his activities for a time but they became too flagrant to conceal.

His downfall came one day after a victim complained to authorities who were waiting for such a chance. A vigilante committee was organized to confront Smith and round up his formidable gang. The group met in the city hall but adjourned to larger space in a warehouse at the end of Sylvester

Dock. One of the leaders was Frank Reid who had left Minnesota for Oregon, serving through the Paiute Indian War and going to Alaska in 1897. He was a sharpshooter with his rifle and went armed at all times as did many in the rough and tumble town.

Smith had spies everywhere and one of them carried news of the meeting to him. Whatever qualities he lacked, one of them was not courage. He took his own gun and walked down the dock, confronting the men at the meeting. Reid told him he was under arrest. Smith brought up his gun just as Reid did, the two shots ringing out together. The mobster's career ended at that moment but Reid lived on for some time and both were buried at the little cemetery above town. A stone placed on Reid's grave was inscribed: "Frank Reid, died July 20, 1898. He gave his life for Skagway." The other grave was marked: "Jefferson R. Smith. Died July 8—aged 38 years." Most of the Smith gang leaders were rounded up and jailed, the unimportant riffraff gradually disappearing and Skagway was a little safer.

Even before the exit of Soapy Smith, church services were held in the town, the first in a tent.

Before 1900 houses of worship for Presbyterian, Catholic and Methodist faiths were established. Even Y.M.C.A. and Salvation Army centers were organized. A skilled photographer, E. A. Hegg, native of Sweden, set up a studio in Dyea. Since the tiny building was built of lumber salvaged from a boat it was anything but light tight and Hegg solved the difficulty by raising a tent inside. Later he moved to the more solid Skagway, eventually taking the trail to the Yukon. He made pictures along the way, developing the plates under all sorts of conditions such as inside small river boats and drafty shacks with the weather far below zero. Hegg has left the best record of people and conditions along the route to the Klondike.

Skagway's most famous resident was a woman, Harriet Smith Pullen, more familiarly known as "Ma Pullen." Purportedly a widow, a long-time woman friend in Skagway said: "Harriet always says she's a widow but she had a lot of trouble with her husband in Washington where they had a ranch and once she told me he had deserted her." Whatever the case, Mrs. Pullen was left with four small children and the ranch including seven horses. When she heard of the gold rush and the wonderful opportunities to make a fortune in the North Country, she left her children in the care of relatives, headed for Seattle, was lucky enough to get passage to Skagway and arrived there in the fall of 1897.

The raw frontier collection of tents had a job for everybody and Mrs. Pullen was hired to cook at three dollars a day. Before long she was making pies of dried apples in off hours at a dollar apiece. Then she was turning them out by the hundreds, accumulating enough money to send for her children who arrived about Christmas.

The tall, red-haired woman kept at her pie baking until she had enough funds to bring the horses to Skagway to run a pack train to the pass. She was at the beach when the steamer pulled into shallow water, watched cranes lift the animals over the side to drop them into the cold brine. As each swam ashore, Mrs. Pullen seized it by the bridle until she had all seven in tow.

With a stout freight wagon purchased out of her pie money, two strong horses hauled miners' supplies to the foot of the pass where they were transferred to the backs of the other horses. As soon as all were loaded, Mrs. Pullen took her position at the head of the train and led the string to the summit where the freight was turned over to the owner.

The building of the narrow gauge railroad over the pass at the turn of the century made the horse freighting business obsolete. Ma Pullen then turned her energies in the logical direction, to her cooking abilities. She bought a house and converted it into a hotel. There is history behind the house.

In 1888 Captain William Moore, sixty-six years of age, and his son J. Bernard, settled at the eastern end of the tiny valley that would soon hold the town of Skagway and built a comfortable home for his family. Being the first permanent whites in the area they enjoyed peace—for a short time. Then the ravening hordes of gold seekers descended on them "like locusts," Moore said later. Over-running his property at the foot of the pass, they ruined his farm. All appeals to shadowy authority proved futile so Captain Moore made up his mind—"If you can't lick 'em, join 'em." He abandoned his place and took off for the Klondike.

The pioneer prospector did so well for himself he soon returned "outside" by dog sled. He took the trail in reverse. Traveling much of the way on the solidly frozen Yukon and the lakes at its head, then over the summit and down the pass to Skagway and his home. Beside his gold he carried with him a large load of letters, among the first to reach a world avidly awaiting news from the interior. One message was an appeal from Captain Constantine of Dawson to the Minister of the Interior of Ottawa —"For God's sake get more police reinforcements to us." Finished with farming, Moore sold the land to several individuals, the home to Harriet Pullen.

The indomitable woman set about remodeling the building near the new railroad tracks. Pullen House signs faced both the tracks and "Broadway," two blocks away. Bath, wash basin and toilet were installed in every room. Some years later, when she expanded the hotel with an addition at the rear, two such facilities sufficed for each floor, rates being less.

By this time Ma Pullen was the best known character in Alaska, the size and quality of her meals famous beyond it. She used no paid advertising but word of mouth carried her renown. She knew what people wanted and what they would talk about. One feature was the rich cream from several Jersey cows. When guests were served large dishes of wild raspberries from the mountains they would find at hand an enormous pan of milk and with a ladle would skim off as much thick cream as they wanted. This sort of thing got around.

Many famous people stopped at the Pullen House over the years, among them Robert W. Service, Jack London, and President Harding. A monument in the neglected garden marks the spot where Warren G. Harding addressed a crowd of citizens.

One of the many stories told of Harriet Pullen is about the small boys who caught trout in the little stream running through the grounds then sold them to Ma. She would pay for them by barter with a doughnut or piece of pie. When it came to settling real debts with cash however, she was not always so prompt to pay. Once she hired Skagway's well known mason, "Charlie" Walker, to build a fine fireplace for the lodge. Charlie did a good job but well aware of her tendencies, left a board across the inside of the flue. When he asked for his money Ma said he would get it in due time. Anxious to show off the improvement, Ma held a celebration and lit the fireplace for the first time. A thick cloud of black smoke billowed out and the guests scattered. Next day Ma upbraided the builder but got a controlled answer. "Ma—when you pay for the fireplace job it will stop smoking." She paid Charlie and he pulled out the obstruction.

Harriet Pullen died a few days before her 87th birthday. She was buried just across the railroad tracks in a lonely grave with a simple white stone marker reading: "Harriet S. Pullen. August 13, 1860—August 9, 1947."

SKAGWAY TODAY — Golden North Hotel shows peaked dome at right. Charming girl at desk wearing "gay nineties" dress, was asked name of mountain towering above. "It's named Mount Harding of course," she replied. "He was the only president to visit Alaska.

ARIZONA
GHOST TOWNS

BY

LAMBERT FLORIN

Drawings
by
DAVID C. MASON, M.D.

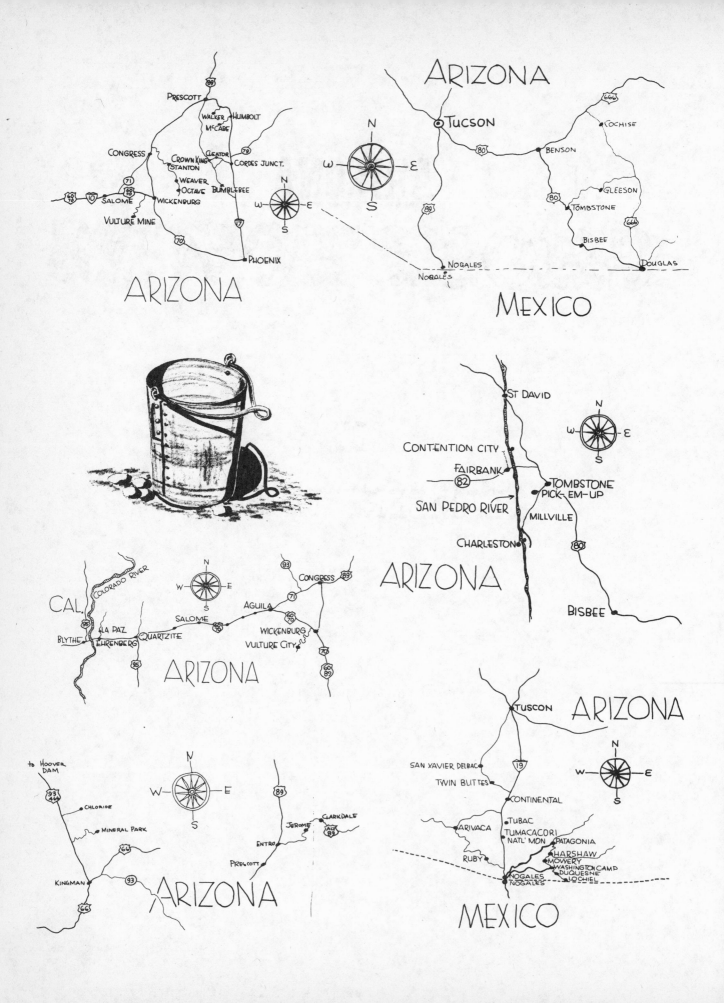

INDEX

CITY	Page
Bumble Bee	77
Calabasas	78
Charleston	81
Chloride	85
Cleator	86
Contention City	89
Crown King	91
Dos Cabezas	92
Ehrenberg	96
Fairbank	100
Gleeson	102
Goldroad	104
Jerome	105
Kitchen Ranch	112

CITY	Page
McCabe	114
Mineral Park	117
Mowery	122
Oatman	125
Quartzsite	126
Salome	128
Stanton	131
Tombstone	133
Tubac	138
Twin Buttes	139
Vulture City	143
Weaver	148
White Hills	150

BUMBLE BEE, ARIZONA

The prospectors were evidently more impressed with bumble bees than with Mr. Snyder for they changed the name of the settlement from Snyder's Station to Bumble Bee. Or it is possible they stumbled into bumble bee nests or as another story has it, they found Indians "as thick as bumble bees".

When W. W. Snyder settled in the valley there was plenty of water in the creek the year around with lots of lush pasture for his horses and cattle. There was also a crude road that penetrated the wild, "Indian infested" land. The term was Snyder's and the other whites', for of course the Indians were marauders for trying to drive the invaders from the Indian lands. And they were making some success of it when a small detachment of U.S. soldiers was sent into the valley to protect Snyder and other ranchers and prospectors to the good soil and water.

A stage line soon began irregular service and Snyder built a small hostelry and stable to accommodate travelers. The stop was known as Snyder's Station for many years. When gold was discovered in the adjacent Bradshaw Mountains, prospectors were soon dipping their pans in the creek.

Most gold discoveries were not made at Bumble Bee itself but in neighboring camps such as those along Turkey Creek — Golden Turkey, Cleator, Gloriana, the enormously rich Tip Top above Gillette, the Silver Prince, Black Warrior, Cougar, New Jersey and many more famous mines along the southwestern fringes of the Bradshaws. The Peck was outstanding. The first ten tons from that mine were sold to Prescott merchants for $10,000, so an old Prescott newspaper stated. Since the stage road to these areas led through Bumble Bee, the town shared a little of the prosperity.

Bumble Bee had gold of its own but the deposits were so rich a man could get no more than a little section the size of a blanket — hence a "blanket claim". From even this small area he might make $100 a day, for a few days. Some of the gravel beds large enough and lasting long enough to acquire names and an illusory fame were Chinese Bar, Portuguese Bar and the Dead Man. Even these were practically exhausted by the early 1900s and remained dormant until depression years when desperate men combed the sands for a few flakes of gold.

All through the years the town has tried to stay "by the side of the road", moving to follow survey realignments three times. At last it was by-passed so far by the Black Canyon highway it could not follow, now remains complacent on a good graveled side road.

PRESENT TOWN OF BUMBLE BEE was offered for sale in eastern newspapers, was purchased lock, stock and barrel by magazine publisher Charles E. Penn and wife Helen, who have restored it to original form.

DISTILLED FROM BLOOD AND COURAGE

Calabasas, Arizona

Oh yes, the old timer agreed, the Apaches were cruel, ruthless, bold and bloodthirsty. But he knew of one case where 200 of them were bitten by white men's bullets and none ever lived to retaliate. Well, there was proof of that too. Don Frederico Hulseman showed Peter Bady a string of what looked to him like dried apple slices, about three feet long. "Ears, my friend," said Don Frederico, "cut from those dead Apaches. See the gold and beaded earrings?"

In this part of southern Arizona and many areas of the southwest travelers take note of curious, spreading vines, each plant usually covering roughly about ten feet in diameter. Early in the season there will be many blossoms scattered along the vines, replaced in late summer by globular fruits about grapefruit size. When dry they are hollow except for seeds that rattle on shaking, leaves and other succulent parts disappearing to leave the hardshelled globes, now pale straw colored, conspicuous on the vines.

These are the wild form of Cucurbita Pepo, an inedible form of pumpkin. They grow in abundance in southern Arizona. Early Spanish explorers found the vines growing everywhere and in the Indians' field of corn, cultivated pumpkins. They called the village Calabasas, either for the little inedible gourds or table pumpkins. The native vines proved far more enduring and still flourish at the townsite long bare of almost any trace of busy life.

For several years following 1691 Father Kino spent most of his time traveling between his mis-

LONELY REMNANT of adobe building, likely last surviving trace of Calabasas with its dark, bloody history. Searching for old town best directions available led author to spot on banks of dry Santa Cruz River where large field of cotton flourished in full bloom. Spanish speaking Mexican workers disclaimed ever having heard of town but said this patch of cotton was called "Calabasas field." Beating thorny mesquite brush revealed this broken relic.

sion at San Xavier del Bac and the head mission at Dolores, Sonora. As a matter of convenience he later established a second mission at Guevavi (sometimes Guebabi). With a priest station here the Indian village of Calabasas became a more readily accessible *visita*.

In 1767 the Spanish government expelled all Jesuit priests from the new world including the area around Calabasas. By 1827 all Spanish, whether priests or ranch owners were expelled by the now dominant Mexican authorities, leaving missions and *visitas* fully vulnerable to murderous Apaches. Calabasas was reduced to little more than a tiny village, a few Mexicans working a gold mine nearby.

In 1842 the square leagues of land comprising Tumacacori, Calabasas and Guevavi were combined into one huge grant which, two years later, the state of Sonora sold to one Francisco Aguilar for $500. A coincidence that Aguilar was the brother-in-law of Manuel Gandra, Governor of Sonora?

During the next decade Gov. Gandra built and fortified a large hacienda at Calabasas, the most attractive site along the generously flowing Santa Cruz River. He stocked it with huge herds of cattle, horses and sheep, the watching Apaches holding back until the rancho was complete, then moving in for the kill. Driving off all stock for butchering and burning, they slaughtered some Mexicans and put the rest to flight. An American dragoon passing by in 1854 stopped there and later wrote, "...at the rancho de las Calabasas are the ruins of an old church with the altar still standing and the bell hanging in the belfry. The road from Tucson lay in the valley of the Santa Cruz as far as this ranch which is occupied by two Germans. A third brother has been killed by the Indians and all their cattle and horses have been stolen by the savages. The two brothers kept an awful old 'bachelor hall'."

Plenty of water for irrigation on good soil brought Indians and Mexicans back to occupy Calabasas during what proved to be only a short lull between Apache raids. Late in 1854 engineer Peter Bady, surveying the 32nd parallel for a rail line, was camped on the Sonoita when he was informed by two Mexicans recently escaped from Apache warriors that their captors were planning to attack Calabasas again and this time kill everybody. Bady took ten men and headed for the

town, meeting on the way sixty Mexican dragoons and forty Apache *mansos* (tamed or domesticated Apaches) who joined his party. Reaching the ranch, now headed by Don Frederico Hulseman, Bady made known the impending danger and instructed Hulseman to his plan, retreating with his forces to heavy brush cover a few hundred yards from the ranch.

About mid-day the watching Hulseman spotted advancing Apaches and blew a high-pitched call on the cavalry bugle as prearranged. Bady and men responded at once, mounting and charging directly into the center of the two hundred Apaches. He later reported, "No cry of mercy was given and no mercy shown." Most of the invaders were killed outright by the Mexican dragoons, the wounded finished off by the mansos, leaving not one survivor. Not long after the slaughter Bady received a dinner invitation from Don Frederico. "Before we eat," the host said, "let me show you something." What Bady saw in the courtyard was the three-foot string of dried Apache ears.

Some protection was being extended by U.S. troops, the territory having become part of the United States the year before. In 1861 the soldiers were removed to fight in the Civil War and the town of the pumpkins was again left to the mercy of the Apaches. In 1864 peripatetic reporter J. Ross Browne wrote to his magazine, Harper's, that he

DRAWINGS are part of promotional spread appearing in New York **Daily Graphic**, Oct. 18, 1878. Variation in caption spelling of Calabasas persists to present day. Form using letter "z" is original Castilian spelling first applied to village. Later Mexican spelling uses "s".

MOUNT WRIGHTSON, FROM CALABAZA, SANTA CRUZ VALLEY.

PLAN OF THE HOTEL AND PLAZA AT CALABASAS AS IT WILL APPEAR WHEN COMPL

had visited the valley, a place of rich soil, ample irrigation and surrounded by mines of copper and gold. "It might be made profitable in the hands of some enterprising American . . . at present, however, military protection in the country is worthless owing to the incursion of the Apaches." He recounted the well known story of Mrs. Page, daughter of early settler "Old Man" Pennington, of how she was captured, tortured and thrown into a gulch for dead, and how after several days of near unconsciousness she managed to crawl to a point where she was seen and rescued.

By 1878 nearby Tucson was in the throes of a boom, fast building up with stores and saloons for travelers arriving at the Old Pueblo. At this time two men from San Francisco chose Calabasas as a delightful place for a luxury hotel. They were John H. Curry, ex-judge, and Charles P. Sykes, newspaper publisher, both visionaries. They went to ex-Gov. Gandra and brother-in-law Aguilar and from them purchased the site for about $6,000.

In late 1878 Tucson papers noted there was much activity at the old town, that the whole area was being surveyed and a hotel building started. Col. Sykes was quoted as saying his hotel would be two-storied and made of brick being fired in the vicinity as the stables and corral would also be. G. W. Atkinson, the best brick man in San Francisco had been hired to oversee the project. Sykes sent out glittering brochures and worked up much enthusiasm for his new hotel. On the negative side the Tombstone *Epitaph* sneered at what it called "Pumpkinville," fully expecting Sykes to

have heavy ocean going vessels plying the Santa Cruz right to the town, unloading world merchandise at its teeming docks.

Yet in spite of these and other spoofing attitudes with dire warnings that the Apaches would stop the building, the hotel was finished. In October of 1882 Sykes arranged for a large delegation from Tucson to come to Calabasas for the grand opening, hiring the Tucson Brass Band to serenade the party all the way. The group left Tucson at 5 a.m. and finally arrived in Calabasas dog-tired in the evening, the account adding, "as only water was available to drink along the way."

Col. Sykes welcomed the party with open arms and uncorked bottles. He fed the delegates roasts of mutton, chicken, beef and game, including wild turkey, quail, plover and British snipe. After supper the party observed floors covered with Brussels carpet, solid black walnut furniture in every room. Plied with more spirits the party danced until midnight. Sightseeing the next day, all returned to Tucson singing praise for Sykes' hotel, "the best between San Francisco and Denver."

Not long after the successful grand opening the colonel began to miss some of his cattle and after several more depredations the losses were traced to the Apaches. One night they were so bold as to enter the brick corral and drag away a pair of blooded black carriage horses. Probably unable to ride them the savages killed the blacks not far from the hotel. Next they kidnaped three members of the Peck family in the area and brutally murdered them. In spite of all this Col. Sykes carried on, filling his registers with the names of some of the most prominent people in the country.

But the end of the dream was coming up sharply. In 1894 the Court of Private Land Claims voided all Spanish land grants along the border. The action wiped out Boston syndicates operating mines leased from Col. Sykes, townsite of Calabasas and hotel. Sykes died on a trip to New York City, his widow living in a room in the hotel until her death in 1910 and the heirs made their homes in houses near it, using some rooms for hay storage after the mother passed away. In 1927 fire broke out in the stored fodder and the entire building burned to the ground, bricks and other unburnables hauled away by Indians and ranchers. Calabasas, distilled from blood and courage, is today almost invisible.

PUZZLING ARRANGEMENT of wooden posts few feet from adobe ruin at edge of Calabasas cotton field. Framed is what appears to be same peak called Mount Wrightson in old sketch. Named for Prof. W. Wrightson, early historian, peak often called Old Baldy now, is highest in Santa Cruz County. One of author's few clues in locating Calabasas was lining up peak as in old drawing of town.

CHARLESTON, ARIZONA

It was Red Dog in Alfred Henry Lewis' fiction, historians called it "a place of bloody violence", to Nell Murbarger it was Devil's Den and Muriel Sibell Wolle said: "If the corpse had a gun on him and the fatal shot came from the front, you didn't look for the killer."

All this and much more was Charleston which was connected to Mexico by the San Pedro River and to Tombstone by a constant stream of ore wagons. The ten-mile stretch of the river supplied the water, which Tombstone did not have, to mill the rich gold ore and for like purpose accounted also for the other adobe-built towns along the river — Millville and Contention City.

Perhaps the first white man to build a shelter here was Frederick Brunkow, a German scientist who left his native land under a cloud and wound up in Arizona doing odd jobs. But the School of Mines at Freiburg, Saxony, prepared him for a job with the Sonora Exploring and Mining Co. and he was valuable in locating several rich silver veins. About 1858 Brunkow found one of his own but his efforts ended with death at the hands of his own peons.

In 1879 Richard Gird and Ed Schieffelin formed the Tombstone Mining and Milling Co. with the help of Gov. Safford. Schieffelin was familiar with the Brunkow location and its advantages as a mill site, having worked for a time in those diggings. Gird agreed with him and a ten-stamp mill was built on the east bank of the San Pedro, water reaching it via a wooden flume from a dam constructed a mile south. Milling activity centered here to be called Millville, the town growing up across the stream known as Charleston.

Strictly a company town, Charleston was solidly constructed of the prevailing adobe material, some buildings with wooden floors and plastered walls.

CHARLESTON is in complete ruin, remnants of once thriving town hard to find. Buildings like these, of stone instead of common adobe have endured in part. Area once supported good stand of pasture grass, now grows drought-enduring scraggly stand of thorny mesquite with spines that often draw blood from too careless ghost town explorer. If and when projected Charleston Dam is completed, San Pedro River's trickle will be converted to vast lake inundating site of Charleston.

MOST IMPOSING RUINS of Charleston-Millville complex are those of Richard Gird's "Big House", standing conspicuously on rise above San Pedro River. Rock foundation may have aided drainage, helping preserve ruins beyond life of others.

Hardly had the town been officially laid out in the winter of 1878-9 when it began its career as head-quarters for bandits, horse thieves, murderers — at least in the public fancy, nourished by many writers of fact and fiction, notably called Red Dog in Alfred Henry Lewis' stories in an Eastern newspaper. Any number of reputable historians refer to Charleston as a place of bloody violence. Alma Ready said the town literally lived and died to the sound of gunfire and quoting Muriel Sibell Wolle in THE BONANZA TRAIL: "No one seemed disturbed when dead men lay in the street. If the corpse had a gun on him and the fatal shot had come from the front you didn't look for the killer. Guns made the law and men had to react in a split second." James G. Wolf who arrived in Charleston in 1883 wrote: "There were four saloons going twenty-four hours a day. All kinds of gambling houses operated continuously. There were lots of naughty girls living close to the saloons. . . When paydays occurred at Fort Huachuca many of the soldiers came to Charleston to drink. . . . . ."

Nell Murbarger says in her GHOSTS OF THE ADOBE WALLS: "Here, if we could believe even half

that has been written about the place, was a second Bodie, an embryo Dodge City, a short-lived Devil's Den where dead men littered the streets and gun-smoke drifted over the land like smog."

The other side of the coin is presented by Mrs. Mary Wood who with her husband moved to the town in 1880. The Murbarger book quotes a Tombstone EPITAPH interview with her in 1929 when she said: "If you came to Charleston looking for trouble there were plenty of citizens who would have supplied you with any amount of it . . . but the honest, law abiding citizen went his way with little if any greater hazards than he faces today in any large city". It may be that Mrs. Wood was unaware of some illicit activities in her community, or as Miss Murbarger suggests, the town came nearer its image of toughness as it grew older. There is one singular fact, according to Mrs. Wood, that while $1,380,336 worth of bullion was shipped out from the mill in one year's time, "not a dollar of it was ever molested by highwaymen."

The two noisy stamp mills ran day and night except when a breakdown occurred, even on Sundays. Eastern backers of the operation heard about

82

this desecration of the Sabbath and protested to Dick Gird and manager Wood. They were invited to come to Millville and watch the results of a trial layoff over Sunday. They came, and on Sunday they watched with horror as miners indulged in all-day sprees in the town's saloons. And on Monday they watched the bleary-eyed miners stagger back to work, noted the difficulties of reactivating the cooled-down equipment and left town, convinced the men should be busy every day. How many of Charleston's carousers took advantage of one unique feature is not known but Alma Ready in an ARIZONA HIGHWAYS article writes of the rare luxury of drinks "on the rocks", the town being the proud possessor of one of the first ice machines in Arizona Territory, even supplying the commodity to Tombstone.

In its busiest period Charleston had four general mercantile stores, meat market, drug store, with two restaurants and two laundries operated by Chinese. Mrs. Hughes' Boarding House, Eagle and Royal Hotels served citizens and transients as did saloons, estimated as five to thirteen. Regular visits to these drink emporiums by such notables as the McLowery bunch, Clanton gang and Johnny Ringo did not contribute to law and order.

The town had no jail and Constable James Burnett apparently paid himself. Just when a drunk was rowdy enough to arrest is not known but when a public nuisance was collared, Burnett held him at the point of a sawed-off shotgun, tried, convicted and fined him on the spot, pocketing the proceeds.

As for the usual lynchings with stories of twitching bodies dangling from trees and derricks, it seems Charleston only came close to one. A disgruntled employee at the Gird mill, Johnny-Behind-The-Deuce whipped out his gun and shot chief engineer Henry Schneider fatally. Rumblings of a lynching were stymied by removing him to Tombstone and later to Tucson where he broke jail and vanished.

There was a school in Charleston and legend has it that pupils were accustomed to carrying guns like papa did. While supposedly studying the temptation was great to wing a buzzard flying by the window or pin a fly to the wall. But one Professor Wetherspoon had stricter ideas than his prede-

YUCCAS GROW at Pick-Em-Up stage stop, appropriately marked by ancient trunk. Tiny mining community between Tombstone and Charleston was stop only if stage passengers stood beside road to flag down drivers who were instructed to "Pick 'em up".

cessors. He installed a shelf in the cloakroom and ordered all boys to park their six-guns there.

Another tale concerns the largest bordello. School children would wander to the place after school to look in the windows at whatever was going on. When several of the girls announced at home they had decided what to be when they grew up, owners of the house were ordered to move it. The new location was near Fort Huachuca. Christmas came often for the soldiers.

Whether Charleston or neighboring Tombstone should rightly be termed the toughest town in Arizona Territory may be debated for years to come. Contender Charleston offers at least one well-authenticated incident for its side — the murder of young M. R. Peel.

Across the river stood the immense adobe structures of the Tombstone Mining and Milling Co. including offices and residences facing the river, one room containing a safe built of brick. One evening in 1882 the popular company engineer — Peel — was sitting in the office talking with three friends when two masked men threw open the door. Both intruders raised their rifles and fired point blank at Peel, one slug entering his body, the other bury-

ing itself in the adobe wall. Still without a word, the two murderers fled to their horses held by a third man and disappeared in the darkness. Peel's funeral was held in Tombstone with burial in its famous Boot Hill.

The killing seems to be explained only as a boner in a badly planned payroll robbery attempt. One of the gunmen, identified as William Grounds, was shot and killed the following day while "resisting arrest". The other, Zwing Hunt, though wounded, lived to be placed in the Tombstone jail, later recovering and escaping.

Charleston, spawned with Tombstone, died with Tombstone. When Tombstone's already declining mines began filling with water in the '80s, production of ore slowed to a standstill, leaving little excuse for Charleston to linger on. On top of that, the smaller town's once highly profitable underground trade with Mexico was now cut off by the border town of Nogales.

But it was a caprice of nature that wrecked Charleston — a major earthquake occurring May 3, 1887. Thirty minutes of continued shocks reduced the adobe buildings to rubble and the town was never rebuilt. Its birth as a company town had been sudden, its destruction complete in one half hour.

THIS ROOM in Tombstone Mining and Milling Co. buildings housed company safe, constructed of fire brick and closed by substantial iron door. Door has long since vanished but location of safe is shown here, marked by bricks differing from larger unfired adobe ones.

CHLORIDE, ARIZONA

Here is a town whose classification is dubious because it has changed its status from living to dead and back again several times. Right now it is in-between, with plenty of the old for interest and with a certain amount of respiration not too noticeable.

In this last category is the little, newish building not more sizable than many a living room. It fronts on the main street and bears the proud sign "Chloride City Library." The movie house, on the other hand, shows a view of sagebrush and cacti through the boxoffice. And so it goes with Chloride. One of its ups was a good turquoise mine, owned by Tiffany of New York. One of its downs was the calamity, common to all silver towns, of the collapse in silver values.

Just when a big silver boom had pumped the veins of Chloride full of blood, the deflation period set in. This began in 1884, and when it ended by the demonitization of silver in 1893, Chloride's collapse was complete, at least as of then.

RELIC OF LATER BOOM was movie house. Through once ornate entrance one now sees a framed view of sagebrush and abandoned shacks.

CLEATOR, ARIZONA

The story of Cleator, the town, is the story of Cleator, the man. It was his enterprise that built it and his right to sell it. You could have bought it in 1947 and it is there today to see.

James Patrick Cleator was born June 12, 1870, in Dhoon, Machold Parrish, on the Isle of Man in the Irish Sea. He went to school for a time but later admitted he "knew it all" when he reached the sixth grade. At 12 he went to sea as a cabin boy on the fishing boats and at 15 he was in the crews of grimy coal boats plying the coast from Newcastle to London. After working in a Thames River ship-yard for several months he signed on, at 16, as able seaman on a ship hauling iron from Spain.

In 1887 young Cleator was a hand on the clipper ship *Arthur Stone* making a voyage around the Horn to Chile, loading nitrates there for San Francisco and flour there for Ireland. Now he was 19 and Jimmie knew the salty sea was not for him but the New World was. As a passenger he took ship to Halifax, train to Winnipeg and worked his way by odd jobs to San Francisco.

There was gold talk in the air and the erstwhile sailor turned to prospecting, finding a gold claim in California in 1898 and selling it for $10,000. Then he headed for Mexico, Chihuahua Province where he found nothing interesting and prospected various sections of Arizona. Attracted to British

OVER ALL VIEW OF CLEATOR—Town is placed in desert country at foot of pine-clad Bradshaws. Highest peak, Mount Wasson, over 8,000 feet, is in background. In center is original store and saloon. Left, nearer foreground, is stone school-house built in WPA days. Original two-room schoolhouse is now home and rock shop of Phil and Audrey Reasoner. Desert growth is abundant, **Opuntia**, known as prickly pear, seen in clumps everywhere. Plant in left foreground is **Yucca**, bearing spikes of beautiful white flowers resembling lilies to which it is related. Author's camper is accidently left in photo.

ONE OF MANY STONE CABINS in hills behind Cleator. Primitive structure is typical of many shelters built of available material before lumber came in. Spiky plant in foreground is **Agave**, each leaf normally armed with stout, extremely sharp spike. Some have been trimmed off as plant has encroached on trail, wounding passers by.

Columbia he found the placers along the rivers long exhausted, so returned to the country he liked best, Arizona. Cleator found the Bradshaw Mountains to his liking and remained among them the rest of his life.

In 1902 a railroad was being built from Mayer to the area near the summit of Mount Wasson in the pine-covered Bradshaws where the fabulous Crowned King mine was being exploited. In the foothills the railroad passed the big Golden Turkey mine named for the many wild turkeys in the state. At the point of convenient access to this mine the rail line established loading platforms called Tur-

key Siding. A considerable crew of men was required to handle freight from and equipment to the Golden Turkey and several other mines along Turkey Creek. Some of the men were stationed there permanently, shacks and bunkhouses being built for them. One "Lev" Nellis set up a saloon and added a store beside it.

On New Year's Day, 1905, James Patrick Cleator walked into the saloon, had a drink and struck up conversation with Nellis. The two men found much in common and before the day was over formed a partnership, Cleator buying half-ownership. Lev had always wanted to raise cattle,

STRANGE "ROCK" is owned by Phil and Audrey Reasoner of Cleator. Object seems to be petrified hornet's nest which it strongly resembles in size, form, even color. Phil Reasoner mined in most of shafts and tunnels of New Mexico and Arizona, was forced to retire from effects of long continued breathing of dust from broken and crushed ore. He and wife now run interesting rock shop in Cleator.

had been too busy with the merchandising but now, with amiable and well-liked Cleator to run the store and saloon, he could turn most of his attention to the small herd he already owned.

In ten years both branches of the business had flourished to the point that both partners decided to separate, each taking over his favorite operation. By this time the settlement had grown to need a post office. Although known as Turkey Siding, the word "turkey" was in common use in the area, a new post office at Turkey Creek not far away. Cleator applied for a post office at his store and authorities gave it his name.

With the mines going well, Cleator also prospered as a supply base for them and its principal citizen took advantage of the situation to include real estate in his business. He built a number of small houses, renting and selling them. In all of them he installed the newfangled element—electricity—and piped in clear spring water. Cleator is in the desert

but close to the high Bradshaws where rainfall is abundant.

At 77, James Cleator made a decision. He had been married years before to Pearl Hunt, the couple having a son and daughter. Now he would retire. Accordingly he advertised his town for sale, lock, stock and barrel, in the ARIZONA REPUBLIC. Other newspapers over the country caught the romance of the town for sale idea, repeating the ad with stories of the colorful life of James Patrick Cleator. A flood of letters came in, sometimes as many as fifty a day, but few of the curious wanted to buy a town and no sale was consummated. One newspaper reporter asked what he would like to do if he found a buyer. "I'd fix up an auto rig," Cleator answered, "and see the country."

The ruddy old gentleman died at 85 without fulfilling this wish. His widow, who also reached 85 in January of 1964, still lives in the town her husband built, retaining a keen memory for names, dates and events.

CONTENTION CITY, ARIZONA

"What is it?" asked the grizzled miner from Tombstone when the waitress in a Contention City cafe set a glass in front of him, informing him it was water. "Oh, that," said the miner. "I've heerd. Even tuk a bath in it onct. Say, miss — will you put it in a bottle or sumpin so I can show it to the boys down home."

Water was scarce enough in Tombstone for ore milling purposes and Contention City was one of the most northerly of the several towns established along a ten-mile stretch of the San Pedro River to process the Tombstone ores and took its name from the big mine owned by partners Ed Schieffelin and Richard Gird. Arizona Pioneer Historical Society records explain the use of the name "Contention":

"Hank Williams was one of the thousands of prospectors who flocked to Tombstone when the word got around that Ed Schieffelin had struck it rich. His camp was close to that of Schieffelin and partner Dick Gird. One of his mules got away and in trailing it he noticed that the animal's halter chains were scraping the dirt off of rich ore. He immediately staked a claim, the location of which was hotly contested by Gird. Williams could not have been very positive about his rights in the dispute; he was persuaded to sell out to Schieffelin and Gird. They developed the claim in question, naming the mine Contention."

As soon as the mill site was established just above the San Pedro on the east bank the town site was bought early in September, 1879 by D. T. Smith and John McDermott. By the middle of the month the partners had surveyed the town, within a week were selling lots and up jumped a hotel, saloon, restaurant, laundry and a hodge podge of shanties. The mill on the bluff, 170 feet long with a depth of 142 feet, was being built and three more expected.

In a year or two the place grew to be a solid city, most buildings of adobe, the available material. By that time there were more businesses with a rash of saloons. The most imposing structure facing the "waterfront" was a railroad station, Contention having achieved the proud distinction of being the railhead for the New Mexico, Arizona and Sonora Railroad. While the line was building, contractors and crews had their headquarters in the town and if there was any danger of Dull Care showing up, the boys kept it safely out in the desert.

When William Henry Bishop visited Contention City in 1882, he wrote of the experience in his book MEXICO AND HER LOST PROVINCES. The section concerning the milling town is reprinted in ARIZONA GUIDE: "We changed horses and lunched at Contention City. One naturally expected a certain amount of belligerency in such a place, but none appeared on the surface during our stay. There were

WHAT BUILDING? While rather extensive, ruins give little or no clue as to nature or purpose of building. Low angle of sunlight brings out surface texture of unfired adobe bricks.

RUINS OF Contention Mining and Milling Co., described as having extended 170 feet along side of rocky cliff. Diligent, thorn-harassed search reveals many remains of wood beams, stamp pistons, rusting tools, cables.

plenty of saloons, the Dew Drop and the Headlight among others, and at the door of one of them a Spanish senorita smoked a cigarette and showed her white teeth.

"Contention City is the seat of the stamp mills for crushing ore which is brought to Tombstone. The latter place is without sufficient water power. The stamps are heavy beams which drop on the mineral on the mortar and pestle plan, with a continuous roar, by night as well as by day. 'That's the music I like to hear', said our driver gathering up his reins. 'There ain't no band ekils it' "

Today Contention is a silent place except at night when coyotes croon their spine-tingling wails,

sounds very different from that of crashing stamps. An unmarked dirt road approaches a small turning area on the west bank of the San Pedro. Peering from the mesquite brush lining the river banks, the ghost town hunter can sight the remnants of the railroad depot on the other side. One swims the stream, wades or jumps over it, depending on the season, crosses several sand bars — and there is what is left of the town. No building remains intact, the depot only partly preserved. Many adobe ruins are encountered and many mesquite thorns. The mill ruins lay back against the bluff, only foundations and rotting beams remaining.

If the weather is wet the advice is to stay away, this reporter learning the lesson the hard way. It is impossible to get traction on slippery adobe and while wheels are spinning, the sticky stuff piles up on fenders and undercarriage. And several dips in the road fill rapidly with any fall of water.

CROWN KING, ARIZONA

Just how was an army officer going to take time to work a gold claim? Maybe somebody smarter than he was had an easy answer but prospector A. F. Place, now an officer stationed at Fort Whipple, couldn't see one. The claim on the slopes of Mount Wasson in Arizona's Bradshaw Mountains did not offer too much but Place had to work it to keep it.

With some diligence he found an idle prospector, provided him with shovels, drilling and blasting tools and against his better judgment, paid him in advance. The man started for the claim through Tiger Camp, later Bradshaw City, and spotted a saloon where the doors seemed always to swing in. So he delegated his assignment and tools to two bull whackers and proceeded to relax.

The pair set to work on the claim and soon got down to hard rock. "Well, I guess it's about time you shot a hole," said one. The other looked blank. "Hell, I though you were the dynamite expert. I couldn't drill a hole let alone load it."

Falling back on the shovels they put in time on one spot and another. Toward evening they gathered up a few pieces of rock and walked back to the Tiger saloon where they found the prospector thoroughly mellow. "Nothing but these here pirates", the bull whackers reported." Jumping out of the fog, the prospector whooped: "Pyrites, hell — that's gold!" Such was the first discovery in the district and others would be richer.

Newspapers of that day gave such news full play and one of Prescott's flung banner lines across its pages, February 6, 1899: "The Richest Strike In The History Of Arizona!" and almost as heavy headlines followed: "Ore that runs $180,000 to the ton." Another mine in the Bradshaws was covered in the next line, only a little less black: "The Riches of The Peck Pale Before The Wealth In The Crowned King Mine!"

This splatter of ink stemmed from a letter written by Lester Jackson of the nearby War Eagle mine, just north of the Crowned King property. Jackson had descended the shaft to the 500-foot level, taken a "grab sample" and the assay had re-

vealed the fabulous values. The newspaper article quieted down to continue: "Mr. Jackson states that the sample was taken from a 10-inch chute of ore. He does not state the extent of the chute. Much excitement prevails all through the Bradshaws over the strike which is the greatest bona fide find in the history of Western quartz mining."

The paper's glowing reports failed to state the difficulty encountered with much of Crowned King ore. From the very first mills had trouble extracting the gold which assays showed was there. The first samplings of ore sent down by burro to the mills by the river proved so obdurate that run-of-the-mine ore was refused, mills accepting only less refractory material. Since burro-back transportation was expensive and slow, much ore was cast aside on the dumps. Later a railroad angled down the mountain as steeply as possible to where the wheels lost traction, then went through a series of switchbacks with the little train reversing itself on every hairpin turn.

By this time ore was being taken out at deeper levels and was improving in quality. Yet much of it

PHIL ANDREWS REVISITS MILL and assay office where he worked thirty-five years ago, was never able to recover gold values in ore discarded long ago as refractory. Scene is in Bradshaw Mountains named for David Bradshaw, pioneer who came to area from California where as member of Bear Flag party he was instrumental in capturing Sonoma, California, in 1846. Bradshaws at these higher levels are covered with dense timber, mostly pine.

was still being thrown aside as too hard to mill. From time to time mining experts would cast covetous eyes at Crowned King ore but even as more modern methods of recovery came into use a big proportion was rejected either at mine or mill. While usage was shortening its name to Crown King piles of "good ore" remained on the dumps and became a legend into modern times. These were the times of Phil Andrews.

Having just graduated from college with a degree in chemistry, Stanley Phillips Andrews was ready for a career. One of his closest friends in San Diego in 1928 was Arthur Kipp, whose father was a mining engineer and friend of the senior Stanley Phillips Andrews. Young Phil was approached by Foster Kipp to take the job of laboratory technician and assistant in the assay office at the Crown King mine. The properties had been closed and abandoned for many years but the dumps of valuable ores were still tempting and Kipp thought he had figured out ways and means of converting them into money. He had backers ready to invest in a quarter million dollar mill at the site, another quarter mil-

lion in equipment and men to work over the old dumps. Previous assays of it ranged from $520 to $540 a ton and now it was estimated there were two and a half million dollars in the dump which could be worked profitably.

Of course the road was a hazard. Years before the railroad had been taken out and an automobile road built over the grade which had some comparatively gentle curves but the same precarious hairpin turns where the switchbacks had been. But it was the old trestles that raised the back hair. Planks were laid on these, barely wide enough for tires of cars which were Model Ts and later Model As. The spindly trestles that spanned deep canyons were but one car width, one of them having a sharp curve in the center, a driver honking his horn vigorously before venturing onto the span. All materials for the

CORNER OF DANCE HALL, Anderson's Saloon. Pancho Villa "got his start" as woodchopper at Crown King mine. When winter snows were deep and wood inaccessible, inveterate poker player Villa sought this cozy spot near stove.

new mill had to be hauled over these death-defying spans.

When Phil Andrews arrived for work he found about fifty people in the reactivated town. He had dinner at the fixed-up mess hall and bunked with several other young fellows in a small frame and sheet metal shack dubbed the "Y.M.C.A." The rest of the crew were all married.

Although actual assay work was new to him the process was familiar and he soon mastered the art of "bucking down" a batch of hard ore on the block, to "quarter" it again and again with a frame with two metal dividers to obtain a "quantitative analysis" by saving one quarter in each operation and discarding the rest. The weight of the sample saved was carefully compared with that of the shining silver and gold "button" which resulted from roasting the powdered ore, giving the values per ton. Silver and gold could be separated for exact measuring.

Life after work was somewhat dull except for Saturday nights in the town where Phil and the other single fellows found a preponderance of girls, as most boys old enough to leave home were at jobs in Phoenix or away at school. There was a weekly dance in the old schoolhouse that attracted the local young people and ranchers from "below" who drove twenty miles or more even over the hair-raising trestles. The school desks would be moved against the wall, floor dusted with wax and Victrola started. There would be "Two Black Crows" and "Yes, We Have No Bananas" until things got going then waltzes and fox trots until the small hours — a family affair rather than a wild west or mining camp dance, everybody having a good time without too much drinking. It could be a man thought he needed a clear head for driving on a road that included two planks on a spidery trestle over a deep canyon.

But things were not going well at the mill. Although Phil Andrews' assays continued to show the same good values, "we just weren't recovering," he says. "The values weren't going into the tailings either and we never did find out why the gold didn't show in the concentrates." The absentee backers be-

gan to think something was wrong and made a series of changes. Foster Kipp was discharged, Tomlinson had a chance to try his method and when nothing came of this, Earl Cranz was made manager and he tried his method which also failed. At this point the entire crew was let out and the operation ended.

Later other companies, or perhaps the same one, tried to extract Crown King's stubborn gold. One possibly had some success, as evidenced by a considerable pile of tailings, but at least three-fourths of the dump remains intact. When the WPB stopped gold mining in 1942 all further attempts at conversion were also stopped. Crown King today is occupied sparsely by a new non-mining group of summer visitors. The mountain refuge is a pleasant spot being about seven thousand feet high, cool in summer and shaded by whispering pines.

STAIRS USED BY MALE CUSTOMERS of girls in Anderson's Saloon. No girls now — hardly any stairs.

COPPER IN APACHELAND

Dos Cabezas, Arizona

The old town of Dos Cabezas lies sleeping in an easy hollow between two low mountain ranges. Conspicuous on the summit of one and directly above the near-deserted camp are the twin granite knobs that give the town and range the name, Dos Cabezas, Spanish for "Two Heads." Hardy Spanish explorers named it as they did many noticeable landmarks in the early 1500s when they scoured the southwest seeking the fabled Seven Cities of Cibola.

Later Mexicans forced the native Chiricahua Apaches from the area and after the end of the war with Mexico and acquisition through the Gadsden Purchase, the country was opened up to white settlers. The first party to camp at Dos Cabezas Spring was composed of soldiers under command of the Capt. Richard Stoddard Elwell who became a Confederate officer of some note. He found the spring of good water directly on the emigrant trail, originally an Indian trail, and camped there before the Gadsden Act was ratified. Later he returned to establish the first stage station in the area, a building erected close to Elwell's Spring of gushing water. Some of the tired emigrants stopped at this sign of civilization and refused to go on.

They were easy prey for the Apaches who pillaged and plundered in a reign of terror that whites seemed as unable to repel as Mexicans had earlier. At the end of eighteen months, sixteen stages and drivers failed to get to the Spring, almost certainly having fallen victims to the savages. The burned remains of one stage was located nearby, the nude body of one man bearing more than a hundred inch-deep burns made by fire brands. The station then closed down. Several others attempted to operate it, Jim Birch being one who held off the Indians until 1858. Then came John Butterfield who made stage coach history. Precious metals were being worked near Cabezas and in 1858 he located his new stage stop a quarter mile from the old spring site, nearer the nucleus of what was rapidly becoming a town.

By this time Dos Cabezas was a center for prospectors, some of them just passing through, others finding traces of metal in the nearby hills. Several small mines were operating and "home made" mills established. With Elwell's Spring no longer adequate for the increased population and too far from the new "city center", a well was dug which proved to be a large success, the water table showing at shallow depths. Every family had a handy supply of water in the back yard, each well equipped with a hand windlass and wooden bucket at the end of a rope.

About 1906 a man known only as "Old Man Mitchell" ran across a rich vein of copper just north of town near the foot of the range. The simple prospector had neither strength nor money to develop his claim, but talk about it reached another man who though also lacking money, had initiative. T. N. McCauley bought the property and then searched out wealthy, influential men who organized the Mascot Copper Company, Inc.

The new company installed the most modern equipment at the mine and built a modern complex near it to house officials and personnel. Dormitories for store employees flanked a movie house, grade school, cafeteria, store, dairy and numerous other facilities. A generator supplied electricity. All structures utilized the easily obtainable adobe and were plastered neatly white. Mexican laborers did the work being familiar with adobe construction. Although development of housing had gone on at top speed, adobe took time and all manner of tents and shacks went up to temporary use of mine and office workers and their families.

For twenty years the Mascot was big news in mining journals. The company built a smelter that cost many thousands, a new powerhouse about a million. Irked at having to haul copper to the nearest railhead at Wilcox, Mascot built its own railroad to that point.

For a time the town had its own post office. Its biggest business was sorting out the daily mail orders with money and checks for stock, and mailing out gilt-edged certificates. Then this stopped abruptly for shortly after the big powerhouse was finished miners came up to daylight with bad news. The rich lode of copper had come to an end. Experts were sent into the mine to survey the situation and they could find no metal, so at a time when prosperity and optimism were at their heights, copper mining at Dos Cabezas was something in the past.

More than 300 employees were told there would be no more checks and to leave town if they

DOS CABEZAS STORE was spared general destruction for unexplained reason when town died as important mining center. Large company dance hall, center of joy unconfined for 20 years, remains as shell at left. Each house in town had own well, this old one with concrete curbing. Shaft now serves as daytime home for large horned owl who sleeps on rocky ledge, shows strong resentment at being disturbed by snapping bill.

could. Those owning the little frame houses sold them for pittances. Wrecking balls were swung against all permanent-type buildings including offices, dormitories and the showplace powerhouse. Dos Cabezas became an instant ghost town.

Several families stll make the town of two heads their home, living there in the hope that some day another copper vein may be uncovered or having nowhere else to go. Nell Merwin is one who likes the town and clings stubbornly to her old home, one of the oldest houses still standing, a museum of relics and artifacts of old Dos Cabezas. She likes people, the town that was and takes pride in entertaining random visitors interested in the history of the one time copper metropolis. She provided most of this story of Dos Cabezas.

ADOBE STRUCTURE reputed to be Butterfield Stage Station, built in 1858. It was erected as overnight stop for Argonauts heading for California gold fields. John Butterfield chose location nearer center of town than near Elwell's Spring where community started. First building there was long used as family residence. After some years residents fled house in terror, saying ghosts chased them away. Another family moved in with same results. The whiteclad spirits were reported hovering near and making unearthly noises. At last historic building was razed, a sacrifice to superstition. This second stage station will soon crumble away, stone foundation prolonging survival.

EHRENBERG, ARIZONA

Whiskey, loose women, pigs and the law were all mixed up in Tom Hamilton's life. He served some of the whiskey over the bar and drank about the same amount to keep it from spoiling. Loose women were no problem as long as he could get enough customers for them. But his pigs caused the judge no end of trouble — and he was the judge.

Hamilton ran a combination store, saloon and brothel in Ehrenberg, a brawling frontier town in the late '60s and through the '70s. The drab cluster of adobe buildings was not a mining town but served as a supply center for the placer activity along the Colorado River's east shore.

As a bartender, Hamilton set up the bottles and glasses, pawed in the money and gold dust and took three fingers himself when anybody wanted to pay for it. And if there were fights and shootings, he was no man to stop the boys from having a little fun. Somebody was bound to be thrown in the calaboose and who would he face in the court in the morning? Tom Hamilton, justice of the peace.

That is, if and providing the j.p. was sober enough to face anybody. If not, he was regaining his strength in bed and further derelict in another duty — looking after his pigs. The porkers had no respect for the flimsy fence around the sty and were not inclined to lead their lives in quiet desperation. They wandered. And most of the time into stores to root around in the leather, lamp wicks and lard and cause general consternation. They also invaded private kitchens and found no welcome greetings from the women trying to get a pot of beans in the oven.

Complaints became so numerous the judge decided he would have to do something but nothing as drastic as staying sober to look after his swine. He simply commandeered a raft, took the pigs across the Colorado and turned them loose. They had to be content rooting around in the willows, until the happy day they discovered a prospector's camp and reduced the food supply to a shambles. The prospector evened things up by shooting one of the vandals and hanging the butchered carcass to a convenient tree branch.

But these goings on were witnessed by one of the Indians in the j.p.'s employ and he reported them to Hamilton. Already unsteady, the owner of the pigs downed a couple more, groped for his gun, crossed the river and found the guilty pig shooter still in camp and very indignant. "This is California," he protested to Hamilton with a show of bravado. "Your jurisdiction is good only in Arizona and you can't force me to cross the river." The judge responded that his gun said he could and he did.

The hearing was held in the saloon immediately. Tom Hamilton lubricated his throat and made a speech to the effect that the prospector was now in Arizona where he was subject to the law laid down by Ehrenberg's justice of the peace. He had stolen and killed a pig belonging to the said jurist and the crime had been witnessed. Nobody could say he had

ALMOST COMPLETE ANONYMITY is lot of pioneers buried in old Ehrenberg cemetery. The good markers of wood have long since weathered away, as many carried off by souvenir hunters, those remaining showing little or no legend, as board at left. Sometimes cacti, such as cholla, right center, afford a sort of temporary monument. One grave is said to have been marked: "J.C. 1867", with brand of the man's horse and year he died of gunplay in street.

not had a fair trial so the penalty was fair — to Hamilton. "I fine you $50 for stealing and $50 for the hog."

In New Mexico Territory in January, 1862, Captain Pauline (born Paulino) Weaver discovered some flakes of gold in a wash called by the Mexicans Arroyo Del Tinaja. The location was roughly halfway between what would later be Ehrenberg and Quartzsite, some 140 miles north of Yuma (then Arizona City) on the Colorado. Weaver is said to have secreted the gold in a goose quill pen for safekeeping but the legend does not explain how he happened to have such an object in his possession as he was illiterate. The yellow granules were taken to Yuma where their glint created a sensation and started a full-scale gold rush.

Jose Maria Redondo was in the vanguard. He found a nugget, called by the Mexicans *chispa*, weighing two ounces. When he spread the news in Yuma a second exodus depopulated the town even more. Then in February Juan Ferra discovered a *chispa* of nearly three pounds.

Now the news spread to the coast and the cities of Los Angeles and San Francisco began to feel the impact with so many hopefuls leaving for the gold fields on the Colorado. But now came an obstacle almost unique in gold rush history — the blazing heat. The climate had been most pleasant in January but by July the hordes of would-be miners ar-

riving from the cool coast found temperatures rising to 120 degrees, with suffocating humidity from the river and its vegetation. There were many heat prostrations and some deaths, particularly among women and children.

Many were discouraged, many returned to the coast, replaced by hardy Mexicans from Sonora. Then a nugget was displayed in the window of a California jeweler, C. Ducommun. The glittering curiosity weighed almost four pounds. This reversed the traffic flow and soon there were so many travelers arriving at the riverbank that enterprising William Bradshaw established a ferry and reaped a harvest comparable to those in the placers where hardly a man made less than $100 a day, some $1,000.

Soon a town came into being as a center for supplies and liquid refreshment — Laguna de la Paz, shortened to La Paz. Olivia, Mineral City and Ehrenberg sprang up nearby, only the latter reaching any size. Laguna de la Paz or "Lake of Peace" was bordered by a quiet backwater of the Colorado when founded, yet the valley became a menace, anything but peaceful, when the floods came roaring down. Olivia was named for "Ollie" Oatman, one of two sisters who were taken into brutal captivity by Apaches near Gila Bend in 1851 when their parents were killed and brother badly beaten. The other sister, Mary Ann, died while held by the

97

Indians but Olivia was released in 1856 and joined her brother who by then had recovered in Yuma. Mineral City was hopefully named when good deposits of gold ore were panned in the nearby wash, booming for a short time and dying as the metal petered out.

Ehrenberg lived longer. Herman Ehrenberg, mining engineer and hero of the Texas Independence War, was a famous figure in early Arizona history, having prospected almost all the state. Right after the Gadsden Purchase he and another well known Arizona pioneer, Charles D. Poston, spent some of 1854 and 1855 looking over the hills above Tubac. Ehrenberg gradually worked his way northwest toward the placers along the gullies and washes.

"Mike" Goldwater, grandfather of the present senator, had a business in La Paz. It flourished with the town but when mud deposits cut it from the river about 1869 the place began to falter and Goldwater established a new store six or seven miles down the Colorado where a number of adobe houses had been erected around an army post installed ten years earlier. He named the new town for his longtime friend Ehrenberg who had been murdered at Dos Palmas.

Until 1877 when the railroad reached and passed beyond Yuma, the store of J. Goldwater & Bro. was supplied mainly by river boats plying the Colorado, returning downstream with many pounds of placer gold for the San Francisco mint. The light boats went down to Puerto Ysabel at the mouth of the river, their cargo shifted to ocean-going vessels for the voyage down the Gulf of California and north to San Francisco. Several of the river boats were owned by Capt. Isaac Polhamus under the name of the Colorado Steam Navigation Co. He and the Goldwater brothers were cronies, for although Polhamus lived in Yuma, he was often in Ehrenberg with one of his steamers.

The town was so well supplied with saloons it could spare one. When forced out of business for lack of patronage, the building was put into use as a school house, the town's first. In April, 1872, bright-eyed Mary Elizabeth Post came from San Diego by stagecoach to Yuma where she waited ten days for the flat-bottomed boat to take her to Ehrenberg as its first teacher. Barely settled in the raw, dusty frontier town, Mary Elizabeth was confronted by fifteen bashful, dark-eyed Mexican children, none of whom could speak a word of English — and she no word of Spanish. She was rescued by the kindly owner of the store next door who took over as interpreter. In addition to formal lessons, pupils and teacher sat outside in the evenings with lights out so as not to attract insects and did exercises in language and poetry.

Living was rugged in Ehrenberg. All water had to be hauled from the muddy Colorado and settled in tanks. Four inches of dust lay in the street and building lumber was imported at great cost, the only local trees being scrubby willows and cottonwoods. Construction was almost entirely adobe and sun-dried bricks whose thickness gave some protection from the hot sun. Insects were obnoxious, especially the stinging, biting types and non-biting black flies that swarmed in black clouds over all food. Part of the plague was due to garbage decomposing at the edge of town in the intense heat and there were always burro and cattle droppings.

Yet as long as gold was harvested nearby and as long as river traffic was important, Ehrenberg continued to thrive. But the $7 million in gold panned out of the arroyos was all there was. When the railroad was completed past Yuma the river boats lost their lifeline and stayed tied to the wharves. Olivia and Mineral City succumbed, leaving almost no trace.

OLD PHOTO OF LA PAZ taken at turn of century shows long abandoned river port as ghost town. Buildings were adobe, only material available. Town was originally called Laguna de la Paz, situated on backwater lagoon of Colorado River. Harbor proved liability, filling with sand when river became raging torrent in unusually high water from melting snows in Rockies. Isolation from vital river traffic proved fatal to port.

Ehrenberg has almost vanished too. Until a very few years ago there were numerous adobe ruins standing forlornly near the river to give some semblance of shape to the once busy port. Then came a trailer park and the historic remains were leveled to the ground, except for one pitiful corner remnant still visible from the road. The cemetery is somewhat more permanent although most markers have vanished and the legends on the few remaining ones are illegible.

La Paz is even more nebulous. It gave up the county seat to Yuma in 1870 and quickly faded out. A few mounds of adobe remain at the edge of the Colorado River Indian Reservation six miles above Ehrenberg, almost impossible to find in the brush and sand.

WAGON HAS STOOD near cemetery many years, protracted weathering making pattern of wood grain.

FAIRBANK, ARIZONA

Fairbank, on the Santa Cruz River and between Contention City and Tombstone, was a supply center for both and way station for drivers hauling ore from mines at Tombstone to the mills at Contention. It was also an important point on the railroad from Guaymas, Mexico and Benson and a stage terminal for mail and express. Generally supposed to be a corruption of "faro bank," the name of the town more likely honors Chicago merchant K. N. Fairbank who had many mining interests in the area. Early Spanish missionaries reported an Indian village named Santa Cruz on the site in 1700. Even today heavy rains will sometimes expose such artifacts as arrowheads and pottery shards.

The river is subject to sudden flash floods, storms on the headwaters in old Mexico will sometimes swell the usually meager flow to a torrent sweeping all before it. One of these floods occurred in September 1890 and the damage was all the more terrifying because it hit in the night when everyone was asleep. The Tombstone EPITAPH reported the flood, the story recounting heroic efforts on the part of a Mr. Salcido owner of a lodging house. He was awakened by the roar of the waters and ran to each room, warning occupants to flee. "He had cleared the rooms and was leaving when the flood struck the front door and filled the house with water before he could get to the back exit to open the door and let the water run through. The water was up to his neck in a moment and he struggled until help arrived and saved him. . . . He was taken to Williams' Drug Store where he recovered from his fright. . ."

But nothing that ever happened in Fairbank was more exciting than the attempt to rob the Wells Fargo car at the turn of the century. Sensational at the time, details seemed to have faded away but were unearthed in a 1912 issue of the long defunct REAL MEN OF ARIZONA. "One affray in which Jeff Milton took part proved not to be scatheless, but resulted in victory for him and the breaking up of a most dangerous gang of train robbers that ever infested the Territory.

"It occurred in February of 1900 in Fairbank. Milton was still in the employ of the Express Co. as a messenger (or guard) on the Mexican run from Benson to Guaymas, and on one of his runs he met Bill Stiles a deputy sheriff of Cochise County. Stiles at that time was joined with Bert Alvord also a deputy sheriff. Both were secretly engaged in depredations of their own, themselves keeping discreetly in the background while they planned hold-ups without being discovered. The dividing line between law breakers and defenders was a weak and shaky one in those days and participants in the one activity might the next day join the other side, or take both parts on occasion.

"Stiles told Milton he had arranged a good deal in the desert southwest of Tucson and was desirous of having Milton join him in promoting it. Milton replied that this was impossible, as he was on his way to Guaymas. Stiles then asked "you are sure of that, are you? Well, when you start north again be sure and telegraph me so I can meet you in Benson." Milton promised and Stiles went on his way to plan a hold-up of the Wells Fargo train at Fairbank at a time when Milton whose readiness as a gunfighter was legend would not be present.

"As it happened, however, Milton received a telegram from W. F. Owen, the Express Co. Superintendent, ordering him to return north to take the place of a messenger named Jones who had fallen sick. In his hurry to return he failed to notify Stiles, so when the car marked for holdup stopped in the dusk of a winter's day in Fairbank the man whom Stiles least desired to run up against was guarding the treasure.

"Fairbank was a much bigger place in those days and there was a considerable number of packages to hand out. Milton noticed a considerable number of men in the offing, but presumed them to be cowpunchers. As he stooped to pick up another parcel he heard a voice shout out 'Hands up, there, you blankety blank so and sos!' 'What's the matter?' asked Milton. 'Oh, I guess some of the boys are having a little fun,' answered the agent. 'That's mighty poor fun. Somebody is likely to get hurt around here,' responded Milton.

"He had hardly stopped speaking when the 'Hands up' command was repeated by several voices. And the next moment a number of the men opened fire on him with six-guns and Winchester rifles. The gang was comprised of the Owens brothers, Bravo Horn and a certain notorious bad man, murderer, horsethief and all around desperado named Three Fingered Jack Dunlap. 'Damn it, boys, line up, there,' cried a voice above the fusilade. Milton was shot at the start by a ball that shattered his arm just above the wrist. Another ball knocked off his hat and grazed his skull. Tumbling back into the car he jumped for his gun which was ready and loaded and returned to the door. It was so dark, with people running about, some shooting, that it was impossible to know which were friends and which were enemies. Lead pelted the air in all directions, a perfect storm of bullets rained toward him and riddled the car.

"One ball knocked a lump of flesh out of the same arm already wounded. Then still another entered the arm, ranged upward through the bone and shattered an artery. At this juncture he managed to raise his gun and deliver what turned out to be the most effective blow of the whole battle, shooting Three Finger Jack fatally, though the bandit did not immediately die. Milton, fearing he would die or at least faint away, took the key from the treasure safe and tossed it outside into the darkness.

"When the bandits entered the car they took him for a dead man, searched him and the car for the key. They had not provided themselves with dynamite, and having fully counted on capturing the messenger without a struggle they were forced to abandon the robbery. Only a short time had elapsed since the start of the robbery but they had already remained too long. The excited town was already gathering men to battle the gang. Three Fingered Jack was lifted onto his horse, lashed to the saddle and the gang dashed out of town.

"Retarded in their flight by their wounded companion, they heartlessly abandoned him to die. He was found in the brush about nine miles away next day by one of the posses that was scouring the country. He lived long enough to make a confession. A general rounding up of the gang followed. Bill Stiles turned state's evidence, the others were given long terms in the penitentiary. Since then there have been no further attempts to rob a Well Fargo car.

"Milton was given the best attention locally, then hurried to a hospital in San Francisco where surgeons decided they would have to amputate the arm in order to save his life. When this news was transmitted to Milton he protested, 'Now Doc, what good would I be without my arm? If you cut it off the first thing I'll do when I get out is kill the man that did the job, that goes!' The arm was not amputated, Milton lived and regained partial use of it. He later joined the U.S. Immigration Service as a rider along the border."

The ARIZONA GUIDE, published in 1940 credits Fairbank with a population of 50. As of now, no such number is in evidence, though the store still operates in a small way, as does the postoffice. There are a few trailer houses parked back in the mesquite brush. But Fairbank now is a very different place from the roistering stage and train stop it was when Three Fingered Jack, Bill Stiles and their gang attempted to hold up the treasure car there.

THIS STORE, still operating, served Fairbank in early days. Of adobe construction, it has changed little from times when travel consisted of mule trains hauling ore from mines at Tombstone to mills at Contention City.

GLEESON, ARIZONA

The robin's-egg magic of turquoise lay hidden in the story of Gleeson but old Chief Cochise and the white man he trusted gave the town a gaudier color—blood red.

The Spanish had originally mined turquoise in the Dragoon Mountains as had a primitive race of Indians before them. The Spanish were a hard lot and subjected the aborigines to a state of slavery but were never able to extract from them the secret of where the real treasure of the blue-green gemstone lay. When the white man came and tried to win over the Indians with double-dealing tactics, Apache Chief Cochise, who had intended to be friendly if his tribe was let alone, rose up in all his savage wrath.

Up to 1860 Cochise had not actually molested any Americans but when he was taken into custody and accused of having conducted a raid on a ranch near the spot where the mining town of Gleeson was later built, he escaped his captors and made up for all the trouble he had not caused, spreading murder, rape and destruction among the ranchers.

For a long time he holed up in the Dragoons in an almost impregnable fortress. He held the U. S. Army at bay for ten years, yielding only through mediation with the one white man he trusted. This was Tom Jeffords who operated a stage on the old Butterfield line, long so vulnerable to Apache attack that drivers never traveled the route without an armed guard always on watch.

Jeffords had lost twenty-two of his men to the Apaches but nevertheless rode alone into the hideout of the old chief to see if he could arrange a peace. Cochise was so impressed with the man's bravery that he did pledge a personal pact with him and made him a blood brother. Jeffords was then able to negotiate a meeting between Cochise and General Howard. This resulted in a treaty, one of the terms being that Jeffords be made an Indian agent.

Shortly old Cochise died and was buried in the Dragoons. Only one white man knew just where and that was Tom Jeffords. He never revealed the secret although he lived forty years longer. The area was abundantly endowed with a type of live oak yielding an edible acorn, called "beyota"

OLD GLEESON GENERAL STORE was buy center of trade and word-of-mouth news when ranching and mining were important. The adobe building has coat of stucco for elegance. Louvre with fan for ventilation was added in days of electricity. Arcade with awnings of corrugated sheet metal was also latter day, luxury for loiterers on benches once lining wall. Live oaks gave shade and *beyotas* — edible acorns gathered by Apaches.

WELLS WERE NOT TOO DEPENDABLE in long dry summer of Dragoon Mountains. Town is filled with adobe ruins such as that of old saloon shown here, fallen to reveal view of Gleeson General Store.

OLD FASHIONED ICE BOX leans tipsily outside ruined house, well preserved in dry air. Shrub in background is mesquite, common in southwest desert areas. Belonging to legume family, nourishing seeds were ground, made into small cakes and baked for Indian's staple food. Plant grows into shrubby tree, is armed with vicious thorns, preventing cattle from grazing, is difficult to control.

by the Indians who gathered them in quantity everywhere but in Stronghold Canyon. It remained inviolate and would indicate this is the spiritland of the old chief.

With Indian troubles fading out the white man's thoughts again turned to the legends and tales of turquoise, gold, copper and silver to be found in the Dragoons. Some of all these treasures were located and the town that sprang up at the site of discovery was named Gleeson after one of the miners.

The town grew but never had a real boom. The area was already on a solid basis with cattle raising and moderate mining prosperity was taken in stride. The biggest boost to the economy came with the entry of Tiffany's of New York. This company proposed to mine turquoise on a big scale but the location of really valuable deposits remained elusive and after some desultory efforts, with only a small quantity of fine turquoise to show, Tiffany's left the scene. So did everyone else in time; even the cattle ranchers gave up as water grew more and more scarce. Only a family or two remain in the area.

GOLDROAD, ARIZONA

Sensible people, and those in a hurry to get from here to there, take the newer U. S. highway 66 from Kingman to Needles. But Ghost Town hunters branch off to the right five miles from Kingman. After a stretch of interesting, flattish desert the old road climbs breathtakingly toward Sitgreaves Pass, 3,500 feet above sea level.

Almost directly, upon starting down the other side, appear traces of buildings, the outskirts of Goldroad. Trickling downward to an only slightly wider stretch of canyon, the small stream of remnants spreads out a little into the main part of what was once an impressive mining camp.

At the close of a bonanza period of prosperity, with the price of gold making all further operations unprofitable, the buildings were sacrificed to avoid taxes. Since many structures were of adobe and stone because of limited supplies of timber, these unburnable ones leave fairly substantial ruins.

Vegetation surrounding them is of the sparsest, but is most interesting. There are many Ocotillos, Chollas and others, all full of thorns. The cliffs form walls all around and even a casual survey reveals mine shafts, heads, mills and dumps dotting the steepest walls, some clinging precariously after the fashion of those in the San Juan Mountains of Colorado.

EVEN THICKEST STONE WALLS crumble under onslaught of years. Pathetic remains were once home to miner's family, now offer scant shade to Gila monsters, rattlesnakes, rodents. Canyon in background holds main town and mines. Distant mountain range extends to Colorado River.

TWO-YEAR BOOM TOWN

Harshaw, Arizona

The Harshaw mining camp in southern Arizona was built on a solid silver foundation in the center of the Patagonia Mountains. Midway between two main river valleys, it lay athwart the path of history, each movement of people passing that way leaving its mark. Indians living along Sobaioura Creek called the area "Enchanted Land" because of streams flowing generously with clear water which provided an ample growth of good grass. Spaniards came later but stayed only long enough to call those Indians "Patagonias" for their reputed large feet.

The padres who arrived next considered all of Primeria Alta a fertile field for conversion, creating devils for the Indians to labor against for more than three hundred years. Then Spain relinquished the country to the Republic of Mexico which put the padres out and their adobe structures untended, to melt away and leave only peach orchards here and there. Mexican families settling in the narrow canyon where the boom town of Harshaw would spring up, found some of the gnarled trees and named their village Durazno for "place of the peaches." With the Gadsden Purchase which made the Patagonias part of the United States came "yankees" with pick and shovel, including David Tecumseh Harshaw.

One of the stalwarts who left comfortable homes in the east to hunt for gold in California, Harshaw was born in New York in 1828 and just 20 when he traveled overland to work in Nevada County mines, probably at Grass Valley. At the outbreak of the Civil War he joined First California Volunteer Infantry mustered at Oakland and was promptly sent to Tucson.

After the war Harshaw traveled around looking for a good place to raise cattle, finally settling in the San Pedro Valley of southern Arizona with about 1000 head. On these forage lands the young veteran found good deposits of gold and silver, in the Santa Ritas, not far south of Tucson. Nell Murbarger in her definitive *Ghosts of the Adobe Walls*, classic of Arizona's mining days, gives reports from the Tucson *Arizona Citizen* in 1875, that "David T. Harshaw brought in a sack of dust and

nuggets weighing $843, the result of four days' labor for three men . . . the Santa Rita placers are entitled to rank equal with the best placers ever discovered."

Perhaps Harshaw's claim petered out, possibly he was run off by Indians, but one thing for sure, he was running cattle on lands properly allocated for use by Chiricahua Apaches. When they complained to Indian Agent Thomas J. Jeffords the official summarily ordered Harshaw to take his cattle and decamp. Forthwith he drove the animals to a section of the Patagonia Mountains not far south of the town. of that name. With plenty of grass and water Harshaw felt he had greatly improved his position, especially when he could get supplies at the Mexican village of Durazno. Again he found metal, his first claims the Hardshell and Harshaw, just south of Durazno which he worked only long enough to prove their potential worth and then sold both in 1879. Having bequeathed his name on the one-time Mexican village he married Maria Jesus Andrada, sister of his partner Jose, and settled down to operate a stage station at Davidson's Springs where he died in September

NEGLECTED GRAVE in one of the two cemeteries at edge of Harshaw, marker not stating and War Dept. unable to determine cause of soldier's death in mining camp. Only one cemetery here is contemporary with Harshaw's brief period of prosperity, 1879-81. Some tombstones are still in evidence, though almost covered by brush, weeds. Cattle around, drop manure on graves of pioneers.

of 1884. His obituary said, "David Harshaw was a typical frontiersman, a man with a big heart, the very essence of noble qualities."

And his name was used with electric excitement when that same year the Southern Pacific entered Tucson and a boisterous boom began at Harshaw nee Durazno. In 1880 James Reilly, editor of *Territorial Expositor* of Phoenix, described it as easily the biggest camp he had ever seen outside of Tombstone. That same year managers of the mines arrived with much needed eastern capital to open a large scale development, their chief investment being in the mine located by David Harshaw, consisting of three parallel ledges from 5 feet to 25 feet wide. A gang of men was hired to grade off a section of steep hillside for installation of a new reduction mill scheduled to arrive in due time by railroad to Tucson.

Within six months the 20-stamp Hermosa Mill was crushing 75 tons of ore every day, making it the largest producer in Arizona. Editor Reilly now wrote that any attempt to evaluate potential wealth of the Harshaw properties would be "preposterous." Silver was soon pouring out to the tune of $365,000 every month. 600 people had arrived to share in the boom, most of them adventurers from 35 states and 3 territories according to the Census Schedule of Arizona Territory of 1880. China, India and Mexico were also represented, several dozen from Ireland.

Only 100 men listed themselves as miners. 24 called themselves grocers, the same number liquor sellers. Restaurants employed 35, laundries 11, the others accounted for in such businesses as livery stables, blacksmith shops, wagonmakers, freighters, barber shops. A few candid individuals listed their calling as faro bank dealers and speculators. There was a "bell hanger," whatever occupation that was. Those were male registrants and as for the 64 females, only two kinds of work were given. Most of them were housewives, 4 forthrightly calling themselves prostitutes. Mexican women predominated, most of them mothers with 59 young children. The Harshaw population was youthful, Mike Fagan, large and powerful ex-peace officer, was the oldest man in town at 45.

A newspaper was started, several hotels and as one Tucson reporter wrote it, "every other establishment in town a saloon." Harshaw was undeniably a real city but this status lasted little more than two years, for two reasons. Silver veins grew thin, then pinched out to almost nothing. The largest mine, the Hermosa, which employed 200 men, closed down, retaining only a skeleton force to guard property and make small exploratory borings for the vanished silver vein. The second disaster was a flood caused by cloudbursts in the Patagonias which poured a huge wall of water down the one street in the narrow canyon. A muddy, boulder-carrying deluge tore out all but the more sturdy stone structures, some of them standing today. The ones destroyed were rebuilt with lumber but a bad fire consumed them, the stone buildings again spared. This gave little incentive to rebuilding and Harshaw died as a town.

The *Arizona Weekly Citizen* of July 7, 1888, reported, "A few of the buildings are still standing in a good state of preservation, though unoccupied for several years. . . . About nine families now live in Harshaw." As of today a census would show about the same population, most of the people Spanish-speaking Mexicans (see Boot Hill).

CATHOLIC CHURCH, one of Harshaw's solidly built stone edifices, commented upon by newspapers of Tucson and other cities. Escaping flood and withstanding less dramatic ravages of time, stone walls are being exposed by cracking plaster coating.

JEROME, ARIZONA

The little movie house was well filled that night some twenty years ago. Every now and then a jolting motion shook the building, an effect to be taken as an earthquake anywhere else. The patrons here paid little attention to shuddering floors and when the show was over they headed for the exit doors. The sidewalk which had been only a few inches above the doorsill when they entered was now nearly two feet higher, or more accurately, the theater floor was that much lower. A few of the more elderly had to be helped up to the higher level but no one was unduly excited, the phenomenon of sliding and moving buildings being too ordinary an occurrence in Jerome.

The jail had started to behave the same way a few years before, settling a few feet downward, the little concrete building pulling away from the sidewalk. Steps were made down to the new level while the now sobered drunks inside talked about their free ride. Then with more slips and slides the jail was so far below the street, a new street level had to be established. As the years went on, successively lower street levels had to be made until the calaboose was closed. However, this was not because Jerome was tired of building new streets for it but because there were no more prisoners among the few Jeromans.

What caused all the shimmeying of the earth?

HIGHWAY BELOW is only "through street" in Jerome. High school on point in middle distance, once filled with local youngsters, is still used by 850 students coming by bus from communities in Verde Valley — Clarkdale, Cottonwood, Clemenceau, etc. Top buildings are 1,500 feet above lowest. Smelter in Clarkdale may be seen in distance, Oak Creek Canyon visible on clear day.

JEROME as seen from below shows fantastic panorama of deserted hotels, theaters, schools. Good stand of pine trees once surrounded city, killed by fumes from smelter which has since been torn down, replaced by huge one in valley. Adobe structures once swelled limits of town, ruins of some seen at center and lower left.

The geological reason was Jerome's situation directly upon the large Verde Fault, a major cause of subterranean movement. Then the town was undermined with a complex of more than 85 miles of mine tunnels.

Add to this the fact that the "overburden" of loose rock and soil on top of a solid layer of rock which lay under the town was penetrated by heavy winter rains and leakage from the aging water supply pipes, with all the water collecting in a saturated layer on the rock. And compounding the natural earth shocks were those from frequent explosions in the mines and one mammoth one in the powder house. Small wonder Jerome progressed downward as well as ahead.

John Figi, custodian of the Art Gallery welcoming Jerome's visitors, says these movements are trivial in light of what went on in former ages. "At one time Mingus Mountain, on the side of which Jerome is built, was 12,000 feet higher than it is today. A prehistoric cataclysm flung the top off and pitched it into the Verde Valley, the sandstone and rock hills you see there being the result. The plant down there is making cement for the dam in Glen Canyon and if removal of material is carried on at the present rate for fifty years, they will reach the layer thrown off from here, the top of Jerome's mines, so to speak, and

it will be a tremendously rich layer of copper as exploratory diamond drillings have shown. The large Daisy mine which used to produce so heavily is probably the top of the decapitated vein."

The earliest use for the colorful ores of the Jerome site was by Tuzigoot Indians in 935 A.D. These aborigines found vivid surface outcroppings in blue, green and brown which, when powdered, made fine war paint and in times of peace was useful for pottery coloring. The first Spanish explorers centuries later were friendly with the natives and shown the deposits. It was tough going up the steep sides of Mingus Mountain but the Spaniards were spurred on by thoughts of gold. When they saw the deposits owed their color to baser metals, they turned back in disgust, giving the country "back to the Indians."

A later visitor to the site was Indian scout Al Sieber, who in 1872 found evidence of Indian mining in the primitive rock tools and crude ladders made of juniper pegs. Sieber, however, was no miner and made no effort to capitalize on his find.

In January of 1876 a small party of prospectors from Nevada headed by Capt. John Boyd and John O. Dougherty arrived in nearby Prescott and listened to the tales of copper wealth on Mingus Mountain. They reached the place but seem to have been unimpressed with the area that was to yield half a billion dollars in copper with gold and silver paying the refining cost. Later that same year came more curious and enterprising visitors, ranchers John Ruffner and his friend August McKinnon. Although the two did stake out several claims, they were primarily ranchers and snapped up a buying offer from Territorial Governor Frederick E. Tritle of $2,000 for the claims, getting $500 cash, the rest to come.

Even now there was no development rush, Tritle finding it took more money than he had to open up the claims and get going. But about the time he was ready to throw up the sponge he met an angel in the form of a New York lawyer, Eugene Jerome (who was the grandfather of England's Sir Winston Churchill). Jerome had money and was willing to sink it in a rocky hole on Mingus Mountain but there was a string attached. He was positive a town would develop there and he thought it would be fitting and proper to have it named after him, and so stipulated in the contract. Tritle was willing, or felt he had no choice if the mine was to be developed.

Yet nothing much happened. It seemed necessary to build a smelter to refine the undeniably rich ore and an impossiblity to get such a thing hauled that distance over rough or nonexistent roads. But in 1882 the Santa Fe came to Ashfork and Tritle, with the lawyer's money, built a wagon road from the railhead 60 miles to his property. Parts for the smelter at last arrived and a fabulous mining town was born.

In 1893 the United Verde Copper Co. was incorporated. At this time the town had four hundred people and six saloons. For years an almost continuous wagon train brought food, water, fuel and mine supplies to the settlement that was progressing as it clung to an all but vertical mountainside. In 1900 a contract was let to supply Jerome with water on a regular basis with a 200-unit mule team. The contractor? Pancho Villa.

The population was cosmopolitan to an extreme. Represented by closely knit groups were Italians, Mexicans, Swedes, Yugoslavs, Bohemians and Welshmen. A large English-speaking section was squeezed into a small space on the red splintered rocks of Yeager Canyon, Slavs filling the Hogback and Mexicans overflowing their adobes along Bitter Creek. No

HUGE OPEN-PIT OPERATION of Phelps Dodge Corp., part of old United Verde workings shown behind buildings in telephoto lens. At left center is "Traveling Jail" which has slid downhill from street above and right. Front center is unique church built by Mr. Sabino Gonzoles, Mexican Methodist minister, who felt "urge" to construct building of any material available including railroad ties, powder boxes and old mine timbers. Construction was from 1939 to 1941. Rev. Gonzoles preached last sermon late in 1952, just before mines were closed down.

975

JEROME
POPULATION
15,000
10,000
5,000
1,000
GHOST CITY

matter what group or location a man lived in, he had a magnificent view of Verde Valley with its red backdrop of Oak Creek Canyon or could look directly down on his neighbor's roof, perhaps scratch matches on his chimney, and on the other side would be the basement of the next house. Only one main street existed, wrapping itself around the crest of the ridge and most cross streets were steep stairways. Some so-called ones were almost impossible to negotiate—and there were no busses or streetcars.

Jerome suffered from labor troubles. The first strike was in 1907, a success for the men which reduced the ten-hour work day to eight and raised wages to $2.75 a day. The next disturbance was not only unsuccessful but took on some comic opera aspects. In 1917, just before the United Verde was bought out by the huge Phelps Dodge Corporation, the I.W.W. started a strike. The men not only ceased to work but staged demonstrations and street battles. The trouble ended when several hundred miners and imported agitators were taken out of the company-owned houses on the hill, loaded on boxcars under the persuasion of guns and other weapons, hauled out into the southeastern Arizona desert and left to sizzle with their sins.

1925 was the top year for Jerome, after which production began to shrivel, closing several of the smaller mines which could not afford operation without rich ore, and then some of the larger ones. In 1953 Phelps Dodge permanently closed the big mine and that was the end of Jerome as a city. Only 100 remained of the 15,000. After this low ebb a few tourist attractions were organized, such as an art gallery, restaurants, etc. The post office is still active, the figure of 300 accounting for all residents now.

Visitors arriving from either end of town, from over Mingus Mountain from Prescott or from Verde Valley, will find the big camp most rewarding. The streets are still such in name only and could lead the unwary motorist into some cul-de-sac of a yard too narrow to turn around in, such as the street leading past the Catholic Church. The automobile should be

JEROME JAIL has slid downhill nearly 300 feet by stages, each new location requiring new street for access. Original level is at upper left, part of street showing. City had ample water supply, enough to keep several swimming pools filled in heyday. Leakage from pipes from artesian springs 14 miles away on Mingus Mountain was partly responsible for unstable ground, a handicap added to natural earth fault and mine explosion.

parked at the bottom of town with wheels against a wall or curb and excursions made on foot, return to the car then being downhill. Otherwise the experience is like descending into Grand Canyon with the return all uphill.

As John Figi said: "Of course if mining should be revived here people would not build on this steep mountainside, but settle on the level ground below. Modern cars would easily reach the mines where the haul up the road used to require at least one team of horses, several with a good load."

In 1884 Senator William A. Clark of Montana showed an interest in the properties since they had begun to pay off. He took a lease on them long enough to assure himself that he had a good thing, then he bought the project, lock-stock-and-barrel. Clark poured a million dollars into the development of the copper mines during the next twelve years.

Now tier upon tier of houses was glued to the 30-degree angle of the hillside, for married men and their families, the immense stone Montana House housing a thousand single men—the largest building in Arizona. Even so, a large number lived in tents and shacky houses of bone-dry lumber. Most of this section went up in smoke in the last series of fire ending in 1899. That same year Jerome was incorporated as the fifth largest city in the state. The mine was to become one of the largest individually owned copper mines in the world.

Near the immense Verde development another vast copper deposit was opened up, the faulted top of what was to be the famed Little Daisy. The ore body was located by George Hull and J. Fisher in 1912 and the richness of the Daisy May was almost unbelievable. Where ore at a value of five percent paid well, here were 300 feet of rock with an assay of fifteen percent at the 1,400-foot level of the mine, then 40 feet of forty percent and at the 1,500 level, five feet of ore with a fantastic copper content of forty-five percent. The Company—The UVX—built a smelter at Clemenceau in the valley and by the end of 1938 production had grossed $125 million.

By 1929 the population of Jerome was 15,000 and included a working force of 2,345 men. More copper was coming out of Arizona than any other state, the Verde operation alone producing as much as $29 million a single year. Gone were the days when building brick was hauled by four and six teams of horses up the single steep road from the kiln in Verde Valley. No longer was it necessary to use the ingenious but inadequate system of converting surplus steam into power to drive the dynamos for electricity. Jerome never had gas. It jumped directly from kerosene to electricity.

Culture was not lacking during the halcyon days.

The miner could attend a lecture by Miss Hollister of Phoenix under the auspices of the W.C.T.U. or a box social put on by the Ladies' Guild of the Episcopal Church. Better attended were the less socially accepted functions.

OLD MOVIE HOUSE slides downhill at rate of inch in two months, may remain stationary for long period, then skid twenty inches in short time.

STATELY COLUMNS STAND at entrance of immense grade school, are slowly crumbling. Structure was closed when large mine operations ceased.

ONE MAN REGIMENT

Pete Kitchen Ranch, Arizona

The Apaches came down "like wolves on the fold" and Arizona ranchers felt the bitter sting of defeat and death. But not Pete Kitchen. He said his hogs looked like walking pincushions with all the arrows sticking out of them and he saw to it they did not stick out of him. "So many men lost their lives in the neighborhood," said Thomas Casanega, who married one of Kitchen's nieces, "if all their bodies were laid side by side like railroad ties they would make a track from Nogales to Potero."

Pete Kitchen was the very essence of stubborn resistance. Although under almost constant attack by Apaches he stood his ground among ranchers who gave up the struggle. The few settlers courageous enough to hold out for a time said of him, "To the Apache he was more terrible than an army with banners."

Frank Rockwood in his book *Arizona Characters* says Pete Kitchen was the connecting link between savagery and civilization. Kitchen left some memoirs showing how clear is this delineation of the man's make-up. He kept much fine stock at his farm near the Mexican border, the fat animals a constant temptation to early cattle rustlers. When

HOME of self-sufficient rancher Pete Kitchen. One of the oldest in Arizona, adobe building was set up in 1850s. It stands several hundred feet from rancher's "fortress" and just left, out of photo, is private cemetery for unknown number of men who dared attack doughty pioneer.

he missed one of his favorite horses and found well-marked tracks pointed toward the border, the outraged rancher got on another good steed and set out after the thief. "I caught up with him some distance south of the line," he wrote, "and put my gun on him, making him return with me. After tying the man to a tree branch overhead with a rope around his neck, I laid down to rest. When I woke up the horse he had been sitting on had wandered some little distance, and much to my surprise, the rope around his neck had strangled him."

Although savage natives killed most of his neighbors, tortured and murdered his favorite herder and slaughtered his stepson, Kitchen fought on. In time the Apaches got the message and left him in comparative peace. He gave all victims of carnage on his ranch decent burial in a private "Boot Hill" near his little adobe ranch home. Not knowing who most were, he did not identify the graves but wife Dona Rose, a deeply devout Catholic, religiously burned candles for them in hope of salvation for their souls.

PETE KITCHEN FORTRESS on rocky knoll with view of fields. Contemporary wrote, "There is a sentinel posted on the roof, there is another out in the cienaga with the stock. The men plowing the bottoms are obliged to carry rifles cocked and swung to the plow handle. Every man and boy, and indeed the women, had to go armed. At the fort there are rifles, revolvers and shotguns along the walls and in every corner. Everything speaks of warfare and bloodshed." When photo was made in 1964 building housed museum operated by owner Col. Gilbert Proctor who kindly allowed author to camp beside it. Historic structure is now operated by Henry Molina family as one of several Casa Molina restaurants in area. Mundane use seems almost sacrilege but occupation of any sort almost guarantees preservation, abandonment leading to swift decay.

McCABE, ARIZONA

McCabe, the Bradshaw Mountains, had its deep-well mystery but there is no cloud of uncertainty about its final demise. And it did not deserve such a fate. It was a family town, suffering a stroke when the gold faded out, was then inundated by an angry flood.

When gold was found in the creek in the late 1860s, there was a rush to get in on the first easy placerings, after which the town was almost deserted until the mother lode was located. A more permanent town then grew up as hard rock mining progressed with several deep shafts bored and a number of stamp mills erected. A two-story brick building on a gentle rise above the creek bed was the largest and most impressive in town. It housed a large general store and several smaller businesses.

Most of the miners were married and as a family town McCabe did not have the usual shootings and scrapes of early Western camps. One old timer described conditions as "dull". "Oh, there was always the hell-raising town of Providence. It was barely over the hill and within easy walking distance. A man could get anything he might want there and some things he didn't, like a broken nose or a slug of hot lead." But McCabe virtuously preserved its reputation as a "clean town."

A good-sized school house stood just above the store and across the road. On the summit of the hill was the immense building housing all the company offices with refinements not found in most camps, including a granite fireplace, showers and flush toilets. A concrete water tank, perhaps two hundred feet across, was built just below the building yet high enough to supply the town by gravity. The water was not palatable because of heavy mineral content and drinking water was hauled up to the town by mule team, one driver in early days a Mr. Conley, helped by his son Earl.

A Swedish miner, Oscar Johnson, was the principal in McCabe's mystery. A loner, Johnson seemed to be doing very well at his claim. He was a hard worker, rising early as smoke could be seen coming from his shack on the north bank of the creek, and almost furtively, said curious observers, Oscar would emerge and head for his well. He had dug it himself, saying the water hauled into camp was too expensive, but the suspicious watchers remembered he had spent an inordinately long time at the digging, that he had removed far more dirt than the comparatively high water table would require.

The morning visits to the well, when Oscar would draw up a full bucket, seemed innocent

UNIQUE MONUMENT stands securely in cemetery on right side of difficult dirt road — first indication that there are traces of Mc-Cabe. Burial ground is deeply eroded by run-off waters, some graves washed entirely away. Monument is cast in one piece from some zinc-like metal, rings when rapped with knuckles. Placed in 1906, marker has enduring qualities but may overturn when foundation breaks down.

LIKE A MONUMENT to past mining glory, granite ruin of elaborate fireplace stands at summit above McCabe. On site stood large office buildings of mining company. Not far away is evidence of showers, granite floor area having drainage hole. Close by are shattered fragments of porcelain flush toilet, a mining camp rarity. Water was available from huge storage tank, circular basin some two hundred feet across. This was for domestic use and mill operations only, drinking water hauled in from stream.

enough, but there were those frequent night trips too, with a lantern. Unable to stand the suspense, one man stationed himself behind a bushy manzanita and waited. After dark Johnson emerged from the cabin with a ladder and a lantern, taking them to the well then returning for a heavy bag. He lifted the well cover and let down the ladder,

OLD SAFE near general store appears to have been blown open. Resting on bed of clean gravel, surrounded by manzanita chaparral, it gives no further clues of violence.

descending with lantern and bag. The watcher waited for a long time it seemed until the miner came up, pulled up the ladder and went to the cabin. Rumor was quick to say Oscar Johnson was hoarding his wealth in the well but the incident was more or less passed by as just another peculiar trait of the recluse.

Then one day someone asked: "Say, where is Oscar Johnson? There hasn't been any smoke coming from his chimney for days." On a Sunday morning several men went to the cabin, found no Oscar Johnson but evidence he had not been there for several days. When a week went by and the man did not put in an appearance, a party investigated the well and reported there was a side tunnel about six feet down. With a lantern a man explored the tunnel and found a large room which showed every evidence of recent use but was entirely empty. Had Oscar been murdered and his wealth stolen? There was no sign of violence at the cabin or around his workings. No answer came. The industrious and secretive Scandinavian was never seen again, the mystery never solved.

One day in the late summer of 1937 black clouds gathered over the Bradshaws. It was the season for

BACKHOUSE was built of scarce lumber, is only frame structure in Leland, small mining community near McCabe.

rain, Arizona's mountain areas getting an annual fall of 25 to 30 inches in fall and winter. But this storm was heavier than most, the deluge concentrated in the several canyons that fed the stream pouring down through McCabe. As the waters rose in their narrow channel, some of the bulkheads against the rocky walls began to give way, timbering being carried far down the stream. As dirt and rock caved in, a temporary dam was formed and when the torrent built up enough pressure, it washed out the barrier and a huge wave came down on the town, brushing aside all buildings. No one was hurt, for no one was there and the damage was not known for months. McCabe was a ghost town and had been for years.

When the waters subsided, many buildings on higher ground still stood. The general store with stout brick walls was almost intact, the shed at the rear still housing a fabulous collection of buggies from earlier days. Groceries and valuable merchandise had been hauled away before the flood but shelves of faded, outdated goods still remained. The school house stood on the rise across the street, blackboard walls still bearing chalked problems and grammar lessons.

Since then time, storm, decay and vandalism have taken their inevitable toll. The general store has been leveled, safe falling into the hole that was the cellar. The school was wrecked for lumber which was hauled down to Humboldt. There are even now a few shacks and many ruins showing where mills and a brick kiln once stood. On the side of one hill above the stream bed is a row of large settling tanks. Another larger tank, excavated from native rock and lined with concrete is high on the opposite side of the gulch and above is all that remains of the office buildings, the ruin of a big granite fireplace. This is the lonely lair of a ghost.

116

MINERAL PARK, ARIZONA

What the Hualpais Indians of this part of Arizona were usually called cannot be printed here. It was only when the early whites felt charitable they referred to the low-grade tribespeople as simply "Wallapais." The Mineral Park *Mohave Miner* constantly complained; "There are more drunken Wallapais women on the street than there are drunken Wallapais men." The best that could be said of them was they were peaceful when sober and never attacked the citizens of the remote mining camp in northwestern Arizona.

Mineral Park's other newspaper, *Alta Arizona*, ran a news item January 28, 1882, concerning a near violent encounter between Wallapais Charley, by way of being a minor chief of his tribe, and Jeff, another Indian. Ordinarily the best of friends, they imbibed too much firewater and when an agrument developed, Charley drew his pistol. Before any blood was shed, Under Sheriff Collins intervened, dragged the pair into his office, gave them a good talking to

HOME-MADE HEATERS were popular in country where stoves were all but impossible to obtain due to expensive transportation. Juniper trees were main fuel, hills near camp cleared of them.

and confiscated Charley's precious gun. The next day Sheriff Robert Steen received this contrite letter:

My Friend Bob Steen

Won't you be so kind as to send me my pistol. I will not carry it into town any more and will behave myself and be a good Indian. Tell me where I can come into town and oblige

Your Friend Wallapais Charley

The first prospectors in western Arizona were soldiers attached to Fort Mohave on the Colorado River or disappointed miners from the California gold fields. Some of them found gold in the blistering foothills, one discovery located where Oatman later mushroomed. The Moss mine developed there and among others those at Gold Road attracted a rush of hopeful, would-be miners. Many found treasure there, others reaching out to make discoveries nearby.

These activities were in the early '60s and a few years later several mines were located at the site of Mineral Park but were not worked extensively as the hostile Hualpais, who were picking out some turquoise, forced the miners to flee. Later some whites took out limited quantities of the semiprecious gemstone.

Ten years later, so many whites had infiltrated the area a truce of sorts was established. Before long, rich silver deposits were uncovered in the Cerbat Range, the mines centered in a beautiful parklike, juniper-covered bench on the western slope, the name Mineral Park as apt as any given to western mining camps. Not only were gold, silver and lead deposits rich and varied in the "Park" but the stream flowing through the town was so permeated with mineral solutions and salts it was unfit to drink. Potable water had to be hauled from a canyon several miles away. By 1874 Harris Solomon was running a regular mule train carrying the supply from Keystone Spring.

Once established, Mineral Park boomed. By 1880

ADOBE RUINS BLEND WITH BACKGROUND, sun-baked bricks matching color of parent earth. This material was much used in areas of scant timber, little lumber available and that high priced. Cerbat Range in which Mineral Park lies is rich in cacti. Shown in foreground is patch of prickly pear, *Opuntia engelmanii,* bearing yellow, water-lily-like flowers, deep red pears which are edible. Behind these are clumps of staghorn chollas (choyas), *Opuntia versicolor,* whose main characteristics are barbed spines with easily detached joints often adhering to stock animals and carried away to start new plants where they drop.

there were four saloons, a restaurant, blacksmith shop, hotel, school and several stores, the earliest influx from less glamorous camps nearby which were soon all but deserted. Anyone wanting to get to the camp

from the east was faced with a formidable problem of transportation. He had to travel across the northern part of the United States on the Union Pacific to San Francisco, get down to Los Angeles and overland to

Yuma. Here he would transfer to one of the flat-bottomed steamers which paddled up the Colorado River as far as Hardyville. If lucky, he would not have to wait more than a week for the stagecoach to Mineral Park. And this ride was not exactly luxurious, the roads only dim trails over sand or rock and cactus-studded hills where in summer it was well above 100°.

Supplies had to be sent over this same circuitous route or transported more than four hundred miles over alkali and sand deserts. It is no wonder commodity prices were so high. Bacon cost $1 a pound, sugar 35 cents, flour 50 cents in a day when the miner earned $3 for ten hours' work.

And occasionally prices were used as weapons by saloons. At one time when most of the saloonkeepers tossed a quarter into a lard can for a shot of whiskey, one rebel was charging only half that, Spanish *real* with a value of twelve for a dollar. These "pieces of eight" were commonly called "bits," accounting for the western use of "two bits."

Two of Mineral Park's merchants were always at each other's throats in this same manner. Krider Bros. openly advertised they would not only equal other prices but undersell anything offered by their aggressive competitors, Welton and Grounds, and carried on a running feud with merchant J. W. Haas. Being postmaster and having the post office in his store from '79 to '86, W. M. Krider had a distinct trade advantage.

In casting around for an excuse to quarrel with Krider, Hass accused the postmaster of withholding his mail, this openly in front of the store. Insulted and infuriated, Krider lifted his cane and fetched Haas a smart one on the cranium. Haas went berserk, drew his gun and fired wildly. Krider returned the fire and also missed. In the post office at the time, Sheriff Steen ran out and grabbed both contestants by their collars, marching them to the calaboose where the pair passed the time arranging lawsuits for assault with attempt to commit murder. Both were released on $3,000 bail. The *Mohave Miner* which chronicled these events failed to tell the rest of the story.

By 1884 there were 500 registered voters in Mineral Park with, no doubt, as many women and children. The Chinatown had several opium dens, as well as stores and laundries. At first the opium houses were ignored, then tolerated with distaste and finally a marked increase in young addicts was detected, the greatest evil being they were spending their money with the Chinese instead of the white saloon and bawdy house keepers. The white madames, some carrying considerable weight in town politics, demanded that boys who smoked the poppy stay away from their girls.

In July of 1884, the *Mohave Miner* was needled into carrying scare headlines: "This Menace To Our Youth Must Be Stopped." It is to be assumed the opium dens were closed, for Wilfred Babcock, who worked and lived in Mineral Park during the period after the newspaper blast, could not recall any.

The town continued to grow by leaps and bounds. Lumber was always scarce and high priced, a great drawback to progress. There was a sawmill in the Hualpais Mountains forty miles west of the Park but by the time this essential material reached its destination, the cost was $125 a thousand. In spite of this, building went on apace and Mineral Park could boast of several hotels and office buildings to house "the many professional people who have moved here from Cerbat, Mohave City and Hardyville," as the newspaper had it. It soon took over as county seat from Cerbat. A fine courthouse was erected and, beside it, the jail. Wilfred Babcock remembers the jail doors did not open or close easily for some time.

First newspaper was the *Wallapais Enterprise*, started June 1, 1876 by John Leonard and Chauncey F. Mitchell and dying soon. Two later ones, the *Alta Arizona* and *Mohave Miner*, were contemporaries for a time and bitter rivals for subscriptions. The former was beset by a plague of drunken printers, the two who

OLD CEMETERY retains original juniper trees spared from axes. Some graves date back to '70s. Enclosure in center is unique in style. On grave in foreground grows beavertail cacti, *Opuntia basilaris*.

drank only water from the spring getting the type set and keeping the presses going. After a few spirited years of refuting each other's statements, the *Alta Arizona* left the field to the *Miner*.

Issues of this paper in '84 stated in glowing terms the many plans for expansion. A new hospital was to replace the one that had burned. It was hoped all patients could be kept and treated under one roof where part of them were cared for in the Palace Hotel. The old school building had been purchased by the school board to make an expansion possible, including a 220-square foot extension for the teacher's platform so she could look over the heads of her older and taller pupils.

Because of the price of lumber, many buildings were made of adobe. The locally popular Sheriff Steen's family had one of these for their home. Early one morning during a rare rainy spell, the Chinese cook at the Palace Hotel passed the Steen house on his way to work and saw it had collapsed in the night. Frantic diggers found the small girl of the family still alive, her younger brother almost doubled up under the weight of the adobe bricks but still breathing, the remainder of the Steens dead. Both children survived.

It cannot be said religious influence was very strong in the Park. There never was a regular church, traveling ministers sometimes preaching in a pool hall or hotel. The community did make one gesture heavenward by organizing a non-sectarian Sunday school. The *Mohave Miner* beamed paternally: "It is very important to the children as well as the community whether they shall be trained to be gentle, kind and good or allowed to grow up in evil, vicious habits, a curse to themselves, their parents and their country."

A bank was also missing from the camp. Miners had a haphazard system of leaving part of their money with storekeepers for safekeeping. In 1883 the *Miner* agitated for a bank with a capital of $50,000 to $100,000 but no bank ever appeared. Another plan for the building of a toll road from Mineral Park to Free's Wash, southwest of the present Kingman, also came to naught. It was to be called the Mineral Park and Wallapais Tow Road, the idea proposed by R. H. Upton and S. Owen who got as far as drawing up a partnership February 1, 1875 but built no road. However, several stage lines were eventually established, two of them running between Prescott and Hardyville on the Colorado River, making Mineral Park a station. Hugh White and Co. ran a small express and passenger service from Prescott to Mineral Park, Mohave City, Hackberry and Hardyville. A. L. Simonds advertised his Mineral Park and Kingman Stage would transport passengers between the two towns for $2, a four-hour, fifteen-mile trip.

The town which had been so hampered by transportation problems was thus overjoyed when in 1880 there were rumors that the Atlantic and Pacific Railroad was being put through northern Arizona. The rumors became facts and in '83 the railroad passed a point within fifteen miles of Mineral Park. Plans were carried out to improve the road to this point so as to take advantage of cheap rates for shipping ore and concentrates. Where the new road ended at the tracks, a depot and loading platforms were built, additional buildings put up for stores and a hotel. Several Mineral Park business concerns moved there, others establishing branches in Kingman, the new station stop.

When Kingman began to be noticeable as a town, the *Miner* predicted caustically the place would "soon be taken over by the horned toads." After a few months it took a neutral attitude and soon it was carrying more ads and news from Kingman than

ORE CAR abandoned beside narrow gauge tracks once carried quantities of rich gold- and silver-filled rocks. Prior to building of stamp mills, ore had to be rich to pay for immense cost of shipping overland to Colorado River, thence by barges to Port Isabel at mouth of river on Gulf of California, down Gulf to Port Arena and up coast to San Francisco where it was shipped to Swansea, Wales. When Selby smelter was built in San Francisco, shipping costs were reduced to $125 a ton. On February 12, 1876 a five-stamp quartz mill was put into operation in the Park, could get high price for crushing. After other mills were built, prices were forced down but never to low level, partly because of water scarcity for wet operation to reduce dust hazard.

NAMES OF MINES around Mineral Park include the whimsical Metallic Accident and Woodchopper's Relief as well as Lone Star and Fairfield. Keystone was first important lode, found in 1870 by Charles E. Sherman, producing gold and silver, giving name to Keystone Springs, only source of good water for town.

from home. In 1887 the paper moved to Kingman where it still operates.

Before long there were many vacant buildings in the Park. Several structures were burned and others vandalized, some adobe buildings collapsed for lack of repairs and Mineral Park took on the aspects of a ghost town. Kingman had been agitating for some time to get the county seat position and in November of 1886 a general election to decide the issue gave 271 votes for Kingman, Hackbarry 132, Mineral Park 99 and definitely out of the running. The town would not give up, however, especially since the supervisors had been so slow in calling for a recount of votes. Official results were not presented until December 31, on demand of County Supervisor Samuel Crozier.

What happened next spelled the final doom of Mineral Park's status as county seat. Shortly after midnight a party of Kingman men, their patience exhausted over the obstinate refusal of Mineral Park to comply with orders to give up the records, piled into a wagon and set out on the four-hour trip to the dying town. Arriving in the early morning hours, they proceeded to the courthouse and broke down the doors. They loaded all essential records into the wagon, returned to Kingman and set up the legal procedures necessary to the operation of the county seat.

Population in the camp was now further depleted and only a little mining activity remained. Even this went out in time and Mineral Park was very dead for many years as all buildings fell away, were burned or wrecked for valuable lumber.

At present one mine is again functioning across the creek of the bitter waters, near the old cemetery so picturesquely hidden in the junipers. These old trees and the fence posts near them, full of hollows and holes, make good nesting places for the profusion of Western Bluebirds which have forsaken so many other areas.

HOW HE WON THE BATTLE AND LOST THE WAR

Mowry, Arizona

It was certainly a duel in the sun and it might have been one to the death. For there was a challenge in the true spirit and tradition of gallantry. It was accepted and seconds appointed. The duelists met and the former lieutenant fired. But it was not a very good rifle and he was not a very good shot and his antagonist was not a very serious enemy. So instead of killing him he went over and shook his hand.

Dramatic discoveries of silver in the Patagonia Mountains in 1736 brought a crowd of treasure seekers and caused King Philip V of Spain to claim the area as his own. According to persistent rumors the mines at Mowry were originally worked by Jesuit priests. If so their efforts were forgotten but still evident when a pair of Mexicans came along about 1857.

These men from south of the border (16 miles away) were sharp enough to discover that working a silver mine was not as easy as panning for gold, that it would require capital and machinery far beyond their means. They sold out at the first offer, from officers stationed at nearby Fort Crittenden. The Americans found the same problems, that they had no cornucopia that would effortlessly pour forth riches in gleaming silver. And when they saw they could not work together they gladly accepted the bid from Lt. Sylvester Mowry, also at the fort.

DANCE HALL, one of best preserved structures in extensive town growing up around Sylvester Mowry's extremely rich silver-lead mines, only metropolitan center in area. It had hotels, saloons, gambling places, stores, almost all built of adobe. When this photo was made in 1963 buildings were good enough to merit listing as "complete town for sale" in Tubac real estate office. By 1967 porch had collapsed, more plaster fallen, but still structurally solid. Tree is one most characteristic of area—interior live oak (as distinguished from California coastal tree). Live oak has evergreen, holly-like leaves, small acorns.

Mowry resigned from the army and devoted his energies to the mine. One of his problems was the roads were little more than trails and there would be no railroad for many years. With a crew of Mexican peons he started deepening the shafts and tunnels and before long his men were ascending ladders with astoundingly rich loads of silver-lead ore. This looked like success and he renamed the Patagonia mine for himself. As the Mowry it would produce over $1 million in one three-year period.

Galena was the ore, at first roughly refined in Mexican blast furnaces at Lochiel on the border, the lead and silver bars weighing about 70 pounds, shipped to Europe and sold in England for $200 per ton. But shortly pure silver was being cast locally into bars worth from $200 to $300 and used as a medium of exchange in an area still lacking in currency.

With the fantastic success of his mines making headlines in Eastern and European press, Mowry received many offers to speak in public at good fees. He turned the management of the mine over to several good men and went on what amounted to a chautauqua circuit. In one speech he declared that all streams in Arizona teemed with fish. However the eastern audience evaluated the overstatement, one Edward Cross of Tubac, Arizona, correspondent of the St. Louis *Republican,* bristled indignantly. In printed comment he ridiculed Mowry's brash utterance, saying he had found a few fish as long as his fingernail, that these must be the "Mowry trout."

Stung by the article, Mowry surprised Cross by demanding satisfaction in a formal duel. Reluctant but game, Cross met his challenger near Tubac (an old town near the Mission Tumacacori). The affair was widely publicized and attended by a gallery largely from Tucson, gamblers from mining camps having a field day placing bets.

Chosen as weapons were Burnside rifles and neither mine owner nor newsman knew much about using them. The first three shots went wild

COMPANY OFFICE interior, deteriorating but for Civil War vintage, still in good condition. Picture taken in 1963 shows usual adobe and plaster construction, streaks on wall seen thru door at left made by water leaking from roof.

MAIN GUARD TOWER overlooking Yuma Territorial Penitentiary. Gatling gun here frustrated most escapes. Water was pumped to tank under platform. During Civil War Sylvester Mowry was confined in this notorious prison, charged with treason, Union government maintaining mine owner provided lead bullets to Confederates. (For story and other photos of prison see **Tales the Western Tombstones Tell.**)

all his energies to them he might have made it through the war but there was talk about his sympathies being with the Confederate forces. A Rhode Islander by birth with no record of antipathy toward the Union cause, his continued public utterances were somehow construed as treachery to the North.

On June 8, 1862, Sylvester Mowry was arrested for treason. Gen. Carlton ordered the accused made prisoner on charges that Mowry had rendered aid and comfort to the enemy by producing for Confederate armies bullets manufactured of lead from his mines. The Union government seized them and confiscated all silver and lead produced.

The prisoner was immediately taken to Yuma and thrown into its notorious, dreaded territorial prison, it being reported he was "closely confined" which indicated incarceration in the "Hell Hole" or dungeon. There he languished until November when he was suddenly released and informed there was not a shred of evidence against him. In spite of complete exoneration Mowry found himself destitute, with no hope of any property being restored to him.

He brought suit against Gen. Carlton and the government for $1 million but all efforts to collect were frustrated especially after the mines were sold at public auction for $4,000. Some historians claim he was paid damages but others dispute this. Most agree Mowry went to London, England, where he died in poverty in 1871.

and then Mowry's gun failed to discharge. The seconds agreed he was entitled to another try but as he raised the weapon he saw Cross with arms folded, bravely ready for the bullet. Firing the rifle into the air, Mowry walked over to Cross and extended his hand. Both declared themselves satisfied, and later both made public retractions of their bitter statements.

Mowry's mines were producing $1,000 a day when the Civil War broke out. Had he devoted

CENTRALLY LOCATED building assumed to be mine company office, photo taken in 1963. Roads wind thru town as main street, visitor continuing along good surface about 1 mile, taking left fork up hill, exploring manzanita brush at left, will bring him to cemetery. Just back of point from which photo was taken is fork leading sharply left and steeply up nearer hill. About ¾ mile up slope are located big Mowry mines and small village dating from World War I days, now as deserted as main town.

OATMAN, ARIZONA

Oatman was named for a family which had camped near Gila Bend in 1851. It consisted of the mother and father, two daughters and a son. The Oatmans were attacked by a marauding band of Apaches, the parents killed, the boy, Lorenzo, beaten to unconsciousness and the girls kidnapped. When a detail of soldiers was sent out to effect their rescue, the sisters, Olive and Mary Ann were hidden by their captors at a small spring a half mile north of town and then spirited away. Mary Ann died later, but Olive was released in 1856 and joined her brother at Fort Yuma. She married John Fairchild in New York State in 1865 and died in Texas in 1903.

In its earlier days Oatman boasted a narrow gauge railway. It ran from the mines to Fort Mojave on the Colorado, to which point supplies were ferried from Needles, California.

During this period of ascendancy, Oatman took $3,000,000 in gold from its sterile, craggy site and boasted two banks, ten stores and a Chamber of Commerce.

"MOST FAMOUS SALOON IN ARIZONA" is proud boast of few remaining residents. Structure was known as "Mission Inn," upper floor once rested on ground, was raised and new section built beneath. Some differences of opinion exist as to purpose of many cubicles, each with one of numbers 1 to 18, upstairs. Some say they were "offices," others "gambling joints" or "apartments." Quartzite obelisk "Elephant's Tooth" looms in background.

QUARTZSITE, ARIZONA

Hi Jolly and eighty camels crossing the desert sands of Arizona furnish the color behind the settlement of Quartzsite at Tyson's Well. The camel caravans did not stay in the country but Hi Jolly did, to act as scout for the army and he lies buried in an unmarked grave in the local cemetery.

The town came into being because gold was found between that spot, Ehrenberg and La Paz. While never a mining camp it was an important stage stop, at first with no name but because of a well there and a man named Tyson the first settler, it became known as Tyson's Well. When the Indians began a series of attacks on the few residents, an adobe fort was installed with a few soldiers and the place became Fort Tyson although it was never a formal army fort.

In time the settlement needed a post office but authorities rejected the name Fort Tyson as having no standing. The white nature of the prevailing country rock suggested "Quartzite" which name was accepted, but somewhere along the line an "s" was inserted and the infant town became officially Quartzsite. This was the area adopted by Hi Jolly who had been Hadji Ali in Syria.

About 1855 the United States Government decided to use camels to open up the road from Fort Defiance to the Colorado River, the country almost all desert. Civilian Gynn Harris Heap was sent to the Middle East to procure camel herds and bring them home. He centered his search in Smyrna, Turkey, and frequented a grog shop called Mimico Teadora near the famous Caravan Bridge where Arabs and Greeks gathered in friendly talk.

Here in late 1856 Heap met his man, one Hadji Ali who had spent most of his life with camels, half of it driving or buying them for others. The first packet of camels had been readied for the voyage and Hadji Ali was ready to leave with them on his great adventure. Instead he was sent into the interior of Asia Minor to secure a second herd and then accompanied it to the United States, arriving at Indianola, Texas, February 10, 1857.

Hi Jolly as he now was called never spoke much of his past but friends and army men knew his

father was an Arabian who had participated in a raid on a Greek island and taken a native girl as a trophy of war. She became Hadji Ali's mother and for a time he went by the Greek name Philip Tetro, later changing it when he embraced the Mohammedan faith.

The two shipments of camels comprised groups of thirty-three and forty-seven, several females bringing forth young aboard ship. The herd was divided into several units and under Arab drivers taken over snowy mountains, through pine woods and over deserts, covering about twenty-five miles a day. The camels did not protest at the heavy packs but the drivers did. One by one they quit but Hi Jolly stayed on to break in new drivers from army personnel.

The camel project seemed to be going well but the Civil War broke out to end it, road building and all. The camels were offered as "surplus" but there were almost no takers. The animals required special handling, were crankier than mules and panicked other stock. Turned loose to fend for themselves they got along with varying degrees of success. Myths and legends about the strange beasts grew rapidly, one concerning "a great, rusty-red animal" seen mysteriously with a dead rider strapped to its back. As the beast roamed the wastelands pieces of the body were torn off against brush and cacti until only the legs and then only the feet remained. At last someone shot the wanderer which by then carried only the rawhide bindings. Another engaging legend was offered by Indians. One camel was foolish enough to defy the spirits of thunder and lightning, was turned into stone and the origin of Camelback Mountain near Phoenix explained.

With the abandonment of the camels, Hi Jolly was out of a job, but not for long as he was too good a man as scout and guide in Northern Arizona with which he was now familiar. He keeps appearing in stories about the subjugation of the Indians by the army and the rounding up of cattle and horse thieves.

About 1871 a band of Apaches stole over a hundred head of horses, mules and cattle from the

Bowers Ranch in Skull Valley, killing the herder in the process. Hi Jolly was working at Fort McDowell and was sent out as tracker for a cavalry company. He came across the trail but could not persuade the commanding officer it was the right one. Disgustedly he returned to the Fort and when the soldiers returned the officer was arrested and courtmartialed.

On April 28, 1880, Hi Jolly was married to Gertrude Serna of Tucson, in that city. The marriage started out well but the Greek-Arab was a born nomad, the trait kept alive by years of scouting and prospecting. In 1894 he reported in Yuma that he had located a rich deposit of tin in the Plomosa district. He had been living in the Tyson's Wells area, he said, and made the discovery in seeking medical aid for a sick prospector who had been working with him. His final wanderings were confined to the Tyson's Well or Quartzsite area where he died, December 16, 1902.

MONUMENT TO HI JOLLY, dedicated January 5, 1936. Built by Arizona Highway Department, copper camel at apex was made in Highway shops at Phoenix. Memorial stands in Quartzsite Cemetery where, in unmarked grave, lies famed camel driver, scout and prospector. Base rocks are black lava of the area, next above snowy quartzite, then band of petrified wood. Rounded log section near right corner is spectacular specimen, ruby red in color, proves vandals sometimes have self-control. In copper container at base are Hi Jolly's government contracts, ashes of Topsy, one of his camels which died at Griffith Park Zoo in Los Angeles, and his total wealth at death — sixty cents.

SALOME, ARIZONA

The Salome Frog, second in fame only to Mark Twain's Celebrated Frog of Calaveras County, was the creation of Dick Wick Hall. He made the frog known locally through the pages of his little weekly newspaper, the SALOME SUN, then in the late '20s broke him into the big time in the SATURDAY EVENING POST. The character was his talisman, symbol of his free spirit and sense of humor as big as the desert itself.

"The Salome Frog is seven years Old," he explained in one of his sketches which was accompanied by a cartoon showing the frog with a canteen on its back, "and even though he can't swim it isn't his Fault. He never had a chance, but he lives in Hope. Three years ago Fourth of July Palo Verde Pete shot off a box of Dynamite and the Frog thinking it was Thunder, chased the Cloud of Smoke two miles down the road, hoping it might rain. He is older and wiser now, and is getting like the rest of the Natives, he just sits and Thinks."

The frog of Salome wasn't born in that town, Hall went on to explain. He found its egg in Owens Valley in California and thought at first it was a wild duck egg, but on the way home it hatched and proved to be a frog. The creature was nurtured on loving care and bottled Shasta and Pluto water which explains why it grew up to be so healthy and active.

If not the founder of Salome, Dick Wick Hall was at least its moving force with his newspaper and service station where he sold "Laffing Gas." As De Forest Hall he was born in Creston, Iowa, 1877. After college he served in a war and collected rattlesnakes in Florida. At a Nebraska State Fair he was so entranced by a display of the Hopi Indians of Arizona, he set his sights on the northern part of the state, arriving there at twenty-one with $14.35 in his pocket. Very soon he was among the Hopis as a census taker and the Indians liked him so well he was taken into the tribe. Wearing Hopi garb, he studied their habits, customs and ceremonies including the sacred Snake Dance. Close observation of their drawings, petroglyphs and symbolic designs may have influenced his later use of sketches in his mimeographed paper the SALOME SUN.

After the Hopi interlude, Hall settled down for a time on a small ranch in Pleasant Valley, the area long the scene of a range feud between cattle and sheep ranchers, theoretically finished with a full-scale battle in 1887. Smaller outbursts continued periodically but Hall, growing vegetables for the community, was never involved. "I was never shot at," he said. "I guess good gardeners were too scarce."

Then came a stint on a construction job, followed by something more fitting to his talents. He was made editor of the WICKENBURG NEWS-HERALD, a paper of shaky stature which did not strengthen

BLUE ROCK INN, operated in days of Dick Wick Hall by Mrs. E. S. Jones and her three daughters. As girls married, husbands provided extra help when business boomed as highway was built by town. Hall wrote free "ad" in his paper: "All inside rooms have Running Water ready to run on Very Short Notice and by coming at the right Season of the Year you can have whichever You Prefer—Hot or Cold (always hottest in summer). Only the Ground and Atmosphere are provided with outdoor Rooms, as no covering is Needed in the summer Season which is often quite Long."

DICK WICK HALL'S MODEST HOME also served as shop where he mimeographed famous little paper, the **Salome Sun.** In 1926 Hall went to Los Angeles "unwillingly" to have dental work done and while there doctors discovered a far advanced case of Bright's Disease from which he died. His body lies under monument in front yard, shaft built of pieces of valuable ore which mining friends contributed. Two small boys guided photographer to spot, took exception to his pronunciation of town's name—Salomay—informed him correct way to say it was—Salom.

financially during his tenure. No doubt he contributed color with such doggerel as:

"The past ten months serve to remind us
　　Editors don't stand a chance.
The more work the more we find behind us
　　Bigger patches in our pants."

During his stay in Wickenburg he used the alliterative "Dick Wick" as his name and was Dick Wick Hall the rest of his days. Also during this period he was bitten by the prospecting bug and the condition became chronic. He wrote home so glowingly of his new love, Arizona, his brother Ernest (later to be Arizona's Secretary of State) joined him and the two started combing the surrounding hills with pick and pan. An acquaintance, one Shorty Alger, lit his fuse in a gopher hole in the area just west of Wickenburg and exposed a pocket of gold assaying $100 to the pound. The news set off a minor gold rush but Dick, being astute and on the spot, filed on 100,000 acres of desert land with his brother as partner.

Shorty's fifteen-foot hole soon yielded $30,000 worth of gold, then pinched out. With almost everyone going home, Dick stayed on and began the drilling of a well, determined to develop a town in

the area. Natural promotion qualities asserted themselves and when the well produced, he formed the Grace Valley Irrigation district.

Having struck some color close by he started a mine called the Glory Hole and as a few buildings sprang up, a town of sorts was born. The railroad was being run through from Wickenburg and he induced a merchant friend, E. S. Jones, former owner of stores in Wickenburg and old Congress, to set up a new one on his property to serve the railroad men and anyone happening along. The location was half a mile below the well and mine, more convenient to the railroad, so the buildings of the first settlement were moved down and new ones added. The tiny hamlet was named Salome for Grace Salome Pratt, wife of one of Dick's mining partners, Carl Pratt.

One addition to the slowly growing Salome was a boarding house and hotel run by Mrs. Jones and her three daughters—Evvy, Lucy and Dorothy. Another was a post office with Hall as temporary postmaster, and a saloon. Salome did not support the latter and it was reopened as a school. The first teacher was one of the Jones girls whose married sister in Wickenburg had several children of school age. When the roster got low the teacher would

129

call her sister to send down the number needed to fill the necessary quota of eight.

Part of this time Dick Wick Hall was busy traveling through Louisiana, Texas, Utah, California and Florida promoting other interests which included mines, oil wells and real estate. When the highway was built close to Salome, paralleling the railroad, he saw possibilities in a gasoline station and garage, and began staying home to develop them. The road was rough and many tired travelers elected to spend the night at the Blue Rock Inn — the boarding house and hotel. Salome had been built north of the tracks and as the highway was run south of them, the store was left "stranded" as it were. Mr. Jones' enterprising sons-in-law, of which there were several by now, tried to prevail on the old gentleman to move the store to the highway. The patriarch was adamant. "Nothing doing. Let them come over here. They know where we are."

It was to publicize the gas station that Hall started his famous one-sheet mimeographed "newspaper" where the Salome Frog found a home. It was only one of many quizzical characters to appear on the pages. As prominent was Salome herself. She was early separated from the lady of the same name, being a ribald caricature of the Biblical dancer. Hall's masthead was varied, most often reading: "The Salome Sun, where she danced," followed by the disclaimer: "It wasn't my fault. I *told* her the Sand would be too hot without her shoes." Many free "ads" were shaped up to the benefit and sometimes embarrassment of the parties involved. One issue said you could always have hot or cold running water at the Inn, provided you came at the right season. Of the fertile soil around Salome, Hall wrote: "The Melons don't do too well here. The vines grow so fast they wear out the melons dragging them over the ground." He also said: "Salome's population has increased 100% a year — 19 people in 19 years", and one of his many comments about the aridity of the region was: "We plant onions between the potatoes, they make the eyes of the potatoes water enough to irrigate the garden." He made crude little maps for his customers at the Laffing Gas Station with a small line under them — "This map doesn't show all the bumps and curves, but don't worry, you will find them all right."

Salome today is still about the same size but many of the buildings are unoccupied. The vitality of the town faded with Hall's death in 1926. But both the town and Dick Wick Hall's spirit come to life each fall, September 10, with an old-fashioned pit barbecue, square and folk dances for the farmers and cattlemen for fifty miles around. They come with their families and relive the times of Dick Wick Hall. The paved roads are about the only difference from the days when he was writing:

"This very old Typewriter I learned to Type on has lost lots of its teeth. It was so Old and so many of its Letters were Gone that I got used to hitting the Capitals where the little ones were gone that I can't get Out of the Habit."

STORE ON HALL PROPERTY was set up by his friend E. S. Jones, former merchant of Wickenburg and old Congress, in 1906. Post office was added shortly, Hall serving as temporary postmaster. Little false-fronts stand silent and empty, slowly falling victims to weather.

STANTON, ARIZONA

"From Monastery To Murder" could have been the title of a biography of Charles P. Stanton if he could have found anybody to write it. By one means or another, always devious, he got what he wanted which was to be "king of the camp" and was the most hated and feared man in the Antelope Valley.

Stanton began his adult life in an atmosphere of rectitude as novice in a monastery but was soon expelled on charges of immorality. Drifting west he passed in and out of many mining camps, always learning some new way of making a "fast buck", preferably by latching on to some innocent's hard-earned cash. Then he struck the Antelope Valley and saw opportunity with a big "O".

The Rich Hill district with the Congress, Weaver, Antelope and Octave mines in Antelope Valley, was one of the several productive placer areas discovered by the Pauline Weaver party in the early 1860's. When the stage line through the Valley established a regular stop there, the place took the name of Antelope Station. The usual saloons, boarding houses and stores grew up along the placer beds, centering around the general store of the popular partners, Wilson and Timmerman.

In Antelope Station Stanton settled in a small cabin near the partners' store. His first intention may have been to pan some of the easy gold in the creek but if so the noble desire was short lived. More to his liking was the Wilson and Timmerman business.

He started a well-planned, three-way plot, pitting the partners against another Antelope resident, William Partridge. Hate was worked up between Partridge and Wilson, then Stanton slipped the word that Wilson was out gunning for the other. Partridge flared up, took the initiative and shot the merchant in the street in true Western style. Partridge was convicted of a murder and sent to the penitentiary largely because of adverse testimony by his supposed friend, Charles P. Stanton.

Smugly, he now began to lay plans to shorten the future of partner Timmerman. Sure enough the man was found dead one day, a coroner's jury unable to say whether the death was suicide from grief over his partner's passing or simply an accident.

Up to now Stanton had not been suspected but when he took over the store and claimed the partners had left it to him, people began to wonder. After a continuing series of mysterious acts of violence, all happening to those who stood in Stanton's way, suspicion became certainty. But his power and influence was so great no one dared to lift a voice— no one except Barney Martin who was heard on several occasions to say: "Something should be done about Charles Stanton."

Then one midnight a stranger knocked at Martin's door and gave warning. "A lot of strange things have been happening in this town, what with people getting killed and all. Get your family out of here before they are all murdered."

131

OLD CONGRESS HOTEL is still in use as private residence. Giant saguaro cacti were planted as small seedlings when town and hotel were flourishing. Holes in upper areas made by woodpeckers as nests are often occupied later by elfin owls. Cactus plant forms hard, air- and water-tight linings around pockets, once used by Indians for water bags. When photographer set up tripod in yard it was filled with milk goats, all scampering out except one curious maverick.

Martin was no personal coward but he knew he couldn't keep guard over his family the clock around. So he sent a man on horseback to tell his friend Captain Calderwood that his family would be arriving at Calderwood Station in a day or two, then he piled his family into a wagon and left town.

Linked with Stanton's nefarious interests were the Valenzuela brothers who were to come up short in the holdup at the Vulture mine. These two desperadoes in company with several others followed the Martin wagon and forced it off the road after it was well away from the camp. The entire family was then murdered, dry brush piled on the wagon and the whole set on fire. When the Martins failed to appear at Calderwood, the captain sent out a search party which traced the wagon tracks to the scene of carnage.

Yet nothing was done to check Stanton's supremacy for fear of reprisal. Instead of suffering

for his misdeeds he now took over the whole town, even changing its name to his own. Feeling secure as "king of the camp", Stanton began pressing his attentions on a beautiful Mexican girl, Froilana, daughter of Pedro Lucero who was leader of a gang of toughs in neighboring Weaver. The girl had different ideas and no intention of submitting to him. Stanton, not used to resistence in any form, forced the issue. The next day in his store, he turned to face what he thought was a customer and quickly saw it was the girl's brother Jose. Before Stanton could draw his gun, Jose put two .44 slugs into the chest of the man who had wronged his sister.

Fleeing from the scene, young Lucero met a friend coming down the trail who inquired the reason for all the hurry. "I have just killed Stanton," he replied, "and I am hurry up to get across the border." The friend caught his arm. "Wait. Don't go. We will get up a reward for you."

"A spiral of gray smoke ... but there was no fire!"

TOMBSTONE, ARIZONA

Edward L. Schieffelin of Tombstone, Arizona, and Bob Womack of Cripple Creek, Colorado, had several things in common. They were prospectors at heart and each had a stubborn faith in the ultimate riches of his chosen locale. Each did, in time, see his dream fulfilled in a fabulous strike but there the parallel ended. Bob never did do much with his strike because he drank too much and could not interest big money for proper developments of his find. Ed, on the other hand, made the proper contacts right away, kept control of the several companies he formed, and was a prime figure in the development and history of his city.

As prospectors found out, locating a rich vein is one thing, mining it is another. In the case of placer gold, a lot of the stuff may be found loose in the creek bed and may be had for the panning, but hard rock mining is something else, particularly in the case of silver. When Ed made his find he had done his searching all over Oregon, California and Nevada, at last bearing down on a restricted area in southern Arizona, the fringe of hills bordering the San Pedro River. For a long time the search was as fruitless as the others but now he didn't move on. Settling down to a dogged, systematic scrutiny, he went over the ground almost inch by inch. It wasn't easy. Plenty of

WEARY OLD SADDLES in harness house of O. K. Corral bear mute testimony to hard usage in days when chief means of transportation was riding horse. These were used by Wyatt Earp, McLowery brothers, Clantons and others of the day.

O. K. CORRAL supported large blacksmith shop, used several anvils. This one saw service over long period in '70s and '80s. Most of auxiliary tools are intact and in their original places.

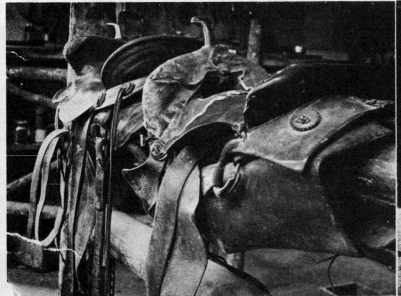

rattlesnakes and gila monsters lurked under every other bush but the most dangerous hazards were bands of marauding Apache Indians. This tribe had more tenaciously and vindictively resisted the white man than any other. And, in fact, the stronghold of the head man of all the Apaches, Cochise, was in the Dragoon mountains, only a few miles from the San Pedro.

Ed tried to work the country under the protection of a group of soldier scouts stationed at Fort Huachuca, but felt too restricted, and informed the men he was going to set out on his own. Asked what he was really looking for, he told them that he expected to find something very useful in the valley. Loud laughter greeted this evasive answer and one of the soldiers said, "Sure you will and it'll be your tombstone."

In approved fashion, Ed persisted in looking for "float" and then searching for the lode or vein from which it came. And finally, there it was, a rich vein of silver, close to the hideout of the Apaches in the Dragoons. The grim joke about

his tombstone had rankled, likely because it could so easily have materialized, and he felt a deep satisfaction in naming his claim "The Tombstone." With help in the form of his brother, Al, and one Richard Gird, a clever mining man, he located several other silver deposits, among them the Lucky Cuss and the Tough Nut. This last had an erratic breaking of the lode in every direction, due to faulting.

A real problem developed in trying to enclose the best of these in the amount of ground allotted to a claim, 600 by 1500 feet, a "tough nut" to crack. Actually, the first find, the Tombstone, proved to be not so rich as he had hoped, and was soon sold for just enough to get a little capital. Then they sold another one, the Contention for $10,000. This last sale was soon regretted, the Contention

OLD CHAINS ARE DRAPED across hitching rail of O.K. Corral Stable. Original building was in bad state of repair few years after famous shooting scrape in yard, was repaired and restored with authentic atmosphere. Visitors can now browse around stable and yard, almost hearing again fusillade of shots.

BOXES IN TINY BIRD CAGE THEATER were taken at $25 a night and often for a whole week during popular presentations. Theater made no pretensions at elegance, shows were frankly burlesque of most rowdy type. Girls doubled as performers, waitresses and anything else requested of them. Opened December 26, 1881, it was never empty, was a place where lonely, thirsty miners or tired businessmen could always be comforted. As girls served drinks to patrons during prelude to performance, they sang the bawdy songs of the day, giving the place its name. Stoutly built of adobe it is well preserved and the visitor today can wander around the tiny floor and stage where performers of another day cavorted.

YARD OF O. K. CORRAL. Adobe wall and big swinging gate are much as they were in days of famous fight here, October 27, 1881. Fight climaxed long standing feud between Ike Clanton's cowboys and three Earp brothers. Clanton's gang had been vowing to "get" the Earps and had so annoyed the Marshal and his brothers that he decided to put an end to it once and for all. As the brothers and Doc Holliday headed for O. K. Corral they saw Sheriff Behan trying to keep the peace by asking the Clantons and McLowerys to disarm. When the Marshal and his party got near enough, he added his order, "Boys, throw up your hands, I want you to give up your shooters." At this Frank McLowery drew his weapon but was a split second too slow, was shot just above the waist by Wyatt Earp. This set off a barrage of gunfire. When the smoke cleared away three men were dead and two wounded. Only Doc Holliday escaped unscathed. The *Epitaph*, Tombstone newspaper of the day, reported that, "The shooting created great excitement, and the street was immediately filled with people. Ike Clanton (who had run from the fracas) was captured and taken to jail. The feeling of the better class of citizens is that the Marshal and his posse acted solely in the right in attempting to disarm the cowboys and that it was a case of kill or be killed."

yielding $5,000,000 in the first five years. This gave them a better idea of the value of what they held, and they refused an offer of $150,000 for the others, deciding they had enough money to go ahead. Big money interests now invested in the operation, as long as they could not buy it outright. This is the point where the careers of Ed Schieffelin and Bob Womack diverge.

By this time, all sorts of stores, offices and saloons had grown up near the diggings, and the motley collection had taken on the status of a city. Because of the slope of the land, streets were laid out at an angle from cardinal compass directions, numbered streets are intersected by Toughnut, Allen, Fremont and Safford. Allen became filled up first and remained the main street. The O. K. Corral, the Bird Cage Theater, Cosmopolitan Hotel, Campbell and Hatch's Pool Hall and many more places of dubious respectability mingled with stores along Allen Street.

The original prospectors, miners, assay men and other hard working gentry now gave way to a new crop of characters. This new crop was made up of men like Wyatt Earp, Doc Holliday, Bat Masterson, Luke Short and Turkey Creek Johnson. Johnson had come from Deadwood with a ready made reputation as a gunslinger, and his confidence in his own aim was such that he invited his opponents to meet him in front of the cemetery. Since he, himself, served as volunteer sexton, he figured to save himself some foot work.

The year 1880 alone saw 110 liquor licenses issued for honky tonks along Allen Street, until every other structure was a saloon. There were fourteen faro joints which never closed.

The biggest tide of population came sometime in the decade between 1880 and 1890, rising to about 15,000. Even with such a large proportion of the lawless, enough remained to support four churches, several dancing schools, along with a Masonic Hall, and quarters for the Knights of Pythias. Catering to culture was the Tombstone Club, this was a sort of library where many periodicals and books were rented, and where meetings were held to discuss plays, politics and the more genteel aspects of life in Tombstone. Somehow, these latter seem never to have been very prominent in the history of the place.

It seemed that there was an inexhaustible supply of silver in the mines, and the shafts went deeper and deeper. Then came catastrophe.

Abundant courses of water were encountered at these lower depths, and the mines filled. Huge pumps had to be installed. One, The Grand Central, stood thirty feet above its foundations and cost $300,000. It worked fine but the water went down slowly, in spite of an enormous outpouring at the mouth of the mine. Only when other mine owners began to celebrate did the horrible truth dawn. The Grand Central was draining all the mines in the district! Not only that, the others refused to share in the expense.

Pumping however, continued until 1885, when the old enemy, fire, struck and razed the pump house. A year later fire hit the Contention operations destroying the pumping works and forcing closure. Then, at long last—cooperation. A consolidated pumping system was set up and in 1901 sunk a main shaft to the depth of 1,080 feet, bringing out 8 million gallons of water a day. Tombstone got on its feet again and resumed the pleasures of the Bird Cage Theater, bawdy houses and saloons.

As the single male population had been increasing so had that of the prostitutes. A fair number of these were employed at the Bird Cage, where the girls acted as performers and danced with the customers "so as to promote friendly relations." Another group worked and lived in a house managed by a madame. Others, more independent or not up to the required standards, kept their own cribs, and sat at the doors to attract busi-

HEARSE MADE FREQUENT TRIPS to Boot Hill, sometimes several in one day as when Billy Clanton and McLowerys were buried there. Vehicle rented for those whose friends could afford it, where undertaker was employed and c a s k e t provided. More victims of bullets or mine accidents were merely laid in pine box and carried over. Even box was of skimpiest construction as lumber was a scarce and expensive commodity. Nearest timber was many miles away in high mountains. Any shipment of lumber had to be guarded as it came into town to prevent highjacking.

ness. Still others walked the streets and went after customers avoiding a split of their earnings with a procurer.

Seldom did anyone hear of a surname for the girls. Nicknames prevailed, such as: Rowdy Kate, Dutch Annie, Blonde Marie, Irish May and Crazy Horse Lil. The land on which Dutch Annie built her brothels was owned by Wyatt Earp and leased to her.

The smaller respectable section, residences of families, etc., tried to edge as far as possible in the other corner of town, still not very far away, as too much expansion would go over the edge of the mesa.

This last flurry of boom and optimism was all too short, and signs of decay began to creep in when the inordinate cost of operating the pump-

ing system began to overtake income. The town was already on its last legs, when in 1914 the big Phelps Dodge Corporation bought equipment of the Tombstone Consolidated Mining Company at a receiver's sale for $50,000, sounding the death-knell of active mining for Tombstone.

The "town too tough to die" still lives, in a sense. It offers much to the visitor, a good many of the buildings so steeped in the rowdy history of the famous place still stand.

Ed Schieffelin lies now on the hill above town, near his first discovery. Over his grave is a stone marked "This is my Tombstone." His funeral was the largest ever held in town. The next largest was that of Dutch Annie, "Queen of the Red Light District," attracting a procession of 1,000 buggies, and most of the business men and city officials.

137

Arizona

NO LAW BUT LOVE

Tubac, Arizona

The story of Tubac is interwoven with those of southern Arizona's three most important missions, San Xavier del Bac, Tumacacori and Guevavi (often spelled Guebabi). San Xavier, poetically referred to as the White Dove of the Desert, has been in almost constant use and is possibly the most beautiful and finest example of mission architecture in the United States. Tumacacori, victim of Apaches and vandals, is a pathetic shell, yet retains a certain nobility. Its ruins are arrested from further decay by its present status as a national monument. Guevavi, older and never as large nor as solidly built as the others, has all but disappeared, its adobe walls melted to mere mounds of mud. Of the seven missions established by Father Kino during his service within the present

boundaries of Arizona, only these three were known to have been in operation at the time of his death in 1711.

Missions and ranches of the Tubac area were constantly exposed to murderous Apache raids during their early years and were all but inoperative by 1851. In that year, Pima and Papago tribes joined forces in an earth sweep just north of the Mexican border. Priests who had failed to escape were killed and Spanish silver-mining equipment, in operation since 1736, was destroyed. The next year a presidio, or garrison was established at Tubac, with soldiers offering a measure of protection to what few farmers remained. By 1753, the priests had returned to their devastated churches.

The earliest history of Tubac as a settlement isn't clear, but its name originated from a Pima

SOME GRAVES in old Tubac cemetery are marked but whole sections lack any identification.

word meaning "a burned out place." Located beside the Santa Cruz River, it is bordered on the west by the Diablito Mountains and on the other horizon by the Santa Ritas. The river, now a trickle at best, was a dependable stream in the days of Tubac's prosperity, even justifying the building of grist mills along its banks. By 1776 the town was the center of an extensive farming, cattle raising and mining community. In that year, Anza chose the fertile spot as a gathering place while he planned his push on to San Francisco. Already distinguished as being the oldest town established by white men in Arizona, Tubac became the first Mormon settlement in the state just 100 years later.

Shortly after the arrival of the "Saints," there appeared a man who later would be called the "Father of Arizona." This was Charles D. Poston, who with his friend Herman Ehrenberg prospected the neighboring mountains in 1854. Poston found sufficient indications of mineral wealth to warrant his being chosen to lead an expedition sent out two years later by the Sonora Exploring and Mining Company, which developed into the Heintzelman mine.

During this period, Poston was put in charge of the town's 800 souls, four-fifths of them Mexicans. Invested by his company with the title of Alcalde, the new mayor instigated a unique monetary system in use at Tubac in 1858. Since almost the entire populace was illiterate, paper money called *boletas*, bearing pictures instead of numbered denominations was used. A pig signified 12½ cents, a calf 25c, a rooster 50c, a horse $1.00 and a bull $5.00.

Poston wrote of the community at this time, "We had no law but love and no occupation but labor; no government, no taxes, no public debt, no poli-

RESTORATION at Tubac has been generally well done, building of this wall not finished where lamp post is inserted. Many other adobe buildings need repairing or complete rebuilding. Insertion of wheel in adobe wall is anachronism not appealing to purists.

FRAGMENT of original Mexican Presidio near modern museum. Soldiers stationed here protected residents from vicious Apaches for comparatively short period.

tics. It was a community in a perfect state of nature." So natural were some of the relations between young couples at Tubac—who merely set up housekeeping without benefit of clergy—that Poston inquired the reason. "It's a long journey to the nearest priest," they said, "and the father charges a fee of $25, which we cannot afford."

Poston then took it upon himself to perform marriages, claiming he was legally authorized to do so because of his government position. Instead of charging a stiff fee, Poston performed the rites free, even presenting the happy couples with a gift. In addition to marrying "new" couples, he married many who had already had offspring and wished to make their children legitimate. So popular did this service become that strange faces from surrounding areas began to show up at his office. "I had been marrying people and baptizing children for two years and had a good many godchildren named Carlos or Carlotta, according to gender, and had begun to feel quite patriarchal," he commented, when the blow fell.

Bishop Lamy sent down to Tubac a priest named Macbeuf, the Vicar Apostolic of New Mexico. According to the Bishop, Father Macbeuf was to "look after the spiritual condition of the people of Tubac." Extremely conscientious, the priest followed the precepts of church law to the letter. The few sheets in town were commandeered to make walls for a confessional; he made parishioners wait until noon for the breakfast blessing, and he or-

dered that his followers have nothing to do with the Alcalde who had been so grossly encroaching upon the rights of the church. But worse yet, he informed his distraught congregation that marriages and baptisms that had been performed by Poston were illegal, that many were living in adultery. Then, going to Poston, he informed him that he had ordered the sinful cohabitors to suspend connubial relations forthwith.

In his journal, Poston says of the situation: "I knew there would be a riot on the Santa Cruz if this ban could not be lifted. Women sulked; men cursed, maintaining they were entitled to the rights of matrimony. My strong defense was that I had not charged any of them anything and had given them a treat, a marriage certificate with a seal on it made out of a Mexican dollar and had forged on an anvil." Still, though the Pope of Rome was beyond the jurisdiction of even the Alcalde of Tubac, he could not see the way open to a restoration of happiness.

"It would never do to let the population of the Territory be stopped in this way," he continued, "so I arranged with Father Macbeuf to give sanctity of the church to the marriages and legitimatize the little Carlos and Carlottas with holy water at a cost to the company of $700." This rectified the matrimonial situation along the Santa Cruz River and all were again satisfied." (Reprinted by courtesy of *Desert Magazine*.)

OLD RAILROAD CAR abandoned among much other rail equipment, mining machinery. Artifacts at Twin Buttes cannot be approached too closely, all sections behind fences. Photo made by special permission. Cactus plant is Opuntia species, this one with slabs of brilliant cerise-purple.

GHOST BEHIND BARBED WIRE

Twin Buttes, Arizona

Copper mining began in what was locally called the Borracho Mines some time in the early 1870s. Located in the mountains 26 miles southwest of Tucson, Arizona, miners named the town that developed Twin Buttes for a pair of nearby peaks. Mining there was sporadic for the first three decades, as little money was available to small-time Mexican operators and digging was done mostly by pick and shovel methods. When the copper veins thickened, activity increased until the deposit pinched out. Then everybody indulged in a siesta.

Near the turn of the century "The Three Nations" began wide-scale operations in the mines. American John G. Baxter, Irish Michael Irish and Scotch John Ellis, seeing what they called "an inexhaustible

supply" of copper ore, began by prospecting both old and new workings. Results were so encouraging and news releases so enthusiastic that a group of Milwaukee financiers bought out the whole thing, incorporating the Twin Buttes Mining and Smelting Co. with assets of $1,000,000 under the laws of Arizona Territory. Before incorporation was fully accomplished, the new company's prospectors made a happy discovery. The Morgan Mine had an ore body 95 feet deep, 25 feet wide and 300 feet long, with ore assaying 10%.

That same year, the company made plans to build a 500-ton smelter and construct a railroad from Tucson to the now roaring copper camp. The railroad would supplant transport by wagon and team and the new smelter would handle the huge amounts of ore pouring from the Morgan Mine and that royal trio, the Copper King, Copper Queen and Copper Prince.

By this time, Twin Buttes had acquired a newspaper, but it wasn't printed in town and it wasn't intended for local consumption. The *Twin Buttes Times*, edited and printed in Milwaukee, was aimed at stockholders. Bubbling with enthusiasm and carrying the Twin Buttes dateline for authenticity, it delivered the glad news that not only would the new railroad carry ores and supplies for Twin Buttes itself, but already applications were being received from other mining districts with requests for spurs. Among these, the *Times* said, were the Helvetia Mines in the Santa Ritas and the Lincoln Mining Company, which consisted of 31 claims in the Sierrita Mountains. The paper continuously stressed forthcoming benefits of the railroad because under territorial law, the Twin Buttes Mining and Smelting Company had to establish a second corporation, The Twin Buttes Railroad, in order to build the railroad. So stockholders, traditionally

OCOTILLO, technically Fourqueieria splendens is widespread throughout warmer sections of southern deserts. This one near Patagonia is in full display of scarlet bloom. Plant is not related to cactus tribe, has own method of coping with scant or nonexistent moisture. In rain, regardless of season, shrub puts forth leaves, flowers. Here foliage has dropped to be replaced by bloom.

dazzled by an aura of rich paying mines, had to be infected by railroad fever, too.

Contrary to dire predictions, the projected railroad was actually built. The new Twin Buttes Railroad, connecting with the Southern Pacific in Tucson, ran in a southerly direction through Santa Clara Valley to Sahuarita. Then, swinging westerly in easy grades and curves, it ascended to Twin Buttes. Shortly after leaving Tucson, travelers on the railroad were treated to a close-up view of Mission San Xavier, that dazzling "White Dove of the Desert." The railroad advertised that it was prepared to accept general freight such as hardware, machinery, milk, cream and meat, the latter three items, it was stressed, at "shipper's risk." For the first few years, the railroad was a huge success. Twin Buttes Mines shipped large quantities of ore of types not handled at the local smelters, freight and passenger business was good, and some of the spur extensions were actually constructed.

Then, around 1907, the line unaccountably laid off employees and some freight shipments were "lost." Dissatisfied customers complained of poor service and high rates. In a few months both mine and railroad companies were overdrawn at the bank. About this time, a Twin Buttes Mining and Smelter stock offer was made of 250,000 shares at 60 cents, the offer almost immediately moderated to 40 cents. There were few takers. Bad times had hit Twin Buttes.

By 1910, the original company was pretty much disbanded. John Ellis, one of the "Three Nation" men who had gone along with the Twin Butte setup, married in Tempe, then returned to Scotland, where he died in 1909. Michael Irish married in Tucson, then took his new bride and copper wealth to the old country. But the other member, John C. Baxter, stepped in when the company closed down operation of the Twin Buttes properties and together with Ed Bush, reopened the Morgan. The start of World War I gave their new company a big boost and the railroad once again carried a car of ore every week. This boom was temporary, however. After the war, things again declined at the Buttes.

As deposits grew thinner, general economic conditions grew steadily worse and soon Twin Buttes became a ghost town. The railroad also faded into a shadowy spectre. Of the town, little is left, and this unreachable behind barbed wire. (Reprinted by courtesy of *Desert Magazine*.)

VULTURE CITY, ARIZONA

In the center of a sun-baked plaza in Vulture City stands an imposing group of ancient stone buildings and in the floor of the central one is a cavernous stone-lined pit covered by a heavy iron door. At the height of activity at the Vulture mine in the 1880s the buildings also housed the general and assay offices and the stone chamber was used to store gold bullion for safekeeping until it could be shipped to Phoenix.

There was the day three horsemen with two pack horses rode up to the front of the bullion room. Two were the brothers Valenzuela, Inocente and Francisco. When they leveled guns and roughly demanded the iron door be raised, a guard and the superintendent protested. They were both shot and killed on the instant. While one of the bandits held a gun on the rest of the office force, the other two went into the bullion room, lifted the conveniently unlocked door, removed $75,000 worth of gold bars and loaded the boxes on the pack horses. Gunfire now broke out on both sides. A bullet hit one of the bandits who dropped to the dust while the other two fled with the gold.

A posse was hastily organized but by the time the pursuers caught up with their quarry the loot had been buried. The leader of the posse shot one of the desperadoes but was held back from killing the other who fled into the mesquite. For two months the fugitive was hounded but eventually he thought it was safe to return to the spot where the bullion was hidden. As he started to lift out the heavy bars, he was shot and fell across them.

For a few years after this the bullion was shipped out by Wells Fargo carriers. The stages were repeatedly held up, drivers killed and the gold carried off. This happened so often Wells Fargo officials declined to haul the cargo and the mining company resorted to packing it on horses over rough and devious routes across the desert. After these safe carries, the gold was sent over the road again and on the very first trip the stage was held up, both driver and guard killed.

This was the way things went at the Vulture from beginning to end. Violence of every sort haunted the mine, its many operators and the men who worked in the tunnels. Danger from raiding Apaches was everpresent, guards with ready rifles being stationed on the knolls surrounding the workings. Even so more than four hundred whites were killed by Indians in one fifteen-year period. Near the point where the road turned toward town, the Wickenburg-Ehrenberg stage was once ambushed, six passengers killed, two escaping. One of these was a woman who later died of her wounds. Robbery, murder and rape were so frequent in the camp itself that at least nineteen men were hanged from the gnarled ironwood tree in the plaza.

It all started with Heinrich Heintzel who had known there was a nice vein of coal on his father's land in Austria and had always wanted to mine and sell it, the family finances seeming ever at the vanishing point. His father stubbornly refused and after his death young Heinrich found out why. He dug some coal and sold it only to learn government agents would imprison him for not turning it over to them. He fled to America, changed

PART OF VULTURE CITY. On descending hill where are located deep shafted mine, shops and mills, much of town comes into view. Group of stone buildings at left faces other direction on central plaza. At extreme left is store, next taller structure contained general offices, smaller one next is bullion room with vault in floor, last is elaborate assay office with almost all equipment still intact. During one period of ore shortage several buildings were torn down, walls put through mill and much gold recovered. Present mine owner estimates "there are 25 to 35 thousand dollars worth of gold in the walls of these buildings remaining." Just beyond is frame building housing mess hall. Others are bunk and tool houses. At extreme right small stone building with vanishing shingles may have served as jail. At its left corner is hanging tree.

his name to Henry Wickenburg, headed for the West and started prospecting in Arizona.

He arrived in Yuma in 1862, having made arrangements to join the party of Major Van Bibber at La Paz to prospect in Peeples Valley. Low water in the Colorado delayed the boat so long young Henry found the major had departed without him. He started out after the party.

Here was a man fresh from a foreign land attempting to penetrate two hundred miles of strange desert land alone. It was an incredible effort but young Wickenburg accomplished it, finding Van Bibber and the others camped in Peeples Valley. They prospected along the Hassayampa River with little or no success and in 1864 several members gave up, the party reduced to six. While they stayed in the river camp to decide what to do next, the young and persistent Austrian headed his burro toward a peak, near which he had heard was a vein of gold.

He stopped a short distance from the peak and set up a semi-permanent camp with a small tent. After several days of prospecting he wanted to sweep out the floor, and since there were many vultures circling around, he shot one to get a wing for a good broom. The wounded bird was thrashing in the dust and as he killed it he saw under the fluttering wings bright glints of gold. Wildly excited, he gathered up several pieces of the rich ore, returned to his companions and filed a claim with them. All went to work on the site but the drudgery and lack of water discouraged the five partners and after ten weeks they decamped.

Wickenburg named his mine and the lonely peak Vulture and set to work by himself. All winter he used pick and shovel to remove surface ore, stuffing it into rawhides and packing it on the backs of two burros to the Hassayampa, twenty miles away.

Mining the ore was not too difficult for at first he did not have to go below ground. The lode was almost pure quartz, actually projected from the ground to a height of eighty feet, the ridges providing roosting places for the vultures, and extended horizontally three hundred feet, sixty to eighty in width. This exposure of such rich, gold-bearing ore was unique and would affect the history of Arizona for years.

Being unable to hand crush his ore and pan it in the river with any efficiency, Wickenburg employed Charles Genung to help him build an arrastra, the crudest type of grinder. After Henry had sluiced some of the product in the river water, he was convinced he really had wealth if he could only mine and recover at the same time. So he engaged several willing men to do the digging, hauling the ore down to him at the stream where he built several more crushers. This was Wickenburg's first mistake and set the pattern for a whole series of heartbreaks.

SUPPER REMNANTS LEFT FOR 21 YEARS. When gold mining was curtailed by government some "bootlegging" was being done here under guise of milling ore hauled in from old copper mine nearby. Informed of illegal gold operations here, U. S. inspectors stopped the men but allowed them to get supper. After hurried meal culprits slipped away to neighboring Bagdad copper mine where they were employed, went to work on morning shift.

144

Since he had never had an assay run, Henry did not know just how rich his mine was. As the prospectors and miners dug into the lode they soon ran into ore worth $100,000 to the ton or better than 25% gold. It was too much to keep men honest and they diverted the richest ore, sending the rest down to the boss.

In spite of this there was enough good ore arriving at the Hassayampa to warrant the building of real stamp mills by various firms. One was erected and operated by the Goldwater brothers who owned the large store in La Paz and later in Ehrenberg. Before long there were four hundred and fifty wagons hauling ore and eighty-five mills to grind it, a far cry from Henry's sledge hammer days a short time before.

Lack of water at the mine was a continuing problem. It had to be hauled from the river and cost ten cents a gallon for both men and mules. The animals hauling the water got very thirsty in the dust and heat and drank most of it. And they also ate much hay which could not be grown in this sterile rocky area. Eventually the water problem was solved by pumping it from the Hassayampa and feed was produced in the fertile Salt River Valley, a small village growing up there. The first building was Hancock's Store and the name of the town became Phoenix.

Wickenburg had sold out his interest in 1865, the price supposed to have been $85,000, $20,000 as a down payment. Almost immediately the buyer, B. Phelps of New York, began to haggle with the Austrian saying his title was not clear, partly because of the long lost partners. Believing he could win the case against the big corporation, Henry hired lawyers and sued, spending almost all his $20,000, but the courts held for the company. Broken in spirit, Wickenburg retired to an adobe house by the river.

During the litigation the company had taken out $1,850,000 in gold, built a huge mill at the mine and was erecting many stone buildings as offices, bunk houses, stores and homes for married workers. Adobe structures also sprang up by the dozens until Vulture City was a city in fact.

After a few years of prosperity B. Phelps sold out, having run up against a fault which cut off the main Talmadge vein. The new owners were furious but helpless, having bought the property on the strength of known richness. After many exploratory thrusts they located the continuing vein but then new faults were encountered and the mine

"MILLION DOLLAR STOPE" was so large miners were forced to leave heavy pillars of rich gold-bearing rock as ceiling supports. When later owners began mining out pillars, thousands of tons of rock collapsed into pit, forming huge "glory hole." While some surface ore has been removed since, artificial crater is essentially due to fall of roof.

changed hands again. Subsequent history of the workings followed this pattern until one lucky owner noticed the vein was widening and becoming even richer. The stope got so wide rock pillars were left to support the ceiling composed of many tons of earth and rock. This section was called aptly "The Million Dollar Stope". Then a new owner, a Canadian named McClyde, found himself running short of ready ore to keep the mills going and started mining out the pillars. Before salvage was completed the entire roof fell in, creating a gigantic "glory hole". Many pillars of high assay ore were lost, as was any possibility of locating the direction of the lode.

In 1931 "Rawhide Douglas" put down a shaft near the present well in an effort to relocate the

"GAY" SECTION of Vulture City (sometimes called Nugget City) was discreetly situated on nearby low hill slightly removed from cabins of married miners. Most cribs were of adobe or combination of mud, bricks and scarce lumber as this one. It was conveniently near one mine so workers might spend lunch hour talking to girls. In lustier days one member of white-shirted group celebrating here was Arizona congressman. When other visitors were heard approaching, statesman's party adjourned to basement room.

main body of ore but without success. The present mine owner, Dr. George H. Mangun says: "No one has ever located it. None of our present fancy electro-magnetic and electronics devices has been able to give us any clue. This makes the seventh time the lode has been lost due to faulting in prehistoric times."

During the life of the Vulture mine it has yielded $17 million in gold. Any estimate as to how much this would be increased by persistent "high-grading" could only be a guess, but some old timers say the true total would be near $100 million.

And the discoverer of all this wealth, Henry Wickenburg, lived out his embittered life in the adobe shack down by the river. His health gradually failed and meager savings disappeared. Early in July of 1905 the Austrian, born Heinrich Heintzel, walked out of his home, stopped under a large mesquite tree and blew his brains out. The weapon, an old style revolver, was very likely the same one with which he killed the vulture that showed the way to it all.

19 MEN MET DEATH HERE. During Vulture's early turbulence most murderers and horse thieves came to gruesome end dangling from stout branch of hanging tree. Fights among citizens or workmen resulting in death were condoned but not shooting of residents by strangers. 19th victim of noose was man whose attentions to comely woman were resented by husband who marched culprit to tree at gunpoint. Limb is conveniently low but as one old timer remarked: "We got their feet off the ground." Tree is large specimen of Olneya Tsota, locally called ironwood, general designation for several tough-wooded desert trees.

WEAVER, ARIZONA

Pauline Weaver was Tennessee born in 1800, the father a white man, mother the daughter of an Indian chief. Pauline was destined to be honored by having the name Weaver used for a mining camp, not because Pauline was some girl wonder of Arizona but because *he* was a military scout and public benefactor. The Indian mother named her baby Paulino which became Pauline in usage. Although a strange sounding name for a rugged character, it was not an uncommon one among half-breeds. Weaver however was to distinguish himself from the ordinary.

The boy started his wandering career as soon as he cut loose from his mother's buckskin "apron strings", ranging from home to Puget Sound and into Arizona. On the great ruin of Casa Grande one can see written on the walls: "Pauline Weaver was here — 1832" but he cannot be blamed for desecration. Pauline could not read or write.

In 1847 General Stephen W. Kearny hired him as military guide to lead the Mormon Battalion from New Mexico to California, rewarding him with a land grant in the area of present Banning. But the man was not a farmer and headed back to Arizona. In common with other "mountain men" he carried several weapons — his long-barreled, muzzle-loading flintlock gun, later a percussion cap type, then there was his bowie-type knife for skinning, butchering and eating.

While many of these men traveled in bands for safety. Weaver, like Bill Williams, preferred going it alone. One memorable exception was his gathering a party including Major A. H. Peeples, Jack Swilling, several other whites and some Mexicans. They were at La Paz after the discovery of gold there but came late and were not satisfied with what they found, pushing on through the arid desert region toward the Bradshaw Mountains. They reached a good stream of water, shot several antelope and made camp. The stream was named Weaver Creek in honor of the guide and the location Antelope Valley. This spot later became Stanton.

Next morning the horses were missing and the Mexican aides were sent after them. Covering the high hill nearby and beyond it, they not only found the animals but an abundance of *chispas*, nuggets the size of pebbles. Gathering a handful, they returned with the horses and told their story. Without waiting for breakfast, Major Peeples rushed over the mountain shoulder and picked up $7,000 in gold before returning to camp.

History says the men soon cleaned up the surface deposits but neglects to state if they ever had

FOUNDATIONS FOR MILL BUILDINGS in Weaver contain much native rock, not much scarce cement. Little adobe structure, center background, is typical of area where lumber was unobtainable. Formerly roofed with brush and mud, new mining activity at turn of century saw sheet metal roof as replacement, and even this has suffered from ravages of time. Building served as store, is lone survivor of business section of once flourishing camp, now only waste of rubble and brush. Tiny cemetery has no headboards standing now but in 1918 thirty-five were counted, all bearing legends: "Died with his boots on."

STONE POWDER HOUSE barely retains heavy iron door. Site is immediately below Weaver, likely chosen as safe distance. Large saguaro cactus may easily be several hundred years old and weigh several tons, is supported vertically by heavy woody-fibered structure, rest is pulp composed mostly of water. Rock intrusion in background is home for countless rattlesnakes, area known as "Rattlesnake Haven."

breakfast. As soon as the news got out a horde of whites and Mexicans burst on the scene in a full-scale gold rush. The mountain became known as Rich Hill, the mushrooming collection of adobes as Weaver Camp, later Weaverville, then Weaver. As men swarmed in, each claim was limited to 200 square feet and claim jumping was common.

When the camp's short life came to an end, the placers alone had given up a total of $1 million and lodes were found both at Weaver and the neighboring camp of Octave. The latter was appropriately named as eight partners found deposits.

Not having a miner's temperament, Weaver departed quickly. In 1867 he was again hired as a guide and attached to Camp Lincoln, later Camp Verde. Refusing a bunk in the barracks he occupied a tent outside the reservation. On the morning of June 21, a soldier was sent to see why the guide had not reported as scheduled and found Weaver dead in the tent. Everything was neatly in order

and the body wrapped in a blanket. Weaver had apparently been sharing the tent with an Apache and a year or so before had received an arrow in the shoulder. The shaft was removed but the head remained and this was thought to have caused his death.

He was buried with military honors by the companies of the 14th Regiment stationed at Camp Lincoln in the cemetery there. In 1892, after the Indian scares had subsided, remains of all military personnel including those of Weaver, were removed to San Francisco yet Weaver was not to rest there but to be a wanderer in death as he had been in life. In 1928 a movement was started in Prescott to bring the remains to the spot where in 1863 he had made as permanent a camp as he ever did. The spot is on the grounds of the Sharlot Hall Museum in Prescott, and is marked by a large stone bearing a bronze plate inscribed: "PAULINE WEAVER — truly a great man."

COMBINATION STONE and dugout buildings served as business section in better days of large gold mining camp of Octave, close neighbor of Weaver. In 1863 rich gold placer beds were discovered in Weaver Creek by party of eight men to commemorate their number.

MILL AT OCTAVE was built in expectation of many years of production by quartz veins, which were exhausted by end of century. Even so, Octave mine, consisting of two shafts 1,300 feet deep, turned out more than $8 million.

MEMORIES GHASTLY & GHOSTLY

WHITE HILLS, ARIZONA

In a truly desert setting, five miles from the highway, lie the scattered remnants of one of the wildest camps in Arizona.

This was White Hills, so named for the backdrop of blazingly white, rocky ridges. The buildings are few and lean toward each other, as if seeking support in their senility.

There is little rubbish in White Hills. The dooryards seem to have been swept recently; the glaring sand is smooth and neat. Many Joshua trees and bisnagas, the barrel cacti, have grown up to form landscaping.

CEMETERY IS OVER-GROWN by "Bisnagas," barrel cacti. These are of type reputed to have saved many desert travelers from death by thirst. If the top is chopped off, the interior pulp mashed into a hollow, copious juice collects and is perfectly p o t a b l e, if somewhat insipid.

"FRONT YARD" OF miner's cottage in White Hills is paved with dazzling white gravel, landscaped with typical desert plants, cacti and gnarled Joshua trees.

The place was not so tidy in the 1890's. There were 1,900 rough-and-ready miners then, not to mention their unsavory hangers-on. Water was brought in from distant mountain springs, but who drank it? Not many, judging from the piles of whiskey bottles on the fringes.

Rats were a serious problem in the town, living sumptuously on the garbage left everywhere. Cats were imported, to become a problem in turn when they multiplied apace, as cats will do. These then became targets for gun practice, their neglected bodies adding to the general stench.

The town suffered a number of cloudbursts, furnishing an embarrassingly large amount of water all at once, to the point of washing outhouses into the open desert.

Wandering around the immediate vicinity reveals innumerable mine headings, shafts and tunnels centered by the mill ruins.

CALIFORNIA
GHOST TOWNS

BY

LAMBERT FLORIN

Drawings
by
DAVID C. MASON, M.D.

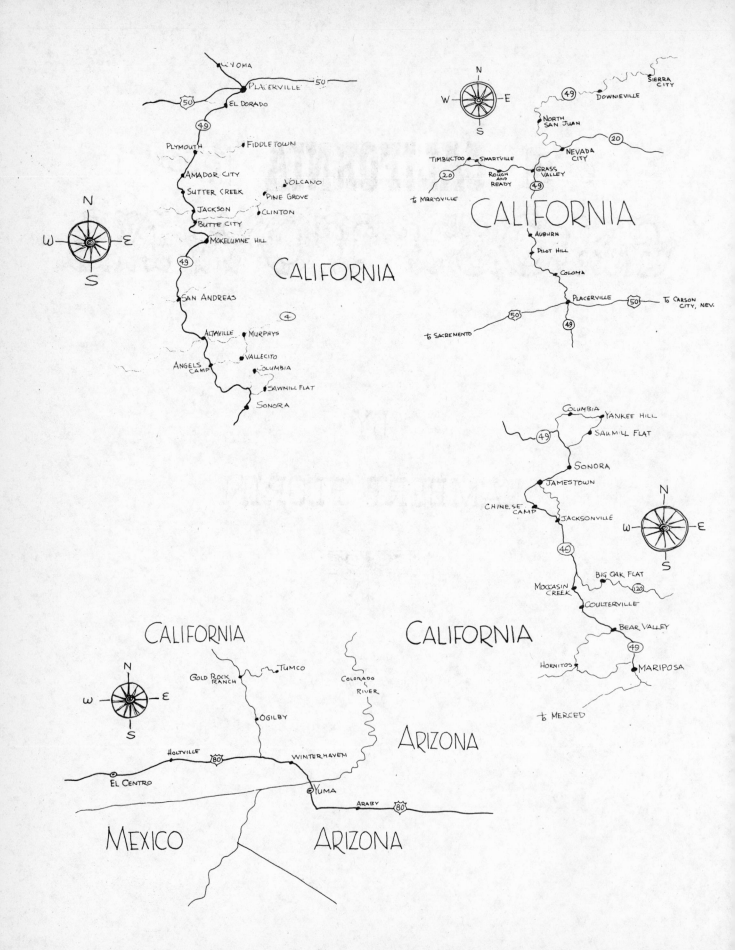

INDEX

CITY	Page
Altaville	158
Amador City	157
Angels Camp	159
Auburn	160
Ballarat	162
Bear Valley	164
Big Oak Flat	166
Bodie	167
Calico	169
Camp Seco	170
Carson Hill	173
Cerro Cordo	176
Chinese Camp	178
Coloma	181
Columbia	186
Copperopolis	190
Coulterville	193
Darwin	195
Douglas City	196
Downieville	198
El Dorado	201
Fiddletown	202
French Gulch	204
Garlock	205
Gold Camp	209
Grass Valley	213
Hornitos	217

CITY	Page
Jackson	222
Jamestown	224
Knight's Ferry	226
Mariposa	229
Masonic	231
Mokelumne Hill	233
Mormon Bar	235
Mother Lode	237
Murphys Camp	238
Nevada City	240
North San Juan	243
Randsburg	245
Rough and Ready	249
Sawmill Flats	254
Shasta	255
Shingle Springs	201
Sierra City	260
Sonora	262
Swansea	264
Timbuctoo	265
Tropico Mine	209
Tumco	267
Vallecito	270
Volcano	272
Weaverville	274
Whiskeytown	278

MINE-RIDDLED BUTTES LOOM above Sierra City. From these heights slid devastating burdens of snow, often burying portions of town. Alarm bell is mounted in tower beside comparatively young Seqouia. It announced disasters such as slides, fires, also arrival of stages and mail. Clapper is actuated by twin pull ropes while bell remains stationary. Several bells of this type persist in gold country, such as one in front of old firehouse in North San Juan.

AMADOR CITY, CALIFORNIA

A small group of Argonauts detached itself from the hordes swarming over the Sierra foothills and started panning the sands of Amador Creek in 1848. The tiny band had great faith in the chosen location even though little gold turned up in their pans to justify it.

Pickings grew ever smaller until the claim was exhausted and the men ready to fold their tents and fade away. Then in 1851 came the big strike. The original miners had been trying to get their gold the easy way, out of the creek gravels, but the bonanza was found in the quartz vein of the Mother Lode itself at the point where it intersected with Amador Creek.

The find was not made by an experienced miner but by a Baptist preacher, a Reverend Davidson. Not being able to do the hard work or handle the finances he took in other members of the cloth as partners. The popular name for the workings was naturally—"The Ministers' Claim." The mine was later consolidated with six other workings, the combine called the "Original Amador," a complex of more than nine miles of crosscuts, drifts and raises. They opened up from a 1,238 foot inclined shaft. Total production was almost $4 million.

Better known and far more productive was the Keystone Mine. It was first dug in '53 and for several early years the ore was crushed in the primitive quartz mills called by the Mexican name of arrastres. Later more modern stamp mills were built and as their capacities increased the underground workings developed a shaft 2,680 feet deep. A large portion of the ore was of an unusual sulfarsenide type but it yielded $25 million.

Amador City is two and a half miles northwest of Sutter Creek and is similiar to it in history and general background. Sutter Creek was named for the man who had once operated the vast agricultural domain of Sutter's Fort where Sacramento stands today. Sutter had set up the sawmill at Coloma to supply lumber for his buildings. Instead, gold was discovered in the millrace and the subsequent rush of gold seekers destroyed Sutter's dream by depleting his help and overrunning his farms. He made a pitiful attempt to follow the "If you can't lick 'em, join 'em" school but failed utterly, principally because he had no aptitude for handling his help along the lines the American miners demanded. They claimed his system was "slave labor" and Sutter was forced to quit his claims at Sutter Creek.

More spectacular was the career of Leland Stanford in the same area. Having made a little money in Sacramento as a merchant he bought into the Lincoln Mine. At first there was nothing but trouble and at one time he was ready to sell out for $5,000. His foreman, Robert Dowes, persuaded him to hang on, the strike at last was made and Stanford was established as a tycoon. With his partners he then built his railroad, became U. S. Senator, then Governor of California and founded Stanford University.

OLD IMPERIAL — finest hotel in Amador City. Bar section operated until fairly recent years, barkeep in fancy vest pouring drinks for fewer and fewer patrons until forced to quit.

157

ALTAVILLE, CALIFORNIA

The question is: Does Altaville owe its place in history to the producing of its gold or its fossilized relic? For here, down 130 feet in the Matison Mine, was found the "Calaveras Skull," subject of controversy and confusion.

When gold in the Mother Lode's easily worked placer streams began to run thin in 1850, miners found more of it in gravel beds above and then in ancient deposits far below the level of active stream beds. This was mighty old gold, as evidenced by the fossil leaves and riffles found with it. Near Altaville several drift mines were developed with shafts as deep as 300 feet.

The Matison Mine was one of these and the finding of the old skull put the Mother Lode in the news more than the gold did. Scientists saw irrefutable proof that man was far more ancient than formerly believed, the public laughed at it as a gigantic hoax and Prof. J. D. Whitney became the man of the hour.

Out of the tangled web of tales about the skull finding is the clear fact that this gentleman, then State Geologist, in January of 1866, had exposed a wildcat scheme of a local financier to foist worthless stocks on the people of Altaville. His act made some bitter enemies but their wrath was blunted by the uncovering of the skull "dating back to Pliocene times."

The whole world heard about the discovery that July. At a meeting of the California Academy of Sciences at San Francisco, Prof. Whitney read a paper confirming the authenticity of the Pliocene Skull. From then on for years the press was full of stories on the subject, many scientists eager to accept the age of the relic, others scoffing. One newspaper reported, "The unscientific public hailed the story as a huge joke on the state geologist perpetrated by the fun loving citizens of the camp." Bret Harte covered the subject in one of his later contributions to the "Californian", the poem "To The Pliocene Skull." In 1903 the American Anthropological Society accepted the skull as a genuine relic but questioned the extreme age which admitted the presence of prehistoric caves in the Sierra Nevada.

And for the light touch is the story that about the time the skull was found, Dr. Kelly, nearby Angel's Camp dentist, failed to find something—the skull of his laboratory skeleton.

HEADSTONE in old section of Altaville cemetery which contains many interesting monuments from gold rush days. Unique in shape, headstone memorializes Alfredo Ribero by portrait cemented to marble. Picture remains unfaded through long years of strong sunshine, was made by converting photographic emulsion to enamel then baked on porcelain base. Uniform is likely that of local Militia during Civil War days.

RABBITS MADE HIM RICH

Angel's Camp, Calif.

Beside a name which strained credulity Bennager Rasberry had a worked-out placer claim, a cranky old muzzle loading shotgun and he was hungry. The rocky rises around Angel's Camp supported a lot of jackrabbits and if the miner could not find gold he could spend time gnawing away on the stringy meat of those sagebrush broncos.

Rasberry shot several and then had trouble with the ramrod. It was jammed in the barrel tightly and neither curses nor muscles could get it out. Losing his temper completely he fired the weapon at a rock a dozen feet away. The ramrod came out right enough and Rasberry saw it had scuffed off the weathered crust of the rock and exposed the yellow gleam of gold.

It may be assumed Mr. Rasberry forgot all about rabbits since it is recorded he picked up nuggets to the value of $700 before it got dark. Come daylight he returned with pick and shovel and that day returned with $2,000. When the following day's work netted $7,000 from the vein he made up his mind he had a gold mine and filed claim to it. Bennager Rasberry soon became the richest man in town and his name is perpetuated in an Angel's Camp street called Rasberry Lane.

George Angel was a veteran of the war with Mexico and went with other footloose, gold-hungry ex-soldiers to the Sierra foothills. He found a likely spot to camp on the bank of a small creek tributary to the Stanislaus but he also found throngs of other hopeful prospectors already working the gravels. Playing it safe, he set up a trading post before picking up shovel and gold pan. So although mining proved a spare time sideline for Angel, he was still able to sift out as much as ten ounces of gold on a good day.

The men Angel joined at the location that would bear his name proved to be the advance guard of the big rush. In those first months every man was friend with an equal chance and there was no need for formal claims. But when reports of the rich harvest reached the outer world and hordes descended on the peaceful community many a prospector found "a snake in his tent." When the solid citizens caught strangers working their favorite locations there was trouble and some killings resulted. Civilization had arrived and it became necessary to legalize claims. Yet this period, loosely called the "Age of Innocence," quickly came to an end when the creek sands gave up the last of the gold flecks.

By 1855 Angel's Camp was "law abiding" with wrong doers duly arrested by a legally appointed sheriff, tried in regular court proceedings varied according to the crime. At least this was supposed to be the procedure and sometimes it did work out that way. Among variations was the case of a miner killing another who called him a "hog thief." Although he had "sort of borrowed" the pig in question, he said, and although he had "et some of it," the slur had irked him to the point of drawing his gun and killing the porker's legal owner.

Some Angel's Campers thought the culprit should be strung up pronto and when lynching rumors spread the law sent to nearby San Andreas for aid in protecting the prisoner, at the same time rushing trial procedure. To a packed courtroom came the word that the San Andreas sheriff and emergency posse were nearing Angel's Camp. As if by pre-arrangement each court officer was seized and bound, the prisoner hustled to the hanging tree and was dangling from the end of a rope when the horsemen of the law rode up.

Today Angel's Camp is better known to the tourist than almost any other town in the Mother Lode. And this is not due to George Angel or the muzzleloader of Bennager Rasberry or to any other bit of verified history, but to an incident nothing more than trivial, if indeed it happened at all.

The area around Angel's Camp was a hotbed for California folklore, nurturing over-fertilized stories about Joaquin Miller, Black Bart, salacious doggerel by anonymous miners and more classic tales by Bret Harte and Mark Twain.

It was in 1865 that Twain toured the Southern Mines. By that time they were "decaying" as a contemporary critic wrote it and it would seem the humorist found little of interest in the mines themselves, preferring, in Angel's Camp, the salubrious atmosphere of the Angel's Hotel bar. It is legend that bartender Ben Coon related to him a local anecdote which Twain jotted down in his notebook—"Coleman with his jumping frog. Bet stranger $50. Stranger had no frog and C. got him one. In meantime stranger filled C's frog full of buckshot so couldn't jump. The stranger won." Twain wove the fragments into a story which he later called a "villainous backwoods sketch" but which was printed and reprinted across the country and beyond in several languages.

AUBURN, CALIFORNIA

In November of 1855 two young easterners arrived in Sacramento. One had been getting some exciting letters from a friend in Downieville and he interested an acquaintance in making a trip west to find out if the letters were truthful or full of hot air.

It was raining hard when they set out for Downieville. Experienced westerners would have waited a few days for the mountain storm to subside, but they took the scheduled stage. At Auburn the drivers said he could not go any farther without endangering the passengers' lives, that the streams were all running full tilt and many would have to be forded.

The young fellows killed time by drinking in saloons and playing poker and when the storm broke, so were they. Deciding to walk back to Sacramento, work awhile to recoup their finances and then return, they took shovels and pans given them by saloon pals together with some advice, and started out.

About two miles out of Auburn, they came to a place where flood waters still covered the road so went up the ravine where the water was cascading to find a place to cross. They noticed a spot where water had cut away the bank and went to work awkwardly,

FLOWERING BRANCH OF FRUIT TREE offers fresh, young touch to old buildings from gold rush days.

but learning fast. In a short time they had three pounds of nuggets and returned to Auburn rejoicing. The find was worth $980.

Claude Chana was one of the workmen at Sutter's Fort who dropped his tools and headed for the gold fields. But instead of going to Coloma as did most of his fellow workers, he picked up some Indian helpers at Sicard's Ranch on Bear River and worked along the arroyos until he found gold. At this place there was no water, it being necessary to take the dirt to the river to wash it, and this seemed to be too much trouble for Chana. He left.

But others more energetic came and stayed. They thought the name should be Rich Dry Diggings or for variety, North Fork Dry Diggings. Finally a miner with some influence made it Wood's Dry Diggings.

Even that name proved impermanent when a bunch of soldiers arrived, stragglers from Stevenson's Volunteer Regiment. Most of them were from Auburn, New York, and referred to the camp as such, the briefer and more refined name becoming official. During the summer and fall of 1848 the take of a miner willing to work averaged from eight hundred to fifteen hundred dollars a day. Small wonder the camp was filled with several thousand prospectors, miners and hangers-on, all of them from California, most from Coloma.

Auburn, feeling like a town, elected an alcalde and drew up a constitution based on generally accepted miners' law. But now it looked to some as though this effort was all for naught, that the dry diggings might be worked out. Some citizens moved away but not the astute Mr. Jenkins. He reasoned there was still plenty of gold here. It just was not paying to haul the dirt to the water. So why not allow the water to come to the diggings?

Jenkins built a flume from a point above the location where the stream came closest. With plenty of water he worked his claim again but with indifferent success. Had it not been for an accident he might have been discouraged and left camp. His water suddenly ceased to flow. Investigating, he found a failure in the flume, a break in the plank bottom which allowed the water to pour out, washing a big hole in the dirt. Jenkins saw the gleam of gold there and abandoned the earlier workings. The new one yielded him a fortune of $40,000 in the next month. Naturally, everybody who had left Auburn now came back, operations shifting in the new direction.

There was a spiderweb of lesser ravines radiating from the town, one of them called Civil Usage for

ONCE PRINCIPAL STREET IN AUBURN, this virtually unchanged section is now preserved at edge of present bustling city. Attorney's offices were concentrated in block giving rise to jocular appellation, "Lawyers' Row." Two-story Masonic Building, dating from 1853 stands at upper corner. Next was hardware store, then old home of *Placer Herald*. Most early-day newspapers in mining towns shipped in four-sheet papers already partially filled with "boiler plate," usually printed in Chicago. This consisted of syndicated hackneyed material. More local, newsier items were then filled in by use of tiny Washington hand press. Earliest issues of *Herald* lacked ready-printed sheets due to difficulties of transportation, soon began receiving them as overland shipping improved.

some unknown reason. A Swiss named Schmidt built a small cabin on his claim here and being industrious, was generally supposed to have accumulated a quantity of dust. Yet when a Chilean shot and killed him, he found no gold. He fled to Amador County where he was lynched for another crime. Miners found Schmidt's body and gave him a decent burial, not looking for hoarded gold as they presumed the murderer had taken it.

The little cabin stood idle for a while and then a Chinaman rented it. He set to work mining with great industry but stopped after a few days to repair the fireplace for cooking his rice. The removal of

one loose stone opened up a cavity in which lay a buckskin bag full of dust. The pigtailed miner showed it to a trusted friend who estimated its value at about $8,000, then he decamped before the public administrator got his hands on it.

Auburn had one big advantage over towns dependent entirely on gold. Strategically placed in the center of a network of roads, it became a hub of distribution, first for mining supplies, later for more durable trade with farmers and orchardists. The present business section is higher on the hill than the old district which is confined to a block or two on the steep slope.

BALLARAT, CALIFORNIA

The names of our old towns, and why they were selected, are interesting facets of history.

Cornucopia is often used, signifying the horn of plenty. Bonanza, Fairview and White Hills are obvious in origin. But Ballarat?

Research shows that gold was discovered in Australia two years after California's big find of 1849. The discovery was made in Ballarat, Victoria, in the southeast part of the country down under. And it was at Ballarat, Australia, in 1869, that the largest nugget in the world was found. It weighed an incredible 2,284 ounces.

The hopeful founders of this California desert town must have baptized it (with whiskey, of course) "Ballarat" for the famous one in Australia. Prospectors, in the 1890's, discovered the yellow metal in several of the canyons leading out of the western flank of the Panamint Mountains.

HOUSE MELTS SLOWLY into earth from which it sprang. View is away from mountains looking east across blazing desert. Dry lake shows as white streak behind shack. Tiny tin-roofed house was home of lonely prospector until fairly recent years.

The Panamint Valley, mostly a glaring white, dry lake bed, butts up against the steeply rising Panamints. These culminate in Telescope Peak, 11,045 feet high above the townsite. There were no trees anywhere, so there was no material for lumber, and consequently Ballarat was literally created out of clay. Its buildings were built of adobe bricks baked in the sun. Some residents added suitable ornaments and additions of corrugated iron, bottles, etc. Enough timbers were imported for lintels, doorframes and sills. In this barren, waterless waste there grew no little flower gardens, or yellow roses, as in other camps, only skimpy sagebrush and greasewood.

The town was actually a center for several mining camps, including the almost inaccessible Panamint City which hardly provided a level spot large enough for a dance floor. In Ballarat were found several dance places as well as the necessary adjuncts such as refreshments and ladies.

After the town died, it had a solitary inhabitant for years. This was "Shorty" Harris. In 1934 he died and Ballarat and he became ghosts together.

The adobe buildings are nearly melted away, but the remnants are well worth visiting, a monument to man's persistent search for gold in the face of almost insurmountable difficulties.

LONELY, WEATHERED REMNANT of business building strikes note of pathos against Panamints. Land is harsh, offering no timber, water, food. All supplies had to be hauled long distances. Yet Ballarat was scene of many gay times, even advertised a "Fancy Dress Ball."

BEAR VALLEY, CALIFORNIA

Col. John C. Fremont was no man for hard work but he knew what his head was for. When he shifted the boundaries of his 44,000-acre grant to cover the newly discovered gold country from Mariposa to the Merced River, he was very successful in getting others to work the extensive and rich placers on his claim. The many experienced Mexican miners in the area who were unwilling to work for wages were given a grubstake and "share" in a claim along the stream. On this basis they would wade into the water and slosh a pan or shovel gravel into a Long Tom like everybody else.

When the placer workings were going good, Fremont discovered the veins scattering loose gold into the creek bed. In 1851 he started hard rock mining in the lode itself and built several stamp mills to crush the ore. Of his operations he favored those at Bear Valley, first called Simpsonville, and decided to build his home here. It was an imposing structure, called "The White House" by the people in the settlement.

A building boom now set in. Fremont's enterprises erected an elaborate two-story wooden structure with wide, gingerbread balconies, the lumber brought around the Horn in 1850. The hostelry served as headquarters adobe the Fremont Company and shelter for travelers including Ulysses S. Grant, its formal name being Oso House. Also going up in this period were a number of saloons, a large livery stable and several stores including the huge general mercantile business of the company.

In 1858 Fremont brought to "The White House" his wife, Jessie Benton Fremont, and the children. In June of that year the famous "Mariposa War" came to a head, threatening for a time the lives of the little family. But Col. Fremont was above all a soldier and had seen trouble coming. He had been fortifying his best-known mine, the Pine Tree, against attack by men of the Merced Mining Co., which firm had taken over two other units of the Colonel's properties by force.

The Merced men surrounded the Pine Tree and prepared to stage a seige. Fremont was wily enough to slip a rider through the solid line

ADOBE STORE BUILDINGS are melting away. This is rear section of walls facing street. Door at left opened into establishment of Nicholas Pendola, an Italian who built structure in 1850. Pendola was expert bootmaker, doing repair work as well. Most prominent customer was Col. Fremont himself who had all his boots made here. Iron doors, shipped around Horn are still in place, $800 for the pair. Walls have unusual construction, adobe c o u r s e s are alternated with schist slabs, quarried in neighborhood. Garbarino Store, General Merchandise adjoins at right.

around the mine who carried a message to the Governor, a desperate plea for help. This was answered in five days by a detachment of state troops which forced both sides to break up, the belligerents were admonished when maneuvered into court.

In 1859 the Supreme Court confirmed Fremont's title and the Mariposa War was officially ended. Later that year Horace Greeley visited Bear Valley, reporting: "The Colonel is now operating two stamp mills and netting $100,000 a year." Whatever the amount, Col. Fremont decided in 1863 it was not worth more gray hairs and sold the entire grant for $6 million. He came out considerably ahead since the original price in '47 was $3,000.

Bear Valley is a ghostly place now. Fremont's fine hotel with its balconies and pillars is gone, set on fire in 1938 by careless campers. Gone also is "The White House." Remaining are many ruined adobe buildings, several schist structures including the roofless jail and a few false fronts on the main street that breathe the atmosphere of the days when Fremont "owned" the town of 3,000 people.

ROOFLESS JAIL stands near schoolhouse on hillside. Built solidly of schist rock set firmly in mortar, structure would seem escape-proof, but further restraint was secured by fastening prisoner by leg-irons to heavy ring of iron in center of floor—common practice when town flourished. Hill behind jail is sparsely forested with digger pines.

BIG OAK FLAT, CALIFORNIA

White women were scarce in the early days of the West and particularly during the first several years of California's gold rush. So it was natural for a lonely white miner to take an Indian wife, not necessarily in legal fashion. James Savage—the same Savage who explored the Yosemite Valley while the head of a party pursuing renegade Indians—is assigned a vast loneliness, for he took five aboriginal wives to his bosom. And more, he retained most of their relatives as servants and laborers.

Savage was prospecting the gulches between Deer Creek and Moccasin Creek in 1849 and he and his retinue camped one night under an enormous oak tree on a wide flat. Next morning found the party panning the gravels of the creek and the showings convinced the leader that here they would stay. News of this kind could not be muffled and in a few months hordes of the gold-hungry, disappointed elsewhere, moved into "Savage's Diggings."

Before it was all over the placers of the immediate area had yielded a total of more than $25 million—one of the richest diggings of the Mother Lode. The name of the spot was changed to Big

Oak Flat in honor of the gnarled patriarch standing alone on the only level part of the camp. The tree was of dimensions out of all proportion to other oaks of the mountains and was thought to be the largest in California, with a diameter of thirteen feet at the base, eleven at a man's head.

The oak was still monarch of the flat when the town grew to 3,000 but was succumbing to a man-made cancer. The miners could not resist the temptation to dig closer and closer to the roots until many branches died. Fire in 1862 which destroyed most of the frame buildings caught the dried or dead limbs and finished the life of the old tree. Unrestrained digging around its base at last toppled it in '69 and in 1901 a fire was set against it, burning most of the trunk and all the limbs.

In 1932 the Boys' Service Club of Union High School in Sonoma gathered the remaining fragments of the old oak and built a monument over them beside the road. In a few years this memorial was so decimated by the hackings of vandals that it was necessary to protect them with iron grillwork.

BIG GENERAL MERCANTILE is one of the finest examples of architecture in entire Mother Lode country and one of the best preserved. Built of dressed schist slabs set in lime mortar, the door frames are made square by the use of bricks. Heavy iron doors, characteristic of gold rush style, were shipped around Horn, had bars and hasp inside for securing at night. Not only did doors afford protection against bandits but kept fire out, or contained within.

THEY REST IN PEACE

BODIE, CALIFORNIA

As early as August, 1865, Bodie attracted such nationwide attention by its wickedness and flagrant disregard of law and order that *Harper's Monthly* sent out a man to "case" the town for a story. He was I. Ross Browne. Having at last arrived there tired and dusty, he was encouraged to sit up and take notice by a slug of snake medicine. His eyes having thus been opened, he looked around him and found the place "destitute of vegetation" with the exception of sagebrush and grass. Mr. Browne missed a few details. There were also Argenomes, a prickly "poppy" and an iris.

For some Fourth of July celebrations trees and shrubs were imported for the day. These "Fourth of July" affairs were indeed important. The entire population turned out, many ladies were in formal gowns. As the day wore on lubrication progressed, and by the time the Grand Ball started in the evening things were really lively even if the imported verdure had wilted.

Dances were held in the Miners' Union Hall which still stands today. Many fights developed and combatants were ejected to continue the often fatal fracas outdoors. If a corpse resulted no one worried too much about it, but the next day a question had to be settled. On the hill close to town there were two burying grounds, one for the "decent respectable folks," the other, larger and more populous, for all the rest, so which one should properly hold the newcomer?

The "Bad Man from Bodie" is a well-founded legend. He is a compounded figure, made up of real-life rascals who infested the town. Among these were two Mexicans who had learned of the planned movement of $30,000 in bullion. They waylaid the coach on the stage road between Bodie and Carson City and got away with the loot. They were caught shortly but the gold was missing. One was killed in the capture, the other died in the Bodie jail overnight. Presumably the bandits cached the gold in the short time between hold-up and capture, but the secret of the location was buried with Pedro on Boot Hill. This was in 1880, but the gold is still there.

Maiden Lane and Virgin Alley were the two streets comprising the "red light" district. Houses ranged from mere cabins with one girl to the elegant high grade salon. Whereas loggers in the northern woods towns brought their girl friends pitchy wood for starting fires, the miners of Bodie filched nuggets of gold for theirs.

As much gold remains under Bodie Butte as was taken out, some $75,000,000 worth, but the vast labyrinth of tunnels and shafts under the Butte and town are collapsing into one another, and water fills the lower levels.

One day, when the price of gold advances, life may return to Bodie. But it is not likely to be the same violent, rowdy and lusty force which once animated the place and its 10,000 people.

The main street, named for *Harper's* Mr. Browne, once lined solidly with commercial buildings, has dwindled to a few blocks of sparsely spaced structures. Some of the most historic ones remain; the Firehouse with its old hose cart, Assay Office and Miners' Union Hall. On side streets are the Methodist Church, the jail, the school and a good many others.

SIDE STREET LEADS to Methodist Church. Funds for building quaint structure were solicited from redlight district, bordellos, saloons and opium dens as well as more legitimate business. The former contributed bulk of necessary funds. Metal roof added in later years has prevented total decay of charming little building.

CALICO, CALIFORNIA

Calico is unique among ghost towns, a reconstructed and restored replica of the original. The man responsible for the feat should know what it looked like, for he worked there in the mines in 1910. He is Walter Knott, who now owns the whole town. The job has been no small project and is not finished yet.

The reason for the name is strikingly evident. The mountains forming a backdrop for the old camp are as brilliantly varied in color as any fabric could be.

Many of the buildings in Calico were made of adobe, sun-dried brick, for lack of sufficient lumber. These had partly melted away, even in this almost rainless country, and have been reconstructed of concrete, roughened and colored in such a way as to resemble closely the original appearance. Every now and then we would spot a frame building in its original condition. No amount of skill could duplicate the beautiful weathering effect only time and the elements can give to exposed wood.

The main street was not called "Main" but "Wall Street." In the 80's there were five saloons, three restaurants, many stores and hotels in addition to the usual boarding-houses, assay offices and school. Cornish miners (as in many early camps) were there in numbers and many of these lived in caves in the hills. These were secure from wind and were no doubt much cooler than the town's man-made structures. Daytime temperatures around the Calico Hills in summer will often reach 110 degrees or more.

Top producing days for Calico Mine were in the 80's. The number of saloons, always an indication of the size and prosperity of the population, was listed at more than twenty at this period.

The town began to die in 1892 and became more feeble until 1929, when it lay down and quit breathing entirely.

LITTLE SCHOOLHOUSE is lovingly rebuilt with original design in mind. Hill behind shows all the colors of calico cloth.

SKILLFUL BLENDING OF OLD with pseudo-old is evident here. Original signs seldom survive, but if these are re-creations they have authentic flavor.

California

THE RIVER WAS FULL OF GOLD

Camp Seco, Calif.

Oregon City, California? No mistake. It was rough and tumble mining camp during early years of the great gold rush to the Mother Lode. Among the first outsiders reaching the strip coursing 150 miles along the lap of the High Sierra were Oregonians barely settled after crossing the plains to the Willamette Valley. Oregon so stimulated them they carried to many gold camps names like Oregon City, Oregon Creek, Oregon Hill and there were several Oregon Gulches, one bisecting a shallow valley not far from the Mokelumne River which was "full of gold."

The population of Oregon City quickly grew

VIEW, looks directly through ruins of store buildings adjoining Adams Express Co. Stones used in construction were undressed but some care was used in selecting flat surface for facing out. Roofs have long ago disappeared. Walls get wet in winter to permit growth of grasses on top edges and long, hot summers dry them to sere, yellow state.

more cosmopolitan, news of riches there attracting men from other areas. Mexicans from Sonora were very numerous along the gold-flecked trail they called Veta Madre. Sonorans soon outnumbered Oregonians and deploring a lack of water, they gave the place a new name, Campo Seco or dry camp.

By 1854 the town had three hotels, many saloons, a brewery and that year a disastrous fire which razed all wooden buildings. With placer gold still flowing and a shallow hard rock mine nearby, inhabitants felt justified in building new hotels, rebuilding saloons and refurbishing stone structures, one the office of the Adams Express Co.

But prosperity had only a year or so to go before it sagged. Placer gold was then exhausted and the quartz veins were pinching out. A few people

moved away, a store closed and almost unnoticeably Campo Seco headed for ghostdom. Then somebody uncovered a deposit of copper nearby, a protruding piece of native, almost pure, copper.

The value of copper, always fluctuating, reached a high point in 1860. A newly organized group of financiers called Penn Copper Co. bought options on the property and soon had a big operation in full swing, gold almost forgotten. From then until about 1924 the fortunes of the dry diggings went up and down according to the price of copper.

In the early 1920s a group of eleven San Francisco Bay communities in need of water united to form the East Bay Utility Co., with the objective of placing a dam across the Mokelumne River to form a long reservoir above. Flood waters would cover many river bars that had yielded millions in

FRAME BUILDING, one of few in Campo Seco. Originally a saloon, some signs of old bar still evident inside, later a meat market, one old picture showing dim outline of steer's head on false front. Still later, contemporary with building of nearby Pardee Dam, enterprising merchant made oblong opening at near end, served drinks to construction workers, some soft by law, most spiked or neat "white mule" by demand.

BELOW BUTTE PEAK, high, conical mountains visible for miles around, is site of Butte City now represented by only solid structure built there. Basin, 1½ miles south of Jackson, was early discovered to be rich in gold, causing immediate growth of town built almost entirely of adobe and wood. One exception is this structure of Calaveras schist fieldstone with doors and windows of fired brick built by Xavier Benoist in 1854. Upper window spaces and ground level doors were fitted with iron shutters, familiar to Mother Lode visitors. After some years Benoist sold out to one Ginnochio whose name relic bears today. Store was built near old trail and when State 49 was put through it stood so close to edge passing cars almost brushed fenders. Then thieves stole heavy iron doors so conveniently close. State erected sturdy cyclone fence with several strands of barbed wire at top to protect historic building against further vandalism, an unsightly but effective barrier. Only other evidence of one time teeming town is cemetery above where bodies of many nameless miners lie.

gold and the corporation was forced to buy many dead claims at inflated prices set when rumors of the project reached the owners.

As work began hundreds of workmen poured into construction camps near old Campo Seco and suddenly a new enterprise sprang up—moonshining. After work laborers came in droves clamoring for something to drink with more authority than near beer. All right, said some Campo Secoans, we'll give it to 'em. They set up a still and shop in one of the old stone buildings, the illicit drink emporium never raided by prohibition agents and flourishing until the Pardee Dam was completed in 1930. Then, according to local legend, the operators of the traffic who had prudently continued to pay insurance premiums, set fire to the wooden interior of the stone building and faded out of history.

$40,000 NUGGET

Carson Hill, Calif.

They were fifteen feet down, four Americans and a Swiss, working their claim at Carson Hill in the Mother Lode country of California. Darkness was falling but the men kept on digging and shoveling and rubbing the dust out of their eyes. Suddenly one of them, generally thought to be Perkins, struck a rock. Failing in an attempt to heave it out of the hole he decided to look at it closer in better light. He could thank his lucky stars he did. It was a big gold nugget. Taken down to Stockton, weighed on the Adams Express Company scales, the chunk of gold made the newspapers all across the land, reports giving the weight as anywhere from 141 pounds to 214 pounds, 8 ounces, depending upon avoirdupois and troy weight plus enthusiasm. In time the true weight was established at 195 pounds.

Mr. Perkins came from Lexington, Kentucky, to the gold fields at the first word of discovery. After mining a few years he still had never owned more than $200 in gold dust at one time but he had joined with four others and still had hopes. The men panned all available gold from their creek at Carson Hill and were working up the lode from which the placer gold had apparently come. They were doing fairly well on that fateful November 29 day of 1854 and were reluctant to knock off but after finding the big rock it is to be assumed they did.

The record does not state how big an argument there was over ownership of the nugget but it was decided that since Perkins owned the biggest share of the claim he was the "principal owner." So he and a fellow miner started for New York with their prize. Neither got that far at that time. At some point along the journey a New Orleans man offered Perkins $40,000 for the nugget which he accepted and promptly dropped from history. The

DETAIL at entrance to wine cellar of James Romaggi house at Albany Flat, built 1852.

MONUMENT stands on bank of Stanislaus River at site of almost vanished Melones, first called Slumgullion, now camp ground operated by owners of nearby tavern. This operates in one of the few buildings remaining from days of ferry and gold camp. First miners, Mexicans from Sonora, claimed to have found nuggets like the seeds of "Melones."

173

THIS BUILDING is one of best preserved and most elaborate in Mother Lode. Pictured in several early publications it is variously termed "Romaggi Fandango Hall" and "Romaggi Adobe." Originally, at least, it was erected as home for James Romaggi, an Italian preferring grapes to gold and setting out vines and fruit trees, nearly duplicating green slopes in homeland. Appellation "Romaggi Adobe" is baffling since walls are constructed of selected, coursed slabs of amphibolite schist. One old photo shows badly weathered roofs of boards, doubtless once covered with shakes or shingles. Nearby road led to Los Muertos, scene of several battles between Mexicans and Americans in fall of 1852.

record follows the mass of gold to New Orleans where it was deposited in the Bank of Louisiana. It was later sold, the new owner taking it to Paris and exhibiting it as the largest nugget ever taken out of California or the United States. Which perhaps it was.

There have been no huge nuggets of gold reported for a long time but during the last half of the 19th century big chunks were being found all over the world, hysterically announced in the press as being the largest wherever found, either by weight or value. The word "nugget" is thought to be derived from "ingot," defined as any lump of

pure metal cast into a particular shape. While a natural chunk of metal, specifically gold, is termed a nugget, it need not be pure metal but could include any amount of the matrix from which it came. Those found in California usually included some quartz as in the case of the Carson Hill find. The famous Welcome nugget found some years later in Australia and roughly the same bulk as the California one, was all gold and therefore holds first place.

There were many other lucky finds on Carson Hill, a man named Hance taking out a 14 pound lump of gold lying at the top of the hill. Scattered around and on Carson Hill were the rich Morgan mine, the Reserve, South Carolina, Stanislaus and others totaling a fantastic yield of $2,800,000 in gold during the most productive year, 1850. Little wonder mining authorities term Carson Hill the "classic mining ground of California." Ironically the man who made the original find and for whom the hill was named shared in little of the wealth produced there.

James S. Carson was a sergeant in Col. Stevenson's New York Volunteers and when the regiment was disbanded at the end of the Mexican War he was stranded in Monterey, California, with many other soldiers. With the news of James Marshall's discovery of gold in the race of Sutter's Mill, Carson joined a company of ninety-two men, mostly ex-soldiers, going to the gold fields. In the party were some who would leave their names for posterity in the Sierra foothills. The Murphy brothers

headed northeast to found Murphy's Camp. George Angel left his mark on a camp later celebrated as the home of Mark Twain's Jumping Frog and Carson, called "Captain," staked his claim and settled down to panning the creek sands, in ten days recovering 180 ounces of gold to excite all members of the party.

They scattered to locate claims but Carson became ill with "rheumatism" or some affliction which incapacitated him. After many months in bed he went back to the creek but again was taken sick, this time even more seriously, and was removed to Stockton. Recovering long enough to be elected to the state legislature from Calaveras County, he was making plans to return to his claim when he was stricken with his final illness. While he lay in his bed millions of dollars' worth of gold were taken from his hill. He died at Stockton in near poverty in 1853.

ACTUAL TRACES of original buildings of Melones are hard to find. These disappearing stone ruins are secluded in grass, brush, few hundred feet from road. Photographed in very early morning light remains seem properly spectral.

CERRO GORDO, CALIFORNIA

The town's mineral wealth was first discovered in 1865 by Mexican prospectors, who applied the name, "Cerro Gordo." Literally translated, this means "Fat Hill."

For two years not much happened, then one of its discoverers showed a few chunks of silver ore to some mining men in Virginia City. That did it. Los Angeles, a small dying cattle town, received one of the first loads of bullion and revived suddenly.

The moving force to get things going at Cerro Gordo needed something more dynamic than the siesta-taking Mexican pioneers. Mortimer W. Belshaw provided the required spark. He had studied engineering and knew just how to do it. He took over the Union Mine which was producing the lead he needed for smelting. Machinery for smelters was hauled in and lifted over cliffs with an ingenious block and tackle system. A road was built and water piped in.

Ore was hauled to the bottom of the grade where a town named Keeler sprang up as a terminus. This was located on the shore of a large lake reflecting the highest part of the Sierra. Owens Lake is gone now, but the steamboats, *Bessie Brady* and *Molly Stevens*, made regular trips across it in those days. The terminal on the far shore, at the very foot of the Sierra, was Cartago. Next the precious stuff went to San Pedro. All this cost more than $50.00 a ton, so development of smelters on the spot was well worth while.

Cerro Gordo had more than its share of violence. For a time there were almost weekly shootings. The daily six-horse stage was frequently held up. So were the wagons hauling Belshaw's "Long Loaves," 85-pound slabs of precious metal from the local smelters intended for the U.S. Mint.

ALMOST ALL THAT IS left of Cerro Gordo is shown here. At extreme left, ruins of upper terminus of tram house, next (in back) is "Waterfall, Gilded House of Pleasure," at right of road (in repair) was residence of big wheel, M. W. Belshaw. Right, in front, is American House Hotel, lower center is livery stable. Above all tower tailings dumps of main shaft, mine head buildings are concealed behind them.

In later years a tram was built from a huge terminal close to the mine down the precipitous mountainside, leaping from crag to crag and alighting at Keeler. On this web of steel rolled the ore buckets, eliminating the mule teams, since supplies came up easily in the emptied buckets, powered by the down-going ones. Machinery was needed, though not for power but to hold back and control the flow down the cliffs.

In 1959 the tram house and machinery were taken down, to be used in new mining operations near Candelaria, Nevada. Some towers and cables, complete with a bucket or two, have been left.

ANCIENT MULE COLLARS hang in groups on pegs in livery stable, now partly open to the sky.

"AMERICAN HOUSE" STANDS nearly 5,000 feet above now-dry Owens Lake. Sierra rises on other side. Hotel did not have private bath in every room, but even so, ran up monthly water bill of $300. Commodity had to be hauled up by mule teams from artesian well near Owens Lake. Guests were admonished to be "sparing with the water."

CHINESE CAMP, CALIFORNIA

It was a fantastic battle—a Pigtail Waterloo. Nine hundred members of the Yan-Wo Tong were pitted against twelve hundred of the Sam Yaps and it was fought with farm tools and venom. And when the air was cleared of yells, the sounds of cymbals and firecracker smoke, the marshals hauled four men to the morgue, two hundred and fifty to the little adobe jails.

The big Tong melee took place in the Mother Lode country before the Civil War. In the preponderantly Chinese population of the camp were several Tong factions, always ready to quarrel with each other. Two of the groups were composed of miners working claims along the Stanislaus River at Two Mile Bar. One claim was held by Celestials belonging to twelve members of the Sam Yap, be-low it another operated by six brothers of Yan Wo.

A large boulder was dislodged on the upper level and rolled down into the camp below, hurting no one but sparking an argument. The only way to settle it, the powers decided, was by formal battle. And this was not a thing to be undertaken lightly. It required thought and judgment, however miscast. Several American blacksmiths of the town were called upon to make the proper weapons for opposing factions to use with dignity and honor, and into the forges went hundreds of hoes, rakes and whatever could be snatched up from the creek bed and farms.

On Sept. 26, 1856 the Yan Wo horde, mostly from Chinese Camp, clashed on the rocky flat with the defending host of Sam Yaps, hailing generally from

ST. FRANCIS XAVIER CATHOLIC CHURCH built in 1855 by popular subscription of funds and labor, was first regular house of worship in Chinese Camp. Even after church was established with Henry Aleric as first Pastor, miners worked at claims as usual on Sundays and the faithful attended service, piling shovels, pans and outer clothing outside door. Structure originally had shingled roof with belfry and small steeple surmounted by cross. By 1949 it had deteriorated badly and steeple was removed, leaking roof covered with sheet iron and several coats of paint. Cross was then replaced at apex of roof.

Pine in background is of comparatively rare species — *Pinus Sabiniana*. Digger Pine is fairly common on lower slopes of California foothills, has dropping grayish needles, uniquely branched trunk, is somewhat tender.

the nearby camp of Crimea House. As the lines drew close, several contraband firearms were found in both groups. No Chinese were supposed to have them, the law said, but in this case the firing was only spasmodic and did little harm. The fighting consisted mainly of noisy clatter, high-pitched yelling and beating of gongs. Since no important event could take place among Chinese without firecrackers, the smoke and popping of these was added to the general confusion.

Just about the time the going was hot and heavy, four American law officers rode in and stopped the proceedings, arresting a small mob of sweating contestants. Four Tong men lay on the ground and did not move, dead of stab wounds, and four others more or less seriously slashed. The Tong War of Chinese Camp had passed into history.

How so many Chinese came to be together at these diggings is not entirely clear. The several versions are no doubt partly true and each episode contributed to the total of some five thousand. One legend has a group of Englishmen arriving in 1849 to make their fortunes in the undeniably rich placer gravels along the Stanislaus. They discovered however that this would take considerable physical labor and to avoid this they made "raids" on several

OLD STORE has been converted to post office with gabbro cobblestones set in mortar and faced with brick. Outside lock boxes are for convenience of few remaining residents but most patrons go inside to pass time of day with postmaster. Plaque on corner of building honors Eddie Webb, born 1880 in Snelling, California, who was "last of the old-time stage drivers." He hauled freight, passengers and mail from Chinese Camp to Coulterville and Groveland. From 1898 to 1902 he drove the first stage over the new Shawmutt Road.

WHEREVER CHINESE MIN-
ERS LIVED they planted *ailanthus* — "Tree of Heaven."
Trees are very self-sufficient,
have persisted and multiplied until they appear native. Photographer made record of Mother
Lode buildings in early spring
before appearance of foliage
which obscures everything behind it.

neighboring mining camps, offering the Chinese workers more money than they had been getting. Altogether they lured away several hundred workers to operate the long toms—enlarged and more elaborate than the rockers in general use after the first simple pan workings.

Then it was said there was the ship's captain who deserted his vessel in San Francisco and headed for the diggings, bringing the entire Chinese crew with him to do the pick and shovel work. Some say the two gangs worked toward each other and when they met, formed and named the town. If this is to be believed, the yellow men must have been members of the same Tong.

In any event the usual evidences of the early day gold camp sprang up—stores, banks, livery stables, honky tonks and brothels. There were enough whites and Mexicans intermixed with the Orientals to erect a fine Catholic church, as well as hotel, Masonic and Sons of Temperance lodges and Wells Fargo Express office. An organization was formed to bring water to the mines, solving the problem by building an elaborate flume from Wood's Creek.

Today most of the buildings and all the Chinese are gone but plenty of relics remain to give the visitor a picture of what life was like in those hectic days of the gold rush.

COLOMA, CALIFORNIA

In any tale of the California gold rush and particularly of Coloma where it all began, Johan Sutter's name looms large even though his part in the discovery was inadvertent and his actions antagonistic. He must have known his troubles were back to dog him when his foreman James Marshall found those fateful flakes of gold in the mill race.

Sutter had trouble in his native Burgdorf, Switzerland, where he was a merchant. Debts and women disrupted his life and he deserted his family, heading for America and landing in Santa Fe, New Mexico. In 1834 he heard glowing reports of wealth to be made in the fertile acres of the pastoral Sacramento Valley.

His course there was roundabout, by way of Fort Vancouver, thence by sailing vessel to the Hawaiian Islands and from there to San Francisco. His record stalled him in that booming city but Monterey gave him a better welcome.

By exercising some imagination he became "Captain Sutter" and was granted a tract of land on the Sacramento River for colonization purposes. An entry in his diary of August 13, 1839 reads: "Today with the help of my ten Kanakas and three white men I founded a colony called New Helvetia." As soon as an adobe fort was built the colony developed rapidly, soon having a bakery, blanket factory, kitchen and dining room for the help and luxurious quarters for the master.

During the war with Mexico Sutter managed to be a friend to each side and when it ended in 1847 and formal transfer of the territory to the United States was consummated by the signing of the Treaty Guadalupe Hidalgo in February, 1848, Sutter's land was left unaffected. He could concentrate on the affairs of his colony which gave the farm the most productive period in its existence.

Six years before, in 1842, Mexicans had found gold in the sands of dry Placerita Canyon near Los Angeles, the first known discovery in California. They "dry panned" the gold-bearing dirt by filling tightly woven baskets and tossing the heavy contents upward in the breezes, deftly catching gold and gravel which were then separated by hand. All this human labor made little impression on history and started no major rush.

Neither did an incident at the mouth of a small stream emptying into the South Fork of the Yuba River. Joseph Aram and wife were members of a party of immigrants who had left New York for San Francisco. Now nearly at their goal, Mrs. Aram went to the creek to do her laundry. The water was too shallow so she scooped out a hole in the bottom and uncovered a small nugget. No one was greatly excited although after the Coloma news, a few staked out claims.

Toward the end of August, 1847, Sutter and James Marshall formed a partnership to build a sawmill at a place called Cullooma by the Indians. It was to supply lumber for Sutter's Fort started about Christmas, 1847, and after seeing it underway, Marshall went to the Fort to oversee the fabrication of mill

EARLY APRIL OF 1851 SAW hotly contested race for honor of El Dorado County Seat between Coloma and Placerville, Coloma winning by act of Legislature April 25th. Until this time Coloma had struggled along with log jail from which prisoners made easy escape. New status demanded more secure hoosegow; $16,000 was set aside for construction, stone jail was built within year. In '57 Coloma was forced to relinquish position of County Seat to more flourishing Placerville, expensive and "escape proof" Coloma jail continued to serve El Dorado County until '62. It was then sold to its former jailer, John Tensher, for building material. Partially wrecked structure still offers imposing and picturesque ruin.

irons, leaving instructions for a ditch to be dug to carry water for the race. On his return he found the job being bungled by inept workers trying to dig the waterway from the upper end instead of the lower, the ditch filling with water as they progressed.

Marshall employed a handyman named Wimmer whose wife was an energetic woman doing much work around the property as well as her household chores. She was later to write: "They had been working on the mill race, dam and mill about six months when one morning about the last days of December, or about the first week of January, 1848, after an absence of several days at the Fort, Marshall took Wimmer down to see what had been done while he was away. The water was entirely shut off and as they walked along talking about the work, just ahead of them on a rough, muddy little rock, lay something bright like

gold. They both saw it but Marshall was first to stoop and pick it up." Doubtful that it was gold, he gave it to the Wimmers' little boy and told him to have his mother throw it in her soap kettle. Later the nugget was retrieved from the kettle untarnished by the "saleratus water" and all had to admit it was really gold.

The fat was now in the fire and Sutter was well aware the event would mean the ruin of his dream of empire. Without much hope his words would have any weight, he asked Marshall to keep the business quiet. Instead, his partner went to Sacramento to display the nugget and was laughed at as a crackpot trying to pass off a chunk of pyrites as gold. Had everyone laughed, the rush might have been delayed, although it was not likely all the gold later found could lie undetected forever. The believing one was

ALEXANDER BAYLEY TOOK UP CLAIM at a site near Coloma, erected two-story homestead with attic and large fireplace at end. Soon rumors were flying railroad would build through then booming Coloma and would establish station near Bayley home. Acting on this hot tip, Bayley spent $20,000 on elaborate hotel, shown here. Railroad was never built, hotel called "Bayley House" and now privately occupied by owners of ranch on which it stands, is only large structure for miles around.

Sam Brannan, a San Francisco publisher on a business trip to Sacramento. Brannan looked at the nugget through eyes trained to minerals and publicity values. He went home, spread the news to the world, and in a year or two the world came to the Sierra and reaped its harvest of wealth with neither Brannan or Marshall getting any of it.

Thousands of wildly shoving men flocked to Coloma and soon were spreading up and down the length of the Sierra Piedmont. On their ruthless way the goldseekers overran the Sutter domain, trampling underfoot all the man's vision of grandeur. Even his Kanakas and Indian help rushed to the hills, leaving New Helvetia to decay.

Forced to join the rabble, Sutter gathered up his pitiful remnant of supporters and moved to a stream in the area in an effort to share in the new wealth. Establishing a settlement called Sutter's Creek, he encountered trouble with the American way of life,

was run out of the diggings for what the Yankees called his system of "slavery."

Back in Coloma, Marshall was also having a bad time. The fact that he was not an employee but a partner of Sutter's gave him the right to claim the ground as his by mineral discovery. It also explained why Sutter went to diggings other than Coloma. The man who should have been revered as the discoverer of wealth that would change the course of history was instead hated and despised because he was forced to post armed guards to keep away swarms of prospectors who disregarded his claims. When he appealed to the courts, friends of the trespassers filled the jury box and even his attorneys turned against him in the hope of getting shares of his claims if he lost the suits.

During the next ten years Marshall was an outcast, spied upon, cheated, abused to the point he gave up mining his own property. He tried to make a

THIS WAS HOME OF JAMES MARSHALL at time of his discovery. It stands on rise directly above Coloma, across road from old Catholic Church. Latter is long abandoned, given over entirely to swarm of bees which is established in walls directly over entrance. Photographer was anxious to obtain record of church interior, nearly intact, was unwilling to climb in through window, even more reluctant to penetrate angrily buzzing bees.

living lecturing throughout the west but this effort to justify his position failed too. Twenty years after the discovery, he returned to the site to find things completely changed. Huge combines of moneyed interests had squeezed most small claims from the original settlers, the law courts upholding the consolidation in many cases. Marshall was left out entirely together with many others who had done the spade work.

In 1872 a sympathetic reporter for a San Francisco newspaper took up the cudgel for James Marshall and wrote a series of articles which so changed the mind of the fickle public the legislature was forced to appropriate for Marshall a sum of $200 a month for two years. By the next session public sentiment had cooled and relief funds were cut in half. On August 10, 1885 James Marshall died a broken pauper, was buried on a hill above and within sight of his discovery location.

DELIVERY WAGON OF "People's Store" is well preserved from early days of Coloma.

184

OLD PHOTO FROM California State Library shows Sutter's mill. Figure in foreground is thought to be that of James Marshall.

BITTER DISCOVERER OF GOLD in Coloma, James Marshall, pushed out of rights to mine own claims and tiring of doing odd jobs for living, went to nearby Kelsey, established new mine, the Gray Eagle. In order to provide funds for pushing tunnel, he started blacksmith shop, doing good work but made little profit. Here he died in abject poverty on August 10, 1885. Body was taken to site on hill above old home at Coloma. In 1890 this monument was erected over his grave by Native Sons of the Golden West. Marshall's figure points finger to spot of discovery so momentous to his state and world, but bitterly disappointing to finder.

ACTUAL SAWMILL BUILT by partners Johan August Sutter and James W. Marshall had long disappeared when period of exceptionally low water in American River revealed bits of timbers sticking out of gravel. Investigation showed enough remains to exactly pinpoint location and even give some idea of ground plan and construction. Other artifacts included axes, bolts and implements, now all carefully sheltered and displayed in museum in State Park at Coloma. Site of mill was permanently marked with monument.

COLUMBIA, CALIFORNIA

John Huron Smith decided he needed one more drink to top off his monumental glow. With bad luck he picked a bar owned by the John Barclays of unsavory reputation. Martha Barclay was alone at the bar and refused Smith his drink. In a violent argument Smith gave Martha a hard shove just as Barclay entered. Drawing his pistol, he killed the belligerent Smith.

The whole matter might have ended there as justifiable had the Barclays not been in constant trouble with the authorities. A friend of Smith's, State Senator J. W. Coffroth, took up the affair and incited the people of Columbia to form a mob and take matters into their own hands. They broke into the jail where Barclay was being held and in the dead of night rushed him to the high flume that carried water to the town. A rope was thrown over the timbers, one end knotted around the prisoner's neck. He was jerked off the ground and one man held up a flaming pine torch to see how the victim was making out. Barclay was holding the rope above his head in a desperate grip, his executioners having neglected to tie his hands. It didn't take long for one of the lynchers to beat the hands loose with the butt of a pistol—and Martha was a widow. The early days of Columbia in the Mother Lode were highlighted with stirring episodes like this.

The glitter of rich gold in the gulch at the foot of Columbia's Main Street was exposed by accident. On March 27, 1850, Dr. Thaddeus Hildreath,

his brother George and several other prospectors, reached this point at nightfall and camped under a large tree, with every intention of moving on in the morning. During the night there was a torrential rainstorm which soaked every blanket. The morning was warm and sunny, the blankets spread out to dry and to pass the time the men took their prospecting tools to the gulch to the foot of what was later called Kennebec Hill. Color of such brilliance showed up in the gravels every man in addition to John Walker, who had made the first find, stayed on. In the next two days the men took out thirty pounds of gold worth $4,680.

The resultant rush to "Hildreth's Diggings," later named Columbia, surpassed almost all others in history. Bursting from a population of nothing to a roaring camp of 5,000 gold-starved souls took

OLD WELLS FARGO EXPRESS COMPANY building, best known of remaining structures in Columbia, architectural showpiece of the Southern Mines. Original office was established in American Hotel lobby. When hotel burned it was moved to Fallon House with William Daeger as express agent. Present structure was erected by Daeger in 1857, with grand opening early in '58, builder continuing as agent until '72.

Brick sidewalks laid diamond-fashion was characteristic of times, have escaped fate of similar ones later covered with cement. Lavish use of bricks in Columbia indicates excellent quality of lateriric clays in locality. Two brickyards operated during boom, were situated on old Dambach Ranch in Matelot Gulch, two miles north of Columbia. Marble-like limestone formations laid bare by sluicing were not utilized as building material although marble quarry here shipped cut stones to San Francisco as early as '54. Delicate, lacy wrought iron balcony grilles were shipped around Horn to San Francisco, hauled to Columbia by mule freight.

only a month. Obviously enough permanent buildings to house this host could not be built so quickly and miners slept under every conceivable kind of shelter—or none at all. April is a mild month in the Mother Lode country and many a miner threw a blanket on the ground when the day's digging was done and collapsed in weariness. He slept in his sweat-soaked clothes and worked in them the next day. When even he could no longer stand the aroma of "ripeness", he would put on his other shirt and hang the first one on a branch to freshen. If it was perchance sprinkled with rain, so much the better. If not, he wore it again when the relief shirt became unbearable.

A lady reporter from San Francisco was said to be interviewing the miners about their lives and habits, asking one bearded man digging in the gravel how he did his laundry. Wiping his brow with his sleeve, he told her: "Lady—we don't use much starch."

The hundreds of flimsy frame structures erected were soon destroyed by fire. Brick buildings replaced them but in the next decade many of these were doomed by the discovery that the ground beneath them held a wealth of gold and the metal could be sluiced out. The first building to go was the first put up and the bricks were sold in other camps. By the time the '60s were over half the buildings in town had been demolished and the materials sold in Sonora and Copperopolis. One stately structure was spared, digging ending at the yard of St. Anne's Church.

Sluicing became such a mania owing to the immense pay-off the entire area around the town was soon a boneyard of bare limestone rocks which stand today as mute reminders of the period. Other towns were also washing soil down the creeks until the valleys were choked with silt and farms covered by mud when the water was high. The mass of soil and debris descending from the mountain camps became such a problem that the State Legislature passed laws banning all such sluicing.

During the boom days prices of commodities reached heights undreamed of in California. Sugar brought $3 a pound, molasses $50 a barrel, flour $1.50 a pound and onions $1, sardines and lobsters $4 a can, candles 50c each and the essential miners' knives $30.

TUOLUMNE ENGINE HOUSE. Columbia h a d history of bad fires, worst on July 10, 1854 and in August '57. After latter committee was authorized to purchase fire engine. Arriving in San Francisco, delegation looked at "sample"—hand pumper made for King of Sandwich Islands (now Hawaii). Rig was named Papeete, gaily decorated with paintings of back-bar type damsels and ready to ship. Enamored citizens of Columbia made successful dicker and rig still stands in Columbia fire house with its hoses of cowhide sections riveted together.
Printing office upstairs published two newspapers, *Columbia Gazette* and *Miner's Advertiser.* Bill Steinfeller's Saloon did business on ground floor. At extreme right was "Doc Parson's" drug store, later notorious Pay Ore Saloon.

187

About 1858 a novel system of furnishing illuminating gas to the town was completed. Large kilns were constructed to roast pitchy pine from the high mountains, the gas carried to houses through wooden pipes. One difficulty after another beset the new company, pipes leaking, the cutting of wood for burning becoming prohibitive in cost. The gas system lasted only a few months and Columbia was back to kerosene lamps, these serving until the advent of electricity at the turn of the century.

The first public high school system began in rented quarters in '54 and six years later moved into its own two-story brick school house. Still standing, the building is one of the oldest schoolhouses in California, classes being held there until 1937.

During Columbia's big, booming years the streets were jammed with traffic. Stage coaches ran on daily schedules. Freight lines operated from Stockton, bringing all sorts of provisions and supplies. The usual gambling rooms, saloons and dance halls were plentiful and houses on the back streets offered their fancy women. An arena was built for a special type of exhibition, fights between bears and bulls.

The contests were advertised as battles between "Wild Bulls from Spain and Savage Grizzlies from the Remote Mountains of California." Often as not the bull was a doltish reject from the Sacramento slaughterhouse and the bear some mangy specimen cornered in the foothills. Usually both animals were interested only in escaping to the free hills and the miners would demand their money back. And even when the bear was gored into a shapeless mass, the miners would still insist on a refund. Horace Greeley, writing about these battles in the New York Tribune is said to have started the use of the terms "bull" and "bear" in relation to the fluctuations of the stock market.

Columbia was needing more and more water for mining as well as domestic use and to meet the demand the Tuolumne Water Company was organized in 1851. It constructed a vast network of reservoirs, ditches and flumes many miles in length. The miners complained the Company was charging excessive rates and needed some competition, and so organized the Stanislaus River Water Company in '54. It's completed aqueduct wound 60 miles through the mountains to Columbia. The project cost over a million dollars and by the time it was finished so were the lush days of Columbia. Surface gold had been virtually exhausted and expensive hardrock mining was under-

COLUMBIA'S LITTLE JAIL was stoutly constructed, had two cells each with opening through which meals were passed to prisoners.

taken reluctantly. The population declined and by 1860 the Tuolumne Company bought out the miners' water works for $125,000.

During its heyday, Columbia had a large Chinatown. This was natural in any West Coast mining town but surprising enough, this one had Italians, French and Irish sections as well as ones called Negro Hill, French Flat, Texas Flat and a neighborhood of Chileans. Most of these sectors were filled with flimsy wooden shacks and as the town began to fade, so did the foreign "ghettos." The same fate befell a double line of cabins extending the whole distance, four miles, to the slightly older town of Sonora. Hardly a sign is left of these shelters. The once sprawling metropolis gradually shrank to its solid nucleus of brick.

But it did not die completely. After the gold rush was over the more substantial buildings did not fall into complete decay nor were they "prettied up" or covered with garish new fronts, as in the case of many of the better preserved towns founded by the Argonauts.

"Recognizing the opportunity to preserve and interpret for future generations a typical Gold Rush town, the state legislature enacted legislation creating Columbia Historic State Park," says a brochure on this Park, "In addition to preserving the remaining historical structures in the main business section of the town, lands are in the process of being acquired in the surrounding blocks in conformity with a master plan approved by the State Park Commission on Sept. 17, 1948, thus assuring the preservation of outstanding historic sites and providing for an adequate setting for this ' Gem of the Southern Mines.' " Due to this studied program there are no modern signs or neon lights and the buildings, while preserved, do not have a stark, "rehabilitated" look, showing instead the effect of a mellowing with age.

EARLY MORNING LIGHT reaches under ornate balcony of hostelry once known affectionately as "What Cheer House," more formally as Morgan's Hotel and later City Hotel. First building on site was frame structure, bought by George Morgan early in July, '54 and remodeled for saloon and was burned to ground ten days later. In '56 he built the first unit of two-story Ale House and Billiard Saloon. this entirely destroyed by fire in '57. Present brick building contained lodgings, theater, bar and Music Hall upstairs, was still operating as City Hotel until 1930s.

MORE BULLETS FOR THE NORTH

Copperopolis, Calif.

The ledge of rock had a greenish-rust color but it sure didn't look to Hiram Hughes like there was metal in it. They said gold was where you found it and gold or silver was what he was looking for and, well, was there any left around here? It didn't seem so after all the digging around he'd done. Now that rusty looking rock—he sure would look like a danged fool taking some of that into an assay office. But what if he did? Only a gimlet-eyed metallurgist and a few Mexican loafers would know. Where's that chipping hammer.., ?

Hiram Hughes was a Johnny-come-lately to the gold country, this Calaveras area on the Sierra's western slope, and he came here believing he just might find some of the yellow stuff overlooked by the others ahead of him. By 1858 most good or promising gold deposits had been located but Hughes while tardy was also persistent. After combing the Calaveras hills he worked north along the Mother Lode and into the Northern Mines. The next year found him in the Washoe silver region but he could find no trace of that white metal either.

So when he returned to Quail Hill where he spotted the greenish-rust colored rock, Hughes was about ready to quit looking for anything but a bottle of whiskey to help him forget all the hard work. But before he stopped in a saloon he took the chunk of rock to the nearest assay office. The report made him want to holler clear back to Kansas. The sample was nearly a third copper and worth $120 to the ton.

Just about this time another prospector, Thomas McCarty, made a similar discovery in the same area. He took as partners W. K. Reed, Dr. Blatchy and Thomas Hardy. The year was 1860, the country full of rumors that a civil war was about to explode and McCarty's discovery was named the Union Mine. In a few months the Keystone, Empire and Napoleon were added to the complex and a town called Copperopolis was growing up around it.

In 1863 W. K. Reed built a toll road, usually referred to as Reed's Pike, a rough trail over which ox teams hauled $1,600,000 in copper ore the first year. Although it had to go all the way to Wales to be smelted, the finished metal provided most of the copper needs of the Union Army during the war. And this gave Copperopolis, with a population of 10,000 a boom bigger than that in any of the gold camps nearby. When Reed sold out his interest in the Union, now the largest producing copper mine in the country, he got $650,000 for it. Shares in the mine, if sold by the foot, brought $200 for that much ground. During this period copper was worth an all time high of 55c a pound. Six mines were going full tilt and a railroad was being brought in from Stockton.

At the end of the war copper dropped to 19c and mines closed or curtailed operation. The Stockton-Copperopolis Railroad came to an ignominious end at Milton, about two-thirds of the way in and the place familiarly termed "Copper" was on the way out. In 1902 the Union reopened with a new smelter and 500-ton flotation mill. It produced varying quantities of copper with surges through the two world wars, then again closed. Since 1861 the mines produced 72 million pounds worth something over $12 million.

One hundred years after the big copper discoveries another product, asbestos, was located not far away. In 1960 Jefferson-Lake Sulphur Co. of Houston, Texas, paid $4,652,000 for a 500-acre tract on which to build a huge asbestos operation. This tremendous enterprise is not close enough to Copperopolis to mar the beauty and charm of the old copper camp.

LARGE STONE CORRAL near Copperopolis is one of several in area, this one of best preserved. Most were built by Chinese laborers during mining heyday.

MARBLE STONE suggests question instead of identifying long-forgotten miner who rests here. Likely it is simply-marked foot-stone, strayed from more completely identifying head-stone.

SOLID BRICK BUILDING served as Union Mine warehouse in Civil War days. Small, frame, sheet-metal-covered structure was successively store, saloon, laundry, etc.

·5 Mo. and 24 days.

Stop traveler and cast an eye
As you are now, so once was I.
As I am now so you must be
Therefore prepare to follow me!
Prepare for death make no delay
I in my bloom was snatched away
When death did call me to depart
I left my friends with acheing heart…

CLASSIC EXAMPLE of "tombstone poetry" carved on marker in Copperopolis cemetery. Burial here was distinctly segregated into four sections—Masonic, I.O.O.F., Catholic and Protestant—separated by 4-foot stone walls.

BUSIEST SECTION of old Copperopolis during Civil War. Left was company warehouse, center building under old oak tree Copper Consolidated Mining Co. offices, right, one of most historic structures in California. Copper produced here was important to Union cause, regiment established to protect mines from possible Confederate sabotage. Soldiers used building as armory for entire period. When news of Pres. Lincoln's assassination reached town "Union Blues" assembled here and formed column on street in foreground, marching north several blocks to Congregational Church for services in honor of martyred war leader. In earlier gold camp of Columbia several brick buildings were torn down to expose rich ground for sluicing. Some salvaged bricks were used to construct this armory. Huge iron doors are considered largest in Mother Lode country.

COULTERVILLE, CALIFORNIA

In spite of the hordes of Chinese and Mexicans in the town, the name Coulterville prevailed. It was originally called Banderita and there are two differing versions explaining the use of the name which signifies "little flag" or "bandana" in Spanish.

When the first whites, who of necessity spoke practical Spanish, arrived in the area they found a goodly number of Mexicans already hard at work. Most of the laborers were wearing small bandanas. In another story when George Coulter left his trading post on the Merced River in 1850 and set up shop on Maxwell Creek, site of the fabulous new "diggin's," he hoisted the only available American flag—a small one—over his tent. The Mexicans took it for the familiar square of colored neck cloth and named the camp Banderita.

The name was of short duration. Coulter's activities were so numerous and varied that his name seemed logical for the town and Coulterville it became. The original Mexican-style plaza, surrounded by nondescript brush "ramadas" and adobes, was maintained but soon outlined with substantial stone and permanent adobes. The influx of more than a thousand Chinese was responsible for many of the latter, this frugal race choosing adobe and rammed earth as being the most economical.

SUBSTANTIAL BUILDING is one of those replacing brush *ramadas* of earlier Mexican occupation. Completed in 1851 it was the second stone and adobe building in Coulterville and among the first in Mother Lode. Built for the Gazolla Store, it was subsequently used as saloon, fandango hall, restaurant and hotel. Ancient umbrella trees, recently beheaded, shade sidewalk.

The first of the pigtails had appeared as early as 1850, establishing a little settlement at the north edge of town. There were the usual twisted streets and opium dives coupled with the inevitable joss house and public bake ovens. These last were built of brick and mortar or mud and were centers for gossip and scandalizing when housewives gathered to do their baking.

Along with the Chinese and half as many Mexicans, there were three thousand American miners and their hangers-on to swell the population of the wildly booming gold camp. The Americans left the placer operations to the foreigners and took to the immediate hillsides to establish the fabulously rich hard rock mines, notably the Mary Harrison. This mine was discovered around 1867 and operated more or less continuously until closed permanently in 1903, after being worked to a depth of 1200 feet by shaft and winch.

The whole area is rich in fine rock, mineral specimens and outcropping, and produces Mari-posite, named for the county. The technical name for the blue-green banded material is chrome mica and it is available everywhere locally. Collectors find white quartz and carbonate minerals such as dolomite, ankerite and calcite. The gold bearing ore consisted of iron pyrites, usually somewhat oxidized.

One completely unorthodox "gold rush" assumed a comic opera aspect, taking place in the middle of the town at the turn of the century. Fire in 1899 destroyed many of the structures. One of the gutted stone buildings was demolished and the rubble shoveled into holes and ruts of the muddy street. A substantial cache of gold, concealed in the wrecked building, was this way buried in the street undetected but the first heavy rain exposed a number of gold coins and nuggets. Almost the entire population turned out to flail the street with shovels and any tool available, leaving it a shambles.

TINY STEAM LOCOMOTIVE was used to haul ore from Mary Harrison mine. Stretch of track was four miles in length, famous as the "World's crookedest railroad." Branches at left are part of Coulterville's "Hang Tree." Dawn of March 16, 1856 saw body of Leon Ruiz dangling from limb. Ruiz was thus punished for slaying of two Chinese miners at Bear Valley and robbing their sluice of gold dust and nuggets worth six hundred dollars. Old oak saw long series of lynchings and "lawful executions."

GHOSTS CROWD AROUND DEATH VALLEY

DARWIN, CALIFORNIA

A group of emaciated, weary men had negotiated fearful stretches of desert and mountains and were camped in the Argus Range. They were hungry and nearly exhausted. The last straw was the discovery that the sight was missing from the only serviceable gun and the killing of any game seemed impossible. An Indian guide, a native to the region, said he could fix the gun, took the weapon and disappeared into the hills. Before long he returned with it. The gun had a new sight of pure silver!

At this point, the main object was to reach the haven of the San Joaquin valley, but the thought of the native silver from which that gun sight had been made stayed with some of the group.

Years later, one Darwin French headed an expedition into the Argus Mountains to search out the lost "Gun Sight Mine." It was never found, but the party did locate mineral deposits worth investigating, and a camp was set up to start mining operations. While Darwin French was the exploring type, not a miner, and soon departed, the embryo town took the name of Darwin and as such developed into a lusty young giant with all the trappings, the saloons, red light houses and roisterous goings-on characteristic of those days.

FIRST SCHOOL IN Darwin was built with funds raised by "passing the hat."

DOUGLAS CITY, CALIFORNIA

When Anderson's riderless mule returned, the settlers knew the Indians had taken him. Constantly harassed by them, the white men were surprised Andy had gone out to the range alone. A search party was formed and sure enough, there was the body, riddled with arrow wounds and no sign of the cattle. There was only one thing to do — find those murderous Indians and kill the lot of them.

The party split in half, the first group trailing the Indians to their camp, near where Douglas City was later settled. The second group rounded up more men, seventy strong and bent on revenge, and caught up with the first bunch of whites. Taken by surprise, almost the entire Indian village of over a hundred and fifty braves, squaws and children was wiped out, even to the few who escaped into Bridge Gulch.

There were three exceptions — two little girls and a boy. The girls were found by a man sickened by all the slaughter. He protected them and one, Ellen Clifford, lived at Weaverville for many years. The other was cared for by a woman whose ideas of charity were warped as she sold the girl to a teamster for $45. The boy lay hidden behind a log and waiting until it was safe, made his way to another Indian camp. Years later, as "Indian Bob", he turned up in Douglas City and told his story.

The history of Douglas City is closely related to that of Major Pierson Reading. He had a part in the Bear Flag Revolt at Sonoma in 1846, later joined Fremont's battalion and finally returned to his ranch four miles east of Cottonwood, between Red Bluff and Redding.

When the big news about the discovery of gold at Coloma broke, Major Reading hurried there to see what the truth was. He found a seething mass of humanity well on its way to start the biggest gold rush ever known, but he himself was too late to find a good claim there. He reasoned that if there was gold in the American River, there must also be gold in the Trinity. He was familiar with that stream through the Trinity Alps, the rugged range of snowy mountains northwest of his ranch. He knew it as Smith River and later renamed it Trinity under the misapprehension that it flowed into Trinidad Bay as noted on old Spanish charts.

In 1858 Major Reading related how very right he had been in deducing there must be gold nearer home, obtainable without the heavy competition in the Sierra. "In the month of July, 1848," he recalled, "I crossed the mountains of the coast range at the head of Middle Cottonwood Creek and struck the Trinity at what is now called Reading's Bar; prospected for two days and found the bars rich in gold; returned to my home in Cottonwood and fitted out an expedition for mining purposes; crossed the mountains where the travel passed about two years ago from Shasta to Weaver.

"My party consisted of three white men, one Delaware, one Chinook and sixty Indians from the Sacramento Valley. With this force I worked the bar bearing my name. I had with me a hundred head of cattle and an abundant supply of other provisions. After about six weeks of work, parties came in from Oregon who at once protested about my Indian labor. I then left the stream and returned to my home where I have since remained in the enjoyment of the tranquil life of the farmer." The major might have added the $80,000 in gold he had extracted from the bar helped him enjoy it.

Lost are the names of the Oregon men who interrupted the major's efforts but Reading's Bar is located on the Trinity River immediately below the Douglas City bridge. More and more Oregon men came to mine the area until it became necessary to build a crude, high-altitude road over the pass to Yreka. The road, nearly impassable at best, became completely so after every heavy snowstorm. The solution to this problem was to drive a herd of oxen to the summit, keep them handy there, and after each storm let them trample the loose snow to firm footing.

During 1850 an even greater number of gold seekers came into the country by way of San Francisco, where they boarded ships for the voyage north to make perilous landings in Trinidad Bay, thence by small boats part way up the Klamath to the point where the Trinity enters that river, then on foot to the diggings. By the end of the next year every stream and mountain pocket had been explored and prospected, and by the end of 1852 the Trinity River, wrapped in solitude only a short time before, was solidly lined with toiling miners, sluices and rockers from Salyer to Garville.

OLD WATER TOWER — only remains of Douglas City, just above site of Major Pierson Reading's epochal discovery of gold along Trinity River. Lower part of tower served as living quarters until recent years. Guardian tree is Ponderosa pine, often called "yellow pine". These timber trees, together with sugar pines — similar in appearance but with very long cones — and Douglas firs, constitute most of the forest cover in the Trinity Alps at this altitude, 1700 feet.

DOWNIEVILLE, CALIFORNIA

Juanita was a good-looking Mexican girl who entertained young miners in her little Downieville cabin . . . until one of her guests pleased her so much she invited him to move in. He jumped at the chance.

A young Australian, Jack Cannon, was not aware of these developments. Juanita had shown him hospitality on several occasions and one morning he was reeling down the street, partly supported by half-drunken companions and partly by thoughts of Juanita's charms. At the door of her cabin he told his friends to go on, that he was going to see a man about a kangaroo.

The others knew about the newly established love nest and tried to argue Jack out of his idea but he pushed open the door and went in. Instead of welcoming him with a loving embrace, Juanita slipped a knife between his ribs. Another version of the legend has Jack opening the door but heeding the advice of his comrades after seeing Juanita had a man, then returning at a later hour to apologize and then getting the knife.

In any event, the result was death for Jack Cannon and the calaboose for the beautious Juanita. The end of the story might have been the funeral but racial prejudice reared its ugly head. Mexicans in Downieville and all California mining camps were barely tolerated. Little excuse was needed to make it rough for them. Forgotten or ignored was the fact of sex and when Juanita was found guilty of murder the same day it happened, she was promptly strung up to a beam of the bridge over the Yuba.

This was mining camp justice but California and the country as a whole reacted with revulsion. Publicity was so unfavorable that lynching even in the California camps became unfashionable for a time.

The first man to pan the water of the Yuba at the forks was Frank Anderson in September, 1949, but he had little success. A few months later there arrived a motley crew headed by one William Downey, a Scotsman. His retinue consisted of ten Negro sailors, an Indian, an Irish boy named Michael Deverney and a Kanaka called Jim Crow.

The group erected several little log cabins above the point where the North Fork of the Yuba joins the main stream. Although snow soon fell and a skin of ice formed on the quiet pools, persistent panning yielded considerable gold. Snow was brushed away from extruding quartz veins, the crevices yielding as much as $200 a day. Most surprising reward came when Jim Crow cooked a fourteen-pound salmon caught in the river. When the eaters got to the bottom of the kettle they found a sizable flake of gold.

Inevitably, a stampede converged at The Forks which was soon renamed Downieville for the leader, now respected and endowed with a courtesy title of "Major." Claims and men spread up and down both streams and by 1851 the camp had a population of 5,000.

Not all of these were miners, one authority claiming "there was only one producer to eight leeches." But the bars were long and shiny with roulette wheels spinning all night. Streets seethed with pack trains of mules, burros and freight wagons. There was no way to haul supplies and prices of commodities proved it—$4 a pound for sugar and boots $100 a pair.

When religion came to Downieville the town had no other edifice for church purposes than the Downieville Amphitheater, located on what came to be Piety

CATHOLIC CHURCH OF IMMACULATE CONCEPTION clings to steep canyon-side, seems to be all steeple, chapel is tiny by comparison. Originally built in 1852, first structure was destroyed by fire 1858. This edifice was erected on site shortly after; Fr. Dalton was first Pastor.

Flat. The intrepid preacher, first to enter the roistering camp and deliver a sermon, was Rev. William C. Pond.

Surprisingly, the miners welcomed Pond and his preaching with an enthusiasm so great funds were provided for a church. It was built in a few months but the week before dedication was scheduled, the building burned to the ground. Thoroughly discouraged and dejected, the minister opened the door of his cabin to a miner with outstreached hand who said he had walked four miles into town. "Here's a hundred dollars, Mr. Pond," he said, "to start a new church." Contributions came thick and fast and in a short time a new fireproof structure of brick and stone was ready for use.

Stories of fantastic finds of gold in and around town would make it appear more churches could have been built in record time. Weirdest is an unverified tale that on August 21, 1856, James Finney found close to town a nugget weighing 427 pounds, Troy. Even allowing for the fact that most California "nuggets" had considerable quartz matrix adhering to them, this one was worth over $90,000. It was sold to bankers Decker and Jewett and sent to the Philadelphia mint where it was displayed for several years. This would be the largest nugget found in California, the the second largest in the world.

In 1858 John Dodge, who was working the forks of the Yuba between '50 and '53, told of an experience plausible enough in view of the highwayman menace. He, said he, Bill Haskins and an unidentified Dutchman were working an abandoned claim on the middle Yuba. Digging in the bank he came to a chunk of pure gold, too large to pick up after being wedged out. Being "very excited" and fearing discovery, the men posted the Dutchman as a guard and went to work on the chunk. On complete exposure it showed some attached quartz, "not over five pounds." This was chipped off, the nugget dragged into the cabin and shoved under the bed.

The men stayed away from Downieville that night and the next day, Sunday, trying to figure out some way of weighing their find, their gold scale being capable of handling only a pound and a half. A novel scheme was concocted, weighing pieces of rock until they had enough to balance the chunk of gold, and it proved to weigh 227 pounds. Any idea of taking it to the express office was ruled out as causing too much excitement and putting the owners' lives in jeopardy. The men spent Sunday working halfheartedly as the nugget held their main attention and a decision was finally made as to disposing of it. Dodge went to town late Monday, bought a cold chisel and the men spent all that night cutting and dividing the big lump. "It seemed like vandalism," he said.

DOWNIEVILLE IS SITUATED in bottom of narrow ravine where North Fork of Yuba enters larger stream. Main street parallel to Yuba is only one somewhat level, others like this one rise steeply by means of switchbacks and terraces of dry-laid schist rocks. Near site of National Theatre was location where trial was held for miner who had stolen pair of boots. Man was convicted, promised release if he returned boots to owner, set up drinks for crowd. Prisoner was glad to comply, was so generous with drinks that judge, jury and witnesses were soon celebrating uproariously. In resultant drunken brawl, culprit re-stole boots, slipped unobstrusively out of town.

When the job was finished they caved down the workings, had a brief nap, cooked breakfast, wrapped the gold in their blankets and boarded the stage for San Francisco. The stage passed Goodyear Hill and Nigger Tent, rendezvous of road agents, without incident and after arriving in the Bay City, they caught a ship for Panama and New York where they sold the gold for cash, about $50,000. The find was made in '53 and in '58, when John Dodge told the story, he was working as a teamster in the Australian gold fields, but "had a good time while it lasted."

A claim on the North Fork of the Yuba was called Sailor's Diggings, being manned by English sailors in '51. The seamen were said to have found many nuggets from a top size of 31 pounds down. When they had enough, they headed back to England with two large canvas sacks of gold.

On a fine Sunday morning of June, 1856, Major Downey went for one of his habitual walks, this time to the top of a hill on slate Creek to look over the country. While enjoying the view, he scuffed his toe on the ground and unearthed a chunk of quartz about the size of a man's hand. He loosened it and let it roll down the slope. Some time later one of the numerous Chilean miners went up the same hill hunting quail. He shot one, the dying bird fluttering into the hole left by Downey's rock. On picking up the quail the Chilean noticed a glint. Half buried was a piece of gold and quartz which, when cleaned by the assayer in town, yielded nearly a pound of pure gold, about $200 worth. The hill was soon covered with claims and more than fifty miners made fortunes there. Far more wealth was almost discovered by Major Downey than he ever found in his claims. Disgusted, he left shortly for the Cariboo fields in British Columbia.

A middle-aged lady in pinched circumstances came to Downieville to start a boardinghouse on a shoestring. A brother there set her up a tent house with board sides but no floor over the dirt. She got a stove, a long table, some chairs and thirty boarders at $12 a week. She was raking and sweeping the "floor" one day when she noticed what seemed like a piece of gold. The chunk she picked up was exactly that and it wasn't the only one. She rushed to tell her brother who helped her move out the furniture and start panning the floor. Before the day was over they had $500 and when the boarders arrived they were told to eat elsewhere. A month later she returned to the east and told the folks her boardinghouse venture had been very successful.

After two summers of working the gravel beds at the edge of the Yuba between Downieville and Goodyear's Bar, the pickings were getting somewhat thin. The miners, confident the middle of the stream bed would yield plenty, contrived to build a flume. It was built in the spring and successfully dried up the stream by diverting the flow, but the first high water from melting snow took out the entire project and it was never tried again.

Hardly anyone was willing to admit the real glory of Downieville was fading but two events in 1865 made the fact hard and clear. Pond's church was closed for lack of a congregation—and the Chinamen came. Mr. Pond went sadly to another call in Petaluma and the church structure was sold. The Sons of the Flowery Kingdom were not tolerated except in menial capacities, such as washing dirty clothes for the miners, as long as gold was plentiful in the creeks. But as the supply grew scant they were permitted to glean the white man's leavings.

The pattern was repeated over and over in the mining camps of the west but in Downieville the Chinese put a different twist to it. They saw how the miners had tried to divert the Yuba by flume so the hardworking Orientals patiently and tirelessly carried large rocks from the edges of the stream to make a new channel. When the exposed gravels were worked out, other parts of the river were opened up likewise. The moved rocks were stacked in piles and many of these cairn-like humps remain today.

DOWNIEVILLE'S MAIN STREET remains much as it was, despite frequent fires and floods. Structure in center is original Craycroft Building, in basement was famous 75-foot bar. At intersection, road turns right one block to bridge crossing Yuba. From beam of original bridge dangled body of Juanita, only woman hanged in California.

EL DORADO and SHINGLE SPRINGS, CALIFORNIA

Mud Springs—a name to conjure with but not to mention to your mother. Yet that was the camp's name. The first seekers of gold there gathered around the water supply in such numbers they trampled the ground into a quagmire—and the camp had a name—Mud Springs.

In addition to attracting an increasing number of Argonauts, Mud Springs was an important stop on the old Carson Emigrant Trail and it soon became a crossroads station for freight and stage lines. At the height of the gold rush the population mounted to several thousands, the town complete with "full quota of saloons, hotels, and a gold production that gave its citizens just cause for pride." It was during this period the town was incorporated and this same civic pride caused a change in the name to El Dorado.

Picturesque place names are also in evidence at some of the neighboring camps which sprang up during the gold rush and have since disappeared —Loafer's Hollow, Deadman's Hollow, Dry Creek, Missouri Flat, Empire Ravine and Shingle Springs.

Though rich while they lasted, the original placer deposits were quickly exhausted. Then the lode mines came into being and for a time there was a continuous line of quartz mills extending south to the crossing on the Consumnes River, the spot then called Saratoga and later Huse Bridge. The stamp mills were of varying capacities, the one at Logtown, a mile or two from El Dorado, having eight stamps.

A good many of the more important buildings were erected on ground later found to be rich in gold and the miners waited impatiently for them to be considered outmoded or "menaces to health and safety," so they could wreck them and mine the sites. Ten thousand dollars in gold was said to have been extracted from the soil where the dance hall stood.

El Dorado's near neighbor, Shingle Springs, gained its cognomen from its shingle mill and a fine spring of very cold water. The Shingle Spring House was built in 1850 of lumber brought around the Horn and had an apparent knack of spawning brawls in the lustier days.

Mining there began that same year, the surrounding gulches filled with cabins, most of them hastily thrown together. For the first few years the miners were forced to get their supplies from Buckeye Flat (named by men homesick for their native Ohio) but by '57 a store was established at the camp. This was a commentary on the slow development of Shingle Springs and of its rather small gold deposits. Most of the gold camps grew so rapidly stores and supply houses sprang up within a few days or weeks of the first strikes.

Prosperity did suddenly smile on Shingle Springs but from an entirely different direction. In '65 the Sacramento Valley Railroad extended its line from the camp to Latrobe. For two years Shingle Springs enjoyed a top place in the ranks of gold towns and then fell flat. The Central Pacific Railroad from Sacramento via Auburn diverted the overland traffic from the Placerville Road and Shingle Springs reverted to the status of a village.

WELLS FARGO BUILDING — most impressive and unaltered remnant in El Dorado — Shingles Springs district. Also housed Phelps Store. Constructed of semi-dressed native stone, it is impressive with deep-set, arched doors in upper and lower stories. Structure once boasted elaborate balcony. Peaked roof, common in gold country, is intact where disappeared from most other buildings. Even brick chimney remains sound.

FIDDLETOWN, CALIFORNIA

The year of first discoveries of gold in the Sierra foothills was drawing to a close when a party of prospectors found rich deposits in the gravel of a creek entering the Consumnes River. So absorbed were they in sloshing out a few dollars to the pan no one noticed darkening skies until the first downpour of the winter season forced them to seek cover. Only then did they think of building make-shift shelter.

The winter was a wet one, continued rains forcing the men from Missouri who made up the bulk of the settlers to stay in their flimsy houses. Most of them had played the fiddle for dances "back home" and they now spent most of their time scraping out "Turkey In The Straw" and other nostalgic melodies. It was "moughty blamed natural" to name the town—Fiddletown.

This was as wild a camp as any in the Mother Lode. Eighty-two-year-old Thomas Davis who lived in Fiddletown many years is quoted by the San Francisco Examiner as saying: "There was plenty of activity and violence. I always remember mother's description of a Saturday night when the miners had come to town after a horse race. One man was leaning against the pillar of the hotel porch when an enemy knifed him. He clutched

the pillar, spinning around several times before he hit the ground, dead." Another incident is related by N. B. Randall who runs the museum housed in Schallhorn's Wagon Shop: "The storekeeper shipped millions in gold out of town. He knew robbers were after him and barricaded his store. But one afternoon when he came back from a trip he found the men inside it. They killed him with a hatchet."

While all this was going on many other camps were springing up in the area fringing on the Consumnes, most of them with names reflecting the circumstances of their founding—French Flat, Dry-town, Loafer Flat, Suckertown, American Hill, Arkansas Hill, Yankee Hill, Plymouth.

Fiddletown itself flourished. Although the placers petered out, hydraulic mining came in and paid huge dividends. Buildings were going up all along the main street, much more substantial than the jerry-built structures of the first winter. A deposit of rhyolite tuff had been discovered close by, and since this material is easily worked when first uncovered, hardening on exposure, it was used extensively. Other buildings used bricks made of clay found nearby and fired in a local kiln. Others went up with schist blocks accurately

RAMMED EARTH ADOBE OFFICE of Dr. Yee near center of Fiddletown's Chinatown. Genial Oriental escaped ostracism suffered by most of race in gold rush days, his sunny smile and expert dispensing of herbs winning hearts of miners. Original roof of shingles was replaced by sheet metal which served in its mundane way to protect venerable structure from usual fate of adobes, melting away when roof deteriorated. Present tenant, Yow Fong Chow, is sole remaining representative of 2,000 Chinese once living in Fiddletown, popularly known as Jimmy. Note original iron shutters at windows, typical of period but not always used on adobe buildings.

cut and fitted. And elegant marble, quarried locally, was given such utilitarian use as lining the basement of Henry Schroeder's Brewery.

Allen A. Woolfolk, old timer in the place, tells of some early structures, most of them now gone. There was a dance hall built by a Mr. Eaurow, two blacksmith shops—Pigeon's and McClary's. Four hotels took care of the transient and some of the permanent residents—the N. S., St. Charles, Flag and the ostentatious Charlesville. Charles Hikinson ran a large livery stable which was destroyed by fire as were most of the frame buildings in this and other towns. The Farnham's lumber yard and their lumber-built home were spared those holocausts and the house stands today. It is owned by George Pacini, an Italian grape grower. This fruit has figured in the history of the town from the beginning of the hydraulic period. The winery in those days was run by Peter Smith and Sons who had their own vineyard. Fiddletown's Chinese population was as high as 2,000 with the usual assortment of stores, medicine shops, joss houses and opium dens.

Two judges held jurisdiction over the community, as colorful as any magistrates in the gold rush country. On one occasion, it is related, Judge Yates listened to a long-drawn-out case in which one of the witnesses was displaying a complete and obvious disregard of the truth. His patience at last giving way, he brought his gavel down hard and thundered: "This court is adjourned!" He allowed the contrasting silence for a moment and then blasted: "This man is a damn liar!" After another pause he lowered his voice dramatically. "I declare this court in session."

The other jurist, Judge Purinton, made frequent trips to San Francisco and Sacramento and became increasingly annoyed at the titters when he wrote "Fiddletown" after his name on hotel registers. When his indignation reached its limit, he pulled some legal strings and had the town's name changed to the more dignified one of Oleta.

The town accepted this gesture to propriety for a few years then the more fitting Fiddletown was restored. The place now drowses in a pleasant bower of grape vineyards, prune and walnut orchards, green pastures where stock grazes. The old wild days are long gone and the camp is by-passed by most tourists. Some of the few remaining residents would like to see more of them stop, the rest wish to retain the peace and quiet which now hangs over Fiddletown like a golden haze on a summer day.

HOME OF MRS. L. E. FRINCHABOY who supplied photographer with much of Fiddletown facts. Beautiful example of frame architecture of the period house was finished 100 years ago, built by young Mr. Chestnut as a home for his intended bride, Patience Neff. Couple moved in later that year. Mrs. Frinchaboy, her husband and three sons (who served in both World Wars) moved into house in 1939. House contains many interesting reilcs such as fireplace of local marble. Famed violinist David Rubinoff, long honorary "Mayor" of Fiddletown, frequently visits old camp with family, staying overnight as guests of Mrs. Frinchaboy.

SCHALLHORN BLACKSMITH AND WAGON SHOP was erected in 1870 of rectangular blocks, 12x18x20, of Valley Springs rhyolite tuff. Source of material is one and a half miles out of town. Builder Chris Schallhorn sawed most of blocks himself, built sturdy wagons in shop for many years. Building now serves as part-time museum, proprietor Randall "closing shop" when mood dictates.

FRENCH GULCH near Whiskeytown once boasted street lined solidly with false front buildings. The few remaining are defaced by posters in front, show atmosphere and age in rear. At left is stone structure serving as bank, other was store with living quarters on upper story. Backyard fence is smothered with ancient grapevines, leafless here in March. First discoveries were made and mining done by Frenchmen in 1849. Later main workings were operated by Washington Quartz Mining Company. When rich veins were discovered in 1852, Shasta **Courier** reported: "Such rich diggings have been struck that miners are tearing down their houses to pursue the leads which run under them."

GARLOCK, CALIFORNIA

The six mills in Garlock separated the gold from the ore hauled down from Randsburg and needed the water in the local wells. So did most of the few hundred souls in the camp. But there were those who scorned water like the plague and kept Cheney's Thirst Emporium in business . . . like "Lily of the Valley" who ran a one man hoisting operation at the bar, then roamed Garlock's street, crooning: "Oh, she's the lily of the valley, the bright and morning star".

A few desiccated cabins stood at the edge of the barren El Paso Range and the people who lived there paid $1 for a 52 gallon barrel of water. It would last the average family a week, with restraint on such things as laundering and dishwashing. Then some enterprising individual came to the cabins and dug a well. He was ridiculed . . . "Why anybody would know there isn't any underground water in an area where the annual rainfall is nothing minus." The digger was deaf to all this and found the water table at a depth of only 28 to 30 feet. He may have become a patron saint of the area which soon became a regular stopping place for prospectors and their wagons. And its name became Cow Wells.

Pioneer Robert Kelly wrote: "Plentiful water was necessary for the stock in the corrals. The large water tank was kept full by pumping with a large rotary contraption, pulled in a circular motion by a large, lazy black mule which needed constant prodding or he would go to sleep in his tracks. With sufficient urging he would stay on his job and pump a sufficient amount of water within a reasonable time to take care of the next day's needs. Then old Mule was turned back to his corral until his services were needed the next day . . . the tank also served for refrigeration in summer time, where my mother kept the butter, milk and other food."

These simple days came to an end with the need to mill the ores from the Rand mines. The poverty-plagued, discoverer-owners on Rand Mountain were determined to keep the mine "in the family" but even though the ores were extremely rich, it cost too much to ship it away for milling and it was out of the question to mill it on the spot as they had no water. Now with water at Cow Wells, a mill could be built there and ore hauled to it by wagon.

Eugene Garlock, always referred to as Gene, built the first — the Garlock Pioneer Mill — and the enlarged cluster of cabins took his name. A load of ore was driven down the grade from the Yellow Aster, at first called the Rand mine, and Dr. Bur-

cham, the physician-wife of one of the partners, came with it to see that none of the ore was carried off — as it often was when shipments were piled around the mills, this taking of specimens termed a polite form of high-grading. The brick of gold resulting from the first milling was worth $800 and to Dr. Burcham fell the task of personally taking it to Mojave, as there was yet no Wells Fargo. She was nervous about bandits but did the best she could to conceal the brick under her skirt.

When the little Garlock Pioneer Mill proved inadequate to handle the increasing amounts of ore, five more were built — the McKernan, Kelley, Smith, Henry and Visalia. Gold was extracted by simple amalgamation, the ore not being refractory, and the power came from steam. Fuel was the big problem in this desert-type country. Brushy, twiggy, fast-burning branches had to do and it was fed to the fires with hay forks.

All ore was hauled by heavy wagons with broad iron tires to stay on top of the sand. The grade down from the Rand was steep with plenty of rough spots in the lower flats and deep washes. The wagons had to be eased down, then pulled by sheer horse or mule power.

The mule skinner's vocabulary is legendary, most drivers working a long string of vitriolic words to a high pitch of profanity as they lashed savagely with the whip. Little Joe did not believe in that kind of brutal treatment. When his team arrived at a bad gully, says Old Jim McGinn, who knew Little Joe in Garlock's good years from 1896 to 1899, he would walk around to the near lead animal, place his mouth close to the ear, whispering words of affection and encouragement. And he made the rounds, whispering in all the animals' ears. Then he got back in the driver's seat, picked up the lines and it never failed. At the signal the animals surged against their collars and took the load right out of the gully.

There were few buildings in Garlock but they made a break in the arid expanse. There was the Doty Hotel, a board and batten, two story structure. Another hotel was the Lilard, where the three daughters of the owner waited on table and later in the evening played the piano and sang for guests. Instead of tagging the girls with the usual "Faith, Hope and Charity", these were called "Tom, Dick and Harry".

The stable, or Big Barn, where horses on the Mojave-Randsburg run changed, was quite impos-

WEATHERED BUILDINGS—all that is left of once busy Garlock. At left is blacksmith shop, complete with forge; at right, livery stable — one end entirely closed for grain storage, rest of building open to weather on one side. Mountains in background are El Pasos, centered by El Paso Peak, 4,500 feet. Comparatively low range runs in east-west direction, is separated at western end from Kiavahs by Red Rock Canyon, scene of many early gold discoveries. Kiavahs, also a low range short distance north, ends at foothills of giant Sierra Nevada.

ing as were the McGinn Grocery, Lew Porter Store and the two saloons — Miller-Montgomery Bar and Cheney's Thirst Emporium. The first "postmaster" was Ida Kelly, wife of Kern County Constable John Kelly. Long after the demise of Garlock he would discover — by proxy — the famous Big Silver mine near Randsburg.

Garlock was fortunate to have a doctor all through its heyday — W. H. Wright. With his wife and three small children, Dr. Wright arrived by train and stage in 1896. One of the children, Sher-

man L. Wright now of Oakland, recalls those days: "The house which father constructed consisted of two rooms with lean-to at the rear. It was made of 1 x 12 inch boards nailed upright to a 2 x 4 framework. The total floor space was about 400 square feet. The front room was used as drug store, doctor's office, dental office and for general assembly of many miners. Later, about 1899 or 1900, half of this room was partitioned off for a post office which was operated until 1903 when it was abandoned for lack of business. The other room and

206

WELL PRESERVED REMAINS of arrastra include wooden parts, unrotted in dry desert air. Crude contraption crushed ore from mines of Randsburg before mills were built there. Ore, dumped unguarded around grinder, presented irresistable temptation to high-graders who claimed they were only selecting specimens. At first practice was condoned by mill owners but when samplers took to carrying off sacks full of jewelry rock, guard was posted.

lean-to were used for living quarters, kitchen, laundry etc., quite a common arrangement in those days.

"Aside from carrying on a general practice of medicine, my father practiced some dentistry consisting mainly of extracting and giving relief to aching teeth. I do not know that he did fillings or other repairs. In his spare time father was also a miner, preacher on Sundays and at funerals, Fourth of July orator, school board member, surveyor and self-constituted authority on anything. . . ."

The three children attended Garlock's little school. Desks were hand made, four feet wide, accommodating two pupils each. Girls were grouped on one side of the room, boys on the other. A wood-burning, cast iron stove stood in the center, gal-

vanized water pail and tin dipper near the front door. At the far end was a platform, teacher's desk and blackboard. The school doubled as church and meeting place for the Garlock Literary Society which was considered an "uplifting influence" to the town morals and a means of recognizing local talent at entertainments.

In the winter of 1897-98, a shadow fell on Garlock. A 28-mile railroad spur was completed to Johannesburg, connecting the Randsburg complex with the Atchison, Topeka and Santa Fe at Kramer. The line ran within a mile of the Yellow Aster and the mine could now ship ore to Barstow for more efficient milling. For a time some poor grade ore was still ground at Garlock, then a screw-pipe water line was laid from the springs at Goler to Randsburg, making possible the construction of a 30-stamp mill right at the mines. When this was followed by a huge 100-stamp mill, the death knell of Garlock was sounded. The little school house, crowded to capacity during boom years, had only the three Wright children in 1902 and 1903.

"We remained at Garlock until 1903." says Sherman Wright, "by which time the population had dwindled to our family and a Mexican, Juan Barsarto, who took in washing. We abandoned our house and asked Juan to drive us in our four wheeler wagon to Mojave. We gave Juan the horse and wagon and took the train for Oakland. . ."

Garlock became a true ghost and except for an occasional tenancy by some wandering prospector, it remained completely deserted until 1911. In that year the Southern Pacific constructed a rail connection from Mojave to Keeler and crews camped in Garlock's weathered buildings. As rails extended they moved on and the little town was again empty.

Then in the early 1920s came a new resurgence. A salt company started mining the saline deposits of nearby Kane Lake. Mine owner and capitalist J. D. Voss and associates made a determined attempt to develop the old Apache mine in nearby Iron Canyon, and a new mining project took form at Mesquite Springs. There was a general occupancy of houses in Garlock, the need for a post office again, a new store was started by John Norton and a boarding house by Sarah "Granny" Slocum.

But ghosts would have the town. The salt project failed and the crew moved away. The men at the Apache mine folded their tents. No one asked for mail and the post office closed on June 30, 1926 — but who can say it was for the last time?

CENTRAL GEARS in museum-piece arrastra shows simple machinery. Turned by another gear operated by steam engine, central rod revolved, turning horizontal beams. Each of these was fastened to granite block, several shown here. These were dragged over ore thrown into pit, crushing it for gold extraction by amalgamation. Crude process wasted much gold, recovered later by mills in further processing by cyanide method, mine owners not sharing in salvage.

GOLD CAMP AND TROPICO MINE, CALIF.

Potter's clay, that humble substance used to make the feet of idols and sewer pipe, had a special meaning for Ezra Hamilton. It not only solved a problem for his Los Angeles Pottery Co. but led to lush living for himself, his goldfish and silkworms.

The need for drain tile in the Los Angeles area was acute around 1878 when booming expansion was eliminating the privy and bringing the plumbing inside, The pottery concern was able to make the tile but it needed better quality clay than the local soil produced. So Ezra Hamilton jumped at the chance to buy a carload of fine clay from the sample submitted by Dr. L. A. Crandall.

This clay was red, conspicuous in the formations of sandstone, volcanic tuffs, dacite and rhyolite in the hills bordering the north side of Antelope Valley, about five miles from the town of Rosamond, which was some fifty miles from Los Angeles. Dr. Crandall had been looking for gold here and thought the clay might have some value.

It did and was soon being dug out of Crandall's hill in huge quantities and shipped to the Los Angeles tile plant. Hamilton balked at the large shipping costs and in 1882 bought the property from the doctor, at the same time taking out two additional mineral claims, labeling these Pottery 2 and 3.

As Los Angeles boomed so did the tile works but in the early '90s both slowed down. Enterprising Ezra took to panning out some of the clay in his desert hill and found some bright yellow particles that turned out to be gold.

Now more excited than he was over the original clay sample, he and his son Truman set out for

Rosamond as a team. At the clay pits they searched diligently on the north side of the hill, washing pan after pan, always finding a few specs of gold. Then in a gully they found several nuggets and then came a pan in which almost all the dregs were pure gold. Ezra said later: "I looked at that gold. It was rough and lay among broken stones, not gravel. I says to myself, it's a native of this place." In 1896, after more searching for the lead from which the float came, he located it in one of the most exposed spots near the ridge of the hill. An assay showed samples around $35 per ton.

Hamilton returned to Los Angeles, quietly closed out his interests, and returning to the Joshua trees in the desert, set about staking claims. Father and son became acquainted with a colored man who had a ranch south of the hill, one Charles Graves. They became close friends and Graves accepted Hamilton's invitation to stake out any claim he might fancy on the eastern quarter of the hill. "We've got plenty," Ezra said, "and we think you would make a good neighbor." Graves, who had left his Kentucky home in 1882, staked out two claims of the usual size near his ranch, 600 by 1500 feet, naming them Home No. 1 and Home No. 2.

With two other sons, Lester and Fred, joining Truman, Ezra Hamilton devoted his entire energies to the prospective mine. The first ore removed from the hard outcropping was that which showed the good assay at the start and the first payment check was for $4,600, spent for further ore removal and a little two-stamp mill, erected at what would be the Lida tunnel. It was powered by a small steam engine and to fire it the surrounding desert was

stripped of sagebrush, Joshua trees and ocotillo stems, the fuel flaring up and dying down like paper. When it was gone the Hamiltons had to import solid wood from the Sierra, hauling it across the Mojave Desert by wagon.

In two years it was clear they had more claims than they could work so they sold one for $100,000. After the Los Angeles TIMES printed a feature story on the big sale, Dec. 12, 1900, prospectors, promoters and legitimate investors flocked to the scene to make hay while Hamilton's sun shone. And instead of the Hamilton's vein pinching out at a shallow depth, it improved as the mine deepened. They bought the old stage station site at Willow Springs where there was a generous supply of water and erected a new five-stamp mill there.

The fame of the Hamilton mine reached St. Louis, for the World Exposition there asked Ezra Hamilton for an exhibit and he sent one to make all eyes pop. Some of the ore specimens had solid gold sticking out of the quartz matrix and would assay at about $90,000 to the ton. The three Hamilton boys went to the fair on funds derived from a ton of ore each from the stope of the Lida — $5,000 for each son.

Hamilton now had time and money to carry out some of the plans for Willow Springs, the first a health resort for those suffering from lung trouble. To the buildings he added a large goldfish pond with landscaping — an oasis contrasting markedly with the uncompromising desert. And the grapevines did so well additional plantings were made to support a small winery. Also planted were mulberry trees, the leaves of which would feed his hungry silkworms.

The next few years saw many changes on the hill. Charles Graves leased his claims to the Hoyt Brothers Company and they in turn sold all rights to the Big Three Mining and Milling Co. which combine then bought several of Hamilton's claims. A J. B. Freeman was president of a firm that "perfected" a new dry wash system which would have saved hard-to-get water had it been more successful. The mill, erected in 1904 to extract gold from the Big Three holdings, operated at a loss for several years and at length the discouraged mine owners allowed the mine workings to stagnate. By this time Hamilton had sold the rest of his holding and things on the hill were very quiet.

In 1907 the mine complex received a temporary shot in the arm, mainly in the form of promotion by J. M. Overshier, president of the Tiger Head Min-

SIMULATED MINING CAMP CEMETERY, another exhibit at Gold Camp, typical of many found in desert mountains around Tropico.

ing Co. He made some pretense of opening the mines while active with stock selling, then quietly decamped.

After the Antelope Mining Co. took a one year lease in 1909 with no results, another company took over. Some of the stockholders came from a small community called Tropico, near the present Forest Lawn Memorial Park at Glendale, and they named their group the Tropico Mining and Milling Co. President V. V. Cochrane, with leading stockholders B. Gross and O. S. Richardson, were successful in consolidating the many past ownerships and in having them patented. The Tropico Company was successful also in finding paying values and operating the mines until 1934 with a one year break in 1923. A J. F. White held the lease for that period.

When the Antelope Valley was being opened up by real estate promotions in 1900, one flamboyant advertisement in FIELD AND STREAM lured at least one family, the Burtons with four sons, one twelve-year-old Clifford. The family settled on a ranch in the valley not far from the present Mira Loma, now site of the county prison.

Young Clifford worked on the ranch with the others but at eighteen took off for the rocky desert hills with a friend, Mel Sanford. The two made a good strike near Ballarat in the Death Valley area and sold it for $4,500 to a well known mining figure, "January" Jones. Clifford used his share to study geology, mining techniques and refining methods, attended a mining and assay school in Los Angeles, returning to Antelope Valley and a job at the Tropico mine in 1912.

Burton was able to suggest methods to improve milling that eliminated many of the worst difficulties and in 1914, as mine superintendent, he sent for his favorite brother Cecil. The Tropico then humped in production, operating profitably until 1917 when the war forced a near closure.

Returning from the service in 1920, the Burton brothers again went to work for Tropico but rising costs and decreasing ore values made the going hard. Many stockholders sold out to the Burtons who eventually had a controlling interest. In the early '30s a number of farmers turned miners began finding small amounts of good ore in the hills and trucked it to the Burton mill for "custom" refining. Then came President Roosevelt's edict raising the price of gold from the prevailing price of $20.07 per ounce to $35. The Burton Tropico mine was on the way to another bonanza.

Clifford Burton was able to see the best gold values would increase in a westerly direction and accordingly stopped all other extensions, opening up new tunnels from several lower levels, proving there was more gold here than even during Ezra Hamilton's heyday. More and more mines in the hills, as far away as Death Valley and Twentynine Palms, were sending in custom jobs until the Burtons were forced to expand their mill facilities to handle ore from four hundred mines.

They also established a "trading post" on the Tropico premises, outfitting and grubstaking prospectors, selling equipment and supplies to established miners. The Tropico mine in 1942 was extending its operations to the Ruth mine near Trona, California, and the Fortuna near Yuma, Arizona,

HILLS AND GULCHES around Tropico mine are included in "Rosamond formation", offer everything from clay to gold. Here on northeast slope of what would be called Tropico Hill, Dr. L. A. Crandall found samples of good quality clay. Discovery of material and timely acceptance by Ezra Hamilton for his Los Angeles pottery works diverted further prospecting for gold until after business recession slowed tile production. Hamilton gophered entire hill, evidence shown here in small dumps scattered over hill. Large excavation in foreground shows enormous amounts of clay were removed and shipped to Los Angeles.

when the whole operation ground to a halt with the government curtailing gold production with order L.208.

Keeping the mines in shape through the second World War was a hard struggle but the glad day did come when the Tropico was allowed to reopen. But now costs had risen to new peaks, machinery had deteriorated, some needing expensive replacement. Miners' wages had risen to a level never before heard of and everything was inflated except the value of the end product, gold being frozen at the price that had seemed so high in pre-war days—$35.

Cecil Burton died in 1947 and Clifford attempted to carry on but was felled by a fatal heart attack two years later. His son, Clifford G. took over, making a gallant struggle to regain the Tropico's former glories but the case was hopeless and in 1956 the Tropico closed down again. This time the pumps were withdrawn and the water level started to rise. Probabilities indicate it will eventually reach to between the 300 and 400 foot levels, flooding all workings below that depth.

The property stood idle until January 1958

when a group composed of Mr. and Mrs. Glen A. Settle, Mr. and Mrs. George F. McNamee and Eric Burton obtained a lease from the Burton Company with the intention of preserving the mine property, keeping it intact and establishing a museum site to bring back the glamorous aspects of early gold mining days. Earlier Glen Settle married Dorene, daughter of Clifford G. Burton, and became assistant manager. The couple has furnished much material for this story of Tropico and the group has moved in many old structures from almost inaccessible old mining camps in nearby desert and mountains. Included are a mine boarding house, railroad section house, freight depot, post office, mine superintendent's home and first school house built in Palmdale. They are grouped along a "Main Street" to create the illusion of a genuine mining camp.

The Tropico Gold Camp is closed to visitors in summer due to extreme desert heat but there are weekend mine tours the year around as the underground levels are always cool. The old mine is intact, almost ready for reactivation should gold values rise to practical levels.

213

GRASS VALLEY, CALIFORNIA

When Lola Montez, the fiery and exotic dancer in the Latin manner, bought a house in Grass Valley and settled down there, the forthright women of the town could be expected to throw up their hands in alarm. Instead they respected her, not because they saw she was going to keep hands off their errant husbands, but because she worked diligently in her garden. It was not a gesture. She liked gardening and was good at it, transplanting such difficult subjects as the native cacti. And too, she was aware even dirty, old, digging clothes looked good on her.

A remote, back-country mining camp was not Lola's native habitat. Her beauty was far more outstanding than any extraordinary talent as a dancer,

SECTION OF GIGANTIC CORE removed from ever-deepening shaft of hard rock mine in Grass Valley during town's golden age of mining. Shaft was bored by machine directed by operator who rode in cage directly over cutting equipment. When section of core was cut, operator and machine were lifted from shaft, section loosened by driving wooden wedges around circumference. Hoist was then lowered, attached to core which was lifted out. Repeated drilling and removal of rock sections sank shaft deep into bowels of earth. This sort of mining with expensive equipment spelled doom for earlier miners with their simple pans and rockers.

yet her time was not booked solid and when she was out of audiences she retired to Grass Valley to think about new dance routines and possible engagements.

Born Eliza Gilbert in Ireland, she eloped with an army officer at fifteen and after quickly shedding him, picked up some rudiments of dancing and walked onto a London stage as a professional—the Famed Spanish Dancer, Lola Montez. Her undeniable beauty brought her to the attention of Ludwig of Bavaria, that monarch being between mistresses. She was said to have caused a revolution in that country, fled back to England and married again. This caused her some embarassment because she neglected to end her first marriage legally, but it enhanced her stage career. She was more popular and earned more money at this period than before or later.

Lola decided on a United States tour. The *New York Times* gave her so many press notices she had a public reception in her hotel suite. Joseph Henry Jackson, said of her: "There was an aura of delicious scandal about her. She was graceful and she was beautiful and that was enough." It was enough to carry her across the country, though with diminishing returns. From San Francisco she drifted to the gold camps, winding up in Grass Valley to lick her wounds and plant flowers.

The dancer liked pets, had in her collection a small bear, several parrots and monkeys. She was slightly bitten by one of her bears which inspired this verse by Alonzo Delano:

When Lola came to feed her bear
   With comfits sweet and sugar rare,
Bruin ran out in haste to meet her,
   Seized her hand because 'twas sweeter.

Legends about her concern an editor who wrote a derogatory story and received a visit from the dancer. She carried a whip with which she taught him a lesson on how to treat a lady. Another is about a preacher who let slip some slighting remark about her in a Sunday sermon. Next evening she knocked on his door, very briefly dressed in costume for her famous Spider Dance. While the "unfortunate" minister watched, she performed the dance on his doorstep.

The most important impression Lola made in Grass Valley was on a little girl who lived with her mother a few houses away—a girl named Lotta Crabtree. She was a constant guest at Lola's and it was natural enough the performer should teach songs and dances to the talented child.

When the exotic Montez left Grass Valley to re-

214

turn to the stage with an engagement in Australia, the residents sincerely missed her. But she returned, the tour a failure, staying only long enough to sell the house, then departing on a lecture circuit. This too was an abbreviated affair and things went from bad to worse. Broke in New York, Lola Montez died five years after leaving the mining town.

In Grass Valley little Lotta Crabtree was growing up the way the flamboyant dancer would have her. The mother, Mary Ann Crabtree, encouraged the dancing and taught her all she could. They started a tour of the mining camps beginning with Rabbit Creek where the bearded miners went wild over the lovely black-eyed child, throwing nuggets at her feet. Success in another camp was punctuated by gunshots, Lotta and her mother lying on the floor while bullets whistled through the walls as a pair of drunken miners shot it out in the street. All this was left far behind as the "darling of the mining camps" went on to

world fame. She lived to be nearly eighty, leaving a fortune of $4 million to charity.

Grass Valley received its name when a party of weary emigrants arrived there in 1849 after a hard journey across country and the Truckee Pass Trail. They allowed their bony nags and cattle to eat their fill on luxurious, waving grass on the well-watered spot. There were white men there earlier but they did not stay, Claude Chana and his party of French emigrants who passed through in 1846.

Late in the summer of '49 a party of prospectors, originally from Oregon, wandered northward from the El Dorado diggings. They searched along the streams and found enough to hold them until cold weather set in, then left for the lowlands. That same fall another party headed by a Dr. Saunders had taken the precaution to build a cabin on Badger Hill near what was to be the site of Grass Valley.

Another party settled in Boston Ravine a short

THIS HOUSE ON MILL STREET in Grass Valley was home to famed exotic dancer, Lola Montez. While licking her wounds caused by recent cool reception of her performances in San Francisco, Lola was a warm hostess to all sorts of theatrical and literary people. Here gathered such lights as Ole Bull, Stephen Masset, and two nephews of Victor Hugo, along with many others less known but equally thirsty guests. Liberal potations encouraged wild applause for Lola's performances in her parlor. New husband dancer had brought to Grass Valley was less enthusiastic, bitter quarrels followed soirees. Lola washed mate out of hair by going to San Francisco for divorce. On return to Grass Valley, parties were resumed on even less inhibited level.

IN BACKYARD OF LOLA MONTEZ residence is picturesque shed topped by dove cote. Little structure sheltered dancer's menage of pets including young grizzly and brown bears. Other members included parrots and a monkey or two kept in the house. Animal pets were less in Lola's affections after divorce gave her greater freedom to fondle succession of young male guests. While photos of Montez home were being taken, crew was laying new pipeline in street. One crash-helmeted worker sauntered over and inquired of photographer, "Say, who the hell was Lola Montez, anyway?".

distance away, the gulch also becoming part of the town. The first Christian burial in Nevada County took place in Boston Ravine. Services were held by Rev. Cummings for an emigrant who had made it this far only to die almost within sight of his hoped-for destination. A dozen smaller camps sprang up nearby, some with names of wonder—Red Dog, Gouge Eye, Little York, Quaker Hill, Walloupa, Sailor Flat and You Bet.

Some of the rich placers in the district were Humbug Flats (first considered a failure), Pike Valley, Grass Valley Slide, Thode Island, Lola Montez and Kate Hardy. Hard rock mining was the mainstay

and the reason Grass Valley lived so much longer than camps having only placer beds. The discovery of a rich lead on Gold Hill in 1850 by George Knight gave impetus to a vast network of later discoveries and many crude mills to crush and reduce ore.

Millions of tons of tailings surrounding hundreds of old shaft heads and mills attest to the huge activity continuing eighty years with a total production of gold amounting to more than $80 million. Under the complex of once-active mining buildings is a vast labyrinth of tunnels and shafts. One vein extends almost two miles and one tunnel drops to 7,000 feet, the bottom 1,500 feet below sea level.

HORNITOS, CALIFORNIA

The origin of Hornitos is clouded in doubt. While the gold rush had a violent impact on the sleepy little village it was not the cause of its birth as in the case of most of the towns along the Mother Lode. The Mexican settlement was many years pre-gold rush, built around a central plaza in approved Spanish style, the adobe buildings low and sprawling. A main street ran beside the plaza and formed one side of the square. In the evenings the strumming of guitars issued from the doorways and gay, though decorous, dances were in sway almost every night—*bailles* that included Las Chapanecas, Fandangos and all the rest. Daytimes saw the Mexican sports—bull fights, bull and bear contests and long-legged fighting cocks pitted against each other. Saints days and fiestas were observed, mass celebrated in the small adobe church.

CHINESE "TREES OF HEAVEN" persist from oriental occupation, grow inside ruins of Ghirardelli store. In 1855 Ghirardelli, who previously had operated a trading post on the Stanislaus River, heard of the boom in Hornitos and felt it would be a good place to start a general supply house. Store was built by him and operated three years, when he moved to San Francisco and devoted himself to chocolate business. Upper floor was added to store and used as I.O.O.F. Hall, then as place to hold dances and meetings until demise of town.

TUNNEL ONCE RAN UNDER STREET from adobe which stood in area shown in foreground. Other end was in saloon across street. On one occasion when "Most notorious bandit in California" was surprised by posse at door of Fandango Hall, he ducked into opening shown here and escaped from pursuers. State soon offered $5,000 for his capture, resulting in Murieta's ambush and killing at the mouth of Arroyo Cantova near Priest Valley by a posse of 20 State Rangers headed by Capt. Harry Love in July of 1853.

Murieta's head was severed and the problem arose as to how to preserve it as proof of the slaying. Capt. Love gathered all bottles of whiskey carried by the men which amounted to a total of three quarts. Paste of flour and whiskey was then smeared over grisly object and it was put in a keg, later being taken to a doctor who cleaned it off and more properly preserved it in alcohol. Head was then brought to Hornitos where Murieta had been so well known and lifted out by hair for identification by erstwhile drinking cronies. After this it was placed in glass jar and displayed all over California.

BURIAL YARD of Catholic Church is heavily populated, casualties in early days many as result of "miner's consumption," frequent quarrels and violence in bordellos and opium dens. Cemetery has many plots with unique ways of arranging graves and stones. Here graves are covered by walk of stone and cement.

The gold rush changed all this. A gold camp called Quartzburg had sprung up not far away and was running in such wide-open fashion with murders rampant that the peaceful element forcibly ejected the prostitutes, gamblers and troublemakers. Hornitos being handy, these undesirables settled there, disrupting the idyllic course of the town's history. It was written: "Gamblers, girls and roughnecks . . . they were a tough lot, the worst in the southern mines. They reverenced nothing but money, cards and wine . . . blood was upon nearly every doorstep and the sand was caked in it." It was during this period the notorious bandit, Joaquin Murieta, moved in and made as permanent a residence as he did anywhere in

his unstable wanderings.

Almost every town in the Mother Lode was said to have been his "hide-out." Some historians have tried to destroy the Murieta legend but facts show there were several Mexican bandits during the period, three named Joaquin—two of these, Joaquin Valenzuelo and Joaquin Carrillo. Blame for the deeds of all was placed on Murieta even though two murders laid at his feet may have been perpetrated many miles apart. It is said Capt. Love and his Rangers were out for a reward and any Mexican would do as a means of collecting the money. It is also reported Murieta's sister made a trip to San Francisco to view the head of her famous brother. If she paid her dollar like other curious spectators she may have felt cheated, as she retorted: "This is not the head of my brother." No one ever claimed to have seen Joaquin Murieta alive after May, 1853.

Gold was plentiful around Hornitos although strictly speaking, the town was about fifteen miles from the Mother Lode proper. Caught with gold fever, the place grew even wilder and the usual entry of Chinese aggravated the situation. The Orientals were the very symbol of peace but they infuriated the whites by their willingness to work for so little on such a low standard of living.

One of these Cantonese was patiently gleaning the leavings of white miners in the gulch one day when a gang of white boys came along to torment him. After taking all this meekly for some time Charley bristled at a particularly mean jibe and fired his gun into the air to scare the boys. The bullet hit a rock and angled into one of his annoyers, inflicting a skin wound. The boy ran home bawling and the resulting hue and cry was so loud Charley tried to run out of town. He was caught and clapped into the tiny jail.

In the middle of the hoosegow floor was (and still is) a short length of heavy chain attached to an iron ring. Ordinarily a rustler or horse thief made no more than a one night stay and to keep him safe, the ring was put over leg irons which were welded together, usually burning the culprit's leg. In the morning, after a quick "trial," he was taken out and hanged.

SLEEPY MAIN STREET shows gap in center where plaza is situated. Building at left was built of adobe and stone in 1852, was originally saloon, ten years later put to use as Masonic Hall, Lodge No. 98. It is said to be the only such hall where meetings are held on the ground floor.

MEXICAN-STYLE PLAZA is at extreme left, old Pacific Saloon at corner. Of simple adobe construction when erected in 1851, it was rendezvous of large cliques of French miners. Purchased in 1862 by Samuel McClatchy, saloon was "dolled up" by removal of old canopy, addition of brick trim around door. Result was so elegant, miners called it "The Bank." Next is thick walled adobe originally built by Mexicans as general store. Merchandise was piled on sidewalk during day where customers pawed over it. In 1860 Mrs. Marck arrived in town from France, bought building for bakery, sold such unlikely items as French pastry which had wide popularity in area.

For some reason, the Chinaman was allowed the freedom of the cell and late that night when he was craving his pipe, he heard voices outside and cringed against the opposite wall. The white men seemed friendly, chatting with him, telling him it was all a big joke and he would be released in the morning. In the meantime they would put his pipe and some tobacco on the ledge of the small window where he could reach it.

When the voices stopped Charley eagerly stepped up on the edge of the bunk to get at the high window. As he reached, his wrist was gripped and he was dragged closer, a noose slipped around his neck. Then several hands took hold of the rope, yanking him against the stone wall of the jail and letting him fall to the floor. This they kept up long after he was killed. None of the gang was ever punished. "It was good enough for the damn Chinks," was the popular opinion.

In spite of constant persecution, the Chinese for a time constituted a major element in the population of Hornitos. Their collection of hovels constructed of odds and ends was located just north of the original Mexican plaza. It was a fantastic labyrinth of basement opium dens with a ground level roof, stores made of packing cases, and some solid adobes. These latter gradually replaced the more flimsy structures and were built above the first "basement" establishments. Several of these remain today, being the first buildings to greet the visitor as he enters the village. The opium den was fitted up in approved fashion, bunks solidly lining the walls. A small opening near the ceiling allowed some of the stale fumes to escape. Here came not only the Orientals but many a white miner who had become addicted to the poppy.

Hornitos had passed through the original phase, the Mexican occupation with its fiestas, the Chinese influx with attendant racial clashes, and now came a new and more peaceful phase. The quartz gold deposits at Quartzburg so rich at first gave out. The white population moved over into Hornitos where the deposits were still productive. These people demanded a measure of law and order, and from then on, children played safely in the streets again.

CATHOLIC CHURCH in center of old burial ground is maintained in good condition, occasional Masses still observed in venerable structure. Note stone buttresses.

LITTLE STREAM WAS FILLED with miners panning the gravels in earliest days of gold rush. In '50s Chinese coolies were employed by hundreds to build stone walls to contain stock on hillsides at 25 cents a day. Remains of these fences extend for miles around Hornitos.

JACKSON, CALIFORNIA

As a ghost, Jackson is lively. It was never rich in diggings but prospered from the swarm of smaller camps surrounding it and as a stopping place for miners on their way to them. Many of those camps have vanished from the earth, some leave a few visible remnants of gold rush history.

Butte City, with its gaunt stone Ginnochio Store, once operated by a Sr. Bruno, is one. Then there is Bedbug, so called by the first miners there. When the gold supply grew scant and settlers raised cattle, they considered the name too inelegant and substituted Freezeout. A few years went by and this name fell to the more romantic one of Ione, after a lady character in Bulwer-Lytton's "Last Days of Pompeii." This name lived and so did Ione, but Shirttail could not last out, leaving only the name to wonder about. It seems a party of prospectors came upon a lone miner's camp. Considering himself alone in the world, he was standing in the stream sloshing his pan in circles and for convenience in this wet work, he wore only a shirt.

Muletown was a stirring little place in the '50s but only yarns about it remain. In one of these a newly arrived Chinaman picked up a piece of gold weighing thirty-six ounces and was so excited he immediately returned to his homeland. Scottsburg had its historic store—the pioneer proprietor of the general mercantile being killed by eight Chinese for the gold in his safe.

Close to Jackson also are the sites of Hogtown, Suckertown and Helltown. And in Big Bar, another episode in the colorful career of Joaquin Murieta. An enterprising Frenchman in Big Bar offered the bandit a fine suit of chain armor for a thousand dollars. Murieta agreed it was a reasonable price if the steel was bullet proof. He forced the Frenchy to don the suit, fired several shots at it, point blank, and the only damage were a few blue and black marks. Murieta took the suit. It is not known why the bandit bothered to pay for it or where it was that fateful night when he met his death at Panoche Pass.

Not far from the tiny new camp of Drytown (which later would have twenty-six saloons) was a spring of good water where travelers between Sacramento and the southern mines would camp overnight. The water was used strictly for laundry and cooking purposes, judging by the accumulation of bottles around the spring, which caused the Mexican miners to call the spot Botilleas Spring.

A settlement grew up around the locality and the spring camp is now the site of the National Hotel in Jackson. The main part of town is largely made up of the old stone, iron-shuttered buildings but they are so altered as to be almost unrecognizable.

In 1850 the camp had grown considerably and demanded something better for a name than Botilleas Spring. Since Col. Alden Jackson had stopped at the original site longer than some and was credited with founding the town, his name was selected even though the gentleman had long since moved on to found Jacksonville, further south on the Tuolumne River.

By 1851 Jackson considered itself ready to become the county seat. It had almost eliminated the lawless element by stringing up ten men from the huge oak on Main Street and could see no reason for delaying the transfer from Double Springs. To expedite proceedings, the Jackson city fathers invited the dignitaries of Double Springs to a party at the largest local saloon. At the height of festivities, two Jackson men drove to the other town, loaded the county records, lock-stock-and-barrel, on a wagon and brought them back home. Next morning when the cold sober Double Springers found out what had happened it was too late to do anything about it.

Jackson was not able to hold the county seat honor very long however. At the regular election the next year it was found there had been a tremendous increase in the population of nearby Mokelumne Hill and the county seat was moved there—even after it was found the large vote had been accomplished by the industrious populace riding furiously from one polling place to another, casting votes like crazy. Mokelumne Hill held on for a decade then the county seat came back to Jackson.

As placer mining faded in smaller communities around Jackson, several deep quartz veins at the edge of the larger town began to yield a steady return. The Argonaut Mine was among the deepest in the world. Discovered in the '50s, it had a long period of discouragements but by the '70s it was established as a good producer. By 1930 it

HUGE TAILING WHEELS at Kennedy Mine, Jackson Gate near town of Jackson, are unique examples of efforts to dispose of silty refuse. Many mines and mills experienced difficulties removing waste—tailings—which tended to accumulate in stream to detriment of water supply and operations downstream.
Built in 1902, wheels are 68 feet high, raised tailings to vertical height of 48 feet. Each wheel was equipped with 176 buckets, belt drive and electric motor. Tops of elevators were connected to elaborate system of gravity flumes carrying liquid debris over top of nearby hill to dumps. Entire operation was once enclosed in sheet metal buildings. Kennedy Mine in background was one of giants of big hard rock days, reached depth of about a mile, making it one of the deepest gold mines in the U.S. according to California Division of Mines. At bottom of shafts are 150 miles of workings which produced gold, pyrites, quartz, galena, fluorapatite, sphalerite, ankerite, chalcopyrite and other carbonates. Mine has been idle since 1942.

had gone 6,300 feet into the earth and yielded well over $17 million.

A deep, narrow fissure in the rocks through which the creek flows gave the name Jackson Gate to the gulch a mile north of Jackson. Here were several rich mines, one of them operated by a woman and this one commanding a healthy re-spect from her masculine contemporaries. Not fully feminine to begin with, she affected pants and a man's red shirt, was known as Madame Pantaloon. Scorning any help from a mere man, except in a strictly business capacity, she accumulated a hundred thousand dollars from her claim and sold it for twenty more.

223

JAMESTOWN, CALIFORNIA

The gold discovery at Sutter's Mill changed the course of history for the state and in a degree for the entire West. But the "rush" was a walk rather than a headlong plunge. Easterners were slow to hear the tidings and when they first came it was by slow boat around the Horn. But even these got to the Sierra foothills ahead of the ones who came across country by wagon.

So it was the opportunists already on the Coast who got to the gold first and had the choice of the best localities. One of the early birds was Col. George F. James and although his stint at mining was short, his name is bright in the memories of one of the picturesque Mother Lode towns.

When the big story broke Col. James was a resident of San Francisco and he was curious to know how much of the talk was true. He had never liked his staid legal profession and was ready to make a switch to adventure. Rumor said it was impossible to get tools at the diggings so he bought what he thought he would need in San Francisco at "hold up" prices. Sellers of pan, shovel and pick were gouging customers with a flourish and prices of salt pork, dried beef, beans, flour and rice had doubled and tripled. James also laid in a few do-it-yourself remedies such as calomel, "blue pills," quinine and laudanum since doctors were almost unknown in the camps and these few, mostly quacks.

James headed for the hills, first by wagon, then horse and finally on foot. He followed the lead of the discoveries at Wood's Crossing, taking samples in each stream he crossed. In the shadow of Table Mountain, about four miles southwest of where Sonora would soon be established, he decided to camp a while.

"Sonora Road" camps sprang up, "thick as hair on a dog's back—Cloudmans, Chinese Camp, Montezuma, Yorktown, Curtisville, Sullivan's Green Springs, Camp Seco and Hardtack.

The gravels of Wood's Creek were rich and James's camp grew to be christened Jamestown.

OLD EMPORIUM has been doing business as usual since Gay Nineties and remains virtually unchanged. Aged Chinaman ambles down street redolent of the days when his countrymen scrambled over tailings to harvest meager crumbs of gold left by careless white men. Many buildings in today's Jamestown retain vintage charm, although town is not a bonafide "ghost," being one of several links in the Golden Chain along Highway 49 which have stayed active after the wild days.

BRANCH JAIL was used again in World War I days, later as home for owner, then abandoned. Brick of construction is typical but cast stone uncommon in Mother Lode. Several cement plants were operated in later years where limestone lenses offered suitable material as in areas along Calaveras Creek, southeast and southwest of San Andreas. Some deposits are dolomitic with too high a magnesia content for good cement.

CURIOUS SHEEP stops to watch photographer make picture of abandoned gateway to old cabin in back street of Jamestown. Mailbox and ancient grapevine are mute evidence of past human habitation.

Jamestown prospered but James did not. He couldn't get along with the other men, partly because so many of them were rougher than his former law associates and partly because he wanted to be boss and these hardy individuals would not stand still for orders. When James departed the diggings in a rage one day he walked right out of the history of the town he founded.

But the memory of the man lingered on and the miners wanted no more of it, changing the name Jamestown to American Camp. This title lasted long enough for tempers to cool, but back came Jamestown, and more familiarly—Jimtown.

One of the best known workings of the James-town area was begun in 1856 when James App and his party became interested in a promising vein on Quartz Mountain. When the mine began to pay off and App felt he could afford to marry, he chose Leanna Donner for his mate. Leanna was one of the six children who had lost their parents in the tragedy at Donner Pass. She outlived her husband by many years, reaching the age of 95. She died on the old App homestead in 1930.

Jamestown today is not a dead ghost but retains much of the charm of its early roistering days even though there are cars parked along the main street and the old buildings are somewhat disguised by modern signs and electric lights.

ALL'S NOT GOLD THAT GLITTERS

Knight's Ferry, Calif.

Well it was in the paper and they sent a reporter probably and he must have seen it . . . there—see the headline in the San Joaquin *Valley Republican?* "THE GREAT KNIGHT'S FERRY DIAMOND . . . here, I'll read it:

"The story goes that a party of miners were working a claim of sluice and hydraulic pipes at Buena Vista almost exactly opposite from Knight's Ferry. One night about dark a pipeman saw an object which he had washed out of the bank glittering on a pile of dirt and stones, about to be washed through the sluice. It's effulgent gleams lit up all the space in the vicinity, causing much astonishment to hardy workmen.

"The miner picked it up and moved along to show it to his comrades, but accidentally dropped it into the sluice where it was carried down by the current of the water into the mass of dirt and stones known as the tailings. A company of spiritualists from Knight's Ferry is now trying to locate the present locality of the jewel which is reported to be larger than the Koh-I-Noor."

All of which must have shown gold rushing settlers in California that newspapers were not just pulp and ink but human after all. With huge gold nuggets and gleaming yellow seams being uncovered every day since James W. Marshall discovered the first in the Sutter's Mill race January 19, 1848,

there was little headline value in ordinary gold finds. So, in the early 1850s the San Joaquin newspaper asked itself, why not jolt the public with a diamond discovery? Aw, it was all in fun, fellows.

In 1841 William Knight left Indiana with the Workman-Rowland party to become a farmer in California. He settled in the Sacramento Valley at a spot where the Sacramento River offered a natural landing place. Presumably he received a grant to the area, building a rude house on top of an ancient Indian mound termed by the natives "Yodoy." The shelter was of willow poles and reeds, tied with rawhide and plastered with mud. He established a crude ferry here and the location was called Knight's Landing.

On April 26, 1848, three months after Marshall's historic find, a San Francisco newspaper carried a story stating, "There are now about 4,000 white people, besides several hundred Indians, engaged in mining, and from the fact that no capital is required, they are working in companies on equal shares or alone as individuals . . . no other implement is required than an ordinary sheath knife to pick the gold from the rocks."

This decided William Knight to go to the Stanislaus River. It was one of the larger streams fed by Sierra snows and along its reach many early battles between Mexicans and Indians were fought, the war brought to a conclusion by a bloody clash in May of 1826. Leading the defeated natives was

EARLY SKETCH of Knight's Ferry shows suspension-type bridge apparently limited to foot traffic. Further upstream is another, possibly earliest covered bridge.

Chief Estanislao who was educated at Mission San Jose but turned renegade and incited his people to revolt. He lost his cause but his name is remembered in connection with one of the most romantic rivers in California's gold country.

The main road to Sonora, center of the Southern Mines, led from Stockton in the valley and crossed several streams of which the Stanislaus was the most formidable. Knight saw the difficulties the would-be miners were having and thought at once of the opportunity for a ferry. Instead of going on to the gold fields as intended he settled on the bank and put together a rude contraption that just did get the miners and baggage across.

He was able to be of service still further. Gen-

erally called "Dr. Knight" because of some education in Indiana, he built a small shelter for an infirmary and gave simple first aid to prospectors suffering from exposure and hardships. Fees for this may have been negligible but ferry fees mounted to $500 a day at height of traffic.

Yet Knight was not able to enjoy his prosperity very long, dying suddenly on Nov. 9, 1849. New owners improved the ferry and river property, enterprising brothers Lewis and John Dent. They also erected a grist mill on the bank and then joined with others to span the river with a bridge.

It was built in 1854 and a second, some historians saying a duplicate of the first, being still in service, completed in 1862. There is confusion here

VENERABLE COVERED BRIDGE still stands secure, author's heavy pickup camper making several crossings in August of 1967. Question: did U. S. Grant have a hand in designing it? This view is made from ruins of grist mill, water in foreground from Stanislaus River coming through penstocks during flood earlier in year.

GRIST MILL erected by Dave Tulloch in 1862 with Englishman T. Vinson as supervising stone mason, after original was wrecked with first bridge by flooding Stanislaus River. Material is locally cut pink sandstone. Well built, structure was still almost intact in 1940s, has since deteriorated with complete loss of roofs.

as old pictures of the town show a suspension-type bridge. And authorities differ about the engineering aid credited to U. S. Grant. One usually reliable source claims Grant "helped draw plans for the second bridge in 1862" yet there was a Civil War raging at that time which fully occupied the general's attention in East and South.

Grant was at Knight's Ferry in 1854. He left Fort Vancouver Sept. 24, 1853, by lumber vessel for San Francisco on his way to Fort Humboldt, site of the present Eureka. While stationed there Grant made several trips to San Francisco where he could indulge in his hobbies, jousting with bottles and handling horses.

His wife Julia, left behind in the East, while Grant served on the Coast, was a sister of the Dent brothers. Sometime during that 1854 summer Grant made a visit to them at Knight's Ferry, a resident reporting in a diary that the captain was seen on one occasion driving down the street in "a peculiarly jovial mood." In front of his buggy were three horses in single file and behind it three empty buggies. Several other such lively incidents are related with no mention of the bridge or of Grant's reputed aid in planning it.

Whoever the designer, this early span was slung too low to allow for such a flood as occurred in 1862 when it was carried away. With the bridge went the grist mill, receding waters leaving a fringe of sacked flour along the lower banks. It was said the contents were quite usable after an outer crust was removed.

"Something wavering?
It could be your imagination!"

MARIPOSA, CALIFORNIA

The miners wanted to work and the Indians wanted revenge and loot. The latter raided the camps in trails of blood and the miners couldn't leave their families long enough to make pay dirt. So the story Charles Smithers heard until he died at 85 was part of the Mariposa pattern.

He was a baby when his father made a trip on horseback from Mariposa to one of the nearby mining camps. 25-year-old father Smithers completed his errand safely but on the way home his horse skittered and looking back, he saw several Indians following him. Spurring his horse he galloped straight into an ambush and as he tried to ride free, an arrow pierced his thigh, pinning his leg to the saddle. Nauseated by pain and loss of blood, he made it back to Mariposa where he fell from his horse, dragging the arrow through his leg.

Shortly after this bands of natives stationed themselves at strategic points around the town and other camps, levying tribute from all white travelers. James D. Savage, who owned three trading posts, one on the banks of the creek at Mariposa, had spearheaded a movement to rid the area of Indians and they retaliated by looting and burning his stores. Now thoroughly aroused, a large group of American miners and others organized a war party and took out after them. They came upon a large band camped on the North Fork of the San Joaquin, threw burning sticks of wood on their tents and as the Indians ran out, riddled

them with a fusillade of shots. Twenty-four, including the chief, were shot.

While this ended Indian forays temporarily, the governor sent Savage and the Mariposa Battalion into the high Sierra to track down any remaining Indians. One of the last of the scattered bands rounded up was hidden in the mountain valley later known as Yosemite and this ended the Indian episodes of Mariposa. The miners now settled down to work.

The jail at Mariposa, still standing, is built of dressed granite blocks from Mormon Bar, two miles south, mined from an intrusion which is the barrier terminating the Mother Lode on the south. Thus Mariposa becomes the end link in the "Golden Chain" stretching northward along Highway 49. Its history goes back some time before the discovery of gold at Coloma.

The first of several enormous land grants, one that was to effect the current of events for Mariposa, was handed out in 1844 by the Mexican Governor of California, Micheltorena. The recipient was Juan Batista Alvarado who, in August of 1849, sold out to John C. Fremont. This was eighteen months after James Marshall found those yellow flakes in the millrace of his sawmill. The original location of the grant was somewhere at the edge of the San Joaquin Valley but by a convenient and accepted process of the day the grant was "floated" to the Mother Lode country when the value of that area began to boom. This was

229

accomplished merely by shifting the boundaries of the grant, which included 44,000 acres of land.

Mariposa Creek runs between "benches," more or less level, about the width of a city block and narrower. As a natural consequence of the panning and placering the town was laid out along the banks and composed entirely of tents, shacks and a few jerry-built frame buildings. When these got in the way of the creek workings a more substantial town was built on higher, drier ground nearby.

Hard rock mining followed close on the heels of the placering operations in Mariposa Creek, although at first this consisted of little more than scraping off the crumbly, gold-bearing quartz from the tops of the veins and running it through Mexican style arrastres. Kit Carson and two of his companions had found the Mariposa Mine as early as 1849, and by July of that year the production had already outgrown the capacities of the primitive method of crushing. Palmer, Cook and Co. built one of the first stamp mills to handle the ore from the Mariposa Mine and were in full operation by '59.

All this time Fremont was fighting not only these "interlopers" but the owners of the Pine Tree, Josephine and Princeton and many smaller workings. He had no legal recourse under American law until he won his long battle in the courts and was given title to the Las Mariposa grant. He then unceremoniously ousted the erstwhile owners of these mines and reaped the harvest of their investments.

The golden years for the Mariposa Mine were from 1900 to 1915. Total production was estimated at $2,193,205. The shaft did not go straight down but inclined at about 60° and penetrated the lode a distance of 1550 feet. Signs of the mine workings may still be seen a mile south of Mariposa.

SCHLAGETER HOTEL built of brick and wood, has wide wooden balconies. Other old buildings in Mariposa are variously built of granite, soapstone from hills immediately east of town. Soapstone blocks are set in mud mortar on inside wall where weathering is negligible. Other interesting original buildings are Trabuco warehouse, present Bank of America, I.O.O.F. Lodge, Butterfly grocery and the jail.

MASONIC, CALIFORNIA

The bones of Masonic lie bleaching in the sun, huddled in a canyon close to the Nevada border. The elevation is enough to allow a sparse forest of small nut pine trees to clothe the hills above the town, supporting a colony of squirrels.

The animals are the only inhabitants now where once nearly a thousand people cast their lot for a few short years of prosperity.

The town is divided into lower, middle and upper sections, the central one being the oldest and largest. Most of the remaining ruins are here. There are some houses in fairly good repair, but most are ready to collapse and are filled with vines and debris. Here stood an enormous mill, now in ruins. It had received its raw material via an extensive tram system from the mines some distance away. The cars still dangle from the cables, and look ready to move at any time.

Gold was first discovered here in the 1860's and the Jump Up Joe mine soon was operating at the site. "Middle Masonic" grew up around the mill which was built at a more accessible location than the mine itself, accounting for the tram.

After the greatest values were exhausted, about 1901, Warren Loose of Bodie bought the claim. Extensive cyanide operations for more efficient extraction employed some fifty men by 1904.

Operations grew steadily less and less after those big days and at last ceased entirely.

Masonic is not well known to anyone now except sheepherders, who sometimes drive a band of "woolies" through the town, temporarily giving an atmosphere of life and sound.

"MAIN STREET," Masonic, California, was busy thoroughfare at turn of century. Pinon pines sparsely cover hill above town, nuts are bonanza to rodents, now the only residents of once roistering camp.

MASONIC'S TINY POST OFFICE was located in "Middletown" section. Window at right of door slid aside for dispersal of mail to eager, homesick miners. Flimsy little flagpole still stands, wired to building.

UNIQUE COMBINATION houses "convenience," left, chicken house, right. Former was lined with carpet and cardboard to help keep out wintry blasts, was "one holer." Hen house was complete with roosts for six birds, hopefully had nesting boxes for four. Tiny chicken run is at right.

MOKELUMNE HILL, CALIFORNIA

The Oregonians almost didn't make it. The fact that they did was due to the persuasive powers of two members of the party insisting they keep on digging after utter discouragement—and these two were forever blessed. The men were prospecting along the Mokelumne River in October, 1848, the pickings slim, provisions slimmer. Then the rich strike in the river sands and no one wanted to leave. Yet someone had to or they would all starve.

A man named Syrec finally made the break, promising himself to make up for all the wealth he would miss digging, by setting up a trading post. This he did with food, supplies and a tent he brought back from Stockton. He set up for business on a hill near the scene of operations.

The place was called Mokelumne Hill and other kinds of business ventures mushroomed around this first tent store, among them a boarding house, also in a tent. Later structures were more sturdy but in August 1854 fire levelled the camp. Subsequently building was largely of stone and several of these structures have survived.

Mokelumne Hill, during the hectic '50s, "enjoyed" a widespread reputation for wildness based on acts of violence of all sorts. Just south of town is Chili Gulch, scene of the Chilean War fought in December, 1849. This affair started over the prac-

MAYER BUILDING erected in 1854, showing beautifully tooled construction, Mokelumne Hill being blessed with local supply of light brown rhyolite tuff. Interior of one-time saloon is filled with "Trees of Heaven," evidences of Chinese population from several hundred to two thousand. At height of Oriental influx there were three joss houses and a "slave market" where young Chinese girls were put on the block.

tice of some mine owners, a Dr. Concha among them, of taking claims in the names of their peon help. Since claims were so rich they were limited to sixteen square feet, often yielding hundreds of dollars a day, American miners bitterly resented the Chilean method of acquiring extra claims. They passed stringent laws against the practice but Dr. Concha led a party of men into a gulch occupied by Americans who had dispossessed him and drove them out with several fatalities. The diplomatic dispute between the United States and Chile which followed was finally settled in favor of the Americans.

In the town itself, during a period of seventeen weeks, as many men were killed in arguments and fights. Then after a period of comparative calm, five more men met violent deaths one week end.

The French War was about as one-sided as any fracas could be. A group of French miners had made a fine strike on a small hill they called "French Hill" and in a burst of pride raised the Tricolor over their camp. Americans claimed this was an insult to their flag, stormed the hill, drove the Frenchies out and took over their claims.

Many other tales are told about life in Mokelumne Hill. There is a waggish one about a negro who entered the camp and innocently asked help in locating a claim. Jokers sent him to an area repeatedly prospected without success. The negro started to dig dutifully. Nothing was heard of him for several days until he came back to thank his benefactors. His bag was full of gold nuggets. Before he could return to the claim, the whites had swarmed in.

There is the Joaquin Murieta legend without which no Mother Lode town would be complete. A young miner named Jack, flushed with gold and whiskey, was playing poker with his cronies when the popular subject of the Mexican desperado came up. Jumping up on the table Jack loudly proclaimed: "I've got $500 here that says I'll kill the———the first time I come face to face with him!" This was the signal for a Mexican, unnoticed till now, to stand up and say: "I'll take that bet." In one swoop he grabbed the poke Jack was recklessly displaying and made for the door, vanishing in the dust of his horse's hoofs. Murieta, of course, in one of his more playful moments.

While American miners objected violently to the peon system of mining, claiming "slave la-

OLD CEMETERY in Mokelumne Hill is sombre with grove of Italian cypress, macabre effect heightened by flock of vultures wheeling overhead at dusk, seeking roosting places in trees.

bor" they condoned another and more vicious form of slave traffic. During the height of the gold rush and before women flocked to the camps, any female willing to share her bed with a lonely miner was worth hard cash, with few questions asked about color or race.

To fill this demand enterprising ship owners in San Francisco bought Chinese girls from poverty stricken parents in Canton and other Oriental ports, loaded them on ships under indescribably filthy conditions and brought them to San Francisco for distribution to the gold camps. Mokelumne Hill's big Chinatown was one outlet for the girls, sold outright to miners or housed in shacks and "rented out." Later the more aggressive white prostitutes crowded them out. The Oriental waifs returning to San Francisco to supply its burgeoning Chinese colony.

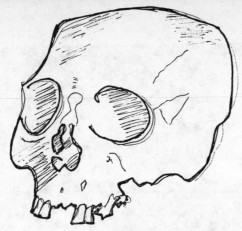

THE LADY FOUND A SKULL

Mormon Bar, Calif.

Mrs. Ellison wanted to plant a garden. "The spot where I wanted to plant my tomatoes," she reported, "was hard and dry. I diverted the spring water to spread over it and let it soak overnight. Next day it was so easy to dig I got carried away and made the planting holes deeper than necessary. At the bottom of one I uncovered a bone that looked human to me. A little more digging uncovered a skull that I was sure was human."

It was but it did not belong to one of the Mormons who in 1849 settled here on the west side of Mariposa Creek, two miles southeast of the old Mariposa gold camp. Mr. and Mrs. Ellison bought property here in recent years and found very little evidence of Mormon occupation. The Saints panned what gold there was in the creek and moved on to richer fields.

The Mormon Bar area is neglected by historians. Technically the spot is not on the quartz seam constituting the Mother Lode proper. The one-time village does not show on maps of the California Division of Mines' book *Geological Guide Book* on the Sierran Gold Belt, these showing the still active town of Mariposa as the southern terminus. Nevertheless the country around and along lower Mariposa Creek was the center of seething activity for a few years.

Just to the west was Buckeye where James Savage had one of his trading posts. A short distance south was Ben Hur and Bootjack lay slightly east. All these shared in the transient prosperity of Mormon Bar. Ranches established here later were fenced by miles of stone walls skilfully erected by Chinese coolies in 1862, each required to put up a rod and a half daily or lose his job. He was paid "six bits" a day, the Chinese contractor receiving $1.75.

Until a few years ago there was a visible Chinese cemetery here. The ruins of several adobe buildings marked the site and still more recently a small frame store, all described in current guides as being viewable relics. They are no longer there. Cemetery occupants were exhumed for shipment to the Orient to be reburied. Grass and brush make the site uniform with the landscape, the adobe ruins gone, the store razed a few years ago.

Intrigued with the skull she found Mrs. Ellison called in Francis A. Riddell, State Park Archeologist from Sacramento. He reported that all evidences indicated a large village once existed here, at least several hundred years before the advent of the whites. Present Mariposa Indians have no knowledge of their predecessors. Exact dates of older occupancy are unknown, no radiocarbon tests having been made. Says Riddell, "I found eight or ten burials and numerous arrowheads during the course of my four days of excavation at the site. More scientific work should be done here."

And Mrs. Ellison has the answer to that. She says many more artifacts than stated were found in her garden, such as beautiful abalone bangles, pottery bowls in good condition. When she objected to giving up these relics for classifying purposes work was abandoned.

SITE of prehistoric Indian village lies at Mormon Bar. Granite outcropping offered conveniently situated **metate**, this multiple version rather unusual. In these holes aborigines ground abundant acorns into coarse flour for food.

ERECTED 1854.

MARIPOSA COUNTY
COURT HOUSE

MARIPOSA COUNTY COURT HOUSE is oldest one still in use in California. Front section, original part, was completed in 1854 at a cost of $12,000. Lumber was whipsawed from trees growing nearby, framework fastened with mortised joints and wooden pegs. Finished lumber was hand-planed, nailed with hand-forged square-cut nails. Fire-proof brick vault for safe keeping of records was added in '61, later enlarged. English-made clock with 267 pound bell was installed 1866, has chimed the hours ever since, musically struck five as picture was being made. Court room was scene of many legal battles, has remained exactly the same, with all original furnishings in place.

236

THE MOTHER LODE

No part of our country has a richer tradition or more fabulous history than a narrow stretch of Sierra Piedmont extending along the western slope from Mariposa to the Yuba River. That rainy day of January, 1848, when James Marshall burst in on John A. Sutter at Sutter's Fort stuttering almost incoherently a tale of his finding gold in the mill-race of Sutter's sawmill at Coloma, meant the end of "the happiest period any country ever knew."

Certainly it spelled the end of Sutter's vast domain, his agricultural empire, depleted of help when almost every man left for the gold fields. This particular incident was perhaps not vital to California as a whole but it signalled the end of a period, of the state's "Golden Age of Innocence." It meant the beginning of another kind of golden age, one which produced some $750 million in actual gold, part of it in chunks weighing as much as 195 pounds.

At first all the yellow metal was found loose in the stream beds, placer gold in the form of dust and small nuggets. When this easily garnered supply dwindled, the Argonauts had to start scratching and in many cases found the veins from which the loose stuff was weathering away. The Mexicans who were working the southern end of the strip called this vein, "La Veta Madre," and so the origin of the term, "Mother Lode," which came to apply more directly to that part of the gold bearing band between Mariposa and El Dorado. There is no geographical division between The Mother Lode, or Southern Mines, and the Northern Mines but an arbitrary line is usually drawn in the neighborhood of El Dorado or Placerville.

The author's treatment of this southern section by no means includes every Gold Rush town but is a generous and typical sampling both of well known ones and others off Highway 49, the main connecting link. The Northern Mines will be similarly covered in another volume and will include Coloma, Georgetown, Colfax, Dutch Flat and others.

MURPHYS, CALIFORNIA

If it is true there are more Murphys in Ireland than people, it could be there were more bandits in Murphys than Murphys. In so many mining camps the name of the first man to find gold was good enough for the camp's name, and it was this way in the case of Murphys, even after the original Murphy was all but forgotten in furor and fooferaw caused by stage robbers Joaquin Murieta and Black Bart.

When news of the gold strike at Coloma reached brothers Daniel and John Murphy, they dropped their hods of bricks as it were and "broke for the mines" with pals Henry Angel and James Carson, arriving in the Sierra foothills in the spring of 1848.

While the Murphy brothers paused to try their luck at the spot where Vallecito would later develop, their companions went on to establish diggings known as Angel's Camp and Carson Hill. This country looked good to the Murphys too and while Henry Angel was still looking for gold, the luck of the Irish brought it to the Murphys in big dollops. Gold-hungry prospectors came to Murphys' Camp and they had time to speak only one name—Murphys.

It is the remains of a town now, full of gold rush atmosphere. Many of the original buildings are standing with little alteration. The town is also full of legends and stories of the roaring '50s, among them accounts of Joaquin Murieta's start upon his notorious career of banditry. The tale may be fanciful but Murieta would not have been the first Mexican unjustly persecuted by the Americans.

Joaquin and his brother were arrested in Murphys, accused of a robbery they had not even heard of. They were tied to a tree (the little jail now standing just below the main street not yet built), a group of American miners dragged Joaquin's wife out in the street and in full sight of the brothers was gang-raped. The brother was then strung up in the tree and while his body still jerked, Joaquin was brutally flogged. With the warning—"Next time you're caught stealing we'll hang you, too!"—he was released and sent packing.

Barely able to sit on his horse yet inflamed with rage, Joaquin Murieta left town to become a professional desperado. Few towns in the gold hills do not have stories of the bandit's visits.

Murphys can also tell you about Black Bart. Proof exists that he at least "slept here", his own signature still on the register in the old hotel, not once but several times—Charles (or C. E.) Bolton, Silver, Montana.

"Black Bart" began his double-dealing career by robbing a stage in 1875, industriously holding up twenty-eight others in the following eight years. He always worked alone and never left a clue, usually completing the deed with the flourish of a piece of verse, such as this masterpiece with its misspelled words:

> I've labored long and hard for bread
>   for honnor and for riches
> But on my corns to long yove tred
> You fine haired sons of bitches

MITCHLER HOTEL. Side entrance shows construction of rough limestone chunks set in lime mortar. Partners John Perry and G. L. Sperry, of flour fame, put up building in 1855. Register contains many names which became great, signatures of Mark Twain, Horatio Alger, Thomas Lipton, Henry Ward Beecher, the Rothchilds, General U. S. Grant, John Jacob Astor and C. E. Bolton, better known as "Black Bart" who stayed several nights while spending daytime robbing stages.

He is not known to have molested old safe, then in hotel office, which held many thousands in gold dust and nuggets. Typical iron doors and shutters of Mother Lode buildings were impassable. Metal also furnished fire protection, although in one case they confined fire so well heat pressure caused building to explode, scattering flaming embers all over the town.

The beginning of his end came on November 3, 1885 near San Andreas when he found the strong box on a stage bolted to the floor. He was wounded while trying to watch the driver and rifle the box at the same time. Although he escaped, he dropped his handkerchief identified with his laundry mark. Wells Fargo detectives found him in his San Francisco apartment where he had been living as a respected Charles Bolton the other part of his life. The trial at San Andreas was speedy, expedited by a plea of guilty. Bolton served several years at San Quentin and was never heard of again.

The skilled engineers among Murphy's miners made real accomplishments in a suspension flume conveying water across Murphy's Creek and a drainage system to dry out the flat where the first claim was located. The main business portion of the camp was consumed by fire August 20, 1859, after which a volunteer fire department was organized. Another picturesque group was the Calaveras Light Guards, started for the purpose of recruiting men for the Civil War.

After the creek beds had given up their supply of gold, the soil-removing and sluicing operations were carried on until forced to stop by law. After that, Murphys tamed down but stayed alive. Although the mines in the area were classed as "never sensational," the camp produced some $20 million.

NEVADA CITY, CALIFORNIA

John J. Kelly was a superstitious Irishman who worked in one of the steeply slanting shafts in the Nevada City mines. Kelly lost his partner in a mining accident and missed him sorely. This day he had been working alone and was now going to check the little wooden storeroom where dynamite and caps were kept. There was a hole in the door and it was Kelly's job to reach in and feel the latch on the inside to see that it was securely fastened.

It so happened one of Kelly's friends was in the powder room where a bucket of water was kept for emergencies, and the water was always cold down in the mine. When he saw the Irishman's hand come groping through the hole, he yielded to the impulse felt by a practical joker, stuck his hand in the cold water and then grasped Kelly's. The Irishman jumped with terror and ran up the shaft in a panic, screaming that the ghost of his dead partner had gripped his hand.

There are ghosts around Nevada City but the town itself is not dead. Its history concerns its place in the Northern Mines and it is full of gold rush color.

The first man to pan for the yellow metal in the area was the same one who first noticed flakes in the race of Sutter's Mill—James W. Marshall. His efforts at Deer Creek were disappointing and he moved on. He would later know that in the next two years there would be a rush of ten thousand miners to the area. Cabins began to go up in Gold Run just above the spot where Marshall dug in September, 1849, the first being that of Capt. John Pennington and his two partners.

A Dr. Caldwell erected a small building for a store on Deer Creek. Then as richer diggings developed seven miles above, he started a store there that became Caldwell's Upper Store, a name applying to the town also. In March, 1850, miners elected a Mr. Stamps to the position of alcalde of Caldwell's Upper Store. He was not one to put up with a name like that and taking his inspiration from the snowy mountains on the horizon, he named the town Nevada or "snowy" in Spanish.

In 1851 the county of Nevada was established with the rapidly growing city as its seat. Ten years later when the State of Nevada was formed, a hue and cry went up from the California city that it had the name first. Government officials said it was too late to do anything about the state's name but the city could add that word to its name. Citizens had to be satisfied with Nevada City.

During the first few months of the town's existence,

strangers along the stream where placering was going on rubbed their eyes in disbelief—a woman was standing knee-deep in the cold water working a rocker right along with the men. The townspeople nodded and went on working. They knew Madame Penn. She worked hard and with some luck got enough gold together to start a boardinghouse, the first in Nevada City. The Union Hotel now stands on the site.

Swarms of hopeful prospectors and miners were pouring in at a record rate with all the excitement of the first placer gold, the loose stuff that could be scooped up from the creek bottoms. But this came to an end and as the old claims were exhausted and new ones impossible to find, the hard rock mining not yet started, some avid miners actually began to dig up the streets in search of gold—and found it.

One merchant, angered at the shambles in front of his store, protested to the man with the shovel: "See here—you can't dig up a public street like this!" The miner maintained he could, that there was no law that said he couldn't. The enraged storekeeper drew his gun to emphasize his words. "Very well, then—I'll make one. You git!" The miner moved operations to the next street.

A short distance from the town on Lost Hill a fantastically rich placering area was discovered. Several miners took out a quart of gold in a single day, worth $6,000. The dry gravels were covered by an overburden of soil and tunnels were necessary to get

DUMP WAGONS OF THIS TYPE were used throughout Sierra gold belt. Tree in background is also characteristic of country, though confined to medium altitudes. Called Digger Pine after native Indians, it does not penetrate loftier mining areas such as Sierra City, where it is replaced by Sequoia and other conifers. Digger Pine is distinctive, having lax, grayish needles and divided trunk. Picture taken in early March shows "candles," new growth starting at ends of branches.

at the gold-bearing material. The area became a maize of burrows and the resulting town was named Coyoteville. When it was swallowed up by the expanding Nevada City, the gravels were exhausted, but during the mad two-year rush a total of $8 million was removed.

One of the last good discoveries in the creek banks was made in the summer of 1859. John Burns, a resident of Nevada City, was walking along a ditch near Deer Creek and in crossing it, slipped on a wet plank and fell in the water. He floundered around and grabbed at the bank, dislodging a piece of decomposed quartz and exposing a yellow gleam. Burns clambered out and went home to change clothes, not because of discomfort but to attract no attention. He took a sack and shovel back to the ditch band and "cleaned out," the yield $2,000. The ditch company took over the new diggings the next day but Burns was happy to have enough nuggets for a string of wild days and nights.

Fourth of July celebrations were big days in mining camps. Two weeks before the holiday, about

NEVADA CITY IS UNIQUE in many ways, repays leisurely stroll on foot. Streets seem to have no set plan, original wandering burro trails may have influenced survey. Steep hills complicate pattern, narrow streets twist and turn unexpectedly; every angle offers architectural surprises like this "conservatory" linking hotel and annex. One house plant visible is Aspidistra, "Cast-Iron Plant" of Victorian times. Not popular or well-known these days, specimen could well have descended from lusty mining days when hotel was built.

1850, Nevada City was delighted to hear there would be a big fight between a jackass and a grizzly bear at nearby Grass Valley. The bear was billed as the most Ferocious Grizzly ever to be trapped in the Sierra, the donkey as The Champion Kicker of California, having killed a mountain lion in Hangtown and a bull in Sonora. On the morning of the festive day some two thousand miners went noisily by horse and foot to the "ring" of brush and stakes in Centerville, just north of Grass Valley.

Considerable dust was being stirred up along the way so a man carried a bottle of something to keep it wet and by the time the crowd arrived it was in a mood for anything. Every man paid his two dollars and pushed inside the stockade. There was the jackass, sure enough, nibbling at the grass at one side and there was the savage bear in a big wooden box. . . . "Don't get too close, gents!"

Then the play was ready to start and at a signal the gate was raised. The bear moved out slowly, a small brown one, timidly sniffing as if reluctant to leave the familiar shelter. A man forced him all the way out with a pole and when he saw the jackass, he ambled playfully toward it. When was the savage rush coming? The spectators waited anxiously.

Now the bear swung its head, obviously wanting to make friends. But the donkey was having none of that. He rolled his eyes, laid his ears back and when the bear got within range, two sharp hooves caught him in the ribs. Fully disenchanted, the bear slunk back and bounded over the barrier, disappearing into the chaparral. While the victor resumed his grazing nonchalantly, a thousand men set up a roar and if the promoters could have been found there might have been a lynching. A few had foreseen the outcome and were long gone for another bottle.

Something had to be done to relieve the tension so the miners who still wanted action took charge of the long-eared animal and led him at the head of a long, disgruntled procession toward, but not directly to, Nevada City. There were a lot of saloons along the way and the new hero would be welcome in all of them. None was passed up and in each he was toasted lavishly. By the time all got to Nevada City, there was only one of the crowd who could walk straight— the jackass.

The advent of quartz mining meant that Nevada City had come of age but with some placers still producing and only a few hard rock operations beginning, the transition was gradual and the camp did not suffer the setback experienced in other gold camps, notably Jackson, another Mother Lode town developing in a similar way.

In June of 1859 news came to the gold country which further depleted population and made an impact on Nevada City. The Nevada City *Transcript* of July 1 carried this item:

"J. T. Stone, formerly of Alpha but now living on Truckee Meadows, has just arrived here and reports the discovery of a vein of ore of extraordinary richness at the head of Six Mile Canyon near Washoe Valley. The vein is four feet wide and is traced a distance of three and a half miles. The ore is decomposed and works easily. It is like that from which silver is sometimes obtained. The discovery was made by a miner working in Six Mile Canyon, who found as his worked his claim, that it became richer as he approached the vein. The news has caused great excitement here."

Then the golden trumpet sounded again—far to the north. The clarion call spelled out "Cariboo" and away went the gold hungry drifters again, while the California camps were left to more decay. But Jackson and Nevada City stood out as examples of having something solid to fall back on when the bubble of loose placer gold broke.

Gold was still coming out of shafts penetrating far down into slide rock veins extending in quartz seams thousands of feet and producing if big companies were at hand to finance. Gone was the day when the individual prospector, equipped with only a pan and shovel, could stand in a stream and slosh riches in glittering gold out of the dripping gravel.

Nevada City, having successfully weathered the adjustment period, was displaying handsomely ornate mansions along Nevada and Prospect Streets, and by 1892 these homes gained further eminence with electric lights. The tiny power plant supplying this new-fangled convenience was the nucleus of the giant Pacific Gas and Electric Company.

French nurseryman, Felix Gillet, started his business in the town, perhaps the first of its kind in the west. He was responsible for the beginning of California's huge English walnut production, introducing these and other nut trees.

Nevada City is a living monument to a fantastic era long gone. If it is not in itself a ghost, it is full of the wraiths of lusty, bearded miners and of sharpies who took their gold the easy way.

FIREHOUSE BUILT OF NATIVE granite and brick about 1851 was at first simple structure, Victorian-type balcony and gingerbread added later. It is likely most beautiful of many buildings remaining from heyday. Traditional iron doors and shutters are frequently encountered, one office building, "modernized" presents shock to history-minded observer; upper floor has several windows complete with ancient iron shutters, brilliantly painted chartreuse, alternated with purple.

NORTH SAN JUAN, CALIFORNIA

The long belt of gold rush towns stretching along the western foothills of the Sierra Nevada begins with Mariposa on the south and ends in a scattered cluster of high-perched camps in Sierra County to the north. The span includes many different geological formations, all having one important feature in common—the outcropping of gold. The belt is cut in two about the middle in the vicinity of El Dorado and Coloma, the southern section usually designated as "The Mother Lode," the northern, "Northern Mines."

Mother Lode towns were often settled by Mexicans, sometimes founded or named by them, as Hornitos and Sonora. Most of the camps farther north were settled or christened by Yankees and this includes North San Juan with its obvious Mexican name.

A German miner, Christian Kientz, did the naming. He had been with General Scott's army in Mexico and was deeply impressed with that country's geography, particularly by the hill on which sat the old Mexican prison of San Juan de Ulloa. When he saw the California gold area hill just north of a bunch of shacks beginning to be a town, he called it San Juan Hill and the town also took the name. By 1857 the place needed a post office, the authorities pointing out a much older town with the name San Juan already existing in San Benito County. They solved

OFFICE BUILDING, BUILT IN 1859 contained headquarters for numerous firms operating hydraulic mines, main source of income for North San Juan after placers were exhausted. When Sawyer Act became law and washing away of mountainsides ceased, prosperity of town ended, offices were emptied. Lower floor — originally large clothing store—was given over to succession of enterprises, in later years garage occupied quarters. At last, building was sold for valuable brick it contained and scaffolding was erected preparatory to wrecking historic structure. Mrs. Amelia Cunningham, long-time resident of North San Juan was outraged, bought structure, saving it from wreckers. However, Mrs. Cunningham died before starting renovation, estate is still in litigation, fate of building hangs in balance. Many hope State will take over, make Park of old town which contains so many relics of California's Gold Rush days.

the problem by simply attaching a "North" before the name.

The famous "Deadman's Claim" also had odd naming history. In January of 1853 two young men, West and Chadbourne, discovered a rich deposit in San Juan Hill. To get a sufficiently steep pitch to carry off tailings from the diggings, they were forced to make a deep cut. They were working at it when the whole bank caved in, burying both under tons of rock and dirt. Since there were no other claims near, and the boys were known for minding their own business and not fraternizing with other miners, they were not missed for several days.

When they were, it took several shifts of men to uncover the bodies. Both West and Chadbourne were found to have brothers, who were located and informed they owned a claim at North San Juan. Neither, it seems, was interested in mining, both selling out to Louis Buhring and Peter Lassen who paid $300 for the legal right to mine the spot.

The new owners had trouble with the water supply which either flooded out the equipment or disappeared and they barely made expenses, selling shares now and then to survive. Then a fluming company brought in a steady supply of water and fortunes changed drastically for the owners, now increased to seven. During the sixteen months ending in December of 1858, they took out a total of $156,000. The men continued to mine the claim by removing and washing the alluvial soil until in '60 nothing remained but bare bedrock.

What was probably the first "gold brick" swindle was perpetrated by a slicker posing as a lucky miner returned to the east from the North San Juan gold area. He announced to the New York assay office he had found a nugget of solid gold weighing 193 pounds Troy, and requested an assay. As he desired to display the chunk, he did not wish to mar its appearance and would samples please be removed at the places he indicated so they wouldn't show. Why, certainly. The assayed samples proved to be of the usual "fineness" of typical California gold.

Then the miner announced he was in a terrible predicament. He had a wonderful offer from a London firm for rights to display the nugget there. Yet he was tempted to cash in more directly by sending it to the Philadelphia mint but, in the meantime, he had to live. Could he have a loan, leaving the fabulous chunk of gold as security? Why, sure thing. The assay office advanced, the nuggeteer retreated. After what seemed a reasonable wait, the assayers dug more deeply into the glittering blob of treasure. Under a coating of gold there was a nice fat wad of lead.

MANY BEAUTIFUL EXAMPLES OF OLDTIME ART of marble sculpture exist in cemetery of North San Juan, most dating from about 1855. During period floral offerings now called "sprays" were made as flat bouquets in style shown on stone. Represented are lilies of the valley, callas, forget-me-nots, roses, morning-glories, lilies, tulips. Roses are "cabbage" type of that period, not high centered hybrid teas of today.

HUGE NOZZLE, CALLED MONITOR spewed streams of water at terrific pressures against hillsides, washing away tons of soil, resulting gold-laden mud to be diverted into sluices where heavier gold lodged against slates or "riffles" at bottom. Several millions in gold are said to remain in hills around North San Juan, hydraulicking being outlawed.

RANDSBURG, CALIFORNIA

Frederick Mooers was a newspaper man but he would never have been able to put the fire and excitement into a paragraph that he did in his eyes when he saw the particles of gold. "Boys!" he yelled to his two partners. "We've struck it! There's no need to look any farther."

This was the gold that started the Rand mine, that gave the name Rand to the mountains and town — "The fastest growing town in the west" — and there was much romance and human interest in the finding of it . . . unless you count the long days under the merciless sun, the desperate search for water with eyes almost glazed shut and the hunger for a kind word remembered from a boyhood in the shade back home.

The men responsible for Randsburg were three who had worked the scattered, played-out gulches around the fringes of the Mojave and had about given up ever making any big money. One was John Singleton, carpenter turned miner, who had gained much experience in the placers and hard rock mines but now was broke and discouraged. One was Frederick Mooers, clever newspaper writer but completely unfit to make a living, let alone a fortune. The third was Charles Austin Burcham, whose chief distinction was having a doctor for a wife. The total assets of the three were a team and wagon, bought with money Dr. Rose La Monte Burcham had earned delivering babies in San Bernardino.

JOSHUA TREES seem to form grotesque Conga line, posturing their way along sandy road in Red Rock Canyon. Several gold strikes brought series of rushes to gulches, leading into brilliant, eroded canyon. During one in 1893, prospector found $150 in four days, celebrated and returned with partner to take out $260 more. Tiny creek dried up and so did his hopes. Others, working on larger scale, did not depend on erratic stream flow, built "dry washers" operating on air blower principle. When all available gold was extracted prospectors left, to return when mountain storms formed Gully Washers in canyons. New beds of gold exposed, cycle started all over again.

Disgusted at finding no paying lode in Summit Gulch in 1895 — where Mooers and William Langdon had found some color earlier — the trio departed in the lumber wagon, heading for the hills where they spent a month until time and money ran short, as Burcham was nearing the end of a two-year limit imposed by his wife.

One night in April they made camp in a dry canyon not far from the Twenty Mule Team road between Death Valley and Mojave. The disheartened Mooers kicked his heels up the wash for fuel and gathered some greasewood stems when his eye caught a glint of yellow in a nearby ledge. Gasping, he dropped the brush and ran back for his pick. The first chunk of rock chipped off showed particles of gold all over it. "Boys!" he yelled, "we've struck it! There's no need to look any farther."

And for once the newspaper man made headlines with resounding effect. The three men secured eight claims and hired an expert quartz mining man to examine the ground, swearing him to secrecy. "You've got a good thing here," he reported. "Get a 100-stamp mill, shovel the whole mountain into it and your fortunes are made. The whole hill is good ore." Then he promptly broke the secret.

The news reached O. B. Stanton in Bakersfield who came running with cash. He liked what he saw and offered to spend $10,000 to get the mine started, erect a stamp mill etc., in return for one half interest. The agreement had the signatures of Mooers and Singleton but not Burcham. He was in Bakersfield giving his wife the good news and signing over to her half of his share, as agreed when she grubstaked him. "Now," Dr. Rose warned him, "don't you dare sign anything when you get back to the mine, at least until we know more about its value." Back at the mine Burcham was handed the document which he refused to sign. The deal fell through but the contract bearing the other two names would later be vital in endless and costly litigation.

Now here came the forthright doctor. In July she took charge of the mine situation while for the next several months the three men dug ore and crushed it by hand using a little water hauled from Cow Wells or Goler. Dr. Rose did the housekeeping and with blind faith of psychic assurance kept books while looking around for some way to finance and expand operations.

The partners got out enough ore to make two shipments to distant smelters in Montana. The rich ore was pulled down the mountain on sleds, transferred to wagons for hauling to Mojave and reloaded on flatcars. When the assay report came there was great rejoicing in camp and the four laid plans to begin mining on a larger scale.

SIDES OF RED ROCK CANYON are spectacularly eroded, giving effect of miniature Bryce. Harder rhyolite and sandstone of bright salmon-pink to red are moulded into fantastic forms, alternating with softer snowy-white clay in fluted columns. Canyon floor is composed of clean sand from walls, supports desert garden of cacti, "desert holly", greasewood, other shrubby growths, mostly prickly. One ampitheater-like area is filled with worshippers each Easter Sunday as first rays of sun enter gorge.

Meanwhile other mines were established — the Gold Coin, Napoleon, Bully Boy, Monkey Wrench, Wedge, Olympus, Trilby and King Solomon. One Swede miner called his claim The Big Norse. Si Drouillard found the rich St. Elmo, five miles from the original Rand, and this set off the big rush to Randsburg. Hopefuls from Los Angeles came as far as Mojave by train, boarding stages for Red Rock Canyon and Cow Wells where extra horses were hitched on for the steep stretch to Randsburg.

Every stage carried mail and a mixed assortment of humanity — miners, prospectors, legitimate business men who expected to open stores, as well as outcasts and riffraff from coast and eastern cities. Enough prostitutes, gamblers, pimps came along to populate a full-blown red light district, but gay and rowdy Randsburg never got a reputation for great violence. There were few killings as compared to those in other camps.

By 1897, Mooers, Singleton and Burcham had received something like $250,000 in payment for ore

RANDSBURG was built on whatever contour ground offered, one end of town much higher than the other. Main thorough-fare makes sharp hairpin curve into and out of town, following available levels. One comparatively level stretch, called Butte Street, intersected central business section. Building shown was famous Rinaldi's Market serving townspeople with meat and groceries over most of town's life.

DURING LUSTY DAYS, Randsburg's brothels were scattered among more reputable businesses, French Marguerite's exclusive bordello being immediately below Rinaldi's. Mothers, living still farther down gulch, forced to bring children past open doors often occupied by painted hussies, protested to civic authorities demanding that bawdy houses be segregated.

and their scraping days were over. Eventually revenues would amount to some $25 million from Randsburg mines. Legal disputes harassed the Rand mine, now called the Yellow Aster, some of them initiated by Mooers' former partner, William Langdon. He lost his case as did others who attacked the validity of the three partners' claims.

It was during this period that Daniel Kelsey struck it rich. A mule team driver, hauling borax for Coleman and Smith from the Harmony Works near Furnace Creek in Death Valley to Mojave, he quit the job because, as he said: "I just couldn't stand seeing those ornery critters go so long without water."

He made one trip with his own team, hauling lumber to the raw mining camp of Randsburg, stood enthralled in the midst of a thousand tents and a few board-and-canvas shacks, then bought some prospectors' tools and supplies. After a few weeks of fruitless picking and panning, he found some float in Yuma Canyon and tracked the ledge to its source. He chipped off a piece, showed it to a friend who invested $20,000 as a partner. The ledge started the famous Blue Daisy mine, which when sold for $170,000, sent the Dan Kelsey family on a grand tour of Europe.

Also during this period Pat Reddy finally gained what he had been refused in Randsburg's earlier days. Reddy was an attorney of sorts, self-educated and keen. He had never been admitted to the bar but made a reputation in the loosely conducted

courts of Nevada in the hectic '60s. In one scuffle at Aurora, he was wounded and eventually lost an arm. Reddy became state senator and then swung through the big mining camps where he fitted his talents into legal squabbles.

In Randsburg he approached the two-fisted Dr. Rose Burcham. "I tell you folks could do with a little cash to start things going," he said. "I'd be glad to advance say a few thousand dollars. Instead of repayment in cash, you can settle with me for a share of your mine." But Dr. B. was not about to see her project divided by even the smallest fraction no matter how much she needed money and no amount of pleading by Pat Reddy moved her. So smarting under the rebuff, he caught the next stage for Mojave.

When he later heard of the Yellow Aster's legal struggles, he hurried back and offered help. This time he found a desperate situation and his offer was accepted for a share of the mine. One phase of the case was won and Reddy's share eventually paid him enough to live on comfortably the rest of his life.

Over the years almost half the world's known minerals were found in the Rand and neighboring mountains. During the first years, if these were noticed at all, they were cast aside as worthless. Gold was all that mattered. But even the Rand's gold supply was not inexhaustible. When it thinned out and Randsburg's miners were scraping the bottom of the barrel, they found they had been overlooking real money in tungsten. In 1895 rich deposits of this element of the chromium family were found five miles from Randsburg, close enough to infuse new life into the fading camp, although the town of Atolia grew up on the immediate site, the name derived from the two men involved in early development, Atkins and De Golia.

With the World War demand for tungsten, excitement ran riot in the gulches, the metal being found mostly in placer deposits. This frantic activity produced in all $65 million worth. Men working in mines were searched and their lunchboxes examined at the portals, and as contraband ore continued to flow, miners were forced to change clothes after work. A shopping bag quickly filled with the ore, scheelite, would bring $350.

Then came the end of the war and almost complete collapse of the tungsten market. With gold mining tapered off at the Randsburg mines, the area went into another slump. The Yellow Aster was in the doldrums and by this time all three of the original partners were dead. Dr. Burcham still held her shares and Mooers' son Edwin retained a part, but law suits, strikes and other labor troubles had brought the famous old mine to a virtual standstill. One strike lasted sixteen years, brought to an end in 1918. With only a skeleton crew of three still employed there, much of the population of the once roistering, booming town had evaporated.

Then in 1919 came the discovery that a ridge of rock running down the slope of nearby Red Mountain was almost solid horn silver. Every former resident of Randsburg who could return to the dead town did so and again it served as in the tungsten boom. Two small centers sprang up close to the Big Silver, Osdick and Hampton, which were soon consolidated and ten years later given the formal post office name of Red Mountain. When the silver boom swelled to over $14 million in 1926, it showed signs of coming to an end. The mine was sold for $50,000 that year, the new owners doing nothing spectacular with it.

The Second World War made no stirring demand for tungsten and gold mining has made no comeback. Once again Randsburg has settled back on a comparative ghost town status. The inevitable tavern still operates, a desert museum is open on weekends displaying many of an almost endless variety of minerals and crystal specimens found in the surrounding hills. It is said of most dormant gold and silver mining towns that only a rise in prices of the metals would bring revival. In the case of Randsburg it would seem possible that one of the many minerals found hereabout and heretofore neglected, might suddenly become indispensable, causing history to repeat itself.

JOHANNESBURG, popularly Joburg, was less glamorous neighbor of Randsburg, contains few reminders of early days. It is busier today, being on highway, filled mostly with shanties and mobile homes. First houses were all frame, were destroyed by repeated fires. Later they were of adobe or as here, as scraps of tin or sheet iron — fireproof if not picturesque. Most prominent structure was 10-stamp mill, dominating town. One large hotel, boxy wooden structure, had about thirty-five rooms, was center of gay social events. Joburg also boasted several stores and saloons but no church, religious services sometimes held in school house.

ROUGH AND READY, CALIFORNIA

The "Great Republic of Rough and Ready" it was to be called. It was only a small mining camp and only a year old in 1850, but people in other towns had to admit the brash camp had ideas of its own and the courage of non-conformity. The scheme? To secede from the Territory of California and the United States, and to declare itself an independent country. The hard-working miners had a point. They had

laws, the mining laws they had worked out and which they figured were good enough to live by. Most of them had left Wisconsin to escape onerous restrictions and now with applications of U.S. laws about to be put into effect through territorial legislation, they were hot under the collar. They could expect all manner of irksome restraints now and, worst of all, they would be taxed the same as back home even though the basis

ROUGH AND READY IS FULL of romantic tales of heyday. Story of secession is well authenticated, less solid is story of Caroline, daughter of "slavegirl" who lived on this site. Caroline loved to ride, on one occasion came up to doorstep on favorite pony, dismounted and with flourish stuck whip into ground. Whip, cut previously from cottonwood tree took root, grew to be venerable giant, was blown down few years ago and part cut away. Caroline, growing up, went to San Francisco to go into "business" on her own. She caught sleeve on fire over lamp chimney while curling hair, rushed out to well for water, in her haste fell in, was drowned. Crumbling remains of W. H. Flippin blacksmith shop show in background.

would be different. They would even have to pay to operate their own claims, their very own by legal staking under miners' law.

Seething with the thoughts of these injustices, tempers suddenly exploded when a spark was unintentionally applied by a smart aleck from Boston. One of the original miners from Wisconsin was sweating at his claim and getting little gold, about ready to quit and "maybe chuck the whole shootin' match, maybe" when he looked up to see a dude watching him intently. On impulse the miner asked: "Say, Mister, how'd you like to buy this claim for three thousand dollars?"

The man in the city clothes shrugged his shoulders, took a step forward and made a counter offer. Nobody could be expected to buy a pig in a poke so he would work the claim all the next day to see how rich it was. Everything he dug over $200 the owner could have. Anything less would belong to him. Then at the end of the day they would decide. An agreement was reached.

The Boston man appeared the next morning still dressed fit to kill but with a helper who was ready to work for a promised $8. No sooner had he begun to fling the shovel at the rock when pay dirt showed up and before the day was over he had brought up $180 in gold. The helper was paid and left. The owner of the claim protested this thing wasn't fair, that he had never found more than a bare wage in a day and he should have a share in this find. The eastern man said no, the contract agreed upon was legal according to U.S. laws and there would be no reneging now. He intended to keep his clear profit— $172.

This reasoning pleased no one in Rough and Ready. Almost every miner sided with the claim owner and got hotter and hotter about it until an indignation meeting was held. Discussion dried men's throats and they repaired to the saloon, the Bostonian conspicuous by his absence. The original group expanded to include almost every adult male in the camp and not only was this most recent grievance hashed over but every other one as well.

When the issue of an impending tax on mines and

ROUGH AND READY SCHOOL, built around turn of century replaced original which was destroyed by fire. Now abandoned because of lack of pupils, it has been put to use as "Trading Post." Identification of little "tails" strung on line baffled curious photographer, even on close examination.

DOUBLE DAFFODIL OF TYPE
popular in early days, probably
Von Zion, still blooms in grass
where house used to stand.

miners was brought up, the crowd exploded. One miner, E. F. Brundage, by way of being a leading citizen because of his ready and sonorous voice, loudly proclaimed—"We've had enough!" Everybody agreed, but what to do about it? Some were for appointing Brundage a committee of one to look into ways and means of combating the oppressive rulings and report a week later, same time, same place. But Brundage already had a solution which he proclaimed with a bullish roar—"Secede!"

After a brief, shocked silence followed by loud cheers, the resolution was passed unanimously and after a long pause for a few shots of Rough and Ready dust layer, a manifesto was drawn up. Climbing on a table, Brundage read the document which set forth a few complaints and ended with the resolution: "We, the people of Rough and Ready . . . deem it necessary and prudent to withdraw from the Territory of California and from the United States of America to form peacefully if we can, forcibly if we must, the Great Republic of Rough and Ready." With loud huzzas the resolution was passed unanimously, Brundage was elected president and all had another round of drinks. A constitution of twelve articles was drawn up and likewise approved.

The new government went into immediate action. Delegates were dispatched to the hotel room of the man from Boston. There was something about the pointed guns of the group that caused him to wilt and hand over the $172. Given five minutes to pack, he was prodded down the stairs, escorted to the edge of town and booted into the Territory of California.

The Republic waited expectantly for some reaction from Washington. Would it be disciplinary after suitable confabs? Would a regiment of soldiers make camp outside the boundaries of Rough and Ready, making plans to attack at dawn? The rebels organized a group of Vigilantes and felt prepared for any emergency—but nothing happened. It felt somewhat miffed at the complete silence, the insulting aloofness of the government—no recognition, no invasion. But gradually the miners settled down to their mundane labors, unhampered by United States law under Territorial jurisdiction.

Spring came and went. The month of June began to brown the green carpet of grass on the rolling hills. Thoughts began to form as to celebrating the Fourth of July in a proper way. Several miners, with others from Timbuctoo, discussed possibilities. Then while plans were sprouting, an appalling realization crashed down on the heads of all. The camp was no longer a part of the United States! Independence Day for it was no longer the Fourth of July. If there were to be a celebration, on what day would it be?

This was a quandary of cataclysmic proportions. No mining camp could hold up its head without a

251

proper Independence Day blow-off. Something had to be done even if it meant restoring the new Republic to the United States. More meetings. More discussion. More whistle wetting. Then decision. Without asking if they might, the people of Rough and Ready voted it back into the Union. With this obstacle out of the way, plans were made for the dad-blamedest lid-lifting Fourth ever held in California.

Putting plans into effect was another thing. When they were going full tilt, on June 28, along came a disastrous fire, sweeping almost everything in town before it. Citizens did what they could with a Fourth of July parade down the little main street now bor-

dered by charred shells of once proud false-fronted businesses.

Rough and Ready was one of the first camps established in Nevada County. A party of men calling themselves the Rough and Ready Company arrived in the area September 9, 1949 under the leadership of a Captain Townsend. He had served under Colonel Zachary (Old Rough and Ready) Taylor, hero of the Mexican War. The men kept their gold discoveries secret for some time, getting out quite a bit of it before the tide of settlers and miners flooded in to make a town of a thousand by early spring, 1850.

A double row of buildings quickly formed, begin-

W. H. FLIPPIN BLACKSMITH SHOP is one of few remaining original buildings of Rough and Ready. At time of taking picture, venerable relic showed strong signs of imminent collapse. Peeks through cracks in walls revealed full complement of blacksmith's implements, forge and all.

ning at the foot of a transverse, oak-covered ridge. About twenty of them lined the camp's one street which had a crook in the middle to conform to the contour. At the end, and considerably elevated, stood an imposing church, complete with steeple and broad flight of steps. As was the custom, this elevation was dubbed "Piety Hill." If any of the founding party which had only "temporarily camped" on the spot ever thought of continuing on to Sacramento, he must long ago have forgotten it for the population remained stable for a number of years.

A Christian Association was organized during the first days holding meetings in one of the little clapboard shanties on the main street. Other religious organizations developed, generally of orthodox nature.

One "church" was headed by a "hell roaring" preacher, James Dinleavy, whose demands were greater than the satisfaction of soul saving and ran a popular and lucrative saloon on weekdays. As soon as he got together enough money, he sent for his wife who waited in San Francisco. Mrs. Dinleavy was the first woman to arrive in camp and excitement stirred the crowd into meeting her at the stage and deluging her with gifts including 21 ounces of gold dust.

The town continued to grow until about 1870. At its best period there were more than three hundred substantial houses, in spite of two crippling fires in '56 and '59. As placer deposits faded, so did Rough and Ready, and little is left of it today except the preposterous legend of secession.

PART OF OLD ROUGH AND READY HOTEL is incorporated in present conglomeration used as post office.

SAWMILL FLATS, CALIFORNIA

Three miles southeast of Columbia, a mile and a half south of Yankee Hill, is a clearing in a once dense forest. The nearly level area is on the banks of Wood's Creek, the same stream that figured so prominently in the histories of Sonora and a dozen other gold camps. Gold however did not bring the swarms of people there in the early 1850s. Here in the center of a bountiful supply of standing timber were established two large sawmills. Lumber was a scarce commodity in the early gold rush days and it brought a good price, creating a boom camp at Sawmill Flat.

At first not many Americans were willing to work in the mills, too many were eager to pan for gold or work for someone who had built a series of Long Toms or was sluicing the beds of the stream. There was always a possibility of pocketing good nuggets while guaranteed a daily wage of $2.50 a day. The first employees at the mills were almost all Peruvians and Mexicans. Being clannish, both races had established "segregated" saloons and stores, nearly every facility in town being duplicated. A population of over a thousand had grown up around the mills when an exciting event was noised around in spite of every effort to suppress it. Only a short distance north of the center of town a good strike of gold had been made.

Yet disappointment was due those who rushed up the creek to stake claims—disappointment and astonishment. The claims were already staked out —and by whom? By no one less than a strikingly beautiful Mexican woman! Her name was Dona Josepha Elisa Martinez and to discourage any too-ardent fortune hunters, she had brought from Mexico a motley crowd of peons, ready to defend their lady boss. The senora was already wealthy and the gravels of Wood's Creek and several shallow surface workings swelled her coffers earlier filled with gems and fancy clothes.

But being wealthy was not enough for the Dona Martinez. She was lonely. So it was opportune that a handsome young Mexican with curly black hair and luxuriant mustache called on her and introduced himself as Joaquin Murieta. He said he was a monte dealer who had fallen into some trouble and would she hide him for a while? Hide him she did and since that all happened before Murieta became notorious, his face familiar to many a victim of robbery and hold-up, he vanished completely from the posse on his trail.

Once he felt safe, he again took the bandit route and soon returned to hide with the lovely senora. This time she was able to conceal him only a short while. His hideout, the first of many to become known, was precarious. Murieta left hurriedly by the back door one night and Josepha Elisa, in her camp now called Martinez, as well as the populace of Sawmill Flats, knew him no more.

In 1857 a disastrous fire almost leveled nearby Columbia, the best customer of the mills. It was the worst but not the first of the fires that destroyed most of the flimsy buildings of the boom town. Columbia ruefully surveyed its ashes and decided that this time rebuilding would be done with brick. This was the death knell for Sawmill Flat and it gently folded. The rich deposits of gold at neighboring Martinez were soon scratched off and that collection of shanties also died, the senora returned to Mexico with her loot and without her swarthy bandit. The camp of Martinez vanished almost from sight and only a few shacks and cabins remained to mark the site of Sawmill Flats.

ONE OF FEW REMAINING CABINS at Sawmill Flats near collapse, with stone foundation and walls probably built of scraps from the sawmills. Ancient grapevine arches over south wall, leaves all but covering structure in summer. Buildings at site were all flimsy, show no sign of stone, adobe or brick walls. This wooden one has survived because high stone foundation kept rot from beams.

SHASTA, CALIFORNIA

Dick Barter might have lived out his life as an honest citizen but the cards were stacked against him. He arrived in California from Canada just too late to share in the first big bonanzas of the Sierra gold rush. His claim was on Rattlesnake Bar, near Auburn, and when he got there with a sister and cousin he found the gravels already depleted. Discouraged, his relatives went north to settle on a homestead at Sweet Home, Oregon.

But Dick stayed on, persistently working his claim. Never admitting its thin yield, he bragged about it so noisily in the Auburn saloons he was soon called "Rattlesnake Dick". If the nickname didn't force him into crime it at least made the rumors about his shady conduct easy to believe.

The first of these came about when a miner, who had taken a dislike to Dick's loud talk, reported he had seen the Canadian stealing from a little store near his claim. Dick was arrested, tried and acquitted, but the seed of suspicion was planted.

Next a Mormon named Crow missed his mule and brought charges of theft against Dick, even stating he had seen the accused taking the animal. This evidence was enough to convict the hapless man but before sentence was passed (which could have been death by hanging) the real culprit turned up, a man resembling Barter.

But now he was a marked man and it seemed to Dick that everyone looked at him with an accusing eye. Completely discouraged with his claim, he left the area for a mining town farther north — Shasta. It was enough removed, he thought, so he could start life again without the hated nickname and its sinister influence. Soon after arrival in the booming camp at the edge of the Trinity Alps he found work to his liking and settled down to what he hoped would be a peaceful existence.

He had two good years before some men from Auburn came to town and spotted him. In no time the information got around that "this man is Rattlesnake Dick, a fugitive from Auburn where he's been in all kinds of scrapes." And now he was looked at sidewise in Shasta. He was later quoted as saying: "I can stand it no longer. I have been driven to a hereafter. Now my hand is against everyone's as everyone's is against me."

Dick Barter lost no time in getting into his new way of life, holding up a man for enough to pay his way back to Auburn and more familiar territory. In best dime novel tradition, he "signed" his first dishonest deed, telling his victim: "If anyone asks who robbed you, tell them Rattlesnake Dick, the Pirate of the Placers".

For the first year or so his crimes were for chicken feed but he was laying plans to intercept a big shipment of gold that would come along the road through Shasta. The bullion would be sent south from Yreka by mules branded with the name of their owner, Wells Fargo. Therefore it would be necessary to transfer the gold to unmarked animals

OLD SKETCH SHOWS SHASTA before fire of June 14, 1853, which destroyed almost entire town in thirty minutes. Adams Express offices, Old Dominion and St. Charles Hotels, largest in town, shown here, were rebuilt within four years as solid brick, fireproof structures.

"TREES OF HEAVEN", grown from seeds brought home by nostalgic Chinese miners, are common sights in most milder climate mining camps. Photo shows bare limbs of early March outlined by low-angled sunlight.

immediately after the holdup. Dick knew where to steal the fresh mules and he would do this part of the job himself. George Skinner would be head of the gang performing the holdup, George's brother Cyrus helping gather up the new mules.

The robbery was committed without a hitch although the train was accompanied by twenty armed guards. George Skinner had only six men but the element of surprise helped him subdue the guards. They were tied to trees as Skinner's men made off with the loaded mules.

Arriving at the rendezvous site above Shasta, the high-spirited highwaymen waited for Rattlesnake Dick and his string of fresh mules. After several days of worry about Dick's absence and the possibility of a misunderstanding about the meeting place, Skinner and his boys were as jumpy as fleas. Expecting a posse from Shasta anytime, scouts combed the gulches and sentries kept constant

watch. In desperation a decision was made to make tracks with half the gold. The $80,000 in bullion represented far too much weight to carry without mules but, Skinner said, they could manage half of it and he would bury the other half alone. As he moved half the gold, a Mexican started to follow him and was shot on the spot. With part of the treasure buried, the gang headed for their hideout near Folsom, south of the American River.

They got there at night and buried the second half of the bullion, then started for Auburn to find out what had detained Dick. The fact was, the Auburn jail was detaining him now for he had been caught stealing the mules — but George Skinner would never know it. At Shasta, Wells Fargo detective Jack Barkley had deduced the job had been handled by Rattlesnake Dick's gang and knowing the location of the hideout, he took his posse in that direction. The two parties met in the moonlight on the Folsom-Auburn road and the first shot Barkley fired killed Skinner. Four men deserted the posse but the rest subdued the robber gang and brought them into Auburn. One of them, Bill Carter, received a pardon for revealing where the second half of the gold was concealed. With George Skinner dead, the first half was unrecoverable. The $40,000 in bullion remains hidden near Shasta to be added to the several other celebrated stories of hidden treasure in California.

Rattlesnake Dick broke out of the Auburn jail and made a brief return to his chosen career. One night, after a holdup, he was shot to death by a pursuing posse. On his body was found a pathetic letter from his sister, imploring her errant brother to give up his life of crime and join her on the farm.

While all this was going on, Shasta was not too much perturbed. The town was full of rough characters and accustomed to events of this sort. Stringing up her own horse thieves and holdup men from the gallows at the rear of the courthouse, she was not too much bothered by crimes outside of town.

STEEP BANK behind brick structures causes heavy runoff in rainy periods, while several semi-permanent springs flow most of year. Provision was made for drainage by bricked gutters between buildings. Here, in early March, rivulet is conducted to street as in 1850s.

LONG ROW OF FADING BRICK REMNANTS mark outlines of Shasta's once teeming business section. Most buildings retain fragments of iron doors and shutters commonly used, intended to keep burglars and fire out, or contain fires starting within.

Shasta was little more to start with than a camp at the gateway to the rich mines in the back country, a stage stop between the level valleys of the Sacramento and the snowy peaks of the Trinitys, the head of "Whoa Navigation" in the vernacular of the day.

Originally called "Reading's Springs" by the first settlers who arrived at the site shortly after Major Pierson Reading found fifty ounces of gold a day nearby, the name was changed to Shasta next year. The mountain for which it is named is not far to the north, is a magnificent old volcano of more than 14,000 feet in elevation, covered with spectacular glaciers on the north and east sides. At its foot is the present day town of Mount Shasta, not to be confused with the roistering old Shasta above Redding.

A hundred mule trains and teams were known to stop in Shasta on a single night. Its strategic position caused a fast growth of outfitters and suppliers. Mule trains heading for the mines in the

layed obtaining full supplies until arrival in Shasta. One of the largest supply houses was that of Bull, Baker and Co. The firm erected a substantial brick building in 1853 replacing a wooden one destroyed by fire. The structure still stands today, a unit in the highly publicized, at that time, "longest row of brick buildings in California." The story is told of one of the Bull, Baker principals being stopped by a mule team owner on his way to breakfast. The latter was anxious to be on his way, joined the trader at breakfast and bought $3,000 worth of goods before the ham and eggs got to the table.

Shasta kept her position of shipping center until 1872 when the California and Oregon Railroad reached the six-mile distant city of Redding in the valley. This was a severe blow and when the neighboring placers became exhausted in 1888, the fading city lost county seat honors and quietly died.

MASONIC HALL shows through gaping doorway. Lodge building has been well cared for, is still in use. Treasured in vault is first charter of Western Star Lodge No. 2 which was brought from Missouri by Peter Lassen. He carried precious document in metal cylinder for protection against fire or water. Lassen made trip by ox train, became well known figure all over northern California, numerous prominent features including Lassen Peak being named for him.

SIERRA CITY, CALIFORNIA

The jagged granite spires of Sierra Buttes frowned down on the huddle of miners' shacks on the broad ledge as though to sound a warning: "Thus far and no farther." The North Fork of the Yuba had willingly yielded its gravels and gold but the peaks were lofty and less charitable. When the lower creeks were raked to meager pickings, the determined miners turned upward to the giant's step on the canyon side and desecrated the mountain with a maze of tunnels and shafts.

The town of Sierra City below was founded on placer gold discoveries in 1849 and was now on the way to becoming a back country metropolis from more substantial though more difficult hard rock mining. But it reckoned without the mountain peaks. In fierce retaliation for the gopherings and pickings of the miner hordes, they held the heavy snows of the 1852-53 winter until they were of prodigious depth in early spring. Then they loosened their embrace and in a terrifying avalanche the village was completely destroyed.

The disaster was so final the place was deserted for about two years. Yet the gold remained in the readymade tunnels and the lure of it was stronger than fear of another inundation. By 1858 another settlement was established on the ledge. All buildings of the first, arrastres and everything above ground had been wiped away but the existing shafts and tunnels were being worked.

In the spring of '50, P. A. Haven and his partner Joseph Zumwalt located among the Indians at the site. They had done some placering and preliminary prospecting on the Buttes but it was a man named Murphy who made the discovery of the Sierra Buttes Quartz Ledge. The mine started here would be one of California's biggest producers, continuing to turn out gold long after most of the Sierra mines were exhausted. This was reopened after the avalanche and another, the Monumental Quartz, was put in operation. This too was to figure in history, in 1860 producing the second largest gold nugget mined in California.

Stories of the finding of large nuggets should be assayed as closely as the metal itself. In the case just mentioned the weight and value are probably accurate. The nugget was found in a commercial mine, officially weighed and recorded at the time. In other instances, nuggets were supposedly discovered by men working for mine owners and perhaps smuggled out to be bragged about at safe distance. Even a nugget found by the owner of a diggings might be kept a secret until it could be transported beyond the danger of road agents, possibly cut into smaller pieces. In such cases no official record would be made.

STURDY OLD BUSCH BUILDING built in 1871 still stands on Main Street, though it has lost former third story which was of frame construction. Construction began with ceremonies on Fourth of July, always big day in Northern Mines. Festivities were under auspices of famed fraternity known as "E.C.V."; full title,— E. Clampus Vitus. Society had been organized in Sierra City in 1857, main headquarters were in upper floors of this building when completed. Originally a burlesque of known fraternities and strictly for fun, brotherhood grew to have more aspects such as aiding widows of miners, though these activities were never published. At top was "Noble Grand Humbug," members gathered at braying of "Hewgag" in "Hall of Comparative Ovations." Initiations were sometimes rough, such as giving intended member blindfold ride in wheelbarrow over such obstacle as length of stepladder. Membership was essential to anyone wanting to do business in town, even traveling theater group found scant acceptance until manager and male actors joined.

OLD BUILDINGS STILL CLING to steep sides of canyon containing North Fork of Yuba. Water supply was never problem here as in many camps. Snows in higher parts of Sierra provided smaller tributaries to Yuba, small one runs past base of house here.

Tales of individual finds should be tested by the integrity of the teller. The word "nugget" is defined as a native lump of precious metal, said to derive from the word "ingot" which is a piece of refined and pure metal, usually cast in some convenient shape. While an ingot would be of pure metal, a nugget might have impurities or be found with part of the matrix attached. Some of the colossal nuggets found in California's early placering period included a considerable amount of adhering quartz or the gold was attached to a much larger chunk of quartz. In the pre-record days many sizable chunks of gold were found, some weighing from five to fifty pounds, containing enough pure gold to send the most phlegmatic miner to spasms of joy.

In the verified case of the nugget found in the Monumental at Sierra City, it was described as a mass of quartz filled with chunks of pure gold. The owners,

including top man William A. Farrish, sold it intact—except for several quartz crystals which were broken off—to R. B. Woodward who owned the Gardens, a popular San Francisco resort. Woodward purchased it for exhibition purposes, paying $21,636 on an estimated value of the metal it contained. After its use as a showpiece, it was crushed and the gold melted out came to a value of only $17,654.

The avalanche that swept over the first Sierra City seems to have been the mountain's only vengeance. The catastrophic fires razing so many other wooden towns never touched this one. Old age and vandalism did, reducing the original buildings to remnants. The spectacular scenery, the Buttes, the forest, the sparkling waters of the Yuba, are still there unchanged for the jagged spires look down upon them with compassion.

261

SONORA, CALIFORNIA

The story of the gold camp with the musically pleasant name, Sonora, is a story of race discrimination and riot. It was a hell roaring boom town with a polyglot population, the dregs of a dozen races. Called Sonoran Camp by the Mexicans who were the sole and peaceful occupants for several years, it was quickly changed to Sonora, as the peace was changed to violence—by the Americans.

Both Sonora and Jamestown were brought into being by gold discoveries along Wood's Crossing by a party headed by Rev. James Woods, and including James Savage, J. H. Rider and Charles

Bassett. The richness of the gravel deposits in the stream was almost unbelievable and the men set to work with feverish energy, and were for some time able to extract about $250 a day by the simplest means. This surface bonanza persisted for several years and the camp called Wood's Crossing was a flourishing, hell-bent settlement.

In less than a year there were more than 2,000 people in camp—an unholy assemblage of Mexicans, Chileans, Chinese and Americans. By the fall of '49 there were 5,000. Shanties had been so hastily thrown up so close together, the narrow

ST. JAMES EPISCOPAL CHURCH, most outstanding old building in Sonora. On "Piety Hill" with four other churches, it survived several fires which devastated most frame buildings at various times. Construction was started in 1859 on a site donated by Caleb Dorsey. Funds for building materials were also donated to finish building the same year. Architect was the Rev. John Gassman of San Francisco who also served as first minister. Beautiful structure stands at head of Washington, the main street, and dominates Queen of the Southern Mines.

Less than a hundred yards from church, also in heart of town is Big Bonanza mine. First worked in 1851 by Chileans who took large amounts of surface gold from the spot, claim was later purchased by three partners for small sum. They operated mine conservatively for three years, then suddenly broke into a solid pocket of gold. Next day they shipped $160,000 worth to the San Francisco mint. During the next week they took out half a million, and another before they sold out.

streets could hardly contain the traffic and were almost impassable on Sundays when everybody was "in town."

The lowest elements flocked to Sonora and violence quickly broke out, murders and street shootings being everyday occurrences. A miners' meeting was held and R. S. Ham selected as alcalde. Some semblance of law and order was achieved but trouble continued to brew in the gambling dives, brothels and opium dens. Although a large portion of the trouble makers were Americans from San Francisco at first, later from the East, the blame fell on the minority groups.

The Americans had gained confidence by the outcome of the Mexican War and being already convinced of their natural supremacy, called the others "foreigners." They decided to get rid of the Mexicans and Chileans but tolerate the Chinese who had proven useful in menial capacities. Under a program of steady abuse, many Mexicans gave up and meekly left their claims for healthier climates but others banded together and rebelled to the point of making guerilla warfare against the Americans, staging skirmishes in which twelve murders were perpetrated in a few weeks.

In June of 1850, the legislature passed a law stating that before any foreigner could operate his mine, even though the claim was established before the Americans moved in, he would have to pay a levy of $30. Since most workings were paying well, this amount could easily have been borne by the Mexicans, but the obvious injustice so rankled that further trouble flared. The Mexican miners organized to defy authorities, refused to pay the tax and continued to operate their claims under protection of armed guards.

The situation had by now become so tense everybody went armed and the potential for an explosion needed only a spark. This was soon provided. A party of whites came upon several Mexicans and Indians engaged in a proceeding which made their tempers jump. The dark-skinned suspects had constructed a funeral pyre of logs and on it were the bodies of two Americans, the wood ready for the torch. Such strong circumstantial evidence of murder seemed ample to those who wished it to be and the foreigners were dragged into town and jailed. A howling mob bore down on the little structure and hauled the men to nearest hanging tree. Nooses were slipped around their necks, the bodies actually off the ground when rescue in the form of an armed sheriff's posse arrived. The same posse also rounded up several hundred Mexican "sympathizers" in order to avoid a mass attack in case the accused were convicted of murder.

The town was jammed with miners from all over the area the day of the trial. Just as court was about to convene somebody accidentally fired his gun and another riot was on. Men poured out of the courthouse by every exit on top of those standing outside to listen to the trial. No one knew what had started the commotion or what the trouble was all about but all were willing to fire their guns in all directions and at anything. A huge business done at the saloons before trial was now showing its effects. When the excitement, dust and smoke had settled, it turned out that only feelings had been hurt, with a minor flesh wound or two. The affair served to blow off steam and the trial was conducted in a somewhat more deliberate manner.

The outcome heightened embarrassment still more. The suspects were found to have been conducting funeral services in their own fashion for the two Americans whom they had discovered dead. The prisoners were then turned loose as were those held in corrals for the "duration."

This affair did not end persecution of the Mexicans, on the contrary probably intensifying it. The Mexicans now realized their position was insecure to say the least and when the order for taxes was enforced by armed collectors, they performed a mass exodus from Sonora. This had a result unexpected by the rest of the population. Their town became a near-ghost with more than half the business potential gone, stores falling upon lean days. After a year of virtual famine, the tax laws were repealed. Some of the exiles returned but the best days were gone for Sonora.

"The Queen of the Southern Mines" continued to operate her many shifts and tunnels—developments that had long replaced the surface operations of earlier days. Hard rock mining was more permanent and paid off to a total of $40 million before it was all over. The "Magic Circle" producing all this wealth was only four miles across, with Sonora at its center.

SWANSEA, CALIFORNIA

Here was a good-sized livery stable, the forge almost intact. There was a boardinghouse with wide porches, once screened. A well-worn path led to a hole in the ground, a vanished "convenience." White talc rocks lined both sides of the trail, whether to satisfy the aesthetic senses or to facilitate stumbling feet in the darkness would be hard to tell. Adjoining the kitchen was a chicken pen of wire. A short trip from the coop to the table!

The town was named Swansea after the famous smelter town in Wales. Mary Austin has given the whole area a fitting name—"The land of little rain."

There is a dry lake a few miles back of the edge of the steep cliff. Its bottom is pure salt, and it's called Saline Lake. The salt was hauled to the edge of the cliff; then run down on a tram cable to the terminus, where it was shipped across the lake to Cartago, from there to San Pedro, thence to Swansea, Wales for refining.

BOARDINGHOUSE STANDS on east shore of vanished Owens Lake (background). Above, to west looms loftiest section of high Sierra, whose once-copious snows nourished lake. Mt. Whitney is above chicken-run at right.

TIMBUCTOO, CALIFORNIA

Jim Denton was a miner in Timbuctoo. His claim on the banks of the Yuba River paid him only the barest minimum in gold dust to keep body and soul together. His little cabin was furnished with only the simple essentials and he ate plain foods sparingly.

Nights along the Yuba even in June are cold and Denton was out of wood. He stopped working his rocker early one evening, June 20, 1860, and cut down the old oak near his cabin for firewood. He had planned to take it down because the aged tree had a badly decayed side and a strong wind might blow it over on his shack. He felled the tree and set about cutting it up. When he split the rotten section, he laid open a large hollow—and in it snugly reposed a buckskin sack.

As soon as Jim took hold of the soft leather, he

RAPIDLY FALLING INTO RUIN is pathetic shell of once busy Stewart Store. Patriotic groups mindful of value of historic relics have made effort to preserve old structure, placed sheltering metal roof over it. Struggle is futile against human vandals who pluck bricks and paint obscenities over old signs on building.

BEAUTIFUL EXAMPLE OF STONE-MASON'S work is crumbling rear wall of only building remaining in Timbuctoo. Native rocks, including river boulders, have been split so as to form facing. Doors and windows are lined with brick, furnished with iron shutters characteristic of period.

knew what he had and his hands trembled as he opened the drawstring and poured some of the contents into his hand. Nuggets they were, hundreds of them, with no quartz matrix sticking to them. He took the sack into the cabin and weighed the nuggets one at a time on his gold scales—total weight thirty-five pounds. He carefully counted the number of *chispas* and wrote down the figures.

An honest man, Jim took the bag to the store for safekeeping and then let out the story. He said all the rightful claimant had to do was give the weight and number of nuggets. No one in Timbuctoo or nearby Mooney Flat or Smartsville came forth and after waiting a reasonable period, Jim took the gold to Grass Valley where he sold it for $7,500. No claimant ever turned up and Jim Denton concluded the rightful owner had met with a fatal accident after pushing the bag into that hollow.

First miners to slosh gravels in their pans along that part of the Yuba camped there in 1850. In the party was a Negro, a refugee slave from the South. He had originally been captured by slavers in the French Sudan of West Africa, his native town being Timbuktu. He worked industriously in the little ravine above where the town was later built and found good colors in his pan. Happy over his discovery, he asked the others if he might call the place Timbuktu Gulch and they were agreeable. The colored man's first strike was followed by many more, news spread and a town grew up where the ground was more level. The name was preserved with American variations.

Getting started in 1855, the town grew steadily but not spectacularly. Then came the hydraulic mining era when the banks of the stream were literally washed away in a flood of thin mud and boulders. Results in gold production were so large that Timbuctoo boomed into the largest town in the eastern part of Yuba County. Churches, theaters, hotels, saloons and stores went up to serve a population of more than 1,200 people.

The flood of debris and mud soon raised another flood, that of protests from ranchers and the valley and the Sawyer Decision, 1884, put an end to this type of mining. The props that had kept up the economy of Timbuctoo were knocked out and the town quickly sank into oblivion.

"Stunted growths...
bleached white...like skeletons!"

TUMCO, CALIFORNIA

Stark desert is the setting for the battered ruins of Tumco. Summers are witheringly hot for humans in the sandy wastes at the edge of the Cargo Muchacho Mountains. The small canyon, holding what is left of the camp, is twenty-five miles from Yuma, Arizona, where the thermometer often reaches 110 degrees or more. Winters offer luxurious temperatures of 60 to 80 with so much bright sunshine a Yuma resort offered "Free meals and lodging any day the sun doesn't shine."

Indians in prehistoric times carved petroglyphs on the canyon rocks near the twin cones of the Cargo Muchachos. The summit of these peaks is a bare 2,000 feet in elevation but they give the illusion of greater height because of the extremely low flat country, much of which in the nearby Imperial Valley is actually below sea level. Early Indians did considerable crude mining, as well as using the blackish "desert varnish" on the rocks. Their comings and goings to the mine sites and "picture galleries" were so constant their bare feet made conspicuous trails on the rocky ground, paths easily traced by the lighter color where the ancient patina has worn off. Along these primitive tracks are sometimes found potsherds and other artifacts.

From 1865 to 1870 Mexicans found gold in the gravels of Jackson Gulch but kept the discovery to themselves, working the area in a quiet and self-contained way. Production was low and not enough gold was brought into Yuma to cause a stir. A spark of excitement came in the early

'80s—news of a find made by a track walker named Hedges. He was apparently more interested in prospecting than sprung rails as his discovery was made in a canyon some distance from the railroad, a few gulches away from the Mexican claims—mica schist heavily laced with gold. Hedges promptly set a stake, quit his job with a small crew, set up mining operations on an enterprising scale.

Several methods of refining the gold were employed, first with crushing mills ranging up from one or two stamps to the hundred stamp mill considered to be one of the largest in the west, if not the world. Final recovery was generally accomplished in cyanide vats. The finished gold bars were hauled to the railroad at Ogilby, shipped to San Francisco mint.

The town growing up at the scene of the diggings was named after its founder and soon had over three thousand people. Water was piped in from Pilot Knob on the Colorado River. Hedges had all the trappings of the boom town except for the usual hotel, the men living in cabins of wood or stone, the natural building material as nothing was more abundant than rocks in this region so barren of soil, water and vegetation. Hedges had its Chinaman—Charley Sam who ran a grocery store.

During the town's period as Hedges it was free of the early day violence but it was responsible for one tragedy it would like to have forgotten. A handsome Mexican boy named Pedro

HOUSE IS QUAINT EXAMPLE of building with material at hand. Lumber for roof, lintels, etc., was imported, walls constructed of stones picked up within few feet, mud from desert floor holding them together, whole plastered with lime mortar.

worked at the twenty stamp mill at the entrance of a small side canyon. The adjacent cyanide plant had turned out three glistening gold bars in the morning but after lunch the men discovered there were only two in evidence. Pedro, being a "Mex" and handy, was promptly accused of the theft, but he vigorously denied any guilt. The men, determined to force an admission, tied his thumbs together and fastened them to the end of a rope thrown over a beam of the stamp mill. The rope was drawn taught. Still the boy protested his innocence. The men pulled some more until he was suspended, screaming with pain. Still no confession was forthcoming and he was lowered, only to have the rope made into a noose and placed around his neck. He was then forced to stand on a beam, the slack in the rope again taken up. Once again he was questioned, and promised that if he would tell where the bar was hidden he would be freed. The boy repeated

WRECK OF HUGE STAMP MILL comprising one hundred stamps, said to be one of the largest in the West. (Another of one hundred stamps stood at Melones in the Mother Lode country until it burned in 1942.) Mill was designed and built by '49ers who profited by mistakes in hard rock mines in Mother Lode where first crushers had square wooden stems and square iron shoes with no way of rotating them, a serious flaw as ore had to be broken by hand and shoveled into mill.

OGILBY, few miles from Tumco, was railroad shipping point for finished gold bars to San Francisco mint. In its heyday Ogilby was wild place, rowdiness not tolerated at Tumco mines. Men came here to spend money in honky tonks. With end of mining activity and close of Tumco, Ogilby languished and died. Buildings were hauled away or wrecked. When this photo was made in '61, only small shack remained near tiny cemetery. In '62 even this was gone and grave enclosures had been used for firewood.

he knew nothing about it. In a rage, several of the men gave the boy a shove and after a few convulsive jerks he was dead. Years later, when the mill was dismantled, a bar of gold was found in the foundations.

When Hedges was satisfied with his profits and tired of mining, he sold the whole operation to the Borden of condensed milk fame. Borden carried on under a corporation called The United Mining Company. He took the initials of the name and made Tumco of them, and so renamed the town. Ore became more and more free milling so that his profits increased as long as expenses were low. Then came the turn in events that caused so many camps to die, increasing costs while the price of gold remained fixed.

Borden closed down in 1909, and sold everything in the place. Machinery was hauled to Ogilby and shipped out, what little good lumber existed there was salvaged, and another ghost town came into being. Tumco today is a forlorn, completely deserted ruin. Particularly pathetic is the cemetery, well populated for a small town. Because of the acute water shortage, many mining operations were carried out dry when the drills and crushers should have been bathed in water. The dust penetrated lungs, resulting in what was called "miner's consumption" and was in time fatal. Excavations for graves were of the shallowest in this rocky terrain—a few inches had to suffice. Then rocks were piled up to form a cover about two feet high. These graves laid out appear in rows on a flat without a blade of grass or vegetation other than a few ocotillos and a little sparse grease-wood. Only one grave now has a splinter of wood which was once a cross. There is no identification on any of them, and a more lonely, barren and desolate resting place cannot be imagined.

"All at once . . . no one was there!"

VALLECITO, CALIFORNIA

The first discovery of gold at the site on Coyote Creek was actually made by John and Daniel Murphy. They were excited by their find and christened the infant camp Murphy's Diggings. But after a few months of panning the stream, the yield fell short of expectations and the brothers moved on to found the bigger camp of Murphy, after which the original location was called "Murphy's Old Diggings." Then the Mexicans drifted in to the Coyote Creek camp and satisfied with smaller amounts of gold dust, established a tiny village which they called Vallecito.

The word is the Spanish equivalent for "a little valley." Any Mexican settlement in such a situation was likely to be so called and there were a good many Vallecitos in California's early days. Only two have survived. One is an old Butterfield Stage station in San Diego county, the other a Gold Rush town in Calaveras county.

In 1850 the Mexicans arranged a little plaza

GILLEADO BUILDING, sole remnant of once boisterous gold town of Douglas Flat, two and a half miles northeast of Vallecito. Constructed in '51 of limestone blocks now stabilized with concrete, was used in several capacities, among them store and bank. At rear is small hole, reputed to be shotgun window for use of guard who watched safe full of gold. Other limestone buildings in Douglas Flat, relics of gold rush days, were torn down for material to build fences.

SHIP'S BELL used to call congregation to church, sound fire alarms, summon children to school, announce funerals and election results. Early in 1854 Vallecito sent delegation to San Francisco where ship had been abandoned when crew headed for gold fields. Ship's bell had been cast in Troy, N. Y. in '53, was purchased and brought to town. Since church had no steeple, bell was mounted nearby in large oak, served through life of Vallecito, then hung silent many years, finally falling to ground when tree blew down in hard wind of Feb. 16, 1939. In October of that year bell was mounted on monument at site by Native Sons of the Golden West. Stump of tree is shown at right. Other stories contradict legend on bronze plaque, insist bell is too large for ship type, not meant to be rung by lanyard connected to clapper.

after the fashion in their home land and put up temporary brush *ramadas* around it. In the next two years a few more substantial adobes were added and life moved along in sleepy siesta fashion.

Suddenly, in the fall of '52, all this was changed. A vein of gold far richer than the stream gravels was found to run more or less through the center of the camp. The Americans moved in and push-ing the original miners out of the way, soon had the plaza plowed up and the buildings razed, establishing another center a block or so away. Saloons went up first, then a miner's hotel, fandango hall and several stores, followed by a bank, express office, school and finally a post office.

After the original burst, Vallecito settled down to a steady existence without much further expansion and had a good period of productivity.

271

VOLCANO, CALIFORNIA

Ill-fated from the start, Volcano went through several periods of travail in its life as a gold camp which may well be characterized by its name. But since the name came before many of its troubles it is explained by the bare rocks resembling lava flow or by the crater-like valley which the town occupied. During the first feverish expansion of the original strike at Coloma, many of Col. Stevenson's regiment of New York Volunteers ranged the hills and valleys of the Sierra Piedmont and found rich deposits in this gulch formed like a volcano.

These first comers averaged $100 a day per pan, the better spots giving up $500. When snow began to fly that fall most of the men prudently retired to the lowlands since no one had taken valuable time to erect shelter. Yet two young soldier friends decided to disregard the ordinarily mild winter climate and stick it out. They left no record of the troubles they endured through the bitter cold but a band of Mexican prospectors found their bodies in the spring. The creek diggings were called Soldiers' Gulch.

That same spring Capt. John A. Sutter, trying to recoup his fortunes, attempted to mine the area with Long Toms manned by a retinue of Indians and South Sea Islanders. He did well for a while with low labor costs and little outlay for equipment but his system had outlasted its day. American miners on the scene raised an outcry that

the captain was using "slave labor," not too far from the truth, and Sutter was forced to decamp or face a noose.

Volcano's troubles had begun. With the first soldier-prospectors, Mexicans, Americans and a goodly number of aborigines were working the gravels and there was only just so much space to work in. The Indians held no regard for the white man's claims, dipping their pans where they saw fit. Tension grew until a quarrelsome white claimed an Indian had stolen some of his equipment. The chief of the Indian camp said he would go to the tribesman's tent and search for the missing tool. When he turned his back, a trigger-happy Texas Ranger, Rod Stowell by name, let fly with his rifle. The killing of the chief precipitated the pint-sized "Volcano Indian War" which ended with several fatalities on both sides.

The next several years were no more peaceful but the camp grew rapidly and soon had a respectable group of buildings, one of the most elegant a Masonic Hall, among the first in California. It had a sumptuous bronze chandelier adorned with no less than twelve "coal oil" lamps. The whole assembly could be lowered to trim wicks and clean chimneys.

The native blue limestone was quarried and blocks dressed to provide excellent building material and this was used for the brewery, Lavezzo and Wells Fargo buildings, two-storied I.O.O.F. building, Adams Express office and wine shop. The handsome brick St. George Hotel with three floors is still in good condition. Unfortunately when the rotting balconies were repaired a few years ago the beautifully turned spindles were replaced by common boards. The little jail is a departure from the prevailing construction, made of sheet iron sandwiched between layers of two-inch lumber.

Volcano's nearest neighbor of consequence is Jackson, still a thriving town. In the '50s the two camps were of similar size with a natural rivalry between them, their respective newspapers not above making derogatory statements about each

FAMOUS "TWO SALOONS" BUILDING was duplex affair, double-barreled threat to sobriety, connected inside. Patrons sometimes became confused, thinking to make exit ran into another bar instead, had to have one more. One of the two saloons, The Jug, was last to close its doors, later acted as store and meeting place.

other. A Jackson visitor in Volcano attracted some attention when he plunked down a $20 gold piece to pay for his lodgings. The local miners gathered around to eye the coin and the Jackson man reported to his home papers that the Volcano populace was so backwoodsy it had never seen such a large piece of money before. The Volcano editor was incensed at this kind of slur and retaliated to the effect that it wasn't so much the novelty of the gold coin that caused so much amazement but the fact that the Jackson man had so much money in his possession and had actually paid his hotel bill instead of skipping town.

During the fabulous fifties Volcano began to show signs of maturity after its roistering days. A Thespian Society was organized and put on performances of such classics of the day as "The Iron Chest" and "She Stoops To Conquer" and wherever it could, often in the hall of the Fraternal Building at the head of the main street. During these first years the miners were starved for any kind of theatrical entertainment and it wasn't long before the amateur efforts were replaced by more practiced ones of traveling theatrical troupes from San Francisco, the actors going where the money was.

Not from the metropolis across the Bay but from Grass Valley came that darling of the miners, the child star Lotta Crabtree, to perform her Highland Fling and other dances under the watchful supervision of her mother, Mary Ann. This one night stand was very profitable, the miners throwing nuggets and coins on the stage in their enthusiasm for the black-eyed charmer, who was to go on from these pick-and-shovel towns to world tours on a career to net her millions.

A group of earnest Volcano citizens felt the miners needed more culture and gave them a lending library, one of the first in California, which lasted until all the books were borrowed and none returned. During the middle '50s a volunteer fire department staged hose drills and parades in the streets but was not too efficient at putting out fires which plagued the town.

Most flashy of the civic groups was a militia company called the "Volcano Blues." Its showpiece was a salute cannon which was merely an emblem until the Civil War broke out. Then the fire department, Volcano Blues and two other organizations banded together to form the Union Volunteers. When a minority group with Confederate sympathies threatened to divert the camp's gold supply to Southern uses, the cannon christ-

LITTLE ASSAY OFFICE was operated by Madera Brothers through busy years of town—except for first few when mining was all by pan, Long Tom or rocker, and gold was self-evident. Later prospectors from hills with ore samples needed assayer's valuation. After Volcano died as mining camp, structure was taken over by Jack Giannini for barber shop. Another Giannini from Volcano founded Bank of America and Angelo Rossi, former mayor of San Francisco was born in Volcano.

ened "Old Abe," was wheeled out into the open. It might have been more of a threat if some Union man had thought to provide cannon balls. Instead some round cobblestones were fired with indifferent success but enough noise to discourage the Rebel cause in Volcano and the great Civil War engagement came to an end.

WEAVERVILLE, CALIFORNIA

Weaverville is a lively wraith now, ghostly only in that it is filled with relics and mementos of its boisterous past . . . of a time when board walks rattled with the clomp of miners' boots . . . when the streets were filled with Chinamen screaming in a tong war . . . of a period when newspapers could report on a Tuesday — "Sunday two persons were killed, yesterday buried and today almost forgotten."

In two blocks on both sides of the street the business section of Weaverville's Chinatown was crammed with 2,500 Chinese. Laundries, joss houses, gambling cribs and opium dens had oriental fronts and when the dives offered more for the customer than the white joints and cut into their profits, there was trouble. The Chinese lived anywhere — in warrens, back rooms of stores or in hovels on the fringes of town.

Most of them came from Canton or Hong Kong and the rival tongs under the two allegiances, were bitter enemies. Hatred built up until something had to give and a battle fought. In 1854 a day was set for it — July 4, popular in Weaverville for hangings, picnics, sporting events and now war.

Preparations went on for weeks, blacksmiths fashioning mining tools into cudgels and tridents, the latter favorite among feuding orientals since pitchforks were not available and guns strictly forbidden to Chinese.

On the appointed day rival forces of some six hundred Chinese gathered on a field above Five Cent Gulch, a mile east of town. Weapons flew and blood flowed until the up-to-now amused white spectators stepped in and stopped the mayhem.

Eight Chinese and one American were killed, many wounded and carried off the flat and a dozen or two with minor injuries limped home. Newspapers next day reprimanded the whites for allowing the bloody scrap but were tacitly reminded that they had encouraged it as a "coming attraction", and as one American defended himself: "We thought it was to be sort of a comic opera." Five Cent Gulch and the flat above it was shortly found to be rich in gold and was deeply mined.

It was in 1850 that John Weaver of Mississippi arrived in the locality, one of the wildest and most remote in California. Nothing disturbed the silence but an occasional scream of a mountain lion or the rushing sounds of the rivers. John (some say William) Weaver found gold to the extent of about $15 a day. The news got out and soon a village of log houses had sprung up. Steady growth was at first slow, so inaccessible was the gold field. Whichever

HANDSOME COURTHOUSE has been in constant use since construction in early days. Kept in good repair (note stucco over bricks), offices modernized but atmosphere of mid-nineteenth century is retained.

GRACEFUL SPIRAL STAIRCASES are unique feature of Weaverville's main street. Greatest building period was in 1850s when, as many wooden structures burned, solid brick ones replaced them. Many had offices and stores on second floors with balconies reached by outside, private stairways. Metal work was done in local blacksmith shops. Original iron doors are still in use upstairs in some buildings.

way the eager argonaut chose to get there he was up against hardships. Especially bad was the route from San Francisco by sailing vessel to Trinidad and the trip up the inner valleys by ox and wagon train, with Digger Indians always a menace. Yet Weaverville did grow and became the county seat of Trinity County very early — a dubious honor since she had no competition.

The Trinity Alps are often compared to the High Sierra but the differences are great. The latter range is strung out lengthwise, the Trinity mountains are bunched. Sierra altitudes reach far above 14,000 feet while most Trinity peaks are between 8,000 and 9,000 feet. The latter group is near the ocean and moisture laden storms pile up snow to depths unknown in the Sierra.

These snows made plenty of trouble for the first miners who were unprepared for them. The winter of 1852-53 was especially severe and flimsy-roofed cabins were crushed beneath the weight. Several homes back against the bases of steep slopes were smothered by avalanches, the slides most prevalent towards spring. To make matters worse, incoming mule trains carrying food and candles for lighting etc. were unable to get through the drifts and prices

on dwindling reserves went sky-high. When the thaws finally did come and trains began arriving, morale had reached a miserable low. It was bad enough to have food stocks reduced to a little grain but the horrible catastrophe was — only a few gallons of whiskey left in the last keg.

Violence flared in Weaverville, with comic opera aspects along with grim results. There was the incident of the traveling man in the pig sty. He had arrived from Klamath in the morning, made calls on several prospects and had his pockets well lined by evening. This called for a celebration and he led the town on a round of the saloons. By midnight, thoroughly drunk, he groveled around for a place to sleep and settled for a cozy pig pen.

The drummer was still there in the morning but what had been in his pockets wasn't. He protested loudly that he'd been robbed and Weaverville's scapegoat, one Seymour, was brought to the sheriff for questioning. On previous occasions, when he had suddenly "come into money", he had headed for the closest bar. This time he had not. He was cold sober and had no money on him. Highly offended Seymour asked: "Why don't you look in the straw in that pig mud?" Sure enough, there was the missing cash. The weekly newspaper had some unsympathetic comments: "The money was found in the hog pen where the sot had found shelter and suitable companionship."

Not so funny was the fate of John Fehly, who also owed his troubles to the bottle. Stoned to the gills, he lunged from the Diana Saloon one day, shooting wildly in every direction. A random bullet caught well-liked Dennis Murray in the head and killed him. Fehly was seized by Dennis' friends and forced to jail. They all had lynch fever but Fehly had sobered up and was not about to let a noose be twisted around his neck without a struggle. He gave it but the hanging committee called for "The Infant", a gangling young giant, six feet six, and used to putting down insurgents. He threw a hammerlock around Fehly and jerked until the murderer gave up. "All right, you!" he panted. "At least put a coal in my pipe." Someone lit the pipe, the noose slipped over it and the trap sprung.

Weaverville got along without a jail for some years by the expedient of quick execution or release. "A man is either guilty or not guilty", the people said. But eventually the decision took longer and a wooden jail was built which was soon set on fire by a prisoner smoking in his bunk. A strong, fireproof one was built of brick and this set the trend for a change in the general aspect of the town, wood giving way to brick as fire forced the issue. Even before

the town was changed, it had some 2,000 people and to serve them were fourteen saloons, four hotels, many stores, the inevitable gambling houses and girl joints.

There was wild jubilation in Weaverville in 1858 when the wagon road came through to Shasta which connected the town to the outside world. Commented the weekly TRINITY JOURNAL, started two years before: "Weaverville now assumes its proper place among the foremost cities of our fair state of California. The opening of the luxurious new wagon road ends our condition of isolation."

PLAINLY VISIBLE from State Highway 299 are evidences of huge devastation wrought by one of the largest hydraulic operations in world. Baron Le Grange mine, opened in 1851, directed powerful streams of water at slopes of Oregon Gulch Mountain, washing away tons of soil, running mud into sluice boxes where heavy gold settled to bottom, caught on slat ridges, was recovered in periodic "clean up". Mud flowed on downstream to spread over farm lands, ruining them. Destruction became widespread in valleys, finally resulted in federal Anti-Debris or Sawyer Act of 1883, putting end to all hydraulic operations. Later, restrictions were eased under certain conditions.

WHISKEYTOWN, CALIFORNIA

A miner could do without tears. He wanted no part of them unless they were tears of joy at finding a rich pocket of gold. But when a mule fell off a rocky cliff and with the mule went two kegs of whiskey, slam-banging down the rocky slope to end up at the bottom smashed to smithereens, the precious liquid dissipated into a stream . . well what could a poor miner do but cry?

This is what happened in the mountains between Redding and the Pacific Ocean, in general the Trinity River country of northern California. And when one miner sobbed: "This is sure one hell of a whiskey creek now", the stream was called Whiskey Creek and the miners revered the memory of the lost hooch by naming the camp Whiskeytown.

Jedediah Strong Smith opened up the country in 1828 on an expedition to Oregon. After pushing up the Buenaventure River (now Sacramento) he found the rocky hills coming so close to the river it was impossible to travel, so moved due west and then north up the Coast. He thus penetrated the Trinity Alps and found the going hard, rocks in the river bed "mangling the horses' feet." Smith's name served as the river's for years and when it was changed to Trinity, "Smith" became the name for another in Del Norte County.

Forced to leave the comparatively easy grade of the cascading stream, Smith's party veered almost straight up the mountainside, scrambling through thick undergrowth. Topping the ridge the party crossed into Humboldt County and eventually met the ocean. Jedediah Smith had opened up a trail that was roughly the foundation of today's roads between the Sacramento Valley and the Coast. In his footsteps followed trappers of Hudson's Bay Company on their travels to and from Oregon. Prospectors also used the route and in 1848 gold in large quantities were found in the Trinity and its tributaries. Although one report had "nuggets lying around in the gravel like walnuts" there was no such rush here as in the Mother Lode. Yet several wildly roaring gold camps sprang up in the Trinity Alps and Whiskeytown was one of the roughest.

At first a nameless clutter of shacks and tents on an anonymous stream, they bred more and got a proper name when the mule toppled off the high trail and the train headed for Shasta City, a camp farther up the creek and noted for its colossal thirst, was short one keg of whiskey.

As Whiskeytown grew large enough to petition for a postoffice, officials scoffed at such a crude name and suggested Blair, which in turn was ridiculed by the miners as was Schilling and Stella. Although called all these names sedately, it was Whiskeytown to the men with the picks and shovels.

OLD ROCK JAIL in Whiskeytown was stoutly built but couldn't resist modern bulldozers which cleared ground to be covered by waters of new lake. Still standing when author-artist Muriel Sibell Wolle took this photo, it was gone in 1963.

It was womanless for years until, said a valley newspaper of 1852: "Whiskeytown's first white woman has taken up her residence there", leaving the reader to guess her purpose. Later that year the paper reported one of the town's several bartenders was "insulted" by a fellow citizen and ventilated him with two bullet holes. The victim had many friends and with a rope over a tree branch they fixed the bartender so he could shoot no more of them.

Late in the '50s a man named Bon Mix erected "a commodious hotel" which embraced a fine saloon and dance hall. The girls employed there were de-

scribed as "young ladies of probable virtue" but at the edge of town in a small row of cribs were several other ladies whose virtue was highly improbable.

Besides washing the gravel of Whiskey Creek, miners were working small hard rock mines, of a type known as "gopher holes." A man would start a horizontal tunnel, working in a prone position, enlarging the hole barely enough to crawl forward. He had just enough head room to hack at the rock and heap the chippings in a gunnysack ahead of him. When the bag was full he wriggled out hind-blind and dumped out the loose rock. There is no record of any of these burrowings paying off much, certainly not enough for the hazard involved. Falling rock could have crushed a man or blocked off his exit.

Official records, always far below actual figures because of "bootlegging", showed $25 million was recovered from the gulches around Whiskeytown. Many other ghostly camps have a few stubborn inhabitants who stoutly maintain that the old place will boom again when the price of gold rises, there being plenty of the yellow stuff around. Not so in the case of Whiskeytown. Two hundred feet of cold mountain water covers the site.

The Bureau of Reclamation has diverted the waters of the Trinity River over twenty miles into the Sacramento by way of the newly created Whiskeytown Lake, formed by the dam of the same name, which was dedicated by President Kennedy in September, 1963, as one of his last official acts. High above, on dry land, a "new" postoffice, built of lumber salvaged from an old saloon in the original town, is plainly marked "Whiskeytown." No one argues about the name now.

RUSTY SKIP BUCKET was safely removed to level above rising waters, still lying in clutter of saloon lumber and other salvaged materials. Heavy container was used to remove ore from mine shaft, raised and lowered by ropes over windlass. When rope became frayed, miners stood clear of load.

COLORADO and UTAH
GHOST TOWNS

BY

LAMBERT FLORIN

Drawings
by
David C. Mason, M.D.

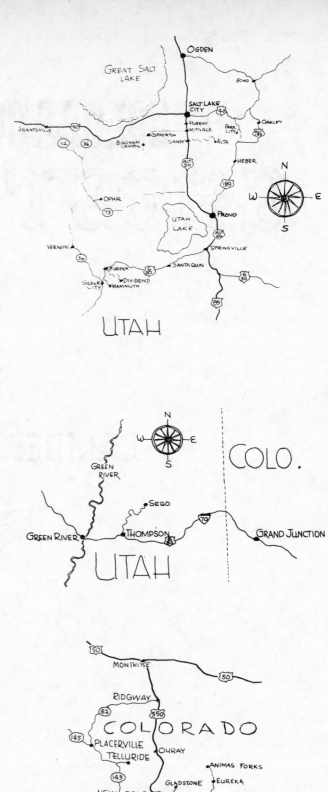

UTAH

UTAH

COLORADO

COLO.

UTAH

COLORADO

COLORADO

INDEX

COLORADO   Page

Alma 285

Animas Forks 287

Apex 289

Black Hawk 290

Bonanza 242

Breckenridge 293

Buena Vista 295

Central City 297

Creede 298

Crested Butte 303

Crestone 306

Cripple Creek 307

Eureka 311

Fairplay 312

Georgetown 313

Gladstone 287

Kokomo 310

Lake City 320

Leadville 323

Ohio City 326

Ophir 328

Pitkin 331

Poncha Springs 336

                                      Page

Saint Elmo 337

Shavano 338

Silver Plume 340

Silverton 341

Spar City 342

Telluride 343

Victor 345

Ward 348

White Pine 350

UTAH

Alta 355

Bingham Canyon 358

Corinne 360

Eureka 364

Grafton 366

Iosepa 370

Mammoth 372

Mercur 373

Ophir 378

Park City 380

Sego 382

Silver City 388

Silver Reef 389

ALMA, COLORADO

In the center of a dozen gold diggings was Alma, which like Silverton, was the place the miners went to buy supplies and what it took to break reality into something livable. One of these camps was called Buckskin Joe, of which nothing is left but a history as ripe as the long unwashed bodies of the miners and their women.

One of its former log buildings was a combination store and boardinghouse, one of several presided over by Horace Tabor and wife Augusta. There were several saloons, three dancehalls and a theatre where, during Buckskin Joe's heydey, a negro minstrel troupe put on a continuous show.

During this period, in the early '60s, Father Dyer, the "Snowshoe Itinerant," was a familiar character in the camps. Constantly on the gospel trail, this Rev. John Lewis Dyer starved, froze his feet, slept in snowbanks but always responded to the call to reform the rowdy "congregations" in Buckskin Joe, Montgomery, Divide, Breckenridge and other spots of sin.

Dyer kept a diary and in it stated he persisted in preaching in Buckskin Joe "in the face of every kind of opposition, at least two balls a week, a dancing school, a one-horse theater, two men shot, and yet, we had a good meeting." When snows were deep, he made his way over the passes on long Norwegian skis, which in those early days were called "snowshoes." His traveling equipment included "a buffalo skin and quilt, some crackers, a piece of bacon, coffee and sugar, with some dried apples, a tin cup, and an oyster-can; in all, thirty seven and one-half pounds

MONUMENT TO FAITHFUL BURRO. Prunes had worked for many prospectors at most of mines in district, was last owned by Rupert Sherwood. When too old to carry burdens he had freedom of town, would panhandle food at any doorway, was beloved by everyone in camp. At his death, citizens buried him beside main street, erected monument. Prunes' last master left request to be cremated and buried in same grave which is immediately behind monument. Colored marbles originally outlined inscription, were pried out by vandal souvenir hunters. Case at left contains Prunes' harness, at right pictures of Sherwood and other mementos. At base are ore samples from mine where shaggy little animal worked.

PRUNES
A BURRO
1867-1930
FAIRPLAY
ALMA
ALL MINES
IN THIS
DISTRICT

CONCRETE CALABOOSE. Prisoners from Buckskin Joe, Mosquito, and Park City, were brought into Alma for incarceration in central, substantial jail. Original building was of log construction but too many escapes took place as building deteriorated. Log house became store, now both buildings are crumbling.

to pack on my back." Four months of his efforts netted him forty-three dollars in collections.

In October of 1861, two Mexicans drove a flock of sheep into Buckskin Joe. They had no trouble selling the animals for mutton and stayed overnight in the camp. One of them woke up violently ill, dying in short order of smallpox. An epidemic gripped the town and many residents were added to the cemetery up among the aspens. The women were evacuated to Alma before things got too bad—all but one, a dancehall girl known as Silverheels.

The real name of this girl has long been forgotten, but her dancing shoes with heels of silver made for her by an adoring miner gave her the name by which she was known to all. When the smallpox

struck this heroic girl who had been so snubbed by the "decent women" of the camp, refused to leave, nursing many of the stricken until they died or recovered. When the worst was over, grateful miners got together a purse of money, nuggets and dust and took it to her door, only to find her vanished. Several years later and regularly thereafter, a heavily veiled woman was seen walking among the graves in the aspen grove, then leaving without speaking to anyone. It was thought she was Silverheels, that she had contracted the smallpox, and would show her once beautiful face to no one.

A mountain, 13,825 feet in elevation and snowy most of the year, now bears the name Mt. Silverheels in honor of the "Angel of Mercy of South Park."

ANIMAS FORKS AND GLADSTONE, COLORADO

By the very nature of the reason for their existence, the old mining camps are often placed in spectacular situations. Among these, Animas Forks holds first place in our experience. Its elevation is 11,300 feet, with craggy, snowy peaks of over 13,000 feet rising in circles around the site. The roaring waters of the Animas leave the town and rush on down the gorge in a canyon, narrow and deep. The snow, even in July, is not restricted to the peaks, but lies in banks in every shaded corner of the town.

The canyon of the Animas is here so narrow that the original road was a real problem to build. And when the little narrow-gauge came in about 1898, there was no place to put it except on the road. Now the tracks and rails are long gone and the road restored.

The remaining buildings are scattered, but give some idea of the plan of the original streets. These were few because of the terrain.

Getting a good start in 1875, Animas Forks soon grew to be the "largest town in the world." The boast was followed by fine print reading "at this altitude."

Avalanches were the bane of the town, wiping out many buildings and frequently stopping travel up the river. Timber was stripped from the steep mountainsides to be used as fuel, shoring, etc. and this smoothed the way for sliding tons of snow. The sides of the canyon are so close together that the wave of snow would not halt at the bottom, but would roll part way up the other side, actually lifting the buildings off their foundations.

SOME OF HIGHEST PEAKS in Colorado tower above remnants of Animas Forks, even though town itself is over 11,000 feet high. Continental divide is in background, stream in foreground is Animas, near its beginning.

JAIL WAS STOUTLY constructed, every window offered spectacular view of San Juans. Structure is almost buried in snow most of year, brush and grass have three-month growing season.

At the farthest end of town were large mines and mills, and conveniently, a boardinghouse. In the kitchen stood a huge cookstove. Those miners no doubt packed healthy appetites! A nearby trap door led down a flight of stairs to what must have been a cold-storage vault. At this altitude and in the short summer, the pit could easily have been the equivalent of a deep freeze unit.

The large room adjoining the kitchen showed empty window sashes opening on an array of snowy peaks.

Here was frenzied activity during the 70's and 80's. Then most of the richer mines began to peter out, the mills closed down or moved downgrade to Eureka and all was quiet again.

From Animas Forks we descend to Eureka, then on down to Silverton, the "hub" of the mining area, and up Cement Creek to Gladstone. The stream is small and not spectacular, and its waters are stained red by iron.

At first Gladstone seems entirely deserted, but a mine on the mountainside is being operated again.

Not many buildings are left standing, but many evidences of foundations and mining equipment attest to those busy times in the 80's and 90's.

288

APEX, COLORADO

Apex is the story of a man who found true gold in the veins of the Pine Creek hills—and none in those of his fellows. The discovery and disenchantment made Apex a part of Colorado mining history, even though brighter parts were played by Black Hawk, Central City and Nevadaville.

Sometime in the '70's, Richard Mackey made a good though not exciting strike in the Pine Creek mining district. He sold it while the selling was good and the new owner soon did the same. This went on until a man named Mountz got hold of the lode—and he was serious about working it. From his mining experience Mountz was sure this was a good vein. Just where it went from its first indication he was not so certain. The main trouble was that he was broke.

Talking up his property, he secured a partner who seemed equally enthusiastic about the Mackey and together they raised enough money to get going. Almost immediately the two struck good pay ore though the main vein still eluded them. In no time the partners had stacked up a tidy $30,000. Then, one fine morning, Mountz woke to find himself alone, his part-

ner and the money vanished. Despondently plugging along alone, he decided to try for the lode and to that end persistently drove his tunnel in what he hoped was the right direction.

One day he was forced to take stock of his situation. He was down to his last dollar, almost out of food and there still was no sign of that vein. His decision was to stack his last several sticks of dynamite in the bore at the terminus of the working, light the fuse and the hell with it.

Next morning he slept late, finished a good breakfast of all the food that was left and went to have a look. The shattered pile of debris was all rich ore—and there behind it was exposed the shining lode! A sample rushed to the assayer in Black Hawk proved out $1800 to the ton but everyone was sure there must be some mistake. A second sampling verified the good news, and the rush to Apex was on. No other such bonanza was ever found there but the Mackey continued to produce so faithfully that it justified the building of a mill, just for the one mine.

EXCITING STRIKE BY MOUNTZ sparked real boom and town of Apex came into being in the '70s. Main street was lined solidly by saloons, stores and hotels in '80s.

BLACK HAWK, COLORADO

Drama rode with every gold mine mule, came bucketing down every crooked lane between the miners' shacks. Black Hawk wallowed in it from 1867 to 1879 and for some years it went under the name of Doe.

Gregory Gulch's first gold was discovered at Mountain City and from this camp grew the settlement of Black Hawk which was soon enough swallowed up by bigger ones above and below. The whole Gulch area produced most of Colorado's gold for three years after 1867.

Black Hawk then began to have trouble. As the shafts went deeper the granites and porphyries grew more obdurate. Soon only 15 to 40 percent of the assay could be saved, the rest swept downstream and lost. Such a situation was tolerated as long as costs of labor, supplies and materials were at a low level, but as these advanced the waste became disastrous. The harder the rock, the better the milling machinery had to be, and this transported over the plains through the hazards of Indian wars. Operations almost ceased, saved from death throes by a Professor Hill who secured the cooperation of Boston and Colorado Smelting Works in putting up a huge smelter at Black Hawk in '68. All good ore was then sent through the smelter, low content rock treated by raw amalgamation in the quartz mills as before. The rehabilitation was further aided by the construction of the Colorado Central Railway up through the mountains to Black Hawk. This sparked life into many neglected and flooded mines.

In July of 1877, a pair of newlyweds arrived at Central City on the narrow gauge—a Mr. and Mrs. William H. Doe, Jr., the husband known as Harvey. The little blond wife had been Elizabeth McCourt back in Oshkosh, Wisconsin, two weeks before, and was already nicknamed "Baby" Doe. She was excited, sure that her Harvey would make a mint of money out of the Fourth of July mine, which his father owned and he was to manage. When time proved that father had all the business acumen, Baby Doe became impatient, donned pants and went to work at the mine to speed things up.

Then father Doe came out to Colorado to take over and ousted the young bride from the mine. Disillusioned and bored, she took long walks around Black Hawk where she and Harvey had taken rooms to save money. During the course of these strolls she walked into the clothing store owned by two Jewish merchants, Jacob Sandelowsky and Sam Pelton. Drama was now hovering low over her head and the handsome, curly-haired one of young Jacob. There were more meetings

DOWN ON FLAT, near Gregory Creek, stands old blacksmith shop. Built after one of Black Hawk's fires to replace wooden structure, it stands precariously, cracks having developed all through brickwork. Door was widened for automobiles, original horseshoe replaced above it.

BLACK HAWK STREET fronting on creek was once solidly lined with ornate houses. This one with fancy carved barge boards is one of few survivors. Baby Doe, on her lonely walks around town, often passed here.

between the two which increased the already rampant town gossip. And when the Does attended the opening night at the Opera House in Central City as the guests of the partners, tongues flapped like shutters in the wind.

Now Baby Doe found she was pregnant and afraid to tell her husband. He learned of it from snoopers and flew into a tantrum. His taunt—"I hear you're going to have a Jewish brat," provoked a furious quarrel and bitter recriminations on both sides. Time passed in this strained manner until the baby was born, prematurely and dead. Harvey's rage was softened at Baby Doe's grief and he relented, a certain kind of peace being declared.

Harvey had lost out at the Fourth of July altogether and was forced to take menial jobs, going deeper and deeper into debt. The gulch itself was

suffering a depression, not so much for lack of gold but because the population was being lured to a brash new camp, Leadville. And this was where debonair Jacob Sandelowsky went, changing his name to Sands and opening an elegant branch store. He was still very much in love with Baby Doe, flooding her with letters entreating her to join him.

One cold day in December, 1879, she walked up the hill to take a long, wistful look at the Fourth of July which had now been declared worthless. To those who saw her she looked dejected and beaten down, yet the next morning she was her bright, vivacious self—when she took the little train to Leadville.

291

BONANZA, COLORADO

Anne Ellis said the road between Bonanza and Sedgwick was a "rare specimen of engineering skill. A vehicle could get over it without upsetting." She was the author of "The Life of an Ordinary Woman" in which she vividly described her life in Bonanza, having "gone up the gulch at six and come down at sixteen."

Once the bed of an inland sea, the San Luis Valley is level, except for occasional rocky upthrusts, islands in those distant times. The silt laid down then makes rich farming soil and it was this fertility which nourished the miners of Bonanza and surrounding camps in the '80s. With an elevation of just under 8,000 feet, the growing season is short.

Near its northern end the San Luis Valley is squeezed closely by the Sangre De Cristo Range on the east and the Cochetopa Hills on the west. In this scenic situation lies the quaint little town of Villa Grove, once the supply center for the mining camp of Bonanza. It was never a big place but it was lively. Its stores offered variety, one sign reading "Fresh Eggs, Rubber Boots, Corsets." Extending from Villa Grove westward and at stretches, almost straight up, is the old road to the camps which have almost disappeared except for Bonanza, itself none too robust. First came Sedgwick and Kerber City, opposite each other on the stream, then Bonanza and above, Exchequerville.

In her book Anne Ellis pictures the Bonanza log cabins, frame buildings and tents, lining the street that followed the creek, the deep snow, mud and dust; miners walking single file on the lower side of the road; strings of burros with panniers packed full, surmounted by bed rolls, drills, picks and shovels; freight teams coming down with ore and going up with supplies; the stage dashing by with its passengers; the "fancy girls" who had their favorite horses to ride up and down the gulch; the saloons where no woman ever went unless she was "fast." The author once tried to peek in, sure there would be "pictures of naked women, shiny glassware and wonderful hanging lamps."

At first the family lived in a one-room cabin, where, in times of heavy snows, they were confined in a welter of drying clothes, socks and heavy, steaming underwear. Every strong gust of wind blew snow through the shack. The next step was into a two-room shanty. It had a canvas ceiling, and moving bulges there showed where the pack rats were running. On one occasion her mother made a successful stab upward with a long meat-fork and blood came dripping down.

When Anne Ellis came to the end of her life in Denver, she was sent back to Bonanza, to rest beneath the aspen trees in the little cemetery on the mesa above the town.

MINERS CABIN IN BONANZA is of sturdy log construction, has endured from days when busy pageant of life in rowdy mining camp passed its door. Some of good mines of day were Rawley, Bonanza, Empress Josephine, latter yielding total $7,000,000. In '70s, population was 1,300, in '90s less than 100. Turn of century saw short revival.

BRECKENRIDGE, COLORADO

Over the continental divide in the summer of 1859 came a horde of gold-hungry prospectors. Their camps along the Swan and Blue Rivers were temporary as they panned the sands of the streams. Then as one pan sloshed around in the Blue, a rich residue showed and this led to a more permanent camp on the little river, with others set up in several gulches, until the whole area was a maze of tents, shacks and cabins—the site of the original strike being built up into a roistering boom camp. Then the original settlers, the Indians who resented the white man's spoiling their streams and killing their game, began a series of attacks on the raw placer camps. Defenses were set at the central point, the place called Fort Meribeh.

As more and more people, businessmen as well as miners, swarmed into the diggings, a post office became necessary. To this end, a town was formed and called "Breckinridge," after John C. Breckinridge, vice-president of the United States. But when the predominantly Union population heard that the Vice-President's sympathies lay with the Confederate cause, the town's name was altered by changing the first "i" to an "e".

Doldrums set in with the exhaustion of placer gold but the development of quartz mining brought a boom. The stamp mills could crush huge chunks of gold-bearing rock into fragments, grind them into powder, the yellow metal separated by raw amalga-mation. As other camps had found, this method was wasteful but more efficient smelters were too costly.

The camp enjoyed a huge prosperity in the '80s, a complete gaggle of gamblers and prostitutes. The miners of all the surrounding camps bore down on the dives of Breckenridge with a bang. Shootings were common but one had a comic opera aspect.

When this case was brought into court, the antagonists were told they would have to fight a European-type duel. The camp was starved for public entertainment and a civic-minded judge thought the idea sportive. The duel proceeded by the book until, at the count of fifteen paces, when each man was supposed to turn and fire, both contestants picked up their feet and fled—one west, one east—never to be seen again around those parts.

The end of hard rock mining again turned Breckenridge into a ghost town and the place slumbered until several dredges began to work the "depleted" gravels of Blue River. Again a resurgence of activity took over and a third boom was on. When the need arose for extensive maintenance of dredge equipment, large shops were built for repairs and fabrication of new parts. But eventually big-time dredging came to an end and the camp by the Blue rested on its laurels, hoping for gold prices to go up.

Owen Freeman was a patient man with an eye to the future, honest and trusting, too—all rare qualities in the slapdash boom world of Colorado gold. He

ORIGINAL FALSE FRONTS mingle with more recent shacks. Where post office now stands, old Denver Hotel sheltered drummers and itinerants for many years. It was across street from grocery store, and one winter, when snow reached depth of 13 feet, tunnel was dug and used until melted.

STABLE END OF OLD FIREHOUSE. Hose carts were in front of structure facing street, horses stabled in rear facing alley. Loft held winter hay. Stable still holds old wagons and fire equipment. Ten Mile Range, spur from continental divide, forms background.

discovered a rich lode but decided to tell no one, to keep working at his mine job until he accumulated enough money to develop his find.

The steep mountainside where Freeman found his vein was cluttered with tents and shanties grouped around the several mine heads. The timber was cut off, tree by tree, for shoring, shelter and firewood. Gradually the water was drained out of the canyon valley and Silver Plume took shape as a town in 1870. About this time, Owen Freeman caught pneumonia after being trapped in a cave-in.

Hovering near death, he asked to see his two best friends and to them revealed the secret of his lode.

Expected to die, he lay in comas and was pronounced tubercular, the end only a pick handle away. Then like a ghost rising from a grave, he made a partial recovery—and a startling discovery. His trusted friends had recorded the claim in their names only and were working the vein.

This mine, the Pelican, turned out good ore containing almost every metal known at that time—gold, silver, lead, zinc and copper. Other mines on the steep mountain slopes were the Payrock, Burleigh, Terrible Dunderburg and others. While their owners prospered, Owen Freeman went back to his sickbed and brooded his life away.

BUENA VISTA, COLORADO

The new railroad had reached only as far as Buena Vista and passengers for the loudly booming silver camps of Leadville and Aspen had to change to stages at that point. This situation soon created still another mushroom metropolis, Buena Vista itself which quickly took its place among a succession of camps claiming the honor of "the most lawless town in the West."

Among the dozens of saloons that sprouted along the single street was one bawdy place with a hastily scrawled sign across its false front — The Mule Skinner's Retreat. A door or two away was the tiny post office and a problem soon developed for the buxom lady serving as postmistress. A sizeable element in the town was "on the lam", drifters operating under a number of aliases. The lady of letters agreed to drop all mail for such names in a special box at the back window which had a pane missing, the questionable characters to reach through and take what they wanted.

The most vivid description of Buena Vista in those days was written by a traveler named Ingham for a book, DIGGING GOLD AMONG THE ROCKIES, published in 1880. He said: "Buena Vista is a new town situated near the headwaters of the Arkansas river. This town five months ago had only three buildings, it now contains from three to four hundred cheap wooden structures, some well built hotels, saloons and gambling houses without number. It claims a population of 1500. The town is in the midst of a park country, surrounded on all sides by magnificent snow-covered mountains. A little southwest is Mount Princeton, rising grandly to a height of 14,196 feet, and a number of other peaks raise their white summits almost as high.

"Tents greet the eye along the streets in every direction. Large canvas covered buildings, tents filled with merchandise and mammoth tents transformed into warehouses crammed full of freight supplies en route to Leadville and the Gunnison country are everywhere seen.

At the depot we saw seven four-horse stage coaches loading with passengers for Leadville, be-sides other vehicles taking in passengers for Alpine, Pitkin and Gunnison City. Eight, and sometimes nine persons are crammed inside the Concord Coaches which look as if four persons would be a sufficient load inside — while four or even five persons are put on top of the box. The fare to Leadville from Buena Vista is $5 for a distance of thirty-four miles. Six and eight mule freight teams, hauling two canvas covered wagons, one hitched closely behind the other, laden with freight

BRIGHT RED BUILDING is one of many still in use in Buena Vista and dating from days of silver rush. Town was founded in 1879 by prospectors, becoming metropolis overnight as temporary end of rail line eventually completed to Leadville. During boom period Buena Vista became headquarters of bunco men, gamblers and prostitutes, situation became intolerable to "respectable element" of town, vigilantes hanged some of most notorious crooks, drove rest out of town.

295

OLD COURT HOUSE bears unique weather-vane. Buena Vista became county seat of Chaffee County later in same year of founding. Granite, former seat was unwilling to give up records, committee of Buena Vista citizens chartered locomotive and flat car, removed records at night from hiding place from loft above brewery in Granite.

of all kinds for Leadville, jacks and mules loaded with their packs for Gunnison were constantly moving out. At the depot tons upon tons of base bullion, (silver and lead), in bars (or pigs) from fifty to one hundred pounds each were closely piled upon the platform for fifty feet in length, which was fairly broken down with the great weight it bore. These bear the stamp of permanent smelters, and are being shipped east, where the silver will be separated from the lead.

"Buena Vista has been a lively town for the past four months, being the terminus of the Denver and Rio Grande Railway, the nearest station to Leadville. But the line will have completed a road up the Arkansas from Canon City past this place to Leadville by July 1st, when this place will have to decline.

"The buildings here, as we stated before, are of the most temporary nature except a few of them. The hotel where we stopped was plastered with building paper tacked to the walls, and ceiled and whitewashed overhead with thin white muslin fastened in the same manner. We got good accommodations, however, and were well fed for two dollars a day. Some hotels, though, ask three."

The town today retains much of the old flavor, the mountains still form the background, many of the old buildings remain in good condition.

CENTRAL CITY, COLORADO

"The richest square mile on earth" was to have a theater. And no less a personality than dancer Mlle. Haydee, with her Troupe, was coming to play in it. Major Hadley told the people of Central City it was all true. That was why he was fixing up his old log hall. And the brothel girls wondered just what kind of troupe this "Mlle." had.

This was Central City in the first summer of its gay day, 1859. April saw John Gregory locate a gold ledge and fight a blizzard. May saw many more claims in the gulches, the boom on its way. June brought 3,000 people and the next month Central City had 30,000.

All this lightning development came after the placer discoveries in Little Dry Creek where Denver would sometime be. John H. Gregory was not satisfied with the "chicken feed" there and with a pick and a prayer, grubbed around in the gulches looking for the source deposits of gold. In a stream flowing down through the Kansas Territory Rocky Mountains, he found grains instead of flakes and was further elated

when he located the ledges they had come from. A snowstorm almost defeated him, but grubstaked by David K. Wall, who raised vegetables for the miners and sold milk from his cow for more than whiskey cost, Gregory organized a party of veterans and green-horns and found his yellow treasure on May 6. The spot was first called Mountain City but it lost its identity as Black Hawk below and Central City above gained attention. Meanwhile, William Green Russell, found grains instead of flakes and was further elated when he made the Little Dry Creek discovery, a rich strike in a gulch parallel to Gregory's. Above Central City the mining locality came to be called Nevada City, then Nevadaville.

The whole area became interlaced with workings and small towns and known as the "richest square mile on earth." Gregory sold his claims by the end of May for $21,000, a small fortune then.

As in all camps when gold was first discovered, panning was the sole method of recovery. Soon rockers were built and, while wasteful, were more

VIEW UP EUREKA STREET shows several famous Central City structures. At immediate left is Teller House, opened on June 24, 1872 with large dinner, and concert of "exquisite music by Prof. Barnum's Orchestra." Publicity stated "the majority of rooms are without transoms, ventilation being obtained by the use of adjustable windows. Guests may therefore lie down to peaceful slumbers undisturbed by apprehensions of getting their heads blown off or having their valuables lifted by burglars." Just above is Opera House, across street is Courthouse (with two towers), next this way is St. James M. E. Church, organized by missionaries first summer of camp's existence. First services were held in home of "Aunt Clara Brown," a former slave. This building was begun in 1864. Next is City Hall, then Williams Stables.

MOST POPULAR STABLE OWNER was big, jovial and beloved R. B. Williams, who was also the sheriff. Williams was murdered in 1896, by a man gone berserk over his wages being garnisheed. Opera House was only hall in Central City big enough to accommodate friends attending his funeral.

productive. Then Long Toms, enlarged versions of the rockers, appeared up and down the streams. By the second summer most of the placer gold was gone and more hard rock mining was enforced. This was where the real wealth lay, in the vertical or nearly vertical, metaliferous veins. In the Central City area these lodes were granite or gneiss, or a combination of both. The upper, exposed ends were more or less weathered and crumbly, were easily worked, but as the mines sank deeper the granite became increasingly refractory and the boys were separated from the men. Quartz stamp mills began to appear, purchased by companies of miners banded together. The day of the individual claim operator was gone.

The first quartz mill to operate here was also the first in Colorado. Set up by Prosser, Conkling and Co., this noisy contraption was small and crude but worked well, and was followed by a rash of similar—larger and more refined—monsters which split the air day and night with their din. Over a hundred mills of five, ten and fifteen stamps were erected in Gilpin County in the first years. Some wore out and their replacements were even bigger and noisier. A system was soon worked out to avoid the stamp mill waste to some extent. The ore of a given mine separated into lots, the few tons of very rich material being sent to the smelter, the remainder, perhaps thirty times as much, crushed in the mill.

The first summer in Central City saw all the excitement of a typical boom town. Almost all the 30,000 in the district were established miners, hangers-on or prospectors looking for a claim and moving on as they found the good ones already taken. Among these last were the Tabors—Augusta, Horace and baby—camping and prospecting in the mountains for many heart-breaking, privation-filled months, then after a short rest moving on toward Leadville and destiny.

When the first flakes of snow fell many decided to return to home and families for the winter, and Central City was down to some 1,500. They worked their claims during open spells, particularly where rockers were still in use, as these did not freeze so easily. One man, left alone, took out some $2,400 during the three coldest winter months. When his partners returned after a winter of ease and carousing, broke and expecting to share in this hard-won wealth, they found it was not being passed around. Next winter they stayed but snows were so deep from November to February no one could work.

But that first year—and Mlle. Haydee's artistic troupe of players. Major Hadley readied the big log building in the gulch, the ground floor of which was fronted by a row of stores, saloons and a barbershop. The theater would be in the upstairs loft where supports for candles were nailed along the walls, one row

298

VISTA DOWN EUREKA STREET shows area almost completely destroyed by fire in 1874. Sidewalk in front of Teller House (next after Opera House on right) was paved with silver bricks on occasion of visit by President U. S. Grant in '73. Silver was borrowed for event, gold being too common in Central. This same gold kept gulch going, even after collapse of silver which ruined Leadville and other camps, but by 1914 Central City was nine-tenths ghost.

placed crosswise near the far end for footlights and before it all the benches in town.

What difference did it make if the "madamoiselle" was from Missouri? Half the men in town fancied themselves in love with her and called her "Miss Millie." She ruled the males of the gulch and that meant almost everybody as there was only one "straight" woman, Mary York, and a dozen prostitutes. Later a permanent theater, The Olympia was built for the players above the Veranda Hotel. When a report got around that gambler Tom Evans had been seen to force Miss Millie into a buggy and depart with her, whipping the horses to top speed, a posse of furious would-be lovers was made up but had no place to go as no one knew where Evans had taken the dancer. A week later came the awful truth. The couple had wed in Denver. The posse was dismissed.

Mary York had been the first woman in the raw young camp and defended her virtue against all comers. She became so adept at this that she set up the first boarding house. Among her guests was a young miner named Billie Cozens. He was the first man she had ever looked at twice and when he proposed Mary gladly accepted him.

Before long Billie was made sheriff, and one of his problems was holding prisoners, there being no jail.

On one occasion, he arrested two men in the evening. Mary had just given birth to a new son, and was still confined to bed. Billie dragged the prisoners into the bedroom, over Mary's weak protest, and chained them to the bedstead. They were forced to lie on the floor, Billie theatening the two with violence if they disturbed the new mother or baby. They were model prisoners and in the morning were hustled off to court. When Mary regained her strength, she made her young husband's life so miserable over the incident that he soon managed to get a jail built.

The next years were ones of prosperity for the gulch inspite of many troubles such as the over-exploitation of mine stocks by New York tycoons who had bought up most of the larger mines. The Gregory lode sold for $1,000 a foot and at this high peak of manipulation, the boom collapsed, plunging the camp into a deep depression. Then came a period when many of these absentee owners came out to run things themselves, only to do further damage through ignorance. But the "square mile" survived, and had some more good years, the best being the '70's and '80's. There were the usual big fires, sweeping flimsy wooden structures before them, but even these catastrophes had good results, solid brick and stone buildings going up—the ones that make Central City the fascinating monument it is today.

CREEDE, COLORADO

"Holy Moses!" was what the man said when he found the rich gold ore and that was what he named the mine. The man's name was Creede and the town was named after him—the town where "Soapy" Smith caught the public fancy and Bob Ford, who had shot Jesse James, came to the same end.

In its lower reaches, where it sprawls out in a shallow trickle most of the year, the Rio Grande is a river famed in songs and stories of the Old West. The stream has another aspect not so well known. In southern Colorado, the Continental Divide, crest of the Rockies, runs east and west for a few miles. Nestled against the northerly buttresses of these snowy peaks is a chain of beautiful mountain lakes where the Rio Grande is born. Flowing east at first, then north about ten miles, it soon makes a sharp bend toward the south. At this point the stream receives the several forks of Willow Creek and near the juncture stands what is left of one of the wildest mining camps of all time—Creede.

Here the Rio Grande is a brawling mountain torrent and Willow Creek no less boisterous though smaller. Prospecting along the banks of these streams in 1889 were Nicholas J. Creede and partner George L. Smith. They had been panning the creek gravels and picking at the rock along the banks all morning. They sat down to eat and Creede, swallowing the last bite, got up to chip off a chunk of rock that attracted him. What he saw on close examination made him stop his wanderings. He had found the ore that was to become "The Holy Moses."

This mine and a second, the Amethyst, found the same summer by Creede, created a boom that had few equals in a state that ate them for breakfast. The first year of the Creede discoveries $6 million had been scratched out of the precipitous rock walls lining Willow Creek. As the motley collection of people from hardworking miners to prostitutes moved in, shelters and stores were hastily thrown together, flimsy from lack of building material and space.

Several canyons debouching onto the slightly wider space where the main part of Creede was built were filled with shanties and hovels crammed against the rocky walls, clinging to them in the clutch of cables or perching precariously on spin-

dly stilts. When the melting snow in spring swelled Willow Creek into a raging torrent many of these structures went swirling down to the Rio Grande. Each collection of buildings, separated by a canyon wall or spaced farther up or down the creek, had a special designation—Upper Creede, Sunnyside, Bachelor, Amethyst, Gintown. This last was also called Jimtown and was more or less homogeneous with Amethyst.

The real estate promoters had a flair for fancy names. Windy Gulch became Zephyr Canyon, Mud Flat blossomed out as Meadow Glade. Lots, once acquired at fantastic prices, often had to be defended and several murders were the result of claim jumping. One man wrote home he had asked directions to the "Palace Hotel" and found it a whip-board shanty, 16x16, with a blanket for a door. Beds were packed like cordwood and brought a dollar with covers and "four bits if you had your own," vermin included either way.

Whatever Creede lacked in virtue it offered plenty of ways to go to hell. Every other shack was a hook joint or dance hall, or combination of both, the ones in between gambling houses and saloons. Here and there was a respectable place but if a grocery store it still sold whiskey.

The place was filled with "characters," among them the notorious Soapy Smith. He got attention first by selling a bar of soap "wrapped up in a dollar," the buyer winding up with the soap and not the greenback. Soapy's most spectacular stunt concerned "The Petrified Man." He and his co-frauders made a human figure of concrete and buried it in the wet gravels of Willow Creek. While "the man" was aging the word was passed around that a miner had accidentally discovered this wonder. Soapy then led a selected party to the site, and with all due ceremony exhumed the relic and hauled it to his saloon where he exhibited it, though not for free. At a dollar a head the profits poured in and Soapy saw to it none of the customers got close enough to examine the gruesome object. Then came word of a visit by a famous scientist to inspect this archeological treasure and overnight the "petrified man" disappeared, with Soapy's outcry at skullduggery louder than anyones. Nothing was heard of the concrete "corpse" again.

Bob Ford, who had shot the Missouri desperado

LOADING BUNKER clings to near vertical rock wall. Crusher was operated by electricity, abundant in Creede where it was generated by ample water power. Lights burned day and night all over camp, inspiring poem, "And There Is No Night In Creede."

Jesse James, built a saloon and enjoyed a phenominal business due to his popularity with the sporting crowd. One night when the town was crowded with celebrants at the opening of a new dance hall, a miner named O'Kelly shot and killed Ford. No one knew what the grudge was, even O'Kelly who said Ford had "done dirt" to his parents. Ford's funeral was one of the largest ever seen in these parts with wine, champagne and liquor flowing

"like water." There was hardly a sober soul in Creede that night in June, 1892.

Gold, silver and zinc were among the metals mined in Creede but silver was queen. In fact Creede led all Colorado camps in silver production during its big years. The silver debacle of '93 dealt the death blow and the place was never the same again. There have been several revivals of a sort. In the 1920s some mines were reopened

301

and in 1939 the Emperius Mining Company re-activated the Commodore-Amethyst east of town. Some 500,000 pounds of silver were then shipped out at intervals of several weeks. In a camp with a less glamorous history of big production this would seem phenomenal but it was pin money to this one.

Cy Warman who came to Creede in its roistering days to start a newspaper *The Candle*, left behind a poem which sets the tone not only of Creede, but all the other boisterous camps of that day.

"And There Is No Night In Creede"

Here's a land where all are equal—
    Of high or lowly birth—

A land where men make millions
    Dug from the dreary earth.

Here meek and mild-eyed burros
    On mineral mountains feed.

It's day all day in the daytime,
    And there is no night in Creede.

The cliffs are solid silver,
    With wondrous wealth untold,

And the beds of the running rivers
    Are lined with the purest gold.

While the world is filled with sorrow,
    And hearts must break and bleed—

It's day all day in the daytime,
    And there is no night in Creede.

RAIL FACILITIES were not long in coming to Creede. Grade up Rio Grande was steep but negotiable. Station is situated on small area nearly level, where rest of main part of town was placed. From here Bob Ford's body was shipped back to Missouri after period of burial in Creede. Slayer O'Kelly served term at Canyon City, was released later.

DISASTER IN THE COAL CAMP

Crested Butte, Colorado

Black clouds still rolled out of the coal mine shaft and a man crawled out with them. He was burned black, far beyond immediate recognition, and for a time seemed the sole survivor. Yet some others did get out, eleven, more dead than alive. One, able to speak coherently, said he was among a group entering the mine for the day's work. He was knocked down and lay unconscious for a while, then started crawling along the floor where the air seemed better. "I know I crawled over several men that seemed very dead to me."

This was the blast that on January 24, 1884, shook Crested Butte to its very foundations. All buildings around the mouth of the mine were demolished, coal cars shot out of the tunnel, debris scattered more than a hundred feet. The new ventilator fan was the first casualty, making it impossible for rescuers to enter the smoky, fume-filled entrance.

There were several coal mines in production at Crested Butte in the early 1880s but one more than equalled the output of all the others. Tunnels stretched farther, shafts went deeper. A natural result was the accumulation of gas and after many complaints the company installed the giant fan to drive fresh air into the depths. Company officials said, "In case of an explosion, fumes and smoke can be eliminated quickly."

This statement was proved wrong. As the news of the January blast spread, miners from Baldwin and other camps quit work and came to Crested Butte on special trains to aid in rescue work. The first group to get in as far as the first level, 200 feet down, found a collection of seventeen bodies. Although it was impossible to penetrate deeper for more than a moment it was obvious many more dead lay at lower levels.

Gunnison historian Betty Wallace, gleaning her

LITTLE RURAL SCHOOLHOUSE beside road from Gunnison to Crested Butte, one of few remnants of one time stopping place for travelers on way to mines in area. At intersection was home of Jack Howe, giving first name to spot, Howville, then Jack's Cabin. Around center grew two hotels, two grocery stores, two saloons, one post office.
Gone now are roistering freighters who stayed here when conveying supplies to mines, ore and coal back to Gunnison. Gone too are all buildings except one-room school house of 80-odd years ago, ranch children still attending classes until very recently. Lush clumps of yellow dandelions make bright spots of color in yard.

303

data from newspapers of the day, wrote, "Huddled around the shattered entrance families of the unfortunate men stood in shocked silence . . . there was no outcry, but muffled sobbing when—thirty-eight hours after the explosion—the first body was brought to the surface, wrapped in canvas, a card of identification pinned to the breast." The process continued until fifty-nine bodies lay in the blacksmith shop pressed into service as a morgue. Several of the victims were teen-age boys on their first job. Most men were found lying on the ground with handkerchiefs over their mouths, indicating deaths by suffocation rather than concussion by the blast.

Although Crested Butte attained its pinnacle of importance in Colorado for its tremendous production of coal, there were placers on Slate and Coal Creeks and some silver and lead. In *Colorado Gold and Silver Mines* by Frank Fossett, published in 1880, are found some pertinent items. The Crested Butte District included such silver-lead mines as the Poverty Gulch group, Independence, Silver, Spence, Renselaer, Wolverine, Silver Queen and numerous others. Considerable ore was treated in Crested Butte, the book states, "A smelter was erected there in 1879, which will probably be steadily employed hereafter." Fossett was derogatory about the quality of Crested Butte coal. "While the veins of North and South are excellent lignite, those of Gunnison are considered anthracite of very inferior quality to that of Pennsylvania." In later years when quality was ignored, it was conceded that the Crested Butte deposits were the only ones of any extent west of the Pennsylvania fields. Very likely the first coal mined here provided the fuel for the smelter mentioned by Fossett. In 1880 there was a collection of tents at the location and after Howard Smith brought in a sawmill, many workers' homes were built.

Before another year passed coal mining was vastly expanded and herds of cattle were pastured nearby, a town built big enough to support a newspaper, the Crested Butte *Republican*, and to be incorporated as a city. By 1882 the railroad was in and coal shipped out more easily. An ultra-modern station was built near where some two hundred burros were still loaded daily with supplies for remote gold, silver and copper mines in the mountains.

Snow at the 9,000-foot altitude of Crested Butte fell almost continually through the winter and by spring often reached twenty-foot depths. Travelers forced to take routes over the passes were in constant dread of the "White Death," as every spring saw avalanches that usually took lives.

In late February, 1891, Edward Clark, superintendent of the Bullion King mine above Crested Butte, went to the city on important business. Before leaving he stopped at one of the saloons for a warmer-upper and as he headed for the door he asked his cronies, "Boys, if I get caught in a snow slide, will you come up to dig me out?" Arriving back at the mine days later he saw the entire complex of boarding houses and offices had been swept cleanly away in a mile-long avalanche. There was no trace of his house where he had left wife and baby.

Fred Germaine tumbled downhill in the shattered boarding house and later told the story. Starting just under the summit of Ruby Peak where snows were deepest, the slide moved down with a tremendous roar. Picking up the boarding house, superintendent's house, engineer's cabin and engine house, the great white wall carried everything to the bottom of the steep slope. Of the personnel, Germaine alone was alive when dug out four hours after the slide. The bodies were brought into

Crested Butte on sleds that required nine men to pull them, so difficult to traverse were the deep snows. The effort of search and rescue was so exhausting and danger from further slides so great, that when several avalanches occurred in March, no rescue crews were sent out until snows melted.

Crested Butte survived as a coal camp even when smelters ceased to operate, but when locomotives turned to diesel fuel, they gave the kiss of death to the town. Some stores still survive here to serve ranchers and sportsmen.

MAIN STREET of old coal camp displays relics of days when town had large population. Buildings shown here are unoccupied but others at western end of street are now used as stores, museum, antique shops.

PANORAMIC VIEW of Crested Butte shows cemetery in foreground, many graves those of mine explosion, avalanche victims. Funeral services, burials for those men dying in 1884 blast required a week, all flags at half mast. 3' of snow lay on ground frozen so hard grave diggers left cavities shallow. Next spring several small boys exploring cemetery found some caskets protruding from ground, fled home to report gruesome discovery. Hasty reburial followed.

CRESTONE, COLORADO

"Sangre de Cristo!"

The prospectors and settlers of the slopes and valleys under the snow-topped range could easily picture the Spanish explorer, Valverde, in the early morning when the sun suffused the white crests with a golden red glow. Reverently, the legend said, he removed his steel helmet and covered his chest, breathing fervently those words. In honor of Valverde and his discovery, the settlers named the range extending from Salida to Santa Fe, Sangre de Cristo—Blood of Christ.

Eight peaks of the noble mountains rise to 14,000 feet and close to the base of them, with the Crestone Needle spiring up to 14,191 feet, the mining camp of Crestone struggled into recognition in the 1880s. The land here was part of the Luis Maria Baca grant, later taken into Colorado by the first territorial governor, William Gilpin.

In 1879 prospectors were pecking at the rocks in these mountains, as along the whole length of the Rockies. Considerable gold was found, a mild boom developed and leveled off, and in 1890 good free-milling gold was found in "gash veins." Before it was discovered these were comparatively shallow, Crestone had been built.

The town took on the shrouds of a ghost but came back to life in '99 when another good vein was uncovered. Having learned no lesson from the earlier fiascos, Crestone again boomed. This time a hotel was built, real estate changed hands overnight and the railroad was extended to the town. The population had reached a new high of 2,000.

Miners were making new strikes in every crack of the Sangre de Cristos and in 1901 the blood count shot up still higher when the exciting strike at the Independent was made. Surely this vein, the miners said, would be a good one. It would yield for years and keep Crestone on the map. But alas, the vein pinched out as the others had and the town lay down in undeniable defeat. Since then only the faintest of heart beats are detected in the shadows of the peaks, and these in the ranchers' houses and vacationers' cars.

KING FERDINAND THE SEVENTH OF SPAIN in 1823 rewarded one of his subjects with title of Don Luis Maria Babeza de Vaca and granted him a trifling few hundred thousand of acres of land in new world. Legal ownership of vast area became serious matter when it was found the City of Las Vegas, New Mexico was included. After many maneuvers and shifting of titles, family was deprived of Las Vegas but in return received four hundred thousand acres extending into Colorado. Grant No. 4 comprises 100,000 acres of land mostly fitted for grazing only. Domain is 12 miles square and contains sources of six streams. Gold, silver, lead, copper and iron were found, several towns established— Cottonwood, Spanish, Duncan Pole Creek and Lucky. Grant owners condoned settlement while development was going on, evicted miners when value of metal finds became obvious. Duncan was saved by re-establishing town as Liberty, just over border.

CRIPPLE CREEK, COLORADO

Bob Womack's first trip to Colorado was not a success. In fact, the whole idea was so repugnant to him that he ran out on his father and started the long journey back to Kentucky walking barefoot. After walking more than a month and reaching a point somewhere in Kansas, he was overtaken by the elder Womack, Sam, and the two returned home together.

Sam had taken the boy to Idaho Springs in the famous gold country around Central City in 1861 for two reasons. He would remove the seventeen year old Bob from danger of conscription into service in the Civil War by getting out of Kentucky and in going to the wilds of Colorado he most likely would find a big strike.

After this first move, Sam saw that he hadn't laid the proper groundwork, and now he started a program of propaganda, about all the wealth to be made in the gold fields of Colorado. This was so successful that the whole Womack family was bitten by the bug, and soon all six of them set out for Idaho Springs.

Here the male members of the family, the two boys and the father went to work in earnest, learning all they could about mining. This must have been considerable, because they piled up some money. With this and experience gained, they worked a claim of their own, a piece of ground that had a rich vein of silver in it. It was in the area that later became Georgetown, and some time af-

ter the tenure of the Womacks, yielded a bonanza of half a million dollars.

Sam and his family did not get in on this kind of money, because he had decided his health could no longer stand mining, and would benefit by a stint of cattle ranching. There was enough cash with which to buy a cattle ranch in the wild area south of Pike's Peak near Mount Pisgah. And this move turned the wheels of destiny for the gold discovery that was to yield more wealth than any other area on earth up to 1930—well over $400 million in gold. Cripple Creek. And how was the spot so named? One of the streams draining the area originated in a spring near the cabin of a cattleman, the first settler. While he was building a shelter over it a helper accidentally discharged a gun, the ball wounding another man in the foot. The commotion frightened a calf which broke its leg jumping over the creek—all of which caused the rancher to exclaim: "Well, this here is sure one hell of a cripple creek!"

Bob Womack wasn't cut out to be a cattle rancher, or farmer of any kind; in fact the only career he was really suited for was drinking himself into one stupor after another, and this he proceeded to do. But there were lucid intervals of devotion to a fanatical belief that a rich lode of gold lay beneath the Mt. Pisgah area, particularly in the ground near the cabin he had bought in what he called Poverty Gulch.

MINING MAGNATE'S HOME.
Most mine owners of Cripple Creek had elaborate homes in more elegant Colorado Springs but some built houses close to "diggings" in earlier days when actual presence at scene of operations was still demanded.

There was no logical basis for Bob's belief. The terrain didn't have the right type of rock and every geological formation was all wrong and the experts in nearby Colorado Springs all concurred that Bob Womack was crazy, drunkenly crazy. If Bob had left the country he himself might eventually have come to that conclusion but he stayed on—and one day found a piece of rock which assayed $200 per ton. This was in 1878 and the find should have set off a boom. It didn't because no one would believe anything Bob said or did, even with the piece of rock as evidence. This was due partly to his carousing, partly to painful memories of a huge hoax perpetrated by one "Chicken Bill" and called the "Mt. Pisgah Hoax" through an error in locale. The spurious "discovery" had been made at Mt. MacIn-

tyre and had produced "ore assaying $2,000 to the ton." There was a frantic rush to the spot, then a complete deflation as the thousands found they had been hoodwinked.

But an angel was brushing Bob Womack's shoulder. A comparative newcomer to Colorado Springs, a dentist named Grannis, borrowed $500 and invested it in the man who thought no more of a bottle of whiskey than he did his right arm.

Grannis had gone into the geology of the ground on the slopes of Mt. Pisgah with an open mind and came to the conclusion that Bob could be right, that this spot was the center of an ancient volcano and had the type of conformation that should show vertical plugs, or gold-bearing veins, especially in view of the regular findings of "float" pieces containing gold that must have broken off from such hard outcroppings.

This reasoning proved to be right and so was Bob Womack. In 1890, after using up a large part of the partnership money on whiskey, he got a little digging equipment and uncovered the top of a rich vein concealed by several feet of cow pasture. But Womack's reputation was always ahead of him. Even though the partners took samples into The Springs and displayed them to all and sundry, nobody cared to do anything about it. After all, wasn't Bob Womack a blowhard? And what about that other hoax?

About this time, James Pourtales of Colorado Springs, a German count and a man of immense social prestige, decided to take a fling at a claim not far from "The El Paso" which happened to be the claim of Bob Womack and Dr. Grannis. He had no trouble interesting big money and soon things were buzzing all over the area, miners as thick as fleas and all claims paying off. Shacks were mixed in with tents and two-story false fronts with no semblance of order, foot traffic and wagons made their way in every direction through mud or dust.

Horace Bennett and Julius Meyers were partners who had bought up a good deal of Cripple Creek land as a cattle range before the gold fever took over. In 1891 they decided to lay out a town, bringing order into all this chaos, and, incidentally make a tidy pile of cash selling lots at the same time. November 6th the new town was laid out on paper in Denver. When the plan was transferred to the actual site, the planners were only a little dismayed to find that the map didn't lay flat on the actual ground, which was all up and down in every direction, with the steepest pitch from high on the north to low in the creek bed on the south. The main east-west streets were, of course, named Bennett and Meyers and the crossing north-south ones were numbered. Bennett Avenue was the main thoroughfare from the start, and soon filled with every kind of business structure, from schools to red-light houses.

Later, the places of less repute were moved over to Meyers Avenue. That street became solidly lined with at least 70 saloons, uncounted large brothels and even more numerous individual cribs. These were placed strictly in order of preference, starting with young white girls at the upper level, ending up with the cheaper, older women and minority groups at the bottom of the hill, near the trestle.

Near these hook shops on Meyers Avenue were many cheap rooming houses and dance halls, their situations and uses often overlapping, and one of these was the Central Dance Palace. On the upper floor were rooms and in one of these started the first big fire in the town. A gambler and his woman, Jeannie Larue, lived here, but not in peace and harmony. One of their more violent fights ended in the overturning of the gasoline stove. In moments the whistle of the Mocking Bird Mine was

CRIPPLE CREEK, SANGRE DE CRISTO RANGE and Rockies in distance. Competing, adjoining townsites, laid out in '91 and '92, were Fremont (for the explorer) and Hayden Placer, just above. Both names and separate identities persisted for a time, but both became "Cripple Creek" shortly. Plans made on paper sagged and humped on ground, one result was split level of part of Bennett Avenue. Old joke—"I hear someone fell off Bennett Avenue last night and broke his leg"—had some basis in fact.

MAIN STREETS OF CRIPPLE CREEK are Bennett Avenue and Meyers Avenue, run east and west, right to left in picture. Catholic Church and Hospital are large buildings at top of first hill. Most other brick structures are along Bennett Avenue. Meyers Avenue, one block south and parallel, was lined mostly by more frail, cheaper houses of extensive honky-tonk lane. These included the establishments of such famous Madames as Mother Duffy, Lola Livingstone, Hazel Vernon and Ellen Holden. These, along with cribs for individual girls and innumerable saloons and dance halls, have largely succumbed to old age and fire, though enough remain to attract the tourists.

shrieking one blast after another. This was the signal that a major fire was burning, calling out volunteer firemen to fight the flames. This one was bad enough, but a few days later a worse conflagration almost destroyed Cripple Creek, and left most of the residents homeless, hungry and freezing. Satellite towns, bitter rivals in normal times, rose to the emergency in a crisis and rushed food, blankets and tents to their neighbors.

This happened in 1896. It marked the end of the era of flimsy wooden structures to a large degree. Buildings constructed to replace those destroyed by fire, were mostly of brick, changing the face of the town.

By 1889 the mines had produced $21,000,000, and in 1900 the year's production was $23,000,000. During these prosperous times several railroads served the city, and the towns in the district were connected by a network of electric trains. 1894 and 1903 saw dark and violent periods brought on by labor disputes, the worst ever suffered by any mining community. Many murders, the blasting of properties by dynamite and other desperate acts of sabotage came to a head in the blowing up of the railway station at Independence, killing a number of men, maiming and injuring many. This act broke the back of the Union, as public reaction brought squads of soldiers and guards to jail many of the agitators and quell further disturbances. 112 men involved in atrocities were deported to Kansas and New Mexico, but these states did not welcome them, and forced many back.

By July, 1904, peace had descended, but other troubles were besetting Cripple Creek and the nearby towns. Water was becoming an increasing menace in the deeper mines, flooding equipment and preventing operation. Many of the older properties were petering out, and it was becoming apparent that the gold in Cripple was not inexhaustible.

Huge projects of tunneling through the granite walls of the bowl constituting the district were undertaken. Water levels dropped and mining was resumed at the lower levels.

Bob Womack died penniless in Colorado Springs on August 10, 1909. He had reached the age of 66 in spite of his heavy drinking, but his last years had been ones of poor health and poverty, as contrasted to the fame and fortune that came to so many of his contemporaries. Cripple Creek's gold had made thirty millionaires, and most of them did not stop at just one million. Winfield Scott Stratton, for example, who had earned three dollars a day before he began his career in the mines at Cripple at forty-four years of age, left over $6,000,000 when he died and this was only a small part of his take, his endowments, gifts and charities amounting to several times this sum.

Production of gold in Cripple Creek in 1903 was $19,000,000. This was $6,000,000 off that of the year before, and the trend was set, continuing until the present time, when all big operations but one, The Carlton Mill and Mine, have ceased.

The place is not dead. There are too many buildings, old mines and other sights reminiscent of Cripple's history for the tourist to see. The roads from Florissant and Colorado Springs, while spectacularly laid out through the mountains, are perfectly safe and the scenery alone makes the visit well worth while.

The Wall Street Journal of December 4th, 1961, reported: "Cripple Creek, Colorado—Golden Cycle Corp. will quit processing gold ore in its Carlton mill here. The plant will be closed and put on a stand-by basis Dec. 31." The president, Merrill E. Shoup, blamed the demise of this plant, which had operated for more than 70 years, on the low price of gold, stating the mill and mines had been kept going at a loss the past three years.

EUREKA, COLORADO

Eureka is suffering more rapid erasure than results from mere decay. Its store buildings are mostly torn down, the lumber to be put to more active service in Silverton. There is now no main street in Eureka, which once boasted the "finest saloons anywhere." This pride in alcohol emporiums had been continuous since 1896 when, of the several buildings comprising Eureka, the "saloon was the finest."

The beginnings of the place were in 1860, when Baker, (for whom Baker's Park, the locale of Silverton, was named) and his party did some digging and panning in the banks of the rushing Animas River. Eureka was no boom-town, but grew slowly and steadily. The Sunnyside mill was easily the leader as a producer of income for the populace. There was even train service to Eureka, beginning in 1896.

Looked at from above, on the road continuing up the canyon, the town is seen to be situated on an "island" extending over the elbow formed by a curve in the river. This got the center of town out from under the terrific avalanches so common in late winter, though fringe areas were devastated.

When the Sunnyside mills closed in 1938, the town died. Now even the mill is gone. Only impressive foundations run up the steep mountainside as reminders of camp town glory days.

ON OUR WAY TO ANIMAS FORKS we come to a wider spot on the narrow steep road. Stopping to look back on Eureka it is easy to see why avalanches crashed down into the valley. Old mine sites are everywhere on precipitous slopes.

BUSINESS BUILDINGS are nearly gone. At left are foundations of giant Sunnyside Mill which produced $50,000,000 in gold, lead, silver, zinc and copper. Tram line is visible, as are tailings and mine heads.

HOMES OF MINERS cluster on tiny level area, far out as possible from steep sides of canyon. Small patch of snow is visible, though picture was made in July, was first of more and larger banks farther up defile leading to Animas Forks.

311

FAIRPLAY, COLORADO

Not all those who responded to the clarion call of "Pike's Peak or Bust" found gold along the eastern fringe of the Rockies. Some restless souls who were not pleased with small pickings there, moved on across South Park and into the fastness of the Rockies themselves. One of these groups found a good show of colors in a stream not far from the South Platte River. Deciding to stay awhile, they named the new camp Tarryall. News of the strike spread, newcomers sought to share the wealth and were bitterly resisted. Smarting with resentment, one larger party of would-be residents moved on to the South Platte itself, found a rich deposit of gold flakes in the gravels of that stream and established a camp of their own which they called Fairplay.

After a few years, the supply of easily obtained placer gold grew less and the town suffered a depression. When capital became interested, hard rock mining began in the lodes that had been dribbling their wealth into the river gravels. This gold was harder to get at and hard to separate from the native rock, but the supply was more steady and Fairplay prospered again. Business picked up in the many dancehalls and saloons and the town's twelve hook-joints could stop having clearance sales.

However, as costs of machinery and labor rose while the price of gold remained fixed, stern difficulties beset the place and gradually decay set in again as mines closed. A large dredge was operating in the South Platte, digging far deeper into the gravels than by other, simpler methods, and while this operation employed a number of men, Fairplay was never the same again. It still breathes and makes a show of its memories and mementos.

SANDSTONE COURTHOUSE, built in 1874, replaced original log building moved from Buckskin Joe after election of 1868. All women and children were herded into structure, in 1879, when false rumor that Indians were burning neighboring Breckenridge and scalping residents threw town into frenzy. About same period brutal murderer was tried here, given life. Irate citizens gathered at night, forced keys from sheriff, took prisoner from cell, hanged him from second-story window over doorway which then lacked present awning.

GEORGETOWN, COLORADO

For many years Georgetown enjoyed the distinction of being the most important silver camp in Colorado, at length deposed by the even more fabulous strikes in Leadville in 1878. Gold, however, brought about the birth of the city and caused one of the biggest booms in the early mining history of the state. The yellow metal was found glittering in the gravels of the several streams gathering in the canyon's depths in 1859 by prospectors dissatisfied with what they found as latecomers to the Denver area. A discovery under similar circumstances and in the same year had started the fabulous careers of the related towns of Black Hawk, Central City and Nevadaville, but there, gold held out and sustained the economy of the gulch.

In Georgetown, on the other hand, large lodes or outcroppings of gold were never found, and although lode mining in the '70s was sufficient to boom the town a second time, this too tapered off. The town went through all the discouragements suffered by other camps in trying to extract silver from refractory ores. Poor communications, the worst kind of terrain and almost impossible travel, kept methods of getting at the shiny metal crude and costly. The margin of profit in silver, comparatively speaking, was never that of gold until several methods were compared and the best features of each combined. Part of this agony had been already toughed out by the camps in Georgetown's category when Leadville's star began to shine, materially stimulating silver extraction methods there.

PROMINENT LANDMARK remaining from days when fire was ever threatening. Shadowy interior still houses antiquated equipment. Tower was built especially for gift of 1,200-pound bell. In 1880 Hose Company won many prizes in State Firemen's Tournaments, including silver tea set and brass cannon. In background at left is Grace Episcopal Church, built by townspeople even before rector was assured. Completed in '69, it was blown from foundations by gale, dragged back, bell anchored in separate belfry beside structure. Bell bears inscription "St. Mark's, Black Hawk, Colo. Terr." Intended for church to be erected there, Georgetown salvaged it when plans fell through.

THIS LITTLE GEM is sole survivor of fire which devastated most of block. When this building was erected, famous Georgetown to Silver Plume Loop was being built. Ore had long been hauled down valley in wagons but had reached proportions beyond capacity of horse-drawn rigs. When railroad was completed it followed a "Loop System" unequaled in its day. Tracks folded over themselves to gain altitude, reaching the Plume and completion thus far in '82.

But while Georgetown struggled to get on its feet as a silver camp, whiskey flowed in a never-ending stream. One saloon proprietor hired a sign painter to embellish the front of his establishment with a sign calculated to stimulate sales. He wanted a good job done but refused to pay what the painter asked, and the resulting legend read, "We sell the Worst Whiskey, Wine and Cigars." Unable to read but pleased with the attention his new sign created, the proprietor paid the painter the rest of his money, later discovering he was being laughed at. Nevertheless, the publicity so stimulated business the sign was allowed to remain for many years. Another story is told that the towns-people felt that they should have a cemetery like any other city, were frustrated by the healthfulness of the climate there, and at last had to hang a man to get things going. Although the camp attracted as many undesirables as did any other, there were fewer killings and other forms of violence.

In the late '70s the following appeared in *The Georgetown Miner.* "For a period of about sixteen years that enterprising individual, the 'honest miner,' has prospected and dug for the precious metal in our county with that energy and tenacity which is a distinguishing characteristic of 'miner men,' and, to some extent, is born of the circumstances under which he is placed. He has lived hard and worked harder, and with an undaunted brow has often faced the bitterest and sternest realities of life. He has gazed down the misty avenues of probabilities until what appeared to others to be the vaguest outlines of chance were to him an absolute certainty of all his hopes. He has acquired a fortune with a few weeks' or months' labor, and often, with a generosity bordering on recklessness, he has squandered it again in but less time than it took to accumulate it. On the one hand, he has toiled incessantly for years without taking out a single

OLDEST FIREHOUSE in town has lacy balcony and elaborate belfry, still retains picturesque emblem of crossed ladders and fire hook. Organized in 1870, Georgetown Fire and Hose Co. stands on Alpine Street, across from Louis Du Puy's Hotel De Paris.

LOUIS DU PUY'S HOTEL DE PARIS was most celebrated hostelry west of Mississippi during '70s and '80s. Born in Alencon, France, Du Puy was a hater of women, yet left all he had to one. He was a despiser of his guests yet made them comfortable in an opulence undreamed of in a wild mountain silver camp. Eccentric, unpredictable, he had squandered an inheritance in France, arriving in Georgetown to recoup his fortunes in '69, and four years later was injured in mine explosion. Displaying heroism in rescue work of disaster, he was rewarded with collection taken up by families. With this, in '75, he bought Delmonico Bakery on Alpine Street, remodeled it into Hotel De Paris. Lavish in furnishings, exotic in cuisine, hotel accepted as guests only people passing close scrutiny of Du Puy, many being turned away for no apparent reason. Only one woman gained his second look — a widow, Sophie Galet. She was taken in at husband's death, made comfortable and was bequeathed entire establishment at Du Puy's death in 1900.

'red,' but his faith still continues unshaken and his perseverance unimpaired. He has accomplished labors compared with which the cleaning out of the Augean stables would be but a before-breakfast chore. He has penetrated to the very foundations of the eternal hills, and the innermost recesses of 'earth's gigantic sentinels' have echoed with the sharp ring of his steel-impelling strokes and bellowed back the infernal roar of his fiery persuasion. He has carved his way through sullen solitude in search of metaliferous wealth, and a liberal and enlightened civilization has followed close on his heels. If he has not discovered the secret of transmutation of metals, he has discovered the secret of their hiding places; while mechanical and chemical science have sprung to his aid and rendered indispensable assistance in their extraction. The brave and persistent miner has accomplished all this and much more, not with the wand of an eastern fairy, but with a striking hammer weighing from six to eight pounds, and other implements necessary to his vocation."

Georgetown could have faded into decay but the town continues to live with pride. Its buildings are kept in good repair and a hard surface road brings many tourists every year to view the monuments to a glorious past.

315

WHERE LIVE THE SILVER SPIRITS

KOKOMO, COLORADO

At Kokomo's elevation, 10,618 feet, deep snows cover the ground between November and May. In 1878 access routes were only narrow trails cut out of the sides of cliffs overhanging roaring streams.

But nothing could assuage the fever for gold that set in with the beginning of 1879. Men came in swarms to improvise shelters of the rudest description. These were set on top of six or eight feet of snow. Since surface indications were absent or out of sight under the snow, shafts were sunk at random on the first unclaimed site the prospective miner could lay hands on. And often, these paid off.

SALOON BEARS TRACES of bright orange paint, with black trim. Bar and tables remain intact. Upstairs "private rooms" were reached by less conspicuous door at side. Narrow gauge railroad passed close by; remains are seen crossing stream just past telephone pole, lower right.

With the opening of summer, Kokomo already had a population of 1,500! Prices of lots compared favorably with the altitude. A city government was organized, a bank built. Then followed saloons, hotels, stores, and sawmills. And before long, a newspaper and smelters.

The Kokomo Giant mine on Gold Hill had actually been producing ore rich enough to ship for smelting before this operation could be produced on the spot. The average assay was 179½ ounces of silver and 17.6 per cent lead. Gold showed only a trace in most of these ores. In this period of mining history standard gold sold at $18.60 per ounce and silver from $1.10 to $1.25.

By the time Kokomo was established, the mine owners had a large advantage over those of 1864, when labor was "outrageously high." Then, a miner, even though "indifferent and lazy," earned as much as $4.00 a day. Now a "more reasonable" scale was estab-

TYPICAL EARLY-DAY construction. House in Kokomo shows combination of log and whipsaw boards. Outdoor "plumbing" is at one side. Roof was steep, to better shed enormous snows of Rocky Mountain winters.

lished with the going rate of $2.00 to $2.25. And other commodities went back on a saner basis, with flour back to $2.25 per 100 pounds, candles $6.25 per box and nails five cents a pound, inflation was ended.

New strikes kept the frenzy unabated. One man who volunteered to dig a grave for a dead friend struck "mineral" and went to file a claim before burying his deceased comrade elsewhere.

Some companies constructed roasting furnaces at the mines, since the neighboring forests afforded fuel for the cutting. A stone wall two and a half feet high enclosed a space ten by twenty feet. In this was placed a floor of pine logs covered with finely split dry wood. About forty-five tons of ore were piled thereon and the wood beneath fired. Combustion continued for two weeks. When the sulphur and other refractory substances were expelled, the ore was then ready for smelting.

MASONIC HALL STANDS alone, facing sun, was even more ornate in Victorian days. "Gingerbread" has largely fallen, though window trims remain among most beautiful examples of art.

HILL ABOVE KOKOMO is honeycombed with mine tunnels and shafts. Two-story school, gauntly tall, dominates town. Just below is rear of Masonic Hall. Still lower is stream where casual panning started all excitement.

This prodigal use of the surrounding forests soon resulted in their depletion and wood had to come from farther away.

In the year 1881, when Kokomo had reached its population peak of 10,000, a disastrous fire raced through the wooden frame buildings of the town. Only a few structures were left standing. Rebuilding was started immediately, and for a time it seemed that the Kokomo of old was off to a fresh start. Much ore was still being taken from the mines and shipped by rail. But somehow the heart seemed to have gone out of the place and several mines faltered in production, it never reached the level of prosperity it had enjoyed before the fire and began gently to fold up.

LAKE CITY, COLORADO

Only a little moonlight entered the house in Lake City that night in April, 1882. Sheriff E. N. Campbell and his deputies waited silently for the pair of saloon keepers who had been robbing the house of its furniture and were expected to return for more loot. Campbell and his men were beginning to grow stiff and cramped when a noise at the door galvanized them to attention. The sheriff called out, "Throw up your hands!" Instead, the intruders fired at the dimly seen shapes, killing Campbell. They then fled in the darkness.

At daybreak next morning a pursuing posse on horseback caught up with the fugitives who were tied up, taken back to Lake City and thrown into jail. Saloons were closed by the Mayor. Dance halls and stores voluntarily shut their doors. A heavy cloud of foreboding hung over the mining camp in the mountains.

That evening men watched as the moon dropped toward the mountain rim and as it set, they began moving toward the jail. "A heavily disguised figure," it is recorded, "carried under his arms the ropes; another bore a heavy sledge hammer; others carried rifles and shotguns . . . a hundred or more unmasked citizens were waiting at the jail . . . then followed the dull thud of the sledge hammer against the strong jail lock . . . the prisoners were

marched to the bridge . . . a rope was thrown over a crossbeam and in less than a minute the men were swinging . . . It was one o'clock. The dark shadows were now creeping up the side of the western wall of the little city. . . The falls under the bridge gurgled and splashed mournfully—silence brooded painfully over the great court and jury and witnesses who stood with upturned faces looking at two figures swinging grimly at the end of the rope of Justice."

An oldtimer of Lake City, a child at the time of this gruesome event, told historian-artist Muriel Wolle that just as the moon went beneath the mountain and the men dropped to the ends of the ropes, a great cry went up from the mob, then all was silent. He also recalled the astonishing fact that next morning all the school children of the town were taken down to the creek to view the bodies swinging there. At the conclusion of this educational display, "Coroner Rapp . . . proceeded to the scene, lowered the bodies and summoned a jury who found that Betts and Browning came to their deaths at the hands of unknown parties."

This episode, gruesome enough, was preceded in 1873 by an even more sordid one. A mile above Lake City is a fairly level area, in this land of steep mountains, called Cannibal Plateau. Here were found the bodies of five men, their skulls crushed, the bodies mangled and cut up. Pieces of flesh were missing from each.

The events leading up to the demise of the prospectors and the apprehension of a sixth member are confused, but all stories agree that the men started out on a prospecting trip through the San Juan Mountains in December, 1875. They had originally come from Utah and now were safely holed up in a Ute Indian encampment. With heavy winter snows imminent, the chief, Ouray, urged the men to stay for the winter. Six who refused the proffered hospitality were Packer, Bell, Humphreys, Swan, Noon and Miller. These pushed on into the snowy mountains. Some six weeks later Alfred Packer appeared at the Los Pinos Indian Agency alone. He told a harrowing tale of how his companions had quarreled with each other and, when he tried to keep peace between them, they turned and severely beat him, left him for dead. He said he almost starved but found a few roots to chew on and killed some small game. He requested a drink of whiskey, but didn't seem as hungry as he should, in fact seemed much too well nourished to have subsisted on roots and a rabbit or two all that time.

A short time later he appeared at Saguache and spent considerable money on drink, gambling and women. In the meantime, just after his departure from the agency, an Indian arrived there with strips and pieces of human flesh which he said he had picked up along Packer's trail. The authorities already suspicious, went after Packer and brought him in. There being no jail there he was chained to a rock but escaped.

Early next spring as the snow was melting a photographer for Harper's Weekly was on his way to Lake City. Crossing the plateau above the town he came upon the remains of the erstwhile companions of Packer. The find set off an intensive search for the man, a hunt that was to last for nine years. The miscreant was finally caught in Wyoming and returned to Lake City for trial on a charge of murder. Convicted, he was sentenced to hang, but gained a new trial and this time got off with 40 years. After he had served only a few years he was pardoned. He died a natural death in Denver in 1906.

Members of Fremont's Party of explorers in 1848 had made the first discovery of gold in the valley where Lake City is situated, but had other things on their minds, such as imminent danger of being scalped by the Utes. This same fear of having "too much off the top" caused a long hiatus of white immigration and it wasn't until the Bunot Treaty

BAPTIST CHURCH has survived with little change, bearing new roof and several coats of paint. Cloud shadows on hill make white church stand out sharply from background. Prior to building of churches in mining camp establishing religion was one man affair. Rev. George M. Darley, later pastor of Presbyterian Church (also still standing) conducted services in any place available, even gambling hall or saloon. He once remarked that a pool table made "best kind of altar." He was a humble man of God, being as willing to preach funeral services for one of the "girls" from Hell's Acre or a bandit strung up from a tree as for one of the first citizens of the town.

DENVER AND RIO GRANDE built extension to Lake City in 1889, relieving acute depression of camp caused by overproduction of ores and metals with lack of facilities for shipping. Arrival of rails reopened many mines. During '90s line did flourishing business, two passenger trains a day rolling in from Sapinero, most of population at station to meet them. Town was already long dead as mining center when rails were taken up in 1937. Spectacular trestles, necessitated by rough terrain were taken down, only visible traces now are roadbed beside stream and relic preserved in front of courthouse. Caboose has for company an ore car on tiny section of track.

STONE STRUCTURE DATES FROM EARLY DAYS of Lake City, was built as meeting place and dance hall. Assembly room occupies three-quarters of building at rear, cloak room and entry hall with ticket booth are in front. Large safe and pot bellied heating stove are prominent objects among stored miscellany in "foyer." Swallows nests add to decorations on already ornate cornice. Section of wooden sidewalk, once extending length of town persists here, though nearly rotted away.

Rear of stone building was "service yard," also enclosed were outdoor "conveniences." Stone and weathered wood offer study in varied textures.

of '74 opened up the valley that a wave of prospectors, long pent up, burst upon the area about which had been heard so many rumors of rich gold deposits. Enos Hotchkiss is generally credited with having made the first big strike, his Golden Fleece.

Before long as the boom expanded, smelters, stamp mills and lixiviation works were being built all around the valley. One of the reduction plants was powered by the energy developed from a seventy foot waterfall.

In 1875 Harry M. Woods started a newspaper called the *Silver World*. The sheet was printed in a log cabin roofed with saplings covered with soil. When the editor would walk across the floor or was operating his little press a shower of dirt would sift down.

1876 and '77 were Lake City's best years. The population had grown to 2,500 and there were about 500 buildings. In spite of this metropolitan atmosphere the menace of the Ute was ever present, and had it not been for Chief Ouray's constant rein on his savages the town's position in the San Juans would have been untenable.

The red light section was confined to a small area on Henson Creek known as "Hell's Acre" which included all the elements of the typical early mining camp, the gambling houses, dance halls and those establishments often referred to as "cat houses." This general term identified both organized parlors and individual cribs.

Lake City began to go down a little before the turn of the century when the richest veins began to show signs of depletion, and by 1902 the population had dropped to about 500. There are now many attractions for the tourist, vacationer, fisherman and hunter and they populate the area in summer, living in cabins and camps on magnificent Lake San Cristobal.

322

LEADVILLE, COLORADO

When the Colorado historian and champion of Leadville, Caroline Bancroft, heard of my intent to include the Cloud City in this book she was alarmed.

I quote her warning, a paragraph of a letter in her always charming style. "But let me warn you, Leadville has 5,000 population. It is not a ghost town and never has been one. The population will blow its top if you call it one."

I wouldn't dare! But I again call attention to our chosen definition of a ghost, "a shadowy semblance of its former self."

And even if the city does not fit this category, how could one write anything bearing on Colorado's fabulous mining history without touching on Leadville, certainly no place in the State is so redolent. Besides, the city is now welcoming tourists with open arms. These will not stay away because of ghosts of those wilder, earlier days.

And so, with some trepidation, we proceed.

"Hang on to the Matchless, it will make millions again!" As the Silver King of Colorado lay dying in the 90's, he whispered those hopeful words to "Baby Doe," but his world had already crashed around him. And so had the luxurious bejeweled dream faded for his still beautiful wife.

The story of Horace Tabor and of his first and second wives, the pathetic, angular Augusta and the voluptuous Baby Doe is inextricably woven with that of Leadville.

The early discoveries of gold in "California Gulch," which supported Tabor and the future Leadville so poorly, the pushing aside of the hated heavy sands and carbonate, the discovery that these contained the real bonanzas, lead and silver, the fantastic returns from the hard rock mining and smelting of these hitherto neglected metals, were the factors that made Tabor and Leadville. The later failure of the early lodes, along with panics and silver crashes broke them.

Tabor, in the early 60's, had listened to the Siren Song of another gold strike in the mountains and had dragged Augusta out of her sickbed in Denver, piled her and their ailing baby into their rickety wagon and set out for the "shining peaks."

LEADVILLE, "THE CLOUD CITY" AS SEEN FROM Fryer Hill, looks as it did to Baby Doe. Fryer Hill was named for Geo. H. Fryer, who, on April 4th, 1878 found carbonates here and named his claim the "New Discovery." Tailings dumps may be seen extending into town.

The cold, the bitter wind, the wails of the sick baby and her own miseries were endured with not too many complaints by Augusta, until they arrived in South Park. She later said it was "gorgeously beautiful." The night here was so cold that a little burro strayed into camp and got so close to the fire that he burned his fetlocks. Augusta cared for him and made him her pet, weeping on his sympathetic shoulder in her wretchedness and longing for her home in Maine.

On their arrival at camp in California Gulch, a cabin was thrown together, the pitiful, scrawny oxen slaughtered, the bag of dried apples opened up and Augusta started taking in boarders. The hard years dragged on, and then suddenly, *Bonanza!*

Tabor's partners, taken on in exasperation to get rid of them and their pleas for a "grubstake," had stumbled onto what would be the famous "Little Pittsburg" Mine. In two months the mine was bringing in $20,000 a week. The hard days were over, and with them, the marriage of Augusta and Horace.

Tabor, now risen to the status of a millionaire many times over, and Lt. Governor of Colorado, had a girl friend in the person of the glamorous Elizabeth McCourt, and certainly had no need for such a "dowdy, straitlaced drudge" as Augusta.

She was shed, not without some compensation financially, and the more rounded "Baby Doe" was wed in pomp and splendor, but sans the approval of the lady members of Denver's 400 of that day. If she felt the chill of this snub, she must have been warmed

IN THIS HOUSE Horace and Augusta lived during the years of his ascendancy. Bone of contention was her determination to remain in unostentatious home, opposing his desire to make more of a display of his ever-increasing wealth. Building at right is early-day assay office.

THE "MATCHLESS" MINE SHAFT opening is covered by grating. At left is cage with just room for man.

THE SHACK ON FRYER HILL where Baby Doe spent her last years and where her frozen body was found. The head house of the Matchless is at the left.

somewhat by her $7,000 bridal dress and the attendance of President Arthur and members of his cabinet.

Their first-born, Lillie, wore for her christening a creation costing $15,000.

A huge mansion rose to house the new family of the now soaring Horace Tabor, and it was surrounded by stables, parks and fountains with elegant statuary.

Tabor had disposed of his partnership holdings and owned scores of mines by himself. His income was more than $4,000,000 a year, and his "pet," the Matchless Mine, alone dumped $2,000 a day into his already bulging pockets.

Typical of his wild extravagances was the purchase of a yacht in New York, and by 1886, it was becoming apparent that even his fabulous income could not keep up with his expenditures. Singly and severally, his mines and other sources of income went into insolvency, failed, or were sold to satisfy creditors. The fabulous Tabor was back where he started.

Now, broken and nearly 70 years old, he went prospecting again for a year, enduring hardships as severe as those of his early days. Then he was given, as a small recognition of former generosities to his party, a job as postmaster in Denver. This he held only a little more than a year, when he died there.

Destitute, Baby Doe soon was forced to move to Leadville, and into the little cabin at the mouth of the Matchless. There she eked out a miserable existence, her daughters gone, one to marry and live elsewhere, and one to die under dubious conditions in a shabby roominghouse in Chicago. She walked down to Leadville at intervals to buy leftover scraps for food, her feet wrapped in gunny-sacks in winter. And, in the cabin, close to the Matchless she died, freezing and alone.

325

OHIO CITY, COLORADO

If friends had not intervened, Reid and Edwards would probably have killed each other in Leadville but in Ohio City, where they had gone separately, they either had no friends or people just loved to see guns blazing and men falling. That was what happened. They saw each other on an Ohio City street in the 1880s. A block apart, their first shots missed, and they continued shooting as they drew closer. When the bullets hit, they were in each others' heart and the men almost touched as they fell.

It was gold that started the excitement at Ohio City, placer gold in the gravels of what would be called Ohio Creek in recognition of the men hailing from that state. The discovery came early in the '60s, making Ohio City one of the oldest camps in the area. When the shallow deposits were exhausted, the men left without searching for the lode that was the natural source. Since the miners had put up only the flimsiest of tents and shacks, all signs of habitation soon disappeared, the small camp slipping back into the wilderness.

Then the big silver boom of 1879 again brought prospectors to Ohio City where they soon found good enough veins to start the camp going again, and more permanently, giving the place the name

LOG CONSTRUCTION of two-story building in Ohio City dates it from silver boom days, before lumber from neighboring Pitkin was available from sawmill there. Corrugated sheet metal roof has saved structure from decay while adjoining dirt-roofed shed is near collapse. Trees on flat in background are cottonwoods bordering Gold Creek, those covering hillside almost all aspens.

ASPENS, the most common and beloved deciduous tree in Colorado's mountain areas, belong to willow family which includes poplars and cottonwoods. Technically **Populus tremuloides**, trees are conspicuous at all times. Leaves have flat leaf-joints, flutter in slightest breeze showing lighter colored undersides. In Fall, foliage turns brilliant gold, some leaves attaining deeper orange. Heavy massing of trees cause whole mountain sides to blaze with color. Snowy trunks, marked by black "eyes," scars left by self-pruned limbs, are attractive at all times.

of Eagle City, then Ohio City. When the boom collapsed in 1893, Ohio City also caved in, becoming a near-ghost town along with other Colorado silver camps. Then in 1896 a party of prospectors found the vein of gold that had been spilling nuggets into the creek, which they now called Gold Creek.

Ohio City's silver-fostered boom spawned some log buildings but with the gold boom the town of Pitkin up canyon was well established and included a sawmill. So the buildings put up in the gold era are dated by whether they are of logs or lumber.

Muriel Sibell Wolle, in her definitive STAMPEDE TO TIMBERLINE, reports the Carter Group of claims on Gold Creek produced enough ore to keep the twenty-stamp mill going full blast for twenty years, producing a gold brick worth $3,000 every two weeks.

Then there was the Raymond mine which produced steadily until its closure at the death of the manager in 1916. About a mile farther up the gulch were the workings of the Gold Link Mining Company. This outfit had drawn on 6000 acres of gold-bearing claims, operated a forty-stamp mill and kept two hundred men on the payroll. Its main 4000-foot tunnel and many ramifications produced almost a million dollars in gold and silver ore.

Colorado

SO RICH IN GOLD

Ophir, Colorado

The first party to explore for mineral veins at the foot of Ophir Needles was a group led by Lt. Howard who founded Howardsville near Silverton. He tarried in Colorado long enough to bestow his name once more, on a stream tumbling down the valley, a branch of the San Miguel River, he called Howard's Fork.

The first legal claims were staked there in 1875 and from then on prospectors dribbled through and sometimes stopped for a while. Nobody stayed all winter at this near-timberline elevation until 1878-9 when seventeen men did hole up there, working their claims whenever weather allowed, which was seldom. Some burrowed under banks of deep snow for some protection from frigid blasts off the 14,000-foot peaks.

The next year the Osceola mine was producing some gold and from others like the Gold King came sack after sack of rich ore. One batch of ten brought the owners $5,000. These miners were able to use arrastras which, though crude, were effective when ore was rich enough. One enthusiastic Howard's Fork miner suggested renaming the place Ophir after the fabled Arabian city so rich in gold.

About the time five hundred prospectors were swarming around Ophir, working up thirsts that required five saloons to put down, carbonate fever struck. At Leadville where gold was growing scarce, miners discovered the heavy rocks they cursed as obstacles to gold mining were loaded with carbonate of lead, and with lead inevitably came silver. This inspired many second thoughts

about areas where other gold placers were exhausted, one of these being Rico, erstwhile heavy gold producer. Sure enough, the place was now found to be "rico" in silver. Since it was near Ophir its miners were caught up in the prevailing excitement and left the camp almost deserted, a ghost town before it was fairly alive.

Where Leadville's carbonate deposits were so extensive as to create the greatest boom of its kind, those at Rico were disappointingly small and soon exhausted. So the tide turned and Ophir miners rushed back to their old claims. With the building

THRU THIS PORTAL passed some of Colorado's ugliest men. Most early mining camps had a few denizens who were fugitives from eastern law.

328

OLD OPHIR JAIL, only building standing in central part of business district which had famous Colorado House, other hotels, stores, saloons, gambling houses. More solidly built for security, jail's heavy logs and beams have resisted gales, snows of nearly century. Town had good water supply, fire protection (note hydrant, right).

In middle distance of photo are scattered remains of business houses, now mercifully graced with blanket of brilliant yellow dandelions. Just right of center in far distance is steep trail to summit of pass up which route many tons of gold rich ore was carried on backs of burros to Silverton before railroad. First mail came in this route. At base of last switchback, mail carrier Swen Nilson was buried in snow slide, body not exposed for two years (see **Tales the Western Tombstones Tell**).

of smelters at Silverton, Ophir miners sent their ore by burro trains over and through the mountains to the city at the foot of Sultan Mountain (see *Tales the Western Tombstones Tell* and *Western Ghost Towns*).

In the summer of 1879 "official" mail service from Silverton was established. Muriel Sibell Wolle relates that the service, though welcome, left something to be desired and cites some items from the Ouray *Times* which had a correspondent at Ophir. "The mail carrier from Silverton . . . has robbed the mail and left the country. The mail bag cut open and with registered mail rifled has been found near Iron Springs." Another item: "No mail for weeks. The Kansas tenderfoot says he wouldn't carry the mail again for $5,000 after one trip." And—"No mail from Rico in ten days. The snow is nearly ten feet deep and there are snow slides in every gulch . . . the mail carrier nearly froze on his last trip."

REMAINING RESIDENCES, only buildings at Old Ophir, these in far better condition than those in New Ophir which was little more than station on highway from which two cars of Ophir mine ore were shipped daily. These houses were occupied until recently. Porches, decorations such as barge-boards have been added in later years, old photo from Fred and Jo Mazula collection in **An Empire of Silver** showing them without porches, etc.

OURAY is one of those Colorado mining camps now much shrunken from rip-roaring center it once was, yet far from ghost. These historic spots can hardly with any justice be omitted from consideration in a pictorial record. Originally called Uncompahgre City for stupendous mountain range hemming it in, later name honoring Ouray, chief of Western Utes, friend to all whites, miners and settlers.

At time when town was terrified by rumors of advancing savage White River Ute tribes, Ouray and wife Chipeta walked up main street with hands upraised in peace gesture. When apprehensive crowd gathered, dignified chief assured citizens he would guarantee their safety from warring segment.

PITKIN, COLORADO

Ladies were rare enough in early mining camps, especially those who backed up their forthright ideas with guns. In Pitkin "Captain" Jack, whose given name was Ellen E., had the temperament of a tarantula and was further poison with a pair of six-guns.

Thoroughly unpredictable, she might appear in men's rough pants and jacket or dressed to the hilt of fashion in women's clothes, complete with bustle. In fact the bustle was most important. "Without pants pockets," she retorted with a sting in the words, "where else am I going to carry my money, stocks and diamonds?"

She drove through the streets at top speed, disregarding corners, until one day her carriage overturned, spilling the lady out into the dirt. There she lay unconscious, bustle up — thirty, blonde and blue-eyed. A passel of eager young bucks rushed to her aid. One cried: "Give her air! Another started loosening her dress and suddenly Captain Jack sat up and spewed forth a stream of oaths that were never spoken in her Quaker church. The question whether the man's touch had been on her bodice or bustle was never answered.

A train of burros came through town one day, the little animals braying painfully, and someone told Captain Jack: "That driver always lets the burros' backs get raw and the packs hurt them. But you dassent go and do anything about it. That jaywhacker's got a violent bad temper." But so did the lady. She jerked out her guns, leveled them at the driver, ordered him to remove the packs and held the guns steady until he did.

Ellen Jack was hospitable — up to a point, such as one she made when a young man moved some supplies to her claim. It was late and when he started to go home, she invited him to stay overnight. The youth saw only one bed in the cabin and whatever hopes or doubts he had were quickly dispelled. "Let's make one thing clear right now," said Captain Jack with the vigor of womanly virtue as she dropped a gun in the middle of the bed. "This is my side. That's yours. See you stay on it."

In his book, DIGGING GOLD AMONG THE ROCKIES, George Thomas Ingham gives an accurate picture of Pitkin in its first hectic years. He arrived in Buena Vista, Colorado, just before the railroad reached that camp on its way to the wildly booming Leadville, and in company with an equally eager friend, visited many of the camps along the East fringe of the Rockies, then went "up and over", emerging at the back door of Pitkin and other camps on the Western side of the range.

"We arrived at Miller's," wrote Ingham, "where there were three or four log cabins about noon, which were the first evidences of civilization, where travelers are lodged and entertained when they wish to stop awhile on their journey. There are two or three mines in the vicinity. The 'Margaret', owned by Miller and Hall, was discovered about a year ago. It seems Miller came along a ledge and camped for the night. Finding float nearby the next morning, he traveled up the hillside for a few rods where he started a tunnel, striking a vein of silver-lead or Galena ore of considerable value. The parties claim to have been offered $20,000 for their find. Quartz Creek is a very rapid stream with a succession of falls and rapids and we descended from

CITY HALL had lower floor carved out of hillside. Upper floor is one large room, was used for lodge meetings, dances, social functions, reached by separate outside stairway. The covered one shown here replaced an older, uncovered one on other side. Building is now unused, the town having only about a dozen residents. Old hotel is at left, service limited to small lunch counter in lobby.

our high elevation to a lower one very fast. When down in the vicinity of Pitkin the mountains rose less abruptly, were not so high and became heavily timbered with a species of yellow pine. . . . . .

"The first evidence of our approach to Pitkin was the site of a steam saw-mill and some log huts in the gulch above town. The valley here widens to ¼ mile or more, and Pitkin is situated on a level grassy flat a mile or more in length. It is a lovely site for a town, being in a grassy park in which there is no timber, yet the surrounding hills are densely covered with spruce, pine to their very tops. Quartz Creek passes on one side close to the mountain, and an irrigating ditch carries the clear

water the entire length of the town along the side of Main Street.

"Main Street is thickly studded with buildings in all stages of erection. Tents and log huts are everywhere to be seen, and for a town of only two or three weeks' growth shows considerable energy in the great number of buildings which have been erected. About five weeks ago three or four log cabins were about the sum total of the buildings in the place. Now corner lots sell for $800. Its elevation is about 9,000 feet.

"One old gentleman who came into town last fall without any means save for his team and less than $100 in cash, purchased nine or ten lots, paying $5 to $10 for each, and holding them until spring, disposal returns ranging from $300 to $750, thereby clearing about $5,000.

"Hotels not being plentiful at the time of our arrival we took quarters at one of the numerous lodging houses which appear to be the fashionable sleeping places of the town. The house in question was a large tent, 18x50 feet; the floor was the ground, which was, however, not level, and was covered with three or four inches of sawdust. A canvas partition divided the sleeping apartment from the rest of the room. There was a stove and numerous boxes and trunks as substitutes for chairs, which constituted the furniture of the room. The bunks on which we slept were made of rough boards,

arranged in a row at the side of the room with two tiers, one above the other, steamboat fashion. The beds consisted of loose hay tossed upon the boards and covered with gray blankets, and comfits were used as covers. No sheets or pillows were to be seen, coats were universally used for pillows. Price of lodging, 50¢.

"We slept well, and in the morning felt refreshed. We went to the 'Bon Ton' for breakfast, where we found two ladies in charge. It was a tent 16x24 with a sawdust floor like our bunk house, and the tables reclining at an angle of about fifteen degrees from the level. However, everything bore the atmosphere of cleanliness and neatness, and we had an excellent breakfast of beefsteak, fried eggs,

BACK YARDS of most abandoned houses are filled with clutter of earlier, busier days.

bacon, fried potatoes, corn bread, warm biscuits, butter and coffee, and in fact everything essential to a good appetite, and well cooked, for a half dollar. We were surprised at such good fare in such a new town, but found it to be the prevailing prices of the place.

"The following day was Sunday, yet the stores and saloons were open; the sounds of the saw and hammer were ringing all day long. Reports of shots from giant powder while blasting in the mines were frequent all day, and the din and rush of travel and freighting through the streets went on as usual. These mining towns have very little regard for the Sabbath.

"Within six weeks there have been erected fifteen hotels, restaurants, lodging houses, and some forty to fifty business houses and saloons. By the 15th of June when a count was taken, there were 1,050 people within the city limits, and doubtless as many more were camping and prospecting within a few miles around the city. There were 168 dwellings, 4 hotels, 8 restaurants, 12 saloons, 50 stores and businesses, a bakery; 80 vacant unfinished buildings, 3 meat markets, several real estate offices and one jail. But with all this population there were but 50 ladies in the town and about 55 children."

Ingham continues with a detailed price list of most commodities in the infant town, including — hay, 5c per pound; butter, 50c; rice, 20c; dried apples, 20c; beefsteak, 20c; coal oil, $1.25 a gallon. He comments that while these prices "may seem high, still it must be taken into consideration that everything must be freighted in from Alamosa." As for the labor and man power situation that first year, Ingham makes it clear that the professional man could not expect to find a comfortable niche, nor could book-keepers or clerks make a lot of money. Carpenters on the other hand, would be welcomed with open arms and purse strings, earning as much as $2.50 for a nine hour day.

By 1880 the town had a newspaper, the PITKIN MINING NEWS, which carried a column of bits and gossip pieces called "Pitkin Pellets". Being of a highly personal nature, not always complimentary to the citizens involved, the editor was often threatened with violent reprisal, but seems to have escaped bodily harm. When the first train came in on July 12, 1882, the paper carried a flamboyant story about the "future growth of our fair city" and witheringly referred to the neighboring camps of Tin Cup and Gothic as being "necessarily temporary since they have no rail service".

The arrival of a train in the mountain camp was indeed something of a miracle. The rails had been extended upward and westward from the eastern slope camps of St. Elmo (then Forest City) and Romley (Murphy's Switch until 1897). As the railroad neared the summit of the range it stopped short of the steepest peaks and dove straight through via an engineering marvel of the day — the Alpine Tunnel. While the tunnel was being bored Pitkin suffered its most violent times. Laborers, released from tunnel work on Saturday night, descended on the saloons and bordellos to whoop it up. They did it so thoroughly citizens locked up doors and windows and went to bed, resigned to the worst.

For a time the rails ended at Pitkin, were later extended to Ohio City, then on down to Parlin where they connected with the Denver and Rio Grande, so that service went all the way to Gunnison. This was a great step forward for the area since the mountain passes were usually closed by snow for eight months. The tunnel itself remained clear but the adjacent slopes presented a constant struggle against snow drifts in fall, winter and spring.

After Pitkin had erected saloons and bawdy houses, someone thought of a theater and built one. Looking around for talent, the owner was informed an engineer in Gunnison, D. J. McCanne, had devised some spectacular stage effects for his amateur production of A DREAM OF FAIRYLAND. McCanne was invited to present the play in the new theater and he accepted without giving much thought to the the matter. An ingenious man, he had rigged up a dynamo powered by a heavy steam pump to provide power for illuminating a series of incandescent lamps. On the stage of the Gunnison playhouse the lighting was successful enough. Concealed in artificial flowers the lamps would light up when the good fairies were on stage, and die down when evil imps appeared. But Pitkin had to get along without all this, the electrical equipment too bulky to transport to the camp. The show must go on, McCanne said, and on the Pitkin stage substituted regular pyrotechnical flares for the bulbs. Everything went fine until the scheduled blaze of light in the flowers. The flash material went off with squeals of delight which quickly became choking coughs as clouds of dense smoke drove the audience outside. Despite theatrical tradition, the show did not go on.

One killing in Pitkin started as a domestic squabble, Tom Sullivan's wife going home to mother. Tom sequestered himself in his home with a bottle to substitute for his wife's affections. "Sullivan tried to drown his sorrows," Betty Wallace,

Gunnison historian observed succinctly, "but succeeded only in nourishing his grievances." The whiskey lasted all day, got Tom roaring drunk and he started for his mother-in-law's with .41 pistol in hand. Deputy Sheriff W. E. Hammon and Jake McWilliams saw him on the run, heard piercing screams in the house. Catching up with Sullivan, they talked him into walking back downtown but neglected to remove his gun.

At first peaceable, Sullivan's mood suddenly made a turn for the worse. He whipped out his gun and fired two shots at Hammon's head, one of them taking deadly effect. McWilliams made a hasty retreat and Sullivan, now master of the situation, paraded up and down Pitkin's main street, chasing everyone to cover. Ammunition exhausted, he fled on horseback up the gulch, pursued by a hastily organized posse. Overtaken in Armstrong Gulch near Tin Cup, he tamely surrendered and since there was a good chance of a lynching if he were held in the Pitkin jail, he was rushed to Gunnison.

In 1891 and 1892 Pitkin hit its peak of prosperity. All mines were producing, the Islet turning out silver bricks weighing 774 ounces and another mine broke into a new vein that poured out still more silver, bringing another influx of miners. Then came the crash of '93, suspending all mining activity. Partial recovery came in '95 when the catastrophe had faded somewhat and Pitkin limped along until a gold strike was reported in the district. When none was discovered nearby, the town suffered another relapse. Pitkin was having a full-fledged depression five years before the general one in the '30s and this was the beginning of a decline that carried into the present time.

Many buildings still stand, the little stream of water referred to by Ingham still sparkling beside Main Street. In the lobby of the otherwise silent old hotel, an enthusiastic young Canadian woman will prepare a meal for the occasional visitor. Surprised by a total of four guests one day recently, she remarked regretfully: "I was thinking this morning of baking a pie. Now I wish I had."

PITKIN IS FULL OF OLD WAGONS, relics of days when all freight was hauled to lofty mining camps by vehicles pulled by as many as ten teams of horses or mules. Pictured in detail is heavy brake shoe used to retard too-rapid descent of wagon on steep hills. Frequently these were augmented by logs dragged along behind.

PITKIN RETAINS many early day buildings, some still occupied in summer. Log construction of this one seems to date it before erection of sawmill, upper facing of boards and battens added later.

335

PONCHA SPRINGS, COLORADO

Although Poncha Springs owed its big development of the mining boom in the late 1870s it was already established as a health resort several years previously. At the site are 99 mineral springs, their temperatures varying from 90 to 185 degrees. The Utes and other Indians had been in the habit of camping here from prehistoric times, claiming that the waters of Poncha Springs were "Good Medicine."

One of the earliest whites in the region was a Mr. McPherson, who had a homesteading claim near the largest springs. In 1874 James True bought the claim and laid out a town. He started a general store which became a bonanza when the rush of miners hit the area. When the railroad came through in 1880 Poncha Springs enjoyed a boom undreamed of by the first settlers. Several hotels were quickly put up including the Jackson which still stands, though greatly altered. It was operated by a retired Memphis steamboat captain, and saw some wild times while the railroad was being extended and trackworkers and crewmen swarmed the town.

In her "Stampede to Timberline" Muriel Wolle quotes the CHAFFEE COUNTY TIMES of January 1, 1881 as saying "The prohibition tendency of the principal owners of town property has caused them to insert a clause in all deeds prohibiting the sale of intoxicating liquor on any lots belonging to them, and the consequence is a small proportion of saloons to other classes of business. We believe there are only two or three in the town. How many drugstores and groceries have private barrels on tap cannot be definitely stated."

There was also a library, a novelty in any boom camp, "a neat, cozy building, containing over 1600 standard volumes and a large number of choice novels, including selections from Harper's half hour series." . . . . . . "This will be a great boon for the army of strangers, young men and others, who, in coming to this mountain town will be provided with a profitable place to spend their evenings instead of frequenting saloons and dancehouses."

Proper or not, Poncha Springs flourished for only a few years, being almost entirely destroyed by fire in 1882. The town was never rebuilt, the boom resulting from building of the railroad having subsided. The Jackson Hotel and the large brick schoolhouse remain as landmarks.

SAINT ELMO, COLORADO

Here is a little town to satisfy anyone. Its environs have fallen away, but this has only served to concentrate what is left into a sort of antique doll town. True, there are gaps, but the short stretch of street offers all that one would expect in an old western town; false fronts, tiny church, log cabins and all.

Several canyons come together here to feed Chalk Creek. Dense woods covered the site in 1878 and the tiny cluster of cabins was dignified by the name of Forrest City.

Soon the collection of houses boasted stores and hotels and was incorporated with a new name, Saint Elmo.

At first, while the population was limited to about 2,000, the town was of high moral tone. Church services were held every few months in one private residence or another when a visiting clegyman would pass that way.

As the place grew, however, it took on all the roistering aspects of a predominantly single male population, with saloons and dance halls going full tilt. Patrons were not only miners but railroad crews from towns below.

Though several camps were established farther up the canyons, notably Romley and Hancock, none surpassed Saint Elmo in size or weekend celebrations.

SAINT ELMO GIVES EFFECT of a town in miniature. Sky is heavily overcast. Moment of sun makes little false fronts stand out against darkly-timbered mountain.

SHAVANO, COLORADO

"Colorado, Its Gold and Silver Mines", published in 1880, has this to say of the mining district straddling the Monarch Pass. "Monarch mining district is located around the headwaters of the South Arkansas river in the southwestern corner of the county. Many of the lodes are above timberline. A district as young as this that can show such promising and valuable mines as the Mountain Chief, Monarch, Smith and Gray, Songbird and Gulch is sure to take a front rank now that the railroad has reached the neighborhood. The towns of the Monarch district are Maysville, Arbourville and Chaffee. The latter is up among the mines and the former nearer the base of the mountain and seem to be the business points. Maysville is 13 miles from the railroad at Cleora, 6 from the mineral springs at Poncho and 8 miles below Monarch Mountain and Chaffee.

"Around the middle fork of the South Arkansas the ore is almost entirely of carbonate of lead or galena, the former predominating. Fine specimens

MARKER INFORMS RARE VISITORS, mostly fishermen that here once stood flourishing Colorado mining camp. Tortuous, steep road winds 7 miles from Maysville on highway at approach to Monarch Pass, is not recommended for average traveler. Side road, not used since mining days leaves at right for Shavano mines, above timberline. Mountain meadows still bore winter's snow drifts at time of photographer's visit, soon to be replaced by sheets of alpine flowers.

of chlorides and silver glance are, however, not entirely wanting, and sometimes the ore is enriched by chlorides to such an extent that it would not be difficult to sort out considerable quantities that would mill out over a thousand ounces to the ton."

It was just such a deposit of galena ore that came to light at the location first called Clifton, seven miles above Maysville. The camp was started in 1879 and was laid out as a town the next year. While the ore was mostly galena, heavy with lead, there was just enough easily recovered silver to sustain optimism and even promote a small boom. Any newcomer was welcome to wood, water and a twenty-five foot building site on the main "street", so long as he cleared and graded his frontage. All buildings were constructed of logs. They formed a double line straggling along a rough thoroughfare which crossed the wildly cascading Cyclone Creek on a timbered bridge.

The creek made a right-angle turn a quarter of a mile below the street, paralleling it, and in a comparatively gentle mood formed a ford where another road could cross. Just below the crossing a three story mill was built, and an access road graded up the steep mountainside to the mines.

It was the fashion at the time to name mining camps after prominent Indian chiefs, and a movement was started in Clifton to rename the camp for the famous leader, Ouray. Then it was found that Ouray was already thus honored, so the town on Cyclone Creek took second choice, the name of Shavano, a sub-chief under Ouray. Although not having the linguistic abilities of the great Ouray who spoke Spanish and English, Shavano was tactful, often presiding at meetings in Ouray's absence.

Re-naming the town was hardly worth the trouble, the vein of lead with some silver rapidly became all lead as it was followed, then not even that. Shavano folded in only a little more than three years of glory, its log cabins and stores already abandoned.

ONLY STANDING BUILDING in 11,000' high Shavano is still partly roofed with sheet metal, contains crude bedstead and other comforts of home. Although picture was taken in mid-June, snow was pelting down, flakes not registering in one second exposure required by red filter and heavily overcast early morning sky. Trip down narrow, rugged, dirt road was accomplished in increasingly heavy snowstorm, which abated only when 9,000' level was reached.

About twenty years later a rich vein of silver was located still farther up the range, the find being made by a Shavano man, Judge J. H. Akin and E. W. Carpenter of Salida. Although it was New Year's Day and three feet of snow covered the ground the men staked out a claim on the spot, calling it the Netsie Castley. A 200 pound sample chunk of rock from this vein contained 119 ounces of silver, a hefty portion of lead and gold assaying $3.50 to the ton.

The discovery revived Shavano as a supply base while the mine was being developed. However, the new vein, while rich, didn't last any longer than the lower one, and after a few years it too was abandoned.

Today, Shavano is almost gone. Only one cabin still stands, and that because a tin roof has preserved it from rotting and collapse. A careful survey through the woods at the site reveals about twenty sites where buildings once stood. Most had stone fireplaces at one end. Considerable care was used in smoothing logs for door and window sills and in placing pegs for shelf supports. In a few years the logs in contact with the ground will complete the rotting process, dissolving into the rocky earth and disappearing completely.

339

SILVER PLUME, COLORADO

Almost the only place in Silver Plume where transients could stay in 1870 was the Pelican House. The charitable proprietors kept a row of beds warm at all times, one sleeper shift flopping on them as soon as another vacated the blankets. These were boom days for the bedbugs, too.

One of the first to come to Silver Plume was a young Englishman named Griffin. He discovered the Seven-Thirty mine and profited greatly. The vein was rich in both silver and gold and the deeper it went, the heavier were the deposits. Yet instead of living in high spirits, the handsome Griffin kept to his cabin each night, making friends with no one. Then he discovered his past was following him. A rumor was circulated that on the eve of his wedding in England, his fiancee had been found dead in his room. Griffin denied nothing, acknowledged nothing.

Getting richer all the time, he did nothing with his money, not even frequenting the brothels of the town. But he did have one project—hewing out a depression in the solid rock facing his little cabin high on Columbia Mountain, directly above Silver Plume. As time went on, people saw this hole grow into the shape of a grave. Each evening, after his stint of excavating the refractory rock, Griffin would bring out his violin to play the melodies and classical music of his earlier days. One June night in '87 the miners thought he played particularly well. Then they heard a shot reverberating in the canyon. Face down in the grave with a bullet in his heart, was the gentleman from Piccadilly.

AT HEIGHT OF BUSTLING DAYS, the Plume boasted two churches, Odd Fellows Hall, Knights of Pythias Hall, shown here at right of church. Also lining street were school, theater and many stores as well as usual quota of saloons and red-light houses. Small community of Brownsville, so close as to be regarded as suburb was overwhelmed by mudslide, never recovered.

GHOSTLY MISTS OF THE MOUNTAINS

SILVERTON, COLORADO

Silverton is not a true Ghost Town, being on a main highway and the hub of an area containing many revived or continuing mining operations.

At the turn of the century it was the supply center, the "metropolitan" area, of a vast network of towns, mines and mills that had flourished in the gold and silver bonanza days of the 80's and 90's. Silverton, along with the rest of Colorado, was staggered by repeated blows in those years. The Federal Government had been buying 4,500,000 ounces of silver a month under the Sherman Act, and India's mints provided a huge outlet for the metal. But suddenly in 1893, India ceased coining silver money and shortly thereafter the Sherman Act was repealed. These events created panic in Colorado, and silver mining was never the same again.

Silverton is located in a "Park," a small area surrounded by towering peaks of the San Juan Range on one side and those of the La Plata Mountains on the other. The elevation is well over 9,000 feet and this means heavy snows for a long period in winter. The streets are lined with many buildings dating from those hectic days when Silver was King. Many are occupied and doing business in a quiet way.

The Denver Rio Grande Railroad still runs its diminutive train up here from Durango. This is the narrow-gauge train now famous for its role in the motion picture *Around the World in Eighty Days.*

The town is a center for trips to a good many deserted mining camps and towns, notably Eureka, Animas Forks and Gladstone.

SPAR CITY, COLORADO

Spar City was young and brash with three hundred people. It began as Fisher City with a systematic plan for streets and city blocks in the spring of 1882, going forward "to assume business proportions, buildings going up on both sides of the thoroughfare. A hack line was established between the young town and big sister Creede. That city's famous newspaper, the *Creede Candle*, felt that Spar City was going to have a newspaper and to avoid competition, started a branch— the *Spar City Spark*.

With a fine sense of smugness, this weekly complained about the Indians who were in the habit of camping along Lime Creek and editoralized: "Great indignation is felt, both at the unwarranted wholesale slaughter of game and the neglect of the Agent in allowing the red pests to be away from the reservation."

The first find of float was made prior to 1882 and led to several good outcroppings which became the Big Spar, Fairview and Headlight mines. With this industry behind it, Spar City went blithely ahead with daily mail service and in 1893 confidently predicted it would soon be second in size to Creede. In June of that year silver was demonetized, paralyzing all the silver camps. In the case of Spar City, with no background of any other kind of industry the effect was catastrophic, many people actually suffering from hunger.

Sam Hyde of Spar wrote to the *Creede Candle* that "people living in agricultural regions or large cities may find it difficult to realize how a community of people in this land of plenty can be placed in such a trying position. While a community may have untold wealth at its doors, it is not directly of a nutritive character. A power beyond our control has made our mineral valueless for the time being, our women and the children must be fed, and in short . . . assistance is necessary. Meat and flour we must have."

Creede came to the aid of Spar City with their publicized plan. "Spar is peopled by honest industrious Americans out of work and out of money. They are proud people but they must eat. Having nothing to exchange for bread and meat, they propose the following plan of the New York bankers and issue clearing house certificates backed by their brawn and industry and offer them in exchange for flour." The beef was butchered and sold in exchange for promises to pay when able and flour passed out on the same plan.

In spite of these temporary alleviations the town of Spar City had received a mortal blow. It was gradually bled of its hungry population and barely kept a spark of life until 1905. Then an entirely unlooked for stream of blood was piped in. A group of 150 strongly prohibitionist Kansans bought the town, lock, stock and barrel and made it over for their own uses.

Each summer now sees these people getting settled in their completely made over cabins, preparing to spend their vacations in the magnificent mountain and canyon scenery, fishing and hunting, and "maybe doing a little prospecting."

"DORMITORY" FOR GIRLS from dance halls, brothels and saloons was this, the only two-storied building in Spar City. Porch originally extended length of big cabin, with roof where little balcony now is. Large interior sees festivities again, of primmer nature than in bawdier days. One of prohibitionist vacationers found cabin assigned to him had bar along side and mirrors on wall, lost no time altering decor. Bar had been moved from Creede, was one behind which Jesse James was shot by Bob Ford.

HOME OF THE FAMOUS SMUGGLER

Telluride, Colorado

The Union and Sherman mines were good producers of silver and other metals in 1876 and in July of that year prospector J. B. Ingram grew curious about them. They seemed farther apart on the mountainside than they should be and sure enough, by measurement he found several hundred feet not legally included in either. So shortly he had a claim, a mine, a fortune.

He named the mine The Smuggler and when it proved to be richer than either of its neighbors, its owner bought out both of them. The name Ingram is perpetuated in a spectacular waterfall dropping many hundreds of feet down a precipitous cliff at the north edge of Telluride.

The name of this old camp was not included in early accounts as it was born when residents of San Miguel wanted to live nearer the mountainside mines, under the towering peaks of the San Juans. And since the ores in the area were mostly telluride, a compound containing tellurium, a non-metallic element analogous to sulphur and selenium, this suggested the word Telluride for the new camp.

The town had its full quota of bad men, those trying to be bad and others trying to keep them subdued, one of its most famous marshals being Jim Clark. Besides carrying the usual number of six-shooters Clark stashed several Winchester rifles in stores strategically located around town. He did not hang around saloons, just glancing in one or the other as he walked his regular beat. And his method worked, Telluride being comparatively peaceful for an isolated mining camp during his rather short regime. The end of it came abruptly one dark night when he was slain by an unknown assailant concealed between two buildings.

Without pasture land, Telluride and other camps in the steep-walled San Juan country, had to import all cattle—often from Texas—as well as hogs, sheep and food staples. The porkers, chickens and sacked goods had to be brought in wagons, at first hauled by ox teams. Hillsides were often far too steep to keep a wagon upright and a teamster would borrow a plow from his load, hitch it behind one of his oxen or mules and run a deep furrow along the up side. Then he might take poles carried for such purposes and place them to extend outwards and uphill. All available men would hang

on the ends as the steepest spots were passed with upper wheels in the furrow.

In the draw to the east of Telluride, near Pandora, there was a small meadow generally used to hold livestock intended for slaughter, abattoir conveniently near. Meat and potatoes were essential food with some bacon, eggs and salt pork. Ham brought about 16c a pound, beef 8c. Long winters at high altitudes kept food without refrigeration. Women were scarce but a few sold bread and pies made of dried apples and peaches. Although miners averaged only $3 to $3.50 for a ten or twelve hour day, food prices were correspondingly low. The single men who ate in company boarding houses were well fed since labor was always in short supply.

Census reports, when taken in remote camps like Telluride, always reported male to female proportions. Typical were such listings as 300 men, 5 women—560 men, 20 women. Many men, while willing to visit cribs, longed for wives and the camp's little 4-page newspapers produced on a Washington hand press, always carried several ads by a lonely hearts club. A woman might travel to

TELLURIDE'S ASPECT from the front is much like other fading but still alive old towns. True character of many old structures is revealed at rear. Here no paint or repairs detract from genuine atmosphere of old mining camp.

343

RED MOUNTAIN with white mantle. Stampede to Timberline is a veritable text book for students of Colorado's romantic mining history. Author Muriel Sibell Wolle includes passage that gives meaning to photo, "From the Million Dollar Highway, these mines cover an area of about four miles in length and behind them Red Mountain looms up like a backdrop to some Wagnerian opera with the mines and buildings as the details in the setting." Two-story boarding house, saloons and other buildings once crowding both sides of Red Mountain Town are gone, most destroyed by series of fires. One old timer recalled that when fire broke out in Red Mountain Hotel everybody carried out bedding, pool tables, roulette wheels, formed huge pile in middle of street. Then wind shifted, turning flames on heap, destroying everything. First activity at scenic location was in 1879 and in 1890s "lights never went out, gambling halls never closed."

the high mountain camp to be shocked at first meeting a proposed mate. Robert L. Brown, in his book *An Empire of Silver*, relates how one such lady, on arriving at her destination, was dismayed at the first sight of her intended, a big raw-boned, homely Swede. She was ready to go back on the train but the man's friends assured her he was honest, industrious, and would be a good provider. The mail-order bride changed her mind.

Telluride today is still home for several hundred people who refuse to leave their mountain aerie. One woman told the author, "I came here with my husband who is dead now. I used to live in Leadville. When I was a small girl there my family lived in a nice house just below Fryer Hill where the Matchless Mine was. Mrs. Tabor, the one people call Baby Doe now, lived up there in a little shack. She often came down to the town and when she walked along the streets the children always teased her because she dressed so poorly. In win-

ter she often wrapped up her feet in burlap sacks. One day I went into our kitchen and there she sat beside the stove, having a cup of hot tea. I was scared because I had often hollered at her along with the rest of the kids and was going to turn and run. Mrs. Tabor said to me, 'Don't be frightened, child. Your mother invited me in because I was cold and I'll leave as soon as I've finished my tea.' I stayed and we began to talk. She really was very nice and not at all like the horrible old woman the kids called her. She got to dropping in often and we became good friends. I told my friends about how nice she really was and from then on they never called her names again."

This elderly lady, janitress at the old courthouse, asked that she not be named. She is one of the few remaining who would remember Colorado's big mining days and who could say they talked with Haw Tabor's wife, Baby Doe.

VICTOR, COLORADO

Victor was never reconciled to being called a suburb of Cripple Creek but its history is so tied up with that of its larger neighbor that it is a component part. Physically connecting the two is a road partly paved with gold ore just a little too low in assay value to be profitably refined when there was such an abundance of richer stuff.

The earliest mines in the neighborhood of Victor included the "Victor" itself and were located in 1891 and '92, but at first there was no thought of a town on the site. When one began to grow there in haphazard fashion a couple of brothers, shrewd promoters, saw the possibilities of getting in on the ground floor.

The Woods boys were looked upon as "Pillars of the Church," "Founding Fathers of Victor" or scoundrels, depending entirely on the viewpoint. It appears they never overlooked the possibility of a "fast buck" in any kind of a deal. The two, Frank M. and Harry E. were deliberately launched on their career by their father, Warren Woods of Denver with a cash advance of some $10,000. The boys first built a reputation for being pious, upright citizens and supporters of the Baptist Church, the Y.M. C.A. and other religious and civic activities. Once the background was established they lost no time setting up a real estate operation on the site for which they had paid $1,000. The location was the Mount Rose Placer which had belonged to a Mr. McKinney and it comprised some 136 acres. The new town was named Victor, after an early homesteader in the area, Victor C. Adams. The brothers advertised that every Victor lot was a gold mine. Now this statement was a strictly promotional gimmick, and not necessarily meant to have the ring of truth. But as the plat was developed it turned out that the blurb was literally true. Not too long after the place got going, an item appeared in the Denver Republican of January 1, 1889 which said "Here you find mining operations carried on in backyards. Gallows frames rearing their heads away above the roofs of houses, thundering giant underground detonations which shake the floor on which you stand and the constant rumble of heavily laden ore wagons through the streets, alleys and vacant lots each seeking the shortest way to the railroad."

As a real estate promotion the laying out of Victor was a fantastic success, but was nothing compared to the profits that poured into the coffers of the Woods boys when they decided to start a hotel,

the Victor. The hotel itself was only incidental. Frank Woods was overseeing the grading operations where the hostelry was to rise when he noticed a gleam of yellow in the dirt. Watching closely he saw the streak widen to an eighteen inch vein definitely auriferous. Frank was one to keep his silence, and even the workmen on the scene didn't suspect what was transpiring. Woods decided the vein was an offshoot of the "Gold Coin," a modestly rewarding mine nearby. He bought the property for a few thousand dollars. Less than a year later his Gold Coin was turning out $50,000 every month for the Woods. Flushed with success, Frank built a brick shafthouse with stained glass windows over the mine.

Shortly after this development other mines were found nearby and even within the city limits. These

ORNATE DECORATIONS BEAUTIFULLY PRESERVED. Building is isolated by past fires, was near home of old Victor Record on Cross Street. Paper was said to be mouthpiece of W. F. M. During Union troubles militiamen invaded offices to haul off editor George Kymer and four employees. Beautiful linotypist named Emma Langdon, the "Barbara Frietchie of Victor," barricaded her door and spent the night setting up paper which appeared in morning carrying banner head reading "Somewhat disfigured but still in the ring!"

included the Portland, Independence, and Strong. The city became covered by claims, many being worked under the streets and buildings. Fortunately the supporting rock was of an obdurate nature, preventing structures from "falling in." As more mines were discovered and developed the economy of Victor began to approach that of Cripple Creek. Then Cripple Creek suffered its most disastrous fire.

In a time like this rivalry was temporarily forgotten. The morning after the fire, Cripple Creek found itself flooded with food and blankets sent over from a sympathizing Victor. And when Victor, in turn was leveled by a mighty blaze, which started in Jennie Thompson's "999" dance hall, it was substantially aided by its big sister. In more normal times there was plenty of back biting; snide allusions were constantly seen in the press and as usual the smaller contender was the more bitter. The Semi-Centennial Celebration was held at Salt Lake City in July of '97. In the parade was a float sponsored by Victor, Cripple having none.

Comment on the situation in the Victor Daily Record was "Victor did the nice thing by Cripple Creek when our representative at Salt Lake invited Miss Gully, the Cripple Creek Queen to ride on the Victor float. We might say that Cripple Creek took a ride on Victor's band wagon, but Cripple has often done that in the past and the habit is growing." And again, when Independence Day had fallen on a Sunday and Victor had celebrated regardless, the Record commented on Cripple's criticism, "The Goody Goody people of Cripple Creek mean to suppress all sorts of patriotic doings on the Fourth, (Sunday). Patriotism must be below par with our neighbors for didn't they close up gambling on Friday and reopen the games on the following Sabbath? Is it more a desecration of the Sabbath to have a drilling match than to go on a Meyers Avenue debauch? Is it worse to play baseball than faro or roulette? Oh, consistency, thy keepers are not the divines of Cripple."

During the big days of Victor the town was

346

served by five railroads. One of them, the Cripple Creek Short Line from Colorado Springs cost its owners $5,000,000 and was completed in 1901. Theodore Roosevelt visited Victor that year, riding on the Short Line. The scenery along the way, he said, "bankrupts the English language." All operations of mines and trams were electrified and a highly complex system of electric trolleys was woven around the camp. The Colorado Mining Resources in 1904 said that the district is the only one "in the world where the miner can go to work in an electric car, descend to the mine in an electric hoist, do his work by electric light, run drills operated by electric air compressors and fire his shots by electricity, from a switchboard remote from the point of explosion."

So much "blossom rock" was encountered in the workings that many miners were tempted beyond their strength and indulged in highgrading. The practice became so general that a society for the purpose of protecting the miners involved was organized, the "Highgraders Association." Exchanges were organized for the purpose of receiving the rich material, but internal disorders developed as miners accused the operators of keeping more than their share of the profits, and several offices were bombed. At least one of the dynamitings was blamed on mine owners who were understandably opposed to the whole thing. Overall losses from the practice of highgrading were tremendous, one mine alone, the Independence, losing $1,000,000. Many measures for prevention were attempted, none being entirely effective. At the Independence the men were for a time compelled to strip naked at the end of each shift and pass inspection. This stringent order was later rescinded and a milder one substituted—the men could keep their underwear on. One can't help wondering whether the rigorous winter climate might not have had something to do with the modification.

The Woods brothers found shortly after the turn of the century that they had overextended their empire without seeing to it that competition was stymied. Troubles compounded troubles. The hardest blow and the beginning of the end for them came in 1908. They had been busy for several years forming a huge combine of more than a hundred Cripple Creek District mines called the United Gold Mines Company. At the same time an autocratic, driving little man from St. Louis, where he had amassed several millions out of his genius for chemistry, appeared in the district. His name was John T. Milliken. He built the Golden Cycle Mill at Colorado City and it was so successful that in

five years it had driven the Guggenheim mills out of business. Catching the Woods brothers in a shaky period, Milliken bought their United Gold Mines Company at a bargain price.

The Woods' financial disaster was only one of a series that now threatened their whole empire. Among other mistakes made, was that of entering the electric street car business in Pueblo, Colorado. The Thatcher family there, firmly entrenched in Pueblo's business since Territorial days, made short work of the Woods' intrusion by seeing to it that some of the brothers' creditors foreclosed on them. Added to this was the ruin of the Hydroelectric Power Company street cars which were to have been a main outlet. In 1910 the Woods Investment Co. was defunct and the brothers moved away. Harry died with small resources in Laguna Beach, California in 1928. Frank lived until '32, dying in Los Angeles so destitute that a collection was taken up for his burial.

STATELY CITY HALL displays old fire equipment. Ever-present menance of fire in severe winters took heavy toll of mining camps. Victor fire of 1899 destroyed business section from First to Fifth Streets and from Portland Avenue to Granite Avenue. It took out two railroad stations, the elegant Gold Coin Shaft House and the Gold Coin Club. Woods boys lost dozen properties, rebuilt immediately, on credit, more lavishly than before. Fire started in "999" Dance Hall. Other palaces of joy were named Bucket of Blood, Crapper Jack's, Great View, Iron Clad, Rose Gordon's, The Red Onion, Red Light.

WARD, COLORADO

Prior to the '60's, prospectors had been pecking around on the steep, heavily timbered sides of Left Hand Canyon, which was named for a south-paw Indian. Every pan dipped in the creek at the bottom of the canyon had yielded a rich residue and there was interest in finding a vein somewhere above. Then Calvin Ward struck it. In his joy at the discovery he called his claim the "Miser's Dream."

Ward's find tended to confirm the belief that a lode must lie somewhere above and the excitement began early the next year when Cy Deardorff chipped off a piece of float that showed the location of the main vein. This was to be the Columbia Mine, which in its period of productivity, turned out $5,000,000 in ore. Later the big producers were the East Columbia, Ni-Wot Utica, Baxter, Boston and Idaho.

Even on foot a prospector had a hard time making his way up the sides of Left Hand Canyon, but that going was easy compared to the troubles encountered when wagons became necessary for hauling equipment. First the trees had to be cut down in a strip wide enough for a road. Rocks had to be blasted out of the way and dirt filled in. Grades were so steep that teams of oxen and horses could just get up the hill with the wagons. The first trees cut were dragged to a sawmill but the mill burned to the ground almost before it had

ONCE WARD WAS LIVELY. Work was started on Congregational Church in same year town was incorporated, 1896. Although Ward's big fire destroyed fifty-three buildings with a property loss of $85,000, the church was seared only on one side. Large false-fronted structure at upper left is C. and N. Hotel. In later years Mrs. Thompson operated hotel in summer only, she herself stayed on in big front room and kept hot fire going in big stove. Artist-Author Muriel Wolle spent part of one winter sketching in Ward, stayed in upper frigid room, slept in sleeping bag on floor, woke up at night to see stovepipe, going straight up through room, "glowed dull red from heat of the banked stove below and vibrated back and forth whenever a particularly strong blast struck the building." Corner of building at extreme left is remnant of store. Long structure in center dates from later period, was Small's Garage.

produced any lumber. A second was built immediately and it turned out the material to shelter the first miners and construct several stores. By 1867 some two hundred people were living in new frame houses in the Columbia district. When the Ni-Wot built its small mill, total population was about six hundred.

By the 90's the town was fllourishing and was incorporated. In 1897 a railroad was brought up to Ward from Boulder. The twenty-six mile right of way climbed 4,100 feet to reach 9,450 feet in elevation. Officially the Colorado and Northwestern, the route was known as the Whiplash and Switzerland Trail. The long switchbacks took the train past one high point called Mount Alta and at this point the company built an elaborate resort with a dancehall in the hope of attracting tourists. June 28th, 1898 saw the "Formal Opening to passengers, traffic and business of the Whiplash Route from the verdant Valley of Boulder to the Cloud Kissed Camp of Ward."

The first train stopped at the mouth of the mine tunnels to allow the passengers the thrill of entering. To make things more homelike for them, boards were laid over the puddles and a long line of burning candles dimly lit the way. About the time the excur-sionists were all inside and more than a little apprehensive, the miners added thrill to excitement by setting off a blast of dynamite in a side tunnel. How were they to know the resulting rush of air would blow out all the candles?

There had been thousands of tons of low assay ore accumulating on the dumps around Ward for twenty years, its value more than offset by the high cost of wagon transport. Now that the railroad had come there was jubilation—the waste would now be converted to cash. But the optimism was not justified as the ores proved to be extremely refractory.

Then, at the turn of the century when the mine production was slackening, disaster was added to disappointment. Fire nearly destroyed the camp. The *Ward Miner* of January 26, 1900 stated that "not a store, hotel, saloon, restaurant or a business house of any sort escaped the flames. If the life of the old town depended wholly upon the profits taken over the counter and the bar, its destruction would be complete, and the little basin in which its business houses once stood might be abandoned for the home of the chipmunk and the coyote."

ONE OF DEARDORFF'S DISCOVERIES was Utica Mine. It became leading workings of camp, began to pay off in 1888 and by next year had made a million dollars. Its stone mill, shown here, is one of oldest still standing, was originally run by water power. Pipeline brought water five miles over hills. Main shaft of mine was destroyed by fire in 1898, forcing temporary closure, suspending monthly income of $10,000. Ore assayed $200 to $500 to the ton.

WHITE PINE, COLORADO

George S. Irwin was White Pine's alert and imaginative newspaper man although he finally went to jail, his most consistent struggle was with the pack rats. When the WHITE PINE CONE printed its last edition after ten years of lively existence, the furry thieves had made away with everything they could carry or drag except the type lice.

When Irwin, his partner and a printer's devil named George Root arrived in the remote Colorado camp in 1883, they spent their first night in a lean-to adjoining the log cabin where the paper would be printed. The rats were big, noisy and bold and banging a shoe on the floor only made them more active. So young Root grabbed his Wesson .44 carbine from the bunk post and handed it to Irwin below him. The editor heard a crunching sound and blazed away, and "no more was heard save strong men struggling for the word." In the morning Root pried up some floor boards near the body of the victim and found a cache of objects belonging to the previous occupants, among them trunk straps, neckties, dish rags, slippers, forks and spoons.

The WHITE PINE CONE enjoyed a regional reputation for genial reflections on the news and morals of the camp, under the heading — "Little Cones" — material like: "The boys all washed their feet in the Hot Springs Sunday. There will be no fish in Hot Creek this summer" . . . . "We will present a copy of the CONE for one year to the first couple that marries in the gulch between the first and last day of February, proximo. Marriage comes high but we must have one occasionally." . . . "White Pine suffered an agonizing famine this week. For two whole days there was not a drop of whiskey in town. Nothing but a liberal supply of peach brandy and bottled beer prevented a panic."

Seldom was the news reported straight. After many months of snowy winter when supplies were hauled into town on ox-drawn sleds, Irwin cheerfully chronicled the end. "The first wagon over the road between Sargent's and White Pine since last fall was the stage last Friday. It was quite a treat for our people to see once again a wheeled vehicle. The stage will hereafter make regular daily trips."

When times were dull and news scarce, Irwin would improvise as with this tongue-in-cheek report of a hold up, February 15, 1889. "BOLD HOLD UP—THRILLING EXPERIENCE OF PASSENGERS ON THE SARGENT-TOMICHI STAGE LINE.

"Ingold Peterson drove merrily day by day through the dark canyon without thought of disaster. But the events of last Monday are calculated to cause the traveler in the near future to traverse the canyon only with fear and trembling.

"Last Monday was most favorable for a tragedy. For a time dark clouds obscured the sun, and a snowfall darkened the heavens. The atmosphere was gruesome and uncanny. A feeling of depression came over the passengers — a silent premonition of approaching danger.

"On the stage besides the driver, Ingold Peterson, were Joe Domandel, a Miss Lilly Dinkins and an alleged drummer. Let us say right here that suspicion attaches to the drummer. It is even charged directly that he was an accomplice of the hold up, an accessory before the fact. There are

WHEN MAIN STREET of White Pine was lined with business buildings, this peak-roofed one was novelty, as others were all false-fronted. Note evidence of outside stairway indicating close crowding of adjoining buildings. Only few scattered structures remain here now, survivors of fires, weather and old age.

several circumstances since remembered tending to corroborate these charges against the drummer.

"When the stage stopped at Cosden he was seen to go into Pat's Place and emerge a few minutes later with a strong aroma tied to his breath, which kept floating out on the morning breeze. Was this the signal to his pals, watching from some high point?

"He frequently glanced at the mail bags, and nervously watched on either side of the road as the stage entered the narrow canyon.

"It was particularly noticed, also, that just before the stage was attacked, the drummer placed his thumb and forefinger to his nose in a most significant manner.

"Evidently the drummer should have been apprehended. Witnesses will swear, we understand, that they saw the road agent throw something which the drummer caught with the dexterity that comes only with long practice. About midway between Cosden and White Pine as the driver hurried the team around a curve, there suddenly came to view a dark, grim sentinel who stood silently by the side of the road. Not a word was said but his actions were ominous, and the passengers shuddered as the stage drew near.

"Joe Domandel, having the safety of the lazy at heart, begged the driver to stop, but the blood of the Northman was aroused, and like the chieftain warriors of his ancestry, he was resolved to do or die.

" 'Up there, Kalma! On, on Ladoga!' With dilated nostrils and trembling limbs, but obedient to lash and rein the horses sprang forward to face the broadside, well delivered.

"A few sharp screams, muttered curses and stifling gasps, and the danger is past. But the holdup had done his work. Peterson and Carr are badly hit, Domandel and the lady are unharmed, however, and the faithful horses bring the load to White Pine. It was known there the moment the stage came in sight an accident had occurred. There was something in the air that spoke of dire catastrophe. A crowd gathered as the stage approached, but no one remained long, the smellability was offended, and the victims were left to their fate.

"The holdup man escaped and the drummer left. Peterson is recovering, but he tells under the seal of strictest confidence that hereafter he will yell at the first sight of a mean, low down, loaded skunk!"

Irwin's newspaper ceased publication when the editor was sentenced to fifteen months in prison in Laramie, Wyoming for some infraction of the postal laws, presumably in the mailing of his papers. The editor's incarceration began shortly after he and other newspaper men had protested the fact that a notorious murderer had recently escaped lynch mobs through protective efforts of lawmen. Irwin had commented: "We suppose that this killer, like all Gunnison County's bad men with guns, will escape the gallows in the end, and possibly be awarded a leather medal as the champion killer. Sad state of affairs."

Irwin's arrest and conviction provoked further caustic editorial barbs to the effect that the course of justice was pursuing strange ends when a man could be put in jail for a comparatively trivial offense, at the same time allowing cold-blooded murderers to go free.

White Pine's rich silver and lead deposits were first worked around 1878. In a couple of years the camp was flourishing. Some silver was in "native glance" form, some in "wire" formation. One locality, Contact Mountain, was said to be "a mass of magnetic iron pyrites carrying silver." Some of the mines developed were Morning Star, Evening Star, Black Warrior, Copper Bottom and Copper Queen.

White Pine held its first election in 1880. Ballot boxes were made up in town, all possible votes were collected in town, then the boxes were carried up the trail to the next camp, Tomichi. Any miner met passing along the trail was invited to cast his vote. At Tomichi remaining voters cast their votes, the results being sent down to Gunnison which by this time was the county seat.

In the fall of the year before, the area had an Indian scare. The Meeker Massacre of 1879 caused panic among the settlers, even though the Indian Agency had been moved to Uncompahgre. Many camps set up guards, at Gunnison settlers built a small fort on a cliffside, maintaining a guard for several weeks, when fear subsided. At White Pine, some seventy miners with only thirteen guns among them established guard stations on the hills above the camp. Onset of winter snows caused abandonment of the posts by mutual agreement. One man, set to guard the gate at a break in the fence at the edge of town jumped the gun by returning to town before the rest, Reproved, he defended himself. "Well, anyway, I put up the bar before I left."

The spring of 1884 was particularly bad because of avalanches, then generally called "runs." At Woodstock, over the mountain from White Pine one of these slides swept away the little railroad station at a time when people were waiting for the train. Carried away and smothered were fourteen people, including Mr. Doyle and his four children, only Mrs. Doyle surviving. In addition to the station, many other buildings were destroyed, boarding house, telegraph shack and many cabins. The awaited train wouldn't have arrived, as it happened, the entire crew was busy fighting a snow obstruction at Baldwin.

The same day, March 10, an avalanche hit the workings at the Magna Charta tunnel, carrying away most of the buildings, but not causing any loss of life. The CONE carried the story. "The wind blew a veritable hurricane, driving the snow with hurricane force. Tom Farrell and Terry Hughes, employees of the Magna Charta, went to work as usual. They were in the blacksmith shop connected with the tunnel, when about eight o'clock, a huge snow slide came down Granite Mountain with a deafening roar, striking the shop with a fearful impact. Mr. Hughes was driven through a partition

then carried out through the end of the shop and thrown about fifty feet down the mountain side. Fortunately he landed in a bed of soft snow and soon extricated himself. Seeing nothing of Farrel he gave the alarm and some twenty or more men hurried to the scene of the accident and began searching for him. A few minutes later he was found imprisoned under the roof of the shop, but the combined efforts of the men to raise the roof were futile until it was broken to pieces. Farrell was unconscious when taken out, but recovered after a time. Examination showed that aside from a few bruises he was alright." The rescue party had just returned to town when a second and even larger slide swept over the Magna Charta, completing the removal of any buildings its predecessor had neglected.

Fifteen years later, again in March, an even more disastrous slide hit the Magna Charta mine

MANY SMALL "SUBURBS" grew up around White Pine. This one on Tomichi Creek has nearly disappeared, leaving only this small group of buildings. One nearest camera is likely unique, owner adding stucco front to old log cabin.

352

buildings. This monster removed all obstacles in its path, including a number of cabins. It killed several people. Young M. C. Smith was buried under the rush of snow, but lived to tell about it. "I was eating breakfast in my mother's kitchen. The first thing I saw was the front of the house falling on me. Instantly all was dark, and soon I found myself in a little place where I could sit up. The snow kept settling down around me until only my hands were free. I felt around and found that I was safely hemmed in. I called out but no response. I decided to take things easy, all the time feeling that I would certainly be rescued. At last I heard a noise up above. I gave the miner's rap on the eating table which was holding the debris off me, with a piece of broken plate. The raps were answered. The workmen seemed to redouble their efforts and soon I was free again. Mother was lying on a cot in the dining room sick when she was hit and killed instantly. I was under ten or fifteen feet of snow and remained there 4½ hours."

Little eight-year-old Perry Sweezy in another house had also been with his mother. As the snow hit, he called out to her, heard a muffled response, a groan, then silence. He had no idea how long it was when he heard rescuers digging above, but when he did, he called out, "Boys, can you get me out?" The men heard him, assuring him that they would, and to remain still. His father and older brother had been outside sawing wood. They never had a chance, being overwhelmed with no protection. Mr. C. L. Stitzer and his son Bert were also cutting wood, but they were working on a rise of ground. The descending avalanche divided at the obstruction, roaring around both sides, reforming at its lower end. It was Bert who skied into town to summon help, fear-

BONES OF ONCE HUGE MILL seem to have been ravaged by time and weather rather than usual enemy, fire. Most such mills took advantage of terrain, receiving ore at top level, passing material downward by easy gravity. First level contained heavy crushers, succeeding stages reduced chunks to powder, usually in ball mill, then material was combined with chemicals in tanks, becoming sludge in which metals floated to top as thick foam to be scraped off by revolving paddles and dried, becoming "concentrates" ready for shipment to smelter.

BOARD-EDGE SEAT and shoulder stop of primitive latrine offered scant comfort, discouraged any tendency of miner to gold-brick or gossip with others on same errand. Structures were common to most mills where large numbers of men were employed.

ful every foot of the way of starting another run. The disaster marked the end of the Magna Charta. It had never been a rich producer and as a Jonah for avalanches was closed down for keeps.

In one respect White Pine was certainly unique. Instead of the usual gunfire, quarrels were settled by fisticuffs, or at least some certainly were. Designated for this purpose was a small area just above town. The spot was known as Battle Park because of its frequent use as a ring. Since the men had to be at work in the mines by eight A.M., the bouts had to be staged before breakfast. First of such encounters was what was expected to be a "slugfest" between Charley Harmon and Tom Mourin. Harmon led off with a hard right to Mourin's chin, but it did not connect because of the extreme near sightedness of the aggressor. While trying to regain his balance, he was an easy target for Mourin's hefty punch, a blow that floored Harmon for the count.

The crowd, eager up to this point, booed the contestants, then turned their attentions to the next event, featuring two men who had quarreled over a girl in a saloon the night before, George Church and James Deck. This one lasted three rounds, affording considerable satisfaction to the spectators, who then left contentedly for work.

One thing White Pine did have in common with others basing their economy on the strength of the silver market, it reeled under the impact when the silver crash came in 1893. Mine owners tried to pretend that things would go on as before. Then one of the best properties, the May-Mazeppa closed down and even the most stout-hearted were forced to admit defeat, with this biggest payroll gone. By 1894 White Pine was deserted, dead.

Then, slowly, life began to flow back. By 1900 some mines were being opened, tentatively. As production increased, the Tomichi Valley smelter, three miles below the town was "blown in", then proceeding to treat 1,000 tons of ore per month. The payroll reached $10,000 a month for a year or two, and optimism soared for a while. But there was not a market for that much silver and things slowed to a halt again. In succeeding years there were sporadic bursts of activity, interspersed with doldrums. The condition of the camp now would seem permanent, that of death and decay. One or two cabins are sometimes occupied by summer vacationers, though on the occasion of a visit in June of 1964, not a sign of life was to be seen.

TIES ONCE SUPPORTED RAILS which conveyed ore cars from mine tunnel (background) to mill. Several large mills and mines near White Pine now show only wreckage.

ALTA, UTAH

In all innocence and guile, one legend says, the lady picked up a piece of ore and asked: "Is this what you are looking for?" The men stood open-mouthed. It was just exactly what they were looking for—a chunk of silver-bearing quartz. And it set off the wildest rush of prospectors Utah had ever seen.

"They"—the gopher-nosed, metal-minded soldiers of Col. Patrick E. Connor's regiment—had been officially mapping the canyon but probing the cliff sides for rich rock was more to their fancy. The canyon and the area around it was a favorite Indian hunting ground until the natives were forced out by white trappers in the 1830s, but they seldom climbed the sides of the defiles as high as this spot where the wife of the party's surgeon found the piece of argentiferous galena in 1864.

This was Little Cottonwood Canyon which drops from its elevation of 8,583 feet to Alta to debouch upon the plain a few miles from Salt Lake City. It cuts a spectacular gorge deep in the Wasatch Mountains, with sides so steep that avalanches are

BEAUTIFUL SLOPES OF LITTLE COTTONWOOD CANYON bear deep scars of mining operations in heyday of Alta. Remains of town are seen at lower right, where lift towers of modern ski resort stand. Skiers are carried directly over what is left of once booming town of 5,000 people. Railroad had just reached camp as death throes took over, failed to share in prosperity, also died. Grade made excellent bed for spectacular road which now carries throngs of skiers to popular Alta Resort.

COVERED TRAM extends from mouth of silver mine to chute. Ore dropped down chute to bunker, collecting until load was ready for wagons and long dangerous haul down precipitous grade to plain below. There smelters awaited where earlier ore had to be shipped overseas for treatment. Alpine area offers much beauty, pointed firs and spruces, spread far apart make parklike scene, spaces between trees filled by wild flowers in short summer season.

frequent, especially early in spring. It is formed of granite of such beauty that the stone for Mormon Temple was quarried from near its mouth.

The first prospectors were almost poverty-stricken, few with any large stakes and the whole group of them was nearly starved out before they could get their claims going on a producing basis. For example, J. P. Woodman, who located what would be the fabulous Emma, which later was sold for $5,000,000, was so hard pressed for capital at the start that he offered a one-quarter interest in the holding for $3,000, and got no takers.

For lack of milling equipment, Woodman and his hungry crew "rawhided" the best ore, wrapping it in green cow hides. Hauling it down the canyon on ox-drawn wagons and "stone boats," thence to Ogden. From there it was shipped to San Francisco, loaded on sailing vessels which carried it around the Horn to Swansea, Wales, where it was milled and smelted. Even after the cost of all this transportation was deducted, there was still $180 a ton left over for Woodman and his men.

Armed with these statistics, he went to Walker Brothers, Salt Lake City grocery firm and sold them one-sixth interest for $25,000, and a Mr. Hussey, a fourth interest for the same amount. What Walker Brothers thought of this deal is not recorded.

After further indication of potential wealth of the Emma, the several partners got together and sold the mine to a firm of investors called Parks and Baxter. The next step in this game of high finance, on receipt of option, was Parks going to Washington, D. C. interesting President Grant and through him gaining the attention of the Prime Minister of England, Mr. Schenk. This worthy bought in for $50,000, thus becoming a director of the combine. Eastern interests eagerly put in $375,000 for a half interest and then everybody got together and formed The Emma Mining Company of New York.

Now the whole operation moved overseas and in England, details of such a prodigous pouring out of silver from the Emma inspired the forming of the Emma Silver Mining Company, Ltd. of London. They purchased the entire interest for the sum of $5,000,000.

All this time the Emma had been faithfully producing its immense quantities of silver. But, almost at the same instant the huge deal was consummated, its output was suddenly cut off. The vein had run up against a solid wall of granite, broken off by faulting.

The outcry of fraud was loud and English investors protested so volubly that a board of investigation had to be set up in order to avoid an international incident.

The board found that there had been no collusion, that no one could have foreseen the pinching out of the lode. The many investors were left

SNOWS **REACH IMMENSE DEPTHS** in canyon high in Wasatch Mountains as shown by tower door for crawling into cabin when regular entrance was blocked. In case one didn't know, door carries lettering, "Winter Enterence."

to unhappily lick their wounds. For a long time after that, American mining stock found very poor sale in England.

Back in Alta, however, less touted mines like the Wasatch, Alta Consolidated, North Star, Prince of Wales and others had been producing steadily, if less gaudy amounts. Their best ore was now processed in new smelters a few miles out on the plain. The '80s produced some $13,000,000 worth of silver.

During all this time a boom had been going on in Alta. By 1872 the town had gathered a population of 5,000. There were 26 saloons, the most popular of which were the Bucket of Blood and the Gold Miner's Daughter. A gallon of whiskey cost $9, but it was one of the necessities of life. The usual "frail sisters" drifted in and out solicit-

ing their trade. Organized houses of prostitution also flourished, presided over by Alta Nell, Katie Hayes and others. These Madams held high places in a community predominately populated by young males, and one of the larger mines was named for Katie.

Snowfall reached extreme depths in this mountain camp, and in order to promptly dispose of casualties in the brothels and saloons where brawls and shootings were common, a tunnel was kept open to the cemetery.

In the '70s, production fell off to a mere $1,703,-068, and the following year Alta was hard put to make a million. Things were already at a low ebb when demonetization of silver hit in '93 and nearly finished the town. Continuing avalanches which killed many and destroyed much property did.

BINGHAM CANYON, UTAH

Brigham Young was not about to have his flock foresake farming for mining. So, when Sanford and Thomas Bingham found gold and other metals in the canyon they had been sent to cultivate, and when news of their dereliction seeped back to headquarters, a proper reprimand was soon dispatched to the boys. "Instead of hunting gold," the message read, "let every man go to work at raising wheat, oats, barley, corn and vegetables in abundance that there may be plenty in the land." The brothers, being good Mormons, covered up their prospect holes, though not without regrets.

This episode transpired in 1848 and about the only visible traces of it are the bare slopes on both sides of the canyon, denuded by busy axes and mills operated by the Binghams.

The next stage in the canyon's history came in 1863, the year Col. Patrick Connor was taking such an intense interest in Utah's mineral wealth. His legitimate business was flushing Indians out of hiding places in the canyons of the Wasatch and neighboring ranges but he could not resist looking for "float" too. The colonel's side line had reached farmers of Bingham Canyon, and one of them sent him a piece of ore thrown out of the early prospect diggings of the Bingham brothers and their friends. This chunk of galena turned out to be rich in silver and gold. That was the smoke signal. The rush was on. In a wave of goodwill, the colonel issued a letter on War Department stationery, informing the general public of the find and personally guaranteeing safety to all who wished to stake out claims in this canyon or any other in the area.

Bingham Canyon history from this point is the reverse of what almost every other mining camp experienced. The hard-rock work was begun first, because of the nature of that first sample, and there was enough encouragement from the results to get a boom town on its feet, though none too steadily. Ores proved refractory in the face of scanty and expensive milling equipment. Heavy losses took place, most of the precious metals "going down the drain." The miners decided to ship the ore somewhere else, like Swansea, Wales, for refining, and some of it actually did go that far. But to make that sort of shipping pay, the raw stuff had to be as rich as it was in Alta, in the Wasatch mountains, and this it was not. So the camp began to die almost as soon as it was born. Then came the discovery that there was a bonanza in the gravels of the canyon, with little expense in the gathering of this wealth. Placering was then started up and down the canyon's length and the town was saved.

Now things began to happen in a big way. One of the placers, the Clay bar, turned out some $100,-000 by 1868, and when the owners stopped at water level they turned their attention to the tailings dumps abandoned in early operations. Each of the men stacked up about ten dollars a day, and every so often a nugget came to light. One was the largest ever found in Utah, worth $128. Altogether, some $2,500,000 in gold was placered out of the gulches by 1870, when the Bingham and Camp Floyd Railroad reached town.

This event brought about some drastic changes, since it occurred about the same time the gravels began to show signs of depletion. Cheaper trans-

LITTLE JAIL AT REAR OF POLICE STATION was popular, full up on weekends, jammed at Christmas. Prisoners were not always drunks. One Rafael Lopez arrived in Bingham as a strikebreaker in 1912, nearly killed a Greek in savage fight over girls. After release from jail, he was again in girl trouble. He shot a rival, Juan Valdez, and took to the hills, evading posse after killing three pursuers, backtracked to town, took refuge in mine. During efforts to smoke him out another officer was killed. After five days, smoke cleared away but fugitive had vanished.

portation changed the picture for hard-rock men and it wasn't long before many tons of good ore were headed for the mills, which by this time had been established on the plain. Again the sagging economy of Bingham experienced an upsurge, the population going from 276 to more than 1,000. Substantial frame buildings replaced flimsy shanties. As earning power increased, easier ways were found to help the miners spend their money. "Share-the-wealth programs" burgeoned in more honky tonks and gambling houses, more hook joints and cribs, than even Brigham Young had feared would materialize when he first heard of metal in the hills. The narrow canyon and one narrow street echoed day and night with sounds of revelry. Shifts in the mines were on a continuous basis and there were always plenty of off-duty men looking for a change of pace. By 1900 there were 30 saloons, and among some twenty brands of whiskey, the top two were "Old Crow" and "16 to 1." The first moving pictures were shown in these dives, Mary Pickford in "Little Lord Fauntleroy" having a long run.

The easing of transportation problems, which made it economically feasible to ship ore out for refining, also made it possible to ship in the materials and parts for mills and smelters. As soon as some of these were completed, ore ceased to flow out of town, being replaced by the finished product. Erection of the Winnamuck Smelter in '72 and '73 by the Nevada-experienced firm of Bristol and Bateman was a big step forward in lode mining, as was A. H. Bemis' concentration plant treatment of lead ore. Biggest strikes were at the Yosemite No. 1, Brooklyn, No-You-Don't, Highland Boy, and Boston Consolidated.

The depression of 1893 almost closed the camp with bottom prices for silver, lead and gold. Bingham miners had always been conscious of some copper in almost all ores taken out of the canyon but it was usually scorned—heavy percentage of copper sulphide caused an upset in orderly extraction of gold. Now, with the old standbys fallen on evil days, with amounts of copper increasing, even up to 18 per cent, that metal could be ignored no longer. Small shipments of copper had been made as early as 1896, but now at the turn of the century, it began to assume a major role.

At this time the Highland Boy merged with the Utah Consolidated. After further deals involving $12,000,000, the now huge copper mines were controlled by one John D. Rockefeller. The next big change was in 1907, when deep shafts were abandoned, since copper was everywhere, and only "scooping" was necessary. (Open pit mining is the practice to this day). A merger with other companies created a new group with $100,000,000 behind it.

The town in the narrow canyon suffered disaster, natural and man-caused. Avalanches of snow and mud slid down the slopes left bare by Brigham Young's men, inundating whole sections of town, and killing many. Fires raged unchecked among tinder dry frame structures and floods rushed down the gulch, washing entire buildings out onto the plain. The town hordes survived all these but now a deliberate annihilation is its certain fate. The old narrow street has not been able to properly carry traffic for several years, so street, houses and buildings all must give way to a broad highway, to carry the flood tide of modern miners.

OLD CITY HALL—POLICE STATION building served Bingham Canyon many years, stood at edge of small parking lot at head of Canyon road. Above are mile after mile of dumps, surmounted by tracks bearing dump cars, endlessly carrying out waste, extending dumps to far hillsides, burying cacti and juniper trees. Operation goes on with complete indifference to day or night.

CORINNE, UTAH

Divorce lawyers were not as greedy in the 80's as they are today. You could even get unhitched by slot machine. The ad in the Corinne UTAH REPORTER said so. "Divorces Secured — Presence Unnecessary — Fee $2.50".

Above the legal firm name of Johnson and Underdunk was the message that any disenchanted mate was invited to use the elaborate and complicated machine in the offices of the firm. The suing party simply inserted a $2.50 gold piece in the maw of the contraption, gave the crank a turn and presto, in hand was a beautifully prepared divorce decree signed by the Corinne City Judge. When the names of both parties were filled in the blank spaces the document was legal.

There was even more. In the event you were too busy to visit the office, you could simply mail the money and necessary names to Johnson and Underdunk. They would turn the crank themselves and mail the papers to you.

It was a grand idea for a while — and then the firm was in big trouble. It seems that as slot-machine divorcees tried to remarry, some found their divorces illegal and those who had married again found themselves living in bigamy. About 2,000 of such divorces were being threshed out in court at one time.

But before divorces, even before Corinne, Mark A. Gilmore and five companions stood on the west bank of the Bear River, looking out over a stretch of grassy, level land. It was in 1868 and inspired by Joseph Smith's visions, Gilmore had some of his own. A thriving "gentile" city would rise here. It would become a throbbing railroad and steamboat center that would overshadow Brigham Young and his Mormon Empire. Even though Gilmore's partners were not endowed with such visions, they could work to create a great future for a city here, one that would have financial benefit for themselves. The group lost no time in securing the land cheaply.

The next step was to lay out a townsite with a business center surrounded by lots. Much dickering with the Union Pacific Railroad resulted in a contract to establish a railway station in the new city in return for railroad ownership of every other lot and free land for right of way and yards.

The Union Pacific saw advantages. East and west rail-laying crews were working and would meet at nearby Promontory next year, but that place was composed of salt flats at the edge of Great Salt Lake and would not do as a loading point for the stock and farm products expected to be produced. The new town, to be called Corinne, was on the banks of the Bear River and so connected to deep water — the lake. Ore from the booming mines at the south end of the lake could also be counted on to swell freight revenues. Mark Gilmore and his cohorts were equally happy. To have the powerful railroad behind them would be a big help in the days ahead when all this progress collided with Brigham Young's resistance.

Within two weeks of founding, Corinne was a town in fact with more than 300 frame shacks and tents, and more being built to accommodate a boom population of 1500, not including the 5,000 Chinese laborers employed by the railroad. The town had been founded on the premise that it would be strictly "gentile", meaning "no Mormons allowed". The field was wide open for any sort of boomer, hustler, gambler, prostitute or any other drifter as long as he or she was not of the Mormon faith. All this created a situation outside the law. When the east-west rail connections were made in 1869, the wild atmosphere was intensified by thousands of "freighters" who swarmed into the "Burg on the Bear", most of them rough, tough adventurers fresh from the Civil War and steamed up with elemental desires.

Corinne was shortly able to accommodate them in all ways. During its most flamboyant period it boasted of 19 saloons, 2 dance halls, 2 theaters, one of which had "the gaudiest stage in Utah," innumerable gambling dens and 80 women sometimes referred to as "soiled doves". With all this going on, Corinne was a thorn in the flesh of Brigham Young. He issued an edict forbidding any of his faithful to go near the place, which may have challenged some stalwart Mormons to visit the seat of iniquity if for no other reason than to satisfy their curiosity.

Early development included smelters to process the rich gold and silver ores shipped in from mines

to the south. Residue, such as slag and tailings, were used to pave the streets. Recovery of the precious metals seldom equaled assay values, a fact to be expected in the days of primitive milling and smelting methods. As processes improved, someone thought of the slag-paved streets, assayed some samples and found them still worth working. So back to mud went the streets and into the mills went the paving materials, which resulted in some gold being recovered. It could be said — "Corinne's streets were literally paved with gold." Everything considered, the mills and smelters proved successful, about the only promotion effort that was with the exception of the exploitation of sin. Almost every effort to "improve our fair city" failed dismally. Brigham Young was behind many of the failures and natural forces spiked the others. The "Burg on the Bear" fought desperately to make itself the junction of the Union Pacific and Central Pacific but the Mormon leader easily influenced the lines to meet at Ogden instead. The "Gentile City" became the butt of crude and sarcastic jokes as business interests departed for Ogden.

Then there was the grandiose plan, far beyond the financial capacities of the town, to found an agricultural empire by creating a huge irrigation system using Bear River water. The promoters petitioned Congress for aid and a grant of public lands for the purpose with the argument: "It is the only

JOINING OF RAILS EAST AND WEST was fulfillment of American dream of spanning continent. On May 10, 1869, Central Pacific's Jupiter rolled over last-laid rails to meet Union Pacific's No. 119. This photo of memorable occasion hangs on wall of Corinne's old depot, now rail museum.

LONELY REMNANTS of Corinne's earliest days are livery stable at right, first bank at left. Front half of latter is of frame construction, rear of brick comprising almost impregnable unit centered by even more solid brick vault. Later growth of town demanded larger bank and increased jail facilities. When new bank was completed, old one was converted to hoosegow, vault serving as security confinement.

place where a purely American community can be brought into permanent and successful contact with the Mormon population whose feet have trodden and who hold in their relentless grasp every other Valley in Utah. . . It is a notorious fact that everywhere in this territory the Mormon Prophet and his coadjutors have acquired control of the water courses issuing from the mountain sides that can be used for irrigation, and of all the canyons that afford any valuable timber within reach of cultivated lands. This monopoly . . . has enabled them to confine immigration to those of their own creed." A bill giving effect to this petition was introduced to the House and Senate but nothing came of it.

Next, in 1871, the town tried its hand at steamboating. The 70-foot, three-decker *City of Corinne* was built and proudly launched that year. It steamed down the Bear and into Salt Lake with a cargo of machinery consigned to Lake Point, returning with a load of ore from the mines in the Tintic and Oquirrh Mountains. The venture was hailed as a huge success but the city fathers had failed to take

into account the fluctuating level of the inland sea. The lake had attained a high after the boat launching and from then on dropped steadily until over 480 square miles of land were uncovered, the water becoming so low the majestic steamer was mired on the bottom time and again. Renamed the *General Garfield,* it became an excursion boat only to fail as that and come to an end as a pavillion at Garfield Beach.

The NEW YORK WORLD in 1870 had this item: "Corinne proposes to remove the capitol of Utah from Salt Lake City to Corinne, which containing but a few Mormons, is deemed a fitter place to put the military corps in." Obviously, from this account, some Mormons had crept in Corinne but the effort came to naught.

Possibly the best known Mormon hater in the territory and one who was not afraid to say so, was General Patrick Connor, the soldier-prospector who had helped found gold, copper and silver towns to the south. Connor headed the Liberal political party which had its stronghold in Corinne. A convention held there in 1870 nominated General George E. Maxwell for Congress. Campaigning speakers and newspaper stories made a point of condemning polygamy, this alienating not only Mormons but the so-called "Godbeites", who although having left the Mormon Church, still retained what they felt were the best features including plural marriage. Maxwell was roundly defeated although as the New York Herald caustically commented: "The gentile town of Corinne polled more votes than it had inhabitants", many such votes were cast by registered but transient railroad workers. Maxwell ran again two years later playing down mention of polygamy but again was defeated.

1872 brought another blow to the hard-luck community in the form of a diphtheria epidemic which caused several hundred deaths and frightened many families away. A few years later Indians were attacking frequently and although the eventual arrival of troops from Fort Douglas drove the marauders away, another share of the population had gone too.

The remaining farmers were discouraged over the effects of irrigation that brought alkali salts to the surface of the soil and laid waste to orchards and fields. A final blow came in 1903 when the road through town was rerouted over the Lucien cut-off to bypass Corinne.

Though shrunken to a remnant, Corinne's tiny population today proudly chalks up a few accomplishments. The town added much to the commercial development of the state and aside from being the first to stand up and "sass" the powerful Mormon Church, it had the first gentile school and floated the first steamboats on Great Salt Lake.

OPEN AIR EXCURSION CAR was used only in summer, Utah's winters being much too chilly. Surrounding mountains retain some snow even in July, although many streams have sources there, most soon sink into salty flats. Exception is Bear River, it originates in north section of Uinta Mountains in Utah, cuts corner of Wyoming, re-enters Utah, again loops through Wyoming and even touches Idaho, finally empties into Great Salt Lake near Corinne.

JAIL WAS BUILT as after-thought against back of fire house. Jail held constant procession of highgraders — men caught carrying off choice pieces of blossom rock in pockets and lunch buckets, even up nostrils — but p r a c t i c e was never stopped. Mammoth mine alone estimated it had lost $150,000 in pilfering. On one occasion whole carload of extra rich ore vanished from railway station. Suspects were jailed but nothing proved. Empty car was finally found in Mexico.

EUREKA, UTAH

Water and life had spiritual significance. The earth was not to be spoiled by digging into it. The spirits would not like that and much harm could come to a man if he angered them.

At least that was the Indian point of view and Tintic was a good Indian, a Ute chief. The valley was well watered by many streams, grass grew thick and tall. Deer and antelope were plentiful and occasionally the braves trapped a buffalo herd. What Tintic and the rest of his village people did not like was the white men poking around in the rocks as if they meant to find something and stay there. He led raiding parties on the white settlers' tents, fired on them and drove them away —but they always came back with twice as many men.

Stage drivers and lone Pony Express riders claimed the valley was the wildest and most dan-gerous on the whole route. Cattle men would have stayed away entirely but for all that fine grass and water. It was good grazing in spite of the cattle thefts by Tintic's warriors. And the white settlement grew so large Tintic finally gave up, and went to Manti where he died in 1859.

The little streams in the valley, clear and lovely, were adequate for watering the natural vegetation but when big mining operations got under way, they were woefully deficient. Certainly there was none left for domestic use and for a long time water was hauled into Eureka and sold for ten cents a gallon. Then a wooden pipeline was built from Jenny Lind Spring. This emptied into a vat in the center of town, from which the water was carried home in pails by householders. This primitive system had to suffice until '93 when a line was installed from Cherry Creek which allowed piping to many individual homes. When water was first turned into the new system there was a celebration lasting all night, and the liquid consumed was not water!

Eureka had its "characters." One of these was one Matteo Messo, born in Sonora, Mexico. He came to Utah with Johnston's army, winding up in the mining camp of Ophir. After a few years of hard work there he "struck it rich" and retired to Eureka. With more money than he could spend he nevertheless couldn't break old habits of economy and continued to "roll his own." As each bag of Bull Durham was emptied it was carefully hung on one of the rafters of his little cabin, "to keep the evil spirits away." But he gave away thousands of dollars to derelicts and beggars, finally dying in the little cabin, broke. The whole ceiling was filled with the little empty tobacco bags.

There was "Buffalo Davis," who made a good stake, soon losing it via the bottle. When every cent was gone he sold his body to a medical so-

HEAD FRAME above one of more recently operated mines in Eureka. At top are sheaves on which ropes and cables lowered or lifted men and ore buckets. Latter caught on tripper above chute, causing bucket to dump contents into waiting wagon. Underground, mile-long drifts required more than manpower to haul one-ton ore cars. Mules were often used. Underfed to reduce weight and legs strapped tightly to sides, animal was lowered in vertical position to workings. Once down it spent remainder of life in darkness.

ciety, and when those funds were also gone he was sent to an asylum in Provo and shortly died.

John Q. Packard couldn't bring himself to spend the necessary quarter to ride the twenty miles from Santaquin to Eureka so he walked, even when the weather was bad. Yet, when he died he left provisions for a library in Salt Lake, the lot to cost $20,000 and the building $100,000. In addition, he left an estate of $20,000,000.

Best remembered for eccentricities, however, is Mrs. Anna Marks. She was a Russian Jewess and came to Eureka in the '80s. Settling herself in the big boarding house on the main street, she attracted no particular attention. Then one night, when a sufficiently large crowd had gathered, she came screaming out, sobbing that the Chinese owner of the boarding house had raped her. Though she had no friends in the town, sentiment against Orientals was so strong that she had no difficulty in getting the embarrassed Cantonese arrested on her testimony. He escaped and fled the town. As soon as he was gone, the crafty lady took over the boarding house operation and did very well with it. Her next door neighbor was John Cronin who made the mistake of stepping on her side of the property line. Her violent abuse made him decide to build a board fence between them. As soon as he had a few post holes dug Mrs. Marks in a fury, grabbed a shovel and filled them in. As he proceeded she got into one of the holes and Cronin calmly dumped dirt on top of her. The affair developed by these means into a knock down, drag out fight, ending when Cronin threw her to the ground and sat on her. The irate woman rushed to court again, but by this time her reputation had preceded her and police refused even to arrest Cronin.

Another unwitting trespasser was Harvey Tompkins, who owned the hotel on the other side. He also attempted to build a "spite fence." Mrs. Marks' recourse this time was to get a gun and start shooting. Fortunately for Tompkins, he was not a smoker; the lady's first well-aimed shot found its mark in a large plug of tobacco in his pants pocket, causing him to temporarily abandon the fence building project. The Rio Grande Railroad was the next victim. The line attempted to build a spur across the corner of her property and was forced to make a heavy settlement on her for the privilege. Although contending the land wasn't legally hers, the company couldn't pursuade its workmen to face the indomitable woman and her gun. Eureka breathed easier when in 1912 Mrs. Marks died, worth $70,000.

Utah

TROUBLE ON THE MORMON FRONT

Grafton, Utah

Young Mrs. Tenny was in labor. Another Mormon was about to appear to draw life-giving air into its infant lungs and add itself to the flock of Brigham Young's helpers. But why in the name of Moroni, asked the men of Zion in the farming community of Grafton, did this contrary female pick this particular time to have a baby?

The Virgin River was carrying with it all the drainage from torrents of rain washing down the red rock walls and the muddy currents were swirling around and into the Tenny cabin. What to do about this woman in pain? There was no choice.

So the men waded into the knee-deep flood, lifted the bed as the baby was born. The boy henceforth carried the name Marvelous Flood Tenny.

At the general conference of the church in Salt Lake City October, 1861, Brigham Young made a pronouncement to 309 "units," northern colonists going out to settle in the south of Utah. They were to raise cotton as a main crop and families as a second. Most of the units consisted of families but all single men were advised to marry—and at once. When they reached Dixie, as the southern area was called, there would be no women available, and even if there were, even if their sweethearts fol-

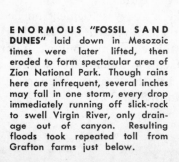

ENORMOUS "FOSSIL SAND DUNES" laid down in Mesozoic times were later lifted, then eroded to form spectacular area of Zion National Park. Though rains here are infrequent, several inches may fall in one storm, every drop immediately running off slick-rock to swell Virgin River, only drainage out of canyon. Resulting floods took repeated toll from Grafton farms just below.

lowed them, no marriage would be performed. They must take place in Salt Lake City.

Following the leader's edict emigrants began leaving homes so recently established, some couples almost strangers, others knowing each other only on the trek from Nauvoo, Illinois. One hastily married pair was Nathan C. Tenny and his bride.

The Tennys and several other settlers eventually found themselves established on land close to the Virgin, about six miles above the town of the same name. One account says the new settlement was called Grafton after the Massachusetts town while an old timer in the area told the author a Mr. Grafton was among the settlers and several of his descendants still live around Escalante, Utah.

To the north across the Virgin towered one of Zion's most splendid peaks, Kinesava, an area which would one day become a national park. Young had informed all settlers this would be their "Zion," a statement taken to refer literally to the surrounding mountains. When he visited the colonies along the canyon later he told them the peaks and walls

were "not Zion." For years afterward the farmers called the area Not Zion.

When garments brought from Salt Lake City began to fall in shreds replacements were made from wagon covers and tent cloth. These protected modesty and gave some warmth but were harsh to the skin, rough seams rubbing against flesh unprotected by underwear. In a few years small foundation flocks of sheep were producing large amounts of wool, the spinning wheels and carding combs brought in the wagons being put to use. Fleeces were sheared, washed, picked and carded, the wool made into rolls, spun into yarn and woven into cloth, all by slow hand labor.

By 1862 cotton had become a staple crop, the larger towns in the new Dixie surrounded by yellow-bloomed fields. Washington, for example, was planting 140 acres annually, the much smaller Grafton with 28 families growing about an acre each. The home spun clothing was a far greater comfort but there was luxury to come.

Brigham Young encouraged any planting which

SPECTACULAR SCENE once utilized by motion picture company as background for current epic. Mock store, saloon were erected between existing buildings, later removed. Virgin River flows immediately behind them. In background is Mount Kinesava, outer rampart of present Zion National Park. Overhanging trees are old Mulberries, planted by early Mormons in effort to produce silk, leaves being natural food of silkworm.

might produce a food product and one "exotic" plant cultured for utility purposes was the mulberry tree, very likely the so-called Russian variety which is more hardy than some. The blackberry-like fruit, while edible, has the disadvantage of dropping when ripe. One Dixie colonist, a Mrs. Jackson, botanist and plantswoman at heart, carried cuttings and seeds of the mulberry to her new home and soon had a small grove of trees.

The settled part of the country was being swept by a "silkworm craze," speculation sending silkworm eggs to unheard of prices. Rumors of easy success and fantastic profits seeped even into remote southern Utah and Dixie settlers wrote to Brigham Young for permission to produce silk. He not only approved of the venture but in 1874 saw

to it eggs were imported from the Orient and sent to St. George, center of the colonies, for wide distribution.

Pinhead-sized eggs arrived in flats of newspapers and were sprinkled on shredded mulberry leaves from Mrs. Jackson's trees. When 1/4" hatchlings grew to 3" they spun around themselves the essential product, cocoons of silk. Scanty instructions sent with egg shipments led to the eventual production of cloth and finally a silk dress. In later years silk production became an essential industry in Washington County but Grafton shared little in wool, cotton or silk success being too busy trying to fight off the ravages of floods and Indians.

The original settlement was washed away the first year, the colonists moving about a mile up-

RESIDENCE dating from 1870s, well built by Mormons. Thought was given to appearance, situated as it was on corner, far side and front faced with plaster, rear and right squared log walls less eloquent, less conspicuous. Tree at left is one of numerous Mulberries remaining from days of silkworm culture.

stream. At first they called the location New Grafton, later dropping the adjective. Here there was a wider shelf of arable ground, the elevation somewhat higher, but bitter experience had taught them to build ditches, levees and canals. Nevertheless the first spring rains and suddenly melting snows on the heights washed away the hand-built levees and filled ditches with mud and sand.

Even when hungry waters were not carrying away crops and homes Grafton settlers could not afford to relax. Indian attacks were so frequent constant guard was required and the rocky cemetery was filled almost entirely with arrow victims (see *Tales the Western Tombstones Tell*). The steady attrition of fields and men so reduced the once independent Grafton that the remains became a part of Rockville Ward two miles upstream. During the worst of the Indian trouble Grafton was entirely abandoned.

In 1868, with an uneasy peace established, the former Grafton settlers returned to plant grain and cotton once more, the sheep and cattle saved starting new herds. By 1877 there were enough Saints to again organize an independent ward with Alonzo H. Russell as bishop. He acted for ten years when he was succeeded by James Munroe Ballard. In 1900 William Isom took over until 1903 when Ballard was returned as bishop.

Although Indian raids ceased to be a problem the Virgin rose each year with increasing destructiveness and in 1907 so many families moved away the ward was again disorganized, only enough people remaining to justify the residence of Philetus Jones acting as presiding elder. When he went to Rockville as bishop in 1921 Grafton ceased to be a unit of the church.

In succeeding years the town retained two or three families attempting to eke out an existence for a year or two, then abandoning the struggle as hopeless. In 1950 the site was used by a motion picture firm to make a film using the ready-made "set" and picturesque background. When actors and crew left Grafton became a true ghost.

LITTLE PRIDE of construction shown in this building used for sheltering stock.

IOSEPA, UTAH

The original inhabitants of bleak Skull Valley were members of the lowly Gosiute Indian tribe. They were scavengers, eating whatever they could find including numerous lizards, horned toads, rodents and snakes indigenous to the arid wastes. When winter cut off even this meager supply, they were reputed to hole up and barely exist in a state of near hibernation until spring. Starvation took its toll, skeletons found by early settlers giving the valley its name.

In 1843 Thomas Farnham wrote "these poor creatures are hunted in the spring of the year when they are weak and helpless . . . and, when taken, are fattened, carried to Santa Fe and sold as slaves." These were the best people this savage land could produce until eager Mormon converts from lush South Sea Islands established a new home in Zion.

The group of Hawaiian Islanders must have looked at their new home in Skull Valley with more than dismay. No landscape could be imagined to contrast more with the one they had recently left. Instead of swaying palms there were a few scattered juniper trees and some sagebrush. In place of curling, foam-crested breakers rolling in on white sandy beaches there was a tiny spring, not even visible to the homesteaders. A few coyotes and jack rabbits made up the animal population. Now and then a black and white magpie would sail low over the rocky ground, its long tail streaming. This was their promised land.

Mormon zeal had spread to the Islands even in 1844, and in a few years the Saints had converted many of the natives. Possibly to demonstrate the success of the Church in gaining converts in such far-flung outposts, some fifty new members were transported to Salt Lake City, there to receive the rites in the temple. The bewildered Kanakas were then displayed throughout the area comprising the Mormon settlements surrounding the Mother Church.

Whether they had been promised lands and homes as an inducement to come to Utah, or whether colonization was in the minds of the natives all along is not known, but they were given land. It was not the lush, irrigated land taken up by earlier settlers under faith but a dreary, barren and rocky site at the edge of the Great Salt Desert. The only redeeming factor was a spring which yielded barely enough water for home consumption, little for watering the meager soil of 960 acres. Later, as the townsite was developed and land put under the plow, a small stream in the nearby Standsbury mountains was channeled to the area for more adequate irrigation.

The only trees able to withstand the rigors of the desert climate were the ubiquitous poplars and cottonwoods, rooted from cuttings and set in rows along the raw streets. Enough houses to shelter the group and enough store buildings were put up as well as a church. The new town was named for Joseph Smith, prophet of the Saints, but the Islanders could not sound the "J", so the word was spelled Iosepa and pronounced something like Yo-see-pa.

Some of the succeeding years were good ones. The Kanakas were industrious to a degree. Their background had never been one of hard labor, for nature had been more provident with fish to be caught, fruit to be cut down, and shelters sufficed to keep warm rain from their heads. Now their days were spent carrying heavy rocks from the fields, directing sparse irrigation water into the ditches, harvesting meager crops. During the best year, crops of hay, grain and cattle were sold for $20,000; the rest of their food was imported from Salt Lake City.

While it sustained itself most times, the colony lost ground in numbers. Deaths from pure hardship outnumbered births and several times new, hopeful converts came from the Islands only to be dismayed

POPULATION OF CEMETERY grew more rapidly than that of colony. Most monuments were of wood, identifications fading under scouring winds. Some few are of more durable marble, one pictured marking last resting place of Kapainue Kalauao, far from palm-bowered, sea-bordered place of birth. Even though directed by tenants of ranch on highway, Mr. and Mrs. J. D. Nebel, photographer had difficulty locating cemetery. It is not accessible by any existing road, was spotted in field glasses, reached by rough hike through sagebrush and rocks, reputedly full of rattlesnakes.

Snowy Mountain in background is Desert Peak 11,031 feet in elevation, third highest in Utah.

and turn back. Hardest blow of all came with the discovery that the dread plague of leprosy had somehow followed them. When several colonists showed unmistakable signs of the disease, they were segregated in a building erected for them. They could see their families and friends working in the fields but could not mingle with them. They had to live out their miserable lives in the gray stone building.

After several crop failures came in a series, dis-

solution among the colonists began to set in. Gold and silver were being mined in nearby mountains, and during the late 90s and early part of this century many men, especially the younger ones, went to work in the mines. Most of these had abandoned not only the colony but their faith which seemed to fail them. When the Latter-day Saints Church was completed in the Islands, the remainder of Iosepa's workers abandoned the project and returned to their homeland.

MAMMOTH, UTAH

Not every day could the pioneers say: "With a bunch of cows the McIntyres made two million." The fortune was not in milk but a mine—the Mammoth. At its peak of production it poured out $1,000 worth of ore to the ton.

But this was some time in happening. Originally staked in 1871, it remained unworked for two years due to the inhospitable combination of Indians, dry weather and barren country. When the owners, Charles Crismon and partners, did make some developments, they had only mediocre success. Discouraged but alert, Crismon saw an opportunity to unload his share on the gullible McIntyre brothers.

Sam and William McIntyre were driving a herd of Texas Longhorn cattle to market at Salt Lake City and were searching for good range land on which to fatten the animals a little before the last leg of the drive. But falling in with Crismon, the brothers were much impressed with the mine owner's glowing description of the wealth that awaited some lucky man who would buy the Mammoth, invest some money in it and sink the main shaft to the point where it would meet with a fabulous lode of silver.

Sam and William decided to trade their cattle for the biggest share of the mine. Crismon continued to market with his animals and the brothers did exactly as they were supposed to do. They did spend some money developing the property, sank the shaft deeper and just as their truthful friend had predicted, met up with the fabulous vein.

Some shady developments with surprising results took place in the district with the legitimate success of the Mammoth. A Mr. Pease, becoming discouraged with his Wyoming mine devised a method of "salting" it for the benefit of a couple of innocent gentlemen who wished "to buy a good mine." Before showing these men the property Pease purchased two carloads of rich ore from the Eureka Hill and dumped the valuable raw material down the shaft. The sale was then readily consummated, Pease to receive $20,000 cash and the remaining balance of $2,000 in a week's time. The new owners saved the final payment, of course— Pease was no longer around to collect. On the strength of the kind of ore they had taken out of the shaft, the operators first constructed a mill. When the rich ore in the hole had been put through it, there was no more to process. As further exploratory probing went on, the owners were forced to take in custom milling to keep from going broke; then suddenly began to break into paying veins, one of which yielded more than $1,000,000.

Another case of salting was performed in reverse. A superintendent placed a lot of worthless ore around the mouth of the mine and informed the owners that the whole thing was hopeless. He would, however, take a lease on it at a very reasonable price and work on it in his spare time. This he did, soon getting down to the lode he knew was there all along.

The turn of the century saw a period of wild living, robberies, holdups and killings. Two miners, William Dryburn and Barney Dunne were spending a quiet Sunday in 1902 getting drunk in their tent. An argument developed as to who was the better shot. Dryburn dared the other to see if he, Dunne could shoot Dryburn's hat off. Dunne proved to be an even worse marksman than his partner had thought, the rifle bullet found its mark in the middle of Dryburn's forehead.

The Mammoth Mine had been performing well. The McIntyres had built twenty-two furnace smelters and Sam had constructed a mansion, a fine brick home in the town of 1,000 that had grown up around his mine.

When the richest ores were exhausted and the poorer ones failed to pay the milling and smelting costs, the mills closed down and people began to move away. Even the Mammoth operations ceased and Sam left his brick house to wandering cowboys and sheepherders. The big schoolhouse was boarded up for many years and finally torn down, the swings in the playgrounds remaining at one side of the rubble and the basketball hoop on the other.

ORE CARS ONCE KEPT BUSY at Mammoth Mine now stand rusting on tracks narrower than regular ore car gauge. Cars, however, are standard one-ton size, so that amount of ore from mine could be calculated.

MERCUR, UTAH

The stranger was regarded with some curiosity. He bore none of the earmarks of prospector, miner or conman. He searched out the city fathers and stated he was the advance agent for the circus which was to come here to Mercur, remote gold camp in the Oquirrh mountains of Utah. Since no such glamourous entertainment had ever been imagined for the place, the agent was warmly welcomed and arrangements for the show speedily made. One little detail, however, was overlooked.

The big day arrived for the circus to pull into town and only then did the citizenry consider the fact that the standard gauge train tracks ended five miles from Mercur, narrow gauge then taking over. Nothing daunted, the circus set up its tents and animals cages on a nearly level spot by the siding. As long as the show couldn't quite make it to town, the town would meet it halfway. There were no passenger cars on their line, but there were flat cars. Boards were nailed around the sides to help keep the holidaying customers from sliding off on the sharp curves. This open-air ride had its disadvantages. Dense smoke and cinders belched from the stack of the engine and, while all passengers arrived safely at the circus, some had holes burned in their clothing and cinders in their eyes.

Lewiston Canyon was a meager, discouraging field for prospectors. When they found a few flakes of gold, there was no water to wash it except in the spring when snow was melting and where water flowed with any degree of regularity, no color showed. Nevertheless, all through the late 1860s a few persistent men searched the boulder- and cacti-strewn gulch, because where there were a few small nuggets, there must be bigger ones or perhaps a lode.

In 1869 L. Greenley found enough to encourage the staking of a claim but when his little dribble of water dried up he quit. This should have been the signal for a complete abandonment of the district, but since silver had been found in paying quantities nearby, persistent prospectors turned their attention to searching for it in Lewiston Canyon and soon found good deposits.

Slowly at first, then more rapidly miners drifted in to work the hills for silver, and almost imperceptibly a boom developed. Mines with names like Silver Cloud, Mormon Chief, Sparrowhawk, Last Chance and Grecian Bend were soon producing real wealth. A stage company saw its opportunity and started a line with six stages a day going up the dry canyon to the new camp in Lewiston. Population zoomed to a couple of thousand, schools were established, saloons

AFTER PINEDO'S DISCOVERY of Cinnabar here and subsequent failure to make ores pay, he vanished; good deposits of gold were found in his claim. Discoverers trailed owner Pinedo halfway around world. Pinedo, who had regarded claim as worthless, now demanded $100,000 for it, settled for $30,000. When gold proved impossible of extraction, all except Pinedo lost shirts. Then, in 1893 came dramatic discovery in Colorado of successful method of extracting elusive metal from refractory ores by use of dilute solution of cyanide in water. After finely crushing ore, powder was mixed with water and small amounts of cyanide, dissolving gold. Soupy mixture was then run through zinc shavings causing gold to precipitate out. Picture shows "thickening vats" where mixture gradually settled to bottom. Center posts carried spokes with canted, snowplow-like blades. As these revolved very slowly, they gently nudged heavier deposits toward center without stirring up remainder. Near-solid sludge was then removed to be refined, ending up as bars of gold bullion.

ALMOST IMPOSSIBLE TO IMAGINE is vast mill building which once covered entire expanse of stone terrace-like levels. Hard, obdurate gold and silver-bearing rocks entered at upper level, gradually descended by gravity through series of succeedingly finer crushers and ball mills until they were at last reduced to powder, when extraction of precious metals was accomplished. Enormous eroded piles of residue, called tailings, extended half a mile below ruins of mill. Narrow road winds upward through scene reminiscent of Bryce Canyon.

thrived and even a church was established. Lewiston bore all the marks of a boomtown for a few short years and then when silver was exhausted, the bubble burst and Lewiston died. By 1880 it was a ghost town without a living soul.

Now came a prospector to the deserted diggings, one more imaginative than earlier ones—Arie Pinedo, a Bavarian. Primarily searching for a richer vein or placer deposit of gold, he kept his eyes open for other metals and was rewarded by discovering good signs of quicksilver, a vein of cinnabar no one had noticed before. Elated, the man of German extrac-

tion called his claim by his word for the volatile metal, Mercur.

Another strange quirk of fate was written for the camp that couldn't decide what metal to settle down to. When the cinnabar ore was assayed, it showed good content of gold, valued at far more than mercury. Not one to keep a secret, Pinedo broadcast the glad news and others flocked in to one-time Lewiston (the former name of the town had been bestowed by the post office on another, newer community) and the site began to come alive again. For a short time there was a lot of gold-bearing ore but when efforts

374

LITTLE CABIN REMAINING from third stage of occupation shows pathetic signs of love and pride in humble home, however temporary. Walls are lined with now tattered wallpaper in flowered patterns. Yard was once planted with rugged types of flowers, vestiges of thorny roses surviving near gate. At left of post may be seen dark green sprouts of hop-vines emerging to face another harsh dry Utah summer. Water to keep flowers alive was hard to come by. John Nicholson owned only spring, a mile distant, and sold water by cup and bucket, giving rise to "Can't afford water" excuse for large-scale whiskey drinking. Later water was piped from nearby Ophir, was still scarce as most of meager supply was demanded by mills for mixing with powdered ores.

were made to get the gold out of the rock, none showed up in the stamps or any of the crude refining machinery available at the site. Again the place was deserted. Yet everyone around knew the gold was there and couldn't leave the area alone. In the next few years one attempt after another was made to mine it and failed. One of the last crude efforts was that of Joseph Smith who wrapped the best chunks in rawhide and transported it by burro to lower levels where it could be more easily attacked. But even that was without success.

Up till now all these efforts had been made by men without capital. About 1890 a group of men with some financial backing decided to go ahead solely on the strength of persistent assay showings of worthwhile gold, planning to get out a lot of ore, devising some way to extract the metal. This somewhat backward method of developing eventually paid off in a big way when a smart young chemist in Denver, where samples had been sent, figured out a way to separate the gold from the rock by using cyanide on it, a method not too well known at the time.

STREETS IN MERCUR STRAGGLED anywhere there was room in narrow canyons. Main business of mining encroached on houses with dumps and tailings. Diggings are shown here on hill above.

A demonstration showed that ninety percent of gold could be "saved" from the ore by this treatment. Now more capital was easily enlisted and Mercur boomed again, in larger fashion than before. By 1885 mining was big business. Not only was the high grade ore giving up its wealth, the low assay stuff formerly cast aside was put through the cyanide mills and made to pay. Soon million of dollars were pouring out of Mercur.

In 1895 another smart young man came on the scene. The owners of the Mercur Mine decided on a big venture, that of building a huge mill to be called the Golden Gate. The concern imported D. C. Jackling from Cripple Creek as engineer. Jackling had

ideas that were contemptuously derided by oldtimers, such as "roasting" the ore before treatment. The owners decided that since they had brought him in for his knowledge they'd give him free rein. The result was that the other ten percent of the ores, the hitherto unproductive residue also gave up its gold under the heat treatment.

Other mine owners soon changed their hidebound views and by 1900 the De Lamar Mercur Mines Co. and the Mercur Mines and Milling Co., giants of the district, combined with smaller outfits to become the Mercur Consolidated Mercur Mines Co, and all ore was put through the Golden Gate Mill.

All this time water in the camp was as scarce as

376

it had ever been. The only civic "water system" was operated by John Nicholson who hauled the precious commodity from the spring and peddled it at a good profit except when there was a new baby in the town, when he made a present of a month's supply to the happy family.

The narrow gauge reached Mercur in 1896 and the camp felt sufficiently important to make plans to incorporate, the big event to coincide with State Admission day, January 6, 1896. While preparations were being made for a combined celebration, fire broke out and almost completely destroyed the town. There was absolutely no means of fire protection. The need had been foreseen but every time anyone wanted to start a volunteer fire department, some detractor would ask, "Where would we get the water?"

Mercur was soon rebuilt, only to be destroyed again by licking flames in 1902. Again rebuilt, the camp was once more going strong by 1905 and in 1910 had a bigger population than ever. About this time the big mill had turned out a batch of bullion worth some $45,000. There were rumors that a notorious gang of bandits would rob the little train that would carry the bullion down to the bank. Several citizens were delegated to put it in an ordinary buckboard, cover it with innocent canvas and drive nonchalantly down the gulch with the valuable load. There were other items stowed aboard, like a couple of bottles of Mercur Firewater. When these were partially consumed, the deadly earnest mission developed into a joyride through the sagebrush where the vehicle was stopped while all hands tried their shooting skill on unfortunate jack rabbits and coyotes. Attempting to get the buckboard back on the road, too much speed was laid on and the wagon was buckled by the heavy load. All hands helped get the vehicle to a blacksmith shop for repairs, nobody apparently too much worried about the precious cargo or its safety. They had no need to be, as no bandits ever put in an appearance.

The current boom lasted until 1913, when deposits seemed to be failing. Things went from bad to worse with Mercur. The Salt Lake and Mercur Railroad removed the rails and ties in 1925 and many buildings were torn down; it was once again a deserted camp.

Seemingly dead "for sure" this time, Mercur surprised itself once more. In 1934 a side canyon, Horse Thief Gulch, ignored until now, was explored and discovered to be rich in gold. In two years Mercur was on its feet again. The Snyder Brothers group, which had discovered and staked Horse Thief Gulch, soon had a 1,000-ton mill in operation and in 1937 there were 150 men at work in it. Tailings and miles of underground workings were being explored and exploited and not far away the Geyser-Marion Gold Mining Company was opening up a "gloryhole" and putting up a cyanide mill to refine those ores. In a year or two the ex-ghost town was the second goldproducing town in Utah.

By 1951 Mercur's pendulum had swung full arc again, mining had become too expensive in the face of rising costs and stable gold prices. That year Mr. Helmer L. Grante, company watchman told authorartist Mrs. Muriel Wolle: "Mercur isn't through yet. She's about due to come back again."

LONELY RUIN OF BIG GENERAL STORE on Mercur's main street, only reminder of hectic, brawling days when street was solidly lined with other stores, saloons, hotels and newspaper with natural name *Mecury Mercur*. Next to this store stood Jack Schaefer's Mercur Hotel. Alert to any opportunity to make a dollar, Schaefer often stopped incipient fights in saloon, next in line of buildings, not to preserve peace, but to stage conflict in ring where he could promote fight, collect gate receipts.

OPHIR, UTAH

Before Ophir were the Indians. They ranged the narrow canyon and made bullets from the silver they mined. In 1865 Col. Patrick E. Connor's far-ranging troops heard about the fancy slugs and routed the redmen at the source of them. The lode was in East Canyon, a slit in the mountains shadowed early and late by tiered, castellated cliffs. The soldiers named the place St. Louis.

By 1870 it became necessary to form a new mining district and plat a town. Both were romantically christened Ophir for the fabulous mines of King Solomon and such individual mine names as Wild Delirium and Miner's Delight indicated high spirits. On August 23, 1870, horn silver was found on Silverado Hill and in rapid order the Silveropolis, Chloride Point and Shamrock lodes were staked out. With the Ophir and Pocatello already producing in a big way, the town zoomed into something resembling a frenzy.

Almost overnight the narrow, dusty canyon trail was lined with tents, saloons, brothels and then stores, a small hotel which was a hybrid of whipsawed lumber and canvas, and two slapped-together restaurants. The first silver ore from the Silveropolis assayed $24,000 to the ton in ten car lots and a dozen new claims were located on Lion and Tiger Hills.

Most often boom camp optimism received a set back when the time came to build a mill and the ore was found to be refractory. Ophir's ores however went through the first mill, built by Walker Brothers of Salt Lake City, with the greatest of ease. The operators saved about eighty percent of the metal where in some early mills all but about twenty-five percent was lost. The first mill was called the Pioneer and its success inspired the erection of several others, among them the Brevoort and Enterprise. Smelters were the next logical step and the Ophir and Faucet were put up.

Tents were replaced by more substantial structures and the easy-going success of Ophir's affairs inspired some fancy stone and brick houses. And years later, when the silver deposits were exhausted and Ophir died, the buildings stood out like mausoleums pointing up the town's short life.

From time to time new life was breathed into the corpse and Ophir sat up again. Copper and zinc in the diggings proved almost equal to silver in value. Some mines here were almost as permanent as the one operated for twenty-five years by Senator W. A. Clark of Montana and Marcus Daly's Zella. In the '30s the International Smelting and Refining Co. built a 600-ton flotation mill at the mouth of the canyon to treat the 400,000 tons of tailings from the old Ophir Mining Co.

POST OFFICE FOR PERMANENT CITY which wasn't. One of solid structures erected when townspeople thought Ophir would be stable. Large sums of money and bullion were handled in one section used as bank, necessitating iron shutters and doors as protection from Indians, bandits. During later, transient boom building served as tavern, bore simple sign reading "Beer."

"A sudden rush of icy-cold air . . . in that heat!"

PARK CITY, UTAH

If the soldiers under Col. Patrick Connor could not find Indians to shoot at, they could always go prospecting. Dig into most of Utah mine history and you will find signs that many of the original discoveries were made by these far-cruising troopers in ragged, blue coats.

The phenomenal boom town of Park City is one that grew out of soldiers' finds. They ran across a bold outcropping of quartz, about two miles south of where the city would be built, and reported: "We tied a red bandana handkerchief to a bush where it could easily be seen to mark the place." The assay report for the chunk they brought to town stated there were 96 ounces of silver to the ton and goodly portions of gold and lead. A whole year passed before miners began working the claim and one conjectures—the soldiers were too busy looking for more to tell anybody what they had until 1870. Then a stampede for the peaceful meadows began.

Tents and brush shanties, always the first shelters in an embryo camp, soon lined the muddy "street" the length of the canyon. By the time the mud turned to dust miners built a boarding stable, meat market and most important, a saloon. The bar was a board laid over two kegs and on it a jug of rotgut and dipper—price of a dipper full, two bits. Later as a refinement a bottle of better quality liquor with a glass or two and a shot of this was twice as much. A year later a mahogany bar was imported from Salt Lake City and with it the customary plate glass mirror and huge painting of a nude damsel reclining on a couch.

In ten years Park City had reached the status of a city in fact as well as name. 1884 saw rapid expansion in building, mining and shipping of ore. And here came the rowdy element. The editor of the *Park Record* complained: "There is too much promiscuous shooting going on in the streets at night." But in spite of shootings, brawls in the bistros and quarrels in the gambling houses, all was not evil in Park City. A Catholic church was built at the end of the first decade. A water system with a small reservoir and one pipe down the middle of the street was installed. Stages linked the town with others and there were signs a railroad, Rio Grande Western, was to run its rails this way.

When rumor of this became established fact, Park City "blew off its dusty lid," people ordinarily abstemious sharing in a great headache the next day. A more lasting worry was over the Chinese population suddenly swelled when the railroad decided not to use them in working crews.

Orientals never were popular with the miners largely because they could get along with so few

OLD HIGH SCHOOL dates back to days of first boom. Classes were still being held when prohibition came in, causing closure of 20 saloons and reducing revenue for city schools by $22,000 yearly. On that July day the miners tried to drink up the entire existing supply of liquor. Stocks were sold out 2 hours before deadline. Bartenders could not serve patrons fast enough so patrons served themselves. Some paid and some stole until at midnight the "grave digging bell" was tolled by the sexton himself warning all prohibition had come.

Frequently the table cloth caught fire, giving the volunteer fire department some practice. Another Chinese who had lived in the city a long time and had owned a business bringing him often in the public eye, rated an obituary in the *Park Record* which ended with some confusion as to his race. "He had been ailing for a long time as though simply to save funeral expenses. He was buried by his fellow 'chinks' . . . with his hat on so he would not catch cold on his way to his Happy Hunting Grounds."

All this time the mining activities had burgeoned to the point where the populace became smug over their future, claiming "Park City is about to become the first city in Utah, will soon outstrip Salt Lake City itself." Then came bad times from an unexpected source.

The first rich workings had been shallow, easily worked and caused the big boom. As the good ores went deeper and became more refractory, miners had difficulty keeping up with the changing conditions. Then as workings reached greater depths

comforts and work for so little money. Some went into businesses of their own, laundries and opium dens the most popular. One laundryman, desiring privacy for his afternoon pipe of poppy juice, always crawled under the table with a lighted candle.

POLICE AND FIRE DEPARTMENT buildings were recently repaired and painted after long period of neglect. Modern alarm was installed on hose tower, replacing old bell. Fires plagued Park City, worst one in 1898. Blaze started in hotel dining room, took most of town, cost $1 million. Arson was suspected, *Park Record* reported: "Should anyone be caught setting fire to a building, his life would not be worth a straw. Murder may be committed, the law allowed to take its course, but the line is drawn on the fire bug and God help the man. . . . A long rope and a short shrift will be his portion as a fate."

OLD SCHOOL stands on higher level street, is slowly being dismantled. Signs warn of falling bricks. Period of reform lasted several years, making deep inroads in revenue for school upkeep; gambling and wide open saloons returned in 1909, easing maintenance of public buildings. Second reform then took over, every den of vice except saloons being closed. Temperance worker told *Record* he "watched the leading saloon and counted the men going in and out, from 7:30 p.m. to 8:30 p.m. The result was 153 in and 164 out."

they got to the water table. One by one the mines became flooded and had to be abandoned. The town was about to die when the big mine owners saw the light; instead of battling each other over conflicting claims, thus supporting an army of lawyers, they joined forces. With combined capital, drainage tunnels were dug, the water removed and Park City got back to work.

At the turn of the century methods of getting at ores had lost most of the grief and sadness of earlier days but the *Park Record* kept the people informed. In 1905 it said: "Twelve years ago two old time prospectors, while exploring a small drift at the bottom of a shaft, stumbled on the body of a man . . . the heavy shoes . . . enclosed gruesomely the shiny bones of the feet . . . a sheet of paper was found upon which was written in a faltering and uncertain hand a short but pitiful story. 'Dear God, I am dying. I have found wealth at the cost of my life. The samples in the bucket are from a ledge on—my hand trembles, my eyes grow dim—I—I am.' Here the record becomes a senseless jumble."

The *Park Record* was always the lead news-

paper. Others had succeeded for a time, the *Call* coming out in 1887 and dying in eighteen months. *The Miner* ran for two years, the *Utah Patriot Miner* holding on for a like period and the *Park Miner* printed its little sheet from 1902 to 1903. Editorials in all the papers were often fiery, sometimes vituperative attacks on people freely identified by name. A customary practice was to air the personal life of some prominent individual or candidate for public office. Libel laws if any were vague but every now and then an infuriated citizen would personally assault an editor in a fusillade of gunfire on the street or in the office of the paper. No staff man seems to have been lost to the *Park Record* however.

One of the services of this stalwart was a hybrid column, a cross between "personals" and "help wanted." During the hard times of 1897, appeared this pathetic plea: "A competent sawmill man wishes a situation. Can run a sawmill and keep it in repair from engine to slab pile. P. S. If I cannot get a situation in a mill, would be perfectly willing to accept a situation with some widow (no matter how grassy) until the roses bloom again."

SEGO, UTAH

Coal had none of the glittering lure the fortune hunters found in gold or in the shining veins of silver. There was no glamor or romance in digging out the dull black stuff that lay in sullen defiance of the miner's pick. Yet above ground coal cast the same spell over men that precious metals did, by using the power of the dollar. In camps like Sego they drank and whored and gambled and murdered. As Walter Ronzio says, they worked close to danger and lived right on the edge of it.

Vast areas in western Utah are stark desert, made up of land more or less level relieved by sections where red rock cliffs predominate. Barrenly picturesque, the country has no water except for the Colorado River that bisects the southeastern part of the state. So it was natural enough for one pioneer named Thompson to settle where he found a generous stream of water, about 45 miles from the Colorado state line and 20 from the river. Although this water source was several miles up a narrow canyon, the small settlement growing up around the homestead was called Thompson's Springs.

In the early 1890's the community was made up of farmers, sheepherders and cattlemen, none of whom had ambitions beyond their immediate needs — except Harry Ballard, of England, a man of far-reaching ideas. In a short time he acquired an extensive spread of sheep and cattle and owned most of the village — hotel, store, pool hall and a few houses, enough to cause the Denver and Rio Grande Western Railroad to stop there and build a small station, calling it simply Thompson's. In time the " 's" went too.

Ballard left his herds and flocks to his help and in roving the country on horseback, made an important discovery about five miles up the canyon near his source of water. Here was a large vein of coal, the seam exposed for yards along the canyon side. Saying nothing of his discovery, he bought up the surrounding land and started mining in a small way.

The coal was first dug by hand and hauled down the narrow canyon by wagon until local customers' wagons came from towns as far away as Monticello and even Bluff, down near the Four Corners. The fame of Ballard's high quality coal spread to Salt Lake City and to B. F. Bauer who owned the Salt Lake Hardware store. Bauer bought out Harry Ballard and formed a corporation, selling stock valued at $1 million. The new company was named American Fuel Co. and the little town around the mines Neslin, after Dick Neslin, new general manager.

Production started in 1911 with ambitious plans, the company erecting a stone store, boarding house and other buildings, all with individual water systems. A coal washer was also constructed, the first west of the Mississippi, and a modern tipple, an elaborate apparatus for emptying coal cars by tipping them.

In 1914 the Denver and Rio Grande Western Railroad built a spur line from Thompson to the coal camp, originally named for Ballard, calling the new line the Ballard and Thompson. In the five-mile stretch the rails crossed the stream thirteen times.

The troubles that plagued the town and mine from beginning to end started with the gradual drying up of the once ample water supply. The level of the water table had been dropping for years but

CENTER OF SEGO, Utah, once busy, rowdy mining camp. At right is company store, walls of sturdy rock still standing though with numerous cracks, ceilings, floors and partitions long gone. At left is boarding house. Few hundred feet below these structures are two others in fairly good condition but rest are in partial or complete ruin. Shown here is one of thirteen bridges once spanning dry gulch which contained lively stream in early days. Bridges, originally built to carry railroad spur, later road, are to be crossed with caution, taking care to keep wheels on lengthwise planks.

was ignored until one summer the spring dried to a dribble, not enough to operate the coal washer. The little "600" steam engine operated by the D. & R.G.W. which pulled four cars of coal to and from the tipple was off the track one fourth of the time or would often go careening down the tracks out of control.

Discouraged with a program yielding little or no profit, majority stockholder Bauer insisted on a general reorganization in 1916. Among officers who got the boot was Dick Neslin, and with his banishment the town became Sego, the Mormon name for *Calochortus Nuttalli*, state flower of Utah. He was replaced by a Mr. Van Dirck and the operation to be known as Chesterfield Coal Co.

Walter Ronzio, now of Grand Junction, Colorado, was only fourteen years old when he went to work in the Sego coal mines. July 18, 1918. He describes some of the financial troubles of the Chesterfield people and their employees:

"The reorganization didn't help much as far as the miners were concerned. Pay days would lag behind sometimes as long as a year. The mine owners would announce a pay day and we would all line up at the pay window. We were supposed to get a month or two of the six or seven months owing. Maybe a third of the line would receive their pay. Then the clerk would say, 'Sorry, no more money'. However no one actually lost any money. To those who didn't get paid the company would issue scrip money. With this you could buy supplies in the company store, gamble or spend it for white mule or home brew. If you needed a little cash maybe you could find some one who would give you $3 cash for say $5 worth of scrip.

"Those were days when it didn't make any difference how provoked you got at the management, you just kept your mouth shut or the boss would say—You're fired! The only thing we could do as American citizens was to quit. But most of us had families that were at least eating." However continuing dissatisfaction at last caused the men to welcome previously rejected organizers of the United Mine Workers Union. Unionization was accomplished in 1933 after which miners were paid regularly twice a month.

Up until 1927 the company supplied its own power for mine operation and electricity for the camp, using a pair of Lance engines which were a constant headache, frequently breaking down. The company knew that if mining were to continue power would have to be secured from some other source. The nearest available electricity was at Columbia, Utah, a hundred miles away, but a line was built by Chesterfield, carrying 44,000 volts, at a cost of more than $100,000, the company forced to guarantee twenty years' use. The first power arrived in Sego November 1, 1927, and exactly twenty years later to the day, the Chesterfield mines were ordered closed, property offered at a sheriff's sale on the courthouse steps at Moab, Utah.

By then the one-time total of 125 miners employed had dwindled to 27. Among them was Walter Ronzio. He had spent almost 30 years working

DESOLATION AND RUIN prevail in Sego. At left is rear of company store where miner could spend scrip, received from mine when payroll was short. At right is one of two "American" boarding houses. Strict segregation of races prevailed in living, if not working quarters. Greek miners had own boarding house as did Japanese, Negroes living in group of shacks in another section. Steady dropping of water table was first evident when vegetable gardens dried up and water supply became inadequate for coal washers. Trees here managed sizeable growth before dying.

DOZENS OF PRIMITIVE DWELLINGS line sides of canyon at Sego. Once home for miner and family, this dug-out now collects tumbleweeds and roof beams rot away. Most of "house" was scooped out of bank, rocks removed used to fashion front wall. Place lacked windows, water and plumbing but in later years had electricity.

in the mines. They were his life. His father went to work there in 1913, the family taking up a home-stead about a mile down the canyon and living temporarily at Green River, Utah. With the father well established in his mine job, he moved his wife and two boys to the homestead, their first shelter an open cave in the cliff side, its roof a ledge protruding from the vertical wall. The children were fascinated by the many Indian petroglyphs engraved on the surrounding red rock walls, a veritable picture gallery. For more comfortable quarters the father set up two tents, dug a well and then built a house of native rock. The ruins still stand about a quarter mile above the point where the railroad is cut through solid rock.

Father and sons raised 60 tons of hay a year and planted a large vegetable garden, selling carrots, cabbages and greens in the camp. During those first years there was plenty of water available for irrigation and all crops raised in the comparatively short season flourished. The Ronzio family literally had its roots in the canyon and the mines.

OLD MINE TUNNEL follows vein of coal shown at left in one of earliest operations, possibly that of original owner, Harry Ballard.

RELIC from old-time kitchen when Sego's coal mines furnished its heat and livelihood for as many as 125 miners, some with families. View looks toward mouth of canyon which widens out here. Most of town was confined between narrow, rocky walls.

The announcement of the closing and impending sale of the mine plant was a staggering blow to Walter and the other men. He called a meeting to discuss what might be done to save the situation. They decided to attempt purchase at the auction, each man to account for an equal number of shares — 1200 at a dollar a share. Not every man had the cash but those lacking it promised to pay what was owing through future payroll deductions. The total cash raised was $18,000 and two banks offered to loan the group the remaining up to $30,000. At the auction the bidding got up to that figure and Walter Ronzio topped it by $10. The entire operation — camp, buildings, equipment and all assets — passed into the hands of the miners for $30,010 and they wisely insisted on a clause giving them mineral rights to all land involved. They formed a corporation under the name of the Utah Grand Coal Co. and elected Walter Ronzio as general manager.

Within a year the Utah Grand Coal Co. was on its feet with all obligations paid. Then, as Walter relates, "things began to happen." The first catastrophe was the July 1, 1949, destruction by fire of the tipple, origin of the blaze never determined. This curtailed production drastically and the railroad notified Ronzio it could no longer profitably operate the spur to Sego. The company, it said, could build ramps for truck loading and haul the coal down to Thompson where the railroad would be glad to pick it up. This meant building a new tipple, purchasing two dump trucks and a boxcar loader. The men made the hard decision to go ahead, closing down for five months for changes and equipment installation. Work started in the middle of December with a general feeling of great optimism but calamity had more evil work to do. In two weeks another disastrous fire struck, starting in the lamp-changing rack, and completely destroying the shops. All spare machine parts were lost as was repair equipment. Any breakdown now meant closure.

Recovery was slow but persistent, the biggest

ONE LARGER HOUSE was built out of whatever came to hand, taking advantage of huge rock to form one wall. Roof is of beams covered with earth which grows scant crop of grass. Flat surfaces in many red rock cliffs were used by vanished Indian tribes as art galleries, larger surfaces for paintings, petroglyphs of heroic proportions showing tribal chiefs with hour-glass figures and triangular heads. Among other paleontological specimens found in mines by Chesterfield Co. were huge dinosaur tracks, one measuring 44x32 inches. Some tracks indicated reptilian stride of 15 feet and animal height of 35 feet.

aid being the stockpile of big lump coal. Readily handled and loaded in boxcars it was rail shipped to mid-west points. The smaller nut and sack coal produced by screening was used by the railroad, sales of this covering the cost of producing the larger sizes. But again came a blow, the fatal one. The railroad changed over to the new diesel fuel for its locomotives. The doom of the coal mines was sealed.

In February of 1955, the Utah Grand sold its holdings to Seaburg Brothers of Dayton, Texas. The amount paid, $25,000, was not for the valueless coal mines but for 700 acres of land with mineral rights. Tests showed both oil and natural gas in the formation including the site of Sego.

Long before this Walter's brother and father had passed away. In February of 1960 he and his mother sold the old homestead in the canyon to a group of sheepmen from Glenwood, Colorado, and moved to Grand Junction. There he operates a hotel-apartment house, his mother at 86 residing with him.

Now, ten years after the sale of the townsite, Sego is a very dead ghost but not a cold one. At least one large vein of coal is burning, the ground hot and crusty, very unsafe to walk on. Several vents, one two feet across which shoots a column of steam and smoke, produce the only tangible wraiths in our experience.

SILVER CITY, UTAH

Silver City was the first real mining camp established in the famous district known as Tintic, after the Indian chief who made so much trouble for the early settlers who were fouling up the Ute's streams and killing their game. For years after it was founded in 1870 it dropped out of importance because more spectacular strikes in Little Cottonwood Canyon and Park City were getting all the attention.

The hopeful but brief life of Silver City began when, in 1869, cowboy George Rust found remains of age-old mines worked by primitive Indians. Without explosive of any kind these early miners managed to penetrate the rocks and dig crude tunnels for long distances, carrying out the ore in skin bags. Evidence seemed to point to a system of fires built against the head of the workings until the rock was hot, then cold water thrown against it to make it crack. One such old mine discovered in the '20s had several large boulders piled against the entrance. When these were rolled away, two human skeletons were exposed.

The Utes, under Chief Tintic, seemed to know nothing about precious metals and care less. But George Rust did. He managed to dodge enough Indian bullets to make a silver discovery. During the summer of the next year a group of five men found promising pieces of float. With assay offices few and far between, it was December before they had a report and this was exciting enough to send them into a blinding blizzard to stake the claim. It was named the Sun Beam and was the forerunner of a dozen or more rich locations in the district.

Laid out at the mouth of Dragon Canyon, the young camp of Silver City dragged its feet for a year or two because of lack of capital. Here were no easy panning and placering methods to return wealth for little outlay of money, but much labor in hard rock mining, blasting out the material and lifting it to the tops of shafts. I. E. Diehl described Silver City and its slow start in his Tintic manuscript, "A billiard saloon, blacksmith shop, grog hole, some tents, several drunks, a free fight, water some miles off, a hole down 90 feet hunting a spring without success, and any number of rich or imaginary rich lodes in the neighborhood. The owners are all poor and poor men work for them. By next spring the poor will be poorer."

Economic conditions slowly improved to the point where about 800 people were making a modest living. About the time their hard-won shafts began penetrating real blossom rock, disaster struck; water began filling the workings, stopping operations almost entirely. William Hatfield managed to get enough water out of the Swansea to salvage ore to the tune of $700,000 and when some of those who had abandoned the town heard about this they returned to see if they could equal the feat in their own claims. But no—pumping cost more than value received and again they quit. That was final and when Hatfield also quit the town was finished. Today not one of the original buildings stands on the site, though several newer ones attest to recent efforts to again reopen the flooded mines.

ONLY RELIC REMAINING FROM EARLY DAYS OF SILVER CITY Tottering head frame and loading bunker. Extensive tailings and refuse dumps attest to large amount of ore removed during active days. Road, now clogged by tailings, used to run under bunker, wagon loads to be conveyed to smelter. Typical desert vegetation covers hill sides. Shrubby trees in background are Utah juniper.

SILVER IN SANDSTONE

Silver Reef, Utah

The lone prospector was wandering over the bleak ridges searching for metallic color. He was sure the sandstone reefs which stretched everywhere were hopeless but he had to keep moving because it was intensely cold and night was coming on. He reached the Mormon settlement of Leeds after dark but a cheerfully glowing lamp in a window led him to a hospitable family who made him welcome and threw more fuel on the fireplace blaze. The wanderer gratefully warmed his chilled body and as he watched the fire closely he was astonished to see a tiny shining stream ooze from an overheated rock. He caught the drops and later confirmed his belief they were silver.

The extraordinary fact that a tremendous wealth of silver was extracted from sandstone ore at the mining camp of Silver Reef has spawned a dozen different stories to explain the original discovery. The above tale is one of the most frequently repeated but early settler Mark Pendleton gives a different version as being more authentic. In 1878 when he was 14 his family moved from the old home at Parowan to the clamoring town of Silver Reef. He lived there thirteen impressionable years, absorbing everything he saw and heard, and in his reminiscences preserved in Utah's history archives is the following version.

Not far across the Utah-Nevada state line was the notorious mining town of Pioche (see *Tales the Western Tombstones Tell*). Among its several assayers was one called "Metalliferous" Murphy for his congenital optimism about values he saw in ore samples, not always proven accurate Pioche prospectors maintained. Over drinks in a bistro one night miners were discussing Murphy and his "exaggerated" assays and one man exclaimed. "I'll bet Murphy would report silver in a grindstone!" Alcohol promoted this idea into action. A broken grindstone was salvaged and smashed into bits which were duly submitted to Murphy for assay.

True to prediction, Murphy reported the fragments contained silver to the value of 200 ounces per ton and the miners exploded. They gave Murphy a choice between leaving town or being strung up to Pioche's hanging tree. Considering the situation untenable, the assayer chose to leave but braved danger by staying long enough to find out where the samples of stone came from. It seemed the grinding wheel was one of those produced by Isaac Duffing Jr. of Toquerville, Utah, and further tracking put the original chunk of sandstone at the spot where the camp of Silver Reef sprang up. If Murphy made a claim the fact is not recorded but he must have drawn attention to the area. The district was "located" in October of 1876 and by February had over 1000 inhabitants. Although miners, geologists and metallurgists confirmed what the Pioche miners stated, "You can't get silver out of sandstone," the camp produced $9 million in silver between 1877 and 1903, this with the price averaging $1.19 per ounce.

It is generally believed that prospector John Kemple was the first man to actually break off and assay a sample of the reef. His little portable furnace showed a tiny button of silver, not a showing to cause him to throw his hat in the air. He continued on to Nevada but could not forget the strange occurrence of even a little silver in this kind of rock. Kemple later returned with friends, filed a claim and started the Harrisburg Mining District.

A few years later, in 1874, Elijah Thomas and John S. Ferris staked a claim near Leeds on the same formation as Kemple's, of red and white sandstone. Their samples sent to Salt Lake City so

REMAINS of old Spanish arrastra are quite well preserved considering antiquity. When in operation rock-paved disc was centered by post holding up one end of bar or pipe. Over this was slipped stone grinding wheel to about midway point, burro-hitched to outer end. Animal plodded in circle, pulled bar, rolling stone over selected silver ore shoveled in path. Though process was crude, this and countless other similar arrastras served to crush ore until advent of stamp mills.

WELLS FARGO & CO. building is best preserved of structures remaining in Silver Reef, partly because of sturdy construction of dressed sandstone, partly because it has been occupied for years. Town has no inhabitant now except horned toads and rattlesnakes. Iron door shutters are reminiscent of those in California's Mother Lode except for rounded instead of square tops.

excited bankers that they staked William Tecumseh Barbee to head a small group including an assayer to investigate the area. Barbee and his men went to work on the reef but back in Salt Lake all experts advised bank officials they were wasting their money in backing the project, that they considered finding silver in sandstone fantastic, impossible. Barbee was told he was on his own but he decided to stick it out for a while.

He hired a man to haul wood, the heavy iron-rimmed wheels of a loaded wagon skidding and scraping off a long layer of the sandstone surface of what was now called Barbee Reef. Plainly visible was a deposit of hornsilver. The teamster rushed to his boss with the story which Barbee soon confirmed. He set up a camp on the flat nearby, calling it Bonanza City, and wrote to the Salt Like *Tribune*, Feb. 7, 1876, "This sandstone country beats all the boys, and it is amusing to see how excited they all get when they go round to see the sheets of silver which are exposed all over the different reefs. . . . This is the most unfavorable looking country for mines that I have ever seen . . . but as the mines are here, what are the rock sharps going to do about it?"

Barbee made another camp on flats near his Tecumseh mine but a merchant, Hyrum Jacobs, who came from Pioche to set up a store, chose a site where roads from Buckeye, White, Middle and East Reefs came together. Other businesses followed and the new center was named Silver Reef.

Mark Pendleton recalled the day he rode with his parents into the town. As the wagon entered the area he was awed. "To a boy from the tiny village of Parowan, Silver Reef was a big city," he wrote. "The brightly lighted stores and saloons, streets filled with peddlers, freighters' wagons loaded with ore or cordwood on their way to the stamp mills, all were exciting. Miners with dinner pails, Americans, Cornishmen, Irishmen, were walking to the mines where they would spend their ten hours a day."

Silver Reef was essentially a "gentile" town though located almost in the center of the large Mormon settlements in southern Utah, collectively called Dixie. Possibly the most remarkable feature in the history of the mining camp is the equanimity displayed in relations between miners and Mormons. An incident in Rockville, as related in the Mormon-controlled *Under Dixie Sun*, indicated the usual attitude in other nearby areas. "Of course in Rockville as in other communities there were men who obeyed the counsel of church leaders and had taken more than one wife. During the 1870s and '80s the United States Government was trying to punish those who were practicing the law of their religion. The Saints felt that they were . . . entitled to live their religion as they pleased. When the Marshal came to Rockville or Grafton a messenger was sent up the river to warn the people so they would have a chance to hide all those who where in danger as second or third wives. . . . On April 21 they came and took Fanny Slaughter. . . . They tried her in court before a jury but could not get a conviction on the charge of polygamy.

"Their hatred of the Saints was so vehement that they were determined to convict her on some

BUSINESS BUILDINGS north of Wells Fargo offices were constructed with less care, are now largely falling into complete ruin. This impressive relic facing setting sun is reputed to have been Chinese Drug Store. Sandstone blocks, erected before days of efficient silver extraction, contain large percentage of precious metal. Such buildings in other mining camps were demolished and run through mills. With present increasing values in white metal these evidences of glory days in Silver Reef could suffer same fate.

charge or other. She was postmistress in Rockville at the time, and when her accounts were gone over it was found they were short three cents. As Sister Slaughter started to walk from the courtroom she was stopped by an officer and again arrested, this time for 'defrauding the United States Mail.'"

In contrast to this bitterness a brief Mormon history told of differences between Silver Reef miners and the people of Leeds just below. When water was suddenly released at Silver Reef, inundating farms at Leeds and washing out ditches, "miners gladly came to assist Leeds people in repairing their ditches, and in turn elders of Leeds would often be called to Silver Reef to preach at funerals."

Indefatigable writer Barbee included an item in the *Tribune*. "They (the Mormons) have a very hard time serving the Lord in this desert, a god-forsaken looking country. It is about time something turned up to take the place of sorghum wine as a circulating medium." He was of course referring to the stream of silver his mine was then pouring forth. The *Tribune's* circulation must have extended to St. George, Mormon center of Dixie. Shortly after Barbee's self-congratulatory letter ap-

peared in print Apostle Erastus Snow observed at Sunday services, "Now that Brother Barbee has turned up something to bring prosperity to Dixie let us pray for God's blessing on him for opening up the mines."

Carrying brotherly love even further, Father Scanlon, priest of the large Catholic Church at Silver Reef, was invited to serve Mass in the Mormon Tabernacle at St. George on a certain Sunday. In unprecedented fashion the congregation learned the Latin ritual chants beforehand so as to assist in the services. And when Federal officers on their way to St. George to arrest polygamists stopped at Silver Reef overnight, the Mormon telegraph operator would order "two chairs" from the furniture store in the county seat, thus alerting the Saints there.

The silver camp's several saloons were noted for fine quality liquor . . . all but one, that is. That was a bargain shop attracting cheap buyers. After complaints about the whiskey it was discovered the proprietor "stretched" the contents of the barrels with a witches' brew of tobacco, strychnine and water.

For a change from whiskey, good and bad,

miners would go down to Leeds to have Sunday dinner at the hospitable boarding house where the famous and potent red Mormon wine was generously served. Regular imbibers took it in stride but incautious miners were often hauled away in what Pendleton describes as "an unconscious condition and waking up to wonder what had happened."

As in most mining camps frequent fires raged uncontrolled and took a big toll. One of the worst razed most of the town in 1879. In double file citizens passed powder kegs from buildings to creeks and back again. The Chinese cook in Kate Duggery's restaurant was credited with saving that building by snatching up an open can of milk and dousing out the sparks.

The town maintained a race track during its prosperous years where visitors from St. George gathered with their blooded horses raised in the Kanab region. Segregated from the elite were Indians in paint and feathers, prospectors in working garb, tinhorn and professional gamblers in ruffled silk shirts. And farthest from the track were the dance hall girls and other mining camp flotsam.

Inevitably the days of big time money drew to an end, the process so gradual few people recognized it. As silver production and values "temporarily" eased off, miners' wages were dropped from a daily $4 to $3. Resentful men organized and retaliated with strikes and sabotage. In 1881 the situation was so out of hand authorities called for help in controlling violence. Sheriff A. P. Hardy rounded up 25 men, assembling them at Leeds. Since most of them were members of the Mormon Church, St. George Stake President John D. McAllister sent a written message of instructions to Hardy:

"We view with alarm the assembly of 25 Saints for this purpose and extend you these cautions. Have total abstinence from anything intoxicating. Studiously observe your posse, should the brethren seem fatigued, a cup of coffee is recommended. Do not stray away from each other, nor visit saloons or gambling halls. Keep together and be on the watch. All attend to prayers in the morning and at night before retiring."

An unusually heavy snowstorm covered readying operations at Leeds allowing Hardy and his men to surprise the insurrectionists at camp and arrest 36 of them. The town's tiny jail being inadequate for the prisoners they were confined in the solid stone dance hall. The next day they were taken to Beaver for trial, the sheriff reporting the trip a "miserable affair," with passengers in open wagons soaked in a cold rain mixed with snow.

Silver Reef experienced the usual murders expected in an unrestricted mining camp (some described in *Boot Hill*). One is commemorated by a beautifully carved tombstone in the camp's cemetery, placed on the grave of Michael Garbis by his son, Michael Jr. The father was slain by a discharged employee who was tried in St. George and found guilty, the execution thwarted by a mob that snatched him from the jail and hanged him at the edge of town. The hanging rope was tied to a bush so that the body was left swinging on the tree. Passing the spot the next morning, the town wag was reported to have said, "I have observed that tree growing there for the last 25 years. This is the first time I have ever seen it bearing fruit."

SILVER REEF is located in area of spectacular desert scenery. Plants here must be of type capable of storing water supplied only in short rainy season. Most conspicuous around old silver camp are cacti of **Opuntia** tribe, this species flaunting satiny blossoms of brilliant chartreuse hue. At right of Wells Fargo & Co. is seen typical plant group, detail of flowers shown here.

MONTANA, IDAHO and WYOMING
GHOST TOWNS

BY

LAMBERT FLORIN

Drawings
by
David C. Mason, M.D.

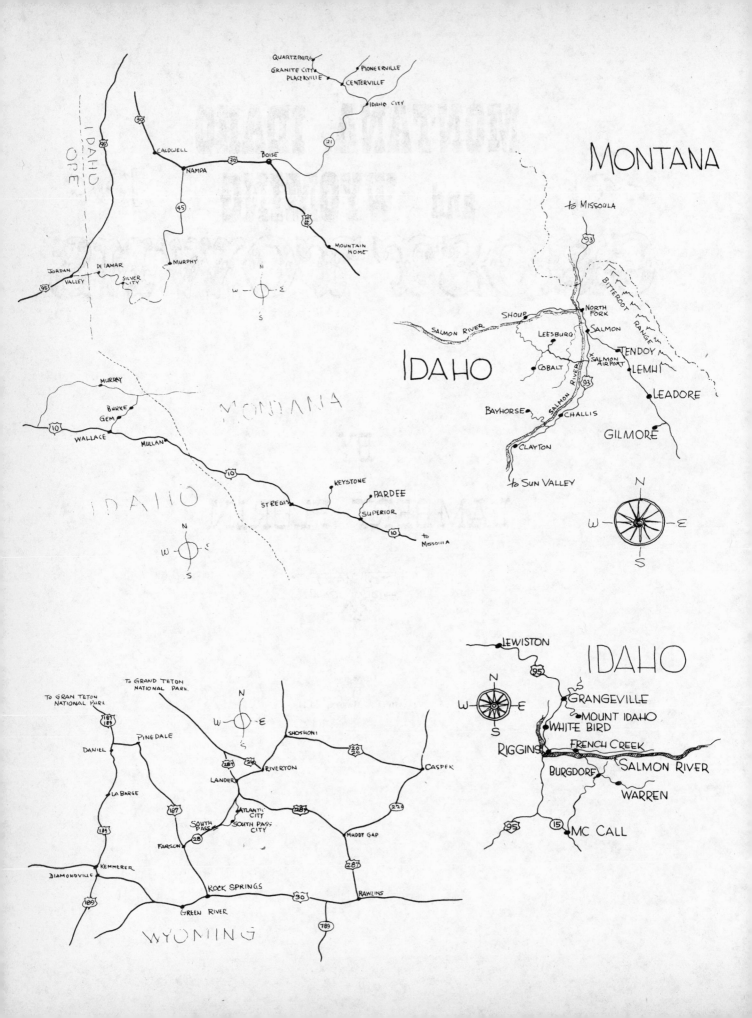

INDEX

MONTANA	Page
Bannack	397
Bearmouth	398
Beartown	399
Cable	400
Castle City	404
Elkhorn	408
Garnet	409
Giltedge	411
Gold Creek	413
Granite	415
Kendall	417
Keystone	419
Landusky	420
Laurin	425
Maiden	426
Mammoth	428
Marysville	429
Melrose	431
Pardee	432
Pioneer	434
Pony	437
Rimini	440
Ruby Gulch	441
Southern Cross	444
Virginia City	445
Wickes	446
Zortman	448

IDAHO	Page
Bay Horse	450
Bonanza	453
Burke	464
Custer	453
De Lamar	460
Gem	464
Gilmore	466
Idaho City	468
Leesburg	470
Mount Idaho	474
Murray	477
Placerville	479
Potosi Gulch	480
Shoup	481
Silver City	482
Warren	484

WYOMING	
Atlantic City	489
Encampment	490
Glenco	484
Medicine Bow	496
Opal	498
Rambler	501
Riverside	502
South Pass City	503

LEFT IS KELLY'S
SALOON, r i g h t barber
shop and drugstore com-
bination.

COLD OF GARNET
WINTERS is attested by
"snuggies" of earlier day.
Relics are from s t o r e
across street; are owned
by Mrs. Dahl.

AT THE RIGHT OF brick hotel is Skinner's Saloon, once hangout of notorious Plummer gang. At right stood building housing first territorial legislature of Montana, now gone.

BANNACK, MONTANA

In addition to being the first capital, Bannack claims several other firsts. Back from the street in discreet seclusion is the first jail, a really primitive one-story, sod-roofed structure. The little false-fronted Skinner's Saloon served both its advertised purpose and as headquarters for Henry Plummer and his outlaw gang. Plummer's masquerade as head of all useful and law-abiding citizens is one of the most incredible episodes in the history of the west.

The stretch of road between Bannack and Virginia City was the scene of more holdups, robberies and murders than almost any other comparable stagecoach route. The outlaw gang made up of ruffians with prices on their heads were strung along the route and relayed information to one another, so that no coach stood a chance of getting through.

This murderous crew had for its mastermind the Sheriff of Bannack! Henry Plummer was also an escapee, having fled from the camps of California and Nevada. In Bannack he started life anew. To the populace he set himself up as a preserver of the peace, guardian of law and order. He soon became official sheriff, built the jail and had rings put in the floor so that prisoners could not escape merely by punching a hole in the sod-roof. His home became a symbol of hospitality, the scene of receptions and dances for the "upper crust" of Bannack. Even the Governor of the Territory of Montana was entertained there.

At the same time, behind this screen of respectability, Plummer pulled the strings that ended in over a hundred murders and a bonanza of money and jewelry taken from unfortunate stagecoach travelers.

At last, a roused committee of citizens formed the Vigilantes which unmasked Plummer and threw him into his own jail. His tenure therein was short. In short order a gallows was erected back of the saloon-rendezvous and the erstwhile sheriff was strung up. So were several of his henchmen, and they remain in close company under wooden headboards close by the gallows.

397

BEARMOUTH, MONTANA

A town dependent upon one industry or source of income is deserted when that source fails. Further, a town serving another depends upon the continuance of its supporter.

So, when Garnet died, Bearmouth also faded away. The fabulously rich ores in Garnet all through the 60's, 70's and 80's poured down the "Chinee Grade" to Bearmouth, to be shipped to smelters.

Garnet had its ups and downs in common with other mining camps, and with each demise and each resurgence, Bearmouth followed suit. It did have one steady business, as a main stop for stagecoaches on the old Mullan Road. This meant an Inn, a beautiful two-story, balconied structure, and at least one large livery stable. In addition to lodgings for man and beast, a blacksmith shop was called for.

The hostelry and livery stable still stand, conveniently near each other.

Time was when the open spaces surrounding these buildings were filled solidly with pleasure houses of various types, all rowdy. It was a treat for the hard-working miners "up on the mountain" in Garnet or Beartown to come down for a weekend spree in "Bear's Mouth," as it was first called.

OLD STAGECOACH STOP and inn. Building is tenanted and in good repair. TV antenna adds modern touch.

THEY BUILT SOLIDLY in old days. Detail of corner of livery stable.

BEARTOWN, MONTANA

Here is a town almost vanished from the sight of man, yet the phrase "as bad as a Beartown Tough" remains potent to the ears of Montanans. The gang known by that name terrorized the citizens not only of their own town, but also of Garnet, at the upper end of the canyon, and Bearmouth at the bottom. They were never really subdued, making trouble over a long period of time.

The canyon is narrow, hardly offering room for more than the gravel road, but at one point not far below the notorious "Chinee Grade," a side stream enters. Here is somewhat more level ground, and here was laid out the collection of stores, saloons, hotels and brothels that was Beartown. The wonder is that the ground suppported the town, so honeycombed it was by mine tunnels. These extended the entire length of the canyon.

The site of the mill is now indicated by scanty foundations and a pile of boards, the center of town can be traced by a board here and there and basements nearly filled with rubble and brush. Across the stream is the only structure anywhere near intact, the jail, formerly a powder house.

Odd that this token of Beartown badmen should survive along with bloody memory of those "Beartown Toughs," who have been so long under the sod that their very headboards have melted away.

THE BEARTOWN JAIL

THE LOST HORSE GOLD

Cable, Montana

"The first place of note is a forlorn looking town with two idle quartz mills, many deserted and torn down houses and but one solitary inhabitant. . . . The hillside below the discovery had been washed bare to the bedrock . . . this alone yielded nearly $100,000." This description from the *Rocky Mountain Husbandman* could well fit many a mining camp as found today but the date on the clipping is September 26, 1878. Gleaned by Muriel Sibell Wolle for her comprehensive book *Montana Pay Dirt* the item shows Cable became a ghost town early. It also points out that ghostly conditions are not necessarily permanent. Cable sat up from somnolence, living on until 1940.

Many a gold mine was located through cooperation of a horse, burro or cow or even as a slain bird as at Vulture, Arizona. In Cable's case, in the early summer of 1867, prospectors Alexander Aiken, James Stough and John E. Pearson made their camp for the night. Next morning the horses were gone and in tracking them the men came across a bed of decomposed, crumbling quartz. Scattered throughout were bits of shining gold, released in the weathering of the top of what turned out to be a nearly vertical chimney of auriferous quartz extending downward about 1000 feet.

As soon as the horses were located the excited men crushed some of the ore in their hand mortars, carried a few pounds of it down to the creek,

BOARDING HOUSE YARD was first place wide enough for author to turn pickup camper around. Cookhouse shown attached to rear. Several photos were hastily made before leaving old camp of Atlantic Cable.

nearly a mile away. They panned it out and calculated they might well make $30 a day per man.

Later when machinery was installed values showed $18 per ton but rich pockets frequently encountered ran it up to between $100 and $1,000. Even so, news of the strike at Cable did not immediately attract the usual influx of prospectors due to the scanty population of Montana spread thinly among other camps.

The three partners had trouble making wages because of the distance to water necessary for sluicing so they agreed to stop panning long enough to build a conduit, part flume, part ditch, and the four-mile waterway was completed by fall.

As soon as snow began to melt in the spring the trio was able to sluice out enough gold for capital to enlarge operations.

The discoverers took the precaution of immediately staking out not only the original claims but five additional 200-foot ones above and five below. Convinced they had something going they delegated one man to go to Deer Lodge, 35 miles away, and record everything in legal fashion, the name selected Atlantic Cable Lode, commemorating the successful laying of the second trans-ocean cable.

The painfully constructed sluiceway proved inadequate for increasingly large operations. With more capital from Helena bankers, a 20-stamp mill

GOLD COIN MINE was one of complex below and around Cable which included Southern Cross, Pyrenees, Stuart, Hidden Lake, Red Lion etc. Old maps showing mine, mill and camp locations give impression they were crowded together. Actual access was hindered by ravines, mountains, gulches. Travel time from one camp to neighbor might be hours or days. Shown here is famous old Gold Coin mill, still fairly well preserved. Ore was handled by gravity system, reason so many mills were built on steep hillsides. Mine dumps shown at extreme right, trestle that carried ore cars to big door at upper end of mill. Rough chunks of material dumped at top of incline fell by stages thru grinding, pulverizing, chemical processes to emerge as concentrates at bottom.

RUINS OF OLD BARN beyond which on road to Cable visitor encounters gate posted against entry. Author was forced to continue since there was no turning space at gate.

was erected on the creek at about the point where the first crushed ore was panned out. Success was indifferent as amalgamation methods were not effective on this particular ore. One man said at the time, "Most of the gold is going down the creek." Even so, with selection of only the richest ore for processing, the mill turned out $30,000 the first year.

Banker William Nowlan thought well enough of results to buy into the claim. According to one authority Alexander Aiken, one of the three original discoverers, did not agree with the new policies and after several furious arguments, instituted suit against the firm. Succeeding legal hassles wiped

out his entire fortune and Aiken left the country on foot, all his belongings in a pack.

Through the 1870s one misfortune after another came to Cable. Good paying leads were lost because of crude, awkward mining methods. With an almost complete lack of ore the main mill was forced to close and then banker Nowlan died, intensifying litigation that had never entirely ceased. Doubt and uncertainty so undermined confidence of other backers they withdrew and things at Cable came to a standstill in 1877.

In that year J. C. Slavery, brother-in-law of Nowlan, began proceedings to straighten out the mess and in some two years acquired clear title to

Atlantic Cable. In 1883 he ran a long tunnel from the hillside in hopes of contacting the vein at a lower level. He felt so sure of doing this that while work on the tunnel was going on he erected a 30-ton mill costing $65,000. Slavery must have been born under a different star than his predecessor for about the time the mill was finished a rich pocket of gold was struck that paid his $150,000 expense within thirty days.

Being a trusting soul he put a man named Jewell in charge as foreman and paid no further attention to details of managing the miners. In time he heard rumors that some of his men were displaying untoward signs of affluence, considering their daily wage of $3. Several had built fancy homes and bought farms down the valley. Many of them were "Cousin Jacks" and Slavery learned of relatives back in Cornwall naming a street Cable Terrace to commemorate the mine that made it possible for so many emigrants to buy fine homes in America. When he did launch an investigation he found some $60,000 in gold nuggets had been "high-graded" in 1883 alone. He then put in effect a rule requiring all workmen to strip for examination when passing out the gate at the end of their shifts.

The Cable produced a fortune in the next few years, then the output began a varied performance that rose and fell until Slavery closed the property in 1891. Total production until then was about $3,500,000. Eventually the workings came to life again in the salvage of ores wasted in previous crude methods. After 1906, brothers H. C. and F. W. Bacon did some development work, running three shifts a day, but these operations ceased in 1940 and Cable again became a ghost town. The properties are now posted against visitors because of vandalism, the present owners very likely hoping gold values will eventually increase enough to warrant reopening.

FRONT ENTRANCE to Cable's old boarding house. Board and batten construction was usual in area lacking proper stone.

CASTLE CITY, MONTANA

It was one thing for a Castle City joy girl to get drunk in a saloon and dance on the bar. That was accepted as normal any night. What did throw everybody off stride was to see one come into the post office cold sober just after the morning mail arrived, peer questioningly into every face and gum her wrath: "Which one of you dirty Cousin Jacks was up in my room with me last night? I lost my choppers and I want 'em back!"

It is not known just who took Mabel's teeth but it was probably not one of the four Hensley brothers who figured prominently in the early days of Castle City. Isaac H. was the first to arrive in the area, going to Fort Benton in 1875 after freighting between there and Helena and wanting to settle down on a farm. Next brother to join him was F. L. (Lafe) who had been working at the N. P. Hills smelter in Black Hawk, Colorado, acquiring some knowledge of minerals and mining. In 1877 he and Ike took up a homestead on the Yellowstone five miles below the present town of Columbus, calling the ranch "The Rapids." Next year the other two brothers joined them.

In those times when you couldn't work at your regular job you went prospecting. When the ground was frozen and the Hensley brothers couldn't farm, they took off separately to "look around." Lafe took his friend G. K. Robertson with him into the Castle Mountains, then nameless. There was little snow that winter, the ground was exposed during the week the pair were there, and one of them picked up a chunk of float which caused them to hurry to the Wickes smelter. The piece of galena was rich in lead and silver when assayed.

The discovery ridge was called Yellowstone by the Hensley brothers who now abandoned their ranch and located a group of mines on the steep slope. The

one proving most successful was the big Cumberland, with the Yellowstone, Morning Star, Belle of the Castles, La Mar and Cholla only slightly less spectacular. On top of the ridge were several domed lava protrusions soon called "The Castles" as were the ridge and town.

In the spring of 1887 the Hensleys bonded the Cumberland claim for $50,000 but when time came to pay up, only half that was available. To cover the rest, a half interest was deeded to the bondsmen, Tom Ash and J. R. King of Billings. Later the brothers disposed of their half to B. R. Sherman and Charles E. Severence.

Ores from the Cumberland and mines still held by the brothers were being shipped to Livingston by freight wagons at the prohibitive cost of $13 a ton. The Hensleys thought they saw a golden opportunity for profits and built a smelter in Castle at a cost of $25,000, but a hard and fast truth soon became evident. Coke for the smelter had to be freighted in, costing as much as to send the ore out. The smelter was forced to close in ten months but during that period it had reduced 13,000 tons of ore, producing bullion valued at $494,906.44—according to some penny-minded bookkeeper.

The usual problem of transportation was made tenable by using oxen for hauling freight. The Indians, having plenty of buffalo to eat, considered the bull teams no great prizes, so did not kill or steal them as they did horses.

Richard A. Harlow, a far-seeing man who had come to Helena a year or so before, envisioned a fortune for himself when he heard of the difficulties of getting the rich ores to and from processing plants. He started a railroad called the Montana Midland to run from Helena to Canyon Ferry on the Missouri River, then east to White Sulphur Springs, Leadboro and Castle. The grade had been completed as far as the river when the Northern Pacific, sensing an extension eastward as a possible competitor, made Harlow a proposition—they to furnish rolling stock, rails and other equipment if he would tie into a place called Lombard, between Helena and the junction of their tracks, with the Butte branch farther south. Harlow accepted and ran tracks up 16 Mile Creek toward the booming lead and silver mines. The new railroad was first termed the "Montana," soon referred to familiarly as the "Jawbone." Financial difficulties and the tough terrain prevented the new line from getting farther than halfway up the canyon and there it ended for many a day.

While all this was going on, Castle was booming in spite of transportation troubles, soon reaching a peak population of more than 2,000. Main business district was centered along a street running parallel with Allabaugh Creek, the residential district of a plateau above. An ample timber supply and good sawmill made lumber available and most residences were of frame construction, many ornamented with fancy barge boards and the gingerbread of the day, all coming from the local mill, with the interior walls of better houses finished with lath and plaster. So rapid was the town's growth such a fancy domicile might have one next to it built of crudely cut and fitted logs dating from the "pioneer period" only two and three years earlier.

Grocers and other merchants took advantage of the returning freight teams to bring in shoes, clothing and millinery. Although Castle had its full quota of saloons and bawdy houses so necessary to mining camp survival, it had its refinements too.

There were so many social clubs editor and publisher Shelby Eli Dillard was moved to remark in his weekly *The Whole Truth* in January, 1893: "It appears that the people of Castle will be compelled to petition to the proper tribunal to have at least two nights added to the week to accommodate various whist clubs and parties, dances, spelling bees and other society affairs in our town."

There was a great deal of gambling and carousing in saloons and dancehalls especially after payday, the 20th, but strangely enough in the entire history of Castle, there never was a fatality resulting from a gunfight or other violence. Many did die from "La Grippe" in cold winters and wet thawing springs and from frequent mine accidents. Deep ruts still show along the hillside, marking the trail made by the be-plumed black hearse on its way to the old cemetery.

One story is told about a new undertaker in Castle. A man in poor circumstances had been killed in an explosion in the Cumberland. A collection was taken up for the widow and a nice funeral which included a suit of clothes for the victim. After the service the undertaker suggested postponing burial until the day following as the road up the hill might be less icy. One curious individual, wondering why another day might be better when it froze every night, slipped in the back door of the "parlor" next to the furniture store and caught the undertaker removing the new suit from the body.

Everyone expected a solid future for Castle. A two-story school was built on the "plateau," the only level spot in town, and staffed by good teachers from Helena and Livingston. Several large hotels and rooming houses went up along Allabaugh Creek, one with a room 20 x 40 feet, furnished dormitory-style with rows of cots each surrounded by netting to discourage petty thievery. This room was called the "Ram Pasture."

Editor Dillard was militant in his optimism concerning Castle and its future. In one issue he stated: "The man who thinks Castle is not destined to be the greatest lead and silver camp in the land has a head on his shoulders as peaked as that of a roan mule." When news of gold strikes on the Klondike began to disturb the even tenor of life in Castle, he apparently was getting ground vibrations that some solid citizens might leave for the gold fields. He wrote: "Castle is the lead and silver Klondike of Imperial Montana. There is no one in Castle inoculated with the virus of Klondike gold." Next week *The Whole Truth* hammered these thoughts home with such gems as: "We had rather be a livid corpse in Castle than to own Alaska and all the sordid gold in the auriferous Klondike Country!"

It was at this period that Calamity Jane came to Castle to run a restaurant. With her was a little girl, daughter of the soldier father in Texas, one of Calamity's many "husbands." Her current name was Mrs. Burke, and she may have had a legal spouse by that name. She had tried the restaurant business elsewhere, losing out because of drunken escapades. In Castle she was determined to lead a circumspect life, putting on the act for the benefit of business and daughter.

Yet she still felt the urge to cut loose and when this compulsion came on she went to some nearby town for a few days. One of these episodes was in Gilt Edge. She found herself a man and was heading for a handy barn when the wife saw the pair and ran them off with a pitchfork. Calamity ended up in a saloon, always a haven, and was soon drunk. The sheriff picked her up and, the jail being full of men whose welfare he was sworn to guard, he locked her up in a shed.

Next morning a small boy came by carrying milk for a neighbor and Calamity called to him, slipping a

BETTER HOMES, built during rush of prosperity, stood in elegant district on "plateau" near level area, in contrast to simple log houses sandwiched in between. Most famous ghost would be that of Lady Rosslyn, born Anna Robinson, daughter of George Robinson, early prospector who settled in Castle in '78. In her late teens Anna worked two years as a waitress in mother's boardinghouse, then before silver crash in '93 family moved back to Minneapolis. With "remarkably sweet voice" Anna went on to sing in Charles Frohman's production of *Shenandoah*, starred in musical comedies, went to London where Duke of Manchester and King Leopold of Belgium paid her court. At height of success, she was friend of Harry Thaw but became bride of Earl of Rosslyn in London in 1905, settling $10,000 on him. Earl lost money at Monte Carlo, Anna divorcing him two years later. She appeared on stage occasionally, losing fortune as she aged. She died in state hospital for insane at Ward's Island about 1912.

silver dollar through a crack in the door, telling him to get her a bottle of whiskey. He let the bottle down to her through a hole above the door and kept the four-bits change.

Released, Calamity returned to Castle, retrieved the little girl from a friend in a bawdy house and settled down to business. And then she had a strong urge to return to Deadwood. Taking her daughter, she hitched a ride to the boom town in the Black Hills. She was welcomed but forced to turn the girl over to the Sisters of St. Martin's Academy at Sturgis. A benefit was staged for her at the most disreputable saloon and dancehall, the Green Front, a purse collected which Calamity spent on drinks for the crowd.

Meanwhile an event was brewing in Washington that had grim forebodings for the silver camp in the Castle Mountains. President Cleveland called for a special session of Congress and after a long and bitter struggle, a bill was passed in October of 1893 which, under the Sherman Act, stopped all purchases of silver. This demonetized the metal and although the struggle for its reinstatement on a bi-metal standard was lengthy and violent and echoed around the world, it was all for naught. Castle began to go downhill.

Yet through this disaster and the accompanying panic, the Jawbone Railroad was completed. One mine in Castle, presumed to be the Cumberland, had more than $240,000 worth of ore on the dump. Jawbone officials saw a good thing in this and interested the owners of the East Helena smelter in sampling the idle ore. The smelter firm agreed to take it at a set price, the ore owners taking stock in the railroad for the same amount.

The Jawbone was thus pulled along on a shoestring and its workers the same, laying rails for meagre wages which they were glad to get when others were starving. When the railroad reached a point near Castle, the ore was loaded and shipped to the Helena smelter.

With a railroad at its front door, Castle now had realized its fondest dream but the victory was hollow. It did not pay to mine silver and only lead was left. Editor Dillard doggedly assured the people that the town would survive and become greater than ever. His brave editorials continued but gradually became less vociferous. "It is serenely tranquil at the present writing but God, in His Infinite Goodness, will take care of us and see that we get our taters and bacon, whether school keeps or not. It is so serene and calm in this great silver and lead camp you can hear your thoughts walk out on your imagination and sit down on the sofa of your brain." Sometime later he wrote: "It is so quiet here in this great future camp that the squeaking noise in the prospector's coffee mill sounds like the rumblings of Old Faithful in the national park—trying to throw up its volcanic liver for the amusement of pink-foot visitors from the effete east." One of the last pathetic items was short: "There are plenty of excellent mining claims in this camp which can be leased on good terms."

When the price of lead dropped, the camp was finished. The last whistle blew at the last mine and even *The Whole Truth*, faced with a deficit of $4,000 was forced to give up. The exodus of population was rapid, every person in town leaving for greener pastures in a few months—except two faithful old retainers who clung to the vain hope that life would return.

Joe Martino was one. He came to Castle as a charcoal burner for the smelter and when it closed down he worked as a freighter out of Dorsey, later returning to Castle. The other was also named Joe—

Joe Kidd. He was a native of Williamsburg, Pennsylvania, where one of his grade school classmates had been Charles M. Schwab who went on to become a steel magnate. Kidd arrived in Castle about 1888, always working in the mines. While Martino had a little log house near the upper end of the gulch, Kidd lived in another at the lower end and was known for years as "Mayor of Castle."

February of 1938 saw the last chapter in the camp's life. Snow that winter had piled up to unusual depths and when it looked as though another heavy fall was on its way, Joe Kidd thought he had better get down to Lennep, six miles away, and stock up on groceries. With his horse he made it safely to the village but on his way back a blizzard caught him, his horse blundering away, Joe staggering on foot to Martino's cabin. He warmed up, divided his food with his friend and pushed on. His body was found in the drifts, frozen hard.

Joe Martino was now Castle's sole surviving resident and he kept up his lonely and hopeless vigil another year, finally consenting to be taken down to the State Hospital at Warm Springs where he soon died. Castle had only ghosts and memories.

CASTLE HAD SEVERAL BROTHELS accepted as necessary adjunct to mining camp. Only well preserved one is shown in background discreetly separated from fashionable residence section. Houses still standing in fair condition invariably have stone foundations as at left. All lumber, shingles and wooden ornaments came from nearby mill; fireplace and chimney bricks also of local origin.

ELKHORN, MONTANA

Here is a real, honest-to-goodness Ghost Town. The main street winds steeply up a rocky slope, to end abruptly at the bottom of huge tailing dumps below the big mine and mill. Beyond that rises even steeper the shoulder of Elkhorn Mountain, covered on its slope with blue spruce, pine and aspen. At the summit the bare rocks above timberline would be early under snow and covered into summer.

On both sides of the street straggle lines of old and weathered buildings. The roofs of some are caved in, the windows mostly without glass, and doors missing or hanging by one hinge.

Several are two stories tall and attics add to their height, giving them a gaunt, cadaverous look. Inside, long strips of imported, once elegant wallpaper hang in tatters to flap dismally in the unhindered wind.

Elkhorn has been dead for sixty years except for desultory flare-ups of activity, and it is hard to picture the frenzy that gripped the area in 1870 when yellow flakes of gold were discovered in the creek running beside the town.

Panning in the stream soon changed to hard rock mining when the quartz lodes were discovered, and the building of the town, its stores, 14 saloons, several churches and lodge halls proceeded at a furious pace.

Transportation was next to impossible and only the barest necessities came in for a long time, but in 1889 the Northern Pacific drove a line up to the 5,500-foot high city, running in three trains a week.

During these productive years, the flow of mineral wealth in gold and silver totaled some $14,000,000.

FALSE-FRONTED "emporium" stands in sagging ruin along Main Street.

WHERE WRAITHS ABOUND

GARNET, MONTANA

Garnet has been resurrected from seemingly permanent ghostliness at least twice. As of this writing it holds a place among the top Ghost Towns of the West, but it could be revived again.

Population: two people and two eager, friendly dogs. The human residents of Garnet are Mr. and Mrs. Clifford Dahl who, with the first flake of snow, move down to Drummond, leaving the town completely to its memories. "The snow comes down like white corn flakes and in no time is ten feet deep."

An imposing three-story hotel lords it over the saloons, stores and other business houses. The warm red coloring of long-weathered wood seems especially pronounced here. Some of the structures lean one way, some another, some seem in imminent danger of collapse, and indeed several have collapsed.

But, it is fairly easy to repopulate the town and imagine the surreys again rolling up and down the steep streets.

Garnet's wealth was in gold and they took millions out in the years following the original discoveries in 1862. There would have been even more, but so many of the men were too drunk to work much of the time. The mine that turned out the richest, the "Nancy Hanks," was owned by two partners, one of whom was much addicted to alcohol. After one protracted spree the other partner bought him out for $50. In the several years following, the "Nancy Hanks" spewed out $10,000,000 in gold. The retired partner had moved down to Beartown, and one day when another load of rich ore from the mine rolled past his door he hanged himself.

F. A. Davy operated the Garnet General Store for 45 years. He was not popular with the children of the town. They hanged him in effigy from the flagpole of the hotel,

HALL OF HOTEL was entrance to t h r e e-story building. Door stands open to weather.

and you can still see some ragged remains of the stingy merchant's proxy hanging there. Mr. Davy also ran the Garnet Stage Line and Garnet Freight Line. He died here years ago. About 1912 a large part of town burned down and never was rebuilt. The "Nancy Hanks" operated off and on, closing entirely in 1954.

The flavor of the town itself is not reminiscent of anything like such a late era. The buildings all date from earlier days.

It was in those times that the combined population from Coloma (above Garnet) down to Beartown was nearly five thousand people. And it was during one of those hard winters the snow came down so hard and so long that supplies ran out. When things began to get really desperate, one brave individual put on his miner's light, went down into the maze of shafts and tunnels, and made his way through one connection after another until he had gone the whole eleven miles to Beartown and arranged for supplies to be sent up. A deed on that high order would seem to make up a little for some of the wildness that was Garnet.

The sharp switchbacks and steep approach to Garnet are called the "Chinee" Grade. The story is that a Chinese miner stached a sizable fortune there, concealed in a five-pound baking powder can. It has never been found.

GILTEDGE, MONTANA

The history of this camp is one of repeated disappointments. The ores gave up their metals reluctantly, labeled "refractory," and while getting them out of the mine was easy enough it was quite another matter to make them pay. This gave rise to a most elaborate plan to disguise gold shipments.

The Whiskey Gulch mine produced well but the amount of gold obtained was so low the superintendent was ashamed of it. He kept the results secret also because some eastern investors were nibbling at an invitation to expand the finances of the operation. He reasoned that if he took the bullion to Billings for shipment to the mint rather than to nearby Lewistown, there would be no leak as to the skimpy production.

This he did and his secret was safe—but now he had another worry. By the grapevine the superintendent had heard certain unsavory characters in town had learned he was shipping the gold on his own, robbing the company at the same time, and they planned to hold him up on some lonely road. So he filled the bags with junk to weigh about the

WHEN JAIL FELL DOWN someone saved stout, barred window frames. Prospect of rebuilding hoosegow seems remote.

same as the bullion and labeled them for the mint as usual—and stashed the real article under the floor of his buggy. He made the next trip without being molested—and all subsequent trips. Whatever happened to the robbers he never knew.

The low ore content resulted also in a spectacular buggy race. The main mine, the Giltedge, was having a particularly bad time at the smelter. Results of the last roasting had been so poor the men didn't get their Saturday pay. They held their protests but when another week rolled around without pay, they revolted, inducing the sheriff to issue an attachment against the bullion ready for shipment.

The man in charge of the mine was Bob Ammon, a New Yorker, and he decided to get the gold to the station in Great Falls for shipment, in spite of the hold out. He loaded it into his buggy and headed out of town, but the watchful sheriff had been expecting some such move and started after him in his own rig. He caught up with Ammon but couldn't overtake him on account of the narrow road. His horse hung on the tail of Ammon's buggy all the way to Great Falls and up to the railroad station. Ammon jumped on the train and the sheriff grabbed his arm. But the New Yorker had his ace card. He had legal training and knew what to do. He smiled calmly at the sheriff and said: "You are now in Cascade County and out of your jurisdiction of Fergus County. Take your hands off me."

Giltedge had not attracted much attention before 1893. Even then nothing too spectacular happened but buildings began to go up and the aspects of a town began to appear. Next year the camp had its first school, young H. A. Moulton its first teacher although he himself had no education. He had a bad time with his "rough neck" pupils, some of whom were older than he was. Moulton wore glasses and came to school one morning to find each boy had shaped wires like spectacles across his nose. By sheer good sense and persistence he eventually won the respect of the pupils and taught the Giltedge school for years. Another young man, David Roberts, started a blacksmith shop, Wise and Co., and owned the butcher shop as well. Sanville Hurvitch was the first postmaster.

By 1895, when neighboring Maiden began to fail, some of the abandoned buildings were moved to Giltedge, one of them the hardware store owned by M. L. Poland. Poland had operated the store in Maiden almost from the town's inception and now all he could do was leave it to his son.

The store was moved to Giltedge on logs used as rollers and Norman Poland who had worked in

HOTEL OR BOARDING HOUSE has stark, lonely quality of old abandoned buildings, emphasized by Montana's "big sky." Giltedge's remaining buildings are scarce, creating open, gaunt look.

the store as a boy was now the manager. A large hotel was put up with a fancy bar replacing the first makeshift one which had a dirt floor. The town jail was substantial, with window bars set in wide casings installed after the first two sets had been pried out by jail-breaking drunks and horse thieves.

During the period of prosperity for the town, shortly after the turn of the century, there were 600 voters and a considerable total population, counting wives, children and the many transients.

The ores, refractory from the first, grew more so as the years wore on and when the biggest smelter failed, the camp began to shrivel. One enterprising miner, losing his job at the Giltedge mill, started a much needed industry, making fence posts to keep stock from wandering too far. The plant had a pool filled with preservative oils in which posts were soaked, running in and out of a crude tramway. The old operation is falling into ruin but today a new one is working, the only visible industry in the town.

412

NOTES ON A GOLD PAN

Gold Creek, Montana

The diaries of early miners who were perhaps conscious of the parts they were playing in history "oft remind us ... footsteps in the sands of time"— and forsooth, in the sands of creek beds. Panning the gold in the diaries of Gold Creek miners turns up some interesting color.

In 1862 the camp was a place where a man could go unshaven, let his hair grow to his shoulders and remain unwashed for weeks, particularly in winter. When his clothing bothered even him, he might wash it, but why hurry? All this was before women and when one or two did appear in camp, he changed his tune—and clothes.

An item in Granville Stuart's diary on July 12, 1862, covers the point. "With the emigrants today is Mr. B. Burchet with his family. . . . Miss Burchet is sixteen years old and a very beautiful girl. Every man in camp has changed and changed his shirt since the family arrived. We are all trying to appear like civilized men."

And on July 23: "Arrived in town today a fine violin player accompanied by his handsome seventeen year old wife. . . . All the men are shaving nowadays and most of them indulge in an occasional haircut. The blue flannel shirt with a black tie has taken the place of the elaborately beaded buckskin one. The white men are wearing shoes instead of moccasins and most of us have selected some other day than Sunday for washday." That same year Granville put an end to his own loneliness by marrying Aubony, a Snake Indian girl whom he described as "a fairly good cook, amiable and with few relatives."

Another Gold Creek miner, James Stuart, brother of Granville and sheriff of Missoula County, recorded in his diary that year, "I brought with me the Indian woman ransomed from Narcisse, the Flathead. She is rather good looking, and seems to be of good disposition. . . . I could do worse, so I find myself a married man." And this Stuart had other pursuits besides the good wife, as he wrote later, "I have lost three hundred dollars today, staking a man to deal monte for me the past three days. I think I will take Granville's advice and quit gambling." The next day he observed, "Our monte sharps are about to take the town. Getting decidedly obstreperous in their conduct," he observed sharply.

The next day two men named Fox and Bull arrived from Elk City in the Clearwater Mountains with the word that they were looking for some card sharps that had been run out of their town but not before they could ride away on horses belonging to prominent citizens. One of the two-man posse carried a double-barreled shotgun heavily loaded with buckshot, the other a Colt navy revolver.

Sheriff James Stuart told them the wanted men might be in Worden and Co.'s store where one of them, Spillman, went to buy a shirt. With the shotgun aimed at his heart Spillman meekly surrendered, Fox and Bull delegating a guard to hold

GOLD CREEK, once so full of violence, is today a mere huddle of ramshackle buildings. Boards and battens conceal original log construction of many relics. Photo depicts crossroads center of town where monte dealer Arnett was gunned down with cards in one hand, gun in other.

him while the sheriff led them to a saloon where the other card sharp and horse thieves Arnett and Jermagin were just about to open a new monte game.

Though dealing, Arnett had his loaded revolver handy in his lap. At the command of "hands up" he reached for the weapon but had no time to raise it, taking a charge of buckshot through the breast. Jermagin ran to the nearest corner crying, "Don't shoot! I give up!" He was quickly tied up and put under guard with Spillman. Arnett died with the monte cards in his left hand, gun in his right, and neither could be wrenched from his grasp after rigor mortis had set in. He was buried with the tools of his trade still close to him.

At a "miners' trial" Spillman testified he and Arnett left Elk City with six horses and found Jermagin walking, so they gave him a horse to ride. Acquitted of horse theft the judge gave Jermagin six hours to leave town. Having little to pack and no stomach for delay, he made it in that many minutes.

In referring to the affair later Stuart wrote, "Spillman, who was a large, fine looking man was found guilty and sentenced to be hanged in a half hour. He made no defense and seemed to take little interest in the proceedings. . . . He walked to his death with a firm step and seemed as little concerned as if he had been a mere spectator instead of the main actor in the tragedy. It was the firmness of a brave man who saw that death was inevitable and nerved himself to meet it."

Gold Creek had a physician who doubled as an "armchair prospector," disdaining the actual digging and panning in the sand and mud. Granville Stuart wrote, "Doctor Atkinson is a most original character. He is always traveling about the country with a pack and horse and one or more companions. . . . He rides up a canyon keeping on the ridge where possible. From some point of vantage he takes out his field glasses and scours the country visible. Then he declares 'I think that section looks good.' Sometimes he will buy a claim and resell it. On the whole he does as well as most of us who dig innumerable holes and pan innumerable pans of gravel, only succeeding in just missing the streak of pay dirt."

Brothers James and Granville Stuart were in Gold Creek after trouble in Yreka, California. Suffering near starvation, encounters with hostile Indians and disappointing results in claims, they moved north to Montana. Wildly optimistic at first, they wrote a third brother, Thomas, in Colorado, to "hurry here before the place is overcrowded." Thomas came but so did hundreds of other hopefuls following the news of gold in the Deer Lodge area. Most of them were disappointed, the deposits at Gold Creek soon showing signs of depletion under the army of shovels. When word of gold discoveries at Bannack, Alder Gulch and Last Chance reached Gold Creek almost everybody was in a mood to travel and in a few weeks the town was virtually abandoned.

The Stuart brothers deserted too when they heard miners at Bannack diggings would turn over their gold for beef after months of stewed rabbit. Thomas, Granville and James drove the cattle they had been accumulating to Grasshopper Creek and spent the winter selling and dealing.

GRANITE, MONTANA

Philipsburg is much too alive to qualify as a "dead" Ghost Town. But it is contemporary with one of the most interesting of Montana's historic camps, Granite, and figures so much in its history that it cannot be ignored.

About 16 miles southwest are the sapphire deposits of the Rock Creek area. These gems are found in gravels of several "Gulches," Anaconda, Sapphire and others. When the stones were first discovered about 1892 the usual exaggerated, excited announcements were made as to size, "rich deep color," etc. The stones actually run rather small, ranging from ¼ to ½ inch, with a sprinkling of larger ones.

The gems were first discovered in routine placering operations for gold, and are still being obtained by variations of hydraulic and sluicing operations.

From 1899 to 1900, 400,000 carats were recovered from the sluiceboxes. Of this amount about 25,000 carats were suitable for faceting, the remainder being put to commercial use, as for watch jewels. For this latter use, the Montana sapphires were in demand as they required less work to ready them and brought $2.00 to $6.00 per ounce.

The bank of Granite has vanished entirely, but the vault remains. Its heavy iron doors have become unhinged and the old records have blown all over the mountaintop site of the town. Among them are many billheads marked "Philipsburg Foundry" with the dates all through the 80's and 90's. Bowen and Thompson were the "Prop'rs" and listed such cryptic items as Battery Shoes, Spiders, R. B. Keys and 5-foot Strate Bars. These items and hundreds more were billed every few days to the Granite Mountain Mining Co., and the concern must have provided the lifeblood for the upkeep of the mines of Old Granite.

Situated almost on the very top of a mountain, Granite affords a splendid view.

Mr. Henry Kistle has lived in this mountaintop aerie since his arrival there in 1899, at the age of nine. He was born in the old camp, Elkhorn. He says that the town hit its peak in 1892, with 3,600 people. "It turned out $60,000,000 in silver," he said, "though other sources do not agree with this. Some people say only $58,000,000."

There was lots of money around, anyway. A Mr. Fisher kept a herd of cows down in the valley and made trips up here every day with milk. This, being a real luxury, brought a good price, and at the end

MINER'S UNION HALL gets early sunshine on mountaintop situation. Stairway to upper floor leads from door at right. Rear of building is approaching ruin.

MINE ACCIDENTS WERE FREQUENT and required large hospital. "Little house" in front seems conspicuous, but there was no room for it in back.

of the month he would make his collections amounting to a lot of money. One time he had $480.00 and was held up by bandits on the way down. He wouldn't give up his money, so they shot him in the chest and took it. But he lived to tell the story.

VAULT IS ALL that remains of Bank of Granite.

KENDALL, MONTANA

In its heyday Kendall turned out a great wealth of gold, the bullion sent to Lewistown for shipment to the mint. There were plenty of road agents ready to appropriate it and plenty of subterfuges used to foil them. All three stage lines out of town were used without a set pattern. Sometimes a passenger would take the gold out in a trunk or it might be in a sack carried openly in a buggy. The ruses were so many and so varied it took a sharp bandit to locate the gold. About all he could count on was the signal. When the smelter was finishing off a batch of bullion in the final "roasting," there would be a roaring noise announcing to all and sundry another load of gold would soon be on its way.

On one occasion a large shipment of about $50,000 was to be sent in to the bank. The stage driver was instructed to take the bag to Brown's Clothing Store instead, when he got to Lewistown, which he did. Brown was busy with a customer but told the driver: "Just leave the bag on the counter.

I'll put it in the safe later." But his streak of brisk business continued and when closing time came he forgot the gold, leaving it on the counter. That night several men who had got wind of the shipment and knew where it would be delivered, broke into the clothing store and blew open the safe. They did get $200 but the gunnysack of gold remained safely and securely on the counter.

In the early days of mining the practice of "salting" was quite common. Kendall had some experts in this line and one of them planted some rich ore in the mouth of a worthless mine and took in an unwary buyer, one Barnes. This man was eager to be a mine owner and didn't look beyond the samples in front, yet was cautious in another respect. As soon as the first deal was closed he staked his three sons-in-law to claims around his mine to protect any extension of the vein. After working the mine for several months he finally decided he had been flimflammed and turned a few desultory efforts toward one of the protecting claims. The

RUINS OF FIRST PRESBYTERIAN CHURCH stand on hill slightly off street surrounded by second growth trees mostly pines.

BANK AT LEFT shows large square vault in center of ruin. Large department store is nearly gone — evidence of both buildings fast disappearing due to vandals carrying stones away.

INSIDE WALL OF DEPARTMENT STORE shows where stairway paused at landing. Lath and plaster covered walls, concealed more handome stone.

result—over $2 million in gold in the next few years, the huge Barnes-King operation.

The first really good mine at Kendall was the Goggle Eye, so named from the way the discoverers looked at the first sight of the gold. It was worked by George Mason but he couldn't stand the expense of getting it started so turned it over to Joe Wunderlin and Bob Woodman. That was about 1899 when Kendall began to boom and several buildings were erected. One of these was a boarding house with a restaurant on the ground floor, owned by Harry Kendall who at that time had no special interest in mining. But the all-absorbing lure of quick riches got him too and he invested some of his boarding house money in a mine just getting started and whose owners needed capital for expansion. He worked his investment up to $450, enough at this stage for the controlling interest. The mine paid moderately but still needed much more money to realize its potential.

Kendall approached Finch and Campbell, mining promoters of Spokane and they were interested enough to send a man to look it over. Kendall was asking $50,000 for the mine and this stopped them. Then one of their experts, a man named R. K. Neal, looked it over on his own and recommended its purchase by the firm. By this time the mine was doing better and Kendall raised his price to $450,000 with a royalty of 10% on the profits. The deal went through and Kendall went back to his boarding house. The mine boomed into heavy

production, Kendall's 10% paying him more than a fortune before it was all over.

One interesting point about the ores at Kendall was "no one ever saw the gold in them." The metal was so finely divided it was never visible in the raw state. Therefore Kendall's refining methods required the cyanide process, one of the first camps to employ it.

The ore was first crushed into fingernail-sized pieces, a strong solution of cyanide run over it. Cyanide was extremely dangerous and there were many narrow escapes from death in the mines and mills. The cyanide dissolved the gold and the mixture was then added to zinc shavings which precipitated the gold, the resulting black sludge roasted in a furnace. When the zinc was driven off the gold was left.

The big cyanide mill started off with 40 men but soon expanded to 194. By this time the town had several pretentious stores, a large bank, two churches and its trade by mule teams and freight lines was a contributing factor in the growing economy of Fergus County.

Kendall was the last mining camp of consequence in the area, its combined mines turning out more than $6,400,000. When they were exhausted the town went into decay rapidly, the demise speeded up by the fact that many mine tunnels ran under the buildings so they later sank into the ground. There is not a habitable structure there now, only gaunt stone ruins through which cattle wander at will.

KEYSTONE, MONTANA

Keystone was first called Carter, when the rich silver lode was discovered in the 80's and was quite a place, "wild as they come," about 1900. But peace certainly reigns there now.

The few remaining buildings are very scattered, but the location of the main street could be figured out by the store and a cabin or two on the other side. Some larger houses, beautifully weathered, stand leaning at various angles here and there. A large barn, partly flattened, is surrounded by nettles and brambles.

KEYSTONE GENERAL Merchandise Emporium marks site of Main Street.

LANDUSKY, MONTANA

From time immemorial Indians in the Little Rockies knew of gold there but it was just some metal too soft to use for tools. Only when the white man showed such eagerness to get his hands on even small bits of it did they pay much attention to the yellow "treasure".

On Thanksgiving Day of 1868, at Fort Browning on the Milk River, the officers' dinner was interrupted by an Indian wanting to see Major Simmons — one Nepee, a familiar figure around the fort. He displayed a pouch filled with gold nuggets and said it was a present to his friend, Major Simmons. Greatly excited, the officers made vigorous attempts to get Nepee to tell where he got the gold but he kept the secret under all promises and threats. If he told it, he said, his people would kill him.

Nepee had a friend, Joe Hontus, with whom he had been camping several summers. Shortly after the incident at the fort Joe got drunk and bragged: "I know where that gold is and I'm going after it." He never returned from the hills, his body was found full of bullet holes along the trail. Nepee died with his secret in 1876.

Powell Landusky arrived in the diggings of Last Chance Gulch as a gangling teenager. Even then he had an ungovernable temper and flew into blind rages. He was joshed about his loose build, his Missouri drawl and one day someone asked him in an imitation of his accent: "Where you from anyhow?" Landusky's reply was a powerful punch that laid the heckler low followed by: "From Pike County, Missouri, by God!" With more respect the people called him Pike.

The man from Missouri was a sworn enemy of any and all Sioux and fell into many encounters with them. In 1880, he and Joe Hamilton were attempting to do some trading with a party of Piegans at a fort the whites had built on Flatwillow Creek. There was trouble, Landusky claiming one of the braves had attacked him with a chunk of wood and tried to stab him in the back. The other Indians were aroused and the two whites fled to the fort kitchen. The window was so small Landusky could just squeeze his head and one arm out to fire at the Indians who were now circling around hurling taunts at the holed-up whites.

The young Piegan Landusky had accused of treachery was hiding behind a bush and now saw the white man's head made a good target, shooting him in the jaw. Landusky jumped back into the room, reloaded his Winchester and started shooting again, this time hitting and killing a squaw. Withdrawing to reload again, an Indian bullet hit him in the body. Staggering with pain and loss of blood from two wounds, Pike clutched at the table edge and before falling, broke off the shattered section of jaw with four teeth in it, still raging as he threw it into the corner. This time he gave up and fell fainting on the bed. The other whites at the besieged fort sent a scout to try to get through to Fort Maginnis for help including a doctor. Scout Healy managed to get through and alerted the army to the situation.

A party of soldiers came with an army doctor who dressed Landusky's wounds and set his broken jaw. The patient lay for days without improvement, raving in delirium most of the time, swallowing whiskey during his lucid moments. His partners knew something drastic would have to be done to save Pike and this was to take him to Lewiston. They made the arduous journey in a week and there

Dr. DePalme told Landusky the jaw had been badly set, would have to be rebroken and reset. "Break it!" roared Landusky. "If I die, I die!" The doctor performed the operation and the jaw began to heal. Landusky recovered although his face was badly disfigured.

In the spring of 1881, he and his partner went to the newly-booming camp of Maiden in the Judith Mountains and started a saloon. He met a widow, a Mrs. Descry, and in spite of his contorted face, Pike Landusky successfully courted and married her. Justice of the Peace "Pony" McPartland performed the ceremony, the first of its kind in camp. Witnesses were the seven Descry children and most of the local population. In 1884 the Landuskys moved to a beautiful valley just where Rock Creek emerges from the south edge of the Little Rockies.

That same year "Dutch Louie" Myers found some color in nearby Alder Gulch. He had just started work on his claim June 15 when he was joined by Frank Aldrich and Charles Brown prospecting up the same gulch. They decided on a partnership, later inviting Landusky in and Aldrich was sent to Fort Assiniboine for supplies. When he returned in two weeks he found the others had panned gold dust worth $109. With food and supplies they now set to work building sluices and each man was soon cleaning up $20 a day.

At this point Maiden was crowded with prospectors arriving too late to "get in on" the best diggings and when they heard of the strikes at Alder Gulch most of them left for the new bonanza. Among them was "Nigger Eli" Shelby and it was he who found the heaviest deposits of gold on a rim high above the gulch, William Shelton finding the largest nugget, worth $83.

During the lull following the first rush, a seventeen-year old boy named George A. Ottowa joined up with a man named Curtis for a prospecting trip in the surrounding gulches. They located a claim, agreeing that one would dig while the other stood guard. The boy stood the first watch and later he was to write: "I stood guard while Curtis shoveled. Shortly after this I saw Pike Landusky coming down the trail, his big .45 six-shooter strapped to his waist. I drew a bead on him and told him to throw up his hands, which he did, as he had not seen us. He said he wanted to talk to us and I told him to unbuckle his six-shooter and throw it on the trail. He did and came over to where we were standing. He said we could keep our ground."

The men figured there must be some good reason for Landusky's unusually agreeable behavior and there was. He and Dutch Louie had just discovered

DETAILED STUDY of old farm building shows nearly regular marks of broad axe used by pioneer carpenter to dress logs used in construction. Simple mud was used first as chinking, later mortar. Montana is full of historic log buildings, most of round, undressed logs. Good examples of dressed log construction, with flattened sides, are frequently seen in Little Rockies mining camps.

a pocket of nuggets upstream — that was to yield them $5,000 very quickly.

The discoveries of these four men started a bigger stampede than the first but there were complications similar to those in the Black Hills of South Dakota. The new diggings were located on Fort Belknap Indian Reservation and white men were barred from mining, even entering. When news of the strikes reached the Government a detachment of soldiers was sent from Fort Maginnis to a point on the south bank of the Missouri where the miners had established headquarters. Periodically the military would make a raid on the trespassers, lecturing them and ordering them to vacate the reservation. The gold seekers complied but returned when the soldiers left. After several repetitions of these bloodless and fruitless maneuvers, the miners were allowed to stay as long as they brought in no liquor. This order was obeyed with tongue-in-cheek agreement, but the army had done its part.

The start of the big rush that would make the towns of Landusky, Zortman and Ruby Gulch boom began by accident. In August of 1893, Landusky and Robert Orman were prospecting along a ridge, expecting to work it to the end. In mid-afternoon of the hot day they dropped down to the stream for a drink. While scrambling up, a hand broke off a chunk of rich ore. On being crushed and washed the rock yielded a "string of gold three inches long in the pan."

Not being sure their claim was on or off the Belknap Reservation, the pair removed their ore at

SEVERAL ORIGINAL BUILDINGS remain in Landusky, most fast approaching ruin. This one is identified by various residents as "first post office," "general store," seems beyond repair but plans are afoot to restore it.

night. This first discovery, rich as it was, turned out to be a "minor miracle" in light of a later one — a vein thirteen feet wide yielding $500 a ton, the ore free milling, gold easily separated by crushing and washing. And that was only the beginning. Soon ore was yielding them as much as $13,000 a ton. When the rumor that they had obtained $100,000 from a single small hole reached the outside world, the biggest and last stampede was on.

By the middle of next year, 1894, the newspapers of Havre, Helena and Anaconda carried many columns about the big strike and were advocating Landusky as the site for the capitol with such flourishes as: "Hurrah for Landusky for Capitol! Helena and Anaconda are not in it" . . . . . "The boys have enough to pay the national debt after making themselves rich . . . all we need is a stamp to make ourselves $20 gold pieces."

The loosely knit camp called Landusky became

the town of Landusky June 9 when a meeting was held and T. J. Throop appointed recorder. Every "bona fide citizen" was allowed two lots, 50 x 100 feet, providing he erect a building 16 x 18 feet with 10 foot ceiling within 90 days. The Havre ADVERTISER issue containing this news had another item about a development that would have a bearing on events leading to Landusky's end. "Jake Harris, better known as 'Jew Jake', is about to embark in the saloon business." It would be in this saloon that Pike Landusky would meet Kid Curry for the last time.

The magnet that drew the Currys to Landusky was not gold but reports of rich, well watered land at the edge of the Little Rockies. The Curry boys had come here as adept ranch hands, having worked for the Circle Bar and Fergus Land and Cattle Co. At the Little Rockies site the Curry brothers took up a homestead at the mouth of Rock Creek and found themselves neighbors of Pike Landusky whose home was just above beside the spring, a mile and a half below the town of Landusky.

Before arriving the brothers had been known as Logan, the reason for the change to Curry unexplained. Henry, the oldest by several years, was not well and after a short time on the homestead went to Steamboat Springs on the Colorado River for a "cure" but died there. Next youngest was Harvey, better known to history as "The Kid" or "Kid Curry". The next was Johnny, the handsome one and then Loney, handy with women and the fiddle.

The boys were friendly with their notorious neighbors for nine years. The first evidence of bad feeling seems to have come when Pike returned a plow he had borrowed. It was broken, Landusky claiming it was in that condition when he got it, the Currys denying it. The feud gained impetus when Landusky discovered lady-killer Loney was ardently pursuing one of his four step-daughters.

When The Kid and his brother John were accused of what they claimed was a trumped-up charge of branding cattle not their own, it was Pike who as deputy sheriff escorted the boys to Fort Benton for trial. While they were in chains in jail Landusky beat them up and the quarrel went beyond any possibility of peace. The brothers were eventually released for lack of proof of guilt and went home shortly before Christmas bound to vengeance.

Christmas was celebration time as active mining was limited by severe freezing weather and the men had time and the inclination to let off pent-up steam. Landusky was determined to celebrate this 1894 Christmas as usual in spite of the feud. The big party lasted two days with men coming to town from all corners of the Little Rockies for the "big free feed and drinks". At the dance, held in the

HIP-ROOFED BARN is one of original buildings on Landusky ranch. While "Montana zephyrs" have blown off some boards and battens they have been replaced with modern, round-headed nails. Others retain old hand-forged type with square heads offering proof of age. Present owner of ranch, friendly, red-headed Pole Thomas Kolczak, attempted to persuade pair of geese to pose properly in center of picture but willful birds persisted in walking out. Tom and wife Jane made author welcome, pointed out where Landusky home stood near spring few hundred feet above barn.

THIS WAS LANDUSKY'S BUGGY. Of it, Tom Kolczak says: "It was stored in the barn and was in perfect shape all these years until this spring. Then one day I found my kids had pulled it outside and almost dismantled it before I caught them. I hope it can be put together because I understand Kid Curry and Landusky often rode together in it before they quarreled."

Curry barn where Loney led the fiddlers, all gunmen were required to check their weapons at the door and they were not returned until the evening of December 26.

The next morning was very cold and snow lay deep. Men drifted aimlessly, most of them drawn to the comforting warmth of the saloons, particularly Jew Jake's. Jake Harris had been in a gun fight with the marshall of Great Falls, losing a leg, and got around with a crutch and sometimes his inverted shotgun. The saloon doubled as a general store displaying all types of merchandise in the rear.

Jake was not surprised to see his friend Pike Landusky come in for a drink but he did look apprehensively toward the store section where Loney and one of the ranch men were looking at a saddle. Landusky ordered a whiskey and was filling his glass when Kid Curry walked in the saloon and slapped him hard on the back.

Landusky twisted around and took a heavy blow on his fragile jaw, falling to the floor. At this point Loney and the hand came up, drew their guns and told the assembling crowd not to interfere. The Kid jumped on the fallen man and began to beat him unmercifully. Pike was unable to ward off the blows clad as he was in a heavy fur overcoat. Although he called for help and a friend, Tom Carter, asked Loney to stop his brother, the Kid continued to beat Pike's face into pulp, then let him up. Somehow Pike managed to draw his gun and pull the trigger. When it failed to fire Kid Curry drew his own .45 and blazed away.

The Kid who might have stayed to plead self-defense, chose instead to flee, thinking perhaps of his shady record. He escaped to join outlaws who were refugees of the Johnson County cattle wars and a gang including Butch Cassidy and the Sundance Kid.

On July 31, 1901, the gang was involved in a sensational train robbery, Kid Curry boarding the train and blowing the safe with dynamite. At least one of the gang was later apprehended and jailed but the rest got away. The Kid began to drink more heavily and was spotted in a saloon in Knoxville, Tennessee. Two officers tried to arrest him but he wounded them both and broke away. Shortly after he was caught and jailed but after several months in a cell he fashioned a noose from a piece of wire, dropped it over the head of his jailer and escaped. The law lost track of him then, presuming he got away to South America to join Cassidy and the Sundance Kid. Or he may have been the Harvey Logan who died of pneumonia in a Denver hospital in 1911.

John Curry remained in charge of the ranch in Landusky, for a while peaceably. Then he — the black-haired and blue-eyed one — fell in love with a widow who returned his affections. The lady attempted to persuade her dead husband's partner, Jim Winters, to sign over to her his share of their ranch. To help matters along, John rode up to Winters' home one day, his gun handy. Winters saw him coming and readied his shotgun. John fired first but missed. His skittish horse began to buck, exposing him to a fatal blast from Winters' gun. John was buried in the regular town cemetery.

Loney had continued to pay court to Landusky's step-daughter now that her protector was dead. In common law fashion the two lived in a cabin in town. When the woman tried to pass a bill in a general store in Fort Benton, it was identified as one stolen in a recent robbery, and Loney made a hurried visit to an aunt in Missouri. Pinkerton men trailed him and surrounded the house, some miles from Kansas City. Loney spotted them and made a dash through the cornfield, receiving a bullet in the head.

Years have passed since Landusky's violent days. Gone with hot-headed gunmen are most of the buildings, lost to decay, fire and vandalism. Enough old structures remain to give some semblance to Main Street but definite identification is doubtful as the few modern residents do not agree. One just knows this was the violent, colorful Montana that was.

LAURIN, MONTANA

Laurin is one of the group of mining camps spawned by the rich strikes of the general area called Alder Gulch. These included the better-known Virginia City and Alder itself.

Old tailings almost the whole length of the gulch attest to the persistent workings of the equipment once operated by Harvard University, so richly rewarded in the several millions in gold extracted from the stream bed.

The original gold discoveries were in May 1863, and the gulch p r o d u c e d $10,000,000 during the first year.

Laurin shared in this bonanza and for a time was the El Dorado of the entire area, but it has now dwindled greatly and the old relics are hard to find among buildings of a somewhat more modern vintage.

Two of the notorious Plummer gang of road agents were hanged here, on July 4, 1864. These two were "Red" Yager and G. W. Brown.

Everywhere you go in the area around Virginia City you seem to find places where members of the unholy terrorists were hanged. This is because frontier outlaws were frequently hanged almost on the spot where apprehended.

LAURIN HAS SOME modern buildings but here and there can be found some dating to turbulent early days. Rain makes flat, grey light on old false front.

"Look! . . . back there in the grass!"

MAIDEN, MONTANA

The Judith Mountains of Montana are misnamed, according to legend. Meriwether Lewis of the Lewis and Clark Expedition wanted to make an impression on a certain girl at home by naming a mountain after her. He remembered her face better than her name. It was Julia.

First discoveries of gold in that part of the state were in the Judith Mountains. Partners David Jones and Skookum Joe Anderson — whose mother was an Indian, his father a Swede — had been grubstaked by Perry McAdow who was crowding them to produce something. Luckily they found a good showing of color in Alpine Gulch but unluckily winter was due. Sure enough, just after they started sluicing a hard snow put an end to all operations and the men had to wait out the winter on the open plain.

They barely made it back to their claim in the spring when a horde of hopeful prospectors who had heard the news began to arrive. One was a man named Maden and he was brusquely informed —"All this ground is taken up. Move on." Maden did move on, up the valley to another gulch which he named for himself and promptly put up a sign: "Camp Maden. Everybody welcome." The spot eventually became the center of a town, the word "camp" dropped from the name and an "I" added apparently by feminine influence, becoming "Maiden."

David Jones and Skookum Joe were ingenious as well as industrious. There being no boards in the gulch, they made sluice boxes by splitting trees into planks for troughs and in the bottom of each put a layer of clay. They ran the gold-laden gravels through these crude V-shaped channels, the heavier gold settling to the clay which was then removed, the gold separated.

This marvelous invention was not in use long for there came a revolting discovery—there was no more gold in the gulch, at least for easy taking. They turned to their backer, McAdow, who made an inspection of the vein in the rocks above the stream and hurried home to scare up more money. He had seen a good thing.

Maiden now came into an era of comparative prosperity. Instead of tree splitting, there were sawmills and boards and buildings went up in a frenzy. By 1883 there were 154 houses and stores in the town with six saloons and by 1888 the population had increased to 1200. Louis Berlanger opened a general merchandise store, taking in a partner until they disagreed too often, Berlanger going it alone and the partner starting another store.

Maiden had its ups and downs, its trials by fire and Indians. Fire took most of the town on several occasions and Indians would come around, ostensibly looking for buffalo but not overlooking animals of some resemblance to them—the miners' cows. Since these animals were hard to come by their loss was serious. In the winter of 1882-3 the Collan mill failed, throwing many out of work and owing several months' wages. The winter was severe and most of the dogs in camp were eaten. The military reservation at Fort Maginnis sent supplies to help out.

Then in 1883 a catastrophe of much larger proportions threatened the very existence of the prosperous camp. Maiden had been inadvertently built on the military reservation centered by Fort Maginnis, the fact studiously ignored heretofore. Like a bombshell came a notice posted in Maiden: "Order 26. All unauthorized persons now residing on the military reservation of Fort Maginnis, working in any mines, prospecting or carrying on any kind of business, are warned to leave the reservation forthwith, removing all property they may

have built or acquired thereon. 60 days are granted for removal."

Reaction was immediate. A mass meeting was held August 9 in Dryden and Essler's Building, presided over by J. Beck, recorder for the Warm Springs Mining Co. The result was a lengthy petition stating the case of the beleaguered miners to the Post Commander, presented on the 11th. Capt. Durand read it carefully, then got out a map of the reservation. He decided that the army could not back down on its decision to remove all unauthorized persons from the reservation but he could, without too much trouble, cut off from the reservation that portion in which Maiden was situated. Maiden was saved.

BERLANGER'S DEPARTMENT STORE is in ruins as are most of buildings in Maiden, earliest of Judith Basin's mining camps.

ASSAY OFFICE was one of most important mining camp functions, had small chemical laboratory complete with retorts, ovens and other equipment for determining value of ore samples brought in by hopeful prospectors.

Perry McAdow had long since taken over the mine he had financed. As his share over and above what he already owned as the grubstaker, he had put in 20 gallons of whiskey and a stock of supplies from the sawmill he was now shutting down. This first big mine was known as Skookum Joe, later Spotted Horse after a friendly Indian chief. As the Spotted Horse the mine became famous throughout Montana. The Maginnis mine was also a heavy producer, the two accounting for about $10 million in gold.

About 1891 things began to go wrong at the mines. Complaints came from the stamp mills that the ore wasn't worth processing any more, the miners admitting the veins were pinching out. Rising costs cut profits so much, in view of the lower grade ores, they could not keep going. Maiden began to fail, the 1200 people faded to 200 in 1896 and more left until the town was entirely empty. But Maiden had given impetus to mining in the Judith Basin and its people had only to move over to newer camps like Kendall.

MARYSVILLE, MONTANA

Here is a town, now almost completely a ghost, which in the 80's and 90's was Montana's leading gold producer and teemed with 3,000 people. It had several streets with one centering a substantial business district, with stone and brick buildings housing the bank, Masonic Hall, drugstore, hotels and the inevitable saloons. At the south end were several imposing frame structures, false fronted, one of which held a large newspaper plant. The remaining two of this group are most picturesque, weathered and worn, but still standing upright, albeit at opposite angles. In front of them is something unique in mining camps, an athletic field with rickety bleachers still standing! Not all of the hard-working, early-day miners spent all their spare time in saloons and brothels. There were bearded western baseball players and bearded western baseball fans too!

The Methodist and Catholic churches stand almost side by side across from the school.

The brick and stone buildings mentioned before line a block on one side and are in fairly good shape, but none does any business. The second floor of the saloon boasts rather large windows, one of which shows an old pool table, long idle.

At one side of the town stands the imposing mill of the old Drumlummon Mine. Its history is the history of the town, although there were others. Thomas Cruse in 1876 discovered the ledge and named it for his native town in Ireland and the town for Mary Ralston, the first woman in the place. Total production from Drumlummon is estimated to have been about $50,000,000.

As usual, the few remaining inhabitants of Marysville still believe there are further rich bodies of gold close by, and chances are good that they are right. Until these are found, and gold advances in price, the town peacefully disintegrates.

IT HAS BEEN LONG SINCE exciting ball games were played on the brush grown diamond. Bleachers still stand.

REMAINING BUILDINGS in Mammoth are of log construction. Central one is saloon, others stores, livery stable at end of street.

MAMMOTH, MONTANA

Mammoth's one street is lined with a number of old false-front stores, the post office, saloon and blacksmith shop. Several log cabins are strung along above, below and on the other side. Some of these latter are kept in repair and a little colony of refugees from hotter areas spend their vacations here in the shadow of the several snowy peaks which tower above the town.

The store buildings remain strictly untouched, and except for weathering, must look much as they did at the turn of the century. At that time the mines were turning out more than 14,000,000 dollars in gold and silver, mostly produced by the Mammoth. This was located on the very steep mountainside above the town, and plainly visible still are the remains of the tramway which carried on a continuously busy procession of cars up and down.

Mammoth somehow missed out on the temporary revival which came to many camps in the 30's and has remained almost unchanged all these years.

MELROSE, MONTANA

Melrose likely would have died entirely long before now, but being on a main highway, many of the old log houses and cabins are still occupied. A store or two and a filling station make up the business center.

The town was not a mining camp itself, but served several big ones as a supply center. Notable among these is Hecla.

Melrose is placed at an elevation of 5,173 feet, and this, with its position in this part of the Rockies some twenty miles from the Continental Divide makes for a heavy snowfall in the winter. The original buildings after the usual tent and shack stage were of logs. They are typical of this part of Montana, and have survived many severe winters. The chinking was done with a snow-white mortar and this, alternated with the dark logs, makes for a striking striped effect.

The Big Hole River, which runs close by, is famed for Rainbow trout and locations requiring some leg work still yield good catches.

In the early days, any conspicuous valley carved out of the mountains was dubbed a "Hole." Melrose is in one of these, larger than most. And, therefore, the name for the area and the river became the Big Hole.

PIONEER LOG AND SOD HOUSE surmounted by television aerial produces ludicrous anachronism. Note also hospitable touch, light fixture at door. Structure is one of earliest homes in Melrose.

Montana

SILVER VERSUS SAFETY

Pardee, Montana

The vein of silver at Pardee was right on top of the ground. There was a rather good deposit of galena throughout but running along the center was a six-foot wide seam very rich in silver. So said the *Weekly Missoulian* of January 1899 in describing the strike in the mountains four miles from Superior. Added almost as an afterthought was the stinger, "It is ten miles by pack train to the N.P.R.R."

At first the silver-laden ore was wrapped in rawhide bags and packed out on mules. Rough trails were blazed over the mountains north of the mine and down to the Clark Fork. There the ore was loaded on barges and floated down to Paradise, the nearest railroad station, and then to smelters.

During the first several years the mine was operated by the Iron Mountain Mining Co. All ore took the slow, expensive route to refinery and large amounts of profit from sales of concentrates went into improving roads and bridges. Finally the situation was greatly improved by the building of a large mill at the bottom of the final steep grade up to the mine on Flat Creek, with only concentrates to be hauled instead of bulky ore. The mill was soon paid for and during the next several years the complex paid investors half a million dollars.

SUBSTANTIAL LOG BUILDING was hotel for travelers to Pardee. White-flowering shrubs are Philadelphus, state flower of neighboring Idaho.

As time and progress continued the Northern Pacific extended a spur all the way to Superior. The Iron Mountain Co. then built a new mill at railhead with a direct connection to the mines by aerial tramway. In 1906 the company had about 125 on the payroll. At the height of mine and mill prosperity disaster struck through a technicality. The State of Montana passed a law requiring all mines to have two openings as a safety measure. For some unexplained reason Iron Mountain failed to comply with the regulation and was abruptly closed down when the laxity was discovered.

During the next several years there were several attempts to operate the mines but most interested operators agreed that even if the state had not closed down the mine, increasing costs of lifting ore from the depths reached over the years would have eventually done so. To get around the problem the Iron Mountain Tunnel Co. was organized and plans laid to bore a tunnel horizontally from the bottom of the hill to the 1,600-foot level of the mine. Stock was being sold about 1910 and a year or two later the men promoting the venture leased several hundred acres of ground adjoining.

Apparently no tunnel was ever constructed though some small-scale gophering continued off and on until 1930 when the town was abandoned. Several individual operators were conducting drilling tests on the property as late as 1958. A visit in 1965 uncovered no traces of recent human activity. A Forest Service sign at the foot of the grade up the old rutted, rocky road to the mine read, "Flat Creek Trail. Next 6 miles steep and narrow with switchbacks."

SHODDY STRUCTURES of Pardee's unsavory section built on narrow bench of level ground above Flat Creek including saloons, gambling houses, prostitutes' cribs. Some buildings have completely collapsed, others totter. All faced sparkling creek that divided disrepute and respectability.

PIONEER DAYS IN PIONEER

Pioneer, Montana

Take pity, Miss Fanny,
  The belle of Pioneer
And grant some indulgence
  To a vendor of beer
Whose heart rending anguish
  Will bring on decline
Oh, God of creation
  I wish you was mine.

The Pioneer bartender who prostrated himself before Fanny and heaven in these blood-letting lines inserted in the *Cedar Creek Pioneer* never got farther into the annals of this gold camp but it is hoped that with all this soul baring he won Fanny's fancy and did not have to turn the muzzles of too many beer mugs on himself.

Lack of female solace was no doubt a problem but the hard workers seem to rise above it. Like W. A. Clark who became a senator and power in Montana, and Mr. Bio on mining company boards. In later years he told how he got his start as a banker in the tiny gold camp of Pioneer. The banker's books were usually carried under his hat, he said, his vaults his buckskin bag of gold dust and a pair of six-shooters. The miner had hazy ideas about the value of gold. With an actual worth of $20 to $25 an ounce, he paid the miner a flat $18 and later sold it at a figure quoted by the Denver mint.

Prospectors who deserted Gold Creek for better pickings went up one creek and down another, pausing in such sparsely settled places as Squaw Gulch, French Gulch, Woods Flat and Wilson Bar. Pioneer was another and it grew to maybe two thousand people.

Henry Thomas was one of the displaced prospectors but not one to wash out a few pans of gravel and then head for the nearest saloon. He sank a shaft to reach bedrock and rigged up a windlass with bucket and sluice boxes. Without lumber or nails the resourceful loner hand-hewed boards from small trees, fastened them together with wooden pegs. The boards used for sluicing were about eight inches wide and seven feet long, necessitating a tremendous amount of labor before he could even begin mining.

Once ready to wash gravel Thomas let the crude bucket down into the hole, slid down the rope, filled the bucket with gravel and climbed out hand over hand, lifting the load by the windlass. Encountering boulders, he trussed them with ropes and used a crude block-and-tackle to get them out. Gravel was washed in the leaky sluice boxes where the riffles caught most of the gold, he hoped. After two seasons of this prodigious labor he found he averaged one dollar a day, never more than a dollar and a half. The same sort of set-up was frequently operated by partners so one man could stay in the hole, but Henry Thomas preferred his own company. Since he never drank or gambled he may have accumulated more gold dust than those who worked and wasted more efficiently.

Pioneer saw its best years in the 1870s, the main

PAT WALL'S DREDGE sits sadly at edge of pond of own making between Gold Creek and Pioneer. Almost any stranger encountered here will be either ghost town buff or ardent fisherman.

street parallel with the creek lined on both sides by cabins and business houses—two hotels, four general stores, blacksmith shops, livery stables, saloons and gambling houses. It was said that in the latter six faro games were kept running simultaneously.

The camp always had a large Chinese population. In 1879 there were 200 Orientals and 500 whites toiling in the gulches. When values began thinning, the latter gradually withdrew and a Chinese contractor named Tim Lee brought in 800 of his countrymen to comb the leavings. They did it the hard way, removing the impeding layer of rocks and carrying it away in baskets. After cleaning the exposed area, the rocks were replaced in order to open new beds. When even this painful process failed to yield a speck or two, the Chinese moved away and Pioneer was a near ghost.

PIONEER BUILDING shattered into rubble. The **Montana Standard** in 1929 predicted what would happen to the old ghost town of Pioneer with advent of Pat Wall's monster dredge. Referring to the several stone structures at lower edge of town, "The old post office will be converted into a bunk house. The bank will be a restaurant, the bank vaults a pantry, for the building of dressed stone is cool enough to keep food fresh without ice." These buildings, spared by dredge operations, stood intact long enough to be sketched by Colorado artist Muriel Wolle and photographed for dust jacket of **Shallow Diggings** by Jean Davis.

Intact in these pictures, the buildings were magnets for this author but in 1965 he found them in ruins. Inquiry of man working for modern concern again digging for gold at Pioneer City, brought explanation, "Our company would have saved the buildings but when money-mad county authorities found we were working here they slammed us with huge taxes for what they called usable buildings, so we deliberately wrecked them."

About 1893 an English firm called Gold Creek Mining Co. Ltd. moved in with a dredge to work the much hand-labored gravels and right away ran into trouble. A few remaining residents resented the big scale removal of gold and obstructed operations by damming the stream above the work field. Rather than force the issue, the company resorted to litigation that dragged on for years.

About 1927 a Butte promoter bought out the English firm which was thoroughly sick of the whole business. The new dredge owner, Pat Wall, now purchased the whole area—town, surrounding land, water rights—acquiring 3,200 acres of hills and gulches. He also bought a monster dredge costing $250,000 and required forty-two freight cars to bring it from California.

A newspaper of the day editorialized, "... with brick and stone and lumber will go apple trees and lilac bushes brought in on the backs of pack animals ... the entire town of Pioneer is about to be fed into the maw of a huge dredge." It almost was. The dredge ran alongside the town which was built on a bench and escaped actual engorgement, but the row of buildings nearest the mine workings was buried in a deep layer of rocky dumps, leaving a single row of now crumbling structures staring at a long ridge of barren rocks.

LOG HOUSE with large roof extension seems unfinished, no marks of usual roofing boards showing. Certainly style would have been practical in country of heavy snowfall, preventing blockage at entrance, usual result of overnight storms (see another view of street with dredge tailings in **Boot Hill**).

PONY, MONTANA

He was less than five feet tall, his accomplishments in proportion. Few people noticed him as he moved from creek to creek, panning enough gold to keep him in beans and get him to the next camp. In 1866 he was crowded out of Alder Gulch and Virginia City by bigger men and made his lonely way to the far-out edges of Tobacco Root Range.

Here in a small creek bed just below Old Hollow Top Mountain he found real gold, lots of dust and several nuggets. Seizing his long-sought chance to shout, he found a partner to help wash the gravels of his new claim. But steady work held few charms for the little fellow and he moved on to what he hoped would be even more glittering chances to shout.

He left very little of himself at the creek. The others who moved in to take advantage of the finds could not even remember his name. Was it Tecumseh Smith? One man was sure that was it. Another said, no, it was the other way around — Smith Tecumseh. Still another insisted it was not Tecumseh at all but McCumpsey. Then somebody remembered the little guy answered to "Pony" and that stuck. The diminutive wanderer, although vanished to other parts, left his nickname attached to a creek, a gulch and what would be a booming mining camp.

In a couple of years after Pony's finds, the gulch was full of men working the gravels with pans, rockers and cradles. Water was in short supply, turning into a muddy soup as it was used over and over again. Then about 1870 George Hadzor and J. C. Hawkins built a combination flume and ditch from neighboring Cataract Creek, bringing in so much water the placer beds were soon worked out.

Searching the hills for the lode which must have been the source of gold supply, George Moreland found the out-cropping in the middle of a patch of wild strawberries. He dug down about fourteen feet and there uncovered his bonanza, ore worth all the way from $20,000 to $100,000 a ton. The claim immediately below Moreland's Strawberry was full of chunks of rocks so thick with, gold it could be mashed out with a pestle.

The rush was quick to swell the population of Strawberry to several hundred and it soon had a post office, store and the usual jerry-built saloons. Moreland had acquired several good claims close by, one of them the Crevice, and close to the mine he built a mill which added to the prosperity of the little boom camp.

The town of Pony itself began to take solid form with the erection of a five-stamp mill which had been knocked down and moved from Sterling by the Mallory brothers in 1875. The little mill was soon swamped by rich ores being dug close by and was augmented by another five-stamper, this moved in from the failing Rising Mill in Norwegian Gulch. Reconstruction was hastily done during the winter, one of the Mallory brothers slipping on ice while carrying a timber and falling to his death.

By 1876 Pony had eclipsed the earlier camp of Strawberry which became merely a suburb, yet in taking two steps forward Pony went back one. The first boom was showing signs of fading when a new burst of activity came in '77, adding another 1,000 in population, several new buildings and a dwindling of ore reserves. Then newer discoveries around Phillipsburg caused a second relapse and Pony was down to a small handful again. Another few

2 PONY'S mines lay idle for many years before persistent hopes for reactivation died. Some remained on standby basis, ready to start at almost moment's notice, others, partly dismantled would need additional equipment.

years and some of the fresh discoveries proved to be bubbles and Pony's more modest diggins looked good once again. The Tobacco Root camp now settled down to its best years, producing steadily if not spectacularly. Such mines as the Boss Tweed, Clipper, Bell, Eclipse, Charity and Summit were turning out hundreds of thousands of dollars in gold ore to be crushed in the many mills around Pony.

A more conventional ghost has been reported seen by Mrs. Hill. She was walking near her home one moonlit night when she was alerted by the barking of her dogs. She saw the shadowy figure of a man walking slowly toward the Grant House, the one-time stage station. As the spectre approached the rear of the building, where legend says a treasure is buried, it vanished. Mrs. Hill found later that several people had reported the same visitation, in each case the ghost disappearing just as it reached the treasure site. Her research

also revealed a story that the supposed treasure had once inspired a Mexican to search the spot, having arrived in town with a map. He tried digging in the only place behind the old station which was not solid rock. At a depth of several feet he unearthed an ancient high-counter boot. He replaced the relic and fled the scene with no explanation. Residents at that time said a murdered witness had been buried along with the treasure.

And then there was the haunt that frequently visited the old spring flowing near the original stage station. This one gave off a "dancing light" and was an accustomed sight to townsmen. Then came the severe earthquake in the spring of 1887 when shifting of the earth's crust destroyed the flow of water in the spring. The water-loving phantom was never seen again but Shakespeare could easily spare a ghost or two and never miss them.

Business houses flourished during the decade. Paul Taft and Potter's Livery Stable, Isdell's and

438

Cramer's stores, Gilbert's Saloon —all doing well. It was said the swinging doors at Gilbert's never stopped flapping. One of Pony's merchants was the druggist, William H. Morris who, with Henry Elling, bought and operated the Boss Tweed-Clipper combination which produced $5 million. Morris had been a druggist in Virginia City before coming to Pony. While his new store there was being built the Vigilantes used an exposed beam to string up five of Henry Plummer's henchmen.

Several things happened in rapid succession at the turn of the century, events that seemed to be launching Pony into big time mining. The Boss Tweed, Clipper and other mines produced well through the '90s but were showing signs of failing in values of ore produced in 1900. That year Henry Elling died and partner Morris offered the property for sale. A Boston syndicate sent a team of mining experts to examine the properties. They went over the ground, descended shafts, pecked at ore dumps and estimated there was easily $10 million worth of ore in the combined mines.

The Eastern concern immediately clinched the deal and set about development in a big way. First it bought a hundred-stamp mill and set it up at Pony. It was operated by electricity, a modern innovation, and in connection were large cyanide tanks for ore reduction. Not until then was the undeniably large supply of ore sampled for values and availability — and found to be of low grade, suitable for roasting methods only. The Boston men folded their tents and stole away without ever stamping a ton of ore. Morris returned from California and took over the property again. He continued to put the ore through his old twenty-stamp mill, making a moderate profit in his remaining years. He died in 1904.

The sale of the mine properties to the eastern concern had the effect of stimulating interest in other mines in the area and for a time Pony enjoyed a period of prosperity not too badly affected by the cyanide plant fiasco. A brick school house costing $12,000 was built. An Episcopal Church was erected but services were spasmodic, the Reverend Lewis blaming the weather for scant attendance. A small Catholic edifice held Mass on special occasions. A Presbyterian church was built in 1894, finally becoming a community church.

In October of 1918, James L. Linn, now of Portland, moved to Pony. Although only thirteen years old at the time he has many memories of the camp. "I went there with my father, Leslie Linn, who worked for the Copeland Lumber Yard there. Mr. Copeland was a brother of J. W. Copeland who now has lumber yards scattered over the west, particularly in Nevada. There were still many signs of past mining around the town. In fact lots of the mill buildings and shaft houses looked as though they could start up again the next day. One big stamp mill had no machinery at all, just the huge 4½-foot fir blocks where the stamps could be set. Possibly it was just a big promotional hoax." (The author is almost certain these were the remains of the mill so hopefully built by the Boston syndicate in 1900).

"There were about 300 people in Pony at the time," says James Linn, "including a number of boys about my age. We used to make lots of short trips around the hills close to town, exploring the old mine shafts, a very dangerous business as I look back. But we learned a lot about mining. We hiked up toward Old Hollow Top Mountain and came to the old camp of Strawberry. It was completely abandoned and the old buildings falling down.

"We got one of the old timers to identify the mines for us. The Clipper was one of the largest and was still getting out gold." (The author concludes from a report of William Barnett, also now of Portland, manager of the Copeland yard after Linn, that the Clipper mine was in its last days of production, as he says all mines in Pony were closed in 1922). "Our guide told us the Boss Tweed mine had produced $2 million in the old days. He said it had the largest system of untimbered stopes in the world and added that they were perfectly safe, being cut out of solid granite."

"The town was still fairly active. The blacksmith shop still had a pile of coal beside the forge, ready to go, it seemed. The old bunkhouse was still well stocked with food that would keep, like canned goods, and the kitchen was still equipped with cooking utensils. The old bank built by Mr. Morris was run by a Mr. Smith, who kept his big Kissel Car parked out in front all the time. We were told he would be glad to keep your money safe, but wouldn't pay you any interest.

"He took us to what used to be one of the saloons. It had a board walk in front, full of cracks between the boards. He said that when the town was in its prime a bunch of miners would gather there and take turns pitching twenty dollar gold pieces at a certain crack, not as wide then as now. When one man's lucky throw placed the gold piece exactly centered on the line, he took the whole pot."

LATE AFTERNOON SUN leaves fronts of old Rimini buildings in shadow. Famous for gold, much silver and lead has also come from mountain towering above town.

RIMINI, MONTANA

The gravel road leading to Rimini from the highway is amazingly level, of the easiest grades and curves. The mystery of this unusual approach to a mountain town is explained by the two Scott brothers who have lived there since 1896. The Northern Pacific had a railroad in Rimini already when Jim Hill got the idea he would run his line in too. He had already graded the whole right of way when he ran into so much trouble with the other line he gave up.

The townspeople built a dam above the town to have a water supply and one night the dam broke. A wall of water came rushing down the canyon. There was only one cabin in its path and it was demolished. Fortunately, the owner was suffering from dysentery and had gone to the backhouse on the side of the hill and so his life was spared.

Rimini now is a true Ghost Town along its main street fronted by a line of false-fronted buildings, all abandoned. There are a few houses on the next street to the west, some of which have the usual quota of summer residents. A very few, including the Scott brothers, are permanent.

RUBY GULCH, MONTANA

Because Ben Phillips was a man of integrity and courage, he buried his two companions killed by the Indians at the risk of his own life. Because his life was spared he sent a letter to the parents of the slain men in England. Because these English people were grateful to Ben for his humane efforts they sent him a check for $2,000 . . . and this tidy sum was the nucleus of the fortune Phillips later made.

The Indian raid took place in the Ruby Gulch area of the Bear Paw Mountains west of the Little Rockies where Phillips and his two partners were prospecting — the same country covered earlier by Tom Carter and John Throop — immediately above the town of Zortman.

With his $2,000 Ben D. Phillips joined forces with Charles Whitcomb and others to buy the August mine at Zortman and the Ruby Gulch mine. Whitcomb's stake was prize money for winning a foot race. The others were Louis Goslin, Coburn brothers, Marlow and Smith, Helena bankers. Whitcomb also developed the Beaver Creek mine farther up the canyon from the Ruby Gulch property and this would become the third largest in the Little Rockies group.

The Ruby Gulch property had a lead 600 feet long, 75 to 127 feet wide, the deposit high on an almost inaccessible shoulder of rocky ground. Finding the vein all but impossible to mine by con-

ORE LADEN CARS emerged from mouth of tunnel to be towed over narrow tracks to mill about ¼ mile distant, route covered by snow sheds. Ruby Gulch is on private, posted property and watchman living in cottage just inside gate graciously gave author permission to explore and photograph relics.

ventional methods, the owners decided on a combination "glory hole" and tunnel method. The vein was exposed in an open pit, ore removed from the side through a tunnel. By this time electricity was available and the haulage tunnel was equipped with electric locomotive trolley line haulage systems.

A typical month saw 19,000 tons of ore mined and milled. Costs were $1.05 per ton, leaving a profit of $15,000 a month and each month seeing dividends paid to stockholders. During the period the last mill operated, prior to its destruction by fire, 1,000,500 tons of ore were put through it, yielding dividends of 1 million paid to Phillips, Whitcomb and a few minor stockholders. During the early 1920s when labor, machinery and material costs began to skyrocket, the mines and mills were shut down. During this period the mill burned to the ground and Phillips died.

His interests then were sold to St. Paul capitalists, who though wealthy, seemed to take no interest in further development of the mine or granting options to men who were interested, at what they thought were reasonable figures. Then Mose Zimmerman, main stockholder in St. Paul died, leaving the First National Bank and Trust Co. as executor. The bank proved slightly easier to deal with and after three months of negotiations, in December 1934, Carl J. Trauerman, Butte mining engineer, obtained an 18-month option on the mine. He wrote: "High grade ore was opened north of the main Ruby glory hole and additional claims taken up. This high grade ore came from a new and unexpected source. The first car contained 16½ tons of clayey gangue, containing more than 20% moisture. This clay contained manganese oxide, fluorite of a purplish color and gold telluride. The 16½ tons gave net smelter returns of $10,183. Further cars of rich ore were shipped and are still being shipped, and a rich body of ore was opened up in the Alabama claim."

The 18-month option was exercised and paid for in five months and in June Trauerman was elected president of the company. In September of 1935 Whitcomb purchased sufficient stock to bring the Whitcomb-Trauerman interests to 98%. A new

tunnel 400 feet long was being driven to tap high grade ore at a depth of 160 feet. The Ruby Gulch Co. was completing a new mill of 300-ton daily capacity with plans to enlarge to 1,000 tons daily. During this optimistic period Trauerman wrote further: "The company has indicated at least 10 million tons and probably closer to 15 million tons of milling ore that should net a profit of better than $1.00 per ton at the present price of gold".

The following summer a disastrous fire started near Landusky, spreading across the mountains and almost consuming the town. The blaze was started by a cigarette-smoking miner who fell asleep in bed. Since there was no phone at Zortman, a fire guard named Otis Pewitt, who had already been on duty twenty-four hours, drove to Harlem, forty-five miles, to get help for the three hundred Indian fire fighters. When the new group arrived it was trapped in a gully when the fire crowned in the tree tops and created a vacuum at the ground. Near suffocation, the men found a cave but only nine men could crowd into it. Left outside were Dr. S. H. Brockunier, Cameron Baker, John Rowles and Pewitt. When a down draught of super-heated air struck the group all but Pewitt were incinerated. His clothes were burned from him and all skin but the soles of his feet scorched. He later died of cancer, attributed to smoke and heat damage to throat and lungs. The fire started July 25 and burning through 23,000 acres of lodgepole pines, was finally controlled on July 27.

Trauerman's predictions of a permanently rosy future for his mines and the camp of Ruby Gulch were never to come true for 1942 brought the U.S. Government order L.208 which forced all gold

ABANDONED ORE CARS, scattered in disarray on spur of tiny rail line, were towed by mules in early days to machine shops (left) for servicing, in more recent times by small electric locomotives, power coming from coal and water plants below near Zortman.

mines to close. The order was catastrophic for such one-industry towns as Landusky, Zortman and Ruby Gulch. With the closure of the mines inhabitants gradually drifted away to other jobs even to the coastal shipyards, the gold camps soon attaining ghost town status. The mines and mills of Ruby Gulch are guarded by a watchman who says the whole setup could begin operation in two weeks if the price of gold would advance enough to make it pay.

OVERALL VIEW OF RUBY GULCH taken from near mill. Spaces between buildings were once filled with stores, houses. Abandoned schoolhouse stands near exact center of picture. At extreme upper left is "glory hole" from which ore was drained out at bottom through long horizontal tunnel opening at left, behind trees. Here also were located mine offices, blacksmith and machine shops, most still standing in fair condition since mine operated until 1942.

Inquiring at Zortman about road up Ruby Gulch, author was told: "Very simple. You just drive down that dirt road there until you reach the gulch which is filled with tailings. Drive out on them and head up the canyon until you see a gap in the trees. Go through that and you'll pick up the road again. It's steep and rough but I think you can make it." Road levels off just below town, is here seen entering at lower right.

THE LAND OF GOLDEN GHOSTS

SOUTHERN CROSS, MONTANA

High on the shoulder of Iron Mountain is the ghostly gold camp called Southern Cross. The name is unique among the old mining towns; surely some sailor, back from sea, must have bestowed the starry title.

It was lively enough in the days when Tillie Riemenschnieder and her husband, Albert, lived nearby. Tillie lives quietly now in Portland, Ore., but remembers vividly those booming times when gold was pouring out of the shafts and tunnels, and the big boarding-house in the center of town was the scene of wild revelry on Saturday nights.

Tillie lived five miles up the canyon formed between Cable and Rumsey mountains. She and Albert occupied a comfortable five-room log house, and if enough cases of food had been stored, they spent the winters in near isolation there. If supplies ran low, Albert donned his six-foot snowshoes and went down to Southern Cross for more.

The train from Anaconda came only halfway in winter and then just once a week. At the end of the line it was met by a large horse-drawn sleigh. This had a covered cab equipped with a little stove. The passengers huddled around this tiny warmth in heavy fur coats, trying to be comfortable in temperatures often 30 degrees below. Winter lasted from October to June, with very heavy snowfalls.

Now the town is reduced to the boardinghouse, the mill and a block of "main street." A large fallen pine blocks the door to the old Post Office, but no one looks for mail, anyway.

STAIRS LEADING NO-WHERE and little false front are part of remains of "Southern Cross."

VIRGINIA CITY, MONTANA

The date was May 26, the year 1863. It was about four o'clock in the afternoon. Bill Fairweather had been "elected" the leader of the group of six miners searching for gold. Bill was young, husky and had "a good personality." He had no trouble giving orders, and now he gave one that made history. "There's a piece of bedrock projecting and we had better go over and see if we can't get enough money to buy a little tobacco." He dug enough dirt to fill a pan, sending Henry Edgar to the stream to wash it out. The spade work done, he poked around some more with a butcher knife and found color enough to make him shout, *"I've found a scad!"*

Henry's pan was only half empty but it was already obvious that he, also, had a bonanza. The group feverishly finished washing it and two others before it got dark. The three pans of gravel produced twelve dollars worth of gold.

VIRGINIA CITY HAS plenty of atmosphere provided by original buildings.

Next day the six panned out $180 and on the next staked out their claim. Then they went to Bannack for supplies. The prospectors fully intended to keep their discovery a deep secret, but the find must have been written all over their faces. Everyone was their bosom friend! They, followed by a cavalcade, started back to the diggin's June 2 and arrived June 6. They named the place "Alder Creek" because of a group of those trees on the bank of the gulch.

The village which sprang up in true early-day, boom-town style was first called "Varina" and then, legally "Virginia."

When millions in gold began to pour out of the gulch, the only road to ship it over was the one to Bannack, infested by Plummer's gang of brigands. It was the robbery and killing of Nicholas Thiebalt for $200 that lit the fuse under the seething townsmen. For this crime, George Ives was strung up. His neck was replaced in the noose by that of another and another until most of the outlaws at the Virginia end were disposed of. Others were hung at Laurin and Bannack, the latter seeing the end of Plummer himself.

The Vigilantes had done a good job, but were "carried away" by their successes and later went too far with their summary carrying out of "Justice" and fell into disrepute.

After this, Virginia led a more peaceful existence with only a few killings, these mostly having been committed in the heat of anger or in self-defense and therefore "excusable."

The town never died entirely, and now likely never will, it having become a tourist attraction.

WHILE THE BUILDING WAS yet unfinished, part of Plummer's notorious crew was hanged from exposed beam.

THIS COULD BE one of the stages harassed by Plummer gang on road between Virginia City and Bannack.

LEFT IS THE livery stable and right the meat market.

WICKES, MONTANA

Here is a town that has had more than its share of disastrous fires having been all but wiped out in the holocaust years of 1901, 1906, and 1910.

The town is picturesque enough in its little group of remaining buildings, but its main interest lies in the ruins of the huge smelters and refineries, the domed coke ovens and piles of cannonball-like grinder used in the ore-pulverizing process.

These operations turned out $50,000,000 in silver and gold. The nearby Alta Mine produced $32,000,000 in silver and gold. The Gregory, with a record of $9,000,000, is in the neighborhood, as are the Nina and Bertha. The early 1890's saw the end of almost all operations.

ZORTMAN, MONTANA

Well documented is the story of Bill Hamilton, noted frontiersman, and his party which found gold in the Little Rockies in the late '60s. One of the men, William Bent, left a written record: "In the fall of 1868 they began hiring men at Fort Benton to build Fort Browning on People's Creek in the Milk River country. This was about the fourth of August. After the fort was finished there were too many men and we were told to look out for ourselves. Bill Hamilton, one of the men said 'Boys, suppose we go into the Little Rockies and hunt for gold.' Bill would not work at the fort, as he would not work at anything like that. He was trapping and hunting most of the time. We formed a party with Bill as the leader. Bill, Joe Wye, Fred Merchant, John Thomas, myself and three other men made up the party. This was in the fall of 1868.

"We went around on the east end of the mountains and prospected Dry Beaver. We found gold, but not in paying quantities, and that was, to my knowledge, the first gold found in the Little Rockies."

"I heard once, through a man named Grinnel, that some men who had been mining in the west, went east, and on their return got off the boat and went into the Little Rockies and were never heard of afterwards. Grinnel later was killed by the Indians.

"We kept on prospecting but the ground froze up on us in the fall of '68 before we could do very much, and we threw everything in the mining line away. Bill Hamilton was not very religious, and when the ground froze up he cussed like I never heard a man cuss before. We killed some elk and packed the skins to Fort Benton. I stayed there and took some supplies back for wolfing on the Milk river. All of us who had been in the Little Rockies, excepting Joe Wye who wouldn't come, went on the wolfing party on the upper Milk river into the Piegan country."

After this there is a long gap in the records until those of the big finds of 1884 that brought 2,000 men into the district. Later, old Billy Skillen the "Sage of Fort Belknap," told that story. "On the third of July, 1884, Bill McKinzie stole 'Spud' Murphy's horse down on the Missouri river and started for Fort McGinnis, 65 miles away. Lee Scott, at Rocky Point, started to look for McKinzie and the blue mare he had stolen. The report of the theft

got to the cowboys, and they got McKinzie close to McGinnis, shot him and hung him up on a big cottonwood tree about a mile and a half below the fort on Hancock Creek.

"About July fourth there happened to be some trouble between a white man and a breed at the races over some betting. The white man's name was Rattlesnake. He knocked the breed down, made him apologize and give back the money he had taken. Then the two rode to Reed's Fort in the Judith, or Lewistown, went into the saloon to get a drink, first tying their horses to the rack outside. When they came outside, the citizens thinking they were a tough outfit, which they were, opened fire on them. Rattlesnake and one bystander was killed. From this time on, the 'strangling' of horse thieves and road agents started through northern Montana and the Missouri river country.

"At this time Dutch Louie ran a ranch on Crooked Creek where these toughs would stop, going from the Missouri River and back and forth. Suspicion fell on Louie and the 'stranglers' as the vigilantes were called, got after him. So he went into the Little Rockies with Frank Aldrich and Pike Landusky. They prospected for gold and found

TYPICAL OF OLD BUILDINGS remaining in Zortman is this cabin, occupied until recently. Hardy hollyhocks persist in blooming unattended, year after year. Members of mallow family, these durable plants have such unlikely relatives as Rose of Sharon, cotton and exotic, tropical hibiscus.

some in a creek which they named Alder . . . . Frank Aldrich, who was with Pike Landusky and Dutch Louie when gold was discovered, says they were not the first to discover gold in the Little Rockies, as near the mouth of the gulch where they were working was a pit 100 feet long, by 150 feet wide, that had evidently been sluiced out years before. This discovery was made on Beauchamp's creek.

"Quartz was soon found and then quartz mining began to take the attention of the miners. Soon large mills were reducing the ore, but little real headway was made until the new process was developed for the reduction by cyanide. That was when real wealth began to pour out of the Little Rockies. Thus it was through the fact Dutch Louie was hiding out from the vigilantes that the wealth of the Little Rockies was discovered."

Pete Zortman entered the picture in the 1890s when he located a rich claim on the eastern side of the Little Rockies, the lode that was to become the famous Alabama mine. Doubt is cast on Zortman's making the discovery in an item in the LITTLE ROCKIES MINER of July 4, 1907: "The Alabama was sold by the original locator for $40 to Spaulding, who later interested Pete Zortman and Putnam,

both of Chinook. They did development work and got some ore yielding as high as $2,800 a ton at the Great Falls smelter and one lot of 1,600 pounds returned $6,000."

Yet facts do show Zortman and George P. Putnam owning the mine in 1893 and that the two brought in promoter E. W. King of Barnes-King Co. and Kendall to aid them in forming the Alder Gulch Mining Co. By the turn of the century the rapidly expanding firm was operating the Pole Gulch complex of mines above the now booming town of Zortman. Many improvements followed rapidly. One of them, a 100-ton cyanide mill, built on the only available level ground, proved to be too remote from the mines and hauling expenses forced its closure after a few seasons.

1906 saw the organization of a new concern, The Little Rockies Exploration Co. which took over the defunct mines and mill. The new operators solved the haulage problem by installing an elaborate aerial tramway connecting the mill to the Alabama mine. The town of Zortman then began a lengthy period of prosperity which was increased and extended by the development of still richer mines in Ruby Gulch above Zortman.

SPACES BETWEEN BUILDINGS in Zortman are now wide, many having burned or fallen down. Little church on hill has been kept in repair, services held periodically. Zortman lies at abrupt edge of eastern Little Rockies, outcroppings beyond church rising sharply from level foreground. Zortman and its mines had abundant electricity after pioneer period, power plant burning 70 tons of coal every 24 hours. Current was supplemented by wheel generator operated by water from hot springs near Morrison Butte.

BAY HORSE, IDAHO

If Leesburg had been able to satisfy all who came looking for riches, Bay Horse might well have been a horse of a different color or not in the running at all. As it was, Leesburg had a disappointed overflow in the early 1870s, a few of whom went sifting the bottoms of Bay Horse Creek flowing into the Salmon River, the "River Of No Return", and they found a little gold.

Hopes for another booming gold camp faded out quickly with the realization that the gold was fading too, and Bay Horse was almost a ghost before it had a body to emerge from. But there in some heavy iron ore deposits was a rich vein of silver, life and hopes springing up anew. Not so glamorous as gold but solid wealth just the same.

How to get capital to get the silver out of the rock, to build mills and smelters? It was going to be a hard job. There were no roads in the area, all hauling of machinery and supplies would have to be done by mule train. But in '79 a toll road was started, coming from Challis and reaching to Bonanza. It was completed in '81, with a spur to Salmon due to the prosperity of Leesburg, and the way was open for big-scale silver mining at Bay Horse.

The first extraction was readily achieved, the white metal being largely "free," pure veins of it running through the ore, a quantity of valuable lead saved the same time. However, to the grief of miners and investors, the silver was more finely divided as the vein grew deeper, the iron ore containing it more refractory—the Bay Horse's easy wealth was little more than a dream.

Its best years were in the '80s and '90s but the mines continued to operate in a desultory fashion until 1915 when the whole town shut down and almost everybody moved away. In 1920 there was a brief revival when a optimistic mining concern thought it had the answer to hard-to-get silver. Rising costs and stable income from silver soon defeated this effort and Bay Horse

ROW OF CHARCOAL OVENS once had seven units, five now more or less intact. Beehive-like structures were used to make charcoal for fuel in large smelter which extracted pure silver and lead from ores mined at Bay Horse. Surrounding hills, once covered with virgin timber were denuded for wood to supply ovens, are now sparsely covered again with second growth trees. Stray cattle use ovens for shelter in severe winter storms and for shade on hot days.

DOOR OF STORAGE HOUSE for blasting powder s h o w s weathering of s e v e n t y years, square heads of hand-forged nails and bolts.

was scratched again, this time to stay out. One man lives there now, making visitors welcome after venturing up the steep road but is "scared to death" when some of them climb over the ruins or scale the coke ovens all of which are ready to crumble at any moment.

There is a tiny cemetery just below the Bay Horse remains. Twenty years ago there were still a few headboards standing there. Those bearing distinguishable markings spelled out sad tales of soldiers killed in battle with Indians. It is a one-sided story, there being no record there of the banishing of the natives from their hunting grounds, their homes and burial places. The markers showing where their attackers died have

gone to dust, and fading are the memories of the original inhabitants.

Most of the vanished dates on those headboards were in the 1860s, the period of the Indian trouble. Another cemetery just above the town and somewhat better preserved, contains some legible markers. These show dates beginning in the early '80s when the mining town was getting started and the first fatalities took place. Natural deaths were few, most resulting from accidents in the mines and violence. The miners spent few evenings pursuing culture, doing their relaxing in the several drinking emporiums on both sides of the one steeply-sloping street. Arguments often started spontaneously and ended with gunfire.

451

Sometimes these affairs had the comic side. One tale concerns a quarrel between Bill Smith, one of the founders of Leesburg, and a Jim Hayden which took place at a nearby camp. The men had been drinking for some hours when hostilities broke out over some trifle. Flaming mad, Smith drew his gun, a "short-barreled pocket pistol," and fired several shots at Hayden. The aim was good but the victim did not crumple. It seems Hayden was wearing a pair of common-type pants made of heavy wool and thickly "foxed" with several layers of buckskin.

PRESENT DAY SCENE ON MAIN STREET of Bay Horse is peaceful, contrasting with boisterous days when silver mining was big industry. Saloons and boarding houses for single miners and smelter workers filled gaps between existing buildings. Tall, false-front structure had pool hall and saloon on ground floor, rooms for rent upstairs. Another saloon and store stood next, then stone shell standing. It was used for many purposes at different times including newspaper office and post office. Although appearing solid in front, it is in state of collapse in rear. Further on were more business houses and across from these at right stood a large pretentious structure described as a "girlie house."

MAIN ENTRANCE of Jaggers Hotel. "Jaggers Annex" at right sported elaborate bar, gambling equipment on main floor, rooms upstairs. Entrance to annex was through vestibule serving in winter as "air lock" against sub-zero blasts.

TWIN TOWNS IN TORMENT

Custer and Bonanza, Idaho

Nobody cared who she was or where she came from as long as she was free and easy and kept her luxurious head of auburn hair, symbol of light and life in Bonanza. And that hair was about all she did keep on her downhill skid to the last ditch. Call her Amanda and if you don't have money just show her a bottle.

* * *

Trappers searching for pelts along the Yankee Fork of the Salmon River often saw gold gleaming in the creek sands. But they were fur hunters and merely reported matters at the supply settlements on the Salmon. In the spring of 1873 such rumors reached prospector John G. Morrison and set his ears tingling.

He packed into the area described and did find gold but returned to the settlements to hire forty-five men, the entire party being in the gold field before snow fell in the fall. The men immediately began drifting shafts to bedrock, taking advantage of the frozen ground that helped keep earthen walls from collapsing. The tools they had were fine for mining but not for building cabins, so in primitive brush shelters at an elevation of well over 6,000 feet, Morrison's men endured a winter in heavy snows and temperatures probably down to 30 below.

The next summer's operations were profitable and other prospectors swarmed in, some finding little gold, more going away disappointed. The next year William Norton from Michigan made a rich strike but it seemed to be limited to the immediate locality. He removed considerable good ore but had no mechanical way of getting the gold out of it since the area was available only by pack horse. He selected the best of it and in a crude mortar crushed it with a homemade pestle, washing the dust in a conventional pan.

At work one day Morrison was accosted by prospector John Rohrer and over a cup of coffee the two became partners, a safety arrangement in a primitive wilderness where an injured man could die alone. Now one man would dig and select the ore while the other pounded and panned it, the pair recovering in one thirteen-day period $11,000.

The year of truth for the Yankee Fork was 1876 when in August a party of three—James Baxter, E. K. Dodge and Morton McKeim—found some good float not far from where Morrison and Rohrer

were working. Content with what he had, Morrison indicated a ledge as being the likely source of the newcomers' samples and there on the 17th was found the mother lode of Yankee Fork.

In that year it was logical the discoverers name the location Custer Mountain and their workings the General Custer Mine. They set up a simple arrastra, crushed some ore and even this crude operation revealed riches to stagger the three men. They realized they had something that would require development far beyond their financial limits and agreed the best course was to sell out to the English-based firm of Hagan and Grayson. Sale price was not released but a much smaller discovery made the same year was sold to this company for $20,000.

By the summer of 1878 the town of Bonanza was started by Charles Franklin (see *Tales the*

SIDE STREET in Gilmore slopes steeply down to residential section. View looks east over valley of south-flowing Birch Creek at point just south of divide from north-flowing Lemhi River, north of scene of Birch Creek Massacre (see Boot Hill). Black cloud here produces dark shadow on foothills in middle distance. Mountains in background are of Bitterroot Range, here forming Continental Divide and boundary between Idaho and Montana. On other side lie Bannack, Virginia City, other famous early mining camps.

Western Tombstones Tell), reputed to hail from Bodie, California. With Morrison and other early settlers, Franklin selected the townsite at a point near where Jordan Creek joined Yankee Fork and platted the township, measuring out lots to sell from $40 to $300.

Among the first crude log structures was a large one intended to be a saloon. With walls up and roof of shakes it was warmed by a big dance, remarkable in that the camp had no women. Yet one man who had experience in other camps was equal to the occasion. The men were divided in halves, each on one side having a red bandana tied around his arm to make him a pro tem woman. Any deficiencies caused by such man-to-man combat on the dance floor were overcome after a few snorts of stingo from the bar. With music from

INSIDE WALLS of old railroad buildings at Gimlet are decorated with "art" clipped from mail order catalogs, magazines.

ABANDONED STATION identifies location of once busy siding. Grassy tracks, rusty rails attest to infrequency of traffic now. Modern highway to Sun Valley, summit of Sawtooth Mountains and head of Salmon River Valley, passes in left background.

banjo and harmonica, Bonanza's first dance lasted till dawn with little mining or building done the next day.

But ere long, the camp did have a woman. When she arrived in 1879 the men had little curiosity about her other than to ask her name and she told them simply, Amanda. But later arrivals learned she was born in Council Bluffs, Iowa, was educated in a convent school up to the age of 8 then very quickly began learning the facts of life.

The turbulent years of gold and silver strikes in the Sawtooth Mountains saw Amanda working in a bordello in Vienna. A tendency to shack up with one or the other of her favorite customers cost her the job and she moved to Sawtooth City only to have this happen again. She was welcomed in Bonanza, then called Bonanza City, and settled herself in a small cabin at the lower edge of town where she carried on a brisk trade.

She proved to have some knowledge of medicine and nursing and in this camp without doctor or hospital she made herself a soiled angel of mercy. A sick or injured miner might suddenly find Amanda spooning out calomel or scrubbing out his cabin. If a prospector or trapper lay ill in some mountain shack Amanda went to him on her horse, medicine bags tied to her saddle, and staying until the man recovered and longer if both were willing and able.

Added to men, Amanda had a weakness for the bottle. She began going on benders that would last for days and in a few years she was spending the night with any man who asked her, and not often being paid for it. One of her most constant friends now was prospector John Bee who had a cabin on the creek bank.

John was a familiar figure in his favorite saloon where he drank and played poker late into the night. More and more often Amanda would be with him, drinking with him and then sleeping by him on her arm. When he lost all his money one night to another prospector, known ambigu-

SMALL CABIN in good condition owes preservation to cedar boards on roof being almost indestructible.

ORIGINAL BUILDING at Bonanza, built of logs as were most others there, shows excellent craftsmanship, careful fitting of corners. Note marks of broadaxe used in hewing and flattening sides of logs. Chinks were filled with clay and moss, sometimes mixed together. Wooden sidewalks were installed when sawmills appeared. On shelf behind cabins is Bonanza City Branch of U.S. Forest Service, only human habitation in once thriving town. Nearby was large C.C.C. camp in 1935.

ously as Pete, he put Amanda up on what he thought was an unbeatable hand. But Pete showed a better one, bought a bottle of whiskey, toted the sleeping girl to his own cabin.

It was just across the creek from John Bee's and all the next day that worthy moaned and mooned and eyed Pete's cabin. In the morning John crossed the creek, loaded the still sleeping Amanda in Pete's wheelbarrow and trundled her home. He left her only to get a bucket of water but Pete was waiting. He had followed the wheelbarrow tracks and caught Pete with a rifle bullet which struck the boulder he dodged behind. When the second came closer he surrendered—both himself and the girl. So Amanda had her second wheelbarrow ride that day.

In the following years Amanda drifted from one camp to another, moving in all directions including downward. She reached the bottom at Challis

where she was admitted to the Custer County Poorhouse infirmary. When she died at about 60 she appeared as an old woman in every way except for her still luxurious reddish brown hair. Amanda, whose surname was never discovered, was buried in an unmarked pauper's grave at Challis.

Bonanza lay south of the General Custer mine and when the huge mill of the same name was built a short distance north, it made necessary another business and residence center which became Custer. By this time several sawmills were operating and new buildings could be built of lumber. As the population of the new town increased the post office was moved there.

The building program included a road to the outside, actually a trail wide enough to allow passage of wagons pulled by ox teams. The route wound over the high mountains to Challis, the grades so steep heavily loaded wagons were often

457

snubbed down with ropes looped around trees. It took teamsters five days to make the thirty-five miles and they paid a toll of five cents per pound of freight. All heavy mining and milling machinery had to be hauled in, adding much to an already expensive operation.

In these days most travelers rode horseback and when stages were put into service they, with teamsters, drivers, stage passengers had plenty of opportunity to drink, eat and sleep at numerous way stations. One hostelry, called Homestead Station, was located just below Mill Creek Summit, 9324 feet in elevation. Then there were Toll Gate, Slab Barn and Eleven Mile Barn. One enterprising young lady named Fanny Clark had accommodations in a deep hollow and it was called Fanny's Hole. Later she opened another higher up the mountain and this was christened Fanny's Upper Hole.

The toll road made great changes in Bonanza and Custer. Married women joined their husbands and curtains went up on the windows. Doctors, lawyers and other professional men came in. In her definitive book *Land of the Yankee Fork* Esther Yarber points up many of the characters living there. One was French Godfrey Poquette De Lavallie who was obsessed with plans for the invention of a machine that once set in motion would run forever by its own centrifugal force. He spent most of his life building such gadgets as a large wheel with pockets into which he dropped lead castings of varied weights. When the wheel stopped turning he would sigh and try again. He lived to an old age still trying to perfect his perpetual motion machine.

Early camp life called for talent and ingenuity and one who displayed them dramatically was Col. James McFadden, blacksmith. Finding himself toothless and unable to eat bear steak, so plentiful in the area, he made himself a set of "choppers" said to be as efficient as ones a dentist would turn out. He made the impressions in soft

FIRST BUILDING constructed in Bonanza after sawmill made lumber available.

LONG DEFUNCT GARAGE, originally store building, is well constructed of squared logs.

native clay and eventually hammered out a set of steel teeth complete with a hinge.

While major mine properties were controlled by the English concern all gold produced was shipped to England via railhead at Blackfoot. Shipments were moderate until the General Custer mill opened when large amounts of gold bullion with lesser amounts of silver went by Wells Fargo, one parcel valued at well over $1 million.

By 1890 the twin cities became one, virtually operated by common officials. One business between the two was the small dairy, the cows almost curiosities. Milk was hauled in a large can on a hand cart, the farmer making his rounds of households, dipping out a quart to anybody responding to his bell with a lard bucket.

Before the turn of the century mines in Yankee Fork and other areas had passed into local or at least U.S. ownership. Towns had been through a depression caused by a slump in quality and quan-

tity of ores, and a second boom when rich material was again found. But in 1903 miners generally admitted the end was in sight. There was plenty of gold still in the mountain, they said, but it would take a fortune to drill the tunnels and shafts to reach it. In 1905 extensive plans for such rejuvenation were made in hopes financing would somehow be found and while diligent promoters were scouring the East for money, the Yankee Fork people lived in some sort of suspended vacuum. At first only the easily discouraged moved away but almost all the others, with nothing to live on, were eventually forced to leave.

By 1910 the population was down to a dozen diehards, one family that of Arthur Leslie McGown whose Deardon and McGown store supplied several mines still being worked. The old pioneer hotel, Nevada House, took in an occasional guest until there were none—and no life in the old carcass.

Idaho

NO PLYMOUTH ROCK FOR SEA CAPTAIN JOE

De Lamar, Idaho

Sailing ship skippers who "swallowed the anchor" and quit the sea were said to be fond of settling down to raising Plymouth Rocks instead of keeping ships clear of them. But Joseph R. De Lamar was one sea captain with a mind for mines.

The camp he built up and named for himself was compressed by Idaho's Owyhee Mountains into a narrow gulch and settled by prospectors on the track of nuggets from the "lost" Blue Bucket Mine. The tales of that 1845 incident of children in the Meek overland party finding nuggets in a stream and carrying them along in a blue bucket which disappeared into legend, spread over the West for a time and then died down. Fifteen years later they sprang up again, fortune seekers still hopeful, perhaps of finding the chunk of gold which was said to serve somewhere as a doorstop.

Some searching parties did find rich gold deposits as in Canyon City, Oregon, and these spurred on others. Rumors of rich finds in the comparatively remote Boise Basin of Idaho sparked prospectors

WITHIN SIGHT of old Tendoy store are several log cabins in various stages of decay. This one, long unoccupied, is still in fair condition. Narrow valley where Tendoy is situated lies enclosed by parallel Beaverhead and Lemhi Ranges. Beaverhead forms Continental Divide and at this point boundary between Idaho and Montana. Lesser Lemhi Range seen here in background exhibits characteristic lack of verdure on east-facing slope, most rainfall being trapped on side catching ocean-born moisture. Famed Salmon River flows on other side of Lemhi.

to take loosely organized parties into the Owyhees. One fanciful story combined the Blue Bucket tale with one of nuggets found in an Owyhee stream and Michael Jordan of Placerville pulled together a group to go look for more. In 1863 the men crossed the spring-swollen Snake River, got over the divide and down to a stream later called the Jordan.

Although intending to camp here overnight several of the more impatient removed only the gold pans from the pack horses and got to work in the gravel at once. In an account later written by member O. H. Purdy, Dr. Rudd "had about a hundred colors" in the dregs of his first panning. "The men were jubilant and excited. They ran from one to another exhibiting their discoveries."

This news spread quickly, sending an estimated 2500 men to the Owyhees. That first camp on the Jordan, called Booneville and later Dewey, was soon surrounded by Silver City, Ruby, De Lamar and others (see *Western Ghost Towns*). Although placer gold was quickly exhausted, tremendous deposits of silver kept up the flow of wealth and activity.

The camp of Wagontown was a stopping place on the stage line between Silver City and Jordan Valley, Oregon, and above it were numerous mines and claims. Here in 1888 appeared Capt. Joseph R. De Lamar who bought scattered properties to form one large mining district named for himself. He immediately expanded the cooperating mines, activated dormant claims and set about developing a town in the narrow Jordan Canyon. De Lamar necessarily grew up as a "string town," two rows of buildings wide, about two miles long.

Having spent some $10,000 for his Wilson and adjacent mines, Capt. De Lamar poured an equal fortune into the building of a mill, large hotel, stores and other town essentials, including red light houses at the lower end, almost joining with the original Wagontown. Naturally called Toughtown, there was nothing shoddy about its facilities, the captain providing the best to attract top talent girls from Hailey, an older town going down hill. One of the madames so lured was Jeannie Mitchel and an oldtimer now living in nearby Jordan Valley, Oregon, fondly recollects, "Jeannie's was the best house they ever had in Toughtown."

Jordan Creek, running the length of De Lamar, was a sparkling clear mountain stream before mining in the Owyhees. Then loaded with mill and outhouse wastes in running through Silver City, it became an open sewer when reaching De Lamar. And there, with a long line of outdoor toilets suspended above the creek, it was something more than turbid.

In 1891 De Lamar's newspaper, the *Nugget* reprinted a news item from Chicago stating that a man from Idaho had deposited a check for $463,000 in a La Salle Street bank, the check accepted without question. The local paper added the comment, "As neither of the editors of this paper has been

LEADORE was early center for mining operations in Lemhi Valley and source of supplies for remotely situated farmers and ranchers. Section pictured was center of town. Small false-fronted structure in center advertising its goods and services, one item remaining legible—"Farmers Telephone Exchange."
Leadore once made national headlines when stagecoach was held up on Gilmore Divide just south of town. Road agents took $37,000, barricaded themselves in cliffs above Hahn's Smelter. Infuriated miners who shipped gold stolen smoked bandits out and killed them. Loot was never located, is presumed still hidden in rocky fastness.

DE LAMAR SCHOOL is imposing even now. Second floor was reached by outside stairways, one at each end. At left in rear are seen pair of privies so situated as to drop wastes directly into Jordan Creek.

in Chicago recently and Captain De Lamar has, our readers may readily guess who deposited the check."

Unquestionably the captain was doing well financially. At a time when his mines were producing half a million dollars worth of bullion a month he sold out to an English company for $1,700,000. And to prove his shrewdness the mines then began a slow decline in production that lasted until final closure. It was estimated the total delivery of silver during the life of the mines in De Lamar was at least $8 million.

FEED TROUGHS in old livery stable handily supplied through chute from loft above.

SHADES OF THE PAST

GEM AND BURKE, IDAHO

Gem shares with its neighbor up Canyon Creek, Burke, a situation so narrow that it is nearly all length and little width. The street, railroad and creek occupy almost the entire space between crowding canyon walls.

Old buildings, some dating from the town's inception in 1886, were squeezed into available spots between the road and cliff.

In the busy and violent days of Gem, each of the larger buildings (and many more since vanished) contained a saloon.

The period before the turn of century was filled with strife between the mines' management and labor. Gem then had a population of 2,500.

The remains of mining and milling machinery stand forlornly rusting on the banks of the stream.

Many old mining towns are strung out in a narrow line, squeezed into the confines of a cramped space along the stream where gold was originally found as "color" in some prospector's pan.

Burke is an example of this sort of construction. In the days when the railroad ran many busy passenger coaches the length of the town, it was said the store owners used to have to hurry out and roll up their awnings before the train could pass by.

Certainly, when the big hotel was built it was forced to straddle the tracks, the trains then running right through the middle of it! The hotel is now gone with the heyday of Burke, as are many of the old buildings. Not that there is any lack of picturesque old false fronts, but one must search them out. The railroad station itself is a gem, with its classic nineteenth century waiting room now full of house plants instead of people.

BRIDGE CROSSED STREAM thick with tailings from H e c l a Mine a b o v e. Red-brick structure faces other way on only, narrow street. It was first p o s t office in Gem, t h e n grocery. Later it served for years as warehouse for Hecla Mine.

NOTORIOUS "PINK-HOUSE," M u r r a y's brothel, used to be some distance away from respectable s e c t i o n, was moved over after original use was discontinued for lack of business.

DOWN, GILMORE, DOWN

Gilmore, Idaho

The first time Peter Amonson, now of Portland, Oregon, saw Gilmore he was 5 and his small hand was held securely in the big protecting one of his father. The mining camp was roaring then, a hell-and-damnation spot on a flat below the high-perched lead and silver mine which had been producing since 1889. The last time Peter saw the camp it had long departed this earth but there was still violence there. He was slugged with a pistol butt.

When grandfather Peter Amonson came to America from Norway he was all for digging up some of the tons of gold reputedly being easily garnered in Leesburg, Idaho. The town then, in 1865, was the largest gold camp in the state (see *Ghost Town Album*). Amonson saw all the good sites were occupied and was further disillusioned by food prices. "Well," the storekeeper said, "everybody wants to dig gold and there ain't nobody to haul supplies up here."

In a few weeks there was. Amonson outfitted a pack train, was hauling goods and provisions up the steep mountain trail from the Salmon River, provisions like cured meat and eggs which brought a dollar each.

As mining at Leesburg passed into the big-time dredging stage Amonson quit the hauling business and bought a spread of land between Leadore and Lemhi in the valley of the Lemhi River flowing into the Salmon. Son Oscar was born into this ranch life and lived here the length of his days, his son Peter born on the same farm.

The nearby town of Lemhi was settled by colonizing Mormons in 1855 and named for a character in the Book of Mormon. The early farmers did some small scale irrigating and were generally successful. Indians were at first friendly but as the Mormon population increased they realized their lands would eventually all be taken over and retaliated with frequent attacks on the settlement in which some settlers were killed. The Saints were ready to give up when a pronouncement came from Brigham Young that the United States was about to attack Salt Lake City and all brethren in outlying communities were to abandon their homes and return at once to Utah.

Later settlers were friendly with the ruling chief Tendoy (see *Boot Hill*). When he died there was a general Indian exodus which left the villages of Lemhi and nearby Tendoy exclusively to the whites.

In 1940 the teacher in the small Lemhi school was an attractive twenty-one year old, blonde Jean Simonson, and the following year she and cowboy Peter Amonson were married. About six months after the wedding the couple took a delayed honeymoon trip up the Lemhi Valley to see what was left of Gilmore and if any of their old family friends were there. At a point near the short spur leading

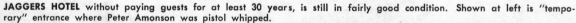

JAGGERS HOTEL without paying guests for at least 30 years, is still in fairly good condition. Shown at left is "temporary" entrance where Peter Amonson was pistol whipped.

to the former camp Peter realized the car was nearly out of gas. Could they make it as far as Gilmore and would the old gas pump he remembered still be in service?

They got there safely, found the town nearly deserted and parked near the gas pump in front of an empty store. Amonson found out from an Indian friend that the pump still dispensed gas, the man operating the "station" being the deputy sheriff who lived in a room on the upper floor of the otherwise abandoned hotel across the street.

Getting no response at the main front entry, Amonson and Indian friend went around to the side and pounded on another door. It was finally yanked open by a man obviously drunk. Scowling and staggering, he pulled out a gun and mumbled, "What the hell do you want?" When Amonson asked if he could get some gas, the gun descended on his head and the door was slammed shut. The Indian helped Amonson find his glasses which had flown into the high grass and commented, "I don't believe he wants to sell you any gas." The Amonsons, coasting most of the way, returned home, crossing Gilmore off their list of places to go.

Gilmore's activity started with the organization of the Texas District named for Texas Creek flowing through the gulch. Six years were spent in attempts to get the operation going, to mill the ore locally. Then the Viola smelter was established at Nicholia and William Kesl was awarded the contract to haul the ore with a string of heavy freight wagons and mule teams. Prosperity reigned until the smelter burned when all Texas Creek operations at Gilmore closed down.

In 1902 the mines were purchased by the Pittsburg Company and attempts made to haul ore to Dubois at rail head. Worn out wagons broke down under the heavy loads on rough roads and with replacements being impractical the company tried a steam tractor outfit. This too broke down and in 1907 the mines closed once more. Three years went by in idleness until the Gilmore and Pittsburg Railway was completed with a large roundhouse at Gilmore. Then all signals were "go" with ore now being easily shipped to Armstead, Montana, where it could be forwarded to large smelters. Production in the last year before the depression beginning in 1929 was $11,520,852, this primarily from the Pittsburg-Idaho mine. All major mines closed down early in the '30s, small ones continuing for a time. The death of the mines meant the end of the railroad and the tracks were torn out for salvage.

BUSY STREET in Gilmore passed many business places, drink emporiums.

IDAHO CITY, IDAHO

The Boise basin area in and around Idaho City produced more gold during its good years than all of Alaska, according to local authority, the total being some $100,000,000. The population of Idaho City during its boom years (1865 to 1888) was 4,800. The town was proud to claim Idaho's first Masonic h a l l, first newspaper buildings, first Catholic church and that extremely necessary item for gold rush towns a jail, also Idaho's first!

There were several elegant theaters with private boxes furnished with chairs having plush seats. The 23 law offices were kept busy with the constant litigation over claims and location boundaries common to boom towns. Four breweries and 41 saloons kept the dust down in the throats of the miners and six livery stables rented hacks and surreys for elegant Sunday trips around the limited roads in the area. The best known of all the buildings of the era is gone, having been built of logs, subject to decay. This was the Territorial jail. It stood in an enclosed acre of ground. Besides the main "cellblock" there were utility sheds, cook-house, storage and a large cemetery. This last handily received the victims of fast-moving justice and hangings, all of which were carried out on the premises. "Road agents," highwaymen who held up and plundered the stages between the several towns in the Boise Basin, were so bad that for a time even Wells Fargo had to suspend operations. Noteworthy was "Teddy White," a terror to passengers and freight haulers. Idaho City's history bears a s t r o n g resemblance to that of Bannack, Montana. It is a coincidence that Idaho City started out under the name of Bannock City!

Several bad fires have removed many

LARGE PINE TREES which have grown up inside grave enclosures attest to distant date of burial.

LIGHTING REVEALS many details of beautiful wrought-iron gate in old Idaho City cemetery.

of the hotels and theaters of early day as well as many other wooden structures. The worst one was called the "Great Fire." Sweeping through the town, the holocaust seemed as though it would destroy the city completely. One of the buildings b u r n e d was the first post office. This had been on Main street. It was rebuilt a block away from there the same y e a r by Postmaster Jas Pinney. Brick used was burned in a kiln on Elk Creek. Most of the brick buildings still standing today owe their origin to these same ovens.

The road from Boise is good, particularly interesting are the old dredge dumps noticeable on Moore's Creek, which rushes alongside the highway.

DREDGE TAILINGS REFLECTED in Moore's Creek show typical structure, clearly delineated by early morning side-lighting.

FIRST CATHOLIC CHURCH in Idaho stands in direct sun against threatening sky.

"Wild flowers had grown there ... and even they were dead!"

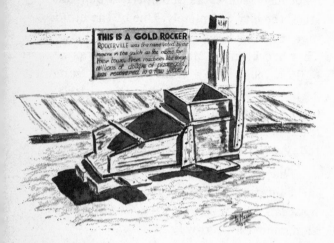

THIS IS A GOLD ROCKER
ROCKERVILLE was the name voted by the miners in the gulch as the name for their town. From machines like these millions of dollars of placer gold was recovered in a few years.

LEESBURG, IDAHO

"We heard a whooping and a shouting and looking up the hill we saw Mulkey waving his hat and hollering like the Indians were after him. We scrambled up the steep, rocky bank to see what the matter was. A big tree had blown over in the previous winter's storms and the roots had dragged up a lot of quartz with them. The stuff was loaded with gold, so rich we were all very much excited and breakfast got all burned up."

So reads the diary of Frank Barney Sharkey, one of a party of six prospectors, banded together for greater safety against hostile Indians. In July of 1866 they reached the banks of the Salmon River, Idaho's "River Of No Return," Lige Mulkey being delegated to cook breakfast that morning and do the camp chores. After he had the food on the fire he set off up the hill after the horses and made the rich find. Once reprovisioned, the men could never find that particular spot again but they did discover one of the richest placering grounds in all mining history, those of the Leesburg basin.

Frank Sharkey was born in Eastport, Maine January 8, 1838. At 14 he stowed away with another boy on the square-rigged brig Black Duck. "We had a hard time of it," he wrote, "having nothing to eat but hardtack but managed to steal some salt pork to go with it. We were 63 days on this trip, saw Cardiff, Wales, and Liverpool before coming back."

Hearing wonderful tales of the gold fields in California he decided to go there. "In the winter of 1854-55, I sailed from New York around Cape Horn and landed in San Francisco, getting my first job in Oroville, delivering meat by wagon around town. It was a team of Spanish horses, wild and hard to manage. I had not worked very long when they ran away with me and smashed the wagon and harness all up." His next job was at the Cape Claim, a mile above town, where he tended the pine knots burning in the dark tunnels so miners could see to work. He got good wages for a job, $3.50 a day, and got acquainted with another youth doing the same work. When the pair grew tired of working regularly, they pooled their knowledge of mining and decided to go into business for themselves.

They went to Compton on the upper Yuba River, invested their small savings and promptly lost them. Their next project in the spring brought them only expenses but they stayed with it two years. Young Sharkey had been getting more and more homesick but after he sailed to Maine, stayed only a few months and took ship again for California, this time by the Isthmus of Panama. He served for a time in the California Volunteers and after being discharged, went to Portland, Oregon, where he spent the winter of 1861-62.

Frank Sharkey had by this time established a pattern of wanderlust that was to prevail the rest

OLD LOG BUILDINGS OF LEESBURG sag toward collapse, one at left serving as post office during years of activity in fabulous gold camp. Until discovery of gold in Leesburg Basin by Sharkey and party, beaver pelts had been medium of exchange. Buffalo, black-tailed deer and elk in Basin were killed for food and hides, mountain sheep retreating to higher elevations. Now with solitude prevailing, they venture into grassy meadows between log houses.

of his life. Working in one camp after another, he "fell in with" Lige Mulkey and William Smith. Outfitting early in the spring of 1863 the trio went up to French Gulch in the upper Columbia country, prospected all summer and gradually drifted toward the Montana diggings. They expected to get over the Coeur d'Alene Mountains before winter set in but on arriving at the old mission at Cataldo, they found themselves snowed in and turned back to spend the winter on the Spokane prairie.

Early the next spring, before the grass had start-

ed, they tried again, making a break to get out by following around Lake Pend Oreille, keeping their horses alive with rushes from the lake, cottonwood bark and young aspen buds. There was a constant plague of Indians but they made their way to Jocko, Montana, where the Indian agent, Angus McDonald, fed them. After resting a few days they pushed on to Bannack, then to Alder Gulch and Virginia City. They worked in various camps until the fall of 1865. "That was the fall they were hanging so many road agents, especially at Bannack," Sharkey recorded.

IMMENSE PILES OF BOULDERS line Napias Creek for miles, residue of dredge which worked stream of gold during years following crude hand methods. Additional millions in yellow metal were salvaged by mechanical monster which worked in a pond of its own making, then moved to another, scooping up mouthfuls of rocks and gravel digesting it for gold, spewing out barren waste behind.

Next summer the adventurers arrived in what would later be known as the Leesburg Basin. There more hardy pioneers joined them—Ward Girton, Joseph Rapp and one Hendricks. "Hendricks," said Barney Sharkey, "Proved to be a very disagreeable partner so we got rid of him at French Gulch." The group had now hardened into the five which constituted the Discovery Party.

As they were coming down the North Fork of the Salmon River, Sharkey noted: "We were surprised to see a man almost naked out in the river. He was jumping around in the water grabbing at something and we found out later he was trying to catch salmon. His name was Mose Miller and he had been prospecting in the central Idaho country. Learning of Quantrell, he had started out to join him but ran out of provisions and clothes. Almost all he had left was a good mule."

The five went on to Napias Creek, named by the Indians for their word meaning "money", because they had found gold nuggets in the gravels which they would exchange for food and trinkets. The prospectors followed up Napias Creek, panning all the way, and thoroughly, since no gold has been found along their route.

While some of the men were pitching camp one night in July, 1866, Sharkey and Bill Smith sank the usual prospect hole. As soon as they struck bedrock a pan of the bottom gravel was sloshed out. There in the bottom were many of the sought after yellow flakes, about a dollar and a quarter's worth. The next panful yielded even more and the men attending to the chores heard the jubilant shouts—"We've struck the biggest diggings ever struck!" All evening routine work was abandoned. Supper had to wait until it was too dark to pan, the meal prepared by the light of the camp fire and hardly tasted.

The spot of the first big find was just above the mouth of Ward's Gulch. Being thorough, even though excited, the men prospected the immediate neighborhood so as to properly file their claims before the news leaked out. Every hole they sank on Napias Creek, in Ward's Gulch, Bear Track and Discovery Bar showed wonderful prospects. Subsequent mining operations proved the claims, several miles apart, had been sunk in the richest ore.

Plans were made to keep the find secret until the men could let their friends in on the good thing, the finders being entitled to only two claims, one by right of discovery, one by right of location. In order to file the claims and lay in a store of supplies, it was necessary to go the Montana diggings, the nearest settled area. Almost immediately Lige Mulkey became very sick and Frank Sharkey was delegated to look after him while the others went on. Mulkey got worse, lapsing into a delirium, calling for his mother. "Here I am, son," Sharkey volunteered. Mulkey turned over, gave him a hard look and asked: "Who are you?" Sharkey said: "I'm your mother," to which the sick man replied with scorn—"Well, you're a hell of a looking mother!"

A party of Indians arrived at the camp next day and asked Sharkey if he had found any napias. When the reply was "No," the spokesman retorted "Ishump!" which meant "you lie!" It appeared the Indians had panned out some of the dirt in the prospect holes and found rich gold and now they said this country was no good for thieving white men and they had better get out or else. Sharkey pointed to the sick man and promised they would leave as soon as he could travel. The braves were appeased to some extent and as soon as Mulkey could walk with Sharkey's help, the pair started off.

The rest of the party had made good time toward the Montana diggings but as they were going up the Lemhi, they were surprised to meet a group heading for "the new diggings at Leesburg," the news having traveled on ahead. The party outfitted, reprovisioned and returned to their camp to find a roaring body of several hundred miners.

472

Sharkey and Mulkey rejoined their partners there and by August 10, 1866, there were several thousand at the new camp of Leesburg. The diary reads: "We worked our claims for several years and took out a lot of gold dust. The average clean up for the first three years was a pan two-thirds full of dust. We hired a bunch of men to work for us and paid them at the average rate of $7 a day. Our discovery party took out the most money during the first two years."

With friendly interest a stranger watched Sharkey at his work one day. The miner scooped up some dirt on his shovel and panned out over a dollar's worth of gold. The stranger let out an excited cry but not over the gold, he explained. His name was Fred Phillips and he had a large stock of merchandise in Helena. He knew now he had found a good place to set up a store. He rounded up his partner, David McNutt, the two of them retrieving the Helena stock to set up the first store in Leesburg.

John H. Wheeler brought in the supplies each fall from then on, but from Salt Lake City. Everything had to come by mule train so a year's stock of food and other needs was packed in each trip. A unique "delivery service" was set up at the central merchandise store in Leesburg. The concern maintained a large bunch of burros in a nearby corral and a miner would cinch his purchases on the back of one and drive it home. After unloading, the burro was turned loose to return promptly to the store.

Leesburg's population was of the roughest sort, most of the men soldiers fresh from the Civil War, and feelings still ran very high between them. Southern sympathizers were in the majority and they had been successful in getting the camp named for General Lee. There was a big celebration with an ample flow of liquor at the "christening," the Northerners conspicuous by their absence. They had removed all their belongings, lock-stock and barrel, to a new site some distance up the gulch and named their town Grantsville. But before long tempers cooled and back came the Northern rebels.

The town boomed to a population of about seven thousand in a few years while operating placers in the stream bed. Some estimates of the amount of gold removed go as high as $40 million, much of this in "coarse gold," some in nuggets. After the wasteful white miners saw the gold was playing out, at least for their hand methods, they allowed an eager Chinese band to move in and start more patient extraction, themselves extracting a stiff fee for the privilege. The section where the Orientals settled became a hot bed of vice, sanctuary for opium smokers and line of crib houses filled with girls imported from the poorest peasant areas of China. In 1879 the Chinese population was massacred and robbed. The one individual remaining maintained the act was done by white men and not the "Sheepeater" Indians who were publicly blamed.

About the time the gravels seemed thoroughly exhausted, a dredge was built on the spot from parts hauled up the steep canyons. This monster chewed up the whole valley, leaving behind it piles of digested rock excrement to make the most enduring monuments to the fast decaying Leesburg.

By 1946 the last two remaining residents of the town had moved down to more comfortable Salmon City, the post office was closed and telephone line taken down. Only Leesburg's ghosts knew the dead streets.

CATALDO MISSION built in 1848 with use of Indian labor. Wooden pegs take place of nails, mud from river spread over walls for plaster. Two paintings beside altar represent Heaven and Hell, were done with Indian vegetable dyes. It was here Frank Barney Sharkey rested in fall of 1863 on prospecting trip to Montana diggings, journey was eventually leading to immense wealth at Leesburg. At mission men were told heavy snows would prevent their crossing mountains until spring. After pause here they returned to "Spokane Prairie" for winter.

473

MOUNT IDAHO, IDAHO

It just don't pay, California Joe said, to trust everybody. Especially when you've got a cabin on a pack train trail to a mining camp, set out victuals and put people up for the night. Now take that halfbreed feller.

California Joe's blooded Kentucky mare was tethered outside the cabin when the halfbreed rode up. He tied his scrawny cayuse next to the mare, had supper and was up early, saying he'd settle his bill after breakfast. The next thing California Joe knew was both the breed and the mare had disappeared. But what the breed didn't know was California Joe, whose real name was Mose Milner. Grabbing a rifle and another horse, he took a short cut to a wooded clump on the trail and sure enough, here came the renegade. Up came the rifle and one bullet into the fellow's skull finished him. California Joe left the body on the trail with a message: "Warning to horse thieves. Mose Milner, Mount Idaho."

About 1860 this wanderer built a log cabin in a meadow filled with beautiful spikes of blue flowers for which Camas Prairie was named, and the bulbs of which were staple food for the Indians. Milner's cabin was a "double" with a second halfstory on the route to the fantastically booming mining camp of Florence. Then with the help of a partner named Francis he brushed out forty-five miles of pack train

LOYAL P. BROWN established home in wilderness that would be town of Mount Idaho. Later, during Nez Perce War which raged around the edges of his town, he turned over his hotel for use as hospital for care of casualties from Battle of White Bird Canyon. (Photo courtesy Idaho Historical Society).

trail and collected tolls for its use, finishing the project in the spring of 1862. As travel increased Milner finished the upper floor of the cabin and added a wing, serving meals to sojourners at a dollar each, giving one away now and then if a man was broke. But Milner suffered permanent damage to his health in an encounter with a mountain lion and was forced to sell his toll road and cabin.

The man who bought the property was Loyal P. Brown who became Mount Idaho's leading citizen for the rest of his long life. Making the trail stop on his way to look into prospects in Florence and hearing the cabin was to be sold, he talked the matter over with another traveler, James Odle, with the result that they went partners, Brown trading his two mares for squatters' rights to the land and hotel, Odle filing on the land just west of it. After three years Brown bought out his partner and on the combined tract most of the town of Mount Idaho was built. The timber-covered mountain at the southern edge of Camas Prairie had been called Mount Idaho since the discovery of the Florence mines and Brown applied the name to his town.

He gave the name Luna to the hotel and Mrs. Brown did the cooking. She did not like the English gang of outlaws that worked the Florence trail although she admitted young Dave English was "right handsome". What bothered her most was their target practice in the yard. One bullet pinged into her kitchen between the logs, scattering chunks of clay chinking into the bowl when she was kneading bread. That kind of nonsense could spoil her reputation as a cook if she didn't get every last piece out.

The gang would run up a sizeable bill at times but Dave English always paid up after a foray on the trail. One traveler related he had been held up just out of town by a lone bandit, a member of the gang. "You're too late," he told the outlaw. "Another robber hit me up the line and took everything I had, even my tobacco money." The man with the gun gave him a dollar and a grin. But the Robin Hoodish "reign of terror" was short lived. An entry in the old Luna ledger of November 9, 1862 noted: "Dave English and his men Peebles and Scott were hanged at Lewiston a few days ago."

A post office was established in the town about 1862, with Frank Fenn as post master, then Loyal Brown. In 1873 a larger building replaced the original hotel of Mose Milner and a stage line established a route from Lewiston to the town. In 1875 Vollmer and Scott started a store to compete with Rudolph's pioneer mercantile. These buildings, with a group of residences, made up most of Mount Idaho when the Nez Perce War broke out.

After many rumors and warnings, to which Mount Idaho became inured, some citizens not even believing a struggle was going on, the dark period came when Chief Joseph carried the war into the White Bird region. About two hundred and fifty terrified prairie people flocked into the town for protection. This was on the evening of June 14 and they remained until Joseph and his hordes of braves pulled out of the area. But now Mount Idaho knew there was war.

The first action was to build a makeshift fort on a small hill at the edge of town. Two parallel rail fences were rigged up to a height of five feet in an incomplete circle about a hundred and fifty feet across, space between rails filled with brush, rocks and even sacks of flour. A narrow access passage toward the west was left open as it seemed no attack would come from that direction.

Some wounded victims of the White Bird raids were brought into Mount Idaho at intervals, among them seven-year-old Maggie Manual, carried in by young Patrick Price. The dead and wounded from the Cottonwood battle flooded the limited facilities and the hotel was turned into a hospital. Mr. Morris of Lewiston arrived to take charge, bringing a number of nurses. The dead were buried in the Mount Idaho cemetery.

Lewis Rice, fifty-nine, friend of all in the Mount Idaho area, who know him as Bude, tells of his grandmother who was called Mona by the Indians, and of her experiences at the time. "She was walking down the road real slow because she was going to have a baby almost any minute when an Indian on a horse came tearing along, his hair streaming out behind him. 'Mona', he hollered, 'get up fort quick! Nez Perce go to war on whites. My friends, no want get um hurt!' Mona hurried as fast as she could to

STONE MONUMENT was erected and dedicated June 31, 1939, by townspeople on site of fort built for protection against Indians in Nez Perce War. Almost every person in small remnant of Mount Idaho and interested former residents of Grangeville contributed to casting of bronze plate commemorating tragedy. Not long after placement on monument it was pried off by vandals. Fort was hastily thrown together—150 foot circle of parallel rail fences, space between rails filled with rocks, etc. It stood in meadow directly behind tree and faint traces can be seen on close examination.

WHEN LOYAL P. BROWN was near death he requested burial under group of trees on his property. His wife was later buried there, marble headstone erected for both. In later years area became pasture, heavily overgrown with brush. About 1955, Mrs. Daisy Smith, daughter of the Browns, distressed over wild condition of graves and constant invasion by cattle, had parents' remains removed to regular cemetery and modern markers installed. Original headstones were left where pushed over at time of exhumation. Mrs. Smith has since passed away, joining her parents in cemetery.

LAST HOME OF PIONEER Loyal P. Brown, "Father of Mount Idaho". While he exerted benevolent, protective influence over town, he did not favor progress, refused to sell his large property holdings. Period of prosperity following Nez Perce struggle was smothered for lack of space for outside investors. Advantage was taken by Grangeville, now thriving town.

warn the other settlers, then walked up the steep hill to the fort. She tried to help the others pile up sacks of flour and it wasn't long before her baby was born, right there in the fort. That was Walter, my father, and I was born here in Mount Idaho too, just at the bottom of the hill where the fort was."

The period following the war, from about 1878 to 1880, the town had its greatest prosperity and highest population. Loyal Brown erected a steam-powered sawmill close to town, logs hauled to it by oxen, and it cut 12,000 feet a day. The Idaho County Courthouse and Masonic Hall were built of Brown's lumber as was a stout jail next to the court-house. In 1896 the sawmill and flour mill next to it burned to the ground.

After 1880 Mount Idaho declined, one factor more than any other being Loyal Brown's refusal to let outsiders buy land. He had been a great benefactor to the community but now was willing to lease only. The town's big opportunity passed by when Brown turned down a request by newspaper man A. F. Parker to buy a central parcel of land and put up a printing plant. Instead it went to Grangeville which forged ahead and is today the leading town in the area. Mount Idaho faded away to a mere remnant, rich in history only.

Bude Rice tells of his little sister "When I was a kid of ten or so, Mount Idaho still had quite a few Chinamen, left over from the old days. They were all pretty ancient by then and one we called Old Cann must have been around eighty. His prized possession was a beautiful diamond ring. He always said he had won it fair and square in a poker game. He was very fond of my little sister Sadie and when she was around five, he gave her the ring. She was never very strong and a year later she died. At the funeral my mother said to my dad: 'We really ought to take that diamond ring off and have it for a keepsake.' Old Cann heard it and spoke right up. 'No takee off ring. I give, she have, she keep.' So little Sadie was buried over there on the hill with her diamond ring still on her finger."

The old cemetery is one of Mount Idaho's most interesting features. Not much else remains. Loyal P. Brown's home still stands, smothered by tall grass, weeds and decrepit fruit trees. On the op-posite hill is a rock monument put up by local citizens to mark the spot where the old fort stood, the original bronze plaque since carried off by vandals. Nearby is the site of the first grade school and the one built to replace it. At the crossroads just below stood Mount Idaho's pride, the court-house, and across the street was the large log build-ing which housed the pack train outfitters store. Next to it was the saloon where drivers took several for the long trail to the Florence mines. This was the bustling center of Mount Idaho but it is very quiet now.

476

MURRAY, IDAHO

It is almost unbelievable how fast a town can burgeon after a big strike of gold. Murray was a good example of this kind of mushroom growth. In 1883 color showed up in a wandering prospector's gold pan which had been dipped in Prichard Creek. There wasn't another soul around on that day, unless you count the prospector's burro! But within two years 2,000 people called the place home.

Flimsy tents were first dwellings and stores, to be intermingled with log cabins with sod roofs; then a sawmill produced whip-sawed lumber from plentiful timber around the site and false-fronts appeared. This motley main street was filled with life, miners, some wives and children, many "fancy women," horses, mules and wagons all competing for space. Then wooden walks were built, separating human and animal traffic. Clouds of dust rose in summer, in fall and spring the wagons sank hub deep in mud and winters saw the snow pile up several feet deep in drifts.

While all this was going on, the stream was being ravaged to its very bedrock bones by dredges and placer hoses. The returns were huge. Gold seemed to fill the spaces between river cobblestones. Then came the inevitable and these rich deposits came to an end in that same decade. Murray, in this short interval since its inception, had become the County Seat but the honor was short lived. With the depletion of gold in Prichard Creek, people quickly moved on to more fertile fields and the seat of county government was lost in 1898. Gaps appeared between buildings where structures burned or were razed. In a last-ditch effort to present a brave front, Murray moved its now scattered structures together, closing ranks in a futile and pitiful struggle to postpone the inevitable end. Depletion continued, however, and not many structures remain now.

THE MURRAY FIRE DEPARTMENT had two of these then modern rigs in the 80's. Murray fire laddies took their hose carts to Spokane, Wash., for drill exhibitions, won prize two years in row. Little bell on top tinkles as cart is wheeled over bumps.

PIONEERVILLE, IDAHO

Accurately named, Pioneerville was the original settlement of any consequence in the famously rich Boise Basin.

The first band of hardy prospectors and miners were so carried away in their excitement over the amounts of gold panned out in the stream-bed, that they didn't lay in supplies enough to get through the winter when deep snows would isolate them.

A stockade of sorts was rudely and hastily thrown together and a delegation sent to the nearest source of supplies. The remaining men hardly dared venture out of the shelter so harrassed were they by hostile Indians.

When the supplies at last arrived, the first cases opened were those containing that heartening staple, whiskey.

The leader of the whole enterprise was J. Marion Moore. His name is still attached to the stream which flows past Idaho City. In fact, the latter was originally called Moore's Creek, then Moorestown.

Ores in Pioneer City, by now Pioneerville, assayed $20,000 to the ton for the richest samples. This was when the town was touted as the busiest camp in Boise Basin.

But somehow the lodes seemed to come quickly to an end and Placerville drew away much of the population, being larger by this time and boasting more and fancier "emporiums" as well as beautiful girls who could be pinched for a pinch of "dust" or a nugget.

Pioneerville shrivelled, though getting a "shot-in-the-arm" later by the introduction of dredges in the streams. These plowed the deeper deposits of gold in the gravels and left the usual desolation. Even now you will pass a huge dredge standing idle in the stream, as you wend your dusty way to Pioneerville.

DREDGE, LONG IDLE, squats in tiny pool of stream below Pioneerville. Miles of dumps downstream attest industrious digestion of gold-bearing gravels.

PLACERVILLE, IDAHO

Mr. Robinson started a store in Placerville in 1874, during the time of Placerville's growing pains and greatest prosperity. Still operating today, the store is run by his grandaughter, Mrs. Henrietta Penrod, who is also postmistress.

Instead of the usual main street, this town had an open square or plaza, such as you might see in Mexico. But instead of adobe brick, these establishments were built of logs and whip-sawed lumber and mostly had false fronts. Several on the north side were built of stone and are in a good state of preservation. Of the original three saloons, the Magnolia still stands.

In early days, it is related, a weary traveler, probably a prospector, came in to Placerville with his string of animals. Seeing the well at the corner of the long porch fronting the Magnolia, he stopped, grateful for the chance to drink. The usual group of idlers sat and stood on the porch watching. One of these, a rowdy who had imbibed more than his share of the beverages served inside, decided to make sport of the stranger, thus showing off to his cronies. Before the thirsty man from the hills could reach the bucket, the rowdy grabbed it and threw the contents in the stranger's face. While the group roared, the wet and dazed man reached for his gun, but was shot dead by the tough before he could see to aim.

There was a trial of sorts, the verdict "Innocent by reason of self-defense." It would have been a lot of trouble to haul the culprit miles to the nearest jail in Idaho City. Besides it was all in a spirit of good, clean fun.

Placerville had 29 places where liquor could be bought in those days, besides the three saloons and three hotels. Currency wasn't always available and a lot of everyday business transactions were done in gold dust by the 3,000 people who once lived here.

METAL ROOF HAS PRE-SERVED Magnolia saloon from fate suffered by many other buildings in Placerville, that of rotting to ground.

479

POTOSI GULCH, IDAHO

Most of the earliest gold discoveries were made in the bottom of a pan which had scooped up some wet gravel from a tiny stream in some "gulch." To the early day prospectors every canyon or small valley was a "gulch" and many a town sprang into life on the spot where "color" showed in the pan. Potosi Gulch was one of these. It quickly burgeoned and almost as quickly it wilted and died. But while it lived, Potosi was a rendezvous for all the usual camp hangers-on. It had a large boardinghouse, a saloon and several business establishments.

Now only a log cabin remains below the tiny cemetery on the point overlooking the once roistering camp. Since there are only two graves, perhaps those early disputes in old Potosi fizzled out before gun play developed.

WHEN THIS CABIN is gone, so will be Potosi Gulch.

SHOUP, IDAHO

In 1881 the Salmon River was so full of those noble beauties "you could almost walk across on their backs." It was a fact mule teams often balked at fording it, finding the swarms of salmon disconcerting to their careful steps in the swift current. Bears, it seemed, liked the situation.

It is not written that Sam James and Pat O'Hara were impressed with the salmon. They had gold on their minds having found the claims around Leesburg quite thoroughly worked out. Their spirits were as low as the canyon walls of the Salmon were high when they camped on one of its banks where Pine Creek tumbled in. The next morning they panned more color than they had anywhere along the stream.

They worked hard and got increasingly large amounts of gold and then very little. Leaving the creek they went up the cliff which overlooked the spot where the gravels had been richest—and sure enough, here was the vein that had yielded the placer grains.

That first hard rock discovery became the Grunter Mine. In rapid succession were developed the Lost Miner, Hummingbird, True Fissure and Spring Lode. Partner James tired of the responsibilities of running a large mine and sold out his share for $5,000. By 1890 more than three hundred claims had been filed in the area, not all of them delivering profit.

As soon as the camp showed signs of permanence, the miners tried to agree on a name for it. The town had developed on the only semi-level spot, the banks of the Salmon, thickly studded with huge rocks. A popular vote decided on "Boulder" and the choice was sent to Washington. Authority rejected the name in favor of "Shoup," as an honor to Governor Shoup who had been extremely prominent in all early Salmon River country affairs.

As in other early day mining camps one of the hardest problems to solve was getting supplies in. The main sources were established camps, Virginia City and Bannack in Montana, Salt Lake City in Utah. When trails became passable in the spring, traders hurried in with loaded pack animals. As soon as the population warranted it, these single mules and burros were augmented by organized strings of assorted beasts of burden, mules favored as being more sure-footed on steep mountain trails and for their load carrying capacity.

Prices for goods brought in fluctuated widely in supply and demand ratio and on the care that had to be taken to deliver the supplies in good condition. The Salmon City *Recorder-Herald* listed sugar at 80¢ a pound, butter $1, tea $3.50, salt $1, soap $1 a bar, yeast powder $1 for a small can, tomatoes $1.50 a can, oysters $1, lard 85¢ and beef 20¢ a pound, coal oil $8 a gallon and tobacco $3 a pound.

Shoup has been dead as a mining town for many years. A fishing resort occupies the site now and interest for the ghost town hunters centers in the area just past the town where there are many remains of the old mills and mines.

MOUTH OF MINE TUNNEL shoots out draft of air at 42 degrees, startling on hot summer day. Little wooden wagon was not usual ore conveyance, iron ore cars more common. Door was kept padlocked to discourage thieves, temptation being strong in heyday of Shoup mining when "blossom rocks"—ore heavily laced with gold—was common. Shovel seems to be ready for use although had stood idle many years.

HERE THE SPECTERS LIVE

SILVER CITY, IDAHO

Here is a dead town still having enough buildings to line the streets and give a semblance of its former robust self. Some are big—the Idaho Hotel, the school and many others. All are weathered and all have the picturesque look of a ghost town. Its history is turbulent, full of shootings between rival mining companies and strife between men and management. As a result of these troubles and many epidemics, the cemeteries above Slaughter House Gulch are well populated and full of the typical wrought-iron enclosures of the day.

The main hotels, the Idaho and War Eagle, seem to have been "assembled" a room at a time with no original plan. The latter is about gone, except for its "Samson's War Eagle Annex" across the street.

The brewery just below the latter could find no room for its storage vats on the same side of the street, so they were built on the other side, underground, and a pipe line carried the beverage under the street.

One of the largest livery stables is on the bank of Jordan Creek; horses were taken to water over a pathway still visible.

The same stream runs right under the middle of the large Masonic Hall, and it was a favorite joke to go in the back door, come out the front. Then one had "crossed over the Jordan."

Some of the mine yields were almost unbelievable. The Poorman mine alone produced ore, assaying $5,000 a ton, so easily turned it could be cut like lead. Until 1875 its production was more than $4,000,000. At that time the secretary decamped with funds and the records were stopped until 1888 when the mine reopened with a new secretary.

Even in 1889, with its main glory dimming, Silver City still had six general stores, a tin shop, two meat markets, the two hotels, four restaurants, a photographers' gallery, the brewery, a bottling plant, a jeweler, the *Owyhee Avalanche* newspaper, two lumber yards, a tailor shop, three barbershops, four lawyers, two doctors and eight saloons. Also there was a section not mentioned in the boasting paragraphs of the newspaper. This was an exceptionally large "Virgin's Alley." Some of the houses in this section were luxurious; more plush than many of the residences. Most of the girls were segregated, but some had little "cribs" of their own on the hill. At least one married man discovered here was added to the population above Slaughter House Gulch by his wife.

Silver City lost its position as county seat in 1935. This was a final crushing blow to a city already flat on its back and the place entered the ranks of the Ghosts.

On the way in after an almost endless series of switchbacks on a narrow dirt road, a splendid view of the city may be had from War Eagle Mountain. Silver City certainly ranks with Elkhorn, Montana; Bodie, California and St. Elmo, Colorado in size and interest.

"SILVER SLIPPER" SALOON to left, drugstore, center, courthouse and jail right. Final shut-down was in 1942.

WARREN, IDAHO

Warren, the man, discovered the gold but the story of Warren, the town, revolves more around Judge Poe, Three-Fingered Jack, Cougar Dave, the slave girl, Polly Bemis, and a sluice box full of other characters in the mining camp who saw life scraped raw.

In August of 1862, a party of three — James Warren, Matthew Bledsoe and one Reynolds — left Lewiston to explore the wilderness of the Salmon River basin north and east of Payette Lakes. In less than a month they were back in town with news that turned the careers of hard working, honest men, news of finding rich placer deposits in a swale. Later the place would be called Warren's Meadows but there in Lewiston they called it Hell, for they were exclaiming: "Hell! I'm going there!" Many of those that did shared in riches amounting to more than $14 million by 1884.

Among the early arrivals was Judge Poe, the "Judge" perhaps a complimentary title but Poe's legal training was unusual enough to give him some distinction in rough-and-tumble times. With his partner Joseph Haines and a man named White, Poe took a look around the site while good ground was still free for the staking. It was White who saw the possibilities in a washout left by spring freshets at the mouth of a creek — later called Slaughter Creek because of the abattoir built there — when a panful of gravel washed out $1.70 in gold. In a week several hundred miners were working the gulch.

Haines hurried "outside" for supplies, returning with a pack train September 8, 1862. This was the first of a steady string of supply trains to the new camp. Poe and party set up a crude store at the mouth of the creek and other rough structures were soon going up around it. Next fall when most of the occupants were discovered to be "Secesh Doctrinaires", the place was named Richmond. Miners at the original discovery site switched the name of their collection of log houses from Warren's Meadows to Washington.

This was war time but Idaho Territory was a long way from Chickamauga and the miners were too busy to exchange shots unless it was on the bar of a saloon in glasses. The claims were proving deeper and richer than most of those discovered in the hectic sixties. Paydirt extended sixteen miles along both sides of the stream, assaying $12 to $17 an ounce, and it was this very richness that caused the demise of Richmond. Gold-laden gravels were found to extend under its buildings, so they were razed and rebuilt in Washington, the ground mined.

In his history of Idaho, Judge Poe related an incident in the camp that came very close to a lynching. "The most serious difficulty which I remember, grew out of a robbery which took place during the winter following the opening of the mines. While Mike Reynolds, one of the miners, was at work near the creek, someone went into his cabin and carried off four or five hundred dollars worth of gold dust. Two men, whose names I cannot now recall, were arrested. I was appointed to defend one and Charles McKay the other.

"That evening while I was sleeping, Three-Fingered Jack, my partner, came to my room and aroused me, telling me that the miners' meeting in which I should be interested was in progress across the street in a saloon. I hurriedly dressed and went to the place indicated. I found it crowded with men eagerly discussing the question of hanging my client. Strangely enough, McKay was one of those ardently supporting this extreme measure. His client was not there, nor was there any talk of punishing him, but when I arrived preparations had already begun for the summary execution of my man.

"I straightway mounted a counter and began an impassioned plea for the poor fellow's life, the re-

ROAD TO WARREN passes along west side of Payette Lake, one of many in area and one of extensive group draining south into Snake River near city of Payette. Warren road passes over drainage divide, entering Salmon River basin near Burgdorf Resort. All of many streams and lakes in Warren district drain generally north into Salmon River. Area is extremely mountainous, heavily timbered, annual snowfall reaching many feet in depth.

sult of which was, that either on my own personal account, or through compassion for the accused, incited by my words, the rope was laid aside and the man held for civil trial. He was afterward convicted and sentenced to a short term in the penitentiary. The discovery of the mines in Montana had drawn away the rough element before the importance of the Warren Mine had been established".

By 1872 Poe had been admitted to the bar and was actively practicing law in Warren, Florence, another big mining camp, and Mount Idaho, its supply center. In '76 he was elected district attorney for the First Judicial District of the Territory and re-elected for the following term. By '88 he had become a member of the Territorial Legislature and had practically given up his working connections with the gold fields.

The autobiography of early day merchant Alonzo Brown sheds some light on how Warren got its groceries. "In the spring there was quite a lot of

miners there and some good mines, and scarcely no provisions there. So Stearns went out to Slate Creek and brought our pack train in over the snow, which would bear a horse in the morning, and we loaded part of the horses with provisions we thought would be needed in Warren's, and Stearns went over with them. He found Warren's a good place to sell our surplus stock and he rented a building and started a store and sent the train back for me to load. We kept the trains running between Florence that summer. Stearns sold goods in Warren's for a fair profit and I sold them in Florence at a loss, sometimes half of the cost and freight. At the end of the second year we came out about even."

Alonzo must have given second thought to his ledger, because in the fall of 1863, he closed out the Florence operation, increased his pack train to a full four-man train, thirty-two pack animals and a saddle horse for each man. He loaded the new outfit at Lewiston, took it into Warren, continuing the run into December when annually heavy snows laid up the outfit.

Prices on all commodities were high in apparent imbalance sometimes. A morning paper from the city brought $1.50 when only two weeks old, but pork was considered exhorbitant at 25c a pound. Hairpins cost Mrs. Schulz, the boarding house proprietor, 75c a dozen, while beef was 15c a pound. Mrs. Schulz charged $3 per meal, and when customers protested this was high, she would bring out her bill for hairpins while not disclosing her butcher bill.

By 1868 the county seat had been moved from its first location at the earlier Florence to "Washington in Warren's Camp." Court records for the next seven years refer to "The Court House in Washington, Idaho County." In 1877 the county seat was moved again, this time to Mount Idaho. Then all use of the name Washington seems to have been discontinued, the camp referred to as Warren's, and a few years later the 's was also dropped.

The camp was filled with picturesque figures, such as Three-Finger Jack, born Sylvester Smith, partner of Judge Poe. While talking with a friend beside a rail fence, Sylvester relaxed by placing his hand over the muzzle of his shotgun, the stock of which rested on the ground. His foot slipped off the lower rail, knee hitting the trigger and firing the gun, changing his name to Three-Finger. Although he made as much as $1,000 a day during his best years in Florence and Warren, he was destitute when he died. Friends cut a section from an old sluice box and closed the ends, making a coffin for him. His son Henry, who recounted these details of his father's life, was the first white child born in Warren, never wore shoes until nearly grown and had only gunny sack shirts most of his life. Henry died in Boise in 1942.

Dave Lewis was a packer who lost so many horses to cougars that he swore vengeance against the depredators and spent the rest of his life killing them. This dedicated warfare lasted until, as he said: "The country got too crowded." As civilization continued to encroach on Cougar Dave, he kept moving to wilder areas. At length he fell ill, hiked from his cabin near Edwardsburg to Boise and entered the veterans' hospital. It was the first time in fifty years he had been in one and he stayed only twenty-four hours, dying of a heart attack. Cougar Dave had reached the age of ninety-two. The previous summer he was asked how many cougars he had killed. "I don't rightly know," he answered. "Years ago I kept track up to two hundred and fifty, then I quit counting."

But most of the stories about Warren characters concern Polly Bemis, the little Chinese wife of Charles A. Bemis. The Orientals here as in most mining camps were industrious and frugal, content to work the dumps scorned by whites and perform-

ing most of the menial jobs like running "wash houses". The Grangeville FREE PRESS often carried items about them. One of Sept. 2, 1887: "The Chinese in Warren camp had a grand festival last Sunday, the occasion being the feeding of the dead. Several hogs and chickens were barbecued and taken to the burying ground and were then brought back to make a repast for the living."—of April 10, 1924: "Wrinkled and bent with age but with the enthusiasm of youth, Goon Dick, veteran Idaho miner, arrived in Grangeville Sunday on his annual pilgrimage to the placer mines near Warren. Every spring he goes to Warren, armed with pick, shovel, pan and grubstake to sift the sands for nuggets and dust." Perhaps the last item about these Chinese was on Feb. 15, 1934: "Ah Can, aged Chinese of Warren, was brought out to the county hospital Tuesday by Chuck Walker, pilot of the McCall-Warren plane. The trip was made in a little over a half hour."

Many of the stories about Polly Bemis are conflicting but as to her coming to Warren, she tells of it in an interview by Countess Gizicka for FIELD AND STREAM of July, 1921. In the writer's words: "She stands not much over four feet, neat as a pin, wrinkled as a walnut, and at sixty-nine is

GENERAL VIEW OF WARREN backstreets from one of many high mine dumps edging town. Several cabins are occupied in summer by vacationers and few attendants in tavern, small grocery, gas pump. Many buildings have survived due to occasional resurgences of mining, when roofs were replaced and repairs made.

DISTINCTIVE ARCHITECTURE of several buildings in Warren is represented in this structure facing main street. It served as grocery store during active period of dredging in '40s, as saloon in earlier days, was reported "fanciest drinking emporium in town."

LITTLE POLLY BEMIS was beloved by everyone in Warren in a day when Orientals were not popular. She came to America as slave girl from China, passed her youth as song and dance girl in saloons of raw mining camp of Warren. As charms faded she married Charlie Bemis, who may have won her in a poker game or fallen in love with her as she nursed his wounds received in gun fight. (Photo courtesy Idaho Historical Society)

full of dash and charm . . . Polly told me . . . 'My follucks in Hong Kong had no grub. Dey sell me, slave girl. Old woman, she smuggle me into Portland. I cost $2,500. Don't looka it now! Old Chinese man, he took me along to Warrens in pack train."

Not mentioned are details of how she met and married Charlie Bemis. One version has it he won a poker game at the saloon where Polly worked, that the dainty miss herself was the prize, that a quarrel broke out between Bemis and an admirer of the girl, John Cox, a halfbreed Indian, that Cox shot Bemis putting out his right eye.

There is a variation to the fight story. Cox and Bemis were playing poker in the saloon, the Chinese girl present when the argument started. Cox fired at Bemis, the bullet entering the eye socket but not

487

the eye itself. Polly immediately took Bemis in charge, "cleaning out the wound with a crochet hook", it is said. A doctor came from Grangeville to tend the wound which Polly had cleaned and dressed. The jolting the doctor got on the rough road put him in a vile humor and he is reported to have taken one look at the eye, proclaimed the case hopeless, denounced all connected with the affair, collected $500 for his trouble and departed in a rage.

Polly then continued nursing Bemis, saved the eye, and in due time married her patient. One old timer reported the whole thing in a nutshell: "Well, poker had something to do with it. Warren was a wild town in those days and gold dust and poker chips seemed to reach out towards each other. . . . I guess the fact was that Bemis did get hurt in a poker game, Polly nursed him back to health, and nature and a minister did the rest."

After some years of living at Warren the couple moved to a ranch on the Salmon River where they welcomed all comers until the death of Bemis in 1922. Next year the little widow was taken on a trip to Grangeville, where for the first time in her life she saw automobiles and movies. Before her death at eighty-one she requested she be buried where she could still hear the roar of the foaming Salmon River.

Only the famous Florence (now reported razed to the ground and the site inaccessible) surpassed Warren as a quartz mining area. Hard rock mining began in 1867, and that same year the Rescue Mine turned out $13,000, mostly in gold, with some silver (present in some degree in most of the deep mines at Warren.)

Around 1870 things were quiet at Warren, activity starting up again about '73, when deep shafts of the Rescue, Samson, Charity and Keystone began producing heavily. At the turn of the century the town was almost dormant again, renewed activity starting in 1915 with a report from the state inspector of mines "A great revival of lode mining activity and interest was manifested at Warren placer district . . . as the result of successful development of ore shoots in the old Rescue Mine at considerable depths through a lower tunnel."

This burst too, died down in a few years, to be reactivated by new type dredging operations, reaching a peak around 1938. There was also some ore removal from several of the old shafts, including the historic Rescue, which was the deepest in Idaho during its peak of production. With the stabilizing of gold prices, Warren like hundreds more gold camps, settled into the doldrums. Reached best from McCall, the camp is well preserved and not too greatly altered.

ALEC BEETON'S PLACE, about 11 miles below Warren, was way station on stage road to mining camp. This was central building of group—hotel, dining room, tavern. Projecting roof enabled stage coaches to drive to front door under shelter from rain, snow. Area was logged off years ago, second growth trees mostly jack pine.

ATLANTIC CITY, WYOMING

Looking down into Atlantic City, it is hard at first to see how such a good-sized town could once have covered both sides of the gulch.

But if you descend to the site and look into some of the quite substantial buildings —the Union Hall, the church, the bank—you begin to see where the rest of the town fitted into the empty spaces.

In 1868 several miners on a "bus-man's vacation" from South Pass City found a rather spectacular amount of color in Atlantic Ledge. In two years two thousand miners and the usual contingent of harlots and gamblers had populated the hillsides.

In another ten years it was mostly over; a few mills and mines kept going, but the bubble had burst and the scavengers moved on.

Now there are still some prospectors around, and summer vacationers, enough to hold occasional services in the tiny church on the hill, a quiet end to those short but hectic years.

THERE IS A "BOARDWALK" in Atlantic City, Wyoming, also.

ENCAMPMENT, WYOMING

On the stream later known as Encampment River, about nine miles above its junction with the North Platte, is a pleasant valley providing respite from the rough going in the mountains. Here prior to the '70s, Indians and trappers made common camp for the purpose of barter. Only tents and the flimsiest of shelters were needed in summer for temporary occupancy. The place became known as Le Grande Encampment.

About 1879 a number of minerals including gold and copper were discovered in the valley and a few settlers moved in. There was no stampede, the amount of gold small and no one was interested in copper. When the Nichols family arrived, with small daughter Lora, her father erected a one-room log cabin quickly before the bitter Wyoming winter set in. Two other branches of the family built their own cabins, to which was added the

MASONIC BUILDING was originally erected in 1899 for Grand Encampment Herald, later shared by Lodge.

Bagget's. Other settlers came and a thrice-weekly stage brought mail from Fort Fred Steele. Eventually a tiny post office and store were established at a point called Swan, four miles down the valley.

In 1897 Ed Haggerty found a copper mine and this was the start of Encampment as a town. Lora Nichols recalls that the first building in the raw settlement was the two-room log office of the mining company. The second was the hotel, also a two-story log affair, then a saloon to be followed eventually by twelve more.

Stage service was started from Saratoga to the north over roads of the most primitive types, barely passable in the deep spring mud, hub deep in summer dust and the worst conditions of all during blizzards.

"Then the wind would blow every which way," Lora recounts. "You couldn't see where you were going. When rumors began to fly that there might be a telegraph line to Encampment, father said it would be a good idea if only because of the poles, for in a blizzard a driver could at least find his way from one pole to another." When the snow got so deep the wheeled coaches could no longer force their way through the drifts, they were replaced by sleighs.

OLD PICTURE by Lora Nichols shows stage operating between Saratoga and Encampment in winter when sleigh was used instead of wheels. Peggy Dougherty was driving rig like this when he became lost in blizzard, was brought in by horse which knew where warm home stable was.

One of the best and most jovial of the drivers was Sam Dougherty. He loved to dance and was one of the first at the socials in the Encampment school. The three rooms would be made into one large hall by pushing back the big folding doors and everybody did square dances and reels. Women were scarce and Sam would grab another man for a partner and pretend he held a beautiful girl.

Until the bad blizzard Dougherty had never had any trouble driving stage. About the middle of December one bad winter, his sleigh was due and people started watching for him, had a good fire and hot toddy ready for him. The rig did not appear and the whirling, blinding gale of snow grew worse. Two hours later one of the horses came stumbling in, a mass of ice, dragging behind it the redoubtable Sam, his hands in a frozen grip on the animal's tail. Sam was unconscious and without help would have died.

Tough and sturdy, he survived although one leg had to be amputated and the hand that clung so desperately to the horse's tail was left with the thumb and only one finger. This would be the end of Sam's dancing, everyone thought, but he had a wooden extension fitted to the short leg and became "Peg Leg" Dougherty, and more affectionately,

MANY OF ENCAMPMENT'S original log houses survive, some covered by whipsawed boards.

"Peggy." And Peggy danced again too. When a square dance was held in the school house the next winter, Peggy was on hand. With a few toddies to get going, he danced with the best of them, singing his own composition: "The neighbors get sore when I dance on the floor, and make dents with my hic-hic-hickory limb."

The town of Encampment was built on shaky foundations. "Its promoters sold ten times the amount of stock they should have," said Lora Nichols. But while the boom lasted, the place, with 5,000 people, was one of the wildest and most boisterous camps in the State of Wyoming. A solid jail had to be built almost at the first, a log structure with a dirt roof, there being no shakes or shingles available, and prisoners had to be chained. A daily stage run was made to and from the railroad terminus at Walcott, one rig starting at Encampment and one from Walcott early in the morning, meeting at Saratoga. Later the railroad was extended to Saratoga and then came the big day when the Saratoga and Encampment Valley Railroad actually pulled into Encampment itself. The day of the stage coach was over.

The town had four newspapers at various times,

the one with the longest life, the *Grand Encampment Herald,* being established in a log cabin in 1898. Two years later it could afford a fine false-fronted building, later shared by the Masons who used the second floor. The *Encampment Echo* and *Encampment Record* had short lives, the *Valley Roundup* even shorter.

The first edition of the *Herald* came out on March 18, 1898, spreading "scare headlines" across the top of page one: "Grand Encampment, the World's Storehouse of Gold, Copper and Cobalt . . . the Coming Metropolis of the Rockies . . . Tangible Golden Wealth that Surpasses the Phantoms of the Klondyke." Banked below in only slightly smaller type: "Wonder of the Age, Grand Encampment has no equal on the globe, says Noah Siever. Days of '49 to be repeated in Wyoming. Thousands soon to take the trail."

The North American Copper Co. was formed and bought the main mine, the Rudefeha, for a half-million and sold thousands of dollars worth of stock. The company also bought and enlarged the smelter, building a fabulous tramway, longest in the world, to carry ore from the mine down to the reduction plant. Construction of it involved some intricate engineering, the tram's twenty miles of length crossing the Continental Divide. Its cables were supported by 304 towers, each bucket holding 700 pounds of ore, and it was capable of delivering 98 tons daily. During the five years after the sale of the mine in 1903, the town grew from a population of a few hundred to more than 2,000.

Encampment's first sign of trouble came in 1906, the year the concentrating mill at the big smelter burned. Two years later most of the remainder was destroyed. Yet for a long time the tram continued to dump its quotas of ore beside the ashes for a ready supply when and if the smelter was rebuilt. The railway came in 1908 but by that time the smelter was closed entirely, the price of copper having dropped. Now came legal troubles for the over-capitalized Ferris-Hagerty Company. It was accused of huge fraudulent stock sales and when this was proved in court, the company was finished.

Encampment continued to dwindle and in 1910 the tram was taken out. The railroad continued to serve the cattle shippers but trucks began to take that source of income away since they could go into the ranch yards and pick up the animals. For a few years more the railroad struggled along, its only job hauling finished lumber from the still-active sawmill near the gaunt station. When the lumber firm ceased operations, so did the railroad, its demise in June of 1962.

THIS WAS LAW, REAL ESTATE and records office of George Kuntzman. Little false-fronted structure is face-trimmed with light sheet metal. Plaque at right corners reads: "G. L. Mesker & Co., Evansville, Ind." Daughter of Kuntzman still lives in Encampment, s a y s: "I wouldn't have that little building torn down for all the world."

GLENCO, WYOMING

Were there a hundred hardy, enterprising young men available who would go on a trapping expedition for three years? General William Ashley hoped so. He and partner Andrew Henry planned a foray into the Rocky Mountain wilderness and to attract men, advertised in MISSOURI REPUBLICAN of March 20, 1822.

Plenty of men wanted to go. In three weeks Ashley had his hundred lined up and ready to start on the great adventure. The "Ashley-Henry Men" included many who would become famous mountain guides and scouts, such as young Jim Bridger, Jedediah Smith and the four Sublette brothers.

The expedition and further explorations were to have a heavy impact on the history of Wyoming and the West, opening the South Pass route to Oregon, navigating the Green River, discovering and navigating Great Salt Lake. It was while crossing from the Green to Salt Lake that the party discovered the coal outcroppings along Ham's Fork of the Green River and Ashley reported: "The coal sticks out of the ground in places and would seem to extend vast distances underground." The general was never to know just how right he was for it was 72 years later that the Ham's Fork district was opened to mining at Diamondville near Kemmerer.

Patrick J. Quealy, coal inspector for the Union Pacific Railroad, interested Mahlon S. Kemmerer of Pennsylvania in organizing the Kemmerer Coal Mining Co., founding the town of Kemmerer and thus starting the vast network of mines in the immediate area. Six years later the mine superintendent of one of these, Diamond Coke and Fuel Co. made a strike in "black gold" on a little prospecting trip of his own.

He was Thomas Sneddon, a Scot not long from the old country. He came to Ham's Fork hoping to start a mine of his own but took a job with the Diamond Co. and did some private prospecting. Southeast of Diamondville he stumbled upon just such an outcropping of coal as Gen. Ashley had described, made a claim, quit his job and started

the mine he had dreamed of. Its name had been in mind ever since leaving Scotland — the little town of Glencoe. As the coal mines developed and the miners needed a town nearer than Diamondville, Sneddon laid out a street running south from the sage-covered hills, sold real estate on both sides for stores and named the new town Glencoe also.

Miners were imported from all parts of the country and foreign ones as well. Their work was hard and dangerous, especially as the slanting shafts penetrated thousands of feet into the hills. They wore kerosene lamps on their caps for feeble illumination and there was the everpresent danger of explosion from black damp. The work was of the heaviest kind, mostly done in winter, and the pay was by the ton, $3 for a ten hour day being about as much as the strongest miner could earn. Coal was hauled out of the stopes by mules in the early days, then freighted down to the railroad by wagons.

Homes were crude, some of boards, more mere dugouts or partially excavated holes extended with slabs of rock or wood. They had the advantage of being warmer in the bitter Wyoming winters when temperatures sagged to thirty below and winds sifted snow through every crack.

Frank Scigliano, now of Kemmerer, was born in Glencoe in 1936. The town was then going down hill fast, the family moving away when Frank was six. He gives a vivid picture of the death throes of the town. "My first memories of Glencoe are of the one street lined on both sides by false-fronted buildings. They were pretty decrepit, I guess, as I think of them now, but they looked pretty grand to me then. I remember our family used to talk often of the terrible explosions in other mines, especially the one in 1927, when 100 men were killed in the Frontier mine and another at Sublet where 39 were killed. Most of the women worried all day while their men were underground. My mother often said she wished father would find some other kind of work than mining but he didn't know anything else. Then one day we heard that awful, ruffled rumble. Smoke belched out of the mouth of the mine,

RUINS OF GLENCOE are few enough, scattered over wide area. Houses, never solidly built, are either in state of collapse or have disappeared entirely. One in foreground of photo was built of slabs and heavy, hand-hewn beams, dates from early stages of town. Other scattered shacks are from later periods.

mother started to scream, then got hold of herself and joined the other women at the shaft. All they could do was wait. When the smoke and fumes cleared away the rescuers began to bring out survivors. Each man was greeted in turn by his wife, but then the men who were carrying them out told all the women to go home. Those women whose men hadn't been brought out knew the terrible truth. It was only then that they broke down and cried, all of them, the ones whose husbands had been saved and the others. My father had been one of the first to be rescued. He said the dust, smoke and confusion was so bad the rescuers were nearly overcome too. I think eight men lost their lives in that explosion."

The disaster, coupled with the fact that the coal was giving out, caused the closing of the mines. In the early 1940s everybody moved away, most of the miners going to work in the Brilliant and Elko mines. "I didn't know it then, but I heard later that the closing of the Glencoe meant finish to another town just below. It was called Bon Rico. There were two saloons there and a dancehall where there were lots of girls. I used to hear my father joke about going 'down to Bon Rico to have some fun' and I never knew why mother always flared up and said it wasn't funny. Actually, I think that the days when the girls earned a living at Bon Rico were gone before we lived at Glencoe. There were some pretty wild times there in the old days though."

MEDICINE BOW, WYOMING

As tough as pine knots and woe be to the weakest, the tie hacks of the Wyoming woods were all that fabled lumberjacks ever were. They had hides like goats and smelled worse with long underwear buttoned up tight from freeze-up to spring thaw. In the woods they called the wild cats cousins and slammed double-bitted axes at the pitchy timber to pile up ties for the transcontinental railroad. In town this lusty vigor went to downing fiery rot gut and rowdy women.

When these men herded swarms of ties down river to the sorting booms and were paid off for the trip, they headed for the nearest saloons where all hell was likely to break loose at the sound of calks on man's shins. Irish, Swede and Norwegian tie hacks with names like Knuckles Ecklund, Deaf Charley, Syrup Strand, Cross-eyed Johnson, Lefty Hjalmar, and Whiskers Einar had money and a place to spend it. Hang tight to the bar!

Soapy Dale was foreman of a gang of them on the upper Medicine Bow River. He knew all the pokeys in towns all over the west, especially the one where they gave him no food for two days and he ate the bar of yellow cell soap.

As soon as Soapy and his fifty men had their ties safely in the corral a mile above Medicine Bow, the legend goes, they drank up their welcome in the first saloon and headed for the next. Wearing this out, they took a fancy to a loaded freight car standing alone on the tracks. Prying the door open, they started unloading when the depot agent heard the noises. He opened his window, letting out a yell, the boisterous tie hacks greeting him with balls of mud. When the agent slammed the window shut, the fun seemed to be over and the roistering crew, feeling massive pangs of hunger, swooped down on the eating house at the eastern edge of town. It was almost time for the train

crews to eat and their meals were ready, steaks sizzling and a big pot of coffee simmering on the wood range. The sides of the building bulged when Soapy and the wild bunch pushed in and loudly demanded all the food. When the cook protested, well-aimed shots punctured the coffee pot, an amber steam pouring out on the hot stove. Tables were shoved catawumpus to suit the whims of the drunken men as the trembling cook brought out the platters. The shooting continued, shattering window glass and chimneys of the swinging kerosene lamps.

Steaks were attacked with a deep-woods gusto. One man held a porterhouse at arm's length and fired several shots through it, yelling: "This critter's still alive! I saw it move!" Before the last bone was flung at the cook's head, he escaped among broken dishes and chairs, running to the depot where a dispatch for help was sent to headquarters. A special car arrived hours later by which time Soapy and his hatchet men were safely away and sobering up. But he was a worried man, realizing the jam they would all be in over the damage caused. His solution was to collect as much money as he could from the crew, dress up in his best clothes and present himself at the scene of carnage. Some railroad officials were there surveying the wreckage. "I beg yore pardon, sirs," Soapy began. "I own a spankin' big spread of sheep over yonder and I just hear some of my herders strayed off the reservation and cut up some last night. What's the damages, pardner?" Neither cook nor agent recognized Soapy in his Sunday clothes and everybody was appeased, if not fully happy. Sheep must have been in as well as on Soapy Dale's mind for at the last report he was herding them at the age of 91 in the Big Bend country.

Medicine Bow came into being when the Central

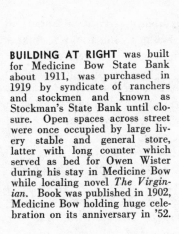

BUILDING AT RIGHT was built for Medicine Bow State Bank about 1911, was purchased in 1919 by syndicate of ranchers and stockmen and known as Stockman's State Bank until closure. Open spaces across street were once occupied by large livery stable and general store, latter with long counter which served as bed for Owen Wister during his stay in Medicine Bow while localing novel *The Virginian*. Book was published in 1902, Medicine Bow holding huge celebration on its anniversary in '52.

Pacific and Union Pacific Railroads were creeping across the vast plains of Wyoming, headed for the inviting bend of the Medicine River. Indians here found "mountain birch" excellent for making bows which were "good medicine" and the mountains were so named.

A railroad station was maintained here so water could be pumped from the river and a tank supply kept handy for the engines. The first agent and telegraph operator at the new depot was Oscar Collister. For several years he watched other buildings spring up around the station and saw a town develop as it became a shipping center for cattle and wool. Indians did not see eye to eye with the settlers and saw the railroad as their worst enemy, despoiling the ranges and streams and bringing more hated white men and their cursed sheep and cattle. Twice the raw frontier town was attacked, one siege lasting so long settlers ran out of food, finally rescued by an army detachment from Fort Steele.

At this period there were two saloons where dry-throated cowboys and herders could get refreshment. Railway men had to enter on the sly as such emporiums were off limits. The first general store was owned by J. L. Klinkenbeard and a small hotel was put up. It had a small dining room, the overflow of customers being taken care of at the eating place in the Union Pacific station. Medicine Bow was incorporated in 1909 with August Grimm as the first mayor, the town having a drugstore owned by Thomas Johns. The Hotel Virginian was erected in 1913, the finest hotel in the state with wall decorations done by cow boy artist C. M. Russell, the opening in September of that year. The main event of the gala affair was

an all-night ball and the next morning saw Medicine Bow with a gigantic headache. A sawmill was built at the edge of town and nearby a lumber yard.

The place seemed to be hold-up prone, among those recorded being a saloon and train robberies. In the first "a big fat man" was drinking with the others in the Home Ranch saloon and he suddenly pulled a gun. He ordered the bartender to hand over all the money in the till, gathered it up, backed out the door and was never heard of again.

Less fortunate was William Carlisle. He escaped from the state penitentiary after serving a few years of a life sentence for holding up two different trains. On November 8, 1919, he tried it again, robbing No. 19 when it stopped at the Medicine Bow station. He got his money and made good his escape. For the next two weeks the town seethed with excitement, curiosity seekers thronging in, taxing the hotels to the utmost as they were already full of law men. Train officials and police tried to get clues with little success and even the army stepped in, a company from Fort D. A. Russell riding up ready to pursue the miscreant. Everybody went home several weeks later when it was learned Carlisle had been apprehended on a ranch in the Laramie Mountains and returned to prison.

Medicine Bow will always be proud that Owen Wister gathered atmosphere and data there for his book *The Virginian*. He rode for the Two Bar ranch long enough to get the feel of the wide open spaces and the background that helped make his book so popular. The town still has some population but the wild old days are gone.

OPAL, WYOMING

WYOMING'S OPAL
A PROGRESSIVE WESTERN TOWN
IN UINTA COUNTY

More cattle, sheep and wool shipped from that point each season than in any other town in the state.

So headlined a lead article in the Cheyenne DAILY LEADER of July 10, 1895. The writer continued:

"The following interesting story is obtained from the impression made on the mind of an eastern newspaper representative while visiting Opal, a thriving town in Uinta County: Scattered on either side of a heavy upgrade of the Union Pacific tracks, leading from a canyon of the Uinta Mountains of Wyoming, are some half a dozen log houses, a saloon and as many corrals. This is Opal. It seems

the height of impudence, writes a tenderfoot correspondent of the Philadelphia Inquirer, that a town so limited in its proportions should occupy a place on the map, but Opal is an important city.

"For that matter, a section house, a sidetracked handcar and a signboard are all that are required to make up a western "city" and a guaranteed license to appear on the map, and in the very same size type as any of its sister cities.

"Opal, with its half dozen houses is a metropolis. It is a railroad center for a district covering 200 miles to the north, embracing a region of sheep and cattle ranches among the wealthiest in Wyoming and the newly discovered gold mines at Cora, the hope of thousands of speculators and miners.

"Opal has many advantages, it is away up, resting some 7,400 feet above the sea level. Then there

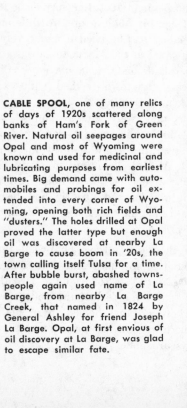

CABLE SPOOL, one of many relics of days of 1920s scattered along banks of Ham's Fork of Green River. Natural oil seepages around Opal and most of Wyoming were known and used for medicinal and lubricating purposes from earliest times. Big demand came with automobiles and probings for oil extended into every corner of Wyoming, opening both rich fields and "dusters." The holes drilled at Opal proved the latter type but enough oil was discovered at nearby La Barge to cause boom in '20s, the town calling itself Tulsa for a time. After bubble burst, abashed townspeople again used name of La Barge, from nearby La Barge Creek, that named in 1824 by General Ashley for friend Joseph La Barge. Opal, at first envious of oil discovery at La Barge, was glad to escape similar fate.

COMMUNITY WATER TANK dates back to Opal's busy days as sheep and cattle shipping center, is still in use for few remaining residents.

is plenty of room and no crowded streets. Four horse teams or bunches of cattle pass each other in the busiest thoroughfare without coming within speaking distance of each other. The only government building in the place is the postoffice which occupies a corner of the little station, while the noticeable absence of jails and police stations strengthens the air of freedom which characterizes this western town.

"The Opalites are as interesting as the place they live in. The man who owns the store is the acknowledged mayor of the city He is not elected to that high office. He doesn't need to be. His position demands it and thrown into contact with every man on the entire range he hears all their troubles while putting up their orders, and is broad minded enough to agree with all, one at a time. In this way he is the confidant of every customer and if he occasionally or invariably charges for a half hour's sympathy in connection with a side of pork, no objection is made.

"The store-keeper at Opal is not only recognized to be, but naturally is, the cleverest man in the place. He is just what the successful western storekeeper must be, a first class business man, a hustler, a true judge of human nature and always to be relied upon in time of trouble, a clever entertainer, cool, courageous, and all in all a man embracing all the true and genuine qualities of that intricately constructed animal. Just such a man is the storekeeper at Opal. Always on the alert to make a dollar, he is quite as quick to drive all night with a doctor from some of the neighboring cities to be at the bedside of a suffering rancher. If he is quick to charge a man coming to the store in possession of his full health he is just as quick to forget to charge a man who is sick or in any trouble. There is an unprinted ordinance in Opal to the effect that 'This is a country where you get nothing for nothing, and damn little for a nickel' but in sickness or real distress the westerner is the quickest to see the wants of his neighbor or any man in the world, and he gives assistance in a roughly delicate way that does not make the receiver read 'charity' in anything he gives him.

"As implied by its name, Opal is very rich in minerals and precious stones, it is from this place that the wonderful specimens sold at Manitou and other Colorado resorts as peculiar phenomena and natural formations of the hot springs are first shipped. Although these curiosities come from the Town of Opal, the town derives no revenue from their sale. The specimens are common property and are to be had for the picking.

In a business way this little town near the Utah line of Wyoming is an example of western push and enterprise. Each year more than 10,000 cattle are shipped to Chicago, as many sheep and one quarter of a million pounds of wool to Philadelphia and other eastern markets. In return supplies for the hundreds of ranches in the north country are sent here for distribution and about the little station there is always a burly crowd of teamsters as there is at the Broadway Depot, even if the number is smaller and of a different kind. Altogether, Opal is a typical western city, a place where the chase after the almighty dollar supersedes the chase after the soft and scented anise-seed bag as a form of entertainment, and the possession of gold is the one ambition of everyman's life."

Opal, along with many other towns stretching across southern Wyoming, owed its birth to the building of the railroads. As Union Pacific rails penetrated west from Cheyenne in the 1860s, shacks, barracks and makeshift restaurants were set up at intervals. Hastily erected saloons, dance halls and various dives were thrown together in ramshackle haste to cater to rail workers. When the tracks had progressed a sufficient distance beyond, all portable company buildings were moved to the new location and again set up. Hanger-on enterprises followed suit, wrecking their flimsy structures and rebuilding where the business was. A large transient population thus moved along with the railhead, surveyors, graders, contractors, track layers and other workers connected with the road building, followed by some reputable business men, and a large proportion of riff-raff. These wild, traveling towns were full of what was called "Hell-on-wheels." Most of them vanished utterly away with the moving on of the tracks, leaving little visible evidence of a lusty interlude. Others would hang on for a time before giving up, others developed into permanence because of having some sort of back ground furnishing goods for shipping, nearby coal fields or oil deposits.

The usual boom camp sprouted at the junction point, called Granger. For a time the population ran into a thousand or so. Three box cars on a siding provided a railway station. The first one was the freight depot, the next was the ticket office and baggage section. The third did duty as waiting room. Men's and Ladies' lounges were divided by a chalk line across the middle, the men were allowed to smoke on their own side, only.

The UP line turned sharply southwestward at Granger, a point west of Rock Springs, heading for Ogden and Salt Lake City, and for a long time the area to the northwest with its rich potential of coal and oil lay without transportation. Then, in 1889 the Utah and Northern built a narrow gauge line through it, connecting to the UP. This line was later called the Oregon Short Line, still later consolidating with UP. The line also had its traveling towns on a smaller scale, one of these remaining permanently as Opal because of the good watering place at Ham's Fork of Green River. So Opal became a flourishing shipping point for livestock. Also, the place was subjected to periods of oil excitement, none of which amounted to anything solid for Opal, although tremendously booming the state as a whole.

There were many seeps of high quality petroleum in the area. Indians had been using the liquid from prehistoric times as an ointment or salve for tired and sore limbs. Early white settlers expanded the liquid's uses by pouring it over dried buffalo chips, making a quick starting fuel. In 1849 Mormons and California-bound gold seekers passing through Uinta County mixed oil with flour as a grease for axles. During the 1860s and '70s much exploratory oil-well drilling was done in Uinta County. Several attempts to find the fluid were made in Opal itself, none of which were successful, but each period of drilling was accompanied by wildest speculation and excitement, all of which would die down as the hole turned out a "duster."

It was during one of these temporary booms that the following incident was reported, also on the CHEYENNE DAILY LEADER. "A ranchman applied for lodging at the section house, operated by a woman. He was accommodated, and when he went to bed he left under his pillow his money, a considerable sum. In the morning he left his room, forgetting to take his money with him. Later he remembered it, and rushing back found the landlady making the bed. He asked her for his purse. She said she knew nothing about it. He was sure she had it and finally caught her by the arm and demanded his money. She screamed, and a lot of men hearing her rushed in, and thinking the man had insulted her, hung him from the nearest telegraph pole without giving him a chance to explain. It was later found that the woman had stolen the money, but beneath that same telegraph pole lies buried an innocent man."

RAMBLER, WYOMING

At the height of the western slope of the Continental Divide where the creeks start for the Colorado River, a vivid green hollow nestles in an alpine setting, a clear blue lake in its center. Around it tall, slimly tapered firs stand like candles and encircling the basin are snow-crested mountain peaks. Near the lake, in a forlorn huddle, are the few remnants of the activity that was Rambler, only two or three buildings still standing of the once bustling city and these sinking fast into the ground saturated by melting snows.

Here was a copper boom town attended by hundreds of people who built scores of stores and houses and through whose efforts half a million pounds of copper were produced up to January 1, 1904. Several carloads of this ore averaged more than half pure metal.

All this ore had to be hauled by mule teams up the steep pitch enclosing Rambler, over the Divide and down to Encampment smelter. Along the route and in the immediate vicinity were several other camps, most of them gone now, a few with paltry piles of rubbish and a beam or two to mark the sites.

Dillon was one, built for pleasure. Liquor was forbidden at the mine but no miner was expected to do without his favorite beverage. To take care of the situation, Malachai W. Dillon, a former soldier under General Crook, opened a house where a man could get anything he wanted by way of diversion. Meals were free to those who drank at the bar. Mary Lou Pence and Lola M. Hosmer, in their book—"Ghost Towns of Wyoming," say of Dillon: "Hundreds of the miners liked the place and sank sturdy foundations under their outhouses to show they'd come to sit a while."

In fact Dillon's main claim to fame seems to stem from its privies. Until a few years ago the first landmarks visible on approach were some strangely tall and thin structures. On closer scrutiny these became outhouses, about twenty feet high, a special arrangement to allow for winter's deep snows.

Dillon hung on even after the copper bubble burst but when the hotel and store burned in 1915 it gave up. The old saloon keeper stared at the dusty bottles in solitude for two years and then departed for Saratoga. Dillon became a shade, along with Coppertown and Elwood which were also in the galaxy of stars that once sparkled around the central sun of Grand Encampment.

"LITTLE HOUSE OUT BACK" sinks to grave in own pit. Boards of walkway over soggy ground in basin around Battle Lake are still in evidence. Nearly circular valley is enclosed by snowy peaks of Sierra Madre Range. Mountains show many bare ridges where snow easily avalanched, particularly in spring when mass settled from weight of season's accumulation.

UPPER STREET on side of canyon shelters these sole remaining buildings of Rambler. Aspens have grown up around abandoned town after pines and alpine firs were cut for boards or firewood, provide "nurse crop" for reforestation by shading young evergreens.

"Trees . . . shrunken into shapes of desperation!"

RIVERSIDE, WYOMING

Riverside was never a mining camp but came into being as a gateway to the mining district and as a neighbor to the more important town of Encampment. Both resulted from the early days of barter from 1851 on. After the trading period ended and ranching started, a man named Dogget started a store and station, a few log cabins and shanties collected around it, the place taking the name of Dogget.

At the turn of the century the town had changed its name to the more fanciful one of Riverside and boasted sixty buildings. One of these was a forty-room hotel which burned and was promptly rebuilt, a matter of questionable judgment as shady dealings of the big copper enterprise at Encampment caught up with the promoters. This with falling copper prices spelled the doom of the big hotel which reflected the whole of Riverside.

FORERUNNER OF MODERN HOUSE TRAILER Sheepherder's home had some "modern" touches—the truck wheels. Otherwise camper is typical of shelters used in past, well designed with many comforts, wood burning stove inside. Sheepmen were often suffocated at night with these overheating.

ABANDONED RANCH AT RIVERSIDE seems to typify popular conception of farmsite in wide open spaces. Central log building has false front—owner did blacksmithing in spare time. Goats from neighboring farm run loose.

SOUTH PASS CITY, WYOMING

The clear and rushing creek called Sweetwater figured prominently in early mining days. Gold had been found as early as 1842. Here the early pioneer-prospectors panned, while Indians watched from the rocks above. As they gathered their yellow flakes together and started East to "organize an outfit that would really develop the Sweetwater," they were often ambushed and killed by the silent watchers.

The white man muddied up the Indian's drinking water with his placerings and killed his food supply. The Indians didn't like it.

Retaliation came swiftly and often, but when the savage Sioux, Arapaho or Cheyenne rode into the now good-sized town of South Pass City, they found no women or children to carry off. What they didn't know was that a lookout was kept on the hill at all times, and at the approach of Indians, the women and children were herded into a cell behind the wine cellar, built into the side of hill, east of the store.

An old gentleman who lives nearby says that an old falling-down building was once a millinery shop. "The ladies liked to have the latest Paris hats then just like they do now. Only in those days it took a lot longer to get the hats out here. But then they stayed in style a lot longer, too."

In 1870, South Pass City had a population of 4,000, and was the county seat of Carter County which took in nearly a third of the whole state of Wyoming. One of the local citizens, William H. Bright, introduced the first bill to give women full right to vote in the state. And, in 1870, the first woman Justice of the Peace held court in South Pass City. She was never able to get hold of the docket from her predecessor, so she set the t o n e for her entire tenure by just starting out with a "clean

new docket." The town's two doctors were part-time miners.

In a few short years, though, the town was deserted and the county seat was moved to Green River.

SAWN LUMBER was scarce in South Pass City.

NOT DATING BACK QUITE to earliest days, truck in old dump still has archaic look.

503

SENTRY WAS OFTEN POSTED on hill above town, to warn of Indian raids which were frequent. Little false front at left was "Millinery Shop" in its good years.

MAIN STREET of South Pass City.

NEVADA
GHOST TOWNS

BY

LAMBERT FLORIN

Drawings
by
David C. Mason, M.D.

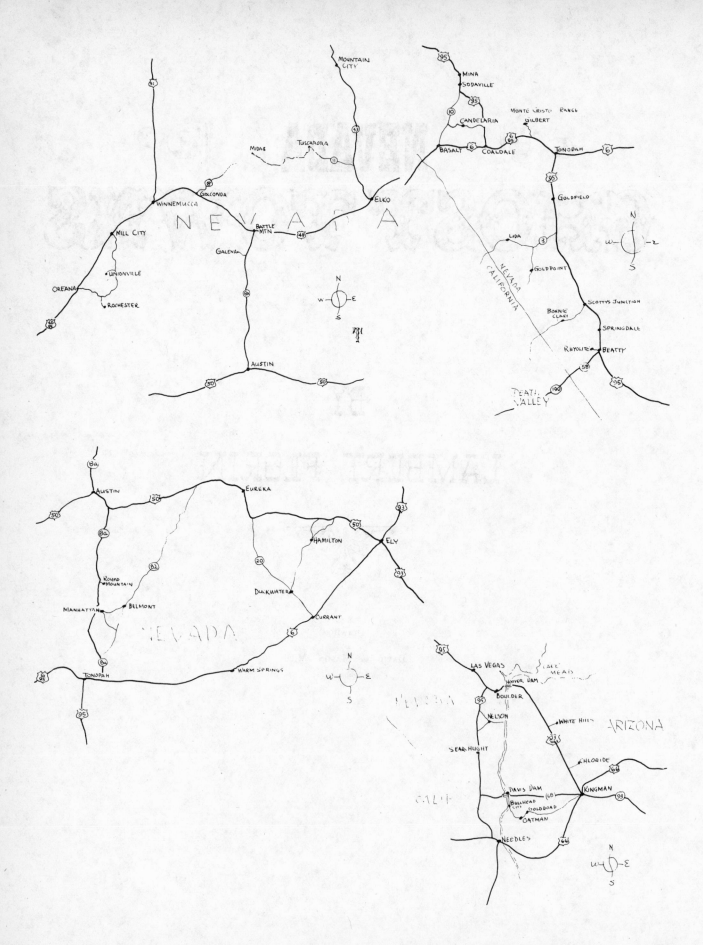

INDEX

CITY	Page	CITY	Page
Aurora	509	Manhattan	559
Austin	514	Midas	561
Belmont	516	National	562
Berlin-Union	517	Nelson	565
Broken Hills	521	Paradise Valley	566
Candelaria	526	Pine Grove	570
Dayton	528	Pioche	571
Eureka	529	Rawhide	574
Fairview	530	Rhyolite	579
Galena	531	Rochester	580
Genoa	532	Rockland	581
Gold Hill	537	Sutro	582
Goldfield	542	Tonopah	591
Gold Point	543	Tuscarora	592
Goodsprings	544	Unionville	593
Grantsville	545	Virginia City	596
Hamilton	548	Wadsworth	597
Ione	551	Washoe City	599
Johnnie	555		

IN THE 70's STEADY STREAMS of customers poured though doors of Unionville "Emporium." Stone is local and varied in color, making beautiful effect.

AURORA, NEVADA

Angus McLeod crossed the plains in 1856-57. The journey lasted six months and included his helping to drive 1200 head of cattle from Dover, Arkansas, working in the California placer mines, farming, clerking in a Genoa, Nevada, store. After this devious circuit he settled on land near Yerington, Nevada, in 1862.

The land extended a mile and a half along the Walker River and he was hardly established before trouble began. Three men — Lee, Mills and Greely — built a flour mill just below the McLeod land, constructing a stout dam and digging a ditch to convey water to power the mill wheel.

As water rose behind the new dam it flooded the land above to a depth of several feet, Angus McLeod's ranch included. Determined to avoid it being turned into a lake, he cut an outlet for the river water to flow around the dam and drain his land. This resulted in the mill ditch running dry and filling with sand.

Lee, Mills and Greely were blazing mad, bringing suit and a year-long legal hassle. The first skirmish ended in success for the mill men but at the conclusion of the trial, McLeod was the victor. Both sides however were drained of cash. Angus leased the ranch to Charles Martin and with his wife went up to the roaring camp of Aurora. He owned an interest in the big Wingate Hotel which had stores and lodge hall on the ground level, and he also owned a lumber yard and the toll road extending from Wellington.

Aurora had sprung up almost overnight. In August, 1860, a prospecting party composed of J. M. Corey, James N. Braley and E. R. Hicks stopped to let their horses forage in a grassy little gulch well watered by Antelope Creek which came out of nut pine covered hills. All three men took their picks to the surrounding rock outthrusts. Braley and Corey had come over the Sierra from San Jose, California, had looked over the ground at Virginia City where they met Hicks. They were too late at the Comstock but not on Antelope Creek. Hicks, a part Cherokee, chipped off the first piece of glittering rock near the top of the hill. Corey found his treasure about the same time and in a day or so the three had located four claims. Next morning when the rising sun colored the entire eastern sky in a blaze of glory, the imaginative Corey tossed out the name of the location — "Aurora, Goddess of the Dawn."

The three founders of the lofty camp did not stay long. Corey and Braley made 357 mining claims, selling them in two months for $30,000, then departed for California to plant fruit trees near Santa Clara. On his departure for home in Arkansas, Hicks carried $10,000 in his poke.

When the three waved goodby to the town they did not leave it deserted. It was already populated with a motley crowd that had rushed in at the first news of the strikes. Almost before these men could start working their claims they had to have shelter and threw together whatever was at hand fast, for at that altitude of 7,741 feet, winter came early and snow sifted down among the pines. Houses were first mostly dugouts with stone fronts, roofed with brush and mud. The first business establishment, owned by one Pat Hickey, was fabricated of "sticks, stones, shakes, canvas and mud." Crude as they

OLD ETCHING OF EXCHANGE HOTEL from "History of Nevada" by Thompson and West. This is same building which Angus McLeod bought about 1880 and was later burned by revengeful arsonists. Front, facing Antelope Street, was fancy, 1910 photo showing plain side and rear.

RARE PICTURE OF AURORA made by "Scotty" McLeod about 1910 while on prospecting trip. Town has nostalgic memories for him, being born in Dunlap house at far end of Antelope Street which angles across lower left in photo. House has dormer, is trimmed white. Road leads right to workings of Esmeralda Lode, discovered on afternoon of Aug. 25, 1860, by J. M. Corey. Below mine is small group of mine buildings, one of which is only brick structure remaining. In central foreground on Antelope Street is burned out shell of Exchange Hotel, that street continuing on down through old Chinese quarter to become road to Bodie, Calif. Route is no longer passable, only entry at left through Fletcher, which road passes Aurora cemetery at top of hill.

were, stores and saloons were well patronized by thirsty miners. A few slugs of Aurora Lightning and nobody worried what the walls were made of as long as they stayed still.

Every bit of food, every pound of explosives, in fact every item necessary to work or life itself, had to come in over rough trails on the backs of mules. Even after a semblance of a road came in from Bodie, wagons were sure to break a wheel on a rock or get mired in deep mud. Prices for everything were sky high and the estimated keep for a mule $3 a day.

The Angus McLeod family first lived at the Dunlap House at the upper end of Antelope Street and later on, April 29, 1878 their son Charles was born there. Now, at 86, Charles or "Scotty" as he is affectionately known all over Nevada, lives in Yerington. He is alert, witty and after a lifetime of mining activity is a mine of information and anecdotes about the state's boisterous early days.

"We lived in the Dunlap House only a short time," Scotty relates, "and then father bought the

Exchange Hotel farther down the street where we lived in upper floor rooms. I was little more than a baby then. One of the roomers had three canary birds, a novelty in that rough town, and went on a short vacation, leaving the birds in mother's care. She went in to feed them once and found me there. Two of the little things were already dead on the floor and I had the third in my fist, squeezing the life out of it. When mother asked me what in the world I was doing, I told her: "I'm making them sing, mama." Scotty proves this with the old hotel ledger. Item in column of expense, dated Dec. 21, 1881 — "Three birds, $30."

Meanwhile the three losers in the lawsuit against Angus McLeod were still smarting with resentment. Charles noticed one day that his friend the Chinese cook for the hotel was missing, a strange white man in his place. That night the family was awakened with the Exchange Hotel in flames. All occupants escaped in time, most of the men in their underwear, leaving six-shooters and ammunition behind. As all stood outside watching flames engulf the

510

hotel, bullets in guns and cartridge boxes began to explode, the air full of flying lead.

Investigation later showed that the Lee brothers and Greely had arranged the substitution of cooks, the new man pouring "coal oil" over the floors and igniting it. The hotel was completely gutted and never entirely rebuilt. The McLeod family moved again, this time to the toll house at the end of the road where Charles' brother Neil was born. The road in those days came in from the notorious Bodie, California, passing through Del Monte on the way and where it entered Aurora at the lower end of Antelope Street was a Chinese section. Asked if it contained the usual joss and gambling houses, Scotty replied: "Oh, no. They were all very fine people, industrious vegetable growers. Of course they may have had those things in another section of town but if so, I was too young to know about them."

Prowling about a shed at the toll house one day, young Charles found a box of dynamite percussion caps on a shelf. He dislodged them with a stick and the box fell to the floor, scattering the caps in all directions.

In playing with them he heard the call to lunch and popped one into his mouth as he ran. When he climbed up in the high chair he spit the cap out on the floor. The hired girl, Josie Hernleben, picked it up took a pin out of her blouse and poked at the white percussion dot in the bottom of the lethal cap. "There was a terrific explosion," Scotty said. "Josie's thumb and forefinger were blown off and stuck to the ceiling. No one ate much lunch that day."

When Charles was a little over eight years old the family moved down to the ranch, remaining there many years. As the boy grew up he followed the prospector's trail as did many other young fellows of the day. One of his buddies was J. C. Bray, with whom he later made the first claims in what was to be the fabulous camp of Rawhide.

Aurora was destined to suffer a long time from a unique problem. It wasn't sure just where it was. No one knew if the town lay completely in California, or in the Territory of Utah or whether it straddled the line. During the first winter a petition was presented to the California legislature, asking for the creation of a new county just for Aurora, so as to "release us from the hated laws and restrictions of Utah." By spring the California authorities concluded that since nobody knew just where the line was, they would arbitrarily include the new county, which held out such juicy prospects for taxes, in the

state. Mono County was created in March, 1861, with Aurora as the county seat, a full set of county officials installed.

By April as weather improved, the real rush for the new camp set in and by June the residential total was 1,400 and increasing each day. When not a year old, town lots were selling for as much as $1,500. Four brickyards were started in the canyon and one of the first brick buildings was a schoolhouse, there being eighty children. That summer the first stamp mill was built, replacing several Mexican arrastras. By 1864 there were eighteen mills.

The summer of 1862 saw several outbreaks of Civil War antagonism. Southern sympathizers gathered in "underground" meeting places while Union organizations were more open, forming two groups—Esmeralda Rangers and Hooker Rifles. The fledgling city also had a newspaper, the ESMERALDA STAR and on August 23, 1862 it reported: "The Dixie group made a complete pandemonium of our town and continued their hideous orgies until late on Saturday morning, cheering Jeff Davis, Stonewall Jackson and the Southern Confederacy." The town was definitely on the Union side however. When the telegraph brought the astounding news of the assassination of President Lincoln, the whole town was "wrapped in gloom and tears rushed from the eyes of young men and old."

One dissenter, A. G. Judeigh, was so bold as to assert—"Lincoln was a tyrant and ought to have been dead long ago." Unfortunately for him the remark was carried to Captain Kelly who asked the Esmeralda Rangers to arrest Judeigh. He was placed in confinement with the immediate prospect of being taken to "Fort Churchill to carry sand." Under this threat he recanted, took the oath of allegiance and was discharged. He made a wise decision as he would have had to carry a fifty pound sack of sand on his back, marching up and down the parade ground in front of a soldier who would have corrected any loitering with the jab of a bayonet.

And all the time the ferment of Aurora's position went on. Far from settling the trouble, the California action only added fire to the dispute. A new group called Esmeralda Union Club spoke openly of being "California secessionists" and fought to get Aurora over the line into what was by this time Nevada, that Territory having been sliced off Utah. The solution of the wrangle caused a situation unlike any other known. Aurora, the seat of Mono

ONLY REMAINING BRICK STRUC-
TURE is mine building directly below Esmeralda Mine on hill of
same name. Little shack at rear is
similar to one at head of Antelope
Street occupied by Mark Twain
during his short stint at mining in
Aurora. His cabin was removed to
Idlewild Park in Reno, has since
been destroyed by vandal souvenir
seekers. Twain's stay was in 1862
when he and Gov. Nye's nephew
worked their portion of Horatio
and Derby claim. It paid off later
but Twain was long gone to Virginia City where he worked on
Enterprise for $25 a week.

County, California, now became the seat of Esmeralda County, Nevada, as well. Mining affairs were
delegated to Nevada courts, litigations connected
with franchises on roads and utilities were handled
under California jurisdiction. Private quarrels
could, at the discretion of those involved, be taken
either to Esmeralda's Judge Turner or Mono County's Judge Baldwin.

Soon after this dual arrangement was put into
effect, a general election was held and Aurora citizens had a choice. A resident could be registered in
California or Nevada or both. He could vote the
Republican ticket at one polling place (for California, the police station) and the Democratic at
the Nevada end of town (City Armory) or vice
versa, or vote the same ticket at both places. The
situation suggests a Roman holiday with twenty-
two stops along the way where a man could refresh
himself. It was remarked the town's bistros did their
biggest business that election day, a fact apparently
more important than being able to vote for a state
and territory at the same time.

The situation, amusing to some, intolerable to
others, was brought to an end by a survey party in
September, 1863, when Aurora was irrevocably
placed on the Nevada side with a good three miles
to spare. Bodie remained securely in California by
a five-mile margin. Finally convinced that their
position was now untenable, Mono officials in
Aurora packed their things and departed for Bridgeport, which replaced Aurora as the county seat.
With them went all money collected and left behind
were all outstanding warrants for some $20,000 in-
debtedness.

Aurora was still behaving like a mining camp.
During the halcyon days of heavy gold production,
bullion was shipped out on stages, duly recorded as
loaded. Even to this day skeptics maintain that the
return stage brought back the same gold to be re-

loaded and rerecorded. If this were so, it was done
by sharp design. High records of production from
certain mines boosted the value of stock. Express
company records list shipments in 1869, for example, as $27 million. This could have been accur-
ate but whatever the figure, there was a lot of bullion
on the move—certainly enough to rouse desire on the
part of highwaymen. Holdups were frequent and
occasionally a stage driver was killed.

There was even a "crime boss" in town, one
John Daley, secure in his position as the head of
a gang of thugs. Not knowing any better, W. R.
Johnson, a vegetable grower on the Walker River,
shot and killed one of Daley's men, James Sears,
for stealing a horse from him. It is not entirely clear
whether Johnson himself did the shooting or sent
one of his hands, John Rogers, to do it. But the
thief was dead and Johnson was responsible. Daley
was not the type to overlook the incident and vowed
to get Johnson.

His opportunity came soon, when Johnson came
into town with a load of vegetables. Daley gathered
his henchmen and waylaid the farmer in a dark
alley. First, Daley knocked Johnson down, then
shot him. Gangster William cut his throat and
"Three Fingered" Jack went through the victim's
pockets while James Masterson poured kerosene
over him and set his clothes on fire. By this time
Johnson's mistake was definitely paid for.

But the executioner had overdone it this time.
Aurora was already a little touchy about its record
of twenty-seven unpunished murderers and this last
atrocity was enough to trigger reaction. Some 350
citizens gathered in a hall in the Wingate Hotel,
organized a vigilante committee which quickly
gathered in Daley and his crowd. All were thrown
into jail and guarded closely while a coroner's jury
deliberated. It was over like that. The four were
found guilty and sentenced to death on the gallows.

All saloons were closed for the affair, mines were shut down and stamp mills ceased to chatter, the gallows was ready and execution only an hour away. Someone decided Governor Nye ought to know what was going on and so informed him by wire. The governor immediately responded that there must be no violence, that law and order must be preserved. Laconic was the telegraphed message to Governor Nye. "All quiet and orderly. Four men to be hung in half an hour." And they were. All the gallery had the help of brandy to sustain them, two being so well sustained they had to be held up. After that day, Aurora was somewhat more peaceful for a few months.

It was reported at one time that Aurora had "seven hundred and sixty-one houses of which sixty-four are brick". In 1864 there were 6,000 people living in the town, the top population a few years later said to be 10,000. There was a fine brick courthouse, the ESMERALDA STAR was joined by another newspaper, the AURORA TIMES, many hotels, rooming houses and stores, almost all built of brick or stone. The first structures used bricks imported from as far as Sacramento, it was reported. Scotty McLeod says that after that a kiln was built and "bricks were baked right there in the canyon."

And Scotty settles another question, was the "Mark Twain" cabin which was sent to Idlewild Park in Reno actually the one occupied by the famous humorist during his short stay in Aurora? He says: "The Dunlap House where I was born still stands at the upper end of Antelope Street. Directly across from it was the Mark Twain cabin. I often played in it as a child before it was removed to Idlewild Park." The defense rests.

When Aurora began to decline it went fast. Golden bonanzas had been genuine enough but shallow. Mines never went very deep, less than a hundred feet. The $30 million in gold and silver had been scraped off by the 70's. Though mining continued after that in desultory fashion, the glory that was Aurora's had faded. The tenure of the McLeod's just covered the waning period for when the family returned to the ranch almost everyone else left too.

Scotty furnishes another bit about the use of brick in Aurora. His friends Vic and James Bernard, whose family had lived in the town, recently visited there and found an opening to the old sewer lines. They were built entirely of brick, arched at the top which was high enough to allow a man to stand up. Unused for years, the lines ran for miles and the "inspectors" concluded many brick masons must have worked on the job at tremendous cost.

For years Aurora was a magnificent ghost town, intact except for some frame buildings lost by fire. But later the blocks of brick buildings, many still holding their contents, were wantonly razed for their bricks. Mrs. Ella Cain, who with her husband, owns most of Bodie and Aurora, told this author a few years ago: "We couldn't keep up the taxes on all those buildings and gave permission for removal of enough bricks to reduce the building valuations. Vandals came in and removed almost everything, entirely wrecking the town."

Today there are barely enough remains to give some vague outlines — foundations, shapeless piles of brick, an iron door. The streets can be seen though overgrown with sage brush. There is exactly one brick building intact and why that was left is a mystery.

"SCOTTY" McLEOD hauls first baby carriage to Rawhide in first rush of 1907. Note bale of hay, bed spring, barrel of flour, box of china and high chair. Of pair engaged in horse play, man at left is Charles B. Holman who named town Rawhide in fit of pique over rebuffs in self-sufficient camp of Buckskin.

TOWNS OF THE CREAKING DOOR

AUSTIN, NEVADA

Austin is one of those historic old mining camps that would be a true Ghost Town but for the highway running through it.

Old brick buildings with collapsed walls and ruins of adobe structures alternate along the street with small stores and gambling houses. The "one-armed bandits" have replaced the real thing in Austin, and probably receive a much larger "take."

The history of Austin began when, in 1862, a horse kicked up a piece of quartz, laced with gold. The owner of the horse was W. H. Talbott and he sent the specimen to Virginia City for assay. Finding that there was silver as well as gold in it, he staked out his claim, others followed, and a silver rush was on.

The locality was inaccessible, but miners and would-be claim owners helped build a road, receiving city lots in exchange.

A brick courthouse was built in 1869, Austin having become the county seat in September of 1863, when some 10,000 people swarmed the town. Already a lumber mill was going full tilt and more than four hundred houses had been built. By the time the courthouse was in use there were many other "permanent" structures including schools, three churches, several hotels, stores and the usual quota of saloons and red light houses.

Austin was composed of so many brick and adobe buildings, clay being more plentiful than lumber, that it suffered somewhat less from fires than did other camps. But floods, especially those of 1868 and 1874, ravaged it.

By 1880 Austin had started the downhill slide and most of its total of $50,000,000 in ore was an accomplished fact.

The railroad, result of so much hard work to acquire, was abandoned in 1938, and this really was the finish of the town as a mining center.

Austin, once so hard to reach, now one of the most accessible of the old camps, is comparatively unspoiled and well worth the study of those interested in the bonanza day of the Old West.

BELMONT, NEVADA

Belmont's history was hectic and brief, with only about twenty frenzied years allotted as the life span for the city. In that time Belmont became the seat of Nye County and produced $15,000,000 worth of lead and silver ore. There were spasmodic bursts of enthusiasm at intervals after the boom period was ended in 1885. Discovery of turquoise in 1909 caused a flurry, but this was short lived. A 100-ton flotation mill was built in 1914 with bright hopes and almost the entire resources of its promoters, but after a couple of years it failed. Another stamp mill was built in 1921 but suffered the same fate in less time.

The Nye County Courthouse, built in 1867 dominates the town, an interesting and picturesque structure. A few feet from the imposing front door is a small stream meandering across the grass-grown street.

In common with other early day mining camps the place saw its difficulties between miners, owners and the unions. Two of the union organizers found such a complete lack of welcome that they were forced to flee. Unfortunately they didn't go far enough, holing up in a mine tunnel near town. Here they were caught, dragged into town and hanged on the main street. One was only a boy of 15.

Across the street from the spot where this brutal episode took place stands one of the most interesting of old-time buildings, the Music Hall, and across the front in old-style lettering is its name, fading but brave, the "Cosmopolitan." Once garishly red and green, time has subdued the brilliance of its paint, and warped its boards to curls. Flagstones, split from nearby rocks, pave its outdoor foyer, under the extending balcony. Remains of fancy lace curtains hang from glass upstairs windows and weeds and sage grow in the doorway. An iron ring to which the driver tied his horse while the star stepped from her carriage, still hangs on one of the posts supporting the balcony.

DESERTED MAIN STREET sees little traffic now, but once was busy parade of buggies, o r e wagons and people in costumes of period from 60's and through gay 90's.

MONITOR-BELMONT MILL is almost gone but stack of smelter stands as monument.

CENTER OF ALL PUBLIC entertainment in bustling era of Belmont's heyday was "Cosmopolitan." Music hall dominated street.

LIFE OF IMPOSING NYE County Courthouse extended from 1867 to 1905. Building had no "central heating"; rooms were heated by stoves connected to many chimneys. Even jail at rear had its own.

ACROSS FROM "COSMOPOLITAN" stands group of typical mining camp buildings. Here were hanged labor organizer and youthful companion. Street becomes road leading down hill to Monitor-Belmont Mill.

ONCE "IMPREGNABLE" JAIL, now open-air affair, is extension of courthouse.

BERLIN & UNION, NEVADA

The past of this ghost town goes back some 100 million years, not to gold but to the amphibious animals, *Ichthyosaurs*. Berlin had gold but along with it the fossil remains of these "fish lizards" or more accurately water creatures akin to whales. Harold and Dorothy Newman will explain them successfully. They are the only residents of Berlin and are responsible for the preservation of the relics.

Berlin is easy to find. Unlike many ghost towns, hidden away in some brush-grown gulch, adobe or rock walls melting into the mother earth from which they sprang, Berlin's bones are gaunt frame structures, worn and weathered but defiantly erect and stand out boldly in a substantial group conspicuous

for miles. Further dramatizing the old camp is the backdrop of Mt. Berlin rising to a height of 9,081 feet above sea level. Set high on the flank of the Shoshone Range and seen from a distance of several miles across a flat, dusty basin the dead town seems still pulsing with robust blood of yesterday. But it isn't. The buildings are only hollow shells without doors, the windows staring without glass. Only these and the Newmans.

The agatized remains of the marine creatures were interesting to the more knowledgeable prospectors from 1860 on. Possibly the first printed mention of the fossil finds appeared in the July 29, 1865 issue of the NYE COUNTY NEWS, published in

PARTS OF SKELETON of huge ichthyosaur, turned to agate-like substance after millions of years of burial, are exposed but left in place by student paleontologists directed by Dr. Charles L. Camp of University of California during four year period following spring of 1953. In foreground are pelvic bones; extreme left is fetus; left center, vertebrae. Tail of twenty-five foot amphibian stretches into background. Altogether nineteen large ichthyosaurs have been uncovered in limey shale. Guardian of deposits, Harold Newman, when asked about future excavations said they are uncertain because of short political tenure of interested officials. "By the time they learn to pronounce 'ichthyosaur' they're out of office."

BUNK HOUSE for Berlin mine workers seems to have been dropped on the ground. In many early mining camps violence often erupted in bunkhouses where drinking and gambling was carried on in evenings, but Berlin seems to have no records of murder or lynching at camp.

Ione, a short distance from Berlin. "Several of the boys have been bringing in to this editor some strange specimens for this country so far from the ocean. They are enough to make one think that perhaps this whole area was once covered with water, even to the mountain tops where the shells were found. They are indeed objects of study for the curious."

It was not until 1928 that the stony bones received official recognition, when a faculty member of Leland Stanford University made public their importance. Later Geologist Margaret Wheat exposed more fossils with simple hand tools. She interested Dr. Charles L. Camp, distinguished paleontologist in the possibilities of an on-site exhibit. The Museum of Paleontology, University of California, carried on delicate but extensive excavation work from 1953 to 1957 and Dr. Camp was successful in

getting the State of Nevada to designate the area a state park.

The name ichthyosaur translates "fish lizard" but the animal was neither. One miner-historian describes the geneology as a "cross between a shark and a whale", a biological impossibility. Actually the animals were entirely warm blooded with some of the characteristics of the modern whales and porpoises, and except for whales and some forms of prehistoric dinosaurs, were the largest form of life known, reaching a length of sixty feet. They swam in warm waters which once filled the great basin, having their existence in the beginning of the "age of reptiles", the Middle Triassic, some 200 million years ago.

The particular group whose petrified remains came to light near Berlin seems to have suffered the same fate of whales today. They were beached and since the animals had a lightly constructed rib cage

SHELL OF COOK HOUSE stands next to mine dumps at Berlin. Large wood burning stove was carried out years ago, possibly to permit other use for building. While photo was being taken Newman's retriever entertained by flushing and chasing dozens of large jackrabbits which bounded back and forth in front of camera as though feeling spirit of game.

and not able to protect the lungs out of water, their enormous weight caused collapse and death. They sank into deep primordial ooze, flesh decaying and bones becoming fossilized. About 60 million years ago the whole area was covered by volcanic flows, then much later the protective stratum split and erosion began, exposing some of the bones.

The deposits lie on a bench directly above a canyon holding other remains —those of the once thriving mining camp of Union, about two miles south and east of Berlin. Union owed its origin to P. A. Haven's discoveries as did Ione, Grantsville and Berlin in 1863. In common also with its sister towns, Union had an initial boom of all too brief a duration, then several spurts of energy equally short.

An item from the NYE COUNTY NEWS of Ione, July 8, 1865, said: "The first lot of bullion from the Union district amounting to about 200 pounds was shipped from the Pioneer Mills. We hope next week to give a larger figure." Next week's issue failed to carry any figure at all but there was a pat on the back for Union, a generous gesture considering the traditional rivalry between the two camps. "There is much doing at Union. It promises to rival our town. We congratulate the Union boys upon their prosperity."

About a year after Union's beginning, a Mr. Shobe, while prospecting the area, came across a large deposit of clay. Shobe could see an indirect glitter of "gold" in the material, found where there

ADOBE BUILDING only substantial ruin at Union. Roof has preserved it from complete deterioration, will soon give way. Search up and down long canyon revealed many fragmentary signs of occupation by hundreds of miners and store keepers.

was no lumber which was always a fire hazard. He abandoned all further prospecting, took a claim on the site and set about getting capital to build a large kiln. His first big job was not for house building material, though, as the NEWS stated: "Mr. Shobe of Union has taken the contract to burn 100,000 bricks for the Atlantic and Pacific Construction Co. to be used in constructing a large roasting furnace for their mill." Several brick buildings using Shobe's product remain at Grantsville, including the school house and mess halls at the mill.

Just below the enclosure containing the ichthyosaur exhibits is the camp set up by excavation crews composed mostly of men students interested in the work. It took advantage of several old buildings remaining from Union's lusty days and added a few ingenious improvements. Coming in from work, covered with dust and perspiration, the men used a unique bathing arrangement. Water from an icy cold spring was conveyed to a metal tank near quarters, the sun heating it during the day to usable temperature. Immediately below the tank a bath tub was placed and connected to the tank. It is included in the park camp grounds and campers are free to use it, if privacy is not required. This fact usually confines the use to small fry whose mothers are glad to remove a few layers of road dust from the young hides.

BROKEN HILLS, NEVADA

Joseph Arthur just stood there staring. He could hardly believe in the reality of the gleaming rock there on the ground, glinting with bright streaks of metallic silver. When he picked it up and turned it over and over, he found he was talking to himself. "This is it! This is it!" And indeed the chunk of float proved to be a fair sample of the wealth soon unearthed in the sagebrush covered Broken Hills.

The discovery was not a haphazard stroke of luck. No burro's frisking heels uncovered it, nor any dying vulture's thrashing wings. It was the just reward of a long conducted search. In fact when Joe Arthur was only a small boy he had stood on a hill with his father who had brought him to Eastern Nevada. He looked out over the vast panorama to the west and asked: "What's over there, dad?" The answer: "Many ranges of mountains with many valleys between. That's where prospectors go looking for gold and silver." Little Joe considered that as he traced the outlines of the ranges sharply defined in the desert air. "That's what I'm going to do," he said with conviction, "when I grow up".

The Arthur family, father, mother, sister and Joe — had come to the new raw country from England. Mr. Arthur got a job in the Ruby mines and on Sundays preached in momentarily quiet saloons and gambling houses. As soon as Joe was old enough to work he too got a job in the mines, all the while listening to talk and reading about mining, metallurgy and prospecting for his own education. As soon as he could he headed out into the mountains — and learned a hard lesson. The first few years he met nothing but discouragement but he learned how to persevere. He kept on prospecting and working in the mines when he had to for money to keep on prospecting.

The gods were on his side for in the same vicinity another Englishman, James M. Stratford was looking for something better to happen. Stratford had made one fairly good strike in the Desatoyas, a few miles north of where the modern day town of Gabbs is. A moderate rush had poured in around the claim and a little town named for him. But the mineral wealth proved to be confined to his claim only and was very modest at that. So the camp melted away and left Stratford to eke out a meager living. Now Joe Arthur came along to check on a claim he had filed in the Stratford area. He found no metal but did find a kindred spirit in Jim Stratford. The two joined forces and that fall headed into the hills together.

They worked all winter and into spring, systematically pecking at ledges, cracking pieces of float, panning samples of gravel in streams. Results? Nothing but discouragement. On the evening of

STORES and other places of business in Broken Hills were modest, this one including living quarters at left. Storage shelter for food supplies is dugout, partly showing at rear corner.

GRAVE OF MATT COSTELLO is lonely one on top of knoll. After life of grinding poverty miner made good strike, sold claim for $1,500. Few days later he was found dead, sitting at his table. Friends buried him near cabin all traces of which have vanished.

April 12 as the two were preparing supper, Jim breathed his discontent. "I'd sure like a cup of coffee when it's ready. Joe — let's call it quits." We'll never find anything this way." Joe nodded — but he hadn't forgotten the lesson he'd learned, keep on trying. "Let's look around just one more day, Jim. If nothing shows up by tomorrow evening, I'll be ready to give up."

The next morning the men separated so as to cover as much ground as possible, Jim taking the ridge, Joe the gully. In the first half hour Joe found several small pieces of promising material and followed the trail, growing more excited by the

foot. He kept picking up more fragments until he saw the large, glittering rock.

He had been almost afraid to let himself believe the signs but now he let his feelings break loose and was shaking all over. As soon as he could get settled down he piled rocks to mark the outcropping from which his silvery find had come, then systematically staked out three claims — the Belmont, Grand Prize and Butler. With his own "grand prize" in his hands he went back to camp and waited anxiously. A pot of coffee was waiting for Jim when he returned dejectedly. "I didn't find a thing. How about you?" In dramatic silence Joe held out the silvery rock.

SMALL, SCRUBBY DESERT GROWTHS persisting in dry gravel cast long shadows as another long, lonely day ends for Broken Hills. Town's life was lively but short, only strike of value being that of man who founded town. Main street was curving gravel road at right. Facing buildings here are a few more across road.

Partners Arthur and Stratford were able to raise money for equipment and supplies to start operation by simply showing some of the ore so rich in gold and silver. Others flocked in, scraping away sagebrush to start a little one street town called Broken Hills. One of the men, Maury Stromer, long afterward told Nell Murbarger, author of "Ghosts of the Glory Trail"; "It was a nice little town, good, decent folks — decent and law abiding. Sure, we had a few saloons, bawdy houses and gambling halls, but they didn't dominate the place."

Joe and Jim stayed with it for five years by which time they had taken out $60,000. They then sold out to George Graham Rice, notorious promoter of Rawhide, for $75,000. Joseph Arthur, still only forty-three, retired to Reno to live with his wife Zua, and Stratford, ten years older, also retired.

In 1921 there was a substantial hotel in Broken Hills operated by partners Daniels and Ross of Yerington, Nevada. "Scotty" McLeod of the latter place tells of the tragedy that took place there. Ross had a beautiful daughter, an accomplished pianist. A single man was greatly attracted to her but the girl did not return his feelings. The man made strenuous advances one evening when they were alone in the kitchen. Repulsed, he raged out of the hotel, first emptying a kerosene lamp on the floor in the hallway and setting it on fire. Neither Daniels nor the girl's father was in the building and first learned of the disaster when they saw the flames. Ross tore himself from restraining arms, dashed into the inferno to find his daughter on her knees in a corner of the kitchen "with her hands folded as if she were praying."

Her father dragged her to the door where he collapsed. "His ears were burned clear off and the flesh fell from his hands," Scotty says. Ross soon died in agony and a double funeral was held in Yerington. "My wife and I went to both service and mass the next morning. It was the saddest thing we ever knew."

Broken Hills was a waterless place. Every drop had to be hauled several miles across the desert from Lodi Tanks, natural reservoirs. Lodi had been a booming camp in the '70s with hotel, saloons, etc. but it died early, leaving only the water. When Rawhide flared into lusty life in 1907, miners had a need for water though despising it for drinking purposes. So Lodi Tanks came to life again and had spurts of activity every time another camp sprang up. It was a spasmodic sort of existence but Lodi

PRICKLY "DESERT POPPY" blooms profusely in lone streets, is properly called Argemone. Various parts of showy annual plant have emetic, narcotic properties. White petals have crinkled, satiny look, are centered by cluster of yellow stamens, flower being about six inches across.

had nothing else. When Broken Hills came begging for water, Lodi was willing to provide it. It was free at the source but by the time it was hauled to Broken Hills by wagon it cost $2.50 a barrel. Later Maury Stromer obtained a truck and hauled the water for $1.

Arthur and Stratford left a 6,000 ton pile of inferior ore on their dump to be worked when and if a suitable mill was erected. It was this potential added to the mines that interested George Graham Rice. His interest was not quite the same as the original owners. He was a promoter only, his methods in Goldfield and later Rawhide only a bare jump ahead of the law. Before he acquired the Arthur-Stratford mine he sent geologist Arthur Perry Thompson to check out the possible wealth in Broken Hills at $60 a day. This was to appear in a fancy prospectus and sometimes a geologist at $60 a day could make things appear very glossy. Sure enough the reports from Broken Hills were very enthusiastic. Cracker Jack, Black Dog, Grand Prize, Belmont, Go-Between and the Broken Hills claims were all of "unusual merit, fully deserving of future development". Governor Emmett D. Boyle, himself a veteran mining man, also seemed to see a rosy future for the camp — "The best potential I've seen in any new Nevada territory for many years." Analyzed, the ambiguous statements did not mean the prospects were good but who wanted to doubt anything that sounded like they wanted it to sound. Much property changed hands and the

Arthur and Stratford holdings were paid for by Rice — with, of course, his stockholders' money.

As it happened the new owners of the claims could not get going, though now and then they did send in a small shipment of reasonably good ore, enough to keep the share holders from screaming too loudly. Altogether production under the new management amounted to a paltry 35 tons worth some $7,000. When some investors compared this with the $75,000 dropped in the mine shafts, they put the glasses on Mr. Rice. His activities led to a full scale investigation and his confinement in the penitentiary.

Smaller operators took over at Broken Hills, the town barely existing. There was a minor burst of activity during the depression years and figures show a production of $197,195 between 1935 and 1940. As people returned to their former jobs, Broken Hills faded away entirely, except for Maury Stromer. He continued to work his mine, the Badger, the hard way, descending to dig ore, loading it in the bucket, hauling it back up. He made about $5 a day at this backbreaking work.

Winters are raw with snow in Broken Hills and Maury finally took some holidays with his daughter in Paso Robles, California. He was taken ill in March, 1956, and died in the hospital. Burial was in his beloved Nevada at Reno. That left Broken Hills, a place deserted except for jackrabbits bounding among the sagebrush and pack rats making homes in the empty shacks.

"HIS" AND "HERS", built straddling worthless mine shaft, offering some hazards as supports barely touch crumbling edges of deep hole. Incidental is beauty of desert —etched wood showing grains and textures.

WRAITHS OF THE WAILING WINDS

CANDELARIA, NEVADA

"Patrick O'Leary, Native of Ireland, Age 25 yrs." So reads an old headboard in the desolate cemetery on a sunbaked knoll above Candelaria.

Patrick sleeps in a setting far different from his cool, green Emerald Isle. There is no grass; no trees shade the little plot filled only with leaning headboards, blistering rocks and rattlesnakes.

Candelaria never had a Chamber of Commerce to boost it as a good place to live. It wouldn't have done any good, anyway. There were several livery stables with big piles of horse manure in back. The flies multiplied by millions and had free access to screenless windows of houses, hotels and boardinghouses.

All water was hauled from a spring nine miles away and cost those who used the stuff a dollar a gallon; whiskey was cheaper!

Even the stampmill dispensed with water in the crushers and the resultant pall of dust settled in the lungs of the miners, who died by dozens of "miner's consumption." Perhaps poor young Patrick O'Leary was one of those.

Mexicans had found silver ore here in 1864, but siesta prevailed until 1879, when a polyglot population of Germans, Slavonians and others, mostly foreign born, took over and built a boom town. Construction was largely of adobe and stone. At this time the big producer was the Northern Belle, credited with a $15,000,000 production in silver.

A narrow-gauge railroad, the Carson and Colorado, connected Candelaria to Keeler on the shores of Owens Lake (which once lay at the foot of Mt. Whitney) and to Mina. Other small towns sprang up along the line; Sodaville, Belleville, and more, but these are nearly gone by now.

After the first big silver boom the town nearly died, breathing only fitfully until about the turn of the century when it revived to the tune of some $1,000,000 worth of gold, lead and copper, along with more silver.

FORTRESS-LIKE STONE STRUCTURE had varied career. It served as a bank, was almost impregnable during raids by bandits and holdup men. Stores, saloons and other business ventures shared quarters at different times. Interior seems dark in contrast to glare of outdoors, windows were purposely omitted as offering weak spots to attack.

HOT SUN SIMMERS GRAVEYARD. Grave enclosures were common in early cemeteries. Ornamentation differed on each. In this picture the one at left protects the grave of Patrick O'Leary. Main street of Candelaria extends beyond. Extensive stamp mills were at point where road curves to left in distance. Most mines were on hill at left, just out of camera range.

DAYTON, NEVADA

Adolph Sutro was a "man with a dream" who conceived the idea of a horizontal tunnel so as to haul out the ore and drain off the water from the deepest shafts of the Comstock, whose mouths opened up near the top of Mt. Davidson, the site of Virginia City.

Almost insurmountable obstacles were placed in his way, especially financial ones. The big mining companies agreed to put up the huge sum of $5,000,000 and the money was eventually forthcoming in the shape of royalties of $2.00 per ton, the water to be free.

Delays stalled completion for thirteen years, so long that the heyday of the Comstock was over. Ore removal continued for years, however, and in 1880, as a sample year, the 20,489 feet of tunnel delivered two billion gallons of water; water almost impossible to remove vertically, which flooded mining operations and was so hot it steamed.

Dayton now has a charming old-time atmosphere with a good many of the original buildings standing here and there. It is not quite dead, however. Complete demise is impossible for any town on a highway. There will, at least, be filling stations and taverns.

YEARS HAVE PASSED since services were held in little church in Dayton. Graceful architecture is evident in doorway. Old church is separated from center of town which offers a typical group of early-day buildings.

EUREKA, NEVADA

Eureka, in 1864, was all set for the explosive rush and boom of other mining camps. Certainly the discovery of lead-silver deposits was as spectacular and important as most, and one of the first big finds of the bi-metallic ore in the country. But expansion of the infant settlement was slowed by the refractory qualities of the material. New methods of smelting had to be devised. The first plant built in 1869 was a failure. Another was erected with different, hitherto unknown grinders and baking methods. This was more successful and pointed the way to still better ways of extracting the metal. Then the boom began in earnest and by 1880 Eureka's population had reached nearly 10,000. But then production began to fall off and things looked bad for the young town. About this time several Comstock-made millionaires built a railroad into Eureka, and because of its central position in the state, the town became a railhead for the whole area.

But the mining boom was over, to revive weakly at intervals, in 1905, during the first world war and in the 30's. The smelters, established under such difficulties, had been closed since 1891. Stamp mills, cyanide plants, refineries and smelters have always meant as much to the economy of these early camps as the actual mining operations. Their end means slow strangulation and such was the case for Eureka. However, there is still life here, partly due to the fact that a paved highway with its tourists passes through. Eureka deserves a day or so of looking around, for it is full of historic buildings, ruins of smelters and mementos of the days when it produced $40,000,000 in silver, $20,000,000 in gold and 225,000 pounds of lead.

OBVIOUSLY NOT A "DEAD" ghost town, Eureka is a museum of mining history. The Main Street, coinciding with the highway, is lively with stores, fire department and other establishments. Balcony of theatre offered cooling breezes during intermissions, was not so popular in winter.

FAIRVIEW, NEVADA

Fairview did not want to stay put; it pulled up stakes twice. The first location was no doubt settled upon because of unlimited level ground on which to build. The view from the site is a magnificent, endless expanse of desert backed up by equally arid mountains. One of these, nearer than the others, has two humps on its low summit. Naturally, the mine gouged out on its side was called "The Dromedary."

The most imposing structure built on site No. 1 was the bank, which included a solid stone and concrete vault. That there were many streets of houses and buildings to shelter and serve the 2,000 people who lived there, is attested by rows of cellars open to the skies. It seems the populace grew weary of commuting so far to the mines and mills, so they moved everything except the bank vault to a spot in the narrow canyon a couple of miles nearer the working area. The ancient vault, standing as the only monument to mark the abandoned location, can easily be seen from the highway.

After a few years in the constricted defile of porphyry rock, the new town again grew restive. Not finding enough space for expansion it was getting longer and longer with the width limited to one block.

So the third and final move was to gather around the mill, and here remain the vestiges of Fairview, its perambulations now long ended.

RAMBLING LITTLE "MAIN STREET" is remaining nucleus of once extensive town. Building at lower right once housed nice flock of chickens, but food for them proved difficult to provide. Buildings at left hold variety of ancient cars. Sagebrush on hills is almost evenly spaced, limited by scarcity of moisture.

GALENA, NEVADA

What remains of this once bustling gold camp forms a satisfying ghostly remnant. Complete desertion is the lot of Galena, where once the population surpassed that of the nearby metropolis, Battle Mountain.

It was laid out in 1869 and in a couple of years had burgeoned into a boom town complete with a park, a rarity in a day when more thought was given to roistering than to the beauties of nature. The most conspicuous feature of Galena, though, was the smelter built to extract silver and lead from the rough material produced by the Dutch Creek Mine. This amounted to some $5,000,000.

The mill itself has long since disappeared, but its site is marked by extensive tailings dumps. These are constituted of flour-fine material which has solidified into piles of something like hard clay. Above these are dumps of waste rock, each heap a different color, the native material being so varied from place to place.

The cemetery is quite large. The earlier dates still discernible on the old headboards are in the 70's. It is close to town, the equivalent of a couple of blocks, and those who died with their boots on were simply carried over and buried with little ceremony. A bottle was passed around afterward, and that was that.

IF THIS WAS "PUBLIC SQUARE," perhaps tiny band played Sousa here on summer evenings, as was the custom in so many towns of era.

MAIN STREET IS SPARSELY fringed by scattered structures. Upper, with fancy railing likely was boardinghouse. Rock in street is mostly galena ore, some glittering with silver, lead.

GENOA, NEVADA

"Fighting" Sam Brown of Virginia City was pure bully, although he bragged he had filled a graveyard singlehanded. For a time he ran things in the mining camp on Mount Davidson and it was at the height of his ascendancy that one of his young henchmen was caught holding up a stage and was taken to the then county seat of Douglas County, Genoa, for trial.

Sam stormed down to the picturesque Mormon town at the base of the Sierra to attend the trial, fully prepared to bluster the judge and jury into intimidation and thereby, free his cohort.

What Sam didn't know was that the county had a new District Attorney, Bill Stewart, and that young Stewart had been informed of what he might expect of the witness. Testimony at the trial had been going against the stage robber, and when it came time for Sam to testify he was boiling mad. Storming up to the stand he was fully primed with the best liquor Genoa had to offer and was prepared to bluster that young lawyer into submission. The edge of his resolution was considerable dulled when he found himself facing the muzzle of a gun held in the steady hand of the man who would one day be U.S. Senator from Nevada. Cowed, Sam gave tistimony at best not calculated to help the case of his friend, who was soon convicted.

As soon as he got out of the courtroom and away from the end of Stewart's six-shooter, Sam, regaining his courage, raging at his failure, and returning to the Comstock, took it out on an innocent Dutch farmer who lived near the road, firing several shots in his direction. His aim being as bad as his disposition, Sam missed the Dutchman, who now understandably got *his* dander up, and with considerably better aim, cut short the career of "Fighting" Sam Brown. A coroner's jury held that "Brown came to his end by the dispensation of a Divine Providence." Van Sickle, once more phlegmatic, paid little attention, having returned to his again placid fields.

Those Argonauts heading for the California gold fields that preferred going overland to an even more dangerous sea voyage again had several choices of route. Some sought to shorten the distance by crossing the terrible Salt Lake Desert to reach the Humboldt. More headed for Fort Hall and Soda Spring, thence south to the river. Some went north around the main part of the great desert, avoiding the greater part of it though still suffering their full share of hardships.

For the first few years of overland travel pioneers could count on shooting game for a food supply. As travel increased, all living creatures soon were exterminated over a wide band adjacent to the route. Those depending on the bounty of the land found themselves hungry to the point of starvation by the time they reached the Humboldt, many had even eaten their dairy cows and some of the beasts hauling the wagons.

It was only natural, therefore, that trading posts would soon be established along the Humboldt Road as the wall of the Sierra grew nearer, the travelers sometimes still having a little cash, not having had any opportunity to spend it. A small settlement grew up beside the first of these establishments. Weary, dirty families often took the rest stop as an opportunity to wash out all clothing still serviceable, hanging the tattered remnants on surrounding bushes to dry. And so "Ragtown" came into being, the name later was changed to Leeteville.

For a time this was the last settlement, then, in June of 1849 Col. John Reese, a trader sent out by Brigham Young, built a log stockade, corrals and a cabin or two at the very foot of the Sierra. At first the place was called, simply, Mormon Station, that being exactly what it was. As others became established this one needed a more identyfying cognomen and a settler with an Italian background called it Genoa. Since the earlier Ragtown never became a permanent fixture, Genoa was the first real town in the state of Nevada, although that state didn't exist at the time of Genoa's founding. For those who fol-

lowed every tenet of Brigham Young it was the state of Deseret. In 1850 the United States Government declared the area to be part of the Territory of Utah, the southern part of what is now Nevada going into the Territory of New Mexico.

An interesting sidelight on the story of Genoa is that when the first gold-hungry men who were heading for the Mother Lode and Northern Mines stopped beside the Carson River near Genoa they panned the stream and actually did find a little gold, but were too filled with dreams of the other side of the Sierra to pay much attention. Later, when the big Washoe Boom hit the Nevada side many of those same adventurers, disappointed in what they found in California rushed back again, proving once again that the grass is always greener on the other side of the fence.

The Sierra was a formidable barrier between east and west travel. Placerville, the fastest growing boom town of the gold rush on the western slope, was the terminus of a rude "road," little more than a path. Genoa was at the eastern end, exactly at the point

STORE DATES FROM EARLIEST DAYS in Genoa. Colonel John Reese, his brother Enoch, and Steven A. Kinsey were among first builders of Mormon town. First lady settler was Eliza Ann Meddangh Mott, the wife of Israel Mott. Their daughter Sarah was the first native, she grew up here and married a Mr. Hawkins.

OLD SIGN ON GROCERY is protected from elements by canopy, has withstood ravages of time. Last item, "Queen's Ware" is flooded by direct sunlight, overexposed in picture.

"SNOWSHOE" THOMSON LIES AT FOOT of beloved Sierra in pioneer cemetery at Genoa. Snow-covered hills rising sharply in background are first easy step in what becomes giant barrier rising to over 14,000 feet at highest elevations, passes over which Thomson hiked averaged 7,400 feet. Thomson's "snowshoes" actually were skis, the first ever seen in West, when the word ski was unknown. Thomson's name is spelled "Thompson" in all available historical references. In face of evidence on stone and fact that Norwegians mostly spell the name without "P," we here follow them.

where the wildly rugged route suddenly flattened out into the desert. Situated as it was, the town could hardly help growing. By 1858 the place even had a newspaper, the first in the Territory. The few inhabitants of the whole area, still less than a thousand, were so hungry for news that a few "newspapers," really only hand-written sheets, had already been attempted. The *Scorpion* and *Gold Canyon Switch* were among these and had a tiny circulation in 1854. So a real, printed paper was an impressive and eagerly accepted innovation. It was called the *Territorial Enterprise.*

The infant paper remained a single sheeter for a time, then when the Washoe Bubble swelled the paper burgeoned into four-sheet size. It soon outgrew Genoa and as population expanded in Carson City the paper moved itself and equipment there. Then came the soaring expansion of Virginia City and the *Enterprise* again moved to what proved to be its permanent home, becoming a daily September 24, 1861.

The at first strictly Mormon settlement of Genoa began to be infiltrated by residents of other faiths in

a few years and among these was a sizable group of adherents to the Catholic faith. These managed to co-exist with the Mormons, but were unable to celebrate masses, confess or participate in any of the rites of the Church except in unconsecrated structures. Then in 1860 with the arrival of Father H. P. Gallagher a simple church was built and consecrated, the first Catholic one in Nevada.

Genoa has an interesting old cemetery with many ornate monuments, some enclosed by elaborate wrought iron fences. A more simple marble stone marks the grave of a Norwegian who was certainly the most remarkable mail carrier known to history. John A. Thomson, born 1827, traveled to the United States with his parents when he was ten years old. The family started farming in Illinois, then moved around through other midwestern states until John was twenty-four. This was in 1851 at a time when the whole country was filled with stories of fantastic gold discoveries in California. The young farmer was so taken with the idea of making a quick fortune he headed for the El Dorado. Arriving at Genoa he climbed over the Sierra along with hundreds of other goldseekers, coming out at Placerville on the California side. He didn't know it then, but the hardy Scandinavian was to retrace this route many times, and more, by himself with a heavy packful of mail on his back.

John worked in the Coon Hollow and Kelsey's Diggings near Placerville for a while, but with poor results. Becoming disgusted with mining he decided to try farming and bought a small place on Putah Creek in the Sacramento Valley. In 1856 he heard about the difficulties the government was having in getting the mail over the mountains in winter when deep snows clogged the high passes and this got Thomson to thinking. He loved the mountains, he had a strong physique and couldn't get lost, having "something in my head that keeps me right."

So he went out to his woodlot, cut a live oak down. He chose a good, nearly straight section about eight feet long and split the stubborn-grained wood into sections. Of the two most even ones he fashioned a pair of skis such as he had seen in Norway, full-sized versions of the small ones he had worn as a boy. They weighed twenty-five pounds. Then came an improvised balance pole. John took his new equipment up to the mountains and practiced on the snowy slopes. Then he showed up at the post office in Placerville and said he'd carry the mail over the snowy mountains, just like that. And carry the mail he did for twelve years, begining in January of 1856.

At first it took him four days to cover the ninety miles between Placerville and Carson Valley, but he soon pared off a day. His pack of mail often weighed

MAIN SECTION OF ORIGINAL TOWN of Genoa shows grocery at right flanked at left by newer, presently used grocery and filling station. At extreme left is inevitable tavern, housed in brick building dating back to 1860s.

eighty pounds so he carried little to eat, a few dried sausages and crackers, and no blankets. When forced to rest, he set fire to a dead pine stump, cut a few boughs and napped with his feet to the fire.

He often played the role of Good Samaritan as well. On one trip, he found a James Sisson half dead and with frozen feet in a cabin on the Nevada slope but nearer Placerville. After making Sisson as comfortable as possible, he returned to Placerville, persuaded several men to don makeshift skis, return to

the cabin with him and take Sisson down to Carson on a sledge. There a doctor decided Sisson's feet would have to be amputated but no chloroform was available. So Thomson retuned over the Sierra to Placerville where he got the precious stuff and again crossed the divide to get the anesthetic to the suffering man in Carson.

After a dozen years of this, the railroad was completed over the pass and Snowshoe Thomson was no longer needed. All this time he'd had no pay and, feeling he should have a little something for his efforts, applied to the post office. There he was told he'd have to go to Washington and make personal application for an appropriation, and this he did. There he got glowing promises of adequate reward, returning home well content. But nothing happened. Later, more promises came along.

He had established another farm in the upper Car-son Valley barely on the California side and here he settled down to agriculture again to await his pay. It never came. Although of the most robust constitution Thomson had suffered much in his snowy journeys, losing so much resistance to infection that when an illness attacked him May of 1876 he lasted only four days. His body was taken down to Genoa and buried there.

IN SHADE OF GIANT LOCUST TREES is restoration of old Mormon Station. Here, on June 10, 1851, Colonel James Reese arrived with 18 men, ten wagons full of supplies, received warm welcome from Hampden S. Beattie, who, with small contingent, had established waystop two years earlier. Combined force built original log Station headquarters, destroyed by fire in 1910. Reconstruction was done of historic building and completed in 1947 by Nevada State Planning Board in cooperation with Genoa Fort Committee.

"HANG ON TO IT, SANDY"

Gold Hill, Nevada

You could say "Old Virginia" Finney had two loves—his home state of Virginia and Forty-rod whiskey. He deserted the first but fell hard for the amber lightning. Once he stumbled at his desert camp, breaking the flask of whiskey in his hip pocket. He gazed ruefully at the dark spot on the ground and decided some use should be made of it. Scattering broken glass over the stain he intoned, "I christen this spot Virginia."

John Bishop's modest discovery of gold up the canyon from Johntown sparked the larger exploration of Nevada which was to some extent still unknown to man. Without Gold Canyon, Nevada's vast stores of mineral wealth might have remained under the ground for many years. Certainly the "fine dust" Bishop saw in the bottom of his pan eventually led to the later discoveries farther up the hill and the founding of Virginia City, most fabulous mining camp of all time, largely instrumental in saving the Civil War for the Union.

Old Johntown, long since utterly vanished, was a cluster of saloons, honky-tonks and shacks near the mouth of Gold Canyon and not far from where Dayton was later established. It was a hangout for prospectors and drifters of all kinds. In the summer of 1859 men were swarming all over the surrounding hills, including Sun Peak (later Mt. Davidson). No spectacular discoveries were made but enough to warrant further search. Autumn brought a heavy freeze followed by continuous cold, all streams freezing solid, stopping all pan-

GOLD HILL BAR AND HOTEL flourished with mine production, ups and downs reflected in patronage, gambling tables. Sustained prosperity was maintained for 20 years, 1868-88. Records show Yellow Jacket mine poured forth $14 million, Crown King $11, adjoining Belcher $15,397,200 in dividends. Old stone and brick structure is still solid. Turned balusters on balcony are originals. Much plaster has fallen from walls, exposing field stone.

ning and sluicing attempts. Everybody retired to Johntown to spend the winter.

Toward the end of January there was a general thaw that sent water running in all the gulches. Men suffering from cabin fever and satiated with the pleasures of the flesh headed up Gold Canyon, the party that included John Bishop having a certain place in mind, a rocky knoll on the west side just north of where Gold Hill would be established.

Bishop later wrote, "Where Gold Hill now stands I had noticed indications of a ledge and had got a little color. I spoke to 'Old Virginia' about it and he said he remembered the locality, that he had often noticed it when out hunting for deer and antelope. He also said he had seen any quantity of quartz, so he joined our party and Comstock also followed along. When we got to the ground I took a pan and filled it with dirt with my foot as I had no shovel or spade." Bishop took the pan to a cluster of willows on the creek. "There was considerable gold left in the bottom, very fine, like flour," he said. "Old Virginia decided that it was a good place to begin work."

The immediate problem was water enough to wash the gold dust and Old Virginia Finney appointed himself the one to go look. He set off up the canyon while, as Bishop told it, "I and my partner meantime had a talk together, and decided to put the others of our party in the middle of the good ground." When Finney returned with the news he had located ample water and learned he had been omitted from these plans he was under-

standably irked. He made some bitter remarks and added, "Well, if you boys are going to hog it all go ahead. I'm going to make my own strike." However he must have changed his mind for when the claims were laid out to be staked, he took his along with the rest. When the men conferred on a name all at first favored Gold Canyon but since the strike was on a hill, the name would be Gold Hill.

Other prospectors sniffed at Bishop's find. The dust was so fine it was hardly worth bothering with, they said. But when the dirt was worked up to a point where a rotted ledge of quartz was uncovered it became evident the boys had a bonanza, foreseen by the astute Bishop. Johntown unbelievers widened their eyes when Gold Hill takes grew from $5 a day per man to $15, then $25. Then came the rush with the men camping under small trees all along the canyon, then in shanties and then log houses. Gold Hill could now be called a reality.

Another celebrated personality of Gold Hill was Allison "Eilley" Orrum Hunter Cowan Bowers who had progressed from her native Scotland to the camp by a devious route. When Eilley reached her fifteenth birthday she became a Mormon convert at the urging of Stephen Hunter who was proselyting in the old country. It turned out Hunter had more in mind than converting the attractive lassie. He ran off with her to Nauvoo, Illinois, the Mormon stronghold in America, and married her in the church.

GOLD HILL city fathers were once so optimistic as to introduce act in Territorial Legislature to put up state capital building on level spot near town. Prosperity in mining camps was largely gauged by price of drinks in saloons. 10-cent shot indicated camp of small respect and when bars in Gold Hill began charging "two bits" for slug of redeye, high rating of town was acknowledged.

Fires periodically ravaged thriving camp, one in Yellow Jacket mine erupting April 7, 1869, most sombre day in town's history. Combined fire fighting forces of communities failed over flames roaring thru underground tunnels. 33 men died, only 27 bodies recovered. Some fires smoldered 3 years.

Another fire in 1873 killed 4, injured 11. These ruins were left when ground level flames gutted interior. Though then doing little business post office managed to operate until Feb. 27, 1943. Years before that drinks in saloons were reduced to 10 cents, Gold Hill News editor remarking, "With nothing but ten cent saloons in town we might as well suspend," and did just that.

All went well with the romance until Hunter took a second wife under the policy of bigamy. Eilley's was an independent spirit not tolerating a second woman in her husband's bed and during preparations for the epic Mormon migration to Utah, the ex-Mrs. Hunter met and married young Alexander Cowan.

The Cowans had barely settled themselves in Salt Lake when they were sent still farther west to help colonize the valleys near Mormon Genoa in Nevada. Then once again plans were interrupted. The United States threatened to send troops against the Mormons and Brigham Young called back all scattered settlers in far flung places. Eilley's new husband was eager to respond but not his Scottish spouse. She was sick of repeated expeditions forced by the church and bade her second husband goodbye. She remained in Nevada.

In Johntown Eilley started a boarding house that was successful from the start because of her good Scotch cooking. She followed the mass evacuation to Gold Hill and set up her business there. Among the boarders was young Sandy Bowers who attracted her despite his being fourteen years younger and she began showing him favors of several varieties, eventually marrying him. It was gossiped about by other boarders that Sandy had run up a big board bill and was vulnerable to the lady's proposal. His present to the bride was a strip of "dirt" alongside his own early established claim.

Married life was just under way when the diggings began to fail generally with the result that the more easily discouraged sold out. Mrs. Bowers persuaded Sandy not to capitulate but rather buy some of the now cheap claims. The rest is history. While others lost their holdings the Bowers sud-

BANK OF CALIFORNIA was branch of main office in Virginia City, short distance above on Sun Mountain. Intense rivalry existed between towns. To escape being overwhelmed by larger VC thru greedy operators who wished to grab Gold Hill's support for building sidewalks, gas, sewers, street lights, other improvements in VC without benefit to GH, it incorporated Dec. 17, 1862 gaining victory over faction in legislature featuring its annexation to VC.
Boundaries were described as "on the north by the southern boundary of Virginia City; on the east and south by the boundary line between Storey and Lyon (Counties); on the west by the boundary between Storey and Washoe." Apparently Gold Hill was ever optimistic about wealth underground, permanence of then booming town.

HUGE BOWERS MANSION was built in 1862 at cost of $300,000, largely furnished with expensive appointments bought by the Bowers on triumphal tour of Europe. On return of new-wealthy pair, Sandy Bowers felt uneasy in luxurious aspect, preferred saloons, housekeeping rooms at Gold Hill. When he died there at 35, members of Gold Hill Masonic Lodge conducted his funeral at Fraternal Hall, and in accordance with last wishes to "Follow me as far as you can," population formed procession on horses, in carriages and wagons extending almost solidly down to Bowers' mansion.
Sandy Bowers was laid to rest on hill few yards behind great house he disdained. Later he was joined in death by adopted daughter Persia. Many years later when owner of Bower house heard of Eilley Bowers' death he had her body brought home, placed beside kin. Graves are in brushy area of high fire danger, access denied by authorities.

denly began to take in thousands of dollars a day from their united claims which hit a bonanza. In a few months Eilley and Sandy were millionaires.

With huge wealth now at her disposal Eilley resolved to build a castle that would put to shame anything previously built in Nevada, an easy thing to do since few miners, even fabulously rich ones, wanted permanent homes there. And Eilley dreamed of a grand tour of Europe staging as a finale audience with Queen Victoria.

The great mansion was erected down on the level land near Washoe City (see *Ghost Town Album*). And off to Europe she and Sandy went, buying splendid furnishings for the great house at every stop, the starry-eyed Mrs. Bowers paying any price asked. She would show those old fogeys in Scotland who had objected to her romance with Hunter what was what, even though Hunter had little to do with her present affluence. The tour was a shining success until she came up against British protocol. Queen Victoria refused to see Eilley, a divorcee.

After two years the Bowers returned home, following a steady stream of marble mantles, gilded French furniture and plush fixtures that had to be shipped around the Horn, then freighted over the High Sierra.

But all this was Eilley's dream come true, not Sandy's. He refused to live permanently in the mansion so lavishly appointed, caring nothing for the glossy society Eilley hoped to gather around her, and rejoined his old cronies in the Gold Hill saloons. Being nothing like astute he allowed his business affairs to become hopelessly muddled and suddenly died in 1868. He was thirty-five years old.

Sadly enough Eilley realized little from the claims when sold due to litigation and accumulated debts, although the properties were potentially very valuable. The widow, once so natively canny, became strangely trustful and careless. Before long it was necessary to mortgage the immense house and retire from public entertaining and ostentatious display. Too late she reversed her spending, making one last extravagant gesture—the purchase of a large crystal ball.

Acting on advice from the sphere she attempted to run the mansion as an elegant resort which involved cook and maid services for the paying guests. When there was no money left to pay them, they left and Eilley reverted to her former status as cook, maid and laundress. When she could talk her guests into it she told their fortunes with the aid of her crystal ball.

Apparently by not interpreting her advice correctly, one man lost a fortune in selling a claim that soon proved an El Dorado. The incident did much to undermine any reputation Mrs. Bowers retained. The activity of seeress and other sources of income fell off to nothing, the one-time millionairess was left broke and starving. She sold the house to a wealthy man who pitied her enough to allow her to stay as scullery maid and janitress, but Eilley was unable to scrub floors any more. She was discharged and drifted away to die in 1903, a ragged, lonely old woman.

BOWERS MANSION had advantage of high-priced architects, builders. Stone cutters were likely Cornish "Cousin Jacks" rightly reputed to be best in world. Stone blocks were so well trimmed little or no mortar was necessary. Cracks shown here were caused by severe earthquake that shook down magnificent ruin of Withington Hotel in ghost town of Hamilton (see Western Ghost Towns).

In 1873 State of Nevada had chance to buy Bowers house and surrounding 120 acres for $20,000, contemplating use as insane asylum but deal failed. Much later house and grounds became county park, with picnic area, swimming pool. In 1967 facilities were enlarged. Fortunately mansion itself remains intact, visitors conducted thru faded splendors for small fee.

GOLDFIELD, NEVADA

In the center of Goldfield is a large hotel. Although all its doors are padlocked, in the lobby there is a grand piano surrounded by leather "settees," and luxurious chairs.

In the dining room everything is set up for a normal, busy dinner hour. Leather-backed chairs are drawn up to the tables spread with linen covers. Silver, glasses and sugar bowl await the diner. Only the heavy mantle of dust gives evidence that these tables had been set up long ago for a repast never served.

Goldfield is dead. This is a city once boasting a population of 30,000 where, in the boom of 1906, lots sold for $45,000. Originally called "Grandpa" when Billy March and Harry Stimler staked out their claim in 1902, the name was changed when "jewelry rock" running $50 to $100 a pound was found.

There were plenty of labor troubles, strikes and disorders of all sorts. Several times State Police troops had to be called in to restore order, an uneasy quiet at best. High grading was common and almost unsuppressed. Miners put rich blosssom rocks heavily laced with gold in their pockets and lunch boxes, peddling them to waiting fences at night.

Uncounted saloons flourished in Goldfield, the most famous one, Tex Rickard's Northern, had a bar so long 80 tenders were necessary.

Tex Rickard made his fortune in the Klondike, lost it in California, and came to Goldfield with the gold strike. His first big promotion was the champion prize fight between Gans and Nelson in 1906. That fight lasted 42 rounds, and put Gans up as the world lightweight champion.

The all-time high in production was $11,000,000, but this phenomenal figure dropped to $5,000,000 by 1912, and those who recognized the signs began to pull out. In 1918 the mines put out only $1,500,000 and this was cut in half the next year. The next three together saw only $150,000 produced. Then even this dwindled and Goldfield joined the ranks of has-beens, but probably few Ghost Towns put on such an impressive front of buildings standing and in good repair. It takes a second look to discern the boarded-up windows, the bars across the doors, the padlocks and nails barring the way into once-busy buildings and stores. The corpse "looks so natural."

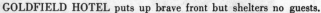
GOLDFIELD HOTEL puts up brave front but shelters no guests.

GOLD POINT, NEVADA

The town really boasts only one group of store buildings dating from the earliest days, the typical tiny structures huddling together, putting on a brave show of false fronts and gingerbread. A couple of blocks above is the Post Office, apparently abandoned. A sign, once hung over it, is now on its side on the porch; it reads *"Gold Point, Nevada live population (so far) 28. Ghost unlimited. Altitude 5,800. Taxes very low."* At *this* date 28 would be a high estimate, less than half that number still live in the Gold Point area.

Originally christened "Hornsilver," it went along with the title until 1929. At that time silver had so languished that investors decided that "Gold Point" would have more value as a name.

Two thousand people once thronged the streets, which provided the usual saloons, hotels and stores, now dwindled to our forlorn little huddle and some scattered shacks.

Poor milling processes in those days which lost most of the values in the tailings, together with constant litigation over rights of the mill to operate, killed the town. It slumbers now, awaiting the resurrection.

GOLD POINT NEARS END of yet another day. Desert landscape stretches beyond, its Joshua trees and buttes soon to merge into darkness.

GOODSPRINGS, NEVADA

"Things are quiet here," Sam McClanahan said, "if people keep on moving away this ain't going to be nothing but a damned Ghost Town."

He had seen the early boom days when Goodsprings was a lusty young camp producing not only gold but a wealth of other minerals, silver, platinum and vanadium.

These are still to be found and, if their recovery could be accomplished cheaply enough, would pay off. But the old mill, an extensive one, is a collapsed mass of ruined ovens, walls and machinery. Sam told the same old story of frozen gold prices, advanced labor and machinery costs. Fondling his ancient gold pan he surmised that "some day, we'll get going again, when gold advances." He showed me some pieces of tufa, a light, foamy type of rock which he had found in the nearby hills. With capital, he said, he could build motels of this material which would provide insulation, "and those tourists in Las Vegas could come up here and get away from the heat."

But old Sam didn't really feel all this would come to pass. Like many other gnarled old-timers of the western Ghost Towns, he was just reluctant to admit that the town he had lived with so long will soon join the ranks of those decaying remnants of another day.

WHERE TIME STANDS STILL and there is no "progress," outdoor "conveniences" are still prominent feature. Even such lowly structure exhibits beautiful textures of weathered wood.

ONE OF EARLIEST RESIDENCES has remaining stone wall propped. Door opens only into more open s p a c e . Goodsprings is center of highly mineralized area, azurite, chrysocolla, malachite, cinnabar are among many prized specimens found on dumps of mines in past. Sources are nearly depleted now.

GRANTSVILLE, NEVADA

On a cold and snowy day in February 1881, a frightened Mexican miner sat in a tunnel shivering. The tunnel was one dug into the mountains at the mining camp of Grantsville which had proved barren of gold and made useful as a jail. It was cold in the tunnel but the Mexican was trembling for another reason. He was charged with the murder of a fellow worker the night before and he was afraid Grantsville citizens, fired up with Shoshone Mountain hooch, would not wait for legal justice.

He was right. The heavy tunnel door crashed in and the roaring mob of miners made for him, the lead man carrying a rope. Pedro was hustled off to the stamp mill, hoisted up on a massive timber, the rope thrown over a higher one, noose slipped over his head. One push and the luckless man was swinging in the wind.

A coroner's jury next day named several persons thought guilty of the lynching. When questioned by the sheriff, the spokesman gave their reason for the

DWELLING IS BUILT of native, uncut stone. Some pains were taken to place flattened side outward for neater effect. Roof was of usual brush construction over poles, thick layer of mud plastered overall. "Airtight" tin heater in center of single room provided heat and cooking surface. Fuel was brush and pine wood.

LITTLE RED BRICK SCHOOLHOUSE supposedly had capacity of sixty pupils, but for this number interior seems cramped. Elegantly proportioned fireplace occupies left end. When supply of pupils dwindled, building was converted into boarding house, with kitchen at left, sleeping space gained by addition of shed at right.

action. The previous August another murderer had been arrested and tried in a legal manner. He was judged guilty but instead of the death sentence he was sent to the state prison where he was serving out an ordinary life sentence. The Mexican had been lynched to avoid his receiving similar soft treatment. The explanation was accepted and the incident forgotten.

The discoverer of gold in Grantsville was P. A. Haven, the same prospector who had located the first vein in Ione. Here he immediately organized a mining district and laid out a town. When eager miners came in droves, Haven was ready for them, selling them lots from $50 to $500. Whatever made the difference in the price, it was not the view, for all the lots had that if nothing else. "Grantsville is laid out," read an early description, "in a beautiful canyon" — a gross understatement. The steep canyon walls were covered with a heavy growth of nut pine trees, the predominant forest cover of the area and altitude. Later all the trees were cut down for fuel, shoring and charcoal.

Haven seemed to be more interested in discovering potential wealth and promoting it than in making any development. His original claim was worked out soon after he left and the place languished almost to a ghost town before it was ever well established. In September 1877, a representative of the Alexander Company, a big mining firm, traveled the seventy dusty miles from Austin and had a look around. He acquired the property for the company, set to work to develop it and Grantsville soon began to look like the town it had started out to be.

There were two general merchandise stores, hardware and tin shop, a livery stable, blacksmith shop, two barber shops and a jewelry store. The town also boasted of two assay offices, a bank, furniture store, two drug stores and a fine restaurant. As usual, saloons outnumbered all others — twelve. Not mentioned in the factual report were bawdy houses but the camp would not have been unique in this respect.

Three weekly newspapers spoke for the area, a succession starting with the NYE COUNTY NEWS in

1867. It made out for about two years, was supplanted by the GRANTSVILLE SUN which lasted only one year when replaced by the GRANTSVILLE BONANZA.

The gold and silver in the Grantsville mining district were found in veins of porphyry, limestone and quartz running northwest to southeast, dipping into the earth at an angle. Other metals were there in variety, such as lead, antimony and copper. Milling was done by crushing and roasting according to information dated 1881, but other methods came in later as is evidenced by old flotation and paddle vats still in the ruins of one mill.

There was plenty of wood, a heavy stand of nut pine trees being ravished for fuel, and plenty of water the year around from several good springs.

All food and supplies were freighted in from Austin at a cost of $40 a ton. Most perishable foods were not obtainable in hot weather because of spoilage or in winter when roads were impassable. Some butter and milk were obtained from Ione where there was a dairy. Occasionally someone would attempt to keep chickens but imported grain was too expensive to make this practical. Also hen houses had to have some heat in winter, otherwise eggs froze in the nest, as did chickens' feet on the roosts at night.

Although Grantsville held tighter to prosperity than did her sister Ione, her death was complete when it came. The town has been deserted for many years, is today one of Nevada's loneliest ghost towns.

EXTENSIVE RUINS of mining operations remain in Grantsville. In extreme foreground is up-ended two-holer. Behind is mess hall for miners and mill workers, with kitchen attached at left. At right of, and behind mess hall, are ruins of stamp mill. Extending upwards are various sections of mill. Recovery here was done at least in part by floatation, vats still in lower section. Principal mines were Alexander which had shaft 1200 feet deep and Brooklyn. Young pines make gallant attempt to reforest denuded hills but progress is slow in short growing season.

"Alone? No!
...there was something else!"

HAMILTON, NEVADA

Hardly a more wind-swept, storm-raked, altogether desolate landscape could be imagined than the one on the slope of White Pine Mountain in 1865. The only living things were the rabbits, squirrels, snakes, owls and other desert creatures.

In that year a group of prospectors from Austin found rich silver deposits there. They banded together with other Austin men of more wealth to form the Monte Cristo Mining Company. The whole thing was kept as quiet as possible and for several years not much happened.

Then, on a bitter cold, stormy day in January 1868 a nearly solid silver deposit was found on Treasure Hill, just across the bowl-shaped hollow in which lay the beginnings of Hamilton. This set off one of those fabulous "rushes" during which people of every sort and description poured into the snowy, inhospitable town which burgeoned till it burst at the seams. Jerry-built and substantial structures rose side by side. A new county was created, "White Pine," a courthouse rose almost overnight. This was used largely as a place to settle constant litigation over conflicting claims.

By now the rabbits were displaced by 25,000 humans scattered over the several ridges contiguous to Hamilton. These people ran the gamut from respectable, hard-working men down to the ever present hangers-on, the sharpies and prostitutes. Several houses for the latter lined a short street near the edge of town.

At 8,000 feet elevation the climate was rigorous, there was no local water, food had to be freighted in from Elko and bandits waylaid the lines of stages and pack mules going out. But the dream of El Dorado sustained the populace. Wasn't the silver lying around in almost pure chunks?

One of the largest and most imposing buildings erected was the Withington Hotel, built of sandstone and Oregon pine and indeed a structure to endure forever.

Then from here and there in small, quiet voices began to come doubts that the silver went very deep, that when the shining surface deposits were scraped off, the future of Hamilton would be something less than the rosy picture painted by the newspapers of the town.

And these voices of gloom were right; the silver was all on top. By 1873 there was a noticeable drop in output. There was a leveling-off process of a few years with small spurts upward, bigger ones downward. In spite of all the glittering prophecies in the early years, 1887 saw the end of the big-scale production. By then there had been shipped out a total of some $22,000,000 in bullion.

RUINS OF Withington hotel dominate Hamilton.

People moved away almost as fast as they had poured in. The "birds of prey" went first to fatten in other, newer camps.

Before many years the town was completely deserted, the buildings fell into disrepair, then ruin. There were two disastrous fires. Stone structures crumbled.

About twenty frame and stone stores and houses remain pitifully scattered about the hollow. Traces of wooden sidewalks partly connect some of them.

DOORWAY OF WITH-INGTON HOTEL laid open to elements frames group of houses almost isolated by past fires.

IONE, NEVADA

"An Ione father who had passed incalculable sleepless nights has immortalized himself by discovering a method of keeping babies quiet. The modus operandi is as follows: set it up, propped by a pillow if it can not set alone and smear its fingers liberally with thick molasses. Then put a dozen feathers into its hands. It will then continue to pick the feathers from one hand to another until it falls asleep. As soon as it awakens again, more molasses and more feathers. In place of the nerve wracking yells there will be silence and enjoyment unspeakable."

Such heart-warming hints as this in the weekly NYE COUNTY NEWS were rarely needed to fill space for things were never very dull in Ione. In the early, flamboyant hectic days one rich discoverer followed another after the first one in April, 1863, by a disappointed Comstocker, P. A. Haven. His strike was made near the center of the Shoshone Range, a string of mountains running north and south as do most of Nevada's ranges. When the camp began to need a name, one erudite miner thought of Ione, the heroine in Bulwer Lytton's novel, "The Last Days of Pompeii".

In only a few short months enough hopeful prospectors had trekked up the Reese River from Austin to make a real town with all the trappings—saloons, stores, and many cabins, all thrown together with adobe, stone, brush or anything handy.

This motley collection grew and the citizens began clamoring to the legislature to have their town made the county seat. The authorities were willing but first had to create a new county for Ione to sit in. This was done by major surgery on two existing ones, Lander, and Esmeralda, carving hefty chunks from each to make the new Nye county. The august and liberal body of lawmakers even made available $800 for a courthouse.

The NYE COUNTY NEWS, published weekly in Ione during the summer of the following year, was a worker for progress in the mountain community. It ran a plug for a new stage line to Austin along Reese River: "The line is well stocked and has accommodating drivers and carries passengers and packages at a reasonable rate. It is not yet definitely settled as to what day it will run. We hope to carry an advertisement next week when we will tell all we know." The line came through with the ad next week. "STAGE FOR AUSTIN. The stage for Austin will leave at an early hour tomorrow, Sunday morning. Passengers, in order to secure a seat should book their names today." The next week, another item. "The stage has established its office at the Bellrude store. It will leave at its usual early hour tomorrow."

Then the lively weekly turned its efforts to securing a bank and assay office for Ione. "A GOOD OPENING" was the headline, and the editorial:

PRIMITIVE CONSTRUCTION dates from 1860s in many Ione buildings. These walls are two feet thick, cracks between roughly cut stones chinked with mud. Roof was covered with clay, mud and layer of gravel.

RAFTERS OF PRECIOUS SAWN LUMBER support heavy horizontal layer of lighter brush which is in turn covered with a thick layer of mud and gravel. Interior was once neatly lined with muslin, vestiges of which interfered with picture taking. Photographer moved aside ancient cloth and got heavy shower of dust on camera and face. Available light came from tiny, deep-set windows and small open door.

"Now that our town is making such rapid strides toward prosperity, we would suggest to some enterprising individual the start of a small banking house in connection with an assay office. There appears to be plenty of money in this community but a scarcity of change, and as work progresses in the various mines rich discoveries are made, which for lack of a competent assay office, their capacity is unknown." And the happy note was sounded two weeks later:

"LONG AWAITED ASSAY OFFICE OPENS by Thomas Cahill, five years assayer in San Francisco mint. We welcome him in our town, having waited a long time for something of this kind. Bring in your specimens!"

There was always room for one more saloon and the newspaper held out the glad hand. "NEW SALOON. W. A. Brophy, Esquire, one of the old settlers returned to our place yesterday with a large stock of liquor. He proposes opening a saloon in the old stand formerly occupied by the Fashion Saloon, next door to the News office. We shall be around, Billy, and 'sample'." And the next week's spread: "INTERNATIONAL SALOON OPENS — BIG FANFARE — FREE DRINKS."

The editor, having accepted payment for this ad

in trade, was incapacitated for several days but rose valiantly to announce: "To Mrs. Michael Kelly we are under obligations for a plate of nice, fresh butter. We carried it to our cabin and our better ? half pronounced it A No. 1. Mrs. Kelly keeps a large dairy and furnishes our citizens with fresh milk and butter. We are glad to learn that she has a large custom."

And then the enterprising editor got apple hungry. "Grocer Bellrude says he has a large stock of fresh apples but as we have not seen any around the office, we have to take his word for it." Apparently Mr. Bellrude was properly rebuked for, a few weeks later came the enlightening information: "Happening into Bellrude's store yesterday we observed a large amount of flour, sugar and such like stowed away as if he was laying in a good winter's supply."

Theatrical news was not neglected. "The beautiful comedy, 'The Swiss Cottage', and a laughable farce, 'The Cobbler and the Lord', will be presented at the Ione Theater. Open 7½ o'clock, start 8, adm. 50c." And always among these lively notes was mining news. "On Saturday last the men engaged in sinking a shaft upon the Olive Ledge discovered a large deposit of gold-bearing quartz which

SOME EARLY CABINS were built of logs formed from nut pine trees and junipers dragged down from higher elevations. Trees are of small size and gnarly growth, logs short and knotty. Chimney is of roughly fired brick, possibly done in hot bonfire. By 1865 commercial kiln was established at nearby Union. Some claim this structure was first courthouse.

will realize $8,000 to $9,000 a ton. The outfit is called the Knickerbocker Mining Co."

The hard working editor evidently took time out occasionally to view the passing parade and voice his observations: "There are many strange faces on the street and it is not unusual to have them pointed out as capitalists" . . . "Emigrant trains still through our town, bound for California. A large train from Davis Cy, Iowa, passed through last night. They are headed for Sonoma Cy. California. They report a very pleasant trip, although there were some delays due to Indian attacks." . . . "Everyone in the city is hard at work. There are no idle men and the streets seem almost deserted in the daytime." . . .

"IONE LIVELY — from the number of teams seen on our streets during the week several times we have blinked our eyes and imagined ourselves on C Street in Virginia before the San Francisco bears got control of the mines." . . . "EVERYBODY COMING, to look at the mines. So many make plans to remain permanently Ione sees a brilliant future ahead."

But it was not to be. Ione's gold proved to be shallow, was soon exhausted and the town with the classic name was just another flash in the pan, as were so many other Nevada mining camps. It had been in the spring of 1863 that the first discovery was made, the spring of 1864 when Ione was made the county seat and the spring of 1867 when that honor was taken away and bestowed on an upstart fifty miles away — Belmont. What really hurt was Belmont's being populated largely with Ione people, miners and prospectors who had defected to the new strike on the old theory that gold is always shinier in the other fellow's claim.

Ione was slow to accept the inevitable. The newspaper of April 6, 1867, reported the county official would complete removal of county records to the new seat at Belmont "as soon as the citizens have reconciled themselves to the fact that they have lost the county seat fight."

Although staggered by the blow, and much shriveled in population, Ione managed to keep from dying entirely, even to the present day. Some small or large discovery has at intervals revivified it enough to hold a few people there. Up to 1880 the mines turned out a million dollars in gold and silver, a small figure compared to the production in the few big years.

One development kept things going for a few years. In 1907 a ledge of cinnabar was discovered in the hills just east of town. Its bright red color should have attracted attention years before but in those days gold was all anyone could see. Silver was recognized grudgingly later, it being so much harder to extract than free gold.

Immediately, upon finding the cinnabar, horizontal roasting furnaces were constructed to melt the mercury or "quicksilver" out of the ore. Fuel was mostly fast burning but plentiful sage brush. More substantial pine was brought down from high elevations after most of the brush had been cleared from slopes nearby. In the several years of operation, some 11.000 flasks of mercury were produced.

Today the town is very quiet, only a few residents hanging on, barely enough to keep up Ione's resolve to "never say die" — and they do miss the old editor.

MANY OLD BUGGIES AND WAGONS indicate remoteness of Ione. In old camps of more convenient access, such relics have been taken by vandals, wheels removed and carried off. Backlighting here brings out details of sagebrush and wheels.

Nevada

SAGA OF THE "LOST BREYFOGLE"

Johnnie, Nevada

Prospector Breyfogle lost a mine he never had. More accurately he could not find the place where he picked up the rich chunk of gold. He made many searches, all to no avail, and broken in health and spirit, he died in the desert. But at least ten rich mines east and north of Death Valley have been identified as the "Lost Breyfogle." Was the real one the Johnnie?

The road up to the large Labbe mine is rough but passable and old time Nevada miner Charles Labbe has been studying the Breyfogle story for many years. He believes he knows about what happened to Jacob (or Louis Jacob or C. C. Jacob or Byron W.) Breyfogle, the events before and after his death.

He says that around 1861 Breyfogle brought a fantastically rich chunk of ore into the thriving mining center of Austin, Nevada. He was barely alive, desiccated and near starvation but was able to say he found the sample somewhere in or near the eastern edge of Death Valley. As soon as he was able to eat and walk he started the first of many searches.

In 1865 a party was following the old Spanish Trail from California to Salt Lake. At a camping ground called Stump Springs, not far from where Johnnie would later be established, they came upon Breyfogle who had barely survived an attack by Indians. He was taken on to Salt Lake where he was nursed by one "Pony" Duncan. He regained a measure of health and took Duncan as partner on another hunt for gold. They had hardly made a good beginning when Breyfogle died, first confiding all he knew of his lost "mine" to Duncan. Later Duncan met the Montgomery brothers who were also looking for it and they pooled information.

In 1890 George and Robert Montgomery were camped at Indian Spring Ranch when they hired Indian Johnnie as guide. The Paiute took them almost directly to some veins with exposed gleams of gold. Excited at first, the Montgomerys cooled down when they found the gold in view was all of it, not enough to warrant the hauling of supplies and equipment to the remote spot. Then Indian Johnnie said something like, "Well all right then, I'll take you about four miles south of here where there is a quartz ledge really loaded with gold." About an hour later the party stood before what Charles Labbe says, "was either the Breyfogle or at least what was the nearest among many versions of the lost mine."

Robert Montgomery later reported the gold in the decomposed surface of quartz was like "plums in a pudding." It was this display of nuggets that gave the location the name "Chispas," literally Spanish for "sparks" or "diamonds," but locally meaning gold nuggets. The mine was rich enough, producing some $250,000 by 1899 when the ledge pinched out. In the meantime another, richer and longer lasting, find was made on the steep hill to

DECAYING HOUSES in Johnnie. Photo made from porch of one directly below, for a few months occupied by Kathryn and Bob West. Tangled remains of chicken wire was once neatly stretched, bore blooming annual vines that gave shade, color to bleak cabins.

the east. The town growing up near the Chispas and the new mine as well were named for the Indian guide. To avoid confusion the village became Johnnie Town, active workings above Johnnie mine.

After treating a hundred tons of ore at the new mine it was evident more equipment would be justified, so a 10-stamp mill was erected, its boilers at first fired by yucca stems. During those first months all machinery and supplies had to be hauled over desert roads 140 miles from Daggett. Later a railroad came to Barnwell, 100 miles to the southeast, a stage line starting from there.

Historian Harvey Hardy writes that sometime around 1900 the Johnnie mining claim was leased by a company with headquarters in Salt Lake City,

the officials mostly Mormons. When their lease ran out, the Montgomery manager whose name Hardy remembers as McArthur, refused an extension. Jerry Langford, manager for the Salt Lake concern, was determined to retain the mine against all comers, including the legal owners.

While armed guards protected them, Langford's miners continued to take out rich ore. One night a force was assembled by McArthur on the hill directly above the mine, among it such gunfighters as Phil Foote and Jack Longstreet. In the early morning light, before guards were stationed, McArthur's men opened fire on the miners going to work, routing and scattering them in every direction as long as it was downhill.

The legal owners then moved in and immediately

556

MAIN STREET of Johnnie mine looking up slope in approximately southerly direction.

began mining operations. When several days passed without incident, the gunmen relaxed vigilance and all guards were taken off. This was the signal for the enemy to take over the same hill from which they had been evicted and start shooting. In the reversed situation McArthur's men ran to the hoist house for cover. After suffering several casualties they were ready to give up but for a time were unable to find something to serve as a flag of surrender. Then the squaw of Jack Longstreet was found among the beleaguered and her white petticoat was tied to a rifle and effective in putting an end to hostilities.

Most seriously wounded among McArthur's men was Phil Foote who was suffering much pain. A man was sent to Johnnie Town to get morphine and after a record trip returned with storekeeper Sam Yount who administered the drug. The suffering man went to sleep, "permanently," as Hardy recalls.

According to this account, the Mormons con-tinued to operate the Johnnie mine for some years, then ran into financial difficulties. Miners were not paid regularly and threatened to quit. With bills for services and supplies mounting the officials sent to headquarters for help.

From Salt Lake City came a man named Gillespie with money to settle outstanding debts which was totally inadequate and in the hassle as to who would get what money there was, Gillespie was killed by a shotgun blast. The town blacksmith was accused and taken to Belmont, Nye County seat, for trial but released for lack of evidence.

Charles Labbe's account of the trouble is terse. "The leasers wanted to jump the claim for themselves and all hell broke loose. Two men, Phil Foote and a man named Gillespie were killed, the mill burned down and office blown up. I picked up the safe, minus the door, 200 feet away." He recalls the dead were buried at Pahrump, not far away and that no trial was ever held.

In 1905 a Los Angeles concern took over the

557

Johnnie mine and production continued moderately until 1908. The "Happy Hunch" whose real name was Ed Overfield, hailing from Goldfield, led an exploratory drilling operation nearby that uncovered a vein three feet wide and assaying $30,000 in gold to the ton. Reporters from Salt Lake's *Mining Review* looked and hurried back to spread the sensational news. Labbe says he saw one chunk from the vein from which $20 gold pieces could be cut. Unfortunately the lead soon ran into Johnnie mine ground and operations ceased.

The Johnnie ran along on an extension of a "pocket zone" until 1940 when the owner died. In a year or so there was further activity by another Los Angeles promoter but when drilling produced no substantial leads, quiet again settled down on the old camp (see *Tales the Western Tombstones Tell*).

JOHNNIE MINE saw several alternating periods of desertion, activity. In 1941 two Hollywood, Calif. men, Joe De Grazier and Walter Knott, promoted reopening of mine with money "invested" for wealthy widow of movie capital. They hired mining expert Robert West, several other knowledgeable men to clean out shaft. "Bob" West and wife Kathryn set up housekeeping in old building still in fair condition. Activity was feverish for 3 months until authorities discovered De Grazier, Knott had mismanaged funds, depleted almost all before actual mining could start. Without waiting for outcome of shady affair, West quit, left for home. Promoters later received jail sentences. Photo of then active post office was made with old Eastman folding Kodak by Kathryn West. After closure office was moved to Pahrump in valley.

MANHATTAN, NEVADA

The town called Manhattan Gulch in early days lay almost on the slopes of Bald Mountain at an altitude of nearly 7,000 feet. This means heavy snows for a long winter, and Manhattan really had them. The ground was out of sight for many months, most winters, with hot summers between.

This sort of climate didn't prevent a hectic boom in the period from 1900 to 1905.

Nearly forgotten is the earlier period of activity there in the 60's. That first stage in the camp's growth was short, and from about 1890 until John C. Humphrey came upon his dazzling chunk of "Jewelry Ore," the town had slumbered. The few people still there awoke with a start at this discovery and so did a lot of opportunists throughout Nevada.

When Charles Phillips, now of Portland, was born there in 1910, Manhattan was a busy place, with about 500 people. Charles was only ten years old when he left with his parents, going to Goldfield, but he has many memories of the town in the Gulch.

"WE WENT TO RIPPY'S Grocery for almost everything, besides food. We went in by door on the corner, I remember." Native of Manhattan, Charles Phillips, says proprietor and family lived upstairs. Route to "outhouse" went down, then up.

"There were several mines going strong in that period," he recalled. "The largest was the White Caps, with its stamp mill and cyanide plant. The La Verde and Big Four also milled their own ore, all of it gold. I remember the White Caps pumped its seepage water into the gulch, water so full of arsenic it was useless. Too bad, since water was so scarce.

"Some of the main buildings along the main street were Oliver Giannini's Saloon, Ziegler's Butcher Shop, Ferguson's Drugstore and Butler's Livery Stable. The jail was close to the stone post office.

"The mule skinners used to throw whatever came handy at their refractory animals, and these missiles were often 'high grade.' I've heard since, that during the depression days, a man and his wife harvested these chunks and sold them for a tidy sum. Those were mostly $5.00 rocks!

"I remember a character who made his living at 'dry placering,' a process using air instead of water. He was called 'Dry Wash Wilson' and had the largest feet ever seen in that part of Nevada. He realized a dream of many years when he bought a 1910 Model T Ford. But his happiness turned to gloom when he found he couldn't put his foot on just one pedal at a time.

The town now can hardly muster up 20 people, some remain from the small-sized resurgence in the 30's. Most are about ready to admit theirs is a Ghost Town, with small hopes for revival. A few feel that if the price of gold would advance, "something good might happen to Manhattan!"

CATHOLIC CHURCH commands imposing position on hill above town. Interior is empty except for altar rail and confessional.

POST OFFICE WAS FOCAL point of all activity; when mail came into town, everybody picked up his own. Jail stood almost against building and was usually well filled with drunks sobering up.

MIDAS, NEVADA

When the populace petitioned for a Post Office in 1908 the desired name was "Gold Circle." The powers that be, however, looked on this name with about as much favor as they had for Raw Dog, Oregon, but for different reasons. There were already too many Gold this and Gold thats in Nevada, so how about "Midas" which, after all, did have a golden touch?

Original discoveries had been made the year before and the town became a reality shortly after. It grew apace, though not with the resounding boom that was being enjoyed at the same time by Goldfield and others. Estimates of peak population vary from 5,000 to 20,000. This will allow a safe margin for errors. There was a Chamber of Commerce, city water system, a newspaper, four big general stores and several hotels and rooming houses. In addition, there existed the usual shady area, dotted at night with red lights, and numerous saloons.

The big mine in Midas was the Elko Prince. About 1910, miners were forced to accept part of their wages in stock, times were so hard, but some sold later for as much as 500 per cent gain.

The Post Office, always a barometer of a town's population closed in 1942 along with the gold mines, the school in 1952, lacking the three pupils required by law to keep it going.

PEACEFUL IS THE WORD now for Main Street in Midas. Little store at right carried everything from corsets to kerosene.

"Branches as bare as bones . . . as white, too!"

NATIONAL, NEVADA

CABIN HAS LONG LACKED human tenants but birds have made themselves at home.

What is left of National is in the Humboldt National Forest. The area was classed, in a time of rich bonanzas, as one of the richest. Its ores contained many "jewelry store specimens," a term used to describe chunks of quartz in which gleamed solid nuggets of gold. The National mine alone produced more than $8 million.

National had a short life but a merry one. Ignored by prospectors in Nevada's early gold discovery period, it did not come into its own until the period called "automobile prospecting days." As evidence that the time of the burro had passed, two of the places named around National were Auto Hill and Radiator Hill.

Soon after the first discoveries of gold on the site by J. L. Workman, blocks of land were leased and the place became a beehive of real estate activity as well as the essential mining. In 1909 the Stall brothers ran into the National vein 40 feet down. Much of the ore removed from it assayed out at $75 per pound, the bulk of the shipped ore $24 per pound and tons were discarded with a value of $2 per pound.

With ore so rich "high grading" was carried on by many of the miners. It is estimated the National alone lost more than a million to these thieves. The worst of it was the citizens seemed to regard the

WORKINGS OF OLD NATIONAL MINE are perched high on mountain above plain, visible in distance. Ore carts ran on rails spiked to ties now only fragments. Hill in background is typically clothed with sagebrush, one in foreground made up of tailings and dumpings of mine.

practice of smuggling out "blossom rock" as being quite legitimate. The company had a hard time prosecuting the occasional miner who was caught at it, public sympathy being with the culprit. Discharging the guilty one only resulted in reprisals by the other miners, sometimes known to blast a tunnel after their safe exit. Even though lunch boxes were searched nuggets were often concealed in body cavities.

During the period of greatest activity the only law in National was that of the company which played searchlights on the mine at night and posted a 24-hour guard around it. But the company didn't give a hoot what the miners did off duty. The one long and narrow street winding up the canyon was lined with a concentration of "houses" bent on ex-

tracting everything a miner had earned or stolen. Such activities weren't always painless, many a man rolled or even killed for his wages.

One of the largest honky tonks stood just above the National mine. It boasted a second story with a hall down the middle between the cubicles where the girls took their customers. Downstairs a grand piano tinkled out its tunes, a long bar at the right sported large plate glass mirrors and mahogany fixtures. Out in back were two tall, narrow structures separated slightly, one "his" and one "hers." Now the house of pleasure has fallen flat and all of its fixtures have decayed away except the frame and wires of the piano. Still standing are the two little "Chick Sales."

Old fort buildings at Fort Churchill, Nevada.

NELSON, NEVADA

Nelson had once been called Eldorado, a name full of Spanish romance and suggestive of riches beyond counting, and indeed Spaniards had made the original discoveries of gold in this spot which now bears the name, Eldorado Canyon.

That was in 1775, but nothing much happened for a hundred years, when things got going under gringo ownership. The main operation became the notorious Techatticup Mine; notorious because wanton killings became so frequent there as to be almost commonplace. These were the results of disagreements over ownership, management or labor disputes, and the canyon with the romantic beginning became as sinister as the black rocks forming its walls.

Even so, the mine and its satellites produced several millions in gold, silver, copper and lead, before lowered values caused general cessation. The row of huge cyanide vats still form an imposing ruin.

HUGE VATS USED FOR PROCESSING GOLD ORE by cyanide treatment stand rotting in blistering heat of Eldorado Canyon. Vats are near cave where Indian "Public Enemy No. 1" named Quejo was discovered dead after 10 years of terrorizing area. His excuse for his crimes always was that he had been ordered by authorities to track down and slay his killer brother and to bring back the head as proof.

PARADISE VALLEY, NEVADA

If Lieut. John Lafferty agreed with scouts who said the only good Indian was a dead one, he had a sound right to his opinion. He spent so much time chasing live Shoshones and Paiutes off settlers' ranches in Paradise Valley, and counting the dead ones, he had little time to go fishing.

And when he did he still had Indian trouble. There was the time in August, 1867, when he went fishing up Cottonwood Creek with Hon. J. A. Banks and Rev. Temple of New York. Banks was a delegate to the Nevada State Constitutional Convention and Speaker of the House at the second legislature. From these labors he took a vacation trip to the fine fishing streams flowing into Paradise Valley from the Santa Rosa Range. Lt. Lafferty, com-

mander of Fort Scott nearby, agreed to go with Banks and the minister.

The three found good fishing but Banks wanted it better. He went on up the creek saying he would return when he had all the trout he wanted. When he failed to return, the lieutenant and Rev. Temple went after him and found his mutilated body in a gully. Lt. Lafferty was enraged, swore vengeance on all Indians and took a party of soldiers after them. They killed several but did not find the murderers of Hon. J. A. Banks.

This was only one incidence in the almost continual strife between whites and Indians in the early days of the town of Paradise Valley. It lay in the grassy, fertile area partly encircled by the Santa

PICTURESQUE BUILDINGS on main street of Paradise Valley. Sun has emerged after hard downpour, fails to reach north—facing side. Structures are among few in West to retain genuine, unspoiled atmosphere of early days. At left is post office established after first was destroyed in fire; next to it tiny shop, meat market at one time—bacon, when available, $1 a pound; next, gambling hall with rooms for girls upstairs, becoming more respectable rooming house later; next, notorious Mecca Saloon, whiskey at 50c a shot, "less for regular customers." Sign is partly discernible behind tree branches.

Rosas. Called Yamoposo by the Indians for its half-moon shape, it earned its English name when in 1863 prospector W. H. Huff climbed to a pass near the top of Santa Rosa Peak, looked out over the land below and exclaimed: "What a Paradise!"

One of Huff's companions was W. C. Gregg. More farmer than miner, the verdant valley so impressed him agriculturally that he brought in a herd of cattle and machinery for cutting and baling hay, thereby setting the pattern for Paradise Valley's future in spite of the hordes of hungry prospectors and miners who swarmed the Santa Rosas over the ensuing years. While some miners did settle in Paradise Valley, and many bought their outfits and provisions there, the real mining towns were Queen City, Spring City, Hardscrabble and the rough and tough Gouge Eye. Spring City was twelve miles away, a typical mining camp spawned in the boom days of the Santa Rosas and boasting of a brewery, seven saloons and a book store.

Gregg, for whom the green of grass was brighter than the glimmer of gold, drew other farmers into the valley. The Santa Rosas handsomely rewarded many with gold but many claims proved shallow or entirely sterile and many miners stayed to grow

hay for the nearby camps, to be used as fodder for riding and work horses.

Richard Bentley and Charles A. Nichols plowed the first furrows for the planting of wheat in the spring of 1864. The settlers put up sod houses and shacks of willow brush, planted large vegetable gardens and cut down the nut pine trees for fuel. And the original inhabitants — Paiutes, Shoshones and Bannocks — watched from the hills. They saw the pastures where game had fed being plowed up and saw the burning of trees which had borne one of their major food supplies, the pine nuts. They watched the sparkling clear streams being dammed, diverted and muddied in sluices and other mining operations.

Then they struck. Small forays grew to mass raids in depredations that lasted for years. The first was an attack on three prospectors just north of the town of Paradise Valley. Dr. H. Smeathman, W. F. White and Frank Thompson were riding out of town when an Indian bullet knocked the doctor off his horse. The other two ignored his cries for help, spurred their mounts on to Rabbit Hole and safety. About two months later a party of four was ambushed near the Santa Rosas, G. W. Dodge slain

STORE AND ORIGINAL POST OFFICE were housed in this structure built around 1870, store established by Charles Kemler, first man to freight supplies into Paradise Valley. Upper floor was dance hall, later boasted hardwood floor mounted on springs, novelty in this sparsely settled section of Nevada. Structure burned in spectacular fire of 1919.

and another man wounded. The next spring, in 1865, Paiute Chief Black Rock Tom organized his tribesmen against the whites, the first casualty being Lucius Arcularius, station keeper on one road and two other whites at another way station. Then came reports the Indians were gathering a war party on the Humboldt. W. H. Haviland of Paradise Valley went to Star City, a thriving mining camp north of Unionville, to ask for help to protect his town from expected attacks.

About the same time two friendly Indians arrived at Aaron Denio's cabin on Martin Creek to warn against an attack intended to slaughter every inhabitant and drive away all stock. Denio spread the alarm and organized plans for complete evacuation.

The fleeing families attempted to reach Willow Point down the Little Humboldt but had difficulty getting their heavily loaded wagons across Cottonwood and Martin Creeks which were running to the banks in spring freshets. Some got the ox-drawn wagons to Hamblin's corral but several stragglers were forced to spend the night in a wayside cabin and awoke to find it surrounded by a party of twenty-two Indians. By a ruse they succeeded in getting away, joining the others at the corral. Then short-

ly this refuge was under attack, the mounted Indians circling and yelling.

The besieged group consisted of ten men, one of whom was Aaron Denio, his 12-year old son Robert, three women and four children. They were armed with three rifles, a musket, two double-barreled shotguns and six revolvers. Everyone seemed agreed that Denio was in command and also that someone would have to go for help.

Whether young Thomas Byrnes was selected or volunteered, there is no doubt of his heroism. He managed to get to the barn without being hit, mounted the fastest horse and headed straight through the lines of screeching Paiutes. Possibly the element of surprise had something to do with the feat but the boy got through, even evading the braves who pursued him, firing as they rode. Thompson and West in their HISTORY OF NEVADA recorded: "It was a race for life. If overtaken by a stray bullet, or the mounted savages, all the lives at the corral would have paid the penalty, and seemingly inspired with the terrible emergency, the noble animal flew like a winged Pegasus out of sight from his pursuers."

The youth must almost have flown as he reached Willow Point at three that afternoon, finding thir-

OLD RED BARN, built by Alphonso Pasquale, early Italian farmer, lover of fine horses and fancy dress, is one of many relics remaining on streets of Paradise Valley. Wagons loaded high with hay were driven directly under projecting balcony, fodder pitched directly into loft. Pasquale built several other buildings along street.

teen men ready and anxious to help. There were only twelve horses and the oldest man named Givens was to be left behind. But as the party started, Givens grabbed one of the saddle pommels and according to the referred to HISTORY: ". . . kept pace with the relief party over the thirteen miles . . . every so often shouting "Heave ahead, boys, heave ahead! The women and children must be saved!', and this while carrying a rifle in his free hand."

The beleaguered group at Hamblin's corral was rescued without a shot being fired. It was just before dark when the Willow Creek party arrived, Given still hanging on. Not sure just how many men comprised the rescuers, the Indians fled. Settlers and deliverers headed for Willow Creek and safety, arriving at three a.m. to find Lt. Joseph Wolverton with a troop of twenty-five men who had responded to Haviland's plea at Star City. Under their protection the Paradise Valley settlers returned to their homes, resuming work in the fields under armed guards.

These and many other Indian incidents resulted in the establishment of two forts in the area — Fort McDermitt at the Oregon border and Fort Winfield Scott a short distance from Paradise Valley. Sporadic Indian fighting continued, with incidents like the fishing party murder of J. A. Banks. It was not until after the winter of 1869 that Indian attacks ceased and Paradise Valley farmers could till their fields without fear.

The protective influence of Fort Winfield Scott encouraged the development of farms and the group of buildings near the fort increased, was in 1866 officially known as Paradise Valley. Charles Kemler who freighted goods into the valley built and operated a store here with a hotel in connection.

The winter of 1867-68 was unusually cold far into spring. Supplies failed to come in and settlers were forced to live on wheat ground in coffee grinders. The next summer A. C. Adams erected his Silver State Flour Mill, putting an end to this. The following year saw the end of the Indian trouble and the start of long, peaceful progress of the agricultural area.

569

PINE GROVE, NEVADA

The best-preserved building in Pine Grove was apparently once a business headquarters, for a rusty safe lay just outside. A ruined picket fence surrounded the house, covered with withered hop vines. One of the vines still showed life, a forlorn sprig in the dead town. At one side of the door was a faded typewritten notice. "You are welcome to live here but please do not tear down."

Another building, the cookhouse, had several layers of paper on its walls, tattered and peeling off. The first layer was of newspapers, mainly the *San Francisco Chronicle* and *World Report*. These carried the dates from 1891 to 1897. Over this was fancy imported wallpaper. Later newpapers covered the torn elegance and the latest of these were dated in the early 30's.

The original discovery of gold in the area was in 1866. Within a year, Pine Grove had 300 people. There were three mills shipping $10,000 in gold bullion every week. The population continued to expand, then dwindled, grew again and, about the time the fancy wallpaper was added, in the 1880's, was at its height. The last small flurry occurred when the latest newspapers were pasted on the walls to keep out the cold winter winds. With the 1930's went the last inhabitants and Pine Grove has become a true Ghost.

IMPRESSIVE STONE RUINS of once busy general store. Occupying central position in original location of Pinegrove, it suffered by later removal of business section half a mile up canyon where boardinghouse and school remain. Portal now stands alone, looking out on hills scarred and torn by mine operations.

NEVADA'S HAVEN FROM HEAVEN

Bartender Faddiman had been warned often enough. Friends told him, "Don't take that job at Pioche." . . . "You're as good as dead if you go to work in Pioche" . . . "No bartender ever lasted longer than a year there." Not one of Faddiman's well wishers wanted to see him go to certain disaster but his reason was simple, his need urgent. "I need a job and I don't care where it is. I can take care of myself". He did go to the most notorious camp in Nevada — and stayed there. In his second week a drunk ordered a drink. "You don't need an-

other drink", Faddiman told him — and those were his last words. The customer objected to them, simple and straightforward as they were, took out his six shooter and Faddiman set up no more drinks.

The killer walked calmly behind the bar, stepped over the barkeep's body and stripped the till. Then he went next door to the butcher shop of buxom "Nigger Liza" and for variation, slit her throat with his knife. He emptied her till too but by this time the sheriff knew about the bartender's slaying and met the murderer at Liza's door with a

LONG ROWS OF GRAVES, barely discernible, makes up famous Murderer's Row at edge of Pioche's Boot Hill. Nearly 100 killers of all types lie here in area fenced off from more respectable occupants of cemetery. During heyday of large mining town, tramline was run over Row, ore buckets clanging constantly. They now hang immobile, except as they sway in often violent winds.

PIONEER BURIED HERE lies in anonymity like many others in Pioche cemetery. Headboard inscription has long since faded away, unusual condition since most painted lettering preserves wood to some extent, outlasting unpainted surface. Perhaps this one was carved, allowing moisture, abrasive sand to erode lettering or could inscription have been chiseled away for some reason? Note horizontal marks.

rattle of lead. And this was the way the single row of unmarked graves in Pioche's Boot Hill grew so long, so fast.

Piochee, pronounced Pee-oche with accent on the last syllable, was developed by Frenchman F. L. A. Pioche, although original deposits of lead-gold-silver ore were discovered by William Hamblin in 1863. Hambin had it easy. Instead of spending years at prospecting, his Paiute Indian friends led him to the highly colored ledges that were to produce $40 million in ore. Hamblin had little money for developing and later sold the claims to the French banker from San Francisco.

By 1870 the camp was considered the wildest in the West, the gun being the only law. The climate was fine enough to keep people from dying of natural causes, unnatural being most popular, the first 75 deaths being from "lead in the head" or

violence of some sort. Not only did bad men drift into town to bully and shoot residents but mine owners imported their own bad men at the rate of 20 a day to fight encroachments. Death rate of these assassins was high and they got the camp's Boot Hill off to a good start, with special sections for various categories.

In Murderers' Row are two desperadoes convicted of the wanton slaying of an old prospector for his money. The sheriff's deputy in charge of their execution was the tidy sort and not wishing to dirty his hands unnecessarily or cause extra work, forced the two hapless killers to stand at graves dug at the end of the row when he shot them.

In 1871 a young lawyer, William W. Bishop, came from Illinois to spend a few hours in Pioche. He later attained some fame by defending John Doyle Lee in the notorious Mountain Meadows Massacre. Bishop brought his bride with him and as they stepped down from the stage, a shot sounded from around the corner, another across the street. By the time they got to the hotel room, says the story, a deputy shot and killed three bad guys on three different corners and the newlyweds had had it, heading back to civilization.

Legend departs from tales of violence to relate that during the Independence Day celebration of

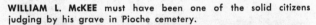

WILLIAM L. McKEE must have been one of the solid citizens judging by his grave in Pioche cemetery.

THE CATHEDRAL, standing majestically few miles below Pioche. That haphazard erosion in chalky clay could produce near perfect replica of European cathedral seems fantastic and could well have inspired composer of "The Cathedral", title song in album named Cathedral Gorge. Cathedral State Park contains many beautiful shapes like this, none as aptly shaped.

1876 the town bell was kept clanging constantly for hours by drunken miners. The people could stand it but not the bell, and it cracked. Dismayed, the townsmen declared another holiday to melt enough metal for a bell that could really take it. A melting pot was fired up at the smelter and a procession of citizens filed by, each contributing dollars or silver bars or jewelry until there was enough mass for a pour. It is said that the new bell had a sweeter tone than any other in the country but no mention is made of its fortitude.

Today Pioche is no longer wild. Many relics of the old days remain, such as the Lincoln County Courthouse. Built of brick in the late 1860s, it cost more than half a million, was condemned as unsafe in 1933, three years before it was paid for.

RAWHIDE, NEVADA

"Rawhide was named by an early prospector who mended his worn out clothes with a strip of that material" . . . "The town was called by that name because some of the first ore was hauled out in raw cowhides" . . . "The first mail box was put up along the trail with a sign that read 'All mail for this camp here'. The box was nailed to a post which had a hide on it, tail still attached."

"All a pack of lies," says Charles A. McLeod. "I went into what is now Rawhide on Feb. 12, 1907 with Albert J. Bovard and prospected around that section and on Feb. 12 I made my first location on what is known as Hooligan Hill. My first claim was named Happy Day and the second Happy Hooligan. My partner Bovard went southwest to Pilot Peak, about four miles from our camp, but did not find anything. Charles B. Holman and my brother Mason arrived at our camp just a few hours after I had made my locations. I had left word at Schurz for them to follow Bovard and myself.

"Charley Holman was very bitter about his recent experience at Buckskin, a new boom camp not far away. They had told him they didn't want any more prospectors making claims around there. He was fuming about this all through supper and finally he exploded. "By God!" he said. "They think they're so darn smart getting that name of Buckskin on the map! We'll go them one better and get a Rawhide on it!' We always called the camp Rawhide after that, and that's what it was after others came in."

The man who relates this incident and other vivid and colorful ones is Charles McLeod who at 86 still makes visits to scattered claims in Rawhide and elsewhere, but living more quietly now in Yerington, Nevada. He is Scotty to his friends which

HERE WAS MAIN STREET of town. In background is Regent Range, composed of rock materials so light colored as to appear snow covered. Derelict buildings are survivors of fire which all but leveled Rawhide at height of inflated prosperity. Vegetation is sparse—dry, hot climate in summer and cold in winter hostile to most plants. Among few ornamental shrubs cultivated was Tamarisk, surviving example at left of small building left of center, still sending out airy panicles of pinkish bloom in spring.

FADED, DESERTED BUILDINGS on street leading to Hooligan Hill are silent only in rare periods of calm weather. When wind blows old structures come to ghostly sort of life, galvanized metal of roofs clanking loudly, metal barrels rolling noisily, loose boards flapping against walls, weeds gyrating wildly.

means everyone privileged to meet him and has a remarkable memory and keen wit. His birthplace was the early day camp of Aurora, Nevada and/or California — the town belonging to two states at one time. A boyhood spent in the never-ending clamor of hundreds of stamp mills and constant talk of assays and values conditioned Scotty to a life closely associated with mines and mining. Even before his family's stay at Aurora, his father owned a ranch at Yerington, the one-time Pizen Switch.

Here at the cross roads of travel west to the Sierra and north to Oregon, an opportunist once set a board on two whiskey kegs and peddled the contents to dusty-throated travelers. Business was brisk and as the whiskey level got low the resourceful samaritan fired up the raw stuff with tobacco juice

and what-have-you, adding water for bulk. So Pizen Switch the spot was, the place where the McLeods settled on the ranch. Other settlers rebelled at the name and called it Mason Valley and later the village took the name of Yerington which today is still a thriving farm center.

Aurora was fading fast when the McLeods left it but Charles had a boy's curiosity and touch of gold fever. Before he reached his majority he was prospecting around Mason Valley and at about twenty-five staked out the claims on Hooligan Hill a few hours before the camp was christened Rawhide.

That was in February, 1907. Ever restless, as soon as the claims were proved to be rich, he and Charley Holman sold out their joint properties of some nineteen claims to Van Doren and Dunning for $20,000 plus 10% of profits. They went prospecting elsewhere but by fall the magnet of the booming Rawhide proved so strong they returned to start working the several claims retained at the north end of Stingaree Gulch. In the meantime Van Doren and Dunning had sold out to the Nat C. Goodwin Co. for $400,000, with McLeod and Holman still getting their 10%. Goodwin was a famous New York comedian enamored of western mining, his company incorporated for $3 million.

The landscape around Rawhide was undoubtedly as stark and barren, yet as fascinating, then as now. A small amount of grass and sagebrush grows along the sides of Stingaree Gulch which bisects the camp but otherwise the mountains, rising sharply on all sides, each of a different color, seem utterly unclothed. But the early inhabitants were likely unaware of such harsh beauty, busy as they were working their claims or prospecting.

Miners on Grutt Hill thought dynamite was necessary to follow a promising vein of gold. The head powder man had imbibed a few too many and placed the blasting material with too lavish a hand — which he was lucky not to lose. The resulting explosion startled the town but nobody was hurt, and a few even helped. The hoped for vein of rich ore was where it was expected to be — until the blast scattered it to Rawhide's far sides. The owners recovered about $14,000 but much was pulverized and lost, much picked up and pocketed by grateful citizens.

Another and less spectacular blast at the Coalition mine sent a chunk of ore through the window of the First National Bank of Rawhide. A bank official, able to "assay" the rock, deducted the value of it from window repair costs and returned a balance of $8 to the owners.

Not all the Rawhide ore was valued for its gold alone. Some material assayed out eight ounces of gold to one of silver, the next batch showing the same values in reverse. Some of the best left indications in the report of $26,000 to the ton. "And it was shallow, easy to get at," says Scotty. "Our claims at the north edge of town produced almost all their good ore between 35 and 94 feet, which was at bedrock."

Rawhide had its sharpies, hangers-on who didn't enjoy working in mines but made their living supplying workers with expensive pleasures of

RAWHIDE HOOSEGOW—most substantial building in town, Roaring waters of flood in Stingaree Gulch threatened foundations but did not undermine them. Part of stone walls caved but cells still held prisoners, roaring days of Rawhide's short prosperity furnishing good supply.

the flesh or extracting even more gold by mine stock manipulation. Rawhide did not seem to care about a man's previous reputation, was not even curious about it, as in the case of one of its more prominent citizens, George Graham Rice. He had done a very good job at promoting the L. M. Sullivan Trust Co. in Goldfield, so good that $10 million had poured into its owner's pockets, almost none in the stockholders'. The whole enterprise collapsed when these stockholders ganged up on President "Shanghai Larry" Sullivan who was thoroughly bewildered to find his erstwhile aide gone with the wind and a considerable chunk of the funds. But Rice hadn't gone far, only to Rawhide where he lost no time in setting up another operation. This was so successful he contracted for a magazine series at three cents a word. With neither caution nor modesty he titled the stories, "My Adventure With Your Money". The series attracted much attention, in-

WONDER LUMBER CO. building is one of monuments to failure in town where many fortunes were made. Founder was soon called "Hard Luck Kenny" by sympathetic townsmen. Kenny had come fresh from fiasco in Portland, Oregon, where real estate venture failed. Scotty McLeod and Barker Butler staked him to have fling at mine which proved a dud. Unfortunate man met end on Black Desert when car broke down. Trying to repair engine, Kenny got gasoline on hands which ignited, burning him to death.

cluding that of federal investigators who eventually confined the activities of the promoter-author behind the discouraging bars of the federal penitentiary at Atlanta.

And there was Tex Rickard who also came over from Goldfield, attracted as others were away from the slightly frayed-at-edge camp to the new bonanza town whose star was blazing. Rickard had been operating his Goldfield Northern Saloon, in which he owned most of the stock, but liked excitement such as his fantastically successful promotion of the Joe Gans-Battling Nelson fight which brought some forty thousand people to Goldfield. His Northern Saloon had been built with money from the stake he made in the Klondike rush where he cut his teeth on the entertainment racket.

Now Goldfield was growing tiresome and Tex sold his interests to one Johnny Mays and staged a farewell party at the Northern. Feeling exuberant on his way to his Thomas Flyer he took cue chalk and scrawled on the door of an abandoned church—"This church closed. God has gone to Rawhide."

A better than average photographer, Scotty Mc-

Leod loved to record the scenes of his early mining days. One of his pictures shows the spot where he and his companions camped at what would later be Rawhide, their little white tent the only sign of habitation in the lonely desert landscape. When Rickard arrived about a year later he bought a lot next to this spot for his new Northern, paying $10,000.

At this time, the peak of prosperity in Rawhide's short but hectic life, the population was estimated at some five thousand. The camp had three banks which stayed open until midnight before there was an official post office. A large portion of a business block shows clearly in a 1909 photograph — the High Grade Bar, G and K Drug Store, Rawhide Clothing House, the Northern and Hermitage, another bar. Not shown are the other thirty-seven saloons and four churches. In addition the town boasted of a school, steam laundry, twenty-eight restaurants, the "Princess" theater, twelve hotels, telegraph and telephone lines. During the first year, it is reported, Sunday masses for Catholics were held in a saloon that closed just before dawn which

577

gave the "church" time to clean up and carry in benches and a crude portable altar.

Then came Elinor Glyn. The lady had recently written the novel, "Three Weeks". Sufficient effort was made to suppress the sensational book to assure its popularity and Elinor G. was riding high. Rickard seized the moment to invite the lady to Rawhide to see how "the other side" lived. Mrs. Glyn accepted, possibly because Rickard had been clever enough to extend the invitation through Nat Goodwin, a friend of the now famous lady author and promoter in Rawhide. Perhaps Mrs. Glyn also saw a chance to gather some publicity while researching the seamy mining camp. She arrived by way of San Francisco with two friends, Sam Newhouse and Ray Baker. All were made welcome with every stunt the ingenious Rickard and Goodwin team could think of.

After several rounds of champagne in Rawhide's best hotel the party was escorted to a poker game in another room. The players were hired to ignore Mrs. Glyn and put on a good show for her, six shooters and all. An argument developed and the guns barked — at the ceiling. La Glyn and her friends beat a hasty retreat, tarrying outside long enough to listen for further gunfire. One horrified glance showed the "bodies" of two players being carried out.

Escorts of the Glyn Guided Tour paused only long enough to make sure she observed the stretcher bearers headed for the combination furniture-undertaker establishment, then proceeded down Stingaree Gulch. Most of the lower end of the Gulch bisecting the town was given over to cribs and the girls had been coached to make every effort to seduce Mrs. Glyn's friends.

At the far end of the street a shack was set afire, the blaze being soon extinguished by the Rawhide Volunteer Fire Department. The fire laddies made up in flashy uniforms and flourishes what the tiny pump cart and meager water supply lacked. That evening another fancy champagne dinner was served for the novelist and the next morning she and her friends left for the East properly impressed with the "innate aristocracy" of the miners of Nevada. Large bursts of publicity in national newspapers both for Mrs. Glyn and Rawhide, made everybody's efforts well worth while though many editors saw through the farce and said so.

On September first rumors came to the town of a rich strike at nearby Silver Lake and Scotty McLeod headed there with his cronies. He was gone just long enough to miss seeing the near total destruction of Rawhide. Three days after he left someone opened a window in a back room of the Rawhide Drug Store, the resulting stream of air blowing a curtain across a gasoline stove on which lunch was being prepared. In moments the room was ablaze and before the R.V.F.D. could get there flames were shooting from several stores. Jerry-built, tinder dry frame structures, they went up like match sticks and flung blazing brands on neighboring buildings and in a few hours nine blocks of the business district were leveled. Tex Rickard watched the flames devour his Northern Saloon, rushed to the telegraph office to order building material for a new one.

The gesture was brave but futile. Rawhide was never the same. Many stores were replaced on their old sites but business failed to get its strength back. The truth, painful as it became evident, was that Rawhide had existed more on promotion, flamboyancy and stock juggling than on the bona fide production of gold and silver. Values in these metals were there but not in sufficient quantities to justify the old, extravagantly-touted Rawhide. Mining by then in Nevada had passed its peak of glamor and as once prosperous businesses failed, ghosts moved in.

Rawhide today displays a large number of picturesque old false-fronted buildings, mostly those which escaped the fire. The ghost town fan who is willing to drive long distances over gravel roads will find atmosphere in abundance in Rawhide, an outstanding example of fast boom and quick bust, of flagrant over-promotion which ballooned it beyond reason, out of all chance for a less flashy but more permanent success.

TYPICAL OF PERIOD is pressed metal sheathing for face of building. This and galvanized roofing saved these structures from disastrous fire. At left was combination store and post office, former owned by Mr. and Mrs. Leonard, wife being postmistress for over twenty years.

RHYOLITE, NEVADA

Towering concrete remnants, dazzling white in the sun, are what is left of a city that expanded almost beyond belief from the day in 1904, when Eddie Cross and the renowned "Shorty" Harris discovered their rich specimen of ore. It was a sample of what the "Bullfrog Mine" to-be would produce, until its collapse such a brief period later.

Here is a depot with no train or tracks, and the vestiges of a school built for an expected population explosion which fizzled. The first school had been ludicrously inadequate, falling far short of holding the juvenile element by the time it was finished. So the next was conceived and planned on a grandiose scale. It was used only a short time and was never filled.

The panic of 1907 shattered dreams that did not have time to become reality. Succeeding financial difficulties, foreclosures, withdrawals of public utilities and pinching out of veins battered at the city whose concrete buildings were newly finished.

By 1910 Rhyolite's 10,000 people had dwindled to a few hundred, then to a few dozen. For years only two buildings have been tenable; the depot and a unique structure made of bottles. These are occupied, and serve as museums. The city that was the "Gem of the Amargosa" is otherwise deserted.

MAIN STREET OF RHYOLITE leads past remains of one of the biggest booms in all history. The school, its future grossly overestimated, stands forlornly in ruins at lower end of street.

HOLES IN FALSE FRONT show where birds are nesting. Scraps of sheet metal have preserved building beyond life of others, warding off weather and sparks of neighboring fires.

ROCHESTER, NEVADA

Rochester is all "uphill," with the center of town occupying the only nearly level area. This is the "old town." A somewhat newer, less picturesque Rochester is first encountered at a lower level.

In what was the business section of upper Rochester only one building still stands erect. It is a typical false front of the day, once the Post Office combined with a store and living quarters.

The little sliding window for dispensing eagerly awaited mail opens from a room filled with debris. Here is an old brass bedstead, and on it a moldy mattress. For a cover it has a motheaten sheepskin coat. Also on the bed is a little booklet, tattered and stained, titled "How to Play the Zither."

All around this building are many foundations and basements giving support to the town's history of 1,500 people. That was at the height of the period between 1860 and 1913. Over all, some $10,000,000 worth of silver was produced. As usual, other metals were a by-product, sometimes paying for the cost of production.

Above the main part of town are extensive mine dumps and ruins of head-buildings. Here also are the remains of a large building, recently collapsed, that must have been a saloon and dance hall on the grand scale. Broken tables are overturned everywhere, as are chairs and carved counters. A prone stairway once led upstairs to pleasures other than gambling, an expected adjunct to any drinking place of that day.

ROCKLAND, NEVADA

Joseph Wilson had an exciting life on the ranches and in the mines of Nevada. He died at ninety-four, leaving voluminous notes and memoirs among them the story of the founding of Pine Grove and its newer, smaller neighbor, Rockland. "On September first of 1863," he wrote, "my father, David Wilson, and uncle William Wilson, bought the squatter's rights to the Wheeler farm, consisting of 4,000 acres, for $2,000."

This was unsurveyed land on which Pat Wheeler and his seven sons had squatted under Utah law in 1860, on the west fork of the Walker river in the extreme south end of Mason valley. The Wheelers had erected earth boundary mounds, three years being allowed to fence the land. Once on it, young William Wilson was eager to go prospecting in the Pine Grove mountains, included in the ranch, but his older brother and family persuaded him to stay, help get part of the land under cultivation and start a herd of cattle. David, however, was just as anxious to find out about mineral wealth and allowed his young brother to saddle a horse once in a while and have a look around.

Of the Paiute Indians who came to the ranch begging food, most persistent was a family trio— Hog-or-Die Jim who sometimes chopped wood, his wife Hog-or-Die Mary who did the washing and their son "Bummer Charlie" who "never did anything useful". To this family, Hog-or-Die meant something like "eat high on the hog or starve."

MILL WAS ONCE much more extensive. Fire, bruising weight of snows, vandals and time have all taken toll. Stone walls date from earliest period, cement foundations coming later.

SUTRO, NEVADA

Sweet are the uses of adversity. Every time a man was killed in the building of the Sutro Tunnel in the 1870s, the other men used it as an excuse for a big time. After the funeral and burial at the cemetery in Virginia City, they hung on a big drinking party and then needed two more days to sober up.

The big hitch in this giddy round was Adolph Sutro. He wanted no delays in the building of this tunnel and did not see why the dead could not be buried right in the new town of Sutro at the mouth of the tunnel. He laid out a burial ground but the men quickly told him it wouldn't work. When a premature blast killed Kelly, they said the burial would be at Virginia City, same as usual: "Because Kelly will be lonely all by himself in that new ground."

Sutro had to swallow one more lay off but shortly a careless powder man left some loose blasting material near a battery. A spark caught it and the explosion killed two men. "Now," said Adolph Sutro in Prussian gutteral, we have the funeral here and start new cemetery." Aching for another bust, the men searched frantically for some next-of-kin to insist on carrying out the final rites on Mt. Davidson. Finding none they were forced to have the services at Sutro and get back to work the next morning.

The story of the ghost town of Sutro is the story of Adolph Sutro. It begins in Aachen (Aix-la-Chapelle) Prussia, when on April 29, 1830, Adolph Heinrich Joseph Sutro was born. One of eleven children whose father Emanuel, and uncle Simon, owned a large woollen factory. Young Adolph had many interests, in machines at the mill, exploring the heavens at night with his telescope and in botany through his many walks at the edge of town. Adolph loved books too and acquired a knowledge of general science far beyond that of his brothers which furnished a grounding for his later interest in California and Nevada mining that led to the building of the tunnel to the Comstock Lode.

In 1848 his father went on a business trip carrying a brace of pistols for protection against bandits. On the way home, not having occasion to use them, he discharged the loads in the air. The horses bolted, throwing him out of the carriage and Emanuel suffered a broken back which paralyzed him. During the year he lived, the family's funds were nearly exhausted and Adolph was compelled to leave school at sixteen.

In 1850 the young man made his big move to America. In New York he was almost immediately caught up in the California gold fever and in two weeks left for San Francisco. His crossing of the

THIS WAS CENTER OF SUTRO. At left is blacksmith shop, complete with forge, in front of it ore car on tracks which lead from mouth of tunnel at left, out of picture. At right is large warehouse. Townsite was surveyed in 1872 in neat gridiron pattern. Streets were 80 feet wide with exception of central one leading from tunnel, 200 feet wide and called Tunnel Avenue. Lots cost $500 up. Cottonwood trees may be descendants of those originally planted along avenue although Sutro preferred more exotic types some of which could not survive climate. Each lot purchaser was required to plant at least one tree and care for it.

Isthmus was the usual battle of mosquitoes, thieving natives in the guise of guides and narrow escapes from dysentery, cholera and smallpox. At Panama City he was lucky in being booked for passage to California in a week where others were held for many.

In San Francisco, where one day he would be its first citizen, he was just another foreigner. Almost starving by the time his trunks arrived, he started at once selling the German cloth and articles they contained. When he had enough money for a few meals and a ticket to Stockton where a cousin

lived, the two set up a store on the levee. He stayed with this a year or so, then returned to San Francisco with enough of a stake to start a tobacco shop and two stores. One was a supply house from which he shipped groceries and mining equipment to the Mother Lode by way of Stockton and to the Northern Mines through Sacramento. When the Trinity Mountain area was opened up at Weaverville and Shasta, Sutro shipped by water up the Sacramento River to Redding, thence to the mines by muleback, or up the Coast to Trinidad Bay where the goods were transferred to small boats on the Klam-

STRING OF ORE CARS still on tracks in middle of Tunnel Avenue. At first cars were drawn by mules, later by small electric engines.

ath River, then in turn to mules for the rest of the way along the Trinity River trail.

Then he made a false move. A year or two later when the gold rush to the Fraser River was in full swing, Adolph left his wife and two children to go north and start a cigar store in Victoria. But the first full migration was over and depression was setting in. He returned to San Francisco to hear of the new gold push to Washoe in Nevada.

He went there, to Mt. Davidson and worked out a new system of greater efficiency for recovery of gold and silver from quartz, not only from virgin ore but in old dump residue. So he settled down at Dayton, at the foot of the mountain, and organized a company, built mills with stamps and roasting ovens and was soon making $10,000 a month.

As soon as the mill was well established he sent for his brother Hugo to run it. For some time there had been a plan in Adolph's head, a plan which was to embrace every thought he had for many years. It was to build a tunnel, a horizontal bore several miles long to start at a level lower than the bottoms

of the deep shafts descending from Virginia City. Those mine shafts were suffering badly from poor ventilation, even with forced air. Temperatures in the depths were so high that water, in itself an ever increasing menace, turned to steam and the high humidity suffocated the already exhausted miners. Sutro reasoned that such an opening to the outside air would drain off the water, ventilate the mines and bring temperatures down. It would also provide a cheap exit for Comstock ores.

With Hugo to take care of things at the mills, Sutro traveled all over the area by horseback, seeking out a logical spot for starting such a tunnel. As a skilled amateur surveyor, he actually lined up the nearly nine-mile tunnel to connect with the bottom of the Savage mine shaft so accurately that 13 years later, when the last charge of powder was set off, it caved in a hole in the side of the shaft.

The hard part was raising the money. Adolph Sutro would never have imagined anyone would stand in the way of such a humanitarian project, one that would benefit everyone, but he proved to be less a logician than he was engineer. He pointed out that with the tunnel completed, the necessity for Virginia City would be eliminated, that all mills and operations would then move to his new town to be named Sutro, where all mining operations and ore refining could be carried out on a level with the present operations.

The interests controlling the wealth of Virginia City would listen to no talk of this kind. The most formidable foe of Sutro and his plan was the Bank of California. It had already foreclosed on a number of Comstock mines, where poor management and less-rich ores had forced insolvency, and it owned many huge mills not only at Virginia City but on down the grade at Silver City and Gold Hill. Furthermore it was planning to build a railway to the city on top of the mountain for prospective patrons of the banks, hotels and restaurants and to haul practically all equipment and supplies to the mines — a veritable monopoly with the wagon roads so steep and rough. If Sutro's tunnel was ever built it would certainly be against the interests of these enterprises.

While William Sharon and other powers of the bank sat at conference planning strategy, Sutro was making contracts with mine owners that he was sure would enable him to start digging. His proposition was simple. He would drain the pesky hot water from their mines and even haul out their ores to the string of mills he would build along the Carson River — all this for free. Then for only $1 per ton he would mill all ores assaying up to $35 per ton, over that $2. The bargain was accepted by many, reluctantly by some, and Sutro agreed to start work by August 1, 1867, spending not less than $400,000 each year to speed completion of the tunnel.

He delayed only long enough to secure additional equipment and mules but the delay was disastrous. Sharon and other big men in the Comstock went to the mine owners, pointing out what to do if they knew what was good for them. So when Sutro was ready to start work, he found there was no money available and there would not be any, that almost every contract was being ignored.

DURING TUNNEL DIGGING DAYS large numbers of mules were used at Sutro, housed in this barn. Drilling and blasting equipment was hauled into dark tunnel by docile animals, each carrying own "headlight". Small building at entrance to tunnel was stocked with collar torches and oil, crew of young boys placing lighted torch in mule's collar as it entered, removing beacon as it emerged. Animals were invaluable to project, were well cared for, had good pasture along Carson River.

SUTRO AS IT APPEARS TODAY from site of mansion. In foreground are fireplace bricks and fancy metal cap which topped chimney. Blacksmith shop and warehouse show at right center. Tunnel opens at point about 200 feet this side of small buildings at extreme right. In distance is Carson Valley, river marked by trees.

Rather than sue, Sutro went to Washington where he appealed in vain to Congress for a subsidy. Sharon had already telegraphed representatives of the Bank of California in the capitol to block any move Sutro might make. Sutro tried to interest financiers William Astor and Commodore Vanderbilt and others only to be snubbed. Back in Nevada he tried to persuade legislators to put up money to start work already ratified by them but again the Sharon shadow stood in his way. As if the Bank of California were not enough to block his efforts, Sutro found another obstacle forming. A group called the "Big Four", Mackey, Fair, Flood

and O'Brien, bonanza kings of the Comstock, was becoming ever more powerful. These men also threw their weight against Sutro, recognizing in the projected tunnel a menace to their whole empire.

Then on April 7, 1869, tragedy struck in the Yellowjacket mine — fire that took the lives of forty-five men. Some members of the crew were rescued by raising them in the open "cage" but others died in the same operation, being so weak they fell against the sides of the shaft and were crushed by the rising platform. The rest, except for three who were actually burned to death, died of suffocation below. The disaster caused great feeling in Virginia City and Sutro took advantage of it, believing firmly that the proposed tunnel would avert future disasters like this by providing a means of escape.

On September 20 he made an impassioned speech for his project at Piper's Opera House. The reaction to the miners was overwhelmingly in favor of the tunnel, some even volunteering to lynch Sharon and the "Big Four". The ENTERPRISE, heretofore reluctant to print anything favoring the tunnel, now broke the speech across the entire front page. Popular sentiment was on Sutro's side and his project now had some backing. The miners even pledged enough funds so construction of the tunnel could begin October 19, 1869.

But even thousands of dollars supplied by miners were only a drop in the bucket compared to the millions needed, and the big money still had its feet planted solidly in the way. Congress eventually sent a commission to investigate the mines and the claimed need to run a tunnel to them. Of course the bank and the four Irishmen saw to it the committee of stuffed shirts never saw the steaming depths, never breathed air made intolerably fetid by heat, humidity, explosive fumes and sweating men. The investigators returned to Washington with the report that there was no real need for a tunnel, especially since the Virginia City powers had finished their railroad. Blow that this was, Sutro held stubbornly to the remaining benefits that would accrue.

Then came the first real money, $2,500,000, from McClamont's Bank in London, where Sutro had applied. Now began the pattern of going broke, getting money again, a succession lasting to completion of the tunnel 13 long years and $5 million later.

Even after the bore itself, twelve feet wide and nine feet high, had broken through to the bottom of the first mine, connecting branches to other mines must be built and a three-foot square trough laid down the middle to carry off the hot water

TOWN OF SUTRO about 1880. At extreme left is Sutro's mansion, rectangle of water beside it called by him an "artificial lake", by scoffers "Sutro's Frog Pond". It was aptly named, Sutro having stocked it first with fish and ducks, then insisted on bullfrogs also. These proving unavailable, not being native to western states, he settled for largest he could get. True bullfrogs have since populated Carson River, having been introduced much later. Warehouse building at right (with four windows on end) still stands as do many others. Courtesy Nevada State Museum.

TUNNEL OPENING 94 years after start of construction. Scene marks head of Tunnel Avenue, 200-foot wide thoroughfare down which passed ore cars headed for mill at foot. Also coming out of opening was steaming stream of water drained from deep mines of Comstock Lode. Water still gushes forth but from spring 2,000 feet back.

as promised. The trough would handle in one year alone, 1880, more than two billion gallons of steaming water.

Completion of the big job dealt a severe blow to the town of Sutro which was started to house and feed workmen. With construction crews laid off away went the town's main support. There was only the mill for processing tunnel-brought ores and the barns for housing mules used to draw ore carts through the bore. And Sutro continued for a time to live in the mansion he had built just above the tunnel.

But the sad fact was, by the time the long delayed Sutro tunnel was completed, the Comstock day of glory was ending. Royalties on ore hauled through it did pay the cost of building but that was about all. Sutro himself soon got out from under, the incentive of struggle gone. He sold his stock in the company and went on to other conquests in the city that was to be his home for the rest of his life — San Francisco.

The only residents of Sutro now are Robin Larson and his family. He writes: "I first saw the Sutro Tunnel site in the spring of 1959 on an automobile trip east with my father. At that time there was a caretaker. In the spring of 1962 I traveled to Nevada to see the Sutro Tunnel again and found it deserted with signs to the effect that it was destined to become a state park. The place interested

MULE PULLS LITTLE TRAIN carrying work crew from tunnel mouth about 1890. During construction days several attempts were made to use other power than mules. Horses failed, proving flighty and not tolerating heat. Mules worked longer in high temperatures until suddenly dropping dead as if shot. Most mechanical contrivances failed because of lack of ventilation causing fatal fumes to accumulate. Courtesy Nevada Historical Society.

CONE OF NUT PINE Pinus Monophylla, showing several "nuts" still attached. Cones are formed during summer, remain as small prickly balls until following season when growth is rapid. Late in second summer green cone is solid, hard and dripping with sparkling, clear, fragrant pitch or resin. In September they begin to open and shed seeds. Nuts were once staple article of diet for Indians who beat limbs with sticks to bring cones down. Fire was built over heaps of cones which caused quick opening of scales and release of nuts. Heat also dissipated small quantity of turpentine which made unroasted nuts bitter and inedible.

me very much and it disturbed me to see that it was deserted. People were breaking and stealing things at such a rapid rate that there was a great change since I had seen it last. I decided to make a personal effort to protect it until it should become a park.

"With the cooperation of the Nevada State Park System and the Comstock Tunnel and Drainage Company (the owners) I took up residence at the tunnel portal and lived there for a year, protecting the place, cleaning it up and campaigning to make it into a state park. The state refused to accept Sutro and rather than see it destroyed and looted and because I had fallen in love with the place, the history and the country, I took up a lease and I intend to preserve the tunnel portal and the existing eighteen buildings as an historical monument. I don't want to restore, only to prevent any further decay."

When they came to the ranch one day, David had no wood to be chopped so brought out a chunk of gold ore showing definite flecks of the yellow metal. He asked Hog-or-Die Jim in a jumble of Paiute and sign language: "Do you know where there is any more rock like this?" The Indian indicated he did and pointed out a location in the hills above the ranch, three and a half miles south of Mt. Etna in the Pine Grove mountains.

David now turned William loose with abandon and after some diligent search he found a gold deposit. The Wilsons then gave their full attention to mining. From the time the find was made in 1866 to about 1871 Pine Grove developed to a population of over 1,000. The three original arrastras owned by Portuguese Joe grew to several power stamp mills using steam from boilers fired by nut pine wood. The ore was known as "free-milling", the easiest type of work, needed only to be washed and crushed in sluices. In later years a mill was built to rework some of the waste, but most of the gold had been recovered by the cruder method.

The town was a boisterous one. (Ed: this information differs sharply from that gathered earlier which declared the Wilsons to be "Blue Nose" meaning intolerant of drinking or gambling, that miners went to nearby Rockland for diversion). See Pine Grove, WESTERN GHOST TOWNS. Joseph Wilson relates that Pine Grove had two sections, that "there were five saloons in the upper part and three in the lower, with a dance hall in the middle". There were also three hotels, Wells Fargo office and a large general store. The barber shop and shoeshine parlor was operated by a colored man who charged fifty cents for a haircut, twenty-five for a shine. The post office charged three cents for sending a letter in competition with the express company which charged an exhorbitant five.

With so many people drawn to an area where a few years before there had been no one, the surrounding hills got a close examination for precious metals. And in 1869 a Pine Grove resident, a Mr. Keene, found a rich vein of silver and gold three and a half miles from his home. As quickly as he could he built a quartz mill in Bridgeport Canyon just below his mine. He called the lively little town that grew up around the mine and mill Rockland, presumably for the fantastic and beautiful red rock cliffs towering over the location.

Keene had trouble keeping his expenses below his money intake. His men were paid irregularly and when no money was forthcoming they set up a howl. One in particular, a Mr. Rhodes, trouble maker at best, threatened to get even and when Keene was away raising money for the payroll, Rhodes set fire to the mill. He was arrested, convicted of arson and sent to the state prison. Keene got deeper in debt, finally lost control of the mine and ex-Gov. Blaisedell tried his hand at operating it and also failed. Then C. D. Lane stepped in, got some ore out but he too was unsuccessful. The mine was deserted and Tom Flynn stayed on as watchman for years, at length buying an interest in the claim and running some ore through the mill.

During this period a boulder showing chunks of gold and weighing several hundred pounds was found nearby. It assayed $500 to the ton and created great excitement. The chunk was definitely a huge piece of float from some rich lode near the area. Hordes of prospectors tried to locate the source but all failed and Rockland settled back to doze again.

The LYON COUNTY TIMES of Nov. 24, 1894, reported this item: FATAL ACCIDENT AT PINE GROVE. Last Monday morning between 8 and 9, John Redding, who was working on the Wilson tailing dump in Pine Grove, was caved upon and buried under tons of dirt. As soon as the accident happened, a force of men began to dig for the unfortunate man. After several tons of dirt had been removed, the body was found but life had been crushed out of it. The deceased was a native of Missouri, aged 26 and came to Nevada about 5 years ago. He leaves a father, three sisters and two brothers. The funeral took place Thursday at the Grove and was largely attended."

By 1948 Tom Flynn was thoroughly discouraged over his property, cleaned his little cabin and headed his old car down the mountain grade to think things over in town — maybe raise money or abandon the pesky thing. Just as Flynn drove into the canyon where the road in the defile is extremely steep, rocky and narrow, a torrent of rain he later termed as a "water spout" struck the rocky walls. The deluge of muddy water took out all semblance of road and carried Flynn and the car down into the gulch. He spent fourteen hours, he said, in reaching the town. No mind searching was needed. The decision had been reached. Tom Flynn kept driving on to leave his now inaccessible perch in the Pine Grove mountains to the buzzards.

LITTLE ROCKLAND LODGING HOUSE, once painted bright red, is faded but still upright. In back is large sleeping porch, open to breezes which at this altitude are considerable and the snows which are deep and long lasting. Nut pines show needle arrangement and bark texture.

TONOPAH, NEVADA

The story of the Mizpah Mine and its discovery has been told in several forms, but the most likely version is the one in which William Hall tried to boot his partner, Jim Butler, out of his blankets one spring morning in 1900, and failed. They had started from Butler's ranch on a trip to Southern Klondyke, a small mining camp. Fifteen miles short of their objective they came to Tonapah Springs and camped there.

Next morning, the early-rising Hall unable to rouse Butler, went on alone disgusted. In his own good time Butler arose, only to find his burros had "vamoosed" over the ridge. After tracking them down, he was pretty much out of sorts and picked up a rock to heave at them, but held on to it, not out of consideration for his beasts, but because the stone was flecked with mineral.

After locating the vein's source, he caught his burros and hurried to overtake his partner. Nothing much was happening in Southern Klondyke, however, and the partners soon returned to Belmont, gathering a few more samples at Tonopah Springs on the way.

It was Butler's wife who really started the ball rolling. She enlisted expert help in the person of Tasker L. Oddie, who was to figure prominently in Tonopah's subsequent history. Oddie, for an interest in the stake, had assays run proving the value of the samples would run $350 per ton.

Mrs. Butler staked a claim near Oddie's, naming it the Mizpah. This was one of the richest producers in the entire area.

There followed the usual influx; the sudden boom. Streets were laid out by Walter Gayhart, who saw fit to make his money in real estate rather than the sweaty job of mining.

Tonopah's heyday was the period centered about 1905, when it wrested the County Seat from Belmont. By 1913 there were definite signs that things were not going too well, and before long the big days were finished, having seen the production of $250,000,000 in gold and silver.

Tonopah is not dead, however. Some mining still goes on. The main street, flanked by the five-story Mizpah Hotel and many clubs, stores and restaurants, is still busy. Features of the town are the high curbs on each side. They rise to the height of about three feet and preclude stepping up just anywhere. The purpose of these is to channel the flood waters of frequent "gulley-washers" that pour through town.

The area is a veritable gem field, full of petrified wood, jasper and other semi-precious material.

STORM BUILDS UP over Tonopah. Town is at base of Mt. Oddie (right) whose sides and summit are eroded by diggings.

TUSCARORA, NEVADA

Nearing Tuscarora one first sees the cemetery, its white headstones and boards conspicuous against the gray-green sage and brown earth. Then comes the red brick smelter stack so noticeable on the hill above the town.

It is surprising to see a little stream of ice cold water running right across the road. How blessed was Tuscarora! Among Nevada mining camps few had an abundance of good water. Not that the miners cared much for the stuff for drinking. And Tuscarora had no wish to be unique, its population imbibing more whiskey than water. It was as wild and rip-roaring a camp as any, and worse than some. Its biggest decades were from 1870 to 1890 when several thousand whites and two thousand Chinese kept excitement going.

The Chinese came to build the Central Pacific Railroad and remained to dispense opium in a dark underground section of the town, concealed by an innocent looking China Town. For a time at least, they also ran most of the brothels and gambling joints. Some of these were behind and under laundries and others brazenly exposed, with red lights hanging at the doors of the cribs.

The town of the euphonius name and beautiful situation on Mount Blitzen produced $40,000,000, in silver mostly, so it must have buckled down to work daytimes.

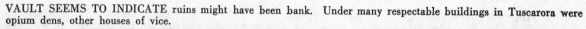

VAULT SEEMS TO INDICATE ruins might have been bank. Under many respectable buildings in Tuscarora were opium dens, other houses of vice.

SHIMMERING GHOSTS OF THE DESERT

UNIONVILLE, NEVADA

Spence Davidson, one of the residents along the creek, allows he arrived in town "quite a while ago!" He gives some data on Unionville.

"Quite a while ago" turned out to be 1890. "Was the town busy then?" "No, it was really dead even then; it had an early start, about 1860." Unionville saw only about ten really good, boom years, and was almost finished by 1880. In this brief period the place had undergone sudden expansion, with 20 new people moving in every day at first. These new residents soon needed, first, nine saloons; then 10 stores, an express office, livery stables and, at the fringe, the inevitable red light district. The girls of the cribs at first did very well, but many families moved to Unionville which, with its water and shade, offered more comforts than starker camps. The proportion of single men shrank and so did the "houses."

But the schools grew, and today the best preserved building is the one on the hill, facing the town. Several ranchers in the valley had as many as six children and these kept the school going until a few years ago. The last teacher was Mrs. Hammersmark, a sister-in-law of Mr. Davidson. She passed away recently in Reno.

Unionville, by virtue of its quick expansion, in the early 70's had become the seat of the then Humboldt County. The Courthouse was in a rented saloon in its early years. During Unionville's period of activity, it had produced some $3,000,000, largely in silver. The Arizona mine above the town had been the big one, with more than a third of the total to its credit.

593

Close by are the ruins of a small mill, and close to them the opening of the gold mine. From this cavern bursts a torrent of air of about 50 degrees, startlingly luxurious in the noonday heat of the Humboldt Foothills.

The cemetery on the way to the main road is large, but with many headboards missing. Those remaining mostly bear dates in the 70's, when the population had reached its peak of some 2,000 to 3,000. Many graves are enclosed in the usual ornate wooden fences. There certainly is a much larger population here now than in Unionville itself.

BUENA VISTA SCHOOL has not sheltered pupils for years but is in good condition. Heating stove stands in center, surrounded by desks graduated in size for different grades. Map of Africa on wall was made in 1887.

SPOOKS OF THE SHIFTING SANDS

VIRGINIA CITY, NEVADA

Virginia City is among the best known of the old camps. The town is neither dead nor abandoned, but nevertheless it is popularly considered a ghost town.

It is situated almost on top of a mountain, offering spreading views of the Nevada terrain in several directions. It has larger buildings than most and more of them. It has as interesting history as any, and since it has never been completely abandoned, most of the past has been preserved in print. The delver into the story of Virginia City can spend days or weeks among relics, books and newspapers on display on the spot where it all happened.

MANY BUILDINGS in Virginia City retain charm of early days.

ORIGINAL ATMOSPHERE still exists away from "C" Street.

IMPRESSIVE RELIC is Fourth Ward School. Located near south end of town on "C" St., it once provided vantage point from which to view spectacular cave-in across street. Sizable area collapsed into cavern created by mines which honeycomb ground under city.

BRICK BUILDING IS often called John Mackay residence. Structure was actually union mine office. Mr. Mackay did stay here whenever he visited Virginia City on business.

RIDERS IN THE SKY

SUPPLY CENTER ON THE TRUCKEE

Wadsworth, Nevada

To those weary travelers plodding toward California's golden El Dorado, the stopping place on the green banks of a river called Truckee was heaven on earth. Many of those who spent searing weeks in crossing the sands of the Great Basin plunged their dehydrated bodies into the river's clear waters. Twenty years later this welcome oasis was the site of a settlement, Wadsworth.

The Truckee is only 105 miles long. Beginning as a clear mountain stream in the High Sierra, over 6,000 feet above sea level, fed by waters overflowing from Lake Tahoe, it ends decimated by irrigation usage as a thick, silt-laden dribble in brackish Pyramid Lake. Famed Chief Winnemucca was said to have a son named Truckee and called the river that in his honor. However the Spanish name for trout is *trucha*, and as the river was called the Salmon Trout by Capt. John Fremont, that may be the true derivation of the name.

The Truckee makes its last sharp turn a few miles south of its end. Just north of Wadsworth it enters Pyramid Lake Reservation, established by President Grant March 23, 1874, for benefit of the Paiute inhabitants of the region. They lived largely on fish, especially the enormous cutthroat trout teeming in the river and Pyramid Lake. What they could not eat they sold to immigrants and later settlers.

The place once called the "Big Bend" is about 2,000 feet below the point where the Truckee emerges from Lake Tahoe. It was here Fremont left the stream he paralleled while descending the steep slopes of the Sierra in January, 1844, and where the pioneers taking this route west stopped, rested and then forded at a point just below the bend, a shallow place they termed "Lower Crossing." Some without the courage to climb over the mountain barricade called High Sierra, stayed and built shanties, living on fish and game while their stock grew fat on luxuriously growing grass. No town or settlement of any size resulted however until the advent of the Central Pacific Railroad.

The spot was a strategic one for the railroad. For the push east across a vast expanse of desert there would be no more wood or water for the engines. So at first Wadsworth served as a supply depot in the building of the line, then in 1868 became a permanent and important station. Settlers there now made a comfortable living cutting and hauling wood from fringes of the timbered mountains and the tenuous town became solid. Stores were established, hotels, saloons and gambling places sprouted like mushrooms as railroad building and maintenance crews roistered. Car shops for the Truckee division, extending from Truckee to Winnemucca, were located at the river's bend. These with work shops steadily employed a large number of men, roundhouse containing twenty stalls.

As soon as the railroad was completed to this point it became the base for supplies to mines then active to the south in Churchill, Nye and Esmeralda Counties. An old *History of Nevada* reads, "The excellent roads leading to Ellsworth, Columbus, Belmont and other towns are lined with long freight teams conveying goods and supplies from Wadsworth. As long as those points are supplied by freight wagons, Wadsworth will get the bulk of the traffic, but as soon as one of the proposed railroads invades that region the freighting business will materially decline. At the present time the population of about 500 are busy and prosperous."

For two years Wadsworth was a bone of contention between Washoe and Lyon Counties because of boundary uncertainties. It had been assumed the line followed the "old emigrant road" but the people of Lyon County discovered traces of a "cut off" which they insisted was the main route. If conceded this would leave Wadsworth in Lyon County which they wanted. Jurisdiction over Wadsworth had always been exercised by Washoe authorities and with Lyon's brazen attempt to take over a rich source of tax money, they took the matter to court. The case was tried twice in Ormsby County without arriving at a solid decision. A third attempt in Humboldt County cleared the matter for Washoe in 1871.

For some reason the section of railroad in the vicinity of Wadsworth was accident prone. The most spectacular near-disaster from the point of casualties was on June 13, 1872. Passenger car No. 1 passed over a broken rail six miles west of town. The two rear coaches jumped the track but plunged on, held upright by the rocky walls of the cut, dragged along to the end of it where they leaped down and were demolished. Had they tipped the other way they would have rolled into the canyon of the Truckee with great loss of life. As it was no one was killed although many were seriously injured.

COLUMBUS HOTEL, long abandoned, and little church with tottering weather vane stand alone in what was busy part of town. It was founded by overland emigrants on their way to California gold fields, stimulated by coming of railroad, nurtured as supply center for booming camps just south of Wadsworth. Collapse came with inevitable failure of mining camps to survive.

WASHOE CITY, NEVADA

Young George W. Derickson, editor of the three-months-old *Washoe City Times* had been getting away with murder in his editorials. This wasn't unusual in the Old West of the 1860s when editors printed exactly what they thought without restraint or fear of libel suits.

Subscriber H. F. Swayze had sent in "a letter to the editor." Derickson printed it and wrote a sarcastic story about it. As soon as the offending issue was on the street the angry Swayze went to the newspaper office and demanded to see the editor. Derickson attempted to soothe the seething Swayze by telling him his printed comment had only been the truth, a remark not calculated to do any soothing.

The heated argument ended in a duel out on the street, both men firing at the same time. Both bullets found their marks, fatally in the case of editor Derickson. Swayze received a shattered jaw and

three years in the Nevada State Penitentiary just out of Carson City.

Washoe City had come into being because it had what was needed elsewhere. The spot where it stirred into life is at the foot of Mt. Davidson on the one side and the High Sierra on the other. Virginia City on top of the hill was suffering for lack of lumber which had to be sawed out of timber from the Sierra slopes from where also its water came. Its ore also had to be sent away for smelting. And so Washoe City sprang up to serve its more glamorous neighbor, the fabulous Virginia City. Timber was hauled down from the high mountains and whipsawed in Washoe. Water was piped in a gigantic syphon from the crystal-clear streams in the Sierra through Washoe where maintenance crews were quartered. And silver ore also came down to it from Virginia City to be smelted.

All this began to happen in the winter of 1860-

BANK AND WELLS FARGO BUILDINGS had iron doors and shutters similar to those in use in gold country on other side of Sierra in California. Photo was made in 1955. Both structures have since fallen to ground.

LAST BUILDING REMAINING in old Washoe City in 1962. It stands at right of sites of structures shown in other Washoe picture. Fringe of bricks can be seen adhering to edge of stone building.

61 when the first buildings were put up. By 1864 when several sawmills were feverishly turning out lumber for the booming Virginia City there was a population of 2,500. Smelters belched smoke from fires which were consuming the Jeffrey pines of the Sierra and refining huge quantities of silver ore coming down the slopes of Mt. Davidson on the Virginia and Truckee Railroad.

When slow death came to the mining camp in the clouds, Washoe City likewise expired, its reason for existence gone. Old Washoe's last shred of dignity was wrested away when in 1871, the upstart Reno, which had sprung up a few miles north, took over as the seat of Washoe County.

More substantial than Washoe City itself is the nearby imposing mansion of Sandy and Ella Orrum Bowers. The couple had started married life almost penniless in the mines on the fringes of Virginia City, then made millions from small investments in mining stock. They spent the money madly, had the huge house erected, to be ready on their return from a trip to Europe. They didn't enjoy either their wealth or their mansion for long. Sandy died at thirty-five, his widow lost all the money and the house, dying a pauper in 1903. The two with their daughter are buried on the hill a short distance behind the house.

NEW MEXICO and TEXAS GHOST TOWNS

BY

LAMBERT FLORIN

Drawings
by
DAVID C. MASON, M.D.

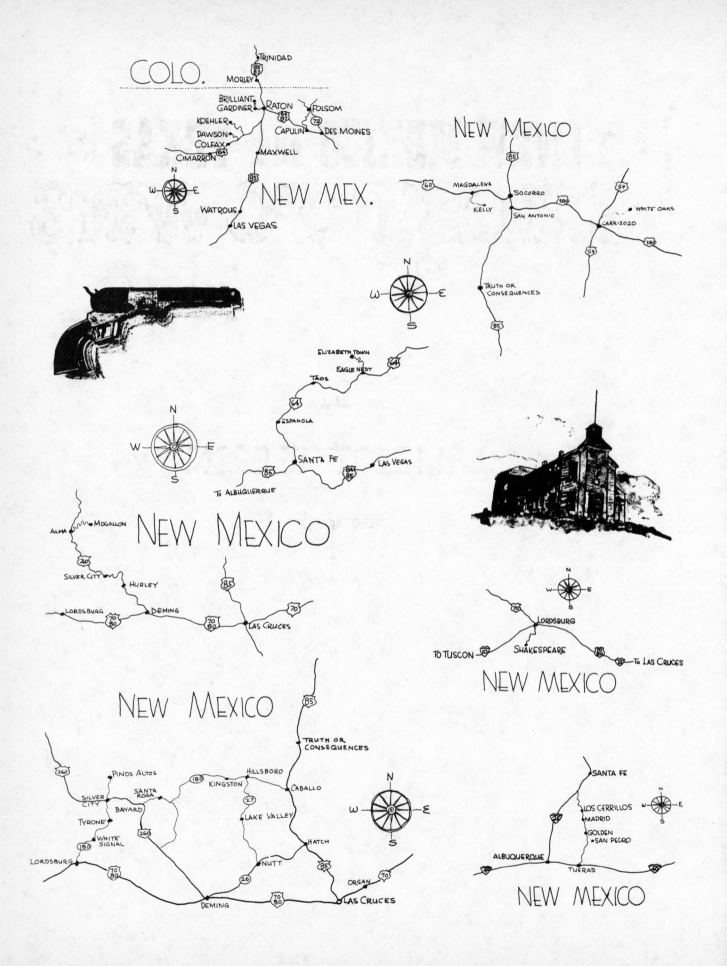

INDEX

Page

NEW MEXICO

Alma 605

Cerrillos 608

Cimarron 609

Dawson 614

Elizabethtown 617

Folsom 620

Golden 623

Hillsboro 624

Kelly 626

Kingston 629

Koehler 631

Lake Valley 635

Madrid 638

Page

Magdalena 642

Mogollon 644

Pinos Altos 647

San Pedro 650

Shakespeare 651

Tyrone 655

Watrous 657

White Oaks 660

TEXAS

Lajitas 664

Shafter 667

Study Butte 672

Terlingua 676

ALMA, NEW MEXICO

Into Alma's brief period of life was crowded more turbulence, murder and bloodshed than fell to the lot of any other comparable town in New Mexico. Apaches almost continually harassed the village; any brief respite from Indian raids was filled with internal strife between ranchers and holdups by bandits.

The original plans for Alma were more than peaceful; in fact, the town was laid out along communal lines. No mining was involved at first; this meant no influx of single men to allow for saloons and brothels. Only families would settle here in the fertile and well-watered "Frisco Valley" and farm the land. Cabins would be built close together for better protection from Indians; the farms would surround the homes; everything seemed ideal.

Maurice Coates, one of the dreamers, was born in Canada in 1856. He was a drifter and in his wanderings became a friend of James Keller who also was heading westward. They stopped in Prescott, Arizona, for a while where they decided that farming was their forte, then retraced their steps to the San Francisco Valley, New Mexico, where they found land that was suitable at the edge of the Mogollon Range, named for Don Juan Ignacio Flores Mogollon, Governor of the Province of New Mexico, 1712 to '15. Together with two other interested men, Capt. J. G. Birney and

Robert Stubblefield, they laid out plans for the town and called the place Mogollon. The same year, 1878, control of Mogollon was bought out by Capt. Birney. Since he had never liked the name Mogollon, he rechristened the infant settlement "Alma" for his mother.

And now the bloody period began. W. H. McCullough, a native New Mexican, was the first man to sell the founders on the idea of settling in the state, and had been one of the original farmers of the valley. Almost immediately after the change in ownership, he, with Birney and Prescott, were slain by a party of sheepherders which included whites and two Pueblo Indians. The sheepherders had learned that the Alma men were going to the Adams diggings in Arizona to see what was going on there, and an ambush was laid for them on the assumption that they would be carrying quite a lot of money. They figured, rightly, that Navajos who had recently been on the warpath would be blamed. The true story came out in '86, when the remains were found and one of the Pueblos, conscience stricken, confessed to the deed. He was convicted of murder by the tribal council and put to death by his own people. Before he died, he implicated the other members of the party and they were pursued by the sheriff but never caught.

Although trouble with Pueblos and Navajos continued, the real terror was furnished by Apaches. One evening five of them made a raid on James Keller's ranch and killed several of his cattle. Infuriated, he swore to kill every one of the Indian party, and started after them, alone. When he caught up with them unobserved, he thought better of it and returned to Alma for help. Reinforced by several men, he took the trail again, and since the Indians had not suspected they were being pursued, they were soon overtaken by the avenging settlers. The tally at the end of the battle, three warriors dead and one wounded. The latter died while fleeing the scene, his body found the next day. The raid had been a costly one for the Apaches, but the significant factor in the whole episode was that one of the slain Indians proved to be Toribo, son-in-law of notorious Victorio. His slaying would not go unavenged.

As soon as the news reached Victorio, the Chief began to lay plans to wipe out the entire settlement of Alma. He went to the camp of a sub-chief called Steve to enlist help. When Steve refused, realizing that slaughter of the whites would soon bring the wrath of a battalion of soldiers on his head, the furious Victorio retreated far enough to assemble his warriors and then attacked his erstwhile friend. The battle of Apache against Apache ended in humiliating defeat for Victorio, and in addition the loss of several of his best braves. Smarting, he killed and scalped the first two white men he ran across. Their names are not known, but two of the same party escaped— George Mehams and Eli Mader. These men made their way to the nearby mining camp of Cooney and spread the news. The founder of this community, Sergeant James Cooney, with a couple of miners named Chick and Brightman and other man unnamed, took off after the Indians. In the meantime, Victorio had found more willing allies than Steve's warriors, the more terrible Geronimo and Nana. Their augmented force was too much for Cooney's party, Brightman and the unidentified miner being killed and scalped. Cooney and Chick fled to Alma, arriving there in the dead of night.

Alma now made preparations for an almost certain attack, and agreed to make a fort of the Roberts home, that being the most likely to resist a siege. Cooney, having alerted the settlers in Alma, was anxious to return to his own town and with one volunteer, left for the camp named for him.

BLACKSMITH SHOP under large trees at outskirts of Alma where travelers stopped to have wagon wheels fixed, horses and mules shod. Dry climate most of year often made iron tires come off wheels. Tire was laid on ground, elevated about eight inches by rocks, fire built under and around. When metal was well expanded, tire was slipped over wheel and hammered on. Blacksmith shop was owned by partners, Dan Russell and William Antrim. Antrim had courted and married Katherine McCarthy, mother of Billy the Kid, in Sante Fe, March 1, 1873. Billy was then 14 years old and extremely fond of mother, resented intrusion of Antrim. Two got along in armed truce. The Kid hung around the blacksmith shop and affection of a sort grew between them so when Garret killed the Kid everyone thought Antrim would go gunning for the killer. He eventually went to Adelaide, California, died and was buried there. Shop was converted to garage in earliest days of autos, "antique" pump added to front of old smithy.

They got safely away about eight o'clock. At ten, Apaches appeared on the hillside east of Alma and opened fire on the Roberts cabin. One wagonload of four whites, the Meador family, had just arrived at the refuge and had not yet entered. They were unable to get out of the wagon because of the firing by the Indians. Suddenly to everyone's astonishment Mrs. Meador grabbed a rifle and began returning the fire. In the resulting momentary confusion, a woman opened the cabin door, and all slipped in, though not before Mr. Meador lost a lock of his hair to a bullet whizzing by. Another missle went through the bonnet of the lady opening the door. The river was on the opposite side and the women managed to get some water collected in kettles and pans before they were spotted and fired upon.

The siege was now on in earnest and firing was general. The first Indian casualty resulted when a brave couldn't resist the temptation of a beautiful horse tethered in the open. When he exposed himself to reach for the bridle, a well-aimed shot from the gun of Jim Keller felled him. One of the men in the cabin, a Mr. Wilcox, made the mistake of standing up to make sure the Indian was really dead and was himself slain by a bullet through the heart.

It seemed necessary to summon aid some way, so Keller and Pete Carpenter managed to slip out as soon as it got dark and made it to Silver City, unharmed. From there a rider was sent to Fort Bayard where a rescue squad was organized and joined by a reinforced group of civilians from Silver City. The men rode the seventy-two miles when they were forced to rest their horses. They then made the distance to Bush Valley where they expected to change horses, but were dismayed to find that Indians had run off all available mounts, some thirty horses. They were now out of provisions as well and managed to collect three days supply while their horses rested. At last they reached the outlying ranches near Alma on May 14th, 1880. The next day they forced the besieging Indians to retreat to the mountains, and the first siege of Alma was over. Altogether thirty-one whites had been killed in the area during the uprising. These figures included Sergeant Cooney and his volunteer, who had been waylaid on the return to Cooney and killed. Their mutilated bodies were found by the rescue party. Cooney was buried in a solid stone "tomb" close to his mine and town.

As soon as Alma had a chance to relax a little it went ahead. July of '82 showed a population of more than three hundred. A school was built, taking care of sixty-eight children. James Meador built the Hotel de Brunswick. An organization called the Minute Men was set up and the men trained regularly so as to be ready for the next Indian attack. Church services were held in the schoolhouse by a circuit rider, and later by ministers from neighboring Cooney and Mogollon. One of the residents wrote a letter to the editor of the *Albuquerque Journal* in 1883, stating "our town is made up of thirty-five houses well constructed of adobe and lumber. We have two business houses doing general merchandising business and in connection with the same a good saloon and card rooms. . . . Two saloons, one owned by D. A. Bechtol who smilingly caters to his many friend's desires in the shape of liquid refreshments; the other mentioned above." Two blacksmith shops and a large general merchandise store in a newly constructed adobe building completed the inventory.

The same year saw another Indian attack. This one was on a ranch near town and Judge McComas and his wife, who had stopped there overnight on a trip from Silver City, were killed and their six-year-old son carried off. The boy was never seen alive again although many stories persisted about him. One was that the boy's head was bashed in when it seemed certain that the party would be attacked by whites, another that the chief of the Indian tribe in later years had red hair and blue eyes and was presumed to be Charley McComas.

In another siege most of the settlers remained awake all night waiting for an imminent attack—all but a Mr. Herr who slept with a large revolver under his pillow. Circumstances, however, weren't conducive to anything but the most restless slumber, and his turnings worked the pistol out from under the pillow. When he arose in the morning, he knocked it down. It fired and sent a bullet through his head.

At various times troops were stationed in Alma to guard against Apaches. During the worst of Geronimo's raiding, two troops of the 8th cavalry made their headquarters at the big W. S. Ranch, remaining for some sixteen months.

Before and after, never during, these occupations the town became the hangout of the notorious "Wild Bunch" made up of Butch Cassidy, Tom Ketchum, Toppy Johnson and the others. William Antrim, father-in-law of Billy, the Kid, was a resident of Alma and the Kid stayed there with him for a time. Another familiar figure in Alma was that of "Mountain Man" Ben Lilly. He was supposed to have killed 110 mountain lions during his time there, earning for himself $55,000 in bounty money.

All these legendary figures, ferocious Apaches, farmers, saloonkeepers, their shelters and places of business are gone with the wind now. Only one adobe building and the tiny cemetery filled with victims of Indians and murder remain.

New Mexico

TURQUOISE TOWN

Cerrillos, New Mexico

No one can say just when Cerrillos (properly Los Cerrillos, "the little hills") had its beginning. Certainly the diggings there are very ancient, gold and turquoise mined in the low mountains around the town since at least 500 A.D. when Basket Maker Indians were in their prime. A few miles from Mt. Chalchihuitl is a huge pit in the solid rock and across Galisteo Creek and up a winding arroyo is the famed Mina del Tiro, "Mine of the Shaft." All evidence is that prehistoric Indians were the miners. History comes into somewhat sharper focus with the likelihood that those gold and silver ores assayed by Spanish prospector Espejo in 1582 came from the Little Hills.

Indian revolutionist Po-pe led his tribesmen against the hated Spanish in 1680, driving those not murdered out of the country. Setting up new quarters at El Paso del Norte Spanish fugitives forgot all about mining or at least made no further attempts to regain the turquoise and gold at Los Cerrillos, all locations being lost.

Three hundred years after Espejo, in 1879, prospecting Americans rediscovered precious metals and blue turquoise at Los Cerrillos and the ancient diggings. A rush followed with more than three hundred men swarming over the little hills. Not long after this the Santa Fe Railroad came through, setting off an even larger boom, satellite towns like Bonanza and Carbonateville mushrooming briefly. It was during this heated period that eastern capital came in to reopen the old turquoise mines, the two largest being the Tiffany and Castilian. An 1899 report listed New Mexico's production of turquoise as worth $1,600,000, most of it coming from Cerrillos, Yankees having dropped the "Los."

With production of metals and blue gemstones lessening, the town began to fail after the turn of the century. There was some activity as long as neighboring Madrid flourished. When tipples there ceased to load coal cars and the railroad curtailed operations, something in Cerrillos died too. It has withered since although a tavern still serves an occasional thirsty rancher or tourist, a general store and restaurant open part time.

OLDEST BUILDING remaining in Cerrillos, it is presumed. Pine logs from mountains were squared with broad axe, laid up with minimum notching, wide chinks filled with mud. Portion at far left received coat of elegant plaster in later years.

CHRONIC DIFFICULTY holding back full development of milling rich ore from mines in high country near Cimarron was lack of consistent water power. Invention of new "impulse type" of water wheel by Lester Allen Pelton in Camptonville, Calif., 1878 was hailed as answer to problem, since wheel required only small volume of water for operation. Although much of metals mining boom in northern New Mexico was already finished by then, some Pelton wheels were imported, proved to be only another disappointment. Though jet of water could be small it had to be directed at cups with great velocity not obtainable at all times.

CIMARRON, NEW MEXICO

"A house is not a home", said a certain madam of distinction, but it is possible to have a home with a house in it. Cimarron land owner Lucien B. Maxwell had one. The mammoth house, as large as a city block, was essentially a hotel containing quarters for Maxwell when he was not riding over his vast domain, as well as gambling rooms, saloon, dance hall, billiard parlor. Then there was the special area reserved for women of special virtue — and they were permanent fixtures. Once a girl was installed in these lavishly furnished rooms she was allowed to leave only if she were not coming back.

The Maxwell estate was three times as large as the State of Rhode Island, comprising 1,714,765 acres. Besides Cimarron, the area included the sites of Springer, Raton and Elizabethtown in New Mexico, spreading well over into Colorado to take in Segundo and other towns. French trapper Don Carlos Beaubien and his Spanish or Mexican partner Guadalupe Miranda, applied for a grant in 1841 and used the land as their own although legal title was held up for 41 years. An ex-trapper, hailing from Kaskaskia, Illinois, Maxwell came exploring, joined General Fremont's expedition and married Luz Beaubien, Don Carlos' daughter. In 1849 the couple settled on the Beaubien-Miranda Grant, and upon the father-in-law's death in 1864, bought out the other heirs, becoming the owners of the largest land grant in New Mexico.

Maxwell's family included four daughters and a son Peter, whom the father despised because the boy would not share his interests and "wasted his time with worthless friends." Maxwell did favor one daughter, Virginia, but when she met Captain A. S. B. Keyes, associated in Indian Agency operations, father objected violently to the romance, but finally did give grudging but unforgiving consent to the marriage. The wedding on the top floor of the estate granary was a brilliant social event — but Lucien Maxwell did not attend.

When he first took over the grant, Maxwell lost no time in getting a herd of cattle established and with complete control of it, industriously increased the herds by setting up individual ranchers with their own cattle, tenants to make payments on a share basis. It was typical of the times that no contracts were ever drawn up, all agreements being verbal.

At about 6000 feet in elevation most of the grassy meadows around Cimarron were assured of ample rainfall for good pasturage and Maxwell's herds flourished. He quickly had a surplus to market, the main outlet a scattered group of accessible army posts. He sold only the extra cattle to their commissaries, keeping his best animals and upgrading the remaining stock. And he maintained a diversity in the stock, saddle and work horses grazing in the pastures, more hilly sections supporting flocks of sheep. There was even a large goat ranch, its manager to be well known in later years as Buffalo Bill Cody.

But Maxwell was not content with agrarian

projects. Noting the many prospectors, trappers and travelers along the Santa Fe Trail who were camping just anywhere, he decided to build a huge stopping place for them. It was not a humanitarian gesture to shelter them from rain and snow. This was business. He would provide amusements for these lonely men, liquor to warm their bellies, faro, roulette, monte and female companionship — to divert the flow of gold to Santa Fe.

The Maxwell House was built in 1864 and was soon the center of social life in northern New Mexico, as well as the principal "wayside inn." The old registers contained some prominent names but if a guest chose not to sign for reasons of his own, he was not refused. Davy Crockett — the desperado, not the legendary character of an earlier era — Kit Carson, Clay Allison and Buffalo Bill, who occasionally came in from the lonely post on the goat ranch to live it up a little, were a few of the famous guests. Cody's visits were not all dalliance as it was in Cimarron he organized the first of his Wild West Shows.

There were some shooting scrapes in the Maxwell House, particularly in the bar and gambling sections, but participants were quickly ejected or carried out, Maxwell not tolerating such nonsense as it was bad for business, he said. But bullets flew freely elsewhere in Cimarron. One man who seemed to attract them was burly Mason Chase, red-headed son of a rancher. On one occasion there was a "shivaree" going on at the Cosgrove house. It had started as a celebration for a newly married couple but had gotten out of hand from too much red eye.

Young Charles Cosgrove stepped outside to run off the demonstrators when Mason Chase came along wanting to know what the party was all about. The infuriated Cosgrove, assuming Chase was the instigator, raised his gun and fired point blank at Chase's heart. But the red-head stayed upright. Recently made deputy sheriff, he made notes on his job in a thick notebook carried in his breast pocket and it received the bullet. Later he complained he could not read some of the writing in it.

Not so lucky was bandit Davy Crockett who had the town of Cimarron and countryside under his control. In September of 1876 he met up with Deputy Sheriff Joe Holbrook. It was a case of which man was quicker on the draw and Crockett was buried on Cimarron's boot hill. Friends placed a headboard at his grave but vandals later carried it off as a souvenir.

Clay Allison was another badman who kept the town in a turmoil. Historian Charles Siringo

OLD CIMARRON JAIL has heavy plank door with tiny barred window. From this opening peered long succession of outlaws, murderers, horse thieves, many emerging only for noose around necks.

"credits" him with eighteen victims, the most modest estimates being ten. J. Frank Dobie, beloved western writer who passed away in 1964, said of Allison: "He was quixotically independent in interpreting what constituted his rights. The more whiskey he drank, the more rights he possessed and sometimes when he came to town he bought a great deal of whiskey. He was generous with it, however, even insisting on his horse enjoying a fair portion."

Allison was twenty years old at the start of the Civil War and he joined the Confederate side. Captured by Union soldiers, he was convicted of spying and sentenced to be shot. He was held in a makeshift prison and although six feet two and weighing one hundred and eighty pounds, he had deceptively small hands and was able to slip out of his handcuffs and escape.

Allison liked off-the-trail types of duels when

610

involved in quarrels. He once got his adversary to stand at one end of a freshly dug grave facing the pit, Allison at the other, winner to cover up the loser. Another was brought on by Allison's killing Pancho Grieg in a flareup over a billiard game in Cimarron's St. James Hotel. He remarked it sure was a hot day and taking off his hat, used it for a fan and with a tricky movement drew his gun under cover of the hat, shooting Pancho dead.

Sheriff Mace Bowman told Allison his actions in the affair were not entirely ethical and suggested the gunman give himself up. Allison had a proposition ready. He and the sheriff would lay their guns on the bar of Lambert's Hotel (officially the St. James). They would stand back to back and at a given signal, walk twenty-five paces. Then at another signal they would rush for their guns. The sheriff allowed this was a reasonable arrangement, possibly because he knew Allison had accidentally shot himself in the foot not long before and might be handicapped. He figured wrong. Allison won the dash and leveled his gun at the sheriff. Bowman then stood straight, exposed his chest and said: "All right, shoot me, you ....!" But Allison admired such courage and answered: "Mace, you're too brave a man to die," placing his gun back in its holster. The two then shook hands and justice, frontier fashion, was done. Allison's death came some years later in ironical fashion. The gunman was full of whiskey and driving a team of four mules

CENTURY OLD GRANARY and grist mill was built to hold and grind grain produced on Maxwell Grant. It seems as solid today as when built in 1864, all floors solid and safe. This view shows north or rear, facing on nearby Cimarron River. Front side once had ramp affording access to second floor. Wedding of Virginia Maxwell and Capt. A. S. B. Keyes was held here.

when the wagon hit a sharp bump. Allison was bounced out and the wheels of the heavy rig rolled over his head, crushing it "like an eggshell," said the freighter traveling with him.

The Las Vegas GAZETTE took a laconic view of the goings on at Cimarron, reporting once: "Everything is quiet at Cimarron. Nobody has been killed there in three days." The town boasted of fifteen saloons where gunmen could get their courage up, four hotels, a post office and a miniature printing plant where a weekly paper, the Cimarron NEWS AND PRESS, was published. The spindly hand-press was said to have been first used by Padre Antonio Jose Martinez to print his little Taos paper, EL CREPUSCULE. One day the NEWS AND PRESS incautiously hit the street with an editorial blistering some of the gunmen terrorizing the town. That night the ouraged outlaws broke into the newspaper office housed in the Indian Agency headquarters and smashed the press, dumping the wreckage and type cases in the Cimarron River.

The mother of Mason Chase was one of the forthright women in Cimarron. On an autumn day when the leaves were yellowing, the apples in her little orchard ripening, she shook the branches and let the fruit fall into her apron. A wildcat on an upper branch suddenly dropped on the woman, clawing and biting her. After getting her hands on the animal's throat, she squeezed the windpipe until the struggling cat went limp. Then Mrs. Chase calmly gathered the scattered apples into her apron and went home.

And it was Mrs. Chase's daughter-in-law, wife of Mason, who was struck by lightning and lived, although doomed to carry a lifetime reminder of the incident. Hope Gilbert, now of Pasadena, California, who lived in Cimarron as a child, heard the story from Tom McBride, born on the Chase ranch. Before she was married, Nellie Curtis Chase traveled with her family to a dance about five miles from home. She rode on the front seat of an open spring wagon beside the driver and her sister. The sky was ominous when they started and during the rain a flash of lightning made a direct hit on the wagon. The mule pulling it was knocked to the ground and the dog running alongside killed. The driver was stunned and Nellie appeared dead, clothes burned from her body, gold necklace melted and imbedded in the skin. Unconscious for several days, the girl survived but all the rest of her life the mark of the lightning-fused necklace remained around her neck.

Lucien Maxwell stayed with stock raising and

MECHANISM ONCE OPERATING grinding stones, still intact on floor above, was powered by generous water flow diverted from Cimarron River. When Lucien Maxwell was made head of U.S. Government Indian Agency, he dispensed flour and provisions to Utes and Apaches from store in granary. Well educated, six feet tall with fair complexion and blue eyes, friendly "White Father" was highly regarded by Indians who felt protective toward Maxwell ranch, on at least one occasion preventing raid by hostile tribe.

inn keeping, and succeeded mightily. He employed five hundred men on the ranches, several thousand acres of rich land producing hay and other crops. His contracts with the government expanded and money poured into his coffers, which was in truth a cowhide trunk in his bedroom, the rancher having little faith in banks.

In the middle '60s gold was discovered on various streams within the Maxwell Grant boundaries. At first these were kept secret, the discoverers fearing ejection and reprisals from the big boss. But when the news did leak out, he took no action and the three men involved in the earliest workings formed a company — head officers: W. H. Moore,

William Koenig and John Buck. Without opposition the outfit successfully mined its claims.

Then even larger deposits were found by two other partners — Brownson and Kelly — in nearby Moreno Valley, but the tiny stream there failed to supply enough water for washing operations. The finders staked their claims, however, and dreamed of obtaining water by diverting some of the flow of Red River in Taos County. Such a scheme would require a big fund but the men set about organizing a stock company to finance the ditch.

First they approached Maxwell with an offer of stock in the company and the man who had done so well at ranching and cattle raising made his first big mistake. He invested heavily in the venture and as the company began to run out of money long before the ditch was finished, he was approached again for further funds. The project took $300,000 for completion and it is probable Lucien Maxwell supplied most of it.

The NEW MEXICO MINER reported: "It was a colossal undertaking . . . a marvelous piece of engineering. The ditch forms three-fourths of a circle in its length of skirting along the edge of the mountains, bridging ravines and gullies." But the article left out some painful details such as the fact that so many leaks developed along the long canal that little water arrived at the lower end. Although extensive repairs were made with expensive maintenance kept up, it was never a success, but considerable gold was extracted with its aid. Some time later the MINER was forced to modify its opinion, stating: "The Lynch Ditch which carries water from Red River to the Moreno placer mines at Elizabethtown is to be sold next month at a sheriff's sale to satisfy a judgment and cost aggregating $7,000."

From one disastrous debacle, Maxwell turned to another. He started the First National Bank of Santa Fe, charter granted in December, 1870. It took him only a year to discover banking was somewhat more complex than stuffing money into a cowhide trunk and he sold out at a heavy loss. Now he was approached by a group seeking to finance the building of the Texas Pacific Railroad and the man born to raise hay and cattle invested $250,000. When it failed, Maxwell retired to his ranch to lick his wounds. In 1870 he sold his grant, lock-stock-and barrel to a group of financiers for around $750,000 and moved to Fort Sumner, which had been demili-tarized and offered for sale by the government. Maxwell bought the part having buildings and other improvements, remodeling the officers' quarters into a luxurious home with twenty rooms. Here he lived in semi-retirement until he died in 1875, leaving his property to his son Peter.

Peter Maxwell was described as a "well meaning, inoffensive man, but very timid" by John W. Poe, deputy of Lincoln County sheriff Pat Garrett. On the hot night of July 14, 1881, Peter had given sanctuary to the notorious gunman Billy the Kid, who was on the run after being convicted of murder and sentenced to hang in April at Lincoln. He escaped from jail there, killing two guards as he fled. Garrett and his deputies tracked him to Fort Sumner and the Kid was slain by Garrett in young Maxwell's bedroom. He was buried in the old military cemetery where Lucien B. Maxwell already lay, and where Peter was buried at his death.

Cimarron had its turn, from 1872 to 1882, at being county seat of Colfax, a county credited with having more of them than any other in the country. Elizabethtown was one, others Springer, Raton and even little Colfax almost made it. By 1880, Cimarron was getting somewhat ghostly, becoming a true wraith after removal of the county seat. Twenty-five years later the St. Louis, Rocky Mountain and Pacific Railroad built a spur line to Cimarron and Ute Park, causing the old town to come to life, particularly the section across the Cimarron River on the north side where real estate operators bought a townsite and erected hotels, stores, selling lots and houses to people who arrived with the rails.

Today there are still two Cimarrons, "old" and "new", divided by the river. All the historic buildings remaining are on the south side, including the jail and the famous 100-year-old granary built to hold the wheat produced on the Maxwell Grant. The notorious St. James Hotel, where owner Herbert Lambert, "had a man for breakfast twenty-six times", still stands in somewhat altered form as does the Don Diego Tavern. Across the street are the all but obliterated ruins of the Maxwell House.

Not far away is the Philmont Ranch, originally Kit Carson's Rayado Rancho established in 1849, later owned by Waite Philips. In 1941 the ranch was turned over to the National Boy Scouts. Now thousands of boys hold their annual Jamborees there, few realizing the aura of history surrounding old Cimarron.

DAWSON, NEW MEXICO

In a day when almost everybody burned wood in their stoves, J. B. Dawson was called a crackpot since he scraped chunks of coal from the surface of his farm land. Then out of curiosity, some of his neighbors asked for samples to burn and were pleased enough at the results to avoid the chore of bucking wood and buy the black fuel from Dawson.

J. B. Dawson, with his homestead, was one of the ranchers with a few hundred acres each who were giving trouble to the Maxwell Land Grant Company which had bought an immense tract from Lucien B. Maxwell. Having neglected to look into the matter of all the ranchers living on the land, they had no way of knowing who was a legal owner and who was merely squatting.

When the company saw the ground was heavily laced with coal, it hankered to develop the vein but the attempted eviction of Dawson brought him up fighting, claiming he had bought his land from Maxwell although admitting the transaction had been purely verbal, sealed with a handshake. Maxwell, he said, always did business that way, and the company officials found he was right.

Dawson was disposed to settle the matter with six-guns but consented to abide by a court decision. He hired attorney Andrieus A. Jones who was well aware of Maxwell's real estate deals. The case was tried in the fall of 1893 and decided in favor of Dawson. The New Mexico Supreme Court held that the company could not prove that Dawson did not own the land, or mineral rights thereof, an important point since the coal deposits were the crux of the whole argument. Maxwell, of course, could not testify as he had died eighteen years earlier.

The trial brought out some facts that further added to the company's discomfort. Dawson stated he had paid Maxwell $3,700 for what he thought was 1,000 acres. The lawyer proved the date and amount were correct but the parcel of land embraced 20,000 acres.

Dawson set about marketing his coal in a big way, with his neighbors the Springers, selling the coal-bearing area to the newly organized Dawson Fuel Company for $400,000 and $5,000 for a township site. He held out 1200 acres on which to build a home, wishing to retain "a little open space around the house." By advice of counsel Dawson had all transactions in black and white with all signatures duly witnessed. But his wife would not sign until she obtained full rights to sell all milk, for a period of ten years, the anticipated town of Dawson would need. J. B. conceded.

Much of the development was under the control of C. B. Eddy, president of the El Paso and Northeastern Railroad, the man who had changed his mind about running his rails to the mining camp

SOLID STONE BARN for sheltering horses and equipment of Phelps Dodge Corp. was retained by company among others for huge cattle ranch when property was sold. This was in 1950 and sounded death knell for Dawson.

of White Oaks, feeling officials of that settlement were holding him up on land for right-of-way and depot. (See Ghost Town Album — Ed.) The railroad had gone to Carrizozo instead to tap coal beds there. These deposits proved shallow and now Eddy was anxious to recoup his losses in the expected deeper veins at Dawson.

On June 17, 1901, the Las Vegas OPTIC reported: "President C. B. Eddy of the El Paso and Northeastern, accompanied by a party of other railroad men, visited Colfax County last week to inspect the Dawson coal lands recently purchased by the El Paso and Northeastern road. Mr. Eddy, in an interview with a reporter with the Las Vegas OPTIC, stated that the money is on hand for the construction of a railroad to the coal fields, and the likelihood is that the railroad will miss Las Vegas a distance of fully twenty miles. A township has been purchased and laid out at the Dawson ranch by the new owners of the Dawson coal fields, as Mr. Eddy is a town builder and boomer who always gets there in his projects. It may be predicted that the new town in Colfax County, through his efforts backed by the railroad he represents, will become one of the most important towns in New Mexico." The company showed a capital of $1,900,000 divided into 10,000 shares with headquarters at Alamogordo where the railroad company already maintained offices.

The same year saw incorporation of the Dawson Railroad Company, also with headquarters at Alamogordo, with plans to build a railroad 130 miles long from Liberty to Dawson, taking advantage of some stretches of lines already constructed or building. Its heads were most of the people who had bought the Dawson coal lands.

Things began happening fast on that ground. By August 1, 1901 a crew of fifty miners was on hand to work the first vein outcropping. A sawmill was busy turning out lumber for houses and by the end of that first year Dawson was well on the way to becoming a city and center of the largest coal mining operation in New Mexico. A post office was established with George T. Pearl the first postmaster. There was a wine and liquor store owned by Henry Pfaff, a large store called the Southwestern Mercantile Co. The town doctor was H. K. Pangborn. By 1902 Dawson's population was 600, with 40 children in the new school. The place had a fine, stimulating climate, there was plenty of work for everyone and Dawson seemed blessed above many other towns. Yet it was doomed to suffer a series of tragedies that shadowed its history to the end.

The first of these struck on September 14, 1903. A fire and explosion in Mine No. 1 took a comparatively light toll, three trapped miners being killed, the bodies shipped away to the nearest known relatives. The worst blow did not come for ten years when Dawson had its cemetery.

1905 brought a newspaper, the Dawson NEWS, with enormous expansion of population and mine operations. There were now about 2,000 people living in the town and many new homes constructed. The Dawson Hotel got a 70-foot addition. Capacity of the coal washer was increased to 250 tons an hour, total number of coke ovens to 124. The mine company owned huge kilns, built mainly to produce bricks for coke ovens and chimneys. Coke, the solid portion remaining after coal is subjected to intense heat in a closed retort, was a major export to smelters and foundries all over the southwest. It burned with a pure flame without gas or smoke, being nearly pure carbon.

About this time the giant, omnipresent Phelps Dodge Corporation began to show a strong interest in what was going on at Dawson. It sent one of its best men, Dr. James Douglas, to the camp with the result the company bought the operation and organized the Stag Canyon Fuel Company, capitalized at $5 million. Under the new management the town expanded even more to a population of 3,500 and the "palatial" Dawson Theater was completed at a cost of $40,000.

Dawson's bawdy houses were forced to build additions to accommodate the large influx of single miners. Trouble ensued, as evidenced in an item in the Raton RANGE, August 15, 1907: "Lizzie Zeller, an inmate of one of the houses in the red light district of Dawson, was shot by Tom Jenkins over the accidental shooting of John Jenkins, his brother. John and Lizzie were in friendly dispute over a gun when the weapon went off and shot John. When Tom heard his brother was wounded he went to the house, called for the woman, called her vile names and shot her. He was placed under arrest. . . The Zeller woman will be taken to her home in Las Vegas for burial."

The camp was largely populated by foreign born workers — Greeks, Slavs, Italian, French, Welsh, Scotch, Mexicans, Germans, Japanese and Chinese. Most of the single men, and those who had to make a stake before sending for their wives, lived in a separate section called Boarding House Row. Greeks and Italians were numerous enough to have their own divisions, presided over by a boarding boss of their own nationality, since many had not yet learned to speak English.

The kilns supplying bricks for construction of coke ovens and chimneys also turned out material for rebuilding and modernizing the old frame school houses, one of the largest being Dawson High School with forty teachers. The Dawson Hospital, with a staff of five doctors, maintained a complete laboratory, with surgery and X-ray equipment. Buildings on the grounds housed nurses and other employees, kitchen, laundry and dispensary with registered pharmacist.

On April 6, 1913, the Raton REPORTER said: "The Phelps Dodge Company that owns the Stag Canyon Mines at Dawson has planned the reclamation of an immense area of land in the vicinity of Dawson by means of a reservoir and a system of ditches and canals, which when completed will be one of the largest irrigation projects in the country. The contract amounts to $350,000."

It was during this period of abundance and prosperity that Dawson suffered its worst catastrophe. On October 20, 1913, a tremendous explosion in Mine No. 2 clogged the entrances and entombed 300 men, killing 263. The blast came at 3 p.m. There were no warnings, no escaping gas or rumblings, only a sudden roar.

Relief and disaster crews were rushed from neighboring towns — Raton, Trinidad, Blossburg, Brilliant, Gardner, Van Houten and Morley. Even a relief car was sent from Denver. By 11 a.m. next day 22 men were accounted for, with 16 alive, and it was hoped this ratio of men saved would prevail, but as the days dragged on the recovered dead outnumbered the living. Rescue crews worked around the clock, rows of bodies brought to the surface grew longer, distraught wives and family members clogged and impeded operations around the mouth of the mine. Two of the rescuers were themselves killed by falling boulders in the shaft. Immense mass funerals were conducted for the victims and row upon row of graves dug, making it necessary to extend the cemetery far up the hill. Wholesale burials were not completed for weeks.

Even after such a calamity life and coal mining went on in the camp and in time, some of the festivities. The camp had always been a good show town and traveling theatrical companies found good audiences even shortly after the disaster.

The NEW MEXICO MAGAZINE, San Diego Exposition Souvenir Edition in 1915, carried a story on Dawson. It included such comments as: "Many a little flower garden surounds the cottage. Sometimes the earth where the cottage stands is hard and stony, and then it is a common thing for the resi-

dent of that house to wall his yard with stones, and then haul in rich earth for his garden. Men do not do these things when their tenure is uncertain. They keep their lawns cropped and the window boxes with their bits of bloom neatly painted. They do good work in the mines and are happy . . . the houses themselves are worthy of comment. There are no shacks. There is no poorer section, although there is a separate quarter for the non-English speaking. . . . .

"The Church, like the schools is financed by the company. There is only one, the Church of All Creeds, but services of several denominations are held in it. Rev. Harvey M. Shields, an Episcopal minister is in charge of regular services, but a Catholic priest holds services in the camp once a month. A Catholic church is being built." The Catholic church was completed in 1917 and dedicated to St. John the Baptist, with the Rev. Joseph A. Couturier, O.M.I. as first pastor.

Safety measures were heavily increased after the disastrous explosion and subsequent accidents were comparatively minor, fatalities few. But in February, 1923, another ruinous explosion took 125 lives. Again the cemetery had to be extended to allow more space for more rows of graves, the mass burial scenes of 1913 repeated.

No further tragedy took place until the one of February 25, 1950. On that date the people of Dawson were told the Phelps Dodge Corporation would close down all operations of the Stag Canyon Mining Co. The announcement meant the death of the one industry town. The reason for the closure was simple — the increasing availability of a new fuel for smelters and foundries, natural gas. Specifically the enormous Phelps Dodge copper smelter at El Paso, Texas, which had been consuming most of Dawson's coke output, now found it more expensive to produce than the handily obtainable natural gas.

When the final blow fell at the actual closure on April 30th, many residents had already left and vacant houses showed curtainless windows. The only surviving operation, and that a temporary one, was the Frontier Power Plant which served Dawson and surrounding area with electricity. It operated until a stock pile of surface coal was exhausted.

On June 6th, the National Iron and Metal Company of Phoenix, Arizona, bought the deserted town of Dawson, wrecking and removing all machinery and buildings. A few houses were spared, these and the land having been retained by Phelps Dodge for a large cattle operation.

ELIZABETHTOWN, NEW MEXICO

This is the country of "The Big Ditch"—and traces of it still show after almost a century. A rare visitor may stand in the deserted ruins of Elizabethtown, where it nestles in the high bowl between the peaks of McGinty and Baldy Mountains, and visualize activity when they brought water to Humbug Gulch.

The gravels of that mountain gash were rich in gold but water was either too scarce to work them or flash flooding in the spring damaged equipment. "We've got to have an even and regular water supply or quit," the miners said. So they did it the hard way, digging the eleven miles of "The Big Ditch" by pick and shovel and a few sacks of blasting powder from the source of Red River. It cost $280,000 but saved the camp.

On July 9, 1869 when the first water hit Humbug Gulch there was a wild celebration but it was short-lived. The flow slowed to a dribble with dozens of leaks showing up along the route. Patching remedied the loss temporarily but crews had to be established at intervals along the waterway with cabins for living quarters to make constant repairs to insure the steady flow of 600 inches. And even then it became necessary to divert more water from Moreno Creek and Ponil River.

Elizabethtown is situated five miles north of Eagle's Nest Lake and some forty miles northwest of Cimarron. The boom began in the middle 1860s when Ute and Apache Indians were relatively peaceful, wandering over the slopes of Baldy and McGinty Mountains. One of them showed up in Fort Union with a specimen of float so rich it set off a rush of the first magnitude, swelling the town on the slopes of Baldy to 5,000 people.

The first men to track down the location where the sample had been picked up were William Kroenig and William Moore, whose small copper mine was named the Mystic Lode. While that first sample of rock was rich copper ore, and the first diggings had been for copper, this find of gold changed the whole scheme of things. The original metal was forgotten and from then on, E'town was all gold.

By the spring of '67, locations had been made at Michigan Gulch, Humbug Gulch and Grouse Gulch,

LOG BUILDING was erected at time of E'town's greatest expansion, when group of five men with sluice 90 feet long were taking out $100 a day in gold for each man, worth $20 an ounce just as it came from dripping gravels. Quartz lode assayed $2,000 per ton and no one bothered with anything skimpier. Almost all frame buildings in town have crumbled away.

the latter containing the phenomenal Spanish Bar. All measurements were made from a large willow tree on the banks of the central stream. The town was named for the eldest daughter of William Moore, Elizabeth, who later became a schoolteacher in the town, shortened to E'town. The camp grew so rapidly it was soon the seat of Colfax County, an honor lost later to Cimarron.

During the best years there were three stagecoach lines, to Springer, Trinidad and Questa. There were saloons and three dancehalls, two hotels, five general stores and later several boardinghouses. One hotel operator was a Henry Lambert who had once cooked for General Grant and Abraham Lincoln. In the fall of '71 he went to greener pastures in Cimarron where he opened the celebrated St. James.

In 1868 the editor of the *Sante Fe Gazette* wrote: "The first house (in E'town) was built by John Moore who furnished the miners with provisions on credit, thereby enabling them to open up the country. Elizabethtown now has 100 buildings." A later article stated: "The new city of Elizabethtown continues on its course. The weather is cold; the cool winds from the snowcapped peaks cause us to huddle around the blazing pitch-pine fires of our fellow townsmen, Messrs. Sears, Pollock, Draper, C. E. Pease and Harburger. Occasionally, we find our way to the Mayflower Saloon, where we warm the inner as well as the outer man. So pass the long winter evenings. Prices are very reasonable for a mining town. New arrivals are an almost everyday occurrence. Denver and vicinity are well represented among the new arrivals. I perceived Doc Howe of prospecting celebrity whose manly form and gentlemanly address is truly an honor to the place he has left. There is very little mining property for sale. Claim owners generally think we have a good enough thing to warrant them to suffer a New Mexico winter in order to be on the ground when the water comes . . . . A stage line has been established between Elizabethtown and Maxwell's by V. S. Dhelby and Co. who intend to commence running a tri-weekly line in a few days." Toward spring came optimism and some advice: "Elizabethtown contains fifty or sixty houses, some of them like the Arkansas Traveler's house, roofless, for the weather is too severe to complete them . . . . There is considerable bustle and business in the air to be seen and especially should you go into Abor's Saloon you will be convinced that it is a stirring place. There are several stores, two restaurants and many saloons, as also a drug store, a billiard table, a barber shop and gambling houses where a miner can deposit all his hard-earned earnings of weeks in a few hours. That house across the street in which you see two smiling faces you will do well to give it a wide berth, as you will be richer in pocket, better in health and wiser in mind."

Those early days of the boom town were filled with such robbery, murder and pillage as have rarely been equalled. One badman was Long Taylor. He stood six foot seven inches, was easily identified but not often caught. In '73, in company with one Coal-Oil Johnny, he held up the Cimarron stage in the narrow passage known as the Palisades, escaping with some $700. George Greely ran one of the most profitable saloons but was constantly in trouble because of a hot temper, taking no "guff" from anyone. On Independence Day, 1886, he called a customer on the carpet for a fancied insult to one of his several "lady friends." Infuriated, the man rushed out, returning in a few minutes with his Winchester. Firing point blank at Greely, he turned to make his escape but was stopped by a flying tackle at the door, later serving time for murder at the penitentiary in Santa Fe.

Perhaps the most gruesome episode was staged at the height of the town's heyday when rooms were scarce and no questions asked about them. A stranger would come into camp, rent a room in the boardinghouse operated by Charles Kennedy on the side of a steep hill, and disappear. Since no one knew such newcomers, they would ordinarily not be missed. But one was and his friends went to Kennedy's place. They were met halfway by the proprietor's distraught wife, a native New Mexican, who had decided to confess everything.

The Vigilantes were sent for and they slipped in the back of the house. There was Kennedy bending over a fire, burning dismembered sections of the visitor's body, his valuables set to one side. The town had a stout timbered jail but when the murderer was taken to the courthouse for trial, the outraged citizens seized him, tied a rope around his neck and threw him to the ground. Then one man got astride a horse and dragged the unfortunate miscreant up and down the dirt streets until long after he was dead.

McKenna, in his *Black Range Tales* recalls: "Myself and three other men who were footloose and without families pitched together and hired a bull team. Loading up what we needed in the way of food and blankets, we pulled out for Elizabethtown, a gold diggings in the main Rockies, a hundred miles west from Trinidad. It took us about fifteen days to get there, the bullwhacker being in no hurry, for the bulls were poor and the grass was good . . . . It was there I panned my first gold . . . learned what was meant by diggings and stored up bits of mining lore from veteran prospectors. I was told that Elizabethtown was tame when compared to the days of the big rush, when shootings were as common as meetings in the street and saloons. I sat for the first time before a golden campfire and listened to blood-curdling tales of raiding Indians, of heartless cutthroats, of daring outlaws, of dashing cowboys, of painted women, of dead shots and regular old sourdoughs and desert rats, some good, some bad . . . ."

And there was the building of the dredge *Eleanor*. In 1901, E'town was still a busy place, its seven saloons always crowded and hotels full. Eastern capital was still interested in organizing companies and gold was still so plentiful it was being weighed out in troy-weight in exchange for such necessities of life as—whiskey. But here and there were reports that a certain placer was petering out, that expensive stamp mills were working on a part-time basis. Some people were even expressing the opinion that E'town might one day be a ghost town. Loud and derisive boos might greet this kind of remark but cold figures gave it credence—that gold production in the camp was not what it had been.

The famous Spanish Bar still harbored as much and more gold in its depths than ever had been removed but getting at the deeper gravels was something else. The answer came in the Oro Dredging Co. and the person of H. J. Reiling of Chicago. He had solved similar problems in the mining camps of Montana and felt the only possible obstacle here would be getting two boilers into the camp. These would weigh a total of ten tons and the existing road from the rail head at Springer was a narrow, winding track that ran almost its entire length up the precipitous Cimarron Canyon. Machinery of lesser weight had been hauled up the road and the inadequate bridges and narrow switchbacks could be remedied.

When the first of the boilers was started on its way, hauled by fourteen head of horses, it soon ran into difficulties, a small bridge at the beginning of the route collapsing like cardboard. With this warning, spans over deeper canyons were strengthened and the first boiler was deposited on the bar in two weeks, the second in one. A side benefit of the job was the widened and improved road for daily trips of the stage. During the period the dredge was being hauled two stages had been shuffled, one running above, one below, since there was no passing.

The camp turned out in a body to dedicate the new dredge in August of 1901. Incongruous were the "outfits" worn by members of the party from the effete East who had shuddered their way up the raw canyon. After all, their money had built the dredge, now so proudly floating on its own pond at the lower end of Spanish Bar, and they felt they should be on hand to see it put into operation.

A bottle of champagne was broken on its bow by Mrs. W. A. Moughy of Wooster, Ohio. Since other bottles had already been opened and emptied in more conventional fashion, champagne for the Easterners and whiskey for the men responsible for the hauling and assembling of the *Eleanor*, the celebration that followed the christening was the wildest in the history of the town.

The first few years of work for the big dredge went according to plan. Values of the gravel in Spanish Bar were about $2 per cubic yard and the machine was capable of biting off 50,000 cubic yards a month. Part of this material was from the bottom of the pond and the rest from the banks. Operations were on a round-the-clock basis to make up for complete closure during winter.

The high and mighty days gradually came to an end with the failure of easily obtained gold in the gravels. Hard rock mining became more and more expensive in proportion to profits, replacement machinery and labor costing more while the price of gold remained static. The fate of the big dredge paralleled the demise of E'town. The *Eleanor* slowed down and for a few years operated on only one shift, then there were complete shutdowns for a month at a time. The company was extending its operations to the town of Breckenridge, Colorado, and needing more money, mortgaged the *Eleanor*. It was gobbling up the gravels but there was not enough river gold to meet expenses. At last the mortgage was foreclosed and the dredge sold at a sheriff's sale to two optimistic gentlemen named J. Van Houten and Charles Springer. For eight years they paid a watchman to live on the gold boat, hoping that one day the metal would advance in price.

As the machinery rusted and the dredge began to settle into the gravel, she was at last abandoned, as was the town itself. Several years later the pilot house was all that was showing above the sand of Spanish Bar. Now even that has disappeared.

FOLSOM, NEW MEXICO

It cost Madison Emery a cow to keep peace with the Indians camped just outside the village. He was trying to explain that neither he nor his stepson had anything to do with the dead buck when there was a sudden rattle-bang of explosions and the peace pipe went out. The "shots" were found to be only rifle cartridges in the stove but the situation was touchy, and well — what was a cow if the Indians would go away?

The town of Folsom, named for President Cleveland's wife Frances Folsom, began as a tiny hamlet close to the present town. Called Madison for the first settler, Madison Emery, the site has disappeared so completely none of Folsom's residents ever heard of it.

When Emery arrived on the scene in 1862 he found the grass in the valley so tall it would hide a man on a horse, the hills covered with a fine stand of pinon pines, streams filled with fish and game abundant. He built a cabin and as more families made homes, stores and other businesses sprang up, he erected a rough hotel.

The frontier town was constantly harassed by Indians and was especially apprehensive when they made semi-permanent camps near the village. On one of those occasions Bud Sumpter, Emery's stepson, found an Indian lying behind the store. He thought the brave was asleep until he turned him over, but he was dead apparently from too much firewater.

Emery feared violence from the Indians who might doubt the manner of the buck's death, invited the chief and council to his home for a parley. Progress was being made when there was a furious fusillade of what seemed to be gunshots and all those present dived for doors and windows. When it was discovered the "shots" were cartridges some prankster had dropped in the kitchen stove, the redmen were persuaded to return and relight the peace pipe. Harmony seemed assured when Emery presented the chief with his fattest cow.

Madison was the nearest settlement to the "Robbers' Roost" just north of Kenton in neighboring Oklahoma. Periodically the notorious Coe and his gang would make a hurried visit to Madison when they scented a raid on the hideout. They would pull up in front of the inn run by Mrs. Emery, order the horses "serviced" at gun point, then repair to the nearest saloon. After tanking up, the outlaws would demand a meal from Mrs. Emery, sleep off food and drink in her beds and sweep away at dawn like so many scavenger crows. Then everybody in Madison breathed easier.

Coe's outlawry got important enough to set the U.S. Cavalry after him. A company from Fort Lyons, Colorado, moved into Kenton, flushed the gang and Coe slipped over to his safe refuge at the Emerys. This time it was not so safe. A detachment from Fort Union, New Mexico, was bivouacked behind a hill. Mrs. Emery fed and wined the bandit and as soon as he was asleep, sent her son Bud on his pony to alert the soldiers. He returned with a guard which arrested Coe. As the badman was led from the house he remarked: "That pony has had a hard ride". To avoid reprisals on the Emerys, Coe was taken to Pueblo, Colorado, to await trial. It never came, his widespread fame proving his undoing. A Vigilante Committee broke into the calaboose at night, snatched the bandit and strung him up, leg irons and all. The mystery of his disappearance from jail remained for years until someone found his skeleton, hardware still attached.

But what lawlessness could not do to Madison, the coming of the Colorado and Southern Railroad did. Because the line bypassed the town just enough to cause it to seek a new site, the original town languished and utterly vanished. At the new location shelters and business establishments were all tents, giving the clutter the name of "Ragtown", but it got a new one — Folsom — when it developed quickly. The rails came in 1887-1888 and by 1895 Folsom had two mercantile stores, three saloons and several other businesses including two houses which were not homes. One reason for the rapid growth was, being on the railroad it had the largest stockyards north of Fort Worth.

But the change in the town was not to the credit of law and order. The first citizen of Folsom was W. A. Thompson, proprietor of the Gem Saloon and deputy sheriff. He came from Missouri under a cloud, charged with the murder of a man and in Folsom racked up a record as lurid as that of any other New Mexico badman, in a state that produced Bill the Kid, Clay Allison and others of that ilk.

One time he shot point blank at an erstwhile friend, killing him and gave as the reason: "The dirty so-and-so had the nerve to get drunk in another saloon." Again, infuriated at a taunt from a local lad in his saloon, he pursued the boy outdoors, firing as he ran. One of the bullets went through the stove of a neighbor but all missed the boy, who escaped. Raging inwardly, Thompson turned his gun on anyone within range including Bill Thatcher, a fellow officer but bitter enemy, and Jeff Kiel who had emerged from King's Store. Thatcher was wounded seriously and Kiel fatally. Thatcher managed to shoot Thompson's gun from his hands, the crazed assailant running into his saloon and barricading the doors.

A crowd bent on lynching quickly gathered outside but short of burning the building and endangering the entire block, they could not get Thompson out. When waiting cooled the mob's temper, Thompson staggered forth dead drunk and collapsed. Authorities took him to the Clayton jail, then to Springer.

Released on bond, he returned to Folsom, sold his saloon and cleared up all personal matters. At the murder trial in Clayton he was acquitted, a verdict that would have been impossible nearer home. He then moved to Trinidad and married the girl for whom he had committed his first murder. The couple later went to Oklahoma where Thompson killed another person and was again acquitted.

In 1908 the town had that new-fangled contraption, the telephone, switchboard being in the home of Sarah J. Rooke on the edge of town. One night in August Sarah answered her buzzer to hear a voice shout that a huge wave from a flash flood was racing down the river and would strike the town in minutes, warning to get people out of town without trying to rescue any possessions. Sarah was too busy to go, but rang one bell after another, as many as she could before the water hit. Her own house was swept from its foundations, girl and switchboard with it. Her body was found eight miles below the town. Most buildings had been carried away and seventeen persons drowned, yet many were saved because of Sarah's heroism. Grateful citizens of Folsom and other nearby towns contributed funds for a granite memorial at her grave.

But Folsom's most prominent citizen was the "Folsom Man", existing only by deduction. Archeologists had long been interested in an arroyo close to the town where they had found superficial evidences of artifacts dating from the Pleistocene or Ice Age, some 20,000 years ago. In 1927 more careful digging revealed a cache of bones belonging to ice age animals, most of them slain by man-made weapons such as exquisitely fashioned lances or spear points, some found among the bones. In several instances a point was imbedded in a bone. Made of flint, they showed careful workmanship, finely fluted along the edges.

Although no human remains were found, the discovery dated the existence of man in North America much earlier than previously estimated, 1000 B.C. It has since been substantiated that these first settlers of Folsom were descendants of wanderers who crossed from Asia over a land bridge, moving on to New Mexico. Although most of the northern lands were still covered by deep ice deposits, there was a corridor of bare ground parallel to the east side of the Rocky Mountains along which men and animals could migrate. Later similar discoveries near the Sandia Mountains, also in New Mexico, suggested an even earlier date for the presence of these immigrants.

BUSY ESTABLISHMENT during heyday of Folsom. Building sheltered Doherty Investment Co., general store, market and early post office. Present one is housed in its own small building, faces imminent closure.

MOST BUILDINGS in Folsom are constructed of stone, have well withstood ravages of time. Water tower, windmill were supported on top of log tripod at left. Folsom is geologically fascinating as Capulin National Monument. Area contains nine small near-perfect craters in addition to Mount Capulin, 8368 feet. Main cinder cone, of recent formation, is one mile in diameter at base, 1450 feet at summit, is considered most nearly symmetrical volcano in this country.

GHOSTS ON THE CREST

Golden, New Mexico

The confirmed "shunpiker" could hardly pick a more rewarding route between Albuquerque and Santa Fe than paved New Mexico State 10. Beginning a few miles east of Albuquerque the road spans a short stretch that leads to highly scenic Sandia Crest, 10,678 feet high, and a chain of some of the most picturesque ghost towns in the state. Here were scenes of successive boom and bust in the frantic search for gold, silver, lead, turquoise and more plebian coal.

The first community reached after turning north from U.S. 66 is San Antonitos, an old village populated mostly by Mexican woodcutters and cattle ranchers. Then comes the ancient site of Paako and gold mining camp of San Pedro where only the old coke ovens remain and these hard to find. After that Golden, the only one now visible of what was a cluster of placer camps.

Adjoining Golden at the north was the earlier town of Tuerto ("one-eyed man," in Spanish) where a boom took place in 1839, ten years before the big one in the California Sierra. But there was an older camp just east, around the shoulder of the cluster of peaks called Ortiz Mountains, 8,928 feet. The city editor of the Albuquerque *Tribune* and writer for *New Mexico Magazine*, Ralph Looney, did much research on the old camps in this area. He reports the fact that Dolores, also called Placitas Viejas ("old placers"), was the scene of the first gold rush in what is now the United States. By way of distinguishing it from the more recent camp nearby, it was at first called Placitas Nuevas and was large enough to support twenty-two stores. Both have utterly vanished and Golden is fast decaying.

When placer gold was exhausted in Lazarus Gulch and Tuerto Creek, miners gradually shifted south, deserting Tuerto and forming Golden, where an old church stood, constructed in the early 1830s. In recent years the structure was restored yet it retains the soft adobe lines of the original (see *Tales the Western Tombstones Tell*). The lady tending the little store in 1966 was quite resentful when visitors called the place a "ghost town" but was quite willing to accept their money. As in all near-abandoned towns considerable vandalism has been perpetrated on buildings and cemetery, but this writer believes those who visit any old town because of its historical interest are not the ones who tear up floors to look for treasure or who smash tombstones. Deliberate destruction is more likely to be the work of casual joy-riders out for a thrill or two, their signatures a scattering of empty liquor bottles and beer cans.

VERY OLD STRUCTURES such as this attest age of Golden. Construction here is primitive, using local materials.

HILLSBORO, NEW MEXICO

Dan Dugan was all for throwing it away and forgetting about it so they could get on with future searching. Dave Stitzel said "No" for a time and then seeing it was no use bucking such Irish stubborness, slipped a couple of pieces in his pocket. The partners agreed on most matters but this April day in 1877 they had run across some float on the east side of Black Range and couldn't see eye to eye on its value.

The two moved on. Discouraged over the poor results of this prospecting jaunt, they were traveling in rough circles intending to return to Santa Rita in the Pinos Altos Range. After more half-hearted poking and picking in the Mimbres Mountains, part of the Black Range, they crossed the valley of the Mimbres River where there was a large stamp mill and the usual assay office. Here they were to rest a few days.

Stitzel slipped away, taking his rocks to the assayer. His partner would only have laughed at him. He was prepared for a delay for even though prospectors were first in line at the office, several days were necessary to run an assay. The pieces of ore must first be crushed into pea-gravel size and ground to powder. A measured amount was then roasted, a "button" of metal melted out and weighed, the comparison to the ore sample given in terms of value per ton. Dugan was impatient to be on his way after hearing what his partner had done. When he got the value news he was impatient to go back. The finished assay ran $160.

The men immediately returned to the float site and established a claim. This first one was called the Opportunity, a second one christened Ready Pay. Both were successful, the first five tons of ore bringing the partners $400. Soon others were flocking in and a name for the new camp was needed. Each man wanted to name the place after his home town. When no agreement was reached, a hatful of names was shuffled and Hillsborough drawn. In usage it was shortened to Hillsboro.

Only seven miles from Kingston, another mining camp, the narrow mountain road through Percha Canyon connecting the two was full of hazards. The road itself was dangerously steep and rough, washouts were common and rocks often rolled down on the coaches, but the most feared danger was that of bandits. There were plenty of

MAIN STREET OF HILLSBORO is unchanged from days when Billy the Kid visited saloons and on one occasion ducked into back room when posse was on his trail.

places along the road where stagecoaches had to slow down to get through and robbers chose these spots for surprise holdups.

Large amounts of gold were often shipped to the railroad at Lake Valley, via Hillsboro, and the return trip was likely to bring the payroll for both mountain camps. Every so often road agents would relieve the drivers of their bullion or money and many were the methods devised for circumventing them. One Bill Holt, a driver for the Orchards Line would make a slit in the collar of one of the horses, remove some stuffing and insert the money in the cavity. Bulky bullion was more difficult to conceal but was sometimes saved by having guards raise their weapons at each narrow pass, ready to fire on any holdup men that might be waiting. The killing of two of them discouraged such surprise parties for a while.

Hillsboro is very quiet now. Enough people remain in the town and surrounding countryside to form small congregations in the two churches, Catholic and Protestant, but very little business goes on and most of the buildings are vacant.

SUBSTANTIAL AND COMMODIOUS JAIL, w a s second to be built in Hillsboro. Original was windowless adobe cell, part of tiny courthouse on main street. This one, built about the same time, 1893, as second courthouse adjoining was erected to take care of flood of drunks, thieves and highwaymen. Latter were constantly holding up the stagecoaches carrying money and gold bullion between Kingston, Hillsboro and Lake Valley, mining towns linked together by common needs. Hoosegow was three weeks' home of Oliver Lee, James Gilliland and William McNutt, in one of most famous murder trials in New Mexico. Prisoners were fed during tenure by Sadie Orchards, retired from stage driving and operating hotel in Hillsboro. Jail is roofless, allowing sun and rain to nourish grass in cells.

MAIN ENTRANCE TO COURTHOUSE, Murder trial for killing of Judge Fountain and his nine-year-old son was held here, although crime supposedly was committed near Las Cruces. Public feeling against the men held for murders was so intense that lynching was feared, and prisoners were moved to Hillsboro under cover of darkness. No trace of missing judge or boy was ever found; for lack of any corpus delicti or evidence of foul play three weeks trial ended in not guilty verdict. Town had been so loaded with curious spectators all hotels were filled and cowboys camped beside their chuck-wagons.

KELLY, NEW MEXICO

The road from Magdalena to Kelly winds steeply up a short canyon and then suddenly becomes a street, narrow and rough, bordered sparsely on both sides by the pitiful remnants of what was once a thriving town of 3,000. Most of these claimed their town was the most orderly in New Mexico. "Gunfighting is out, here. Fights are to be settled with fists, bricks or rocks."

Kelly's beginnings concerned a Civil War soldier marching with the Union Army, he stooped to pick up a rock that interested him. He couldn't conveniently keep it with him, so sent it to a friend, J. S. Hutchason. This friend was so excited about the sample that he immediately went prospecting in the Magdalenas, hoping to find the outcropping from which the float had come. This he never did, not even finding another piece to match the original. But he did stake out a couple of claims, naming them the Graphic and the Juanita.

Hutchason was an industrious man. In addition to blasting out his own ore (oxidized lead-zinc) he built a crude smelter of adobe. He had to ship the resulting lead pigs all the way to Kansas City by oxcart over the Santa Fe trail, but still made enough money to keep going. He sometimes took a little time off and on one occasion was pecking around at the rocks some little distance from the Juanita mine. While studying these interesting specimens he was joined by a friend who had a sawmill nearby, Andy Kelly. Kelly was intrigued but didn't show his interest. When Hutchason returned to work, Kelly staked out a claim to the spot and called it after himself. He worked it for a time, but one year failed to do the legal amount and Hutchason who had kept his eye on the project, stepped in and took over, keeping up the assessment work himself. The ore produced by this mine was carbonates with galena, averaging 50 to 60 per cent of lead, 10 ounces of silver and some copper.

In 1870 miners laid out a townsite, long and narrow in the canyon and named it Kelly for the mine now producing well. In the next period of development, a Col. E. W. Eaton decided to put some money into the mines of Kelly, and leased the Juanita. Almost immediately the more extensive workings ran into a rich vein of silver so good that when the news leaked out, a boom was on its way. Now things happened fast. Hutchason took advantage of the fever and sold his Graphic claim to a firm called Hanson and Dawsey for $30,000, and the Kelly to Gustav Billings

LITTLE MISSION CHURCH of Saint John the Baptist still stands on steep street of Kelly. Once private residence, it was remodeled for church purposes. Mission never had a priest of its own, was attended from Magdalena. Although Kelly is now completely deserted, each feast day of Saint John the Baptist, June 24th, sees little chapel filled with about seventy-five people from all over countryside, gathered to attend Mass.

EXTENSIVE RUINS OF BOARDING HOUSE disintegrates beside quiet street once teeming with activity. Adobe, sun-dried brick, was standard building material in southwest where timber is scarce, stiff clay always available. Sometimes adobe was mixed with chopped straw for added strength. Also optional was finishing coat of stucco which could be of mud or plaster. Either way, thick walls provided protection against heat, cold. Indians could not set fire to structures to force evacuation as often happened in case of frame buildings.

for $45,000. To roast his own ore, Billings built a smelter at the edge of nearby Socorro in 1881 and operated it for twelve years. During this period the village in the Magdalena mountain canyon produced most of the lead mined in New Mexico.

Until about 1885 Indian troubles beset the camp. Every so often they would come swooping down the canyon, to be repulsed only at heavy cost. Or they would sneak to the edges of the camp at night, stealing horses and cattle. When at last the railroad reached Magdalena, several cars were kept handy to carry the women and children to safety in Socorro in case of an outbreak.

But Kelly flourished. There was now a Methodist church as well as the original Catholic one, seven saloons, several rooming houses and three stores. The three dance palaces supported a goodly number of "frail sisters," some kept in a regular "house," the more independent ones having individual cribs farther down the canyon. Both hotels kept three shifts going on the same beds, the saloons and dance halls on a "we never close" basis.

Jonas Nelson got a short term lease on the Hardscrabble mine and worked it for all it was worth in the time allotted. When he received a check from the smelter, it was so large he was inspired to throw a party the likes of which Kelly had never seen. He built a platform in front of

REMAINS OF LARGE, ELABORATE MILLS, roasting ovens still stand at head of street. Ores were loaded into vertical ovens with alternate layers of fuel, either wood, coal or charcoal. Here, "newer" oven of concrete stands next to original one of brick, show funnel at bottom for emptying accumulated metal, melted from ore by intense heat. In background are mills for reduction of l a r g e chunks of ore to ready material for smelters.

the mine workings, ordered a special train from Los Angeles. It was a "surprise package" containing such goodies as champagne and beautiful girls. The party cost Nelson every cent he had and he had to go back to the pick and shovel, but he always maintained "It was worth it."

In the '90s, sharp-eyed Cony Brown wondered about the greenish rocks so common everywhere in Kelly and sent some samples for analysis. When the report came back, he took a lease on the old dumps and all available workings not in active operation before he made details of the paper known. He had found the "worthless" green rock to be Smithsonite, zinc carbonate, a rare and valuable ore. This discovery set off another boom.

In 1904 the Sherwin-Williams Paint Company bought the old Graphic for $150,000 and the Tri-Bullion Smelting and Development Company bought the Kelly from Billings for $200,000, building a smelter on the spot. Zinc recoveries made Kelly the leading producer of that metal, output between 1904 and 1928, $21,667,950.

1931 saw the end of the Smithsonite deposits and a few more years ended the workings of the lead-zinc sulphides. While some of the population held on, refusing to believe the town had died, most moved to other camps, or to Magdalena below on the plain. At last even the old die-hards gave up. and today Kelly does not have a living soul to shelter.

KINGSTON, NEW MEXICO

A single piece of float exhibited in Denver in 1882, created such a boom in the place where it was found that a whole town was born on the site in a few weeks. The camp was first called Percha City, after Percha Creek, where Jack Sheddon had first found the chunk of rich silver ore. It was surveyed for a town in October of 1882 and by the end of that year 1800 men and some women had moved in. The men consisted of miners and merchants with a sprinkling of gamblers and pimps. The women were mostly the latter's stock in trade, a few others, miners' wives. As the camp settled down to a more steady existence more families became established.

In Kingston's first hectic years, the buildings were of the flimsiest nature, large tents or some combination of fabric and whipsaw lumber. One of the first hotels had walls of canvas and a roof of boards, the cracks in the latter battened to keep most of New Mexico's infrequent rains out. Three tiers of bunks lined the walls. Prices varied, ranging from cheaper shelves above to the more convenient and costly ones below. All patrons were reduced to the same level, however, when frequent shooting scrapes outside sent bullets flying through the fabric walls and everyone dived to the floor and comparative safety. Food served in the kitchen and dining room "annex" came from an outdoor kitchen. Meats on the menu were purchased from the butcher shop near by advertising beef, bear, venison, pork, wild turkey and goat.

At first the camp had no jail, prisoners being tied to a post, gagged if too noisy and at the convenience of whoever was serving as "sheriff," hustled off to the jail in seven-mile-distant Hillsboro. There were no churches for a long time. When the idea of building one occurred a man passed the hat in the saloons and brothels and soon had it filled with nuggets, rings and currency to the tune of $1,500, enough to build a stone structure. One church to 22 saloons was not considered too bad a proportion.

Before the Civil War, the old New Mexican town of Mesilla on the Rio Grande had a little weekly newspaper. The *Mesilla Times* was printed on an old Washington hand press which had been hauled in over hundreds of miles of desert. When that town was captured by Confederates the press was a victim of the general carnage and wound up in the bed of the Rio Grande. There it lay for several years until an itinerant printer who wanted to start a paper in the now flourishing Kingston thought of it. He got help enough to extract the relic from the sands of the river bottom and hauled it to town. Miraculously, it functioned after some repairs and served to get out a crude newspaper and odd job printing for several years. One of the hand bills produced read:

Ho! For the Gold and Silver Mines of New Mexico
  Fortune hunters, capitalists and poor men,
Sickly folks, all whose hearts are bowed down;
  And ye who would live long and be healthy,
and happy; come to our sunny clime and see
  For Yourselves.

About this time Kingston began having Indian troubles. One day the town found itself entirely surrounded by a ring of the dreaded Apaches on horseback, led by notorious Victorio. Unfortunately for the Indians, they had picked a day some miners were ready to go on a hunting expedition to augment the meat supply. Remingtons were handy and loaded, the aborigines were routed in a blaze of rifle fire in a matter of minutes. The defeat caused a long respite in further attacks, but the miners knew that another attempt to sack the camp would sooner or later be made and kept a constant watch. When Victorio and his men did come whooping in and were again repulsed with heavy losses he called the whole thing off, permanently. To show how big they could be, the miners named their newly completed three-story hotel after the vanquished chieftain calling it "The Victorio."

At its height Kingston was well supplied with hotels, with a smaller one and another built later. In addition there were several dance halls, many stores, the Percha Bank, a G.A.R. Post and Masonic, Knights of Pythias and Odd Fellows halls. By this time there were enough families to require a schoolhouse. All these buildings lined up on both sides of the single street above Middle Percha Creek made a fine effect, Kingston was on its way.

"Pretty Sam" had finished a Casino and Dance Hall during this period of prosperity and the whole town was eagerly awaiting the grand opening, since all drinks were to be on the house. The elegant falsefronted building was on the side of the street next to the creek, and as the ground sloped sharply away, only the front was on the level, while the rear of the bistro rested on stilts above the stream. Since this rear section was not finished in time for the festivities, "Pretty Sam" had a man put a few nails in the door leading to a bridge planned for future construction.

Came the big night and the celebration was at its height. Sam had shrewdly set the date on Christmas Eve. An orchestra had been imported from El Paso, the girls from all but one of the various hook joints were dancing and available. The only reason one brothel was not represented was that Big Annie and her Girls from the Orpheum planned to make a big entrance when the party was at its height, and this they did. There was one miner who was not at the party. Drunk, he had forgotten about the opening and had other plans in mind. Banging on the door of the darkened Orpheum he got madder and madder. It suddenly dawned on him where everybody was and he turned and ran all the way to where the glittering casino was swelling to the joints. Bursting in the front door, his guns blazing, he made even more of an entrance than had the Madame and her girls. Big Annie, however, broke for the back door, followed by the rest of the frolickers. The few small nails might had prevented the headlong plunge of Big Annie, buxom though she was, but the pressure from behind was terrific. The Madame was precipitated headlong into Percha Creek, with a few other celebrants to keep her company.

OLD PERCHA BANK stands just below foundations of Show House where Lillian Russell and her troupe once performed. Bank was center of all business in Kingston, transactions were involving sales of mines and claims. Bank furniture, teller's windows are still intact in structure, but all floor space is taken up with storage of mine equipment. Little ore cart has position just inside front door. Bell was used many years to sound fire alarms and announce arrival of mail. Small trees in front of bank are young specimens of ubiquitous "Tree of Heaven." (Ailanthus altissima). This fast growing, self sufficient tree was originally introduced by Chinese miners homesick for some reminder of their homeland. Seeds blow in wind and suckers spread underground, resulting in widespread propagation. Plants are rapid growers, reaching height of twenty feet in three or four years.

KOEHLER, NEW MEXICO

The swastika, ancient symbol of good luck, seemed to cast its benediction on all of Koehler and its huge coal mines. The emblem was a part of life in the camp, seen on every building and all business correspondence, natural enough as the mining company was named Swastika Fuel Co. All this was pre-Hitler and while all signs and symbols were removed in war time, ghost town seekers may still be slightly puzzled at outlines and evidences of the swastika on some of Koehler's weathered boards.

In the spring of 1909 when the town's spectacular growth was attracting national attention, the Des Moines (Iowa) REGISTER sent reporter Tracy Garrett west to write a feature on it. The article was reprinted in the Santa Fe NEW MEXICAN, June 13, 1909, and later included in the works of historian F. Stanley, pseudonym of Francis L. Stanley Crocchiola. Native of New York, teacher of English, history and other subjects at St. John's College on the Hudson, Crocchiola came to New Mexico for his health, amassing a great store of the state's history and writing many books about it. He cites the REGISTER's story as containing the most vivid picture possible of life in Koehler, particularly on pay day.

"The miners are paid once a month, and though no credit is given, no one need go hungry or thirsty between paydays. This is avoided by a system of scrip money. After a miner has worked three days he can go to the mine office and draw a portion of his "time" in scrip. The scrip is elaborately lithographed paper in denominations of from ten cents to five dollars in scrip and good only for merchandise at the company store or saloon.

"From Raton comes the paymaster on the afternoon of payday. With him is a chest containing about $24,000 and three or four armed guards with six-shooters and Winchesters. The chest is carried into the company store and there closely guarded until 7:30, when the line that has been forming since early evening is permitted to enter.

"At the pay window, or directly in front of it sits Bill Bolden, marshall of the camp, deputy sheriff, gun man, a sure shot, a man who is always cool in danger, mild of voice, quick of action. At Bill's side hangs a six-shooter, but he seldom has to reach for it. Every man in camp knows that he can reach for it with lightning quickness, and no one dares to provoke him into action. A word from Bill Bolden will stop the line of march or a fight. He is all powerful at Koehler.

"For pay day and night and the day following several extra deputies are sworn in. Their badges of office are well filled cartridge belts, six-shooters and rifles. These men are much in evidence around the stores when the $24,000 is being handed out to the laborers. . . The cashier counts out the money, currency, except for the last four to seven dollars, this being paid in silver so the man may have some change handy when he leaves the window. . . .

"On the outskirts of the crowd, pushing and

STOCK PILE of coal at Koehler seems tremendous now in face of little demand, would be mere drop in bucket in days when all locomotives on lines of Atcheson, Topeka and Santa Fe were burning coal. Now little used spur line visible in middle ground runs to mine short distance above.

ONCE HUGE MINE OPERATION just above Koehler is still in limited production. Skeleton crew removes some valuable coal, guards valuable machinery. Sometimes former miners bring children here for visit, try to explain working of tipples, cars, washers, usually meet with lack of interest.

jostling to keep as near the line as possible, are women of all nations waiting for the breadwinner money, that they may secure their share for the purchase of supplies or perhaps a ribbon or a piece of dress goods. Some, especially the Mexican and Italian women, are gaily dressed, green, red and yellow being the favorite colors, and she who can contrive to have all these colors on wears the happiest smile. One girl of fourteen, who was pointed out as a bride of one week, appeared on payday night in a green satin skirt reaching to but a few inches below her knees, red shoes and stockings, yellow waist, and a hat that combined all colors. As she was waiting for her newly wed husband to draw his wages a withered old lady forced her way through the crowd whispered to Bolden, and the payline was halted. The woman presented a time check for $7.50 and hurried over to the butcher

shop. Again the line moved on. Soon after another woman slipped up to the marshall and the performance was repeated. Every few minutes this occurred, with never a word of complaint from the waiting miners. For these women were the wives of miners who were ill or had been injured. . . .

"The throng of recently paid representatives of a dozen nations left the women and picked their way up the track to where the saloon door stood invitingly open. The saloon is tremendous barn-like structure running more than one hundred feet down a side. Crowded three and four deep about the bar were negroes, Chinamen, Slavs, Greeks and Mexicans, in fact all nations except Japs. The other side of the room is lined with card tables and these two are crowded with players of everything from stud poker to cooncan. Before them sat their mugs and glasses and among them hurried sturdy waiters, selected for their jobs as much for their ability to bounce disturbers as for filling empty glasses. A babel of languages rose from the tables and bar, and could be heard across the prairie and towards the ranches long after the lights of the town were left behind and only the glare from the coke ovens marked for the eye the place where payday night was at its height.

"Sunday the day following pay night was quiet at the town. Riding through the gate that surrounds the camp, there were, however, many silent evidences of the revels of the night before. Empty and broken bottles, articles of clothing and pieces of harness. In the middle of the road, his coat folded carefully over his arm, his hat missing, lay a man, or the wreck of one. The sun shone brightly on his face, but though the hours passed, he did not move. Riders and drivers turned their horses aside, but none touched him. He was not dead, the marshall or one of his deputies would pick him up. 'Every-

thing passed off nice', remarked the chief officer of the camp, as he kicked his boots on the store steps. "There wasn't a killing, or even a big fight, we have an all-fired peaceful outfit here in the lay-out.'" The writer expressed himself as confident however that any lack of fights and killings could be credited to Bill Bolden and his pair of six-shooters rather than to any inherent restraint on the part of the miners.

Koehler had no more fire protection than any of the mining camps and time after time large sections of the town were destroyed, one of the last disasters, in 1923, leveling the large two-story school building that served for twenty years. By the start of the new year the community hall or other structures were sufficiently remodeled to serve as pro-tem school houses.

Yet the town might have saved itself the trouble. The mines closed down in 1924 and that meant desertion of the camp. Koehler became a ghost town

KOEHLER had cosmopolitan population of about 1,200. Houses were heated with free coal, lit by kerosene in early days. When electricity became available company insisted on electric lights, forbade old lamps clung to by many foreign born workers and families. Times also changed shopping habits, residents forsaking local stores to travel to large centers at Raton and Trinidad, Colorado, when rapid transportation became available.

COLFAX PREDATED most of coal towns in Colfax County, was only a stop on the old road to Cimarron, a flourishing supply center while Dawson, a short distance up the canyon, boomed with its coal production. When railroad was built directly to coal mines at Dawson, Colfax declined. Town is now deserted except for family living in old Frederici store, built and operated by father of Fred Frederici, District Judge of Raton, now deceased. Senior Frederici migrated to America from Italy in 1903, remembered when coke ovens glowed at nearby Starkville, Colorado, now "suburb" of Trinidad.

and remained empty for twelve years. Then with some returning demand for coal the owners decided to reactivate conservatively. Mr. J. Van Houten, head of the company made a public statement to stockholders. "As this property has been idle since 1924 many repairs to tracks, buildings and pipelines will be necessary. Considerable new equipment will have to be purchased. For this purpose the sum of $200,000 has been appropriated by the board. By adding production of this mine to that of existing operations, the company's producing capacity will be maintained for many years to come." Mr. Koehler's report went on to stress new expenses added to the company's outlay, such as increased taxes, unemployment contributions, social security costs. "The recent increase in oil prices will help some," he said with a qualifying note, "to what extent remains to be seen."

That was in 1938 and actual reopening of the mine was still postponed. The Atcheson, Topeka and Santa Fe, previously the largest single purchaser of coal for its locomotives, was rapidly converting to oil. More, government control of coal processing was not favorable to mine owners.

Finally, for a few years, the company produced coal again but on a very limited scale. Production in 1954 was only 57,000 tons, almost all used for fuel in neighboring towns. "The railroads are now almost completely dieselized as far as locomotive power is concerned," wailed the president. "We have been unsuccessful in securing any government contracts of consequence. We have tried to interest the authorities in shipments of coal to Japan and other foreign destinations but to no avail."

The neighboring coal camp of Van Houten, one of the largest in the northern New Mexico complex, closed down February 2, 1954. At first related camps felt the closure would improve their own situations but creeping paralysis set in. Brilliant, where investment was over $1 million at one time, was soon affected as was its close neighbor Gardner. It was only a matter of time until Koehler, already ailing, would receive the kiss of death. The same fate was in store for Catskill, Yankee, Blossburg, Carisburg and Morley, just across the line in Colorado.

The common denominator in the death of New Mexico's coal camps was the failing usefulness of solid fuels, variations being only in detail. Where coke was the major product as in Dawson, its use in foundries was replaced by natural gas. Where raw coal was the big export, as in Koehler and other camps, it was diesel oil that rang the death knell.

LAKE VALLEY, NEW MEXICO

On the map of New Mexico, Lake Valley lies at the bottom or south end of an inverted L. Kingston is at the other, western end and Hillsboro at the junction. These three towns in the wild and wooly days of the 1880s and '90s composed the stage route of the Orchard Line.

Sadie Orchard knew it well. She ranks among the most colorful characters of New Mexico's early days. She came to the Territory in 1886 and seeing the advantages of having the only stage line in the region, she and her husband assembled two Concord Coaches and an express wagon as a nucleus. She drove one of the coaches, making the full run from Kingston to Hillsboro to Lake Valley. It

was her proud boast that her coach had never been held up while she held the reins. This could not be said of the stage line as a whole for bandits and Indians waylaid the stage and freight wagons with discouraging regularity. Sadie is said to have shaken her head about the worst stretch on the route, narrow Percha Canyon. "It sure was troublesome for us stage drivers. Indians lurked along the way and the road was surely trying."

Lake Valley hadn't always been the important terminus of a stage line. In the '70s it was only a tiny settlement and few people knew of it. More did very quickly after the August day in 1878 when cowboy George W. Lufkin rode along the

IN OLD LAKE VALLEY CEMETERY some graves like this one of Sarah Collins are fenced. Those graves without protection from digging coyotes became project of Christian Endeavor. Society raised money to place heavy stone slab cover over graves. C. E. also built fence around entire graveyard, keeping out cattle, other large animals. George Lufkin, first discoverer of silver in camp lies here, died penniless, was buried by county.

MAJOR MORGAN MORGANS, veteran of the Union Army ran rooming house in little false front and "annex." By '96 Lake Valley had lost much of population but remainder felt need of religious influence. Town never had church but ladies organized Christian Endeaver Society, bought rooming house, covered walls with oilcloth, hung up seven kerosene lamps, placed chairs in rows. Annex was furnished for convenience of any preacher who might stay overnight. Ordinarily a leader was chosen from members to conduct each Sunday's services. These were non-sectarian; members included Presbyterians, Methodists, Baptists, Quakers, Mormons and Catholics. Dues were ten cents a month, modest sum realized was augmented by bazaars, basket socials. Society was even able to contribute to famine relief for stricken China, flood victims in Monticello, Sierra County, offered food and lodging to any needy persons traveling through Lake Valley by wagon and team.

edge of Black Range, rifle cradled in one arm and loaded for Apaches, his prospector's pick in the other. At lunch time he stopped under a pinon tree. Among the stones scattered about was a piece of float so interesting he put it in his pocket. Later he had it assayed and was told the value of the sample came out several thousand ounces to the ton. Excited, Lufkin got his friend Chris Watson to join him in partnership and the two relocated the source of the sample. They found the spot but no more float. However they did locate several promising claims, one of them near the town of Lake Valley.

Money dwindled and no good vein was forthcoming. The partners sold out to the Sierra Grande Mining Company, made up of a group of Philadelphia capitalists, receiving $100,000 for the claim. This was a good price considering the prospects. The location actually consisted of several shafts and tunnels; one of the latter had hardly penetrated the side of the hill. A lease was taken on this one by a blacksmith named John Leavitt. Two days after the original finders had sold their

claim Leavitt broke through into the most fabulous lode of silver the world has ever known.

It consisted of a hollow in the hillside, a "room" nicknamed the "Bridal Chamber." The cavern had walls of solid horn silver. The total silver removed was 2,500,000 ounces bringing $1.11 an ounce at that time. Before it was all scraped out a spur from the railroad had been extended right into the Bridal Chamber and the rich stuff was shoveled directly into the cars.

Naturally this kind of thing could not be kept a secret, and a rush of prospectors, miners and hangers-on poured into a forty-mile strip along the edge of the Black Range, presided over by Kingston, Hillsboro and Lake Valley.

The Black Range Mining District was officially organized in 1881. Most of the population came that same year, when the Apache troubles were at their peak; no miners cabin or settlers hut was safe from raids by Victorio, or his henchmen, Loco and Nana. In spite of their continuing raids, total production in the period up to 1894 was close to $25,000,000.

One of the smaller towns in the area was Chloride. During the period of intense badgering by Indians, a sentry was kept on constant duty there. Old timers gloried in telling about the time the watch fell to one Schmidt, a German fresh from the old country. He had never handled a rifle but was carefully instructed in its use and reminded that a single shot from the weapon would warn the town that an Apache raid was imminent. About the middle of the night the ominous shot was heard, throwing the camp into the usual panic; women and children were hustled off to the blockhouse built for this purpose. Nothing happened. Pretty soon Schmidt came walking sheepishly into town explaining, "I shot her all right, but I don't mean to do it."

In 1883 Kingston was a hotbed of rustler activity. Organized gangs of cattle thieves became so brazen that they even flaunted their identity to the ranchers they had robbed, as no recourse was possible, short of murder. Ranchers finally appealed to Territorial Governor L. A. Shelton to send a full company of militia, armed to the teeth. The governor ordered Major A. J. Fountain to proceed from Mesilla to the Black Range area. Fountain headed for Kingston with almost his entire battalion, leaving only a skeleton force to guard

the jail at Mesilla. Arriving at Kingston, Fountain found that the ringleaders of the rustlers had fled to Lake Valley. Taking a detail of five men he proceeded toward that town arriving there at five in the morning. He arrested one of the most wanted men without any trouble. This was "Butch" whose real name was William Leland. The other of the desired duo, John Watts, made a run for it, and when cornered lifted his rifle. When he saw that he was outnumbered he put up his hands.

"The two prisoners," Fountain wrote in his report, "were mounted on one horse, unbound. At about 4:30 a.m. after the moon had gone down and before daylight the command arrived at the *cienaga* known as Daly's . . . There I halted the command and ordered the men to dismount and prepare coffee . . . I had the prisoners dismount and asked Watts how he was getting along, he replied 'I want a drink bad'. I told him the men would have coffee in a few minutes. He answered that he didn't want coffee, but whiskey and asked me to allow him to go to a nearby tavern to get some. I told him I could not give him permission and rode off and dismounted."

There was a good deal of confusion while the men were unsaddling the horses and unpacking the mules and in the midst of it someone noticed that the prisoners were hightailing it up the road. The men seized their carbines and fired a volley of shots after them. "I directed Capt. Salazar to take a sufficient detail and follow the fugitives. He took six or seven men and proceeded up the road about 200 yards and came upon the bodies of Watts and Butch lying in the road. They were both dead. I ordered their bodies be covered with loose earth in order to prevent them from being disturbed by coyotes . . . I telephoned Lake Valley the fact of their death with the request that their bodies be sent for."

Eventually the cattle rustling ring was broken up, most of its members fleeing toward the Mexican border. Some were intercepted but most escaped. Thus ended rustling on a big scale in that section of New Mexico.

MOST REMAINING RELICS show a d o b e construction, fronted by whipsawed lumber; this one shows unique combination of adobe and stone. Adobe was not of prefabricated bricks as usual but extension of mortar.

HE BROUGHT LIGHT IN

Madrid, N.M.

Nobody thought a nice fellow like Lloyd, clerk at the Albuquerque and Cerrillos Coal Co., would ever be put in jail . . . and there was the sheriff going to the Cerrillos railroad station after somebody else. Well after all, this was Madrid, New Mexico, where anything might happen. It did, that night. They let Lloyd out of jail on the promise of a keg of beer, the sheriff brought Marjorie in and the miners threw a big party for the bride and groom.

Coal was found at Madrid as early as 1839 and probably used at the nearby Cerrillos gold mines. When Gen. Stephen Watts Kearney came through New Mexico in the 1840s he used Madrid coal for his army. And it is said that at one time ox teams hauled the coal all the way to St. Louis.

Legends grow more factual when the Madrid mines were opened by a subsidiary of the Santa Fe Railway in the early 1880s. In 1899 when the town had a population of 3,000 the Colorado Fuel and Iron Co. took control, later selling to the Albuquerque and Cerrillos Coal Co. In 1910 Oscar Huber went to work for the company, eventually buying them out, the property still owned by his heirs in 1964.

Marjorie Lloyd came to the coal camp as a bride in 1913, she recalled in a *New Mexico Magazine* article. Her new husband was very much concerned about the charivari that might greet them when they arrived from Denver as bride and groom. He was employed in the camp as mine clerk and well aware of rowdy welcomes of the sort. He arranged to have the Madrid sheriff meet their train in Cerrillos, three miles distant, and spirit them into his home unobserved.

The miners however discovered why the clerk went to Denver and the next day through a ruse managed to lock him up in the town jail. Kept a prisoner until dinner time, Lloyd was glad to buy his freedom with a keg of beer and the traditional charivari was staged after all.

At that time, as now, the residential district consisted of four long, dreary rows of houses sadly in need of paint. They faced the company store, offices, tavern and other business, a row of shade trees bordering both sides of the main street. The population was about 3,000 and there were no vacant homes, the Lloyds being forced to live at one of the three boarding houses, the one having the only green lawn in Madrid.

The company employed one doctor, the entire medical facility for the town without hospital or nurses. Every man paid a dollar a month for any medical care he might need. When his wife had a baby he paid extra for the delivery. The town's water supply was a sometime thing. Railroad tank cars brought water from springs five miles away, siphoning it into a reservoir. Sometimes the supply became exhausted and pipes were dry for a whole day until another tank came in. Mrs. Lloyd wrote, "Dishes, laundry and baths just had to wait. If you got too thirsty the tavern wasn't too far away."

Electricity was unavailable for homes in 1913. Generated in a powerhouse the current was sufficient only for company houses. Families had to rely on kerosene lamps and candles. Cooking was done on coal fires, the fuel bought "reasonably" from the company. Sometimes a dynamite cap lost in the coal would liven things up in the stove.

CHRISTMAS CITY of New Mexico. Below are most of the buildings remaining in Madrid, all vacant. On hill at right still stands cross that centered electrically lit "replica" of Bethlehem with large cut-outs representing Biblical figures, display one of many completely surrounding town. Surmounting each of 12 hills on both sides of Madrid was huge Christmas "tree"—pine pole with iron bars for limbs, each generously strung with colored light bulbs. Tree in foreground alone remains erect.

638

Fire was always a hazard, some houses burned through the use of lamps and candles, the company finally wiring them for electricity but limiting them to a single bulb hanging naked from the ceiling, the "juice" turned on only at a given time after nightfall. In time daytime electricity was allowed, for ironing—one day a week.

The men made their living at the company mines and were expected to spend it in the company store. But the drygoods section offered little more than jumpers, overalls and a few women's house dresses. When wives ordered more frilly items from mail-order houses, they had to do it secretly and hope no company official would see her carrying the package home.

All this was before Oscar Huber. He changed everything, literally brought light to shine on Madrid. He became superintendent after working there for several years, bringing his wife and children from Albuquerque. Marjorie Lloyd says of him, "I used to enjoy watching him stride up the street each morning. You sensed in his quick decisive step that he was definitely going some place." Huber planted flower beds in his yard, the only

ones in town, and soon had a showplace, with flower boxes under the windows. When others admired the effect, he made available water flowing from one of the mine tunnels, piping a convenient supply to each section of houses. That summer there were splashes of color in almost every yard.

Huber had the main street paved and new houses built in all lots made vacant by fires. Then came a six-room hospital, first grade and high schools to replace old residences used by students. An employees' club was organized, baseball diamond and bleachers built, Madrid becoming famous for its ball team, the company paying its transportation to compete in other towns. Yet no change in the gloomy, soot-blackened town was as spectacular as allowing all residents unlimited use of electricity.

In the first winter after this innovation, Huber helped the people put on a Christmas display, the like of which had never been seen in New Mexico. Huge figures were created—of Mary, Joseph, the infant Christ, shepherds and wise men. Miners enthusiastically painted and wired them for electrical illumination. The nativity scene, utilizing

OLD CEMETERY on hill above Madrid contains many markers and enclosures individually hand-crafted from local materials. Not all graves are fenced, or wooden pickets have disappeared, many graves marked only by piles of stones.

CACTI "ask but little here below," growing happily on dirt roof of stone house. Plastered inside with mud, it is one of the oldest relics in Madrid, dating from days before large companies took over coal production.

COMPANY HOUSES—4 long lines of nearly identical units—presented dreary sight to residents but now of interest as ghost town relics. Originally standing in Kansas, houses were sawed in quarters, shipped to Madrid on Santa Fe Railroad. Reassembled they were plastered to make windproof but storms soon seeped through. Most had living room, kitchen on main floor, 3 bedrooms upstairs. Danger of fires was always present from overturned kerosene lamps or candles. In absence of water firemen dynamited burning buildings to prevent spread of flames.

live sheep, burros and oxen was set up on a hill overlooking the town, followed by a Bethlehem scene with central cross and many buildings. As each Christmas came, new ones were added until in a few years both sides of the canyon were covered with brilliantly lighted Biblical scenes. Every building in town displayed strings of colored lights and in the ball park was a display for children featuring Santa Claus and mechanically lighted toyland figures.

The magnificent pageant drew thousands of visitors from other parts of the state, the show of lights maintained from early December through New Years. The program set in motion by Oscar Huber gave the miners initiative to organize choral clubs with many fine voices and during evenings of Christmas week various groups were stationed at strategic points, breaking into coordinated song with the words "Let There Be Light." At that instant the main switch was thrown on and the dark old coal town broke into a blaze of glory and glad voices.

In the '30s the town that shipped millions of tons of coal annually began to show signs of slowing down. Gradual conversion in railroading and industry to other fuels slackened coal production.

OLD BEDSTEAD and climbing vine offer composition on wall of old Madrid house.

COMPANY OFFICES near north end of city on road to Los Cerrillos and Santa Fe. Close inspection reveals strings of lights still clinging to structure.

World War II brought it up some temporarily, 20,000 tons going to Los Alamos to help build the first A-bombs. But Madrid's Christmas lights were turned on for the last time in 1941. When the switch was thrown off at the end, the choraleers sang "Auld Lang Syne" while almost everyone wept openly.

641

MAGDALENA, NEW MEXICO

Socorro is the town where one turns west for Magdalena and Kelly. The old shipping center isn't dead, though sleepy, and has a plaza authentically Mexican. The church of San Miguel is one of the oldest in the country. The town, during the old, wild days, was the current hangout of Russian Bill. Not actually a killer, Bill only liked to pose as one. He suffered from a compulsion to stay in the public eye and the only way he knew how to do it was to keep up a constant stream of practical jokes. The town's patience grew thin, and by one Christmas Eve, reached the breaking point. The main hotel boasted a card room as well as dining hall, and it was there Bill played his last game of poker. He got drunk, and bragged about his marksmanship, proving how good he was by expertly shooting one finger from the hand of one of the players. The rest of the gamblers grabbed him by the scruff of the neck, read a charge against him of "being a damn nuisance" and hanged him right then and there in the hotel dining room.

Some twenty-seven miles west is the old camp of Magdalena, still having life but showing its age in the many false fronts scattered through the town. Alice Morley Cleaveland in her book "No Life For A Lady" gives a vivid picture of her advent there. "We arrived in Magdalena in February, 1886. The town sprawled in the sun at the foot of Lady Magdalena Mountain, a bare and defiant monolith in the midst of her decently pine-clad sisters. . . Halfway up the mountainside, Lady Magdalena herself gazes into the blue sky resting upon far mountain peaks, her face turned away from the town. . . There is a legend that Lady Magdalena Mountain was a sanctuary respected by the Indians, where fugitives, whether deservedly or not, found refuge from pursuing enemies. The legend did not hold after the paleface came shooting his way into the land. Many a pursuer fell before his enemies in the streets of Magdalena.

" 'Please give us a room that is not directly over the barroom,' my mother stipulated to the hotelkeeper the night we arrived. 'I'm afraid those bullets will come through the floor.' It was years later before Magdalena gathered herself together and made it a misdemeanor to shoot within the city limits."

In the 1880's when Kelly was already a boom town, Magdalena was hardly more than a watering place at Pueblo Springs. There was a station of sorts there as a convenience of the stage line from Socorro to the western part of the Territory. There the cattlemen watered their stock on market drives and cowboys unlimbered their legs while they had the chance. The present town of Magdalena didn't occupy its present situation until '85 or so, when it began to grow into the place where "the lights were repeatedly shot out by ebullient buckaroos." It was then getting its water the hard way, hauling it from Pueblo Springs at a cost of ten cents a barrel. Kelly nourished the place by sending down her miners who wished to carouse but found insufficient space to spread out in the narrow confines of the canyon in which Kelly is cramped. On the plain there was room for saloons and dance halls of generous proportions and these promptly took shape. Other factors contributed to the economy, such as the railhead and the sheep and cattle ranches which sprang up in the surrounding ranges. The railroad's purpose was to serve the booming mining town of Kelly, up the steep canyon from Magdalena. One look at the canyon's grade, however, and the engineers gave up, saying in effect to the "city fathers" of Kelly, "If you want a train, come and get it." And this Kelly did, rolling its ore and bullion down the short but precipitous wagon road to the station.

When Kelly died, so did a large part of Magdalena, that part having to do with the shipping of supplies for a vast area of cattle ranches and sheep ranges, but days of the old reckless shootings on the main street are gone and the town drowses.

PYTHIAN HALL, BUILT IN 1907 at height of Magdalena's development, is one of New Mexico's best examples of architecture of the time. Decorations are ornate but lack gingerbread effect of other structure of period. Tiny building at right once housed newspaper office, served many later purposes. Eyebolts above door seem to indicate one time sign or awning. Magdalena's prosperity depended upon that of Kelly, mining camp two miles up canyon. Before railroad came to Magdalena, Kelly's ores were shipped 29 rough and rocky miles in ox-wagons over Blue Canyon road to Socorro. Closeness of railhead enormously amplified output made practical by easy disposal. Many mines in district had euphonious names, as Ambrosia, Cimmaron, Alhambra, Little Louella, Iron Mask, Legal Tender, reflecting literary, political or practical leanings.

643

MOGOLLON, NEW MEXICO

Young Sergeant James C. Cooney was one to keep his eyes open and his mouth shut. When, in 1870, on a scouting expedition out of Fort Bayard he found a rich ledge from gold bearing float was crumbling, he kept the discovery secret until his hitch was over. This feat is unparalleled in the history of most mining towns. Whiskey usually loosed the tongues of those finding gold.

As soon as Cooney was mustered, he confided in several men he could trust, among them Harry McAllister, forming a partnership to explore the possibilities of his find. The area was in the mountains called the Mogollons (pronounced muggy owns), thickly infested by hostile Apaches. Cooney's party was attacked by Indians so continually that, after establishing several locations, the prospectors retired to Silver City to nurse their wounds. Two years later, with augmented defenses and supplies, the men again set out for the claims. Two ox-drawn wagons carried their equipment and food.

The first place to be established as a camp in the Mogollons was Claremont but this one was short-lived. Then a camp in Cooney Canyon was started and flourished as a typical rough-and-ready camp for a brief period of glory.

Indians were a constant menace and on one occasion when it was rumored the redskins were about to attack the camp was evacuated as usual. A couple of miners named John Lambert and George Doyle were hiding in the bushes just above the houses when the Indians came down the trail. The white men had their little dog with them and he began to growl. Fearful of attracting attention, they choked the animal to death. The Indian party ransacked the house, one squaw coming out with a full length mirror tied to her back. She was followed by a retinue of delighted youngsters who vied for positions to see their reflections.

At about this same period nearby Alma was established and shared attacks by Apaches. In one of these, James Cooney was killed and his camp at Cooney taken over by his brother Captain Michael Cooney.

In the spring of '83 the Captain grubstaked a man named Turner. Rumors persisted that Turner found a bonanza but the man himself vanished. In '89 his body was found in Sycamore Canyon, waylaid by

PLANK PORCHES ALSO SERVED as sidewalks over stream bed, show wear and tear from use and weather. At about this point on one street of town, during Presidential election in fall of 1896, large picture of William McKinley was suspended from wire stretched across street by Republicans. Returns began to come in indicating candidate was losing. Portrait was lowered by Democrats, black cloth draped over it, and again elevated. Late evening stage came in with word that McKinley had won. Everyone, regardless of affiliation, got drunk, then went home to sleep it off.

644

ever-present Apaches. Captain Cooney determined to find the supposed wealth that was legally his if it existed. He started out in the fall; next spring *his* body was found where he had frozen to death, only about 100 yards from where that of Turner had been found.

In the meantime, the new camp of Mogollon had been started in the bottom of Silver Creek Canyon, a short distance from Claremont and Cooney. The first mines developed there were the Maude S., Deep Down, Little Fanny and Last Chance. It is the history of the Little Fanny that permeates the history of the camp itself.

Mr. Friolo was a resident of Mogollon all through its best years and still lives in the crumbling old camp, the only "bona fide" resident, the few others being summer campers. The old gentleman tells of how miner's consumption, so called, and "miner's con" in

his words, took a ghastly toll of men working in the Little Fanny. The jack-hammers used in breaking the quartz for removal from the mine made a cloud of gritty dust which affected the lungs, some miners lasted only three years or less. If they did not die outright they were relegated to lighter jobs, but even this did not save them. Water hoses were provided them by the company for wetting the rock to reduce or prevent the dust, but this procedure soaked the men too. They refused to work wet all the time, perferring the dust. Finally, in desperation, the company worked out a system where the water was squirted along with the air-pressure. From then on the toll from "miner's con" was cut down and the town's three physicians, Drs. Feel, Kern and Parm, had a respite.

At the time the Little Fanny was developed the population of the camp was about 2,000. That was in 1909. Two years later the number of people had

FACING J. P. HOLLAND GENERAL STORE is group of buildings constituting main business center of camp. At extreme left is tiny saloon, next is Mogollon Mercantile, then Annex to larger Holland store, specializing in furniture and "notions" after period as post office.. Large stone structure at extreme right was Howard's Drug Store, with doctor's offices above. Upper floor was gained by outside stairway, now smothered by "Trees of Heaven." Structure served as grocery store later, as town declined and adobe buildings disintegrated. Patch of mullein weeds in foreground is at edge of area once constituting red-light district.

IMPOSING ADOBE served Mogollon as roominghouse, was "respectable" since brothels were segregated, confined to flat at lower edge of town. Smaller "dobe" at left was grocery store. One road to mines wound up gulch back of buildings and many small cabins still perch along route.

expanded further and there were fourteen saloons, seven restaurants, five stores, two hotels and the usual brothels.

The sixth annual edition of "Mogollon Mines" pointed out that "there is room for and an absolute necessity for the establishment of a Society for the pre- vention of Cruelty to Animals in Mogollon. Scarcely a day passes but what a cruel and heartless driver abuses his animals. Whether in a team or a burro heavily laden with wood, both are subjected to knock- out blows with cordwood or loaded whips. It is not uncommon to see an animal devoid of one eye, and frequently this is in a bleeding condition, and the poor, suffering brute has no way to relieve itself of the constant annoyance of myriads of flies. . ."

By 1915 the camp's payroll was between $50,000 and $75,000 every month. Gold and silver bullion were shipped out regularly to Silver City. The distance was ninety miles and in bad weather the ore teams required ten days for the trip. Even in the most favor- able weather, fifteen miles was a good day's average because of the frighteningly steep grades encountered. Ordinary harnesses were not used for the long line of 18-mule teams. A center chain ran the entire length, each team harnessed with hames and collars, belly bands, back bands and chain tugs, with the ex- ception of the two wheel horses. Metal doubletrees were hooked to each section so the teams could pull. The teamster rode the right wheel horse with a saddle, and guided the teams with a jerk line which extended the entire length and was snapped to each team. On

the steep curves the mules stepped right or left over the chain as it rubbed against their legs. Ordinary brakes were ineffectual. Rough locks with heavy timbers were dropped by a lever in front of the rear wheel of the train wagons. On the steepest grades the strings of wagons were separated into smaller groups.

The end of the haul at Silver City would see the 300-pound bars of gold and silver stacked in front of the Silver City National Bank, the return trip made with heavy loads of crude oil for the diesel engines at Mogollon. In 1912 when a flywheel weighing 12,400 pounds was hauled up to the Little Fanny, a 24-horse outfit was employed. The rigs were owned by W. A. Tenney, and operated from 1910 until the opening of World War I. Trucks took over but the camp was tired and beginning to drag its feet.

There was less and less of that famous "blossom rock" from which little nuggets could be shaken. What remained assayed poorly, was refractory and hardly paid costs of milling and refining. Several mines closed down entirely, others operated on a part- time basis. When the Little Fanny quit, so did the town. The Black Jack Gang, so belligerent at the turn of the century, was already long since tamed, holdups along the steep and rocky road to Alma and Silver City had become less frequent. Gunshots ceased to echo from Jimmy Johnson's saloon or the similar emporium of Pedro "Pete" Almeraz where the notori- ous Cosmo Zapata had been killed. Mogollon shriveled as people moved away, sighed and lay down to sleep.

PINOS ALTOS, NEW MEXICO

In the realm of legend is the story of a long vanished settlement on the site of the present town of Pinos Altos. Prior to known discoveries of gold in 1837 Mexicans were said to have found rich deposits of the metal in a stream at the foot of an enormous cottonwood tree. They erected an enclosure for protection against marauding bands of Indians, the barricade constructed of materials at hand — adobe, stone and logs, built in horseshoe shape. Men and animals were safely quartered inside at night while by day the men placered the gravels, the horses grazing on the hillside close by. In time all their rawhide panniers were filled with treasure and the decision must be made as to who was to take them to distant Chihuahua in Mexico. Here the men fell out. Everyone wanted to stay with the gold and return home. No one wanted to remain at the diggings and guard the stockade.

Here the tale becomes even more gossamer. There would seem to be two outcomes possible. The men all returned to their homes with the golden *chispas* or they fought among themselves and were overpowered by Indians.

Three items in this story are borne out by facts. There were running streams of water even though these flow now only in times of rain. Correlated is the fact that an ample stand of tall pines, *"pinos altos,"* existed before the slopes were wantonly logged off. Gone now is the forest and the streams of clear water once stored by a generous groundcover. Remaining are faint signs of horseshoe shaped ruins, outlined by enduring stones.

More substantial history begins in 1860, when a party of twelve scouts left Tucson for the Rio Grande. A long rest was taken at Mesilla, N. M. Here the men heard rumors, always flying, that there was gold in "them thar hills." Re-routing to Santa Rita they stopped again, this time to stock up on supplies and split into smaller parties. The group made up of three men named Hicks, Snively and Birch made their camp on the banks of Bear Creek and eagerly rushed to begin sifting the gravels of the creek bed. Birch is credited with having been the first to find a couple of nuggets, the *"chispas"* of earlier Mexicans. Frenzied search rewarded each man with a handful of gold. All found it hard to sleep that night and rose early for a council as to what was to be done. The obvious problem was to get provisions and tools if they were to stay

on. But how to keep the discovery a secret? It seemed wisest to go to Santa Rita, confide their secret to trusted friends who would purchase food and supplies so as to rouse no curiosity. The confidants were the Marston brothers and one Langston all of whom swore secrecy. The three discoverers then slipped unobstrusively back to their diggings.

Arising bright and early next morning to begin work, they made another discovery. They were not alone. A party of three Americans had crept in and staked several claims close by. All day and for weeks and months thereafter a motley assemblage of Mexicans, Americans, hard working miners, soft-handed gamblers and con artists streamed in to swell the population of the infant camp called at first Birchville.

The original discovery by Birch had been on May 18 and by September there were 700 men panning the streams. Santa Rita now boomed, supplying staple groceries, as did Mesilla the source for tools and clothing.

At first all gold recovery was done by panning and sluicing in the stream bed, but as rewards grew slimmer, the sources of loose dust and nuggets were found in rich lodes on the hillside. At first these needed only scraping, plenty of ore was easily obtained and crudely refined in primitive "arrastras." A low circular rock wall was built. About twenty feet across, it was centered by a short pole topped by a spike holding the end of a beam that reached outside the wall. A horse or mule, sometimes a burro for small outfits, was tied to the outer end to walk in a circle, dragging a heavy rock around inside the wall. Ore was dumped into the enclosure to be more or less pulverized. At intervals the larger, harder chunks were thrown out and the fine material treated as usual in rockers, Long Toms, sluices, or even in some small operations, panned out.

The town grew to the point where the Mesilla *Times* was running little news items about it. Some of these, gleaned by Dorothy Watson in her *"Pinos Altos Story,"* read: "Thomas J. Marston is pushing ahead his work of grinding quartz, although constantly annoyed by Indians." "The Pinos Altos Hotel serves bread and meals." "Samuel G. and Roy Bean (prominent in Law West of the Pecos) are dealers in merchandise and liquors, and have a fine billiard table." "Thomas Marston wants 200 quartz miners." Marston added that he was willing to pay top wages, up to two dollars a day.

Following this cozy period came a long spell of strife, involvement in the fringes of the Civil War and constant harassment by Apaches. When the Confederacy was established, the area including Pinos Altos was claimed by the South. On August 1st, 1861, Col. John R. Baylor, governor at Mesilla, proclaimed the area to be part of the Territory of Arizona. He then afforded some small protection from Apaches for the settlers and miners by sending Snively, now promoted to captain to help control Cochise's savages, and making another captain of Thomas Birch to watch over his mining camp. About the same time the Apaches made up their minds to get rid of the whites, once and for all. They gathered on September 14, for a concerted attack. Cochise as usual, was in the forefront with his warriors from Chiricahuas, and joined by Mangas Colorado and his band of Mimbrenos, led 400 yelling braves down upon the whites from the forested slopes of the continental divide upon which the camp lay straddled. The attack was begun at dawn and raged until afternoon. The toll of retreating Apaches was fifteen, one of these was killed by a dog belonging to a Mexican miner named Carlos Norero. Two Americans were killed outright and Marston was so severely wounded he died a few days later. He was buried beneath a juniper tree in the little Pinos Altos cemetery.

Although the Indian attack had been successfully repulsed, the miners compared the relative values of gold and their scalps, then decamped in large numbers to engage in what they thought might be the comparative safety of the Army. Some chose the Union side. Others were more in sympathy with the South. The remaining residents felt their numbers were so decimated as to make them targets for further attacks and screamed for help. Governor Baylor responded with a detachment of 100 men under Major E. Waller for their protection.

Even with this another Apache attack occurred in which forty miners were casualties. This one was executed in crafty manner, with a full understanding of the emotions lonely young men must be feeling after such a long time in camp without women. Mangas Colorado stationed a group of his more attractive young squaws on the hillside above the camp in full sight of the miners. The girls languidly combed their hair and otherwise displayed their feminine charms.

At last the men could stand it no longer and most of the shrunken male population made a mad rush up the hill. Apaches ambushed them on both sides and cut off any retreat. Other Indians united and drove off the horses. Additional parties of Apaches seized a number of whites who were hunting game in the hills. One of the hunters who escaped the terrible slaughter reported the hills "full of Indians."

Mangas Colorado had been subjected to many indignities and treacheries by the whites, blaming them as the reason for his continued attacks. General Carlton sent out word that Mangas Colorado must be captured "by any means deemed necessary." Captain Shirland and Jack Swilling located the chief in the Pinos Mountains and conveyed the message to him that the whites were anxious to negotiate and would guarantee his safety if he would accompany them to Fort McLane. In spite of all previous experiences with whites and "negotiations" with them, the chief went willingly and alone with the emissaries. On January 18, 1863, he was shot to death "while trying to escape." With the chief out of the way, the soldiers found courage to "capture" his wife who was taken to Pinos Altos and killed.

The last act of treachery on the part of the whites came in the summer of '64 when a partially successful treaty had established a certain amount of confidence on the part of the Indians, at least enough so that they came peacefully into camp for barter. One of the settlers owned a house larger than the rest. He asked some of the Indians to invite their friends to a sumptuous dinner he would serve them in celebration of the signing of the treaty. Some sixty guests responded. When all were seated the host opened fire on them, killing many, maiming many more. From then on it was not safe for a white to venture out of camp bounds alone or unarmed.

At the end of the war and with the return of most of the men, Indian harassments became less, though were never really absent for any length of time. A Navajo band drove off more than thirty yoke of oxen and were promptly pursued by about fifty men. In the ensuing clash thirteen Navajos were killed and a number taken prisoner.

After the establishment of several military forts in the vicinity in '69, such incidents were replaced by others of a more homely nature. A Sr. Ancheta, resident of Pinos Altos, made a visit to the hacienda of his old friend in Mexico. While there he fell in love with the wife of his host. He talked her into running away with him and as soon as the couple reached Pinos Altos, Ancheta made haste to reinforce the defenses and made port holes in the walls in case the bereft husband should pursue them.

Other men were content to take Indian or Mexican women as common law wives, to build log or adobe homes and start planting garden seeds. Orchards and vineyards were established and except for an occasional murder in the saloons or a miner being killed in a premature mine explosion or attacked by bears while hunting, life in the camp became almost prosaic.

Historian Dorothy Watson paints an idyllic picture of early day Pinos Altos. "They made of their homes a garden spot, there were fields of alfalfa, corn and beans, and smaller plots of garden truck and flowers. Besides his terraced grapevines and fruit trees Mr. Stanley had a rose garden. The Mexicans planted almond and peach trees around their homes and invariably had oleanders in tubs. During the summer they blossomed beside the doorways and somehow room was found for them in their small dwellings when frost came. They took fledgling mocking birds from nests, carefully tended and trained them. They were kept in large cages hanging outside on the walls where they called and exchanged confidences with the neighboring wild birds or complimented the guitar music. Each home had a small corral for a burro. Chickens and cows roamed at will and here and there goats would clamber over walls and roofs. Every day the yard was swept as clean as the mud packed earth floors of their dwellings. Peter Wagnor and John Simon brought wild roses from the canyon and planted hedges of them around their homes. Although the buildings were crude, the effect was pleasing."

The camp flourished for a long period but began to show signs of decay toward the turn of the century. Silver City had in the meantime come into prominence and in 1879 one newspaper there referred to Pinos Altos as "an abandoned camp in Silver City's back yard." The "abandoned" town had a population of 9,000 in the '80s and '90s, boasted a drug store, two hotels, barber shop, clothing stores and even a Turkish bath.

In spite of a downward trend there were several spurts forward, one in 1906 when the long dream of narrow gauge came into camp, enormously expediting the shipment of ores to Silver City. Excursionists were thrilled to ride on the tops of loaded ore cars. On one such trip, returning cars on the steep grade got away, failed to make a sharp turn and landed in the gulch. After this no one but employees was allowed on the cars.

Great excitement was caused in 1911 when Ira Wright and James Bell struck rich deposits in their newly leased Pacific Mines. One lot of 1800 pounds of ore brought them $43,000. As was to be expected this set off a wave of high grading; miners were thought to have taken out as much for themselves as did the owners. All recipients were relieved of temptation when the shallow pocket gave out. Bell and Wright did not renew the lease, marking another downward step in the economy of the town.

During depression days idle men flocked to the diggings, scratching around once-rich shafts and tunnels, trying to eke out a living. Others were operating as many as seventy rockers in the stream beds so that the scene resembled the aspects of early days.

Altogether, The Bureau of Mines estimated, over $8,000,000 in gold, lead, silver and copper were produced in the camp once so blessed with tall pines and streams, now so barren and dry.

GOLD AVENUE METHODIST CHURCH w a s dedicated May 18, 1898. First Pastor was Rev. Henry Van Valkenburgh. Church was built on part of Good Enough Mining claim, the owners donating the site. Methodist ladies gave church suppers, basket socials to raise money for building fund. Phoebe Hurst, member of wealthy mine owner family, offered to help on condition reading room was provided. When edifice was completed it was found that separate room had not been provided, so front of church was stocked with magazines. 1942 picture shows bell surmounting frame tower at right. Earliest church activities were Catholic, diocese was in Mesilla. Priest visited parish, baptized children, blessed casual unions entered into since last visit, said Mass for those who had died.

TWO BOOMLETS FAILED

San Pedro, New Mexico

Just south of the mining camp of San Pedro are the ruins of an ancient Indian village called Paako, the language spoken there either Keres or Tewa. In 1598 the explorer Onate called the pueblo Tano. The houses were built of native rubble and generally two stories high. There were three kivas, those circular holes in the ground, paved with rock and used as places of worship. Early historians state the pueblo was still occupied as late as 1626 but by 1670 all Indian inhabitants had vanished.

With Spanish occupation a mission was established on the site in 1661 and named San Pedro de la Cuchilla after the patron saint. The University of New Mexico did some excavation at the site in 1936, uncovering traces of stone walls and kivas. Adjoining the remains on the north was the early mining camp also called San Pedro as was the huge Spanish land grant including Indian ruins, mission church and hundreds of acres of pasture land.

The exact date of gold discoveries at San Pedro camp is uncertain but in 1846 army Lt. J. W. Abert visited there. In his report to Congress he said, "In the evening we visited a town at the base of the principal mountains here, mingled with the houses were huge mounds of earth thrown out of the wells so that the village looks like a village of giant prairie dogs. Nearly all of the people were at their wells, and were drawing up bags of loose sand by means of windlasses. Around the pools men, women and children were grouped, intently pouring over their bags of loose sand, washing the earth in wooden platters or goat horns...."

The fevered days of washing and panning by hand did not last long because particles of gold had to be a little larger than "dust" to be discovered in sediments, specks smaller than flakes of coarse pepper usually going undiscovered. Also water had to be available where the gold was. Primitive hand panning was replaced in 1880 by big time hydraulic operations when the San Pedro and Canyon del Agua Company set up equipment. Overlooking the area is the now famed tourist attraction, Sandia Crest. Up there the company found ample water with a steep drop down to San Pedro.

Officials spent $500,000 for a pipeline to carry it into monitors or hydraulic nozzles that would wash whole hillsides into waiting sluices. While the pipeline was being constructed, the company made real estate hay by laying out a town for sales to credulous buyers who were told there would be a big city here. Then the company was beset by extensive litigation, pipeline and town building held up in the courts. Construction became so entangled the company was forced to quit. Again quiet settled over the San Pedro foothills.

A few years later another company moved in, putting up buildings on empty lots and in 1887 the *Golden Nine* was so optimistic as to proclaim, "Everybody is coming to San Pedro and the rest of the world will be used for pasturage,"... "Newcomers should bring a tent. There are no vacant houses here, there are families living even in the coke ovens...." But that boom died too. There were more recent spurts of activity, for a time during World War I some copper being taken out, but no big time mining has been done for years.

STONE COKE OVENS are only remaining tangible evidence of once roaring gold camp. Coal was hauled by ox team from Madrid to the north, roasted in ovens to drive off easily removed soot, smoke, leaving residue of highly efficient fuel for smelter. With roof already collapsed even this relic will soon become a mere pile of rubble.

SHAKESPEARE, NEW MEXICO

It was Christmas of 1882 in Shakespeare and the town was celebrating with a big community party. The tree was a symmetrical pine brought down from the mountains. It was lavishly decorated, most of the ornaments home-made but not the most conspicuous one. This was a doll, about two and a half feet tall with arms and legs of cloth, a sawdust body and head of china, the prized possession of eight-year-old Emma Marble. She had brought it from Virginia City, Nevada, when she came with her mother and sister to join her father who had established a home for them in the raw mining camp.

The doll was admired by everyone, especially little Jane, the daughter of Mr. and Mrs. Nick Hughes. Jane could not take her wide eyes from the china beauty and talked of it all the way home. Not long afterward she fell ill and in her delirium constantly called for the doll. Her sister Mary went to the Marble home and asked Emma if she could take the doll to Jane, offering a five dollar gold piece for the favor. It was gladly granted and Jane had her doll — for a few days. When she died she was placed in a simple board coffin and her arms tightly clutched the doll with the china head. The coffin was placed in the little cemetery already holding so many who had met tragic or violent death in the camp.

Two of the cemetery's occupants were Pony Express riders slain by renegade Indians under Cochise and Geronimo. The site of what would be Shakespeare was decided by the presence of a good spring a few miles from the site of Lordsburg. The Butterfield Stage Station called Barney had been nearby, failing when the Butterfield Lines met disaster from effects of the Civil War. As soon as it ended a new line called the National was established and John Evensen was sent out to refurbish the station, now called Pyramid after the nearby range of mountains. The next name change came when Evensen, impressed by the current popularity of General Grant, bestowed the officer's name on the tiny group of adobe buildings. A year later the county was also named Grant.

About this time a government survey party, of which one member was W. B. Brown, was working in the area. Brown was a prospector at heart, not vitally interested in surveying, so the rocky ground received more attention than did his transit with the result that he found a spectacular specimen crisscrossed with veins of silver. He deserted the survey party and rushed to San Francisco with the sample.

A believer in going straight to the top man, Brown obtained an interview with Bank or California magnate William C. Ralston simply by showing his chunk of silver ore. Although Ralston was fighting Adolph Sutro's attempts to bore a tunnel to the bottom of Virginia City's mines, he was not too absorbed to overlook a good thing in Brown's offer of a partnership in exchange for capital to develop the New Mexico silver property. The financier personally had the ore sample assayed and when results showed 12,000 ounces of silver to the ton he formed a company to stake out further claims and set up a mining district to be called the Virginia Mining District with the little stage station as its center. With the consequent influx of workers and drifters a town soon developed at the hub and was rechristened Ralston.

The company made a miserable attempt to recover values and quickly failed. Blame was placed partly on absentee ownership, Ralston being too busy with Bank of California interests in the fading Virginia City to pay much attention to a far

LOOKING DOWN AVON AVENUE from intersecting old stage road. Long unused branch line of Southern Pacific runs along middle of street. Tin version of "covered wagon" stands bereft of wheels at left. Behind is old saloon. Right is Grant House, then Stratford Hotel where George W. Hunt, late great Governor of Arizona waited table as youth. At right, on near side of street is General Store.

away New Mexico mine. Then Ralston's bank was forced to close its doors in the financial panic and Ralston resigned as officer of the bank. He went out for his customary swim in cold San Francisco Bay, was apparently seized with cramps and drowned, some sources claiming it was suicide. With this event the town and the nine-by-four mile mining district in the Pyramids took a new name, that of the new owners, the Shakespeare Co., a concession to a large block of British stockholders. One of the two little adobe hotels was also named Shakespeare and a most natural title of Stratford House settled on the other.

The town was subjected to many short booms and sharp declines, the result of over-promotion. An editorial in the MINING NEWS, July 26, 1881, said of the situation: "Work at Shakespeare is being pushed ahead systematically. Shakespeare has had no little to contend against. When the district was first opened up it was puffed and lauded to the skies by a series of mining speculators who wished to dispose of their claims before doing any work to show there was anything in them to warrant investment by capitalists. . . . The mine owners of this

camp have begun to realize this fact and have thrown aside the puffing policy and gone to work in earnest."

F. Stanley, New Mexico historian, gives a vivid picture of the place in his SHAKESPEARE STORY: "The houses were built of adobe. The walls were thick to withstand Indian attacks, the windows small so they could be boarded up in a hurry. Victorio and his warriors were still making the rounds during the early days of Shakespeare history. The town was unique among mining towns of New Mexico, if not the Southwest, for it boasted no plumbing, no club, no church, no school, no fraternal organization, no bank. Even the dance hall girls who came in from Deming and Lordsburg were permitted neither residence or domicile in Shakespeare. The same carriage that brought them also took them back the same night."

Later no doubt, when the town had reached its peak of about 3,000 people, such extreme restrictions on the girls' activities were relaxed with the opening of Roxy Jay's Saloon. Its bar ran the length of the building, the longest adobe in the area. Made of polished mahogany, it was brought from St. Louis,

DINING ROOM of Grant House, scene of hanging of Russian Bill and Sandy King. When management offered no such diversions as cutting down bodies, diners amused selves shooting at flies on wall.

part way by eighteen-mule freight wagon. Also freighted in, and even more precariously, was the wonder of the town, an enormous mirror for the back bar. It was held in such awe and respect by habituees that although the doors were so full of bullet holes "they look like lacework", the mirror was never hit by flying lead.

Although Shakespeare was considered to be an extremely "honest town", one prominent citizen known to keep as much as $30,000 in a baking powder can, there was no lack of excitement. Most deeds of violence were perpetrated by out of 'town-ers. Frequent raids and shooting scrapes occurred when such "prominent" personalities as Curly Bill, Johnny Ringo, Dave Rudabaugh, Sandy King and Russian Bill came to town. The activities of these gunmen were so frequent the nerves of citizens finally snapped into action. They organized the Shakespeare Guards which were recognized by the Territorial Government in 1879. The Guards summary treatment of two of the more persistent tor-

mentors was followed by several peaceful years.

One was Russian Bill, fugitive from Russia where, as Count Feador Telfrin, member of the Imperial Guards, he had been involved in some shady money deals. Fleeing to Arizona he went to work on the McLowery ranch and also became associated with the equally notorious Clantons. Finding himself without a horse near the Speer ranch one day, he took one, but was spotted by a ranch hand. Apprehended in Deming, Russian Bill was brought to Shakespeare's shiny new jail which had been heralded in the Santa Fe NEW MEXICAN on September 28, 1881: "Shakespeare is to have a substantial calaboose. Its cost is estimated to be about four hundred dollars."

Flung into this proud structure, Russian Bill found he was not in solitary. One Sandy King had the honor of being the jug's first guest. Sandy had refused to pay for a gaudy silk handkerchief in Smyth's haberdashery, then literally added injury to insult by whipping out his six-shooter and clipping off the index finger of the clerk's out-stretched hand.

The NEW MEXICAN reported the events that followed: "You doubtless have heard of Russian Bill and Sandy King, two noted horse thieves and desperados. They were brought to Shakespeare a few days ago and lodged in jail. Yesterday they were loud and demonstrative against the citizens, declaring that the people of the town would have a chance to dance to their music in twenty-four days. During the small hours of the night the jail was visited by an armed force, the guard was overpowered and in an hour or so two pulseless bodies, stiff and cold, could be seen suspended by a cord to a girder in what was formerly the barroom of the old Shakespeare Hotel . . . Shakespeare is on its mettle and woe betide the unfortunate who raises the next row at this place. A coroner's jury ruled that the men met death by suicide."

Other reports fill in some details lacking in the newspaper statement. The reason the beam in the room was selected as a gallows was the scarcity of trees. The bodies were not cut down immediately. A large number of passengers was expected on the noon stage and it seemed a shame to deprive them of the edifying spectacle, so the bodies were left in place until after their arrival. One of the passengers offered to help carry the body of Russian Bill to the cemetery in exchange for the fine boots he wore. He said he thought they would fit him and they did. A final note was sounded by the NEW MEXICAN a few days later. "Shakespeare has not been annoyed by ruffians since the last necktie party. The friends of the two men who were lynched there a week or so ago have not avenged the death of their comrades as they threatened to. There is nothing that lessens the zeal of the average desperado than a conscientious vigilante committee." This story of Russian Bill's demise differs sharply from one credited to a member of the School of Mines at Socorro. (See GHOST TOWN ALBUM).

Then there was the affair involving the handsome "Arkansaw". Young Robert Black, who bore the nickname because he had come from that state, was carrying on an affair with the wife of a prominent citizen of the town, the outraged husband said, when he urged the vigilantes to action. They

GRANT HOUSE. Old stage station and dining room was named when whole town was called Grant for Civil War general. Windows were unusually large for day, more cheerful than most, but presented hazard in times of Indian attacks. Supply of rocks was kept piled inside under windows, stacked on sills in case of raid, providing protection from arrows, holes for extending rifles.

were reluctant but finally the wandering Romeo was caught and given the rope treatment. His feet had just left the ground when the saloon keeper, Roxy Jay, grieved at an obvious waste of an efficient mine worker, called out: "He's too good a man to hang. Let the woman and her husband get out of town."

Hangings and near hangings were interspersed with sporadic Indian raids, most of them without fatalities. At each alarm however, one of the women, Mrs. W. D. Griffith, would rush to the closet where she kept her treasured wig. She said that if and when she was scalped the Apache would get her "falsie" and not her own locks.

Ghosts have made their presence known in Shakespeare where in most deserted towns they remain secluded. Several spectres have become familiar through reported appearances, one preferring to attract attention to his sulphurous aroma. This one "lives" in the basement of the adobe residence of Mr. and Mrs. Frank Hill, used as a school about 1905. During a lunch hour the children amused themselves by digging in the dirt floor of the basement, unearthing a number of bones which the teacher identified as human and ordered them reburied immediately. Since then, at intervals of several months, the ghost comes upstairs, companionably emitting faint sulphur fumes "like the odor of a struck match."

"Be wary of the shadows!"

TYRONE, NEW MEXICO

The unprepared ghost town hunter, arriving in Tyrone, can hardly be blamed if he rubs his eyes in disbelief. Palaces in Spain must have been the models of the dazzling, rococo mansions and public buildings lining both sides of the street in opulent splendor. It is a dusty and deserted street. The ornate arches along shady corridors are crumbling and there are long cracks on the plastered walls of the depot. Patios and pavilions are centered by stone fountains long dry. Where emerald lawns bordered by flower beds once flourished, dry clumps of desert grasses and sage brush now share the courtyards with shriveled corpses of trees and shrubs. Behind these crumbling shells, once so splendid, the hill rises sharply then levels off just enough to give space for an impressive assemblage of imposing Mediterranian-style homes, stuccoed and tiled. Here again are the signs of ruin and crumbling decay, broken windows and fissured walls show that this is no lush resort on the Riviera. Tyrone is indeed unique among deserted towns.

When white men came to the Burro Mountains in the early '70s, they found a marvelous climate, beautiful scenery and Indians busily engaged in the mining of turquoise and copper. Winters in the valleys at the base of 8,035 foot Burro Peak are mild and sunny, summers are warm, there is just enough rain to nourish the typical desert vegetation consisting of juniper, pines, live-oaks and clumps of bear grass. June and July see the magnificent white plumes of "Our Lord's Candles" (yucca radiosa) rising ten or more feet above the valley floor.

But the early whites were interested only in mineral wealth. Their first burrowings were scattered all over the hills, in time became consolidated in larger mines as companies with capital took over. The major operation by 1904 was the Burro Mountain Copper Co. About this time the giant Phelps-Dodge Corporation became interested in the manifestly rich copper deposits in Tyrone and bought an interest in the Burro outfit. Pleased with the results produced under improved methods the Phelps-Dodge people infiltrated the workings until they were the major owners of the whole operation.

There had been two distinct settlements haphazardly growing up near the two main groups of diggings, Leopold and Tyrone. These now became one. Although there were good showings of zinc and lead, they were by-passed in favor of the more available copper. The fact that turquoise existed in the Burro seems to have been kept under wraps —nothing must interfere with King Copper. Ore had been shipped laboriously by wagon and ox team to Silver City where the smelters were, but now a railroad spur was extended from the Deming-Silver City line.

Up until this time Tyrone looked like any other mining camp of that day. The dream of making Tyrone the most beautiful mine town in the world was born in the brain of Mrs. Dodge. The New Tyrone would rise like Phoenix from ashes of the little frame buildings with typical false fronts that had been Tyrone. Her first step was to invite to this New Mexico wilderness the famed architect Bertram Goodhue from his home on the French Riviera. Goodhue also designed the famous buildings of the Panama-Pacific Exposition, San Diego, in 1915. The same fundamental plan was worked out for Tyrone with long arcades along the main boulevard. These were actually covered walkways giving access to stores and public buildings. Mrs. Dodge envisioned a resort town with a large steady population, augmented by a huge influx of tourists in the delightful winters of the valley. The T. S. Parker Hospital was constructed on a rise above the "downtown section," it was amply large and well equipped to take care of several hundred patients. The depot would handle a large volume of traffic and the stores were to carry the largest and most modern line of merchandise to be found anywhere in all New Mexico.

The principal buildings beside the hospital and depot were four large commercial structures, a handsome school with ample capacity, a Catholic church and an office building for the company headquarters. All these structures were planned and built on the grand scale, with no consideration of expense.

A large residential section was laid out on the bluff above the town and filled with handsome homes, many of them imposing two story structures, all in the same old world style. They made a brave and colorful showing in pink, cream, blue, tan and white, each with a tiled roof of red.

More than a million dollars had been spent building the new town and now in 1915 all was ready for occupation. But something was obviously wrong. While a few people bought houses on the hill and others rented several of them there was no influx. There were alarming rumors being circulated that the rich copper deposits were not so rich as before, and some mines were frankly depleted. Rumors became established facts and no one wanted to move to a failing operation. Added to these calamities was the depression following the war, and in 1921, only six years after Tyrone was completed, the mines closed down and everyone moved away. Everyone, that is, except a skeleton crew in the now shrunken office of the Phelps-Dodge Co.

Tyrone's palatial buildings have been crumbling for more than forty years and have long since ceased to be useful or safe for occupancy. At intervals tiles come tumbling down from the roofs, chunks of masonry or stucco break off from the walls to come crashing down on the paved but cracking walks. Because of the extreme danger, visitors, while welcome to look from the safety of the road, are forbidden access to the buildings. Some of the houses on the heights are occupied by summer vacationers, rentals range from $17.50 per month to a top of $35.00 for the most luxurious homes. There is abundant water and electricity. Tyrone harbors the thought that its ghostly aspect would disappear if it were near a big city.

"PORTALES" — COVERED WALK — ceilinged by exposed beams—"vigas"—runs along entire length of two-story, imposing building planned to house general store, other commercial establishments. Street is at left, view looks toward railway depot.

WATROUS, NEW MEXICO

Soldiering "Out West" was all right, except for the twenty-four hour leaves. Most of the time all you had to do was see you didn't sleep next to a rattlesnake or let some Apache get close enough to put a hole in your ear. It was those floozies in town that put your foot in the gopher hole.

Soldiers on leave from old Fort Union were offered a choice in places for hell raising. Las Vegas had more kinds of bordellos but it was twenty miles farther than Watrous. The correspondent in that town contributed this item in the Las Vegas OPTIC of November 28.

"One of the soldier boys from Fort Union came to our town to have the pleasures of gambling his money at our saloons. After four or five hours he came out without much success, and insisted on our citizens to loan him money, which they did, and after having success on borrowed money failed to divide up, after which harsh words ensued between parties and causing our soldier to receive one eye loss. Our doctor claims the eye is ruined. We feel sorry for his losing his eye, and also his money. Would not consider it a safe and pleasant place for boys to come and spend their money."

When the boys wore out their welcome in Watrous, they turned to even smaller Loma Parda which soon got tired of roistering soldiers, boarded up all business places and closed up. Then back to Watrous went the soldiers and back in the news they came, just after Christmas. "On Christmas Day," wrote the OPTIC correspondent, "there was horse racing at Watrous as well as at Tiptonville. The school children went from Watrous to Tiptonville (where the Mission school was located) to sing Christmas carols. All was quiet until the body of a soldier from Fort Union was found in the Mora

TWO WELLS about six feet apart showing water table was near surface and well digging easy. Watrous was built on point of land at junction of Mora and Sapello Rivers, first settlement called La Juncta de los Rios. Well nearest camera served cabin behind photographer, house shown one of group built in earliest days of town, all fashioned of logs, brush, anything available, then covered with thick layer of "stucco"—hard-setting native clay.

River. Since the excitement caused by the visit of four drunken soldiers and the finding of the dead body of one of them in the Mora River a few days afterwards, nothing has happened to disturb the quietness of our town until last Sunday. On that day a rumor reached us that soldiers from Fort Union were coming to raid our town in revenge for their comrades. But they didn't come which was fortunate for them as our citizens were prepared for anything of the kind and any visitors on any such errand will meet with a hearty reception, and find they have not got another Loma Parda to deal with. It is but justice to state that the better class of soldiers at the fort, together with the officers, condemn any such demonstrations, and the perpetrators of the last outrages will be severely dealt with."

In the early days Watrous was known to Indians and Mexicans as La Juncta de los Rios, the name describing the location of the village at the junction of the Mora and Sapello Rivers. Originally a meeting and barter place for pueblo and plains Indians, it became the gathering area for sheep herders from Las Vegas, Mora, Abiquiu, La Questa, Antonchico, Albuquerque and Manzano. Nearby were camps of transient comancheros, Comanches, Utes, Kiowas, Cheyennes, Arapahoes, Navajos and Apaches.

By 1801 the spot was where mule trains of all sorts stopped, most of them carrying cargo valuable in a land where comforts of civilization were few. They attracted bandits who could sell stolen tobacco, jewelry, furs and other luxury items. Yet in spite of constant depredations, the beauty of the locality with ample water supply and extensive green pastures for stock was so appealing many merchants — drivers tarried and even settled down to stay.

New Mexico was still under Spanish control for not until 1821 did it become independent, then a province of Mexico and in 1848 a part of the United States. It was the age of land grants and Governor Armijo was known to be generous in bestowing vast acreages upon prospective settlers. At Juncta de los Rios a group of farmers banded together, drawing up a formal petition to Armijo for the surrounding lands. While legalities were pending, raids by

STONE HOUSE, walls covered with clay mud, then finished with finer clay and painted. Long unused, building served many purposes — saloon, dance hall, store. During '80s it was remodeled for livery stable, blacksmith shop. Many other original buildings remain in Watrous.

marauding Jicarilla Apaches discouraged some petitioners but the steadfast were eventually rewarded with deeds to the property.

When Samuel B. Watrous arrived on the scene he was footloose and fancy free, not interested in land grants. When he did decide to settle down he was too late for the free land deal and was forced to buy his farm from one of the original grantees. Born in Connecticut, orphaned at an early age, Sam was sent to live with an uncle in Vermont. The boy resented what he thought was undue discipline imposed by the uncle together with very early rising, before breakfast chores and day long hard labor. He fled, joined a wagon train heading west, arrived in Taos, New Mexico, to work as clerk in a store. Young Sam quickly caught the popular fever and headed up the Rio Grande with a gold pan at every chance. The virus hung on and he gave up the clerking job for the booming placer mines of San Pedro. The good ground was all taken and finally discouraged with mining, he married and went back to storekeeping, this time on his own, in the village of San Norios.

In a few years he fell ill and forced outdoors by doctor's warnings, he left wife Josephine to run the store and took off for the hills. He spent much time with various Indian tribes and acquired knowledge of their ways which was to prove valuable in later years of frequent clashes with raiding Apaches.

Now the wanderer made up his mind to earn his living on a farm and cast his eye on part of the parcel called La Juncta de los Rios. After years of legal delay, title was finally cleared and in May, 1846, Sam Watrous bought out Richard Dallam's interest in the grant. Josephine joined her husband, the farm and business affairs of Samuel Watrous flourished and he became a leading member of the community.

One of the larger enterprises was the general mercantile, operated by partners Watrous, Thomas Rice and Sam's son-in-law, William Tipton. This was broken up in 1865, Sam's son Joseph becoming the new partner, the store operating as S. B. Watrous & Son. It was about this time the Watrous herds and flocks pastured near Tucumcari were being repeatedly run off by Comanches and Kiowas, Watrous' locally good relations with Indians apparently not extending to that area.

Then in 1879 came news that the Santa Fe Railroad would build through La Juncta de los Rios and public spirited Sam and son promptly donated land for right-of-way, station and yards.

But Sam was most surprised of all to see WATROUS on the new depot's name board. Officials told him it was the least they could do and moreover there was already one station named La Juncta de los Rios in Colorado.

S. B. Watrous & Son also donated land for a park, fenced it, planted trees, all providing if and when the county seat came to Watrous, the courthouse would be erected on it. When neighboring Mora got the prize the Watrous interests did not sulk but set about getting a fine new school house, donating land and initiating a campaign for building funds. At first the project seemed to be a success but it fell through when pledged money failed to materialize. The disappointment to Watrous was all the more bitter because the upstart neighbor Tipton, which did get the school, was founded by son-in-law William Tipton, Sam's ex-partner.

There might have been biological reasons for the school going to Tipton. Its founder also started a population explosion sufficient to fill it. A roster of pupils in 1881 shows two Watrous descendants, Charles and Rose, followed by Lizzie Tipton, Susan Tipton, Martin Tipton, Louise Tipton, W. B. Tipton, Tom Tipton, Charles Tipton, Ella Tipton and several less numerous representatives of other pioneer families.

Another newspaper item, this one dated February, 1888, shows that life at Watrous and environs continued to be as interesting as in earlier days. "James Lafer, who was arrested at Watrous, was wanted for a murder he committed in Olean, New York in 1882, for which his twin brother served two years imprisonment but was pardoned when he turned out to be the wrong man. This Lafer was run out of Las Vegas as a bad character. He worked as a cowboy and was known as a rustler. He would shoot on the slightest provocation. On more than one occasion he cleaned out the town of Watrous, riding in and terrorizing the people by firing revolvers promiscuously through the streets. He once rode into Fort Union in the middle of the night and tried to assault the sentry who was walking post but was captured and slightly wounded in the melee. In Loma Parda he is still remembered as the man who picked up a New Mexican woman in the street, placed her across the horse in front of him, and rode into the saloon, making the bartender set up drinks for the whole party, and because his horse would not drink, he shot him through the head, lifted the woman from the saddle before the horse fell, and walked out, leaving the horse dead on the floor."

"... being drawn forward as though by an invisible cord!"

WHITE OAKS, NEW MEXICO

John J. Baxter was a disenchanted '49er. For every one who got rich in Calaveras county and other gold diggings in the Mother Lode, a thousand got only broken picks. Many of them left California for the glitter of other fields and Baxter was one of them, wandering eastward into the territory ruled by the Spanish and Mexican military. He found natives from San Antonio, Luis Lopez, San Marcial, Valverde and Socorro escaping the watchful eye of soldiers from the presidios and searching for gold. And there were rumors that some of them found it.

Baxter was curious and vigilant. He tracked one of the peons down a gulch, part of the shallow canyon running east from a mountain to the arroyo which later would form the western boundary of White Oaks. Having had experience with the rigors of solitary digging, washing and panning, Baxter took into his confidence John H. Wilson and John Winters and proceeded to the spot with whatever primitive equipment they could scrape up without creating too much attention.

They did find gold there—lots of it. What they did not find was water. The camp had to be two and a half miles away where the springs were. There were two flows, generous ones for so dry an area, surrounded by a grove of white oak trees. In the morning after breakfast, the men would set out for work at the diggings taking as much water as possible on the backs of several mules. This they would use as sparingly as possible to wash their pans of gravel. At night the

process was reversed, pay dirt went home with them and was washed where the water was.

Hard work paid off. Even little nuggets turning up to cheer the laborers. News of their find got around and when the summer was nearly over they had a visitor. He offered no information except his name was also Wilson. Some said he was from Arizona, others Texas. Most agreed, judging from his furtive manner, he must have a price on his head and wouldn't tarry long. The miners put him up for the night and fixed him a lunch for the next day.

Instead of going along with them to the gravel bed, the new Wilson set out for a walk up Baxter mountain to survey the country. While resting and eating his lunch he idly chipped off some interesting rock and put it in his pocket. He then took a good look around from his vantage point and returned to camp. At supper time when all were assembled, the chips were displayed. Excitement grew as the more experienced miners confirmed what Wilson had only guessed. The whole group hurriedly took lanterns and retraced Wilson's steps, finding the spot without too much trouble.

Early next day stakes were set out and Wilson was asked how much he wanted for his share. He said that gold was of no use to him, he'd have to go, and whatever the others wanted to give him would be all right. He took the offered $40 in washings, $2 in silver, a pistol and another lunch and was on his way, disappearing from the pages of White Oaks history. The others realized $300,000 apiece not much later when the mine was sold as the Homestake. The original claim returned a total of more than $3,000,000 during its useful life.

The early days of gold discoveries in White Oaks were somewhat frenzied even allowing for the florid style of reporting in the newspapers. The *Albuquerque Journal* for April 6, 1881 touches on some of the finds. "One pocket being found from which in one day there was taken by the men over three hundred dollars. For several weeks thirty dollars was average for each man . . . on March 1 was struck another body of ore with gold visible to the naked eye all through the rock . . . An assay of a piece of ore from the last find, showed no free gold, was made on March 24, resulting $17,000 per ton, flour gold. Surprise to relate, the float from this vein, on the side of the hill and the bottom of the canyon, near where the last gold was found on the last soil being washed from it, shows free gold sticking to it on all sides and on breaking gold appears all through the rock. . . The Old Abe seems to be an immense deposit of gold bearing rock. The deposit is about a hundred feet in width."

The town itself grew up on a flat of about 160 acres beside the stream bed. The founding date was August 15, 1879—a tent city growing up even before saw mills could be built or lumber freighted in over almost non-existent roads. Tents gradually gave way to shacks. The first real house was completed July 17, 1880 and occasioned a big celebration. Population in the camp was then about 800 (it was later to grow to 4,000). The growth was so rapid the burgeoning town was splitting its seams, it couldn't absorb all elements in orderly fashion and some sections acquired cognomens of their own. There was Hide Town where buffalo hunters spread their odoriferous wares for curing and tanning. Hogtown was composed of cantinas, gambling dens, brothels, dance halls and like places where the miner could be parted from his money.

The camp was a fertile breeding ground for newspapers, some of which lasted a while, others got out one or two issues. First to come out was the little sheet modestly titled *The White Oaks Golden Era.* A year later partners Fenn and Morse

EXCHANGE BANK OF WHITE OAKS — l a s t survivor on main avenue. Town had 213 houses in 1885. First President of bank was editor of White Oaks Eagle, John Y. Hewitt, whose crumbling mansion also still stands. One historian calls city "attorney ridden" because of plethora of lawsuits over ownership and profits of cattle, horses and mines. Total list of lawyers is long, those having offices over bank were Hewitt himself, W. C. McDonald, later first Governor of New Mexico under Statehood, and H. B. Ferguson, later delegate to Congress.

planned a new paper, *The White Oaks Scorpion*, but this one never even got going. Then came *The Lincoln County Leader*, *The Old Abe Eagle* and the *New Mexico Interpreter*. Each lasted several years. An ad in the *Interpreter* extolled the qualities of a commodity strange in a rough mining camp—Ah Nues Song Birds, "The best in the country, and his cages the most beautiful. Those desiring a lovely singer should give him a call. His prices are very low."

The water problem was solved by the discovery that the moisture table was only about fifty feet down. For more serious drinking "the cantinas supplied various brands of gutrot at fifty cents although quality stuff was higher. After you drank enough of the putrid liquid that had been mellowed by dead rodents, snakes and birds, the quality stuff tasted like poison."

Then there was the more enterprising drinking establishment which put on stag shows in its enlarged building and booked traveling companies such as the famed "Wallace Sisters." The place was called the Starr, after a popular prospector of that name. Not all troupes made a killing at the new Opera House. Sometimes performers were compelled to remain for further shows to get sufficient funds to move on to Socorro.

The least excuse called for a celebration in White Oaks, and such occasions as Independence Day necessitated a real rip-snorter. The whole town turned out to eat at a table "130 feet long, loaded with all the good things of life." Beer and liquor flowed freely and the usual quarrels flared up, though with not too many casualties.

Outlaws of every description left their mark on the town. Among these were Dave Rudabaugh, Joel Fowler, Jim Greathouse, Toppy Johnson and Billy the Kid, attracted to the camp's larger saloons, better entertainment and fancier women. Tall tales of cattle rustling centered in White Oaks. Those episodes in which Billy the Kid and his pal Rudabaugh were involved are bloody episodes in the history of White Oaks. These two had their hang-out at the livery stable belonging to West and Dedrick; many of their depredations stemmed from there. The Kid's contact man in White Oaks for the sale of stolen horses was a man named Wheeler. He was caught trying to handle too large a job, the disposal of thirty head turned over to him by the Kid and Rudabaugh.

JUNIPER-RINGED SCHOOL is imposing structure, best preserved in town, cost community $10,000. Teacher of earlier, smaller school was Mrs. McCinnis, who took over as principal when more elegant structure was completed.

SILVER TONGUED SALES-MAN made pitch for Singer Sewing Machine during week's stay in White Oaks, left most homes equipped with gadgets. House is built of adobe with annex of hand-adzed timbers with plenty of adobe mortar. Building materials, native to site were used in construction of many structures in camp like bistro where Jose Leal was master of ceremonies. On one occasion when *baille* was in progress there, Jose M. Ribera, full blooded Yaqui Indian crashed party. Guard had been posted at entrance for just such contingencies, attempted to stop Ribera, was succeeding when intruder was reinforced by friend Justo Salas. Indian entered, one shooting six-gun, other brandishing knife. General melee developed, ending with cracked skulls for several participants, death for Leal, Ribera and Salas. Mass funeral was celebrated next day.
Short time later Salcedo, full of White Oaks' special brand of rot-gut threw wild shot at M. Leecher in latter's home. Leecher picked up club, k n o c k e d weapon from attacker's hand, dispatched Salcedo with gun. Rash of killings continued, avoided in such smug items as story in New Mexico Interpreter for June 24, 1887, "There is no more orderly city west of the Allegheny than White Oaks . . . Our Supreme Court, M. H. Bellomy held a session on Wed. and Thurs. White Oaks is too peaceable to make this court a financial success and we hope it may continue."

In 1887 clamor for a railroad grew more intense. The *Interpreter* stated that "White Oaks is bound to be one of the best towns in the Territory. It has the precious metals and immense beds of coal right at its own doors and when the railroad reaches that portion of the country, White Oaks will grow rapidly." In 1888 rumors flew thick and fast, "it is generally understood that the Sante Fe road will . . . push from Socorro to White Oaks . . . The Kansas City, El Paso and Mexican Railway known as the White Oaks Line is being pushed with great vigor."

Property owners were called for a special meeting to allocate land for the anticipated right-of-way and station. Instead of making things easy for the railroad company, however, the town's business men decided that since the road "had to build into the city" they would make a killing and put a stiff price on the property, making no concessions of any kind. To their dismay, rails were laid through Carrizozo instead. Although the local worthies begged the company to come on any terms, it was too late. White Oaks had cut its own throat. The effects of this fiasco were far reaching; the town actually died of disappointment, at least it started downhill then and never came back. Family after family moved away and the remaining ones began to tear down vacated houses for fuel. Whole stretches of store and business buildings became empty and roofs fell in. White Oaks was on its way to becoming the ghost town it is today.

663

SOME ADOBE HOUSES in Lajitas were repaired, covered with new tin roofs during small uranium boom, others exposed to infrequent but heavy downpours, are already melting away. Adobe bricks vary from place to place in binders, extenders, but all have two common characteristics: basic material is native clay and bricks are unfired except by sun. Usually mixed with clay are stones (as here), chopped straw, weeds. These hoed into mixture with water, packed into wooden forms much larger than fired-brick shapes. Partial drying shrinks adobe enough to allow removal of form for further "baking." Adobe building stands solidly as long as roof is intact, walls weathering in rain only slightly. Once roof goes entire building melts rapidly away.

Texas

A BANDIT LIVENED IT UP

Lajitas, Texas

He was said to be a peaceful lad until he killed an official who raped his sister. Then the teenager Arango took another name and started a career of banditry and revolution. He made many raids on the Texas side of the border, some of them from the easy crossing at Lajitas, and set the state on edge, the army on point. This was Mexico's colorful bandit, Doroteo Aranga, better known as Francisco (Pancho) Villa.

It was naturally, before Pancho Villa, a peaceful village, lying on the Rio Grande River where it flows tranquilly in shallow reaches over easily crossed sand bars just before it plunges into the spectacular Santa Elena Canyon. Aborigines traveling the old Comanche War Trail stopped to rest or camp here overnight, water not being so readily available for many miles farther on. Perhaps some stayed longer, built adobe houses and planted gardens. Vegetables thrived in this region of mild winters, warm summers and plenty of water from the river. Spanish and Anglo explorers found Lajitas (meaning "little flagstones") a village of Indian and Mexican farmers and goat herders drowsing peacefully on the banks of the Rio Grande.

Although on a dirt road Lajitas was a port of entry and the United States took the precaution of sending army troops to protect the rich mining camps of the Big Bend area, by far the largest being Shafter and Lajitas. Gen. John J. Pershing and Lt. Gen. George Patton were there, their tenure

just before the advent of World War I. Villa was murdered in July of 1923, his death ending a period of prosperity of sorts for Lajitas.

It sprang to some activity as the main importation point of a plant growing in abundance on the Mexican side, useful in the manufacture of chewing gum. Locally called "candelia cactus," it was the source of a wax which supplied 45% of Wrigley's

CRACKED, FALLING PLASTER makes pattern on old adobe wall. Finishing plaster coating is simple mud, water mix, smoothed on and often whitewashed. Area in upper left of photo shows detail of brick and same-material mortar construction.

665

NATURE WRITER Donald Culross Peattie once said of those easterners who starved in western deserts, "These courageous greenhorns, these corn and beef fed farmers, these small townsmen whose food came out of barrels, sacks and boxes— how could they guess that the Lord had appointed any manna in the valley and shadow of death?"
Peattie was referring specifically to Bennet-Manley party in desperate circumstances, lost in Death Valley in 1849, but point could apply to thousands of pioneers who went hungry while succulent, sweet and nourishing pods of Mesquite bushes hung over their heads. "Mesquite" comes from Nahuatl Indian **mizquitl**, most common species in southwest **Prosopis juliflora.**
Bean pods of plant growing as shrub or small tree can be eaten in green state or ripe seeds can be ground into flour. Roots hold soil, trunk makes good fuel, fence posts, blossoms making excellent honey. Against these are vicious thorns, aggressive takeover of forage lands. Thorn shown here, upper left, explains why careless treatment of thicket is likely to draw blood.

need. Actually a relative of the Christmas time poinsettia and properly *Euphorbia antisyphilitica,* the plant has slender, rodlike branches about three feet high, almost leafless and growing vertically. Around 1949 there was a big boom in candelia but it ended when Mexico placed a ban of exportation of it.

Then came the atom bomb and the frantic search for uranium. Believing a fortune could be found in the Big Bend country, prospectors bought their supplies in Lajitas. The climate tended to dry their throats so the bistros there flourished. With dreams of uranium fortunes fading, the prospectors drifted away and Lajitas was quiet again.

The near ghost town is situated in Brewster County, largest in Texas and one of the most thinly populated. The community was without electricity until 1964 when all of fifteen meters were put into service. Lajitas has the reputation of being several degrees hotter than Presidio which often reports the highest summer temperatures in the United States. Spring, fall and winter months are the best time to explore the Big Bend country, preferably February to June. Even in summer months many high-elevation foot-and-horse trails in the Chisos offer cool comfort.

666

SILVER IN BANDIT COUNTRY

Shafter, Texas

The sun was good to John Spencer. He probably cursed the glaring, dazzling spot in the sky all day as its heat burned into his back and bounced up from the stony cover to blind him. Water was little solace as it disappeared so fast and his thoughts dwelt so bitterly on the damn foolishness of a Rio Grande rancher to go prospecting when he ought to go to town and get food for his kitchen. He was just about to quit and go back to camp when he saw, glinting in the dusty shafts of the near-setting sun, a shiny streak in a rock. It was nearly pure silver.

He looked around and found other pieces of float, deciding he had surely enough located a projecting lead of silver. Pocketing the sample he strolled back to his camp where "tame" Apaches were preparing supper, saying nothing of his find. The party got an early start for Fort Davis where Spencer purchased his supplies.

Some historians say John Spencer was one of the "original settlers" in the area but there is proof of white men being in that part of Texas in 1571. While some of these first Spaniards were "explorers," some remained to live along the Rio Grande, then called Rio Bravo del Norte. And before that

SEVERAL FAMILIES still live in few adobe cottages remaining more or less intact. Senora Lupe Munoz is lady alcalde of old mining camp, operating store, only business here. She attends to twice daily mail call at post office a block away. Spanish is prevailing language in village, only few of about 20 residents understanding English. Rocky foothills of Chinati Mts. seem entirely barren but support wealth of plants appearing exotic to northern strangers—many kinds of agaves, more cacti species than most southwest sections.

an advanced Indian civilization flourished there as long ago as 8,000 B.C.

Until Fort Davis was established in 1854, Milton Faver was the only Anglo-American to settle in the Big Bend country. Fluent in several languages, Faver was thought to have fatally wounded a man in one of the southern states and escaping to Mexico, joined a cattle train traveling north on the very long established Chihuahua trail. Crossing the Rio Grande at Ojinaga he dropped out to set up a ranch-fort at a point later called Cibolo. At that time the water table was much higher than now, creeks flowing abundantly and steadily to make a lush growth of grass. Faver ran cattle on his ranch and later at other nearby locations, Cienaga and El Morita. It was generally supposed to be impossible for a white man to hold out against marauding Apaches for any length of time but Faver did and others were encouraged to follow. Some lost their lives in Indian attacks but one who lived to thrive was John Spencer, his ranch a few miles from Cibolo as was the place of his silver find.

Adjacent to the military establishment of Fort Davis was the little town of the same name. As Spencer suspected, the assay office there reported

OLD SHAFTER CEMETERY lacks softening influence of green grass, shrubs, trees, is typical of burial grounds in arid sections. Area at right rear is "populated" by descendants of earliest settler Milton Faver. He died in 1890s, is buried on his Cibolo ranch, now inaccessible. His son Juan had daughter Francisca who married Ira Cline and still lives at Shafter, giving this reporter much of mining town story. "Many victims of mine accidents rest under those stones in cemetery," she said in Spanish. Identifying descriptions on wooden crosses are completely weathered away.

his sample to be heavily laden with silver but he kept his secret well. He was not known as a prospector, simply a rancher laying food supplies.

At the time there was an outburst of the always smouldering hatred between the original dwellers on the land encompassed by the Big Bend of the Rio Grande and the white settlers. Ranches were pillaged, buildings burned, women carried off. Could Spencer, in the face of widely scattered attacks, safely start and carry on a mining operation? To make sure he could Spencer shared his secret with Major Shafter, in charge of cavalry, and Indian fighter Lt. John L. Bullis.

Major Shafter, later made full general, must have been something of a financial genius. In San Francisco he raised enough capital to start the Presidio Mining Co., then joined his cavalry with the Seminole-Negro scouts of Lt. Bullis. Although the Chinati Mountains were teeming with lurking Apaches they had little chance against a concerted attack by trained soldiers and were soon all killed or put in full retreat. That left the field clear to start mining.

Everything needed for it was hard to come by being so far away from source of supplies. Machinery was at first shipped from the east by Southern Pacific to the rail crossing of the ancient Chihuahua Trail, thence to camp by freight wagon and assembled at the mill site on Cibolo Creek where there was an ample water supply. Furnace fuel was delivered on contract by a wood-cutting firm which stripped the fine oak and sycamore groves along water courses and pines from high elevations—which have never regrown due to lack of water.

Mexicans from both sides of the border nearby were employed as laborers, most of them honest and reliable. One who was not caused a small scale riot in Shafter a few years after the town was started. Always a drinker, he spent a good share of his payday dollars in one of the several cantinas and then declared he wanted a woman. Si, si—he

RUINED BUILDING is near mill site, was likely residence or office of mine, mill officials. Photo shows structure in brilliant, head-on morning sunshine. Accompanying photo shows building in late afternoon light with near-setting making star pattern in door opening.

could have one of those handy at the *burdel* on a back street but he wanted class. On the main pike he openly propositioned every senora and senorita he met and then attempted to rape a girl in the middle of the street. Free and easy citizens thought this edging beyond good reason and had the local constabulary grab the miscreant and tie him to a tree until he could be taken to the nearest jail, in Marfa.

During the night several miners untied the man, took him out of town and shot him to death. Fearing further trouble the company called in the Texas Rangers. The famous early law men arrived, quieted all outward signs of violence and departed without the actual culprits being identified. At a dance held soon afterward a quarrel broke out between those who sympathized with the lynch mob and those who favored the law. Gunfire and stabbings caused authorities to call the Rangers back which neither faction liked as they felt they could settle their own squabbles. Joining forces all gathered in a barricaded building and when the Rangers approached they were met by a blast of rifle fire which killed one and wounded several. The Rangers returned some fire, inflicting casualties on the rebels inside and held them trapped. Reinforcements arrived and they surrendered, allowed to return to their jobs after a short cooling off period.

All wood supplies for mill furnaces were exhausted by 1910 but oil was then available and hauled in by truck from Marfa. Mine shafts penetrated the limestone to pockets of silver at depths of 700 feet. Writing for *True West*, Robert Graham says some of the silver concentrations yielded as much as $500 per ton of ore. By 1913 mules used to haul ore from mine to mill were replaced by tram and in 1914 came the exciting period of the Mexican Revolution and Pancho Villa.

Villa, deeply involved in the revolution that deposed dictator Don Porfirio Diaz and installed as president Francisco Madero, retired on funds supplied by Madero. He went to live in Juarez, El Paso on this side of the border not offering the luxuries he wanted, but leisure was not Villa's "kind of country." When President Madero was assassinated by Don Victoriano Huerta, Villa planned a coup against Huerta. He had friends in Ojinaga, Mexico, but could not go there safely with Huerta in power, so he looped around by way of El Paso, Valentine and Shafter. He rested at the mining camp and went on to the border, marshalling willing forces at Ojinaga.

At once Villa set out to attack his bitter enemy Gen. Orozco who had once sentenced the bandit to death for horse stealing, a fate escaped through help from Madero. Orozco and forces were routed, fleeing into Texas, a flagrant violation of neutrality laws. According to common rumors he knew the area around Shafter, had in 1913 escorted Gen. Luiz Tarrazas to an abandoned mine shaft there to conceal a fortune in gold and silver the absconding general had spirited across the Rio Grande. And this time Orozco was carrying some $80,000 in bills of large denomination.

Encountering a party of Americans he exchanged gunfire with them, hurriedly buried his loot somewhere on Eagle Mountain and slipped into Shafter to hide out with old friends. According to the tale once the heat was off, Orozco retrieved his fortune and added it to the hoard in the mine tunnel. Then he recrossed the Rio Grande, hoping to return eventually and secure his treasure to live the life of leisure in Mexico. What he had not counted on was the implacable hatred of Pancho Villa who was hot on his trail. He died while still running from the bandit without revealing the location of his cache of riches.

At its peak operation there were 4,000 people in Shafter, 500 men in the silver mines, prosperity for town and company lasting until 1931 when the price of silver dropped to 25c an ounce which brought mining to a grinding halt. During Pres. Roosevelt's time silver values rose to reactivate it.

In WPA days Shafter was said to have a population of 300. "It is a far cry," says the Texas Writers' Program, *Guide to the Lone Star State*, "from urban luxuries to this village of adobe houses tucked away in this mountain wilderness. Hidden trails to the south are still frequented by smugglers and raids by Mexican bandits occur. Life is often lonely for officials of the mines. Free barbecues are a favorite pastime, but owing to the difficulty at times of freighting in sufficient refreshments for the guests, invitations for such festivities have borne the initials B.Y.O.B. (bring your own beer)." This level of activity lasted until 1942 when mines were again closed, this time the machinery removed which seemed to ring the death knell.

But in 1954 the few people left in town were thrilled to see surveyors and prospectors employed by Anaconda Lead and Silver Co. working in town and the surrounding Chinatis. Rumors circulated that the firm would resume mine operations, that ore would be hauled to Marfa for refining since no water existed in Cibolo Creek except in unpredictable floods. Anaconda said only that its men had located vast reserves of high grade lead and silver in the Chinatis, but their men went away and never came back.

Today Shafter is very quiet industrially. There is no grind of tramway cables or noise of revolving ball mills, and there are no Mexican mine workers singing ballads in their homes in the evening. Yet an inspiring medley of sounds does reward the ghost town scout who camps overnight in some thicket of mesquite trees on a deserted back street. Morning brings cascading bird songs and calls unequalled in the west. Chirps, trills and cadenzas are linked together by the varied overtones of mocking birds, more numerous than any other. Not too intrusive is an occasional challenging rooster crow from the yard of one of the ten families remaining to remember a lively past.

ARID SOUTHWEST AREA generally is lacking in timber. Early builders here erected structures of material available, the earth underfoot. Clay was mixed with water, often combined with straw, weeds or other binder, then shaped into large bricks and laid in hot sun to dry. Walls made of adobe blocks were almost proof against heat and cold, but vulnerable to rain, lasting until protection of roof failed, then slowly succumbing to weather.

ADJACENT TO OLD HOSTELRY were stables, "parking places" for wagons. Study Butte has had minimum amount of vandalism, possibly because old store was more or less continuously occupied.

GENERAL VIEW of Study Butte shows company offices in foreground, stables in middle distance left, still operating store near center. Fringes of hills, mountains in background, lie across Rio Grande in Mexico. Photo was sent author by Texas State Highway Dept. with information, "Considerable activity has recently been noted at Study Butte, but information as to nature is unavailable and property is now posted. Assumption is that quicksilver mining will be resumed soon."

SIMMERING in one of U.S. hottest spots are ruins of adobe buildings that housed company offices at Study Butte. With protective coating of plaster gone historic building is not long for this world.

THREE TONGUES — THREE TOWNS

Terlingua, Texas

Old Terlingua was situated at the junction of 50 mile long Terlingua Creek and the Rio Grande. When the first Spanish speaking travelers arrived there well before 1800 they found a village of adobe huts and corrals built of spiny ocotillo canes. The natives were peaceable Indians but savage Apache tribes attacked at intervals, driving out both Mexicans and Indians. The natives invariably returned to find homes destroyed, domestic animals driven off or killed for food.

About 1859 a troop of U.S. Cavalry arrived with supplies on backs of mules and camels. They did not remain permanently but the threat of unexpected return had a restraining influence on the raiders. Yet the menace of them was not removed until 1880. The name Terlingua almost certainly corrupted from the Spanish *tres lenguas* but what were they, the three languages? Originally the name referred to a tiny Indian village on the banks of the Rio Grande just above its plunge into the narrow-walled Santa Elena Canyon. Early Spanish explorers are said to have found the Indian inhabitants of Terlingua speaking three distinct idioms. Another theory is that after some Spanish and later Americans settled in the area, the three languages were Indian, Spanish and English.

When cinnabar was discovered in the hills just

IMPOSING MANSION on hill was placed to allow superintendent's observation of entire town and mine workings. Built by owner Howard Perry but not used continuously by him. He spent most of his time in Chicago after Terlingua mines were well established. Smaller adjoining structure at far right served first as stable, later as garage.
During period when Pancho Villa was raiding border towns, Perry made hurried visit to Terlingua, ordered superintendent to sandbag and barricade parapets of house, keep guards posted with order to fire on any suspicious strangers. "Constable" Bob Cartledge soothed excited owner, argued that constant presence of U.S. troops not far away would be enough protection.

LONG, BRICK-PAVED CORRIDOR follows entire east length of house. View here to southeast shows old store framed in second arch from left. Barren Hills at rear are still in Texas, those at extreme right part of Sierra Mulato, Chihuahua, Mexico. Mansion has no inner hallway, all offices and first floor rooms opening on walk. Each has fireplace and wall-recessed shrine.

above the old village, the town growing up around the mines was also called Terlingua, or Terlingua-Chisos, the name of the largest and oldest mine. In further complication, when these mines were flooded out underground in 1942, what was left of operations went near the still-producing Mariposa mine, a post office named Terlingua established there. So there were three towns of the name too.

Just who found the first cinnabar in the area? There is no record but a modest amount of the brilliant red, softish, mercury-yielding rock was mined around old Terlingua. The cattle wranglers, Devine McKinney and Jess Parker, who accidentally found a red outcropping while rounding up some stray cows were not aware of its potential value. They secured the cows and went back to do enough digging to believe the deposit was extensive and perhaps worth claiming.

Discreet inquiry revealed the property had recently been acquired by a man completely unknown in the area, Howard E. Perry. McKinney and Parker learned he was in the lumber business in Portland, Maine, and wrote to ask if he would sell his Texas property. Not hearing for several months they wrote again and still heard nothing.

There was a reason. Perry was thinking. Described by Texas historian Ed Syers as "tight-fisted, close-mouthed," he suspected a reason behind the unusual interest and hired lawyer Wingfall Van Sickle of Alpine, 90 miles distant, to get the facts. Van Sickle rode a horse to the Indian village, pronounced the reason as cinnabar and by urgent message advised Perry to secure title to the property firmly and start mining. Perry heeded the advice, went to Terlingua, set up full scale operations and hired experienced Robert Lee Cartledge of Austin to manage the property.

677

The quicksilver operations started under extremely primitive conditions. All equipment was hauled the 90 miles from Alpine over a sandy trail in the river washes, wagons of the old Studebaker freighting type hauled by twelve Spanish mules used to profanity. And the finished product, mercury, was shipped north by the same means.

While sometimes found in the pure state the metal is almost always combined with sulphur to form cinnabar, mercuric sulphide. The Terlingua area ore is brilliant vermilion, soft enough to rub off on the hands and for use by Indians as war paint. Piles of ore, ready to be roasted for separation of quicksilver, still stand near the old Rain-bow mine at Study Butte near Terlingua, appearing like heaps of glowing coals in the hot sunshine.

Terlingua was always plagued by water trouble—too little above ground, too much in the lower levels of the mines. For a long time a tiny spring was piped downhill to a town tank, the precious liquid rationed at two pailsful per day per family. These were carried uphill by shoulder yoke to some tiny tin-roof adobe or ocotillo cane, mud-plastered shack. Or if the family owned a burro a carreta could be hauled to the Rio Grande for a full cask of that kind of water. Most of the time it was as said, "Too thick to drink, too thin to plow." Later, when ground water became a menace to the mines,

HEADFRAME in background. Built of bolted 12x12s, structure supported cable system operating two cages allowing continuous up and down traffic. Shaft drops 600', laterals at 50' intervals. Horizontal tunnels, interlacing, connecting total 50 miles in length, some reaching under old cemetery where miners killed in accidents were buried. At left background is waste dump, comparatively small due to richness of Terlingua ore. Rock houses, now roofless, were homes of better-paid miners, some officials. Ordinary laborers lived in tin or adobe shacks.

it was pumped out for the mills and domestic use.

The town was strictly company owned, right down to the little jail with iron rings in the floor. An industrious Mexican laborer could earn up to $2 a day and whether he spent it for food at the company store or tequilla at the company cantina, Howard Perry got it in the end. If an over-thirsty peon got drunk and was thrown in the company's own *carcel*, he could bail out with a fine. The company "court" got this too.

Ed Syers, author of *Off the Beaten Trail*, asked Bob Cartledge, retired in Austin, about the jail's leg irons. "We didn't use them," Cartledge said. "Just the sentence, 'report to jail on Saturday!' If he had a sick wife he could come when convenient." "Constable" Cartledge may possibly have forgotten

a few disagreeable incidents in Terlingua's history. The rings in the floor show signs of some use.

Perry's Chisos and Terlingua Mining Companies hardly paid their way at first. The demand for mercury fluctuates to an extreme. Gold discoveries in California in the late 1840s and '50s created a sudden need for the liquid metal used in gold amalgamation, mercury later driven off as steam, cooled and saved. At that time the only source was Spain, shipping a near impossibility. Luckily cinnabar was found in California at just the right time. In Terlingua the demand for mercury was moderate over the years, prices generally low, until World War I started when the demand boosted the town's economy to the point where $2,000

SEVERE BUILDING, strictly utilitarian, served as assay offices where steady stream of core samples drilled from deep-down bedrock were analyzed. Fading or expanding values in cores controlled direction of penetration in rock. Short distance from photographer is yawning shaft opening, many hundreds of feet deep, no head structure or barricade to warn of danger. In background is rear of officers' quarters.

REFINERY MILL, one of several almost open to the sky. Cinnabar, mercury ore, composed of metal combined with various sulphur compounds, was roasted for separation. While both mercury and sulphur are volatile, latter vaporizes first, is driven off without opportunity to cool, solidify. Quicksilver follows at slightly higher temperatures, (357°C - 675°F) is vapor-cooled and condensed into normal liquid form.

Finished mercury, named for speedy Greek god, was packaged in "flasks", steel cylinders. Threaded at one end, when filled they were sealed tight by steel screw-in plug. Fit must be perfect, quicksilver making way through tiniest opening, as hairlike tube in thermometer, and no sealing compound could be used for stopper because of danger of contaminating product. Flask weighed fraction over 76 pounds, equalling weight of pottery containers Romans used for mercury. They called heft **quintal,** 100 libre. Quart of heavy liquid would weigh 28 pounds.

was rolling in every day. These were Terlingua's golden years.

During this period the Chisos Company greatly expanded all facilities including the store. A six-pew church was built, brick factory, large hotel, several cafes, even an adobe movie house. Local baseball and basketball teams were said to equal all rivals in the area. About this time a company of infantry in the Texas State Guard, says Texas historian Dick King, was made up entirely of Terlingua men.

The decline that followed the end of the war brought panic to Terlingua. Perry over-extended his Chisos operations in a desperate attempt to maintain war-time prosperity, and lost all he owned. The property stood idle for a few years and some families remained in hope things would

pick up, most of these gradually moving away to leave but a half dozen houses occupied. In 1946 all residents were ordered out, homes dismantled and all valuable mill machinery removed, Terlingua becoming a deserted city.

Today it is a fascinating ghost, completely deserted except for a caretaker at the old store making welcome the few visitors who reach this remote area. A sign, posted conspicuously near the open gate, warns sternly of open, dangerous shafts. The warning is not over-emphasized. Everywhere there are yawning holes where a person could drop hundreds of feet. Running children and pets should be confined to the car. Summers are likely to be hot, with temperatures often highest in the nation, but a dry atmosphere relieves oppression.

OREGON
GHOST TOWNS

BY

LAMBERT FLORIN

Drawings
by
David C. Mason, M.D.

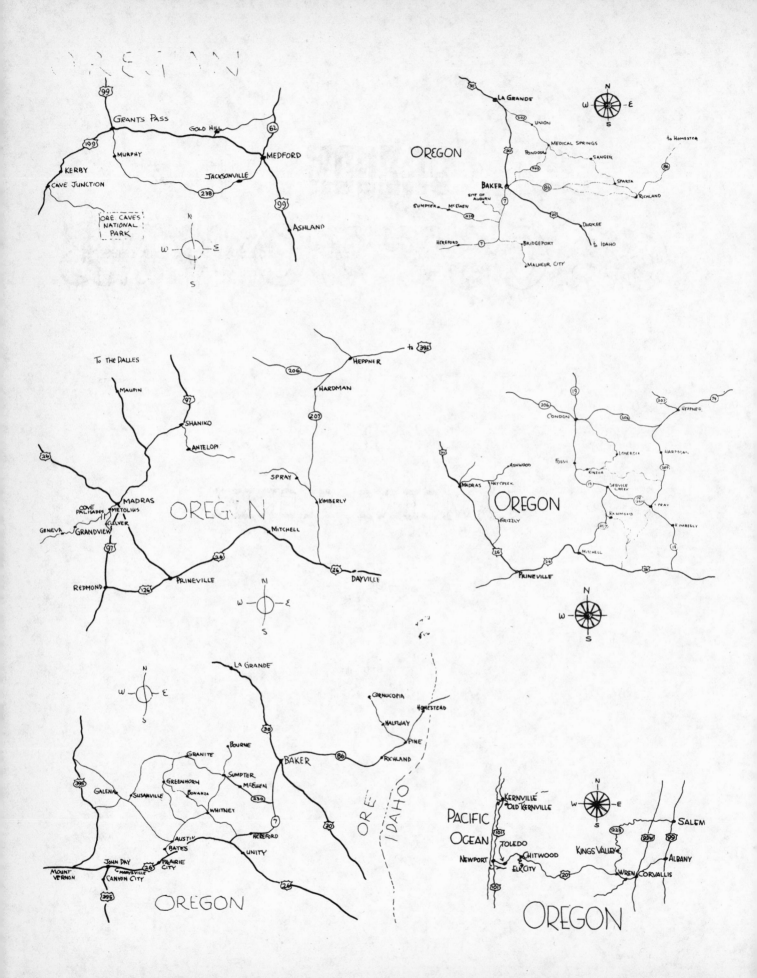

INDEX

CITY	Page	CITY	Page
Antelope	685	Kerby	783
Apiary	684	Kernville	734
Ashwood	688	Kings Valley	736
Auburn	691	Lonerock	740
Aurora	694	Mabel	742
Austin	697	Malheur City	744
Bonanza	699	Marysville	747
Bourne	700	Mitchell	748
Butteville	701	Narrows	751
Canyon City	704	New Era	754
Champoeg	707	Ortley	756
Chitwood	712	Paisley	760
Cornucopia	718	Richmond	763
Elk City	722	Sanger	765
Grandview	723	Shaniko	767
Granite	724	Shelburn	769
Greenhorn	725	Sherars Bridge	771
Hardman	727	Sparta	773
Hoskins	729	Sumpter	774
Jacksonville	731	Whitney	775

HISTORIC OLD HOUSE was built, in part at least, in 1888 by William L. Brown in Apiary, now nearly vanished. It was named for beehives of early resident David M. Dorsey. William Brown had married Irene Lowman in Olive Hill, Kentucky, in 1885, and the couple came to nearby Rainier in 1887, taking homestead claim the next summer. When house was built, the Browns had one child, their first one having died earlier. In house shown thirteen more children were born to them, eight sons and five daughters. The father died here in 1932 and until 1964 the house was still occupied by a bachelor son.

ANTELOPE, OREGON

The gay 90's were not only gay in Antelope, but punctuated by shootings and brawls in the best western town tradition. And in common with so many tinder-dry and nearly waterless towns, it suffered trial by fire in 1898 and was nearly wiped out.

Antelope is situated in a small valley of the same name, so called first by someone in the party of Joseph H. Shearer, who was engaged in packing supplies to the John Day mines in 1862.

The road to Antelope consisted of two ruts through the sagebrush in the 60's and for a long time thereafter. Stagecoaches bumping along over rough terrain ran more smoothly when they entered the little valley where so many antelope fed and watered. Passengers were glad to stop and eat or stay overnight at the stage station, newly erected. This entailed a little hotel and a blacksmith shop. Also, inevitably, came a saloon. This was owned and operated by F. W. Silvertooth, who had driven a stage from The Dalles to Canyon City and decided to settle here.

By the year 1871, the place expanded to the point where a post office became possible, and on the seventh of August it was opened.

A prime figure in the history of Central Oregon was appointed first postmaster, intrepid Howard Maupin, who left his print on so many places in the state. It was he who, tiring of having stock stolen by Chief Paulina, tracked that wily Indian down and killed him near Paulina Basin, putting an end to depredations that had harassed the pioneers in the valley for years.

The town grew apace, being a natural center for cattlemen and later sheepmen. It was a convenient stopping place for supply wagons and enjoyed prosperity for a few years. More saloons went up. One of these was run by partners named Benjamin Pratt and Ed Gleason. All was not harmony between them, however, as rumors were rife that Mr. Pratt fancied the wife of his partner. One fine morning in '85, as Pratt was unlocking the door of their business establishment, Mr. Gleason, a believer in gossip, walked up and shot his partner dead with a rifle.

The trial was a cursory Kangaroo Court sort of affair. It was decided that the outraged husband was justified in eliminating Mr. Pratt from the scene.

TINY STAGE AT END OF dance hall once looked on gay balls, Christmas parties, lodge gatherings and just plain dances.

R. J. Pilkington was Antelope's first doctor, serving the town all through the 90's. In addition to his practice, Dr. Pilkington operated a drugstore in the old saloon building.

The disastrous fire of '98 started in Tom Condon's Bowling Alley, above which were his family living quarters. After he had seen the women safely down, Condon's escape was cut off by flames. Outside the window was the pulley and rope by which water was raised to the apartment. Fortunately the bucket was at the top and ready. The resourceful Condon straddled the bucket and let himself down the rope. The town itself was not so lucky. After the holocaust, only one of the original buildings on the main street was left standing, as it still does today, at the far end of the street.

The town was rebuilt almost immediately, and things went pretty much as before. The little main street with its one surviving structure was solidly lined again, but this newer phase of the town's history was to end also. The town of Shaniko had been born only eight miles north as terminus of a railroad from the Columbia River. The new town drained off the population of Antelope and eventually left it an empty shell.

LITTLE CHURCH SERVED Antelope for many years. Now idle, its doors stand open and town's few children romp up and down aisle. Tiny filigreed organ waits near pulpit, is in working order, birds nest in walls, their nesting holes can be seen in clapboards.

THE JAIL HOUSE, standing west of the dance hall was convenient place to hold rowdies.

THE SILVERTOOTH ESTABLISHMENT also boasts a barbershop with business being conducted among relics of mining, cattle. Extensive rock collection completes resemblance of room to museum. Area is famous as source of agate of fancy quality, once abundant in huge chunks as "nuisances" in plowed fields. Gem stones are now much harder to find.

JAIL ITSELF WAS FRAIL, but "cell block" within was stout, and safely held most belligerent drunks, one of whom set fire to his thin straw mattress, hoping to escape in resultant confusion. However, fire hose was inserted through little window, drenching mattress *and* occupant, suddenly subduing the latter, completing the sobering-up process.

ASHWOOD, OREGON

"A volcanic butte and an early day family gave the ghost town of Ashwood, on Trout Creek in Jefferson County, its name," relates Phil F. Brogan, whose father owned a stock ranch seven miles east. "Near the site of the bustling village of the Oregon King mine days is Ash Butte. Settling close to it in the 1870s was Whitfield T. Wood and when the post office was established in 1898 the name of the butte was combined with that of the pioneer. The town grew on both sides of Trout Creek, spanned by a footbridge occasionally washed out by freshets, and into it for supplies and mail came ranchers from the range country.

"I remember all this as it was shortly after the turn of the century, with memories of riding into town from the east as a small boy to get the mail and pick up a few groceries. I can still hear the echoes of my horse's shod feet as we entered the big livery stable where the pony was rested and fed before starting home. When I walked past the open doors of saloons on warm summer days, I saw inside men standing at bars back of which were big mirrors. I have other memories of freight trains moving through town, headed for the end of the rails at Shaniko."

This part of central Oregon has a turbulent geological history. The area was covered at different times by lava flows and deposits of volcanic ash, layer by layer. As erosion progressed, many remains of long-extinct animals have been recovered which add to the store of valuable fossils in museums throughout the country. At the edge of one vast expanse of juniper trees, sagebrush and scanty grasses stands the prominent eroded cone which is Ash Butte, its sides covered by caked pumice and ash.

At the base of it, a promising region attracted pioneer Wood into settling there. The first spring

TYPICAL FALSE FRONTS of Ashwood's day. Saloon at left was one of several serving thirsty miners, ranch men and cattle drivers. Street once had small newspaper plant, printing weekly Ashwood *Prospector,* one of chain owned by Max Lueddeman. Editorials were embellished by florid prophecies of future wealth and productivity of Ashwood's mines and ranches. Town would grow to be "the metropolis of central Oregon . . . greatest producer of mercury ever known."

ASH BUTTE GRANGE for many years center of community affairs and even yet swept out for rare dances or celebrations. Was originally largest saloon in area, ground floor having bar on one side, small dance floor on other. Saturday nights saw wild times when cowboys, ranchers and miners "blew her in." Traces of windows upstairs can be seen. These opened into rooms for occupancy of short duration.

the little stream close by was a bountiful source of good water, the skies sunny and the soil soft and easily worked. But as spring became summer, hope became disillusionment. The stream shriveled and disappeared. The soil, composed largely of clay, turned as hard as concrete. Frosts persisted until late in the spring, freezing nights began in late summer. Discouraged at trying to farm in the face of these difficulties, Wood turned to raising cattle, a venture somewhat more successful, and soon the solitary rancher had neighbors, some as close as ten miles away.

"On a blustery March 27, 1897," recounts Phil Brogan, "Thomas J. Brown, herding sheep in a gulley

leading into Trout Creek picked up a piece of quartz from a brushy, rocky slope. It proved rich in silver and free gold. Soon a mine boom town, with its frontier saloons, hotels, livery stables and stores, took shape on the floor of Trout Creek about three miles from the mine, and became Ashwood. It was not a wild pioneer town. On Trout Creek to the west, a lonely cove reminded the villagers that pioneer days were past. In that cove, the raider chief Paulina died under gunfire many years before to end the Indian unrest in the area."

The Oregon King mine gave Ashwood its start but there were other big producers in the Morning Star and Red Jacket as well as several lesser ones. With no smelters or milling facilities at hand, the ore was shipped out. There was talk of building a stamp mill and smelter, the weekly Ashwood *Prospector* pushing the project, but signs of the veins pinching out appeared and no backers were to be found. As ores became lower in assay values, and in quantity as well, the town settled into a period of doldrums, enlivened only slightly by occasional periods of mining.

Then came the discovery and working of a vein of cinnabar over Horseheaven way and since Ashwood was the supply center, it revived and sat up. But quicksilver in paying quantities did not pour forth for long. The company pulled out all its machinery, leaving the building to shrivel in the sun. The blight spread to Ashwood, which never recovered.

Brogan feels a bit wistful when he realizes Ashwood holds few of its buildings of pioneer days. "Gone are the livery stables, the hotels, stores and homes built close to the edge of Trout Creek. Most were lost in fires. Ashwood was a town of one main street with winding roads serving as side streets. One led past the Woods' orchard to the Axehandle highlands. One headed upstream to the T. H. Hamilton ranch and the big ranches near the head of the creek. Still another was routed down creek to the Columbus, Friend and Howard Maupin ranches, and up Little Trout Creek to Prineville."

Today the town has an open, sun-washed look. Magpies fly across the dirt road which is the main street and coyotes close in at night.

BLEAK, FORLORN ASHWOOD SCHOOL stands on knoll, surrounded by typical junipers, only trees of desert regions of Oregon. Cupola had bell which rang well in advance of schooltime, its peals reaching far across sagebrush hills, warning tardy pupils walking several miles. Schoolyard, surrounded by barbed wire fence, once held usual two outhouses.

"Alone? No!
...there was something else!"

AUBURN, OREGON

"Sweet Auburn! Lovliest village on the plain,
    Where health and plenty cheered the laboring
    swain."

These lines from the poem, "Deserted Village," inspired the naming of many towns and villages in the eastern states and at least one in California's Mother Lode country. Then when a group of restless prospectors from those diggings christened the first collection of shacks in the new Oregon gold fields Auburn was again a sentimental choice. And prophetic enough, this Auburn has long since been deserted and nearly vanished.

Early in 1861 a party headed by Henry Griffen and his partner David Littlefield, on the way to the Orofino diggings in what is now Idaho, paused in Portland for rest and supplies. In one of the bistros a man named Adams was loudly claiming full knowledge of the fabled Bluebucket Mine. He referred to the tale of the Meek Party which in 1845 was said to have camped by a creek in eastern Oregon while children of the emigrants amused themselves picking up yellow pebbles in a blue bucket. On the way again this dangled under the wagon for a while and then was lost. Later, on hearing tales of gold found in the mountains the pioneers had a sinking feeling they had likely overlooked a bonanza and now knowledge of the place was gone. They remembered only vaguely the stream, thought it probably a tributary of the John Day or Malheur Rivers.

Now here was a man claiming he knew the exact location! Gold conscious Griffen and Littlefield, imagination warmed by liquor, could not get to the man fast enough. They engaged him to lead them to the Bluebucket site in exchange for keep and a percentage of the gold found. Setting out in high spirits, the small party reached the arid central portion of Oregon in good time and after an extended rest, started for the location Adams claimed to have pin-pointed.

Now the guide changed directions erratically. Griffen and Littlefield thought little about it until Adams made an about-face twice and told them to camp in a dismal place without wood or good water. After more uncertain movements, the partners had a conference, called a halt near the head of Burnt River and demanded an explanation. Adams was forced to admit he had not the slightest notion where they were or where the Bluebucket might be. The man was summarily sent out of camp without food, arms or blankets and told he would be shot if found following the party. One soft-hearted member did get some food to him to save his life.

Unable to agree on a traveling plan, the party split, the majority deciding to retrace their steps as nearly as possible. Shortly after crossing Blue Canyon at noon, October 23, 1861, they reached a good camping spot in a gulch. While Littlefield shot some game and made supper Griffin sank the inevitable prospect hole at the creek. Next morning they worked the hole further, panning when

HEADFRAME is only standing remnant of town, surmounts shallow mine. Hard rock mining was secondary to panning and sluice operations, amounting to so little usual piles of waste dumps are almost absent.

down to bedrock. Suddenly Henry Griffen was swirling and sloshing the sands faster and faster as though glints of the yellow metal were showing before the dross was poured off. When the residue came clear it was of such value excitement broke like a rocket. Pan after pan was finished with about a dollar's worth of dust in each, with even small nuggets here and there. At a feverish pitch the partners and others staked out claims, twenty-two that fateful day. Even the forlorn Adams, trailing at a discreet distance, was called up and allowed to peg out a claim of his own.

Four of the men—Griffen, Littlefield, William Stafford and G. W. Schriver spent the winter at the diggings, just able to build a cabin before a terrific storm blew up. With three feet of snow

piled up, the weather suddenly turned warmer and rains melted the snow so fast flooding was general in the mountains and valleys. The men found they could not work without rubber boots and in the middle of December set out for Walla Walla for supplies.

They carried a poke full of Powder River gold dust which was not only accepted by merchants but sent by them to Portland and exhibited in a store window with a story that two men working on Powder River half a day had cleaned up two and a half pounds of gold dust! Almost by the time the four miners got back to the diggings a gold rush had set in. By spring thousands of gold-mad prospectors were panning every stream in the area. The ubiquitous William Packwood headed

RUINED STONE WALLS are sole remains of building in hell-for-leather gold camp of Auburn. Thickets of brush and weeds obscure site of town, once one of largest in Oregon. Living apple tree near ruins testifies miners sought respite from sowbelly and beans.

a group that laid out the town of Auburn on Blue Canyon Creek in April, 1862.

A population of 6,000 quickly made it the largest town in eastern Oregon and one of the largest in the state and it became the county seat in September of that year. It had all the trappings of boom town tradition—saloons, hook joints, dance halls. Murders and lynchings were part of it. In November of that action-packed first year miner Jack Desmond and gambler Henri Larabee became involved in an argument with an underworld character, Spanish Tom. The gambling debt quarrel simmered for several days and finally erupted in a shooting that ended with the deaths of Desmond and Larabee. The dead men were respected citizens where Spanish Tom was not and he was promptly snatched from custody to be strung up in a pine tree. All three victims were added to the growing population of Boot Hill. Next year Henry Griffen died at 59, was buried there. The stone now over his grave credits him as being "discoverer of gold in Eastern Oregon."

Auburn aged as rapidly as it grew, going into such a speedy decline its importance in 1864 was less than the upstart Baker, 14 miles northeast, and in June, 1868, a state election voted the county seat to that city. Sometime that spring the records were spirited away "very early one morning" and hauled to Baker in a wagon. Auburn citizens woke up to realize the town had reached the final step of ignominy, was fast headed toward oblivion and decay.

SITE OF OLD AUBURN

ONE QUARTER OF A MILE NORTH OF THIS SPOT ON BLUE CANYON CREEK IS THE SITE OF OLD AUBURN, EARLY MINING TOWN AND FIRST COUNTY SEAT OF BAKER COUNTY FOUNDED IN APRIL 1862 AFTER DISCOVERY BY MEMBERS OF THE "ADAMS PARTY" THIS WAS THE GOAL OF THE FIRST HISTORIC GOLD RUSH INTO EASTERN OREGON.

THE POPULATION AT ONE TIME WAS OVER 5,000 ONE OF THE LARGEST TOWNS IN THE YOUNG STATE OF OREGON

SIGN ERECTED 1941 BY CO.644 CCC
WHITMAN NATIONAL FOREST.

SIGN ERECTED BY C.C.C. BOYS marks nearest approach of good road, rocky track leading steeply down into Blue Canyon to few remnants of Auburn's heyday.

AURORA, OREGON

If Cheyenne Chief Shot In The Hand saw the desert cavalcade he must have said to his medicine man in whatever way he said things to his medicine man — "Well, old herbs and skulls, I've seen everything now." Yet whatever the Indians did think of this "far out" procession on the Oregon Trail, they let it alone. Dr. Wilhelm Keil had a safety factor working for him.

The outfit would have startled any good honest settler. Leading the string of covered wagons were two mules pulling a hearse, inside it a lead-lined casket filled with alcohol in which was preserved the body of a nineteen-year-old boy. Beside the hearse rode several German band musicians playing doleful Teutonic hymns which were sung by others riding behind. Then followed the wagons with women and children and supplies of a large party head-

ing for the Willamette Valley. This was the wagon train of the fanatical religious leader, Dr. Wilhelm Keil and his followers.

Born in Bleicherod, District of Erfurt, Prussia on March 6, 1812, young Keil emigrated to the new world in 1836. Tailor by trade, he worked in a New York clothing factory and being diligent he would have done well but for his constant exhortations on religion among his fellow workers. They protested and Keil was discharged. German Methodism now took over his whole being and moving to Pittsburgh, he was ordained a Methodist preacher.

For a time dispensing gospel in the conventional manner satisfied his zeal but soon his radical tendencies set him in open revolt and he cut himself off from his church and moved to Shelby County, Missouri, where in 1845 he formed a colony of sym-

DR. WILHELM KEIL BUILT HUGE HOUSE in 1872 for favorite son and bride, architecture closely styled to "Das Grosse Haus" built for leader and family earlier. Mansion was stately but offered few comforts. Each of two floors has two large rooms, at end of each a large fireplace, only provision for heating and cooking. Resting on cedar stumps, practically indestructible as foundations, house is solid to this day.

FOUNDER OF COLONY is buried in family plot. Nearby is grave of daughter Aurora for whom village was named.

Willapa, Washington Territory, the originally planned destination, and Willie was buried there. After a short stay, however, Dr. Kiel became dissatisfied with the place as a permanent site for his colony and again pulled up stakes.

Arriving in the Willamette Valley, the Doctor selected a location on the west bank of Mill Creek, just above its junction with the Pudding River and near the Willamette which received the waters of both.

It was share and share alike for everybody except Dr. Keil and many of the names of the colony founders might have come straight out of the Prussian army — Rapp, Steinbock, Wolff, Koch and Koenig. All members were to live by these tenets: "From every man according to his capacity to every man according to his needs, is the rule that runs through the law of love. Every man or woman must be a brother or sister to every man and woman in our family under the law of God."

The autocratic leader set standards of modesty for the homes of colony members yet his own, one of the first to be erected, was three stories tall. It had four very large rooms, two on each floor. There was no central heating system, large fireplaces at each end sufficed for heating and cooking. Two large balconies with railings of turned spindles graced the front of the imposing mansion.

pathetic believers. Some six thousand acres were acquired, the center of it to be called Bethel, House of God. For a time the colony prospered but then came trouble — antagonism on the part of neighbors, several seasons of bad weather for crops and general discouragement.

By 1855 Keil had acquired the title "Doctor" and many ideas. The real New Jerusalem, he said, must be in the much talked about Oregon Territory and that was where the colony was going. The faithful gathered up their belongings, said farewell to loved ones and prepared to leave.

Also by this time the Doctor had five sons, the eldest named for his father and called Willie. He was nineteen and enthused about the trip west but was suddenly beset by malaria. Before he died he begged his father not to leave him in Missouri but take his body on the caravan and bury it in the new land. Following his promise, Keil placed the boy's body in the sealed casket with the alcohol and placed it on the lead wagon.

After four months of travel the party arrived at

ELIAS KEIL, born in father's house two years after it was built, two years before death of grandfather Keil, lived in structure all his life, never knew electricity or inside plumbing. Picture shows back porch covered by old grapevine.

Communal activities were varied and included working in the fine orchards and selling the fruit to neighboring settlers. A large furniture factory was set up, its products sold up and down the valley as were bakery goods. A fine band was organized, playing concerts from the balcony of one large building and for celebrations in neighboring towns. Dr. Keil was quite willing it should be so — for $50, of course. Proceeds of all projects were divided for the benefit of all — or so it was believed by devout members. Some detractors outside the colony claimed the funds went into a stout trunk which reposed under Dr. Keil's four-poster.

However no one in the colony seems to have suffered from want, especially of food. This item seems to have been all important in the progress of Aurora in true old country folk tradition. At all summer celebrations long tables were set up in the open and lavishly spread with German sausages, roasts, pies and pastries — all the rich indigestibles of peasant land. The band played loudly while everyone ate, the record says, and it is assumed the musicians had already eaten.

At Christmas huge baskets of cakes, fruits and candies were distributed to the colonists. Two large fir trees were trussed up in the forty by eighty church, where the altar was built in the shape of a star. Preaching and band concerts went on almost constantly, gifts accumulated under the trees until New Year's when they were passed out to the children.

Outsiders, even complete strangers, were welcome at all celebrations and came in droves. It was good business, spreading the good word of Aurora's products. When the railroad came through it stopped for meals at Aurora rather than at Portland which was much larger and only a few miles farther on. Schools operated the year around, allowing no such nonsense as summer vacations. Nor were any educational frivolities tolerated. Reading, writing and arithmetic were the only studies with the exception of music.

Dr. Keil's despotic rule prevailed for twenty-five years, then an undercurrent of change was felt. Many of the original colonists were aging, as was the leader himself. A younger generation was exposed to the outside world and this influence was working its way in. As long as the word of Dr. Keil was undisputed, the colony held together as a unit but he was failing, his word weakening, his grip loosening.

There was a reorganization, a deviation from the credo "Equal service, equal obligation, equal reward," yet still tempered to the older order while Dr. Keil lived. Upon his death in 1877, the colony was dissolved, all communally held property divided between members according to length of service. And as the years passed evidence of the original colony began to disappear, old buildings and houses falling victim to fire and slow decay.

Across the stream, on the highway, a town of Aurora grew up, somewhat as a development of the colony. It was a thriving community for years during the early twentieth century when it was on the main Pacific Highway and a center of the huge hop growing industry of the valley. It had at least one newspaper, the weekly AURORA BOREALIS, starting in 1900 and lasting eight years. Now the Portland-Salem freeway has bypassed the town which retains many reminders of more flourishing times. The community is beginning to realize the importance of its history and is making an effort to preserve its old buildings and visible reminders of its past.

SOUTH END of venerable house shows basement entrance at ground level. Elias Keil, grandson of colony leader, was born here August 17, 1875 and occupied it all his life. He played in famous Aurora Band most of these years, even participating in program at Aurora's Centennial in 1956 at over 80 years of age.

AUSTIN, OREGON

Austin was not itself a mining camp, but a supply depot for the many busy gold towns in the Blue Mountain area. The little narrow gauge railroad from Sumpter had its terminus here for many years in the earliest days, later being extended to Prairie City.

During this bustling period Austin was supposed by everyone to have a brilliant, permanent future. There were three large sawmills going full blast, turning out lumber for Greenhorn, Bonanza and other flourishing towns higher up in the densely forested mountains. A substantial jail was necessary for the many rowdies, drunks and more serious offenders. Several stores and office buildings for doctors, lawyers and real estate operators were built.

Already long established was the hotel and stagecoach way-station started by Mr. Newton. It was later bought by Mr. and Mrs. Minot Austin and called the "Austin House," giving the now growing community its name. The post office was incorporated in the building in 1888. The station was still being used as a hotel for hunters as late as W.P.A. days.

The decline of the gold camps spelled the death of Austin which had depended upon their existence. The population which had totaled about 500 at its height dwindled to 50 at the close of the second World War and is at the vanishing point now.

AUSTIN HOUSE LOOKS BETTER now than in photo of 1900. Wing extending south is long gone. Square structure on adjoining section shows at left. Original loghouse stands to right, out of range of camera.

LOAD AND PASSENGERS seem mostly to be on outside of stage in picture taken 60 years before our record. Picture was kindly loaned us by present tenants, the Alton E. Roods.

CENTER OF CITY GOVERNMENT in Austin heyday was this gaunt building. Inside on main floor are two stout cells with heavy doors with strong iron hinges and hasps. Upstairs were offices of city fathers.

ANCIENT LOG STRUCTURE dates back to earliest days of gold discoveries in Blue Mountains. Standing near Austin House, it antedates that building, is now regarded as "just the woodshed."

BONANZA, OREGON

Frank Roberts was an eager young man when he arrived in the rowdy mining town named after its main mine, the Bonanza. This was in 1900 and he planned to make teaching the mine roughnecks their three R's his work. And he did it, too, for a year or so. He had 25 to 30 scholars of all grades in the tiny Bonanza school.

At that time the big Bonanza mine had been operating since 1877 with a final depth of over 1,200 feet, and a thriving camp had grown up about it. Fifty men were employed in the mine alone and several were required to operate the aerial tram with its 20-to-30-foot towers suspending the cables well above deep winter snows. A constant stream of rich gold ore flowed down this web in buckets to be processed in the 20 stamp mills near the town, giving employment to another 40 or so.

Even this huge capacity could not process the increasing quantities of materials and the mill owners, about 1905, made the bold move of doubling the stamps. This was no simple job in such a remote mountain wilderness.

Pioneer Bonanza teacher, Frank Roberts, is now retired, living in Yamhill, Oregon, but he vividly remembers the various phases of that operation. "The snow was almost gone that spring when those 18 span of horses came up the hill from Whitney. They pulled two large pine logs laid parallel and on them was mounted the boiler necessary to steam power the 20 new stamps. They would come in a rush of 100 feet or so and then have to stop and blow."

During those days anyone could get a job and many did so, for the express purpose of "highgrading," pocketing "blossom rock," ore so heavily laced with gold that its theft paid more than wages. The practice was never wholly controlled and it was felt that many thousands of dollars were lost to the rightful owners this way. Even so, the estimates on total production ran from $1,500,000 to $5,000,000 and it is agreed that the Bonanza was one of the richest in the Baker sector. In addition, extensive placer, sluicing and dredging operations went on in the streams below the town, adding much to the total gained in "hard rock" methods.

Big operations closed down about 1910. Then Frank Dodson and his father took a lease on the property and worked it with more or less success for several years, after which the place died entirely.

MAIN STREET OF BONANZA is lined with ruins. Store on south side, near complete collapse, was center of commercial activity.

BOURNE, OREGON

Cracker was an honest, genuine gold mining and placering town in the 1870's and it had all the earmarks of the typical camp. A "Maiden Lane" section adjoined the several saloons and gambling houses; a large general store and hotel helped line the steeply inclined street. The main street was the only one, because the canyon sides all but squeezed out even that. At the upper end, however, there were several short, interesting "pieces" of streets perched here and there on the ledges. Each had its quota of businesses and residences in the days of Bourne's golden prosperity.

At the turn of the century Cracker began to deviate from honest mining and began to speculate. Somehow this more or less coincided with the change of name, although the new title honored a respected U.S. Senator, Jonathon Bourne. The Post Office of Bourne was established in March, 1895.

As Bourne, the place became a hotbed of inflationary get-rich-quick bubbles, all of which burst in short order.

Two newspapers emerged each week from the same printshop. One contained legitimate news. The other, meant for the outside world, promoted the myth that the town of Bourne was only a thin skin over a lode equal to the world's greatest bonanzas.

The closure of the post office in May, 1927, indicated the approaching end of this era and ten years later a cloudburst sent a wall of water down Cracker Creek and Main Street marking the finish of Bourne.

Enough remains to make a visit well worth while. Bourne is only about seven miles from Sumpter over a road typical of the more remote sections of the Blue Mountains, not good, not bad, not as steep as many, and lined with mementos of the boisterous days of gold placering along Cracker Creek.

UPPER END OF MAIN STREET of Bourne. Extensive foundations of large buildings are in background. Traces of all periods of former activity are scattered through town.

HYDRAULICKING GOES ON in small way along Cracker Creek below Bourne. Gold recovery still pays if not too much cost is involved. Here powerful head of water from small dam upstream is directed at gold-bearing mud and gravel; resulting thick liquid is channeled into sluice to settle out gold.

BUTTEVILLE, OREGON

The paddle-wheel steamer SHOALWATER was no more but her bones had been reshaped, her decks relaid, her defects covered with thick white paint. And there was her owner pointing proudly to her new name — FENIX. Funny name, people of the Willamette Valley said. What's it mean? "Why that," explained the owner, "that's the bird in the fable that rose up out of the ashes to fly again. See the point? I know how it should be spelled but this way I could make the letters bigger."

And what had happened to the SHOALWATER? One day in May, 1853, making her landing at the Butteville dock, above the falls where Oregon City is now, the Willamette River swollen by spring rains and flowing savagely, the skipper laid on all the steam she had and called for more. The SHOAL-WATER had the spirit but her flues were weak and a great blast rent the boilers. On deck ready to disembark, the passengers suddenly found themselves in the cold currents. All were in luck to be saved from drowning but none of them ever wanted to hear the name SHOALWATER again.

Etienne Lucier planted the first crop in French Prairie, a flat, treeless area along the Willamette about 1830. The crop was wheat and from then on, until about the turn of the century wheat was almost the only agricultural product of the area — this in a land where the soil was capable of producing anything suitable to a temperate climate. Wheat found a ready market and that was enough. The only real difficulty at first was getting the crop to that market since there were no roads, only the river, and cargoes had to be portaged around large falls and rapids at Oregon City and transferred to

OLD BUTTEVILLE — picture taken from opposite bank of Willamette River about 1890, judging from fact concrete dock has replaced wooden one on pilings. Most buildings shown have vanished but white frame house upper right, ornate one center right and plainer frame with porch extreme left, still remain. Section of deeply rutted road leading to dock gives some idea of difficulties wagons encountered on most roads in western Oregon's rainy season.

ORIGINAL LANDINGS were built on pilings, some remarkably preserved after 100 years or more. Level of river shown here is average. Willamette has become much more tractable in recent years with flood control in main river and such tributaries as Santiam which originates in Cascade Mountains, although even now it goes on rampage when snows melt rapidly or during protracted rainfall.

other craft for the rest of the trip to Fort Vancouver.

All this effort caused a rash of little towns to spring up along the Willamette between the present Salem and Oregon City. Butteville, at the extreme northern end of the wheat belt called French Prairie, was one of these. It was primarily a river landing and never progressed much beyond that although it did boast a church, schools, stores and several saloons during the golden period of wheat shipping.

Joel Palmer, the man who had pioneered a route for the first wagons over the shoulder of Mt. Hood, mentioned the settlement in his journal in 1845; "Eight miles from Pudding River is a village called Butes. It was laid out by Messrs. Abernathy and Beers. There were but a few cabins there when I left. The proprietor had erected a warehouse to store wheat they might purchase of the settlers, who should find it convenient to sell their crops at this point. At this place are some conical hills called Butes, which arise to considerable heights; the sides and tops of them are covered with tall fir trees which can be seen from the valley for sixty miles." All this was essentially true, the exceptions being one butte of noteworthy height and that only 427 feet, hardly noticeable except locally. His spelling of Bute was common enough in those days.

The village that grew up beside the first crude river landing about 1840 was first called by the preponderately French settlers La Butte but Americanized a few years later. When George Abernathy and Alanson Beers drove pilings at the edge of the river and laid out a simple town, they had big ideas of a metropolis that would outshine the rival Champoeg. For instance they planned to handle the buying and shipping of the settlers — almost to a man retired French Canadian trappers of the Hudson's Bay Co. — and later they would sell real estate, establish stores and saloons. Since there was little or no gold and business was done in trade, the rancher would get his pay in groceries and spend the rest of what he had coming for liquor or wine, Abernathy and Beers making a profit at every turn.

However this was not to come about. Abernathy became involved in the simple politics of the day and was so dedicated to seeing the provisional government get off on the right foot he was elected first governor of Oregon in 1845 and had no time to promote his interests in Butteville. The facts about Beers are obscure but it is known the first real store at the landing was started about 1850 by one Francis Xavier Mathieu, who talked the vacillating Etienne Lucier into casting his vote with the Americans at Champoeg (see Champoeg story).

Mathieu was one of the early French Canadian trappers who with the decline of the fur industry had settled on French Prairie in 1842. He lived with Lucier two years, making himself generally useful as a builder of wagons and houses, then married Rose Osant, daughter of another ex-trapper. Two years later he took a donation claim at La Butte. Mathieu had "a way with people" and after his successful persuasion of the deciding votes in Champoeg, he was elected constable, often settling disputes by inviting contestants to dinner and the difficulty was usually settled amicably over a bottle of French wine.

Mathieu decided against a comparative retirement to run the store. He cut trees on his claim and laid the logs for the lower half of the building and had some whipsawed for the upper section. Hand-adzed planks served for a floor and split cedar shakes for the roof. From then on for fifteen years Mathieu's Store was the most important place in Butteville. One good customer was Robert Newell of Champoeg, another the Hudson's Bay Co. emissary, Michael Framboise. For two years he had a partner, a George La Roque. A plat of Butteville in the Historical Atlas Map of Marion and Linn Counties, 1878, shows the La Roque claim as entirely surrounding the townsite of Butteville and seems to include it.

In 1860 an Episcopal Church was built, prudently quite high on the bank. Funds for construction came short of a bell but the congregation felt that God, in time, would provide. Next year the big flood that washed through so many river towns inundated Champoeg, wrecked the sister church there and carried its belfry, complete with bell, down to Butteville and depositing it in a thicket along the creek bank. Champoeg, utterly destroyed, had no more use for the bell, so it was joyfully reclaimed, cleaned of mud and hung in the Butteville steeple.

As long as there were few roads, and these almost impassable in wet weather, Butteville flourished. When rumors circulated that the Oregon and California Railroad would stop there, it was hoped farmers would continue to haul wheat in and that it would be shipped by train. But the rails by-passed Butteville and the town gradually faded. Today it is still alive, a tiny and picturesque hamlet with only one business, a modern little grocery store in one of the old, revamped buildings.

LITTLE OLD BUTTEVILLE SCHOOL shown here all prettied up and moved to grounds of Newell home at Champoeg, restored by D.A.R. While exterior of old structure has been renewed, interior is almost unchanged. Original flooring is of whipsawed planks, walls of lighter boards also showing whipsaw marks. School has two rooms, upper and lower grades in former days, is presumed same building as that of "Butteville Academy" incorporated at state legislature in 1869, Francois Xavier Mathieu being one of trustees. Howard McKinley Corning, in his definitive book, **Willamette Landings**, says the Academy "probably was a large name for a small public school." Dolores Purdue, now of Portland, remembers the time she attended graduation exercises at school; "There were three graduates from the 8th grade. After they received their diplomas there was a picnic followed by all kinds of games and races."

Oregon

GOLD — AND A GENIUS

Canyon City, Oregon

While its diggings yielded many millions in gold, Canyon City's history is colored more vividly by the character of one of its citizens. This was the bearded poet Cincinnatus Heine Miller, more familiarly known as Joaquin Miller who doubled as squaw man, prospector, printer's devil, supply packer and who as county judge claimed he "dispensed justice in Canyon City with a six-shooter in each hand."

In the early 1860s an unknown number of men combed the canyons and gulches of eastern Oregon, most of them on the trail of the mysterious Blue Bucket Mine. Although that location was never positively identified many other rich diggings were located. No one can say how much gold may have been or still is in the Blue Bucket but certainly Canyon Creek gave up a whopping $8 million in dust and nuggets. Among many stories of the original discovery in 1862 is the one that has the unlikely elements so often founded on fact. One of these is that in the first party camping on Whiskey Flat, a scant half mile north of where the town would grow, was one Billy Aldred who strayed from the others to make his own explorations. Spotting a location he liked across a creek, he waded over and found the gravel promising. Being without a pan or container for samples he stripped off his long underwear and by knotting the ankles and wrists, made four long bags which he filled

HERE LIVED JOAQUIN MILLER, described as "a bit of a charlatan . . . a restless, spectacular character, capable of writing an occasional poem with a vigorous lilt." Arriving here with wife Minnie and baby in 1864, controversial poet brought first fruit trees, ornamental shrubs to raw mining camp on pack animals. Double white lilacs shown left and right could be survivors of original shrubs.

Chair, hand cut from single section of log is on porch of Joaquin Miller cabin at Canyon City. Long extended periods of sitting in it would seem to invite case of curvature of spine.

with gold laden sand. Three days later a saloon was erected on the spot and other structures followed it. Canyon City was on its way. At the peak of the rush some 10,000 people of every description thronged the narrow main street called Whiskey Gulch.

Breaking through the crowds were numerous trains of oxen, mules and horses bringing in supplies from The Dalles by way of the old Military Road, animals and wagons having crossed swollen rivers, stretches of desert sand and rocky mountain defiles. Indians lurked at several points, the danger increasing as they learned the value of gold coming back with the teams.

With the influx of packers, miners and traders came the inevitable gamblers and prostitutes. One of the former was a notorious card sharp known as Black Dan because of his swarthy complexion. The story told about him is the one credited to some gambler in almost every mountain camp, yet it could have happened to him. Caught by a bullet, Black Dan could see his end approaching but requested his saloon buddies to "lay him out" as already dead and bring in some of the girls. The going away party got rolling with a toast to the near-departed when it was discovered he had

been so inconsiderate as to spoil everything by not waiting for the glasses to be drained.

Independence Day celebrations in early mining camps were rated next to Christmas in importance and featured sack races, football games and volunteer fire department drills. In 1863 Canyon City staged a Fourth of July affair that got somewhat out of hand. With the Civil War raging there was some violence between miners, prospectors and hangers-on who had Confederate or Union sympathies and on this occasion with saloons filled quarrels sprang up quickly. Supporters of the South, largely from California, and Union men from Oregon, Washington and Idaho, let their feelings and tempers grow hotter as the day went on.

Shortly after noon rebels climbed the hill above town and raised a large Confederate flag, firing off a defiant volley. When the banner was seen from the street Union men quickly organized and armed themselves, stormed the hill and tore it down. Although some shots were fired in the melee, more were downed in the saloons. There were no fatalities but bitterness and resentment lasted for years. Lest anyone forget the incident the bluff, actually part of the rim rock above town, was named "Rebel Hill."

At the time of the party on the hill Col. Henry E. Dosch was on his way to Canyon City from St. Louis, Mo. Born in Germany June 17, 1841, and arriving in St. Louis in 1860, he lived there less than a year when he enlisted in the Union Army. By way of California young Dosch arrived at The Dalles on the Columbia River in 1864. There he set up an enterprise to pack supplies into roaring Canyon City. In later years, after he became a prominent citizen of Portland, with a road named for him, he wrote an account of his adventure along the old Military Road in Eastern Oregon.

His partners John Snively and William Claffin furnished the money, Dosch wrote, and he the experience gained on his trip north. The packers carried about $25,000 worth of supplies to the camp, selling them at double the cost. "We didn't include flour in this, selling the staple which everyone must have, at cost—55 cents a pound. Nobody got rich but we made wages." The return load paid better. Canyon City gold was exceptionally pure without the infusion of copper that reduced value elsewhere. At $17 per ounce Dosch's pack animals were most attractive to road agents.

At this time Grant County had just been organized, the first election naming W. L. Laird as county judge and Tom Brents county clerk. After a short term the latter was replaced by saloon keeper Mike Goodwin and Dosch relates, "Mike didn't know the first thing about the duties required, so he named me as his deputy. I took over his job and served under C. H. Miller who had been elected county judge."

He refers to Cincinnatus Heine Miller who came across the plains in a covered wagon in his early teens. After a short stay with his parents he began a wandering career, fighting briefly in the Modoc War, traveling to the gold camps of northern California. As a youth of about eighteen he found life among the Digger Indians of the McCloud River country near Mt. Shasta very much to his liking because of the amiable Indian girls so easily available.

Going native, he shed his regular clothes for the fringed buckskins he was to affect during much of his life. Flitting from one acquiescent squaw to another he settled down with one whose "flowing hair," he wrote, "only partially screened the rounded young breasts of maidenhood." His white friend Jim Brock wrote later, "I should say a man would be crazy to live with one of them . . . the sight and smell of most would turn the stomach of any but a poet."

Of Miller's dalliance was born a daughter whom he named Cali-Shasta, then deserted both mother and child. Later he returned for the little girl and put her in the care of a friend in San Francisco. Moving to Eugene, Oregon, he worked on a newspaper which soon went out of business because of the editor's Confederate sympathies.

Some time later Miller and white wife Minnie and their small child joined a pack train for Canyon City, some of the animals carrying fruit trees, berry vines and ornamental shrubs. In the rough mining camp the family settled down in a cabin and Miller began writing the poetry that would bring him world fame. Dosch wrote of Miller, "He was an ardent admirer of Lord Byron, even affecting his idol's slight limp caused by a deformed foot. He wore his hair down to his shoulders and wore high boots, one of which was usually covered by a pant leg, the other leg being tucked inside. He loved to be conspicuous." Dosch, who often had to share the same office, complained that "Miller would often corner me so he could read me his stuff which I didn't much care for. I thought his wife Minnie wrote better, though her verses were never published."

But much of Miller's was, some of it in the Dalles *Times-Mountaineer*, sent out under a pen name—John Smith, Jr. Emboldened by success Miller submitted more material to his home town paper, the *Blue Mountain Eagle*, under his real name, Cincinnatus Heine Miller.

His marriage, ill-starred from the beginning, was dissolved and he moved to Portland where he continued his writings under a name that would be permanent—Joaquin Miller. Then came a European tour and in England his spectacular garb and flamboyant air "made a big hit," Dosch records. In 1907 Miller returned to his Canyon City home as a celebrity and there wrote "A Royal Highway of the World," actually a form of "letter to the editor." It was reproduced many times and sent to Grant and Harney County papers, commissioners and any other authorities he could think of. It protested the condition of the road from Canyon City to Burns. Miller claimed the "highway" was so clogged with brush that stage drivers had to carry axes and saws and cut their way through.

The road, now part of U.S. 395, is a modern paved highway, full of sharp curves as it skirts scenic Strawberry Mountain and many narrow canyons. It was formerly termed "Joaquin Miller Highway" but now the designation does not appear on maps.

MAIN STREET of Canyon City shows plunder taken by market hunters. Birds beaten out of swarming marshes bordering some sections of John Day River were ruthlessly slaughtered, even rare swans. Hunters pose with guns, butcher in apron. (Courtesy Oregon Historical Society).

CHAMPOEG, OREGON

"A ball was given on the floor of Dr. John Mc-Loughlin's mill in Oregon City. Lt. Peel bet the wine with the late Dr. Robert Newell that most of those present would take the British side in case of a contest. Lt. Peel lost the bet and showing some chagrin in his manner, offered to bet another bottle of wine that a man he indicated sitting right opposite to him across the floor would fight under the British flag. Dr. Newell took the bet. The man was asked to cross the floor when the question was put to him. 'Sir, which flag would you support in case of a war for this country?' The answer was quick and clear. 'I fight underneath the Stars and Stripes, myself'. The man was Willard H. Reese."

This incident was related by S. F. Chadwick a number of years later. It gives a vivid glimpse into the way events were building up to trouble with Great Britain over the Oregon country, as to whose flag was to fly over it. "Oregon" at that time was a vast territory extending from Pacific Ocean to Rocky Mountains, between parallels 42 and 54-40. The controversy centered in a rolling, grassy "prairie" area extending from the Indian village of Chemeketa, near where the State Capitol at Salem now stands, northward to a point just south of the Willamette falls at Oregon City. Possibly this land had once been covered by the same dense forests that mantled the surrounding country but native

OLD PICTURE, said to have been taken at Champoeg is undated but scene is typical of early days in busy river town. River is low, exposing bare banks where normal highway would bring it near grass. Phenomenal flood which destroyed Champoeg sent waters high above any point shown here.

"DOCTOR" ROBERT NEWELL, whose title was given for courtesy and affection, was one of earliest and most picturesque of Oregon pioneers. All his buildings and property in Champoeg, except home on higher ground, were washed away in disastrous flood of 1861. Newell persisted in trying to rebuild town for time but became disheartened and moved to Lapwai, Idaho, in middle '60s. Indian friends donated land to him in what became the heart of Lewiston. Portrait here was made on visit to Washington with Indian group to agitate for betterment of their situation.

Indian tribes, loosely grouped as Calapooias, had long been in a habit of setting fire to the grass and brush each fall, to corral game for easy killing and discourage forest growth.

To the earliest settlers in the 1820s the land seemed waiting to be planted to wheat. Etienne Lucier, born in the District of St. Edouard near Montreal, came to this part of the Willamette Valley in those years. He had been a recruited member of the Wilson Price Hunt Expedition overland to Astoria, arriving there in 1812. The arduous trip was part of Astor's great venture to establish a branch of the Pacific Fur Co. at the mouth of the Columbia River. Lucier became a trapper and guide, saw the fertile fields of the Willamette Valley and decided to settle there, planting wheat he brought from the post at Fort Vancouver, Lucier was Oregon's first farmer.

During the '30s more French Canadians gave up trapping, "married" Indian girls, termed "infidel women" by the priests who established missions at nearby St. Louis and St. Paul. Inept at farming to begin with, these "Mountain Men" were soon producing wheat in a golden flood, using it to pay for all manner of food and supplies in place of money.

A system was established to get the grain to market. Many of the farms centered on the banks of the Willamette River at a point called "Encampment du Sable". A landing and warehouse were built there, "batteaux" loaded with grain and floated to the falls at Oregon City where larger boats reloaded the cargo below the falls. Dr. John McLoughlin at Fort Vancouver found a good sale for the crop in Russian settlements along the coast.

Encampment du Sable took on the more convenient name of the Indian village nearby—Champoeg. The origin of the name, according to one version is that it is a combination of two Indian words for "weed" — "champoo" and "coich", pronunciation similar to "shampooik".

By 1840 there were fifty families on the "French Prairie", most of them near Champoeg. At first all were French Canadians with Calapooia or Nez Perce wives and numerous progeny, but later Americans joined the community so that Protestants, particularly Methodists, mingled with the Catholics. There was little friction since in this remote country every man had to rely closely on his neighbor.

Yet there was a storm of vaster implications brewing in high levels — the dispute between the United States and Great Britain as to who would control these fertile lands of the entire Oregon area. On October 28, 1818 a treaty of joint occupancy had been signed in London. In 1827 this was renewed but now more and more American settlers began to chafe at the idea of a possible English government. When the discontent finally reached an explosive stage, it was less a quarrel than the need to settle a private estate amicably.

Ewing Young, who became one of the wealthiest settlers, died in 1841 without an heir, his lands, buildings and stocks unclaimed. Now in place of the social and religious meetings the settlers were accustomed to have, they gathered to appoint an executor. At the same time another kind of meeting was called to cope with losses of livestock from wolves and other predatory animals, specifically losses of cattle and horses running wild on the Young place after his death.

On February 2, 1843 the farmers met again and levied an assessment of five dollars on each to pay bounty for carcasses of marauding wolves, mountain lions, lynx or bear. It was aptly termed a "Wolf Meeting" and the phrase applied to others following. A second Wolf Meeting was held on March 2 but this time wolves were not discussed.

The Americans, now about equal in number to those of foreign origin, were in some ferment over fear of British control and it was agreed by all that a local government of some kind must be established. A committee of twelve was appointed to "take into consideration the propriety for taking measures for civil and military protection of this colony." The committee met at Willamette Falls within a few days and arranged for a general gathering at Champoeg on May 2 to vote on the situation.

That meeting was the most momentous and dramatic in the history of the Oregon country, resulting in a bloodless decision that the vast territory should be under the control of the United States rather than Great Britain.

It was called to order in a corner of the wheat warehouse, used as an office by the Hudson's Bay Co. The first resolutions, calling for organization into a self-governing body, generated such excitement and confusion in the confined quarters that many voters went unheard and many of those who did hear voted improperly, even for the opposing side. The whole gathering then moved outdoors to the middle of a field and while the situation was

NEWELL HOME about turn of century, prudently built on high ground above Champoeg. House fell rapidly into disrepair after abandonment and when it collapsed, D.A.R. made project of restoring it. Present house on site is relic-filled museum, containing some original boards and fireplace bricks, is maintained as historical shrine.

OLD CHAMPOEG CEMETERY was on ground too high for flood-waters. Section shown here was planted with lilacs, now gnarled, lichen-encrusted, but still blooming in spring. Contrary to fate of some old cemeteries, this one is maintained for historical significance.

improved, a voice vote was hopeless. Trapper Joe Meek, tall, dark-eyed and black-bearded, raised his penetrating voice against the uproar, urging the men to "side up" in the field and declaring he would start things by taking the American side. French Canadian G. W. LeBriton made the formal motion that this be done and it was seconded by American William Gray, a Methodist mission worker. Joe Meek stepped out and called on all those of the one hundred and two present who wanted an American government established to gather around him.

With a loud hallooing forty-nine men went to the American side to make fifty in all. And fifty remained where they were. The other two? They were Etienne Lucier and F. X. Mathieu, standing in the middle, hesitating. Everyone waited impatiently for them to make up their minds. Lucier said he had

heard that under American rule, the very windows of his house would be taxed. Mathieu, who owned much land and property in nearby Butteville where he was surrounded by American sympathizers, suddenly decided to go with them and persuaded Lucier to do the same. They joined Meek and swayed the vote. The immense area sandwiched between Mexican California and Canada, so tenuously held by England, was now safely under the flag of the United States — at least as far as the inhabitants were concerned. Succeeding events soon made it official.

A group of nine was named to set up the beginnings of the infant government and a short time later Champoeg was declared "The Capital." A crude State House was erected of split cedar slabs and poles, roofed with cedar bark.

England was not willing to go along with all this quite so easily and in 1844 was still contending with Washington although it had ceased any activities in the Oregon country, the issue seeming dangerous to everybody but the Oregonians. There was even talk of war but the increasing influx of American immigrants to the Willamette Valley over the Oregon Trail made it obvious to the British that their cause was lost.

Champoeg began to take on the appearance of a permanent town, largely through the efforts of Robert Newell. Two places in Ohio, Putnam and Zanesville, are mentioned as his birthplace, in 1807. At eighteen he became a Rocky Mountain trapper, then as the fur trade declined, he teamed up with Joe Meek on a trip to the Oregon country, spending some time in Idaho and acquiring Nez Perce wives. They were sisters, daughters of sub-chief Kow-e-so-te. With a third man they brought the first wagons from Fort Hill into Oregon, although half dismantled. When they stopped at the mission in Walla Walla, Marcus Whitman congratulated the young men, saying: "You will never regret your efforts. Now that you have brought the first wagons, others will follow."

Newell, often referred to as "Doctor" or more familiarly as "Doc", took up residence in Champoeg and began to raise a family. He bought and fitted up two batteaux, starting a regular run between the town and the falls above Oregon City. They were called MOGUL and BEN FRANKLIN, power provided by Indian paddlers.

By 1851, when steamboats reached the town, Newell abandoned his primitive vessels and turned to real estate. Having taken up the 360-acre claim of Walter Pomeroy at the southern edges of Champoeg, he laid out a sub-division and sold lots. When need for land access became acute, he persuaded the provisional legislature to survey and construct a stage road from Salem to his property which he called Oxford. The Salem-St. Paul-Champoeg road is essentially the same route today.

By the 1850s there were about a hundred and fifty buildings in Champoeg including adjoining Oxford where Newell had built a fine home on a higher level above the Willamette. Peter Skene Ogden and James Douglas reported in 1847 that the Hudson's Bay Co. property in Champoeg was worth about $8,500 and the concern sold out in 1852 for some $17,000. Values and building continued to increase until the catastrophe of 1861 which all but wiped out the progressing city.

The Willamette had risen in 1853-54 to the point where water flowed through the edges of Champoeg and nibbled at the foundations of buildings. The stream subsided with little damage but Champoeg citizens were not alert to the warning.

In 1861, September and October passed with almost no precipitation. Then it began to rain in earnest and November brought an unending deluge which turned to snow. Temperatures rose, rain continued and the snowbanks melted.

Every tributary of the main stream, particularly the raging Santiam, swelled the Willamette almost a foot an hour until by December 2 the river was fifty-five feet higher than summer stage and twelve feet above the level of the '53-'54 flood. This time the murky, roaring waters swept over the town seven feet deep with terrific force, large logs acting as battering rams, and one by one Champoeg's buildings were carried away. The river stayed up for several days then slowly subsided to reveal a townsite "bare as a sandy beach". Three hundred and fifty houses were washed downstream yet the destruction was not quite total. Two solidly constructed structures remained standing — the two saloons.

The higher bench where Robert Newell had his house remained dry, the house intact. Newell, however, was financially ruined, his holdings in town entirely swept away. His Indian wife had died long before and now he took his new white wife and many offsprings to Lewiston, Idaho, the scene of his youthful dalliance.

Attempts were made to lay out a new town on the old site but with its moving spirit gone, once so strong many people thought of the place as Newellsville, nothing much happened. The green

meadow where the fateful vote was taken is now marked by a granite shaft, its exact location determined in 1900 by the last surviving voter, Francois Xavier Mathieu. It is emblazoned with the names believed on best authority to be of those siding with Meek and the United States. Surrounding all is Champoeg State Park where thousands hold summer picnics. The author visits there often, one such occasion in November when heavy rain was making a lake of the picnic grounds, tables and benches floating. The Willamette will continue periodic rampages; present and future dams along the tributaries such as the Detroit and Santiam appreciably restraining flood levels.

UNIQUE MONUMENT in Champoeg burial ground shows full maiden name of wife in accordance with Catholic custom. Object is partly to maintain evidence of accuracy of birth, baptismal records. English ivy, established and growing wild in much of Willamette Valley, clambers around base of marker. At least one marker in cemetery dates back to 1853. It is thought long-vanished wooden ones were first placed by settlers in '30s.

CHITWOOD, OREGON

Grace Davis left her telephone switchboard only once. It taught her a stern lesson. Now Mrs. Collins of Portland she thinks back to 1906, to her life in the rugged, timbered mountains of the Oregon coast.

There were only about twenty telephone subscribers but their calls kept Grace Davis busy almost the whole twenty-four hours she was on duty. Although she loved the job there were jangling interruptions while she was busy with other necessary duties that "got on her nerves" some days. This one day she made up her mind she would finish her lunch, buzzing or no buzzing. She tried to shut her ears until she finished eating and then sweetly answered the signal.

The voice was that of Chauncey Trapp, conductor of the eastbound train, telling her it had been wrecked below Chitwood and he had been trying to get her for fifteen minutes and he was about crazy, that she must get out there and stop the westbound train when it passed through Chitwood to avoid a terrible collision. Grace jumped and barely had time to warn the engineer as the train was pulling out. "That was the only time I ever ignored the switchboard," Grace says now. "And I haven't really felt safe in telling the story until now, almost sixty years later."

The area was a primeval wilderness in the 1860s when M. L. Trapp and his wife settled on a land claim a short distance below where the town would be. Life was lonely for the solitary woman until the Barney Morrisons took the next location. In a few more years more hardy pioneers came to cut the trees and till the soil. Some had families, more children were born and the need for a school arose. A house with one large room a half mile west of Chitwood was pressed into service, a fireplace at one end being the only source of heat. No one seemed to have time to cut firewood of proper length so the teacher, Thomas J. Brannan, poked the ends of large branches in the blaze and moved them farther in as they burned. There were no desks or tables so the pupils sat on benches and did their sums on slates in their laps.

After a few years of hardships some of the settlers gave up and moved away, taking their children with them, so education languished for a while. Then Mr. Trapp, one of the persistent ones, offered the use of a room in his home and hired a teacher who "lived in."

It was not until 1887 that a real school was built, its location near Chitwood and built by donated labor. It became the center for all community affairs — box socials, committee meetings, farm group get-togethers, Christmas parties and even weddings. Sometimes itinerant evangelists would hold revival meetings in the little "hall". A collection of books donated by residents, became the nucleus of a growing library shortly after the turn of the century and the "hello girl," Grace Davis, served as librarian.

During the early years many adherents of the Seventh Day Adventist faith wanted a church which could double as a school, but lumber was scarce and the dream had to be postponed. Then a little farm building in nearby Elk City which was already fading was dismantled and the material hauled to Chitwood by a sturdy pair of oxen—Lep and Lion. Lep was conspicuously spotted and was first called Leopard until it proved cumbersome. Oxen were best for hauling on the deeply rutted, muddy roads, but their doom was spelled when at last the railroad came—and with it P. A. Miller.

He had been Per Anderson in Sweden but that country's army complained there were already too many Andersons and would Per please change his name? The young Swede borrowed one of his cousin's and became Per Moeller. After the army service he took his new bride, Marie, to Chitwood and they lived in a section house while the Corvallis and Eastern Railroad was being built. And his name got "in the road" again. His daughter Lillie tells about it. "My father was quick to embrace new ideas, new things. As soon as he realized his name was awkward to American tongues he abbreviated Per to P, then inserted an A for the original Anderson and simplified Moeller to Miller. For the rest of his life he was P. A. Miller."

He was soon transferred to Mill City in the Willamette Valley at the very edge of the Cascade Mountains and helped build some of the bridges for frequent crossings of the Santiam River which

TRACKS OF CORVALLIS AND EASTERN, later branch line of Southern Pacific, run close by old George Smith store at right. Line ran from Corvallis in Willamette Valley over Coast Range to Yaquina on bay of same name, connecting agricultural area to coast, was started in 1880. Trains were first composed of flat car or two, a few box cars and about three coaches, hauled by puffing, wood-burning engine. Number of farmers added to income by cutting fuel on private wood lots, stacking it beside track. When train crew saw a pile ready, they would stop train and load it on tender. Passenger service was finally discontinued, tracks taken up between Yaquina and Toledo. Covered bridge is 96 feet long, was built in early 1920s, replacing hand-hewn span.

SNOW IS RARE in coastal area of Oregon, helps to delineate buildings shown in picture made about 1900. At extreme left is store built by Lafayette Pepin, rented to Rogers two years, then run by Pepin. Next right is old bridge of hand-hewn beams, above it Seventh Day Adventist Church. Large house with surrounding porch was originally owned by Mr. Durkee, later housing telephone office and switchboard, and still stands but long unoccupied. Next right is post office, shown in modern photo without porch. Next is railway depot, back of that old Whitney store, later operated by George Smith. Above is old Chitwood family home. Forest fire nearly denuded hills now covered with luxurious growth.

twisted down its narrow canyon. But he was dissatisfied because the job kept him away from home where his young wife was expecting her first child. He applied for the job of track maintenance on the Chitwood line where he could have permanent residence with his family. His request was granted six months after the baby girl was born, so the little family moved to a train stop called Morrison Station just below Chitwood, close enough for Lillie to go to school when ready.

Young Miller did well at his job and managed to improve his small home too but with the birth of two sons he started building a much larger one. Lillie's memories really begin with this house. "It had lots of bedrooms and a huge kitchen with a big wood range. Just above it, on the side of the steep hill was a woodshed which seemed as large as the house and appeared attached to it. One of the many people who stopped with my folks remarked: 'This

is the first time I ever saw a two-story woodshed'. There was always company at our house, salesman or drummer, itinerant preacher and, of course the school teacher. Everyone seemed to think it was expected he stay with the Millers, and mother, on whom the largest share of the extra work fell, never protested although it must have seemed she was running a boarding house."

The wagon road was a sea of mud in winter, with dust a foot deep in summer. Much later when the first automobiles began to filter in, it was said: "One car would raise so much dust that another couldn't follow it for a long time." In the muddy season the road was completely impassable but this did not handicap the section foreman. He had access to a hand car — a tiny, four-wheeled platform that ran on rails, powered by a handle bar worked up and down. It was a back-breaking job for one man but was easier when two used the rig, one facing forward and one backward, each man

714

alternately lowering and raising the handles like the operation of a see-saw.

Just as the patient Mrs. Miller was relied upon to "put up" all stray visitors, so was P. A. trusted to take care of any emergency such as fetching the doctor when someone was desperately ill or an imminent childbirth. When called upon he would jump on the hand car and pump madly to Elk City where the doctor lived and with that worthy's help on the other end of the handle, speed to wherever needed. Since most of these calls came at night when the trains did not run, there was little danger on the rails. When Elk City declined and could no longer maintain a doctor, Miller was forced to pump his rig all the way to Toledo.

The right of way ignored most of the twistings of the Yaquina River along which it was built with spidery trestles and tunnels through projecting points of rock. When Lillie started going to school in Chitwood, she and other children walked the ties to avoid the muddy road. "We got very expert at hurrying over the trestles," she says, "so as not to be on one when a train came." In a year or two she was joined on the walk by her little brother whose twin had died in infancy.

Coming home from school one day the children came to a pile of glowing embers where the section crew had been burning old ties. The children put more wood on the dying fire and fanned it to a blaze. As Lillie stooped low over the flames her dress caught fire. In a panic she ran back to the school house and fortunately the teacher was still there. She tore most of the clothes from the little girl's body and rolled her in a coat. Lillie was a long time recovering from her burns, the scars still showing faintly.

It was about this period that a "prospector" from San Francisco discovered a fine vein of sandstone nearby, the material deemed most suitable for construction of the mint and post office in his home city. The Corvallis and Eastern ran a spur line into the quarry, the sandstone cut and loaded by hand on flat cars hauled to Yaquina, the lower terminus on Yaquina Bay, and trans-shipped on vessels to San Francisco. The industry caused quite an influx of workers for a time, "inflating" the tiny community to some extent.

In 1905 a movement was started for a telephone line to serve Chitwood, P. A. Miller in particular feeling the telegraph was not adequate. It was his responsibility to see that the long stretch of track was kept in good repair and he needed better communi-

cations with those who lived along the route. So on December 14, 1905, the Rural Telephone Co. was organized with A. L. McDonald as chairman, George T. Smith as secretary-treasurer. The list of signed members starts with P. A. Miller, includes most of the responsible residents including the Pepins, Wilsons, the younger Trapp and W. N. Cook. The office and switchboard was set up in the Durky house, owned by Miss Jean Robertson. It was here Grace Davis took over as switchboard operator. At first the line went only to Morrison Station but was soon expanded and eventually connected to the outside world for long distance calls, at first a big thrill for Grace Davis.

The coming of the Corvallis and Eastern changed things for Chitwood more than any other factor. When travel was confined to the wagon road, the stages sometimes got through and sometimes did not. The first fall rains turned the heavy dust into a quagmire in which wagons and stages were bogged down to the hubs.

CHITWOOD POST OFFICE was for years in George Smith store with Smith as postmaster. Later it was transferred to this little building. After it was closed out, door was enlarged and building served as garage. This business also has gone but pigeon-hole racks still hang on walls where they held letters. Huge chestnut tree once shaded front, was cut down some years ago, new growth springing up, as shown here in bloom.

When stages did get through they were useful. A man with a freshly killed deer carcass who lacked flour could wrap up a hind quarter in a sack, take the stage to Corvallis, make a trade in the store and return by stage with his flour.

When the puffing, wood-burners started pulling trains from Corvallis to Yaquina, Chitwood became an important stop. The little depot was close by George Smith's store and post office and train time always stirred the town into a frenzy. Grace Davis, in addition to her switchboard and library, saw that the mail sack was thrown on board, the incoming one taken off.

Since George Smith was the butcher as well as grocer there was always a smelly bale of cowhides ready for shipping. There would be sacks of dried and crushed cascara bark gathered in the woods where the trees abounded and carried out in bundles strapped to the pickers' backs. Cord upon cord of wood would be stacked beside the tracks for train crews to load as fuel for the boiler. Cutters got 90 cents a cord delivered on right-of-way. And trains brought large shipments of goods for George Smith's store.

The store had its beginnings in a small building put up by Joshua Chitwood who served as first postmaster as well, selling out later to a Mr. Whitney. George Smith worked in the store and later married the owner's daughter, taking over ownership after Whitney's retirement.

You could buy anything you needed at George's store. If it was not on hand it would be "sent for" from Corvallis and come in on the train. Bee keeping was an important part of the economy, Smith himself having an apiary and selling his neighbors a complete line of supplies, hives, supers and even queens on occasion. He sold meat but allowed customers to use his facilities for their own slaughtering.

Growing up and going to school here was Smith's son Morris. When he was old enough to work he did many jobs and then at 24 was elated to get steady work at another, later stone quarry. The stone was regularly blasted out of the solid vein by chipping out a "coyote" hole, placing the charge, then plugging up the hole with tapered rock with the wide ends out so they would jam tightly with the explosion, causing the full force of the blast to go upward instead of out the hole. Morris had gone to the cook shack for lunch one day which had been delayed for the scheduled twelve o'clock blast. This time a shower of badly placed rocks arched high overhead and came hurtling down through the roof of the shack, pinning Morris to the floor by his leg, crushing it from the ankle to above the knee. After a year of hospitalization, the knee was left rigid and ankle almost so.

GAY TIMES WERE HAD in olden days at Chitwood's dance hall.

PHOTO TAKEN FROM CHITWOOD'S covered bridge looks toward U.S. 20, shows old Pepin store. At other end of bridge was George Smith's, both stores necessary to service Chitwood in heyday, were friendly rivals. Lafayette Pepin came to Chitwood about 1878, married Flora Akey who bore him four sons. He built store in 1908, first rented it, took it over two years later. He died in 1917, Flora continuing to operate store. One son Archie, who had worked as logger 22 years, returned to care for ailing mother. When she died in 1948, Archie ran store in same old-fashioned way until about 1959 when he retired to Salem Nursing Home.

When Morris left the hospital he found the depression in full swing. With few jobs available he was happy when his father offered to take him into the store and as he kept busy, the leg improved. He cultivated berries and orchard fruit near the store, sold the produce there or with honey to the coast resorts at Newport.

When Lillie Miller graduated from the Chitwood grade school she went to high school in Toledo, thirteen miles away. It was hard to get there and lonely staying there so after the first year she took courses at home. When ready she taught in several of the small area schools and saving her money, took a summer course at Oregon Agricultural College at Corvallis, western terminus of Corvallis and Eastern. She had a stint of teaching at West Linn across the Willamette from Oregon City, graduating from the University of Oregon at Eugene. After a few years she married Charles A. Nutt and moved to Portland where she now lives, a widow.

When the old wagon road was rerouted and paved the improvement was hailed in Chitwood as a great thing. Automobiles, coming rapidly into popularity, used the new, short route to the coast. Soon no one was riding the train and with increasingly large tonnage of freight shipped by truck, the railroad reduced service to a minimum, discontinuing passenger service. The depot was torn down and many people moved away. Business was so slow at the Pepin and Smith stores, now that larger stores and markets were so readily reached by automobile, both owners quit trying. Chitwood, although retaining a few residents who love the place, is now a virtual ghost.

717

RIDERS IN THE SKY

CORNUCOPIA, OREGON

Cornucopia was once a rip-roaring gold mining camp with over a thousand people. It boomed not once but several times, as each new lode of fabulously rich gold ore was followed up. Some of the ore was so full of free gold that nuggets could be shaken out of it. Eight saloons provided refreshment and entertainment to hundreds of rough miners, many of them from Cornwall, England and called, for some obscure reason, "Cousin Jacks."

The first big boom years were from 1884 to 1886. The Union Companion Mine was the big one then, but several others ranged on up the rugged slopes, the Last Chance being at 7,000 feet. As for the name of the town, Cornucopia, with its connotation of wealth and abundance, has always been a popular name for mining towns. Some of the early miners here had come from Cornucopia, Nevada, and named the new camp for the old.

Erma Cole was a child of eight when she arrived with her father and mother in Cornucopia. Her father had been mining in the Yellow Jacket near what is now Sun Valley, Idaho, but had been told to quit the mines as he suffered "miner's consumption." The little family traveled on horseback to Weiser, then to Red Bluff, California. Here Mr. Cole heard that a Mr. Shipman, who had been the bookkeeper of the Yellow Jacket, was now in charge at the mines at Cornucopia. Not having found work elsewhere, he decided to cast his lot in the mines again. The family set out in horse and buggy for Cornucopia, a long and arduous trip in those days.

When they arrived there in October, 1898, Cornucopia had already shed its first site and moved farther up the slope to be nearer the mines, although the school, several saloons and office of the only physician, Dr. O'Conner, remained on the old townsite.

The little girl and her mother sat in their buggy on Main Street for half an hour. "When father returned," Erma remembers, "he told us that he had a job at top wages; $3.50 a day. He had already rented a tiny house and bought a stove so we would be warm." Mother Cole was not happy; Joseph ought not work in the mines again, but there was no choice. The family was destitute. And sure enough, "Father lasted just 15 days and came down terribly ill with pneumonia." The Irish physician, Dr. O'Conner, was summoned from the lower town and reassured the frightened family by telling them he had never yet lost a pneumonia patient. Joseph Cole did get well, but could not return to the mine.

At this time the one street was lined on both sides for several blocks by the typical false fronts and many cabins. There was a livery stable across from the post office. The meat market boasted two floors, the residence of the proprietor being over the shop. Mr. Estes was the butcher, a huge man with very short legs. He went everywhere on his mule named Becky, pulling himself up into the saddle by sheer strength. A good-sized general store was on the west side of the street, owned by Tom Turner in those early days. Later he took in a partner named Brown.

One of the buildings was a hotel and, at that critical period in the fortunes of the Coles, it needed a cook and manager. "Mother was a wonderful cook and Father was able by now to take over the duties of clerk and manager. Together they made a go of it and for a time it seemed as though this would be permanent. The hotel was always full, as living quarters were scarce and Mother's cooking attracted business."

Winter snows were and are of a prodigious depth in that section of the Wallowa Mountains. Total depth in winter often reached 30 feet, or a settled depth of 10 feet. The two stages which came daily, one from Baker and the other from Union, used sled runners instead of wheels. All winter the little street lay buried deeply and the trail rose higher and higher, much above the level of the doorways.

"Father cut a tunnel from the door up to the trail, and carefully made beautiful steps in the hard-packed snow. As soon as he turned his back we kids used them for a delightfully bumpy ride on our sleds and it soon took the sharp edges off the steps and Father would have to make them all over again. Little brother, Robert, who was five, would never come down stairs the conventional way, but jumped out of his upstairs window onto the snow, often with all too few clothes on his small body. This particular winter he became ill with rheumatic fever and mother had to devote her full time to nursing the boy.

BARBERSHOP AND "CANDY STORE" are among buildings on Main Street of Cornucopia. Barbershop was post office before tonsorial conversion. Space between buildings was boarded up during winters and soon filled up with snow. It packed and was handy during summer for making ice cream treats.

EARLY-DAY BARN of logs still stands. Shake roof was steeply pitched to shed enormous winter snows. Even so, snow piled up and had to be removed by hand.

The cooking had to be turned over to hired help, an unsatisfactory arrangement which resulted in the sale of the hotel to George Herbert, who later was sheriff of Baker County."

At this time the mines were using huge amounts of timber for shoring up the tunnels and shafts, for sluice trestles and many other purposes. Although the town was surrounded by an immense stand of virgin timber, wood and timbers were in short supply for lack of cutters. So Mr. Cole turned to this occupation and it proved to be successful.

Things became easier for the Coles and another strike helped produce a new boom for the town. Had the rich streaks of gold been mined systematically the situation would have been more stable, but some companies gutted them, and miners had to be searched on leaving to go home at night. Their pockets and lunch boxes would sometimes be found to have golden linings.

Mine accidents were frequent. Men were blown to bits by premature blasts, tunnel walls caved in or were flooded. Fire took its toll and avalanches were frequent. Huge slides of snow sometimes buried buildings entirely, entombing luckless inhabitants.

An explosion made fatherless one of the playmates of the Cole children. He was Christopher Schneider, and at 12, he had to get a job to support his mother and sisters. He was industrious and well liked and soon was doing the important work of sharpening drills.

Erma and other camp children usually played near where Chris was working. They ranged the mine tunnels and, since there was little room left when the ore-filled cars came rolling along, they flattened themselves against the walls whenever this happened. Shafts hundreds of feet deep connected to the tunnels, but strangely, no child ever fell down one of them.

FORGOTTEN WAG nailed shoes to weathered pump house.

EARLY-DAY CONSTRUCTION shows interesting wood textures. This is corner of huge barn which sheltered large part of important population of mules and horses, used mostly in hauling of firewood, shoring and stope timbers for mines.

Cornucopia lacked the wild shooting frays and killings so characteristic of other mining towns in early days, but in common with them, had the usual quota of women who lived in a couple of buildings by themselves. Miss Cole delicately refers to these as "Sporting Ladies."

The madam of one of these was familiarly known as Fanny, and she took her meals at the hotel where the Coles stayed. Around the corner from the dining room was a closet in which was a barrel. The hotel's official mouser, a big white cat named "Snowball," had selected this as a nursery for her new litter of kittens. Came dinner time and Fanny swept in with one of her girls named Nelly. They were followed by her several dogs whose custom it was to wait attentively on the chance of a bone. But now the dogs were irresistibly attracted to the barrel. When Snowball exploded in their faces, the resulting confusion in the dining room was such that both Fanny and Nelly jumped up on the table and held their voluminous skirts well up out of the way. To quote Erma Cole again, "I was somewhat bold in those days and I couldn't help laughing at them, but they were very upset."

As Erma grew up she also worked, usually helping wait table for the single men, in the company mess hall. "It was all I could do to carry those enormous platters heaped high with steaks, and the tureens of soup, each with a big ladle. The men helped themselves and ate like beasts. They piled up outside the door, and at the signal, fell over each other in their haste to get into the dining hall. And, while they looked at us girls, it would have been as much as his life was worth for one of them to so much as touch us. The company saw to that."

Now Cornucopia is slowly reverting to wilderness, sagging and empty buildings sparsely line the main street. Trees grow up through collapsing porches and cedar shakes rattle in the winds, playing a wild tattoo on steeply pitched roofs. Pack rats frolic where miners and gay ladies danced on rough plank floors, and where games of "21" lasted all winter.

TRESTLE LED DOWN FROM mill and carried pipe line to pump house. Tailings in soupy sludge dropped by gravity and then were lifted to top of huge pile by pumps. House was near to being engulfed by its own dumpings when town died.

ORE CAR STANDS WHERE it was left at mouth of Coulter Tunnel. Mines, whose upper workings were many hundreds of feet higher on mountain, dropped their shafts to level of tunnel which was well lighted in later years and had a restaurant for miners carved out of solid granite and gold ore a mile and a quarter back in the mountain. Blast of icy air emerges from mouth.

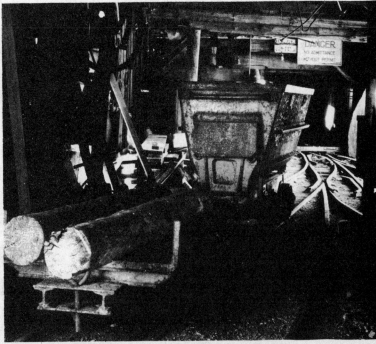

ELK CITY, OREGON

Mary's Peak is the most prominent mountain in the Coast Range as it crosses Benton County. Down its western slope flows a clear, sparkling stream typical of those in coastal Oregon. Near its banks, in 1856, was camped a party of explorers in search of grazing land. Food supplies were low and supper was expected to be beans as usual. Then one man saw a fine bull elk standing on a hill, an easy mark for his gun. In memory of this provident event the stream became Elk Creek.

About four years later, where this stream flows into the Yaquina River, a small settlement grew up. It was named Newton for the man who laid out the plat, Albitha Newton, and placed it as far up the Yaquina as boats could go. During normal low water periods the stream was quite narrow, branches hanging low and sometimes brushing the heads of boat passengers. Water-soaked snags lurked on the bottom of the none too deep waterway to scrape bottoms or rip holes in them. At times of high water the menace of low trees and branches became worse but the influence of ocean tides became noticeable.

As Newton grew and more travel came up the river from Toledo, Yaquina and Newport below on the bay, efforts were made to clear the waterway by removing snags and cutting branches. A small dock was prefabricated at Toledo, brought up on a barge and installed on the bank. Then it was possible for small steamboats to tie up at the town and regular service was instituted. A flat-bottomed stern wheeler was the first to make regular runs, down the bay one day and back the next. The railroad was also completed through Newton and on to bay points.

Two saloons, a hotel, store, Odd Fellows Lodge which was shared by other fraternal orders, many cabins and houses — all grew up on the site, giving the place the appearance of a real town.

The first post office had been established in 1868 with E. A. Abbey the postmaster. Marshall Simpson held the job next, was out of the office for a while and then returned November 23, 1888. He came full of ideas about advancing the status of the little town and one of the first efforts he made was getting the name changed from Newton to Elk City to conform to the name of the post office.

The town flourished until automobiles took away the need for river traffic. And as logging in the area declined so did Elk City. Another blow was the abandonment of the rock quarries which had provided a live industry with workers living and buying supplies in the town.

The old grocery which for years housed the post office is the only business still going in the town by the Yaquina. The Scovilles now operate it and a gas pump. They tell of frequent floods when the only traffic through the main street was by boat. "All these coastal rivers are short," says Mr. Scoville. "Our heavy winter rains of sometimes two and three inches a day quickly swell them to flood heights. In early days there was a sawmill and hotel here. One time when the river was exceptionally high the water took a lot of lumber piled in the sawmill yard and slammed it against the hotel, turning it on its side so it had to be torn down. It was never rebuilt and neither was the wrecked sawmill. That seems to be the way the old town went, little by little."

Elk City still has at least one resource, says Mr. Scoville. "We have extra good fishing here, especially in the middle of summer when steelhead salmon and blueback are running. Then fishermen bring their families over from the Willamette Valley and stay a while. We keep those little cabins there rented all the time."

PICTURESQUE COVERED BRIDGE once carried passenger traffic to depot which still stands on other side but falling into ruin. Spanning Yaquina River it is almost smothered under dense vegetation typical of Oregon coastal country. Town is only three miles in air line from Toledo, largest town in area, nine miles by river, only means of access at one time. Elk City's covered bridge, built about 1922, is 100 feet long.

GRANDVIEW, OREGON

The road to Grandview descends into a deep, precipitous canyon, crosses two turbulent streams, and climbs out again to a typical, high plateau of central Oregon.

The snow peaks looking down on the site are even more spectacular and include a half dozen of the tallest in Oregon. The name "Grandview" does not exaggerate.

But there was exaggeration in the promises to the farmers and homesteaders who settled the place. There would be "plenty of water," "the land is good." They settled to work and found that the sharp rocks on the land were more than enough to make high stone fences all around the fields. The rocks were endless and dulled farm machinery.

Schools were built, homes, barns and a store which served also as a mail distributing center. The letters were hauled across the canyon from Madras.

Optimism was boundless. The settlement extended several miles toward the south and a second school was erected in the Geneva district.

But there was not enough water for this arid place. The junipers encroached upon the farms, the stones continually came to the surface. By the time the tiny cemetery held a dozen graves the town was being deserted, and by 1932 only a handful of people remained, their children going all the way to Culver to school.

Grandview is empty now, the schoolhouse filled with sheep hides, the fields covered with juniper trees and sagebrush.

LITTLE SCHOOLHOUSE served as church on Sundays, now stands deserted. Rusting farm machinery in schoolyard shows defeat in face of rocks, sagebrush and drought.

LARGE JUNIPER TREE shades dooryard of combination store and mail-station. Mail was hauled across canyon from Madras, distributed from here. Junipers and sagebrush are natural "flora" of area, jack rabbits, coyotes and ground squirrels the "fauna."

GRANITE, OREGON

When the original prospectors and settlers arrived at Granite in 1862, they realized the date was July 4th and accordingly named the future town Independence. But the postal authorities said no, there already was an "Independence" in Oregon. Further consultation produced "Granite," for the prevailing rock of the region.

Until about twenty years ago the general store had a good supply of derby hats, black corsets with beaded tops, heavy "snuggy" underwear and brilliantly spangled women's garters.

Now the faded buildings stand empty and deserted, their ranks thinning by fire and collapse under winter snows.

IN FRONT OF OLD CEMETERY stands tiny schoolhouse. Later it served as polling place, a sort of "city hall." Pine-covered hill in background is typical of Blue Mountains. Seen from a distance through haze, heavy stands of ponderosa pines take on bluish look. Ancient headboards totter over forgotten graves behind plank fence at right.

NICKELODEON FACES drugstore across street. Until rather recent years structure also served as store and filling station. Grass-grown streets attest to lack of traffic now. Road carries cars to going mine in mountains and small private claims.

GREENHORN, OREGON

The two young men fresh from the East were as ignorant as they could possibly be on mining lore. They were determined, however, to strike it rich with a gold mine. They had heard that almost anywhere "Out West" they could simply strike a pick in the ground and there would be gold in unlimited quantities. Why they picked on this tiny camp high in the Blue Mountains of Oregon no one knows. But they did, one day, about 1890, walk brashly up to the bar of the little saloon and ask the barkeep, "Where can we dig for gold in this place?"

After the man with the towel recovered his composure, he turned to some of the more seasoned customers and in turn inquired, "Well, where would *you* say these boys might hit a vein of gold?" One of the "regulars" seeing an opportunity for a joke, took them outside and at random pointed to the side of the hill above town, saying, "There's a likely looking spot to dig!"

And dig they dutifully did. In a moment they came back down to the now uproariously merry group lugging a chunk of rock, with the naive question, "How does this look?" Laughter died among the gathering. The piece of rock was "blossom" stuff, richer than anything yet discovered in the camp.

Ridicule vanished, the old-timers in all honesty directed the innocents to stake their claims immediately, but the mine's discoverers didn't get the chance to name their find. The wiseacres had already christened it, "The Greenhorn Mine." The camp changed *its* name to Greenhorn and as such burgeoned and grew into a real, full-scale town, complete with several hotels besides the big one called the "Red Lion." Inevitably, several saloons were established and a newspaper, *The Greenhorn News,* was published every Friday.

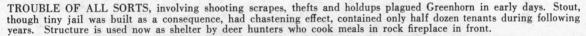

TROUBLE OF ALL SORTS, involving shooting scrapes, thefts and holdups plagued Greenhorn in early days. Stout, though tiny jail was built as a consequence, had chastening effect, contained only half dozen tenants during following years. Structure is used now as shelter by deer hunters who cook meals in rock fireplace in front.

A water system was built, possibly unique among mining camps in that every house had its water piped directly to the kitchen. The source was on Vinegar Hill and the water company laid wooden pipes bound with wire to conduct the supply. Everything worked fine, except that elk wallowed in the spring and frequently broke the pipes.

By 1895, some 3,200 people were living their lives in this green wilderness and the nearby forest slopes boasted several large mines besides the Greenhorn, among them the Phoenix, I.X.L., Humbolt and Virginia.

The place had no regular post office until May, 1902, with Burton Miller as first postmaster. The town is divided by the line between Grant and Baker Counties, with the post office in the latter. Why postal facilities were not established for so many years after the original gold rush in the 1860's is a mystery.

The Greenhorn Mine was purchased by Richard Baird in 1914 and was operated by him until 1925. Some years after that, with increasing cost of mining and non-advancing price of gold, this and other mines became unprofitable to work and Greenhorn died a slow death.

Its people moved away and many of its buildings fell into decay, to be replaced by the magnificent White Firs, *(Abies Conocolor)*, of the area.

ORIGINAL CLAIM CABIN stands in small clearing. Section marker is visible in front of house. Here in infant mining camp lived Mr. Carpenter, the first miner to build a permanent home. Staking out homestead claim he did his necessary "improvement work," mined his discovery and built his cabin long before Greenhorn attained its status as town.

WHERE SPIRITS ROOST

HARDMAN, OREGON

In the days of stagecoaches two small Oregon towns were bitter rivals for the stage depot in their area. They were Raw Dog and Yellow Dog, about a mile apart in Morrow County, Oregon.

In the 1870's many stagecoaches and wagon trains traveling north and south through eastern Oregon and Washington, found one or the other of the two towns a convenient overnight resting place. This business was much more lucrative and easy than the regular ranching and cattle operation. Passengers found themselves shunted from one place to the other as drivers were favored or even bribed to stay the night.

Then, late in the decade, the rivalry became even more intense because it became known that a post office would be established in the area.

The whole thing was settled when Raw Dog was found to have several more people than Yellow Dog and was declared to be the metropolis and a fitting location for a United States Post Office. This move also decided the location of a more permanent stagecoach station and the demise of Yellow Dog was complete. Its remaining inhabitants moved over to the town that "had everything'" and their abandoned stores and buildings, such as they were, completely disappeared.

Now, as a veritable kennel of "dog towns," Raw Dog became just that . . . Dog Town and was so known for many years. When the post office was officially established in 1881, however, the dignitaries frowned on the name Dog Town and instead called the newborn

GENERAL VIEW OF TOWN from cemetery on hill above town. Clouds sweep in from south, but promise of rain is false in summer, usually dry. Two painted buildings are permanently occupied, others temporarily or not at all.

post office Hardman, after the man who had homesteaded the site. So Hardman it was officially known, but the dog tag hung on it for many years.

The town flourished and grew. A large hotel was built just south of the Odd Fellows Hall, and smaller hostelries sprang up along the main street.

There was even a jail, built of 2 x 6 inch lumber laid flat, and considered impregnable. One morning after a particularly boisterous Halloween, however, it was found tipped over on its side. It stayed that way until the following Halloween, when it was set afire, and "made a very hot blaze" according to an old resident.

Parker's Sawmill was located about 15 miles southeast near the pine woods, and contributed much to the economy. More important to the more lively element was the big all-day celebration and dance held every Fourth of July. These annual events were not always conducted with as much decorum as they might have been.

A large flour mill did a good business grinding the local wheat. It stood at the extreme south end of town. A drugstore with the typical false front of its day was built just north of the present grocery store. In front, in the middle of a wooden platform extended from the board sidewalk, was a handpump for water. Since there was no central water system and many people had no well, the pump was a community affair, and news of the townspeople spread rapidly from there.

With the decline of the stagecoaches and wagon trains, and as travel speeded up, the main usefulness of Hardman began to fade away and the town pump served fewer and fewer people. The community slid into a decline from which it will never recover.

HARDMAN MARKS southern edge of wheatfields. Drugstore in background once stood on Main Street.

HOSKINS, OREGON

The remains of Hoskins nestle in a hollow at the edge of the Coast Range, just where the mountains merge with the level flood plain of the Willamette River.

Due to a concentration of Indians at Siletz Agency in 1856, Fort Hoskins was established on the Luckiamute River near the mouth of what is now Bonner Creek, on July 26th of that year. The Fort was named for Lt. Charles Hoskins who had been killed in the battle of Monterrey, Mexico, ten years before.

Lumber was king in those days and the timber to be sawed grew densely there. Virgin forests were so dense as to shut out the light of day except at noon. Sawmills sprang up all along the coast range.

As the woods were depleted close by, short logging railways were extended to the diminishing forests. About 1918 the Valley and Siletz Railroad laid tracks through Hoskins displacing the old store, a relic of the 1880's. The venerable building was moved to a new location a few hundred feet down the slope and beside the tracks.

Mr. Earl Lonie, who now owns the store, says, "But I guess they had some wild times upstairs in the old days." It is easy to imagine the ladies and gentlemen, perspiring from the performance of a lively two-step, walking out on the little balcony for a cooling breath of air.

A number of abandoned houses and cabins are scattered about, no pattern of streets exists any more for Hoskins, and as Mr. Lonie sadly remarked, "The place seems to be a thing of the past."

COVERED BRIDGE LEADS to Hoskins. Many of these structures may be found in back ways of area. Luxuriant foliage of maples and firs is in sharp contrast to stark bareness of towns of "Great Basin" recently visited.

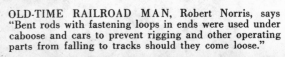

OLD GROCERY PRE-
SENTS architectural study
from rear. Front has bal-
cony extending from upper
story.

ANTIQUE CABOOSE dates from 1870's. Crossed bars
on sides were for reinforcement. Probably even they
would not hold venerable car together now. Repair
shops with walls full of parts is in background.

OLD-TIME RAILROAD MAN, Robert Norris, says
"Bent rods with fastening loops in ends were used under
caboose and cars to prevent rigging and other operating
parts from falling to tracks should they come loose."

PHANTOMS OF THE FAR WEST

JACKSONVILLE, OREGON

Original discoveries of gold were on Jackson Creek, in December, 1851. By the middle of the summer the place was already swarming with prospectors and miners of claims already staked out and the city of Jacksonville was on its way.

This frenzied activity was interrupted for a time when the Rogue River Indian wars of 1855 broke out, but resumed at the cessation of hostilities.

A smallpox epidemic in 1868, a flood in 1869 and fire upon fire ravaged the village, but never seriously discouraged the populace.

Advent of the Civil War split the people into factions, however, and did more to cause of dissension and strife than all the natural disasters put together. But that too, passed away and left the town in the peace it still enjoys today in a somnolent but living atmosphere.

Jacksonville is not a dead ghost, but neither is it a lively one, except for the tourists who visit this fascinating monument to Oregon's mining history.

CROWDED GRAVES ARE SUBMERGED in dense grove of cypress and madrona. These last are indigenous to area and are striking with peeling red trunks and evergreen leaves, clusters of orange-yellow berries.

FIRST PROTESTANT CHURCH west of the Rockies. Covered wagon is "prop" of Oregon's centennial year.

WELL-FORTIFIED AGAINST bandits and Indians was this building, dating from 1856.

PETER BRITT STANDS OUT among early-day photographers. His studio is set up in the museum located in the old courthouse. Beautiful structure was built in 1883. Courtroom upstairs is preserved intact.

KERBY, OREGON

James Kerby (or Kerbey) spelled his name first one way, then the other, and confusion still hovers over the spelling, not only of his name, but that of the town named for him. The town seems to have first been called Kirbey's Ranch, then Kerbyville. Then for a time it was named Napoleon! In 1857, D. S. Holton got control of most of the town and decided, since it was in Josephine County, Napoleon would be an elegant and appropriate title. The name was popular only with him and the town soon reverted to plain Kerby.

Kerby was well established by 1850, and in 1858 took over the position of county seat. As usual, gold was the main attraction, but many other minerals have been mined in the area, including iron, quicksilver, cobalt and ilmenite. Infusoria earth and quartz have had their day, too.

At its best, Kerby had a population of 500 or more miners and the usual proportion of hangers-on.

About this time, a neighboring mining town contracted for an elegant pool table, to be packed in in sections on the backs of mules. The expedition started from Crescent City, California. On camping one night near Kerby, one mule with the most important part of the table turned up missing. When found in the morning, he was dead. The packer decided he had gone far enough, buried his mule and established his pool hall in Kerby.

The town populace has dwindled to a mere handful, but a typical group of buildings remains, including the Masonic Temple, a tiny store, and several false fronts.

Across the street is a huge oak which is supposed to have been the inevitable "Hanging Tree," for the only ghost town without a "Hanging Tree" is a town with no trees at all. In this case, since the old Courthouse stood in its shade, and convicted prisoners were dragged out and hanged immediately, the tree certainly would have been convenient for this grisly use.

"HANGING TREE" broods over remnant of Kerby.

KERNVILLE, OREGON

All that glitters in ghost town lore is not gold. It can even be the silver horde Rex Beach wrote about — the silvery sides of salmon establishing an industry and a town. It happened that way at Kernville.

The man who started it was Daniel Kern, born in Menominee, Michigan, on September 12, 1856. He came west at twenty-one, working at one odd job after another in Portland, Oregon. They taught him how to get along with people and lead them and in a short time he was a contractor on jetty projects at

the mouth of the Columbia River, at Bandon, Coos Bay, Yaquina, and Grays Harbor on the Washington coast. Kern was particular about the type of rock used in the jetties and prospected for the material personally. He discovered the quarry at Elk City, Oregon, and the sandstone from it was sent down the Yaquina River to build the breakwater in the bay.

A man working along the Washington and Oregon coasts in those days could not help being involved with salmon in one way or another. In

OLD BUSINESS CENTER of Millport, as Kernville was confusingly called in hectic days of first world war, surrounded by stranded and neglected fishing boats. Building in background housed general offices of mill company. Beyond, now collapsed, were bunkhouses called "bachelors' halls." Fish boat on side is typical of thousands plying coastal rivers, most of them in war years equipped with famous Regal engines. Two-man crews laid out gill nets across stream and let them drift with current, catching whatever type of salmon was running, with sturgeon and other fish.

1896, Dan Kern enlisted his brother, John H., as partner and built a large fish cannery on the north bank of the Oregon coastal river called the Siletz. Wildly remote from civilization, the spot became the first white settlement in North Lincoln County.

Two years later a youth, Warren Pohle of Salem, took a trip to the coast to fish the Siletz. He later wrote — "The river was full of Indians fishing for salmon to supply the cannery there." He said the Indians got 25¢ apiece for Chinooks and a dime for "silversides", regardless of size. The Kern Bros. Packing Co. was later sold to Mat P. Kiernan and J. W. Cooke of Portland and eventually Sam Elmore of Astoria took it over.

Elmore wrecked the building, using the lumber to rebuild a short distance from the Siletz. The "new" Elmore Cannery employed a large number of Chinese laborers in the plant, bunkhouses being built back of the main building. Rice was their staple food, imported by the ton, the straw bundles coming in by boat. Eventually the cannery became a boat building plant.

Elections were held in the cannery, the precinct being called "Kern." A number of other industries, including a sawmill, were developed on the south side of the small river, the short crossing made by boat. The post office was also established there, July 6, 1896, with John Kern as the first postmaster, succeeded by Mat Kiernan. There were some dark, slack periods in Kernville history when the post office was listed as "Not In Service."

Daniel's daughter Grace, who now lives in retirement in Portland, recalls a trip to Kernville in the early days before there was a road along the coast. "We spent a summer at the cannery, hoping the sea air would be of benefit to my brother Arthur who was suffering from rheumatic fever. I was two years younger but well remember the interesting trip from Portland. We went to Corvallis, transfering to a line called the Corvallis and Eastern. It was pulled by a wood-burning locomotive and ran only to Yaquina on the coast. We got off at Toledo just this side of Yaquina and again transferred, this time to a buckboard. We rode on this to a place called Olsen's Landing, then completed the remainder of the trip to the Siletz by rowboat. There were four young men there on a fishing trip, one of them a medical student named Lee Steiner. All the young men had beautiful voices and would serenade us every night. Then one day Arthur had a very bad attack of the fever. Mr. Steiner carried him to the salmon boat which was to get us to the steamer for Astoria and he stayed with us, helping mother take care of Arthur. At Astoria we got on the train going up the Oregon side of the Columbia River to Portland where we met my father who took us to the hospital there. My brother recovered and about 1943 met Dr. Steiner who remarked — "You don't look much like the sick boy I carried out of Kernville years ago."

Kernville's busiest years were those when Kaiser Wilhelm was so close to winning the First World War. Oregon's coastal spruce was found to be the best material known for making airplanes. The Sitka spruce reached its finest development and heaviest stand along the lower Siletz. An average acre of these trees yielded 150,000 board feet. A sawmill, the Kernville Spruce Division Mill, with a capacity of 30,000 feet a day had to "hump it" to cope with the War Department's estimate of 3 billion board feet accessible from tidewater. The mill maintained a schedule with creditable consistency, considering all the difficulties of production. There was no dependable wagon road reaching the place. Wet weather made a quagmire of the only road there was and high tides covered it. The Siletz was crossed by a "drift and pull" ferry, since no bridge had been built, and this river was only one of many along the route north.

Except for a few supplies brought in by wagon in the summer when roads were dryer and tides lower, all materials depended upon boat shipments and there were plenty of troubles with these too. The depth of the Siletz bar was only about seven feet in a changing channel.

When a drawbridge was finally completed over the Siletz in November of 1926, it was a major link in the coastal highway system, so impeded with tidal flats, rivers and canyons. Kernville was already a ghost town and the new bridge only hastened the removal of almost all the remaining residents and old machinery from the mill to the new Kernville on the highway.

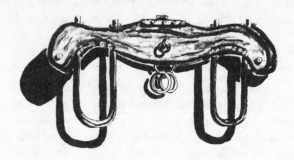

KINGS VALLEY, OREGON

The words had a deep and tragic significance. Samuel Parker, the wagon master, wrote them as they sounded. "We tuck what is called the Meek cut of", and later in view of what happened, he added: "A bad cut of fore all that tuck it." It was indeed a bad cutoff for all who took it.

Destiny interfered with the crunchingly slow progress of the wagon trains at Fort Boise. A number of them bound for Oregon's Willamette Valley met there, the emigrants exhausted and dispirited, yet trying feebly to answer the question — "Shall we keep on and if we do, do we go by the established Oregon Trail or follow this Steven Meek and pay him $5 a wagon? Maybe he's right and maybe he's wrong. All we know about him is he's a brother of Joe Meek who is a trusted mountain guide."

One party did follow Meek, the train of Nahum King, his young daughter Sarah and her husband Rowland Chambers. And then deep trouble began. The ox-drawn wagons were in the country named by French trappers "Malheur", meaning "evil hour", and so it proved. Sarah died, near the place the hamlet Beulah appeared forty years later, and a crudely lettered stone was set to mark the grave — "Mrs. S. Chambers   Sept. 3, 1845."

The procession toiled on at a maddeningly slow pace. In two days it stopped at a stream, a much disputed spot where, legend says, the children picked up gold nuggets and played with them in a little blue bucket which they hung under the wagon when it began moving. When the long journey ended its contents were discovered and the wild excitement caused many searches for the spot on the stream and many tales about the mythical Blue Bucket Mine, which was never found. The weary emigrants did not join in the hunt or lift their spirits in wondering. They were just thankful to be

YOUNG LT. GARBER just couldn't win, even at the end. Tombstone, paid for by collection among soldiers stationed at Fort Hoskins came from stone-cutters with "r" in name transposed to "s," was erected anyway.

GRIST MILL, built in summer of 1854, is among oldest in Oregon country. Located on banks of Luckiamute River, it utilized water power generated by overflow from rock dam built by partners Rowland Chambers and A. H. Reynolds. Upper story was storage space for grain to be ground.

able to settle down in the peaceful valley with no wish to return to the place of tribulation even if they found it.

The fertile little valley the Nahum King family and widowed Rowland Chambers selected was separated from the Willamette Valley by a low line of hills. It came to be called Kings Valley and the apostrophe, if any, has long since disappeared.

The lonely Chambers wooed and won another of King's daughters. He built a little house and planted a large acreage in wheat as did most early settlers there. But instead of shipping out his grain, he built a grist mill on the creek called Luckiamute. By means of a stone dam he was able to get enough fall in the slow moving creek to turn an old-fashioned water wheel which transferred power to the

mill higher on the bank by means of huge, hand-made leather belts. Chambers had an able partner in the project, A. H. Reynolds, whose lately discovered diary records the time of construction "We started work on the grist mill in June, 1854."

On April 13 of the next year the Kings Valley post office was established with Rowland Chambers as first postmaster. From then on the town grew rapidly, supporting a sawmill, store and several saloons. Although a log school house dated as early as 1849, a church had to wait for popular subscription to get a frame building, 36 by 58 feet.

Indian troubles ended with the surrender of Old John, one of the main trouble makers, the last chief to come to the treaty grounds on the Rogue River. He set his gun against a rock during negotiations

UPPER FLOOR of grist mill had V-shaped floor, divided by partition, bottom on each side having opening for chute through which either of two kinds of grain could be fed to grinding stones. These photos were made in spring of 1963 when historic mill was due to be burned. Dam in river remains, impounded pool still providing neighboring children with swimming hole.

risings. The land was at the southern end of the town of Kings Valley and belonged to Rowland Chambers who sold it willingly enough.

At the rear of the bench and set against the hill was the largest building, the barracks. Immediately to the left was the latrine, then the commissary, water tower and bakery. The guard house was placed at the right of the barracks and farther down, near the foot of the bench, a hospital with Dr. D. G. Campbell of Corvallis in charge. The building still stands. At the left of it were the several buildings serving as officers' quarters which completed the square. In the center was a spacious parade ground.

Lt. Philip Sheridan, active in the Oregon wars in 1859, was the first in charge of Fort Hoskins but he was soon promoted to higher rank in the Civil War which followed. Taking his place was Capt. Augur, the unfortunate who had to take the brunt of complaints from neighboring farmers as to the behavior of his soldiers. One such protest was strongly worded. "The garrison at Fort Hoskins has a strong predilection for wine, women and song. Details are so indelicate they will not bear repeating." The report obviously lacked the savory details some wanted but ended with the definite statement: "The soldiers are a menace to the peace and prosperity of the community."

The captain is reported to have been "upset". He wrote letters to the farmers and neighbors ranging from Kings Valley itself to the little town on the other side of the fort called Fort Hoskins requesting

and at one point grabbed it to shoot down the officer reading the terms. When fifty soldiers aimed their rifles at him he gave up, temporarily, and surrendered his weapon. He was first sent with other Indians to the reservation at Grande Ronde, northeast of Kings Valley. When the neighboring farmers complained "the ground here is too good to waste on redskins. They ought to be thrown out so we can farm it", the Indians were transferred to the Siletz agency, farther south and near the Coast. A fort was ordered built at the western gate of the reservation, not so much to protect the settlers from the Indians as to guard the natives from being debauched by the whites. In this lofty aim the authorities were not entirely successful.

The site selected for Fort Hoskins was on a bench of a gently rising hill overlooking the lower part of the Luckiamute Valley, beautifully serene but considered the most likely spot for Indian up-

ROWLAND CHAMBERS with some of brood. Picture is thin, positive film on cracked glass, provided some problems in copying by this photographer. It is about 100 years old.

FAMILY GATHERING photo was taken after Rowland Chambers passed away but not before he had started population explosion. First wife died on journey to Oregon, second probably woman at right of infant in center, eldest daughter at left. Relationship of others vague. Many now rest in old Kings Valley cemetery not far away.

them to state their feelings on the matter. As reports came in Augur held a plebiscite with Rowland Chambers, L. Norton, O. King — son of the late Nahum — and other parties concerned. The somewhat surprising consensus was stated: "Either the farmers have had a change of heart or else the chief complainant, Mr. Ross Browne, was a liar." True, one farmer did say that although he had made good money selling the soldiers milk and eggs, the profit was nullified by their thefts of his hogs which they butchered and added to the commissary as a change of diet.

There was also continual trouble from Indians who insisted on coming over from the Siletz reservation and getting into trouble with the white settlers. One was caught peeking into the bedroom window of a farm house. The owner swore he would kill the next Indian Peeping Tom and he promptly did. This caused an uproar but the bereaved family was quickly placated with a payment of $200 by the army.

Then there was the incident concerning the beautiful Indian girl and young Lieutenant Garber. On duty at Fort Hoskins, he became acquainted with the girl in the early spring of 1850. She was soon visiting the reputedly "very handsome" officer in his quarters and then moving in, apparently tolerated by fellow officers until her parents complained, not so much on moral grounds as they needed her at home. Hoping to put an end to the affair, Augur sent Garber to Fort Vancouver to cool off, but reckoned without the persistence of the young squaw who walked all the way to the fort on the Columbia River to rejoin her lover. Garber was returned to Fort Hoskins and brought before Captain Augur for a dressing down and a warning to stop seeing the girl. This was supposed to end the matter but the Indian maiden was again discovered in the lieutenant's rooms. Again sent for by Augur, tempers flared on both sides and Garber made some insubordinate remarks. He was sentenced to six months in the guard house but died of unstated causes in a few months. He was buried in the Kings Valley cemetery, his grave identified only by the regular army marker for a time. Then his fellow soldiers contributed funds for a marble marker which stands today. Ironically, as though pointing up his ill luck, his name is misspelled.

OCCASIONAL BEAR was killed by soldiers and civilians at Fort Hoskins. Comment of one soldier: "It was a treat to get something we could eat once in a while." This and other very old pictures were loaned by descendant of Rowland Chambers.

LONEROCK, OREGON

Scotland's greatest export is Scots and the newly married Spaldings were two of them, making the incongruous jump from the fishing village of Banff, Aberdeenshire, to the raw and bleak wilderness of Lonerock in 1898.

At 17, David Spalding went to the arid eastern section of Oregon to establish a ranch home for his intended bride, Sophia Essom, choosing the locality near Trailfork in an almost barren area of sagebrush and juniper trees. The nearest large settlement was Condon, some 20 miles away but a smaller one, Lonerock, was only five miles distant and David felt Sophia would not be too lonely with such near neighbors. After five years of improving the ranch he returned to Scotland and claimed his bride. She had been taking nurses' training, a skill of inestimable value in a land so far from doctors and hospitals.

On arrival at the lonely farm the young couple set to work in earnest to establish a few of the comforts, and these were few indeed. One deprivation was being almost completely cut off from the outside world. Both were eager for news from Scotland but getting mail was a chore. Their small home was some distance from the mail route and a temporary system was set up that gave the ranch its name. When the mail carrier came by the road intersection he would put the Spaldings' mail in a heavy paper bag and stuff it in the crotch of a large juniper. Before long the Spalding place was the "Paper Sack Ranch."

Sophia and David worked their place for a number of years, then moved to the comparative comfort of Lonerock. This town had been settled as a crossroads gathering place for ranchers and sheepherders and being on the main emigrant route a supply center was needed. Two ranch partners, R. G. Robinson and Albert Henshaw, laid out the town in 1881, seeing to proper platting the next year. Prior to this, in '72, a post office

TINY JAIL held last prisoner, drunken Indian, 25 years ago, once was crowded when sheep were moved to higher pastures by sheepherders who celebrated at crossroads settlement. After last tenant was freed, fire hose cart was moved in. Little shed at right held wood supply for stove. Just past corner of jail is seen edge of early hotel, the Williams.

was established, with Robinson carrying the mail from The Dalles in a buckboard or on horseback.

The arrival of the Spaldings was an occasion for rejoicing, both young people being popular in this new country as they were back home, and social life enjoyed a lift. Since David was an accomplished musician with accordion and piano, and Sophia with a pleasing voice, an entertainment group was started at their ten-room home with neighbors gathering in the evenings for songs and dances.

The couple had two children, Lovena and Cecil. Their mother would make a batch of cookies and leave the lid off for all nearby children to help themselves. She and David became close friends of the Robinsons, Hardies, Maddens and Campbells. Sophia's nursing ability stood her in good stead as she aided in many an emergency as unofficial midwife. She often helped a birth before the only doctor, overworked George Gaunt who might be miles out in the country, could get to the scene.

Busy as she was, Sophia planted a row of little trees along the side of the house and in dry spells carried water from the creek to keep them alive and pumped water from the well when the creek dried up.

People began to move away from Lonerock about the end of the first World War. Water was getting scarce to the point of crop failures every few years, the climate always rigorous, reaching 16 degrees below zero and 100 above. The Spaldings stayed on and even after David's death in 1935, Sophia kept the big house tidy and the front yard full of flowers, still administering to the needs of her dwindling neighbors.

In 1956 she fell, fracturing her hip, was taken to a Portland hospital. Upon recovering she stayed with her married daughter Lovena in Condon. Another fall two years later resulted in breaking her other hip requiring more hospitalization. From her wheelchair she cheered other patients as she ignored her own pain. In July of 1961 she died and was returned to the little Lonerock church for the funeral.

By this time the town was almost completely deserted but on that Sunday, July 29, the church was filled beyond capacity, more than three hundred people coming from far and wide to say goodbye to the woman who had held such an important place in their lives.

IMPOSING SCHOOL was once alive with children, even housed higher grades in one room 2 to 5 years ago, high school later moved to Condon. Sophia Spalding's daughter, Lovena Palmer, taught here between 1934 and 1942, another teacher, Ruth Potter. Only seven pupils remained in '60-'61 taught by Geraldine Overhulse. Old school is now entirely deserted, cupola still holding silent bell.

LONEROCK M. E. CHURCH dates from before turn of century, saw regular services for many years. Now worshipers gather only on rare occasions when minister of Assembly of God Church of Condon makes visit. Huge rock behind church gave town its name. Funeral services for pioneer, Mrs. David Spalding were held here.

MABEL, OREGON

When the Ritters arrived in Mabel in 1912 they were aghast. The little town was wide open, as the minister understood the term, composed of about five hundred roistering loggers and sawmill workers, most of them single, to whom a church meant one place where you couldn't blow off steam.

The Mabel men lived in bunkhouses and ate in several big chow houses supplied by the main cookhouse. When a meal was ready the head cook would send a flunky with an iron bar to beat a tattoo on a triangle hanging outside the door, called the "gut hammer." Then the fellow would have to jump back like a chipmunk or have boot hobs up and down his spine. One flunky, it is said, varied the humdrum three notes by some jazzy tune. They were more careful of him when they rushed the door and he lived long enough to set chokers.

This was the ungodly setting the Herman H. Ritters were called upon to enlighten. He and Mary Elizabeth Nedrow were married in Illinois in 1894 and moved to Pennsylvania where Herman had his first job teaching in a country school. At the start of his four-day week, he walked nine miles to the little building, boarding with one farm family and another and then walking home Thursday evening. He taught sixty-one pupils on a salary of $25 a month. Each four days away from home cost $1.50 so it was a meagre existence.

In search of something better, the young couple migrated to Kansas, then Oklahoma and on to California. Teaching in small schools barely kept body and soul together but somehow young Ritter managed to study for the ministry and was ordained in the Church of the Brethren. His first call was the little

CHURCH OF THE BRETHREN. Brother Herman H. Ritter, with wife Mary Elizabeth, lived in Mabel 42 years, preaching last sermon in little church in September, 1953. Following January, couple was honored by community at nearby Mohawk Grange. Party planners were hard put to decide on gifts as Ritters lived austerely and luxury items would be out of place. *Eugene Register-Guard* story was written at this stage of uncertainty and item on January 31, 1954 read: "Their tastes are simple, their needs few indeed, since they have abiding faith, happy hearts and health surprising for their years, besides their own snug home and garden, fowls and a cow. (At the latest the committee seemed to favor an electric blanket.)" Reverend Ritter was ordained at early age of 18.

church in the raw timber town of Mabel and he preached there for nearly fifty years.

The place boomed during World War I, hitting a stride never again equalled. The Coast Fork Lumber Company ran two eight-hour shifts in the mill and turned out up to 180,000 feet of lumber in each. This was the wildest period in Mabel's history for the hard-working, hard-living, well-paid loggers and sawmill men were going to relax when they felt like it, especially on Saturday nights, come hell or high water. Some went to Eugene a few miles south "to get their teeth fixed" but they could do a passable job of "blowing her in" right at home. The more genteel loggers who had regular girls in Mabel would save choice pieces of pitchy wood to take along on a courting cruise. Somehow an armful of fat pine seemed more appropriate than a handful of wild flowers and if they got the cold shoulder they could always throw more wood on the fire and keep warm.

Once settled into the community, the Ritters enjoyed learning about its history. The heavily timbered valley saw its first whites when a small party headed by Jacob Spores pursued a band of marauding Indians into the area in 1849. Losing their quarry, the men stood on a hill and surveyed the virgin stands of Douglas fir running down to the shining river. Spores, a native of Montgomery County, New York, was reminded of the Mohawk River back home and named this new one for it.

In 1870 a small clearing was hacked out of the wilderness about three miles above the entrance of Shotgun Creek into the Mohawk and a sawmill was built to turn out boards for cabins along the stream. By 1878 a community had grown up around the small mill, large enough to require a post office, the first official being Alfred Drury. His second daughter was named Mabel and so was the little town.

R. W. Earnest, now of Marcola nearby, remembers the first site of the town. "Around 1906 my parents took me as a small child to pick blackberries around the ruins of the old Fields mill." By that time the timber had been cut out and Mabel was moved to its present location. Mr. Earnest treasures memories of the area, among his keepsakes the "gut hammer" from the cookhouse.

In 1957 U. S. Congressman Norblad announced plans for closing six small Oregon post offices to save money. "A good example," he said, "is the one at Mabel, Lane County, where there are only six families to serve. The post office receipts are about $280 a year and the cost to the government $2,300."

In addition to his work as minister, Herman Ritter had taken care of the postmaster duties. When

he relinquished these at 70, he turned them over to a woman who held the job for a year. Then Mrs. Mildred Gwynn took over and had been postmistress for fifteen years when the closure came. She took down the Mabel Post Office sign from the small lean-to at her residence, thus ending a service unbroken for 78 years.

MASSIVE RUINS OF POWER PLANT of huge Coast Fork Lumber Co. operated during World War I. Furnace remains, boiler and other metal parts salvaged for war effort. Built about 1910, mill was closed in '28 when Robert Dollar Co. foreclosed, third mill on this site. Earliest was Hyland, started before turn of century. It burned, was followed by Sunset Lumber Co. mill. Closure of Coast Fork operation spelled doom to Mabel's prosperity. Several other mills were active in area at various times, some with water power, one with wheel in Shotgun Creek. Larger one had saws driven by water of Mohawk River.

MALHEUR CITY, OREGON

There is a story that Malheur City received its name in the early days of mining there when a tunnel caved in trapping a French miner who died of his injuries. "Tam" McArthur, in his book "Oregon Place Names" thinks this is highly improbable, that the name came from the same source as did Malheur River. His version concerns Peter Skene Ogden, a Hudson Bay trapper, who made an expedition into the Snake River country and noted in his journal: "Tuesday, Feb. 14, 1826. We encamped on *River Au Malheur* (unfortunate river) so called on account of property and furs having been hid here formerly, discovered and stolen by natives."

As for Malheur City itself, it is not on the Malheur River but the much smaller Willow Creek close by and it was in this stream that gold was discovered in 1863. A group of miners who had left the exhausted El Dorado nearby, were prospecting for other diggings and made their find about the time they were ready to give up and go back to California.

The gravels of Willow Creek had plenty of gold and at first, when miners were easily satisfied, they panned and sluiced the stream when there was water in it and quit when there wasn't —which was often. Getting impatient at these enforced delays they made efforts to get water to the diggings and this resulted in the El Dorado Ditch, in that day an immense undertaking. The largest of its kind on the West Coast, it was planned and carried out by W. H. Packwood who engineered the Auburn and Sparta ditches.

The project was started in 1863 and was at first

FIRE LEVELLED ALL WOODEN HEADBOARDS in Malheur cemetery. Identification of these graves was lost, partially restored by memory, a few new markers erected. Some are pathetic in their brevity, such as: "A Mother and Her Three Children."

744

MANY YEARS HAVE PASSED over Malheur City since any mail was placed in box. Malheur is hot in summer, cold in winter and dugout style of home building had advantages besides making use of available materials. Rock and dirt walls had excellent insulating qualities, were only type to survive fire.

called the Burnt River Ditch since it was to carry water from that stream. The digging got off to a slow start but by '67 eleven miles had been built; forty-six more in the next two years. In 1870 the project was bought by an Illinois firm which speeded things up by putting 1,000 Chinese laborers on it. By some default the ditch was back in Packwood's hands in '74 and he kept at it four more years.

When the channel was carrying water it was 134 miles long and cut through many a big hill on its way to El Dorado and Malheur City, costing between a quarter and a half million dollars. An issue of the *Portland Oregonian* of that day report-

ed: "El Dorado Ditch in Baker County is now carrying . . . about 800 inches of water, from which is realized about $600 every 24 hours, over and above running expenses." This was below its capacity, as historian Isaac Hiatt wrote. "The main ditch was five feet wide at the bottom, seven at the top, with a carrying capacity of 2,400 miner's inches." But it was large enough to float logs for building purposes and proved to be a boon to Malheur City for five years, even if it did not pay for itself.

In 1887 Malheur County was formed and the town found itself out of Baker County and in the

FIRE IN 1957 started in tinder-dry grass, swept unhindered through Malheur, destroyed all wooden buildings remaining from mining heyday.

extreme northern end of the new one. El Dorado was dead, placer mining unproductive there and going out in Malheur. The ditch was no longer used by miners and its owners tried to find new uses for it. In 1911 the Eastern Oregon Agricultural Co. was formed to convert it to irrigation purposes but Baker County farmers were not willing to share the water with those in Malheur County and the costly project was dropped. And as the ditch dried up, so did Malheur City. On August 16, 1957 a disastrous grass fire devastated the few lingering remains of the town.

MARYSVILLE, OREGON

Nostalgia must have soon taken over the little group of prospectors from California. They had discovered traces of gold in Dog Creek near John Day, traced them to a good ledge on the hill and there founded a little town. This was in April of 1862, and they christened the infant camp Marysville after their home town.

In two years the place already had a population of several hundred and the juvenile element needed, though likely did not desire, a school. With contributions and a poll-tax one was built, this being the second school district in Grant County. It started off with twenty-one pupils and one teacher. This brave soul was a girl named Elizabeth Chope. The community spent $97.34 that first year.

The town was started so early, the buildings were so impermanent and have been abandoned so long that tracing its plan is difficult. Almost all of Marysville has melted away, leaving only the collapsed shell of the schoolhouse. Before long this, too, will have vanished.

PATHETIC REMAINS of little school crown bluff above canyon of John Day River. Rimrock scene is typical of eastern Oregon where low elevation and rainfall do not permit stand of timber.

STAGE LINE BLUES

Mitchell, Oregon

It did not take long for Canyon City to boil over after the news of the gold discovery spread east and west. There were no facilities for the people who thronged the place, no way for mail to get there. A mail route was a prime necessity and one was hurriedly established from The Dalles on the Columbia River, mainly over ancient Indian trails, twisting over flats and hills.

Mail was put in tightly strapped saddle bags. Daring riders carried letters at 50 cents each, newspapers, even though outdated, at $1. Some riders were waylaid and killed by Indians but dangers were accepted as part of the job.

Dust and nuggets in the veritable flood of gold from Canyon City were shipped to Portland by way of Sherar's Bridge and over the Barlow Road, or to The Dalles by the mail route. As Indian attacks along the way became more acute, the Federal Government improved the latter route to expedite the movement of soldiers to base camps and it was thenceforth called The Dalles-Canyon City Military Road.

Pony express and pack train were soon followed by regular stage lines, the first one operated by the man for whom Wheeler County would be named, Henry H. Wheeler. On May 1, 1864, he placed stock, wagons and coaches on the 180-mile run between the Columbia River town and the gold camp in the John Day Valley. Later he often related the next four years were the most exciting ones of his life.

Wheeler's first trip conveyed 11 passengers to Canyon City, about as many on the return, each paying a fare of $40. Then regular trips three times a week were established, Wheeler driving his rig with four horses. In 1865 he was awarded the mail contract. Encounters with Indians were varied and frequent, enough of them, Wheeler said, to fill a book, one in particular being a bloody hair-raiser.

On Sept. 7, 1866 he was driving the route between Dayville and Mitchell, accompanied by H. C. Page, Wells Fargo agent. Among the valuables were the usual mail, $10,000 in greenbacks, $300 in coin and several diamond rings. Near Mitchell a band of about twenty Indians appeared on horseback, opening fire almost at the same instant, the first bullet going through both

of Wheeler's cheeks and taking out several teeth with a section of jawbone. Unable to speak he signaled Page to hold the Indians at bay as long as possible and jumping to the ground he managed to unhitch the horses. Then the two mounted a pair of animals never before ridden and got away to the road house at the Meyers ranch.

After Wheeler's wounds were dressed, he and Page returned to the scene of the attack to find the mail bags ripped open and contents scattered about. Valueless to the Indians they had strewn the greenbacks to the winds. Except for a small part of the currency all valuables including rings were recovered.

One of the several stopping places along the Military Road was named for J. H. Mitchell, former U.S. Senator from Oregon. By the time the place became large enough to be platted it already had two stores, blacksmith and hotel. Its location was not chosen but happened to be a good camping place. A stream called Bridge Creek afforded year around water and cottonwood trees shaded the small level area. The fact that the spot was at the bottom of a narrow canyon coming out of

BRONZE PLAQUE marks site of stage driver Wheeler's most notable encounter with Indians.

DOORWAY to old homestead cabin near Mitchell.

barren mountains was overlooked while the town grew.

In the summer of 1884 Mitchell was flourishing, its many buildings crowded into the narrow confines of the canyon mouth. The season produced numerous heavy thunderstorms in the nearby mountains and one of them dumped a deluge concentrating in a tributary to Bridge Creek canyon. Ignoring the small watercourse at the junction, a nine-foot wall of water burst over a cliff and inundated the town. Damage was tremendous in proportion to the size and isolated situation. Entire buildings were carried away, the street covered with several feet of mud, boulders and debris. This flood, the first in a disastrous series, failed to take any lives. Having made such an ominous roar in going over the cliff all residents were warned and able to escape.

In 1904 another and even worse flood hit the community, sending down a thirty-foot wall of water that took out a total of twenty-eight buildings and killed two citizens. Phil Brogan, well-beloved historian of his area, writes in *East of the Cascades*, "Those who escaped to the hills watched the heavens blaze with lightning and heard the crash of thunder echoing from cliffs that were once ocean ooze." Most recent was a disastrous flood about 1960.

Calamitous fires were added to the unusual drama of Mitchell's existence. One blaze on March 25, 1896, destroyed nine buildings and ten more were lost in August of 1899.

Although the days of gold and pony express are long since finished, Mitchell did some rebuilding from destruction time and again, and still lives. Strategically located on U.S. 26 it provides supplies for far-flung ranches and gas for the traveler between Willamette Valley points and Eastern Oregon and Idaho.

BUILDINGS dating from Mitchell's early days of gold and stage coaches are few. This one of stone survives a few feet back of the row of main street stores. Solid metal door attests its use as a vault in early days. Canyon walls rising directly behind gives hint of narrowness.

FAST DECAYING REMNANTS of barn in Ochoco Mountains above Mitchell shakily survive elements. Gate post, well rubbed by stock, is near collapse.

750

THE RABBITS ALMOST HAD IT

Narrows, Oregon

In the sparsely populated area south of Burns the now defunct village of Narrows was built on an unusual site, unusual in that the two lakes between which it lies are twins except that one contains fresh, potable water, the other being brackish and undrinkable.

One of the lakes, its French name "Malheur" meaning "evil hour" since early day trappers discovered there a valuable cache of furs stolen by natives or other trappers, is fed by fresh water from Donner und Blitzen River. It appears this stream was crossed by a troop of cavalrymen engaged in the Snake Indian War in 1864, a furious electrical storm raging at the time and leader Col. George B. Curry gave it an apt German name.

Harney Lake is by nature isolated from any supply of fresh water, receiving only scanty rainwater and in times of flood a supply from its twin Malheur which overflows into a channel connecting the two. Harney's water, its salts gradually concentrated by evaporation, has become unusable for any purpose.

In 1892 on the narrow strip of land Charles A. Haines built a home centering a cattle ranch he hoped to establish. The single house turned out to be the nucleus for a good sized town because of its isolated position, the only stopping place in a vast lonely land south of Burns and north of Frenchglen where famed Peter French had his domain.

Haines put up several buildings to serve travelers in the otherwise uninhabited 80 miles of desert. In five years the settlement required a post office, in a few more a hotel, several saloons, livery stable and gambling house. A large store did a good business in merchandise brought by freight wagons from Burns. One oldtimer in the area, a rancher from Happy Valley recalls, "I was born at Narrows. It wasn't that my parents were living here, there was a midwife in the place and where else could a woman go to have a baby in this country?"

The only boom or rush Narrows had was on the side of the rabbits. The story is well remembered by Ray Novotny, county extension agent. There were always plenty of rabbits around but during the '20s not particularly troublesome to ranchers.

SCHOOLHOUSE from rear with corner of stone jail visible, about all left of Narrows' town center. No forest exists in this arid section except sparsest growth of junipers, few seen in right distance.

DESERTED SCHOOLHOUSE stands alone on treeless plain. Only family now living at Narrows is that of property owner, Henry Church, whose father came here in 1916. "I was a student in that schoolhouse until 1941," he says. "I was only in the fifth grade then but they had to close the school for lack of pupils."

Then unexplainably there was a population explosion among the long-eared, long-geared jacks. They made such inroads of forage and crops that the county placed a five cent bounty on each pair of rabbit ears brought in. Not in the habit of bothering much about such small game, ranchers now found some profit in shooting the pests and on the next trip to Burns collecting the bounty. Some, with only a few dozen pairs to turn in, were glad to do business with the Narrows storekeeper who paid three cents a pair in trade and who collected a nickel in Burns. When the depression came its effects seemed to extend even to the Narrows rabbits, keeping population down to a minimum.

Other fauna fared better. Both Malheur and Harney Lakes are bordered by lush growths of aquatic plants. From pre-historic times immense flocks of water birds have bred in thickets of reedy growths. Migratory fowl including herons, pelicans, egrets and geese gathered in such flocks as to temporarily obscure the sun. In 1908 the area just south of Narrows was set aside and dedicated by President Roosevelt as the Malheur Migratory Bird Refuge, the original area later expanded to 159,872 acres.

In the 1930s the road to Burns was paved and nearly all the ranchers around Narrows owned cars. They drove handily to the larger town to find more variety in the stores and Narrows was as good as doomed, its demise conceded when the hotel burned down.

Henry Church and his family are now the only residents. He owns the property adjoining the bird refuge, raising cattle on the vast acreage. The Churches live in a picturesque old house in the middle of the deserted town. They are interested in antiquities and during the last 20 years have uncovered over 100 arrowheads and other Indian artifacts around the farm. An obsidian knife they found was checked out at the University of Oregon which established its age as about 1000 years. Almost certainly the material came from Glass Buttes deposits of obsidian not far west of Burns.

The Churches find that owning a ghost town has its drawbacks. Some visitors have displayed a regrettable lack of respect for private property. When interviewed in 1966 by Robert Olmos, Portland *Oregonian* writer, Church said, "People have damaged and almost carried off the old buildings. I put up no trespassing signs in self-defense, but they are ignored, so I have had to tear down some of the old houses and expect to raze the rest."

PONDEROSA PINE is familiar tree in Ochocos, intricate textural pattern of plated bark shown here.

SOLIDLY BUILT JAIL, only stone building in Narrows. Not far from jail Mrs. Church found nearly buried Colt pistol. Although stock was rotted away serial number 107335 is still clearly visible.

753

NEW ERA, OREGON

New Era. The name held promise, hope. Maybe, thought Joseph Parrott, that would be just the name for the community springing up around his store and grist mill on Parrott Creek flowing into the Willamette River above the falls. It was the name of the religious group on the hill overlooking the farm he settled on in 1855 — The New Era Spritualist Society which printed a little tract, THE NEW ERA. Maybe with the railroad coming now in 1869, the settlement would be inspired with that name — New Era.

In 1892 a five-year-old girl saw this new land with big, wondering eyes. Now Laura Ellen Thompson, she looks into the past when her father turned his back on the wild and wicked mining country around Dillon, Montana, and brought his family to the mild climate and rich soil of Oregon.

As activities of the spiritualist society broadened its members acquired more land and buildings, starting a regular summer program of camp meetings. They must have been very successful, Laura believes, as she remembers "long lines of wagons full of people waiting to buy tickets for camping privileges. We attended some meetings although my folks never actually joined. They were very interesting, stressing the return of one's spirit after death."

By this time the little store of Joseph Parrott was inadequate and outdated. Laura's father saw his

OLD HERMAN ANTHONY FARM on hill above railroad, across from grounds of New Era Spiritualist Church and campgrounds, half-mile from site of Catholic Church and cemetery, Anthony, immigrant from Germany, was familiar with "Lichgate" (old English "Lychgaet") and decided one could well serve as portal to his farm. This type of gate had a somber origin in Europe, was covered entrance to burial grounds where preliminary services were held at bier. Cupolas and other old world touches adorn old outbuildings dating from about 1880. Anthony was enthusiastic beekeeper, had own ideas about care, such as large bee house to shelter hives in winter, not successful in mild Oregon climate. Bee house is still intact as are other structures, livery stable at right now serving as garage.

opportunity and built a larger one beside the road paralleling the river and railroad tracks. He was appointed postmaster and at one side of the store the Wells Fargo Company had its offices. His daughter says: "There was a great deal going on all the time. Father would be selling groceries, weighing postal parcels and relieving the Wells Fargo man all at the same time."

The valley soil was every bit as rich as newcomers expected — black, loamy stuff that grew great quantities of top quality potatoes. The farmers soon were growing more of them than could be consumed locally and shipped them to Portland. Because of the falls at Oregon City, the crop was hauled in wagons to that point, transferred to boats below the falls. After a system of locks was built, boats could load at New Era and when the railroad came through, produce was shipped by train.

A year after Laura's arrival at New Era she started school in the little one room schoolhouse which taught all grades. Another pupil was a boy of her age, John Thompson. They grew up with an "understanding" and when John got a job on the river steamer IRALDA, which plied the Columbia River with terminal dock at Rainier, Oregon, John moved there. He did not see much of Laura for a while, only on trips to New Era with his parents.

They were both eighteen on one of these trips and were married. John went to work for the railroad and the couple moved to Portland. He was with the railroad the rest of his working years, eventually retiring with Laura to a home on the banks of the Willamette near Milwaukie, not far from their old New Era haunts.

LITTLE FALSE-FRONTED GEM in picture made about ten years ago, torn down in August of 1964. It had distinction of once being Wells Fargo station as well as containing general store and post office.

755

ORTLEY, OREGON

The Cascade Mountain range, extending in a north and south direction through Washington and Oregon, exerts a very strong climatic effect on the western and eastern sections of both states. The barrier causes most marine storms common to the area to deposit most of their moisture on the westerly slope and holds back much of the colder air prevailing in winter on the eastern side. But there is a rift in this wall, the gorge cut through the Cascades by the Columbia River. Terrific winds whistle through the gorge much of the time at some seasons, their direction depending upon the location of high and low pressure areas. Strangely enough, this geographical peculiarity had a direct effect in making a ghost of a thriving, growing town.

On an exposed plateau on the eastern side of the summit of the Cascades high above the Columbia huddle the few remnants of Ortley, once bustling with 300 people dedicated to the dream of making a fortune growing Ortley apples.

About 1908, a group of business men in Hood River, Oregon, began to work on the idea of establishing a European type of community for the purpose of establishing a large orchard of apples and of creating a world-wide market for them. They selected comparatively level fields on a bluff surmounting high cliffs facing the Columbia — a spec-

tacular setting offering a view of many miles up and down the river and of several snow-clad mountain peaks.

In 1911 the plat was filed in Wasco County for the Town of Ortley by the Hood River Orchard and Land Co. Business buildings were to be centralized near the only source of water, a small stream. Close to these stores were to be the residences of the settlers, who would have to radiate out some little distance to their orchards, which would surround the whole. Lots for homes were an acre in size, orchard space was laid out in 5 and 10 acre plots.

As soon as building was begun the need for expert carpenters and other artisans became apparent and ads were inserted in the Portland newspapers.

A Mr. Hallyburton was one carpenter who responded, his skill so evident he was put in charge of the whole building operation. A school was erected, several stores, a fancy two-story hotel elegantly fitted with bath both upstairs and down, and a saloon. In the rear was a huge barn capable of sheltering 200 horses for working the land.

People moved in eager to set out their little apple trees. Early arrivals had to go down the steep mountainside to Mosier, 7 miles away, for mail but on April 9, 1912, the post office was opened with L. D. Firebaugh as first postmaster. As soon as the new Ortley Hotel was completed the post office was moved into the lobby. The hotel also housed a fine dance hall and Saturday nights people came from Mosier, The Dalles and surrounding farms to relax in a big way.

Kerosene lamps provided the only illumination at first but the developers invited the power company in The Dalles to come up and see what was going on. Duly impressed the purveyors of power invested $10,000 in the up and coming community which soon had electric lights.

A garage was built near the hotel to house two elegant new automobiles, a Franklin and a Cadillac. Prospective settlers were met at the train in style and carried up the twisting mountain road to the town on the heights. Here they were put up at the hotel, wined, dined and importuned to buy an apple orchard. And buy they did until young trees

NATIVE TREES on high windswept plateau are hardy pines, firs and oaks, well adapted to fend for selves. Oaks were left around barns and buildings for shade, removed in areas where apple trees were to be grown.

LITTLE SCHOOL HOUSE stands almost intact but long ago converted to shelter for farm machinery. Water stands in road in foreground. Snowy Cascades show in distance.

flanked the whole countryside. By this time the land company had sunk $200,000 in the project, and had the settlers paid cash for their property, it would at least have broken even. But they had not paid even a fraction of what they owed.

Then some painful truths began to appear. Many apple trees died from lack of water in summer, drowning in an excess of it in winter, there being little or no drainage. And the trees that lived were having their troubles. There were many large fir trees along the bluffs with branches on only one side due to the strong prevailing winds blowing up the river in the growing season. So eager were the settlers to cultivate their ground and get their trees started, they did not question the reason for the lopsided firs until the apple trees began to be distorted the same way.

This discouraging state of affairs caused the orchardists who had bought on contract to quit and move away. Before long the population had dwin-

HOUSES AND BUILDINGS not razed or salvaged for lumber soon disintegrated among native trees which formed grove around nucleus of town. Soil is almost impermeable, rains of winter stand as surface ground water. In summer ground dries into something resembling adobe bricks, cracking and killing roots of susceptible apple trees.

dled to a low point and the post office was closed in November, 1922. Ortley was getting to be a very lonely place for Mr. Hallyburton, the builder, who had decided to hang on, no matter what. And remain he did until he was the sole resident.

The power company was anxious to take its poles and lines down, salvaging what it could from the fiasco but old Hallyburton paid his electric service bill of $1.10 per month regularly and promptly and all the company could do was sit on its hands, hoping for a slip up in the payments. The Community Hall, hotel and other buildings were torn down and the old man held on tenaciously until 1946. Then even he abandoned the place, the light poles and most of the apple trees still living pulled up and desolation in Ortley was complete.

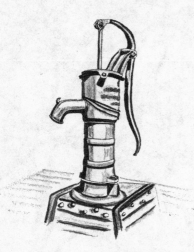

PAISLEY, OREGON

All is quiet on the Paisley front. With the saw-mill shut down, the general lethargy of the little town was sharpened to the edge of frustration. Credit at the general store became a problem although people did seem to have enough money to drink at the tavern. But idleness was only incidental the day big trouble came. It started at the post office, shattering the quiet with gunfire and murder.

Postmistress Mrs. Anita Bannister, a grandmother at forty-one, saw the two men come in the door. "They were dressed like cowboys," she said, " and seemed drunk, asking silly questions. They both carried guns and I was worried."

The men staggered through the knot of loungers, then suddenly one of them stiffened, shifted his gun and demanded the "payroll." The second man, Jesse Thurman Hibdon, who had formerly worked in the Paisley sawmill and was unaware that it had closed and there was no payroll, moved back toward the door. One of the trapped onlookers was too quick, breaking outside.

"The first bandit was still threatening me," recalled Mrs. Bannister, "and kept shouting, 'I'm goin' to blow yer brains out.' I told him there was no payroll and I guess he finally believed it, poking me and saying—'You want to see yer family again? Give us all the the money you got.'

"He jabbed the gun barrel into my head and told me not to look at his face. I gave him everything, our V.F.W. money and even the postal orders. He handed it all to Hibdon who ran to the door and

yelled—'Let's get out of here! One of them's escaped already.' But the man holding the gun at my head didn't go. He said, 'I'm goin' to think about this a few minutes' and I was sure I was going to be killed."

Now there was a shotgun blast outside and Donald Lee Ferguson who was still holding his gun at Mrs. Bannister's head, dropped it and ran outside. A man lay bleeding in the doorway and from the car with motor running Hibdon screamed—"Come on, hurry up!" Ferguson piled in and the car took off.

The man who had escaped from the post office earlier saw 65-year-old Troy Lawson with a rifle. It was the deer season and the plumber, like every other man in Paisley, was never far from a gun. Lawson ran toward the post office and, about to go in, turned to warn a woman—Mrs. Norman Carlon with baby Lana in her arms—"Get away or you'll get hurt!" The hesitation was fatal. As Lawson turned, he exposed himself to Hibdon in the car and received a shower of lead pellets in his abdomen. As he dropped, a second blast from Hibdon's gun ripped a big hole in the side of the building. Mrs. Bannister had followed Ferguson outside and later recounted: "Although the women inside were crying all the time of the holdup, I didn't—until I went outside and found Troy dead."

All available townsmen quickly gathered into a posse, every member armed with a deer rifle. One remained in town to telephone Summer Lake Lodge, thirty miles up the road the car had taken, to arrange for a roadblock.

When the bandits came to the makeshift barricade

they swung the car off the road in a desperate effort to clear it, but crashed into the boulders below the rimrock about a hundred yards from the highway. Then the posse arrived, swarming up the hillside. Logging truck driver Doug Houston, 25, sent a shot that nailed Ferguson behind a boulder. "I told him to come out but he fired and almost got me. Then he stepped out and I let him have it in the arm. He was thirty yards away and I could have killed him but didn't have the nerve."

Houston then ran up to the wounded man who had dropped in a pool of his own blood and was trying to reach his gun. Houston kicked it away as his grandfather came up. "Ferguson made a pass for grandpa's rifle and I hit him over the head with the butt of mine. He didn't go down so I hit him again. That's all there was to it."

Hibdon had escaped into the sagebrush and disappeared into the juniper-covered, boulder-strewn hills. Next day at dawn an armed group made a systematic search of Paisley on the chance Hibdon had circled back to get some shelter and food. The hunt widened into the surrounding area, every farm combed, every haystack stabbed with pitchforks. Famed bloodhound man, Norman Wilson, brought his dogs from Dallas to help and once one of them seemed to have picked up a trail but no lead developed.

All this time Hibdon was slogging over the hills to the northeast, keeping out of sight of the highway. Nearing exhaustion and starvation, he reached the Jack Pine Motel about ten miles south of La Pine. He asked the proprietor, William Schabener, if he could rent a cabin, saying his car had broken down. Suspicious of his appearance and actions, Schabener refused and alerted the State Police. Officer William Aveline tried to follow Hibdon's trail through the brush but lost it.

The robbery and murder had taken place on Thursday. The next Tuesday, Harold J. Broderick, 50, fire chief of Hammond, was hunting deer in the area with his two sons, Harold, Jr., and Pat. They had worked north from Paisley where they learned of the trouble. Broderick was about three-quarters of a mile from the Jack Pine Motel when he saw a man walking furtively among the pine trees. "He must have heard me," Broderick said of his experience, "and started going faster, almost breaking into a run. I had my rifle aimed at him and shouted to him to halt." Hibdon did and, surrendering, allowed himself to be walked back to camp where he was given the drink of water he asked for.

"He must have gulped down a quart," said Broderick, "like a horse in the desert." The fire chief had a siren on his pickup and wound it up. The boys came running. Tying Hibdon to the tailgate, they drove to the motel and called the State Police. Hibdon

MAIN STREET OF PAISLEY conforms to State Highway 31, only road through town. Peaceful setting was scene of violence when post office (center) was held up and citizen shot to death. Jagged hole in wall made by second blast can be seen in lower boards at left of deposit box. Post office saw lighter incident later. For more than 20 years after-hours patrons had dropped mail in slot in building front. Some letters, instead of sliding completely through, fell to floor between walls, accumulating until October, 1961. Then R. G. Greene was hired to modernize mail deposit and on opening wall, discovered old cards and letters. When Anita Bannister, postmistress, was told of it "she darned near fainted" said Greene. Her comment: "I thought everyone in town would be mad at me but they took it right good." Postal authorities made effort to deliver lost mail even though postage had become insufficient. At least one letter would be late, regardless. It was from a mother who wrote her daughter 20 years earlier just before Thanksgiving Day: "Please bring the cream for the pie."

offered no resistance, obviously at the end of his endurance. He had walked over 150 miles in common oxford shoes over a rugged terrain. When asked what he had eaten, he said: "I had a quart of milk" but that was the only question he would answer. That evening he was back in Paisley where he was identified by burns on his legs received in a gasoline fire some years before.

He joined Ferguson in the jail at nearby Lakeview and later confessed it was he who had fired the shot that killed Lawson. Both men were sentenced to life imprisonment. After its brief excursion into violence, Paisley dropped back into its rut of peace. The townspeople still patronize its general store, post office and tavern and do not expect to see another holdup.

WALL OF PAISLEY POST OFFICE is still scarred by effects of shot gun blast, one of two fired by would-be bandit. First was lethal, second hit wall.

TOWER CARRIES BELL rung in all emergencies, particularly fire. Paisley Mercantile is only store and, like old Chewaucan Hotel, shows signs of decay. Town was plagued by spring floods when rising temperatures released ice-blocked Chewaucan River. Ice would jam against bridges, divert rising waters into farms and town. *Morning Oregonian,* Portland newspaper of Feb. 4, 1951, said: "The ice-jammed waters of the Chewaucan River have been channeled back into the river bed and this Lake County community is totaling the flood damage. The Forest Service blasted a channel from near the Adams Mill bridge to the Z.B. ranch, . . . Icy waters that covered pasture lands and flooded homes did considerable damage, Bob Parker of Paisley Mercantile said."

MILL STREET runs at right angles to Main, between post office and Chewaucan Hotel. Hostelry, long unused, was named for marsh and the river emptying into it. Word "chewaucan" derived from two Klamath Indian words — *tchua,* a swamp root variously known in Oregon and Washington as *wapato,* sagitaria and arrowhead, and *keni,* a general suffix meaning locality or place. At right is post office with fraternal hall above serving several lodges. Ubiquitous poplar trees stand bare in early March, lit by near-setting sun.

"Some wings fluttering . . . yet the room was empty!"

RICHMOND, OREGON

In 1889 a number of ranches were settled in the rolling sage-covered hills of Wheeler County, Oregon. Ranchers had to go all the way to Mitchell, about 19 miles to the south, or to Spray, about the same distance north, for their supplies. Their children were growing up without education except a little home instruction and many of the settlers felt the need of public worship. A meeting was held in one of the farmer's homes to see what could be done about a population center.

Among the earliest settlers here were the Gilliams, Donnellys, Keyes and Walters. These families attended the meeting as did several interested men from nearby communities, representatives of the cattle firm of Smith and Waterman from Waterman Flat and Caleb N. Thornburg who ran stock at Spanish Flat in the John Day area, was receiver of the land office at The Dalles and for whom the little community and post office at Caleb were named.

The meeting was successful in establishing plans for a town and all agreed the first building would

OLD COMMUNITY CENTER almost swamped by sagebrush and poplars. Starting as a residence, building expanded into general store, post office with T. B. Elrod as first postmaster, and general cracker barrel meeting place.

LITTLE M. E. CHURCH was a m o n g earliest structures in Richmond, steeple an architectural gem. Weathered walls are riddled with woodpecker's holes. Hill behind is sparsely dotted with junipers and sagebrush, typical of the eastern Oregon terrain.

be a school. The name for the new city was not so easily settled, the effort almost breaking into hostilities. R. N. Donnelly and William Walters disagreed over the school site, Walters objecting to everything Donnelly proposed. Even the Civil War got into the controversy and Donnelly called Walters "Jeff Davis" because of his rebellious tendencies, vowing that if things ever did get ironed out the town would be called Richmond after the capitol of the Confederacy. When tempers cooled, Donnelly donated three acres of land for the school. And the name of the town agreed upon? Richmond.

Construction of the small schoolhouse was started as soon as lumber could be hauled to the site. This had to come from the sawmill at Six Shooter owned by E. M. Howell. A store was built and immediately prospered, people coming from many small outlying communities such as Waterman to trade at the new Emporium. Next was the Meth-

odist Church and a large I.O.O.F. Lodge Hall. Other buildings followed and Richmond was a real town.

The biggest gathering ever held here was the get-together of the Wheeler County Pioneers. 450 attended and the festivities lasted a week. This was in 1901 and is still remembered by a few old timers.

Many factors contributed to the slow decay of Richmond. The "Tin Lizzy" and better roads made it possible for the farmers and cattle men to get to larger cities to buy their goods. The younger generation was not enthusiastic about ranching or the isolation involved and the older land owners died or moved away. Gradually the buildings were deserted and fell into disrepair, many collapsing or were burned. The few remaining ones, gray and shabby, present a picturesque and bona fide ghost town.

SANGER, OREGON

The little Wallowa Mountain community of Sanger, built on the flat just below the Sanger mine, and the mine itself, were originally named Hogum as a commentary on the nature of some of the earliest placer mines in the area. After the joke grew stale and the town sought a more dignified title, in 1871, the name of Augusta was selected, honoring Miss Augusta Parkwood, the first unmarried resident. After a year another change was made—to Sanger, the name of an early mine owner. The Sanger post office was established August 17, 1887, with William Aldersley the first postmaster. What the miners did for mail distribution for fifteen years, remains a mystery.

The Sanger mine on the road between Medical Springs and Lilly White was the largest producer in the district. The old placer camp operated for many years before the mine was started, yielding some half a million in easily obtained nugget and dust gold, separated from the granite gravels by panning, sluicing and Long Toms—when there was water. This was before ditches were so frequently constructed to bring water from Eagle Creek.

In 1870 the vein from which most of this loose gold came was discovered and named the Summit Lode. In 1874 this mine produced $60,000 from ore assaying $16 to the ton. A mint report shows it turned out $813,000 from '89 to '92. It closed in '97, opened for a short interval in 1900 then shut down for good with a total production of a million and a half.

The Sanger is on the west side of Eagle Creek and close to an older placer camp which had been a good producer. The Sanger had a long period of activity, closed for a time, opened again at the turn of the century, was then defunct. In 1915, the Oregon Almanac reported there were thirty people in the community. There was a little prospecting at Lilly White in 1930 with no result.

In the summer of 1936 there was a short reopen-

OLD SANGER HOTEL later occupied for many years by Charley Marks and his eighteen dogs. Cabin is placed in meadow among pines and deciduous trees of Wallowas. In summer wagons could be driven under upper floor for cool shade. In time of heavy snows sleighs were pulled directly to front door. In rear clear stream of cool water flows year around and spring house over it kept milk and perishables fresh.

ing of the Sanger. Baker druggist E. B. Cochrane with partner Harry Belden worked here all season but when the snow came to the Wallowas, they decided the results were not worth the effort and the mine died. The Wendts of Baker, its present owners, have placed a new roof on the old mill and hope to revive the workings when and if the price of gold goes up.

A large and impressive log cabin still standing on the flat below the mine has a varied and obscure history though it seems to have been a hotel at one time, the spring house just above the building being much too large to have served a private house. The first tangible story of it is, it was occupied for years by Charley Marks.

Old Charley graduated from Stanford, it is said, and went to Alaska with the gold rush using a dog team of Alaskan huskies. When he came to the Sanger cabin after the mines were down, he brought some of the sled dogs and bought others until he had eighteen. They all lived and ate with him in the house. On one of his rare visits to the biggest town in the area, Baker, he heard of a police dog which had bitten a child and might be destroyed. Charley brought the dog, Rex, home, made the huskies accept him, which they did after some fights.

The Wallowas see a heavy fall of snow every winter and Charley built up a complete dog team to haul a modified toboggan Alaska-style. In the winter trapping season he carried supplies to several line cabins and on one occasion he was following his marten traps when he came to an open spot in a frozen stream. There were several large fish

stranded here and Charley hankered to get one and change his diet.

As he walked out his snowshoes broke through the thin ice and he took a bad fall, his gun flying out of his hand and a bullet going through his knee. He crawled back to the line cabin, made a makeshift splint from a snowshoe and crawled on the sled. His lead dog was a veteran husky but the German shepherd Rex held the most important position, that of turning the sled. The dogs had been to the large Basin Mine workings many times and understood the word "Basin." Charley told them to head there and weak from loss of blood, blacked out. The timber was heavy and the snow deep but the dogs struck out and Rex carefully maneuvered the sled away from low-hanging branches. They reached the mine after several hours and the men there rushed Charley to a doctor.

He recovered from the ordeal with only a slight limp. He is 82 years old and lives in the same area at Keating. He has only four dogs now but they live with him in his little two-room shack and eat their bones there too.

VIEW THROUGH BROKEN WINDOW shows living room and fireplace of old log hotel.

ABOUT 100 FEET FROM LOG HOUSE is pile of beef bones where Charley Marks did butchering for dogs. Mr. Wendt of Baker, present owner of Sanger mine says: "I was out there once when I was a boy. It was in the summer and the smell from the pile of bones was pretty strong."

SHANIKO, OREGON

"Shaniko is the wool center of the world" proudly boasted its citizens of an earlier day. Cornered, they might admit, "Well, if not of the world, at least of the Pacific Northwest." And this came very near the truth.

Shaniko owed its birth to wool, and to wheat. No accidental gold strike or gradual accretion of farmers produced the town. Shaniko's was a planned birth.

Central Oregon, in the 1890's was, in effect, one huge sheep ranch. Wool was produced in enormous quantities and the only outlet for these thousands of bales of fleece was The Dalles, Oregon. Then in 1898, in order to expedite the shipment of wool from the countless bands of sheep which extended to Lakeview and the California line, a railroad was constructed from Biggs Junction, on the Columbia River.

Since a railroad couldn't be useful without some kind of terminal, Shaniko was built for that express purpose. It was the brainchild of a group of bankers and businessmen in The Dalles and Moro and was first laid out as a tent town, but by 1900 many permanent buildings were put up, including the hotel, a combination City Hall, Fire Hall and jail, and a general store, all of which still stand. In rapid succession followed many other structures. Many of these have succumbed to time, fire and vandals. A school was built with funds raised by popular subscription.

Actually, Shaniko was preceded by another settlement, or rather a small community, gathered around a stagecoach station called Cross Hollows, because of the two gullies

OLD SCHOOL WAS BUILT in 1902 with funds raised by "passing the hat" according to Frank Wagner who lived there 43 years. Any school children now must make trip to Maupin schools.

HOTEL WAS BUILT AT turn of century, still serves excellent home-cooked meals at long table, "family style." Tall "City Hall" across street had council chambers upstairs. Fire hose-cart and jail cells occupy ground floor. Structure is surrounded by empty spaces once filled by business buildings.

PRESENT POST OFFICE was established in this building about 1906. Structure in background was drugstore, smaller one leaning against it was pool hall. Rotting wooden sidewalks extend many empty blocks beyond in sagebrush.

having their intersection there. The spot was a natural stopping place for stagecoaches on their way from The Dalles and other points. The station was owned and operated by John and Elizabeth Ward. In 1874, a German immigrant named August Scherneckau arrived and bought out the Wards. Being industrious and possessed of many other good qualities, he prospered. A post office was established for the expanding village on May 23, 1879 with the benevolent and bearded head man as first postmaster.

By 1887, Mr. Scherneckau was well off financially and decided to retire, and spend the rest of his days in California. All the Indians in that part of central Oregon were fond of him and regretted his going, although none of them could correctly pronounce his Germanic name. And so they called the place Shaniko. Having sold out to one Gustav Schmidt, Scherneckau departed to Astoria to catch a ship south. But the city of Astoria so appealed to him that he stayed there until 1923, when he decided to take a long deferred trip to California. This he did, but his stay was short. He died in 1925 and was returned to Astoria, where he is buried.

The site for Shaniko had been chosen for the same reason the original station was built there. A good reliable water supply existed on the spot.

The Cross Hollows post office ceased to exist in 1887 with the departure of its Postmaster. With the establishment of Shaniko Post Office on March 31, 1900, with John D. Wilcox as postmaster, the era of the original Cross Hollows settlement was officially ended.

Shaniko now is only a faint shadow of its former self. Wooden sidewalks run out to nothing and are bordered only by grass and weeds.

SHELBURN, OREGON

In the old graveyard on the hill there are stones dating back to the 1850s, more from the '60s, the decade in which a cholera epidemic carried away so many of the early settlers in this section of the fertile Willamette Valley.

By the time the '90s arrived, the need for some sort of centralization of stores, school and a post office became obvious and several buildings were erected around the old blacksmith shop. This authentic gem of the false-front period of western architecture is still standing though the roof leaks and windows lack glass. With the establishing of a post office in June, 1890, a name for the town had to be selected.

Two of the leading citizens, Shelton and Washburn, were honored by having parts of their names spliced together to form the title, Shelburn.

Sawmills sprang up in this land of virgin fir and spruce and the railroad came to haul out their products as well as potatoes and farm produce. A large hotel was built and operated by Stanley Strylewicz who, for some reason, was simply called Stan. J. R. Moses was the lone barber for several years and if there was anything going on he didn't know about, "it hadn't happened yet," as one oldtimer puts it. A large dancehall was erected and on Saturday nights the sawmill hands and farmers performed the two-

ED ZINK, now gnarled and grizzled, was born on farm in 1879 before Shelburn was a town. With his older brother Eph, he lives in small shack built from lumber salvaged from old home which had begun to disintegrate and was hard to heat. "Eph and I worked in the sawmills as long as they were running," he says, "then did some farming on the old place. We used to think we could get jobs in Shelburn but the old place is sort of going downhill now."

769

step and Black Hawk waltz with their ladies. The perfect serenity of this was altered by the weekly thirst build-up. Because of a rash of accidents in the sawmill, hard liquor was forbidden there and the men slaked their thirsts at the Saturday night hoe down. Dances were often interrupted by drunken brawls and several bullet holes in the wall of the hall remain as evidence of broken romances.

When the surrounding timber was cut out, the mills began to close down. The once healthy potatoes developed a scabby disease and train stops were made only for passengers to buy bread and cheese for lunch. With the coming of the automobile, Shelburn residents went to Salem or Stayton for many of their needs and the local stores dropped away.

Today the place is almost deserted. The dance-hall, having suffered ignominy as a chickenhouse, now stands empty. And yet not silent. Metal feeders, hanging on their wires, creak and groan with the vagrant winds sweeping through the glassless windows.

BLACKSMITH SHOP, oldest building in Shelburn, dates from early 1890s. Many horses in logging and farming made it one of busiest in new community. Concern also sold and repaired harness gear, saddles and bridles, later became supply center for farm equipment, growing into general store when mechanized equipment and "tin lizzie" caused blacksmithing to fall off. Little "wing" served as millinery shop, early phone office and residence. Roof is deteriorating in heavy rain of Willamette Valley, building having small chance for long survival.

THE RIVER WAS A CHALLENGE

Sherar's Bridge, Ore.

In 1826-7 Peter Skene Ogden took an exploring party down the long miles of arid territory east of the Cascade Mountains, a major portion of "Oregon." One large river he encountered, tumbling in falls and rapids most of its length, was termed by the French Riviere aux Chutes and Riviere des Chutes, and by Lewis and Clark, the Clark. Ogden wrote of his crossing, "On Thursday September 26 we reached the River of the Falls and found an Indian camp of about 20 families. Finding a canoe and a bridge made of slender wood, which we began crossing, 5 horses were lost through the bridge."

Years later, John Y. Todd, whose father, John Y., built the first substantial bridge over the cataract, wrote, "It is difficult to believe that there could have been much of a bridge there when Peter Skene Ogden crossed it. It seems as if Ogden must have been blinded by the snow, because it is hard to think the Indians could possibly have built a structure that would support a horse."

The first John Y. Todd was born in Missouri,

Nov. 30, 1830. Determined to join the forces going overland to fight the war with Mexico in 1846 and refused enlistment as being too young, he went along as driver of an ox team. Once in Mexico, however, young Todd was "drafted" as a regular soldier and returned to his home in Missouri in 1848, a veteran at 18.

When he heard the news of gold in California he went to the West Coast to try his luck at finding a bonanza. Denied this and depressed by summer's dry heat in the gold country, he went to San Francisco and boarded a steamer for Portland. At Astoria he was transferred to the steamboat *Lot Whitcomb* (see *Tales the Western Tombstones Tell*).

He sold wheat harvesting machinery up and down the Willamette Valley for several years and then turned Indian fighter, joining the Yamhill Company which attempted to subdue the Yakimas. After that the young Missourian went into the cattle business and eventually settled in Oregon's Tygh Valley on the eastern flank of Mount Hood.

Some pioneer wagon trains bound for the Wil-

OLD PHOTO gives hint of town-like settlement at crossing, no trace of Indian fishing village which developed more recently. After Todd built first bridge in 1860 most weary immigrants abandoned dusty Oregon Trail, taking short cut by way of Grass Valley and the Wamic approach to Barlow Road over Cascade Mountains. Location is narrowest defile in entire course of Deschutes River, deeply cut channel crowding river into black, swirling torrent rather than white rapids and cascades generally characteristic of river. Tolls of $3.75 for each yoke of oxen or team of horses plus $1 for driver were charged. Users beside immigrants were miners or freighters passing to and from Canyon City and John Day gold mines.

lamette Valley and nearing the goal, chose the Columbia River route for the last push. Others pressed on by land and encountered several difficult river crossings, the tumultous Deschutes by far the worst. Todd saw he could help his fellow pioneers and make money at it so in 1860 he built a bridge over the stream at a point where it deepened and narrowed between waterfalls.

For two years the bridge served well, then came a winter of heavy snows in the nearby mountains and hard spring rains which caused severe flooding, a surge in the Deschutes carrying away the span. Since Todd had put all his money into his buildings and logs necessary for rebuilding would have to come from mountain forests as before, he was forced to take in two partners, Ezra Hemingway and Robert Mays, before he could build a new bridge. When the new firm was organized and second span built, Hemingway bought out the

other two and shortly, in 1871, sold out to a man named O'Brien who in turn sold to Joseph Sherar, the bridge bearing his name since.

Born in Vermont in 1833, Sherar also arrived in the West via the California mines, his digging done in the northern section and later the John Day mines of eastern Oregon. He saw in the bridge far greater opportunity for investment than had Todd and the other owners. Paying only $7,040 for the structure itself, he invested $75,000 in building approaching roads. Then he put up a stage station which soon developed into a 33-room hotel, large and elaborate for those primitive parts.

In 1868 a post office was established at the site with Hemingway as postmaster and now Sherar improved the building to succeed him. In addition to hotel and postal facilities the location had a store, livery stables and many other buildings.

MODERN "SHERAR'S BRIDGE" is part of State Highway 216. No trace exists of village once established here for early immigrants to Oregon Country. Instead large but transitory Indian village stands along both banks. Existing only during salmon runs, settlement consists of habitations ranging from stinking, garbage-surrounded tent shacks to luxurious campers. Indian fishermen erect temporary and seemingly precarious platforms suspended above water from which they wield long-handled nets. Salmon are particularly vulnerable here while resting after leaping falls just below and before ascending equally difficult one immediately above.

SPARTA, OREGON

At the southwestern edge of the snowy peaks in Oregon's Wallowa Mountains which nearly fill the northeastern corner of the state, is the Eagle Creek area of old mining camps. Here on a small "island" of granite in the center of a rather recent lava flow is Sparta, where in 1863, Squire Morris and his partner Neales Donnelly, made their Shanghai Gulch strike of small gold nuggets and dust in the stream gravels. A short time later Tom Koster made his find at the head of Maiden Gulch.

There was great excitement. These new finds were just what was needed to take up where the depleted mines of the area left off, and the town of Koster sprang up on the slope. Friends of the first discoverers renamed it Eagle City but authorities found the new name a duplication and the post office was established as Gem, after one of the larger mines. This was on August 7, 1871 and the name lasted over a year.

William H. Packwood, pioneer prospector, farmer, engineer and civic leader in Gem, proposed the town to be renamed in honor of his home town—Sparta, Illinois. Three other pillars of the community had home towns and weren't willing to go along without a struggle. The four inscribed their choices on the sides of a square top and needless to say the side showing up was Sparta. Even if the others had heard of loaded dice, they accepted fate peaceably.

Sparta flourished. Gold dust up to $15,000 a week was sent through the mails, other large amounts by express and individuals. E. E. Clough and his father took $25,000 in dust and nuggets to Baker by horse and wagon.

But the water supply was inadequate for the placering equipment and Packwood backed a daring venture called the Sparta Ditch. Raising capital, he had the survey made and the 32-mile ditch built in two years. The placers had plenty of water but now the gold supply was thinning out.

With the richest mines abandoned, the Chinese workers from the completed transcontinental railroad moved in, content with placer gleanings. The luckless Orientals were harassed by wrathful whites, robbed, murdered and finally ejected. In 1915 all hard rock mining ceased and most of the shafts caved in. About two years later even the placering came to a stop.

SPARTA STORE only remaining business structure was solidly built to resist robbers. Erected in 1873 by W. H. Heilmer. 24x50'. Opening was celebrated with ball, attracting everyone in whole area, many from "metropolis" of 'Baker, 30 miles away. Store was operated for many years by Joseph Wright.

SUMPTER, OREGON

The railroad came to Sumpter in 1896 because of the new veins of ore being opened and developed . . . or maybe it was the other way around. In any event, the population zoomed to 3,000 in no time. This was a big increase from the few hundred pioneer-type individuals who had patiently panned in the Powder River, and pecked away at the hard rock streaks of gold in the previous 20 years.

In 1862 three men from North Carolina built a log cabin on the site. They intended to farm the land, an ambition later swamped by the tide of gold mining.

They found a spherical rock almost like a cannonball nearby and were inspired by this discovery, along with severe nostalgia, to call their new home "Fort Sumter," a name prominent in those Civil War days.

The "Fort" was lost, but the "Sumter" remained, picking up a "P" somewhere along the way. Spelling in those days was regarded lightly.

For a good many years Sumpter flourished, feeding on new lodes opened by improved methods and the substantial returns from the huge dredges in the river. As these sources died out, so did Sumpter. Several disastrous fires took heavy toll as evidenced by parts of brick walls and exposed bank vaults.

Dredging operations have continued until the whole valley is in ruins, tailings occupying the creek bed and both banks. But since 1916 the town has declined. A few newer buildings are scattered among the ruins, and Sumpter would have had a chance to become a farming community, but for the preponderance of granite tailings over good soil.

VAULT IS ALL THAT remains of old bank, burned years ago in Sumpter. White Masonic Hall is on hill in background, was one of few wooden structures spared in holocaust.

WHITNEY, OREGON

Whitney was never a mining camp, though it lived in company with many gold towns. It was strictly a center for logging operations, the surrounding Blue Mountains having heavy stands of Ponderosa Pine and, at higher elevations, Alpine White Fir. The place is wild and wooly, though murders were not as frequent as in some. There *was* a lynching in the spring of 1915 some eight miles south of Whitney. The case involved the rape of a girl and murder of a boy, and the aroused populace had taken justice into its own hands. Law officers, later trying to track down those responsible, met a tight-lipped silence, and soon gave up.

Our same Miss Erma Cole, who figures in our Cornucopia story, taught school in Whitney in the winter of 1919-1920. She had all the children of the first five grades in the tiny schoolhouse on a small knoll near town. Although she started with 28 pupils in the fall and finished with 28 in the spring, only two were continuous, so transient was the logging population.

"I boarded in one of the small hotels near the saloon on the east side of one street," she relates. "The walls were just boards with battens more or less covering the cracks. I had a little sheet iron stove, a bed and a little table for furniture in my 9 x 10 foot room. That winter was extra cold; the thermometer stayed at 55 degrees below zero for a spell, and although the little stove was bright red all the time, I was still cold. When the temperature rose to only 50 degrees below, it seemed almost balmy."

MAIN STREET OF WHITNEY, once thronged with roistering loggers, is now almost silent. Cattle graze in meadow beyond.

HUGE SAWMILL STANDS ROTTING on shore of log pond. Logs were snaked up chute to upper floor to emerge on ground floor at other end as sawn lumber. Spur of narrow gauge ran close by, busily hauled product to all northeastern Oregon.

Each Saturday saw a big dance, and the hotel man made a trip to Prairie City on the narrow gauge earlier each week to replenish his supply of bootleg booze so the festivities would be a success.

That old narrow gauge, the Sumpter Valley Railroad, figures prominently in all the history of our Blue Mountain group of towns. Ahead went the tiny engine, then the little box cars and, trailing behind, a passenger car or two. The trestle crossing a deep canyon between Sumpter and Whitney had a short life, but it is said by the editor of the Sumpter newspaper to have been the second highest in the world, surpassed only by one in the Bavarian Alps. Due to its impressive height it was too shaky and dangerous and was removed in 1915; the grade run around the mountain instead. The little station in Whitney was a neat, well-kept building.

A nearly level meadow is centered by the weathered buildings that are Whitney now. There is no school, depot, hotel or saloon, but a dozen or so residences remain scattered along the main street. Here and there are the ties of the little railroad. At the south end of town is a really imposing sawmill, or the shell of one, the height of a three-story building. A large log pond adjoins it.

EXCEPT FOR HAY, crops did poorly in Whitney. Summers were too short, frosts came late in spring, early in fall, sometimes in August. Machinery stands long idle, rusting away in barnyard.

WASHINGTON
GHOST TOWNS

BY

LAMBERT FLORIN

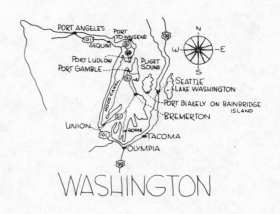

INDEX

CITY	Page	CITY	Page
Altoona	781	Nighthawk	829
Bakers Bay (or Chinookville)	782	Northport	832
Blewett Pass	785	Orient	834
Bossburg	786	Oysterville	835
Claquato	788	Port Blakely	840
Conconully	792	Port Gamble	843
Copper City	799	Port Ludlow	846
Curlew	800	Republic	849
Frankfort	803	Riverside	850
Home	807	Roslyn	853
Index	812	Ruby	858
Knappton	813	Skamokawa	859
Liberty	817	Sultan	864
Loomis	818	Trinity	865
Maryhill	822	Union	868
Monte Cristo	826	Vader	870
Nahcotta	828		

ALTOONA, WASHINGTON

If you were a salmon fisherman living in Altoona, mused a newspaper reporter, on the north shore of the Columbia River near it mouth, you would be one of a hardy breed. You rode out into that turbulent, treacherous river, usually out over the bar where she spreads murkily into the heaving Pacific and where a storm can blow up like the temper of a shrew. You tossed out your small gill net and staked your life on the catch. It was a hard life but a glad one and you didn't complain. But the going got really tough when that old devil river choked herself on ice and your isolated village was cut off from the outside world for two weeks and you got so hungry you could eat your oilskins.

The Portland OREGONIAN of January 23, 1930 carried a dramatic story of relief for the near-starving residents of Altoona. The whole Pacific Northwest shivered in below zero temperatures for thirteen days, the worst weather in forty years. Even the lower Columbia region, usually subject to no more cold than occasional frosts, was in deep freeze with temperatures as low as 10 above, and the river was covered with an unbroken crust of ice.

Altoona, like several other communities on the river with no roads, depending entirely on water traffic, began to get hungry when boats did not dock. Then on the 21st a freezing rain started to fall, soon coating wires with ice, the weight of it threatening to ground the single telephone line to the outside. Before it came down the people sent out a distress call which got to Astoria, Oregon, across the river.

Next day the Arrow Tug and Barge Co. of Astoria dispatched a sturdy tug loaded with food. It broke ice successfully in the faster running channel but was unable to get nearer than 350 feet from the North Shore. So the hungry Altoonans walked out on the ice to where the supplies were dumped from the tug, five of them fighting the numbing cold river water to get aboard the vessel, wanting to see Altoona never again. The others worked their way back and the emergency was relieved.

Pillar Rock in the Columbia River just east of Altoona, is an historic landmark around which much of the lower river activity has centered. A rugged column rising some twenty feet above deep channel water level, it was noted by British explorer Lt. William Robert Broughton in 1792 when he sailed up to it in the armed tender *Chatham* and commented it was "a remarkable pillar of rock." Later Lewis and Clark made notes about the rock in their journal.

Around 1840 the Hudson's Bay Co. established a salmon barreling operation near Pillar Rock and the local Chinook Indians caught salmon in their

WAHKIAKUM COUNTY COMMUNITY of Altoona was largely built on docks. Pilings supported huge cannery operations, space for drying and repairing nets, segregated housing for Chinese workers and general store, Altoona Mercantile. Closed for many years, store was last operated by W. L. Smith who turned to fishing. Cavernous cannery buildings sit on more solid section of same wharf.

COVERED BRIDGE over Gray's River close to mouth at Gray's Bay, is unique in having no windows. Gravels of stream yield agates and rock specimens especially after spring freshets.

willow weirs and nets, packing them down with salt, sailing vessels loading the barrels as cargo for London. Ships heading upriver to Vancouver would tie up at the rock to wait for favorable winds and tides. The respite from a long voyage was so welcome to the sailors they usually ended the breather with black eyes and broken noses in brawls over the Indian women fish packers.

In the 1870s a large fish cannery was operating just west of the Pillar, the locality called Altoona. In expanding its activities at the river mouth, the New England Fish Co. took over the cannery and enlarged it. For several years large numbers of Chinese were imported to gut and clean the salmon, their usefulness ending with the introduction of the Iron Chink, mechanical marvel that did all the cleaning and cutting.

As salmon runs diminished and canning became unprofitable, the company changed over to fish oil reduction and then in the late '40s closed down entirely. During these busy years the hamlets of Altoona and Pillar Rock were accessible only by boat, no great handicap when hundreds of gill netters swarmed the river and steamers made regular stops. But with the cannery closed, boats fewer and river steamers no longer running, the communities were cut off from the world. It was not until the early 1950s that a road was cut through to them — to all but Brookfield. The cannery there burned and the deserted town never did get more than a rough dirt track through the

timber. It is now used as a log dump by Crown Zellerbach, access not available to the public.

Just off Altoona Head, rocky point projecting from shore at the western edge of the village, lies the wreckage of the British steamer *Welsh Prince*. At 11:10 P.M. on May 28, 1922, she met the American freighter *Iowan* head on in a grinding collision. In the dense fog common to the lower river, neither vessel could see the other even after the crash until the British ship sent up an orange flare which showed her to be on fire. Her fore quarters were nearly severed, seven seamen crushed to death and she was settling fast. Responding to distress signals, the *Oneonta* set out from Astoria, feeling her way through the fog and removing the bodies of five men, two trapped in the sinking forecastle.

When the vessels were separated it was found that the *Iowan* could be towed even with her crushed bow and she was taken to Portland for repairs. When the fog cleared the upper decks of the *Welsh Prince* could be seen just above the water as she settled to the bottom. After several attempts to raise her, agents Frank Waterhouse and Co. notified the Furness Line of London that their ship was a total loss.

In that position close to the main channel, the hulk was declared a menace to navigation and M. Barde and Sons were employed to break it up. The firm brought ten tons of super-power gelatin dynamite from Olympia, Washington, blew off the top deck, then blasted the hull apart.

782

THE BLOOMS WERE A BEACON

*Baker's Bay (or
Chinookville, Wash.)*

A sailing ship bound for the shifting shallows of the Columbia River mouth was completely at the mercy of wind, tide and luck. Where was the channel? There were no markers, no lighthouses, no break to be seen in the low, timbered headlands obscured by fog or haze or spume from the sea pounding on the rocks and beaches. The skippers set their course by guess and St. John, put the sail gangs on point and sometimes escaped the sand spits and shoals to cross the bar into the river's yawning mouth.

The bark *Isabella* had no such luck. Out of England, bound for Fort Vancouver in the fall of 1829, she sighted the bar but lost headway in a lull, let her slack sails be caught in a sudden gale and was washed up on the sands. Capt. Thomas Ryan ordered her abandoned and all hands made shore through mountainous seas to watch the *Isabella* be pounded to kindling.

Her second mate and boatswain, Essexman James Scarborough, was one so stranded but being an experienced seaman found employment with the Hudson's Bay Co. and for ten years was master of the *Cadboro*. After his shipwreck experience he had deep compassion for skippers trying to enter the Columbia and upon taking up a homestead on the bluff above the bay where the *Isabella* came to grief, he immediately planted a grove of fruit and hawthorn trees. In succeeding years,

"THE CHINOOKS" wrote Capt. Lewis in his journal, "are low in statue, rather diminutive and ill-shapen possing thick broad, flat feet, thick ankles, crooked legs wide mouths, thick lips, nose moderately large fleshy, wide at the extremity with large nostrils, black eyes and coarse hair, their eyes are sometimes of a dark yellowish brown the puple black. The most remarkable trait in their physiognomy is the peculiar flatness and width of forehead which is artificially obtained by compressing the head between two boards while in a state of infancy and from which it never afterwards perfectly recovers" . . . (Photo Smithsonian Institution).

OLD PRINT of British ship **Tonquin**, anchored in harbor then called Haley's Bay, officially Baker's Bay, in 1811. John Jacob Astor sent out two parties, one overland led by Wilson Price Hunt, one by sea captained by crusty Jonathan Thorn. Latter was one of several to select site of what would be Astoria. **Tonquin** sailed from here to Clayoquot Sound, Vancouver Island, where it met disaster through attacks by Indians and explosion (Photo Smithsonian Institution).

LEWIS AND CLARK CAMPSITE

MERIWETHER LEWIS AND WILLIAM CLARK
WITH MEMBERS OF THEIR EXPEDITION CAMPED
IN THIS AREA FROM 16 TO 25 NOVEMBER 1805.
FROM THIS POINT THEY SAW THE BREAKERS
OF THE PACIFIC OCEAN AND KNEW THAT THEY
HAD COMPLETED THE MISSION ASSIGNED TO
THEM BY PRESIDENT THOMAS JEFFERSON.
THEIR OVERLAND JOURNEY ESTABLISHED
A NEW CLAIM FOR THE UNITED STATES TO
THIS REGION.

STATE PARKS AND
RECREATION COMMISSION

MARKER AT BAKER'S BAY (Chinookville). Capt. Clark noted in his journal. "The tide meeting of me and the emence swells from the Main Ocian raised to such a hite that I concluded to form a camp on the highest spot I could find . . . in the upper part of Haley's Bay . . . This Chinook Nation is about 400 Souls inhabited the country on Small rivers that run into the bay directly below us . . . I directed all the men who wished to see more of the main Ocian to prepare themselves to set out with me early on tomorrow morning. The principal Chief of the Chinooks came to see us this evening." The "Chief" would have been one-eyed Concomly (see **Boot Hill**).

when the trees were in full bloom, the sheet of white blossoms on Scarborough Head was conspicuous for many miles on the lower river, a beacon seen even out at sea.

At the base of the Head near the beach was a Chinook Indian village of perhaps 300 to 400 natives, the community existing many years before advent of the white man. Among the first of these were men named Svipton, "One-Eyed" Skelly and Haley, an adjacent inlet first called after him, Haley's Bay.

When Capt. Bruno Heceta sailed up the Columbia about the time of our American revolution he indicated the bay as "Bahia de la Ascuncion". Thirteen years later Capt. John Meares named it "Deception Bay". Lewis and Clark had other ideas and it became "Rogue's Harbor". Later Capt. Baker of the brig *Jenny* anchored there and no doubt unaware that the water was topheavy with names, bestowed yet another on it—his own. And Baker's Bay it has remained.

By the custom of most white men alone in Indian country, Capt. Scarborough in 1843 married a Chinook woman, Ann Elizabeth, a member of the tribe in the village on the site of Chinookville, across the river from Fort Astoria. At one time the tribe was headed by famous one-eyed Chief Concomly (see *Boot Hill*).

The young couple took up a donation land claim of 640 acres which included part of Concomly's

domain as well as Scarborough Head or Hill. Besides his fruit trees and shrubs the captain raised stock animals picked up on his voyages. He built a house shared with his Indian wife, contrary to custom, and to them were born four sons, only two surviving.

During these years Capt. Scarborough had his hand in many business ventures such as shipping fish to England and serving as river pilot. A mystery begins with the story of his having been paid for these efforts over the years in gold ingots amounting to $60,000, and that he buried the fortune somewhere on the hill. In February of 1855 the captain died suddenly without divulging the location of the ingots. James Burney of Cathlamet took the two boys in, one of them, Ned, living to be 80, dying at Cathlamet about 1925.

In 1864 the government bought the Scarborough estate as being a strategic location for defense of the Columbia. About 1894 Fort Columbia was built on the site, becoming a state park after the end of World War II.

Presumably the treasure is still somewhere about, apparently not discovered in the building of the fort or highway through the park. There remains a large area still undisturbed, too large for a search without a clue. Ruby El Hult, author of *Lost Mines and Treasures,* estimates the present value of the gold ingots to be about $120,000.

BLEWETT PASS, WASHINGTON

Blewett Pass in Washington was not so much a town as a continuous string of little towns, mines, mills and settlements, now faded away. There are many visible traces and in some cases a substantial reminder of those roaring days when thousand-dollar gold nuggets were not uncommon.

The most impressive of these is the Blewett Stamp Mill, north of the summit of the Pass. While much of the building is collapsed, enough stands to give a pretty good idea of what it once was.

An old gentleman lives in a tiny cabin across the road, his name is Anton Newbauer. Although the mill is completely useless now, he loves it still, having worked there as a young man. "You would never guess to look at the old mill now that there were hundreds of men working here in the 80's. Gold was what we mined here, and the lode was rich. There is still a lot of it down in that shaft and the tunnels that go clear back into the mountain. But the main vein pinched out about 1905, and the mill hasn't operated since. Now and then someone gets the idea of mining here again, but gold would have to be worth $200.00 an ounce to make it pay now."

Old Anton's estimate of a profitable price is far too high, according to later talks with other old hard-rock miners, but most are agreed on from $75.00 to $100.00. Everything depends on how much labor and machinery is needed for the amout of the yellow metal extracted. Simple, inexpensive placering operations are still paying off even at the present low price.

ORE LOADING chute is almost buried in rank vegetation typical of mountainous area. Even so, rainfall is much lighter on this east-facing side of Cascades. Timbers and logs would long since have rotted away on western rainy side.

OLD BLEWETT STAMP MILL reduced large chunks of rich gold ore into more manageable size for extraction. Weight was hauled to top of t o w e r (right), allowed to fall with crushing force on ore.

BOSSBURG, WASHINGTON

Although twice in the history of the State of Washington the annual value of silver produced has exceeded that of gold, the yellow metal has held first place in the dreams of prospectors and the imaginations of those interested in old mining camps. The mines of Republic turned out millions in gold, those of Blewett Pass some, yet fully half of the old camps and ghost towns of the state have histories bound up with metals of another color.

Old Trinity was strictly a copper producing camp. The golden product of the Swauk district, including the Blewett Pass, was so alloyed with silver its color was definitely paled to a light yellow. The Ruby silver mines near Conconully were going full tilt in 1890 and at least a thousand miners were working in the camp at its height. The lead-silver mines of Colville produced large

amounts of ore, the biggest being the old Dominion. For lack of roads or railroads the output was carried to Spokane at a cost of $100 a ton.

Five years later the Young America and Bonanza deposits were opened up at what is now called Bossburg, its first name Young America. The galena ore here was so rich some of it was "specimen" material and for some time the mines were going at top speed. The village grew up a short distance from the mines, just off the banks of the Columbia River.

The summer of 1892 saw 800 people at Young America and a quartz mill was erected. There were also stores, a good-sized school, the inevitable saloons and honkytonks. The next year the town was formally platted and rechristened Millington. A Congregational Church and large meeting hall were added and again, in 1896, the town was

ROTTING REMNANTS OF VEHICLES of another day lie in grass and weeds around old town.

CRUMBLING FALSE-FRONTED store in Bossburg had living rooms upstairs. Columbia River is just beyond, hills once heavily timbered with Ponderosa pine now show sparse cover.

rechristened—Bossburg in honor of the first citizen, C. S. Boss.

After mining operations tapered off Bossburg attempted to recoup its failing fortunes by establishing a ferry across the Columbia. Fruit orchards were set out and produced apples and pears, vines growing top quality berries. A sawmill had been put in working order and some lumber was shipped. The prevailing limestone formations were tapped, stone was shipped in building blocks as were lime products.

None of these efforts lasted long. The old zip was gone, silver mining collapsed under the low prices and Bossburg died on the vine. Nearly all the old buildings are gone. A store, a few sheds, substantial schoolhouse still stand, the latter occupied by a family who had topped the old structure with a TV antenna.

FLAG IN THE TALL TIMBER

Claquato, Wash.

All that scary talk! Why these northern Indians in Washington Territory were so friendly they were going to show him how to put up a temporary camp in the forest against the wet winter weather and even help him and his boys build it. The plains Indians were warlike and troublesome but these fellows pointed out a big fir tree where he could put up the camp and by Jupiter, he'd call it the "Pioneer Tree"!

So did the first family start life on the hill called Claquato, a high place, by the Indians on the south side of the Chehalis River. They hacked out a crude road to a shallow place in the river where they could ford it and haul in the household goods brought up from Portland.

This was the Lewis Hawkins Davis family from back east. He was born in Windsor County, Vermont, and went west to Fort Wayne, Indiana, becoming a partner in a sawmill venture. He married Susan A. Clinger and fathered five sons and two daughters. In 1852 it seemed the whole country was headed westward for the fertile Willamette Valley in Oregon. On fire with the idea of carving out a new home in a new country, Davis and family joined a wagon train out of Independence, Missouri, and arrived in the village of Portland near the end of the same year. Some twenty-two months of casting around the area convinced Davis it was already too crowded, some farms being within a mile or two of each other.

Hearing much talk of good farm lands available farther north, he and family set out again, this time on a boat going down the Willamette to the Columbia River. At its junction with another tributary, the Cowlitz, the party went upstream to Cowlitz Landing, then a pioneer settlement. The surrounding country looked good to Davis but he selected an area centered by a rise of land and took out a donation land claim.

By 1855 the Indians had turned bitter, realizing that unless the increasing white tide was stemmed, they were doomed. Skirmishes with settlers all over western Washington caused the government to authorize the building of stockades and blockhouses as protective measures. At Claquato Davis got the local contract, providing manpower and logs. The structure was built on the brow of the hill just west of the town center, the always hungry workers fed by Mrs. Davis from a kitchen set up on the site. When the building was finished all families moved in but after many quarrels natural to strangers in cramped quarters, they returned to their homes.

The first settlers built cabins of logs cut from the smaller trees. The hill was not solidly forested and opening it up increased pasture area. In 1857 Davis built a whipsaw sawmill at the bottom of the hill where little Mill Creek flows into the Chehalis. A pool was enlarged to hold logs skidded in by ox team. A dedicated Methodist, Davis used his first produced lumber to build a church.

Fortunately for the community a good craftsman was available, one who easily doubled as architect— John Duff Clinger, brother of Mrs. Davis. He planned the structure in entirety and personally

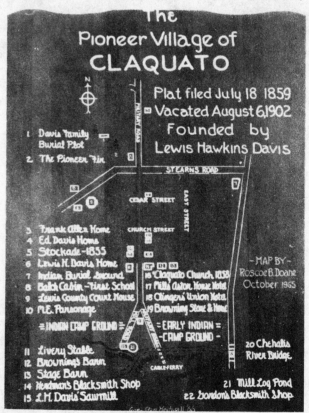

"BILLBOARD" near Claquato Church gives quick run-down on one of most historic towns in state.

788

SUNDAY SCHOOL, occasional services, were held in old building until mid-'30s when slow destruction by vandals began, doors then padlocked, windows boarded up. Restoration was begun in early '50s by Chehalis Post No. 22, American Legion and county officials. No structural changes were necessary, all original materials left in place with few exceptions. New wallpaper utilized old pattern as used in churches a century ago. Renovated church was rededicated Aug. 16, 1953.

made door and window casings. He built the unusual steeple, framing it with mortise and tenon work of finest quality. Even the lookouts supporting the roof projection on the gables were mortised and wedged into the end rafters. As the oldest building still standing in the State of Washington the unique church is a monument to John Clinger.

The crude little mill was pushed to its limit, its lumber snapped up for more construction. In a short time the hill was crowned by two hotels, blacksmith shop, carpenter and cabinet shops, livery stable and church parsonage which with several houses constituted Claquato, the largest village between Monticello and Olympia.

Davis was astute in realizing the growing town

must have more systematic planning and hired Henry H. Stearns, surveyor and one of the original immigrants, to legally lay out the site. The resulting plat was filed with the county clerk on July 18, 1859. It shows the location of the church already built and four lots deeded to the county by Davis on which he intended to build a two-story courthouse and deed that to the county too.

By the next year when construction started an extra set of gears had been added to the shaft in the mill so water power could be used for grinding wheat and corn. In the spring with ample stream flow both operations could be handled simultaneously. The trouble was, most grist was made shortly after late summer harvest when water was low. Some farmers were forced to cool their heels while enough lumber was cut to keep courthouse builders on the job and on occasion they were forced to wait until grain growers were satisfied. In spite of these and other delays the structure received the finishing touches early in 1862.

The Civil War was raging now and while it hardly whispered into the northwest corner the Claquato women were resolved to be patriotic and make a flag that would be a credit to the new courthouse. John H. Browning, son-in-law of Davis and owner of the general store, was in San Francisco buying supplies when he received a letter from his wife telling him to bring home materials for a flag 18 by 36 feet. Although convinced the size given was in error he returned in mid-April with $90 worth of cloth and thread. In his home the women hand stitched thousands of feet of seams to complete the giant emblem. A crew of men scoured the forest to find a big tree of proper proportions. Trimmed, peeled and brought home, it was placed in a 20-foot hole, then standing 120 feet tall.

And then for the dedication of the courthouse. The war demanded immense quantities of medical materials called "sanitary supplies." An inspired suggestion was approved—to call the planned affair the "Sanitation Ball," all proceeds to go to the war effort. The big day came on the Fourth of July, 1862. At 10 a.m. minister John Harwood opened the ceremony with prayer. Then thirteen men, one for each of the original colonies, fired four volleys and the flag was slowly raised to the top of the pole while the townspeople sang a hymn. After a picnic by the river, Mills Brothers orchestra arrived from Olympia and the dance was begun, to end in a blaze of "Old Glory." Tickets sold at $5 each and after all expenses, such as $50 in gold for the band, there remained a grand total of $250 for the sanitation fund. The flag was flown daily for the remainder of the war but on one sad day, October 22, 1864, it was lowered to half-mast for Lewis H. Davis.

The town's founder had suffered a bad fall in his mill and he lingered in agony for several weeks without recovering. The funeral was held in the little church he built, his body borne past the courthouse and on up the hill to the small cemetery and laid to rest not far from the Pioneer Fir.

With the patriarch's death some changes came to Claquato. Most of his activities were taken over by his grown sons but the Davis stage line, initiated by Henry Winsor and Rice Tilly of Olympia in 1861 and which ran from Monticello to Olympia with Claquato as an overnight stop,

was sold to a Mr. Coggins who was killed by Indians later. In 1865 the big flag was again lowered in mourning for Abraham Lincoln.

The Indian scare of the middle '50s that brought tragedy and death to other Washington communities never directly affected Claquato and the building of the fort was entirely futile. Local Indians became friendly and cooperative as in the founding days, small groups camping nearby for many years. Probably the best remembered native was "Queen Susan," wife of a powerful chief in the area. She was still young and attractive when he died and could have married a brave of high rank, instead falling in love with a slave. When she married him outraged members of the tribe rejected her but, as royalty, permitted her to remain, with the same lowly status as her mate. When he died the middle-aged and fat widow lived among the whites at Claquato. Dressed in brilliant cast-off clothing she went from house to house doing any kind of cleaning or laundering chores for a living. Her cheerful nature was a bright light in the community.

Susan died in 1868 and the citizens gave her a funeral as imposing as one the tribe would have given her as queen. Most townspeople attended and schools were closed for the day. Even the passengers of two stages which stopped for a change of horses witnessed the rites. All Indians living within several miles also came, having forgotten their queen's descent from grace. Susan's body was taken to the foot of the hill and placed in the Indian burial ground. No marker remains on her grave or that of any other native.

The town on the old Military Road, then the main traveled artery between the Columbia River and Olympia, was shrugged aside when rails were laid in 1874. The line now ran through Saundersville, where Davis camped when locating a homesite. With subsequent growth that town became Chehalis and eventually took the county seat from Claquato, which was officially vacated in county records of August 6, 1902.

HISTORIC PIONEER FIR, identified by bronze plaque fastened to trunk. Gigantic specimen sheltered immigrants 116 years ago, was huge then. This form of branching rare in fir. Location is near center of Claquato cemetery.

CONCONULLY, WASHINGTON

It was high drama even for the raw West. Sheriff's deputy, Pete Barker did not like the looks of the stranger watching the L. L. Work Bank in Conconully. He told Sheriff Fred Thorp the fellow was far too interested in the bank's workings. Thorp took a good look at the man but could not get worked up over the idea of arresting him for doing nothing. By chance a man-wanted poster came in the next day depicting Frank LeRoy, wanted in the east for burglary. The face was that of the stranger.

Thorp found him in the Morris Saloon playing pool with his back to the door. With his .45 at the man's back, he said quietly: "I'd like to search you, if you don't mind." LeRoy swung around and said: "Sure." Then starting to open his jacket, he jerked a pistol from a shoulder holster and fired. The bullet went wild and LeRoy went into a fast dance, making himself such a difficult target Thorp's first shot also missed, his second taking off a finger, making LeRoy drop the pistol.

He broke for the door, drawing another gun from a second holster with his left hand. Another shot from Thorp caught the fugitive in the right shoulder. He spun around and dropped. While the sheriff was grabbing another gun, LeRoy gained his feet and ran staggering up Salmon Creek. He quickly collapsed, blood running from his mouth. He was carried to the jail on an old barn door.

While waiting for Dr. Polk, a search of the man and his belongings revealed two more guns, a set of burglar tools and some loot from a recent robbery in Brewster nearby. The doctor reported the patient would live but recommended he be locked up. The "maximum security" cell was without heat and as a bed patient, LeRoy was put in an outer room and given watchful care for about nine days. His guard was then lightened but in reality the burglar was feigning extreme weakness. Aware of tools in a closet, he got into the sleeping jailer's room one night, stole shoes, overalls and a blanket which he wrapped around himself Indian fashion and faded into the night. This was November 7, 1909.

LeRoy got safely to the nearby mining camp of Ruby, got a long-bladed butcher knife and at the home of Casper Miller demanded an outfit of clothes and probably some food. During the next three days Sheriff Thorp tracked him to a clump of sagebrush near the little community of Malott, leveled his rifle at the fugitive and gave him a choice: "Come out with your hands up or be blown to Kingdom Come." LeRoy stood with his hands high cursing: "If I had anything but this knife, I'd kill you right now!" Tried for burglary, he was adjudged a habitual criminal and sent to the state penitentiary at Walla Walla for 99 years. He was later paroled.

Although the Conconully jail later developed many weak spots, it was planned for strength. At one of the first county commissioner meetings careful details were specified for the detention of future prisoners. The jail was to be built of "two by six scantlings, spiked together—spikes to be not more than six inches apart." Orders were placed for 24 pairs of hand-

JURY PANEL at trial in 1906 on front steps of courthouse, photo owned by Helen Rice. Her brother George, top row, third from left, worked for freighting outfit, hauling logs on sled through town when load overturned on bridge over Salmon Creek, was tapped for jury duty while ruefully surveying wreckage. Standing at extreme left, top row, is Judge Hartew. Next, Mr. Gibson, then young Fitch, next to him, Bill Sproul. Next is unidentified, then Ham Pinkerton. Man leaning against post is unknown, next and final two are Ed Sayles and Bill Gamble. Of the front row only two are identified — at left, standing with hand on rail is Mr. Jay. At right, man with interlaced fingers is Joe Pinkerton.

"STREET SCENE ON SUNDAY," another of Frank Matsura's vivid pictures of Conconully in bygone era. Note raised sidewalk giving pedestrians some protection from mud and snow. No protection was possible when Salmon Creek flooded down main street. Wave more than 50 feet high was known to come down canyon after mountain cloudburst.

In May of 1892 one such disaster swept many buildings down street ending up as wreckage on huge delta of sand also carried by waters. Safe was washed out of one building, never found. One woman, safely out of home, missed her glasses, rushed back to get them, was swept away with house, body later found in wreckage, hand still clutching precious spectacles.

cuffs and three pairs of shackles complete with chains and 24-pound balls.

Nevertheless, from its building about 1891 to the time the courthouse was wrecked about 1915, the pokey suffered ridicule and abuse because of frequent escapes. Early one spring when snow was beginning to melt and the ditch under the lockup was filled with icy water, two thieves were incarcerated and told they could build themselves a fire in the stove. Instead, they built it on the floor and when the flames had eaten into the boards enough to weaken them, the men took a plank and poked out an opening over the ditch. The first man got down with no difficulty but the second was so fat he stuck midway. His friend came back to poke the hole bigger and pull the fat man down through.

One Sam Albright heard two of his friends were lodged in the famous calaboose and came to Conconully with another friend, Clint Williams, to have a chat with the prisoners. The visitors found the jailer absent, unlatched a window and climbed in. The reunited foursome had a friendly game of stud, after which the callers gave the inmates some books and candy and departed the way they had come, relatching the window.

Proprietor Gibson of the store of that name in Conconully tells of a jail break with a different twist,

when Ben Snowden was jailer. "Old Ben had three fellows in there, one named Kallentyne. When Ben took their food in, one of the men was doubled up on the floor like he was sick and Ben set the food down to go and see what was the matter with him." It seems the jailer always kept a rifle hanging on the corridor side of the door and the prisoners knew it. When Ben bent over, the two on their feet ran for their gun while the one on the floor held Ben. The rifle came cracking down on his skull, almost killing him, and the three took off, hiding in the brush at the edge of the lake. Sheriff Thorp quickly organized a posse and surrounded the patch of willows and aspen trees.

When he demanded the fugitives' surrender, the man with the gun threatened to shoot anyone who moved closer. Thorp was a man of courage and strode forward, but there was no shot—the gun had jammed in the beating of old Ben. The three walked out meekly and were returned to jail.

Then there was the day in January, 1891, when Indian Steve was jerked from the same jail by a howling mob of drunken miners. They tied his hands behind his back, blindfolded him and forced him down the road to a large tree. A heavy limb stuck out horizontally about fifteen feet up and a rope was thrown over it, the other made into a noose which was

793

PICTURE MADE IN 1962 shows town in opposite direction of early-day photo. Historic courthouse stood in grove of pines at bottom center. Comparatively new church is at right on site of earlier one destroyed by fire. Indian name of Conconully meant "clouds" or anything threatening, in this case monster supposed to live in lake of same name. Sparsely pine-clad hills are typical of Okanogan Highlands, large section of north-central Washington, extending into British Columbia. Modern camp ground and State Park are at right of picture. Lake teems with regularly planted trout, mostly rainbows averaging 8 to 11 inches.

looped around Steve's neck. The lynchers hauled him into the air, jerking him up and down. The body swayed there a day or two and then the rope was cut off, the tied end remaining until the tree was cut down in 1938.

This lynching and other incidents were part of the "Conconully Indian Scare." The government restricting of the Indian population to the nearby Colville Reservation was difficult or impossible to enforce, the natives making sporadic forays into Conconully and neighboring Ruby, Tonasket and Loomis.

They were suspected at once when the dead body of C. S. Cole, driver for the freight line between Okanogan and Conconully, was found near the road near the close of 1890, wagon rolled over the cliff and horses gone. There were no clues until a squaw who loitered around Conconully began spreading rumors that Indian Johnny and his friend Indian Steve had done the deed. Asked why she would inform on Johnny, her "fella," she said she had tried to get him to marry her but he would not. She said one reason he had picked Cole, aside from stealing the horses, was that the freighter had poked fun at the Indian about his feeble attempts to raise a mustache.

794

Deputy Ives took off after the pair of braves who he heard were at an encampment near Chilliwhist. Johnny saw him first, drew a gun and fired, the bullet grazing Ives' cheek. The deputy's shot was more deadly, hitting the Indian in the head and killing him.

During the gunfires a squaw was wounded, which further angered the sullen tribesmen. Bad feeling was so strong Ives decided not to look for Indian Steve and get out as soon as possible. He said later that as he rode away he could imagine guns aimed at his back, making his flesh crawl, but he escaped unmolested.

Word was soon sent to the camp that Steve had better give himself up before there was more trouble, and on January 5, 1891, he surrendered to the sheriff in Conconully. He was placed in jail and Judge Price, who knew Indian ways and thinking, started an investigation before trial. The next week the Ruby *Miner* was to print this ambiguous note:

"Last Thursday morning twenty horsemen galloped through Ruby, the soft white snow muffling the sound of their horses' hooves and the slumber of the camp was not disturbed by their movements. Death was in their hearts and they sped remorselessly onward." Jailer Thomas Dickson had been warned by the judge of the strong possibility of a lynching and when he saw the mob approaching, he hid the cell key under his mattress. The mob soon found it, opened the door and dragged Indian Steve to his death. This item appeared in the Ruby *Miner* the following week:

"Trouble is on foot and danger stalks abroad. It is principally owing to the lynching of Steve that this condition exists—but there are many supplemental reasons. George Monk accompanied by Smitkin started to convey the body to the Indian Mission. The Indians claim that Monk, when he started out, was sitting on the corpse which was wrapped in a blanket and carried on a single bobsled. The appearance of the body was the signal for the start of a big dance. For two days the body was kept while the Indians stimulated themselves at the bier."

The lynching did intensify matters. It was now rumored Indians were gathering in the mountains for mass attacks on Conconully. Another report had it that every man, woman and child would be killed and scalped in vengeance for the deaths of Johnny and Steve. Alarm grew to the point that citizens appealed to the U.S. Army for help.

In response, on January 17, 1891, Gen. A. P. Curry arrived with a detachment of soldiers and an arsenal for use of residents in case of attack. One hundred eighty rifles and 3,000 rounds of ammunition were stacked in the courthouse. When no raid developed, the guns were stored in an unused room where they gathered dust for many years.

In the beginning, Indians trapped beavers in the area, selling the pelts at a good profit and calling the valley Sklow Outiman or Money Hole. The first whites were prospectors who founded Salmon City on Salmon Creek.

In March of 1888 the newly organized board of Okanogan County Commissioners met in a log barn

OVERALL VIEW OF CONCONULLY taken about 1905 as shown in old newspaper, Conconully *Record* in real estate plug with list of merchants. Main business section is at lower right, courthouse at base of hill, left of center; public grade school at left. Salmon Creek is seen flowing parallel to road in lower right. Site of hanging of Indian Steve is along same road at extreme bottom center. Church shown here just below courthouse was destroyed by fire, replacement built on same site shows at lower right of modern photo.

RUIN OF VAULT, once impregnable, built in connection with courthouse for keeping of records, now fast disappearing remnant of wild days in Conconully. Remains of bars protecting windows are visible in center of picture. Mrs. Andrew Nickel, wife of early county treasurer and his deputy, once remarked: "I was afraid to go into vault mornings after that bank bandit LeRoy was searched and the nitroglycerine found on him."

on the farm of John Perkins at the head of Johnson Creek near the booming mining camps of Ruby City and Salmon City, four miles apart. George Huley, later mayor of Ruby City was one member, Guy Waring, pioneer merchant of Loomis, another. Next day, the 7th, another meeting was held at which members read petitions from both towns pleading the right to be the county seat. Ruby City won out and the committee left the log barn to meet in Ruby. By November, Salmon City had changed its name to Conconully and, the population of both towns having swelled enormously, an election was held to decide which city should now have the county seat. Conconully got 357 votes to Ruby's 157, and the commissioners again switched locations.

About 1900 there was a strong movement to change the seat to Riverside, that town doing the promoting and Conconully sitting back. The latter town had an elegant courthouse, built by the famous Steven Cloud and sheltering a safe that weighed a ton and a half with a time lock unequalled in the country. The Riverside effort failed.

One of the first county treasurers was Andrew J. Nickel, earning $125 a month, his wife having campaigned with him and getting $75 as deputy. Mrs. Nickel had spent several months driving around the county in a light buggy drawn by ponies Peter and Peggy, had talked to every man encountered on the road, passing out campaign literature and a card. After

the election, she related her embarrassment when the newspapers in 1914 with the local high school footponies continued to stop at the sight of every man on the road.

A freighter named Brown used a buggy with two horses when the load of supplies and mail was light. On the road steeply descending to Conconully by a series of switchbacks, his progress was blocked by a snowslide. As he unhitched his horses to lead them around, one struggled into the deep snow and vanished. Brown led the other one down the hill and just before arriving in Conconully, met the other animal which had floundered safely down.

A stage line ran between Conconully and Oroville with bearskin coats and foot warmers as standard equipment to keep passengers from freezing to death in winter. But in November of 1904 which had been deceptively warm, the driver did not take the coats and warmers along. A large group of teachers took the stage in Oroville for Teachers' Institute in Conconully, all wearing light clothes. During the meeting the temperature plummeted to below zero. On the way home men and women teachers had to huddle together under a few blankets and at each way stop to change horses on the eight-hour trip, they were taken into the stage depot and thawed out.

Disastrous floods and fires plagued Conconully as well as avalanches and Indians. Superstitious residents recalled the invective screamed from the knoll above town by a bitter miner who had been rolled in a bawdy house. "Curses on you, damned Conconully! May you burn, be drowned and burned again!"

In spite of the silver panic of 1893, the town kept going in a limited way. It made headlines in area newspapers in 1914 with the local high school football team called "Terror of the Okanogan" but other headlines the same year proclaimed the end of the old camp. The proud position of county seat was surrendered to the now more prosperous town of Okanogan.

The old courthouse was torn down, the lumber used to build a little city hall. The jail was removed, leaving on the site the two concrete and rock vaults— and now even these have crumbled to a large extent. One has visible evidence of bars which were used as added protection for legal documents. Visitors and prowlers for historical remains are usually happy in

the delusion they have found the famous Conconully jail which actually was a frame structure.

A third substantial vault remaining near the present little post office belonged to the bank which bandit LeRoy was so intently watching before he was caught. The huge livery stable stood until about 1958 when it was razed. A tiny, false-front, one-room building which served as a plant of the Conconully *Record* was torn down about the same time.

The area is now a State Park with a fine campground having all modern facilities even to automatic laundry machines. It is situated in an aspen grove on sand brought down the canyon by Salmon Creek in flood times. In the center of a landscaped park is a replica of the little log cabin in which the original county commissioners met. Trout fishing in the lake and reservoir is rated among the best in the state.

FAMOUS HOOSEGOW in Conconully, long since vanished, was butt of ridicule because of frequent prisoner escapes but did keep many prisoners in custody. Was located near courthouse which can be seen in overall photo of town. Section at left confined prisoners; quarters for jailer, at right.

RT HOUSE, CONCONULLY, WN. FRANK MASURA, PTS.

ORIGINAL PHOTO OF CONCO-NULLY COURTHOUSE was picture post card taken in 1905 by little Japanese photographer, Frank Matsura; property of Mrs. R. Brunke who still lives in old silver camp. View from balcony was superb, looking out over piney mountains and Conconully Lake. In winter, when frozen, lengthy stretch of water served as part of highway to "outside," eliminating difficult and dangerous avalanche-beset road.

STONE HOUSE dates from Conconully's early roistering days as does tenant. He walks down steep trail to tavern each day, wearing pair of six guns as he has for fifty years. These are checked at door, returned when old gentleman leaves.

COPPER CITY, WASHINGTON

Mr. Fred Eaton has lived in the area of Copper City for nearly fifty years, and the town was already old and abandoned when he came. There had been a good strike of gold and copper, creating great but short-lived excitement. The great "Yacolt Burn," an enormous forest fire in 1902, stopped everything for a time and the mine was never worked profitably again. Mr. Eaton surmised that the vein had run out.

Some years later, a Sam Pumpelly conceived a plan to revitalize the mine and sell stock. "Sam drank a lot and would do anything to make a fast buck." He hauled good, rich ore from another mine and scattered it all over the diggin's. But his reputation was his undoing and the scheme fell through. He died not long after. Since then, the mine has been completely abandoned except for a few fishermen who cast their flies on the tumbling waters of Copper Creek.

LITTLE GROUP OF CABINS is swamped in rain-nurtured verdure.

CURLEW, WASHINGTON

Always a bridesmaid, never a bride—that was the story of Curlew. It was named for a water bird and a lake where they abounded but it never had a name for gold.

Curlew had its beginings in a very modest way in the '80s with a few trappers' cabins. Since the soil was rich and comparatively free of trees and stumps, a few farmers built homes and fenced some fields. A school and a few stores were built.

During the early years life in Curlew was peaceful. Occasionally some prospector would come into town claiming he had struck gold in the hills and there was a flurry of excitement. The news was readily accepted each time since the wish was there and lots of gold had been found in Republic and other nearby camps. But alas, nothing ever materialized from these claims except grubstakes by the gullible storekeepers.

Curlew had settled back into a succession of naps when the actual bombshell exploded. "The railroad is coming!" The Spokane and British Columbia announced plans for a line through Republic, Kettle Falls, Curlew and Grand Forks in Canada. The Great Northern already had an option on the only logical right-of-way but that did not deter the S. & B. C. from making a great show of surveying another one alongside. An elaborate station was built on the hill above Curlew—then the long, empty pause. The investors

J. C. KIEHL who has lived in Curlew since before the days when the "Hot Air Railroad" made numerous false starts toward construction which never materialized. He stands here at side door of Ansorge Hotel where he now resides. Small false-front stood here first, erected by Ansorge and used as restaurant. To make room for hotel it was moved around to side, facetiously referred to as "Ansorge Annex."

COPY OF OLD PICTURE loaned by J. C. Kiehl shows Ansorge Hotel in days of first World War. Jitney service operated by Kiehl was in full swing, taxis shown here lined up and ready to go. Several loungers on porch seem not too interested in proceedings.

ANSORGE HOTEL at right, now more than commodious home for Mr. and Mrs. J. C. Kiehl, two of Curlew's oldest inhabitants. Mr. Kiehl remembers: "There were many times in the old days when the hotel was so full they had to put extra cots in the hallways. Those were the war days and I ran a jitney service for drummers and prospectors. It seems like they wanted to go everywhere, around town and out to the neighboring towns, even to Republic. Those boys were always good pay and sometimes gave me tips." Building at left was old Maxwell Meat Market.

MANY BOARDED UP FALSE-FRONTED STORES line streets of one-time flourishing Curlew. Most breaks in ranks caused by fires which took heavy toll in days when frame structures were tinder dry, water pressure low.

were wondering where their money had gone when more surveys were ordered and the "notch on the hill" was deepened to a more respectable cut. Now, everybody thought, we are really on our way to having a railroad through town. Real estate values advanced and property changed hands.

Again the interminable wait. The grumbling of citizens grew louder. "That new railroad is nothing but a lot of hot air!" was shouted and the Spokane and British Columbia was always called "The Hot Air Railroad" through the years, the line never being completed. Eventually the Great Northern exercised its option and Curlew did have trains, but it was too late. All hopes of a big gold discovery had long since vanished and Curlew was just a whistle stop.

ST. PATRICK'S CATHOLIC CHURCH built in 1903 and kept in good repair now has scant congregation. Barren hills surrounding town once had good growth of timber, were stripped to provide wood and lumber.

FRANKFORT, WASHINGTON

"Curiosity unveils marvels" and no one knows it better than Dr. Ralph Isaac of Portland, Oregon. He spends much time in the outdoors of his free days, eyes and ears open, feelers tuned to a sensitive pitch. One summer day in 1960 he and his son-in-law walked along the beach of the Columbia River, at Knappton on the north or Washington shore. The tide was going out and they looked for a trail to skirt the headland which appeared to block the way.

"We came to a group of weathered houses," the doctor told the author later, "some just above high water level, some well up the bank. At first we thought all the houses were vacant, although most of them were still furnished. We looked through one window into a kitchen and saw dishes and silverware still on the table, as if the people living there had just finished a meal. Exploring further we discovered the settlement wasn't entirely deserted, that it had two inhabitants, a German who lived alone at one end and a lonely Swede at the other. We talked to the latter, commenting it was fortunate he had company in the otherwise deserted place. His reply was: 'We got mad at each other a couple of years ago and ain't spoke since.' " Mindful of the returning tide which would block their return the two explorers were forced to leave, not relishing a climb over the intervening headland with its mantle of tangled vines and brush native to Washington's coastal regions.

Dr. Isaacs lead was tantalizing to this inquisitive photographer but—how to get to Frankfort with camera equipment when the light was right (all the buildings faced south and the Columbia) and not be at the mercy of ebbing and flowing tides? After several futile attempts to reach the spot, information came in the late summer of 1964 that the firm of Crown Zellerbach was logging on the bluff above Frankfort, that dirt roads had been knifed through the heavy timber to a point a mile above it. So an over-night camp was made and in the early morning a climb down an old overgrown trail.

Here was the classic deserted village—a small one almost isolated, never reached by road of any sort, without telephone, electricity or wheeled vehicle larger than a wheelbarrow. Frankfort's only exchange with the outside world was by fishing boats, the nearest towns mere settlements, the nearest city Astoria across the broad mouth of the Columbia River with its formidable bar and almost constant threat of storms. River traffic with Frankfort tied up at a wharf which extended out across the mud flats to deep river and which was now rotted and wrecked by heavy battering of waves, making Frankfort accessible only by small boats that could reach the bank at high water, or by foot. What was the story behind the desolation?

Early in 1890 two promoters, Frank Bourn and Frank Scott, took a long look at the small clearing they found on Gray's Bay. It seemed a likely spot to start a city, a river metropolis protected from fierce winter storms by a prominent headland. Maybe they could induce a railroad to build a line to the site or at least promise to. At any rate the two Franks could call their city Frankfort.

803

FRANKFORT RESIDENTS when Lawrence Barber visited isolated community in 1947. He found 11 people, 6 of them shown here. At left is Fred Hansen, who with 9 brothers and sisters, was raised in Frankfort, all attending one-room school presided over by teacher Ulrika Brandt, daughter of Swedish sea captain. She stands next in line, partly concealed by Hugo Claeson. Next is Mrs. Claeson, then Charles Lawrence and Mrs. Lawrence.

Rumors were soon spreading like wildfire, hinting that the Northern Pacific Railroad was actually surveying a route down the north bank of the Columbia to connect with ocean shipping points. Further, said the "overly Frank" reports, the line would pass directly along the edge of Gray's Bay, a station to be built where Bourn and Scott indicated.

The promoters built a flimsy landing float at the river's edge but its usefulness was limited, as lower reaches of the Columbia advance to the ocean only on the ebb tide, being forced backward on the flood. This meant that if prospective purchasers were dropped from boats on the wharf at low tide they were faced with a mile or more of oozy mud flats.

Yet buyers came on the heels of promises and the picturesque bay front seethed with activity. Bourn and Scott took in another partner, L. O. Chemault, and on May 15, 1890, filed the original plat of Frankfort, plans calling for 1226 lots. Streets and alleys were laid out with fine disregard of terrain, much of it swampy with only a narrow bench of solid ground, this terminating at the bottom of a steeply rising bluff.

Nevertheless many of the lots were sold. The promoters ploughed their increasing funds back into Frankfort's boggy soil, building a hotel, general store and sawmill, and all these signs of a city to be, encouraged more lot sales. A newspaper was soon in print, a saloon and then two more doing business. But it soon became apparent to the most

optimistic that with all this no railroad tracks were being laid. While a committee of inquiring citizens gathered at the front door of the real estate office, two of the partners faded away at the back, leaving Bourn to face the music.

Well, it was like this, he said—the railroad had decided against building the line. He had been informed of the change in plans only yesterday. However, nobody would regret his investing in the future of Frankfort. The site was perfect for a salmon cannery and think of that tremendous stand of timber at the very door of the sawmill. The committee went away and if its members were not placated, they grumbled without protest.

Bourn was still there ten years later when Axel Nelson arrived but the population had fallen to about 150. The salmon canneries were interested in Frankfort as Bourn had predicted but not to the extent of building plants. Two of the larger concerns, New England Fish Co. and Anderson Packing Co., had built substantial wharves where they could load fish netted by Frankfort fishermen and these companies had hired Nelson as agent to facilitate the buying and loading. He bought the long unused hotel built by Bourn and partners and rebuilt it as a substantial home.

At this time the *Mayflower, Pioneer, Julia B.* and other steamers plying the river made regular stops at Frankfort docks. When the *Mayflower* was condemned as unseaworthy she was replaced by the *Shamrock.* Five years later a smart new steamer, the *General George Washington* made its maiden voyage on the Columbia and began regular stops at Frankfort. The vessel had been built by its owners, William Anderson, Ed Simmons and Ed Shatto, was destined to be the most familiar steamer on the run, the best remembered by old timers.

Early in January, 1947, Lawrence Barber, marine editor of the Portland OREGONIAN, visited Frankfort and found only 11 residents, among them Axel Nelson. The community was even more isolated than in earlier days, having no mail delivery or regular boat service. Nelson complained that Frankfort was cut off from the rest of the world, that in case of emergency it had no way of getting word out. A man needing medical attention would die before any aid could be summoned. He said he had gone into the matter of getting the county to build a road, either from Knappton, a stretch of only three miles but over the steep intervening headland, or from Deep River to the north, three and a half miles over the mud flats. Either way the cost would be between $35,-

000 and $50,000 for a single lane graveled road and the county could not consider it.

Barber's story and pictures appeared in his newspaper January 12. On the 17th there was a news item from Astoria headed: "Navy To Help Isolated Area." The announcement read: "The navy Wednesday came to the rescue of Frankfort, Wash., the tiny community on the north shore of the Columbia." The item stated that Capt. L. B. Ard, commanding officer of the Tongue Point Naval Station would send a crash boat to Frankfort at the request of the Astoria Chamber of Commerce, and if any emergency condition was found to exist the navy would provide temporary weekly service until regular commercial boat service could be restored.

And a month later, on February 12, the OREGONIAN carried this dispatch: "Doctor Rushed To Isolated Area—The isolated community of Frankfort . . . called on the navy Sunday for assistance when one of its 12 inhabitants became suddenly ill. The navy command at Tongue Point dispatched a picket boat to carry Dr. J. B. Lund from Astoria to Frankfort to treat Leo Nelson who was seriously ill with intestinal influenza. . . . The navy has been sending a crash boat there occasionally as an emergency service."

Frankfort's ultimate usefulness was mentioned in the OREGONIAN'S issue of January 14, 1953: "Logger Acquires River Townsite — The forest grown townsite of Frankfort, across the Columbia River from Astoria, has been sold at auction by Pacific County, Wash. for $74,918. E. J. Mell, Shelton, Wash. logger bought the bulk of the property . . . several independent buyers took lots on the waterfront that might be capable of development for resort purposes. The sale put an end to the dreams of real estate promoters of more than fifty years ago who platted the townsite in the hopes it would develop into the metropolis of the lower Columbia."

HOME OF AXEL NELSON, native of Finland, who arrived in Frankfort at turn of century. House was built of lumber salvaged from hotel made useless when plans for railroad collapsed. Most of furnishings remain, although badly damaged by vandals. Piano still stands in parlor but needle point settee dumped on front steps has been ruined further by rains which often total 15 inches a month in winter at near-ocean site. Moisture and mild climate foster heavy verdure which will soon engulf Nelson home and entire village.

VIEW FROM DESERTED VILLAGE of Frankfort across broad mouth of Columbia River. Early morning mists rise from water, partly obscuring Oregon coastal range in distance. Large public dock was wrecked in violent winter storm in 1933. Mud flats in center foreground are exposed by low tide which strongly affects Columbia here near ocean. Volume and power of water at flood are evidenced by stranded logs at shoreline.

LAST REMAINING RESIDENT of Frankfort was Swedish fisherman, Sven Hovic, who was taken to rest home in helpless condition in 1962. Sven had used most of his winter's wood, rest remaining to rot, as apples on tree. Wires were strung above fence to discourage marauding deer and elk, other residents using more effective fish net barricades 8-feet high.

HOME, WASHINGTON

"Home", said the indignant editorial headed "The Nudes and the Prudes" in the colony's newspaper THE AGITATOR, "is a community of free spirits who came out into the woods to escape the priest-ridden atmosphere of conventional society. One of the liberties enjoyed by Homeites was the privilege to bathe in evening dress or with only the clothes nature gave them, just as they pleased. . . But eventually a few got into the community and proceeded in the brutal unneighborly way of the outside world to suppress the people's freedom. . . ."

The community of free spirits included two who lived in a tree. Joe Kapolla and Franz Erkelems arrived in the idyllic colony on the shore of Joe's Bay in 1908, attracted by the well-publicized tolerance of Home's people toward ways of living that might be considered odd elsewhere.

The site Joe and Franz selected for a home had a ready-made water supply, a bubbling spring, but the same plentiful waters made the ground too soggy for a house. The problem was solved by cutting off the top of a large, forked tree nearby and building their domicile on the several high stumps. They put up a tent on the ground below for use as a kitchen and since it straddled the cold spring, a natural ice box was provided. Dish washing was eliminated, the dirty dishes merely placed in the flowing water where minnows nibbled off scraps of food. Among the many stories told about the partners is one about a "dinner party" given for two lady guests, one of whom brought her small boy along. He amused himself grabbing at the little fish swimming among the dishes and unexpectedly caught one. Joe Kapolla told him to put it back immediately. "That's our best dish washer."

Home's history of individualism, discontent and frustration is recorded in its series of newspapers or more accurately in the several revivals of the same one. Beginning as the NEW ERA, the little paper was successively brought out as the DISCONTENT — MOTHER OF PROGRESS, THE DEMONSTRATOR and the AGITATOR, all printed on a portable press. The NEW ERA, started in June of 1897 by O. A. Verity, stated in one of its first issues: "Liberty we have, so far as *we* are concerned, but. the laws of the state — of course — the ever-present thorn in the flesh — are the great barriers to the realization of Liberty. Now, one may, at Home, keep within the pale of the law or completely ignore it, just as he pleases. Most of us prefer the latter course and teach others to do the same." An issue or two later came forth with the illuminating premise — "The love principle of our nature is a natural one, and to defy it is to defy nature."

More exciting was the coming of Halley's Comet, the arrival scheduled for four o'clock in the morning. Joe and Franz were out scanning the heavens and Joe spotted a glow at the brow of a hill. "There it is!" he shouted but Franz said it couldn't be, that the comet was supposed to appear over a hill in the opposite direction. In the next moment they realized they were looking at Joe Brewster's cabin and it was ablaze. They were eager to help put the fire out but the only source of water was a deep well and neither of them knew how to operate the windlass. Joe managed to get the bucket down and excitedly wound the handle as fast as he could, the full bucket coming up with a jerk and banging against the head of the open-mouthed Franz. The water spilled out and by the time more concerted team work brought up another bucketful, the fire was hopelessly out of control. Halley's Comet had meanwhile made its fruitless trip across the sky.

The paper attracted plenty of attention but costing only a dollar a year, with most copies being mailed free to outsiders as propaganda, the NEW ERA soon died. One of the last issues fell into the hands of an alcoholic printer named Charles Goven in a Barbary Coast saloon in San Francisco. He recruited friend James F. Morton Jr. to go with him to Home with the idea of improving the paper and at the same time enjoy the purported freedoms. They arrived to find the NEW ERA defunct and Goven set about to revive it.

Volume 1, No. 1 of the new paper, dated May 11, 1898, was headed: "DISCONTENT — MOTHER OF PROGRESS, Successor to NEW ERA — Dedicated to Anarchist Communism — Price 50¢ Yearly." On the 29th a summary of Home history was included. "Our progress in the two years we have been here has been slow. The Mutual Home Association was started by three comrades whose combined cash was one $20 gold piece each. They came from the Socialist Colony at Glennis in a boat they built themselves."

The three referred to were George Allen, O. A. Verity and F. F. O'dell who had indeed built their own boat, toured the maze of waterways adjacent to Tacoma and made their selection of Joe's Bay, a small intrusion from Von Geldred Cove, which in

VIEW UP TINY JOE'S BAY, roughly twenty miles from Tacoma. Life in Home was tied closely to waterways, only means of transportation and access to outer world, which though scorned in theory, supplied many of daily needs. Wharf housing totters precariously on barnacle-encrusted, rotting piers. Other structures in background also date from colony days. Long dock was later convenience, ship passengers for Home in first years landed unceremoniously on small raft and ferried ashore. Low tide here has given access to beach for low angle photograph, exposing oysters in plenty, many 7 inches long. They are escapees from those planted commercially in Dabob and Quilcene Bays. For about ten days after hatching, larval form called "spat" floats freely in water, may drift long distances in free-swimming stage. Early Home settlers likely would have welcomed added item to meager food supplies but they were many years too early.

turn is an arm of Carr's Inlet. There were twenty-six acres of land there, available to the colonists at a price of $2.50 per acre. The trio and their families set to work digging clams and cutting wood, selling these products to neighboring townspeople. In the spring of 1897 they bought the land and for-mally set up the Compact of the Mutual Home Colony Association.

O'dell continues the story in DISCONTENT: "We came here, got our land on time and went into debt for the lumber, $100, to build houses, unable to pay freight entirely on our goods. Allen (an honor student of Toronto University) taught school and with the proceeds we lived while the other two built houses and cleared land for the gardens. After the short space of 16 months we were practically out of debt. Incoming members aided us with payments for land and membership fees. Today we have 22 members, 14 adult male workers, have 11 houses erected and another cost $300 well under way; bought and paid for two teams of horses, but sold one recently. This success is the result of our labors as none of the incoming members had means to aid them."

Allen went on working hard said the item of January 1, 1899: "Comrade Allen has his hands full these days teaching singing classes, writing copy for advertising in DISCONTENT, all voluntary and without pay. Yet, there are those who say that in Anarchy where money is eliminated there would be no incentive to labor." In another issue was this bit: "Comrade C. W. Fox has rheumatism. He says it is nobody's business, though, that he can be sick if he wishes." And every issue carried this note: "How to get here. Parties inclining to visit us will come to Tacoma and take steamer *Tycoon* for Joe's Bay, leaving Commercial Dock every day except Saturday and Sunday at 2:30. Ask Captain to let you off on Joe's Bay raft." Presumably, someone in the colony would row out and bring the visitor ashore.

By 1900 Home's population was seventy-five, including thirty school children. DISCONTENT had claimed a circulation of twelve hundred, it being obvious the paper was intended for outside propaganda. One of these readers was Emma Goldman, feminist radical, who wrote essays for the publication on free love in which she invariably blamed the organized church for prostitution.

Although Home was getting a reputation for being a retreat for those who advocated free love, sin and anarchy, there was no serious focus of attention on the doings there until the assassination of President McKinley in 1904. Home could not be suspected of harboring the actual assassin, Leon Czolgosz, but it was a known refuge for anarchists like him. In the hysteria following the President's death, a group calling itself Loyalty League held a mass meeting in Custer Hall in Tacoma. Members formed a Vigilante Committee whose express purpose was to go to Home and "subdue" the colonists. The Tacoma LEDGER reported that the Committee should charter a steamer, go to Home, run off the members and burn their town.

While the excited Committee members were discussing ways and means, the pastor of the German Evangelical Church of Tacoma, Rev. J. F. Doescher, made a trip to the colony, interviewed members in their houses and preached a sermon in their Liberty Hall. When he returned to Tacoma he went straight to the LEDGER office and demanded that the paper see to it that any raid on the colonists be prevented. "They have made clearings", he said, "planted orchards, made gardens. The people are sober, industrious and friendly. Their neighbors give them good witness. They are better citizens by far than those that have been shouting 'Exterminate the vipers!'"

The newspaper did discourage the raid, possibly because destruction of the colony would ruin a good news source. But Home was not out of the woods. The postal authorities took over, sending the United States marshall over to arrest Goven and his helpers for "depositing obscene matter in the U.S. Mails."

As a gesture of passive non-resistence, Home members greeted the marshall at the gangplank, made him a guest of honor at a dinner and later at a dance. The marshall dined, danced and next morning escorted his prisoners to the Tacoma jail. The LEDGER had a large type heading next day to the effect that the intrepid law officer had single-handedly attacked, subdued and arrested the miscreants at great personal danger to himself. The DISCONTENT cried out at the injustice, attempted to have the LEDGER retract the statements and when it failed to do so, the newspaper was branded in the colony's own as "not being interested in simple truth."

The trial was held on March 11, 1902. Goven and his associates were acquitted but authorities held one more trump. In April the Home post office was removed by order of the Postmaster General. Shortly afterward the DISCONTENT was deprived of its mailing privileges and that finished the paper.

Following a new established pattern, another new publication was created from the old, THE DEMONSTRATOR, with Morton listed as publisher and Goven as printer. The appearance was familiar and so was the approach. It also reminded outsiders: "If you should consider coming to us to live you should consider several things. There is much hard work to be done. We have cleared rough streets but still lack sidewalks. While there are eleven cows here now, there still is not enough milk for our needs. Most important consideration however, is that you will be able to live under the anarchist plan, that you may do just as you please as long as you do not infringe upon the natural rights of others."

Indicating some satisfaction in the way things were proceeding, was this item: "How does a com-

EARLY COTTAGES built by colonists stood in open, old growth trees having been cut for wood. Lusty, brushy second growth has all but covered some houses falling into decay through abandonment. This house provided excellent view of harbor entrance, is not now visible except to searchers of relics of colony days.

munity of eighty people, with two newspapers, one weekly, one monthly, a school with two teachers, no saloons, no churches, no policemen and no jails compare with what you have been used to ?"

But now transportation troubles beset the colony, the newspaper reporting: "The steamer *Tycoon* has been laid up for repairs and our sole communication with Tacoma has been by means of the Dadisman and Adams launches.". . . "Our path along the shore toward Tacoma is being extended and improved and it is beginning to take on some of the aspects of a real road."

Morton did very well with THE DEMONSTRATOR for a time, as long as he paid strict attention to business. He was susceptible to outside interests, such as helping promote his friend, Henry George,

for mayor of New York. While in that city Morton neglected his newspaper and it died like the others.

What bothered Home the most or what gave the Tacoma LEDGER the most ammunition to fire at Home was nude bathing. The reports that the colony's beaches were filled with assorted human forms cavorting gaily in the altogether caused more than raised eybrows. Hundreds of LEDGER readers visited the place "just to make sure the truth or falsity of the reports."

What started most of the rumors was Henry Dadisman's purchase of two hundred acres adjoining Home. He opened the land to settlers, the first of whom were a number of Dukhobors from Russia. Members of the sect were accustomed to being undressed at home and naturally the same when bathing. Home colonists who had enjoyed such bathing privileges but had been discreet or in semi-seclusion, were now emboldened to the same openness. But there was a complication. A small neighbor village named Lake Bay did not share in these liberal views. Residents there protested that four people, two men and two women, were bathing in the nude across the bay. Arrested for indecent exposure, the quartet was brought before Justice Tom Larkin in Lake Bay court. One witness was asked how she could be sure the bathers across the bay, nearly half a mile from her home, were nude. She replied: "I have a good pair of binoculars and I know how to use them." Worst of all, it turned out the complaining witness was a resident of Home.

By this time there was a new newspaper in the colony, the AGITATOR, run by Jay Fox and it was he who wrote the editorial mentioned earlier—"The Nudes and the Prudes". The Tacoma LEDGER made much of the editorial and drew attention to the various "atrocities" committed in Home in recent years, implying that Home was capable of allowing anything. In the winter of 1910-11 the plant of the Los Angeles TIMES was bombed by anarchists, Home was immediately suspected of harboring the guilty men. William J. Burns, head of his detective agency visited the colony under the guise of a book salesman. The evidence he picked up there led to further investigation and eventual arrest of two of the men involved in the bombing. One, Matthew Schmidt, had actually lived in Home at one time. The other was David Caplan, apprehended in New York on information given Burns by a boy named Donald Vose living in Home.

Burns later wrote a book enlarging on his experiences. The volume had a wide circulation and it did Home no good. It included such distorted paragraphs as "Home Colony is the nest of Anarchy in the United States. There are about 1200 of them living there without regard for a single decent thing in life. They exist in a state of free love and are notoriously unfaithful to the mates thus chosen, and are so crooked that even in this class of rogues there does not seem to be a single hint of honor."

A few months later Fox's editorial boomeranged. He was arrested for "tending to encourage or advo-cate disrespect for law or for a court of justice. The trial, held in Pierce County Courthouse, excited much comment in newspapers nationally. Every detail of life in Home Colony appeared lurid when reported in the LEDGER. Nothing was said of the industry, frugality and general peacefulness of the settlers.

Fox was convicted, the jury recommending leniency. He was sentenced to two months in the county jail and while serving the time, the State of Washington elected a new governor, Ernest Lister, who pardoned Fox unconditionally. The editor returned to Joe's Bay, but things were not the same. Unfavorable publicity had been too much for the colony. The Association was broken up and people began to move away.

Jay Fox and his wife remained with a number of other faithfuls. Fox died a few years ago but his wife still lives in the old home across the bay with an interest in painting. The colony area is again populated, sparsely enough, by summer residents and a few permanent homes. Home's post office was never reinstated under the same name but the area is served by another at the crossroads about half a mile away. It bears the name of the colony's old antagonist, Lake Bay. In retrospect, all things considered, there was no place like Home.

SOME COTTAGES closer to water front have been kept in repair, are occupied by summer residents. Apple trees, here in full bloom, attest agricultural proclivities of settlers. Venerable specimens are small remnants of orchard of seven hundred assorted fruit trees planted on this bench above Joe's Bay. Beach below was site of many stories told of residents in days when reputed nude bathing caused big furor in Tacoma press. One was about two young girls called to mother's knee. "You're getting to be big girls now and shouldn't go swimming without your bathing suit." Girls, later observed sun bathing on sand in nude, protested: "We **did** wear our suits while we were swimming."

811

INDEX, WASHINGTON

Index still has a few interesting buildings remaining from its lusty boom days, but they are fast disappearing. The most impressive still standing is the Fraternal Hall. The Red Men, the Masons and the Odd Fellows, tend to hold dear the old Hall.

The town is spectacularly situated, in what the pioneers called a "Hole." Surrounded by towering peaks in a wild section of the Cascades, it is bounded further by the rushing Skykomish River. Mt. Index with its pointing rock needles dominates as high a horizon as a town could have, and deep timber crowds close.

The post office was established in 1891, at which time the town was well underway and several mines were taking out a high grade copper ore called Bornite.

Amos Gunn's saloon was one of the largest during the town's boom days, but by no means the only one. Several more faced the main street running parallel to the river. Growth was slow until about 1897, when new veins were opened and the Sunset Copper Mine was being operated at such pressure that many men were killed in its tunnels and shafts. Hotels, drugstores, a newspaper and more saloons were established. Many more minerals were found, some only in traces, gold, silver, antimony, arsenates and even the "modern" molybdenum. When the copper deposits wore thin and attempts to exploit some of the others failed, the town died.

There are lots of open spaces now from which one can gaze up at the encircling peaks.

STEEP, TIMBERED SLOPES crowded old Index. Much virgin timber was cut for mine use, second growth was killed by fire. Now new growth is taking hold; in t w e n t y years new forest will cover naked hills.

KNAPPTON, WASHINGTON

Cement making started it, fishing and trapping added to its growth, sawmilling made it tick and fire put an end to everything—Knappton on the Columbia.

For two years, after the end of the Civil War, Job Lamley and George Hopkins lived alone on a narrow strip of land on the north shore of the Columbia River near its mouth. If they were not talking to each other, the arrival of six more people relieved the tension. The newcomers were R. N. Knapp and wife, their sons Amen and Jabez, Amen's wife and J. H. Burl.

Young Jabez was interested in minerals and geology, exploring the timber-covered hills that ran steeply up from the tiny settlement on the shore, and he found an outcropping of lime rock, a rarity in this predominately basaltic area. Experimenting with the material, he found it would

make good cement and with partners Burl and Hopkins, started the small plant which gave the community its first name—Cementville.

The industry attracted workers, fishermen and trappers came to live there and a post office was established in 1871 with Jabez Knapp the first postmaster and the family name used in renaming the settlement. It soon became evident cement would not shape Knappton's future. The limestone rocks were being used up, outcropping confined to the surface, and the plant cut down operations.

Sawdust however was in the path of destiny. Flanked by a bountiful supply of virgin fir, spruce and cedar, the men who started the sawmill were sure it would succeed—Jabez Knapp, S. W. Backus, H. F. Williams, N. W. Spaulding and D. W. Grant, with James Vaughn hired to clear the land for the mill. Vaughn, born and raised in Keatesville, Missouri, enlisted in the Union Army with the Indiana

OLD KNAPPTON QUARANTINE STATION served 56 years. Four and a half acres of ground adjacent to docks site were logged off in 1899, wharf and buildings constructed same year, operations by U.S. Public Health Service started May 9th. Here were detained immigrants (mostly Orientals imported to work in New England Fish cannery) suspected of carrying communicable diseases. Fumigation of ships required two day period in early days when sulphur fumes were employed, operation being much expedited later with use of cyanide. Detained "guests" sometimes overflowing hospital buildings on wharf were accommodated in hull of old Navy cruiser Concord tied up alongside. Viewpoint here is western extremity of Gray's Bay, eastern arm shown in distance. Columbia River at this point is about seven miles wide.

Volunteers and at the end of the war came northwest to Old Chinook at Point Ellice near Knappton to fish for salmon. Between fish runs he worked at the cement plant, displaying an eagerness and ability for the land clearing job.

Engaged also by the sawmill company to build the mill was craftsman Samuel Everhart Barr, Pennsylvania born and migrant to Portland, Oregon, in 1859. Like Vaughn, Barr brought a young wife with him and the two families built a house to occupy jointly. It had a common kitchen with a board across the center, used to separate warring factions among the rapidly growing brood of children when they were less than amicable.

James Vaughn became chief log supplier for the mill. Close in timber had been cut for building of stores and houses but an almost limitless supply of trees extended in three directions from the river. Vaughn had homesteaded a 160-acre tract of timber at the mouth of near by Deep River and now with twelve men and eight yoke of oxen, he became one of the first "contract" loggers in the area. Some of the first trees could be felled directly into the river and rafted to the mill. As the stand receded from shore, short skid roads were laid down, oxen dragging the big logs from woods to river.

Until 1875 the Knapp family was predominant in the town, then a commanding figure appeared — Asa M. Simpson. He was a Maine man, born February 21, 1826 in New Brunswick, apprenticed to a shipbuilder at 14. On his tenth birthday his father gave him a one-thirty-second interest in the four-masted bark *Birmingham* and at 23 he shipped as her supercargo, sailing around the Horn and arriving in San Francisco in the midst

of gold fever in 1850. Going directly to the gold fields, Asa made a small strike and with New England frugality invested it in the ship *H. F. Gray,* first ship built in San Francisco Bay. Later the ship was lost and so was Simpson's money.

Then he persuaded the owners of the *Birmingham* to haul lumber to Stockton, the venture recouping his small fortune. He bought a share in the *Potomac* but this ship was disabled and nearly wrecked off the Columbia River in 1852. While waiting for her to be repaired in Astoria, he built a sawmill only to have it lost in a sudden business depression. With what money he had left he bought into the ship *Harriet* and began hauling lumber down the coast. While at the mouth of the Umpqua River, awaiting a cargo of piling, he heard Indian tales of the immense stand of timber around Coos Bay and made an overland trip to see for himself. This area supplied the nucleus of his later successes, providing cargo for his ships.

That year, 1875, he built the first full-rigged ship launched on the Pacific Coast, *Western Shore,* at his shipyard in North Bend, Oregon. It was on her maiden voyage to Knappton for lumber that Asa Simpson recognized the possibilities in the little sawmill. He bought it — lock, stock and barrel — installing Melville P. Callendar as superintendent. "For the next thirty years," relates Carlton E. Apello of Deep River, local historian, "The Callendars, Melville and Charlie, ran the mill."

It was the only important industry in a remote, almost isolated area and had a strong impact on people in surrounding villages — Deep River, Salmon Creek, Frankfort, Crooked Creek, Naselle and Grays River — which depended on the lumber activity as well as fishing and farming. When winter stopped normal ways of making a living, many

ROTTING BONES of partially constructed 120' vessel lie in muddy slough near Knappton. One story says wreck is that of transport ship floated off the ways at Columbia City by flood waters during World War I, winding up on beach many miles down river, that end of war precluded salvage. Better substantiated is information supplied by merchant-historian Carlton Appelo, Deep River. He says that a Mr. Callendar of Knappton purchased half-built boat from shipyard at Astoria with intention of finishing it for own use, abandoned project when it proved impractical and too costly. Situation of derelict was once exposed to open river, now is enclosed by dike carrying modern highway, water still ebbs and flows with tides and seasons through culvert under dike.

DEEP RIVER, Washington, looks much as it did in early days when loggers gambled wages away in saloon of Shamrock Hotel, right. Building went up in 1900 as store with living quarters above, built by Charles Schwegler whose father, Christian, came from Germany to Deep River as homesteader about 1862. Structure was remodeled into saloon, hotel upstairs, by new owner Mr. Reikkola in 1904.

Activity began when Bell Logging Co. cut nearby timber, hauled logs to dump by ox teams. By 1898 Olsen Brothers had taken over, found trees too far back to haul on skid road, built first logging railroad in area. All logs were floated to Knappton Sawmill until it burned. Deep River Timber Co. built booming grounds in late 1920s, were able to raft 450,000 board feet per day in logs worth $19,000.

men moved their families to Knappton and went to work in the mill.

Ships from all nations called at Knappton for lumber, one of them, the *Rival*, American bark of 299 tons. At Knappton the vessel took on hay, lumber and shingles in September of 1881. Like hundreds of ships before and since, the *Rival* stranded on Peacock Spit, notorious sand bar at the Columbia mouth called the "Graveyard of the Pacific." Caught in a dying wind while on the bar, then driven onto the spit by a change in the wind with both anchors dragging, the hull ploughed into the sands. The tug *Astoria* managed to get a line on her but the hawser snapped. The storm swung the vessel completely around, breaking the anchor chain and carrying the *Rival* high on the beach between Cape Disappointment and McKen-

zie Head. Her master, Capt. Thomas B. Adams, wife, and crew, took to the boats which careened on the beach but landing all safely. The $8,000 bark and $6,000 cargo were a total loss.

On Saturday, July 12, 1941, the Knappton mill which had served the town for seventy years, burned to the ground and pilings. The blaze started in the planing mill, destroying a million feet of dressed lumber. Casper Korpela, working atop the refuse burner, was able to get down and make his escape only a few feet ahead of the flames. Burned were the main mill buildings, office, oil house and yard office. In its early stages the fire ate through the wooden water main, draining storage tanks so fire fighters were completely helpless.

Coast Guard lighthouse tender *Manzanita* crossed the Columbia from Astoria to ply water

815

on the flames, saving some lumber on the wharf and a portion of the wharf itself. Two barges loaded with 9 million feet of lumber were saved as were two automobiles driven onto the stacked lumber.

And the town of Knappton died, too. Eighty-five permanent jobs were wiped out and the post office closed November 15, 1943. Abandoned homes and the few buildings remaining from the holocaust began to weather and collapse. In 1960 a new state highway slashed through the nearly deserted site, eliminating most evidence of what had been Knappton. Today the old quarantine station buildings remain on their wharves, as does a tiny cluster of gray, weathered houses. At the river's edge are the stubby pilings, concrete and brick foundations of the huge boilers that once generated steam to power the screaming saws of the Knappton mill.

PADDY McGOWAN from the Auld Sod, later from Portland, Oregon, came to the north shore of Columbia river where it enters Pacific Ocean in 1852. He established a thriving business of catching and salting salmon for foreign shipment. Indians from nearby settlement of Chinook made temporary tent village at fishing site, returning home in winter. Paddy built first salmon cannery on lower river, operated at first by Indian help. He married New York girl, Jane Huntley, had four sons, one of them Henry Silas marrying and continuing to live nearby. Henry's widow, now 92, still resides in this almost vanished community named for father-in-law. Ornament draped from window is string of "corks," fishing net floats referred to in sketch of Wauna, Oregon.

LIBERTY, WASHINGTON

The reason for a lively town's becoming of ghost status, in the case of Liberty, is quite simple. When news of big strikes in the Yukon reached camp, the entire population left for those greener pastures.

There were later gasps of life for a brief time. Some who had failed in Alaska came back and worked the creek bed for a time, but eventually left entirely. There was a brief revival in the 30's, but that too failed to bring any real stimulus to the dying town and at last it lay peacefully back to slumber in winter snows and summer sun.

Next to the school stood the only dance hall for many miles and people gathered "even from Montana" for the big dance of the year which was held at the opening of the deer season. Mostly, the dance deteriorated into brawls and fights. The lady who kept store across the street "used to come over and raise hell because she couldn't sleep." This went on for years, but she never got used to it.

Liberty is so high and so cool, while the nearby lowlands of eastern Washington are roasting, that several people take refuge in its old cabins during the summer. But this doesn't spoil its charm, or status as a bona fide Ghost Town. No business is transacted there, no children go to its old school and no gas is sold from the broken old pump which in the latest days of Liberty's existence served the Model T's.

The gravels of Swauk Creek are still worth $1.00 a yard, even at the present price of gold, but costs are too high to work them.

LIBERTY'S QUIET Main Street. School is at far end.

LOOMIS, WASHINGTON

The first question the judge asked the mammoth lady was: "Did you intend to kill these men?" Her answer put an end to the proceedings. "Hell, no! If I had wanted to kill them, they'd be dead."

It all came about because sheepherders were anxious to get their woolies to summer pasture. Just above Loomis was a regular route by which the animals were moved but obstructing it were several ranches from which permit of access had to be obtained. One of these ranchers was a lady reputed to weigh some four hundred pounds, with a temper to match. One band of sheep moved too slowly across her property and she told the herders to hurry them along. When they still didn't go fast enough to suit her, she got her .30-.30 and sent several shots over the men's heads. They filed a complaint of attempted murder and the sheriff, unaware of the lady's bulk, went after her in his little buggy only to return to town for a dray wagon. After she was released, it was used again to take her home.

The first settlers in the Loomis area operated a large cattle station owned by Phelps Wadleigh and Co. in the early 1870s. In the bitter cold winter of '79-'80 their entire herd of 3,000 head perished, wiping the enterprise out of existence.

While the cattle station operated, helpers had started small farms on the side and when the station was gone, some of them stayed on. One was Alvin Thorpe, a man of experimental nature, a unique type in a day when harsh realities forced pioneers to take the accepted course. He got his supplies the hard way like everybody else, freighting them in, and one bad spot on the route was the crossing of the Columbia River. At this point a "ferry service" was operated by one "Wild Goose Bill," a fleet of three canoes conveying passengers and mail, cattle and horses swimming. On one of his trips Thorpe bought some peanuts to put in a crop. He planted them carefully but none ever came up and he later discovered the nuts had been roasted. He tried it again with green ones, grew several crops at a profit.

A rancher who made a more lasting imprint on history and gave the town its name, was J. H. Loomis who started what became a trading post and then a large general store in a somewhat accidental way. Seeing that many of the ranchers ran out of supplies before fresh shipments came in, he thought he would help them out by laying in extra goods for himself. When his shortsighted neighbors ran out, he would let them have what they needed at cost. Later, when joined by a partner Gus Waring, he was induced to

raise the selling price a little and buy larger amounts next time. The system proved the beginning of a long and profitable business.

Waring was a man of many talents. Educated at Harvard, friend and contemporary of Theodore Roosevelt and Owen Wister, author of *The Virginian*, he tried making a success at architecture in his father's office, gave it up and left for Portland, Oregon, with wife and three children. He worked on a railroad there for a short time and then headed for the Okanogan country, working first as a cowman, then barber, cook and carpenter before settling down as successful partner of Loomis. Their trading post became the largest business in town. Many "characters" of the Okanogan range were customers, two of the most famous being friends of Waring—"Okanogan" Smith and a missionary, called saintly by many, Father de Rouge.

Between Loomis and Oroville are the remains of a home, built in 1860, and orchard of Hiram F. Smith. He was prominent in local affairs, friendly with the Indians who gave him the name, "Okanogan." Elected to the legislature in 1865, he had to go through British Columbia, down the Fraser River by steamboat and cross Puget Sound to reach Olympia, the territorial capital. Returning to the Okanogan, he brought apple and other small fruit trees and peach seeds. These trees still grow at the site, are over forty feet tall, were the first orchard trees in an area now world famous for apple production.

During the early period of ranching in the area, various mines were discovered which gradually preempted farming in importance. A variety of metals was found in the hills around Riverside, the Solomon group working on a "huge body of ore" yielding as high as 50 percent lead with silver 25 to 70 ounces per ton along with some copper and gold. Tungsten was also found but ignored until the first World War when that metal came into demand. Other mines included Black Diamond, Whiskey Hill, Bull Frog, Golden Zone, Kit Carson, Six Eagles and Why Not?

Among the more famous was the Pinnacle which had a strange beginning. Original discoveries were made at the site in 1880. The first men to work it got out a lot of gold, took the metal outside to have it melted so it could be sold and never came back, leaving foreman James O'Connel to wonder about them. He waited a decent interval, then relocated the mine. When it was legally his, he named it the Pinnacle and he was soon called Pinnacle Jim. He was a strange, stubborn man. Where others carried six-shooters,

he carried a bowie knife and occasionally brandished a heavy gold-headed cane.

John O'Hearne was a close friend who became Pinnacle Jim's partner and they got along well except when drinking. One of their bitter arguments started in the saloon of the Wentworth Hotel and Jim rashly asked John outside to settle it. The latter carried a gun and it proved superior to the knife, Pinnacle Jim lying dead at the end of the battle. O'Hearne was tried for murder but freed as having shot in self-defense. Shortly after this came inquiry from a lawyer as to James O'Connel's whereabouts, an uncle having died and left him a large sum.

Such affrays were not uncommon in Loomis. Children sent to the grocery store had strict instructions to walk down the center of the street, not on sidewalks where they would encounter drunks weaving out of saloons and "those terrible painted ladies." They were to continue in a straight line until opposite the grocery and then to make an abrupt turn and go straight in.

Walter Allen who still lives in Loomis tells a story of those early days. "When I was a young man there was a district at the foot of the hill where there were several 'houses.' One of them, the best known, was called 'Big Edith's'. I had a friend who dared me to ride my cayuse right into the parlor and in those days I never backed down from a dare. We went down there on our horses and I rode up the front steps and through the front door with no trouble. Then I rode through the hall and came to a sort of screen of strings of beads hanging in front of the parlor and started to ride through. When my cayuse felt those beads swishing across her shoulders, she bolted. We went on through the parlor and through the back door that wasn't even open. There was a porch in back, quite high from the ground. My horse turned a somersault and I landed partly under her. Didn't break any bones, but was pretty shaken up."

Mail service encountered some difficulties getting started. The last distribution point was Marcus and when anyone left there for the Loomis area he was given what mail there was and was expected to carry it to town and dump it where it would be claimed by addressees. One young man made the trip rather often and went to the trouble of personally delivering letters, collecting 25 cents for each. It was soon noticed a large amount of the letters were worthless advertisements and inquiry revealed the enterprising youth was furnishing a mailing list to advertisers in Marcus.

Loomis had an official post office after 1888. Judge H. Noyes, who had come out from Springfield. Massachusetts, and bought an interest in the trading post of Waring and Loomis, was first postmaster. A branch office was established for ranchers on a farm owned by Jess Huntley. He was a busy man, abrupt and irascible, and although holding a mail franchise he was unwilling to take the time to wait on people

GAUNT CONCRETE SHELL identified as early power generator for mines, sawmills and crushers, incongruous in now unpopulated area near Loomis. Water provided ample power, was carried down to plant from mountains above by flume, remains showing above structure. After passing through generators inside building, water was carried away through now yawning hole in floor. Small settlement grew up around plant, even a jewelry store operated by Bill Kepp. A laundry was established by Henry Decent so close to the stream it was washed out in the first heavy spring freshet.

819

or deliver letters. When a bag of mail came in, he would dump it in a large box on the counter and let everyone dig through it. One day he was getting ready to plow and a man asked him to look for a letter he was expecting. Jess retorted sharply—couldn't any damn fool see he was busy and couldn't he look for it himself? The man took offense, reported the incident and the postal authorities wrote a caustic letter to Huntley, ordering him to deliver all letters to patrons and give no back talk. Gathering all mail and equipment into a bag, he drove to the office at Loomis and angrily dumped the contents in the middle of the floor. "There's your damned post office!" he fumed.

There was social life of an elevating sort in Loomis and one cultural influence was a fine band. It was made up to a large extent of men employed in the Palmer Mountain mines. The Company provided tailored uniforms, the band practiced in the Eagles' Hall and performed at affairs in neighboring towns as well, being paid $100 per performance.

While all the mining excitement was going on, there was a steady amount of ranching in the surrounding hills. This did not provide the same sort of thrills that mining did but it had its compensations. There was young Joseph Rice in Spokane who yearned to be a rancher and had ideas of homesteading on Palmer Mountain. He hesitated to ask his sweetheart Helen Fitch to marry him and go to such a wild country but she was willing. They were married in 1903 and homesteaded on Palmer Mountain four and a half miles from Loomis.

At first Joe had to work in Tillman's Sawmill to get started but this was a stroke of fortune as he fell heir to a lot of cull lumber and with it built their first home. Later the couple got enough money for a more pretentious place and the first home became a chickenhouse. Funds for improvement came slowly but Helen and Joe were hard workers, determined to make a success. They planted wheat and in the fall a thresher crew would arrive at the farm on its rounds, the threshers' wives in at the big dinner and carrying

DECAYING RUINS OF CABINS built in 1890s high on Gold Hill above Loomis. Great excitement prevailed when first discoveries were made but cooled somewhat when difficulty of moving ore to mills became evident. John Reed and "Irish" Dan McCauley found gold in a piece of quartz on the steep mountainside about 1890. They had no capital for hard rock mining and sold out to a company naming itself Gold Hill Mining Co. It started operations, had great difficulty getting ore down mountain to mills at Loomis. Road was constructed but washed out at every rain or when snow melted. First enthusiasm generated building of small settlement just prior to turn of century. Gold return was finally judged too small to justify better road or building of mill at site, entire project abandoned around 1910. At present, steep winding road to ruins is badly washed, long hike required to reach remnant of short-lived gold rush. Almost all trees are second growth; virgin stand cut when mining was carried on, was spruce, larch, pines with scattering of Douglas fir.

LOADED FREIGHT WAGONS pulling into Loomis from Oroville — photo in collection of Walter Allen of Loomis. On driver's seat are Mr. and Mrs. Frank Schull. Dick Sutton says: "Frank did a lot of freighting, mostly of ore to Spokane. On the return trips he carried lots of whiskey and wine for the saloons. Some of the saloonkeepers were Jack Long, Jimmie Kenchlow, Johnnie Woodard and George Judd." Man on ground holding dog is identified as Al Carroll. Perambulator is mounted on rear wagon.

away tales of the Rices' baked beans. Helen had her own recipe and grew her own beans from a "start" brought along from Spokane. The variety name for these succulent beans, a little larger than ordinary, was never known. They were just "Helen's Beans."

After wheat was threshed, Helen and Joe made frequent trips south to Tonasket with loads of grain, starting about four in the morning to get to market early. And Helen made thirty loaves of bread at a time, selling them around the area. She kept a large flock of chickens, a six-foot fence protecting them from marauding coyotes. The eggs and churned butter also helped out in income.

The water supply was a spring at the bottom of a very steep slope from the house. After staggering up the bank a few times, Joe rigged up a contraption to ease the situation. He equipped a large wheel from a broken washing machine with a cable to which a bucket was attached. When the wheel was turned, the cable took the bucket down hill and overturned it in the spring. Continued turning of the wheel brought the full bucket back.

The distance to Loomis was usually covered by buggy in summer, sleigh in winter. If the snow was frozen hard, the latter with no brakes could not be used on one steep hill. So Joe would have to walk for the mail. He carried a shovel to open the trail below and to put it to good advantage on the steepest pitch, he sat on the scoop and slid down.

There were other breaks from drudgery. In winter, a little lake higher up Palmer Mountain froze practically solid. The couple cut ice and stored the harvest in an icehouse they built. In summer, ice cream parties were often held, either at the Rice home or neighbors.

Sometimes Helen took horseback rides around the country when she felt the need to get away for a change. Her favorite mount was a mare named Tootsie, brown with three white stockings, and no one else could ride her. The two would have a wonderful time, leaping over logs and low fences.

And the dances at Loomis were the best of all. They danced the favorites like "Black Hawk Waltz" and "Three Step" but there were enough Swede loggers wanting some Hambos and Schottisches. Helen says when one of these Norsemen with a few drinks in him would whirl her around in a Hambo, she could hardly stand for dizziness at the finish.

Once there was a masquerade and she wanted Joe to dress as an Indian. There being no costume rental in those days, she cut a picture of an Indian suit from a mail order catalog and copied it as best she could. She insisted he have long black hair and she achieved this by cutting off the luxurious tail of a white horse, dyeing it black and sewing it to a skull cap. Joe won first prize.

But the homestead was increasingly a burden and after both Joe and Helen had long spells of sickness, they abandoned the old place in 1914. Long years later they realized $120 by selling the property to a sheepman. By then the buildings had fallen into decay and Loomis was declining to the point where all property values were next to nothing.

The last ores were taken from the Palmer Mountain Tunnel mine in 1927 and this marked the finish of Loomis as a going town. It is quietly peaceful today with only a handful of people. Helen Rice, now a widow, lives in Portland and furnished the author with much of the information about the Okanogan area.

821

MARYHILL, WASHINGTON

In its journey to the sea the Columbia River makes its final turn west through timbered mountains and then a desert of barren rocks and cliffs. No spectacle could be more astonishing than the immense gray castle sprawling high on one of the river's bordering palisades.

The pile is best viewed from across the river on the Oregon side. The observing traveler up the Columbia gorge may well ask: "What, for goodness sakes — is that?" That, the traveler's guide will usually say, is Maryhill Castle. "It was built by Sam Hill, son of the railroad tycoon, Jim Hill, as a monument to his mother." However, Samuel was not the son of the "Empire Builder", James Hill, but his son-in-law. He was a trusted employee of Jim Hill at first, then in 1888 married the oldest daughter of his boss — Mary Hill. Jim did have a son Louis, but the brothers-in-law were not overly compatible. The unanswered questions are — did Sam Hill build the castle as a memorial for his wife, as a palace-residence, or did he foresee its ultimate use as a museum?

Samuel Hill majored in law at Harvard and was admitted to the bar in 1880. Jim Hill engaged young Sam to help him fight some legal battles, then admitted him to his giant railroad combine, allowing him to carry on his own legal practice and make some profitable investments. He traveled extensively, making friends in high places everywhere. One of these was Queen Marie of Roumania, who would later dedicate his castle on the cliffs.

Samuel Hill was personable, shrewd and eccentric. Shortly before the end of World War I, he bought some 7,000 acres of rock and sagebrush which surprised no one who knew him but did intrigue them. When Sam announced he was going to set up a colony for Quakers from Belgium, he raised more questions than he answered. Was the project a purely benevolent gesture or was he planning to add more millions to his coffers with cheap foreign labor?

The ground planned for the colony on the Washington side of the Columbia was opposite Biggs Junction in Oregon. The site included a long established village called Columbus, an agricultural center, the gently sloping ground on the river's shore deep and fertile — a bench extending about half a mile to suddenly rising cliffs of barren rock and scanty soil only a little less arable. A wagon road wound up a steep gully to the summit and along this the colonists would be quartered in cottages Hill would build. On both sides of the steeply sloping valley rose vertical cliffs, partly separated into palisades, each surmounted by a rounded dome of rocks, soil and sand. On the top of the highest one, Samuel Hill, in 1913, started construction of what would be the most conspicuous structure anywhere along the Columbia, an imposing feudal-type castle, such as those that stand along the Rhine.

LITTLE CHURCH was serving community of Columbus when Samuel Hill appeared, turned town into supply center for building of Maryhill Castle, changing name of town to Maryhill. Tycoon kept church in good condition during "occupation" but it has deteriorated. Building is set on low bench of river bank, grass and trees showing fertility of narrow band of soil, barren hills making up background.

SIMULATED STONEHENGE—one of Sam Hill's projects in connection with castle—"exact" replica of mysterious place of ancient worship or astronomy near Salisbury, England. In original only few of pillars retain connecting slabs, only two of original five gigantic trilithons surrounding central altar or sacrificial stone. Hill sent engineer, astronomer, other workmen to England to measure and make plaster casts of original rocks, bringing back molds for duplicating them. Hill's interest in Stonehenge stemmed from visit to original where guide informed him flat rock in center was used for human sacrifice. As a Quaker, he was particularly impressed, comparing such useless slaughter of human life to that of war. It was then he conceived idea of erecting similar structure as memorial to war dead. Legend on horizontal slab in center reads: "In memory of Soldiers and Sailors of Klickitat County who gave their lives in defense of their Country. This monument is erected in the hope that others inspired by the example of their valor and their heroism may share in that love of liberty and burn with that fire of Patriotism which death alone can quench."

During the next several years parcels of Quakers came from Belgium and other European countries to look at the rocky ground, searingly hot in summer, swept by icy winds in winter — looked briefly and went away. A scant few did settle for a while, making some effort to coax a crop from the stark land, but they also departed.

While the Samuel Hills lived in a stately mansion in Seattle, construction of the castle went on regardless of the failure of the colonization plans. It was known almost from the start that it would be called Maryhill. Was it named for the wife, Mary Hill? One point seems a fact — although Mary never saw the pile at any time, even from a distance, gossip had it she was a resident, almost a prisoner, a woman with a failing mind.

While the exact purpose of the vast building was never known, possibly even to Sam Hill, it was almost completed by 1926 and in the fall of that year came Queen Marie to dedicate Maryhill Castle. Before leaving Portland for the ceremony, the Queen attended the International Livestock Exposition, sitting with her royal party in a special box. The group made a worthy subject for the newsreels and the royal lady was not above making pin money by endorsing beauty products.

And at Maryhill she found ready a platform erected in front of the gaunt, gray shell. From it one could look east up the Columbia, south into the gorge and down many miles of the river's westerly flow. After the outdoor ceremony everyone hurried indoors for more convivial celebration, then departed to allow workmen to continue plastering walls.

Construction went on a few more years and when completed the interior included electricity,

SAM HILL'S CASTLE dedicated by Queen Marie of Roumania on a dreary, gray early winter day as indicated here. This is conventional rear of structure, more ornate facade commanding almost limitless view of Columbia gorge, shown dimly in background.

plumbing and other refinements foreign to the traditional castle. Samuel Hill died February 6, 1931 in Portland, his ashes taken to Maryhill and deposited in a tomb on the rocky cliff. It was supposed he had not made up his mind to what use the castle would be put, yet in his will he left a handsome endowment in the hands of trustees of the state to perpetuate the building as a museum.

In 1940 Maryhill Museum was opened to the public. It attracts an increasing number of visitors each summer, offering extensive and varied exhibits of painting, sculpture and Indian artifacts. The Throne Room is displayed, complete with furniture including the royal throne itself, all transported from the now vanished Kingdom of Roumania.

PEASANT SHELTER at Maryhill. It was Samuel Hill's wish that the countryside surrounding his feudal castle be filled by Belgian Quaker immigrants. Many did come, a few remained to eke out miserable existence on stony, dry soil of hillsides. Then even these were forced to go elsewhere. Land affords few near-level spots, bluffs in background descending to Columbia River in giant stair steps.

HE WENT DOWN WITH HIS SHIP

Young Jimmy Kyes seemed to feel a great compassion for the small seedling. He loved to spend his summers roaming the snowy-peaked Cascade Range in northern Washington and this day in the 1920s he stood at the edge of a tarn, a tiny high country lake, snow still mantling its fringes. Growing there was a little alpine fir, its foliage displaying the blue coloring sometimes found in this species.

Jimmy wanted to nurture the struggling little tree and he lifted it from the earth very carefully so as not to disturb the roots, carrying it down to the old mining town of Monte Cristo where he was staying. He planted it in the garden of the hotel there and it was his to care for. In 1923, while in the U.S. Forest Service as lookout on the summit of Mt. Pilchuck, he met Mr. and Mrs. H. A. Annen of Everett, Washington who would later carry on Jimmy's protective efforts by building a fence around the tree.

James E. Kyes was born in Everett and educated in grade and high schools there. He studied at the University of Washington, specializing in mining engineering, and a year later was appointed to the U.S. Naval Academy at Annapolis, graduating in 1930.

After serving on the carriers *Saratoga* and *Ranger* he returned to Annapolis to complete a two-year postgraduate course in engineering and then assumed command of the U.S.S. Destroyer *Leary*, taking it on convoy and patrol duty. On Christmas eve 1943, the vessel was returning to port where Kyes would be given a new command. A message was received that an aircraft carrier in the North Atlantic was under attack by German submarines. The *Leary* was ordered to go to her assistance.

As the destroyer drew near the carrier she was struck by two torpedoes fired from the enemy wolf pack, the vessel breaking into three sections and sinking rapidly. Commander Kyes was donning his preserver when he saw his negro messboy was without one. Kyes put his around the boy and went down with his ship as it foundered.

James Kyes, who held the rank of full commander for two years at the time of his death, received posthumous honors including the Navy Cross for heroism displayed during the sinking of his ship. Already held were the Purple Heart, Bronze American Defense Service Medal, European-African Campaign and Middle East Area Campaign honors. Another mark of recognition for his courage was the naming of the destroyer *Commander James Kyes* in 1946, which was christened by Kyes wife Frances, their son David beside her. An even more enduring memorial is the 7,239 foot mountain seven miles west of Monte Cristo named Kyes Peak, Jimmy and a companion making the first recorded ascent of the rocky spire in 1920.

And the alpine fir still grows in the old hotel grounds.

NEAR FLATTENED RUINS of hotel on Dumas Street in one time mining camp of Monte Cristo, stands fir tree planted by James Kyes in boyhood. About time of his death picket fence was placed around tree and later this monument erected memorializing heroic death of Commander Kyes at sea.

826

OLD TIME PHOTO of Monte Cristo. Extensive mines, mills were served directly by railroad. Present day Monte Cristo, while no longer important as gold mining center is mecca for campers, fishermen, mountain climbers.

ALPINE PHLOX, botanically Phlox Douglasii, forms dense mats of deep pink to white flowers, spreading color over large areas of Cascade Mountains at altitudes of from 4,000 to 7,000 feet.

LETTER IS FRAMED and secured to picket fence around tree.

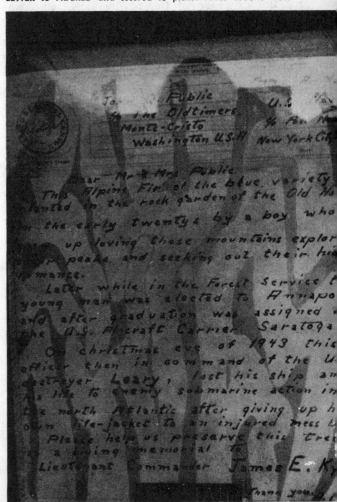

TIDEFLAT TABLEAU

Nahcotta, Wash.

"Folks, you are now in Oysterland, U.S.A."

"I don't care about oysters. I can't eat the slithery things."

"Well, I'm sorry, lady. If I was anything more than the conductor of this train I'd get you some crepes suzette."

"When does this train get to Nahcotta? It's over an hour late and my sister will be frozen to death waiting for it."

"Oh I don't know. She's probably keeping warm and happy eating oysters. They're fine for the blood."

Some such spirited conversation might have taken place on the Ilwaco and Shoalwater Bay Railroad or was it the Ilwaco Railway and Navigation Co. or maybe this week the Oregon and Washington Railway and Navigation Co.? Sometimes the "noon" train would come puff-puffing into the tiny station at Nahcotta on time but more often it would arrive at 11 or perhaps 1. While travelers got nervous, residents understood that schedules depended upon the ocean tides at the mouth of the Columbia River since the main reason for the existence of the narrow-gauge line was its connection with the ferry from Astoria, Oregon.

The Chinooks were the original settlers at Nahcotta, their villages once dotting the entire North Peninsula. An ample food supply was guaranteed them by the millions of oysters growing wild on the flats of the harbor. Innumerable food middens still evident today show oyster shells their main content. No primitive tools are found with them as oysters require only to be picked up at low tide and pried open.

The abundance of bivalves and fish attracted whites too, the first to arrive at Nahcotta as a resident being J. A. Morehead in 1890. He was shortly joined by James R. Morrison and eight other men, some with families to form a fair-sized village. With later settlers came a store, Morehead building one to contain the post office, Morrison being the first to handle the mail. There was unanimous agreement in naming the town for old Chief Nahcotta who was still camping on the outskirts. While lacking the power of Chief Concomly at nearby Chinookville, Nahcotta displayed the same friendly attitude toward the whites.

In 1899 the town became the terminus of the short line railroad running on narrow-gauge tracks which over the years had so many names the Nahcotta station master A. P. Osborne sometimes forgot just who he was working for. By 1908 the train was running on a regular schedule and continued to until 1930. Until recently traces of trackage were visible in places along the line.

Once boasting a weekly newspaper edited by John Phillips, Nahcotta is today a resort settlement with two small industries—a sweater knitting "factory" and one punching and stringing oyster shells for nurturing baby shellfish.

OLD OYSTER BARGE, one of once large fleet at Nahcotta beached away from water except during flood tides. Flat-decked vessel took large empty baskets to anchorage over oyster beds. Baskets were filled at low tide and reloaded on barges which floated at high tide and were towed to oyster plants. In background is Willapa Bay, early termed Shoalwater Bay. In middle distance are rotting pilings, all that remain of large railroad terminal dock. Body of water, considered to be prehistoric channel of Columbia River, offered exact condition of alternating fresh and salt water demanded by oyster. While tide is out bay is freshened by flow from many rivers. Returning tides obstruct streams temporarily providing high salinity. Sometimes strong offshore winds and high tides force in oversupply of salty water, preventing breeding, even killing some stock.

OLD POSTCARD shows Nahcotta when narrow-gauge railroad had terminus here. Hotel at end of rails was important then, has vanished now. Water supply was pumped by windmill and stored in tank left.

NIGHTHAWK, WASHINGTON

Hiram Smith, called "Okanogan Smith" by friendly Indians of the Similkameen Valley, was elected to the territorial legislature of Washington in 1860. After serving one term he settled on his ranch near Chesaw, tended his orchard for 40 years and died peacefully, surrounded by his many white and Indian friends. He left a considerable estate with no will in evidence and his affairs were in such a confused state a lawyer was engaged to untangle them.

He did and made a good thing of it—attorney James M. Haggerty of Portland, Oregon. He completed the legal work, established headquarters at Loomis and started a systematic search for mineral prospects.

Not a man to work with his bare hands, Haggerty planned to become a wealthy miner by his wits and he was right. Newspapers of the day stated: "Haggerty appropriated three mining claims which turned out to be good producers." These mines were strung along the Similkameen in an area where nighthawks, sometimes called "bull bats," were very prevalent and the supply center that sprang up here was named for the birds.

The Ruby, Kaaba and the more famous Six Eagle mines were among those developed by Haggerty. Had he confined his activities to them and not let his tongue wag so much when he was drinking, he would have been spared some grief. He had moved from Loomis but liked to visit his former haunts and brag about his success as a mine operator. And if he had only stopped there, accepted some scorn and let it go at that, he would have gained some stature. But he made a fatal mistake one evening in his cups at a Loomis saloon, an ill-timed comment about a mine on the hill above Loomis.

The Palmer Mountain Tunnel mine was of more than doubtful merit and all the local gentry were aware of it. In spite of this, the owners had sent a John Wentworth to Portland to cajole innocent investors into sinking money into the property. The population of Loomis and the mine owners rationalized that selling this stock was not really dishonest, that further development so financed would certainly turn up a rich vein that might be the making of everybody in the town. Gilbert Alder was one of the residents who, while waiting for this to happen, had put in his time farming and raised a crop of sugar cane. The long hot summer matured it enough for Alder to make some molasses and he proudly brought a jug of it to the saloon to show it off.

OLD BARN, says Leo W. Andrus of Nighthawk, was built by father known in community as "Daddy" Andrus. Dating from 1900, venerable structure still serves purpose. International road runs past barn, crosses Similkameen on bridge close by.

RUINS OF OLD NIGHTHAWK MILL are composed, in general, of rusting machinery. Town itself lay in valley in middle distance beside Similkameen River. Surrounding hills are typical of Okanogan Highlands, those near town are sparsely timbered, with heavier stands farther away.

This night he stepped up to the bar, ordered a drink and displayed his jug of black molasses as an example of what the area could produce. Haggerty felt a great urge to push his importance into the conversation and pompously declared:

"Well, it's a good thing Loomis can produce molasses. It'll never turn out any gold from that damn mine."

It would have been better for Haggerty if he had tried to shoot somebody. At his words several men jumped up, threw him to the floor while Alder poured the contents of his jug over the spread-eagled form. Another man rushed upstairs to the business quarters of one of the girls and grabbed her pillow. The cotton slip was quickly split and the feathers shaken in snowy humiliation over the sticky coating of blackstrap.

OLD PICTURE reproduced in Okanogan *Independent* shows group dressed in Sunday best gathered outside Log Cabin Saloon in Chesaw, few miles from Nighthawk. Sign on Chop House at right advertises meals at all hours, 25¢.

Chesaw was mining and farming center, never very large. Main feature was hostelry Bungalow run by hospitable Chinese who gave town name. Bungalow was open to all travelers, owners respected in a day when Orientals were generally despised.

Log Cabin Saloon in Chesaw

NIGHTHAWK HOTEL was built by Ed McNull for drummers in boom days. Later when Nighthawk Mill was running "full blast" Ewing family took it over as boardinghouse for mill workers. It stood vacant for many years near the little grocery store operated for 25 years by Mr. and Mrs. Lynn Sullivan who now live on Palmer Lake a few miles south.

Haggerty was allowed to slither to his feet but was jerked off them and put astride a hitching rail that had been yanked loose and given a rough ride out of town. His face was never seen again in Loomis. Whenever he had business in Spokane, he avoided the town and went by way of Oroville. When he died years later, he asked that he be buried at Nighthawk—"But don't take me through Loomis."

Nighthawk had been built where the ground was level but the main producing mine was across the Similkameen. A footbridge was good enough for the early traffic but when it became inadequate, a ferry was put into operation by William Berry, an observing and enterprising man. After several passengers had asked him: "Where can a fellow get a drink in this town?" he started a saloon with financial help from his brother Joe. It was a success in summer when the dry and dusty wind blew, a success in winter when at forty below a man needed warming.

About the turn of the century the Vancouver, Victoria and Eastern ran its line through Nighthawk and the town looked forward to a rosy future. For a time it seemed to be coming true as all heavy equipment for the mines including that for twelve-mile-distant Loomis, was rail shipped to Nighthawk. This meant freighting lines were based here, large livery stables maintained, as well as hotel, store and several more saloons.

When business of transporting mine equipment and passengers was flourishing, the rail line, a branch of the Wenatchee, Oroville and Great Northern, ran from its connection at Spokane through Danville, Molson, Chesaw, Nighthawk and Hedley, B. C., terminating at Princeton where it connected with the Canadian Pacific. By 1950, the line had been cut to a spur fifty-odd miles long from Oroville to Hedley. Freight was limited to a small amount of farm equipment and produce with a passenger or two now and then, the train coming to Nighthawk twice a week, the engineer always on the lookout for a flag signal that someone wanted to get on. A tiny one-room customs office stood beside the single track.

Now even the Tuesday and Friday arrivals of the train have ceased. The tracks are gone, so is the customs house. There is only one business in Nighthawk now—the little general store.

NORTHPORT, WASHINGTON

A few miles below the United States-Canada line the Columbia River flows past the sleepy old town of Northport, once one of the most roistering mining camps in the state of Washington. At this point below Silver Crown Mountain the Columbia is wider than it used to be, now forming Roosevelt Lake by waters backed up from Grand Coulee Dam.

In April of 1892 the only means of travel here was along a mountain trail and at the future site of Northport there were only three homesteaders' cabins. Yet a few short months later the place had a newspaper, the *Northport News*, its little press hauled in by ox team and set up in the huddle of tents and shacks. The first issue came out on July 4th, greeting the community: "It is already a town. Tomorrow—a few tomorrows hence, at any rate—it will be a city."

A forest fire threatened the dry buildings that first summer, only a change in wind saving them. In September the railroad reached town and Northport was on its way to become "the future mining, milling, smelting and agricultural city of north-

eastern Washington. There followed a series of disastrous fires and after each the town was rebuilt, each time more permanently so that today the buildings remaining are of brick. One striking exception is the huge frame brothel.

After fire came flood. With the spring freshets of 1894 the Columbia rose far above normal. All of Northport down along the flat was swept away, the main portion higher on the bank left untouched. All future building was above the reach of high water.

British Columbia was speeding along with its mines and some of the biggest producers were having a hard time getting ore smelted and finished. One was the huge Le Rio operation just off the Rossland Trail and the owners decided to build a large smelter in Northport. Although the Canadians put up a spirited fight to have it on their side of the border it was plain the necessary materials for smelting, such as limerock for flux, existed in enormous quantities in Northport and the smelters could work the ore much more

BRICK TUNNEL at old Northport smelter which carried off gases and dust from furnaces.

OLD SMELTER AT NORTHPORT is in ruins, one stack standing, others having collapsed. International difficulties were headache during life of reduction works in U.S., mines in Canada.

HORSE TROUGH was scene of violence shortly after turn of century. Argument developed in saloon across street, one Penrose claiming another man, Jackson, owed him money. Jackson denied this and both "lickered up," tempers grew hot. Jackson drew his gun and Penrose fled across street behind watering trough. By this time he had his own gun unlimbered and when Jackson imprudently showed himself, Penrose "let him have it."

SCENE ON QUIET STREET in Northport shows old meat market in foreground. Next is town's notorious house of ill fame. Town had large proportion of single men who worked in mines and smelter and plenty of ways to spend their money were available.

cheaply there. The B. C. concern interested American capital and a U. S. company was formed to build the $250,000 smelter. The Northport Smelting and Refining Company plant was "blown in" in '97.

Labor troubles beset the company almost from the start. The owners bitterly resented any efforts of the Mill and Smeltermen's Union to organize the workers. In 1901 they went on strike, demanding they be allowed to join the union. The company retorted that any employee doing so would be fired and imported a large crew of non-union men from the east. As the strike continued sixty-two more men arrived and this started riots requiring the efforts of the Colville sheriff to quell. The strikers made things so tough for the new men, thirty-five quit.

At the end of nine months with nothing settled, the Western Federation of Miners with headquarters at Denver decided to cut the aid it had been extending to striking Northport men. One morning the strikers found the union's free eating place closed and many went hungry. A mass meeting was held, the strike called off, the union was abandoned and its charter surrendered.

Now international difficulties arose and for a time the smelter company was so harried it shut down entirely and the town became a ghost before its time. Accused of being aliens at the core, the company incorporated under the laws of Idaho and began accepting ores from the Coeur d'Alene districts in that state. Had the entire output of Kellogg, Mullen, Gem and other mines in that area been available to the Northport smelter the action would have meant a continuing life but the Idaho smelters took most of their ore. Once again the Northport plant closed down and the town was almost deserted.

There was a ray of hope when the rumor spread that the American Smelting and Refining Co. had bought the plant and people began to move in. Then the final, devastating blow fell, spelling Northport's doom. The buyers had no intention of opening the smelter. The machinery only was wanted and when this was moved out the source of Northport's life blood was an empty shell.

Today a large sawmill stands at the edge of the old smelter, taking up some of the employment slack. It is so close in fact, sawdust lies in deep drifts among the falling brick walls and cavernous roasting ovens. A large quarry working a fine quality of limestone-marble operates south of town.

ORIENT, WASHINGTON

Gold had been discovered on the shoulder of First Thought Mountain and there was a certainty something big would come of it. Alec Ireland platted the town of Orient in 1900 and Mr. and Mrs. George Temple drove a wagon there from Bossburg which was then a thriving place, establishing a homestead the following year.

Gold hopes were slow being realized. There were no loose placer grains in the stream and it took time to interest big money for hard rock mining. Ireland, Billy Stiles and the Temples were at first the only residents of Orient, the latter proving up their claim and in 1904 receiving their ownership papers signed by President Theodore Roosevelt. They worked hard on the farm and Temple started a stage line from Bossburg to Republic, and up to Greenwood and Phoenix—a big mining camp in Canada—and Grand Forks, also across the border.

As the mines developed in a big way, Temple got much business hauling machinery, particularly for the Easter Sunday and Little Gem Mines. There were several other prosperous operations, one named after the mountain looming over the town—First Thought. This mine was also the main course of the economic development of Orient although its name came from another mine, the Orient.

Two quartz mills were set up, one at the First Thought, the other at the Gold Stake. By this time Orient had grown into a bustling town. "It was a very lively place," says Mrs. Leslie Gourlie, daughter of the Temples, "We had five saloons, two big livery stables, several stores and three hotels. These were whipsaw-shacky places, called by their owners names — Mrs. Reynolds, Mrs. Hayes and Mrs. Arnold. All three were pretty good cooks, doing the best they could under the circumstances. The best food, however, was available to the men at the mine cook houses. Most of the single ones ate there, slept in the bunk houses and lived quiet lives during the week. But on Saturday nights they'd come down to town and cut loose. What wild times they had, spending most of their money just that one night. There were plenty of loose women and lots of hard liquor to help them do it, too."

When the Great Northern Railroad made plans to run its line to Republic, George Temple ceded the right of way through his land, as he did later for the highway. During the hectic days of railroad construction there was a boom, the hotels full and Mrs. Temple feeding many of the men in the tiny homestead cabin.

When asked if Orient is permanently finished, Mrs. Gourlie replied: "Oh, no. There is lots of gold in the mines yet. They have barely scratched the surface. Most are down only about a hundred and fifty feet, none more than three hundred. All we need is an advance in the price of gold. Of course the machinery is getting all rusty and likely will be badly out of date. But the people who are still living here are hopeful that something good will happen to the town. We really haven't had any activity since the first World War."

ORIENT FIRE DEPARTMENT did its best when fire broke out in Orient but best was often not enough. Many buildings burned because of tinder dry condition and insufficient water pressure. Fancy tower in background is crowning glory of school which once held several hundred pupils. Structure was fixed up several years ago and is in good repair but now serves only handful of children.

834

THE TOWN THAT OYSTERS BUILT

Oysterville, Wash.

The pilot of the river steamer looked with disdain at all the industry displayed in harvesting the flat, curly-edged shells in the low tide mud. "It's sure a good thing I don't like oysters," he said, "or I'd eat 'em and I hate the damn things!"

There are deeply etched opinions about the succulence of oysters but the early workers on the Pacific Ocean beach cared little about that. They had a tide flat gold mine in millions of the bivalves lying there defenseless in the oozy muck just waiting to be picked, shipped to market and opened before eyes bulging in anticipation. "Too good for Indians," they said.

When the white man first came to Willapa (then called Shoalwater) Bay he found its south arm one vast field of oyster beds. The native marine bivalves were the small, delicately flavored *ostrea lurida*. For them and the later introduced Pacific oysters, the bay offered perfect conditions for reproduction and growth. The oyster requires an almost exactly formulated mixture of fresh and salt water and the saline content must vary at specific intervals. Willapa Bay, like very few harbors on the Washington coast, offers the right mixture, an inflow of fresh water supplied by the Naselle and other rivers while the tide is at full or receding, supplying an alternating flood of salt water from the ocean. Native Chinook tribes had long made the shellfish a major item of food but this local consumption had hardly dented the supply.

The first white to see commercial possibilities here was very likely young Virginia-born Charles Russell. For several decades the United States had been on an oyster binge, consuming huge quantities in all forms, appetite whetted by rumor that oysters would enlarge or resuscitate the libido. Russell was aware that during the time the non-ambulatory oyster was exposed by outgoing tides it closed its valves tightly, excluding desiccating air. He also knew this normally short hibernation period could be extended.

The only entrance to Willapa Bay was at the north end, some 30 miles north of the Columbia River from which Russell would ship his oysters to San Francisco. In prehistoric times the Columbia had at least partially emptied its waters into the now separated northern estuary, the old channel now low and watery or marshy in spots. This route was used by Indians for centuries as a portage connection from the Columbia. In the summer of 1851, with a partner, Russell took a canoe over this route to the bay and at low tide walked over the flats, easily collecting a load of oysters which he took back to Astoria. The cargo reached San Francisco in good condition and was sold at a good price. When gourmets there clamored for more they expanded the life purpose of *ostrea lurida*.

Heartened by visions of success Russell put into action ambitious plans to improve the southern access route to the source of supply. Meanwhile he learned that a Capt. Fielstad had run a schooner direct from San Francisco to Willapa Bay, entering

OLD POSTCARD version of Oysterville's famed courthouse, forcibly entered by rival residents of South Bend across bay to remove county records.

PACIFIC HOUSE, Oysterville's largest hostelry of which no trace remains. Likely not all people in old photo were patrons though hotel did big business while town flourished.

835

LINES OF PILING, weathered to silvery gray, indicate location of wharf where sailing ships loaded live oysters for San Francisco markets. Here also were tied barges that placed empty picking baskets, later retrieving filled ones at next high tide. Long unused baskets now rust away, half-filled with sand, oyster shells. Willapa Bay is in background.

by the easy but farther north entrance south of Cape Shoalwater. Hard on his stern were the schooners *Sea Serpent* and *Robert Bruce*, other ships following. One was delayed by a storm when sailing south, the cargo spoiling, and one burned to the water's edge by a mutinous cook. The oyster rush was on.

In 1854 R. H. Espy of Wisconsin arrived at the bay to locate and supply logs for pilings. A man of strong religious principles he invited I. A. Clark, of similar background and who had some money, to become his partner. While scouring the shores of the bay they became enthused with the possibilities of commercially canning the abundantly available oysters. Abandoning the piling venture Espy and Clark built a log house on the spot where the town of Oysterville would develop, the location between sea and bay near the northern tip of the peninsula.

Then came the brothers John and Thomas Crellin to share in the oyster profits, John establishing a mercantile store. With rapid growth the little town was demanding mail service and got it in 1865, the post office set up in a corner of Crellin's store. Mail had to be carried over devious Indian trails from Chinookville.

After a few years of such primitive service Lewis Loomis, who was to become a big man in Oysterville's history, secured the mail contract. In 1875 he and his partners built the 110-foot, screw-drive *General Canby* at Willapa at the northern end of the bay, the vessel undoubtedly named for the ill-fated army officer who died at the hands of Captain Jack in the still fresh Modoc War (see *Tales the Western Tombstones Tell*). As soon as launched, the ship was put into service carrying mail and passengers from Astoria, Oregon, to Ilwaco, Washington, where they were dumped on the beach.

OLD ANCHOR AND BUOY are few of marine items in machine repair shops of near-defunct Columbia River Smokery.

If time and tide were right, a stagecoach that was humanely called "clumsy" picked them up.

Powered by eight broncos the wooden vehicle was closed at the ends, passengers admitted from one side. There were seats inside for five but what was that when twenty people climbed in? Two would cling to the mail-loaded boot at the rear, others perched on top and when all were aboard the coach bumped and swayed onto the wet sand recently vacated by the Pacific, then headed north.

In recent years the North Jetty at the mouth of the Columbia River has diverted river-born sands northward, building up a beach far-famed for length and width. In the 1870s the beach was narrower and the stagecoach was sometimes forced to take to the dunes, humping itself over the sandy hillocks and small pieces of driftwood. The region has a heavy annual rainfall and when frequent ocean storms lashed the coast those unlucky passengers on top must have deeply regretted embarking for Oysterville.

The village had become seat of Pacific County some time before the first schoolhouse was erected, lumber for which was California redwood shipped north on a schooner that returned with canned and smoked oysters. The arrival at Oysterville of the ship was celebrated by a general holiday. When all sobered up the entire town joined with the hired carpenters in putting up the little schoolhouse and painting it bright red. The first teacher was James Pell.

Ten years later, with growing pains subsiding, residents began to think of social festivities, something more dramatic than box lunch suppers and community dances. With all that water around why not stage a yacht race? After several small but successful annual events, the town went all out in 1876 with a well advertised regatta that attracted such famous racers as the sloop *Artemisia* owned by wealthy Ed Loomis. The affair attracted the entire population of the coastal area, and a large contingent of "city folk" arrived from Portland on the specially-chartered steamer *Gussie Telfair*.

Shortly after Oysterville became a village much of Washington was being harassed by rampaging Indians, the troubles threatening to explode into a full scale war. Towns and settlements along the west coast were thrown into panic, most of them erecting blockhouses. Oysterville did so, hastily building a log fort near the water. While the structure still lacked a roof, townsfolk realized their placid, friendly Chinook neighbors were laughing at their efforts and sheepish carpenters left the project unfinished.

In the expanding community by the bay the main street was called "Front," built largely on rocks brought in as ship ballast and piled along the edge of the harbor to be close to canneries and vessels. The village so near the water was vulnerable to extremes of high tides which all too often demolished whole buildings when high winds combined with high water. One storm took away the roofless fort.

Oysterville was the seat of Pacific County very early but for years no actual courthouse was built. In 1860 a man named Dupenny was accused of murdering the Indian wife of a neighbor, William McGunnegill. Constable Espy was forced to board the suspect in his home temporarily before transferring him to the more secure Army barracks jail at Fort Vancouver. Even so nothing was done about the situation until 1869. Then the county erected a substantial two-story structure set on a foundation of squared logs.

During the decade of 1880-1890 Oysterville enjoyed its greatest days of glory. The first really adequate wharf was extended into deep water in

'84, another built in '88. A newspaper, first in the county, was established in 1887. Called the *Pacific Journal*, it was edited by "Alf" Bowen.

The 1890s were not "gay" for the oyster center of North Peninsula. The shellfish were found elsewhere on Willapa Bay and rival town South Bend had grown up on the shore opposite. The upstart had the unfair advantage of being on the mainland at a strategic point in the stagecoach system, and close to forests, it soon had a large lumbering industry.

In the fall elections of 1892 South Bend was declared the new seat of Pacific County and all records were ordered delivered there. Oysterville ignored the summons, the town's hardy, brine-soaked citizenry refusing to give up the honor of county seat, claiming the South Bend electorate had illegally included residents of all surrounding communities. Authorities were successful in obtaining an injunction but before this could be put into effect, ambitious promoters of the rival town forced the issue.

On February 5, 1893, a cold day dawning over a snowy scene unusual for the peninsula, two steamboats docked at Oysterville. Eighty-five men swarmed off and converged on the courthouse. Auditor Phil D. Barney was the first to assess the invasion and when South Bend leader John Hudson kicked in the courthouse door, the enraged Barney broke off a chair leg and valiantly attempted to defend the records by cracking several enemy skulls. A witness to the fracas was 6-year-old C. J. Espy who says, "I hid behind the door and was scared to death but I saw the action." Overpowered, Barney was forced to watch the removal of all paper except that in his vault, the key to which he steadfastly refused to give up. Later, however, other Oysterville authorities persuaded him that further resistance would be futile.

Although later investigation proved the South Bend election was highly irregular, counting ballots of transient loggers and other non-registered voters, the situation was by now irreversible. Staggered by the blow Oysterville mourned the loss of the courthouse for two years then decided to put the

LITTLE BAPTIST CHURCH was built in 1870s by Oysterville's founder, R. H. Espy, photo made some years ago. When author returned to Oysterville in 1967 to make more recent one, he found church being restored. Repairs are being made by son C. J. Espy who reported that services were held until "community interest dwindled to a point that continuance of regular services seem inappropriate. Sunday School was maintained until about 1942. Since then occasional funerals and weddings have been held there. There seems to be no immediate or early rejuvenation of service activities, only a hope by the writer and his family who, for sentimental reasons are giving some attention to the upkeep of the physical edifice."

INTERIOR of Baptist Church in Oysterville. No one, including builder's son C. J. Espy can explain why pews are divided in center. He does report structure never had electricity except temporarily in recent years when church was lit for wedding by extension cables powering borrowed light fixtures. Original light came from two large chandeliers with circles of lamps, suspended from ceiling on ropes, lowered for filling with kerosene and wick-trimming. After years of faithful service one crashed down on pews. Though accident happened in midweek, potential danger to worshippers caused removal of chandeliers and use of small wall lamps seen here. When founder-builder R. H. Espy died his casket was squeezed into tiny sanctuary leaving little space for passage.

OLD COLUMBIA RIVER SMOKERY is now mostly idle, small crew operating part of equipment in winter, smoking and canning limited catch.

empty building to practical use. In 1895 a brash sign announced it was the new "Peninsula College." Courses scheduled studies in grade and high school subjects, the initial enthusiasm bringing in forty students. Tuition was $30 for nine months. A faculty of six was hired and the institution opened. At the end of the first year the student body dwindled to half, the second showed fewer. The college closed and the building suffered ignominy as a cow barn, in recent years collapsing through heavy weather and neglect.

Little is now left to indicate the existence of a town large enough to support several hotels, saloons, stores. In addition to being remotely situated, Oysterville's prosperity was based on a single industry. When the once ample supply of oysters vanished, so did the economy.

The few present residents of the town are mostly descendants of pioneers, notably C. J. Espy. He recalls that during the period of prosperity every out-of-town visitor was sooner or later regaled with a bit of doggerel:

Said one oyster to another
  In tones of pure delight,
"I will meet you in the kitchen
  And we'll both get stewed tonight."

BEAUTIFUL HOUSE might be termed Victorian, displaying uniquely elaborate barge boards. Built in 1869 as home of pioneer Tom Crellins, it became home of Harry Espy, elder son of founder, who grew up here and was father of Dr. R. H. Espy, Gen. Sec. of Nat. Council of Churches, N.Y.C. Next door is 1871 house built by town's founder and birthplace of C. J. Espy who, now in his 80s, sleeps in room of nativity.

PORT BLAKELY, WASHINGTON

When the Port Blakely Mill was put into operation in 1863, the fir and cedar forests seemed to stretch endlessly behind it. But the saws chewed their way through the logs so fast it became obvious that the island on which the mill was located could not supply enough trees for very long. Then the mill men got Sol Simpson out of Nevada with a reputation for railroad building. He took over the Puget Sound and Grays Harbor line which had been built across the neck of the Olympic Peninsula from Grays Harbor on the ocean, cutting through "enough timber 'til kingdom come" as the saying went.

Simpson extended the line into Port Blakely and to several other mills that needed logs. The official name of the railroad was the G. S. Simpson and Co. but it was familiarly referred to as the Blakely Line and its rails were the first to be extended so far east in Washington.

Simpson did not confine his activities to railroad building, making many improvements in yarding logs, cutting time and cost in getting them from woods to mills, waterways or his rails. Ox teams had been the only method used for pulling the big logs along the greased skid roads but Simpson said horses would be better and proceeded to prove it over the opposition of the old timers. But his satisfaction was short lived as along came that revolutionary new contrivance, the Dolbeer donkey engine, that ousted both oxen and horses as log dragging power.

WHEN PORT BLAKELY WAS A PORT. Sailing ships jam the harbor in days when Washington lumber was number one cargo. The K. V. Kruse, Malahat, Mowtor, Oregon Fir, Forest Friend, Conqueror were a few of the old lumber carriers that tied up at the big Skinner and Eddy mill dock. The Alice Cook and Commodore were two of the sailing vessels built at Port Blakely.

HERE WERE DOCKS that fronted town of Port Blakely and its mill. Rotting stubs have replaced wharves once covering acres of tidelands. Gone also is imposing hotel which fronted on dock. Tide is shown here at low ebb but at flood, water line reaches nearly to trees at left. Town no longer exists, is replaced by scattered suburban cottages and permanent homes. On clear days view of city of Seattle is seen between headlands marking entrance to bay.

Of prime importance to every sawmill is the log pond. Its function is to corral the logs in live storage, to hold them until the selected logs are conveyed into the mill, kicked onto the carriage which moves forward to meet the saw. Port Blakely's narrow bay was usually so cluttered with sailing ships from all over the world there was no space for an undisturbed log pond. But the mill owners had their eyes on the extreme end of the bay which was a mucky flat of mud at low tide.

The problem was neatly solved by throwing a dam across the bay, trapping a quarter mile half-circle of water. Near the center of the earth-fill dam, gates were installed which would admit the flood tide from the outer bay, then close to prevent the filled pond from emptying. The log spur of "The

Blakely Line" was built alongside the pond so logs were dumped into it.

During the heyday the Port Blakely mill was said to be the largest in the world. It employed 1,200 men and cut 400,000 feet of lumber a day. A shipyard was built on the bay not far from the mill and constructed among other ships was the largest stern-wheeler in the Northwest, the S.S. *Julia*.

When the United States bought Alaska from Russia, it acquired a few bonus items, one being the gunboat *Politokofsky*. Offered at one of the country's first "surplus sales", the vessel was purchased by the Port Blakely Mill Co. Its guns were removed and the ship put into service as a cargo carrier to ply Puget Sound.

841

OLD BLACKSMITH SHOP built of bricks from local kiln. It was established early to construct first "permanent" buildings, all of which are now gone except this one. In cool, moist climate of Puget Sound, English ivy luxuriates, thriving like native plant as shown here.

Until '79 the importance of Port Blakely seemed to be ignored by some of its neighbors. Tacoma, for example, suddenly became aware of lost opportunities when its LEDGER spoke up in an editorial February 29, 1879: "Blakely is the smartest town of its population in these parts, and a little trade with it would help New Tacoma immensely. Olympia now furnishes the bulk of the beef that goes in there to supply ships, steamers and townspeople, a new trade, by the way, gained by that city at the expense of Seattle." Also of Tacoma, the item conceded three inches later.

The port reached its peak period during and shortly after the end of territorial days. By the beginning of the World War it was almost dead, picking up somewhat during that conflict, then again lying back never to recover except as a suburban area for ferry commuters to Seattle. All shipbuilding and sawmill structures are long gone. Rails have been taken up, short sections being used for gate posts. Except for the stubs of teredo-eaten pilings, remains of the old dam and a brush-concealed brick smithy, few signs of the once booming town remain.

The town was described in the late '70s as being long and narrow, confined at the rear by the steeply-rising hills, on the front by the bay filled with so many sailing vessels it sometimes had the appearance of a "woods of killed and bleached trees". While the townsite had been cleared of timber, stubborn stumps remained and wagons going down the one "street" had to meander around the obstacles.

Other than the post office, school and several saloons, the most imposing building in the village was the new hotel. It had two stories and was proudly claimed to be painted. The gay structure faced the bay, fronted by a roomy "porch" which was really a dock built on pilings over the edge of the bay and connected to the wharf where passenger ships tied up. Disembarking passengers were easily influenced to walk the few remaining steps to the hotel where they could promptly alleviate thirsts and sign the register.

RUINED FLOOD GATES once controlled ebb and flow of tides to create stable log pond of small bay at right. With gate gone, all water flows out on extreme low tides, final dregs seen here spilling into outer part of bay. Dam has nearly disappeared, was built along lines of pilings seen in background, constructed mostly of soil, mixed with bricks from early kiln. Walls of gates are of cut stone, iron gates long since vanished, perhaps salvaged for metal during first world war, by which time Port Blakely was nearly defunct as town.

PORT GAMBLE, WASHINGTON

When Captain Talbot and Cyrus Walker left the schooner *Junius Pringle* in June, 1853, in small boats, after sailing all the way from Maine, their object was to find a suitable site for a sawmill. It had to have its back set against many years' cut of timber and it must be flush to deep water instead of the mud flats prevailing along most of these inner shores. When they came to a small bay edged by an Indian village called Teekalet, "Brightness of the Noonday Sun", they knew they had found the place.

The oval-shaped harbor about two miles long had a narrow entrance to protect it against winter gales and many other advantages. Knowing the first white men here had been members of the Wilkes Expedition who had visited the waters in 1841, they named it Port Gamble in honor of Robert Gamble, naval officer and veteran of the War of 1812 in which he had been wounded.

Talbot and Walker recognized the value of the location immediately, and with the same dispatch returned to the *Pringle* which speedily sailed into the bay. Hardly had she dropped anchor when a crew of ten men was sent ashore with tools to construct cook and bunkhouses and other buildings, the lumber for which had been brought from California. The first native materials used were the cedar logs cut from the site to clear it, and squared for mill foundations. By a quirk, almost unbelieved by later sawmill men, the first lumber actually sold from the mill was white pine, brought from Maine by the *L. P. Foster* which arrived in September. There were 60,000 feet of the imported, "coals-to-Newcastle" lumber and the lot brought over $100 a thousand. This was the first profit made by Pope and Talbot in Washington, although their families were cutting trees and shipping lumber from their home area in East Machias, Maine, as early as 1767.

The *Foster* also carried to Port Gamble the machinery for the mill, which by that time was almost ready to be outfitted. It was 45 by 70 feet in size, built just above the high-tide mark. The boilers were fired and saws started turning not long after the *Foster* was unloaded and the first boards were "plowed back", being used to side up the mill until then open to all breezes.

The mill was not the first in the area. Mentioned in the Port Ludlow account is Captain William Sayward's little mill at that point. There was a sawmill at Fort Vancouver, owned by the Hudson's Bay Co., one run by Michael Simmons at Tumwater, Henry Yesler had one on the Seattle waterfront and there was a small operation at Port Madison on Apple Tree Cove owned by J. J. Felt. But these were all small businesses, the Pope and Talbot mill at Port Gamble being the real start of the Sawdust Saga in the Pacific Northwest.

Port Gamble's first little "muley" saw was able to cut about 2 thousand feet a day, that being eleven and a half hours. Logs were hauled into the mill by cable and drum, then hand-spiked onto the carriage to be pushed up against the up-and-down saw. In another year production had been increased six times by improved machinery. Four years later there was a new mill with modern twin circular rig having 56-inch saws which could cut logs up to 9 feet in diameter. It was soon producing ship spars and timbers 60 feet long.

LOST TO TIME and vandals is surname of young man buried in old cemetery at Port Gamble. Tombstone shows Indian name of town, Teekalet, was then in use, also that Washington was still territory, not achieving statehood until 1889. March of year 1863 when stone was erected did see reduction of area which previously included Idaho Territory, to present size.

It was dark inside the mill early in the day and toward evening, especially in winter. Illumination was by "teakettle lamps" which had spouts for wicks on both sides and burned dog fish oil bought from the local Clallam Indians. Results were a small amount of light, plenty of smoke and smell.

The monotony of long work days, broken only by Sundays, Christmas and Independence Day, was relieved by the "Indian War" in November of 1856. In the dusk of November 18, seven high-prowed, black war canoes entered Teekalet Bay. They were filled with Haida warriors from the Queen Charlotte Islands who made camp on the opposite shore, ostensibly preparing to attack the next morning. The sawmill crew hastily threw together an eight-sided fort of planks and at dawn waited inside for the expected raid. The 19th and 20th went by with nothing happening. In the late afternoon of the second day of "siege" the *U.S.S. Massachusetts* entered the bay. It sent a few shells into the Haida camp and the Indians departed as quickly as they had come. The next morning the sawmill workers were back on the job as usual.

Most of the white men came from Maine, a few of the crew being Indians. They were undependable workers, unused to discipline, with a habit of working only when the salmon were running, when they needed deer meat or when berry picking was good. Even with a steady job at the mill an Indian could be expected to take off for the woods or streams when he felt like it. Being expendable they were replaced when more Americans were available. Pay was $30 a month for eleven and a half hours, six days a week and the men got it weekly, in silver half dollars.

In 1858 the company announced it would "have the town surveyed and laid out into lots for the accommodation of all those who wish to make permanent residence here." In 1860, with a population of over 200, another notice was posted on the big bulletin board. The company planned "to erect buildings for all those who desire Public Worship, social enjoyment or fraternal communion".

1870 saw 326 people in the town. By now a hall had been built for dances and public meetings. In two more years Port Gamble ranked fourth among cities on the Sound and for the first time attracted a circus, in the summer of 1872. That same year the PUGET SOUND DISPATCH reported: "The town, which is owned almost entirely by the Mill Company, includes beside the mill and warehouses, many neat and tasteful residences and presents quite an attractive appearance. There is the Masonic Hall and a school house. The only real estate in town owned outside the Mill Co. are the houses of A. S. Miller and John Condon and two large, well furnished and well kept hotels owned by John Collins, The Teekalet House is kept by Miller and Condon who minister to the necessities of the thirsty traveler."

By this time the school had about 40 pupils being taught by two teachers. The "exhorbitant" salaries paid the "principal" teacher, $90 a month, and his assistant, $50, were the cause of a bitter controversy. One resident wrote "There is much ire over this expenditure. It is thought by many that the school board faces bankruptcy, and that the school directors are trying to give their children a college education at the expense of the poor man's children who, because of lack of funds, will not be taught even to read and write. The large salaries are attracting many teachers to Port Gamble, there being 30 applicants in 1872 as against 2 in 1870."

Luella Buchanan in her History of Kitsap County, records that "February, 1874, a library was established through the agency of the preacher, school principal and Cyrus Walker and on Christmas of that year it received a gift of 200 books. Also the Amateur Theatrical Club gave a play which netted enough to buy an organ for the Hall."

That same year Port Gamble's steady growth faltered somewhat in a business depression when many men "left for the mines" but soon steadied and went ahead until by 1876 it was reported: "The Exchange Saloon and Lodging House has 25 rooms and the grist mill is now chopping 60 tons of grain a month, enough for use of the mill and logging camps. There is also a good barber shop. Though not the county seat, the Superintendent and Justice of the Peace live here. Traveling dramatic companies find this a good place for shows." 1879 saw Port Gamble hailed as the largest sawmill town in the county, a position it held until 1885 when all had to admit the place was "fading somewhat".

The mill still operates, although on a greatly reduced rate. The main company buildings still stand, much as they did at the peak of operations. They are well kept and painted a neat, "New England white", still retaining the appearance that justifies the reference to "Little Boston." The structure prominently labeled "Port Gamble Post Office" houses also the barber shop and library which opens only on Tuesdays.

ST. PAUL'S EPISCOPAL CHURCH in Port Gamble was built by mill owners as duplicate of Congregational edifice in home town of East Machias, Maine. All imported was original landscaping. In face of abundant verdure offered locally, New Englanders brought from Maine various trees such as eastern maples. Most of these, planted near church grew crowded, were replaced by others.

PORT LUDLOW, WASHINGTON

"At Port Ludlow a man could be sure of $30 a month for a twelve hour day. He could have a roof over his head and hot meals. But he would have to work for them. The mill whistle split the foggy gray chill at twenty minutes past five. Twenty minutes later it blew again and the men sat down to a breakfast of boiled beef, potatoes, baked beans, hash, griddle cakes, biscuits and coffee. At six o'clock whistle saws were turning, logs and boards booming along the rolls in the wet, sawdust-filled air. And twelve hours later — every day — the men were paid spot cash at the company store." Thus does Ralph Andrews vividly describe a day at Port Ludlow in his HEROES OF THE WESTERN WOODS.

The first sawmill at Port Ludlow seems to have been that of red-headed Captain William Sayward and J. F. Thorndyke who had come out from Maine in the fall of 1853 and built a simple mill overlooking Admiralty Inlet. In June of the following year the schooner *Junius Pringle* arrived off Cape Flattery with Captain William Talbot and A. J. Pope who had organized the Puget Mill Company, and a Maine surveyor, Cyrus Walker, hired on a temporary basis. Pope remained on board. The other two explored the shorelines of the waterways to locate a suitable site for a sawmill, Talbot in the ship's longboat, Walker in an Indian dugout canoe.

They stopped at Captain Sayward's mill to exchange Maine pleasantries and marvel at the great expanse of fir forest, then found among the coves and inlets an ideal mill site at Port Gamble. But they did not forget the advantageous location Captain Sayward had.

By 1862 the big Pope and Talbot mill at Port Gamble was underway with a will. The partners were planning expansion when their manager, Captain J. P. Keller died. Cyrus Walker, still on the temporary basis, was offered the position on a permanent salary. He accepted only when offered the opportunity to buy a one-tenth interest. The operation grew rapidly with mills at Port Gamble and on Camano Island and in 1878 the company decided to build one at Port Ludlow. Captain Sayward's interests were purchased and a huge plant replaced the small one. It measured 65 by 394 feet and could turn out 100 thousand feet of lumber every day it operated.

With this mill well established Walker set about buying up immense amounts of standing timber, known as "stumpage", never more than a mile or two away from tidewater. The problem in logging was not in cutting the trees but in getting the logs to the sawmills. Much of the timber was acquired by taking advantage of the Timber and Stone Act,

REMAINS OF DOCK on which Cyrus Walker, Pope and Talbot's manager, welcomed visiting dignitaries who came on sailing vessels to the mill town. Much larger docks were located quarter of a mile to right adjoining giant sawmill, long since wrecked. Port Ludlow was situated on small deepwater bay on Admiralty Inlet, waterway providing access to Puget Sound and Hood Canal. In foreground lies twisty-grained log resembling stranded sea lion.

passed in 1876, which enabled any person declaring his intention of becoming a citizen to buy 160 acres of timberland at $2.50 an acre. The Pope and Talbot men, as well as other mill owners, made a practice of having sailors from their ships walk into the timber, then each making a legal purchase of 160 acres. They then sold it to the company at a nominal profit. It was a standing joke along the waterfront that the seamen never bought land very far from their ships for fear of getting lost in the woods.

For several years Cyrus Walker had been paying court to Emily Foster Talbot, daughter of the captain. She finally accepted him and in 1885 they were married, the couple setting up housekeeping in the manager's house at Port Gamble. When the building caught fire and burned to the ground, Walker laid plans to build the fabulous mansion at Port Ludlow.

FOOTHILLS OF OLYMPIC RANGE (opposite page) look down on old log pond of Puget Mill at Port Ludlow. Trees are mainly Douglas fir making up "second growth" which has sprung from slash of early logging. Bound groups of piling, termed "dolphins" in marine parlance, remain from sawmilling days, floating logs shown being stored temporarily in today's "contract" logging.

The new home, called Admiralty Hall after the inlet it faced, was nearly a block long, built of the material so readily available, red cedar and fir. The bathrooms set the scale for all else — said to be "as big as kitchens". During the fifty years Walker was a power in the Puget Sound lumber industry three generations of Chinese cooks held forth over the enormous kitchen range at Admiralty Hall. There was a well-stocked wine cellar for the benefit of guests, Walker himself abstaining.

For most of the years Walker reigned at Admiralty Hall, Port Ludlow was the lumber capitol of the world. The position was attained after a shutdown, when lumber was being over-produced and causing prices to drop to unprofitable levels. Walker accepted a subsidy of nine hundred dollars a month to keep the mill closed and the company town had its first experience at being near a ghost during the several years when almost all employees moved to other mill towns. When prices rose, the mills again rolled and Port Ludlow gained a new and greater prestige. Its lumber and shingles were shipped to every corner of the world including South Africa where Cecil Rhodes was building a grape arbor.

Industry at Port Ludlow was not confined to sawmilling. A large shipyard was kept busy building such vessels as the three-masted schooner *Courser*, barkentine *Katherine Sudden* and the *Moses Turner*. Built for the Hawaiian trade were schooners *Waehue*, *Lihuluho* and *Luke*. Among steamers built were *Augusta* and *Hyack*.

Cyrus Walker and his associates cut trees from purchased stumpage as long as it lasted, then started cutting into their own extensive holdings, kept for years for the purpose. When at last that source of trees was exhausted, the mills were dismantled and many of the houses barged over to still operating Port Gamble. The colossal, soft wood mansion was turned into a hotel, at first elegant, then increasingly shoddy as time took its toll. Forced to close for lack of patronage it stood idle, transients "camping" in the once plush rooms. Then one night it caught fire and in hours little but ashes was left. Today the ghost town hunter searches in vain for any sign of the building itself. Still growing where the lawn used to be are old holly trees, maples and shrubs brought around the Horn to grace the grounds of a lumber baron's castle.

ENORMOUS MANSION built by lumber baron Cyrus Walker stood on slope immediately above docks and mill. Grounds were landscaped with shrubs and trees brought on ships from Maine, centered by brass cannon, veteran of War of 1812. It boomed on 4th of July and whenever company's ships sailed into Admiralty Inlet. Visitors welcomed into the huge center hall found walls paneled with native fire and cedar. House was filled with massive pieces of furniture also brought from New England. Highboards of carved bedsteads reached almost to ceiling, every bedroom having marble-topped dressers. Sideboard in main dining room was of walnut, hand-carved in Germany. Room and closet doors slid back and forth like those on ships. Widow's walk surmounting cupola afforded Walker unobstructed view of domain and access to flagpole of Sitka spruce. House was used as hotel in later years and became completely covered with ivy. After abandonment it burned to ground. (Photo courtesy Stewart Holbrook.)

REPUBLIC, WASHINGTON

John Welty was discouraged after a whole summer of prospecting along the streams in northeastern Washington. When winter snows covered the ground he got a job for the winter, glad of a respite from clawing over the rugged mountains. But wanderlust and the ever-present hope of a good strike pulled him out along the streams at the very first break in the weather. In the middle of February, 1896, he did make that strike, and in the same stream he had worked the fall before —Granite Creek.

The resultant boom was such that by the first of May that year, Republic had a name and newspaper—the *Republic Pioneer*. On the 14th of the month it reported with a glow: "Here is a little city that is moving right along. Large quantities of whiskey, flour and other necessities arrived during the week."

By fall the camp had fifty log and canvas shacks, five stores, three blacksmith shops, four restaurants, two hotels, two fruit and cigar stores, two meat markets, three livery stables, three bakeries, three assay offices, tailor, shoemaker, doctor, jeweler and the usual lot of saloons. The Miners' Union sponsored big dances held in Patsy Clark's big boarding house. No cemetery existed until a young woman was found strangled "by persons unknown" and her body was the means to a permanent burial place on the steep hillside. The first school was a tent in the brush of the creek bottom, soon replaced by a log building. Indians were welcomed in the school and at first outnumbered the white pupils.

By 1900 a large part of Republic's growth was in the direction of brothels and saloons, the latter numbering up to twenty-eight, with six dance halls going strong, night and day. As late as 1940 an elaborate Opera House remained from those days. It was described as having an "elegant false front, copiously ornamented with balconies, each of which had a railing supported by fancy turned spindles." Republic now serves the surrounding farmers and vacationers, the days long vanished when the roistering miners found many easy ways to spend their money.

ORIGINAL ALTAR is intact in old Church of the Immaculate Conception in Republic, Wash. Edifice stands on steep hillside, conspicuous for miles around.

849

RIVERSIDE, WASHINGTON

Gun-toting, cattle-rustling Frank Watkins rode at the head of a string of stolen horses. He had run away from the rope in Oregon, chased by a mob and now, in 1903, was arriving in fresh territory and headed for Williams' Saloon in Riverside.

What Watkins liked was hot toddies such as Tom and Jerrys and he had heard how good Jack Williams could make them. He stomped in, pounded on the plank bar and demanded one of Williams' specials.

Watkins' reputation, not for consuming hot drinks but for confiscating hot horses and cattle, had preceded him. The tea kettle was steaming away but the bartender thought it was out of the cowboy's line of vision. He was not about to indulge cattle thieves' whims. "Ain't no more hot water," he sang out. But Watkins had heard the simmering kettle even though he couldn't see it. "Well," he drawled, "no more use for that thing then." And he moved out to sight the kettle and shoot the spout off.

The rustler hung around Riverside all winter. He seemed to think he rated the protection of the law, unaware that the townspeople were wary of him. Twice he went to the sheriff with complaints he had been shot at, once exhibiting a hole in his hat to prove it. "Too high," the sheriff may have said.

One evening the next spring he rode into Riverside, bedded his horse in Kendall's Livery Stable and after supper climbed into the loft to sleep in the hay. As other sleepers in this early day flophouse were wak-

ing and shaking the grass seeds and nits out of their ears, they noticed Frank Watkins was not stirring in his nest. He was dead with a bullet in his head.

At first it was called suicide but Watkins' gun was found beside him unfired and there were no powder burns on his skin. Nobody cared much how the cowboy had died and the questions asked of the other sleepers and witnesses at the inquest were desultory. No one appeared to press further inquiry and the business was settled. Watkins was buried without ceremony beside the road entering town. The grave can still be seen and may even have the little fence around it.

Richard Sutton tells this story, especially if you call him "Dick." His father, Robert W., brought the family to Riverside from Genesee, Idaho, in a covered wagon in 1890 and Dick grew up here, marrying in 1908 and rearing a family of five boys and five girls.

The early prosperity of Riverside was due entirely to its road position, freight teams and boats using it as a convenient stopover for loading or unloading. The actual year-around head of navigation was Brewster, where the Okanogan River meets the Columbia. Most of the year the former, which flowed past Riverside, was too shallow for steamboats, even the shallow draft paddle-wheel vessels, but in spring it swelled with melting snow from the mountains. That was a period of feverish activity and a fleet of loaded steamers brought a steady stream of supplies to Riverside, the center for a vast area of mining and farming communities. Merchants stocked up for the whole year and mine owners replaced equipment parts. As soon as flood waters subsided, river traffic was finished for another year and shipping activities began. Goods were moved to outlying points and Riverside was the headquarters.

At the turn of the century, the town decided it deserved the honor of being the county seat. Growing pains were about over and things were booming. A large store operated by C. E. Blackwell and Co. stood proudly on the waterfront near a big hotel, the Occidental. A bank was doing a flourishing business and the interest was 12 percent on loaned money. For a while it was squeezed in one corner of Pat Carney's saloon but the enterprising banker, Arthur Lund, quickly expanded into a separate building and even established branches of the bank in neighboring towns. With all this the populace thought Conconully had been on the top of the Okanogan heap long enough.

Heading the ensuing county seat fight, one-sided with Conconully sitting smugly on its prestige, was the fiery editor of the Riverside *Argus*. Outspoken, vituperative, Wallace Struble spared no dirty words in supporting the proposed shift. This was the same

period county elections for officials were scheduled and although most candidates were vigorously for or against the change, all kept their opinions buttoned up for fear of losing votes. When the election was over, Riverside was right where it started. Conconully held the county seat until 1914 when it went to Okanogan.

Struble put up another good fight but another losing one over the matter of a bridge over the Okanogan River—at Riverside or Okanogan? Final disposition was made in secret and editor Struble sounded a bitter blast in the *Argus* of Dec. 8, 1908. "On Monday last the retiring board of county commissioners awarded a contract to the Puget Sound Bridge Co. for the sum of $10,500 for the erection of a 'steal' bridge across the Okanogan at the village of Okanogan. The contract price does not include approaches which will probably swell the total $500 or more making the cost of the structure at least $11,000." The next paragraph was set in capital letters. "The awarding of this contract was done, the *Argus* is informed, with extreme secrecy. In a star chamber session at which only the commissioners and one Harry J. Kerr, 'Mayor' of Okanogan village, were present. Even the people of Conconully, except those in on the deal, were not aware of the proceedings and expressed surprise that

LIVELY SCENE ON WATERFRONT about the turn of the century — photo copied from calendar of Dick Sutton, pioneer resident of Riverside, showing large shipment of wool arriving from ranch of Clay Fruit to be loaded on sternwheelers tied up on Okanogan River bank.

Driver of wagon at left is Bert Winnick, his lead team Baldy and Jake; on next wagon is driver William G. Reeder, owner of freight line with headquarters at Brewster. Reeder had small terrier which nipped at heels of out-of-line or laggard horses. On driver's seat of third wagon is "Six-Shooter Andy" Southworth who habitually carried gun and bowie knife. Standing on ground at Andy's right, sporting boiled shirt, is ship's captain of Griggs Steamship Line. Loose horse in foreground is Nespelum, privileged race animal which didn't have to work and turned rump to photographer.

such a high-handed course should have been taken by a retiring board of commissioners."

The Okanogan *Independent* of Oct. 10, in a resumé of the historic battle said it had remained independent but did point out the advantages of the Okanogan site, prophesying that "the pendulum of development will swing in favor of Okanogan, that the bridge will have marked convenience in the transportation of trade to the growing communities of the Tunk Creek and Omak Creek areas," further pointing out that the railroad would be coming along in a few years and would likely bypass Riverside.

Riverside and the *Argus* editor must have sensed the truth of the prediction but to see it in the public prints was a punch below the belt. And Struble must have felt a certain satisfaction when the bridge was finished and proved to be eleven feet higher than needed to clear the tallest stack on any sternwheeler, which made the cost excessive and the approaches too steep to use in icy weather.

Riverside settled down to enjoy what it did have, its famous week-end dances in the big hall at the south end of town. These were held on Friday nights instead of Saturday because of the Sunday races at a fine track near the river. And also due to the Sunday racing, Authur Lund reaped a harvest by keeping his bank open.

True to the ominous prediction, the railroad did bypass Riverside when it came through in 1914, a blow to the town depending on road and river traffic. It was left sitting on the banks of the Okanogan to grumble and nurse the stray wagon freight. And the final stroke of destiny came when a modern highway was built to the north of the town.

In 1958 Stanley Hixon, a rancher in Tunk Valley, with "a small fortune tied up" in a museum on his ranch, decided something must be done about Riverside's retrogression, pointing out the 1896 population had dwindled to 186. He put over the plan of selling the town as a ghost town, building on its heritage to attract tourists the way the two famous Virginia Cities had. He enlisted the aid of the two grocers, tavern, dairy and roofing companies, about the only merchants remaining, and formed the Riverside Historical Association. Memberships were sold for $5, ground broken and plans made for a fine museum town utilizing the large collection of Hixon's ranch.

Mrs. De Tro, of H. De Tro and Co., general merchandise, said, when interviewed in 1963; "Oh, that all fell through. The thing was too optimistic. They planned too big. They spent all their money but couldn't do enough and no tourists came. Mr. Hixon and his wife separated and he moved to Arizona. The ghost town venture is a thing of the past."

OLD RIVER SCENE is often attributed to Riverside but structure showing in right background is Bureau Hotel in Okanogan. Owner Capt. Charles Bureau, more efficient as shipbuilder, constructed steamer *Enterprise* shown at right, piloted by Jack Brown. Other boat is *Chelan*; pilot—Capt. Grey. This picture, as most other old ones in this group, was taken about 1907 by Frank Matsura. He was pathetic little Japanese, arriving in Conconully in 1905. Developing a knack for photography, he gathered simple equipment, recorded hundreds of happenings. He moved to Okanogan in 1907, expanded interest into livelihood, was a lonely figure under racial prejudice. Early one cold Sunday morning about 1913, he was walking down street when he saw open window at back of store and was suspicious. Alerting sheriff, was told to fetch owner living some distance away. Storeman, responding to knock at front door, found Matsura dying on step. Suffering from tuberculosis, he had run all the way and had hemorrhage. Little photographer left behind invaluable heritage of historic pictures.

OLD KING COAL IS DEAD

Who ever heard of a coal rush? Yet Roslyn had several—the sudden influx of miners in 1886, rushes in and out of town when it was beset by fires, strikes, explosions and competition from nearby Ronald. There was "never a dull moment" in this coal center of the pine woods.

The railroad set off the first blast. The Northern Pacific needed a west coast source of good coal and this area was only four miles north of its main line. The first coal was packed out of outcroppings by horses in 1883 and three years later the Northern Pacific Railroad sent a corps of experts in to probe the protruding black ledges along Smith Creek east of Stampede Pass. What they found was coal of a quality and quantity that encouraged a survey for a branch line up the creek bed from Cle Elum. By act of Congress the company already owned every other section of land in the region which included this coal and within weeks more than a hundred men were working at the outcropping veins. Some brought their families and the result was an almost instant town.

Logan M. Bullitt platted it and with a romantic gesture named it Roslyn after a sweetheart in a Delaware town of that name. Dedication papers were filed in Minnesota September 22, 1886, with local legalities for Kittitas County taken care of six days later. Most streets were laid out sixty feet wide with Pennsylvania eighty. By December 13, it was evident an addition would be needed and this was platted at the northeast corner of the original townsite. Almost immediately still another became necessary to accommodate all the new arrivals.

The first iron horse brought a wave of them, mostly miners from Italy, followed by others from Austria and Slavic countries and Negroes in quantity. That first winter saw some four hundred men congregated in camp.

Company officials were well aware that a percentage of them would be rascals, male and

SPIRALED STRIPS OF STEEL are long undisturbed shavings from machine shops at lower edge of Roslyn.

853

female, and since it was a company town they were determined to keep it as peaceful as human nature would allow. Gambling dens were strictly prohibited and officially absent for many years but that did not prevent some clandestine poker games and cock-fights.

To curb excess drinking the company set up its own saloon, which with a general store were the first business structures in town. One individual lot buyer erected a building across the street from the company enterprise, getting little trade until the word "Saloon" was painted on its false front. Then the owner got the Sunday punch and a padlock on the door. He was instructed to read the fine print in his deed, a clause strictly forbidding manufacture or sale of intoxicating liquors.

Inevitably another saloon went up, but on private land just outside the town limits in the "tall uncut." Two more followed it and then another, so labeled but actually a spot where a lonely coal miner could find a warm embrace for a price.

Rumor had it several men not reporting for work had been rolled and dragged into the heavy forest. All this forced the town bosses to allow legitimate saloons within town limits where they could be regulated.

Other pioneer buildings were the hotel (corporation owned) that housed a hundred men, boarding house and two livery stables. All were built of lumber cut in the company owned sawmill from company owned timber.

The first half of 1888 saw a briskly flourishing Roslyn with some 1200 population. On June 22, about four o'clock in the afternoon smoke was seen coming from a building between First and Second. The alarm was sounded, a futile gesture with so little fire protection available, for within two hours all buildings were in ruins. Loss was about $100,000 and that meant loss for most property owners felt the 10% insurance premium was exhorbitant.

In a few months Roslyn was on its way to recovery, many new buildings springing up from

NO. 3 MINE, altho part of Roslyn complex, warranted separate town of Ronald for convenience, businesses, rooming houses, saloons. Although later mines like No. 9, 10, were fairly good producers, none ever surpassed production, importance of old No. 3.

PARTLY OCCUPIED, partly boarded up house is typical of many old homes in Roslyn, once flourishing coal camp, deterioration now well under way.

the ashes and an era of prosperity prevailed. Then in August came the first of several labor uprisings, An organization called the Knights of Labor was organizing unions all over the country and in July of 1888 almost all Roslyn miners were made "brothers," the few dissenters made miserable. The town was fertile ground in which to plant and cultivate seeds of strike against the Northern Pacific mine owners. Wages were small, working hours stretched to ten, miners working under constant threat of explosions and collapsing tunnels.

The ensuing strike was long and bloody incidents frequent. Most workers had little or no backlog on which to subsist and some had to leave town. Mine officials imported crews of Negroes as "scabs," many remaining after the settlement to account for much of Roslyn's population to its very end. Among scanty details of the strike is the item that officials called for martial law but the settlement was reached before soldiers were sent in.

By December of 1890 all miners were working full time, the monthly payroll $84,000. Then when the owners lost the Union Pacific contract the payroll shrank to $63,000 and lean days came until new contracts were secured. Then the famous producer, Mine No. 3, one mile away, was opened and all was rosy again, the town of Ronald growing up around the new mine, named after Alexander Ronald, a mine superintendent.

In the midst of happy prosperity came the disastrous explosion of May 9, 1892. A noontime underground blast took the lives of forty-five men. A relief committee was quickly organized and gathered $7,000 from outside communities, $2,000 from Roslyn citizens, the fund aided by supplies collected by Knights of Pythias and other organizations. 36% of it went to widows, the remainder to the fatherless children.

That same year on September 24, bandits got away with a small fortune from the town's bank, Ben E. Snipes Co., and more money was spent in a futile attempt to solve the crime. The bank may have been thinly financed for on June 9 of the next year its doors were closed in the face of a clamoring mob of depositors who lost $100,000. The blow was a crippling tragedy as the sum represented all savings in the community. Some depositors eventually received certificates of indebtedness, "good for framing," as one man said. The next year saw a strike in May over wages which lasted several months, greatly depressing business and working hardships.

Yet things brightened up at the end of 1896. One reason seems to be the progressive ideas of B. F. Bush who came to Roslyn as manager of the coal company's operations that year. He put into practice a more liberal policy which increased the number of working days to six per week which was still not enough to supply the coal in demand. For the next seven years the town enjoyed the full dinner pail, fat pocketbook and comfortable home.

OLD MINE CAR stands idle with others in lots once occupied by business buildings, long made empty by series of destructive fires.

POWER HOUSE, generating steam, part of complex of once busy warehouses, machine shops etc., adjacent to old railroad yards.

A murder shocked the town on the morning of Friday, March 20, 1896. The brutally bludgeoned body of the well-liked company doctor, J. H. Lyon, was found a few feet from his own doorstep. The apparent weapon was a table leg lying a few feet away, covered with blood and hair, pocketbook and jewelry untouched on his body. The last person to see Dr. Lyon was his long-time friend, merchant Samuel Isaacs. Enraged townspeople collected $400 as reward for the murderer's arrest and conviction to which was added $500 by the state governor, $300 by Kittitas County and $300 by the city of Roslyn.

Suspicion eventually fell on two brothers known to have made threats against the doctor, accusing him of what amounted to malpractice in treating a third brother. The evidence was slim and they were released after a preliminary hearing, the record stating, "Mystery still enshrouds one of the blackest crimes ever committed in the history of the State of Washington."

In the same period the town was struck down by an epidemic of diphtheria. After several deaths all schools were closed, all public gatherings banned. On the heels of this came another. Smallpox spread rapidly, blame placed on admitted poor sanitary conditions in the town. When this scare subsided, Roslyn again went forward.

In 1904 the population was some 4,000 made up mainly of Slavs, Negroes, Italians and Germans. By this time the mines were privately owned, 1898 legislation denying railroads the right to operate mines of any kind. In 1909 another mine explosion took ten lives. By 1930 the population was down to 2,289, the decline continuing steadily. Today the town, not entirely dead, displays many examples of Victorian elegance in its surviving buildings, some of them still occupied.

POWDER HOUSE building solidly built of stone and iron-shuttered, still stands at Ronald, "suburb" of Roslyn. It held large supplies of blasting powder for coal mines but stored well away as accidental explosion might collapse mine shoring.

RUBY, WASHINGTON

At the height of Ruby's success as a boom town, the Ruby *Miner*, on June 2, 1892, editorialized: "As Virginia City is to Nevada so is Ruby to the State of Washington. Ruby is the only incorporated town in Okanogan County. It is out of debt and has money in the treasury. Public schools are open nine months of the year and are under the management of competent instructors, these furnishing unsurpassed advantages. LET US MAKE SOME MONEY FOR YOU IN RUBY. THIS DISTRICT IS APPROPRIATELY TERMED THE COMSTOCK OF WASHINGTON."

Ruby's first butcher, W. A. Newcomb, was a jolly, friendly man who was popular with the citizens, a fact that served him well later. He was known to have an ample supply of fresh meat and one day somebody found out why. The butcher was a rustler on the side and when cattlemen came into his shop with a rope, he was put under protection of the sheriff and hustled off to Conconully for trial. The guards were friends and being friendly, all got drunk as lords and on the trip Newcomb made an easy escape.

County commissioners held a special meeting, the second in Ruby's history, to vote a reward of $500— and hoped the townspeople would match it—for the capture of the butcher-rustler. Notice of the reward was posted in Ruby, advertised in the Portland *Oregonian*, Seattle *Post-Intelligencer*, Walla Walla *Statesman* and Victoria (B.C.) *Colonist*.

Whether or not the reward was responsible, Newcomb was apprehended and brought back to Ruby. Tempers of cattlemen had now cooled enough to try him in a local court, where he was judged not guilty and freed, jurors being friends of the affable Mr. Newcomb. His experience apparently chastened him and he afterward bought his beef.

As a silver town Ruby had a series of booms and relapses as new discoveries were made and old ones faded out. It was a raw-edged town with little regard for law and order. On one occasion a few town toughs were idling on a bench outside Billie Dawson's hotel when the stage pulled in with a stranger on top. He was wearing a white plug hat, the like of which had never been seen in these parts. Lounger Len Armstrong bet Al Thorpe, considered a crack shot, that he couldn't put a bullet through the trick top piece without hitting the head under it. Without hesitation Thorpe drew his gun and fired, putting a neat hole in the upper crown. When the visitor protested at the violent reception to Ruby, Thorpe apologized and set up the drinks.

The same hotel was the setting for another shooting incident when Jonathan Bourne, who had spent half a million in his silver mine which was currently in low production, found he couldn't meet the payroll. A crowd of irate miners assembled outside the hotel and, not knowing which room Bourne lived in, shot out all the windows.

Bert Comstock ran a saloon in Ruby; John Bartlett, a store. The former had eyes for Bartlett's wife and she responded. The pair left town together; in a few days Bartlett's body was found in his store, dead apparently by suicide. The fleeing couple had take the Bartletts' baby daughter with them and when she reached fifteen, Comstock deserted the mother and married the child.

Ruby shared Indian troubles with Conconully. Walter Brown had a dairy between the towns, delivering milk to both. He attended a Fourth of July celebration in Ruby, arriving just in time to witness an atrocity. An Indian brave name Pokamiakin, as handsome as he was bold and brash, came into the crowd with a fast horse he had stolen, well-known race horse, Nespilim. Sheriff Bill Tiffany ordered the Indian to dismount and submit to arrest but the brave refused and spurred the animal into a spurt. Tiffany galloped alongside him, grabbed Pokamiakin by his long, black hair and dragged him along the ground. Dairyman Brown, in telling the story, said the crowd was sure every bone in the Indian's body was broken but he got to his feet running. In the hail of bullets, both he and the horse were killed.

Winter snows were cruel to towns in the area, avalanches frequent and crippling the mining camps situated at the bottom of steep slopes. One such slide in Ruby crashed down on an engineer named Magee and his two helpers who were pinned under a flume, which fortunately allowed them to breathe and saved their lives. Not so lucky was a young Ruby man who taught school in Conconully. He was buried in a slide on his way to the school, found dead in the big snow pile.

Richard Price, later scheduled to preside over the never-held trial of lynched Indian Steve, was sent into the area by the Indian service to make a survey on all white men who had Indian wives. He was to determine nationality, tribal connections of women, number of children, wealth and social standing of couples. It was never revealed what purpose the survey was to serve, but it gained good results for Price. He was justice of peace in Ruby and a well-versed counsellor on Indian affairs.

HOTEL BUREAU in nearby, hated rival city, Okanogan, was long time in building since builder, Charles Bureau, described as "handsome Frenchman," was too busy with many girl friends in Portland. Started about 1900, hotel was still unfinished in '20s when Bureau died. Four-horse stage regularly covered route from Oroville to the north, calling at Riverside as last stop before Okanogan.

LOG CABIN ON JOHNSON CREEK, where in 1888 first Okanogan county commissioners held meetings under confusion due to fact county seat was undetermined. Delegations from Ruby and Conconully gathered in separate camps outside cabin to carry on campaigns, Ruby delegation promising office space free from taxes, Conconully five acres of land for county buildings. Stimulating refreshment caused boisterous demonstrations, Ruby people forming circle around cabin, dancing and shouting —"Ruby for County Seat!" Decision went to Ruby, lasted for 11 months, then to Conconully until 1914.

BANK ROBBER LEROY, alias Charles Ray or Andrew Morgan, shown in newspaper photograph with Sheriff "Baldy" Charles McLean after capture by Sheriff Fred Thorp. Prisoner shows desperate gleam in eyes even in poorly reproduced photo, also wounded finger. Likely LeRoy was even then planning escape which took place soon after.

OLD RUBY pictured in only known photo, has been completely ravaged by time, fire and vandalism. No building remains in lusty, boisterous town called "Babylon of the West." Ruby was early county seat, had no office buildings or safe. County treasurer found himself in tough town with county funds of $1,800, placed money in can, buried it at his ranch. Although some gold and considerable copper were mined here, Ruby depended on silver and silver crash of 1893 sent camp rapidly downhill. Remaining residents moved to one-time rival, Conconully.

ONCE THERE WAS LIFE

SKAMOKAWA, WASHINGTON

Until the year 1915 the town of Skamokawa had no land connection with the outside world. Surrounded on three sides by rocky cliffs and dense virgin timber, on the fourth by the broad lower Columbia River, the inhabitants took to the water.

Situated in Wahkiakum County in the state of Washington, Skamokawa is less than 80 miles northwest of Vancouver, yet is unknown to many Portlanders. It will repay the one-day tripper with its blend of Ghost Town atmosphere and live fishing and farming community.

It would be hard to say exactly when the town got started. Since there have been Indians, there has been some sort of village there, made up of fairly permanent aborigines. Fishing then, as now, has always been good along the lower river, the most desired fish being the Chinook Salmon, because of its delicately flavored red meat. The earliest whites found the peaceable Chinook Indians catching their staple food in the most primitive of nets and weirs, made of willow stems bound together with twine of twisted cedar-bark fibers.

Shortly after the Hudson's Bay Post was established at Fort Vancouver in 1825, other posts were strung along strategic routes. One of these was less than three miles from Skamokawa. A labyrinth of waterways, sloughs and creeks intersect the area. A peculiarity of the waterways funnels fog into the place, causing the Indians to give it the name, meaning "Smoke-on-the-water." (Pronunciation is Ska-mo'ka-wuh.)

The natives built up a steady trade in supplying the new Hudson's Bay Post with fish. Up until then they had always dried their catch (a dubious accomplishment in this damp atmosphere), ground the result into powder and stored it for the winter. A deerskin full of this stuff must have been a hard thing to live with, especially if the shelter grew warm and the air close. But now the post introduced the method of salting down, an only slightly less odoriferous method of preservation. The casks full of fish were sent up the river to Fort Vancouver, from whence they were shipped to England.

860

All went well until one day the Factor was found murdered and everything of value at the post stolen. Soldiers were sent down from Fort Vancouver to deal with the culprit, who, it was naturally assumed, would be found among the Chinooks. But these people were not given to deeds of violence, and were outraged. In effect, they said, "We didn't do it, but we know who did, and we'll bring him in" and they did, too.

Some time previously, a ship had been wrecked on the shores of the Olympic Peninsula, to the north. The crew had chosen a bad spot to be shipwrecked, because here lived the savage Hoh Indians. The entire crew was slaughtered, the ship pillaged. It was a member of this rapacious tribe who had wandered south and committed the crime at the post. He didn't enjoy his ill-gotten gains long; the indignant Chinooks, eager to prove their innocence, tracked the luckless Hoh down and returned him to their village. On the spot where one day the present schoolhouse would be built, he was tried and summarily hung. The noose had been knotted before the trial was finished. This headlong rush of justice was in striking contrast to later laxity among white settlers on the site.

Mr. L. E. "Les" Silverman, who was born in Skamokawa in 1897 and lives there still, provides much information.

When Mr. Silverman's father, C. L., arrived there in the 80's, there was quite a little town along the inner waterway called Skamokawa Creek. The creek is submerged in tidal water backed up from the river and is actually more like a canal. Along this waterway for perhaps a quarter mile stood a line of small buildings on each side. One side held most of the business structures; at least two of which, a saloon and a meat market, still stand precariously. In those days elk steak "tender and juicy" sold for eight cents a pound. The saloon, soon eclipsed by a fancier one, became the office of a tiny steamboat company called "Bobbidge & Holt." The name along with the words "Steamer Efin" are still faintly discernible on the front of the little building. The

FALSE FRONTS line this watery "Street." Many of the buildings are the original ones included in a painting of this scene made by T. S. Weedell, along in the 1880's.

name *Efin* was made up of the initial letters from the given names of the owning family. These were Edmond, Fred, Ida and Nellie.

All these structures faced the water, their rears the wilderness.

No man was ever tried for murder in Skamokawa since Indian days. This was in spite of not a few killings. One man, standing on the dock, whipped out his pistol and shot to death a man approaching in a boat. Presumably there had been bad blood between the two. The killer fled to the county seat, Cathlamet, gave himself up to the Sheriff, who turned him over to the Justice of the Peace. That worthy extracted 500 dollars from him as bail and pointedly suggested that he fade away for a while. He did so, moving to the Oregon side of the river. Every few weeks he came back to town on the early boat, visited his relatives and departed next day. He was never molested.

Skamokawa reached its peak in the first years of this century. About 1910 there were about 400 to 500 people, a fine schoolhouse had been built and three large shingle mills operated full tilt. The first co-operative creamery in the state was operating. A

PICTURESQUE HOTEL stood partly on wharf, partly on bank: was home to travelers who came to Skamokawa by river steamer. In times of high water in spring when snow in upper reaches of Columbia melted, hotel and wharf were surrounded by flood.

TIDAL EFFECTS ON LOWER Columbia are strong, as are fluctuations in seasonal levels of water. Walks on hinged connections and floating docks keep fishing boats accessible. Vat in foreground holds "blue vitrol" cupric compound in which nets are soaked, killing algae which would rot twine. Note roller, over which long gill net is fed into tank.

newer section had sprung up closer to the river itself. New docks, an imposing store and a three-story hotel faced the water. To them came, several times daily, the steamboats of the day. Sidewheelers and sternwheelers they were; the *Lurline*, the *Harvest Queen*, the *T. J. Potter* and all the rest.

But when river traffic died, so did something in Skamokawa. The big hotel emptied and faded, the store windows now stare on a sagging dock, the planks of which are rotting away and returning to the river. Empty, gray and weathered residences line a once busy steamboat slough, and the old school is forlornly a meeting place for the Redmen Lodge.

Mr. Silverman hopefully maintains the town is not dead and it never will become a true Ghost Town because there are still the fish and the fertile farmlands. Many docks are still draped with drying gill nets. Fish boats still ply the canals of once busy "Little Venice." A modern school stands at the edge of town where the guilty Hoh once swung at the end of a rope.

863

SULTAN, WASHINGTON

Sultan, as were many Washington towns in the heavily timbered Cascades, was a combination mining and lumbering town. Some industry still persists, but the place doesn't begin to enjoy the color of the early days.

Sultan is now about as accessible as a town could be, barely off the highway. But in 1870 when prospectors found scattered flakes and a few nuggets of gold in the Sultan River, no roads existed, and timber as heavy as anywhere in the world covered the area. Indian trails made their way through the woods, and beside one of these John Nailor and his Indian wife established a claim ten years after the first discoveries.

Their place became a rough and tough hangout for all sorts of undesirables, thus setting the tone of Sultan's earlier days.

Prosperity was well established when the first light-draft river steamer, the *Mama*, reached the place in 1888.

Sultan really boomed when the Great Northern built its tracks on through the Cascades, one of the most staggering jobs in railroad history, and a separate story. The effect on Sultan, however, because of basing the men and materials there, was to expand an already rowdy mining camp into a sprawling mass of shacks housing all the hangers-on of a construction camp.

Sultan now is a quiet, respectable town. The buildings remaining from that wild, early period are on a back street.

TRINITY, WASHINGTON

Trinity is situated on Phelps Creek, in a wild, remote section of the Cascades. Heavy virgin timber crowds close.

Before the turn of the century there was prospecting, then placering nearby. Later, a rich vein of copper was found about five miles from the present site, and the first mine sank a shaft into the side of the mountain about 1900.

About 1914 the Royal Development Co. was formed and the town was built. A power plant was erected near the upper end of the main street. Large frame buildings followed; a mess hall, commissary, rooming houses and all the other structures necessary to a booming mining camp took shape. Another lesser street ran at right angles, fringed with smaller houses and cabins for the married men and their families. Above the power plant was the large mine building with the usual huge pile of tailings extending from it. On the older section of the latter was built a sawmill. Narrow gauge tracks led everywhere, and the dump ore cars ran back and forth between the openings of the shafts and tunnels and the mill.

Copper was the mainstay, although enough silver showed to pay actual cost of mining, 80 cents to the ton of ore. As costs increased and returns did not, operations began to slow down. There had been about 275 men working in the mines and the mill, but the number dwindled until at last everything stopped and everybody moved away, except one old man, a Mr. Foster, who stayed as watchman. Now even he is gone and the buildings stand silent and deserted. Many are crushed to the ground by the weight of winter snows totaling 30 feet some years. Dump cars are rusting on little rails, which look as if they were made for a long-gone toy engine. The skeleton of a deer lies inside the mill where the animal must have taken shelter in a winter storm and starved to death. The stream rushes through town, taking first one path and then another as the flushes of melting snows in spring urge it on.

OLD ORE CARTS stand rusting near mill.

OLD CABLE SPOOL reveals details in cross lighting.

THESE WERE MESS HALLS and dormitories for single miners. Structure at right has been crushed by weight of snow.

SPECTACULAR PEAKS of some of wildest parts of Cascades rise behind remains of Trinity as backdrop. Dense timber covers hills. Fuel and lumber were never problem here.

UNION, WASHINGTON

Lumbering has been of prime importance in the Puget Sound country of Washington since 1788 when Captain John Meares left it with his sailing vessel loaded with spars for China. The load never reached there, the ship running into a heavy storm and the cargo jettisoned. Several years later when Captain George Vancouver's ship lost a spar, he had his men cut a tree in the Washington woods to replace it. Then fur trading became well established and the need for log cabins created a new industry. Millwright William Cannon set up a whipsaw platform at Fort Vancouver in 1825. He sawed boards with this crude hand-device for a year, replacing it with a sawmill built with machinery from London.

The Fort Vancouver mill operated until about 1847 when the machinery was sold to Colonel Michael T. Simmons who set it up at Tumwater, bringing sawmilling close to Puget Sound. In 1852 residents of the Alki Point settlement, later to be part of Seattle, cut trees on the hills back of the village for use as pilings. They brought oxen from the Puyallup Valley to haul the logs to the water, this probably being the first operation of its kind. A sawmill owned by Nicjolas De Lin in Tacoma sawed 2,000 feet a day. De Lin's boards sold only while there was no competition for his saws invariably cut them "on the bias", tapered from end to end or in both directions from the middle.

Henry Yesler's first steam sawmill in 1853 at Seattle was the beginning of the big time in the lumber industry and mills now spread along Hood Canal, actually a natural inlet from the Strait of Juan de Fuca. The Olympia COLUMBIAN reported in 1853: "There are now no less than fourteen sawmills run by water power and one steam sawmill in process of construction on Puget Sound. A large number of our citizens are getting out cargoes of hewn timber, piles, shingles and cordwood faster than the number of vessels engaged in that trade can carry them to market."

The shores of Hood Canal were becoming dotted with logging camps and small sawmills, with no central source of supplies. In 1858 partners Wilson and Anderson set up a trading post on the south shore of the Canal at the narrow neck of land connecting the Kitsap Peninsula to the Olympic Peninsula and the mainland. This strategic situation commanded a view of Hood Canal and ships in both northeasterly and northwesterly directions, the Canal making a right angle bend at that point.

As soon as the trading post was well established, the Rush House was built. It was a grand affair, two stories high with six bedrooms (guests supplying their own bedding) and most important, a bar where all sorts of potables could be had. The dining room served "elegantly complete" meals. To make sure no guests were absent when dinner was served, the cook went out on the balcony and sent out a couple of blasts from a cow's horn fitted with a shrill-sounding reed.

After a few years Anderson tired of keeping up his end of the trading post work and sold his share to F. C. Purdy. In a few more years the enterprise was transferred to the ownership of John McReavy, until then a lumberman. By 1876 there were at least fifty logging camps in the area, most of them buying all their provisions at the trading post. By 1889 the land around the store and hotel was becoming so well settled it was platted as a town and christened Union City. Growth had been slow but steady yet Union City was to regret things could not stay that way.

Around 1890 rumors were rife that Union City would be at the crossroads of several railroads — the Grays Harbor and Puget Sound, the Union City and Naval Station, and Port Townsend and Southern Lines. As a consequence Union City boomed so fast lots that had been worth next to nothing now sold for $1,000 each. So many people moved into the town there was no place for them to live, in spite of earnest efforts of the one sawmill, brand new, to turn out enough lumber for new houses. Tents blossomed everywhere, even along the beach. More than one greenhorn from the midwest pitched his tent when the tide was out, only to find his domicile flooded a few hours later. Meals were cooked over communal fires until stoves could be obtained.

Further inflation came with the arrival of construction crews, horses and Union Pacific equipment. On the very day work was to start came devastating news. Baring Brothers Bank of London refused further payments on its outstanding debts

HOME OF JOHN McREAVY who bought and operated town's early day trading post, platted and named Union City in 1889. Sawmill built by McReavy cut cedar boards lining interior walls of house. Building, erected in 1889, was once painted bright yellow, is now mellowed by age. It has ground level basement at rear where hand laundry was once operated by Indian women. House is now home of Mr. and Mrs. Lud Anderson. Mrs. Anderson was Helen McReavy, daughter of John, has written history—**How, When and Where on Hood Canal.**

of twenty-one million pounds, obligations assumed in a fantastic web of international finance. The panic of 1893 was on and all railroad work was immediately canceled. Union City's dream of becoming a rail terminus at salt water skittered away, the boom at an end. In embarrassment the town quickly dropped the "City" from its name and as plain Un-

ion, settled back to the simple existence it has since led. In recent years, with rapid transportation available, summer residents have built cottages along the shores of Hood Canal. Restaurants, stores and other small businesses have sprung up at Union, causing small scale prosperity, likely to prove more permanent than the first.

VADER, WASHINGTON

Vader, in the heart of the great Washington logging area south of Olympia, where Swedes and Finns and bull teams were trying to "get daylight into the swamp," had its share of shooting scrapes and murders. But while old-timers, including keen-minded Norman "Pat" Hitchcock, have trouble recalling the full details of them, sharp and clear is the memory of Husky Dog. Everyone who lived in Vader around 1906 will tell you about the town's most proficient alcoholic.

George Gale, now of Olympia, heard the story from Bill Dickenson who lived in Vader for several years. Husky Dog was brought down from Alaska by some prospector who wandered on, leaving his sled dog as a public charge. Bill Dickenson adopted the animal and always took him along when he had one or two in Vader's several bars. One evening as he stood up to the bar in the Spangler Hotel, Bill thought Husky Dog might be thirsty too, ordered an extra glass of beer and set it on the floor. Husky Dog sniffed but turned his head until a little of the brew was poured on the floor. He eagerly lapped up the sample and the rest in the glass when it was poured out. The husky's several admirers "set 'em up" for him all evening and when Bill left the dog walked as he never had at "40 below in the Arctic snow."

The next evening bartender Pat Hitchcock opened up and who but Husky Dog was waiting

VADER'S OLD CITY HALL is crowded by trees, grass, brush. At left are council chambers and shown under cedar tree barred windows of two-cell jail. Most occupants of hoosegow were drunks but it also held murderers. At right is fire station once sheltering two-wheeled hosecart pulled by hand by volunteer fire-laddies, sometimes in 4th of July parades. Hose-drying tower was surmounted by belfry, fire bell weighing more than 800 pounds. Present Vader resident John Groleau remembers when supporting timbers were judged unsafe and bell was removed. He says: "We attached ropes to it and pulled. It made a big crash when it came down, the belfry along with it. It landed behind the building. We always intended getting it out on the main street and mounting it some way as a momento, but never did."

OLD VADER HOTEL, last one to go and was under wrecking hammer when photo was made in 1962. Vader had at least five saloons, two housed in hotels. Near this building was newspaper office where GAZETTE was published.

at the door. Pat poured him a drink on the floor before serving anyone else, recognizing the hangover. The dog stayed in the bar all evening and when it closed he had to be ejected — but not like the men. The "cork-booted" inebriates had to be helped or carried out but Husky Dog was cooperation itself, letting himself be gently guided out. Then his aplomb deserted him. He headed for Bill's cabin but collapsed beside the road to sleep it off.

And so in truth Husky Dog became the furry face on the barroom floor, his progress downward being rapid because of an amiable nature that could not say "no." Several years of guzzling, says George Gale, "soon ruined Husky Dog's beautiful physique, turning him into a 300-pound monster with a gut like a beer barrel. His meaty jowls meas-

ured 24 inches from ear to ear. He became famous as the only dog in the country who could smile" . . . and that was about all. When forced to leave any bar at 2 a.m. he usually tried to make it to the nearby livery stable or blacksmith shop, Bill's cabin having long proved out of range. If he fell short of either he simply slept there, carrying his own blanket against the coldest weather.

And alas, retribution reaped its reward—Husky Dog fell seriously ill. His many friends came to his aid, guaranteeing care by the local doctor who immediately placed his patient on the water wagon. The dog lived a few months, then died in his sleep. Again quoting George Gale: "For Husky Dog the cork had been pulled, the bung knocked out of the barrel."

In the early 1850s flat-bottomed boats nego-

NEAR NEIGHBOR was town of Olequa, named for nearby stream. Was mostly farming community, depending largely on production of hops. With increasing expense of growing and lessening demand for hops, industry declined, most residents moving away. At one time several buildings stood at crossroads, center of Olequa, grocery store last to go. This photographer found only ruins of recently wrecked structure, settled for only remaining evidence of Olequa's one-time lively industry, fast-decaying hop drier.

tiated the Cowlitz River as far as Toledo, a land route, "military road," roughly paralleling the waterway. Near the small falls on Olequa Creek, a Cowlitz tributary and conveniently near the highway, the small village of Little Falls came into existence by the early 1880s, thought to be an outgrowth of an earlier Indian village, with post office, one-room school, general store, hotel and several houses.

When the Northern Pacific Railroad came this way it stopped not at the hamlet but at a point about a mile south, advancing no reason for naming the stop Sopenah. One old-timer in the area says a shipment of soap addressed to the general store in Little Falls, Wash., was sent instead to Little Falls, Minn., and the railroad wanted no more such mistakes. In any event, for many years mail came to the town addressed "Little Falls," rail shipments tagged "Sopenah."

Businesses found it more convenient to move closer to the rail point where others were already established, and took the Little Falls name along with them, the station alone retaining the word Sopenah. The community boomed in the latter part of the century, one large industry the Little Falls fire clay factory, using local high quality clays, and the Stillwater Logging and Lumber Co. Several hotels did a thriving business — Bannon, Spangler, Stillwater, the latter a three-story structure as was the school house. The town was also proud of its Opera House where thespians emoted from the heart to audiences of the bustling metropolis, then the busiest between Portland and Tacoma.

Among employees in the Stillwater mill was a Kentuckian. He liked his job on the edger so well and wrote home so glowingly many of his friends in the Blue Grass State joined him, resulting in a formation of a clique at the plant. Member stood by member on any and all occasions, as the time one of the southerners got into a quarrel with Ed Bertrand in one of the saloons. The two exchanged a few blows, the man from Kentucky getting the worst of it. He backed out the door vowing to get even, borrowed a gun at a friend's house, returned to shoot point-blank at Bertrand.

The killer waited for trial in the City Hall jail, facing almost certain conviction since the shooting had been witnessed by many. But his fellow Kentuckians collected a purse large enough to hire a clever lawyer to defend the prisoner. At the trial, self-defense was claimed with the contention that Bertrand attacked first, was even wearing brass knuckles. The accused was acquitted and released.

During Little Falls' best years there was continuing argument about the name of the town and station, railroad steadfastly refusing to conform. Finally a conference between townsmen and railroad officials brought the positive promise that the line would change the name, but not to Little Falls. So citizens huddled at City Hall and decided to call the town after a long time resident—Mr. Vader. The railroad went along with that.

Vader is today a near ghost. Gone are the hotels, saloons, industries. Quiet streets see little movement — of live people, that is.

872